Food: In Context

Food: In Context

Brenda Wilmoth Lerner & K. Lee Lerner, Editors

VOLUME 2

JUNK FOOD TO YEAST AND LEAVENING AGENTS

GALE
CENGAGE Learning™

Detroit • New York • San Francisco • New Haven, Conn • Waterville, Maine • London

Food: In Context

Brenda Wilmoth Lerner and K. Lee Lerner, Editors

Project Editor: Elizabeth Manar

Editorial: Kathleen Edgar

Rights Acquisition and Management: Margaret Chamberlain-Gaston, Leitha Etheridge-Sims, Robyn Young

Composition: Evi Abou-El-Seoud, Mary Beth Trimper

Manufacturing: Wendy Blurton, Dorothy Maki

Imaging: John Watkins

Product Design: Kristine Julien, Jennifer Wahi

Indexing: Dow Jones & Company, Factiva, Inc.

For product information and technology assistance, contact us at **Gale Customer Support, 1-800-877-4253.**
For permission to use material from this text or product, submit all requests online at **www.cengage.com/permissions.**
Further permissions questions can be emailed to **permissionrequest@cengage.com**

Cover photographs: Image of earthquake survivors reaching for boxes of food reproduced by permission of AP Images. All others used under license from Shutterstock.com: Image copyright Dmitriy Karelin, 2010 (cow); Image copyright Tan Wei Ming, 2010 (dairy plant in Switzerland); Image copyright Vishal Shah, 2010 (Indian woman cleaning grain); Image copyright Certe, 2010 (olives); Image copyright Sandra Caldwell, 2010 (corn cob); Image copyright apdesign, 2010 (wheat); Image copyright @amp;erics, 2010 (grapes); Image copyright Sveta San, 2010 (poultry farm); Image copyright Anna Jurkovska, 2010 (fishermen); Image copyright Laurent Renault, 2010 (rows of lettuce).

While every effort has been made to ensure the reliability of the information presented in this publication, Gale, a part of Cengage Learning, does not guarantee the accuracy of the data contained herein. Gale accepts no payment for listing; and inclusion in the publication of any organization, agency, institution, publication, service, or individual does not imply endorsement of the editors or publisher. Errors brought to the attention of the publisher and verified to the satisfaction of the publisher will be corrected in future editions.

LIBRARY OF CONGRESS CATALOGING-IN-PUBLICATION DATA

Food: In Context/Brenda Wilmoth Lerner & K. Lee Lerner, editors.
  p. cm.
  Includes bibliographical references and index.
  ISBN-13: 978-1-4144-8652-9 (set) ISBN-10: 1-4144-8652-9 (set) ISBN-13: 978-1-4144-8653-6 (v. 1) ISBN-13: 978-1-4144-8654-3 (v. 2) [etc.]
  1. Food. 2. Nutrition. 3. Food supply. I. Lerner, Brenda Wilmoth. II. Lerner, K. Lee.
TX354.F6657 2011
641.3--dc22   2010054584

Gale
27500 Drake Rd.
Farmington Hills, MI, 48331-3535

ISBN-13: 978-1-4144-8652-9 (set)   ISBN-10: 1-4144-8652-9 (set)
ISBN-13: 978-1-4144-8653-6 (vol. 1)   ISBN-10: 1-4144-8653-7 (vol. 1)
ISBN-13: 978-1-4144-8654-3 (vol. 2)   ISBN-10: 1-4144-8654-5 (vol. 2)

This title is also available as an e-book.
ISBN-13: 978-1-4144-8655-0 (set)   ISBN-10: 1-4144-8655-3 (set)
Contact your Gale, a part of Cengage Learning, sales representative for ordering information.

Printed in China
1 2 3 4 5 6 7 15 14 13 12 11

Contents

Advisors and Contributors xv

Introduction xvii

About the *In Context* Series xxi

About This Book xxiii

Using Primary Sources xxvii

Glossary xxix

Chronology lvii

VOLUME 1

Advertising Food 1

African Famine Relief 5

Agenda 21 9

Agribusiness 12

Agricultural Deforestation 16

Agricultural Demand for Water 20

Agricultural Land Reform 25

Agriculture and International Trade 30

Agriculture Brings Hierarchical Societies 34

Agroecology 37

Aid for Agriculture to Replace Illicit Drug Production 40

Alice Waters: California and New American Cuisine 43

America's Second Harvest/Feeding America 46

Aquaculture and Fishery Resources 49

Asian Diet 53

Avian Influenza 57

Baking Bread 61

Banana Trade Wars 65

Biodiversity and Food Supply 69

Biofuels and World Hunger 74

Bioterrorism: Food as a Weapon 78

Bisphenol A 81

Bottled Water 84

Botulism 88

Breastfeeding 91

Building Better Ovens 95

Bushmeat 98

Caffeine 102

Calories 106

Cannibalism 109

Cartagena Protocol on Biosafety (2000) 112

Celebrity Chef Phenomenon 115

Center for Food Safety and Applied Nutrition 119

Changing Nutritional Needs Throughout Life 122

Chocolate 125

Cholera 128

Climate Change and Agriculture 132

Codex Alimentarius 135

Coffee 138

Commission on Genetic Resources for Food and Agriculture 142

Community Supported Agriculture (CSAs) 145

Confectionery and Pastry 149

Consumer Food Safety Recommendations 154

Convention on Biological Diversity (1992).................................. 157

Cooking, Carbon Emissions, and Climate Change.................................. 160

Cooking Fats.................................. 164

Corn.................................. 169

Culinary Education.................................. 173

Cult Diets.................................. 176

Dairy Products.................................. 179

Decollectivization.................................. 183

Desertification and Agriculture.................................. 187

Diet and Cancer.................................. 191

Diet and Diabetes.................................. 194

Diet and Heart Disease.................................. 198

Diet and Hypertension.................................. 201

Dietary Changes in Rapidly Developing Countries.................................. 204

Dietary Guidelines for Americans.................................. 208

Dietary Reference Intakes.................................. 212

Dietary Supplement Health and Education Act of 1994 (DSHEA).......... 215

Disasters and Food Supply.................................. 218

E. Coli *Contamination*.................................. 222

Eating Disorders.................................. 225

Ecological Impacts of Various World Diets.................................. 229

Edible Schoolyard Movement.................................. 232

Eggs.................................. 236

Embargoes.................................. 239

Ethical Issues in Agriculture.................................. 243

Ethical Issues in Food Aid.................................. 246

Extreme Weather and Food Supply.................................. 250

Factory Farming.................................. 254

Fair Trade.................................. 257

Family Farms.................................. 260

Family Meal Benefits.................................. 263

Famine 266

Famine: Political Considerations 271

Farm-to-Table Movement 275

Fast Food 279

Fermentation: Alcohol 282

Food Additives 288

Food Allergen Labeling and Consumer Protection Act of 2004 291

Food Allergies 294

Food Alliance 297

Food and Agriculture Organization (FAO) 300

Food and Body Image 303

Food and the Internet 306

Food as Celebration 309

Food Bans 312

Food, Conservation, and Energy Act of 2008 316

Food Critics and Ratings 319

Food, Drug, and Cosmetic Act of 1938 323

Food Fads 326

Food First 330

Food Inspection and Standards 332

Food Irradiation 335

Food Packaging 339

Food Patents 343

Food Phobias 347

Food Preparation Methods 351

Food Price Crisis 355

Food Recalls 359

Food Rheology 363

Food Safety and Inspection Service 365

Food Security 368

Food Sovereignty 372

Food Styling 375

Food Webs and Food Chains 377

Foodborne Diseases 381

Foodways 385

Free Trade and Agriculture 389

French Café Culture 393

French Paradox 396

Fruits 399

Functional Foods 403

Fusion 406

Gastronomy 409

Gender Equality and Agriculture 412

Genetically Modified Organisms (GMO) 416

Gluten Intolerance 422

Gourmet Hobbyists and Foodies 425

Government Food Assistance for Citizens 428

Grains 432

Green Revolution 436

Gulf of Mexico Oil Spill Food Impacts 440

Head-to-Tail Eating 443

Heifer International 446

Hepatitis A 449

Herbs and Spices 452

History of Food and Man: From Hunter-Gatherer to Agriculture 456

History of Home Cooking 459

Human Gastrointestinal System 463

Humane Animal Farming 468

Hunger 472

Hydrogenated Fats and Trans Fats 475

Hydroponics 478

Immigration and Cuisine 481

Contents

Import Restrictions...484

Improving Nutrition for America's Children Act of 2010.......................488

Indigenous Peoples and Their Diets...491

Infant Formula and Baby Food...495

International Federation of Organic Agriculture Movements....................499

International Food Aid..503

International Fund for Agricultural Development................................507

VOLUME 2

Junk Food 511

Lactose Intolerance 514

Land Availability and Degradation...517

Latin American Diet 520

Legumes 523

Listeria 526

Livestock Intensity and Demand..529

Locavore..534

Macrobiotics..537

Mad Cow Disease and vCJD..540

Malnutrition 544

Meat Inspection Act of 1906..548

Meats...553

Mediterranean Diet 557

Michael Pollan: Linking Food and Environmental Journalism...................561

Migrant Labor, Immigration, and Food Production 564

Molecular Gastronomy..568

Monounsaturated and Polyunsaturated Oils.....................................571

Movies, Documentaries, and Food..574

MREs 577

Neighborhood Food Cooperatives..580

Norovirus Infection 583

Nutrient Fortification of Foods..586

Nutrition..589

Nutrition and U.S. Government Food Assistance....................................592

Nutrition's Role in Human Evolution..595

Nuts and Seeds..598

Obesity..601

Oral Health and Diet..606

Organic Foods Production Act of 1990..609

Organics..613

Paleolithic Diet..617

Paralytic Shellfish Poisoning..620

Pasta..623

Pasteurization..626

Pesticides and Pesticide Residue..630

Phytochemicals (Phytonutrients)..634

Pica..637

Political Food Boycotts..640

Population and Food..644

Poultry..648

Poultry Products Inspection Act of 1957..652

Preservation..655

Processed Foods..660

Produce Traceability..663

Protein and Carbohydrate Metabolism..666

Pure Food and Drug Act of 1906..669

Raw Foodism..673

Raw Milk Campaign..676

Religion and Food..679

Reportable Food Registry..683

Rice..686

Rome Declaration on World Food Security (1996)................................690

Salmonella 695

Salt 699

Salt, Nitrites, and Health 703

School Lunch Reform 706

Seafood 710

Shark Harvesting 715

Slow Food Movement 718

Social Media and Food 721

Spice Trade 724

Standard American Diet and Changing American Diet 727

Staphylococcal Food Poisoning 733

Street Food 736

Subsidies 741

Subsistence Farming 744

Sugar and Sweeteners 747

Sustainable Agriculture 750

Sustainable Table 754

Tasting Food 757

Tea 760

Television and Food 763

Texas Beef Group v. Winfrey 766

Therapeutic Diets 770

Truth in Labeling 773

UN Millennium Development Goals 776

Undernutrition 779

Urban Chicken Movement 782

Urban Farming and Gardening 785

U.S. Agency for International Development (USAID) 790

U.S. Department of Agriculture (USDA) 793

U.S. Food and Drug Administration (FDA) 796

USDA Food Pyramid 800

Veganism 803

Vegetables 806

Vegetarianism 810

Viniculture 814

Vitamins and Minerals 819

Wage Slavery in Food Production 823

War, Conquest, Colonialism, and Cuisine 827

Waste and Spoilage 830

Water 835

Water Scarcity 839

Whaling 842

Wholesome Meat Act of 1967 846

Women's Role in Global Food Preparation 850

World Food Day 854

World Food Prize 857

World Food Programme 860

World Trade Organization (WTO) 864

Yeast and Leavening Agents 867

Organizations 871

Sources Consulted 879

General Index 947

Advisors and Contributors

While compiling this volume, the editors relied upon the expertise and contributions of the following chefs, scientists, scholars, and researchers, who served as advisors and/or contributors for *Food: In Context.*

Andrea Abel, MPAff
Independent Scholar and Food Writer
Austin, Texas

Susan Aldridge, Ph.D.
Independent Scholar and Writer
London, England

Steven J. Archambault
Department of Economics
University of New Mexico
Albuquerque, New Mexico

Stephen A. Berger, M.D.
Director, Geographic Medicine
Tel Aviv Medical Center
Tel Aviv, Israel

Melissa Carson, Ph.D.
Sustainability Expert
London, England

Bryan Davies, J.D.
Independent Scholar and Science Writer
Whitby, Ontario, Canada

Sandra Dunavan, M.S.
Journalist
Saline, Michigan

Emily Walden Harris
Writer, Cook
Portland, Oregon

Brian D. Hoyle, Ph.D.
Microbiologist
Nova Scotia, Canada

Tiffany Imes, M.S.P.H.
Congressional Hunger Center International Fellow
Arlington, Virginia

Phillip McIntosh
Science Journalist and Writer
Colorado Springs, Colorado

Pamela S. Michaels, M.S.
Independent Scholar and Writer
Santa Fe, New Mexico

Matthew Munsey
Independent Scholar and Writer
Tucson, Arizona

Caryn Neumann, Ph.D.
Visiting Assistant Professor, History
Miami University
Middletown, Ohio

Anna Marie Roos, Ph.D.
Research Fellow in Modern History
University of Oxford
Oxford, England

Blake J. Stabler, M.A.
Policy Analyst, Agriculture and Food Security
Washington, D.C.

David Brennan Tilove
Independent Writer and Chef
Hollywood, California

Melanie Barton Zoltán, M.S.
Independent Scholar
Amherst, Massachusetts

Acknowledgments

The editors are grateful to the global group of scholars, researchers, and writers who contributed to *Food: In Context* as academic advisors: Andre Able, Steve Berger, Melissa Carson, Brian Hoyle, Anna Marie Roos, Blake Stabler, and David Tilove.

The editors also wish to thank John Krol, whose keen eyes and sound judgment greatly enhanced the quality and readability of the text.

The editors gratefully acknowledge and extend thanks to Julia Furtaw, Janet Witalec, and Debra Kirby at Cengage Gale for their faith in the project and for their sound content, advice, and guidance. Without the able guidance and efforts of talented teams in IT, rights and acquisition management, and imaging at Cengage Gale this book would not have been possible.

Deep and sincere thanks and appreciation are also due to Project Manager Elizabeth Manar who, despite encountering the usual myriad of publishing hurdles and woes, managed miracles with wit, skill, grace, and humor.

Introduction

As memorialized in the opening chapter of his book *A Moveable Feast,* the American writer Ernest Hemingway sets out on one of most renowned walks in literary history, a walk that takes him from his humble apartment in Paris to eventually write in a "good café on the Place St. Michel."

Nearly ninety years later, one can still, as Hemingway recalled, walk past the Lycée Henri-IV and the ancient church Saint-Étienne-du-Mont, into the Place du Panthéon. The wind is still bitter on cold, rainy days, and shelter can still be sought by cutting right and slipping behind a remnant of the Université de Paris to reach the Boulevard St. Michel. Turning right and walking down the slight grade toward the river Seine, the Musée de Cluny and Boulevard St. Germain still mark the journey.

Just shy of the Place St. Michel itself, the boulevard flattens, as do the hopes of finding a café similar to those that existed in Hemingway's day. Such cafés exist in many other parts of Paris, but in this heavily touristed area, the only café open early one morning was a Starbucks coffee shop—albeit one culturally assimilated enough to have Parisian-style café tables outside.

In the Place St. Michel proper, there are now only high-traffic cafés that have signs and menus in multiple languages. Looking left and downstream along the river in the direction of the Louvre museum, a blue awning advertising "Pizza" and "Pasta" shades the opposing corner café. Wheeling back to look across the river to the Île de la Cité and then over a bit to view the westward façade of the Cathedral Notre Dame de Paris, the view of a flying buttress of the famed Gothic cathedral is partially obscured by signs perched on top of the closest corner: a café advertising Ben and Jerry's ice cream, along with an Italian brand of coffee that brews beans grown and harvested from farms around the world.

In the most important and profound ways, Hemingway's words remain true. Paris is a movable feast for the soul, but globalization has, for better and worse, also moved the feast of the world to Paris.

Food: In Context is not, however, a book about gastronomy or the impacts of globalization on cuisine *per se*. It is, rather, a book dedicated to offering a first course in food-related science, politics, and issues. While food is art—its history and expression both mirroring and articulating subtle cultural differences—its provision in some areas devolves to more sharply drawn struggles with outcomes measured in health or sickness, life or death.

The editors are humbled and fortunate that a lifetime of work covering science and disease-related issues has taken us, quite literally, around the world. We must more humbly, however, also confess to hubris, hunger, and family-driven folly regarding food choices. We know parental pangs of paying far too much for unremarkable sandwiches at tourist-trap cafés in Venice's Piazza San Marco and the profound shame of indulging in a celebratory seafood feast in Chennai, India, when only meters away, people scavenged for food. We know the joys of seeking out wonderfully intimate back-alley restaurants run by families in Bonnieux, France, Girona, Spain, Cairo, Egypt, and in the Moslem quarter of Xi'an, China. In addition to experiencing the cultural diversity of food, these intimate encounters invariably led to long discussions about food set in the context of the local geography and politics held by the owners, chefs, servers, and local patrons. Perhaps more influential in shaping *Food: In Context*, however, we have too often and too closely seen the devastating impacts of malnutrition and the folly of government policies that provide food to a fortunate few while others are left to undernourishment. We have seen food, separated from hungry people only by bad policies and inept distribution, allowed to rot instead of benefiting a population. Nothing expresses the frailty of the human condition more than a malnourished mother determined to feed a starving infant with what little milk her body will yield.

In the West, we are normally privileged to fight food wars with less dramatic outcomes. Regardless, matters of nutrition, food integrity, labeling, equitable treatment of workers, lunches for school children, etc. are also vibrantly debated and vital to creating healthy and sustainable societies. Although headlines are often consumed with the potentially deadly impacts of higher food prices or famine globally, it would be imprudent to simply ignore what are often local issues in order to focus only on more fully global issues. The motivation to tackle global issues can often come from awareness and involvement at the local level. Moreover, many of the lifestyle and sustainability issues have vital overlaps with energy and ecology issues critically important in an increasingly environmentally challenged world. Lastly, many of the health related issues are profound. While not as immediately deadly as famine, diabetes and obesity are akin to modern plagues in the West and growing in importance globally.

We also know the passions aroused when local cultures deeply entwined with local foods are imperiled. We raised children along the Gulf Coast of the United States and have long sailed the waters between New Orleans, Louisiana, and Pensacola, Florida. We lived and worked on the Gulf Coast through the worst parts of the 2010 *Deepwater Horizon* oil spill, experiencing first-hand the mounting anxiety of people fearful of losing their unique resources, cuisine, and culture.

Similarities and differences in context and perspective are an essential component of *Food: In Context* entries. Talking with farmers or workers in a market in Cambodia translates surprisingly well to similar uncertainties about keeping and maintaining family lands voiced at struggling roadside family markets in Alabama. Struggles to carve out and preserve a local niche in markets dominated by large food companies are, given minor differences in context, similar for both a family dairy in Georgia and a family farm in Ireland.

Concerns over food safety can dominate discussions with public health officials in Berlin or Kuala Lumpur.

These personal insights are important because food is not a dispassionate topic. No topic we have ever tackled has so deeply stirred passions among writers, editors, and advisors as have the issues explored in *Food: In Context*. Provided that opinions were supported by well-established science or policy, our disposition as editors was to best serve students by allowing the widest divergence of expert opinion. There were however, tough editorial calls to be made.

For example, the treatment and depiction of agribusiness is often quick to inflame passionate debate. After weeks of internal debate over which material to cover in a ballooning entry on agribusiness, we decided to retain older material related to the Nestle baby formula scandal even though more modern issues rage in the press. While the current issues were well covered in other topics (e.g., seed monopolies, GMO issues, treatment of migrant workers, child labor, etc.) we made difficult space-related choices about including the "textbook" Nestle scandal. In the end, we felt it was vital to developing a base for critical thought that we include the classic material. Such material may be classic to more advanced readers, but it is often foundational to younger students.

Accordingly, if a reader were only to read the one entry of agribusiness, we would expect to brace ourselves for a charge that we failed to more fully explore the market power of agribusinesses. As before, there are treatments of related issues throughout *Food: In Context*. We also specifically retained the Nestle baby formula example, because as one advisor advocated, he could not think of "anything worse to accuse agribusinesses of as being responsible for infant deaths." At times, providing the "textbook" example is vital.

On the other hand, we also tried to acknowledge that there is a wide diversity of opinion, especially outside the West, on the value of agribusiness. As scientists attempting to provide introductory material for students, we made a deliberate attempt to heavily rely on vetted material and avoid the inclusion of material that, although abundantly supported, did not rest on established science, or was subject to extreme, highly speculative, or conspiratorial interpretations. As editors, we considered it prudent to initially provide a diverse, but solid base of issues that will allow students to build toward their own conclusions as their studies progress.

The editors acknowledge and take responsibility for the fact that our personal experiences and perspectives from around the world have shaped *Food: In Context* to a far greater extent than our other science-related and "In Context" work. Although we attempt scholarly balance within each topic, the selection of topics—limited by space— was more subjectively driven than, for example, the topics one might cover in a book on infectious disease or climate change. Regardless, as editors, we attempted to select those topics that provide a solid foundation for beginners and a reference for more advanced students. To the extent that there are omissions, or where topics seem too briefly covered, the editors accept full responsibly. Much good material went to the editing bin.

We respectfully submit that while *Food: In Context* is more subjective editorially, it is most decidedly not self-indulgent. There are many assertions made by expert authors with which we as editors disagree or might modify if the article was in our voice alone. If the authors could, however, substantiate their positions with peer-reviewed supporting evidence, we welcomed and included divergent viewpoints and assertions.

Accessibility is a key concept for the book. Rather than detached scholarly discourse, our personal experiences drove us to seek experts with "hands on" experience grappling with an array of food issues, especially in developing nations. While we attempted to make *Food: In Context* readable for a wide audience, we also attempted to allow experts to challenge a range of student abilities, and did not shy away from promoting awareness of those causes that likely will stir a reader's own intellect and passions.

As different styles and interpretations of art, music, and literature are manifestations of the need to communicate and connect, so the many viewpoints regarding food and food issues reflect and reveal communal beliefs, deep differences, and the manifest complexities of civilization. We will consider *Food: In Context* a success if it leaves readers hungry to learn more about the vital issues covered in these pages.

To a man with an empty stomach, food is God.
—Mohandas Karamchand Gandhi (Mahatma Gandhi)

K. Lee Lerner & Brenda Wilmoth Lerner, Senior Editors

PARIS, FRANCE, DECEMBER 2010

Although grateful for the assistance of colleagues working around the world, *Food: In Context* was also a dedicated family effort within a family-run company. The senior editors wish to extend profound thanks to our senior assistant editors on this project, Joseph Patterson Hyder, J.D., and Adrienne Wilmoth Lerner, J.D., who tirelessly tackled the enormous challenges of reconciling internationally disparate food related policies. Our editorial intern and assistant editor, Adeline Wilmoth Lerner, a student at Auburn University (now also studying at *Le Cordon Bleu* in Paris), provided a solid selection of photos and helped ensure that the text remained accessible to our target audience.

The Lerner & Lerner/LernerMedia portfolio includes award-winning books, media, and film that bring global perspectives to science related issues. Since 1996, they have contributed to more than 60 academic books and served as editors-in-chief for more than 30 books related to science and society. Their book *Infectious Diseases: In Context* was designated an ALA Outstanding Academic title, and their book, *Climate Change: In Context,* both published by Cengage Gale, was named a ALA RUSA Outstanding Reference Source for 2009.

About the *In Context* Series

Written by a global array of experts yet aimed primarily at high school students and an interested general readership, the *In Context* series serves as an authoritative reference guide to essential concepts of science, the impacts of recent changes in scientific consensus, and the impacts of science on social, political, and legal issues.

Cross curricular in nature, *In Context* books align with and support national science standards and high school science curriculums across subjects in science and the humanities and facilitate science understanding important to higher achievement in science testing. The inclusion of original essays written by leading experts and primary source documents serve the requirements of an increasing number of high school and international baccalaureate programs and are designed to provide additional insights on leading social issues, as well as spur critical thinking about the profound cultural connections of science.

In Context books also give special coverage to the impact of science on daily life, commerce, travel, and the future of industrialized and impoverished nations.

Each book in the series features entries with extensively developed words-to-know sections designed to facilitate understanding and increase both reading retention and the ability of students to advance reading in context without being overwhelmed by scientific terminology.

Entries are further designed to include standardized subheads that are specifically designed to present information related to the main focus of the book. Entries also include a listing of further resources (books, periodicals, Web sites, audio and visual media) and references to related entries.

Each *In Context* title has approximately 300 topic related images that visually enrich the content. Each *In Context* title will also contain topic-specific timelines (a chronology of major events), a topic-specific glossary, a bibliography, and an index especially prepared to coordinate with the volume topic.

About This Book

Food: In Context is a collection of entries on topics designed to provide an introduction to the global diversity of viewpoints on a broad array of food related issues. In addition to life-and-death decisions reflecting the fundamental importance of food, policies related to food issues both reflect and shape societies, social justice, and social change. While the entries contained in *Food: In Context* include treatments of traditional food related issues grounded in peer-reviewed science, they also provide insight into the development and implementation of polices shaped by history and contemporary geopolitical realities.

General Structure

Food: In Context is a collection of entries on diverse topics selected to provide insight into increasingly important and urgent topics associated with the study of food science and issues.

Intended for a wide and diverse audience, every effort has been made to set forth *Food: In Context* entries in everyday language and to provide accurate and generous explanations of the most important scientific terms. Entries are designed to instruct, challenge, and excite less experienced students, while providing a solid foundation for reference for more advanced students. *Food: In Context* provides students and readers with essential information and insights that foster critical thinking about food science and policy issues.

In an attempt to enrich the reader's understanding of the mutually influential relationships of history, science, and culture, as space allows, the editors have included primary sources that enhance the content of *In Context* entries. In keeping with the philosophy that much of the benefit from using primary sources derives from the reader's own process of inquiry, the contextual material introducing each primary source provides an unobtrusive introduction and springboard to critical thought.

- Entries are arranged alphabetically, rather than by chronology or scientific subfield.

- The **chronology** (timeline) includes many of the most significant events in the history of food. Where appropriate, related scientific advances are included to offer additional context.

- An extensive **glossary** section provides readers with a ready reference for content-related terminology. In addition to defining terms within entries, specific Words-to-Know sidebars are placed within each entry.

- A **bibliography** (citations of books, periodicals, and Web sites) offers additional resources to those resources cited within each entry.

- A comprehensive **general index** guides the reader to topics and persons mentioned in the book.

Entry Structure

In Context entries are designed so that readers may navigate entries with ease. Toward that goal, entries are divided into easy-to-access sections:

- **Introduction:** A opening section designed to clearly identify the topic.

- A **Words to Know** sidebar contains essential terms that enhance readability and critical understanding of entry content.

- A **Historical Background and Scientific Foundations** section provides the historical context of the topic.

- An **Impacts and Issues** section relates key scientific, political, or social considerations related to the topic.

- More than 200 sidebars added by the editors enhance expert contributions by focusing on key areas, providing material for divergent studies, or providing evidence from key scientific or official agency reports.

- If an entry contains a related primary source, it is appended to end of the author's text. Authors are not responsible for the selection or insertion of primary sources.

- A **Bibliography** section contains citations of books, periodicals, Web sites, and audio and visual material used in preparation of the entry or that provide a stepping stone to further study.

- **"See also"** references clearly identify additional content-related entries.

Food: In Context special style notes

Please note the following with regard to topics and entries included in *Food: In Context*:

- Primary source selection and the composition of sidebars are not attributed to authors of signed entries to which the sidebars may be associated. Sources for sidebars containing external content (e.g., a quote from an Intergovernmental Panel on Climate Change (IPCC) report related to the entry) are clearly indicated.

- Equations are, of course, often the most accurate and preferred language of science. To better serve the intended audience of *Food: In Context*, however, the editors attempted to minimize the inclusion of equations in favor of describing the elegance of thought or essential results such equations yield.

- A detailed understanding of nutrition, physiology, or chemistry is neither assumed nor required for *Food: In Context*. Accordingly, students and other readers should not be intimidated or deterred by the sometimes-complex names of chemical molecules or biological classification. Where necessary, sufficient information regarding chemical structure or species classification is provided. If desired, more information can easily be obtained from any basic reference.

Bibliography citation formats

In Context titles adopt the following citation format:

Books

De, Dipak; Basavaprabhu Jirli; and K. Kiran. *Empowerment of Women in Agriculture.* Varanasi, India: Ganga Kaveri, 2010.

Hovorka, Alice, Henk de Zeeuw, and Mary Njenga. *Women Feeding Cities: Mainstreaming Gender in Urban Agriculture and Food Security.* Warwickshire, UK: Practical Action, 2009.

Jacobs, Susie M. *Gender and Agrarian Reforms.* New York: Routledge, 2010.

Kristof, Nicholas D., and Sheryl WuDunn. *Half the Sky: Turning Oppression into Opportunity for Women Worldwide.* New York: Knopf, 2009.

Periodicals

de Brauw, Alan, Qiang Li, Chengfang Liu, Scott Rozelle, and Linxiu Zhang. "Feminization of Agriculture in China? Myths Surrounding Women's Participation in Farming." *China Quarterly London* (2008): 327–348.

Giarracca, Norma, and Miguel Teubal. "Women in Agriculture." *Latin American Perspectives* 35, no. 6 (2008): 5–10.

Gill, Jatinderjit Kaur, M. K. Dhillon, and Muninder K. Sidhu. "Women in Agriculture." *International Journal of Rural Studies* 14, no. 1 (2007): 2–6.

Motzafi-Haller, Pnina, and Paul J. Kaldjian. "Geographical Reviews—Women in Agriculture in the Middle East." *Geographical Review* 96, no. 4 (2006): 721–722.

Ngowi, Aiwerasia Vera Festo. "Women's Work in Agriculture." *African Newsletter on Occupational Health and Safety* 18, no. 3 (2008): 48–49.

Web Sites

"Agriculture and Achieving the Millennium Development Goals." *International Food Policy Research Institute.* http://www.ifpri.org/publication/agriculture-and-achieving-millennium-development-goals (accessed September 18, 2010).

"Asia's Women in Agriculture, Environment, and Rural Production." *Food and Agriculture Organization of the United Nations (FAO).* http://www.fao.org/sd/wpdirect/WPre0108.htm (accessed September 18, 2010).

Using Primary Sources

The definition of what constitutes a primary source is often the subject of scholarly debate and interpretation. Although primary sources come from a wide spectrum of resources, they are united by the fact that they individually provide insight into the historical *milieu* (context and environment) during which they were produced. Primary sources include materials such as newspaper articles, press dispatches, autobiographies, essays, letters, diaries, speeches, song lyrics, posters, works of art—and in the twenty-first century, web logs—that offer direct, first-hand insight or witness to events of their day.

Categories of primary sources include:

- Documents containing firsthand accounts of historic events by witnesses and participants. This category includes diary or journal entries, letters, email, newspaper articles, interviews, memoirs, and testimony in legal proceedings.

- Documents or works representing the official views of both government leaders and leaders of other organizations. These include primary sources such as policy statements, speeches, interviews, press releases, government reports, and legislation.

- Works of art, including (but certainly not limited to) photographs, poems, and songs, including advertisements and reviews of those works that help establish an understanding of the cultural milieu (the cultural environment with regard to attitudes and perceptions of events).

- Secondary sources. In some cases, secondary sources or tertiary sources may be treated as primary sources. For example, if an entry written many years after an event, or to summarize an event, includes quotes, recollections, or retrospectives (accounts of the past) written by participants in the earlier event, the source can be considered a primary source.

Analysis of primary sources

The primary material collected in this volume is not intended to provide a comprehensive or balanced overview of a topic or event. Rather, the primary sources are intended to generate interest and lay a foundation for further inquiry and study.

In order to properly analyze a primary source, readers should remain skeptical and develop probing questions about the source. Using historical documents requires that readers analyze them carefully and extract specific information. However, readers must also read "beyond the text" to garner larger clues about the social impact of the primary source.

In addition to providing information about their topics, primary sources may also supply a wealth of insight into their creator's viewpoint. For example, when reading a news article about the effects of biofuel production on the 2008 world food crisis, consider whether the reporter's words also indicate something about his or her origin, bias (an irrational disposition in favor of someone or something), prejudices (an irrational disposition against someone or something), or intended audience.

Students should remember that primary sources often contain information later proven to be false, or contain viewpoints and terms unacceptable to future generations. It is important to view the primary source within the historical and social context existing at its creation. If for example, a newspaper article is written within hours or days of an event, later developments may reveal some assertions in the original article as false or misleading.

Test new conclusions and ideas

Whatever opinion or working hypothesis the reader forms, it is critical that they then test that hypothesis against other facts and sources related to the incident. For example, it might be wrong to conclude that factual mistakes are deliberate unless evidence can be produced of a pattern and practice of such mistakes with an intent to promote a false idea.

The difference between sound reasoning and preposterous conspiracy theories (or the birth of urban legends) lies in the willingness to test new ideas against other sources, rather than rest on one piece of evidence such as a single primary source that may contain errors. Sound reasoning requires that arguments and assertions guard against argument fallacies that utilize the following:

- false dilemmas (only two choices are given when in fact there are three or more options);

- arguments from ignorance (*argumentum ad ignorantiam*; because something is not known to be true, it is assumed to be false);

- possibilist fallacies (a favorite among conspiracy theorists who attempt to demonstrate that a factual statement is true or false by establishing the possibility of its truth or falsity. An argument where "it could be" is usually followed by an unearned "therefore, it is.");

- slippery slope arguments or fallacies (a series of increasingly dramatic consequences is drawn from an initial fact or idea);

- begging the question (the truth of the conclusion is assumed by the premises);

- straw man arguments (the arguer mischaracterizes an argument or theory and then attacks the merits of their own false representations);

- appeals to pity or force (the argument attempts to persuade people to agree by sympathy or force);

- prejudicial language (values or moral goodness, good and bad, are attached to certain arguments or facts);

- personal attacks (*ad hominem*; an attack on a person's character or circumstances);

- anecdotal or testimonial evidence (stories that are unsupported by impartial observation or data that is not reproducible);

- *post hoc* (after the fact) fallacies (because one thing follows another, it is held to cause the other);

- the fallacy of the appeal to authority (the argument rests upon the credentials of a person, not the evidence).

Despite the fact that some primary sources can contain false information or lead readers to false conclusions based on the "facts" presented, they remain an invaluable resource regarding past events. Primary sources allow readers and researchers to come as close as possible to understanding the perceptions and context of events and thus to more fully appreciate how and why misconceptions occur.

Glossary

A

ACT: A statute, rule, or formal lawmaking document enacted by a legislative body or issued by a government.

ADAPTATION: Adaptation to global climate change refers to projects and initiatives designed to reduce the vulnerability of agriculture, infrastructure, and other human and natural systems to the effects of global climate change.

ADDITIONALITY: The extent to which food aid reaches those who would not otherwise have access to food and to which additional food is not available in the targeted area and must come from the outside. Additionality refers both to the food deficit of a region or country and to the food deficit within a household.

ADOLESCENT: A person who has started puberty and continues to mature by experiencing a period of physical and psychological development. Also known as a transitional period of development between youth and maturity, this period usually starts at age 12 or 13 and lasts until 18 or 19 years of age. This time period is informally referred to as the teenage years.

ADULT-ONSET DIABETES: Also known as non-insulin-dependent or Type-2 diabetes, a form of diabetes that is often associated with obesity and often can be controlled by diet, exercise, and oral medication rather than daily injections of insulin.

AEROPONICS: A hydroponic method of growing plants in which a well-aerated root environment is maintained by enclosing the root zone in a container and pumping a steady mist of nutrient solution directly onto the roots.

AFICIONADO: An ardent follower, supporter, or enthusiast.

AGE OF DISCOVERY: A period from the late fifteenth through early seventeenth centuries, during which European maritime powers explored, mapped, and claimed previously unexplored parts of the world.

AGRARIAN: Rural, agricultural, or relating to the land. Also, a person who follows agrarianism.

AGRARIANISM: A philosophy that advocates rural living, agriculture, and equitable distribution of land.

AGRIBUSINESS: Any business involved at any point in the value chain in agriculture, livestock production, or the food industry. The term is also narrowly used as a synonym for corporate farming or industrial farming by opponents of large, corporate-run farms.

AGRICULTURAL COMMODITIES: Variable quantities of grain, livestock, poultry, fruit, timber, or other items produced from agricultural activities. Agricultural commodities are frequently traded on commodities exchanges.

AGRICULTURAL SUBSIDY: Financial assistance paid to farmers or agribusinesses by the government to supplement income or to affect the price of agricultural commodities.

AGRICULTURE: The production and management of crops and livestock, primarily for the production of food.

AGROECOLOGY: The study of how agricultural systems react with and integrate into the natural environment.

AGRONOMIST: A researcher who applies various agricultural sciences to improve soil management practices and improve crop production.

AGRONOMY: The science of cultivation of land, soil management, and crop production.

AGROTERRORISM: A subset of bioterrorism that involves the use of pathogens or pests to infect or destroy livestock or crops.

AID: Aid (also known as international aid, overseas aid, or foreign aid, especially in the United States) is a voluntary transfer of resources from one country to another, given with the objective of benefiting the recipient country.

ALEURONE: The thin layer just beneath the outside of a grain that is rich in proteins, oils, vitamins, minerals, and fiber. The aleurone layer is the outer layer of the endosperm.

ALGACULTURE: The branch of aquaculture that concerns the cultivation and harvesting of algae, the aquatic plant species. All forms of algae are produced through photosynthesis. Micro-algaculture involves the production of various types of plankton, the tiny organisms that are the foundation for virtually all aquatic organism food chains. Macro-algaculture products are more complex plant forms such as seaweed and kelp. Algae have a number of important commercial uses.

ALLERGEN: Any substance that causes an allergic reaction. Typically, various proteins are the most common food allergens.

ALLERGY: An abnormal immune reaction to an allergen introduced into the body by ingestion, inhalation, or contact with skin. The reaction produced, which can take many forms, is commonly known as an allergic reaction.

ALMS: Money or food given to the poor, typically by religious groups or by individuals for religious reasons.

AMYLOPHAGY: The consumption of uncooked starches, such as cornstarch, flour, or rice grains.

ANAPHYLAXIS: A severe, multi-system hypersensitivity reaction requiring immediate treatment to avert life-threatening symptoms such as vascular collapse, respiratory distress, and shock.

ANIMAL RIGHTS MOVEMENT: Individuals and groups concerned with protecting animals from perceived abuse or misuse. Supporters are specifically concerned with the use of animals for medical and cosmetics testing, the killing of animals for furs, hunting for pleasure, and the raising of livestock in restrictive or inhumane quarters.

ANOREXIA NERVOSA: An eating disorder in which the patient intentionally restricts eating to the point of near starvation with the purpose of weight loss and control over weight.

ANTHROPOGENIC: Being caused by, or coming from, human activities.

ANTHROPOPHAGY: Cannibalism; eating humans.

ANTIBODIES: Antibodies, or Y-shaped immunoglobulins, are proteins found in the blood that help to fight against foreign substances called antigens.

ANTIGENS: Antigens, which are usually proteins or polysaccharides, stimulate the immune system to produce antibodies. Antigens can be the source of infections from pathogenic bacteria and viruses. Organic molecules detrimental to the body from internal or environmental sources (such as allergens) also act as antigens.

ANTIOXIDANT: A substance that inhibits oxidization or slows the progress of oxidization. Biochemical reactions involving oxygen within the cells of the body produce substances called free radicals that can damage both genes and proteins. Over time, this free radical damage increases the likelihood of chronic diseases such as cancer and heart disease. Antioxidants are compounds that are thought to block free radical damage.

ANTISENSE TECHNOLOGY: The use of DNA to generate RNA molecules that bind to a target RNA and prevent it from being translated into protein.

AQUACULTURE: The process of raising fish, crustaceans, mollusks, and other aquatic plants and animals in confinement.

AQUAPONICS: A method for producing both fish and plant crops using the same water supply.

AQUIFER: An underground bed or layer of permeable rock, gravel, sand, silt, or clay that contains groundwater.

ARCHAEOBOTANY: Also known as paleoethnobotany, this is the identification and interpretation of plant remains from archaeological sites. Zooarchaeology is the related specialization that focuses on animal remains.

AROMATIC OIL: Plants used as herbs and spices synthesize oils with compounds that have distinctive aromas and flavors and result in aromatic oils. The aromatic oils are used not only in cuisine but also for medicinal purposes. Several natural essential oils may be combined to make aromatic oil, or plant material can be combined with oil to make an aromatic oil.

ARRONDISSEMENT: In France, an administrative division or compartment. The city of Paris is currently subdivided into 20 municipal arrondissements. There are also national departmental arrondissements, dividing France into 100 departments.

ARTISAN: One who is skilled in a particular trade that typically involves making products by hand using traditional methods.

ARTISANAL: Any product made by hand by an artisan or skilled craftsperson.

ARTISANAL FOOD: Handcrafted, often gourmet, food that is usually made from high-quality ingredients by traditional methods.

ASCETICISM: A way of life characterized by self-restraint, abstinence, and the rigorous self-denial of earthly pleasures, such as certain foods.

ASEPTIC: Free of agents that could cause disease.

ASSIMILATION: The process by which one ethnic group is absorbed by another, losing or altering unique cultural traits, customs, and attitudes, including those about food. Less pervasive changes associated with colonialism and migration are more accurately described as acculturation, with cultural groups remaining distinct but altering each other's cultures.

AUROCHS: Aurochs, or urus (*Bos primigenius*) is a species of wild cattle that existed across Eurasia and North Africa, from which modern cattle breeds were derived. Humans hunted wild aurochs into extinction, with a hunter killing the last known aurochs in Poland in 1627.

AUSTRALOPITHECINE: A member of the genus *Australopithecus*, australopithecines are the extinct ancestors and side branches of humans that lived 4 million to 1.4 million years ago in Africa, preceding the genus *Homo*.

AUTOTROPHS: Organisms that make their own food.

B

BAN: To prohibit something.

BARREL (OF OIL): The traditional unit of measure by which crude oil is bought and sold on the world market. One barrel of oil is equivalent to 42 U.S. gallons (159 liters).

BATTERY CAGES: An industrial, agricultural confinement system used primarily for egg-laying hens. The battery cage has generated conflict between industrial egg producers and advocates for animal welfare and animal rights due to the restrictions on movement these high-density cages impose on the hens.

BIG PHARMA: This refers to the largest multinational pharmaceutical companies, often reported in the media as having the financial ability to exert considerable influence on governments and other decision-making bodies.

BILE: A bitter, greenish fluid secreted by the liver and stored in the gall bladder that aids in the digestion of fats and oils in the body.

BINGE EATING: An eating disorder that is commonly described as continuously snacking or eating large amounts of food in a short period of time. To be considered binge eating disorder, a person must binge eat two times per week for at least six months.

BIOACCUMULATION: A progressive increase in the amount of a substance in an organism due to the inability of the organism to clear the substance from the body faster than it is accumulated.

BIOAVAILABILITY: The degree to which an ingested substance, including a vitamin or mineral, can be absorbed and used by the body. For instance, iron in meat is more bioavailable than iron in spinach, although both foods are rich in the mineral.

BIODIESEL: A biofuel produced from vegetable or other plant oils that is used to power diesel engines.

BIODIVERSITY: The number, variety, and variability of living organisms, including diversity within a species, between species, and among ecosystems. Agricultural biodiversity is particularly important for food security.

BIOFUEL: A fuel derived from biomass, which may be any living organism.

BIOMASS: Plant material, agricultural debris, or animal waste that is used as a fuel or energy source, most commonly by burning.

BIOPIRACY: Claiming patents for existing plant and animal species in order to restrict their use.

BIOTECHNOLOGY: The manipulation or use of organisms for industrial or agricultural purposes.

BIOTERRORISM: A form of terrorism that uses bacteria, viruses, or other organisms to attack people or disrupt societies.

BIOTOXIN: A toxin that is a component of, or is produced by, a living organism.

BIPEDALISM: The ability to walk upright on two feet.

BLACK CARBON: A pollutant emitted during the burning of biomass, coal, diesel, and other fossil fuels; a component of soot.

BLIGHT: A plant disease inflicted by a pathogen that causes the plant to brown, wither, and die.

BLOG: A weblog, or journal, maintained on an Internet website.

BLOOD ALCOHOL LEVEL (BAL) OR BLOOD ALCOHOL CONCENTRATION (BAC): The amount of alcohol present in the bloodstream, determined by the number of ounces of alcohol consumed per hour, the period of time in which drinking occurred, and gender and weight of the individual.

BLOOD PRESSURE: The pressure exerted by circulating blood upon the walls of the blood vessels. Blood pressure is measured in millimeters of mercury (mm Hg), and a reading is composed of two figures. The lower figure is the diastolic blood pressure, which corresponds to blood pressure in the resting phase of a heartbeat. The higher figure, the systolic blood pressure, is the blood pressure when the heart is actually contracting.

BLUE WATER: A term used to refer to all bodies of groundwater and surface waters together: rivers, lakes, and aquifers.

BODY MASS INDEX (BMI): A measurement of body fat based on a person's height and weight.

BOTULISM: A deadly form of food poisoning, botulism is caused by the bacterium *Clostridium botulinum*, which produces a potent nerve toxin. Spores of the bacterium can survive cooking. Although botulism has become rare, its most common cause in Europe is cured pork; in Japan it is salted fish; and in North America it is home-canned vegetables.

BOVINE SPONGIFORM ENCEPHALOPATHY (BSE): Also called mad cow disease. A fatal, slow-developing, prion disease affecting the nervous system of cattle. It is thought to cause a variant form of Creutzfeldt-Jakob disease (vCJD) in humans.

BRAN: The hard outer layers of a cereal grain, bran is high in fiber and also contains micronutrients.

BREMSTRAHLUNG: Electromagnetic energy given off by an electron that passes near a positively charged nucleus.

BRIGADE SYSTEM: A system of kitchen organization in which each person in the kitchen is assigned a specific station and task.

BROILER CHICKEN: A chicken intended for slaughter for food, the broiler chicken has been bred to have bigger thighs and breasts, as these are the most popular parts for consumption.

BROWNING: The color change that occurs when some foods are heated, progressing from yellow to brown, then black. The chemical reactions responsible for this color change produce new flavors. The dehydration of sugars in food, known as caramelization, and the reaction between proteins and sugars, called Maillard reactions, are the two main browning processes.

BROWNING AGENT: A chemical that causes food to turn brown to give it the appearance of having been cooked.

BUCKWHEAT: A grain prominent in the macrobiotic diet that is unusual in being a complete protein source, supplying all essential amino acids. Buckwheat also contains a compound called D-chito-inositol, which plays a role in insulin signaling and is deficient in some people with type 2 diabetes.

BULIMIA NERVOSA: An eating disorder in which the patient eats large volumes of food (binge eating) and later purges the food via forced vomiting, the use of diuretics and/or laxatives, and/or excessive exercise.

C

CALORIE: The energy value of different foods is measured in kilocalories (kcal) or calories. One kilocalorie is 1,000 calories, and one calorie is the amount of energy required to raise the temperature of one gram of water by one degree Celsius. When talking about diet and nutrition, the word calorie actually refers to a kilocalorie.

CANNING: A method of food preservation in which food is heat processed and sealed in a vessel.

CAPITALISM: An economic system in which private owners control the means of production and operate trade and industry for a profit.

CARBOHYDRATES: Molecules composed of carbon, hydrogen, and oxygen. For many animals carbohydrates are a primary source of energy, mainly in the form of starches and sugars. This term can also be used to refer to foods that are high in carbohydrates such as bread and grains.

CARBON FOOTPRINT: A measure of the amount of carbon dioxide released into the atmosphere by a single endeavor or by a company, household, or individual through day-to-day activities over a given period.

CARCINOGEN: A compound that increases the risk of cancer. Carcinogens found in food include nitrosamines, heterocyclic amines, and polycyclic aromatic hydrocarbons and acrylamide that occur in red meat or from cooking meat and other foods at high temperatures that produce charring.

CARRYING CAPACITY: The ability of an ecosystem to sustain a certain population of a species. The carrying capacity defines the maximum load of population the ecosystem can support without disrupting other species' populations.

CATALYST: A substance added to a chemical process that remains unchanged throughout, but which speeds up the rate of the reaction.

CELIAC DISEASE: Celiac (or coeliac) disease, also known as gluten-sensitive enteropathy or gluten intolerance, involves an autoimmune reaction to the gluten found in wheat and some other grains. It causes an acute inflammation of the lining of the small intestine that leaves the intestinal villi unable to absorb nutrients from food that passes through the digestive tract. Symptoms of celiac disease include chronic diarrhea, fatigue, and in infants, failure to thrive.

CELLULOID: A tough, highly flammable substance consisting essentially of cellulose nitrate and camphor, used in the manufacture of motion-picture and x ray film and other products.

CERTIFIED ORGANIC: In the United States, the states manage and regulate the use of the label "certified organic" and associated claims by supervising programs designed to give consumers confidence that products claimed to be organic meet certain standards.

CETACEAN: Any member of the marine mammal order Cetacea, including whales, dolphins, and porpoises.

CHEMOSYNTHETIC AUTOTROPH: An organism that uses carbon dioxide as a carbon source but obtains energy by oxidizing inorganic substances.

CHEMOTROPHS: Animals that make energy and produce food by breaking down inorganic molecules.

CHOLESTEROL: A waxy lipid found in animal foods and also produced in the body by the liver. Cholesterol is needed for essential bodily functions such as synthesis of cell membranes and hormones. Excess cholesterol may clog the arteries and lead to coronary heart disease and stroke.

CHROMOSOME: In higher plants and animals, discrete structural bodies composed of DNA, supporting histones, and proteins that exist in the cell nucleus and divide genetic material into entities and regions bearing specific genes.

CHUTNEY: A type of sauce originating from India with many different styles of preparation. Traditionally, a chutney is made by blending fruits, vegetables, spices, and oil.

CINEMA: The art or business of making films.

CISGENIC ORGANISM: A genetically modified organism that contains genetic sequences from the same, or closely related, species that have been spliced together in a different order.

CLOACA: The cavity into which the intestinal, genital, and urinary tracts open in vertebrates such as fish, reptiles, birds, and some primitive mammals.

CODEX ALIMENTARIUS: A collection of standards, guidelines, and codes of practices related to food production, hygiene, and food safety produced by the Food and Agriculture Organization (FAO) of the United Nations.

CODEX ALIMENTARIUS COMMISSION: Formed as a joint effort between the Food and Agriculture Organization (FAO) of the United Nations and the World Health Organization (WHO) in 1963, the Codex Alimentarius Commission works to supervise international cooperation for safe food practices across borders.

COEVOLUTION: The joint evolution of two different species, interacting with and changing each other in turn. Human societies and domesticated plants and animals evolved together, with human actions altering the other species, and the domesticated species in turn altering human cultures. Coevolution is generally seen as the unintentional consequence of long-term interactions.

COLLECTIVE AGRICULTURE: The organization of agricultural production wherein farmers jointly work on a large farm. Collective agriculture typically involves state ownership of the means of production, including the land.

COLLECTIVIZATION: The organization of the economy, or some sector thereof, on the basis of ownership by the people as represented by the state.

COLUMBIAN EXCHANGE: The products and ideas that were traded between the Americas and Europe as the result of Christopher Columbus' voyage to the Americas.

COMMENSALISM: A relationship involving two organisms, in which one organism benefits, and the other is not affected.

COMMENSALITY: The act of eating with other people.

COMMODITY: A uniform good about which it is difficult to make distinctions based on quality in the market. In agriculture, grains and oilseeds are often referred to as commodities, as are some meat and dairy products.

COMMON AGRICULTURAL POLICY (CAP): The European Economic Community (EEC) and then the European Union (EU) systems of agricultural subsidies, tariffs, and controls designed to create a single agricultural market without giving advantage to particular countries within the customs union are examples of common agricultural policies.

COMMON POOL RESOURCE (CPR): A resource that is open to use by many individuals. Pastures, fisheries, and irrigation systems can all be organized as common pool resources. Unlike a pure public good, additional users do have a cost. These users can negatively affect the resource, but unlike a public good, they can be excluded from using the resource.

xxxiii

COMPARATIVE ADVANTAGE: Efficiency in production of one good over another that makes trade possible even if one country lacks absolute efficiency in either good. Even if one country is more efficient at producing every product, it can gain from specializing in the products it is comparatively more efficient at producing. Then the country can move out of producing products in which it lacks comparative advantage and trade with other countries for those products.

COMPLETE PROTEINS: Protein sources that contain all eight amino acids in adequate amounts. Animal foods are complete proteins but many plant foods are not.

CONCENTRATED ANIMAL FEEDING OPERATION (CAFO): Agricultural facilities (or "factory farms") where a single facility confines a large number of animals. The animals, waste, and production are highly concentrated in a small area of land. Legally, in the United States, the Environmental Protection Agency (EPA) defines a CAFO as a farm that has at least 1,000 beef cattle, 700 dairy cows, 2,500 hogs, or 125,000 broiler chickens.

CONNECTIVE TISSUE: The tissue between muscle fibers in meat and between muscle tissues and other tissues, such as bone. Connective tissue is made up of three proteins—collagen, elastin, and reticulin—and contributes to the texture of cooked meat.

CONQUISTADOR: A conqueror, especially one of the sixteenth-century Spanish soldiers who defeated the indigenous civilizations of Mexico, Central America, or Peru.

CONSUMER ADVOCACY GROUP: An organization dedicated to protecting consumers from corporate abuses, including unsafe products and false advertising.

CONSUMER PRICE INDEX: A measure of price changes, or inflation, through the monitoring of the average price of a set basket of goods.

CONTAMINATION: The unwanted presence of a microorganism or compound in a particular environment. That environment can be in the laboratory setting, for example, in a medium being used for the growth of a species of bacteria during an experiment. Another environment can be the human body, where contamination by bacteria can produce an infection.

CONVENTION ON INTERNATIONAL TRADE IN ENDANGERED SPECIES (CITES): The Convention on International Trade in Endangered Species of Wild Fauna and Flora, often known as the CITES agreement, is a voluntary international agreement to restrict trade in animal or plant products from endangered or threatened species.

COOKING: The transfer of heat to a food by conduction, convention, or radiation. The heat brings about chemical reactions between food molecules that transform the food's texture and flavor.

COOKING SHOW: A type of food-related television programming dedicated to providing instruction to home cooks on food preparation.

COPING STRATEGY: A way in which a household seeks to avoid the negative consequences of a reduction in income, agricultural production, or livestock production.

CORN SYRUP: An aqueous solution composed of glucose chains of different lengths derived from the acidic or enzymatic breakdown of corn starch, a glucose polymer.

CORONARY HEART DISEASE: In atherosclerosis, which is the main cause of coronary heart disease, fatty material, including cholesterol, forms a deposit called plaque on the inner walls of the arteries. This causes them to narrow—slowing or even stopping the flow of blood to the heart.

COSMETICS: Products that by direct application to the skin, nails, lips, or hair of a person are intended to promote attractiveness by cleansing, enhancing, or otherwise altering one's appearance.

COTYLEDON: The seed leaves that form part of a seed, storing its food supplies. Most nuts and seeds consist of two swollen cotyledons packed with oil, protein, and other nutrients.

COUNTRY OF ORIGIN LABELING (COOL): Labeling on a food item that shows the country in which the product was farmed, grown, or raised.

CREOLE: Refers to both the people and the culture of French settlements in the Caribbean and Louisiana beginning in the fifteenth century.

CROP ROTATION: An agricultural practice that involves growing different crops in sequential seasons or letting fields lie fallow for a season in order to preserve soil fertility.

CROSS-CONTAMINATION: The movement of a pathogen or potentially dangerous or uncooked material from one surface to another. For example, if a cook uses the same knife to cut raw chicken and a tomato, the tomato may become cross-contaminated with a pathogen from the raw chicken.

CULTIVAR: A variety of a plant that has been created or selected intentionally and maintained through cultivation.

CURING: A method of food preservation involving salt, smoking, and dehydrating that works by drawing water out of the food so that bacteria are less likely to grow on it.

CURRY: A technique for making a stewed food dish common in India and South Asia that can be made with meat or vegetables with curry spices.

D

DEBEAKING: Also called beak trimming, this is the partial removal of the beak of poultry, especially chickens and turkeys. Most commonly, the beak is shortened permanently, although regrowth can occur. The term debeaking implies that the entire beak is removed during the trimming process, though in reality only half or less of the beak is generally removed. Debeaking is done in order to reduce instances of cannibalistic pecking among birds in dense populations, where such behavior is more common.

DECOLLECTIVIZATION: The process of moving from collective agriculture to private land ownership or removing state control over agriculture.

DECOLONIZATION: The process of transforming from a colony to an independent nation.

DECOMPOSITION: Breakdown of cells and tissues.

DEFICIENCY DISEASE: A disease caused by a lack of a specific nutrient, whether that nutrient is missing from the diet or is unable to be absorbed or metabolized by the body.

DEFORESTATION: The clearing of forest cover through human activity.

DENTAL CARIES: The condition when the enamel or outermost surface of a tooth is eroded or damaged to the point at which food particles and bacteria can pass through the protective enamel covering and into the living tissue of the tooth where blood vessels are stored. Signs that a person may have caries include sensitivity or pain to foods that are cold, hot, sour, or sweet.

DESERTIFICATION: The degradation of fertile, habitable land, typically semi-arid dryland, into arid desert, usually due to climate change or misuse of the land. Desertification is identified as a main barrier to food security and sustainable livelihoods.

DETRITUS: Dead organic matter.

DIABETES: Diabetes mellitus is a disease of glucose metabolism that is defined by blood glucose levels. There are three types of diabetes: insulin dependent diabetes mellitus, IDDM (type 1), non-insulin dependent diabetes mellitus, NIDDM (type 2), and gestational diabetes (onset occurs in women during pregnancy).

DIET: The word *diet* really has two meanings. It can mean simply what a person happens to eat, and diets are influenced by many factors, such as access to food, culture, personal preferences, and beliefs. Diet can also mean eating with a certain goal in mind, such as a reducing food intake to lose weight.

DIETARY GUIDELINES FOR AMERICANS: The *Dietary Guidelines for Americans* contains science-based, nutritional advice for Americans and outlines the U.S. government's nutrition policy and education initiatives. The U.S. Department of Agriculture (USDA) and U.S. Department of Health and Human Services (HHS) jointly publish the *Dietary Guidelines for Americans* every five years.

DIETARY REFERENCE INTAKES (DRIS): Developed by the Institute of Medicine of the National Academy of Sciences, Dietary Reference Intakes (DRIs) are intended to plan and assess nutrient intake for healthy people. DRIs include the recommended daily allowance (RDA) and also the tolerable upper intake level (UL), which is the maximum daily intake unlikely to result in adverse health effects. DRIs are intended to plan and assess nutrient intake for healthy people.

DIETARY SUPPLEMENT: A product, such as a vitamin, mineral, or herb, that is intended to be consumed in addition to the regular diet in the expectation that it will improve health.

DIETARY TABOO: A prohibition of a food or a type of food preparation.

DIGESTION: The physical and chemical processes that transform the food a person eats into nutrients that the body can use.

DIOXINS: A group of highly toxic, carcinogenic compounds produced during the manufacturing process of various substances, such as herbicides.

DIRECT FOOD AID: The provision of food or rations of food to individuals. Direct food aid can also include providing the infrastructure for delivering and distributing food aid.

DISASTER RECOVERY: Distinct from disaster management, disaster recovery encompasses the processes, policies, and procedures related to preparing for recovery or continuation of technology infrastructure critical to an organization after a natural or human-induced disaster.

DISEASE SURVEILLANCE: Routine monitoring of important diseases conducted by state health departments. Salmonellosis and *E. coli* 0157:H7 bacteria are foodborne illnesses subject to surveillance.

DISPARAGEMENT: A communication that belittles, undermines, or damages the reputation of someone or something.

DOCUMENTARY: A factual film or television program about an event, person, etc., presenting the facts with little or no fiction.

DOMESTICATION: The process by which humans selectively alter plant and animal species, resulting in new varieties or new species with different behaviors and physical characteristics. This may done consciously, through controlled breeding, or through repeated interactions with unintended consequences in a coevolutionary fashion. Domesticates rely on humans to reproduce themselves; without human aid they will go extinct or revert back to wild forms.

DRY NURSING: The term for the practice common in the 1800s and 1900s of feeding of infants, via spoon, finger, or bottle, any mixture of animal milk and other foods as a substitute for breast milk.

DRYLAND: Arid desert or semi-arid xeric shrubland biomes.

DUMPING: Food aid that consists of free, subsidized, or below market price food, which undercuts local farmers and can lead to the destruction of local farming and economies and to an ongoing cycle of poverty and hunger.

DYSPHAGIA: Dysphagia refers to experiencing difficulty swallowing.

E

E. COLI: *Escherichia coli* is a form of bacteria found in the lower intestine of humans and many warm-blooded animals. Many *E. coli* forms are harmless; the *E. coli* strain O157:H7 is associated with food poisoning, and its presence has precipitated numerous food product recalls in North America and Europe.

EATING DISORDERS: Eating disorders include anorexia nervosa, bulimia nervosa, and binge eating. Individuals suffering from bulimia and anorexia exhibit excessive control over their body weight by controlling their food intake. Anorexia nervosa and bulimia nervosa are disorders that are more prevalent among young women in industrialized countries where food exists in abundance yet there is pressure to diet and to achieve a perceived ideal, thin body.

EATING HABITS: Describes what foods people eat, why and how people eat, and with whom they eat. Individual, social, cultural, religious, economic, and environmental factors can influence people's eating habits. Acceptable and learned eating behaviors can vary by cultural group and are reflected in a person's meal and snack patterns, portion sizes, and food combinations.

ECONOMIC STATECRAFT: The use of economic power by one country to influence how other countries behave.

ECONOMY OF SCALE: A reduction in the cost of the production of a product attained by producing more. Economies of scale also refer to cost reductions accrued by geographic concentration of an industry.

EDIBLE: The ability to be eaten or used as a source of nutrients.

ELECTROLYTES: Compounds that ionize in a solution; electrolytes dissolved in the blood play an important role in maintaining the proper functioning of the body.

ELECTROMAGNETIC RADIATION: A phenomenon consisting of oscillating magnetic and electric waves existing at right angles to each other. Waves with shorter wavelengths (higher frequencies) have higher energies.

ELECTRON BEAM: A focused stream of electrons emitted from the hot filament of an electron gun.

EMERGENCY RELIEF: The aspect of humanitarian assistance that seeks to directly preserve life, health, and safety and directly protect livelihoods and dignity during a crisis.

EMULSIFIER: A chemical used to suspend oils in water.

ENCEPHALOPATHY: A disorder or disease of the brain.

ENDOCANNIBALISM: Eating people from within one's own group, usually as part of a religious rite involving dead ancestors. In contrast, exocannibalism is defined by eating outsiders, usually the enemies of the one's group.

ENDOCRINE SYSTEM: A system comprising glands that secrete specific hormones into the bloodstream to regulate body functions.

ENDOSPERM: The central and largest portion of a grain, filled with starch granules embedded in a protein matrix.

ENGEL'S LAW: As a household's income increases, it will spend a lower percentage of income on food though its actual food expenditures may increase. The increase in spending is due to a shift in the diet away from grains to more expensive foods such as meats, dairy products, fruits, and vegetables. Engel's Law is named after Ernst Engel (1821–1896), the German economist and statistician who first noted the tendency.

ENTERAL NUTRITION: Feeding through a tube that goes in through the nose and down to the stomach. Long-term enteral nutrition may involve a gastrostomy tube being inserted into the stomach through an incision in the abdomen.

ENTERIC: Involving the intestinal tract or relating to the intestines.

ENTEROTOXIN: Enterotoxin and exotoxin are two classes of toxin that are produced by bacteria.

ENTITLEMENT PROGRAM: A program that uses government resources to provide assistance to needy families.

ENTITLEMENTS APPROACH: An approach to understanding famine, hunger, malnutrition, and poverty based on understanding how a population acquires food and on what resources a population has available to acquire food. Pioneered by Amartya Sen, the approach looks at the right to food and other goods and to changes in exchange conditions to explain sudden deprivation events such as a famine.

ENVIRONMENTAL LITERACY: Basic knowledge of environmental connections, ecology, and the environmental issues that are important in the early twenty-first century.

ENZYME: Proteins found in living cells that act as catalysts for chemical reactions, including digestion. Some raw food advocates argue that cooking kills the enzymes found in freshly harvested foods that are beneficial to human health.

EPHEDRA: An herbal supplement, derived from the plant *Ephedra sinica*, which is a stimulant that may increase blood pressure and heart rate. Ephedra-containing supplements were banned in the United States in 2004.

EPOXY RESINS: Short chain polymers or monomers formed by the reaction of bisphenol A (or other compounds) and epichlorohydrin. When mixed with a hardener, the resin forms a very tough epoxy copolymer.

ESSENTIAL AMINO ACIDS: All the proteins in the body are made from 20 different amino acid building blocks. Humans can synthesize 12 of these but eight need to be obtained from the diet. These eight are known as essential amino acids.

ESSENTIAL OIL: A concentrated liquid containing volatile aromatic compounds extracted from plants.

ESTROGENIC: Having an effect similar to that of the female sex hormone estrogen.

ETHANOL: A term often used to refer to bioethanol, a type of ethanol (ethyl alcohol) derived from plants and used as a fuel.

ETHNOBIOLOGY: The study of the interrelations between people and the plants and animals in their environment, including cultural classifications and perceptions of other species, as well as traditional ecological knowledge and the utilization of plants and animals. Researchers may specialize in ethnobotany or ethnozoology.

ETHNOECOLOGY: The study of how people, agriculture, economics, and the environment interact with an emphasis on culture.

EUTROPHICATION: The depletion in water of oxygen available for fish and other animals resulting from the rapid growth of algae and other organisms in the presence of excess nutrients in the water system.

EVAPO-TRANSPIRATION: Loss of water through both evaporation from the surface and the transpiration of moisture from the aboveground parts of plants.

EVIDENCE-BASED: Using scientific method and research studies to determine the best practice in a specific discipline.

EXISTENTIALIST: A philosopher who argues existential philosophical principles, typically (but with many variations) emphasizing the uniqueness of the individual and the isolation of the individual imposed by mortal existence in an indifferent natural world. The philosophy stresses freedom of individual choice and responsibility for personal actions.

EXOCANNIBALISM: Exocannibalism is defined by eating outsiders, usually the enemies of the one's group.

EXPERIENTIAL LEARNING: A form of education that emphasizes learning by doing, or through direct experience.

EXTERNALITY: Something external to a production process for which the producer does not pay or get paid. An externality can be negative, such as pollution for which a producer incurs no cost. It can also be positive, such as bees from one farm pollinating other farms' crops in an area for free. Externalities are external to the accounting and decision making process of the producer.

EXTINCTION: The state or process of a species or larger taxonomic group ceasing to exist.

EXTRA VIRGIN OLIVE OIL: Olive oil derived from the first press of the olives and not chemically processed.

F

FAD DIET: A specific food regimen, typically restricted to no more than five foods or to one food group, designed to create extreme, short-term weight loss.

FAIR TRADE: A process that incorporates equitable distribution of profit, environmental and ecological consequences, human rights, and cultural issues into capitalist markets. In the late twentieth century, advocacy groups pushed for fair trade in the coffee industry.

FALAFEL: Ground chickpeas formed into a ball or patty and fried, sometimes served in a pita sandwich.

FAMILY FARM: Defined by the U.S. Department of Agriculture (USDA) as any farm organized as a sole proprietorship, partnership, or family corporation. The definition excludes co-operatives and farms with hired managers.

FAMINE: A generalized and extreme scarcity of food, prolonged extreme hunger, undernourishment, or lack of food.

FARM BILL: A comprehensive omnibus bill adopted by the United States Congress that sets the agricultural and food policy of the United States.

FARMER'S MARKET: A local, decentralized produce market in which farmers sell directly to the public, without the middleman of produce brokers or grocery stores.

FARM-TO-SCHOOL PROGRAMS: Local partnerships that public school districts, or individual schools, can form with area farmers to deliver agricultural and nutritional curricula to students while serving local produce and crops. These programs often include field trips to farms, cooking classes that incorporate local crops, and unit studies on nutritional composition and growing conditions for local foods.

FAST FOOD: Food that can be prepared and served rapidly, usually involving precooked or preheated ingredients. Fast food is usually taken away, rather than eaten where it is prepared.

FAT: A type of lipid or chemical compound used as a source of energy, to provide insulation, and to protect organs in an animal body.

FATTY ACIDS: A group of organic chemicals consisting of a carbon backbone linked to a carboxylic acid group. The length of the carbon backbone varies. The simplest fatty acid is acetic acid, the main ingredient in vinegar, which has a backbone consisting of just one carbon atom, bonded to three hydrogen atoms. Naturally occurring fatty acids have carbon backbones containing up to 35 carbon atoms.

FEAST: A large and usually elaborate banquet, often prepared for many people, and often in recognition of a celebratory event or religious occasion.

FECAL-ORAL ROUTE: The transmission of minute particles of fecal material from one organism (human or animal) to the mouth of another organism.

FERMENTATION: Biological process performed by many microorganisms in which sugars are converted to carbon dioxide and alcohol.

FERTILIZERS: Fertilizers are soil amendments applied to promote plant growth and are usually directly applied to soil and also sprayed on leaves.

FIBER: Fiber is not always defined as a nutrient because it is not digested. Yet it plays a useful role in maintaining good bowel function. Diets high in fiber may also protect against diabetes and certain types of cancer.

FIXED MENU: A style of restaurant service in which instead of having a list of dishes from which the diner can choose, there is only one list of courses that every diner receives.

FLORA: In microbiology, flora refers to the collective microorganisms that normally inhabit an organism or system. Human intestines, for example, contain bacteria that aid in digestion and are considered normal flora.

FOIE GRAS: A traditional French product, the name of which in English means "fat liver." It is the liver of overfed ducks or geese and contains about 65 percent fat. Foie gras production is banned in some countries because the method of overfeeding the animals is considered inhumane.

FOOD ADDITIVE: A substance, not normally consumed by itself, that is added to a food product to increase shelf life, appearance, or taste.

FOOD AID: Emergency food aid is distributed to victims of natural or human-made disasters. It is freely distributed to targeted beneficiary groups and usually provided on a grant basis. Food aid is channeled multilaterally, through nongovernmental organizations (NGOs), or sometimes bilaterally, given by one country directly to another.

FOOD ALLERGY: An allergy is an adverse reaction to a substance called an allergen that is usually harmless. In food allergy, the allergen is contained in one or more foodstuffs. Allergic reactions always involve the allergen triggering a response from the immune system.

FOOD ALLIANCE CERTIFICATION: A comprehensive certification program for sustainably-produced food in North America.

FOOD ASSISTANCE: Any intervention to address hunger and undernutrition (e.g., food stamps, WIC, food subsidies, food price stabilization, etc.). It is distinct from food aid in that it is not related to international sourcing of resources tied to the provision of food, whether by a donor or to a recipient.

FOOD BANK: An organization that stores and distributes food to the hungry.

FOOD CO-OP: A member-owned and run grocery store.

FOOD CRITIC: A person who writes reviews of dining experiences at restaurants for publication in newspapers, magazines, or on the Internet.

FOOD EMULSIFIERS: Emulsifiers are chemicals that facilitate the complete mixture of substances that naturally separate when they are added one to another, such as oil and water.

FOOD GUIDE: A book or website that contains information on restaurants, often including restaurant ratings.

FOOD INSECURITY: A situation that exists when people lack secure access to sufficient amounts of safe and nutritious food for normal growth and development and an active and healthy life. It may be caused by the unavailability of food, insufficient purchasing power, inappropriate distribution, or inadequate use of food at the household level.

FOOD INTOLERANCE: An adverse reaction to food that does not involve the immune system.

FOOD JUSTICE: The concept that society should arrange its relationships so everyone can have sufficient food.

FOOD MILES: The distance that food products or the raw ingredients used in food travel between the farm gate and the final producer. Food miles are used as a comparative measure of the environmental impact of transportation in the food industry.

FOOD PRESERVATION: Techniques of food handling, processing, or packaging that slow down the decomposition of the food.

FOOD QUALITY PROTECTION ACT OF 1996: Also known as the FQPA, this act changed the way the Environmental Protection Agency (EPA) regulates pesticides and set stricter standards for acceptable exposure levels for infants and children.

FOOD RECALLS: In a recall, the Food Safety and Inspection Service (FSIS), a Food and Drug Administration (FDA) agency, asks the public to return products from a specific batch produced by a manufacturer or farm, for reasons such as contamination by foodborne illness. Most FSIS-originated recalls involve voluntary recalls, in which the manufacturer works proactively with government agencies to remove a product from shelves and to educate consumers to return or destroy defective products.

FOOD SAFETY MODERNIZATION ACT (FSMA): Passed by the U.S. House of Representatives in 2009, FSMA authorizes the Food and Drug Administration (FDA) to order the recall of any contaminated foods commercially available in the United States.

FOOD SECURITY: Access to sufficient, safe, and nutritious food to meet dietary needs and food preferences for an active and healthy life.

FOOD SOVEREIGNTY: The right of peoples and sovereign states to determine democratically their own agricultural and food policies.

FOOD STAMPS: A form of government assistance to low-income citizens that enables the recipient to acquire food from grocery stores, markets, or other locations.

FOOD WASTE: Food that is not consumed, from domestic and commercial food scraps not eaten at the table to harvested foods rotting before they are delivered and everything in between.

FOODBORNE ILLNESS: An illness caused by the consumption of contaminated food that has usually been improperly stored, handled, or prepared.

FOODIE: A person who follows food fads and trends for interest or entertainment.

FOODS FOR SPECIFIED HEALTH USE (FOSHU): A legal term in Japan used to regulate the health claims made by functional foods. FOSHU producers can receive a seal and verification of their health claims from the Japanese government.

FOODSHED: A foodshed is defined by the area within which one's food is produced, as a watershed defines where water drains. Modern foodsheds may be global in scale, but locavores' foodsheds are much smaller and regionally restricted.

FOODWAYS: Customs and traditions that accompany the production, selection, preparation, consumption, and culture of food.

FOUR BASIC FOOD GROUPS: The four basic food groups were part of nutrition education in the United States from the 1950s until the development of the Improved American Food Guide Pyramid. These groups were meats (including poultry, eggs, nuts, and legumes), dairy, fruits and vegetables, and grains.

FOWL: Often used to describe birds in general, but more accurately applies to the orders Galliformes, which includes chickens, turkeys, pheasants, partridges and quail, and Anseriformes, which includes waterfowl such as ducks and geese.

FRANCHISE: Many restaurants and other outlets serving fast food are franchises, or branches, of a chain in which the food is delivered from a central location and is standardized.

FREE AND REDUCED PRICE LUNCH: Students from families with incomes below 130 percent of the federal poverty line generally qualify for free school lunches through the National School Lunch Program (NSLP), with the fee for lunch reduced for children from families earning between 131 percent and 185 percent of the federal poverty line, per United States Department of Agriculture Guidelines.

FREE RANGE: A food-source animal that is permitted to pasture graze for food rather than being confined to a feed house or feed lot.

FUNCTIONAL FOODS: Also known as nutraceuticals, functional foods are foods, beverages, or nutritional supplements that contain additives with purported medicinal or health benefits.

FUNGIBLE: The condition of one unit of a commodity being absolutely identical to another unit of a commodity and thus being a perfect substitute.

FUSION CUISINE: Food that contains combinations of traditions, techniques, and ingredients of varying cultures.

G

GAMMA RAYS: Electromagnetic radiation of wavelengths from about 0.003 to 0.03 nanometers.

GASTROENTERITIS: Gastroenteritis is an inflammation of the stomach and the intestines. More commonly, gastroenteritis is called the stomach flu.

GENDER MAINSTREAMING: The incorporation into organizations, development programs, and research of concern and understanding about how women and men work, live, and earn money differently.

GENE: A loosely defined term describing a DNA sequence that contains a discrete coding unit for a single protein or RNA molecule.

GENETIC ENGINEERING: General term for using a wide variety of techniques to introduce specific changes in an organism's DNA.

GENETICALLY MODIFIED (GM) FOODS: Foods derived from genetically modified organisms that have had changes introduced into their DNA by techniques in genetic engineering to introduce a new trait that does not occur naturally in the species.

GENETICALLY MODIFIED ORGANISM (GMO): Any living organism, including plants, animals, and bacteria, in which the genetic material has been altered so the organism expresses desired traits.

GENOCIDE: According to the United Nations (UN) Convention on Genocide of 1948, "any of the following acts committed with intent to destroy, in whole or in part, a national, ethnical, racial or religious group, as such: killing members of the group, causing serious bodily or mental harm to members of the group, deliberately inflicting on the group conditions of life calculated to bring about its physical destruction in whole or in part, imposing measures intended to prevent births within the group; forcibly transferring children of the group to another group."

GENOME: The total genetic material contained in a single cell of an organism.

GENRE: A class or category of artistic endeavor having a particular form, content, technique, or the like: the genre of epic poetry; the genre of symphonic music.

GEOPHAGY: Also known as geophagia or geophagism, this is the consumption of substances taken from the earth, such as dirt, clay, and ground stone. Certain types of smooth clay, such as kaolin or "white dirt," are often preferred. In some parts of the world, clay that has been processed for eating is sold at markets and convenience stores.

GERMPLASM: Genetic material, especially in a form that that can be used to reproduce an organism. Seeds, tubers, cuttings, breeding colonies of living animals, and frozen sperm and embryos are all types of germplasm.

GESTATION CRATE: A metal pen typically two feet wide and seven feet long in which a pregnant sow is kept during its four-month gestation period. The use of these enclosures is controversial because they often do not include any kind of bedding material, and the cramped conditions within the pen do not allow the animal to turn around or even to lie down comfortably. Most sows in factory farms are kept in a lifelong state of impregnation and birth and will therefore spend most of their lives in these crates.

GINGIVITIS: A mild form of periodontal or gum disease that causes inflammation or swelling of the gums. If a person's gums bleed when being brushed, gingivitis is a likely cause. Daily brushing and flossing of the teeth can help to prevent this disease.

GLOBALIZATION: The integration of national and local systems into a global economy through increased trade, manufacturing, communications, and migration.

GLUCOSE: A type of sugar that serves as the body's fuel. Other sugars include sucrose (or table sugar), lactose, and fructose.

GLUTEN: Elastic protein molecules specific to certain cereal grains. It is found in high concentrations in wheat and in smaller concentrations in barley and rye.

GOITER: A swelling of the thyroid gland, located in the neck, that is caused primarily by iodine deficiency.

GOLDEN RICE: A variety of rice that has been genetically modified to contain beta carotene using genes from corn.

GOURMET: A connoisseur of fine food and drink.

GRAIN: The edible part of a cereal grass plant. A grain is a whole fruit, containing a seed and a thin, dry layer of ovary tissue.

GRAM CALORIE: The small calorie; the amount of heat energy necessary to raise the temperature of one gram of water by one degree Celsius.

GREEN COFFEE: The dried berries from the coffee bush. Green coffee has a long shelf life, and beans are sold in large volume as green coffee. Leaving the beans in their green state prolongs the life of the berries. Coffee cannot be brewed until the green coffee beans are roasted and ground.

GREEN CONSUMER: A consumer who puts the environment at the top of his or her shopping list by buying products made from natural ingredients that cause minimal or no environmental damage. The term was made popular by a book called *The Green Consumer Guide* written by sustainability pioneers Julia Hailes (1961–) and John Elkington (1949–) in 1987.

GREEN WATER: A term used to refer to rainwater.

GREENHOUSE EFFECT: A process by which atmospheric greenhouse gases absorb radiation from the Earth's surface and reemit the radiation—some of which returns to the surface—instead of allowing the radiation to escape into space. The greenhouse effect results in an increase of the Earth's surface temperature.

GREENHOUSE GAS: A greenhouse gas (GHG) is any gas that contributes to the greenhouse effect by absorbing and emitting radiation within the thermal infrared range. Carbon dioxide, methane, ozone, nitrous oxide, and water vapor are the most common greenhouse gases.

GROUNDWATER: Water that exists underground in aquifers, streams, soil, or rock.

GUSTATORY: Relating to the sense of taste.

H

HABILINE: An early human ancestor in the genus *Homo*, particularly *Homo habilis* but also including such fossil species as *Homo rudolfensis, Homo georgicus*, and some transitional forms of australopithecines. Habilines evolved into *Homo ergaster* and

Homo erectus and several other species during the Pleistocene, including Neanderthals.

HALAL: Foods that adhere to Islamic dietary laws.

HALVAH: A Middle Eastern and Mediterranean confection made by grinding almonds into a sweet paste and combining them with other ingredients and flavorings.

HARMONIZATION OF FOOD STANDARDS: Harmonization occurs when all member nations adopt the same standards to the same degree.

HAZARD ANALYSIS AND CRITICAL CONTROL POINT (HACCP): According to the Food and Drug Administration (FDA), HACCP is a "management system in which food safety is addressed through the analysis and control of biological, chemical, and physical hazards from raw material production, procurement and handling, to manufacturing, distribution and consumption of the finished product."

HEAT: A form of energy that makes molecules travel faster. When heat is transferred to a food, it causes physical and chemical changes that transform the food into a palatable dish.

HEIFER: A young female cow that has not yet given birth to its first calf.

HEIRLOOM: A variety of plant or breed of animal that has not been subjected to industrialized modification. Heirloom chickens, for example, include mostly free-range breeds that are slow-growing, as opposed to the fast-growing chickens that are used in conventional poultry operations.

HEIRLOOM VARIETY: A particular cultivar of plant that was previously grown in agriculture, but experienced decreased cultivation with the rise of industrialized agriculture.

HERB: A plant with aromatic leaves, seeds, or flowers that are used, fresh or dried, to flavor food, scent perfume, or as an ingredient in medicine.

HERITAGE BREED: Traditional, genetically distinct livestock and poultry breeds that were raised by farmers in the past before the reduction of breed variety caused by industrial agriculture.

HETEROCYCLIC AMINES (HCAs): Potentially cancer-causing compounds that are formed on meat when it is charred or cooked at high temperatures.

HETEROTROPHS: Organisms that do not make their own food.

HIERARCHICAL SOCIETIES: Social groups characterized by an inherited political hierarchy (ruled by few, with many agricultural producers below), and different levels of social inequality. In anthropology, complex chiefdoms, states, and empires are classified as hierarchical societies. More egalitarian societies may be organized into tribes or bands.

HIGH-FRUCTOSE CORN SYRUP (HFCs): High-fructose corn syrup is a sweetener and preservative that is commonly used in baked goods, soda, dairy treats, and many other processed foods. It is made by converting the glucose in corn starch to fructose, and then adding more glucose.

HILUM: The small pore in the center of the curved edge of a bean that allows water in during soaking to make a dried bean edible

HOLISTIC DEVELOPMENT: Sometimes used interchangeably with sustainable development, holistic approaches involve agroecology and development that does not compromise future generations or cause environmental damage.

HOLOCENE: The current geological epoch, which began approximately 12,000 years ago.

HOMININ: A taxonomic term used to describe humans, their ancestors, and closely related species, including all members of the genera *Homo* and *Australopithecus*. Hominid, which anthropologists previously used to describe humans and their ancestors, now includes chimpanzees and gorillas as part of the family Hominidae.

HOMOGENIZATION: Milk is an emulsion of fat in water, and if left standing will separate into two layers. Homogenization involves passing the milk through a fine nozzle, which breaks up its fat globules into smaller particles that form a uniform liquid with the watery component of milk.

HORIZONTAL INTEGRATION: Controlling a single step or stage of a value chain.

HOST: Organism that serves as the habitat for a parasite, or possibly for a symbiont. A host may provide nutrition to the parasite or symbiont or simply a place in which to live.

HUMAN TRAFFICKING: To move a person, often from one country to another, for the purpose of exploiting that person.

HUNGER: No internationally recognized legal definition of hunger exists. However, it is widely accepted that it goes beyond a minimum calorie intake sufficient to prevent death by starvation. The term "starvation" refers to the most extreme form of hunger; death by starvation is the end result of a chronic, long-lasting, and severe period of hunger.

HUNTER-GATHERERS: People whose subsistence depends on hunting and gathering or foraging for their food. In the Paleolithic period, all humans were hunter-gatherers, but in the early twenty-first century most of the world's population eats an agriculturally based diet.

HYDROCARBON: A chemical containing only carbon and hydrogen.

HYDROGENATED FAT: The fatty acids in fats and oils may contain carbon-carbon double bonds that are capable of reacting with hydrogen. The hydrogenation of a fat, as in the manufacture of margarine, increases the degree of saturation of a fat.

HYDROLOGIC CYCLE: The hydrologic cycle, or water cycle, is the cycle in which water circulates between the earth's oceans, atmosphere, and land. During the hydrologic cycle water falls to the surface as precipitation, flows as runoff into streams and rivers, and returns to the atmosphere via evaporation and transpiration.

HYGIENE: Actions that help maximize health, particularly by controlling the growth of bacteria on surfaces.

HYPERTENSION: Long-term elevation of blood pressure defined by two readings, systolic and diastolic blood pressure, that are above the normal of 140 and 90 mm Hg, respectively. Hypertension risks damage to the blood vessels and complications including stroke, heart attack, and kidney failure.

I

ICSR NUMBER: The Reportable Food Registry issues Individual Case Safety Report (ICSR) numbers when a responsible party inputs a reportable food to the registry. Responsible parties and the Food and Drug Administration (FDA) then use this number to track developments in the case.

IDEOLOGY: A system of knowledge, myths, and beliefs guiding the behavior of a group.

IMMUNOGLOBULIN: Globulins are a type of protein found in blood. The immunoglobulins (also called immune globulins) are Y-shaped globulins that act as antibodies, attaching themselves to invasive cells or materials in the body so that they can be identified and attacked by the immune system. There are five immunoglobulins, designated IgM, IgG, IgA, IgD, and IgE.

IMPROVED AMERICAN FOOD GUIDE PYRAMID: The formal name for the food pyramid, the Improved American Food Guide Pyramid, was introduced by the U.S. Department of Agriculture (USDA) in 1992.

INACTIVATED VIRUS: Inactivated virus is incapable of causing disease but still stimulates the immune system to respond by forming antibodies.

INDEPENDENT CONTRACTOR: A person who contracts do a specified project or type of work for another person using his or her own resources and processes to accomplish the work; an independent worker rather than an employee.

INDIGENOUS: Native. The definition of indigenous peoples varies across the world, but usually refers to those whose ancestors were born in a particular area and who retain traditional knowledge of their environment and culture (including food). Indigenous peoples may be also be described as ethnic groups, and aboriginal, tribal, or First Peoples.

IN-KIND DONATIONS: Donations that are made in goods and services rather than money (or cash).

INSTITUTE OF MEDICINE: Founded in 1970, the Institute of Medicine is non-governmental organization established under the U.S. National Academy of Sciences that advises the government and policymakers on issues related to medicine and health.

INSULIN: A hormone produced by the pancreas after eating that carries glucose in the blood to muscle, liver, and fat cells after a meal. Too much insulin makes blood glucose levels too low, whereas insufficient insulin results in high blood sugar that is stored as excess glucose. The right amount of insulin is needed to keep blood glucose levels under control.

INTEGRATED PEST MANAGEMENT (IPM): A pest-management technique that involves balancing the need to increase crop yield and protect crops from damage with the desire to protect the environment and cause the least damage. Rather than never using pesticides, or always spraying regardless of need, IPM seeks a middle ground to reduce the pesticide load as much as possible.

INTELLECTUAL PROPERTY RIGHTS (IPR): Rights to produce or reproduce intangible property such as music, written words, ideas, or processes that are protected through patents, copyrights, and other means. In agriculture, recent disputes in IPR include controversies surrounding patenting genes or seeds in biotechnology and the effort to grant IPR to indigenous or traditional knowledge.

INTENSIVE PLANTING: Planting seeds more densely than traditional methods to increase yields.

INTERGENERATIONAL EQUITY: The principle that the actions of one generation must take into account their impact on subsequent generations, and that some resources must be preserved for use by future generations.

INTERNATIONAL COFFEE ORGANIZATION (ICO): Founded in 1963, the ICO works to coordinate coffee trade worldwide and to set industry standards for farmers, middlemen, and large manufacturers. The ICO has a loose association with the United Nations (UN).

INTERNATIONAL MONETARY FUND (IMF): An international non-governmental organization that supervises the global financial system with the objectives of stabilizing exchange rates and facilitating economic development through liberal economic policies.

INTESTINAL MOTILITY: Intestinal motility refers to the movement of smooth muscles in the small and large intestines that aids in mixing, digestion, absorption, and movement of foodstuffs.

INTOXICATION: The point at which the amount of alcohol consumed causes impaired judgment, behavior, and decision-making.

IODINE: A chemical element required by the thyroid gland in the body to produce thyroid hormone. Iodine is commonly added to table salt to help prevent goiter development.

IRRIGATION: The agricultural practice of artificially supplying land with water, usually for the purpose of growing crops.

I-TAL: The Rastafarian food code, which specifies that foods should be eaten unprocessed, whole (uncooked and unchanged), or minimally cooked.

J

JAUNDICE: Jaundice is a condition in which a person's skin and the sclera (whites of the eyes) are discolored a shade of yellow due to an increased level of bile pigments in the blood resulting from liver disease. Jaundice is sometimes called *icterus,* from a Greek word for the condition.

K

KASHRUT (KOSHER): Jewish dietary laws.

KILOGRAM CALORIE: The heat energy necessary to increase the temperature of one kilogram of water by one degree Celsius.

KNEADING: The process of rolling dough made from wheat flour to develop and align the gluten molecules.

KOSHER: Foods that adhere to Jewish dietary laws.

KURU: An incurable, degenerative type of transmissable spongiform encephalopathy (TSE), a fatal brain disease transmitted by infection with prions (abnormal protein particles). Kuru is found in New Guinea and was mainly contracted by the Fore people during endocannibalistic funeral rituals. A gene protecting its carriers from kuru (and possibly other TSE diseases) has been discovered among the Fore.

L

LA LECHE LEAGUE INTERNATIONAL: Founded in 1956 in Franklin Park, Illinois, at a time when breastfeeding rates were close to 20 percent in the United States, La Leche League International supports on-demand breastfeeding for mother and child pairs, with monthly meetings for women seeking breastfeeding support in 68 countries.

LABOR UNION: An organization of workers formed to negotiate terms of employment with employers.

LACTASE: An enzyme that hydrolyzes lactose. It is found in the intestines of most young mammals.

LACTOSE: The sugar in milk, lactose, is not found in any other food. It is a disaccharide made up of glucose and galactose and requires the enzyme lactase to break it down into molecules that the body can utilize as fuel.

LAND TENURE: A system under which land is acquired, used, and possibly bought and sold. A variety of land tenure systems exist, including legal land titles, land use rights without land ownership, untitled family farms, and shifting cultivation.

LANDRACE: A traditional crop variety.

LEAKAGE: In international food aid, the use of food by someone other than the targeted recipient. Leakage can occur through sale, barter, or use of food as a gift by a recipient to another party.

LEAVENING: The volume expansion of baking dough caused by the formation and inclusion of gas bubbles.

LIBEL: The negligent or intentional publication of a defamatory statement.

LIBERALIZATION: In trade, the reduction or removal of tariffs and other barriers to trade. In agricultural policy, liberalization refers to reduction or elimination of domestic subsidies, price and production controls, export subsidies, and other agricultural support programs.

LIPIDS: Molecules that include fats such as oils from plants, animal fats such as butter and lard, and fat-soluble vitamins.

LIPOPOLYSACCHARIDE (LPS): Lipopolysaccharide (LPS) is a molecule that is a constituent of the outer membrane of Gram-negative bacteria. The molecule can also be referred to as endotoxin. LPS can help protect the bacterium from host defenses and can contribute to illness in the host.

LISTERIA: A genus of bacteria that includes the pathogenic species *Listeria monocytogenes.*

LISTERIOSIS: An infectious disease caused by ingestion of food contaminated with *Listeria monocytogenes* bacteria.

LIVELIHOOD PORTFOLIO: A collection of strategies a household uses to earn income or otherwise obtain goods and services.

LIVING MODIFIED ORGANISM (LMO): Any living organism that has been genetically modified through the use of biotechnology.

LOCAL AND REGIONAL PROCUREMENT (LRP): The purchase of commodities for food aid either within the recipient country or in a nearby country as opposed to the shipment of food aid from the donor country.

LOCAVORE: Someone who attempts to eat a high proportion of foods that are grown or raised locally. Local food can be defined as that produced within a certain radius (e.g. 50 or 100 or 250 miles), a geographic region or a foodshed, or even a state or a country. The term localvore may also be used.

LONGLINE FISHING: Longline fishing is a technique used extensively in the commercial swordfish and tuna fisheries. Monofilament lines equipped with hundreds of baited hooks and flotation devices are extended for up to 100 miles (160 km) over open ocean waters. Longline fishing is controversial because of its indiscriminate bycatch of other fish species.

M

MALNUTRITION: A condition in which a person is not consuming or absorbing adequate and balanced nutrients in order to sustain a healthy, active life. Diets with caloric deficits, deficits of protein or fat, or deficits of key vitamins and minerals cause malnutrition. Obesity is also sometimes considered a form of malnutrition if it contributes to a state of decreased health or disease.

MARBLING: The internal fat in meat, which can often be seen as white veining within the red muscle matrix. Marbling differs from the adipose fat on the outside of a cut of meat, which can be trimmed off. It contributes to the flavor of meat but is saturated fat and may raise cholesterol levels.

MARICULTURE: Mariculture is the aquaculture variant in which seawater is used to cultivate desired aquatic life forms for harvest. Mariculture is practiced in open ocean environments through the use of specialized protective nets and enclosures or in natural or artificial sea water ponds.

MARKET ACCESS: The ability to get goods to market and sell them to willing buyers of the seller's choice.

MARKET ECONOMY: An economy that permits the open exchange of goods and services and relies on market forces to determine price, production, investment, and savings without government intervention.

MARKET POWER: The ability to influence price through increasing or decreasing production in the market or choosing customers.

MARZIPAN: A type of confection made from almond paste. It is often made into fruit or animal shapes as a stand-alone treat. It can also be used as a topping for cakes and pastries.

MAXIMUM SUSTAINABLE YIELD: The maximum extraction of a species from an ecosystem by humans that can occur without reducing the long-term average population of the species.

MEALTIME: The period of time at which a meal is habitually or customarily eaten. All meals, whether at home or in a restaurant, are usually structured events. Current standard meals include breakfast, lunch, and dinner. The components of a meal vary across cultures, but generally include the consumption of two or more foods.

MEAT: The edible parts of an animal, usually excluding the skin and bone. The term meat often excludes poultry and fish, and refers to beef, lamb, pork, and veal. However, these meats are sometimes known as red meat, whereas poultry may be referred to as white meat.

MEATPACKING: The process of slaughtering animals and preparing meat for sale to consumers.

MELAMINE: Melamine ($C_3H_6N_6$) is a synthetic chemical that is primarily used to produce commercial resins, laminates, and glues. Prohibited for use as a food additive, melamine attained world-wide notoriety in 2008 when a number of Chinese milk products were found to contain the chemical. When added to food products, melamine will tend to disguise low levels of protein and other nutrients in milk adulterated by adding water.

MERCANTILISM: An economic theory that advocates increasing capital through beneficial, government-controlled balance of trade with other nations, often through the imposition of import restrictions.

MESOAMERICA: A region extending south and east from central Mexico to include parts of Guatemala, Belize, Honduras, and Nicaragua.

METABOLIC SYNDROME: A group of risk factors including elevated blood pressure, insulin resistance, increased abdominal fat, elevated lipids in the blood, and overweight or obesity, that together are linked to future development of heart disease and/or diabetes in an individual.

METABOLISM: The total of all the chemical reactions that keep the body alive. Metabolic reactions include the breakdown of proteins and carbohydrates to their constituent parts and their use in various bodily functions. Metabolism depends upon action of enzymes to achieve reactions at a rate compatible with life.

MICRO-COMMUNITIES: Groups of people who communicate on the Internet and via social media that come together based upon a shared interest, regardless of the physical distance between them; for example, people in different countries who are car enthusiasts or fans of an artist that communicate on a public message board.

MICROCREDIT: Loan programs that give people, many times women, access to small sums of money by developed-nation standards (often less than $100), enabling people who are unable otherwise to access capital to buy equipment necessary for creating surpluses to sell in a small business or at market.

MICROLOAN: A small sum of money loaned to persons living in poverty in order to promote entrepreneurship and alleviate hardship.

MICRONUTRIENT: A vitamin or mineral necessary for growth, metabolic functions, and other biological processes in humans, other animals, and plants.

MICRONUTRIENT MALNUTRITION: Different from general malnutrition, micronutrient malnutrition occurs largely in women and children in developing countries with low food security and with low food variety, evidenced by conditions such as anemia and vitamin A deficiency.

MIDDLE-INCOME COUNTRY (MIC): A country that when compared to other countries in the world is neither very poor nor very rich. According to the World Bank, a middle-income country has a per capita gross national income (GNI) between 996 and 12,195 U.S. dollars. In 2010 middle income countries included Botswana, Brazil, Chile, China, Fiji, India, Indonesia, Jordan, Kazakhstan, Mexico,

Nigeria, Russia, Senegal, South Africa, Thailand, and Turkey among others.

MIGRANT WORKER: A person who moves from one region to another to find or follow employment. Migrant workers are used extensively in agriculture, moving frequently during the course of the year to follow the harvest seasons.

MISO: A traditional Japanese seasoning paste made from fermented soybeans, which can be used for sauces, soups, pickling vegetables, and many other dishes.

MONOCULTURE: The agricultural practice of cultivating only a specific crop within a given area.

MONOMER: A small molecule used as a chemical building block. Monomers can be linked together to form much larger molecules called polymers.

MONOSODIUM GLUTAMATE (MSG): Monosodium glutamate (MSG) is one of the best known food additives, used widely as a flavor enhancing agent since the early twentieth century. In addition to the general health concerns associated with excess sodium consumption in modern human diets, such as high blood pressure and increased risk of stroke, MSG symptom complex is a condition experienced by persons who have MSG intolerance.

MONOUNSATURATED OIL: Oil with a fatty acid carbon chain containing one double or triple bond per molecule. Peanut oil, canola oil, and olive oil are examples of monounsaturated oils, which are thought to help lower LDL cholesterol levels in the blood.

MOUTHFEEL: The textural properties of a food when it is perceived in the mouth. Mouthfeel includes qualities such as crunchiness and creaminess and is an important concept in food technology.

MUCKRAKERS: Late nineteenth-century and early-twentieth century journalists, authors, and photographers who sought social change by featuring injustices in such a way as to create maximum interest and action in the public.

MULTI-CROPPING: The practice of growing two or more crops on the same plot of land during one growing season.

MYOGLOBIN: An iron-containing, oxygen-transporting protein in red blood cells that gives meat its red appearance.

N

NaCl: The chemical formula for sodium chloride, or table salt.

NARCOTERRORISM: The use of terrorist techniques to promote, protect, or fund the trade of illicit drugs.

NATIONAL SCHOOL LUNCH PROGRAM (NSLP): The National School Lunch Program is a U.S. government-assisted program that provides low-cost or free lunches to American schoolchildren in public schools, non-profit private schools, and residential child care institutions.

NEOLITHIC: The archaeological period during which agriculture first appeared, no earlier than 12,000 years ago in the Middle East. The Paleolithic (or "Stone Age") and the Mesolithic (or "Middle Stone Age") preceded the Neolithic, and in Europe, the Neolithic is followed by the Bronze Age. The Neolithic Revolution refers to the changes in human societies correlated with agricultural economies.

NEUROTOXIN: A poison that interferes with nerve function, usually by affecting the flow of ions through the cell membrane.

NITRITES: A group of salts, including sodium nitrite, which are derived from nitrates by either chemical or bacterial action. They play a role in curing meats through stopping the growth of bacteria, preventing oxidation of fat, preserving color, and adding flavor.

NO ACCESS–NO FOOD: The principle that humanitarian food aid will be distributed only under regimes in which the distribution and storage can be monitored by humanitarian relief workers, usually by foreign humanitarian relief workers. Food refers to food aid, and access refers to the ability to travel to the locations where food aid is stored and distributed.

NOMADIC: Individuals or groups who do not have a static place of residence; a lifestyle or culture characterized by periodic relocation without a permanent dwelling. Herding cultures are frequently nomadic.

NONGOVERNMENTAL ORGANIZATION (NGO): This generally refers to organizations that are created and directed outside of any governmental affiliation. Often, NGOs are involved with human rights and health-related issues. They are typically dedicated to development and service.

NON-TARIFF BARRIER: Any barrier to trade other than tariffs. Usually refers to quotas and restrictions on trade or to rules and regulations that affect trade but may be set for other reasons.

NOUVELLE CUISINE: A culinary trend beginning in the late 1970s that pulled away from classic French cooking to find new, lighter techniques and more artistic presentations.

NUT: The strict botanical definition of a nut is a one-seeded fruit in which the fruit tissue is dry and tough rather than juicy. A broader definition is any large seed of certain long-lived trees.

NUTRACEUTICAL: A food that may treat illness or prevent disease due to its nutritional qualities.

NUTRIENT: A component of food that has some useful role in the body's functioning. Macronutrients are required in larger quantities and consist of carbohydrates, protein, and fat, whereas the micronutrients, the vitamins and minerals, are required in much smaller quantities.

NUTRIENT FILM TECHNIQUE (NFT): Hydroponic technique in which a thin layer of nutrient solution is continuously passed over the plant roots, which are enclosed in a tray or pipe.

NUTRIENT FORTIFICATION: The process of adding concentrated micronutrients to processed foods.

NUTRITION: The process of providing or obtaining the nourishment necessary for health and growth.

NUTRITION LABEL: A listing of all ingredients and nutritional information, including calories, fat, sodium, protein, and carbohydrates, contained in the product.

NUTRITION TRANSITION: Process of change that is occurring more in low and middle-income countries, whereby people are transitioning to a more sedentary lifestyle with decreased activity patterns and access to more high-fat, high-sugar, and low-nutrient based foods. The combination of these lifestyle changes results in an increase in conditions such as heart or cardiovascular disease, diabetes, and high-blood pressure.

O

O157: A recently emergent strain of *E. coli* that causes mild to severe diarrhea and, in advanced cases, brain and kidney damage that may be fatal.

OBESITY: Excess amount of body fat; usually defined by a body mass index (BMI) measurement of 30 or more, based on age and gender. Obesity is a risk factor for developing heart disease, high blood pressure, high cholesterol, type 2 diabetes, and other chronic diseases.

OFFAL: The internal organs of animals prepared for consumption.

OIL: A fat that is liquid at room temperature. Oils generally come from vegetable sources, and a wide range of oils are available for cooking.

OMNIVORE: An animal that derives food from both plant and animal sources.

ORAL DISEASE: May be any of a number of diseases and disorders that affect more than just the teeth.

This group of diseases refers to an infection or ailment affecting the mouth, throat, tongue, lips, the salivary glands, the chewing muscles, and the upper and lower jaws.

ORGANIC AGRICULTURE: Agriculture and livestock production that uses no chemical, mineral, or otherwise artificial inputs. Organic agriculture is thought to be more natural and to have less impact on the environment than the conventional methods associated with the input-dependent technologies of the twentieth century. Certain human-made fertilizers, soil amendments, herbicides, and pesticides are prohibited by organic standards that define organic agriculture.

ORGANIC CHEMICAL: Any compound containing carbon is technically referred to as an organic compound, which includes most chemical pesticides. This use of the term organic should not be confused with its use with respect to farming methods.

ORGANICALLY GROWN: This term means that no synthetic fertilizers or pesticides are used in the growing of a particular food. Biological pesticides are permitted for food labeled "organically grown" according to U.S. Department of Agriculture (USDA) standards.

ORGANISATION FOR ECONOMIC CO-OPERATION AND DEVELOPMENT (OECD): An economic forum of 33 countries focused on promoting democracy and market economies.

ORTHOREXIA: An unhealthy obsession with healthy eating, modeled by an analogy with anorexia nervosa. Orthorexia is not a medically recognized diagnosis, but may be useful in describing individuals who are fixated on eating only certain types of food.

OSTEOPOROSIS: A loss in bone density that may be the result of a chronic calcium deficiency, early menopause, certain endocrine diseases, certain medications, advanced age, or other risk factors.

OUTBREAK: Occurrence of disease. Most cases of foodborne disease are individual or sporadic, but sometimes a group of people will eat the same contaminated food, and several or many will become ill. Such incidents are defined as outbreaks and may need further investigation to stop them from spreading.

OVARY: The part of a plant that produces a seed and nourishes it until it is ready to grow into another plant.

OVERWEIGHT: Defined as having a body mass index (BMI) of 25.0–29.9, based on age and gender.

OWNER-MEMBER: A member and employee of a food co-op.

P

PADDY: Rice in its unprocessed, raw form without the hull removed, which is also called paddy rice or rough rice. Can also mean the flooded field used in rice growing.

PAGOPHAGY: The excessive consumption of ice, especially common during pregnancy, which is highly correlated with iron deficiency anemia.

PALEOLITHIC: Also known as the Stone Age, this archaeological period of time began when human ancestors and their relatives began making stone tools and ended with the transition to agriculture, from about 2.6 million to 12,000 years ago.

PANDEMIC: Pandemic, which means "all the people" describes an epidemic that occurs in more than one country or population simultaneously.

PAPILLAE: Small projections on the upper surface of the tongue that give it a rough appearance. Each papilla houses 25 to 250 taste buds. Papillae are also located in the throat, sides of the mouth, and soft palate.

PARENTERAL NUTRITION: Parenteral nutrition is nutritionally complete feeding delivered directly to the stomach, by means of a tube. For short-term nutritional replacement, the tube is generally inserted through the nose. In patients with severe gagging issues, the tube may be surgically placed into the abdomen, connecting directly to the stomach.

PASTEURIZATION: A process by which food is heated to a high-enough temperature for a specific period of time to kill bacteria. Pasteurization is named after French bacteriologist Louis Pasteur (1822–1895), who developed the process in 1864. By the early 1950s, most milk in the United States was pasteurized, leading to a significant decline in milk-related food-borne illnesses.

PATENT MEDICINES: Tonics, remedies, compounds, and drugs of untested effectiveness that were popularly sold in the nineteenth and early twentieth centuries. Ingredients were most often kept secret from consumers, and manufacturers advertised "patented formulas." Many of the so-called patent medicines were in fact trademarked instead of patented because the application for patents required revealing ingredients and quantities.

PATHOGEN: A disease-causing organism.

PECTIN: A glue-like compound located between plant cell walls. Pectin forms a matrix that traps water into a smooth and viscous gel. It is an essential component in making jams and jellies to preserve fruit.

PERIODONTAL DISEASE: Diseases of the gums that can result in tooth loss. When a bacterial infection starts in the mouth, the gums become inflamed. The tissue that supports and holds the teeth in the mouth breaks down, and the teeth are loosened. One of the main causes of this disease is a buildup of bacterial plaque on the surfaces of the teeth.

PERMACULTURE: A method and philosophy of local land management stressing integration of people and the land in harmony with natural biological patterns and cycles.

PHENOLS: A broad group of alcohol-like compounds.

PHENYLETHYLAMINE: Informally known as "the love drug," phenylethylamine raises blood pressure and blood sugar slightly, causing a state of alertness.

PHOBIA: A phobia is a fear of an object or situation that is sufficient in intensity to cause an individual considerable distress and result in avoidance not only of the feared object but of situations associated with it.

PHOTOSYNTHESIS: The process by which plants use chlorophyll, their green pigment, to capture sunlight and carbon dioxide in the atmosphere to make glucose. Photosynthesis is the primary source of energy for both plants and the animals that eat them.

PHOTOSYNTHESIZING AUTOTROPHS: Animals that produce their own food by using sunlight to convert other substances to food.

PHYTOCHEMICALS: Trace chemicals found in plants that often perform some biological function, such as protecting the plant from predators. Some phytochemicals, such as the purple anthocyanins, have antioxidant properties in humans that may help protect against disease.

PHYTOESTROGEN: Phytochemicals that mimic the action of human estrogen and so may block its role in activating cells, potentially preventing the development of some cancers.

PLAINTIFF: A person, group of people, or legal entity that brings suit against another party in court.

PLEISTOCENE: The geological period of time from 2.58 million years ago to 12,000 years ago. By the end of the Pleistocene epoch, which was also the end of the archaeological period known as the Paleolithic, or "Stone Age," human hunters and gatherers had spread across the world. The Pleistocene was preceded by the Pliocene and is followed by the current period, the Holocene.

POACHING: Illegal hunting and killing of animals, often to sell their meat, skins, tusks, or other parts.

PODCASTS: Spoken word shows, similar to talk radio shows, that are recorded and posted on the Internet for download. The word is derived from the name of Apple's "iPod" mp3 player. Whereas many podcasts are homemade, some traditional radio stations record their shows and post them as podcasts on the Internet for fans to download.

POLYCARBONATE PLASTIC: A versatile, transparent, malleable polymer with many commercial applications, synthesized by combining bisphenol A and phosgene.

POLYETHYLENE TEREPHTHALATE (PET): Also known as PET, polyethylene terephthalate is a lightweight, rigid polymer resin that is widely used for food and beverage containers.

POLYMER: A molecule of relatively high molecular weight, consisting of repeated chemical subunits that are linked together by chemical bonds.

POLYUNSATURATED: Substances such as oils composed of molecules containing more than one carbon-carbon double bond are said to be polyunsaturated.

POLYUNSATURATED OIL: Oil with a fatty acid carbon chain that contains multiple double or triple bonds in each molecule. Corn oil, safflower oil, soybean oil, and sesame oil are examples of polyunsaturated oils. Polyunsaturated oils are thought to help reduce LDL cholesterol levels in the blood.

POPULATION: A group with similar demographic characteristics such as geographic location, species, gender, age, habits, nationality, ethnicity, productive requirements, or needs.

POTABLE: Potable water (or drinking water) is water fit for human consumption. Water that is not potable may be made potable by filtration, distillation, or by a range of other methods.

POULTRY: General term describing all birds raised for their meat, feathers, or eggs, including chickens, quail, turkeys, ducks, geese, doves, and pheasants.

POVERTY TRAP: A level of poverty below which a household no longer has the means to increase income over time, especially a decreased level of productive assets such as livestock, land, or tools. Once a household is in a poverty trap, the household lacks the tools to escape poverty or to improve its condition in any way.

PRECAUTIONARY PRINCIPLE: A principle that any product, action, or process that might pose a threat to public or environmental health should not be introduced in the absence of scientific consensus regarding its safety.

PREHYPERTENSION: A term that reflects increased risk through mildly raised blood pressure. Prehypertension is defined as having systolic blood pressure greater than or equal to 120 and/or diastolic blood pressure greater than or equal to 80.

PRESERVATIVES: A type of food additive that preserves the life of a food. The use of preservatives increases the range of foods available to the consumer by extending their shelf lives and improving food safety.

PRION: A proteinaceous infectious particle, or prion, is a deformed protein that converts other proteins into the same form, resulting in a buildup of abnormal proteins causing one of several types of transmissible spongiform encephalopathy (TSE), a type of fatal brain disease, such as BSE (bovine spongiform encephalopathy, or "mad cow disease"), scrapie in sheep and goats, and Creutzfeldt-Jakob Disease (CJD) in humans. Variant CJD (vCJD) is usually contracted by human consumption of BSE-infected beef.

PRIX FIXE: A menu style in which there is one price for a meal consisting of many small courses.

PROCESSED FOOD: A food that has been modified during production to transform raw ingredients into different forms of food.

PRODUCER SUPPORT ESTIMATE (PSE): A commonly used measure of the impact of agricultural subsidies and other agricultural policy measures. The PSE combines estimates of government spending in agriculture along with the higher prices consumers in a country may pay due to agricultural trade policies and the price effects of subsidies.

PROGRESSIVE ERA: A period of social and political reform in the United States from the 1890s to the 1920s. Progressive Era reforms included labor, education, food safety, and anti-corruption laws.

PROOFING: Allowing dough that has risen once to rise again.

PROSPECTIVE STUDY: A research study that starts with healthy people and gathers information about factors such as diet or medication intake and then follows up their medical history for a number of years to deduce the influences of these factors upon health. A prospective study generally has high scientific validity if well designed and carried out.

PROTECTIONISM: The theory or practice of protecting a nation's domestic industry or agriculture from foreign competition through the imposition of trade barriers or regulations that discriminate against imports.

PSYCHROPHILES: Organisms that live and grow more efficiently in moderate temperatures between 14–68°F (–10–20°C).

PULSES: Legumes dry well, and the dried versions are known as pulses. They consist mainly of starch and protein, and their water-resistant, hard coat makes them easy to store.

PUNCHING DOWN: Pressing on risen dough to expel excess carbon dioxide.

PURE FOOD AND DRUG ACT OF 1906: This Act created the agency that is now known as the Food and Drug Administration (FDA); the Center for Food Safety and Applied Nutrition (CFSAN) operates under the authority of the FDA.

Q

QUOTA: A trade restriction that limits the number of goods that may be imported into a nation within a certain period.

R

RAMADAN: The ninth month of the Islamic calendar year and a period of fasting, prayer, charity, and family celebration.

RATION: Ration, when used within a military context, refers to a daily food allowance designed to meet the dietary and nutritional needs of service members.

RAWIST: A person who consumes a diet of mostly plant-based foods in an uncooked state.

READY-TO-EAT FOOD: Prepared food that can be consumed as soon as it is purchased.

REALITY-BASED COMPETITION: Television shows in which contestants compete against each other in mock, real-life situations.

RECALL: In a recall in the United States, the Center for Food Safety and Applied Nutrition (CFSAN) asks the public to return products from a specific batch produced by a manufacturer, for reasons such as contamination or foodborne illness. Most CFSAN-originated recalls involve voluntary recalls, in which the manufacturer works proactively with CFSAN to remove a product from the shelves and to educate consumers to return or destroy defective products.

RECOMBINANT BOVINE GROWTH HORMONE (rBGH): A genetically engineered hormone given to cattle to increase milk production.

RECOMBINANT DNA: A form of artificial DNA that contains two or more genetic sequences that normally do not occur together, which are spliced together.

RECOMMENDED DIETARY ALLOWANCE (RDA): Sometimes known as the recommended daily allowance, RDA is the level of intake of a vitamin or mineral required to prevent deficiency disease. In real life, people will tend to consume more of a vitamin or mineral on one day than another, so it is probably best to think in terms of average, rather than daily, intakes.

RECOVERY: The aspect of humanitarian assistance that seeks to prevent further deterioration of an affected area and to restore basic living conditions, services, livelihoods, security and rule of law, and national capacities.

REDUCTION: Thickening or intensifying the flavor of a liquid by evaporation.

REGULATION: Controlling behaviors, business practices, or industrial practices through rules, restrictions, or laws to encourage preferred outcomes or prevent undesired outcomes that may otherwise occur.

REPORTABLE FOOD: Any food item that, if consumed by humans or animals, may be believed to cause serious health problems or death.

RESPONSIBLE PARTY: Any registered food facility or manufacturer, processor, or packager that manages food for human or animal consumption.

RHEOLOGY: The science of deformation and flow when a force is applied to a material, including a food. Materials vary widely in their rheological behavior.

RHIZOBIA: Species of soil bacteria that form a symbiotic relationship with legume plants, living inside nodules in their roots.

RIPENING: A series of chemical processes occurring in a fruit that make it more attractive to animals. Ripening includes increasing sweetness and decreasing starch and acid content, as well as characteristic color changes from green to red or yellow and the development of texture and aroma.

RURAL DEVELOPMENT: Rural development refers to actions, programs, or projects designed to increase the living standards of people living in rural areas, typically through agricultural improvement or poverty reduction.

S

SALMONELLA: The genus *Salmonella* includes more than 2,500 types of bacteria. Salmonellosis, a common form of food poisoning, is the illness that results when food contaminated by this bacterial strain is consumed. *Salmonella* causes a variety of illnesses in humans, animals, and birds; poultry are especially vulnerable to *Salmonella* outbreaks.

SALTATION: The process by which sand or soil particles move across an uneven surface when carried by the wind.

SANITARY AND PHYTOSANITARY (SPS) MEASURES: Laws, rules, and regulations intended to help protect human and animal health (sanitary) or plant health (phytosanitary). Regulations regarding food safety, animal diseases, plant diseases, and pests are referred to as SPS restrictions.

SAPROPHYTE: Saprophytes are organisms that obtain nutrients from dead and/or decaying matter in the environment. They are important decomposers of organic material.

SATAY: Marinated, grilled meat on a kabob skewer often served with a dipping sauce, a dish that originated in Indonesia and Thailand.

SATURATED FAT: Fat in which the fatty acid chain contains only single bonds between carbon atoms in each molecule. Saturated fats are usually obtained from animal products, including lard and butter, but are also derived from plants, such as coconut oil and palm oil. Saturated fats are thought to increase LDL cholesterol levels in the blood.

SAXITOXIN: A neurotoxin that is the basis of paralytic shellfish poisoning.

SCIENTIFIC RELIABILITY AND VALIDITY: Reliability refers to the consistency or replicability of a measurement across repetition. A reliable instrument is one that gives the same results for the same object measured at different times. Validity is concerned with the accuracy of a measure and the determination of whether a result accurately reflects what was being measured.

SEA LICE: A naturally occurring aquatic parasite. These small creatures prey on the blood, skin, and mucous membranes of juvenile or adult fish hosts, causing damage to the flesh and immune systems of its targets. Salmon farms have been identified as key sites where sea lice proliferate. From the farms the lice migrate to nearby wild salmon populations, causing widespread destruction. Pacific salmon and sea trout are fish species that are especially vulnerable to sea lice infestations.

SEED: A compact package containing a plant's embryo and the food stores it needs to develop into a new plant.

SELF ESTEEM: A state of being that is grounded in self acceptance and self respect. In the context of body image and food, a person with high self esteem feels good about his or her body and has a positive self perception about their size and shape. Individuals with low self esteem will most likely be unsatisfied with their body image and size. Unfortunately this could result in a repetitive pattern of self deprivation, followed by bingeing, weight gain, and worsening self image.

SEMOLINA: A rougher, uncooked durum wheat product made as a precursor to the final grinding of flour or for use in pastas, breads, or cereals.

SEROTYPES: Serotypes or serovars are classes of microorganisms based on the types of molecules (antigens) that they present on their surfaces. Even a single species may have thousands of serotypes, which may have medically quite distinct behaviors.

SEVEN Ms: Money, muscle, motivation, milk, materials, manure, and meat.

SHARK FIN SOUP: Shark fin soup, *yu chi* (translated Mandarin for shark wing) has been regarded as a delicacy in Chinese food culture for centuries. This soup was a dish traditionally available only to the very wealthy due to the scarcity of shark fins needed for its preparation. The emergence of a consumer middle class in late twentieth century China broadened the soup's appeal as a status symbol. Chinese consumer demand for shark fins helped spur a dramatic decrease in world shark populations.

SHELF LIFE: The amount of time a food product can be stored without noticeable changes to its quality or significantly increased risks of foodborne illness.

SILT: Fine particles of clay, sand, or other matter that are carried by running water and deposited as sediment.

SLASH-AND-BURN: A deforestation technique in which trees and other vegetation are cut and burned to clear land for planting crops or grazing livestock.

SLOW FOOD: A movement promoting traditional and regional cuisines, deliberately (and often slowly) prepared, eaten at leisure with friends and family, and opposed to corporate-produced fast food consumption.

SLOW FOOD MOVEMENT: Founded by the Italian writer Carlo Petrini (1949–) in 1989, the international Slow Food Movement acts as an antidote to fast food, with its campaigning for the pleasure of food, preservation of traditional dishes, and respect for community and environment.

SMALLHOLDER: A farming or livestock-raising rural household with small amounts of land or otherwise limited access to land. Smallholders typically have less than two hectares of arable land, and many have access to far smaller plots.

SMOKE POINT: The temperature at which a cooking fat breaks down into visible gaseous products.

SOCIAL SAFETY NET: A public program designed to prevent households from falling into extreme poverty or reducing their consumption of necessary nutrients, medical services, and education.

SOIL EROSION: The process by which soil is carried away by wind or water.

SOOT: A particulate air pollutant, primarily composed of carbon, produced by the incomplete combustion of biomass and fossil fuels.

SOVEREIGNTY: Supreme and independent power or authority in government as possessed or claimed by a state or community; rightful status, independence, or prerogative; a sovereign state, community, or political unit.

SPECIES: A taxonomic group of living organisms capable of exchanging genes or interbreeding.

SPICE: The fragrant roots, barks, fruits, seeds, or nuts of a plant. Often found in tropical regions, spices can be dried and transported. They develop their characteristic flavors and aromas on drying, but can be used both dried and fresh.

SPORE: A dormant form assumed by some bacteria, such as anthrax and *Clostridium botulinum*, that enables the bacteria to survive high temperatures, dryness, and lack of nourishment for long periods of time. Under proper conditions, the spore may revert to the actively multiplying form of the bacteria.

SPRING ROLLS: A traditional appetizer in several Asian countries. Often they consist of vegetables or seafood rolled in rice paper, but the finishing varies from country to country. Some countries, such as China, fry their spring rolls, whereas in Vietnam the rice paper of the spring rolls is dipped in water, and the spring rolls are served cold.

SPRING WATER: Spring water refers to groundwater that emanates from a spring.

STANDARD AMERICAN DIET (SAD): The standard American diet includes large amounts of red meat, eggs, and refined grain products that are generally high-fat, high-sugar, and heavily-processed foods.

STARVATION: The most extreme form of under-nutrition, in which there is a partial or total lack of nutrients for a long time. Total starvation, in which no food is consumed, is usually fatal within 8 to 12 weeks.

STERILIZATION: Refers to any procedure that kills all of the microorganisms in or on a product. May be done with high temperature and pressure, by use of chemicals, or by irradiation.

STRAIN: A subclass of a particular tribe and genus.

SUBSIDY: A form of financial assistance granted by the government to assist a particular business or industry, usually so that the price of a commodity remains competitive.

SUBSISTENCE: Methods of obtaining food. Subsistence was based on hunting and gathering until relatively recently in human prehistory.

SUBSISTENCE FARMER: A farmer who grows food primarily to feed his or her family, with little or no surplus remaining for selling at market.

SUBSTITUTE: In economics, any good that can be used instead of another good with little or limited reduction in consumer satisfaction.

SUBSTRATE: In hydroponics, the root supporting medium used to grow plants. Substrate may consist of any inert material that does not directly supply nutrients to the plants.

SUGAR: The common name for the smaller molecules of the carbohydrate family, known as the monosaccharides and disaccharides, composed of one sugar unit and two sugar units respectively. Glucose is the monosaccharide that is used as the body's fuel. Sugar is also the common name for sucrose, a disaccharide composed of glucose and fructose, which is also known as fruit sugar.

SUPPLY CHAIN: All of the steps between a raw material and the final consumer.

SURPLUS FOOD: Food that is near or past its expiration date but remains edible, as well as an oversupply of food.

SUSTAINABILITY: Often defined as being able to meet the needs of the present without compromising the needs of future generations. Sustainability is an important concept in environmental protection.

SUSTAINABLE AGRICULTURE: Methods of producing food that can be sustained without depleting resources for future generations.

SUSTAINABLE DEVELOPMENT: Sustainable development involves economic development and the fulfillment of human requirements in an environmentally responsible manner.

SUSTAINABLE FOOD: Food that is grown in a manner that is profitable for the farmer, nutritious for the consumer, and preserves the environment.

SWADESHI: The Swadeshi movement was a facet of the Indian independence movement that advocated boycotting British goods in favor of strengthening domestic production.

SWEETNESS: One of the five basic tastes, long associated with pleasure. There are taste buds that detect sweet-tasting molecules on the tongue, and these relay messages to the brain, creating the sensation of sweetness. There are many sweet-tasting compounds, both natural and synthetic.

SYNTHETIC FERTILIZER: A commercially-prepared chemical mixture containing plant nutrients, such as nitrates, phosphates, and potassium.

SYNTHETIC PESTICIDE: A commercially-prepared chemical mixture designed to kill or repel insects.

T

TANNINS: Astringent chemical compounds found in the skins, stems, and seeds of wine grapes that produce a sense of bitterness and tactile drying sensation in wine. As a wine ages, tannins form long polymerized chains resulting in the wine "mellowing" its taste and mouthfeel.

TAP WATER: Tap water refers to water produced by a municipal water system and transported to consumers through home plumbing systems.

TARIFF: A duty or tax imposed on imports or exports.

TASTE BUD: A group of cells that are responsive to taste molecules. Taste buds consist of a barrel shaped arrangement of alternating taste receptor cells and supporting cells, the latter acting as a source of new taste receptor cells.

TEIKEI: The Japanese word for "cooperation," a connection between consumer and farmer to form an economic relationship similar to that of community supported agriculture (CSA). *Teikei* was part of the foundation of the international CSA movement.

TEMPERATE CLIMATE FRUITS: Fruits that grow on trees, bushes, and vines and need a period of cold before they flower.

TERMS OF TRADE (TOT): The relative prices of goods or of goods traded between countries.

TERROIR: The special characteristics of soil, weather, and techniques of farming that contribute to the unique qualities of wine.

TEXTURE: The qualities of a food, or other material, that can be felt with the fingers, tongue, palate, or teeth. Foods have many different textures, which contribute to their imparted sensation of taste.

THEOBROMINE: A vasodilator and a diuretic, theobrimine is found in the cacao bean.

THIRD-PARTY CERTIFICATION: A system in which an organization independent of all the companies in a supply chain certifies that a good reaches particular standards or has particular attributes. Most international organic standards, fair trade standards, humane animal treatment standards, claims of being not genetically modified, and a variety of environmental claims are substantiated by third-party certification.

TOFU: Curdled soy milk, made by heating soy milk and adding salts to solidify its protein content. Tofu is often used as a meat substitute in macrobiotic and vegetarian diets.

TOXIN: A poison that is produced by a living organism.

TRACE ELEMENTS: Elements such as copper, molybdenum, boron, selenium, chromium, iron, and manganese, the trace elements are the minerals that the body requires in much smaller amounts than calcium, for instance, or phosphorus. There are only a few grams of each trace element in the body.

TRACEABILITY: The ability to follow a product through each step in a supply chain.

TRADE AGREEMENT: An accord or contract among participating nations or trade groups that establishes rules for trade, including taxes, import fees, tariffs, duties, levies, subsidies, or restrictions on the exchange of goods and money.

TRADE BARRIER: Anything that impedes or distorts the movement of goods between countries. Examples of trade barriers include tariffs, export taxes, export subsidies, quotas, country of origin rules, safety regulations, licensing requirements, and product standards.

TRADITIONAL FOODS: The Traditional Foods Movement is a byproduct of the Weston A. Price Foundation and the book *Nourishing Traditions* by Sally Fallon Morell, the co-founder of A Campaign for Real Milk. Using principles from Price's research, Fallon advocates a diet of raw milk, grassfed meats, raw liver, coconut oil, and sprouted grains.

TRADITIONAL KNOWLEDGE: Sometimes called indigenous knowledge, traditional knowledge is information related to practices that are often preserved and passed on by methods other than through academic study or formal writings. Although components of beliefs and practices may not be fully tested by scientific experimentation, many experts argue that traditional knowledge and practices contain useful insights about the environment, medicine, and agriculture.

TRANS FATS: Hydrogenated, unsaturated fats often present in processed foods that lower the HDL (good) cholesterol and raise the LDL (bad) cholesterol in the blood and are, therefore, associated with an increased risk for developing heart disease.

TRANSGENIC ORGANISM: A genetically modified organism that contains genetic sequences from multiple species.

TRANSMISSABLE SPONGIFORM ENCEPHALOPATHY (TSE): Transmissable spongiform encephalopathies, or prion diseases, are incurable brain diseases transmitted by infection with prions, protein-based infectious agents.

TRANSMISSION: Microorganisms that cause disease in humans and other species are known as pathogens. The transmission of pathogens to a human or other host can occur in a number of ways, depending upon the microorganism.

TRIGLYCERIDES: The chemical name for the form in which most fats exist both in the body and in foods. Higher levels of triglycerides in the blood, resulting from a high fat diet, are a known risk factor for coronary heart disease.

TROPHIC LEVEL: The division of species in an ecosystem by their main source of nutrition.

TROPICAL PRODUCT: An agricultural product that can be cultivated only in a relatively warm climate. Tropical products include tea, coffee, cocoa, cotton, pineapples, bananas, and a wide variety of other tropical fruits.

tTG TEST: tTG is the standard diagnostic blood test performed when gluten intolerance is suspected. Short for anti-tissue transglutaminase antibody, the tTG test measures the presence of antibodies to gluten in the blood. Higher results indicate a likely gluten intolerance disorder.

TURBIDITY: A condition in which water (or another liquid) becomes opaque due to suspended particles of clay or other matter.

U

ULTRA HIGH TEMPERATURE (UHT) PROCESSING: A food processing procedure in which the product is heated for a very short time to a temperature higher than the setting used for pasteurization, which accomplishes a result close to sterilization.

ULTRAVIOLET: Electromagnetic radiation of wavelengths from about 100 to 400 nanometers.

UMAMI: Sometimes known as the fifth basic taste, umami is a savory taste triggered by the presence of amino acids in meat or aged cheese.

UMBRELLA ORGANIZATION: A federation or other grouping of organizations for a single purpose. An umbrella organization unites many organizations, often from various countries, to represent a cause or movement on a broader level or internationally.

UNDERNUTRITION: Undernutrition describes the status of people whose food intake does not include enough calories (energy) to meet minimum physiological needs. The term is a measure of a country's ability to gain access to food and is normally derived from Food Balance Sheets prepared by the United Nations Food and Agriculture Organization (FAO).

UNDOCUMENTED (WORKER): A person of unverified immigration status; someone who entered a country without advance permission, entered without required paperwork, or who cannot prove that he or she legally entered a country under its immigration laws.

UNITED NATIONS FOOD AND AGRICULTURE ORGANIZATION (FAO): Organization that leads international efforts to defeat hunger. Serving both developed and developing countries, the FAO acts as a neutral forum where all nations meet as equals to negotiate agreements and debate policy. The FAO is also a source of knowledge and information and assists developing countries and countries in transition to modernize and improve agriculture, forestry, and fisheries practices and ensure good nutrition for all.

UNITED STATES DEPARTMENT OF AGRICULTURE (USDA): A department of the United States government, the role of which is to provide leadership on food, agriculture, natural resources, and related issues based on sound public policy, the best available science, and efficient management.

UNITED STATES FOOD AND DRUG ADMINISTRATION (FDA): The Food and Drug Administration (FDA) is an agency of the U.S. Department of Health and Human Services (HHS) that is responsible for regulating and ensuring the safety and effectiveness of foods, drugs, cosmetics, tobacco, and other products.

URINARY INCONTINENCE: Inability to retain urine in the bladder until the person chooses to empty it.

USDA NATURAL LABELED FOOD: Food that is minimally processed with no artificial ingredients or coloring according to USDA standards. This does not include genetically altered food.

USDA ORGANIC LABELED FOOD: A food that is at least 95 percent organically grown or produced product according to USDA standards.

V

VALUE CHAIN: A series of steps between a raw material and a finished good that reaches a final consumer.

VARIANT CREUTZFELDT-JAKOB DISEASE (vCJD): A fatal neurological disorder that is transmitted by prions, or protein-based infectious agents, contained in the brains or spinal cords of cattle infected with bovine spongiform encephalopathy (BSE).

VEGAN: A person who does not eat any animal products, including eggs, milk, cheese, and honey (as opposed to a vegetarian, who does not eat meat).

VEGETABLE: A culinary term, which excludes fruits, describing the edible part of a plant. In a botanical sense, both fruits and vegetables are edible parts of plants.

VIGNERON: A person who cultivates grapes for winemaking.

VINICULTURE: The science, art, and social customs that surround the practices of growing grapes and making wine.

VINTNER: A person who makes wine.

VISA: A certificate or other evidence of permission to enter a country legally for work, residential, or visiting purposes.

VOLATILE: Easily vaporized at moderate temperatures and pressures.

VOLATILE ORGANIC COMPOUND (VOC): Any organic liquid that changes easily (volatilizes) to a gas.

W

WAGE SLAVERY: The practice of being dependent on a wage from hiring out of a person's labor. For some critics of capitalism, all workers who receive wages and live by hiring out their labor are wage slaves. For others not opposed to wage employment *per se*, wage slavery usually denotes forms of indebtedness or other forced systems in which a worker is unable to leave a poor work environment for fear of the consequences.

WATERSHED: The surface waters or streams, rivers, deltas, wetlands, and lakes that share sources of water from both above and below the ground.

WEIGHT CONTROL BEHAVIORS: Behaviors exhibited when someone is trying to control his or her body weight. Some of these behaviors include skipping meals, using diet pills, self-induced vomiting, excessive exercise, and dietary restrictions.

WET NURSING: A term for a woman, not an infant's biological mother, who breastfeeds an infant due to the biological mother's inability to breastfeed. Wet nurses were typically women who had recently had an infant, whose infant had died, or women who maintained lactation easily and charged a fee for wet nursing services to provide economic support for their families.

WIC: The Special Supplemental Nutrition Program for Women, Infants, and Children (WIC) provides nutrition assistance to more than 45 percent of all infants in the United States. WIC supplies specific foods via a voucher system to pregnant women, postpartum women, breastfeeding mothers, infants, and children through age five for families with incomes below 185 percent of the federal poverty line.

WORKSHARE: A type of community supported agriculture (CSA) share in which the shareholder pays a reduced price to the CSA farmer in return for spending an agreed-upon number of hours working on the farm.

WORLD BANK: The World Bank is part of a group of international financial institutions that provides loans and other financial assistance to developing nations to promote economic growth and reduce poverty.

WORLD FOOD PROGRAMME (WFP): The front-line food agency of the United Nations (UN), the World Food Programme (WFP) is the largest food aid organization in the world dedicated to hunger issues, delivering aid to more than 90 million persons in more than 70 countries per year.

WORLD TRADE ORGANIZATION (WTO): An international non-governmental organization that implements and supervises international trade agreements.

X

X RAYS: Electromagnetic radiation of wavelengths from about 0.03 to 3 nanometers.

Y

YEAST: A naturally occurring single-celled fungus that ferments sugar to produce carbon dioxide bubbles to leaven dough and to produce alcoholic beverages such as beer and wine.

YIELD: The amount of a crop produced per planting or per growing season.

Z

ZOONOSIS: A zoonosis is a disease of microbiological origin that can be transmitted from animals to people. The disease may be caused by bacteria, viruses, parasites, or fungi.

ZOONOTIC DISEASE: A disease transmitted from animals to humans.

Chronology

A chronology of events related to the history of food and agriculture.

c.18000 BC

Nile valley sees rise of agricultural techniques; cereal grains are specifically cultivated.

c.10000 BC

Neolithic Revolution: transition from a hunting and gathering mode of food production to farming and animal husbandry, the domestication of plants and animals.

c.9000 BC

Sheep and goats domesticated in Mesopotamia, other livestock in Persia.

c.8750 BC

Pumpkins and other members of the squash family are known to have been cultivated in what is now Persia and Central Asia.

c.8000 BC

Settled agriculture occurs in the Near East and other centers of human habitation.

c.8000 BC

The first forms of fired clay are used by Neolithic people to keep track of agricultural products. They are unmarked and have geometric shapes.

c.8000 BC

With the beginning of settled agriculture come the first simple digging and harvesting tools.

c.8000 BC

Beer is brewed in Mesopotamia.

c.8000 BC

Potatoes are cultivated in the Andes of Peru.

c.7000 BC

The water buffalo is domesticated in eastern Asia and China.

c.7000 BC

Durum wheat is cultivated in Anatolia (Turkey). This important variety is used to make alimentary paste-like foods and much later becomes a staple for pastas.

c.7000 BC

Wheat, barley, and millet are cultivated in the east Mediterranean basin.

c.7000 BC

Pigs and cattle are domesticated in what is today Turkey.

c.6500 BC

A primitive plough called the ard is used in the Near East.

c.6400 BC

Beer is known to be brewed in the Andes at this time.

c.6000 BC

Millet is cultivated in Africa. These various types of grasses produce small edible seeds that are used as forage crops and as food cereals. High in carbohydrates, millet becomes an important food staple.

c.6000 BC

Peaches are known to be grown in central China, and citrus fruits are cultivated in Indonesia.

c.6000 BC

Bread-making wheat called *Triticum vulgare* is cultivated in southwestern Asia. This is the most important variety of wheat, because it is used for bread making; it becomes a major source of energy in the human diet.

c.6000 BC

Wine-making begins in northern Mesopotamia and in the Levant (along the eastern Mediterranean shore).

c.5600 BC

The saddle quern is used for grinding grain. A type of mortar and pestle, it consists of a flat stone bed and a rounded stone that is operated manually against it.

c.5000 BC

Date palms are grown in India, and rice is cultivated in the Yangtze Delta in China.

c.5000 BC

Iraq develops formal irrigation methods and tools.

c.4500 BC

Fired clay tokens are used for agricultural record-keeping.

c.4000 BC

Maize or corn is cultivated in what is now the Tehuacan Valley of Mexico.

c.4000 BC

Grapes are grown around the Caspian Sea and the coastal regions of the Black Sea.

c.4000 BC

With the appearance of the plow in Mesopotamia, planting can be done in rows or furrows instead of in holes, allowing more crops to be planted in less time and more food to be produced.

c.4000 BC

The Sumerians make cheese in Mesopotamia.

c.4000 BC

The yoke is used possibly for the first time in the Near East. It is a wooden bar or frame that rests on the shoulders or withers of draft animals and is tied to the neck or horns to assure that they pull together.

c.3500 BC

The edible olive is grown on the island of Crete. It is eventually used primarily for its oil.

c.3500 BC

Sumerians describe methods of managing the date harvest.

c.3400 BC

Opium is first cultivated in lower Mesopotamia. The Sumerians called the poppy Hul Gil or the "joy plant." The art of poppy cultivation subsequently spreads from the Sumerians to the Assyrians, and from the Assyrians to the Babylonians and Egyptians.

c.3100 BC

Peanuts and sweet potatoes are domesticated and grown on the west coast of South America in what is now Peru.

c.3000 BC

Making sugar from sugarcane in India is known to be practiced at this time.

c.2700 BC

Certain cereal and forage grasses, now classed as millet, form one of the chief sources of food in China. The Chinese claim that wheat used as food during this period is a direct gift from Heaven.

c.2700 BC

Tea drinking begins in China.

c.2500 BC

Apiculture or beekeeping begins in Egypt around this time. One of the oldest forms of animal husbandry, it involves the care and manipulation of colonies of honeybees (of the "Apis" species) so that they will produce and store a quantity of honey above their own requirements.

c.2400 BC

Food is known to have been stored by primitive man below ground in pits during winter months in what is now Eastern Europe. This is an early form of cold storage and food preservation.

c.2000 BC

The shduf or shadoof, a hand-operated device for lifting water, appears in Egypt and Mesopotamia. It consists of a long, tapering pole mounted like a seesaw with a skin or bucket hung from one end and a counter weight at the other end. It is still used in India and Egypt today.

c.1500 BC
A primitive seed drill for planting seeds is introduced in Sumer.

c.1500 BC
The beam press is used in Greece to squeeze olives and grapes mechanically. It is a considerable improvement over the old manual "bag press."

c.1400 BC
Fatty matter (animal and vegetable oils and fats) are used to lubricate the axles of chariot wheels.

c.1350 BC
The Rollins papyrus, containing elaborate bread accounts, is dated to this time. It indicates how large numbers are used in everyday, practical ways.

c.1100 BC
The rotary or true quern for grinding grain appears in the Mediterranean area. It uses a handle that rotates one stone atop a stationary stone. It is the precursor of the heavy querns used later by the Greeks and Romans that are operated by slaves or donkeys.

c.1000 BC
Oats are cultivated in central Europe. This important cereal plant is used primarily for livestock feed but also is processed for human consumption. It is not used for breads.

c.1000 BC
The Chinese preserve their foods by salting, drying, smoking, and fermenting them in wine vinegar.

c.1000 BC
Flax is known to have been harvested by people living in what is now Switzerland. It is not known if it is used solely for food.

AD

35
Marcus Gavius Apicius, Roman epicure, writes what many consider to be the oldest cookbook. Titled *De Re Coquinaria* (On the Subject of Cooking), it contains glimpses of Roman cooking and eating habits as well as recipes.

75
Pliny (23–79) recommends eating animal testicles to improve the sexual function of men.

1000
In Naples, a food called "pieca" is eaten and is regarded by some as the forerunner of modern pizza.

1100
In western North America, the Hopi tribe of Native Americans uses coal for both heating and cooking purposes.

1200
Buckwheat is introduced into Europe from Asia. It becomes a staple grain crop for poultry and livestock and is also cooked and served much like rice. It is not considered suitable for bread-making.

1202
King John of England (1167–1216) proclaims England's first food law. The Assize of Bread prohibits adding undisclosed ingredients such as ground peas or beans to bread.

1560
Jean Nicot de Villemain (1530–1600), French ambassador to Portugal, sends tobacco seeds from the New World to Paris and introduces tobacco into France and the rest of Europe. Tobacco is already being smoked in Portugal and Spain.

1600
French agronomist Olivier de Serres (1539–1619) publishes *Theatre d'Agriculture et Mesnage de Champs*, a textbook on French agricultural practices. He is also the first to practice systematic crop rotation.

1609
The first yield of corn that is produced by American colonists is harvested by the Jamestown colony in Virginia. The Jamestown settlers learned how to grow corn from the Native Americans two years earlier.

1623
Flax is first introduced in America and is cultivated solely for its fiber, from which linen and yarn are made. The seeds of the plant are called linseed from which linseed oil is made.

1650
Glass bottles replace stoneware for conserving wine and beer. They are made by the mouth-blowing technique and are surprisingly standardized.

1670
The first cookbook written by a woman is published. Written by Hannah Woolley (1622–c.1675) of England, *The Queen like Closet; or, Rich Cabinet* sees several editions.

1679
French physicist Denis Papin (1647–1712) develops a steam digester that is the

forerunner of the pressure cooker. Work on this device leads him to later experiment with steam pushing a piston.

1701   English agriculturalist and inventor Jethro Tull (1674–1741) invents a seed drill that sows seed in neat rows, saving seed and making it easier to keep weeds down. His horse-drawn hoes destroy weeds and keep the soil between the rows in a friable condition.

1716   The first unambiguous account of plant hybridization is given by the American writer Cotton Mather (1663–1728). He describes a case involving red and blue kernels of *Zea mays* (corn).

1727   English botanist and chemist Stephen Hales (1677–1761) studies plant nutrition and measures water taken up by plant roots and released by leaves. He states that something in the air (CO_2) is converted into food, and that light was necessary for this purpose. His work *Vegetable Staticks*, published in this year, lays the foundation for plant physiology.

1728   Italian physician Jacopo Bartolomeo Beccaria (1682–1766) discovers gluten in wheat flour. This is the first protein substance of plant origin to be found.

1731   English agriculturalist and inventor Jethro Tull (1674–1741) publishes *Horse-Hoeing Husbandry*; its advanced ideas help form the basis of the modern system of British agriculture.

1742   The first cookbook published in the American colonies is *The Compleat Housewife; or, Accomplished Gentlewoman's Companion*, published at Williamsburg, Virginia. It was first written by a cook and published in London in 1727. Following this first edition, this popular work went through a total of 18 editions.

1747   Agricultural seeds are first sold commercially in the American colonies.

1747   One of the most popular cookbooks of the eighteenth century, *The Art of Cookery Made Plain and Easy* is published. It is reprinted in the first year and goes through 20 editions, continuing to be in publication until 1843. Its author is Hannah Glasse (1708–1770), though it was published anonymously.

1752   French physicist and physiologist René-Antoine Ferchault de Réaumur (1683–1757) studies the physiology of digestion and obtains gastric juice.

1753   Scottish physician James Lind (1716–1794) first publishes his *Treatise of the Scurvy*. This vitamin-deficiency disease, which killed more sailors on long voyages than did battle with the enemy, was finally eliminated in the British Navy some years after Lind's book. The Navy's practice of giving lime juice to their crews resulted in British sailors being called "limeys."

1768   Italian biologist Lazzaro Spallanzani (1729–1799) concludes that boiling a sealed container prevents microorganisms from entering and spoiling its contents. (See 1795.)

1770   Swedish chemist Karl Wilhelm Scheele (1742–1786) discovers tartaric acid. One of the most widely distributed of the plant acids, it eventually assumes a wide variety of food and industrial uses.

1780   Swedish chemist Karl Wilhelm Scheele (1742–1786) discovers lactic acid. Found in the soil, in the blood and muscles of animals, and in fermented milk products, it eventually is used in food processing and for tanning leather and dyeing wool.

1783   Chinch bug is first noted as a pest of wheat in the United States in North Carolina.

1784   David Landreth opens the first seed business in the United States in Philadelphia, Pennsylvania.

1785   The first organization of American agricultural societies convenes in Philadelphia, Pennsylvania.

1795   French inventor and chef Nicolas François Appert (1752–1841) discovers how to hermetically seal food and creates what becomes known as canning. He devises a method of putting food in corked glass bottles and immersing them in boiling water. This destroys microorganisms in the food (although bacteriology has not yet discovered this). Appert sets up a bottling plant at Massy, south of Paris, in 1804. (See 1810.)

1801   American legendary figure John Chapman (1774–1845), called "Johnny Appleseed," begins planting apple seeds throughout

Indiana and the adjacent territory. He uses the broadcast or scatter method of seeding, and he lives to see 100,000 acres with apple trees in them.

1802 The sugar beet is first introduced as a field crop into Germany where it becomes a commercial success.

1804 The soybean is first cultivated in the United States. It becomes a major crop after World War II (1939–1945).

1804 The first agricultural fair in America is held in Washington, DC.

1805 French agriculturalist Antoine-Augustin Parmentier (1737–1813) produces the first powdered milk.

1810 French inventor Nicolas François Appert (1752–1841) publishes *L'Art de Conserver les Substances Animals et Vegetables* (The Art of Preserving Animal and Vegetable Substances), which founds the commercial canning industry. He describes how to preserve food over long periods of time by putting it in corked and sealed bottles and submerging them in boiling water. He applies heat to kill anything that might cause spoilage and then excludes air. Appert also develops the bouillon cube.

1810 Peter Durand of England patents an improved version of food preservation by using tin-plate canisters instead of glass. He does not offer an easy method of opening the cans, however. (See 1811.)

1810 Scottish physicist and mathematician John Leslie (1766–1832) is the first to create artificial ice when he freezes water using an air pump.

1810 The first farm magazine in the United States, *The Agricultural Museum*, begins publication.

1811 Bryan Donkin (1768–1855) and John Hall of England buy Peter Durand's patent for canning food and establish the first cannery in England in 1812. They supply canned goods to the Royal Navy and to various Arctic expeditions.

1811 French industrialist Bernard Courtois (1777–1838) discovers iodine in the ashes of seaweed. The ingestion of burnt seaweed was recommended as a treatment for goiter by Spanish alchemist Arnold of

Villanova (c.1235–1311) around 1300 and is known to have been used by the Chinese around 1600 BC.

1811 A horse-drawn version of a circular-blade reaper is patented by an Englishman named Smith. Reapers are used to harvest mature grain crops.

1815 The secrets of the new canning methods are introduced into the United States by the Englishman Ezra Daggett, who begins a business hermetically sealing food in containers.

1819 The first distinctively agricultural journal in America, *American Farmer*, is published in Baltimore, Maryland.

1819 The canning industry in the United States begins in Massachusetts and New York. In Boston, Thomas Underwood packs fruits, pickles, and condiments in bottles, while in New York Thomas Kensett and Ezra Daggett pack seafood in bottles.

1820 The "wheat belt" in the U.S. Midwest begins its successful spread. Seventy-two percent of the U.S. population who are gainfully employed are engaged in agriculture.

1822 A wheat and barley reaper that uses a serrated horizontal bar moving side-to-side is developed by two Englishmen named Ogle and Brown.

1823 French chemist Michel-Eugène Chevreul (1786–1889) publishes his classic work *Recherches sur les corps gras d'origine animale* (Research on Animal Fats), which deals with oils, fats, and vegetable colors. He shows that fat is a compound of glycerol with an organic acid. This is one of the first works addressing the issue of the fundamental structure of a large class of compounds, and it has a revolutionary effect on the soap and candle industries.

1824 First preservation of meat in cans is made.

1827 French inventor and chef Nicolas François Appert (1752–1841) first condenses milk to make it keep better. Seven years later he invents the method of evaporating milk.

1827 The first slaughterhouse in Chicago is a log structure built by Archibald Clybourne. This marks the beginning of Chicago's meat packing industry.

1827   English chemist and physiologist William Prout (1785–1850) first classifies the components of food into carbohydrates, fats, and proteins. He uses the words saccharinous, oleaginous, and albuminous for the three respective groups.

1832   German chemist Heinrich Wilhelm Ferdinand Wackenroder (1798–1854) discovers carotene (carotin) in carrots. This organic compound is usually found as a pigment in plants, giving them a yellow, red, or orange color, and is converted in the liver of animals into vitamin A.

1835   German physiologist Theodor Schwann (1810–1882) discovers pepsin, the active digesting principle in the stomach.

1837   American inventor John Deere (1804–1886) develops a steel plow that he fashions from a circular saw blade. It is able to cut through the difficult prairie soils. He also realizes that a successful self-scouring steel moldboard depends upon its shape. His steel plow plays a large role in opening the western states to agriculture. His company becomes a leading maker of farm equipment.

1840   German chemist Justus von Liebig (1803–1873) publishes *Die Organische Chemie in ihrer Anwendung auf Agrikultur und Physiologie* (Organic Chemistry in Its Application to Agriculture and Physiology), in which he shows that plants synthesize organic compounds from carbon dioxide in the air, but take their nitrogenous compounds from the soil. He also says that ammonia (nitrogen) is needed for plant growth and introduces the use of mineral fertilizers.

1842   English agriculturalist John Benne Lawes (1814–1900) patents a process for treating phosphate rock with sulfuric acid to produce superphosphate. He also opens the first fertilizer factory this year, thus beginning the artificial fertilizer industry.

1845   The Irish potato famine begins and lasts for 15 years. Called "late blight," this fungus disease of potato and tomato plants destroys plants in two weeks' time and results in more than 30 percent of the population of Ireland either dying or being forced to emigrate.

1846   Robert Reid of the United States develops a new variety of corn known as "Reid's Yellow Dent" that eventually comes to dominate the Corn Belt.

1856   American surveyor and inventor Gail Borden (1801–1874) cans his sweetened, condensed milk using a heat and vacuum method. In 1858 he establishes the New York Condensed Milk Company.

1859   The Great Atlantic and Pacific Tea Company (A&P) is founded and eventually becomes one of the largest food chains in the United States.

1862   President Abraham Lincoln (1809–1865) signs legislation that creates the U.S. Department of Agriculture (USDA).

1864   French chemist and microbiologist Louis Pasteur (1822–1895) invents the process of slow heating that kills bacteria and other microorganisms. Called pasteurization, it is used first as a way of keeping wine and beer from turning sour.

1864   F. S. Davenport of the United States invents the sulky plow, which offers the farmer a seat to ride on behind his team.

1869   French chemist Hippolyte Mege-Mouries (1817–1880) patents his "oleomargarine" and wins a government prize given to the inventor of the best "cheap butter." His product consists of liquid beef tallow, milk, water, and chopped cow's udder churned into a solid form. It is first produced commercially in 1873 as "butterine."

1870   Superphosphates begin to be used as fertilizers. This soluble mixture is made from mineral phosphates treated with sulfuric acid, and its use as a rapid-acting fertilizer boosts agricultural production.

1874   German physician Adolf Kussmaul (1822–1902) explains diabetic coma as due to acetonaemia and describes the labored breathing or air hunger that accompanies that condition. It becomes known as "Kussmaul's respiration."

1877   Swedish inventor Carl Gustaf Patrik de Laval (1848–1913) invents the first cream separator. Operated by a steam engine, his device centrifugally spins milk and separates out the heavier cream from it.

1877   Frozen meat is packed in ice and successfully shipped from Argentina to France.

1878   Joseph Lister (1827–1912) publishes a paper describing the role of a bacterium he names *Bacterium lactis* in the souring of milk.

1879 A bread slicing machine is manufactured in England.

1883 A machine for making a self-opening, pleated, flat-bottomed grocery bag is patented by Charles Stilwell of the United States.

1886 Franz von Soxhlet (1848–1926) first suggests that milk given to infants be sterilized.

1888 Meat is shipped in railroad cars cooled by mechanical refrigeration for the first time in the United States.

1890 American agricultural chemist Stephen Moulton Babcock (1843–1931) perfects a test for determining the buttermilk content of milk and offers a standard method of grading milk.

1892 Scottish chemist and physicist James Dewar (1842–1923) improves the Violle vacuum insulator by constructing a double-walled flask with a vacuum between the walls. He then coats all sides with silver so heat will be reflected and not absorbed. His Dewar flask keeps hot liquids hot and cold liquids cold. This flask eventually becomes the first Thermos bottle.

1893 The first ready-to-eat breakfast cereal, "Shredded Wheat," is introduced by Henry D. Perky (1843–1906) of the United States.

1894 Max Rubner (1854–1932), a German physiologist, makes accurate caloric measurements of food and discovers that the energy produced by food being consumed by the body is the same amount as if that quantity had been consumed in a fire.

1895 Refrigeration is introduced for commercial and home food preservation.

1896 English engineer William Joseph Dibdin (1850–1925) and his colleague Schweder improve the sewage disposal systems in England with the introduction of a bacterial system of water purification. These improvements greatly reduce the number of waterborne diseases like typhoid fever.

1898 American agricultural chemist George Washington Carver (1860–1943) publishes his first agricultural paper. During his long and productive career, he develops hundreds of products from sweet potatoes, peanuts, and soybeans that prove valuable

alternatives to cotton and tobacco as staple crops. He also emphasizes crop rotation and diversification.

1901 Prince Edward Island, Canada, becomes the first province to enact prohibition legislation banning alcohol.

1902 The Horn & Hardart Baking Company of Philadelphia, Pennsylvania, creates an early automat that offers food for a "nickel in a slot."

1904 Russian physiologist Ivan Petrovich Pavlov (1849–1936) is awarded the Nobel Prize for physiology or medicine for his work establishing that the nervous system plays a part in controlling digestion and by helping to found gastroenterology.

1906 English biochemist Frederick Gowland Hopkins (1861–1947) first argues that certain "accessory factors" in food are necessary to sustain life. This theory of trace substances becomes the starting point of further work on vitamin requirements.

1906 Freeze-drying is invented by Jacques Arsène d'Arsonval (1851–1940) of France and his colleague, George Bordas. This food preservation process works on the principle of removing water from food. It is not perfected until after World War II (1939–1945). (See 1946.)

1906 Japan begins the production of monosodium glutamate (MSG) as a flavor-enhancer for foods. By 1926, production reaches industrial proportions.

1906 The Pure Food and Drug Act of 1906 and its companion bill the Federal Meat Inspection Act are passed in the United States. The two pieces of legislation sought to remedy the adulteration of food, addition of intoxicating ingredients, and unsanitary conditions in the food processing industry that had been exposed by Progressive Era reformers.

1908 George H. Shull (1874–1954) proposes using self-fertilized lines in the production of commercial seed corn. This results in highly successful hybrid corn programs.

1912 American biochemist Casimir Funk (1884–1967) coins the word "vitamine." Since the dietary substances he discovers are in the amine group, he calls all of them "life-amines" or "vitamines."

1913   Swedish inventor Carl Gustaf Patrik de La-val (1849–1913) perfects a vacuum milking machine. Despite its efficiency, it is painful to the cows.

1913   American biochemist Elmer Verner Mc-Collum (1879–1967) discovers that a factor essential to life is present in water-soluble fats; it is soon named vitamin A.

1914   Pasteurization of milk begins in many large cities.

1917   American inventor Clarence Birdseye (1886–1956) begins to develop a process for freezing foods in small packages suitable for retailing. His process is highly efficient, and he founds the General Seafoods Company in 1924.

1917   German organic chemist Adolf Windaus (1876–1959) extracts cholestrin (later known as vitamin D) from cod liver oil and formulates it.

1917   Canada enacts legislation restricting the import, sale, and manufacture of alcohol. Several provinces have total bans on alcohol by this time, but the union government permits the importation of beverages with 2.5 percent alcohol or less into Canada for sale in those provinces without bans.

1920   The Prohibition Era begins in the United States as the nationwide alcohol ban enacted the previous year takes effect.

1922   The first canned baby food is manufactured in the United States by Harold H. Clapp of New York.

1922   American biochemist Ernest Verner McCollum (1879–1967) discovers and names vitamin D as a substance found in cod liver oil that prevents the deficiency disease rickets.

1922   Herbert McLean Evans (1882–1971), an American anatomist, embryologist, and physician, and his colleagues discover vitamin E.

1926   American pathologist Joseph Goldberger (1874–1929) and his colleagues discover the cause and cure of the disease pellagra. This disease leads to a severe skin condition, diarrhea, and eventually coma and death. He discovers that it is caused by a diet totally deficient in niacin (vitamin B3) and protein.

1926   Dutch biochemists Barend C. P. Jansen and Willem F. Donath first isolate vitamin B1.

1927   Hungarian-American physicist Albert Szent-Gyorgyi (1893–1986) discovers ascorbic acid or vitamin C while studying oxidation in plants.

1927   The first stainless steel cookware is made in the United States by the Polar Ware Company.

1928   Hungarian-American biochemist Albert Szent-Gyorgyi (1893–1986) first isolates and describes ascorbic acid. In 1931, he shows this to be identical to vitamin C.

1929   Dutch physician Christiaan Eijkman (1858–1930) is awarded the Nobel Prize for physiology or medicine for his discovery that the disease beriberi is the result of a nutritional deficiency. He is also the first to experimentally establish a deficiency disease. English biochemist Frederick Gowland Hopkins (1861–1947) is also awarded the Nobel Prize for physiology or medicine for his discovery of growth-stimulating vitamins.

1930   The first sliced and packaged bread, "Wonder Bread," is introduced in the United States.

1930   The first stationary electric food mixer, the Mixmaster, is introduced in the United States by the Sunbeam Company.

1930   The first modern supermarket is the chain of King Kullen food stores operated in New York by Michael Cullen of the United States.

1931   Erma Rombauer's *The Joy of Cooking*, a modern comprehensive cookbook intended for homemakers, is first published. The book becomes the bestselling cookbook of the twentieth century.

1932   American biochemist John Howard Northrop crystallizes trypsin, a protein-splitting digestive enzyme of pancreatic secretions.

1933   Prohibition of alcohol ends in the United States, reintroducing the legal manufacture, importation, and sale of liquor, beer, and wine.

1934   German biochemist Philipp Ellinger (1888–1952) and Walter Koschara discover vitamin B2 (riboflavin) and establish its chemical formula.

1934   Danish biochemist Carl Peter Henrik Dam (1895–1976) discovers vitamin K and finds it to be a factor in blood clotting.

1937 Shopping carts are made available to food customers at Humpty Dumpty Stores in Oklahoma. They are a basket attached to a folding chair on wheels.

1937 English chemist Walter Norman Haworth (1883–1950) is awarded the Nobel Prize for chemistry for his investigations on carbohydrates and vitamin C. Swiss chemist Paul Karrer (1889–1971) is also awarded the Nobel Prize for chemistry for his investigations on carotenoids, flavins, and vitamins A and B2. Hungarian-American physicist Albert Szent-Gyorgyi (1893–1986) receives the Nobel Prize in physiology and medicine for his work on vitamin C.

1938 Austrian-German chemist Richard Kuhn (1900–1967) first isolates vitamin B6 (pyridoxine) from skim milk.

1939 Food stamps program is introduced in the United States.

1940 American biochemist Vincent Du Vigneaud (1901–1978) identifies a compound called biotin as being what previously had been known as vitamin H.

1940 The first MacDonald's and Dairy Queen restaurants open in the United States, sparking the spread of fast-food culture worldwide.

1941 *Gourmet* magazine publishes its first issue.

1942 American food manufacturer Wrigley Company develops packed rations military personnel serving overseas during World War II (1939–1945). Typical ration packets contained items like graham biscuits, canned meat, cigarettes, sugar, pickles, flavoring sauces, and chewing gum.

1943 Danish biochemist Henrik Carl Peter Dam (1895–1976) is awarded the Nobel Prize for physiology or medicine for his discovery of vitamin K. American biochemist Edward Adelbert Doisy (1893–1986) is awarded the Nobel Prize for physiology or medicine for his discovery of the chemical nature of vitamin K.

1944 The worldwide introduction of mechanized agricultural practices and bioengineered crops in developing nations struggling with food insecurity begins, sparking what becomes known as the Green Revolution.

1945 Earl Tupper (1907–1983) invents Tupperware plastic food storage containers.

1945 The Food and Agriculture Organization (FAO) is formally organized as part of the United Nations (UN). It is the oldest permanent specialized agency in the UN, and its objective is eliminating hunger and improving nutrition.

1946 American bacteriologist Earl W. Flosdorff (1904–1958) demonstrates that the process of freeze-drying can be used to preserve coffee, orange juice, and even meat. When food is flash frozen in a vacuum, the water in it sublimates or changes directly from a liquid into a vapor. Because the water sublimates rather than melts, the food's tissues do not collapse.

1946 The Culinary Institute of America, dedicated to educating professional chefs and restaurant owners, opens.

1947 The microwave oven is introduced. The first commercial model is known as the Radarange.

1948 American biochemist Edward Lawrence Rickes, with N. G. Brink, F. R. Koniusky, T. R. Wood, and K. Folkers, first crystallizes vitamin B12.

1948 Prince Edward Island is the last Canadian province to repeal its prohibition laws.

1963 The United Nations Food and Agricultural Organization (FAO) and the United Nations General Assembly establish the World Food Programme (WFP) on a trial basis. The WFP provides food aid and agricultural development assistance to developing regions.

1964 Automated irrigation systems are field-tested for agricultural use in the United States.

1965 Dwarf, high-yield rice is introduced in India and other Asian nations. It requires higher-than-usual amounts of fertilizer and insecticides. It also contributes to what becomes known as the Green Revolution.

1965 After a successful trial period, The World Food Programme (WFP) is made a permanent agency.

1967 The U.S. Wholesome Meat Act of 1967 requires the inspection of meat that stays within state lines. Meat must be certified as truthfully labeled, sanitary, unadulterated, and free of disease.

1968 The Poultry Products Inspection Act passes, requiring the inspection of most poultry sold in the United States. The law also creates a unified inspection division for all meats subject to federal inspection.

1970   American agronomist Norman Borlaug (1914–2009), dubbed the "Father of the Green Revolution," is awarded the Nobel Peace Prize for promoting food security by increasing the global food supply.

1970   The U.S. Food and Drug Administration (FDA) orders the recall of canned tuna fish after mercury levels above 0.5 parts per million are discovered in it.

1971   American chemist Robert Burns Woodward (1917–1979) first synthesizes vitamin B12.

1981   The artificial sweetener aspartame is approved for general use by the U.S. Food and Drug Administration (FDA). Discovered in 1965, it does not have saccharin's bitter aftertaste.

1986   The U.S. Department of Agriculture (USDA) approves the release of the first genetically altered virus as well as the first outdoor test of genetically altered plants. The virus is to be used to combat swine herpes, and the plants are high-yield tobacco plants.

1986   Italian advocate Carlo Petrini founds the International Slow Food movement.

1992   Nutrition fact labels indicating nutrition information such as calories per serving appear on all manufactured or processed foods sold in the United States, as directed by the Nutrition Labeling and Education Act of 1990.

1994   The first genetically-altered food for human consumption, the Flavr Savr tomato, gains approval by the Food and Drug Administration (FDA) and is sold in U.S. food stores.

1993   The Food and Drug Administration (FDA) approves bovine somatropin (BST), a genetically-engineered synthetic hormone that increases the amount of milk given by dairy cows.

1994   The Dietary Supplement Health and Education Act declares supplements a food ingredient, thereby permitting regulation. The law establishes specific labeling requirements, manufacturing practices, and evaluation of claims or use of a disclaimer that the product is evaluated for effectiveness.

1996   Olestra, a calorie-free fat substitute, is approved by the Food and Drug Administration (FDA) for use in processed foods, despite reports that its ingestion can cause gastrointestinal side effects.

1997   A record El Niño develops in the Pacific Ocean, altering the typical hurricane pattern and causing severe drought in Australia, Northern Africa, and Southeast Asia.

1997   The Food and Drug Administration (FDA) revises its recommendations for vitamin intake, replacing the recommended dietary allowances (RDAs), with dietary reference intakes (DRIs), intended to support optimum health.

1997   The Food and Drug Administration (FDA) permits manufacturers of low-fat, oat-rich cereals that are found to lower cholesterol in the blood to advertise the claim.

1997   A study argues that women who eat whole-grain foods and other rich sources of phytoestrogens are found less likely to develop breast cancer.

1998   The Food and Drug Administration (FDA) approves a bacterial spray for newly hatched chicks laden with beneficial bacteria which prevent their picking up *Salmonella* and other bacteria that cause food poisoning.

1999   The United States leads the world in corn production, a crop grown on every continent except Antarctica, due to scientists' development of diverse hybrid varieties that suit growing conditions and locations worldwide.

1999   A U.S. federal study reveals that dioxins in breast milk can permanently weaken children's molars, and repeated occupational exposure to dioxins can increase a person's risk of developing fatal cancers.

1999   Scientists develop plants that infuse crop soils with biodegradable pesticides.

2000   The Cartagena Protocol on Biosafety is adopted in Montreal, Canada. The protocol, negotiated under the United Nations Convention on Biological Diversity, is one of the first legally binding international agreements to govern the trade or sale of genetically modified organisms of agricultural importance.

2000 Food irradiation is endorsed by the United States Food Protection Agency, the American Medical Association, and the World Health Association, and over 40 countries sterilize food by irradiation.

2000 The Institute of Medicine of the U.S. National Academy of Sciences increases the recommended daily consumption of dietary antioxidants, such as vitamins C and E.

2001 European countries, including France and Germany, push for tough European Union rules regulating the sale of genetically modified foods. The U.S. State Department brands the new rules without scientific merit.

2001 New food labels will identify choline-rich foods. Choline is a nutrient essential for learning and brain health.

2002 The United Nations holds an Earth Summit in Johannesburg, South Africa, to focus on international regulations that address environmental problems: water and air quality, accessibility of food and water, sanitation, agricultural productivity, and land management, that often accompany the human population's most pressing social issues: poverty, famine, disease, and war.

2002 Drought conditions again threaten eastern Africa, with an estimated 15 million people in Ethiopia, 3 million in Kenya, 1.5 million in Eritrea, and 3 million in Sudan facing the risk of starvation as a result.

2002 Reports surface that scaremongering concerning genetically modified foods causes several African countries fighting starvation to reject genetically modified food supplements that may have reduced starvation and death rates.

2002 The agricultural chemical atrazine, used in weed control, is thought to be partially responsible for the dramatic global decline in amphibians, as it is found to disturb male frog sex hormones, altering their gonads.

2002 Biochemists discover that starchy foods become contaminated by the animal carcinogen acrylamide when fried, and scientists

attempt to find the threshold for human exposure and risk.

2003 An obesity working group is established by the U.S. Commissioner of Food and Drugs to study ways that food and advertising regulation could help address the U.S. obesity epidemic.

2004 The Food Allergy Labeling and Consumer Protection Act requires food labels to disclose whether a food contains any protein derived from peanuts, soybeans, cow milk, eggs, fish, crustacean shellfish, tree nuts, or wheat—the eight most common sources of food allergies.

2004 The Food and Drug Administration (FDA) bans dietary supplements containing ephedrine.

2004 A joint advisory by the Food and Drug Administration (FDA) and Environmental Protection Agency (EPA) suggests limiting consumption of tuna and certain other fish by children and women of childbearing age after findings show low levels of mercury contamination. Coal-fired power plants are suspected to release into lakes and streams up to half of the mercury that eventually makes its way into oceans and contaminates fish.

2004 Amid the worst drought in over 100 years, Australian scientists warn that the continent faces an environmental crisis unless scarce water resources in the world's most arid inhabited continent are carefully managed.

2006 Norway announces plans to build a "doomsday vault" in a mountain close to the North Pole that will house a two-million-crop seed bank in the event of catastrophic climate change, nuclear war, or rising sea levels.

2006 The Oakland, California, city council passes a measure to ban Styrofoam packaging for restaurant takeout food.

2006 Researchers report that carbon dioxide from industrial emissions is raising the acidity of the world's oceans, threatening plankton and other organisms that form the base of the entire marine food web.

2007 The World Wildlife Fund (WWF; also known as the World Wide Fund for Nature) conservation group states that climate change, pollution, over extraction of water, and encroaching development are killing some of the world's major rivers, including China's Yangtze, India's Ganges, and Africa's Nile.

2008   Oil and food prices rise sharply on a global scale, increasing widespread dangers of famine and poverty. Critics contend increased prices for petroleum lead to the diversion of food crops to biofuel production.

2008   Global agricultural experts issue a warning that UG99, a plant rust fungus that kills up to 80% of current wheat strains, threatens crops (most immediately those in developing countries). The spread of UG99 raises the specter of widespread wheat crop destruction on a global scale. Such destruction would, of course, result in massive poverty for farmers, widespread economic damage, increased global wheat prices (at a time when wheat prices have already experienced sharp increases), and possible famine.

2008   Despite initial studies suggesting that vitamin C and vitamin E supplements might offer some protection against prostate cancer, two major separate studies published in the *Journal of the American Medical Association* argue that taking vitamin C and vitamin E supplements fails to reduce risk of any cancers. Public health researchers also argue that improper use of vitamins can lessen the importance of following a healthy diet known to reduce cancer risk.

2009   The last issue of *Gourmet* magazine is published in November. Publishers cite decreased readership and the global economic crisis as reasons for ceasing publication.

2009   Falling prices and reduced U.S. demand for dairy products prompt dairy farmers to sell hundreds of thousands of dairy cows, up to 15 percent of the U.S. herd, for meat slaughter.

2010   The Food Network, the most popular cable channel devoted to food and cooking themes, reaches almost 100 million homes.

2010   A trans fat ban takes effect in California, the first state to ban trans fats in restaurants and retail food establishments. Several U.S. cities, including New York, had previously enacted similar bans.

Junk Food

Introduction

There is general agreement that junk food is typically high in fat, especially the unhealthy saturated or trans fats, has added salt and sugar, is likely to be high in calories and highly processed, contains artificial ingredients, and has relatively little nutritional value. Junk food is generally tasty, satisfying (at least temporarily), appears to be inexpensive and easy to eat, can be addictive, and contributes to obesity. It is often said that "the more junk food you eat, the more junk food you want." Junk food has been likened to illicit drugs in its addictive capacity, and a number of scientific reports indicate that frequent consumption of junk food alters brain chemistry, shutting off the alarm system that tells the body it has had enough food. In another study, involving rats that were fed a diet of high-calorie junk food, the rats preferred to starve rather than switch to healthy food, additional evidence of the powerful, addictive effect of junk food on the brain.

Obesity through the lifespan has risen dramatically around the globe, and it has been termed a world-wide epidemic for children and youth. According to figures published by the World Health Organization (WHO), in 2010 approximately 42 million children under five years of age are overweight. Of those children, 35 million live in developing countries. In the United States, First Lady Michelle Obama's (1964–) primary social cause involves educating the public about the seriousness of childhood obesity in America and decreasing the child and youth obesity rate significantly within a generation.

Historical Background and Scientific Foundations

The United States is generally credited with the refinement and mega-marketing of junk food. Categorically, junk food mainly consists of sugar-added sodas, sweet desserts, heavily processed snack foods, candy, gum, and many types of fried foods.

Cracker Jack is generally considered the first commercially available junk food. Created by Frederick (1846–1934) and Louis Rueckheim (1849–1927), it was sold for the first time at the 1893 Chicago World's Fair. By 1896 the Rueckheims had refined their packaging and begun a national marketing campaign.

In 1905, in New York City, Tootsie Rolls were the first junk food to be individually wrapped for convenient sales. The popsicle, inadvertently invented in San Francisco in 1905 by an 11-year-old boy named Frank Epperson (1894–1983), was patented by him in 1923. In 1928 a Fleer Chewing Gum employee named Walter Diemer (1904–1998) invented bubble gum. It was sold by Fleer and marketed under the name Dubble Bubble. The original Twinkies, created by baking plant manager James Dewar (1897–1985) in 1930 were small shortcakes filled with banana cream. The banana was replaced by vanilla cream during World War II (1939–1945).

By the late 1970s, junk food was mass marketed and readily available, particularly at so-called convenience stores, across America. The Seven-Eleven convenience store chain introduced the idea of super-sizing when they branded a 32-ounce soda called the "Big Gulp." The Big Gulp was followed by the 64-ounce "Double Gulp" in 1998. Portion sizes continue to grow; what was once a large portion size has since become small, and super-sizing portions for fast foods has become the norm.

The United States Centers for Disease Control (CDC) has reported that more than 60 percent of adults and roughly 15 percent of the children and youth in America are either overweight or obese. There is a strong causal link between exposure to marketing and ease of access to junk food and likelihood of being (or becoming) overweight or obese. The WHO has recommended that children have limited exposure to television advertising of junk food, and that all schools and play areas be prohibited from marketing or advertising any form of junk food.

WORDS TO KNOW

OBESITY: Excess amount of body fat; usually defined by a body mass index (BMI) measurement of 30 or more, based on age and gender.

OVERWEIGHT: Defined as having a body mass index (BMI) of 25.0–29.9, based on age and gender.

TRANS FATS: Hydrogenated, unsaturated fats often present in processed foods that lower the HDL (good) cholesterol and raise the LDL (bad) cholesterol in the blood and are, therefore, associated with an increased risk for developing heart disease.

■ Impacts and Issues

In 2008 the CDC reported that more than one-third of American high schools allowed students to purchase junk food, either during lunch or at other times of the day. Some schools contracted with fast food suppliers to sell their wares as part of the school lunch program. Many permitted junk food sales outside of the lunch period as a means of fund-raising, citing that the money made could be put directly into school programs. The CDC study encompassed 12 cities and 36 states. In a large subset of the study, the CDC reported that the percentage of high schools selling junk food to students at lunchtime declined from 53 percent in 2004 to roughly 37 percent in 2006. During the same time period, there was no change in the percentages of schools selling junk food outside of the lunch period.

Teens are attracted to the convenience of tasty packaged foods, economically priced and readily available through school vending machines of snack sales areas. They are cited as unlikely, in general, to be close readers of nutritional labeling. A hamburger can be healthy, if a freshly prepared low-fat cut of beef is broiled or grilled. Conversely, a high-fat, heavily processed cut of meat, perhaps mixed with meats or fillers other than beef, that is fried or cooked on a griddle surface where fat cannot drain off, is considered junk food.

According to the journal *Pediatrics*, the prevalence of overweight among American children doubled

County and state fair food stands advertise junk food items like sno-cones, funnel cakes, candy apples, popcorn, peanuts, and pretzels.
Image copyright Laura Stone, 2010. Used under license from Shutterstock.com.

The majority of American school children drink at least one soft drink per day. In each 12 ounce soda there are 150 calories—the equivalent of 10 teaspoons of sugar. *Image copyright Felix Miozinikov, 2010. Used under license from Shutterstock.com.*

between 1984 and 2004, with almost a third of all American children meeting criteria for "at risk of overweight" and roughly 17 percent diagnosed as clinically overweight. In 2004, overweight was the most common medical condition of childhood in America. The dramatic rise in obesity brings with it a host of medical problems, among them juvenile-onset type 2 diabetes, high cholesterol, fatty liver, high blood pressure, formation of coronary plaques, and myriad behavioral and psychosocial stressors.

American children and youth who consume junk food are taking in an average of 40 percent fat and processed sugar calories daily. The bulk of those extra calories are assumed to result from the consumption of sugar-added sodas and soft drinks. The *Pediatrics* article cites an increase in soft drink consumption among American youth of 300 percent since 1980. With the advent of super-sizing, the size of each soft drink serving rose from 6.5 ounces in the 1950s to more than 20 ounces by the end of the century. According to the United States Department of Agriculture, between 56 and 85 percent of American school children consume one or more soft drinks daily. As soft drink consumption increases, milk and dairy intake decreases. A potential side effect of overall decreased milk intake, particularly among adolescents, is lower bone mass, leading to a higher risk of fragile bones and fractures later in life.

Early in 2010 PepsiCo announced that it would remove its full-calorie sweetened beverages from sales at schools around the world by 2012, replacing sodas and

soft drinks with bottled water and other, more healthful beverages. The Coca-Cola Company announced a similar plan for elementary school sales worldwide unless specific schools request that they remain, but reported that the company will continue sales of sugar-sweetened drinks at secondary schools.

SEE ALSO *Advertising Food; Diet and Cancer; Diet and Diabetes; Diet and Heart Disease; Diet and Hypertension; Dietary Guidelines for Americans; Dietary Reference Intakes; Fast Food; Improving Nutrition for America's Children Act of 2010; Obesity; Processed Foods; Sugar and Sweeteners; Truth in Labeling.*

BIBLIOGRAPHY

Books

Smith, Andrew F. *Encyclopedia of Junk Food and Fast Food*. Westport, CT: Greenwood Press, 2006.

Spurlock, Morgan. *Don't Eat This Book: Fast Food and the Supersizing of America*. New York: G. P. Putnam's Sons, 2005.

Witherly, Steven A. *Why Humans Like Junk Food*. New York: iUniverse, 2007.

Periodicals

"Addiction: Junk-Food Junkies." *Nature* 464, no. 7289 (2010): 652.

American Academy of Pediatrics Committee on Nutrition. "Prevention of Pediatric Overweight and Obesity." *Pediatrics* 112, no. 2 (2003): 424–430.

American Academy of Pediatrics Committee on School Health. "Soft Drinks in Schools." *Pediatrics* 112, no. 1 (2004): 152–154.

Web Sites

Fernandez, Manny. "Let Us Now Praise the Great Men of Junk Food." *New York Times*, August 7, 2010. http://www.nytimes.com/2010/08/08/weekinreview/08manny.html (accessed October 31, 2010).

Horovitz, Bruce. "Pepsi Is Dropping Out of Schools Worldwide by 2012." *USA Today*, March 17, 2010. http://www.usatoday.com/money/industries/food/2010-03-16-pepsicutsschoolsoda_N.htm (accessed October 31, 2010).

Nebehay, Stephanie. "WHO Targets Childhood Obesity with Market Curbs." *Reuters*, May 20, 2010. http://www.reuters.com/article/idUSTRE64J6A520100520 (accessed October 31, 2010).

Pamela V. Michaels

Lactose Intolerance

■ Introduction

Lactose intolerance, although not formally defined until the early 1960s, has been anecdotally described in historical writings for thousands of years. At birth, mammals (with rare exceptions) are able to consume the milk provided by their mothers in order to acquire nutrition. In the case of human infants who are unable to be breastfed, substitute formulas are required. The most commonly prescribed alternative formulas are cow-milk based. Nearly all mammalian milk (with the notable exception of lions) contains a complex sugar molecule called lactose. Human milk contains about 7 percent lactose; cow's milk contains between 4 and 5 percent lactose. Human infants produce an enzyme called lactase that breaks the lactose down into simple sugars, which can then be digested by the majority of babies. Those who are unable to absorb lactose and who develop a range of physical symptoms after ingesting cow's milk are termed lactose intolerant.

When lactose is ingested, the lactase enzyme breaks it down and converts it into the complex sugars glucose and galactose. Galactose is then processed by the liver, acted upon by the enzyme galactokinase, and converted into glucose. As with lactase, the human body produces progressively less galactokinase across the lifespan. When individuals who no longer produce lactase ingest dairy products, especially cow's milk, the lactose is fermented by enzymes in the intestines, leading to the physical symptoms of lactose intolerance: bloating, flatulence (gas), cramping, abdominal pain, and diarrhea. The more lactose ingested, the more severe and uncomfortable the resulting physical symptoms.

By mid-childhood, the production of lactase has dwindled significantly, and many human adults are unable to absorb lactose readily. There is significant ethnic and geographic variation in lactose tolerance. Nearly all Asian and Native American peoples, and the vast majority of Africans and Aboriginals, are lactose intolerant to some degree. In contrast, the majority of Scandinavians and Northwestern Europeans are highly lactose tolerant. The age at which lactase production diminishes sufficiently as to cause physical symptoms of lactose intolerance follows the ethnic variation in overall lactose intolerance. Those with the highest degree of lactose intolerance typically show symptoms at much earlier ages than the majority of lactose tolerant groups. Although statistics vary by research institution and location, the consensus appears to be that roughly three-fourths of the world's human population develops some degree of lactase deficiency by early adulthood. Despite the scientific evidence to the contrary, common parlance suggests that lactose intolerance is a deficiency disease, and that lactase persistence is the normative condition. The social implication, therefore, is that individuals or groups who exhibit lactose intolerance are somehow less healthy or less evolved than lactase persistors.

■ Historical Background and Scientific Foundations

The ancient Greek physician Hippocrates (c.460–370 BC) has been credited as the first person to write about his observation of physical symptoms evidenced by individuals after consuming raw milk. Early Romans drank little milk, but consumed significant quantities of aged cheese, which has minimal lactose content. Early Northern Europeans were described as large consumers of milk and non-aged dairy products. Early non-roving Asians did not drink milk, whereas their nomadic counterparts consumed it regularly, particularly in the form of horse milk. The Fulani peoples of Africa have traditionally herded cattle, sheep, and goats, have been nomadic, and have been significant consumers of milk and milk products.

Although there have been numerous written accounts dating back as far as the early Greek and Roman civilizations in which the physical symptoms associated with lactose intolerance have been described, it was not the subject of scientific research until technology had advanced enough for the development of tests to study intestinal enzyme activity, in the 1960s. By the late 1970s global data had been collected, and it had been determined that significantly decreased lactase production in adult humans was the norm.

There is a school of thought regarding racial and ethnic prevalence data concerning development of lactose intolerance: Nomadic, agrarian, or herding peoples whose dietary practices involved the lifelong consumption of milk and non-aged dairy products were more likely to remain lactose tolerant. Conversely, those whose cultures did not involve milk consumption developed early onset, broad-spectrum lactose intolerance. The theory suggests that it was advantageous for the survival of the species in cultures based on dairy farming to be able to continue to produce lactase into adulthood.

Another, less popular theory suggests that lactase persistence was genetically selected for in areas where

there was less daylight, leading to an increased need to acquire vitamin D from sources other than the sun. Because there is strong evidence that lactase persistence began in southern regions and gradually evolved northward in Europe, this theory has been largely debunked.

A mother and son drink tea with their dinner instead of milk because both are lactose intolerant. *AP Images.*

Yet another evolutionary or adaptation theory suggests that the persistence of lactase production was selected for both on the basis of proximity to an abundance of milk and milk products and a scarcity of potable water.

■ Impacts and Issues

Conventional wisdom has long suggested that cow's milk is a healthful and important part of the human diet in developed countries. Much has been made of the calcium present in cow's milk, and it has been touted as essential in order to develop and maintain strong bones throughout the lifespan. In fact, it is possible to obtain all of the nutrients present in cow's milk from other readily-available sources.

The lactase enzymes needed to digest lactose adequately are present in the vast majority of humans before birth, as nearly all lactating mammals produce lactose as part of their milk supply. Because human infants are programmed for survival, they are able to produce sufficient quantities of lactase through infancy until early toddlerhood, when most breastfed infants are weaned. Shortly after age one, lactase levels begin to decline, with levels falling throughout childhood and adolescence. In addition to containing the nutrients requisite for development of adequate early infant immunities, brain development and rapid growth, human (breast) milk also contains a bacteria called *Bacillus bifidus*, which assists in the digestion of lactose.

Based on several decades of scientific and survey research, it has been determined that the majority of adult humans are lactose intolerant. The groups with the highest rates of lactose intolerance are Native Americans, Aboriginal people, and Asians, followed by individuals of African heritage, those of Jewish ancestry, Hispanic people, and those whose ancestry includes Southern Europe. Northern Europeans and Scandinavians have the highest rates of lactase persistence (they are the least likely to be lactose intolerant).

Although there are laboratory tests available for determining lactose intolerance, it is most often self-reported. Individuals notice a causal or temporal relationship between ingestion of cow's milk or non-aged cheeses and the onset of gastrointestinal symptoms.

Overall, it appears that rates of lactase persistence are at least causally related to geographic origin: Those whose ancestry can be traced to early pastoral and herding cultures, such as the Scandinavians, northwestern Europeans, some areas of the Middle East, far northern Africa, and the nomadic and Bedouin cultures whose ancient livelihood involved the use of horses, camels, reindeer, and cows are most likely to retain lactose tolerance. Early cultures that did not involve herding and the drinking of mammalian milk, such as the Asians, Aboriginals, Native Americans, and most African tribes, did not retain the trait of lactase persistence.

SEE ALSO *Breastfeeding; Dairy Products; Food Allergies; Raw Milk Campaign.*

BIBLIOGRAPHY

Books

Carper, Steve. *Planet Lactose: Reports from the Worlds of Lactose Intolerance, Milk Allergies, and Dairy-Free Alternatives: The Best of the Planet Lactose Blog.* Rochester, NY: Planet Lactose Publishing, 2009.

National Dairy Council. *Lactose Intolerance and Minorities: The Real Story.* Rosemont, IL: National Dairy Council, 2005.

Wilt, Timothy J. *Lactose Intolerance and Health.* Rockville, MD: Agency for Health Care Policy and Research, U.S. Dept. of Health and Human Services, 2010.

Periodicals

Heyman, Melvin B. "Lactose Intolerance in Infants, Children, and Adolescents." *Pediatrics* 118, no. 3 (2006): 1279–1286.

"Lactose Intolerance and African Americans: Implications for the Consumption of Appropriate Intake Levels of Key Nutrients." *Journal of the National Medical Association* 101, no. 10 (2009): S5–S23.

Lomer, Miranda C., Gareth C. Parkes, and Jeremy D. Sanderson. "Review Article: Lactose Intolerance in Clinical Practice—Myths and Realities." *Alimentary Pharmacology & Therapeutics* 27, no. 2 (2008): 93–103.

Shaukat, Aasma, et al. "Systematic Review: Effective Management Strategies for Lactose Intolerance." *Annals of Internal Medicine* 152, no. 12 (2010): 797–803.

Suchy, Frederick J., et al. "National Institutes of Health Consensus Development Conference: Lactose Intolerance and Health." *Annals of Internal Medicine* 152, no. 12 (2010): 792–796.

Taylor, Cathy. "Lactose Intolerance in Infants." *Nursing Times* 102, no. 17 (2006): 43–44.

Voelker, Rebecca. "NIH Panel Tackles Lactose Intolerance." *JAMA: The Journal of the American Medical Association* 303, no. 13 (2010): 1240–1242.

Web Sites

"Lactose Intolerance." *National Institute of Diabetes and Digestive Disorders.* http://digestive.niddk.nih.gov/ddiseases/pubs/lactoseintolerance/ (accessed October 25, 2010).

Lee-Thorp, J., and B. R. Ackerman. "Lactose Intolerance is Normal!" *Science in Africa*, June 2002. http://www.scienceinafrica.co.za/2002/june/lactose.htm (accessed October 25, 2010).

Pamela V. Michaels

Land Availability and Degradation

■ Introduction

Land degradation is the process by which human activities decrease the productivity of land by negatively affecting soil, water, and vegetation. Land degradation may result in decreased agricultural productivity through lower yields. If land degradation is severe, however, the land may lose all productive capacity. Land degradation does not refer only to the loss of agricultural productivity; it may also involve the loss of productive forest land or other non-agricultural lands that suffer a decline in the ability to support vegetation or other life.

Both improper agricultural practices and the destruction of the existing physical environment can degrade the land. Deforestation, overgrazing, over fertilization, improper irrigation, depletion of soil nutrients through agricultural practices, and urbanization all contribute to degradation. Soil erosion, soil salination, and soil acidification are common after-effects of land degradation. Through improved agricultural practices and conservation, degradation may be slowed, or degraded lands can often be restored to productive use.

■ Historical Background and Scientific Foundations

Although the rate of land degradation has accelerated over the last several centuries, land degradation has been a significant issue since the rise of civilization approximately 7,000 years ago. Land degradation and agricultural collapse has contributed to the decline of numerous civilizations, including Mesopotamia, Egypt, Greece, and China. In *Essay on the Principle of Population* (1798), British political economist Thomas Malthus (1766–1834) describes the relationship between agriculture and population. Malthus illustrates how population could outstrip agricultural production if disease and famine do not keep population in check. Post-Malthusian political philosophers asserted that if population growth outpaces agricultural production for too long, without external checks on the population, a civilization would eventually collapse because of its overstressed agricultural system.

In "Tragedy of the Commons," an influential article in *Science* magazine in 1968, American ecologist Garrett Hardin (1915–2003) describes how people could overexploit natural resources to the detriment of the entire community. Hardin demonstrates that independent individuals, acting rationally and in their own self-interest, could deplete a shared resource to the point that the resource becomes degraded and unproductive for the entire community. Common examples of the tragedy of the commons include deforestation by a community in search of nearby wood for fuel or building materials, and overgrazing of communal land. If exploitation of these natural resources goes unchecked, then the community will ultimately deplete the natural resource.

Poor agricultural practices, including those involving a tragedy of the commons, combined with natural factors contribute to land degradation. Land degradation involves one or more human activities producing a negative effect on soil, water, or vegetation condition. Soil degradation is the deterioration of beneficial soil properties, usually through the loss of topsoil or nutrients. This degradation restricts agricultural production, and, if the degradation is severe, results in desertification.

Numerous human-related activities stress land and lead to soil degradation. Deforestation, the cutting of forests for timber or to clear land for agriculture, removes plants that hold soil in place, which results in soil erosion and possible desertification. Overgrazing by livestock also removes plants and leads to soil erosion and possible desertification. Poor agricultural practices, including failure to rotate crops, degrade the land by removing nutrients from the soil faster than they can be replaced. Improper irrigation can also lead to land degradation. All water contains dissolved salts. High levels of salts in the soil may reduce crop yields or make the land completely unsuitable for agriculture. Irrigation increases soil salinity in areas with poor drainage and in areas of high evaporation if the salts are not flushed out of the land later in the season. Overuse or improper use of fertilizers and other agricultural chemicals may also degrade land by increasing soil acidity or alkalinity.

■ Impacts and Issues

Land degradation decreases the agricultural productivity of land and, if the degradation is severe, may result in the complete loss of arable land. In 2008, the Food and Agriculture Organization (FAO) of the United Nations released the results of a 20-year study of land degradation around the globe. According to the study, approximately 1.5 billion people—roughly one-quarter of the world's population—depend directly on land that is currently being degraded. In addition, the FAO determined that land degradation is accelerating. The FAO estimates that 20 percent of agricultural land, 10 percent of grasslands, and 30 percent of forests are undergoing degradation. Whereas degrading land in arid and semi-arid areas is lost to desertification, land in humid areas also faces degradation. Globally, 22 percent of degrading land is in arid and semi-arid areas, and 78 percent of degrading land is in humid areas.

The causes of land degradation vary considerably among regions. Programs to slow or reverse land degradation, therefore, must be designed to address the causes of land degradation in a particular region. Globally, overgrazing is the leading cause of land degradation and accounts for about 35 percent of the problem.

Farmland destroyed by drought, overgrazing, and erosion in Central Tasmania, Australia. United Nations World Summits in 2002 and 2005 identified reversing the degradation of agricultural land as a major step towards protecting the environment and alleviating hunger.
© National Geographic Image Collection / Alamy.

In Africa, however, overgrazing accounts for about 50 percent, and in Oceania, overgrazing is responsible for approximately 80 percent of land degradation. Deforestation is responsible for 30 percent of global land degradation, but accounts for about 40 percent in South America, Asia, and Europe. Agricultural production is responsible for 28 percent of the world's land degradation, but accounts for nearly two-thirds of land degradation in North America.

The loss of agricultural productivity on degraded lands remains a major area of concern. As much as 40 percent of the world's agricultural land is already degraded, which reduces agricultural production and decreases food security. Between 1985 and 2000, the most recent years for which reliable statistics exist, the world lost 285 million hectares (704 million acres) of arable land. Less than 1.5 billion hectares (3.7 billion acres) of arable land is used for global agricultural production. Urbanization accounted for the loss of 150 million hectares (370 million acres) of arable land, followed by 60 million hectares (148 million acres) lost to soil salination and nutrient loss. Soil erosion removed an additional 50 million hectares (124 million acres) of arable land from production. Desertification claimed 25 million hectares (62 million acres) of arable land.

Despite the accelerated degradation of land around the world, farmers and governments can take steps to slow degradation or restore lands. Better urban planning and forest management can lessen or prevent land degradation caused by urbanization and deforestation. Lightly degraded soil may be restored by improved agricultural practices by farmers, including improved tillage, better irrigation, and crop rotation. Moderately degraded land requires the implementation of national programs such as drainage and large-scale soil conservation plans, combined with improved agricultural practices by farmers. Severely eroded land requires an enormous input of labor and capital to restore the land to productive use. Such investment generally is not economically feasible, especially in developing nations.

SEE ALSO *Agricultural Deforestation; Agricultural Demand for Water; Agroecology; Biodiversity and Food Supply; Biofuels and World Hunger; Climate Change and Agriculture; Desertification and Agriculture; Ecological Impacts of Various World Diets; Ethical Issues in Agriculture; Food and Agriculture Organization (FAO); Food Security; Sustainable Agriculture; Water; Water Scarcity.*

BIBLIOGRAPHY

Books

Chisholm, Anthony H., and Robert Dumsday. *Land Degradation: Problems and Policies.* Cambridge, UK: Cambridge University Press, 2009.

Clay, Jason. *World Agriculture and the Environment: A Commodity-by-Commodity Guide to Impacts and Practices.* Washington, DC: Island Press, 2003.

Johnson, Douglas L., and Laurence A. Lewis. *Land Degradation: Creation and Destruction.* Lanham, MD: Rowman & Littlefield, 2007.

Siva, Kumar M. V. K., and Ndegwa Ndiang'ui. *Climate and Land Degradation.* Berlin: Springer, 2007.

Wild, Alan. *Soils, Land and Food: Managing the Land during the Twenty-First Century.* Cambridge, UK: Cambridge University Press, 2003.

Periodicals

Dauvergne, Peter, and Kate Neville. "Forests, Food, and Fuel in the Tropics: The Uneven Social and Ecological Consequences of the Emerging Political Economy of Biofuels." *Journal of Peasant Studies* 37, no. 4 (2010): 631–660.

Kummerer, Klaus, Martin Held, and David Pimentel. "Sustainable Use of Soils and Time." *Journal of Soil and Water Conservation* 65, no. 2 (2010): 141–149.

Web Sites

"Food and Soil." *Global Education Project.* http://www.theglobaleducationproject.org/earth/food-and-soil.php (accessed October 30, 2010).

International Soil Reference and Information Centre (ISRIC). "Degraded Soil." *United Nations Environmental Programme.* http://maps.grida.no/go/graphic/degraded-soils (accessed October 30, 2010).

Wiebe, Keith. "Linking Land Quality, Agricultural Productivity, and Food Security." *U.S. Department of Agriculture (USDA),* June 2003. http://www.ers.usda.gov/Publications/AER823/ (accessed October 30, 2010).

Joseph P. Hyder

Latin American Diet

Introduction

The Latin American diet benefits from the rich biological diversity of the region and has been augmented over time by people from Europe, Africa, Asia, and the Middle East who became part of the ethnic fabric. Tomatoes, potatoes, chilies, pineapple, corn, quinoa, cassava, avocados, squash, chocolate, and guinea pigs: What do all these have in common? They are all foods that are native to Latin America.

Latin America is generally considered to be the countries in the Americas where Spanish or Portuguese is the predominant language, from Mexico south to Central America and South America, as well as a few Caribbean islands. With nearly 20 countries and a total population of more than 565 million, Latin America is made up of different native cultures and ethnic groups, each with its individual culinary traditions. Diet in the region also has been influenced over the centuries by African, European, and Asian peoples who came to Latin America as conquistadors, colonists, slaves, and laborers.

In the United States, people of Latino descent comprise the largest ethnic minority, an estimated 16 percent of the total 310 million U.S. population in 2009, according to the U.S. Census Bureau. They are the country's fastest growing minority. Latin culinary influences, once found only in urban ethnic communities, are pervasive in every area of American food from haute cuisine to school lunches to fast food—so much so that salsa, a condiment popular in Mexico and other Central American countries, has become one of the most popular condiments in the United States, along with ketchup and mustard.

Historical Background and Scientific Foundations

Dozens of indigenous groups inhabited Latin America about 14,500 years ago. The Aztecs and Mayans of Mexico and Central America and the Incas of South America are thought to have been the most populous. Many of the foods of the early twenty-first century can be traced back to early cultivation by these indigenous groups.

Estimates vary from about 5,000 to 9,000 years ago as to when maize (corn) first was cultivated from the plant teosinte (*Zea mays*) in the Central Highlands of Mexico. Over time, thousands of different corn varieties were developed, providing a rich biological diversity. Maize, beans, and squash comprised the basis of the ancient Aztec and Mayan diets.

Historical evidence of chocolate or cacao (*Theobroma cacao*) has been found among the Olmecs, an ancient group predating the Aztecs and Mayans, who lived in the tropical lowlands along what is now a portion of Mexico's Gulf Coast. First used as a currency and as a bitter ritual beverage, the pod was cultivated throughout Mesoamerica.

Farther south, in the Andes Mountains of South America, the Incas began cultivating potatoes (*Solanum tuberosum*) about 7,000 to 10,000 years ago. Thousands of potato varieties with unique shapes, colors, sizes, flavors, and textures belong to this one plant, and more than 200 wild species are documented from Argentina to the Southwestern United States in nearly every kind of climate including cold mountain climates, coastal valleys, and subtropical forests.

Chilies (*Capsicum*) generally are assumed to have originated in Bolivia though archeological evidence shows cultivation from about 6,000 years ago to the present on Caribbean Islands south to the Andes.

Tomatoes (*Solanum lycopersicum*) originated in an area that is now Chile, Ecuador, Bolivia, Peru, and Colombia. The wild fruit appeared in tiny clusters. Whether the tomato first was cultivated in Mexico or Peru has not been definitively determined, but the food became a staple in the ancient Incan, Mayan, and Aztec diets.

At the same time that conquistadors shared Latin America's agricultural bounty with the world, they also introduced the New World to other culinary influences. The Spanish and Portuguese colonizers were the first to introduce European foods to the New World. Remnants of these cuisines are evident throughout the region.

Distinct cuisines developed in Latin America as trade, slavery, and modernization occurred. Large numbers of Italians immigrated to Argentina beginning in the 1870s up until the 1960s, making Italian cuisine prominent and introducing a wheat-based diet. In Peru, Chinese slaves brought to work on sugar plantations in the 1850s added cooking techniques and ingredients to the local traditions. In the early twenty-first century, Chinese-Peruvian restaurants called chifas remain popular. African slaves brought to Cuba added their own preparations and spice palette to the native ingredients.

■ Impacts and Issues

The staples of the ancient Latin American diet, such as corn, beans, chilies, cassava, tomatoes, and potatoes, continue to be prevalent throughout Latin America. However, they have come to represent some of the most universally consumed foods in the world. Globally, corn is consumed more than any other grain. Total energy derived per capita from corn is more than wheat and nearly twice that of rice. Per capita, Eastern Europeans eat the most potatoes, more than quadruple Latin American consumption figures. Africans rely

> ### WORDS TO KNOW
>
> **BIODIVERSITY:** The number, variety, and variability of living organisms, including diversity within a species, between species, and among ecosystems.
>
> **CONQUISTADOR:** A conqueror, especially one of the sixteenth-century Spanish soldiers who defeated the indigenous civilizations of Mexico, Central America, or Peru.
>
> **CULTIVAR:** A variety of a plant that has been created or selected intentionally and maintained through cultivation.
>
> **LANDRACE:** A traditional crop variety.
>
> **MESOAMERICA:** A region extending south and east from central Mexico to include parts of Guatemala, Belize, Honduras, and Nicaragua.

heavily on cassava, also known as manioc or yuca, for their caloric intake. Chilies are a mainstay of the Asian and African diets.

Yet increased demand and trade liberalization have netted unintended consequences. In their native

Vendors offer a variety of potatoes, a key component of the Latin American diet, at the Mercado Central in Sucre, Bolivia.
© *Mike Finn-Kelcey / Alamy.*

habitat, thousands of corn, bean, potato, and tomato varieties once existed. As production has spread throughout the world, fewer and fewer cultivars are planted. Often, large scale production of genetically similar mono-crops replaces smaller fields of more diverse traditional crop varieties, called landraces, and agricultural techniques.

Loss of plant biodiversity is one outcome. Biodiversity loss can affect food security. With fewer plant varieties cultivated, crops are more susceptible to drought and pest infestations. Researchers have a smaller pool of plant varieties from which they might develop hybrids with desirable qualities such as natural disease resistance. Biodiversity loss also affects delicately balanced ecosystems that have developed over millennia.

In Mexico, for example, small-scale farmers are the guardians of more than 40 distinct maize landraces. Researchers at El Colegio de Mexico's Program on Science, Technology, and Development (PROCIENTEC) examined the effects of trade liberalization on maize biodiversity in the Mexican state of Chiapas. Their 2007 report found that due to economic pressures, small-scale farmers are shifting away from up to 12 different native maize landraces in 1960 to three landraces combined with eight commercial hybrids and two mestizos, or a mix of a native variety and a hybrid. Researchers found overall plant diversity in a three-hectare plot to have diminished from 32 different types of plants in 1960 to at most eight in 2007.

Just as foods native to Latin America have had a major impact on the world's diet, so has the world had an impact on Latin Americans' diet. Latinos living in the United States have adopted American dietary habits, leading to alarming obesity rates and other unhealthy outcomes such as diabetes, high cholesterol, and hypertension. Data compiled by the U.S. Centers for Disease Control revealed in its July 17, 2009 *Morbidity and Mortality Weekly Report* that 28.7 percent of U.S. Hispanic adults are obese, compared to 23.7 percent of non-Hispanic whites and 35.7 percent of non-Hispanic blacks.

Free trade and a more global economy also have accelerated the availability of American food trends throughout much of Latin America, particularly in large urban centers. In Latin America, McDonald's posted nearly 32 percent revenue growth in the second quarter of 2007, making it the company's strongest growing market worldwide. Burger King and Wendy's also reported robust growth in the region. Combined with other factors such as a more urban lifestyle and access to cheaper food, this influence has contributed to a rising number of obese and overweight adults in Latin American countries such as Brazil, Chile, Mexico, and Peru. The rate of overweight and obese Mexican adults is now on par with those in the United States with a combined rate of nearly 70 percent in each country.

SEE ALSO *Dietary Changes in Rapidly Developing Countries; Ecological Impacts of Various World Diets; Foodways*

BIBLIOGRAPHY

Books

Janer, Zilkia. *Latino Food Culture*. Westport, CT: Greenwood Press, 2008.

Presilla, Maricel E. *Cooking from Sun Country: A Cookbook of Latin American Cuisine*. New York: Scribner, 2009.

Wood, Andrew G. *On the Border: Society and Culture between the United States and Mexico*. Lanham, MD: SR Books, 2004.

Periodicals

Fonseca, Vanessa. "Nuevo Latino: Rebranding Latin American Cuisine." *Consumption, Markets and Culture* 8, no. 2 (2005): 95–130.

"New Twists on Latin American Foods: Latin American Cuisine Is a Mix of Worlds, Old and New, Near and Far, Native and Imported." *Prepared Foods* 172, no. 7 (2003): 57–64.

Uauy, Ricardo, Cecilia Albala, and Juliana Kain. "Obesity Trends in Latin America: Transiting from Under- to Overweight." *Nutrition* 131 (2001): 893S–899S.

Web Sites

Latin Fast Food Growth, Latin Business Chronicle. http://www.latinbusinesschronicle.com/ (accessed October 17, 2010).

U.S. Census Bureau. http://www.census.gov/ (accessed October 17, 2010).

USDA Foreign Agricultural Service. http://www.fas.usda.gov/ (accessed October 17, 2010).

Wise, Timothy. "Policy Space for Mexican Maize: Protecting Agro-biodiversity by Promoting Rural Livelihoods." *Tufts University*, February 2007. http://ase.tufts.edu/gdae/Pubs/wp/07-01Mexican Maize.pdf (accessed October 17, 2010).

Andrea Abel

Legumes

■ Introduction

Legumes are the second most important group of plants in the human diet, after grains and cereals. They are also the third largest family of flowering plants, after the orchids and the daisies. Their seeds, commonly known as peas and beans, are two to three times higher in protein than grains, and are also rich in both B vitamins and iron. They have long been a primary protein source and alternative to animal protein. The proteins in legumes contain all of the amino acids, unlike other vegetable proteins. They can also be readily dried and stored, then soaked before eating. In the early twenty-first century, legumes play an important part in the cuisines of Latin America, the Mediterranean, and Asia. They are also beneficial for agriculture, because they add nitrogen to the soil through their symbiotic relationship with Rhizobia bacteria. Planting legume crops therefore enriches the soil, whereas cereals deplete it. In crop rotation a cereal crop is followed by a legume crop, which keeps nitrogen levels steady. There is increasing interest in the health properties of beans; for instance soybeans contain phytoestrogens, which are under study for possible benefits in preventing prostate and breast cancers. Other beans are potent sources of antioxidants, such as the anthocyanin pigments in the coats of kidney beans and other colored beans.

■ Historical Background and Scientific Foundations

The lentil, native to southwest Asia, dates back around 9,000 years and is therefore probably the oldest cultivated legume. It was often grown with wheat and barley. The pea is almost as old and spread from the Middle East to the Mediterranean, India, and China. It became a very important protein source in Europe in the Middle Ages, particularly among the poor. Chickpeas (also known as garbanzo beans) and broad beans have been known, too, for around 8,000 and 6,000 years, respectively. In ancient Greece and Rome, citizens used black and white beans to indicate voting intentions. The common bean and lima bean of Latin America go back around 8,000 years, whereas the soy bean and mung bean of Asia appear to be more recent introductions.

Legumes cover several different botanical families, including peanuts, pigeon peas, chickpeas, lentils, beans, and broad beans. The familiar pods are fruits with seeds inside. A few can be eaten fresh if picked young, such as green beans and sugar snap peas, but mostly the legumes require soaking and cooking. Generally, the fruit is stripped away to reveal the seeds, whose coats are hard and non-porous. Water enters the seed only through the hilum, so it can take several hours for the seed to fully hydrate and be ready for cooking. Lentils are an exception, because they do not need to be soaked.

Although legumes are nutritious, being a good source of fiber, protein, and vitamins, they do have the potential to cause some health problems. They contain carbohydrates known as oligosaccharides, which consist of short chains of basic sugar units, bound with hemicelluloses and pectins, none of which can be digested by the human gut. These molecules pass into the bowel, where gut bacteria feed on them, producing flatulence. For some people, eating legumes leads not just to embarrassment, but also abdominal pain and bloating. The problem can be alleviated somewhat by rinsing legumes free of their soaking water before cooking. There are dangers in consuming raw or undercooked red-skinned kidney beans because they contain a toxin called phytohemagglutinin, which is broken down on thorough cooking. Another legume-related disease is favism, which occurs among some people in the Middle East or Mediterranean when the body breaks down vicine and convicine, amino acids in fava beans, to compounds that can damage red blood cells, causing a potentially fatal anemia. It has also been found that hyacinth beans and

WORDS TO KNOW

HILUM: The small pore in the center of the curved edge of a bean that allows water in during soaking to make a dried bean edible.

PULSES: Legumes dry well, and the dried versions are known as pulses. They consist mainly of starch and protein, and their water-resistant, hard coats make them easy to store.

RHIZOBIA: Species of soil bacteria that form a symbiotic relationship with legume plants, living inside nodules in their roots.

tropical strains of lima beans are high in cyanide-generating compounds that may be ingested if the beans are not cooked properly.

■ Impacts and Issues

Legumes are important in agriculture, nutrition, and cuisine. They are important in nutrition because they are high in protein and in agriculture because of their nitrogen production. Both of these functions are possible because legumes form a symbiotic relationship with Rhizobia bacteria in the soil. The bacteria enter the root hairs of a legume and establish a community inside the root nodules of the plant. Here they trap nitrogen from the air and fix it, by a series of biochemical reactions, into ammonium ions, a form that the plant can use to make amino acids and then proteins. The bacteria are unable to fix nitrogen on their own but can do so when they use the plant as a source of energy. The Rhizobia produce more nitrogen than the legume plant needs so the extra is deposited back into the soil, enriching it. Because cereals draw nitrogen out of the soil, it is good agricultural practice to carry out crop rotation, where legumes are planted on the same land following a cereal crop to restore nitrogen levels. Crop rotation has been known since Roman times.

Legumes are popular in cuisines worldwide because they lend themselves to drying and canning. This means they have become a staple, stored cupboard item. The way legumes are used in cuisine varies from the tinned baked beans of the Western world to hummus in the Mediterranean and Middle East and the soy products of Asia. Soybeans are probably the most significant legume crop in the world. Soy is processed into many different

One of Lebanon's leading chefs, Ramzi Shweiry, center, celebrates with others after preparing a massive bowl of falafel, a Middle Eastern dish made from chickpeas and beans, seen in the background, weighing 11,380 pounds (5,173 kg), in Fanar, east of Beirut, Lebanon, in May 2010. *AP Images.*

524

foods, including soy sauce, tempeh, tofu, miso, and even soy milk. Asian women have much lower rates of breast cancer than Western women, and some researchers have attributed this to their high consumption of soy, which contains phytoestrogens. Although these compounds are not fully understood, it may be that they can somehow block the action of human estrogen, which may confer an anti-cancer effect. Studies in the first decade of the 2000s offered conflicting results about any potential protective effects of soy; later studies, in contrast, point to a role in cancer prevention. The area of soy phytoestrogens in cancer prevention, therefore, remains an active area of research. Soy protein is also a useful alternative to animal protein and may be recommended to those who want to cut their saturated fat intake to avoid heart disease.

SEE ALSO *Agroecology; Diet and Cancer; Diet and Diabetes; Diet and Heart Disease; Diet and Hypertension; Dietary Guidelines for Americans; Dietary Reference Intakes; Mediterranean Diet; Protein and Carbohydrate Metabolism; Vegetarianism; World Food Programme*

BIBLIOGRAPHY

Books

Du Bois, Christine M., and Chee B. Tan. *The World of Soy.* Urbana: University of Illinois, 2008.

Food and Agricultural Organization (FAO) of the United Nations and the World Health Organization (WHO). *Codex Alimentarius: Cereals, Pulses, Legumes, and Vegetable Proteins.* Rome: WHO/FAO, 2007.

Lewis, G. P. *Legumes of the World.* Richmond, UK: Royal Botanic Gardens, Kew, 2005.

Lumpkin, Thomas A., et al. *Proceedings of the 1st International Conference on Indigenous Vegetables and Legumes Prospectus for Fighting Poverty, Hunger and Malnutrition: Hyderabad, India, December 12–15, 2006.* Leuven, Belgium: International Society for Horticultural Science, 2007.

Ojiem, John O. *Exploring Socio-Ecological Niches for Legumes in Western Kenya Smallholder Farming Systems.* Wageningen, The Netherlands: Wageningen University and Research Center, 2006.

Prakash, M., and S. Murugan. *Legumes, Their Production, Improvement and Protection.* Delhi, India: Satish Serial Pub. House, 2009.

Rao, Mamatha. *Legumes in India: Applications in Food, Medicine, and Industry.* New Delhi: Ane Books India, 2008.

Singh, Ram J., and Prem P. Jauhar. *Grain Legumes.* Boca Raton, FL: Taylor & Francis, 2005.

Periodicals

Duffy, Christine, Kimberly Perez, and Ann Partridge. "Implications of Phytoestrogen Intake for Breast Cancer. *CA: A Cancer Journal for Clinicians* 57, no. 5 (2007): 260–277.

Web Sites

Linus Pauling Institute. "Micronutrient Center: Legumes." *Oregon State University.* http://lpi. oregonstate.edu/infocenter/foods/legumes/ (accessed September 29, 2010).

Susan Aldridge

IN CONTEXT: CHICKPEA PASTE FOR CHILDREN IN PAKISTAN

When unprecedented flooding in 2010 left millions of people dependent on food aid in Pakistan, stocks of the World Food Programme's ready-to-use supplementary foods (RUSFs) were already weakened by multiple humanitarian crises around the world. A highly nutritious paste based on legumes, including the chickpea, made in Pakistan from local ingredients and according to local tastes, helped fill the RUSF gap, and became the dietary staple for thousands of Pakistani children affected by the flooding. After the emergency, more stocks of the new chickpea paste will be added to the World Food Programme's RUSF supply.

■ Introduction

Listeria is a genus of bacteria that have an important role as decomposers in the environment. Most species are harmless to humans, but one species, *Listeria monocytogenes*, is a dangerous foodborne pathogen. The infectious disease caused by ingestion of *L. monocytogenes* is called listeriosis.

The U.S. Centers for Disease Control (CDC) reports approximately 2,500 serious cases of listeriosis per year, of which about 500 are fatal. People with immune systems weakened by HIV infection or by immunosuppressive drugs, cancer patients, and pregnant women are more susceptible to the disease than the general population. Listeria can cause gastrointestinal disease, invasive septicemia (bacteria proliferation in the blood), or meningitis in susceptible individuals. Pregnant women who contract the infection are at elevated risk of experiencing spontaneous abortions.

Listeria monocytogenes is a common species in soil and water, and it is quite easy for it to find its way into products destined for human consumption. This includes vegetables as well as meat and seafood products. Although listeriosis is not as prevalent as other diseases contracted by eating contaminated food, the lethality of *Listeria monocytogenes* makes it an organism of significant concern for both food producers and consumers.

■ Historical Background and Scientific Foundations

The genus *Listeria* contains at least eight species of gram-positive rod-shaped bacteria. All members of the genus are motile by means of flagella distributed over the bacterial cell surface. *Listeria* is a common saprophyte in the environment, and it is present in the normal gut flora of a small portion of the human population. It is also associated with a number of animal species.

The first confirmed isolation of the organism now known as *L. monocytogenes* was from a meningitis patient in 1918, but the isolate was not correctly identified until many years later. The species has been known by many names, but gained its current name in 1924. The relationship of *Listeria* to other bacteria was not clarified until the 1970s with the development of numerical, chemical, and molecular methods of analysis.

Outbreaks of diseases attributed to *L. monocytogenes* have occurred in animals sporadically, but the species was recognized as an emerging human pathogen in 1979. Cases of listeriosis are in decline as a result of improved awareness, detection, and food processing quality control.

The infectious dose of *L. monocytogenes* is variable, with healthy individuals probably able to ingest many thousands of bacteria without ill effect. In people with risk factors for the disease, less than a thousand may be enough. *Listeria monocytogenes* is an intracellular pathogen that, after exiting the digestive system, can be transmitted throughout the body inside infected blood cells. An unusual trait of the species is its ability to use a host cell's actin network (part of the cell cytoskeleton) to propel itself inside the cell.

Although *L. monocytogenes* is tolerant of harsh conditions, it can be killed by proper heat sterilization, pasteurization, or by temperatures routinely reached during cooking. *Listeria* bacteria do not form heat-resistant endospores, but are able to withstand high temperatures, and foods must be cooked to steaming temperatures to insure safety. It also survives at refrigerator temperatures. *Listeria* is remarkably resistant to freezing, drying, osmotic stress (resulting from high salt concentration) and high or low pH.

Symptoms of listeriosis range from mild to severe and can manifest anywhere from two days to more than a month after exposure. Mild gastrointestinal cases present flu-like symptoms with fever, headache, vomiting, and diarrhea. If the bacteria become invasive by entering the bloodstream, they can infect organs, the nervous system in particular, or cross the placenta in pregnant women to infect the fetus.

■ Impacts and Issues

Consumption of foods eaten or drunk without cooking such as leafy salad vegetables, raw milks and cheeses, and ready-to-eat (RTE) meats (commonly called lunch meats) is the principal cause of listeriosis. Processed RTE foods may be contaminated after cooking and during or before packaging. Hot dogs are also of concern if eaten undercooked or raw. From 1 to 4 percent of all foods tested are positive for the presence of the organism, although it is usually at a very low level. RTE meats often harbor the organism at a much higher rate.

Once established in a food processing facility, *Listeria* is difficult to eradicate, sometimes resulting in low levels of food contamination at the plant for many

years. A major contributing factor in this persistence is the organism's ability to form difficult-to-remove biofilms on the surfaces of processing equipment. According to a review article published in the *Journal of Food Protection* in 2002, some processing plants have harbored *Listeria* for up to twelve years without being able to eliminate it completely.

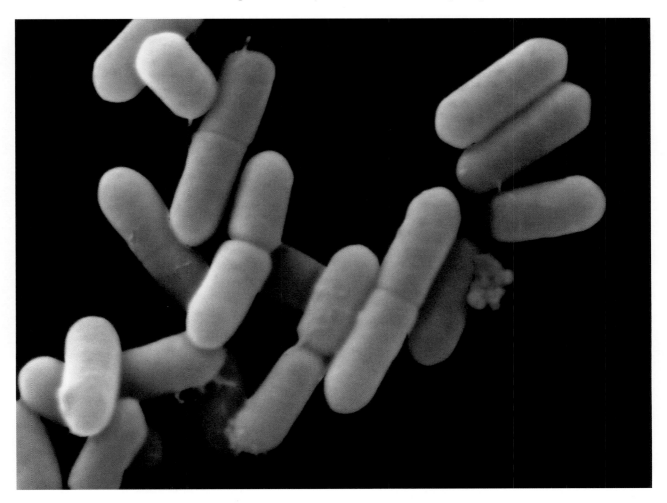

A false color image from a scanning electron microscope (SEM) shows *Listeria* monocytogenes, the bacteria that causes listeriosis in humans. © *Mediscan / Alamy.*

Nearly all cases of listeriosis (99 percent) are contracted by eating contaminated food, with the remainder caused by the breathing in of bacteria, or contact with animal carriers. Listeriosis is seldom contagious, but in rare cases infections have been transmitted in neonatal facilities.

Healthy adults need take no special precautions to avoid infection. Certain populations are more at risk, however, and should be mindful of the foods they eat. This includes the very young, the elderly, people taking immunosuppressive drugs after transplant, human immunodeficiency virus (HIV)-positive individuals, acquired immunodeficiency syndrome (AIDS) and cancer patients, and pregnant women. Pregnant women are approximately 20 times more susceptible to the disease than non-pregnant women, with nearly 30 percent of all serious cases occurring in pregnant women. The third trimester is the time of greatest risk for listeriosis complications for the mother.

The risk of contracting listeriosis is reduced by avoiding foods that are known to present the greatest possibility of being contaminated with *L. monocytogenes*. Unpasteurized dairy products should not be consumed by pregnant women. The CDC also recommends pregnant women avoid soft cheeses such as Brie; feta; Mexican varieties such as queso blanco, queso fresco, and panela; and blue-veined varieties. Hard cheeses, semi-soft cheeses (cream cheese and cottage cheese), pasteurized cheeses, and cheese spreads are considered safe. Hot dogs should be heated to at least 160° or avoided altogether. Sandwiches containing lunch meats should be avoided because they are usually not cooked before serving.

Although listeriosis is not as common as other food-borne illnesses caused by bacteria such as *Salmonella* and *E. coli*, invasive cases of the disease have a high fatality rate (approximately 20 percent). Pregnant women and people with weakened immune systems can reduce their chances of contracting listeriosis by avoiding high-risk foods.

SEE ALSO *Consumer Food Safety Recommendations; Dairy Products;* E. Coli *Contamination; Food Inspection and Standards; Food Safety and Inspection Service; Foodborne Diseases; Meat Inspection Act of 1906; Meats; Pasteurization; Processed Foods; Raw Milk Campaign;* Salmonella; *Staphylococcal Food Poisoning*

BIBLIOGRAPHY

Books

Goldfine, Howard, and Hao Shen. *Listeria Monocytogenes: Pathogenesis and Host Response.* New York: Springer, 2007.

Walker, W. Alan, and Courtney Humphries. *The Harvard Medical School Guide to Healthy Eating during Pregnancy.* New York: McGraw-Hill, 2006.

Periodicals

Carrasco, Elena, Fernando Perez-Rodriguez, Antonia Valero, Rosa M. Garcia-Gimeno, and Gonzalo Zurera. "Risk Assessment and Management of *Listeria Monocytogenes* in Ready-to-Eat Lettuce Salads." *Comprehensive Reviews in Food Science and Food Safety* 9, no. 5 (2010): 498–512.

Khatamzas, Elham, et al. "The Increasing Prevalence of Listeriosis—What Are We Missing?" *QJM: An International Journal of Medicine* 103, no. 7 (2010): 519–522.

Rodriguez-Marval, Mawill, Patricia A. Kendall, Kenneth E. Belk, and John N. Sofos. "Inactivation of *Listeria Monocytogenes*." *Food Protection Trends* 30, no. 1 (2010): 16–24.

Snow, Michelle. "On the Lookout for Listeriosis." *Nursing* 39, no. 7 (2009): 59.

Web Sites

"Listeriosis." *U.S. Centers for Disease Control and Prevention (CDC).* http://www.cdc.gov/nczved/divisions/dfbmd/diseases/listeriosis/ (accessed October 21, 2010).

"Protect Your Baby and Yourself From Listeriosis." *Food Safety and Inspection Service (FSIS), U.S. Department of Agriculture (USDA).* http://www.fsis.usda.gov/Fact_Sheets/Protect_Your_Baby/index.asp (accessed October 21, 2010).

Philip McIntosh

Livestock Intensity and Demand

■ Introduction

Demand for livestock products increases both as the world's population grows and as that population becomes more affluent. Since the 1930s, intensive animal production systems have been developed primarily in the United States and have spread to additional industrialized and developing nations. These concentrated animal feeding operations (CAFOs) have reduced the amount of grain or feed necessary to raise the livestock that produce meat, eggs, milk, and other livestock products. Their efficiency gains result from selective breeding, from economies of scale, and from advances in understanding veterinary medicine and animal nutrition. However, these larger intensive livestock operations pose new risks to food safety, animal health, the environment, and animal welfare.

Whether intensive animal production systems can meet growing demand for livestock products without posing unnecessary threats to the environment and health remains a major challenge in contemporary agriculture. Alternately, extensive systems that are less concentrated and use more land would need to experience more productivity gains to provide the livestock products currently supplied by CAFOs to meet growing world demand for meat, eggs, milk, and other livestock products.

■ Historical Background and Scientific Foundations

The increased demand for livestock products such as meat, dairy products, and eggs has two primary driving sources. The first driver is a growing population: As a population increases, generally, it will consume more livestock products. The second source of increased demand for livestock comes from dietary changes. According to Engel's Law of Consumption, as income increases, a falling percentage of that income will be spent on food. However, increased spending on food will be used to buy higher-value foods. These higher-value foods replace grain-based foods with fruits, vegetables, dairy products, and meat. So as the world's population becomes more affluent, it will, in general, consume more meat and other livestock products.

Intensive animal agriculture began on farms in the Midwest region of the United States in the 1930s. More mechanization in slaughterhouses demanded more uniform animals. As grain yields increased due to technological advances, all grains, but especially corn, began to be used more for animal feed. By scientifically breeding animals for particular characteristics, controlling feed, and changing veterinary practices, the animal agriculture sector experienced huge productivity gains to parallel the increased productivity of grain. Between 1960 and 2009, meat production in the United States more than tripled. Processes also take less time and fewer resources: To raise a chicken to five pounds took 84 days in 1950, but only required 45 days by the 1990s. The weight of feed necessary to produce a pound of meat on a hog decreased by 20 percent between 1992 and 1998 alone. These jumps in productivity have lowered the cost of meat as a percentage of income, meaning consumers can purchase more meat with less of their income. The changes have also led farmers to take advantage of economies of scale: By concentrating more animals into a single operation, producers save costs, which can be passed on to the consumer to increase sales volume. Primarily originating in the United States, these technologies have spread to both developed and developing countries around the world.

The concentration of animals into larger operations meant fewer farms with small numbers of animals but

WORDS TO KNOW

CONCENTRATED ANIMAL FEEDING OPERATIONS (CAFOs):
A single facility that confines a large number of animals. Legally, in the United States, the Environmental Protection Agency (EPA) defines a CAFO as a farm that has at least 1,000 beef cattle, 700 dairy cows, 2,500 hogs, or 125,000 broiler chickens.

ECONOMY OF SCALE: A reduction in the cost of production reached by producing more. Economy of scale also refers to cost reductions accrued by geographic concentration of an industry.

ENGEL'S LAW: As a household's income increases, it will spend a lower percentage of income on food though its actual food expenditures may increase. The increase in spending is due to a shift in the diet away from grain to more expensive foods such as meat, dairy, fruits, and vegetables. Engel's Law is named after Ernst Engel (1821–1896), the German economist and statistician who first noted the tendency.

EXTERNALITY: Something external to a production process for which the producer does not pay or get paid. An externality can be negative, such as pollution for which a producer incurs no cost. It can also be positive, such as bees from one farm pollinating other farm's crops in an area for free. Externalities are external to the accounting and decision process of the producer.

an increase in livestock farms holding huge numbers of animals. From 1994 to 2001, the number of U.S. hog farms fell by 60 percent, but the total hog population remained the same. In chicken, egg, hog, and beef cattle production, farms began to specialize in certain stages of an animal's life.

One farm might produce day-old hatchling chickens that are then sold to other farms to be raised. With chickens ("layers" as chickens used in egg production are known), and also hogs, this specialization in one phase of production has been accompanied by vertical integration by processing companies. The processing company, sometimes called an integrator, will own the chicken throughout its life, but send it to several farms, each of which will raise the chicken at different stages. The integrator takes advantage of the reduced costs that come from economies of scale and negotiates contracts to work with many farms at once. For dairy and beef cattle, vertical integration has not been as prevalent. During the majority of an animal's life in this system, it lives at a farm designed to feed it, usually with purchased feed grown away from that farm. These feeding farms, called feed lots for cattle, are known as concentrated animal feeding operations (CAFOs), a term legally defined in the United States. Because the vertical integration and the concentration on economies of scale resembles many manufacturing processes at factories, some critics of CAFOs refer to them as factory farms.

A commercial poultry farm raises chickens in a broiler barn. *Image copyright Sveta San, 2010. Image used under license from Shutterstock.com.*

IN CONTEXT: RINDERPEST

The global eradication of smallpox remains one of the leading achievements in public health. Rinderpest, a viral disease that once ravaged cattle herds and resulted in famine and economic hardship around the world, is widely expected to join smallpox as a globally eradicated disease sometime in 2011. British veterinary surgeon and scientist Walter Plowright (1923–2010) died just before the official announcement that his vaccine had helped eliminate a disease threat that repeatedly destabilized economies and food supplies in many developing nations.

Rinderpest (a word derived from the German for cattle-plague) is also known as steppe murrain. Although rinderpest is not capable of causing disease in humans, rinderpest infection results in highly lethal fever, diarrhea, and tissue necrosis (wasting) in cattle. The rinderpest virus (RPV) is genetically close to the measles and canine distemper viruses. All three are species of the Morbillivirus genus of the family of Paramyxoviridae viruses. The virus is spread by direct contact and though contaminated water. Airborne transmission has also been documented.

Although virtually eliminated in Europe more than 100 years ago, rinderpest continued to be a scourge to African ranchers and farmers, often killing most of the cattle and buffalo in infected herds. The cattle and buffalo that survived were often too sick to be used to produce dairy products or as food. An outbreak in Nigeria during the 1980s resulted in famine and billions of dollars of economic damage to Nigerian cattle and dairy farmers. One rinderpest outbreak in the 1980s is credited with killing more than 80 percent of the cattle in all of South Africa. Prior to the development of Plowright's vaccine, the only way to control the spread of the virus was by killing (culling) potentially infected herds.

Plowright was one of the first to use tissue culture techniques to successfully prepare an effective vaccine. Plowright's laboratory used cell-culture techniques developed by polio vaccine researchers to produce a live attenuated (weakened, non-pathogenic) virus as an antigen for the rinderpest vaccine. A single dose of Plowright's cell-culture produced rinderpest vaccine (TCRV) provides a low cost and easily administered method of generating permanent immunity against rinderpest.

According to the United Nations Food and Agriculture Organization, Plowright's rinderpest vaccine helped produce much needed food, especially in Africa and India, and increased production for subsistence farmers around the world. In 1999 Plowright was honored with the World Food Prize.

■ Impacts and Issues

CAFOs present special risks to health. Livestock living closely together can infect a large proportion of the animals with a disease in a short time. Herd health can be difficult to maintain for a large operation, and some operations have been criticized for liberal use of antibiotics or preventive use of antibiotics to control infections. Antibiotic residue in meat has been a concern of many citizens' groups in developed nations. At the same time, the isolation of chickens in the enclosed houses usually found on CAFOs actually protects them from the many common avian diseases spread by wild fowl.

The environmental externalities of CAFOs are another concern. In economics, an externality is a side effect or side product whose cost is not paid by the producer. In this case, the CAFO does not pay for its external product, animal waste. Some neighbors of CAFOs complain about smell, but the most serious threat to the environment from animal waste is that it threatens water sources and bodies of water. In an extensive livestock operation, where livestock wander over a wide area of land, manure ideally poses no environmental problem as it fertilizes the land, which has the capacity to absorb the nutrients from the manure. However, by intensifying the number of animals and decreasing the land, CAFOs and larger livestock operations exceed the capacity of the farm's land to absorb these nutrients. In some cases, the extra manure is stored on site or is sent to other places to be spread on land, but the manure poses environmental risks if it spills in storage or during transport. One spill in 1995 in North Carolina released more than 20 million gallons of animal waste into a nearby river. When large amounts of manure enter waterways, aquatic animals may be poisoned with ammonia and excess nitrogen and phosphorus can deplete levels of dissolved oxygen in the water. In addition, contaminants such as *E. coli* enter watersheds or localized water resources, raising bacterial counts to levels that make water unsafe for recreation or drinking. The economies of scale that bring many large CAFOs together into a small geographic area exacerbate the manure problems and create the potential for large scale environmental and health risks.

In addition to environmental and health risks associated with CAFOs, some critics express concern about how animals are treated on CAFOs. Animal welfare concerns have engaged more European consumers than consumers in other parts of the world, so in the European Union CAFOs face a variety of regulatory constraints attempting to address animal welfare, food safety, animal health, and environmental concerns. CAFOs in other countries may also be subjected to environmental, food safety, and animal health regulations, but in general other countries have not implemented widespread regulation concerning animal welfare. However, regulations do not always lead to the intended result. Producers, farmers, and managers of CAFOs may not have enough incentives to share all information with regulators. Hidden actions can be undertaken without the regulator's knowledge. Also, some critics argue that regulations may reduce incentives to exceed the required environmental or health standards for certain producers, since the producers merely give the minimum standards required by law.

■ Primary Source Connection

When the following primary source perspective was first published by the Food and Agriculture Organization (FAO) of the United Nations, the author, Robin Mearns, served as a Fellow of the Institute of Development Studies. Mearns is also a founding member of the IDS Environment Group and a geographer specializing in the impacts of climate change, natural resource management policies, and community-based risk management analysis for developing countries. Working with the World Bank gave Mearns a globally diverse base of experience with food and agricultural policy impacts. Mearns holds a Ph.D. in geography from the University of Cambridge and is a widely published author on topics related to the environment and sustainable development practices.

Mearns paper—the introduction to which is published below—along with links to the complete paper—discusses both positive and negative facets of livestock production, with a fuller explanation of facts and arguments that, in Mearns' view, demonstrate positive environmental and market-based benefits associated with livestock production.

When Livestock are Good for the Environment: Benefit-Sharing of Environmental Goods and Services

More than half of the world's land surface is used for livestock production, encompassing landscapes of extraordinary natural beauty and of global importance to the biosphere. The environmental consequences of livestock production vary widely, depending on the opportunities and constraints afforded by different production systems, institutional and policy contexts. But it is now increasingly recognised that such environments are characterised by multiple uses and multiple users, all with legitimate claims on goods and services derived from the environment. These claims cannot be compatible with one another all of the time, and relationships among competing claimants can at times become highly conflictual. The notion of "benefit sharing" is here understood to refer to the fact that goods and services derived from the environment provide benefits to a wide range of potential users, among them

livestock producers, which need to be balanced. But since balancing contested claims is inherently a political act, the "appropriate" distribution of environmental benefits among users cannot be defined objectively. The task of policy analysts must be to expose these multiple, contested claims on environmental goods and services; to make explicit the political choices involved in the design of instruments and mechanisms for benefit sharing; and to seek out those that offer most promise of "win-win" or at least "win-no regret" solutions.

Market Failure in Distribution of Environmental Benefits

The prices paid for livestock products world-wide fail to reflect fully the environmental costs associated with their production. Government subsidies of various kinds, whether for animal feed, for land clearance, or for fossil fuel energy used in industrial livestock rearing, and tariff barriers to trade in livestock products, yet further distort market prices and exacerbate the environmental costs of livestock produced under certain conditions. The consequences are well documented. . . .

It is less widely appreciated, however, that there are also positive environmental externalities associated with livestock production, which go equally unaccounted in market prices for livestock products. In a wide range of livestock production systems, from pastoral grazing systems to integrated crop-livestock systems, livestock production confers certain environmental benefits which are not well captured by the market mechanism. In some cases the underlying causal processes are not well understood by policy makers and, as a result, livestock producers are wrongly castigated for environmental problems that could be avoided with more appropriate institutional, pricing and policy arrangements. . . .

Robin Mearns

MEARNS, ROBIN. "WHEN LIVESTOCK ARE GOOD FOR THE ENVIRONMENT: BENEFIT SHARING OF ENVIRONMENTAL GOODS AND SERVICES." FOOD AND AGRICULTURE ORGANIZATION (FAO) OF THE UNITED NATIONS. FTP://FTP.FAO.ORG/DOCREP/NONFAO/LEAD/X6184E/X6184E00.PDF (ACCESSED NOVEMBER 3, 2010).

SEE ALSO *Agricultural Deforestation; Agricultural Demand for Water; Agroecology; Bushmeat; Dietary Changes in Rapidly Developing Countries; Ecological Impacts of Various World Diets; Ethical Issues in Agriculture; Extreme Weather and Food Supply; Factory Farming; Farm-to-Table Movement; Food and Agriculture Organization (FAO); Food Inspection and Standards; Humane Animal Farming; Meat Inspection Act of 1906; Meats; Organics; Population and Food; Sustainable Agriculture.*

BIBLIOGRAPHY

Books

D'Silva, Joyce, and John Webster. *The Meat Crisis: Developing More Sustainable Production and Consumption.* London: Earthscan, 2010.

Krasner, Deborah. *Good Meat: The Complete Guide to Sourcing and Cooking Sustainable Meat.* New York: Stewart, Tabori & Chang, 2010.

Niman, Nicolette H. *Righteous Porkchop: Finding a Life and Good Food beyond Factory Farms.* New York: Collins Living, 2009.

Periodicals

Cox, Andrew, Daniel Chicksand, and Martin Palmer. "Stairways to Heaven or Treadmills to Oblivion?: Creating Sustainable Strategies in Red Meat Supply Chains." *British Food Journal* 109, no. 9 (2007): 689–720.

Fairlie, Simon, and Richard Young. "Meat: Eco Villain or Victim of Spin?" *The Ecologist* 38, no. 8 (2008): 14.

Febriani, Yossi, et al. "Association between Indicators of Livestock Farming Intensity and Hospitalization Rate for Acute Gastroenteritis." *Epidemiology and Infection* 137, no. 8 (2009): 1073–1085.

Ilea, Ramona Cristina. "Intensive Livestock Farming: Global Trends, Increased Environmental Concerns, and Ethical Solutions." *Journal of Agricultural and Environmental Ethics* 22, no. 2 (2009): 153–167.

McMichael, Anthony J., John W. Powles, Colin D. Butler, and Ricardo Uauy. "Food, Livestock Production, Energy, Climate Change, and Health." *Lancet* 370, no. 9594 (2007): 1253–1263.

Web Sites

"Concentrated Animal Feeding Operations (CAFOs)." *Environmental Health Services (EHS), U.S. Centers for Disease Control and Prevention (CDC).* http://www.cdc.gov/nceh/ehs/Topics/CAFO.htm (accessed September 20, 2010).

Media Centre. "Towards a More Sustainable Livestock Sector." *Food and Agriculture Organization of the United Nations (FAO),* February 18, 2010. http://www.fao.org/news/story/pt/item/40117/icode/en/ (accessed September 20, 2010).

Blake Jackson Stabler

Locavore

■ Introduction

Until the past hundred years, almost all food was locally obtained. There was trade in exotic foodstuffs, especially in spices and seeds, but the bulk of what almost everyone ate everywhere in the world was—by necessity—produced near where they lived. A large part of the population was engaged in getting food, whether they were hunter-gatherers, herdsmen, farmers, or villagers. In the not so distant past, even urban dwellers were intimately acquainted with where most of their daily bread, rice, corn, or millet came from and how it was prepared.

A shrinking percentage of the population actually raises or collects their own food in the early twenty-first century. In many industrialized countries, people do not live near where their food is produced, and many do not even know where it originated. Technological advances in food processing and preservation, coupled with global networks of corporate production and trade, make it likely that the ingredients for a given meal come from several different countries, and even different continents. The local food movement seeks to draw attention to this aspect of modern life and counter it with local food networks. Locavores attempt to find food from nearby gardens, farmers' markets, ranches and fisheries, and prefer to use fresh, seasonally abundant, and organic or sustainably raised foods that support the local economy.

■ Historical Background and Scientific Foundations

In *The United States of Arugula*, David Kamp describes how an increasing number of Americans began to appreciate fresh food in the 1960s and 1970s. Led by gourmet chefs such as Alice Waters, there was a push for more farmers' markets, organic produce, humanely raised lean meats, and a greater diversity of food choices. This trend intensified in the following decades as more people began writing about food, investigating traditional cuisines and culinary history, and scrutinizing patterns of food production and distribution. In 2002 ethnobotanist Gary Paul Nabhan published *Coming Home to Eat*, an account of the year he spent growing, collecting, and buying food from neighbors within 250 miles of his home in Arizona. Nabhan's book exploring "the pleasures and politics of local foods" was an inspiration to many, including four women who challenged the people of San Francisco to eat only foods produced within a hundred miles for a month. One of these women, Jessica Prentice, coined the term *locavore* for this 2005 challenge.

The following year, Michael Pollan's book, *The Omnivore's Dilemma*, became a bestseller, compelling more people to think critically about where their food was produced and processed. In 2007 *Animal, Vegetable, Miracle*, Barbara Kingsolver's description of her family's

---

WORDS TO KNOW

FOOD MILES: The number of miles a particular food travels from production to consumption, or from "farm to fork."

FOODSHED: A foodshed is defined by the area within which one's food is produced, as a watershed defines where water drains. Modern foodsheds may be global in scale, but locavores' foodsheds are much smaller and regionally restricted.

LOCAVORE: Someone who attempts to eat a high proportion of foods that are grown or raised locally. Local food can be defined as that produced within a certain radius (e.g. 50 or 100 or 250 miles), a geographic region or a foodshed, or even a state or a country. The term localvore may also be used.

SUSTAINABLE AGRICULTURE: Methods of producing food that can be sustained without depleting resources for future generations.

relocation to a Virginia farm—where they ate mostly food they raised on the farm or bought from neighbors at the county farmers' market—became even more popular. Alisa Smith and J. B. MacKinnon published *The 100-Mile Diet* (titled *Plenty* in the United States) in 2007, an account of a year eating foods from around Vancouver and their cabin in northern British Columbia. *The New York Times* and *Time* magazine delivered enthusiastic accounts of the benefits of food that was "better than organic" that saved fuel and farmland. Near the end of 2007, Oxford University Press declared that the word of the year for the *New Oxford American Dictionary* was locavore. In 2009, Smith and MacKinnon starred in a television show produced by Food Network Canada, which followed the lives of six families as they ate local foods for 100 days. Local food remains popular, as shown by a marked increase in farmers' markets, options for CSA (Community Supported Agriculture) shares, restaurants offering locally produced dishes, and advertisements and supermarket signs showcasing regional offerings.

■ Impacts and Issues

Local food initiatives are still evolving, and it is unclear how large the effect on diet and trade patterns will be in the industrialized nations where they are popular. Many more American shoppers buy highly processed convenience foods at Wal-Mart than buy carrots and cabbage from local farms. By linking themselves with other regional and environmental campaigns, however, such as the Slow Food Movement, the Edible Schoolyard, and the worldwide push for more sustainable agriculture, activists have kept the importance of eating locally in the public eye. There have been some efforts to integrate institutions into local food networks, such as the Farm to School plan, and the USDA's new "Know Your Farmer, Know Your Food" program, which assists school administrators in buying more local produce. Groups such as the Center for Environmental Farming Systems of North Carolina and the Community Food Security Coalition of Oregon provide local food to colleges, military bases, and other large institutions. A high proportion of locavores use the Internet to organize, communicate, and tell consumers where local food can be obtained on sites such as www.locavores.com, www.foodroutes.org, and www.localharvest.org. A new iPhone app provides shoppers with information on what is in season nearby.

The benefits of eating locally produced food are widely acknowledged. Local foods are usually fresher, and generally retain more nutrients and flavor. Fruits and vegetables can be picked when fully ripe, and more varieties, including many that cannot withstand shipping, are available. Bacterial and viral contamination is less common and more easily contained, and bioterrorism is less of an issue. Locally produced foods are commonly grown organically, or at least sustainably, and many consumers

Chef Cat Cora (1967–) harvests vegetables with students from Hollin Meadows Elementary School in Alexandria, Virginia, from the White House Kitchen Garden in June 2010. *AP Images.*

appreciate seeing how the food they eat was raised— perhaps even picking it themselves—and talking to producers. Shoppers feel closer to nature, connected to the seasons, and a part of their local communities. A hundred years ago, eating imported food displayed wealth; in the twenty-first century, local foods connote higher status than eating industrially produced junk foods.

Locavores also argue that agribusiness food transportation uses fossil fuels and produces pollution that could be drastically reduced. Although not all locavores still argue that "food travels an average of 1500 miles" (debunked in *Slate* in 2008), most are concerned with food miles and maintain that industrially produced foods carry hidden environmental and social costs. Some locavore critics acknowledge advantages to eating local foods, while pointing out that that food miles may not be the best criterion of sustainability or social justice. An alternative measure of the energy used in producing, processing, shipping, selling, buying, and cooking particular foodstuffs was introduced in 2008 and called the LCA (Life Cycle Assessment). It suggests that eating less meat and shopping less frequently might have more positive environmental effects than eating locally. Locavores have also been criticized for ignoring economies of scale, being elitist, and fetishizing local communities that may be sources of inequality. Some authors also suggest that food regionalism or "locavore isolationism" may damage the economies of developing nations that may be uniquely well-suited for producing and exporting certain foods.

For an increasing number of people, however, it is clear that the future of at least some of their food lies closer to home than it has for several decades. In addition to locavore literary contributions, the local food movement continues to be an important aspect of the current trend that views eating as a deliberate act with political and social implications.

SEE ALSO *Alice Waters: California and New American Cuisine; Edible Schoolyard Movement; Farm-to-Table Movement; Michael Pollan: Linking Food and Environmental Journalism; Slow Food Movement; Sustainable Agriculture; Sustainable Table.*

BIBLIOGRAPHY

Books

Hewitt, Ben. *The Town that Food Saved: How One Community Found Vitality in Local Food.* Emmaus, PA: Rodale, 2010.

Kamp, David. *The United States of Arugula: How We Became a Gourmet Nation.* New York: Broadway, 2006.

Kingsolver, Barbara. *Animal, Vegetable, Miracle: A Year of Food Life.* New York: HarperCollins, 2007.

McWilliams, James E. *Just Food: Where Locavores Get It Wrong and How We Can Truly Eat Responsibly.* New York: Little, Brown & Co., 2009.

Pollan, Michael. *The Omnivore's Dilemma: A Natural History of Four Meals.* New York: Penguin Press, 2006.

Smith, Alisa, and J. B. MacKinnon. *Plenty: One Man, One Woman, and a Raucous Year of Eating Locally.* New York: Harmony Books, 2007.

Periodicals

Charney, Madeleine K. "FoodRoutes Network and the Local Food Movement." *Journal of Agricultural and Food Information* 10, no. 3 (2009): 173–181.

Weber, Christopher L., and H. Scott Matthews. "Food-Miles and the Relative Climate Impacts of Food Choices in the United States." *Environmental Science & Technology* 42, no. 10 (2008): 3508–3513.

Web Sites

Black, Jane. "What's in a Number: How the Press Got the Idea That Food Travels 1,500 Miles from Farm to Plate." *Slate*, September 27, 2008. http://www.slate.com/id/2200202 (accessed July 31, 2010).

Locavore Network. http://www.locavorenetwork.com/ (accessed July 31, 2010).

Sandra L. Dunavan

Macrobiotics

■ Introduction

The macrobiotic diet was brought from Japan to the United States in the early twentieth century. Its guiding principle is that both health and happiness depend upon the food people eat. The macrobiotic way aims to promote the physical and spiritual health of the individual, and the health of the planet, by eating in harmony with the seasons and focusing upon certain types of food. Grains are the staple of the macrobiotic diet, along with locally grown vegetables, soy-based products, and a little fish or seafood. Other sources of animal protein are avoided, along with sugar. The most extreme version of the macrobiotic diet consists merely of brown rice and water. Whereas the macrobiotic diet contains many components of a healthy diet, such as high fiber and no saturated fat, strict adherence to it could create various nutritional deficiencies. Various claims have been made that the macrobiotic diet can prevent or cure cancer and acquired immunodeficiency syndrome (AIDS), but these have not been proven by clinical research. The macrobiotic emphasis upon eating locally and seasonally echoes the concerns of environmental and other groups about the impact that the global food trade has upon the environment.

■ Historical Background and Scientific Foundations

The idea of macrobiotics, which means "long life" or "large life," originated with a Japanese army physician. Sagen Ishizuka (1850–1910), in the late nineteenth century. He wanted to combine the traditional Asian diet with modern Western science and claimed that his diet cured his own ill health. He began to prescribe macrobiotics to his patients. Japanese educator George Ohsawa (1893–1966) became a student of macrobiotics and went on to write 300 books on the subject. Ohsawa, and later Japanese-born lawyer and peace advocate Michio

Kushi (1926–), did much to popularize the macrobiotic diet in North America.

Macrobiotics aims to integrate physical, spiritual, and planetary health through the application of its principles. Considered the foundation of both health and happiness, foods are classified as to their yin and yang properties. The idea of yin and yang is an essential concept of Daoist philosophy; the two elements are often interpreted as male and female elements that should be kept in balance. Therefore, balance in a macrobiotic diet means balancing yin and yang foods. Grains are the staple food of a macrobiotic diet, and foods should be unrefined, whole, and natural. Another principle of macrobiotics is that food should be grown locally and eaten in season.

Ohsawa devised a macrobiotic diet with ten progressively restrictive stages. The last stage of his diet consisted of only brown rice and water and is no longer recommended by macrobiotic counselors. In a modern macrobiotic diet, whole grains will make up 50 to 60 percent of each meal. Whole grains permitted include buckwheat, brown rice, barley, millet, rye, and corn. Oats, noodles, pasta, and bread and baked goods are eaten only occasionally. One to two cups per day of miso or shoyu soup are consumed. Vegetables make up another 25 to 30 percent of the diet, of which up to one-third are eaten raw. Beans comprise 10 percent of the macrobiotic diet and include bean products such as tofu and tempeh. A small amount of seafood or fish is consumed several times per week, but meat, poultry, eggs, and dairy products are avoided. The fish or seafood are eaten with wasabi, a kind of horseradish, and ginger, or grated daikon. These are thought to detoxify the body of the effects of fish or seafood. Local fruit is eaten, but not tropical fruits such as mango or pineapple. The macrobiotic diet permits desserts, but these are very different from typical Western desserts: They are naturally sweet foods such as apples, aduki beans, or dried fruit, sweetened with natural sweeteners such as barley malt or rice syrup. Sugar, honey, and chocolate are avoided. Cooking is accomplished with unrefined vegetable oil. Dark sesame oil and mustard seed oil are often used. Macrobiotics employs a range of seasonings, some of which are unfamiliar to the American palate. These include natural

Whole grains, beans, and fresh vegetables are an important part of a macrobiotic diet. © isifa Image Service s.r.o. / Alamy.

sea salt, fermented pickles, roasted seaweed, umeboshi plums, and brown rice vinegar. The macrobiotic diet varies with season and climate and is individualized according to age, gender, state of health, and level of activity.

■ Impacts and Issues

A macrobiotic diet contains several elements that echo more conventional healthy eating advice. Its emphasis on whole grains, vegetables, and beans supplies ample amounts of fiber, which could help fight cancer and other chronic diseases. The lack of animal protein means the macrobiotic diet is low in saturated fat and so provides some protective effect against heart disease and certain cancers. The emphasis on soy-based products provides a high intake of phytoestrogens, which are thought to help balance female hormones and may protect against breast cancer.

However, following a strict macrobiotic diet may lead to some serious nutritional deficiencies. Whole grains are not, in general, complete proteins, so deficiency in one or more of the essential amino acids may result. Avoiding meat altogether may lead to deficiencies in vitamin B12 and iron. Deficiencies in other micronutrients such as calcium and magnesium are also possible. Claims have been made that the macrobiotic diet can cure cancer and AIDS. There is no current scientific evidence for this, although a diet rich in fruits and vegetables has been shown to have some protective effect against the development of cancer. There is a danger than naïve or desperate persons with cancer could embrace these claims and abandon conventional treatments in favor of a macrobiotic diet. According to the American Cancer Society, the macrobiotic diet is unsafe for cancer patients and can deny the body essential nutrients at a time when it especially needs nutritional support and balance.

The seasonal, local nature of the macrobiotic diet coincides with current concerns for the environment. Importing from around the world so that consumers have access to a wide range of food all year leads to carbon emissions that could be avoided if food was sourced nearer to home. However, reducing international trade in food would hurt the interests of farmers abroad who depend upon their exports to make a living.

SEE ALSO *Asian Diet; Diet and Cancer; Functional Foods; Phytochemicals (Phytonutrients); Veganism; Vegetarianism; Vitamins and Minerals.*

BIBLIOGRAPHY

Books

Brown, Simon, and Dragana Brown. *Macrobiotics for Life: A Practical Guide to Healing for Body, Mind, and Heart.* Berkeley, CA: North Atlantic Books, 2009.

Periodicals

Di, Genova T., and Harvey Guyda. "Infants and Children Consuming Atypical Diets: Vegetarianism and Macrobiotics." *Paediatrics & Child Health* 12, no. 3 (2007): 185–188.

Kirby, Midge, and Elaine Danner. "Nutritional Deficiencies in Children on Restricted Diets." *Pediatric Clinics of North America* 56, no. 5 (2009): 1085–1103.

Mullin, Gerard. "Popular Diets Prescribed by Alternative Practitioners—Part 2." *Nutrition in Clinical Practice* 25, no. 3 (2010): 308–309.

Web Sites

George Ohsawa Macrobiotic Foundation. http://www.ohsawamacrobiotics.com/ (accessed October 15, 2010).

"Nutrition and Special Diets: Macrobiotics—Detailed Scientific Review." *The University of Texas MD Anderson Center.* http://www.mdanderson.org/education-and-research/resources-for-professionals/clinical-tools-and-resources/cimer/therapies/nutrition-and-special-diets/macrobiotics.html (accessed October 15, 2010).

Susan Aldridge

Mad Cow Disease and vCJD

■ Introduction

Bovine spongiform encephalopathy (BSE) is a progressive infection of the brain and nervous system found in cattle. It is often known as "mad cow disease" because of the way affected animals stagger. There is overwhelming evidence that BSE can be transmitted from cattle to humans via the consumption of infected beef, resulting in an invariably fatal brain disorder called variant Creutzfeldt-Jakob disease (vCJD).

An epidemic of BSE in the United Kingdom (UK) starting in the 1980s was linked to cases of the human form of vCJD, mainly among younger people. The impact of BSE on Britain's farmers and beef industry was severe, as countries rushed to boycott imports of meat that might have come from infected cows. By 2010 the assessment of epidemiologists and public health officials is that the BSE-related epidemic is in rapid decline. However, occasional cases continue to appear, with an increasing global distribution.

■ Historical Background and Scientific Foundations

BSE is a relatively new disease of cattle that was first identified in the United Kingdom in 1986. It proved to be one of a group of diseases called the transmissible spongiform encephalopathies (TSEs). On post-mortem examination with a light microscope, the brain tissue of an animal with a TSE shows a characteristic spongy appearance because the pathology of the disease creates holes within the brain tissue—hence the term "spongiform."

TSEs affect other animals, including humans. For instance scrapie, a TSE found in sheep, has been known since the eighteenth century and is found at a low level in many parts of the world. The name comes from the tendency of animals with the disease to scrape their fleece against trees and bushes. TSEs have also been found in mink (transmissible mink encephalopathy) and

in mules, deer, and elk (chronic wasting disease). CJD is the most significant TSE in humans; it is very rare, usually occurring at a rate of around one per million of the population. The cases that arose from exposure to BSE in the United Kingdom from the mid–1990s represent a new form of CJD.

BSE occurs in adult animals of both sexes. The incubation period—the time lag from exposure to the appearance of symptoms—of TSEs is usually measured in years. Therefore the disease is rarely seen in very young animals, even though they may be infected. Animals with BSE exhibit abnormalities of movement and posture and changes in mental state that an experienced veterinarian or farmer would be able to detect. The disease lasts for several weeks and is invariably both progressive and fatal.

TSEs can be transmitted from one animal to another. However, there is a species barrier, which means that transmission within species is more likely than transmission between species. For instance, there are no known instances of scrapie being transmitted to humans.

It is widely (but not universally) accepted that BSE arose in cattle from exposure to feed derived from sheep infected with scrapie. Adding protein from the carcasses of ruminants (sheep and cows) to animal feed is a long-established practice. The UK BSE Inquiry, which was set up to look at the underlying causes of the BSE epidemic, concluded that changes in the way the feed was processed probably allowed infectious material to survive and infect the cattle consuming it. From the time the BSE epidemic first took hold there were fears that the disease might be transmitted to humans through exposure to meat and meat products (such as hamburgers) from infected animals. These fears were realized with the announcement of the first case of variant CJD (vCJD) in 1996.

Although the mechanisms of prion transmission are the subject of intense research and not fully understood, experts argue that the best evidence currently points to prions as the infective agent in transmission of BSE to human cases of vCJD. Research on infected tissue has shown that prions are not destroyed by either heat (which would destroy bacteria) or ultraviolet light (which would destroy viruses). Prions are an abnormal form of a protein that is found normally in the brain. When it infects the brain, the prion "corrupts" the normal prion protein molecules. These newly-formed abnormal prion protein molecules go on to corrupt further normal prion molecules, beginning a cascade effect. The accumulation of more and more abnormal prion molecules triggers the brain damage that produces the symptoms of TSEs.

By September 1, 2006, approximately 133,139 cases of BSE had been confirmed in the United Kingdom, according to the Department for Environment, Food and Rural Affairs. The epidemic peaked in 1992, with 36,680 confirmed cases in that year. In 2006 there were only 15 cases.

The World Organization for Animal Health collects data on BSE. Although BSE has reached epidemic levels only in the United Kingdom, it has affected other countries in Europe including France, Germany, Ireland, and Portugal. There have been confirmed cases of BSE in both Canada and in the United States.

There is no treatment for BSE, and so quarantine and culls are the most effective measures to prevent its spread—both to other cattle in a herd and to humans. The government of the United Kingdom has introduced a number of measures to keep BSE under control. In July 1988 it imposed a ban on feeding cattle with potentially infected material. This measure kept animals that were not already infected from becoming infected and has been adopted in many countries, including those that are currently BSE-free. This measure alone made a major contribution to halting the growth of the UK BSE epidemic. However, because BSE has a long incubation time, there was a lag between introducing this ban and a fall in the number of cases. This is why the number of cases continued to rise from 1988, despite the ban. In 1997 the United Kingdom also began selective culls (i.e. selective slaughtering those animals at high risk of contracting BSE).

In 2000, 28 deaths were attributed to vCJD (the peak year of the outbreak). By July 2010, 169 total deaths were attributed to confirmed or probable cases of vCJD. The number of deaths per year has significantly diminished since 2004. In 2009 three deaths in the United Kingdom were attributed to vCJD, strengthening arguments that the UK outbreak was in decline. Two fatalities attributed to vCJD took place in the first half of 2010. As of September 2010, four additional persons remain alive following presumptive diagnosis of disease.

■ Impacts and Issues

The BSE epidemic caused substantial economic losses to ranchers and restaurateurs in Britain. In addition to direct losses to British farmers and the UK meat industry, there was wider lack of confidence in beef products and

A butcher weighs beef at his premises in central London. British beef exports resumed to Europe in May 2006, finally ending the ban brought in more than a decade earlier to stem the spread of mad cow disease (BSE). *AP Images.*

IN CONTEXT: THE DISCOVERY OF VARIANT CJD (vCJD)

Variant CJD (vCJD) is the human form of bovine spongiform encephalopathy (BSE) disease that emerged in Britain in the mid–1990s. The vCJD outbreak in Britain echoed the emergence in the 1950s of a strange and invariably fatal condition called kuru (meaning "trembling with fear") among the Fore people of New Guinea. After years of living among the group, American doctor Carlton Gajdusek (1923–2008)—who went on to win the Nobel Prize for Medicine or Physiology in 1976—came to the conclusion that the disease was transmitted in the ritualistic eating of the brains of the deceased, a Fore funeral custom. He suspected that one of these brains, at least, must have belonged to someone with sporadic or familial CJD. There were some striking parallels between the emergence of vCJD and its links with the earlier epidemic bovine spongiform encephalopathy (BSE or mad cow disease), one of the transmissible spongiform encephalopathies (TSEs) found in cattle. The latter prompted a public inquiry to investigate the cause of the outbreak.

The picture that emerged from the inquiry was, briefly, that vCJD is, indeed, the human form of BSE. The inquiry concluded that infected material—either from sheep infected with scrapie (a sheep TSE) or from BSE-infected cattle—was incorporated into cattle feed. Further, it was found that changes in the processing of carcasses used for animal feed were the likely cause of this contamination. Fortunately, the epidemic, though tragic for the victims and their families, was limited by steps such as the wholesale slaughtering of infected cattle and a ban on imports of British beef.

The inquiry led to a variety of developments. For example, in an attempt to restore public confidence, a Food Standards Agency was set up in the United Kingdom to advise on food safety issues. Regulatory authorities are moving towards eliminating animal products from the manufacture of medicines and other items destined for human consumption. The BSE Inquiry also led to changes in the supply of blood and blood products, in an attempt to screen out donors that are, unknowingly, carrying vCJD.

fear of vCJD that continues to fuel fears of beef imports and spur transitory bans and boycotts. The spread of BSE to humans has been limited by restricting imports of meat and meat products that might be infected. In 1996 cattle over 30 months old were no longer allowed to enter the food chain—instead, they were incinerated after slaughter. This ban has now been lifted and replaced by BSE testing—only meat that tests negative can enter the food supply.

In 1996 the government of the United Kingdom admitted a link between BSE and variant CJD, and shortly afterwards France and many other European countries announced a ban on imports of British beef and related products. South Africa, Singapore, and South Korea soon joined in. The Meat and Livestock Commission stated that the bans had caused half of the UK's slaughterhouse workers to lose their jobs. The import bans were gradually lifted over the next few years, as the BSE epidemic began to die down, but it has taken many years for British beef sales to begin to recover, both at home and abroad.

In 2000 the government of the United Kingdom set up the Food Standards Agency, a department that looks after public health and consumer interests with respect to food. Formerly, food and agriculture had been the responsibility of the same department, which many felt marginalized the interests of the consumer.

Beginning in 2001, several nations restricted the import of American beef products, concerned that the United States beef industry lacked sufficient testing and identification methods for BSE. In 2003, when the U.S. Department of Agriculture announced that BSE had been discovered in one cow in Washington state, approximately 60 nations temporarily banned the import of U.S. beef. The infected cow was later traced to a herd in Canada, but the discovery of BSE in the North American herd resulted in approximately $4.7 billion in beef industry losses that year.

The vCJD epidemic also prompted fears about the safety of the international supply of human blood, plasma, tissues, and organs. Many nations excluded, or continue to exclude, donors who resided for several months in parts of Europe and the United Kingdom from 1980–2000. People who received transfusions or organ or tissue transplants in the United Kingdom are also excluded as potential donors in several countries. The three cases of transfusion-associated vCJD in the UK came from a pool of 23 recipients of blood from the infected donor. One person developed vCJD symptoms eight years after receiving the transfusion.

In late 2008, researchers warned that a new wave of vCJD disease in the UK has the potential to bloom within the next three decades. Researchers discovered that a person admitted to a London hospital with signs of vCJD in 2008 had a genotype more common in the general population but that was previously unassociated with individuals contracting vCJD. Experts debate whether this is technically the first such case or whether another individual with the more common genotype contracted vCJD in 2004 to 2006. Regardless, the occurrence of disease in the more common genotype group is troubling to physicians, researchers, and public health officials.

SEE ALSO *Agribusiness; Consumer Food Safety Recommendations; Embargoes; Food Bans; Food Inspection and Standards; Foodborne Diseases; Meat Inspection Act of 1906.*

BIBLIOGRAPHY

Books

Yam, Philip. *The Pathological Protein: Mad Cow, Chronic Wasting, and Other Deadly Prion Diseases.* New York: Springer, 2006.

Periodicals

"Blood Risk of vCJD Highlighted." *New Scientist* 2582 (December 16, 2006): 7.

Web Sites

"Bovine Spongiform Encephalopathy." *World Health Organization (WHO).* http://www.who.int/entity/mediacentre/factsheets/fs113/en/index.html (accessed October 21, 2010).

"BSE (Bovine Spongiform Encephalopathy, or Mad Cow Disease)." *Centers for Disease Control and Prevention (CDC).* http://www.cdc.gov/ncidod/dvrd/bse/ (accessed October 21, 2010).

"Safer Food, Better Business." *U.K. Food Standards Agency.* http://www.food.gov.uk/foodindustry/regulation/hygleg/hyglegresources/sfbb/ (accessed October 21, 2010).

"vCJD (Variant Creutzfeldt-Jakob Disease)." *Centers for Disease Control and Prevention (CDC).* http://www.cdc.gov/ncidod/dvrd/vcjd/ (accessed October 21, 2010).

Susan Aldridge

Malnutrition

■ Introduction

Malnutrition is the result of a person not consuming or absorbing sufficient nutrients to live a healthy, active life. Malnutrition often results from undernutrition, which means that a person is not routinely consuming sufficient calories or sufficient amounts of fat or protein. In common speech, undernutrition is often a synonym for hunger, the condition of not having sufficient food to eat or not having access to sufficient food. Malnutrition is a broader term: It also describes a condition in which a person suffers from micronutrient deficiencies. A micronutrient deficiency is a lack of an adequate amount of a vitamin or mineral in the diet that leads to a wide variety of health problems including increased susceptibility to disease and even death from starvation in extreme cases. As of 2010, the Food and Agriculture Organization of the United Nations (FAO) estimated that 1.02 billion people worldwide suffered from undernutrition.

■ Historical Background and Scientific Foundations

The term malnutrition has been used since the late nineteenth century. Modern government-run and charitable programs to fight malnutrition and undernutrition emerged in modern times primarily in reaction to the Irish potato famine that occurred between 1845 and 1851. Dietary guidelines by national authorities began to appear in the late nineteenth century. However, the modern study of nutrition owes much to the discovery of vitamins in food by chemists during the 1910s and 1920s. As various vitamins were discovered and better researched, the link between specific diseases and micronutrient deficiencies emerged. For example, anemia in pregnant women and children is associated with a lack of iron. Vitamin A deficiency causes night blindness; in young children it may cause complete blindness. Iodine

deficiency causes goiter. Many of the deficiencies are combated by fortifying other foods with the necessary micronutrients.

In addition to specific diseases linked to lack of specific micronutrients, advances in understanding the human immune system in the 1960s led to research examining the links between diet and infectious diseases. American food scientist Nevin Scrimshaw (1918–) of the Massachusetts Institute of Technology (MIT), in conjunction with the World Health Organization (WHO), was one of many scientists working in this emerging field during the 1960s. At the same time, government employees in the United States began to develop proxy measures of malnutrition and hunger within the population. These measures were used to run government programs designed to combat hunger and poverty. On a worldwide basis, the Food and Agriculture Organization of the United Nations (FAO) began to collect comparable country statistics on undernutrition in 1970.

As understanding of human development over the lifetime has increased, malnutrition has been blamed for a wide variety of health problems. Some even cite malnutrition and the associated impaired brain development as a cause for reduced lifetime earnings and income. Without an adequate diet, children may fail to grow to their full potential weight and height. Many studies suggest that adequate nutrition in the first two years of life may prevent many lifelong health and growth problems. Children under the age of five are also considered to be more vulnerable to the health consequences of malnutrition than older children and adults. Another group especially vulnerable to malnutrition is pregnant or lactating women. During pregnancy and while breastfeeding women have specific nutritional needs for additional calories and for some micronutrients. Lack of these nutrients may lead to poor health outcomes for their children. Malnutrition during pregnancy may lead to greater risk of maternal complications during childbirth, low birth weights, and stillbirths.

■ Impacts and Issues

Measurement of the number of malnourished and undernourished people has been a key debate both in academic studies and in policy making. Malnutrition tends to be estimated for national populations using social science techniques and scientific sampling methods. Few studies try to estimate the number of malnourished based on identifying malnutrition itself, as most studies rely on proxy measures, measurements of more easily measured traits associated with malnutrition. One of the most common proxy measures uses cash incomes to estimate the ability to purchase food for each household. In the United States, this method was pioneered in 1963 during work on household budgets for the Social Security Administration. To this day, the U.S. Department of Agriculture (USDA) uses this technique along with a basket of commonly purchased foods to determine eligibility for food assistance programs.

Other common methods of estimating the extent of malnutrition in a population include food diaries, food intake surveys (FIS) conducted by the FAO, and dietary diversity surveys such as the Household Dietary Diversity Score developed by the U.S. Agency for International Development's (USAID's) Food and Nutrition Technical Assistance Program (FANTA). These surveys require that households write down, or relate by spoken word, what they ate in the last day or last week. The surveys provide information about which foods households actually eat so that information can be used to show both a lack of general diversity in the diet or to highlight suspected deficiencies of particular micronutrients.

Sometimes physical measurements are also a way to measure the extent of malnutrition in a population. Birth weights are one frequent measure. Another common physical measurement is though surveys that estimate the extent of malnourished children by weighing children and measuring their height at school or a variety of other settings. Also, some surveys may sample iron in blood or seek other physical measurements of micronutrient deficiencies.

Whereas measurement presents many issues for the study of malnutrition, the very definition of malnutrition can be debated. Malnutrition has generally been a focus on undernutrition and in regard to diets that lack adequate amounts of key micronutrients. However, the health problems of overweight people and obesity are increasingly being noticed both in the developed and the developing world. By the 1990s, even organizations such as the FAO included obesity as a consequence of malnutrition. Though clearly different than undernutrition and protein-energy malnutrition (PEM), overeating and obesity may also be linked to a poor diet. Some consider diets that have led to obesity to be nutritionally insufficient diets because they may lack key micronutrients, or poor diets could, like undernutrition, be

associated with poverty. For these and other reasons, some researchers, organizations, and policy makers want to include obesity as an effect of malnutrition. Others

A Burmese refugee holds her malnourished child while in a hospital in Bangladesh. © *Liba Taylor / Alamy.*

IN CONTEXT: UNDERNOURISHMENT INCREASING

In October 2009, the United Nations Food and Agriculture Organization (FAO) issued a report detailing increases in world hunger since 1995. Analysts predicted that higher food prices and a decline in funding for agricultural aid programs will cause substantial increases in undernourished people. The global economic recession greatly reduces the possibility of reaching 2015 targets in hunger reduction. The report produced data showing that whereas the number of undernourished people declined in the 1980s and early 1990s, the number of undernourished people has increased steadily since 1995 to number more than 1 billion people by 2009.

want to have studies of the health problems associated with obesity separated from those of undernutrition or hunger. This debate is especially acute for developing countries whose health systems must simultaneously deal

A severely malnourished man sits in his home in Eritrea. © *Mike Goldwater / Alamy.*

with the health problems associated with obesity, under-nutrition, and with micronutrient deficiencies.

■ Primary Source Connection

The Food and Agriculture Organization (FAO) of the United Nations has its headquarters in Rome, Italy. Facets of the FAO's position on the spectrum of global malnutrition impacts are clearly articulated in the factsheet excerpt that follows. The FAO asserts that almost one-third of the world's population suffers some form of malnutrition. The lack of proper nutrition has far-reaching health impacts and creates "incalculable loss of human potential and social development." In recent years, FAO experts have also started to address the fact that developing nations are not immune from food-related perils found in advanced economies, that developing nations are "quickly joining the ranks of countries dealing with severe health issues at both ends of the nutritional spectrum."

The Spectrum of Malnutrition

Hunger, which afflicts one in five of the developing world's people, is a profound impediment to the advancement of individuals and societies. Without proper intervention, undernutrition and the death and disease it causes are repeated with each generation.

The hungry suffer in silence and are often invisible: to the casual observer, many of them show no outward sign of the severity of their hunger.

Chronic hunger increases susceptibility to disease and leaves people feeling weak and lethargic, reducing their ability to work. This is reflected in economies and contributes to a devastating cycle of household hunger and poverty. Vitamin and mineral deficiencies in children lead to stunted growth, blindness and compromised mental development. Iron-deficiency anaemia contributes to 20 percent of maternal deaths in Africa and Asia.

Malnutrition, however, is not limited to the poor, nor is overnourishment a "luxury" of the wealthy. Poor nutrition crosses economic lines and leads to health problems caused by eating too little (under-nourishment), too much (overnourishment) or an unbalanced diet that lacks essential nutrients for a healthy life (micronutrient deficiencies).

High energy intake, poor dietary habits and faulty metabolism lead to an entirely different set of problems. Obesity and chronic diseases such as heart disease, diabetes and hypertension are quickly becoming a social and economic burden in developing countries. Recent evidence also suggests that susceptibility to these diseases may be linked to undernutrition during pregnancy and early childhood.

While the specific health consequences vary, both the underweight and the over-weight share high levels of sickness and disability, shortened life spans and diminished productivity. The result is that developing nations, their resources already stretched to the limit, must now cope increasingly with serious health issues at both ends of the nutritional spectrum.

"THE SPECTRUM OF MALNUTRITION." FOOD AND AGRICULTURE ORGANIZATION (FAO) OF THE UNITED NATIONS. HTTP://WWW.FAO. ORG/WORLDFOODSUMMIT/ENGLISH/FSHEETS/MALNUTRITION.PDF (ACCESSED NOVEMBER 2, 2010).

SEE ALSO *African Famine Relief; Biofuels and World Hunger; Dietary Changes in Rapidly Developing Countries; Famine; Famine: Political Considerations; Food and Agriculture Organization (FAO); Food Security; Hunger; Nutrient Fortification of Foods; UN Millennium Development Goals; Undernutrition.*

BIBLIOGRAPHY

Books

Fogel, Robert W. *The Escape from Hunger and Premature Death, 1700–2100: Europe, America, and the Third World.* Cambridge, UK, and New York: Cambridge University Press, 2004.

Food and Agriculture Organization (FAO). *The Double Burden of Malnutrition: Case Studies from Six Developing Countries.* Rome: Food and Agriculture Organization of the United Nations, 2006.

Hussain, Azmal. *Malnutrition: Issues and Combat Strategies.* Hyderabad, India: Icfai University Press, 2007.

Stanford, Claire. *World Hunger.* New York: H.W. Wilson Co, 2007.

Vesler, Lyman W. *Malnutrition in the 21st Century.* New York: Nova Science Publishers, 2007.

Waterlow, John C., Andrew Tomkins, and Sally M. Grantham-McGregor. *Protein-Energy Malnutrition.* New Barnet, UK: Smith-Gordon, 2006.

World Bank. *Environmental Health and Child Survival: Epidemiology, Economics, Experiences.* Washington, DC: World Bank, 2008.

Periodicals

Kuehn, Bridget M. "Aid Groups Target 'Silent' Malnutrition." *Journal of the American Medical Association* 300, no. 17 (2008): 1983–1985.

"Malnutrition—the Starvelings." *The Economist* 386, no. 8564 (2008): 56–57.

Stephenson, Joan. "Malnutrition in Darfur." *Journal of the American Medical Association (JAMA)* 299, no. 7 (2008): 755.

Web Sites

"Malnutrition." *World Health Organization (WHO).* http://www.who.int/child_adolescent_health/ topics/prevention_care/child/nutrition/malnu trition/en/index.html (accessed September 6, 2010).

"World Food Insecurity and Malnutrition: Scope, Trends, Causes, and Consequences." *Food and Agriculture Organization of the United Nations (FAO).* ftp://ftp.fao.org/docrep/fao/010/ai799e/ ai799e02.pdf (accessed September 6, 2010).

Blake Jackson Stabler

Meat Inspection Act of 1906

■ Introduction

The Federal Meat Inspection Act of 1906 (34 Stat. 674) mandates that the United States Department of Agriculture (USDA) and other government agencies regulate and inspect all meatpacking facilities, including slaughterhouses and meat processing plants, that conduct businesses across state lines. At the time the act was passed, four large companies—Armour, Swift, Morris, and National Packing—owned a significant majority of the nation's meatpacking facilities. All four companies sold meat products and operated facilities in several states.

The Federal Meat Inspection Act was enacted on the same day as its companion bill, the Pure Food and Drug Act (34 Stat. 768). The two pieces of legislation sought to remedy unsanitary conditions in the food processing industry that had been brought to light by worker strikes, Progressive Era reformers, journalists, and authors.

■ Historical Background and Scientific Foundations

In 1904 workers in union stockyards and nearby meatpacking plants in Chicago went on strike, demanding better working conditions and higher pay. The strike was ultimately unsuccessful, but the news caught the attention of American journalist and author Upton Sinclair (1878–1968), who was then writing for the Socialist journal *Appeal to Reason* in New Jersey and looking for ideas for a new political novel.

Sinclair visited the Chicago stockyards for two months, spending most of his time in the tenement neighborhoods that surrounded meat-processing plants. Technological advances such as ice boxes and refrigerated railroad cars enabled meatpacking to transition from seasonal winter employment to a year-round industry. As stockyards and meatpacking plants grew, so too did their need for workers. Mechanization and the advent of assembly lines provided jobs for unskilled laborers and recent immigrants

with little command of English. Sinclair spent time with workers in their homes and talked with them about how a meatpacking facility worked. He noted that small children and women were also employed in some parts of the facilities in the same 12-hour shifts, but made a fraction of the wages as adult male workers. Sinclair found illness was rife in both the workers and the animals being slaughtered.

Sinclair's book about the meatpacking industry, *The Jungle*, was first published by Doubleday in February 1906. The story follows the plight of the main character, Lithuanian immigrant Jurgis Rudkus, as he and his family live and work in Packingtown (the nickname of the area around the Union Stockyards). Sinclair intended his bestselling story to serve as a socialist allegory, but journalists, politicians, and the public largely ignored most of the book, focusing instead on eight pages that graphically described the meatpacking industry.

Sinclair described the pervasive stench of the stockyards and the surrounding area, noting that workers returned home covered in animal remnants. Inspectors were easily bribed. Diseased animals were knowingly taken to slaughter, processed, and packaged. Ill workers, including those with tuberculosis, were forced to work for fear of being blacklisted from employment in spite of the potential danger of contaminating meat. Workers would relieve themselves near their work stations. Potted meat and sausage products were contaminated with insects, rats, hair, hide, sawdust, human urine and blood, and animal remnants that had been swept from the floors. Practices such as these were later documented by government inspectors, but Sinclair added a particular element of horror to his novel when he recounted a tale of Durham's Pure Leaf Lard, which occasionally contained the remains of men who fell into the large lard processing vats.

Sinclair's book quickly became popular with the American public. Magazines and newspapers ran panicked stories of "tubercular beef" and meat industry practices. Sales of U.S. meat products plummeted.

U.S. President Theodore Roosevelt (1858–1919) later admitted to being sickened when he had read an advance copy of *The Jungle*. In response to the public outcry raised by Sinclair's book and the work of other muckraking journalists, Roosevelt sent labor commissioner Charles P. Neill (1865–1942) and social worker James Bronson Reynolds (1861–1908) to conduct a secret inspection of the nation's meatpacking industry. The large meatpacking companies were tipped off about the inspections. They ordered all facilities to be cleaned, and instructed English-speaking workers not to talk to inspectors without a supervisor present. However, Neill and Reynolds ultimately confirmed the existence of unhealthy practices within the meatpacking industry. The complete Neill-Reynolds Report indicated that Sinclair's novel may have underrepresented the scope of the hygiene and corruption problems in food processing at the time. Roosevelt later invited Sinclair to the White House and solicited his advice on how to reform the industry.

■ Impacts and Issues

On June 30, 1906, Congress passed the Pure Food and Drug Act and the Meat Inspection Act. Also created at Roosevelt's request was the Food and Drug Administration, charged with oversight of the regulation and inspection of medicines and foods.

The Federal Meat Inspection Act required four main reforms. First, livestock must undergo a mandatory

---

WORDS TO KNOW

MEATPACKING: The process of slaughtering animals and preparing meat for sale to consumers.

MUCKRAKERS: Late nineteenth-century and early-twentieth century journalists, authors, and photographers who sought social change by featuring injustices in such a way as to create maximum interest and action in the public.

PROGRESSIVE ERA: A period of social and political reform in the United States from the 1890s to the 1920s. Progressive Era reforms included labor, education, food safety, and anti-corruption laws.

REGULATION: Controlling behaviors, business practices, or industrial practices through rules, restrictions, or laws to encourage preferred outcomes or prevent undesired outcomes that may otherwise occur.

A NAUSEATING JOB, BUT IT MUST BE DONE
(President Roosevelt takes hold of the investigating muck-rake himself in the packing-house scandal.)

An early-twentieth century cartoon features U.S. President Theodore Roosevelt taking control of the investigation into the meatpacking scandal. © *North Wind Picture Archives / Alamy.*

IN CONTEXT: NANO-SCALE BATTLE AGAINST FOOD POISONING

Nano-scale technology can be used to protect food from poisonous microbial infections. Scientists attending the Institute of Food Technologists' annual meeting in Chicago during July 2010 announced recent advances in reducing levels of food-poisoning bacteria in foods by means of bactericidal nanoparticles. Bacteria killing and resistant nanoparticles can also be embedded in packaging. Nano-scale particles of zinc oxide, for example, take on new properties at such a small scale. The nano-scale zinc oxide can act to disrupt bacterial membranes, including potentially deadly *E. coli* O157:H7 membranes.

Independent experiments of packaging with embedded zinc oxide particles and coatings with nano-scale zinc oxide mixed with food-grade polylactic acid were tested against *Campylobacter, Listeria,* and *Salmonella* microbes. The nanoparticle-containing linings and coatings both showed increased resistance. The addition of Nisin, an antibacterial agent derived from bacteria (a bacteriocin), further enhanced resistance to the potentially deadly food-poisoning bacteria.

inspection before slaughter. Though several stockyards and slaughterhouses conducted inspections to exclude diseased animals, corruption, bribery, ineffective training, and lax enforcement undermined such protocols. Second, every carcass must again be inspected after slaughter, but before processing. Third, meatpacking facilities must abide by government regulations dictating cleanliness standards and sanitary practices. And finally, the U.S. Department of Agriculture (USDA) is authorized to regulate, monitor, and inspect all processing operations.

The original Meat Inspection Act has been amended several times, most significantly in 1967. Several companion laws have strengthened regulations on the meatpacking industry to ensure food safety, purity, and quality. In addition to focusing on meat processing, subsequent laws set forth standards for slaughterhouses and mandated more humane methods of killing animals.

Regulation of the meat industry continues to be controversial. In 2001 Congress overturned reforms intended to reduce repetitive stress injuries among meatpackers. In 2005 the international watchdog group Human Rights Watch concluded in their report "Blood, Sweat, and Fear: Workers' Rights in U.S. Meat and Poultry Plants" that working conditions in the U.S. meatpacking industry violated labor laws and basic human rights. The report cited dangerous working conditions, long shifts, repetitive work, unfair wage practices, anti-union actions, and abuses towards the significant population of recent-immigrant workers in the industry. In 2006 the U.S. Bureau of Labor Statistics reported an average injury and job-related illness rate among full-time meatpacking plant employees that was twice as high as the national average of all manufacturing jobs.

After a series of food recalls occurred in the first decade of the 2000s, including several instances of large amounts of contaminated meat that reached consumers, U.S. President Barack Obama in March 2009 called for re-evaluation of current meat inspection processes and regulations. By 2011 the Food Safety and Inspection Service expects to focus on increasing beef inspections particularly, in order to identify and prevent hamburger meat contaminated with *E. coli* O157:H7 bacteria from reaching consumers. Currently about 70,000 Americans per year experience illness due to eating foods, mostly ground beef, that has been contaminated with *E. coli.*

■ Primary Source Connection

Upton Sinclair wrote *The Jungle* to describe the life of the working class in 1906. He details the meatpacking industry, from the horrible working conditions to the corruption of the officials in power. Sinclair, a writer and reformer, was born in Baltimore, Maryland, in 1878. After attending graduate school at Columbia University, he began to publish novels. Sinclair ran for public office several times as a Socialist candidate, including runs for a U.S. Senate seat from New Jersey and the governorship of California. In 1934, as a Democrat, he nearly was elected the governor of California by promising government-owned factories an elaborate pension plan. In addition to *The Jungle,* Sinclair wrote two other muckraking novels. In 1943, he won the Pulitzer Prize for the novel *Dragon's Teeth,* which addressed the rise of Adolf Hitler. He died in New Jersey in 1968.

The Meat Inspection Act of 1906 mandated federal inspection of all livestock (cattle, swine, sheep, goats, and horses, but not poultry) destined to be sold overseas or in another state. The legislation is generally credited to public disgust at the meatpacking processes that were revealed in the pages of Upton Sinclair's *The Jungle.*

The novel provided readers with stomach-churning descriptions of the unhealthy and corrupt conditions in the Chicago meatpacking industry. Sinclair's protagonist is Jurgis Rudkis, a Lithuanian immigrant who firmly believes that hard work will lead him to success in America. He perseveres despite one setback after another before finally becoming disillusioned. Rudkis comes to see that the forces of the meatpacking industry are too massive to be overcome by one individual. He becomes a socialist.

Sinclair expected the novel to promote socialism. Most Americans paid little attention to the book's political message because they were too horrified by descriptions of what went into sausages and cans of lard. According to Sinclair, canned meat products contained rats, rat droppings, expectorations, floor filth, and the occasional unfortunate worker who fell into a vat. As Sinclair himself declared, "I aimed at the public's heart and hit it in the stomach."

Despite Sinclair's claim and the oft-told story of *The Jungle* converting President Theodore Roosevelt into a supporter of an inspection law, the book is not solely responsible for the 1906 inspection law. The United States had been moving towards some sort of wide-ranging federal meat inspection legislation for some years prior to the publication of *The Jungle*; however, the book brought the issue to the forefront of American consciousness.

The first meat regulation appeared in Boston in 1692. These early regulations were not aimed at protecting the consumer from bad meat. Instead, slaughterhouses, with their noise and pollution, were public nuisances. The regulations aimed to stop or reduce these nuisances. By the late nineteenth century, increasing knowledge about bacteria led to an attempt to understand the causes of disease. This development prompted the rapid expansion of municipal health departments in the early twentieth century. However, these departments were badly understaffed and the few inspectors they employed were not professionally trained.

Meanwhile, the first federal meat inspection act passed on August 30, 1890. It mandated the inspection of salted pork and bacon intended for export. The law was a response to strict European import laws aimed at diseased American meat. On March 3, 1891, in reaction to continued European restrictions, Congress approved a law that mandated inspection of all cattle, sheep, and swine prior to slaughter only if the meat was to be shipped in interstate commerce. Goats, horses, and poultry were not included, since such animals were rarely sold by processors.

Congress did not protect the local meat buyer and did not guarantee the quality of meat after the initial inspection of the live animal. As Sinclair discovered, human food was prepared under the most revolting conditions. Meat inspectors sent to Chicago in 1906 by President Roosevelt after the publication of *The Jungle* discovered numerous processing problems. Workers, categorized by inspectors as "indescribably filthy," would typically climb over diseased carcasses thrown on the floor and stand with dirty shoes upon tables used to process meat. Supervisors were unconcerned with such unsanitary practices, indicating that the practices were common.

The Jungle

With one member trimming beef in a cannery, and another working in a sausage factory, the family had a firsthand knowledge of the great majority of Packingtown swindles. For it was the custom, as they found, whenever meat was so spoiled that it could not be used for anything else, either to can it or else to chop it up into sausage. With what had been told them by Jonas, who had worked in the pickle rooms, they could now study the whole of the spoiled-meat industry on the inside, and read a new and grim meaning into that old Packingtown jest—that they use everything of the pig except the squeal.

Jonas had told them how the meat that was taken out of pickle would often be found sour, and how they would rub it up with soda to take away the smell, and sell it to be eaten on free-lunch counters; also of all the miracles of chemistry which they performed, giving to any sort of meat, fresh or salted, whole or chopped, any color and any flavor and any odor they chose. In the pickling of hams they had an ingenious apparatus, by which they saved time and increased the capacity of the plant—a machine consisting of a hollow needle attached to a pump; by plunging this needle into the meat and working with his foot, a man could fill a ham with pickle in a few seconds. And yet, in spite of this, there would be hams found spoiled, some of them with an odor so bad that a man could hardly bear to be in the room with them. To pump into these the packers had a second and much stronger pickle which destroyed the odor—a process known to the workers as "giving them thirty per cent." Also, after the hams had been smoked, there would be found some that had gone to the bad. Formerly these had been sold as "Number Three Grade," but later on some ingenious person had hit upon a new device, and now they would extract the bone, about which the bad part generally lay, and insert in the hole a white-hot iron. After this invention there was no longer Number One, Two, and Three Grade—there was only Number One Grade. The packers were always originating such schemes—they had what they called "boneless hams," which were all the odds and ends of pork stuffed into casings; and "California hams," which were the shoulders, with big knuckle joints, and nearly all the meat cut out; and fancy "skinned hams," which were made of the oldest hogs, whose skins were so heavy and coarse that no one would buy them—that is, until they had been cooked and chopped fine and labeled "head cheese!"

It was only when the whole ham was spoiled that it came into the department of Elzbieta. Cut up by the two-thousand-revolutions-a-minute flyers, and mixed with half a ton of other meat, no odor that ever was in a ham could make any difference. There was never the least attention paid to what was cut up for sausage; there would come all the way back from Europe old sausage that had been rejected, and that was moldy and white—it would be dosed with borax and glycerine, and dumped into the hoppers, and made over again for home consumption. There would be meat that had tumbled out on the floor, in the dirt and sawdust, where the workers had tramped and spit uncounted billions of consumption germs. There would be meat stored in great piles in rooms; and the water from leaky roofs would drip over it, and thousands of rats would race about on it. It was too dark in these storage places to see well, but a man could run his hand over these piles of meat and sweep off handfuls of the dried dung of rats. These rats were nuisances, and the packers would put poisoned bread out for them; they would die, and then rats, bread, and meat would go into the hoppers together. This is no fairy story and no joke; the meat would be shoveled into carts, and the man who did the shoveling would not trouble to lift out a rat even when he saw one—there were things that went into the sausage in comparison with which a poisoned rat was a tidbit. There was no place for the men to wash their hands before they ate their dinner, and so they made a practice of washing them in the water that was to be ladled into the sausage. There were the butt-ends of smoked meat, and the scraps of corned beef, and all the odds and ends of the waste of the plants, that would be dumped into old barrels in the cellar and left there. Under the system of rigid economy which the packers enforced, there were some jobs that it only paid to do once in a long time, and among these was the cleaning out of the waste barrels. Every spring they did it; and in the barrels would be dirt and rust and old nails and stale water—and cartload after cartload of it would be taken up and dumped into the hoppers with fresh meat, and sent out to the public's breakfast. Some of it they would make into "smoked" sausage—but as the smoking took time, and was therefore expensive, they would call upon their chemistry department, and preserve it with borax and color it with gelatine to make it brown. All of their sausage came out of the same bowl, but when they came to wrap it they would stamp some of it "special," and for this they would charge two cents more a pound.

Upton Sinclair

SINCLAIR, UPTON. *THE JUNGLE.* CAMBRIDGE, MA: R. BENTLEY, 1971.

SEE ALSO   E. Coli *Contamination; Factory Farming; Food Recalls; Food Safety and Inspection Service; Humane Animal Farming; Meats.*

BIBLIOGRAPHY

Books

Becker, Geoffrey S. *USDA Meat Inspection and the Humane Methods of Slaughter Act.* Washington, DC: Congressional Research Service, Library of Congress, 2008.

Kallen, Stuart A. *Is Factory Farming Harming America?* Detroit: Greenhaven Press, 2006.

Singh, Vijender. *Meat Inspection for Public Health.* New Delhi: Maxford Books, 2007.

Wilson, William. *Wilson's Practical Meat Inspection.* Chichester: John Wiley & Sons, 2007.

Periodicals

Ciftcioglu, Gurhan, et al. "Survival of *Escherichia Coli* O157:H7 in Minced Meat and Hamburger Patties." *Journal of Food, Agriculture and Environment* 6, no. 1 (2008): 24–27.

Razzaq, Samiya. "Hemolytic Uremic Syndrome: An Emerging Health Risk." *American Family Physician* 74, no. 6 (2006): 991–996.

Adrienne Lerner

Meats

■ Introduction

Meat is an important part of the diet in many cultures. It is an important, but not essential, food because it is high in protein and calories. People like meat for the complex flavors it develops during cooking, which depend on many factors such as how the animal is reared and slaughtered, and how the resulting meat is cured, stored, and (finally) cooked. It is the protein, fat, and water content of meat that account for its flavor and texture on cooking, and older animals tend to be more flavorful than younger ones. Meat was formerly something of a luxury in the human diet but in the early twenty-first century it is an everyday commodity for many, particularly with the rise of fast foods such as burgers and sausages. There is medical evidence that people who consume more meat are more likely to develop heart disease and some cancers compared to those who consume little or no meat. Modern meat production also has an environmental cost in terms of water, energy, and grain crop usage, which increase greenhouse gas emissions. The widespread use of antibiotics in cattle also encourages the spread of antibiotic resistant bacteria, which is a growing public health issue.

■ Historical Background and Scientific Foundations

Early humans were hunter-gatherers who would eat meat when it could be obtained, which was not often. The domestication of animals such as sheep, goats, pigs, and cattle probably started with agriculture, around 10,000 years ago. However, meat would have been a luxury to most people because plant foods would have been much cheaper to grow. Meat was popular in Europe in the Middle Ages because there was plenty of land available for pasture and the population was relatively low. Meat has always been abundant in North America too, with early settlers living on game followed by the development

of cattle ranching. Urbanization meant that meat had to be preserved by salting to supply those not living on or near farms, but the development of refrigeration and railroad transportation revolutionized the industry and made meat a part of most Americans' daily diets.

Cattle and other food animals are fed either grain or grass. Intensive farming prefers grain as the animals' diet, and their meat is more uniform. But the flavor of cattle fed on grass is very popular. For example, Argentinian grass-reared beef is much in demand; in addition to being grass-fed, these animals are usually slaughtered in a humane way, which avoids exposure of the meat to the stress hormones and accompanying biochemical

WORDS TO KNOW

CONNECTIVE TISSUE: The tissue between muscle fibers in meat and between muscle tissues and other tissues, such as bone. Connective tissue is made up of three proteins—collagen, elastin, and reticulin—and contributes to the texture of cooked meat.

HETEROCYCLIC AMINES (HCAs): Potentially cancer-causing compounds that are formed on meat when it is charred or cooked at high temperatures.

MARBLING: The internal fat in meat, which can often be seen as white veining within the red muscle matrix. Marbling differs from the adipose fat on the outside of a cut of meat, which can be trimmed off. It contributes to the flavor of meat, but is saturated fat and may raise cholesterol levels.

MEAT: The edible parts of an animal, usually excluding the skin and bone. The term *meat* often excludes poultry and fish, and refers to beef, lamb, pork, and veal. However, these meats are sometimes known as red meat, whereas poultry may be referred to as white meat.

MYOGLOBIN: An iron-containing, oxygen-transporting protein in red blood cells that gives meat its red appearance.

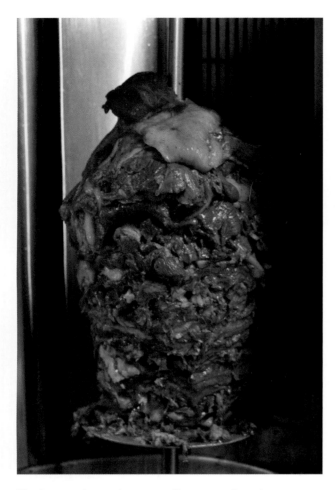

Hand-prepared meat shawarma grills on a rotating spit at Karam's, a family-owned Lebanese restaurant in Jacksonville, Florida. *Adrienne Lerner / Lerner & Lerner / LernerMedia Global Photos.*

flavor compounds, many of which are fat-soluble, enabling them to reach receptors in the mouth when the meat is eaten. Meat contains a lot of water, which makes it juicy, and the water eventually runs out of the meat during cooking. Overcooking will make the meat dry, particularly pork, which is only 52 percent water, compared to beef's 60 percent water content. Pork is well suited to drying, because it dehydrates easily due to its relatively low water content. As meat is cooked, its protein content begins to coagulate and the meat becomes more opaque and darkens. People have their own preferences as to whether they like their meat rare, medium-rare, or well-done, but the longer meat is cooked, the more likely is the formation of carcinogenic compounds such as heterocyclic amines.

■ Impacts and Issues

Heavy meat consumption, especially red meat and processed meats (such as bacon, ham, hot dogs, and lunch meats) may not be good for human health. A study supported by the National Cancer Institute (NCI) published in 2009 in the *Archives of Internal Medicine* that involved 500,000 people aged 50–71 suggested that those with the highest meat consumption had an increased risk of death from all causes, particularly heart disease and certain cancers, during ten years of followup. A link to colorectal cancer has been debated. The results of the Fukuoka Cancer Study, published in 2007 and carried out in Japan showed no link between meat consumption and colorectal cancer, but other studies in the United States and Europe have contradicted this study. A study by the NCI published in 2010 in *Cancer Research* followed 300,948 people for seven years and found that people whose red meat consumption was in the top fifth of those in the study had an increased risk of developing colorectal cancer when compared to those in the bottom fifth of red meat consumption. Contributing factors that are likely responsible for increased health risks associated with heavy red meat intake include: the saturated fat and cholesterol content of the meat; the iron in red meat, which may increase oxidative cell damage; nitrates and nitrites in processed meats; and the presence of carcinogens in cooked red meat, which are increased in meats cooked at high temperatures (as when frying, barbequing, or broiling). Though there are health risks associated with heavy intake of red and processed meats experts suggest limited portions of lean meats cooked at lower temperatures, when balanced by non-starchy vegetables and fruits in the diet and physical activity, can help decrease health risks.

In addition to health risks, meat production has a high environmental cost. It takes eight pounds of grain to produce a single pound of beef. In the United States, the majority of the grain crop is dedicated to feeding cattle, and these grain crops occupy 80 percent of agricultural land, accounting for about half of the nation's

processes associated with fear. This is said to improve the flavor of the meat. The carcass is hung to drain away most of the blood, then the hide is stripped away and the organs removed. Further hanging allows the muscles to stretch and enzymes begin to break down some of the proteins in the flesh, which makes the meat more tender. The meat is then sectioned, vacuum packed, and shipped. Fresh meat has a limited shelf life but it can be frozen for months or even years. Meat is a red color because of the oxygen-carrying protein myoglobin content. Some animals contain more myoglobin than others, which is why beef is redder than veal or pork. Parts of the animal that have been used for support, such as the shoulder, chest, leg or thigh, tend to be tougher and more flavorful than those parts that do not move much, such as the rib or the loin between the ribs and the hips. These parts have a more tender texture.

When meat is cooked, whether by grilling, frying, roasting, or some other method, many different physical and chemical processes happen. Browning reactions occur on the surface, which produce hundreds of different flavor compounds. The marbling fat melts and dissolves

A worker at a slaughterhouse in Brittany, France, prepares hogs for processing. © *FORGET Patrick / SAGAPHOTO.COM / Alamy.*

water usage. Meat production also adds to greenhouse gas production. In 2006, the United Nations Food and Agriculture Organization estimated that at least 18% of all greenhouse gases were related to meat production. In addition, the FAO states that other environmental effects, such as the clearing of rainforests for expanding livestock production, land degradation due to overgrazing and erosion, water pollution from animals' excrement, and loss of biodiversity are also associated with the meat industry. Finally, animals are routinely dosed with antibiotics to stop the spread of food-poisoning bacteria. This practice, however, encourages the spread of antibiotic-resistant bacteria among the human population.

SEE ALSO *Bushmeat; Diet and Cancer; Diet and Diabetes; Diet and Heart Disease; Diet and Hypertension; Dietary Changes in Rapidly Developing Countries; Dietary Guidelines for Americans; E. Coli Contamination; Factory Farming; Food Inspection and Standards; Heifer International; History of Food and Man: From Hunter-Gatherer to Agriculture; Humane Animal Farming; Import Restrictions; Livestock Intensity and Demand; Mad Cow Disease and vCJD; Meat Inspection Act of 1906; Organics; Salt, Nitrites, and Health; Texas Beef Group v. Winfrey; USDA Food Pyramid; Wholesome Meat Act of 1967.*

BIBLIOGRAPHY

Books

Friend, Catherine. *The Compassionate Carnivore: Or, How to Keep Animals Happy, Save Old Macdonald's Farm, Reduce Your Hoofprint, and Still Eat Meat.* Philadelphia: Da Capo Lifelong, 2008.

Horowitz, Roger. *Putting Meat on the American Table: Taste, Technology, Transformation.* Baltimore: Johns Hopkins University Press, 2006.

Toldrá, Fidel. *Safety of Meat and Processed Meat.* New York and London: Springer, 2009.

Periodicals

"Grilling Basics: Don't Char the Meat." *Consumer Reports* 73, no. 8 (2008): 52.

Holmes, Bob. "Meat-Free World." *New Scientist* 207, no. 2769 (2010): 28–31.

"Meat Cutback Could Prolong Life." *Science News* 174, no. 9 (2008): 17.

Stokstad, Erik. "Could Less Meat Mean More Food?" *Science* 327, no. 5967 (2010): 810–811.

Web Sites

Doheny, Kathleen. "Eating Red Meat May Boost Death Risk." *WebMd*, March 23, 2009. http://www.webmd.com/diet/news/20090323/eating-red-meat-may-boost-death-risk (accessed September 28, 2010).

Harvard Medical School. "Red Meat and Colon Cancer." *Harvard Medical School Family Health Guide*, March 2008 update. http://www.health.harvard.edu/fhg/updates/Red-meat-and-colon-cancer.shtml (accessed September 28, 2010).

"Meat and Meat Products in Human Nutrition: Meat and Health." *Agriculture and Consumer Protection Department, Food and Agriculture Organization of the United Nations (FAO)*. http://www.fao.org/docrep/t0562e/t0562e05.htm (accessed September 28, 2010).

"My Pyramid.gov: Inside the Pyramid: Meats and Beans." *U.S. Department of Agriculture (USDA)*. http://www.mypyramid.gov/index.html (accessed September 28, 2010).

National Cancer Institute. "Red Meat Consumption." *U.S. National Institutes of Health*. http://progressreport.cancer.gov/doc_detail.asp?pid=1&did=2007&chid=71&coid=731&mid=#cancer (accessed September 28, 2010).

Susan Aldridge

Mediterranean Diet

■ Introduction

Twenty countries, one principality, and several territories surround the Mediterranean Sea, each with its own agriculture, foodways, history, ethnicity, and economy. The 135 million people who live along the Mediterranean coast, however, each share many of the basic components of a diet that scientists claim is among the healthiest in the world. According to a 2007 study published in the *Archives of Internal Medicine*, adherence to the Mediterranean diet reduces the chances of overall mortality, as well as lowering the risk of developing heart disease, cancer, Alzheimer's disease, and Parkinson's disease. Since the popularization of the Mediterranean diet in the mid-1990s, extensive studies have supported many of the identified benefits of this diet, and therefore it is among the diets most often recommended by physicians and nutritionists for persons interested in pursuing a healthy lifestyle.

■ Historical Background and Scientific Foundations

Along the Mediterranean seacoast, ancient civilizations tended fertile soils to harvest vegetables, grains, and the grapes for wine; caught fresh fish year round in abundant seas; and picked pomegranates, figs, and other fruits from orchards that grew in the moderate climate. The olive tree features heavily in both the ancient and modern Mediterranean diet, as it adapted to the region's long, hot, and dry summers and cool, damp winters. Ancient Minoans, in fact, traded olive oil for metals and timber. Seafaring trade among the ancient Greeks, Carthaginians, Phoenicians, Arabs, and Romans widened the diversity of the Mediterranean diet, although regional differences remain within the diets of people currently living along the Mediterranean coast in the Middle East, Africa, and Europe.

The modern Mediterranean diet is most identified with food patterns typical of Southern Italy, Spain, and Greece. In 1958, American physiologist Ancel B. Keys (1904–2004) began the "Seven Countries" study, which continued until 1980 and ultimately linked a population's diet, and particularly saturated fat intake, to arterial plaque formation and cardiovascular disease (CVD). Keys studied 12,000 healthy middle-aged men living in the United States, Italy, the Greek Islands, Finland, Holland, Yugoslavia, and Japan. Study participants in Greece were found to have the lowest rates of CVD and heart attacks, although almost 40 percent of their caloric intake came from olive oil. Keys published results from the study in book form in *Eat Well and Stay Well the Mediterranean Way* in 1975. Although the book was immediately popular, a philosophy that low-fat or ultra low-fat diets were more beneficial pervaded the 1980s. It wasn't until 1994, when Walter Willet (1945–), physician and researcher in nutrition and public health at Harvard University, rediscovered and redefined the currently accepted Mediterranean diet that the diet became popular again.

Four main characteristics define the twenty-first-century Mediterranean diet: high consumption of fruits, vegetables, grains, legumes, nuts, and fish; low or moderate consumption of dairy products, eggs, and meat; moderate consumption of wine; and reliance on olive oil to provide most of the dietary calories derived from fats. Grilling, sautéing in olive oil, or stewing are the most common food preparation methods.

■ Impacts and Issues

Scientists at Harvard University published findings in 2003 suggesting that close adherence to a Mediterranean diet results in better survival rates after a myocardial infarction (heart attack), and that overall longevity is increased as well. Followup studies have suggested that the monounsaturated fatty acids in olive oil are likely help prevent cardiovascular disease by lowering walls of blood vessels more elastic. In the United States, the Food and Drug Administration (FDA) allows olive oil and olive oil-based products to carry a heart-healthy label. Oil obtained from the first pressing of the olives and not chemically processed is termed extra-virgin olive oil and has been shown to have the most health benefits.

The Mediterranean diet tends to be higher in salt than current American Heart Association recommendations suggest for daily sodium intake. High salt intake is often associated with hypertension. Current evidence indicates, however, that the Mediterranean diet lowers blood pressure in persons with existing hypertension, and that people with hypertension benefit from following the Mediterranean diet. Much of the salt in the Mediterranean diet comes from processing olives or fish, which are eaten in small quantities and are both beneficial foods, so nutritionists speculate that the increase in salt is compensated for by the overall benefit of the healthful Mediterranean diet. Additionally, fair weather, hilly terrain, and cultural habits such as enjoying walks before and after meals also encourage physical exercise,

low-density lipoproteins (LDL, or bad cholesterol) and raising high-density lipoproteins (HDL, or good cholesterol) in the blood. In addition, evidence suggests that phenolic compounds contained in olive oil also make the

Greek Orthodox monks look through a recipe book at the chapel of Mylopotamos, near the monastery of Great Lavra, at the Orthodox sanctuary on Mount Athos. Food cooked at the sanctuary—billed as a strict form of the Mediterranean diet—has enjoyed a wider appeal among Greeks who have become increasingly health conscious. *AP Images.*

A Mediterranean diet rich in olive oil, fruit, vegetables and fish provides "substantial protection" against diabetes, according to a 2007 study. Eating such meals helps keep people healthy and wards off Type-2 diabetes, which is linked to lifestyle factors like diet and obesity. *Image copyright Certe, 2010. Used under license from Shutterstock.com.*

and along with diet, likely contribute to lower blood pressure and overall health.

Viniculture is a pervasive and important part of the Mediterranean region. Wine is usually consumed in moderation (a glass or two), and only with meals. Red wine contains resveratrol, an antioxidant substance that scientists suspect helps play a beneficial role in preventing inflammation and blood clots. Grapes for making wine are harvested in September and October, and festivals, along with agricultural tourism, have become especially popular along Mediterranean winemaking routes.

SEE ALSO *Aquaculture and Fishery Resources; Asian Diet; Biodiversity and Food Supply; Climate Change and Agriculture; Diet and Cancer; Diet and Diabetes; Diet and Heart Disease; Diet and Hypertension; Dietary Changes in Rapidly Developing Countries; Food Security; Fusion; Genetically Modified Organisms (GMO); Immigration and Cuisine; Latin American Diet; Legumes; Monounsaturated and Polyunsaturated Oils; Seafood; Vegetables; Viniculture.*

BIBLIOGRAPHY

Books

The Food of the Mediterranean: A Journey for Food Lovers. London: Murdoch, 2009.

Heinrich, Michael, Walter E. Müller, and Claudio Galli. *Local Mediterranean Food Plants and Nutraceuticals.* Basel, Switzerland: Karger, 2006.

Helstosky, Carol. *Food Culture in the Mediterranean.* Westport, CT: Greenwood Press, 2009.

Klapp, Emilia. *Your Heart Needs the Mediterranean Diet: Learn How Mediterraneans Have Kept a Healthy Heart for Centuries.* South Pasadena, CA: Preventive Nutrition Press, 2007.

Quiles, José L., M. Carmen Ramirez-Tortosa, and Parveen Yaqoob. *Olive Oil and Health.* Wallingford, UK: CABI Pub, 2006.

Periodicals

Alonso, Alvaro, and Miguel A. Martinez-Gonzalez. "Mediterranean Diet, Lifestyle Factors, and Mortality." *JAMA: The Journal of the American Medical Association* 293, no. 6 (2005): 674.

Feart, Catherine, Cecelia Samieri, Virginie Rondea, et al. "Adherence to the Mediterranean Diet, Cognitive Decline, and Risk of Dementia." *JAMA: The Journal of the American Medical Association* 302, no. 6 (2009): 638–648.

"Health Effects of Olive Oil and the Mediterranean Diet." *Nutrition Reviews* 64, no. 10 (2006): n.p.

"Mediterranean Diet: Good Snacking." *Consumer Reports on Health* 20, no. 3 (2008): 7.

Nauänez-Caordoba, Jorge M., Faelix Valencia-Serrano, Estefanaia Toledo, Alvaro Alonso, and Miguel A. Martinez-Gonzalez. "The Mediterranean Diet and Incidence of Hypertension." *American Journal of Epidemiology* 169, no. 3 (2009): 339–346.

Sofi, Francesco, Francesca Cesari, Rosanna Abbate, Gian Franco Gensini, and Alessandro Casini. "Adherence to Mediterranean Diet and Health Status: Meta-Analysis." *British Medical Journal* 337 (2008): a1344.

"Summaries for Patients: The Effects of a Mediterranean Diet on Risk Factors for Heart Disease." *Annals of Internal Medicine* 145, no. 1 (2006): 1–11.

Web Sites

Childs, Dan. "Take It or Leave It? The Truth about 8 Mediterranean Diet Staples." *ABC News*, June 24, 2009. http://abcnews.go.com/Health/MensHealthNews/story?id=7911505 (accessed November 4, 2010).

Mayo Clinic staff. "Mediterranean Diet: Choose This Heart-Healthy Diet Option." *Mayo Clinic.com.* http://www.mayoclinic.com/health/mediterranean diet/CL00011 (accessed November 4, 2010).

"Mediterranean Diet." *American Heart Association.* http://www.americanheart.org/presenter.jhtml?identifier=4644 (accessed November 4, 2010).

Brenda Wilmoth Lerner

Michael Pollan: Linking Food and Environmental Journalism

■ Introduction

Michael Pollan's book on the food chains that feed most Americans, *The Omnivore's Dilemma: A Natural History of Four Meals*, surged to surprise popularity in 2006, followed quickly by *In Defense of Food: An Eater's Manifesto* in 2008 and *Food Rules: An Eater's Manual* in 2009. All three books topped *The New York Times* best-seller lists and won numerous awards, garnering praise from such diverse groups as environmentalists, historians, cooks, book club readers, and popular comedians. Pollan's columns on American nutrition, organic agriculture, cooking, and government policy have popularized formerly obscure issues and become a powerful voice for many activists, and *Time* magazine listed him as one of the world's 100 most influential people in 2010. Although Pollan's effect on people's food choices cannot be directly measured, it is appreciable. If readers are following any of his advice, they are consuming less high-fructose corn syrup (HFCS), eating fewer highly processed foods, more fruits and vegetables, and less meat, especially from animals raised in concentrated animal feeding operations (CAFOs) or factory farms. Even readers who have not altered their eating habits have become more knowledgeable about what is in their food, their foodways, and how their food comes to them.

■ Historical Background and Scientific Foundations

Michael Pollan (1955–) started his career as a journalist and an editor, publishing articles about gardening and the interaction between culture and nature for *The New York Times* and *Harper's* in the late 1980s. His first book, *Second Nature: A Gardener's Education* (1991), collected many of his essays on the changes he made to the land on a piece of a former dairy farm in Connecticut; the book was popular among gardeners and naturalists who enjoyed Pollan's ruminations on history and ideology. Pollan's

next book, *A Place of My Own: The Education of an Amateur Builder*, was published in 1997 and chronicled his experiences designing and building a cabin-like office on his land. This was not as popular as his next book, *The Botany of Desire: A Plant's-Eye View of the World*, which appeared in 2001 and examined the domestication and history of apples, tulips, marijuana, and potatoes.

Pollan continued writing essays, especially for *The New York Times Magazine* along with these books, in addition to moving to California and becoming a professor of journalism at the University of California at Berkeley in 2003. Many of his essays, such as those on sustainable farming, CAFOs, feedlot cattle, and corn, foreshadowed more detailed examinations of these topics in *The Omnivore's Dilemma* in 2006. The surprising popularity of *The Omnivore's Dilemma* was at least partially due to Pollan's skill at describing the history and processes behind many popular American foods, a growing interest in culinary history and alternative food chains such as farmer's markets and organic farms, and increasing American anxiety over food, which Pollan articulated as a dilemma between the different choices humans face as omnivores. Pollan's discussion of industrial agriculture, pastoral agriculture (including an examination of "organic industrial" vs. local farming alternatives, or Whole Foods vs. Polyface Farms in Virginia), and "neo-Paleolithic" or hunted and gathered foods was revolutionary for many readers who had not thought about the idea that "eating represents our most profound engagement with the natural world" and how eating industrially produced foodstuffs may obscure these connections.

Pollan's success with *The Omnivore's Dilemma* led directly to two shorter books addressing people's questions about what they *should* eat. He answered this rather succinctly in 2008 with the first sentence of *In Defense of Food*, which suggests that people should "Eat food. Not too much. Mostly plants." Pollan goes on to describe how nutrition scientists and advertisers have become the authorities on food in American culture, replacing traditional values on cuisine with

WORDS TO KNOW

CAFO: Concentrated Animal Feeding Operations are agricultural facilities (or "factory farms") where animals, waste, and production are highly concentrated in a small area of land. Pollan examines the economics and problems inherent in these enterprises in *The Omnivore's Dilemma*.

FOODWAYS: Food-related behaviors that relate to or identify a culture.

HFCS: High-fructose corn syrup is a sweetener and preservative that is commonly used in baked goods, soda, dairy treats, and many other processed foods. It is made by converting the glucose in corn starch to fructose, and then adding more glucose, a process that Pollan describes in some detail in *The Omnivore's Dilemma*.

OMNIVORE: An animal that eats both plants and animals; a dietary generalist, as opposed to a specialist that can eat only a few types of food.

ORTHOREXIA: An unhealthy obsession with healthy eating, modeled on an analogy with anorexia nervosa. Orthorexia is not a medically recognized diagnosis, but may be useful in describing people who are fixated on eating only certain correct foods. Pollan describes Americans as "a nation of orthorexics" in *In Defense of Food*.

Author and professor Michael Pollan (1955–) gained notoriety for his writings on industrial food production and its impact on human health and the natural environment. *AP Images.*

inexplicable or ever-changing dietary advice and the pernicious marketing of "edible foodlike substances." Pollan touches on many of the topics described in detail in *The Omnivore's Dilemma* in this book, without quite as much history and science, although he does examine orthorexia and the pitfalls of the Western industrial diet.

Food Rules, the shortest of Pollan's books, takes some of the ideas from *In Defense of Food* and more current essays and blogger contributions, and condenses them into 64 short pieces of advice accompanied by a few explanatory paragraphs. His rules include such counsel as "Don't eat anything your great-grandmother wouldn't recognize as food" (with the note that if your great-grandmother was a terrible cook or eater, you might want to adopt a French or Sicilian great-grandmother), and "Avoid foods you see advertised on television." Pollan also published *The Omnivore's Dilemma for Kids: The Secrets behind What You Eat* in 2009, which some adults found more accessible than his 2006 book.

■ Impacts and Issues

Michael Pollan's books and articles have generated continued and enthusiastic discussion on the topics he has brought to pubic attention since 2000, including a couple of documentary films and citations in almost every new book published on food or agriculture. Local food networks, such as farmers' markets, community supported agriculture cooperatives (CSAs), grass-fed beef producers, and organic bakers who don't use HFCS have undoubtedly profited from his work. At least some people altered their diets after reading his work, and many are more thoughtful about their food choices, perhaps checking food labels and selecting less processed alternatives.

Although Pollan is generally lauded for consciousness-raising on food-related issues, his books and articles have not gone without criticism. Some feel that he gave vegetarians short-shrift in his books; others argue that his work (and the modern food movement in general) is overly elitist. Others, like Julie Guthman, argue that he hasn't used his popularity and position to call for greater structural and political changes in the American food chain. Some of Pollan's more recent articles have been quite politically pointed, however. In 2008 Pollan addressed President-Elect Obama in an article titled "Farmer in Chief," arguing that "the health of a nation's food system is a critical issue of national security." Pollan called for Obama to "make the reform of the entire food system one of the highest priorities of your administration" and asserted that his party could not make significant progress on the health care crisis, energy independence, or climate change without addressing the problems embodied in American food. He addressed the different factions in the contemporary food movement and their varied political and social goals in his article "The Food Movement, Rising" in 2010, noting quite explicitly that "… the food movement's strongest claim on public attention today is the fact that the American diet of highly processed food laced with added fats and sugars is responsible for the epidemic of chronic diseases that threatens to bankrupt the health care system." Pollan continues to educate and advocate on food issues by linking to other writers' articles, proposed policy changes, and new books through public appearances and on Twitter and his Web site (http://michaelpollan.com/).

SEE ALSO *Alice Waters: California and New American Cuisine; Farm-to-Table Movement; Foodways; Locavore; Organics; Processed Foods; Slow Food Movement; Sustainable Table.*

BIBLIOGRAPHY

Books

Berry, Wendell. *Bringing It to the Table: On Farming and Food.* Berkeley: Counterpoint, 2009.

McKibben, Bill, and Albert Gore. *American Earth: Environmental Writing since Thoreau.* New York: Literary Classics of the United States, 2008.

Pollan, Michael. *Food Rules: An Eater's Manual.* New York: Penguin Books, 2009.

———. *In Defense of Food: An Eater's Manifesto.* New York: Penguin Press, 2008.

———. *The Omnivore's Dilemma: A Natural History of Four Meals.* New York: Penguin, 2006.

Weber, Karl. *Food, Inc.: How Industrial Food Is Making Us Sicker, Fatter and Poorer—And What You Can Do about It.* New York: PublicAffairs, 2009.

Periodicals

Guthman, Julie. "Commentary on Teaching Food: Why I Am Fed Up with Michael Pollan et al." *Agriculture and Human Values* 24, no. 2 (2007): 261–264.

Web Sites

Pollan, Michael. "The Food Movement, Rising." *Michael Pollan.com.* http://michaelpollan.com/articles-archive/the-food-movement-rising/ (accessed August 24, 2010).

Sandra Dunavan

Migrant Labor, Immigration, and Food Production

■ Introduction

Migrant laborers are people who move from one region to another to secure employment. Many of the world's migrants earn their livings by working in agriculture. The U.S. Department of Labor's Occupational Safety & Health Administration (OSHA) and the United Nations Development Programme (UNDP) both list agriculture among the most dangerous occupations worldwide.

Most migrant laborers are adult men who work in a location geographically remote from their homes and families. They frequently send a majority of their earnings back home to support relatives. The typical pattern of migrant worker movement is from less-developed nations to wealthier nations or from poorer rural regions to wealthier urbanized areas. In regions with fluid borders or for migrant farm workers who remain in their home nations, many return home at the end of the agricultural season. However, agricultural migrant workers who cross borders without documented immigration status or who obtain long-term work visas often do not return to their places of origin. Some migrant agricultural workers move from job to job with their families, with multiple family members working in the fields or processing plants.

Agricultural interests, especially in developed nations, assert that migrant farm labor is an essential element in reducing consumer food costs. In the United States, various studies estimate the potential cost of staple vegetables (such as tomatoes) would likely rise by 25 to 40 percent without the current supply of migrant agricultural workers. Debates over migrant labor in food production concern issues of immigration, human rights, fair wages, child labor, and food security.

■ Historical Background and Scientific Foundations

In the United States, Congress passed the Fair Labor Standards Act (FLSA) in 1938. The act guaranteed a minimum wage, outlawed almost all child labor, and capped the number of hours in a standard workweek. The act, however, exempted agricultural workers. By 1945 there were 550,000 hired farm workers in the United States who migrated around with the harvest schedules of popular crops. On average, these workers worked less than 75 days per year and made an average annual family income of less than $1,000.

The U.S. government introduced the Bracero guest worker program during World War II (1939–1945) to help replace agricultural workers who had joined the war effort. The program permitted Mexican agricultural workers to legally work and reside in the United States. When the program ended in 1964, 5 million Mexican workers had come to work in the United States. Migrant workers for other nations entered the United States under the Guest Worker Program that created the H2 visa program. After Bracero ended, demand remained for migrant labor in agriculture that outstripped the number of H2 visas set aside annually. The supply of workers did not abate, but an increasing number of migrant workers were of undocumented immigration status.

In 1960 journalist Edward R. Murrow (1908–1965) drew attention to the plight of migrant agricultural workers in the United States with his documentary *Harvest of Shame*. The special television program aired just after Thanksgiving Day in order to highlight American's dependence on the people who picked their abundant food. Murrow stated that he hoped the graphic pictures of how migrant farm workers lived and the working conditions they endured would "shock the conscience" of his audience.

In the mid-1960s a grassroots movement among farm workers began demanding better pay, safer working conditions, and better housing. Activists César Chávez (1927–1993) and Dolores Huerta (1930–) led the unionization of some migrant farm workers, protesting working conditions and forcing employers to bargain with unions by instituting large-scale boycotts of some foods. In August 1965 a strike of Mexican and Filipino grape workers in Delano, California, was supported by Chávez's United Farm Workers of America (UFWA), resulting in a five-year consumer boycott of grapes by supporters. The grape boycott ended when employers agreed to recognize and give concessions to unionized farm workers.

Debate over illegal immigration and the rights of undocumented farm workers became a fixture of U.S. politics. The 1983 Migrant and Seasonal Agricultural Worker Protection Act (MSPA) provided pay, housing, transportation, and working-hours protections to migrant and seasonal agricultural workers. However, it exempted a large portion of the migrant agricultural workforce that the law considered independent contractors. In 1986, the U.S. Immigrant Reform and Control Act granted amnesty to undocumented Mexican migrants who could prove they had at least 60 days of employment in the United States during 1985 and part of 1986. The law extended legal permanent resident status to more than 1.2 million agricultural workers.

Migrant agricultural work is not limited to farms in the United States. During the twentieth century, more of the global population moved to seek employment than at any other time in modern history.

■ Impacts and Issues

China and India have the world's largest populations of migrant workers. However, migrant workers in India and China are typically leaving agricultural employment and agricultural regions to seek employment in cities. In China, as machinery has replaced millions of jobs on state-run collective farms that once ran on an abundance of labor, Chinese workers have left farming villages in record numbers. Migrant workers in China are typically unemployed agricultural workers who seek out urban jobs in construction, manufacturing, or sanitation. They comprise 9 percent of China's population, almost 150 million people. The migrant labor force in China is expected to reach 250 million by 2015 and 300 million by 2025.

Crop failures, low crop prices, and depressed agricultural wages drive India's migrants away from agriculture. India has 100 million migrant workers, approximately 10 percent of whom seek employment outside of India. Those who settle abroad typically work as farm workers in Canada and Australia or in service sector jobs in Europe or the United States. Whereas agricultural production has not declined in either India or China since 2000, some experts worry that abandoned farmland and rapidly expanding, typically poor, urban migrant worker populations could threaten food security.

In the European Union (EU), migrant workers tend to be both leaving agricultural work and migrating to take agricultural employment. As the EU expanded to include former Soviet-satellite nations in Eastern Europe, migrant workers sought employment in Western European nations. Agricultural migrant workers in the United Kingdom, France, Spain, and Germany tend to be from the EU's newest member countries.

WORDS TO KNOW

INDEPENDENT CONTRACTOR: A person who contracts to do a specified project or type of work for another person using his or her own resources and processes to accomplish the work; an independent worker rather than an employee.

MIGRANT WORKER: A person who moves from one region to another to find or follow employment. Migrant workers are used extensively in agriculture, moving frequently during the course of the year to follow the harvest seasons.

UNDOCUMENTED (WORKER): A person of unverified immigration status; someone who entered a country without advance permission, entered without required paperwork, or who cannot prove that he or she legally entered a country under its immigration laws.

VISA: A certificate or other evidence of permission to enter a country legally for work, residential, or visiting purposes.

The EU offers cross-boundary employment opportunities among member states. However, the EU also has a sizable population of undocumented migrant farm workers, predominantly from African nations. Whereas migrant farm workers throughout the EU have been found to be living in difficult conditions and working for low pay, African migrant workers, who predominantly work in Italy and Greece, often live in makeshift encampments with no food or electricity. A 2008 EU study found that African migrant fruit pickers in southern Italy earned the lowest wages, often less than 20 euros per day. African migrant agricultural laborers, regardless of their immigration documentation status, have experienced harassment by employers and authorities, had their encampments razed, and been deported. Many agricultural businesses in the region admit that they depend on migrant labor to bolster profit margins, harvest the entirety of their crop, and keep consumer food prices lower.

In the Americas, migrant farm workers predominantly come from the Caribbean, Mexico, and Central and South American nations to work in the United States and Canada. The 2007 National Agricultural Workers Study, conducted by the Department of Labor, found that 75 percent of migrant farm workers in the United States were from Mexico and that as many as half were of undocumented immigration status. U.S. agriculture needs 2 million seasonal or migrant workers per year; however, the United States offers only between 5,000 and 20,000 agricultural worker visas per year. Since 2000, the median annual income for Latino migrant farm workers in the United States has remained around $10,000.

The International Labor Organization (ILO) contends that a worldwide rethinking about the economics and human costs of migrant farm labor is needed.

A Mexican migrant worker culls, prunes, and weeds grape plants by hand in a Kern County, California, vineyard. *Image copyright Richard Thornton. Used under license from Shutterstock.com.*

Despite the proliferation of national laws protecting the health, safety, and wages of some agricultural workers, many others remain in precarious employment conditions. The ILO asserts that all migrant workers have several fundamental rights: the right to voluntary and unforced labor, freedom from child labor and access to education, adequate wages, access to medical care, freedom from violence or intimidation, the right to join a union and collectively bargain for improvements in pay and working conditions, and the elimination of discriminatory hiring and employment practices.

Critics of international migrant labor contend that an influx of migrants willing to work for substandard wages drives down wages for everyone in the agricultural industry. Others contend that immigrant laborers are taking jobs that might otherwise be filled with residents of the host nations. In 2010 the United Farm Workers, a U.S.-based union of agricultural workers, announced the Take Our Jobs program. The program invited unemployed Americans to work in the fields alongside migrant farm workers and was intended to counter immigration critics claim that migrant workers take jobs away from U.S. residents. Few people accepted the challenge to work in the fields; most could not handle the physical demands of the jobs. U.S. television personality and comedian Stephen Colbert (1964–) worked in the fields picking beans and packing corn as part of the Take Our Jobs program, filming parts of the workday for a segment on his late-night show. Colbert later testified before Congress on the need for better visa programs, improved wages, and better living conditions for migrant workers on U.S. farms.

Worldwide, child labor remains a problem among agricultural migrant worker populations. The international nongovernmental organization (NGO) Human Rights Watch (HRW) reports that most children of migrant farm workers work in the fields alongside their parents at least part of the year. Children in migrant labor populations suffer from abundant safety hazards, exposure to pesticides and chemicals, disrupted schooling, and are more likely to be the victims of violent crimes and sexual assaults. HRW considers migrant agricultural labor a threat to childhood, which they assert—in accordance with the Universal Declaration on Human Rights—is a fundamental right. In the world's poorest regions, child labor on a farm can be an economic necessity for a household. Child labor in agriculture is not limited to the developing world: U.S. regulations permit children as young as 12 to do limited work with parental permission. Globally, children of migrant laborer parents who work in agriculture are the most likely children to work and are among the least likely to attend school.

SEE ALSO *Foodways; Fusion; Immigration and Cuisine; Latin American Diet; Wage Slavery in Food Production; War, Conquest, Colonialism, and Cuisine.*

BIBLIOGRAPHY

Books

Burton, Alvin W., and Irwin B. Telpov. *Farm Labor: 21st Century Issues and Challenges.* New York: Nova Science, 2008.

Martin, Philip L., Michael Fix, and J. E. Taylor. *The New Rural Poverty: Agriculture & Immigration in California.* Washington, DC: Urban Institute Press, 2006.

Stone, Dori. *Beyond the Fence: A Journey to the Roots of the Migration Crisis.* Oakland, CA: Food First Books, 2009.

Periodicals

Anderson, Bridget. "Migration, Immigration Controls and the Fashioning of Precarious Workers." *Work, Employment and Society* 24, no. 2 (2010): 300–317.

Borre, Kristen, Luke Ertle, and Mariaelisa Graff. "Working to Eat: Vulnerability, Food Insecurity, and Obesity among Migrant and Seasonal Farmworker

Families." *American Journal of Industrial Medicine* 53, no. 4 (2010): 443–462.

Maldonado, Marta M. "'It Is Their Nature to Do Menial Labour': The Racialization of 'Latino/a Workers' by Agricultural Employers." *Ethnic and Racial Studies* 32, no. 6 (2009): 1017–1036.

Melillo, Edward D. "Kathleen Mapes, Sweet Tyranny: Migrant Labor, Industrial Agriculture, and Imperial Politics." *Business History Review* 84, no. 2 (2010): 390.

Shah, Dimpy J., et al. "Hand Problems in Migrant Farmworkers." *Journal of Agricultural Safety and Health* 15, no. 2 (2009): 157–169.

Waugh, Irma M. "Examining the Sexual Harassment Experiences of Mexican Immigrant Farmworking Women." *Violence against Women* 16, no. 3 (2010): 237–261.

Youn, Hyewon, Robert Woods, Xun Zhou, and Christian Hardigree. "The Restaurant Industry and Illegal Immigrants: An Oklahoma Case Study." *Journal of Human Resources in Hospitality & Tourism* 9, no. 3 (2010): 256–269.

Web Sites

"NOW with Bill Moyers: Migrant Labor in the United States." *PBS.org*, May 28, 2004. http://www.pbs.org/now/politics/migrants.html (accessed November 3, 2010).

Stoddard, Ed. "Agriculture Dependent on Migrant Workers." *Reuters*, July 23, 2007. http://www.reuters.com/article/idUSN1526113420070723 (accessed November 3, 2010).

Adrienne Wilmoth Lerner

Molecular Gastronomy

■ Introduction

Molecular gastronomy refers to the branch of scientific research that studies the chemical and physical changes that happen to food as it is cooked, e.g., the complex development of sugars as food caramelizes or the interplay of volatile organic acids as grapes are fermented into wine. In common usage, however, the term molecular gastronomy also refers to a style of cooking in which the chef uses unusual techniques or tools to create an artistic and challenging meal. Often the techniques utilize modern science, such as using gas-pressurized carafes to create flavored foams, or using liquid nitrogen to freeze food or create extreme temperature differences. This style of cooking became known as molecular gastronomy because of its high-tech methods. Although there are only a few restaurants that fall into this category, the cooking has had a wide-reaching impact on the culinary world as these chefs create new techniques and dishes that challenge convention.

■ Historical Background and Scientific Foundations

As modern cooking developed, there have been many trends and fads. One of the most significant trends was the *nouvelle cuisine* movement of the 1970s, led by chefs such as Paul Bocuse (1926–) and Pierre Troigros (1926–). The nouvelle cuisine movement focused on lighter cooking techniques and more artistic plate presentations than in traditional French cooking. As the chefs experimented with different techniques, they started incorporating modern equipment that did not exist in classic cuisine, such as microwave ovens, non-stick pans, food processors, and steam ovens. The concept of experimenting with new tools and techniques, along with the artistic plate presentations, led eventually to the current trend of molecular gastronomy.

In the early 1990s, the cooks of this school of thought focused on two tenants of nouvelle cuisine, artistic presentation and utilizing ultra-cooking techniques and tools. The chefs expanded on these ideas to create a style of food that is unique, but also challenging to most diners. As with nouvelle cuisine, often a meal cooked in this style will be *prix fixe*, also called a tasting menu. This means that the diner pays one price for a meal consisting of multiple small courses so the guest can taste many different dishes. In regard to plate presentation, classic French cuisine presentation called for plates to look full and appealing with little empty space. In nouvelle cuisine, chefs leave empty space on the plate, and stack food in very particular ways to create an image of height off of the plate. In molecular gastronomy, plate presentations are often a striking mix of colors and shapes, sometimes stretching the imagination as to how the dish was created.

For a molecular gastronomy chef, each course is an opportunity to surprise or challenge the guest's preconceptions. For example, Ferran Adrià (1962–), chef of the restaurant El Bulli near Roses in Catalonia, Spain, will sometimes serve his food with instructions as to how it should be eaten, such as a glass of pea soup layered by temperature that is to be drunk slowly but without stopping. Adrià's guests experience a study of the same food at different temperatures as the heating soup slowly engages their olfactory sense and intensifies in flavor. Food that is hot releases more vapors and aroma, and a person's sense of smell is an essential factor in taste. By having the guest drink the pea soup without stopping, Adrià creates the sensation of the soup's flavor gaining intensity while it is being eaten,

---

WORDS TO KNOW

NOUVELLE CUISINE: Culinary trend beginning in the late 1970s that pulled away from classic French cooking to find new, lighter techniques and more artistic presentations.

PRIX FIXE: A menu style in which there is one price for a meal consisting of many small courses.

demonstrating both the challenges of managing temperature but also the way one's senses respond to the same food at varying levels of heat. This combination of meal and science experiment is quintessential molecular gastronomy.

■ Impacts and Issues

Molecular gastronomy has been the recipient of much praise and much critique. It has been praised for its cutting edge viewpoint and its inventiveness. Adrià is a prime example: His restaurant is only open six months during the year and Adrià, his kitchen staff, and a few food scientists spend the other six months in a kitchen-laboratory experimenting with new techniques and new preparations. The critiques of molecular gastronomy are that it is too esoteric, too inaccessible for the average diner to appreciate or enjoy. Detractors say that the point of food is to comfort and nourish, to provide a pleasant and enjoyable experience to one's guest, something that most people will not find in a molecular gastronomy meal.

Proponents of molecular gastronomy argue that the chefs at its forefront are forging new ground, creating meals and techniques that never existed before, such as Adrià's warm jellied consommè, which exists in direct opposition to the fundamental understanding of how gelatin operates at higher temperatures. Despite the controversy, some of the new techniques that have been developed have spread throughout the culinary world. One of Adrià's most famous creations is his use of foams: By filling a nitrogen-fueled whipped cream charger with various sauces, Adrià was able to create flavorful foams to use in his meals. This relatively simple technique quickly became a very popular fad, and soon foams could be seen on menus throughout the world.

When nouvelle cuisine was a new and groundbreaking trend, one of the common critiques at the time concerned the plate presentations. The nouvelle cuisine presentation trend consisted of serving a small amount of food on a large plate to include empty space, as well as shaping the food into an artistic design. This garnered the criticism that nouvelle cuisine looked unappealing and did not sate the appetite. In the end, nouvelle cuisine's plate presentations became more standard, and the *prix fixe* style countered the critique that the meal was not filling. Molecular gastronomy takes plate presentation to a more artistic level, oftentimes challenging the guest to wonder how the chef was able to achieve his or her finished product. For example, Wylie Dufresne (1970–) of wd~50 in New York City has a dish that includes "scrambled egg ravioli," which seems straightforward on the menu. However, what arrives on the table is a smooth, unblemished yellow cube, seemingly defying the laws of physics. Grant Achatz (1974–) of Alinea in Chicago also creates dishes that inspire wonder. The menu might read "Short Rib: Beets, Cranberry,

Heston Blumenthal, chef and proprietor of The Fat Duck restaurant in Bray, England, works in his food laboratory. He has written an educational textbook on chemistry in the kitchen for children. *© Peter Titmuss / Alamy.*

Campari" but by cooking the Campari into a flexible sheet and using the beets to create six different colorful preparations and garnishes, the finished plate looks like a Dali painting, a shimmering landscape of stretched and poised oddities.

Like nouvelle cuisine before it, molecular gastronomy is a controversial topic among food professionals. There are those who find it awe-inspiring and groundbreaking, and those who discredit it as mere shock value. However, the fact that several of the techniques associated with molecular gastronomy spread throughout the world culinary scene so thoroughly indicates that many chefs find the innovations inspiring enough to follow suit. History may eventually show that molecular gastronomy was just as important to the state of modern cooking as nouvelle cuisine was in the 1970s.

SEE ALSO *Celebrity Chef Phenomenon; Food Critics and Ratings; Food Fads; Food Rheology; Food Styling; Gastronomy; Gourmet Hobbyists and Foodies.*

IN CONTEXT: TREND, INNOVATION, OR BOTH?

Food trends can be seen as either homage to an innovator or copying someone else's success. For example, Ferran Adrià (1962–), chef at El Bulli restaurant in Catalonia, Spain, invented a method for making culinary foams. Specifically, Adriá would prepare a sauce and then put it in a nitrogen-charged whipped cream carafe, which when activated would produce a light, whipped foam of his sauce. Immediately after news of this technique spread, foams started popping up on menus all over the world. Soon however, the popularity of foams began to wane, for although one could make foams of almost any sauce or flavor, the uses for foams were somewhat limited. Also at issue was that this particular fad involved a technique created by one particular chef, and as such, the use of foams started to seem less like simply following a popular fad and more like stealing from a noted chef. Adrià took foams off of his menu a few years after he invented them, and chefs now rarely use them. Just as fads are present in the worlds of art, film, and fashion, the culinary industry is equally as susceptible to fads as any other creative industry. In 2010 Adrià confirmed previous speculation that he planned to close El Bulli, famous for its innovation in molecular gastronomy, permanently in 2011.

BIBLIOGRAPHY

Books

Chartier, François, and Levi Reiss. *Taste Buds and Molecules: The Art and Science of Food with Wine.* Toronto: McClelland & Stewart, 2010.

This, Hervé. *Molecular Gastronomy: Exploring the Science of Flavor.* New York: Columbia University Press, 2006.

Periodicals

Barham, Peter, et al. "Molecular Gastronomy: A New Emerging Scientific Discipline." *Chemical Reviews* 110, no. 4 (2010): 2313–2365.

"Chemistry in Cooking: Molecular Gastronomy." *The Economist* 385, no. 8560 (2007): 140.

Cousins, John, Kevin O'Gorman, and Marc Stierand. "Molecular Gastronomy: Cuisine Innovation or Modern Day Alchemy?" *International Journal of Contemporary Hospitality Management* 22, no. 3 (2010): 399–415.

de Solier, Isabelle. "Liquid Nitrogen Pistachios: Molecular Gastronomy, Elbulli, and Foodies." *European Journal of Cultural Studies* 13, no. 2 (2010): 155–170.

"Food to Blow Your Mind: 'Molecular Gastronomy' Has Attracted Chefs and Plain Foodies with an Appetite for Extreme Experimentation." *Business Week New York* 4000 (September 11, 2006): 104–105.

Linden, Erik, David McClements, and Job Ubbink. "Molecular Gastronomy: A Food Fad or an Interface for Science-Based Cooking?" *Food Biophysics* 3, no. 2 (2008): 246–254.

Ruhlman, Michael. "Forget Molecular Gastronomy. Michael Ruhlman Explains What's Really Going on in Cutting-Edge Kitchens around the Globe." *Restaurant Hospitality* 91, no. 5 (2007): 26.

"Taste a Food Fight in the World of Molecular Gastronomy." *Maclean's* 119, no. 25 (2006): 60.

This, Hervé. "Food for Tomorrow? How the Scientific Discipline of Molecular Gastronomy Could Change the Way We Eat." *Embo Reports* 7, no. 11 (2006): 1062–1066.

Yek, Grace S., and Kurt Struwe. "Deconstructing Molecular Gastronomy: Part Food Science and Part Culinary Art, Molecular Gastronomy and Its Offshoots Are Revolutionizing Food Preparation, Presentation, and Eating and Sensory Experiences." *Food Technology* 62, no. 6 (2008): 34–45.

Web Sites

Abend, Lisa. "Debating the Merits of Molecular Gastronomy." *Time*, January 23, 2009. http://www.time.com/time/arts/article/0,8599,1873579,00.html (accessed September 21, 2010).

Gadsby, Patricia. "Cooking for Eggheads." *Discover*, February 20, 2006. http://discovermagazine.com/2006/feb/cooking-for-eggheads (accessed September 21, 2010).

David Brennan Tilove

Monounsaturated and Polyunsaturated Oils

■ Introduction

Fats and oils have many functions in cuisine and diet. They are a major ingredient of numerous sauces, dressings, and dishes, and are often used as a cooking medium. Plants, fruits, nuts, and seeds may store substantial amounts of oils that can be extracted for culinary use. The major chemical components of fats and oils are fatty acids, and the chemical nature of the fatty acid affects the melting point of the fat or oil, as well as its impact on health. Solid fats tend to contain saturated fatty acids, whereas oils contain unsaturated fatty acids. In general, saturated fats and oils are bad for health because they may increase the risk of heart disease and some cancers. Unsaturated fats and oils have a positive effect on health, mainly because of their content of omega-3 fatty acids. Diets rich in oily fish, one source of omega-3 fatty acids, have been shown to protect the heart and brain, and olive oil has long been valued for its health benefits. Fats and oils are good energy storage compounds, releasing about twice as much energy as the equivalent amount of carbohydrate, which is why a high-fat diet may lead to weight gain.

■ Historical Background and Scientific Foundations

Oils for culinary use can be obtained from plants, nuts, and seeds, either by mechanical extraction or solvent extraction. The source of the oil influences its flavor, color, texture, and smoke point. The latter is the temperature at which an oil begins to smoke and break down during heating. Oils are good for cooking food because they transfer heat much more quickly than air or water. They also enhance the enjoyment of food because many flavor molecules are soluble in oil. Moreover, the presence of oil makes flavor molecules stay in the mouth longer, enhancing the experience. And oil lubricates food, making it easier to chew.

Olives have been cultivated for their oil for at least 5,000 years and were brought to the New World by the Spanish in the fifteenth century. Canola oil, however, is a modern invention. It comes from the seeds of a cruciferous plant that was developed at the University of Manitoba in 1974. This was bred from rapeseed, but has lower levels of erucic acid, which had been linked to increased risk of heart disease. Corn oil was first extracted from the germ of maize in 1898 and is valued because it is light and easy to use for frying due to its high smoke point.

■ Impacts and Issues

The fatty acid component of oils plays some important roles in human health. Saturated fatty acids, such as stearic acid, which are found in animal fats, tend to promote deposition of plaque in the arteries and have been linked to an increased heart disease risk. The monounsaturated fatty acid oleic acid, which is found in olive oil, tends to have the opposite effect and has long been valued for its role in heart health.

Most of the fatty acids that the body needs to synthesize hormone-like substances that regulate blood clotting and immunity are made within the cells. Those that cells cannot make are known as essential fatty acids and must be obtained from the diet. These polyunsaturated fatty acids include omega-3 fatty acids and omega-6 fatty acids. Oily fish are particularly rich in two important omega-3 fatty acids called eicosapentaenoic acid and docosahexaenoic acid. Both can reduce inflammation and blood clotting that could otherwise lead to a heart attack or stroke. Eating fish twice per week has been shown to reduce the risk of stroke by up to 50 percent. However, the omega-6 fatty acids, in which the double bonds are in a different place on the molecule's carbon backbone, have been associated with increased inflammation. It is the proportion of omega-6 to omega-3 fatty acids in oils and in the diet

WORDS TO KNOW

MONOUNSATURATED: Carbon backbones in organic molecules contain either single carbon-carbon bonds or double carbon-carbon bonds, or a mixture of both. A substance, such as an oil, whose components contain just one double bond, is said to be monounsaturated.

POLYUNSATURATED: Substances such as oils composed of molecules containing more than one carbon-carbon double bond are said to be polyunsaturated.

TRIGLYCERIDES: The major constituent of natural fats, triglycerides are a class of molecules composed of three fatty acids, which may be the same or different, chemically bonded to a glycerol backbone.

that is important. For most of human history, this ratio has been about two to one, but since the 1950s it has changed to the point that in many diets, particularly in the West, it is as much as 20 to one. Corn oil has quite a high omega-6 to omega-3 ratio so should not be consumed in excess.

A further health concern has been the overconsumption of so-called trans fatty acids, which are common in margarines and processed foods. The term trans refers to the geometry of double bonds in a fatty acid molecule's backbone. These fatty acids have been shown to increase total cholesterol, which likely increases the risk of heart disease and stroke. That is why many manufacturers are making efforts to reduce or eliminate trans fatty acids from their products. New York City enacted regulations that took effect in 2008 to eliminate trans fatty acids in foods served in the city's restaurants, and Chicago is considering a similar ban. The U.S. Food and Drug Administration as of 2007 requires all products containing trans fats to identify and quantify this information on the food label. Also, according to the American Heart Association, any consumption of trans fatty acids is unhealthy, and identifies unsaturated vegetable oils including canola, peanut oil, olive oil, flax seed oil, corn oil, safflower oil, and sunflower oil as heart healthy, as long as they have not been subjected to the process of hydrogenation.

SEE ALSO *Cooking Fats; Diet and Heart Disease; Diet and Hypertension; Dietary Guidelines for Americans; Hydrogenated Fats and Trans Fats; Mediterranean Diet.*

A man makes olive oil using a traditional olive oil windmill press in southern France. © *niceartphoto / Alamy.*

BIBLIOGRAPHY

Books

Kaufman, Sheilah, and Sheri Coleman. *Canola Gourmet: Time for an Oil Change!* Sterling, VA: Capital, 2008.

Preedy, Victor R., and Ronald R. Watson. *Olives and Olive Oil in Health and Disease Prevention.* Amsterdam and Boston: Elsevier, 2010.

Quiles, José L., M. Carmen Ramirez-Tortosa, and Parveen Yaqoob. *Olive Oil and Health.* Wallingford, UK, and Cambridge, MA: CABI, 2006.

Periodicals

Alonso, Alvaro, Valentia Ruiz-Gutierrez, and Miguel A. Martinez-Gonzalez. "Monounsaturated Fatty Acids, Olive Oil and Blood Pressure: Epidemiological, Clinical and Experimental Evidence." *Public Health Nutrition* 9, no. 2 (2006): 251–257.

Fito, Montserrat, Rafael de la Torre, and Maria-Isabel Covas. "Olive Oil and Oxidative Stress." *Molecular Nutrition & Food Research* 51, no. 10 (2007): 1215–1224.

Foster, Rebecca, Claire S. Williamson, and Joanne Lunn. "Briefing Paper: Culinary Oils and Their Health Effects." *Nutrition Bulletin* 34, no. 1 (2009): 4–47.

Sanders, Tom A. B. "The Role of Fat in the Diet—Quantity, Quality, and Sustainability." *Nutrition Bulletin* 35, no. 2 (2010): 138–146.

Web Sites

"Meet the Fats." *American Heart Association.* http://www.heart.org/HEARTORG/GettingHealthy/FatsAndOils/MeettheFats/Meet-the-Fats_UCM_304495_Article.jsp (accessed September 2, 2010).

United States Department of Agriculture (USDA). "What Are Oils?" *My Pyramid.gov.* http://www.mypyramid.gov/pyramid/oils.html?debugMode=false (accessed September 2, 2010).

"Unsaturated Fats." *American Heart Association.* http://www.heart.org/HEARTORG/GettingHealthy/FatsAndOils/Fats101/Monounsaturated-Fats_UCM_301460_Article.jsp (accessed September, 2010).

Susan Aldridge

Movies, Documentaries, and Food

■ Introduction

Artists have incorporated food into their works for as long as artistic expression has existed. Early civilizations documented the bounty of the hunt or the harvest in primitive cave drawings, or carved likenesses of food onto ritual bowls and other items. As civilizations developed, so did various art forms from rudimentary cave paintings and personal adornments to the late nineteenth century technological breakthrough of film.

Since film's very beginning, food has played a role. Whether as film's focal point or as a metaphor, food can demonstrate without words social class, health, ethnicity, religion, power, passion, sorrow, pleasure, sensuality, or heartache. The director can incorporate food to make political or environmental statements or to symbolize consumption in general.

Food has been the focus in a spate of food-related documentaries encompassing aspects such as agricultural production, school nutrition programs, eating disorders, and childhood obesity, as well as individual foods such as asparagus or corn. More recently, a handful of film festivals has been dedicated solely to screening food documentary and fictional movies.

■ Historical Background and Scientific Foundations

More than a century of technological advances led up to the birth of modern cinema, beginning with the seventeenth century magic lantern used to project images onto a screen with a light source such as a candle. A rapid succession of inventions, including the 1869 development of celluloid and the 1879 first public exhibition of an incandescent light bulb, brought forth near simultaneous film projection inventions in France, Germany, England, and the United States in the late nineteenth century.

French brothers Louis (1864–1948) and Auguste Lumiere (1862–1954), with their invention of the patented Cinematographe, were the first to present a commercial projected motion picture show to a paying audience on December 28, 1895, in Paris, France. Of the ten brief films presented, each depicting an aspect of everyday life, one depicted Auguste feeding his infant daughter. Thus, the first food movie was born.

Food played a rather minor role in movies for more than half a century. It mostly served as a prop to add movement to a scene, to further a conversation, or bring a focal point. In the 1960s and 1970s, growing concerns over rapidly deteriorating environmental conditions in the United States led to the birth of the environmental movement. In response, Congress passed the Clean Air Act (1963) and the Clean Water Act (1972), and by executive order President Richard Nixon (1913–1994) formed the U.S. Environmental Protection Agency (EPA) in 1970.

Science fiction films mirrored the nation's nascent environmental conscience. Set in corrupt, polluted, and overpopulated New York City circa 2022, science fiction thriller *Soylent Green* (1973) depicts complete environmental and moral degradation brought on by humans, including the secret behind the engineered foods that the masses are forced to eat. In another ecological science fiction film, *Food of the Gods* (1976) portrays the horrors as a food that bubbles up from the earth acts as a growth hormone violently working its way up the food chain.

Food began to play a different, more literary, role in the late 1980s, becoming its own cinematic genre. In the 1987 Danish film *Babette's Feast*, based on a short story by Isak Dinesen (pseudonym of Karen von Blixen-Finecke, 1885–1962), a French woman is brought in as a housekeeper and cook into an austere Danish household composed of two sisters after her husband and son are killed during the French Revolution. When she wins the French lottery, she spends it all on creating a multicourse sumptuous meal to show her gratitude to the sisters. Unbeknownst to the crowd, the woman had been an accomplished Parisian chef. As the menu of turtle soup, caviar, quail, truffles, foie gras, and rum cake are served, food becomes the vehicle to renew friendships, restore love, and bring harmony to the community.

Mexican author Laura Esquivel's (1950–) novel *Like Water for Chocolate* is translated to film in the 1992 movie by the same name. Forbidden by tradition to pursue her love, the main character expresses her passion through her gift of cooking. The clash between Old World and New World sets the stage for the Italian food that serves as a backdrop in *Big Night* (1996), revealing betrayal, passion, and the unbreakable bond between brothers. These films sparked a trend of combining film screenings with menus based on food prepared in each movie.

Adapted from Julie Powell's (1973–) autobiographical book about her endeavor to cook her way through Julia Child's (1912–2004) epic French cookbook, the 2009 film *Julie and Julia* weaves back and forth between Julie's and Julia's attempts to master the art of cooking.

■ Impacts and Issues

For much of the twentieth century, food functioned merely as sustenance. American culture placed more importance on convenient preparations and low costs than on the pleasure of cooking and eating. Cookbooks stressed quick recipes with few ingredients relying on processed, prepared foods and kitchen gadgets such as microwave ovens and can openers. During this time, food played a minimal role in all film genres.

The environmental movement that began in the 1960s brought an awareness of how practices such as industrial agriculture were polluting air, water, and soil. Science fiction films portrayed food as noxious and dangerous, reflecting the growing environmental consciousness. At the same time, renowned cookbook author and cook Julia Child (1912–2004) introduced mainstream America to the pleasures of French food and time-honored culinary techniques. Chefs such as Alice Waters (1944–) brought to the forefront the concept of eating in season using fresh, local, and organic ingredients and the impact that this can have on health, the economy, and the environment. Food in film went from tainted science fiction killer to representing a passionate ideal as society placed more importance on enjoying food.

Since the turn of the twenty-first century, food also has become frequent fodder for documentary films. Documentaries examine every aspect of the food system, even extolling the virtues of a single food such as asparagus, oysters, or bread. Morgan Spurlock's (1970–) 2004 documentary *Super Size Me* led the food documentary revolution. Spurlock paired a 30-day diet based solely on fast food with disturbing facts about the fast food industry and its impact on the nation's health.

Also in 2004, Deborah Koons Garcia's *The Future of Food* explored the prevalence of genetically engineered foods. She pointed fingers at multinational corporations and industrial agriculture and argued that these practices

are having an irrevocable impact on sustainable farming and human well-being.

In *King Corn* (2007), director Aaron Woolf follows Ian Cheney and Curt Ellis as they move to Iowa and plant an acre of corn following agro-industrial methods. They follow their crop from the field to the food system, raising questions about how we eat and farm. The 2008

Documentary filmmaker Morgan Spurlock (1970–) poses with French fries in his mouth. In *Super Size Me* (2004), Spurlock documented his one month quest to consume only food from McDonald's. © *Photos 12 / Alamy.*

documentary *Food Inc.*, directed by Robert Kenner, also explores corporate farming in the United States. In three separate segments, Kenner focuses on the production of meat, grains and vegetables, and the power of food companies, illustrating unsustainable practices, inhumane animal treatment, and the ways in which Americans' diets and health are affected by the marketing of unhealthy food products.

But not all current documentaries portend the demise of health and environment. Films such as director-producer Christopher Taylor's *Food Fight* (2008) chronicle the positive impact of the California food movement championed by Alice Waters. The 2009 film *Fresh* directed by Ana Sofia Joanes lauds American leaders who are reinventing the nation's food system, communicating their vision for the future of food and the natural world.

In addition, a number of film festivals devoted solely to food have surfaced in recent years. Begun in 2007, the New York City Film Festival pairs documentaries, features, and short films with thematic food events. The 2010 festival, for example, screened the documentary *It's Grits*, exploring the southern corn staple with brunch and featured more than 30 different grit dishes prepared by New York amateur chefs. The concept has spread to cities such as Nashville, Chicago, Anchorage, Kalamazoo, and Portland.

From mere prop to starring role, food's changing prevalence in film mirrors its elevated position in American society.

SEE ALSO *Alice Waters: California and New American Cuisine; Food and the Internet; Food Fads; Food Styling; Foodways; Gastronomy; Social Media and Food; Television and Food.*

BIBLIOGRAPHY

Books

Bower, Anne L. Reel, ed. *Reel Food: Essays on Food and Film*. New York: Routledge, 2004.

Web Sites

Dirks, Tim. "The History of Film." *AMC Filmsite*. http://www.filmsite.org/pre20sintro2.html (accessed October 21, 2010).

"Food on Film." *Gastronomica*. http://www.gastronomica.org/foodfilms.html (accessed October 21, 2010).

"Fourth Annual New York Food Film Festival." *NYC Food Film Festival & Grease Bomb LLC*. http://www.nycfoodfilmfestival.com (accessed October 21, 2010).

Handman, Gary. "Food and Eating in the Movies." *University of California, Berkeley, Library*, updated November 29, 2010. http://www.lib.berkeley.edu/MRC/foodmovies.html (accessed October 21, 2010).

Parkhurst, Priscilla. "Babette's Feast: A Fable for Culinary France." *University of Chicago Press*. http://www.press.uchicago.edu/Misc/Chicago/243230.html (accessed October 21, 2010).

Andrea Abel

MREs

Introduction

The Meal, Ready-to-Eat—or MRE—is the main operational field ration for the United States military. A field ration is a prepackaged meal that may be transported easily by military personnel and eaten with minimal preparation when away from food service facilities. An MRE is a self-contained, relatively lightweight meal designed to meet the nutritional requirements of service members in combat or other demanding situations. The MRE replaces the Meal, Combat, Individual (MCI) rations used by the U.S. military during the Korean War (1950–1953) and the Vietnam War (1955–1975).

In the early twenty-first century, MREs include a selection of 24 entrees and more than 150 additional items. MREs are produced in varieties to accommodate food preference and religious considerations, including vegetarian, halal, and kosher meals. The military faces numerous challenges in designing MREs including nutritional, storage, and transportation considerations.

Historical Background and Scientific Foundations

Feeding an army on the move has always been a major problem for military leaders. Before the development of modern food preservation methods, armies were limited in the manner in which to provision soldiers. Supply lines could provide an army with food, but could not stretch too far, due to the personnel required to sustain supply lines and the vulnerability of supply lines to enemy attacks. For short campaigns, armies could take some food supplies, consisting primarily of salt-cured meats, hardtack, or other items that do not spoil quickly. Primarily, however, advancing armies had to live off the land through foraging or seizing supplies from civilians or enemy troops.

During the U.S. Civil War (1861–1865), the military began supplying soldiers with rations that employed modern food preservation. The U.S. Army distributed

canned rations of meat to soldiers along with flour, yeast, potatoes, dried beans, and coffee. By World War I (1914–1918), many nations developed different rations to meet the nutritional requirements of soldiers in different situations, including trench rations and emergency rations. During World War II (1939–1945), countries continued the specialization of rations to meet different dietary needs. The United States even developed Mountain Ration, known as the M-Ration, and Jungle Ration, known as the J-Ration, to meet the unique dietary and logistical conditions presented by these environments. The Jungle Ration was one of the first military rations to utilize dehydrated food, including beef, peaches, and milk.

In 1963 the U.S. Department of Defense began developing a lightweight ration along the lines of the Jungle Ration that would serve as the military's standard field ration. Within a few years, the military issued the Long Range Patrol (LRP) ration to special operations forces in Vietnam. The expense of the LRP ration led the military to seek a cheaper alternative. In 1975 the Department of Defense began developing a similar dehydrated ration. In 1981 the U.S. Armed Forces began distributing the modern MRE as a special issue, and the MRE became the standard issued ration in 1986.

Impacts and Issues

Meeting the nutritional requirements of soldiers maintains energy, mental alertness, and morale. A statement commonly attributed to the French Emperor Napoleon Bonaparte (1769–1821), "An army travels on its stomach," illustrates the importance of maintaining adequate nutrition during war. MREs are designed to supply soldiers with proper nutrition in almost any setting, including combat and emergency situations. American businesses that contract to provide foods for MREs must meet demanding and exacting standards. The mandated instructions and standards for brownies alone are contained in a 26-page-long document.

The modern MRE is designed to provide optimal nutrition. Each of the dozens of varieties of MRE contains approximately 1,200 calories. According to the U.S. military, soldiers should eat three MREs per day for a

An Iraqi boy carries two MREs given to him by U.S. Marines near Haditha, Iraq. © *Ed Darack / Science Faction / Corbis.*

maximum of 21 days. The U.S. Armed Forces relies on the Dietary Reference Intake of the Institute of Medicine in formulating the nutritional requirements that each MRE must satisfy. While the military invests a great deal of money and effort into designing nutritious MREs, the military has discovered that many service members do not consume their full rations, which decreases service members' nutritional and caloric intake. This problem is exacerbated during combat. A study by the Institute of Medicine discovered that the average service member consumes approximately only 2,400 calories per day during combat instead of the 4,200 calories per day required to meet the physical and mental demands of combat.

In addition to meeting certain nutritional requirements, the U.S. Armed Forces require MREs to attain additional storage and performance standards. Each MRE is designed to have a minimum shelf life of three and one-half years when stored at 81°F (27°C) and approximately nine months at 100°F (38°C). Furthermore, each MRE must be able to withstand a parachute drop from 1,250 feet (380 m) and a non-parachute drop from 98 feet (30 m). Since 1992, MREs have included a flameless ration heater, a water-activated exothermic heater, that is required to warm an eight-ounce (227-gram) entree to 100°F (37.8°C) within 12 minutes.

The United States government developed Humanitarian Daily Rations (HDRs) for use by government agencies and non-governmental organizations (NGOs) as emergency food aid. HDRs are designed to meet the religious and dietary needs of a wide variety of people. All HDRs, therefore, are halal, vegetarian meals with limited or no dairy products. The U.S. government designed HDRs to withstand airdrops without a parachute to allow their deployment in more remote or rugged locations. Avoiding parachute pallet drops also lessens the likelihood of hoarding. HDRs have been used as emergency food aid during the conflicts in Bosnia and Afghanistan.

In the United States, both MREs and HDRs temporarily provided the substantial source of food and nutrients for thousands of Gulf Coast residents after hurricanes Katrina in 2005 and Ike in 2008.

SEE ALSO *Calories; Center for Food Safety and Applied Nutrition; Dietary Reference Intakes; Disasters and Food Supply; Extreme Weather and Food Supply; Food Inspection and Standards; Food Packaging; Foodways; Nutrient Fortification of Foods; War, Conquest, Colonialism, and Cuisine.*

BIBLIOGRAPHY

Books

Kutz, Gregory D. *Investigation: Military Meals, Ready-to-Eat Sold on Ebay.* Washington, DC: U.S. Government Accountability Office, 2006.

Periodicals

Feagans, Jacob M., Darius A. Jahann, and Jamie S. Barkin. "Meals Ready to Eat: A Brief History and Clinical Vignette with Discussion on Civilian Applications." *Military Medicine* 175, no. 3 (2010): 194–196.

Masamitsu, Emily. "Apocalypse Chow—Hungry Taste-Testers Scarf MREs—Meals Ready-to-Eat—to Find Out If Survival Grub Can Fuel the Body and Boost Morale." *Popular Mechanics* (October 2009): 78.

"Meals, Ready-to-Eat—Innovations in Food Chemistry and Packaging Provide Soldiers on the Battlefield with Tastier, More Nutritious Food." *Chemical and Engineering News* 88, no. 18 (2010): 40.

Web Sites

"Meal, Ready-to-Eat (MRE)." *Defense Logistics Agency.* http://www.dscp.dla.mil/subs/rations/programs/mre/mreabt.asp (accessed October 9, 2010).

Soldier System Center. "Nanotechnology Applied to Ration Packaging." *U.S. Army,* June 4, 2004. http://www.natick.army.mil/about/pao/2004/04-21.htm (accessed October 9, 2010).

Joseph P. Hyder

Neighborhood Food Cooperatives

■ Introduction

Food cooperatives (co-ops) are grocery markets that are owned and run by the employees who work there. Co-ops can be either private or public and are considered to be a community of people united for a common cause and dictated by democracy. They are jointly owned and run, so responsibilities are divided equally amongst the owner-members. Food co-ops are typically nonprofit organizations and are often concerned with being a responsible part of the community in which they operate. Co-ops often support local businesses and sell locally- or seasonally-grown food. Some or all of the money the co-op acquires may be returned to the community in the form of daily specials, classes, and public events. Co-ops often pride themselves on providing healthy and natural food from local sources at affordable prices. Customer education is also an important aspect of co-ops and is something that differentiates them from other, larger food corporations.

■ Historical Background and Scientific Foundations

Food co-ops are based on a democratic system of cooperation that has helped societies exist since ancient times. Communities of people learned that if they worked together to achieve a common goal, the outcome would be greater than if they worked separately. Early agriculture especially would have been difficult if it hadn't been for a cooperative state of thought.

The first co-ops, or systems known in the twenty-first century as co-ops, were seen in Europe in the eighteenth and nineteenth centuries. Originally co-ops were created to protect the working class and allow people a say in the products they were offered and could afford. Store owners during this time had the power to adulterate products to be able to achieve higher profit from

them. Working class members of the community eventually decided to pool their money and buy a larger quantity of food wholesale and then divide it equally among themselves. People realized that they were getting better product this way and saving money.

The birthplace of the modern food cooperative was in Rochdale, England, in 1843. Workers in textile mills there had attempted to strike and the strike had failed. Instead of organizing another strike, they looked for other ways to improve the quality of their lives. They argued that opening their own food store as an alternative to shopping at the company store would save money and improve their diets. Twenty-eight people banded together to open their own co-op in December 1844; after a year of saving, the Rochdale Equitable Pioneers Society was up and running. At first the cooperative's offerings were limited to sugar, flour, butter, and oatmeal. When the gas company refused to donate the co-op's lights, however, they were forced to buy candles in bulk, then sold off the extra to their members. Although the Rochdale Pioneers Society was not the first co-op, they were successful and sustainable in what they accomplished. By learning from previous cooperatives that had failed, and by passing on a list of principles and organization, they formed the basis for what future cooperatives would use to perpetuate themselves.

■ Impacts and Issues

Although the idea of food co-ops is not new, its popularity has waxed and waned since the nineteenth century. From the 1960s into the 1970s, there was a resurgence of food cooperatives in America, whereas in the 1990s the number of cooperatives declined severely. Studies have shown that an increase in the popularity of food cooperatives is often linked to times of economic turmoil, when there is a concern for food safety, and when a community of consumers shares a desire for an ethical society. In the twenty-first century, however, there has been an intense rise in consumer interest in the cooperative movement mainly due to niche marketing.

The industry of retail groceries has become highly competitive, and food cooperatives have become an efficient way to stand out among the competition. Labels such as fair trade and organic are becoming increasingly appealing. Critics sometimes lament that current food co-ops are more about labels, trends, and niche markets than they are about the original principles they set out to perpetuate. Cooperatives by definition are intended to benefit the working class, but in the early twenty-first century many cooperative shoppers are either highly motivated or wealthier consumers willing to pay more for organic, heirloom, or other specialty foods. Cheaper food prices are often found in large corporate package stores where foods are bought and sold in bulk.

While food cooperatives usually sell locally sourced food, it is sometimes difficult for them to sell certified organic products. Smaller local farms often cannot afford the large investment fees to obtain an organic certification from the U.S. Department of Agriculture (USDA), and therefore their products might not sell as well as those from the larger farm that is certified. A smaller farm could therefore experience more difficulty

WORDS TO KNOW

FAIR TRADE: A system of direct trade put in place to balance the cost of food versus the cost to produce it and to ensure equity for producers.

FOOD CO-OP: A member-owned and run grocery store.

FREE RANGE: A food-source animal that is permitted to pasture graze for food rather than being confined to a feed house or feed lot.

GARDEN SHARING: An agreement between a landowner and a laborer to share land and product.

OWNER-MEMBER: A member and employee of a food co-op.

SUSTAINABLE FOOD: Food that is grown in a manner that is profitable for the farmer, nutritious for the consumer, and preserves the environment.

USDA NATURAL LABELED FOOD: Food that is minimally processed with no artificial ingredients or coloring. This does not include genetically altered food.

USDA ORGANIC LABELED FOOD: A food that is at least 95 percent organically grown or produced product.

The Latino Farmers Cooperative community garden in New Orleans, Louisiana. The project teaches community residents about urban farming while making healthy fresh food available for the city s growing Hispanic community. © *Jim West / Alamy.*

A baker sells his fresh-baked breads at a neighborhood cooperative market in the United States. *Brenda Lerner / Lerner & Lerner / Lerner-Media Global Photos.*

in sustaining itself. Co-ops often try to educate consumers about the source of their local products in order to encourage consumers to support local farmers.

SEE ALSO *Agroecology; Alice Waters: California and New American Cuisine; Community Supported Agriculture (CSAs); Edible Schoolyard Movement; Ethical Issues in Agriculture; Farm-to-Table Movement; Michael Pollan: Linking Food and Environmental Journalism; Organics; Sustainable Agriculture; Sustainable Table.*

BIBLIOGRAPHY

Books

Madden, Etta M., and Martha L. Finch. *Eating in Eden: Food and American Utopias.* Lincoln, NE: University of Nebraska Press, 2006.

Radbill, Amy. *The Davis Food Co-op Cookbook.* Davis, CA: Davis Food Co-op, 2007.

Periodical

"The Co-op's Innovative Drive to Promote Fresh Food Sales." *Grocer London*, June 5, 2010: 8–11.

Web Sites

"Food Coops." *Local Harvest.* http://www.localharvest.org/food-coops/ (accessed October 4, 2010).

"Putting It All Together for Food Co-ops." *National Cooperative Grocers Association.* http://www.ncga.coop/ (accessed October 4, 2010).

Emily Walden Harris

Norovirus Infection

Introduction

A Norovirus infection is a type of stomach ailment known as viral gastroenteritis. The infection is also commonly (and incorrectly) known as the stomach flu and is not related to the respiratory symptoms caused by the influenza virus. The infection is caused by Noroviruses, which have also been termed Norwalk-like viruses and caliciviruses.

According to the Centers for Disease Control and Prevention (CDC), food workers infected or sick with norovirus gastroenteritis pose a risk to their patrons' health. An infected food handler may contaminate food that is consumed by others, causing a transmission of the norovirus and illness in others. Norovirus gastroenteritis outbreaks often take place in communal settings including restaurants, cruise ships, hospitals, retirement and nursing homes, schools, summer camps, and other settings where groups congregate and eat food from the same source. CDC estimates that more than half of all food-related illness outbreaks can be linked to norovirus transmission by food handlers.

Historical Background and Scientific Foundations

Noroviruses are named after the Norwalk Virus, which was the cause of a gastroenteritis outbreak in a school in Norwalk, Ohio, in 1968. Once called Norwalk-like viruses, they have since been officially designated as Noroviruses.

An infection caused by a Norovirus is usually not life threatening, but can certainly cause a person to feel miserable. Typically, a person develops the symptoms of infection suddenly and becomes ill for several days. Vomiting and diarrhea occur many times during the illness; the loss of fluids can cause dehydration. Dehydration can be serious in infants, elderly people, and people whose immune systems are not functioning efficiently.

Recovery is usually complete, with no lingering symptoms or infection. However, because different strains (types) of the Norovirus exist, repeated gastrointestinal infections throughout a person's life are possible.

Noroviruses are found in the intestinal tract. A Norovirus infection can occur when fecal material is transferred to food, liquid, or an object. Most often this occurs when food has been handled or an object such as a doorknob is grasped by someone who has not properly washed their hands after having had a bowel movement. The virus is ingested by eating the contaminated food or handling the object and then touching that hand to the mouth—this is called the fecal-oral route. A person becomes contagious from the moment that symptoms appear to as long as two weeks after the symptoms have ended. There is no evidence that the virus can by transferred by inhaling virus-laden air, even though it has been shown that vomiting does release virus particles into the air.

A wide variety of foods can be contaminated, including salad dressings, deli-style meats, bakery items, cake icing, fruits, and vegetables. Seafoods such as oysters can become contaminated and can concentrate the virus in high numbers when they filter Norovirus-laden water, and eating raw oysters can transmit the virus to people. Drinking water can also be contaminated with Norovirus.

Norovirus infections occur anywhere in the world. Indeed, because the virus is easily spread among persons, difficult to kill, and contagious, the probability exists of repeated, large-scale outbreaks.

WORDS TO KNOW

GASTROENTERITIS: Gastroenteritis is an inflammation of the stomach and the intestines. More commonly, gastroenteritis is called the stomach flu.

IN CONTEXT: FOOD SAFETY, PERSONAL RESPONSIBILITY, AND PROTECTION

Norovirus infection is common. Most of the foodborne outbreaks of Norovirus gastroenteritis are due to the handling of food by someone whose hands are contaminated with virus-laden fecal material. With regard to the disease burden of Norovirus gastroenteritis, the Centers for Disease Control and Prevention (CDC) estimates that:

- Annually there are about 21 million cases of acute gastroenteritis due to Norovirus infection, and it is now thought that at least 50 percent of all foodborne outbreaks of gastroenteritis can be attributed to Noroviruses.
- Most foodborne outbreaks of Norovirus illness are likely to arise though direct contamination of food by a food handler immediately before its consumption. Outbreaks have frequently been associated with consumption of cold foods, including various salads, sandwiches, and bakery products. Liquid items (e.g., salad dressing or cake icing) that enable the virus to mix evenly are often implicated as a cause of outbreaks. Food can also be contaminated at its source, and oysters from contaminated waters have been associated with widespread outbreaks of gastroenteritis. Other foods, including raspberries and salads, have been contaminated before widespread distribution and subsequently caused extensive outbreaks.
- Waterborne outbreaks of norovirus disease in community settings have often been caused by sewage contamination of wells and recreational water.

With regard to preventing Norovirus gastroenteritis the CDC states:

- "Many local and state health departments require that food handlers and preparers with gastroenteritis not work until 2 or 3 days after they recover from an illness. In addition, because the virus continues to be present in the stool for as long as 2 to 3 weeks after the person feels better, strict handwashing after using the bathroom and before handling food items is important in preventing the spread of this virus. Food handlers who were recently sick can be given different duties in the restaurant so that they do not have to handle food (for example, working the cash register, or as host or hostess)."
- "People who are sick with norovirus illness can often vomit violently, without warning, and the vomit is infectious; therefore, any surfaces near the vomit should be promptly cleaned and disinfected with bleach solution and then rinsed. Furthermore, food items that may have become contaminated with norovirus should be thrown out. Linens (including clothes, towels, tablecloths, napkins) soiled to any extent with vomit or stool should be promptly washed at high temperature. Oysters should be obtained from reputable sources and appropriate documentation kept. Washing raw vegetables thoroughly before eating and appropriate disposal of sewage and soiled diapers also help to reduce the spread of norovirus and prevent illness. In small home-based catering businesses or family owned or operated restaurants, sick children and infants in diapers should be excluded from food preparation areas."

SOURCE: *Centers for Disease Control and Prevention, National Center for Infectious Diseases.*

Treatment for a Norovirus infection consists of keeping a person hydrated and as comfortable as possible while waiting for the infection to subside. Good personal hygiene is the best prevention strategy. Proper handwashing is crucial. Similar to the viruses that cause the common cold and influenza, having an infection does not produce an immunity to future infections because there are many, slightly different versions of Norovirus. An immune response to one version is not protective against other versions of the virus.

Washing fruits and vegetables before eating them, especially those labeled organically grown, is wise, as some organic produce is fertilized with manure. Because virus particles require a host cell before they can replicate, Norovirus particles that adhere to produce can remain capable of causing an infection for a long time.

■ Impacts and Issues

The intensity of the symptoms of a Norovirus infection is of most concern. This is because the rapid loss of fluid that occurs with repeated bouts of diarrhea and vomiting can be quickly dehydrating. In an infant or an elderly or immunocompromised person, the combination of the infection and dehydration can be dangerous.

The consequences of the immune catch-up response that occurs when a new version of Norovirus appears can be enormous, especially when the infection occurs in settings in which many people are in close quarters, such as a day care establishment, cruise ship, school, or hospital. An example involves the high number of Norovirus infections that occurred in the United States and Europe in 2002 with the appearance of a new Norovirus variant. The majority of cases occurred in hospitals, cruise ships, and nursing homes. In some cases, patient and surgical wards and the emergency room were temporarily shut down, crippling hospital services and escalating medical costs. Cruise lines cancelled cruises, quarantined ill crew members, and kept ships out of service for cleaning and sanitizing. Outbreaks of Norovirus occurred in 25 cruise ships bound for U.S. ports in 2002, affecting almost 3,000 passengers. Cruise ships sailing into U.S. ports are required to notify the CDC of each case of gastroenteritis diagnosed aboard ship 24 hours prior to arrival. If the number of affected passengers or crew reaches 2 percent, the ship must file an alert informing U.S. health authorities of the outbreak. The CDC monitors reports of outbreaks of gastroenteritis aboard cruise ships on a daily basis, and helps to identify the causative agent. Outbreaks reduce consumer confidence and can be economically devastating to cruise lines.

Outbreaks of Norovirus can also occur following natural disasters where people may be forced to live in close quarters in rescue shelters. For example, in September 2005 the Reliant Astrodome in Houston, Texas, was used to house evacuees from Hurricane Katrina. Approximately 1,500 evacuees and relief workers subsequently received treatment for gastroenteritis. The causative agent was later identified as a Norovirus, and despite the rapidly changing population of evacuees, the outbreak was contained within one week by isolating persons with symptoms within one area of the complex, distributing hand sanitizer, conducting handwashing awareness campaigns, and installing additional portable sinks in the facility.

Even the most established institutions can be vulnerable to norovirus outbreaks. In 2010 the Harvard Faculty Club was closed for several weeks following a norovirus outbreak sickening more than 300 members and guests.

Norovirus infection also has consequences for the military. The debilitating and contagious natures of the infection can lessen soldier and unit combat readiness.

SEE ALSO *Disasters and Food Supply;* E. Coli *Contamination; Hepatitis A;* Salmonella; *Staphylococcal Food Poisoning.*

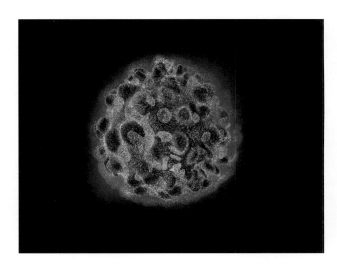

A 3D image shows a norovirus, a common cause of gastroenteritis. © *medicalpicture / Alamy.*

BIBLIOGRAPHY

Books

Anderson, Rodney P. *Outbreak: Cases in Real-World Microbiology.* Washington, DC: ASM Press, 2006.

Matthews, Karl R. *Microbiology of Fresh Produce.* Emerging Issues in Food Safety series. Washington, DC: ASM Press, 2005.

Percival, Steven, et al. *Microbiology of Waterborne Diseases: Microbiological Aspects and Risks.* New York: Academic Press, 2004.

Periodicals

Maunula, Leena. "Norovirus Outbreaks from Drinking Water." *Emerging Infectious Diseases* 11 (2005): 1716–1722.

Palacio, Herminia, et al. "Norovirus Outbreak among Evacuees from Hurricane Katrina—Houston, Texas, September 2005." *Morbidity and Mortality Weekly* 54 (2005): 1016–1018.

Web Sites

"Norovirus Infection [Calicivirus]." *Centers for Disease Control and Prevention (CDC).* http://www.cdc.gov/ncidod/dvrd/revb/gastro/norovirus.htm (accessed September 6, 2010).

"Norovirus: Technical Data." *Centers for Disease Control and Prevention (CDC).* http://www.cdc.gov/ncidod/dvrd/revb/gastro/norovirus-factsheet.htm (accessed September 6, 2010).

Brian Hoyle

Nutrient Fortification of Foods

■ Introduction

Fortified foods can serve an important public health function by helping prevent or correct micronutrient deficiencies, a form of malnutrition. Micronutrients, vitamins, and minerals essential for biological functions are lacking or occur in insufficient amounts in many world diets. Micronutrient deficiencies can lead to diseases and other health problems such as poor growth. Nutrient fortification of foods is the process of adding concentrated micronutrients to processed foods. In the twentieth century, nutrient fortification of foods was instrumental in control of human diseases such as goiter, neonatal hypothyroidism, and rickets. Some micronutrients that are lost in processing, such as in the milling of wheat flour from whole grain wheat, are added back during fortification, whereas in other cases micronutrients that were never present in the whole food in raw form are added to the processed food product. Vitamin A, Vitamin B1, Vitamin B2, Vitamin C, Vitamin D, calcium, niacin, iron, iodine, zinc, and folic acid are routinely added to fortified foods such as flours, cereals, rice, salt, fruit juice, milk, and sugar. Although fortification can have many public health benefits, some food processors and some groups of citizens oppose mandatory fortification. Also, as a public health measure, fortification alone may not be an entirely effective method to prevent micronutrient deficiencies.

■ Historical Background and Scientific Foundations

Nutrient fortification is one of three strategies for preventing micronutrient deficiencies. First, dietary change can increase the overall diversity of micronutrients in the diet or encourage consumption of foods rich in a particular micronutrient. The second strategy is the use of supplements, concentrated micronutrients in a non-food form. The third approach, nutrient fortification of food, increases micronutrients in the diet without requiring dietary change. Nutrient fortification requires no additional effort on the part of individuals. However, unlike supplements, the amount of micronutrients is difficult to target, as different people will eat different amounts of the fortified processed food. Supplements, on the other hand, can be targeted specifically to those at risk of a micronutrient deficiency. Some processed foods are intended to specific groups, such as special fortified cereals for consumption by infants, foods used in emergency situations, and foods to treat specific medical conditions. However, many fortified foods target the entire population, not only the groups most at risk of a micronutrient deficiency.

Based on evidence that iodine deficiency was the cause of goiter, iodized table salt was proposed in the 1920s after successful trials of iodized salt for livestock. Iodized salt first appeared in Switzerland in 1922 and later in the United States in 1924. Michigan, a U.S. state along the Great Lakes, was the center of the push for iodization of salt in the United States. The Michigan health department conducted a study of the effect of iodized salt on goiter prevalence that demonstrated a huge drop following voluntary introduction of commercially produced iodized table salt. During the 1930s Vitamin D began to be added to milk in the United States and Canada to prevent rickets, a disease that softens children's bones. Around the same time, Vitamin A fortification of margarine was introduced in Denmark, a country in Northern Europe, and later this practice was implemented in the Philippines, a country of islands in the Western Pacific Ocean. Also in the 1930s and 1940s, wheat flour fortified with iron and a variety of vitamins was introduced first in Great Britain and then in the United States.

Nutrient fortification has not been limited to Europe, the United States, and Canada. In 1974 Guatemala began fortification of sugar with Vitamin A, a practice that spread throughout Central America. In the 1980s concern grew about the health effects of micronutrient deficiencies in the developing world, especially iodine deficiency. Instead of focusing solely on undernutrition or insufficient consumption of the macronutrients of protein and fat in these countries, advocates pushed for nutrient fortification to prevent micronutrient deficiencies. Efforts to iodize salt or even to add both iron and iodine to salt followed. Like many technologies, nutrient fortification must adapt to local diets. On a trial basis, iron fortification has been tried for fish sauce in Vietnam, soy sauce in China, and curry powder in India.

■ Impacts and Issues

Among the issues surrounding nutrient fortification has been whether fortification should be mandatory. Early fortification efforts such as iodized salt were not required by national laws but were established through partnerships between the public and private sectors. For areas with voluntary fortification, both fortified and unfortified processed foods are available. Luckily, the cost of these foods tends to be the same or very close, because fortification adds very little cost for larger food processing companies. The low cost has held true in many successful fortification programs such as Vitamin A fortified sugar in Central America. When the price is the same, consumers will often choose fortified foods. However, prices may differ

in areas where food processors incur high startup costs or high importation costs for ingredients for fortification. The poor are often the target of nutrition campaigns, and they may not know about the benefits of fortified foods, not consume large amounts of processed foods, or not be able and willing to pay extra for a fortified food. Mandatory programs have been advocated as one way to reach the poor, but this strategy may create a black market for unfortified foods or force the poor to rely on other foods. Mandatory programs also have their own administrative difficulties such as the costs of enforcement and testing for many smaller processing facilities.

The Chinese Ministry of Health and the Global Alliance for Improved Nutrition worked together to introduce affordable, iron-fortified soy sauce in China to address widespread iron deficiencies. *AP Images.*

Some consumers express concern about the amount of micronutrients in fortified foods. Others argue that fortified foods are unnatural and not as healthy as whole, unprocessed foods that provide many other health benefits because they contain fiber, essential amino acids, and micronutrients. The problem of amount stems from the fact that fortified foods are often targeted to specific segments of the population. For example, iron deficiency is the most common nutrition problem in the world and may affect up to 40 percent of the world's population according to the World Health Organization (WHO) in 2006. However, this deficiency usually is present in young children and women, particularly pregnant and lactating women. Women and children, in general, consume less food than men though they have greater need for micronutrients such as iron. Thus concentrations of micronutrients in fortified foods for these groups need to be higher than for the general population. At higher levels in fortified foods, those who already consume sufficient quantities of micronutrients in their diets may be harmed by excessive quantities. For example, high iron levels may be linked to cardiovascular diseases and cancers. For this reason, the European Union regulated upper limits on fortification in 2006. Likewise, the 14 countries that regulate fortification of wheat flour may name both lower and upper limits for micronutrients to be added during fortification.

SEE ALSO *Dietary Guidelines for Americans; Dietary Reference Intakes; Dietary Supplement Health and Education Act of 1994 (DSHEA); Nutrition; Processed Foods; Vitamins and Minerals.*

BIBLIOGRAPHY

Books

Allen, Lindsay. *Guidelines on Food Fortification with Micronutrients.* Geneva: World Health Organization, 2006.

Bagchi, Debasis. *Nutraceutical and Functional Food Regulations in the United States and around the World.* Amsterdam and Boston: Elsevier, 2008.

Periodicals

Haas, Jere H., and Dennis D. Miller. "Overview of Experimental Biology 2005 Symposium: Food Fortification in Developing Countries." *The Journal of Nutrition* 136, no. 4 (2006): 1053–1054.

Horton, Sue. "The Economics of Food Fortification." *The Journal of Nutrition* 136, no. 4 (2006): 1068–1071.

Mills, James L., and Tonia C. Carter. "Invited Commentary: Preventing Neural Tube Defects and More via Food Fortification?" *American Journal of Epidemiology* 169, no. 1 (2009): 18–21.

Solomons, Noel W. "Food Fortification with Folic Acid: Has the Other Shoe Dropped?" *Nutrition Reviews* 65, no. 11 (2007): 512–515.

Web Sites

"Fortification of Foods with Micronutrients." *Food and Nutrition Division, Food and Agriculture Organization of the United Nations (FAO).* ftp://ftp.fao.org/docrep/fao/005/y8346m/y8346m10.pdf (accessed September 11, 2010).

Blake Jackson Stabler

Nutrition

■ Introduction

Nutrition is the study of the components of food that are needed to keep the body functioning in a healthy manner. Food should be enjoyed, but equally as important, it plays a major role in the body's state of health. Carbohydrates, fats, and proteins are the macronutrients that provide the body with energy and the means for tissue growth and repair. Vitamins and minerals are the micronutrients that make an important contribution to the thousands of biochemical reactions going on in the body's cells. Although fiber is not, technically, a nutrient, it helps keep the colon healthy and may help prevent diseases such as diabetes and cancer. Water is an essential part of the diet because it is the solvent in which biochemical reactions take place, and it is lost by the body every day, so it must be replaced. Eating a widely varied and balanced diet is the best way of ensuring adequate supplies of nutrients. There is plenty of nutritional advice to allow people to become informed about how to eat to keep themselves healthy, however there are many individual differences in nutrient requirements, and there is still much to be discovered about the science of nutrition.

■ Historical Background and Scientific Foundations

The foundations of nutritional science were laid in the late eighteenth century, when French chemist Antoine Lavoisier (1743–1794) realized that oxidation of certain foods could provide energy, and that chemical reactions were important in breaking food down into its components. Before this, it had been assumed, from the ancient time of Hippocrates, that food contained only one kind of nutrient and that, therefore, all foods were essentially equal. During the nineteenth century, the macronutrients carbohydrate, fat, and protein were identified. It was German chemist Justus von Liebig (1803–1873)

who laid down the first theory of nutrition, stating that nitrogen-containing proteins form tissue and are consumed in mental and physical activity, and that sugars and fats are consumed in order to provide energy. His student, Carl Voit (1831–1908), proved him wrong about proteins being a source of energy, and gradually the roles of the three macronutrients were clarified. By the turn of the nineteenth century, most of the amino acids that make up proteins had been identified. Attention then shifted to the micronutrients, with Frederick Hopkins (1861–1947) in England, Christiaan Eijkman (1858–1930) in the Netherlands, and American E. V. McCollum (1879–1967) identifying the vitamins and working on vitamin deficiency diseases.

Nutrition describes, in increasing detail and concurrent with advances in scientific knowledge, what people need to eat to live, maintain health, and prevent disease. Diets can be designed to meet a specific health goal, which may focus upon ensuring adequate supply

WORDS TO KNOW

DIET: The word *diet* really has two meanings. It can mean simply what a person happens to eat, and diets are influenced by many factors, such as access to food, culture and personal preference and beliefs. Diet also means eating with a certain goal in mind, such as a reducing diet to lose weight.

FIBER: Fiber is not always defined as a nutrient, as it is not digested. Yet it plays a useful role in maintaining good bowel function. Diets high in fiber may also protect against diabetes and certain types of cancer.

NUTRIENT: A component of food that has some useful role in the body's functioning. Macronutrients are required in larger quantities and consist of carbohydrates, protein, and fat, whereas the micronutrients, the vitamins and minerals, are required in much smaller quantities.

of specific nutrients or cutting down on others. For instance, a high-fiber diet may be used to help prevent diabetes, whereas a low-salt diet may be prescribed to people with high blood pressure. The most important diet, however, is the balanced diet that supplies adequate amounts of both macronutrients and micronutrients. In 1940 British scientists Robert McCance (1898–1993) and Elsie Widdowson (1908–2000) compiled the first edition of *The Composition of Foods*, which listed the macronutrient and micronutrient content of many common foods and formed the basis of wartime rationing plans. The most recent edition contains the nutritional content of more than 1,200 foods and continues to be regarded as the classic reference work of nutrition.

Most carbohydrates come from plant foods. They are a large group of compounds, of which starch and sugar are the most important. Carbohydrate-rich foods in the diet include cereals, bread, potatoes, and desserts. The main role of carbohydrates is to provide energy. Protein comes from meat, fish, nuts, legumes, eggs, and dairy products. It is used for growth and repair of tissue. Fats and oils, from butter, vegetable oils, meat, and dairy products, are also used for energy and help form cell membranes.

Vitamins and minerals have many roles in the body, such as helping enzyme function, building strong bones and teeth, and maintaining body fluid balance. Fruits and vegetables are important sources of micronutrients, but vitamin B12 and iron are most readily available from meat rather than plant sources. Fiber is a collection of complex carbohydrates—such as cellulose, pectin, oligosaccharides, and gums—found in whole grains, fruit, and vegetables. Although fiber is not absorbed like the other nutrients, it does help maintain the health of the colon, and it may also have other health benefits. Finally, water is an essential part of a balanced diet. Water is the solvent

A nutritionist with Action Against Hunger examines children in Dalaad, Ethiopia, to gauge their level of malnourishment. *AP Images.*

for all the biochemical reactions carried out by cells. The human body is about 60 percent water. As water is continually lost through sweating and urination, regular daily intake is essential. The body can survive for much longer without food than it can without water.

The body extracts the nutrients it needs from food by the process of digestion. Thus, carbohydrates are broken down to glucose, which is converted into energy by a complex chain of reactions in cells involving oxygen. Proteins are broken down to their component amino acids, which are then built up again into the specific proteins that cells need for functioning. Fats are broken down into fatty acids and glycerol. Food is broken down by the action of enzymes in the mouth, stomach, and small intestine, and then absorbed into the bloodstream through the walls of the small intestine. Non-absorbed components of food pass into the large intestine and are eliminated from the body.

■ Impacts and Issues

There is no shortage of expert advice on nutrition. For example, dietary reference intakes from the U.S. Institute of Medicine provide a guide to how much of different micronutrients are required, and there are also recommendations of how much energy should come from saturated fat and what the upper salt intake limit should be. All of this is based on scientific evidence and can change in the light of new evidence. However, these recommendations are meant for large groups in the population and therefore should be regarded as a guide to nutrition rather than an individual prescription. Nutritional needs also vary over time, depending on age, level of activity, state of health or pregnancy, and other factors. It is possible to suffer from malnutrition even when sufficient calories are consumed, if the diet is not balanced. And even where food is present in abundance, nutritional deficiency is still possible if a person cannot absorb food or experiences appetite loss.

SEE ALSO *Calories; Center for Food Safety and Applied Nutrition; Changing Nutritional Needs throughout Life; Diet and Cancer; Diet and Diabetes; Diet and Heart Disease; Diet and Hypertension; Dietary Guidelines for Americans; Dietary Reference Intakes; Malnutrition; Nutrient Fortification of Foods; Nutrition and U.S. Government Food Assistance;* *Nutrition's Role in Human Evolution; Obesity; Vitamins and Minerals.*

BIBLIOGRAPHY

Books

Duyff, Roberta L. *American Dietetic Association Complete Food and Nutrition Guide.* Hoboken, NJ: John Wiley & Sons, 2006.

Farrell, Marian L., and Jo A. L. Nicoteri. *Nutrition.* Quick Look Nursing series. Sudbury, MA: Jones and Bartlett Publishers, 2007.

Nestle, Marion. *What to Eat.* New York: North Point Press, 2006.

Otten, Jennifer J., Jennifer P. Hellwig, and Linda D. Meyers. *DRI, Dietary Reference Intakes: The Essential Guide to Nutrient Requirements.* Washington, DC: National Academies Press, 2006.

Pollan, Michael. *In Defense of Food: An Eater's Manifesto.* New York: Penguin Press, 2008.

Periodicals

Barrett, Jennifer. "The Gurus' Guide to Daily Nutrition." *Newsweek* 147, no. 3 (2006): 64–69.

"Nutrition and Health: Food, Glorious Food." *The Economist* 393, no. 8655 (2009): 103.

"Nutrition—Food for Thought." *The Economist* 378, no. 8461 (2006): 14.

Web Sites

"Lifecycle Nutrition." *U.S. Department of Agriculture (USDA).* http://fnic.nal.usda.gov/nal_display/index.php?info_center=4&tax_level=1&tax_subject=257 (accessed October 17, 2010).

Nutrition.gov. http://www.nutrition.gov/nal_display/index.php?info_center=11&tax_level=1 (accessed October 17, 2010).

U.S. Department of Agriculture (USDA). "MyPyramid.gov: Steps to a Healthier You." *mypyramid.gov.* http://www.mypyramid.gov/ (accessed October 17, 2010).

Susan Aldridge

Nutrition and U.S. Government Food Assistance

■ Introduction

The United States federal government has several programs aimed at assisting low-income families, the elderly, and disabled individuals to meet their food needs. The largest U.S. government program is the Supplemental Nutrition Assistance Program (SNAP), formerly known as the Food Stamps Program, which provides families with monetary credit that can be used specifically for purchasing food. The Woman, Infants, and Children (WIC) program provides nutritional supplements to low-income mothers and their children up to age five. The School Meals Program and other childcare assistance programs supply children with free or reduced-priced meals at schools and childcare centers.

Although these programs constitute a food safety net, there is some concern that the food consumed in these programs has inadequate nutritional value. Policies place some limits on the items that can be purchased within the programs and what types of food can be prepared for children. Components of the government food assistance programs also focus on educating children about healthy eating habits and the importance of physical activity.

■ Historical Background and Scientific Foundations

The SNAP/Food Stamps Program is considered an entitlement program, providing and transferring resources from the U.S. federal government to individual households. The quantity of money for which households are eligible depends on income status, household costs, and the size of household. Typically, a family cannot have more than $2,000–3,000 worth of resources in cash, bank accounts, or other property. The amount given to households is adjusted based on changes in a family's financial circumstances, and with changes in the Consumer Price Index (CPI). The CPI gives an indication of the costs of living for a household.

More than 41 million people, representing nearly 13 percent of the U.S. population, participate in the Food Stamps Program. Each recipient receives an average of $101 per month, or $227 per household. Approximately 31.3 million children participate in the National School Lunch program. The average monthly household income of individuals in the Food Stamps Program in 2006 was $640. Approximately 51 percent of participants are children under age 17, with 65 percent of these living in a single-parent household. Of the total resources, 79 percent goes to households with families. The elderly make up 9 percent of Food Stamps participants, receiving 7 percent of benefits. Fourteen percent of recipients are disabled. Forty-one percent of participants are white, 36 percent are black, and 18 percent are Hispanic. There is very limited access to the program for people who are non-U.S. citizens. The Food Stamps Program does not allow recipients to purchase alcohol or tobacco, vitamins, pet food, food to be eaten in the store, or warm foods with food stamps.

The first Food Stamps Program began in 1939 toward the end of the Great Depression (1929–1941) when there was high unemployment. Orange and Blue stamps could be redeemed for food. The program was designed to assist families with meeting food needs, while also providing markets for farm surpluses. The initial program reached up to 4 million people, costing $262 million. This first program was discontinued in 1944, when unemployment and agricultural surpluses decreased with U.S. involvement in World War II (1941–1945). The National School Lunch Act was passed in 1946 to give federal assistance to school lunch programs, primarily as a way to boost the nutritional levels of potential soldiers in the military. A new Food Stamp program began when President John F. Kennedy (1917–1963) used an Executive Order to call for larger food distribution. The program gained traction under the Food Stamp Act of 1964 and was initiated nationwide in 1974, with 14 million participants. Cutbacks to the program were implemented in the 1980s, making the eligibility requirements more restrictive. Additional changes in the 1990s included limiting access to Food Stamps for most legal immigrants. Much of the legislation was passed to determine allowable income levels for participation, including the use of medical costs and housing expenses as deductions to determine eligibility for the program.

■ Impacts and Issues

Some sociologists and economists assert that food support programs help keep participants poor, not enabling them to move out of government welfare programs that give cash to households struggling financially. Researchers have concluded that the SNAP/Food Stamps Program has the reverse effect, keeping former welfare recipients from rejoining welfare programs. Another concern is fraud in the system, or the ability of recipients to overstate their eligibility to receive assistance. Food Stamps administrators have made some improvements to address overpayment in the program, which was found to be close to 10 percent in the 1980s. Instances of overpayment are not necessarily considered cases of intentional fraud, but occur because of mistakes made by recipients, eligibility workers, and data entry workers

when determining eligibility levels. Computer programs are used to catch cases of intentionally misstated eligibility. There are strict penalties, including imprisonment, for transferring Food Stamps credit and for using benefits to purchase items that are not allowed under the program.

There are also concerns that individuals using food support do not consume the most nutritious products. Several studies have shown that the nutritional status of those using food support is not any different than those not using food support. There is an argument that if the most needy individuals did not have access to food support, their nutritional status would drop. Children participating in National School Lunch program are documented to have improved nutrition.

USDA-supplied rolled oats and walnuts await distribution at a food pantry in Wilmington, Vermont. *AP Images.*

School lunches must meet federal dietary guidelines, with school lunches to provide a third of recommended daily consumption of protein, vitamins A and C, iron, calcium, and calories.

An issue for those in poverty, and particularly those in the Food Stamps program, is the need to stretch the household food budget to buy the largest quantity of food. To do this, households purchase cheaper foods, which are often the least nutritious. In many cases, these are processed foods, which often contain high levels of processed sugars, fat, and sodium and lack essential vitamins and minerals. Media reports have focused on whether or not food stamp participants should be allowed to purchase sugary sodas and other less nutritious foods. Evidence has shown that lower income individuals often live far from grocery stores that sell the most nutritional foods. Without reliable personal vehicles or readily available public transportation, these individuals must shop at convenience stores that stock predominantly unhealthful foods. Some convenience stores, including Walgreen's Pharmacy, have made attempts at stocking nutritious alternatives such as fruits and vegetables.

SEE ALSO *Dietary Guidelines for Americans; Dietary Reference Intakes; Food Security; Improving Nutrition for America's Children Act of 2010; School Lunch Reform; U.S. Department of Agriculture (USDA); USDA Food Pyramid.*

BIBLIOGRAPHY

Books

How to Use Your SNAP Benefits at Farmers' Markets. Oklahoma City: OK-SNAP, Supplemental Nutrition Assistance Program, Oklahoma OKDHS, 2010.

Kaushal, Neeraj, and Qin Gao. *Food Stamp Program and Consumption Choices.* Cambridge, MA: National Bureau of Economic Research, 2009.

Roush, Margaret. *U.S. National Debate Topic, 2009–2010: Social Services for the Poor.* New York: H.W. Wilson Company, 2009.

SNAP Can Make a Big Difference in Feeding Your Family. Salem, OR: DHS, Children, Adults and Families Division, Supplemental Nutrition Assistance Program, 2010.

SNAP: Supplemental Nutrition Assistance Program. Indianapolis, IN: Family and Social Services Administration, 2010.

Periodicals

Christian, Thomas. "Grocery Store Access and the Food Insecurity-Obesity Paradox." *Journal of Hunger & Environmental Nutrition* 5, no. 3 (2010): 360–369.

Issar, Sukriti. "Multiple Program Participation and Exits from Food Stamps among Elders." *The Social Service Review* 84, no. 3 (2010): 437–459.

Wilde, Parke E., Lisa M. Troy, and Beatrice L. Rogers. "Food Stamps and Food Spending: An Engel Function Approach." *American Journal of Agricultural Economics* 91, no. 2 (2009): 416–430.

Web Sites

"Food Stamps and Other Nutrition Programs." *Social Security Administration.* http://www.ssa.gov/pubs/10100.html (accessed October 30, 2010).

"SNAP/Food Stamps." *Food Research and Action Center.* http://frac.org/federal-foodnutrition-programs/snapfood-stamps/ (accessed October 30, 2010).

"Supplemental Nutrition Assistance Program (SNAP)." *Food and Nutrition Service, U.S. Department of Agriculture (USDA).* http://www.fns.usda.gov/snap/ (accessed October 30, 2010).

Steven Joseph Archambault

Nutrition's Role in Human Evolution

■ Introduction

Nutrition and the efforts of human ancestors to obtain food play a fundamental role in most scientific hypotheses explaining human evolution. Changes in hunting, meat-eating, and scavenging behaviors; the collection of new types of plant foods; and new methods of processing and cooking foods have all been proposed as major factors underlying the origins of humanity and the genus *Homo*. Historic alterations in subsistence and diet appear to have played an instrumental role in the beginnings of bipedalism, increases in brain size and intelligence, language, technological advances such as tool use, human longevity, and unique forms of human social organization and family structure. An understanding of the past several million years of evolutionary history with food may also be important for understanding modern nutritional needs, desires, and the "diseases of civilization" such as obesity and metabolic syndrome that are increasingly common worldwide. Modern diets are obviously drastically different from those of humanity's pre-agricultural ancestors of 20,000 years ago, the earliest modern humans of nearly 200,000 years ago, or that of foraging Pleistocene forerunners, and some researchers question whether genes have had a chance to keep pace with the cultural and nutritional changes of the past millennia.

■ Historical Background and Scientific Foundations

In the 1950s and 1960s, anthropologists studying non-human primates, modern hunter-gatherers, and hominin fossils suggested that hunting was the major evolutionary change that separated early humans from their ape-like ancestors. "Man the Hunter" was put forth as the basis of the sexual division of labor among humans, with males hunting animals and provisioning and protecting females who collected plant foods, insects, and smaller animals and cared for children. American anthropologists Sherwood Washburn (1911–2000) and Chet S. Lancaster (1932–) summarized that "the habitual sharing between a male, a female, and their offspring becomes the basis for the human family." Although ideas about male hunting as the source of the modern family had been around since the nineteenth century, this was the first time that new evidence on human origins and nutrition was examined scientifically, in the context of adaptation and natural selection.

This widely accepted "hunting hypothesis" was seen as the impetus behind the increased intelligence, communication skills, cooperation, and tool use that differentiated hominins from their ancestors. Later, scientists suggested that walking upright freed australopithecine hands for more effective hunting and for carrying food, which was shared in a manner that was markedly different from that of chimpanzees and other primates. Archaeological evidence from Pleistocene sites in Africa supported the hypothesis that human ancestors shared food at home bases.

By 2000, some paleoanthropologists noted that women provided the bulk of the nutritional resources for subsistence amongst many groups of historic and modern hunter-gatherers, and that there was little evidence for a rigid division of labor between the sexes in the early Pleistocene. American anthropologist Hillard Kaplan theorized that the evolutionary changes attributed to hunting could also be explained by advances in collecting, carrying, and sharing many types of "high-quality, nutrient dense, and difficult-to-acquire food resources" that may have included nuts, seeds, roots, and tubers as well as meat.

Hominin meat consumption remains an important focus of research, however, especially as techniques for reconstructing prehistoric diet and the understanding of human nutrition become increasingly sophisticated. What had been interpreted as evidence of hunting was re-examined for signs of scavenging, for instance. Researchers came to agree that opportunistic hunting and aggressive scavenging may have been important

WORDS TO KNOW

AUSTRALOPITHECINE: A member of the genus *Australopithecus*, australopithecines are the extinct ancestors and side branches of humans that lived 4 million to 1.4 million years ago in Africa, preceding the genus *Homo*.

BIPEDALISM: The ability to walk upright on two feet.

HABILINE: An early human ancestor in the genus *Homo*, particularly *Homo habilis* but also including such fossil species as *Homo rudolfensis*, *Homo georgicus*, and some transitional forms of australopithecines. Habilines evolved into *Homo ergaster* and *Homo erectus* and several other species during the Pleistocene, including Neanderthals (*Homo neanderthalensis*) before the appearance of modern humans, who are classified as *Homo sapiens*.

HOMININ: A taxonomic term used to describe humans, their ancestors, and closely related species, including all members of the genera *Homo* and *Australopithecus*. The Tribe Hominini does not include chimpanzees or gorillas. Hominid, which anthropologists previously used to describe humans and their ancestors, now includes chimpanzees and gorillas as part of the family Hominidae.

METABOLIC SYNDROME: A group of risk factors including elevated blood pressure, insulin resistance, increased abdominal fat, elevated lipids in the blood, and overweight or obesity, that together are linked to future development of heart disease and/or diabetes in an individual.

PLEISTOCENE: The geological period of time from 2.58 million years ago to 12,000 years ago. By the end of the Pleistocene epoch, which was also the end of the archaeological period known as the Paleolithic, or "Stone Age," human hunters and gatherers had spread across the world. The Pleistocene was preceded by the Pliocene and is followed by the current period, the Holocene.

SUBSISTENCE: Methods of obtaining food. Subsistence was based on hunting and gathering until relatively recently in human prehistory.

strategies for obtaining meat and fat in the Pleistocene. As American anthropologists Craig Stanford and Henry T. Bunn noted in 2001, however, "There is little doubt that meat-eating became increasingly important in human ancestry, despite the lack of direct evidence in the fossil record of how meat was obtained, or how much was eaten, or how often, or how exactly increasing importance of meat-eating may have contributed to the rise of the genus *Homo*."

Other scientists stress the nutritional importance of meat and the concurrent importance of hunting as hominins first migrated out of Africa a little less than two million years ago. Increases in brain size and the brain's expensive energy requirements are inversely related to animal gut size. This relationship shows that the relatively small digestive systems of humans needed high-quality, easily digestible food, and that an increase in the consumption of animal products was essential to the evolution of large human brains. Analysis of chimpanzee, gorilla, and human gut anatomy similarly shows that nutrition from animal matter of some kind is essential in explaining human evolution. Human ancestors who ate meat could also intensify their use of previously marginal plant foods such as tubers and grains, which may be rich in calories, but lack essential nutrients. Meat may also have played an important role as a weaning food, increasing child survival rates, and reducing birth intervals among early hominins.

Sharing food with newly weaned children also plays a role in the "grandmother hypothesis" put forth in 2003, which suggests that human longevity, especially that of post-menopausal females, may be related to the nutritional advantages that females provide to their families after their own reproduction is finished. Like the hunting hypothesis, the grandmother hypothesis assumes that changing ecological circumstances favored a shift in foraging strategies. An alternate theory known as the signaling mode or the "show-off" hypothesis suggests that males hunt primarily to gain social status, and that sharing meat translates to increased mating opportunities and reproductive success. Recent research notes that these factors may reinforce hunting behaviors, but argues that the food obtained from hunting was also nutritionally significant.

Most recently, the British biological anthropologist Richard Wrangham suggested in 2009 that "the transformative moment that gave rise to the genus *Homo* . . . stemmed from the control of fire and the advent of cooked meals." Wrangham agrees that dietary increases in root use, meat-eating, and processing techniques may account for the evolution of austrolopithecines to habilines around 2.5 million years ago, but argues that the "cooking hypothesis" is a better explanation for the biological and behavioral changes almost two million years ago that resulted in *Homo erectus*. He demonstrates that cooking increases the amount of energy that can be extracted from most foods, looks at the nutritional and archaeological evidence, and contends that "the design of the human digestive system is better explained as an adaptation to eating cooked food than it is to raw meat." Wrangham also points out that cooking can explain the origins of the division of labor and human pair-bonding as well as hunting does.

■ Impacts and Issues

In the first decade of the twenty-first century, sophisticated analyses of tooth and jaw morphology; the wear patterns on teeth, bones, and tools; trace elements and isotopes in bone; and detailed studies of artifacts and plant and animal remains at Pleistocene sites have produced more data for debating the competing hypotheses

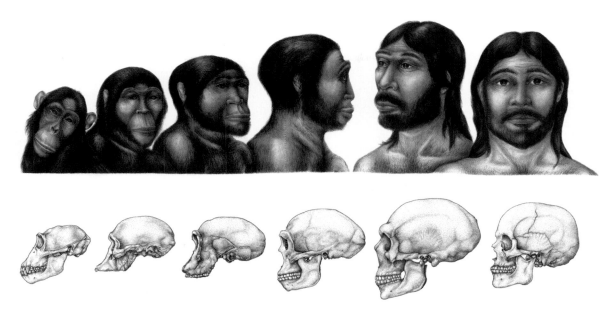

An illustration shows the evolution of the human skull.   © *Medical-on-Line / Alamy.*

for human evolution. Microbial ecology, comparative genomics, and the study of parasites from humans and their close relatives have also provided new insights into the mechanisms and timing of changes in hominin diet and behavior over the last five to six million years.

Some scientists theorize that modern diets are not appropriate for people who evolved as hunter-gatherers eating wild plants and animals (which may or may not have been cooked) for several million years. The argument that the human genome has not had time to adjust to the new diets that followed the adoption of agriculture and new techniques of food processing over the last ten thousand years has become a tenet of evolutionary or Darwinian medicine, which seeks to explain the prevalence of chronic diseases of civilization and affluence, such as obesity, diabetes, some cancers, and atherosclerosis. A few researchers and many other less well-informed enthusiasts have promoted "Paleolithic" diets and exercise patterns, more or less based on pre-agricultural lifeways, as an antidote to these issues. Although the lifestyle changes that are being promoted may prove beneficial, many anthropologists note that these diets may bear little relation to the diets of ancestors in a given period, while pointing out the theoretical and empirical fallacies of current "Paleo diets." There is certainly a wide disconnect between the scientific and the popular literature on prehistoric food and nutrition, with many experts acknowledging there is much that is still simply unknown (and perhaps unknowable) about human ancestors' diets.

SEE ALSO   *History of Food and Man: From Hunter-Gatherer to Agriculture; Meats; Paleolithic Diet.*

BIBLIOGRAPHY

Books

Cordain, Loren. *The Paleo Diet: Lose Weight and Get Healthy by Eating the Foods You Were Designed to Eat.* New York: Wiley, 2002.

Hublin, Jean-Jacques, and Michael P. Richards. *The Evolution of Hominin Diets: Integrating Approaches to the Study of Paleolithic Subsistence.* Dordrecht: Springer, 2009.

Ungar, Peter S., ed. *Evolution of the Human Diet: The Known, The Unknown, and the Unknowable.* Oxford: Oxford University Press, 2007.

Wrangham, Richard W. *Catching Fire: How Cooking Made Us Human.* New York: Basic Books, 2009.

Periodicals

Gurven, Michael, and Kim Hill. "Why Do Men Hunt? A Reevaluation of "Man the Hunter" and the Sexual Division of Labor." *Current Anthropology* 50, no. 1 (2009): 51–74.

Stiner, Mary C. "Carnivory, Coevolution, and the Geographic Spread of the Genus *Homo.*" *Journal of Archaeological Research* 10 (2002): 1–63.

Web Sites

"Kibale Chimpanzee Project." *Harvard University.* http://www.fas.harvard.edu/~kibale/ (accessed August 1, 2010).

Sandra Dunavan

Nuts and Seeds

■ Introduction

Since the prehistoric days of hunter-gathering, nuts and seeds have been part of the human diet. Nuts and seeds resemble grains in their protein and vitamin content, but are higher in fat content and lower in carbohydrates. Their importance declined with the cultivation of grains and legumes. Nuts and seeds have much in common, with both containing food stores intended to nourish the embryonic plant. However, they come from a diverse group of plants, from the walnut tree to the coconut palm. Nuts require little preparation other than shelling, and can be eaten raw, although roasting and salting improve their flavor. Nuts are often used in processed products such as marzipan and peanut butter, are often found in baked goods, and are also a popular snack. Research suggests there are health benefits in giving nuts and seeds a more central role in the diet, replacing some of the animal protein. In addition, nuts and seeds are important commercial crops for the production of oil for cuisine and other applications. Most nut and seed oils promote health because they are highly unsaturated and some, such as hemp seed oil, are high in omega-3 and omega-6 fatty acids, which are thought to protect against inflammation, heart disease, and stroke.

■ Historical Background and Scientific Foundations

Nuts and seeds were among the earliest foods consumed by humans, because they represent a compact food source that requires little, if any, preparation. Nut-bearing trees such as the walnut and coconut have been on earth longer than many other food plants. The worldwide distribution of nuts and seeds is a hallmark of their antiquity. Acorn and chestnut, which have a high carbohydrate content, were often ground into flour and used as a staple when grain was scarce.

There is no strict dividing line between nuts and seeds, because most nuts are seeds of one kind or another. Mostly they consist of two swollen cotyledons packed with nutrients, joined together with a tiny stem. Because the cell walls of nuts and seeds do not contain indigestible fibers like the cell walls of grains and legumes, they do not need to be soaked or cooked. However, roasting and toasting nuts and seeds will help improve their texture as well as bring out flavor. The cotyledons are usually covered by a thin protective skin that has a high content of phenolic compounds, which have antioxidant properties. However, these often taste bitter so the skin is usually removed. Because of their high fat content, nuts are prone to becoming rancid through oxidation, which impairs their flavor. They should be stored in a cool, dark place. Unshelled nuts maintain freshness longer than shelled ones.

The nuts and seeds are, botanically, a fairly disparate group. Almonds and cashews are actually the seeds of drupes. Almond is in the plum family and cashew belongs to the ivy family. Almond is a commercially important nut crop for its oil and processed products such as marzipan and cakes. Bitter almonds are wild and contain a compound called amygdalin, which forms hydrogen cyanide, a potent and well known toxin when crushed. They are used only as a source of oil and should not be consumed whole. Sweet almonds are cultivated and safe to eat in any form. Brazil nuts are native to the Amazon basin, as the name suggests; they are actually swollen embryonic stem rather than cotyledon. Coconut, the largest nut, is the seed of a drupe fruit from a palm. The milky fluid in the center of the nut, high in electrolytes, is useful as a sports drink. The walnut, second to the almond in worldwide consumption, is also the stone of a drupe, with its edible part being its two irregularly shaped cotyledons.

The peanut is actually the fruit of a leguminous bush, rather than a true nut. Asia is the largest producer of peanuts, most of which are processed into oil. There are four varieties of peanut grown in North America, and they are used mainly for consumption in raw, shelled, or unshelled forms. The variety called Runner is often used to make peanut butter or baked goods because it is relatively resistant to rancidity.

Pine nuts are the naked seeds of many different pines and are harvested from the scales. They have a characteristic pine flavor that is brought out by toasting, although they are prone to burning because of their high fat content. Sunflower seeds, the only significant native North American plant to become a major world crop, are actually a complete fruit like the seeds on the outside of a strawberry.

■ Impacts and Issues

Because nuts are high in fat and calories, excess consumption may promote weight gain. But there is also evidence that nuts can be a healthy component of the daily diet, especially if consumed instead of, rather than in addition to, animal protein. This is because nuts are high in protein, and the fat they contain is unsaturated fat. Some nuts have specific health benefits: Walnuts contain omega-3 fatty acids, and Brazil nuts contain more selenium than any other food. Selenium is an important antioxidant, and eating two to three Brazil nuts per day provides an

> ### WORDS TO KNOW
>
> **COTYLEDON:** The seed leaves that form part of a seed, storing its food supplies. Most nuts and seeds consist of two swollen cotyledons packed with oil, protein, and other nutrients.
>
> **NUT:** The strict botanical definition of a nut is a one-seeded fruit in which the fruit tissue is dry and tough rather than juicy. A broader definition has a nut as a large seed of certain long-lived trees.
>
> **SEED:** A compact package containing a plant's embryo and the food stores it needs to develop into a new plant.

adequate intake of this mineral, as well as the protein equivalent to that of a boiled egg. Studies have suggested that regular intake of walnuts, peanuts, and almonds may help protect against heart disease. Seed oils such as hemp and flaxseed are also high in omega-3 and omega-6 fatty acids; they can be used as a substitute source of these valuable nutrients for those who do not like oily fish.

Nuts are often processed into oils. Peanut oil plays an important role in Asian cuisine, while the aromatic oil from walnuts is used to flavor vegetables and salads in

A variety of nuts and seeds available at a market.   *Image copyright Mircea Bezergheanu, 2010. Used under license from Shutterstock.com.*

Almonds grow on an almond tree in California. *Image copyright XuRa, 2010. Used under license from Shutterstock.com.*

France and Italy. Coconut oil is used widely in industrial frying, but is less healthful than other nut oils because it is more saturated, a property that also makes it more stable and less prone to rancidity.

Finally, Brazil nuts could play a part in saving the Amazonian rain forest, because they are being planted there as an increasingly important commercial crop. Brazil nut trees grow only in canopied rainforests, where they contribute to the canopy by reaching heights of up to 150 feet (46 meters). When Brazil nuts are profitable for growers to produce due to consumer demand, it becomes economically desirable to preserve more acreage of rainforest. The Brazil nut tree depends on the carpenter bee to pollinate its flowers, along with the agouti, a sharp-toothed rodent, to spread its seeds to the rainforest floor. As the tree can produce mature nuts only in a healthy rainforest ecosystem, Brazil nuts provide a natural link to conservation.

SEE ALSO *Biofuels and World Hunger; Chocolate; Food Allergen Labeling and Consumer Protection Act of 2004; Food Allergies; Raw Foodism; Veganism; Vegetarianism.*

BIBLIOGRAPHY

Books

Burns, Diane L., and John F. McGee. *Berries, Nuts and Seeds.* Cincinnati: Paw Prints, 2008.

Burrows, Ian. *Food from the Wild.* London: New Holland, 2005.

Mintel, Int. *Nuts, Seeds and Dried Fruit.* London: Mintel, 2008.

Steinman, Harris. *Legumes, Nuts & Seeds: Allergy—Which Allergens?* Milnerton, South Africa: Allergy Resources International, 2008.

Periodicals

Gonzalez, Carlos A., and Jordi Salas-Salvadó. "The Potential of Nuts in the Prevention of Cancer." *The British Journal of Nutrition* 96, suppl. 2 (2006): 87–94.

Marcason, Wendy. "What Is the Latest Research Regarding the Avoidance of Nuts, Seeds, Corn, and Popcorn in Diverticular Disease?" *Journal of the American Dietetic Association* 108, no. 11 (2008): 1956.

Nettleton, Jennifer A., et al. "Dietary Patterns and Risk of Incident Type 2 Diabetes in the Multi-Ethnic Study of Atherosclerosis." *Diabetes Care* 31, no. 9 (2008): 1777–1782.

Web Sites

"Honduras: Cashews Create Stable Income For Poor Communities." *World Food Programme.* http://www.wfp.org/stories/honduras-cashews-create-stable-income-poor-communities (accessed October 2, 2010).

Spiller, Gene A., and Bonnie Bruce. "Nuts and Healthy Diets." *Vegetarian Nutrition: An International Journal* 1, no. 1, 1997. http://www.fao.org/inpho/content/documents/vlibrary/ac307e/pdf/ac307e05.pdf (accessed October 2, 2010).

Susan Aldridge

Obesity

■ Introduction

Obesity is the accumulation of excess body fat to the degree that it may negatively impact health and life expectancy. Since the early 1980s there has been a dramatic increase in obesity in the United States and in many Western European countries. The rapid increase in obesity rates is blamed on a number of factors, including genetic predisposition, improper eating habits, and reduced physical activity.

In the United States, the Centers for Disease Control and Prevention (CDC) reports that the prevalence of obesity grew substantially starting in the 1980s. When analyzed in the context of height and age, the CDC estimates that by 2010 approximately 65 percent of Americans were overweight and 30 percent of adults above 20 years of age were clinically obese. Obesity-related conditions are the second leading cause of preventable death following smoking.

■ Historical Background and Scientific Foundations

Despite the myriad of diet fads, gimmicks, and claims, the essential elements of weight loss and control are simple in terms of general physiology: Weight is maintained when the calorie intake is balanced by calorie expenditure. An excessive intake of calories leads to a storage of fat and results in weight gain. Weight loss occurs when the expenditure of calories is greater than caloric intake. However, genetics and lifestyles add enormous complexities to the manifestation and remediation of obesity.

Genetic factors influence how the body regulates appetite and the rate at which it turns food into energy (metabolic rate), but a genetic tendency to gain weight does not automatically mean that a person will be obese.

There many characterizations of obesity, and there is disagreement as to how obesity should be defined in terms of the physical size, the percentage of body fat, or

physical capabilities of a person. One of the least accurate estimates is derived from simple individual comparison with standardized height and weight charts used to characterize large populations.

For adults, the most widely used indicator for obesity is the body mass index (BMI), a mathematical ratio of weight and height. In children and adolescents, obesity is determined by BMI in conjunction with age and growth charts.

The terms *obesity* and *overweight* are both used to describe weight ranges that are greater than what scientists consider healthy for a given height. The body mass index (BMI) has been the medical standard for obesity measurement since the early 1980s, when government researchers developed it to take height into account in weight measurement. BMI equals a person's weight in kilograms (kg) divided by that person's height in meters (m) squared (kg/m^2). In 1998 the U.S. federal government changed its guidelines for BMI, making a BMI of 18.5 to 24.9 a healthy weight/height ratio. A person with a BMI of less than 18.5 is considered underweight. In BMI terms, the overweight range is 25.0 to 29.9 for both men and women. Experts usually consider a person obese if the BMI falls between 30.0 and 40.0; a person is considered morbidly obese if the BMI is over 40.0. Depending on where a person is positioned within this BMI range—and depending on whether the person's waist size is below or above 40 inches (102 centimeters) for men, or below or above 35 inches (89 centimeters) for women—then that person can be at increased, high, or extremely high risk for health problems related to obesity.

According to established guidelines, a person who is 5 feet (1.52 meters) in height and weighs 155 pounds (70.3 kilograms) has a BMI of 30.3 and is considered obese. Someone who is 5 feet 4 inches (1.62 meters) in height and weighs 155 pounds (70.3 kilograms) has a BMI of 26.7; this person is considered overweight, but not obese. A person who is 5 feet 11 inches (1.80 meters) and weighs 155 pounds (70.3 kilograms) is in the healthy BMI range, with a BMI of 21.7.

Although BMI is a useful indicator of body fat it does not directly measure it. Another problem with BMI estimates is the tendency to overestimate the body fat in athletes, who are heavier due to increased muscle mass. It can also do the opposite and underestimate body fat in older people, who lose muscle due to the aging process. The most accurate body fat estimates can be determined by a number of measuring and examination methodologies, including estimates obtained from tomography or magnetic resonance imaging (MRI).

Data and studies show that diets have changed since the end of the nineteenth century. There is an increased consumption of convenience foods (ready-made or frozen) as well as fast food from various sources (such as hamburgers or fried foods). An important difference between most convenience foods and homemade alternatives are generally a higher fat and sugar content found in commercial foods. Other factors contributing to poor eating habits include increased workload and financial pressure due to workplace "productivity" demands (e.g. people working longer hours under more stress). On top of consuming more calories, according to CDC data from 2000 more than 26 percent of Americans are not exercising sufficiently to maintain proper weight and health.

Public health officials most often recommend approaches to weight loss and maintaining a healthy weight that are based on a lifelong commitment to regular exercise and sensible eating habits. Up to 85 percent of dieters who do not exercise on a regular basis will regain their lost weight within two years. In five years, the figure rises to 90 percent. Exercise increases the metabolic rate by creating muscle, which burns more calories than fat. When regular exercise is combined with regular, healthful meals, calories continue to burn at an accelerated rate for several hours.

Obesity has become so prevalent that, since 1980, the study of obesity and its causes has evolved into a distinct medical specialty, bariatrics, a term derived from the Greek word *baros*, meaning weight.

■ Impacts and Issues

Obesity is traditionally considered a public health concern in wealthy, highly developed countries. The World Health Organization (WHO) indicates, however, that obesity is also a growing problem in developing countries, particularly in regions of Africa, South America, and the Caribbean, where large migrations of rural populations have crowded into densely populated urban areas. The WHO estimates that more than 400 million people worldwide are obese, and that the number could grow to 700 million by the year 2015.

In developing countries and among poor populations in industrialized countries, obesity can coexist with malnutrition. In Africa, traditionally considered a continent with crushing poverty and hunger, the numbers of overweight and obese people are fast approaching equality with the number who are undernourished—about 200 million people. As mega cities continue to explode in Africa and other areas of the developing world, obesity levels are rising among city dwellers who walk less and no longer engage in strenuous agricultural work.

Asia is not immune from the rising obesity rates found in America and Europe. WHO officials cite rising obesity and diabetes rates across Asia. In a 2005 study, about 30 percent of the population of Asia was estimated to be clinically overweight. WHO officials predict that obesity levels in Asia could grow to levels rivaling the United States and Europe by 2015. A study released in 2009 concluded that approximately 23 percent of the population of China could be considered overweight. In some areas of India—especially major urban centers and areas of rising income due to technology-related jobs—approximately one quarter of the population can be considered clinically obese.

The looming dangers and cost of obesity alarm public health officials in all countries. An increased number of people are at risk of developing serious medical conditions due to their excessive weight. The significant consequences of the obesity epidemic are increases in the level of chronic or life-threatening diseases such as adult-onset diabetes (also known as non-insulin-dependent or type 2 diabetes), heart disease, hypertension, stroke, osteoarthritis, infertility, menstrual irregularities, some cancers (endometrial, breast, and colon), high cholesterol levels, respiratory problems, and other medical problems. An associated consequence of the obesity epidemic is an increase of direct and indirect medical costs in the billions of dollars.

In October 2009 a team of European researchers speaking at a joint meeting of the European Cancer

Organization and the European Society for Medical Oncology in Berlin declared that obesity was poised to become the leading cause of cancer in women in developed Western nations during upcoming decades. Obesity is linked to about 8 percent of cancers in Europe, but the percentage is expected to rise. Cancers linked to tobacco use and hormone replacement therapy are expected to decline due to antismoking campaigns and changes in hormone treatment programs. The researchers also base their projections on studies showing that the number of cancer cases linked to obesity nearly doubled between 2002 and 2008. Some studies in the United States suggest that up to 20 percent of cancer cases in the United States are related to obesity.

In February 2010 a *New England Journal of Medicine* essay published information on the relationship between childhood obesity and a shortened life span. Some obese children identified in the study had a mortality rate prior to age 55 that was double that of non-obese children. Children with pre-diabetes also had nearly double the risk of death prior to age 55.

The CDC released a study in August 2010 containing data derived from the 2009 Behavioral Risk Factor Surveillance System; the study indicated that all U.S. states failed to meet preexisting targets for obesity reduction. Moreover, self-reported obesity rates among U.S. adults continued to rise, up more than 1 percent in 2009 from 2007 levels. About 27 percent of U.S. adults reported height and weight data that classified them as obese using body mass indices. Among demographic groups, approximately 37 percent of non-Hispanic blacks described themselves as obese. About 31 percent of Hispanics described themselves as obese. Among states, Mississippi had the highest level of self-reported obesity (34.4 percent) and Colorado had the lowest level of self-reported obesity (18.6 percent). Obesity determinations were based on BMI calculations relying on self-reported weight and height data.

Although in the United States, Canada, and European Union it is unlawful to discriminate against people on the basis of race, religion, gender, sexual persuasion, or ethnic group, overweight people often find it more difficult to get and keep a job; almost half those who are 100 pounds (45 kilograms) or more overweight are unemployed. For those who do have jobs, obese workers are often overlooked because they do not present a stereotypical corporate or professional image. Heavy people historically have been discriminated against by insurance carriers who refused to provide scientifically validated therapy.

Appetite-suppressant drugs are sometimes prescribed to help people lose weight. For people who are severely obese, diet and lifestyle changes may be accompanied by surgery to restrict, reduce, or bypass portions of the stomach or small intestine. There are a wide variety of non-clinical weight-loss programs available. Behavioral programs are often commercial franchises that offer program materials that may or may not

An obese man eats junk food in Leicester, England. © *Ashley Cooper pics / Alamy.*

be produced with guidance from health care providers. Critics of what is often characterized as the "diet industry" contend that many programs simply prey on the vulnerabilities of overweight and obese people to make profits on unscientific and potentially dangerous remedies, some of which border on consumer fraud.

Most experts agree that the best way for an overweight person to achieve and maintain weight loss is a lifelong commitment to regular exercise and sensible eating habits. For a person who is obese, evaluation by a health care professional will identify weight-related medical concerns along with the safest, most effective ways to resolve them. The CDC has labeled American society as "obeseogenic," encouraging an environment that promotes unhealthy food intake in both composition and amount of foods, along with physical inactivity.

■ Primary Source Connection

The incidence of childhood obesity in the United States has increased at an alarming rate over the past thirty years. Since 1980, the percentage of children who are considered obese has more than tripled. Childhood obesity has implications for both current and long-term health, including an increased risk of cardiovascular disease, bone and joint problems, sleep apnea, and social and psychological problems such as stigmatization and low self-esteem. Obese children are also more likely than youth of normal weight to become overweight adults, and therefore more at risk for associated adult health problems, including heart disease, type-2 diabetes, stroke, several types of cancer, and osteoarthritis.

In her role as First Lady of the United States, Michelle Obama has committed to solving what is now widely recognized as a childhood obesity epidemic. On February 2, 2010, she unveiled the "Let's Move" Childhood Obesity Action Plan. This plan includes requiring food manufacturers to include better information about ingredients and nutrition on food packages, encouraging doctors to provide routine BMI checks during annual checkups and spend more time counseling parents and children on healthy eating early on, working with public schools to provide more nutritious lunches for their students, encouraging more physical activity in children by doubling the number of Presidential Active Lifestyle Awards, and spending $400 million dollars per year to bring more grocery stores and more healthful food options to poor areas.

As a part of a television segment on the "Let's Move" action plan, First Lady Michelle Obama appeared on PBS's *NewsHour* on February 9, 2010, to talk with host Jim Lehrer on the subject of childhood obesity.

Michelle Obama: Team Effort Needed to Halt Childhood Obesity

JIM LEHRER: Why did you choose childhood obesity as your major project?

MICHELLE OBAMA: I think I connected with it as a mother because I remember so clearly life before the White House, and it was a life that most working parents are dealing with, where you're juggling jobs and trying to get kids to and from and you're trying to make life easier. You're eating out more and you're probably moving less because you're carpooling and you're sitting and kids are watching TV and as a result of this lifestyle, this busy, hectic lifestyle, my pediatrician pointed out some changes in my kids' body mass index that he just sort of checked us on. And I hadn't even thought about it—hadn't thought about our lifestyle. But the beauty of that situation, for me, was that I made some pretty minor changes over the period of months, and saw what the doctor said were pretty remarkable changes, that he usually didn't see in his practice, which is a predominantly African-American, urban practice.

So he was pretty floored by how quickly you could turn the tide on this issue with—by just removing juices from lunchboxes and cooking a little bit more, maybe one or two more meals, turning the TV off a little bit more, limiting desserts to the weekends. I mean these were really not major lifestyle overhauls. So when I came here, I thought, if it can be that simple, it's all about lack of information and lack of focus on the issue. So I wanted to use the first lady spotlight to shine the light on this issue for many families that are struggling with this issue.

JIM LEHRER: Did you consider other causes? Something more related, say, or directly related to the recession, unemployment, that sort of thing?

MICHELLE OBAMA: Well, there have been several issues that I've developed over the course of my first year. Children's health and nutrition is one; with planting the garden—that was really sort of laying the foundation and using that year to learn more. But I have and will continue to focus on supporting our military families; national service will continue to be something that I'm promoting around the country.

So I'm still multitasking. It's really with childhood obesity that we saw an opportunity to really launch a major initiative that we thought could move the ball. So a lot of this effort results from the belief that this is something that we can do something about.

JIM LEHRER: Do you feel that because you have made the decision to do it and you're going to get involved in this that you really can change where the trends are, all the things that you have lamented and others have lamented, that are going on among young people?

MICHELLE OBAMA: Well, I know I can't do it alone and the solutions are not going to come from any one single solution. But I do have the platform to lead an effort to pull all of these resources together and, again, shine a spotlight on this issue in a way that I couldn't do as a regular mom on the South Side of Chicago.

So I don't think that me alone will solve this, but I think if we're working with the governors and mayors all across the city, highlighting important initiatives; if we've got our pediatricians, the American Academy of Pediatrics working to improve their practices around this issue; we've got the school lunch providers that are on board; athletes and the entertainment industry engaged, as well as elected officials in Congress and around the nation that, yes, if we're working with parents who ultimately have the responsibility that we can move the ball.

JIM LEHRER: What about this word, "obesity?" It's been suggested that that's a very accusatory, negative word. It's not a comforting word at all.

MICHELLE OBAMA: No, not at all.

JIM LEHRER: Do you use it that way when you—

MICHELLE OBAMA: Well, you use it to describe the issue because the trends are obesity-related trends: 30 percent, or one in three of our kids, are overweight or obese; that's a real statistic. So it's a real word that's important to describe the problem. We're spending over $140 billion a year on this country dealing with obesity-related illnesses like heart disease and cancer and type-2 diabetes.

So you have to use the word to talk about the reality of the situation. But I agree; this isn't about looks. And it's not about weight. It's about how our kids feel. And those are really the implications of the problem and the words that tell a fuller picture of the challenges that we face; you know, kids struggling in ways that they didn't a generation ago. . . .

OBAMA, MICHELLE. "MICHELLE OBAMA: TEAM EFFORT NEEDED TO HALT CHILDHOOD OBESITY." INTERVIEW WITH JIM LEHRER ON *PBS NEWSHOUR*, FEBRUARY 9, 2010. HTTP://WWW.PBS.ORG/NEWSHOUR/BB/HEALTH/JAN-JUNE10/FIRSTLADY_02-09.HTML (ACCESSED NOVEMBER 29, 2010).

SEE ALSO *Calories; Diet and Cancer; Diet and Diabetes; Diet and Heart Disease; Diet and Hypertension; Dietary Guidelines for Americans; Dietary Reference Intakes; Fast Food; Food Packaging; French Paradox; Junk Food; Processed Foods; School Lunch Reform; Standard American Diet and Changing American Diet.*

BIBLIOGRAPHY

Books

Davies, H. Dele, Hiram E. Fitzgerald, and Vasiliki Mousouli. *Obesity in Childhood and Adolescence.* Child Psychology and Mental Health series. Westport, CT: Praeger, 2008.

Fairburn, Christopher G., and Kelly D. Brownell, eds. *Eating Disorders and Obesity: A Comprehensive Handbook.* New York: Guilford Press, 2005.

Kopelman, Peter G., Ian D. Caterson, and William H. Dietz, eds. *Clinical Obesity in Adults and Children.* Malden, MA: Blackwell, 2005.

Lopez, Gail Woodward, ed. *Obesity: Dietary and Developmental Influences.* Boca Raton, FL: CRC/Taylor & Francis, 2006.

Mela, David J., ed. *Food, Diet, and Obesity.* Boca Raton, FL: CRC Press, 2005.

Oliver, J. Eric. *Fat Politics: The Real Story Behind America's Obesity Epidemic.* Oxford, UK: Oxford University Press, 2006.

Wolin, Kathleen Y., and Jennifer M. Petrelli. *Obesity.* Santa Barbara, CA: Greenwood Press, 2009.

Web Sites

"Obesity." *National Institutes of Health (NIH).* http://health.nih.gov/topic/Obesity (accessed November 3, 2010).

"Obesity and Genetics." *Centers for Disease Control and Prevention (CDC).* http://www.cdc.gov/genomics/resources/diseases/obesity/index.htm (accessed November 3, 2010).

"Obesity and Overweight." *Centers for Disease Control and Prevention (CDC).* http://www.cdc.gov/nccdphp/dnpa/obesity/index.htm (accessed November 3, 2010).

"Obesity and Overweight." *World Health Organization (WHO).* http://www.who.int/mediacentre/factsheets/fs311/en/index.html (accessed November 3, 2010).

Oral Health and Diet

■ Introduction

The connection between oral health and the body is one that often goes unnoticed, but the correlation between dental diseases, illness, and quality of life is something that should not be overlooked. Teeth are a unique part of the body because they enable humans to talk, eat, and chew food, and they play a role in individual appearance. When dentists examine a person, the presence or absence of gingivitis, enamel erosion, tooth loss, gum disease, and sores in the mouth can reveal a lot about that person's medical history and health. The World Health Organization (WHO) reports that oral diseases, heart disease, cancer, chronic respiratory diseases, and diabetes all share the same risk factors. Diet contributes significantly to overall dental health. Oral hygiene practices such as flossing, using fluoridated water, brushing daily, and being frequently examined also play a role in protecting people from dental diseases.

Over the past few decades, highly developed or industrialized countries have witnessed a decrease in the number of children with cavities or dental caries. In contrast, children living in lower-income and developing countries often experience more tooth pain, dental caries, tooth loss, and gum or periodontal disease. Researchers have linked these high rates of oral disease to the nutritional transition that some countries may be experiencing. Risk factors for developing oral disease include having an unhealthy diet, smoking or tobacco use, heavy alcohol use, and poor oral hygiene. Dental diseases are a major public health issue that can be addressed through proper education about prevention.

■ Historical Background and Scientific Foundations

Historically, little attention has been paid to oral health status because many other areas of health were given priority. The progression of dental status in the United States illustrates the achievements in this area of health and how oral health has become much more accepted. One hundred years ago, tooth loss at the age of 40 was a normal part of aging for most Americans. Tooth pain and infections were typical aspects of getting older.

After a system of public health promotion and disease prevention was established through the Public Health Service Act of 1944, awareness began to increase about the impact of oral health on quality of life and well-being. In 1945 the fluoridation of community drinking water was introduced as a way to reach much of the American population and help to prevent cavities. When added to water, fluoride works to strengthen a child's tooth enamel, protecting against dental caries. For individuals with weakened or eroded enamel, fluoridated water can repair this damage. By the 1970s, most Americans suffered from significantly fewer cavities than had been the case in the early twentieth century. Researchers also began to realize that cavities and oral diseases are caused by various types of bacterial infections.

The role of diet and nutrition in oral health and disease is something that has been thoroughly researched over the years. Studies show that during the early years of life a child's nutritional status can affect the development of the teeth and enamel. If a child is deficient in vitamins A and D, the child's teeth will be more susceptible to erosion and subsequently dental caries. As cavities develop in the presence of both bacteria and sugar, regular brushing and flossing can prevent cavities even if a person eats large amounts of sugars. According to a study in the *American Journal of Clinical Nutrition*, undernourished populations experience accelerated periodontal disease. Another 2004 study validates the impact of the nutrition transition on oral health, finding that the combination of undernutrition and an increase in the amount of sugar consumed can make a person more susceptible to cavities.

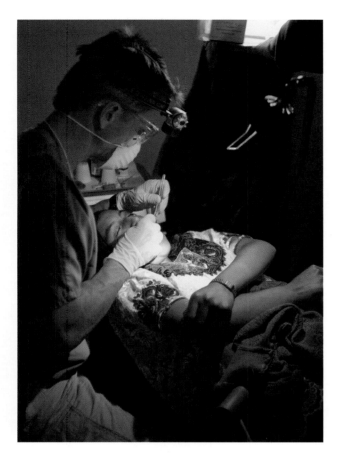

A medical mission volunteer dentist fills cavities of a young Mayan woman in a Cuchamatanes Mountain community in Guatemala.
© *Tina Manley / Central America / Alamy.*

■ Impacts and Issues

It is widely recognized that oral health is a mirror of an individual's general health. Studies are showing that tooth loss in older women can be a sign of osteoporosis or low bone density. Individuals who suffer from anxiety and post-traumatic stress can develop canker sores and lesions. They may also be at higher risk of developing cavities and periodontal disease. The mild form of gum disease, gingivitis, can put a person at risk for developing heart disease because sometimes bacteria around the teeth and gums can enter the bloodstream, contributing to inflammation and plaque formation in the coronary arteries.

The high costs associated with dental exams and procedures around the world have greatly contributed to disparities in oral health. The WHO estimates that in some highly developed countries, oral caries are a rare occurrence, whereas in most of the world, 60 to 90 percent of all adults and children have dental caries (cavities). In addition, access to dental services in many low-income or developing countries is rare. The WHO also lists poor living conditions, low education levels, and lack of traditions or beliefs that support oral health as characteristics that put individuals at high risk for developing oral disease.

One of the most powerful tools for improving oral health status is preventative education. By learning to brush their teeth, floss regularly, and eat a balanced diet, young children are able to develop healthier oral habits. These improved oral habits can act as a safeguard against the development of diseases such as cancer and diabetes later in life.

SEE ALSO *Undernutrition; Vitamins and Minerals; Water.*

BIBLIOGRAPHY

Books

Palmer, Carole A. *Diet and Nutrition in Oral Health.* Upper Saddle River, NJ: Pearson, 2007.

Wilson, Michael. *Food Constituents and Oral Health: Current Status and Future Prospects.* Oxford: Woodhead, 2009.

Periodicals

Auad, Sheyla, and Paula S. Moynihan. "Nutrition & Oral Health—Diet and Dental Erosion." *Quintessence International* (February 2007): 130–133.

DePaola, Dominick, and Riva Touger-Decker. "Nutrition and Dental Medicine: Where Is the Connection?" *Journal of the American Dental Association* 137, no. 9 (2006): 1208–1210.

Medina, Widman, et al. "Dental Caries in 6–12-Year-Old Indigenous and Non-Indigenous Schoolchildren in the Amazon Basin of Ecuador." *Brazilian Dental Journal* 19, no. 1 (2008): 83–86.

"Methodological Issues in Oral Health/Diet Linkage." *Dental Abstracts* 54, no. 5 (2009): 262–263.

Morgan, Maria, et al. "A Content Analysis of Children's Television Advertising: Focus on Food and Oral Health." *Public Health Nutrition* 12, no. 6 (2009): 748–755.

Moynihan, Paula, et al. "Researching the Impact of Oral Health on Diet and Nutritional Status: Methodological Issues." *Journal of Dentistry* 37, no. 4 (2009): 237–249.

Touger-Decker, Riva. "Diet, Cardiovascular Disease and Oral Health: Promoting Health and Reducing Risk." *Journal of the American Dental Association* 141, no. 2 (2010): 167–170.

Web Sites

"Global Consultation on Oral Health through Fluoride." *World Health Organization (WHO).* http://www.who.int/oral_health/events/Global_consultation/en/index.html (accessed October 15, 2010).

"Oral Health." *World Health Organization (WHO).* http://www.who.int/mediacentre/factsheets/fs318/en/index.html (accessed October 15, 2010).

Tiffany Imes

Organic Foods Production Act of 1990

■ Introduction

The Organic Foods Production Act of 1990 (OFPA) is a law that regulates the production, processing, handling, packaging, and labeling of organic agricultural products in the United States. The OFPA establishes clear, national standards for organic agriculture and aids consumers by requiring simpler, standardized labeling of organic products. It also protects consumers and legitimate organic producers by setting fines and punishments for producers and marketers that make false or misleading claims about organic agricultural products.

Generally, organic products do not contain ingredients produced with the use of synthetic fertilizers, synthetic pesticides, or other chemicals. The OFPA and subsequent regulations require that all organic producers and handlers be certified under the standards set forth under the OFPA and the U.S. Department of Agriculture (USDA). Once organic producers and handlers have been certified, they may produce and market agricultural goods as "organic," if the good meets all organic production and handling requirements.

■ Historical Background and Scientific Foundations

Prior to the passage of the Organic Foods Production Act (OFPA), the United States did not have a uniform standard for certifying or labeling organic foods. Organic agriculture in the United States originated in the 1970s as a small group of consumers began demanding organic produce and meat. Without any regulation over what foods could be labeled organic, unscrupulous growers and retailers began selling non-organic goods as organic products. In 1973 Oregon passed the nation's first organic certification law. Other states followed during the 1970s and 1980s.

By 1990, 22 states had passed organic certification laws, but the laws varied widely. Some state certification laws allowed private certification agencies to certify organic food, whereas some state laws did not provide for organic certification at all. In states without organic certification laws, producers and retailers could make claims about organic food without any certification or oversight. Even among products certified by state agencies, products labeled as "organic" could contain between 20 and 100 percent organically sourced ingredients. This system of multiple organic certification standards confused consumers. Organic producers and consumer advocacy groups called for the creation of a uniform, national organic certification system.

The U.S. Congress responded by including the OFPA in the Food, Agriculture, Conservation, and Trade Act (FACT) of 1990, a five-year omnibus farm bill that addresses agriculture and other issues under the purview of the U.S. Department of Agriculture (USDA). OFPA establishes national standards for the production, handling, and labeling of organic food in the United States. The Act allows states to maintain organic certification programs that are stricter than the federal standard with the approval of the USDA, but states may not discriminate against products that qualify under the federal organic standard.

To advise the USDA on standards for the National Organic Program (NOP), the OFPA established the National Organic Standards Board (NOSB), a program to establish and oversee organic certification standards. The NOSB consulted the public and industry representatives in developing organic certification standards for the NOP. In April 1995 the NOSB adopted a definition of "organic," which states: "Organic agriculture is an ecological production management system that promotes and enhances biodiversity, biological cycles and soil biological activity. It is based on minimal use of off-farm inputs and on management practices that restore, maintain and enhance ecological harmony." Generally, under the NOP, organic products may not contain synthetic pesticides or fertilizers.

WORDS TO KNOW

ORGANIC AGRICULTURE: The production of food or fiber crops, livestock, or livestock-related products without the use of synthetic fertilizers, pesticides, or hormones.

SYNTHETIC FERTILIZER: Commercially-prepared chemical mixtures containing plant nutrients, such as nitrates, phosphates, and potassium.

SYNTHETIC PESTICIDE: Commercially-prepared chemical mixtures designed to kill or repel insects.

THIRD-PARTY CERTIFICATION: A system in which an organization independent of all the companies in a supply chain certifies that a good reaches particular standards or has particular attributes. Most international organic standards, fair trade standards, humane animal treatment standards, and claims of being not genetically modified, as well as a variety of environmental claims are certified using third-party certification.

■ Impacts and Issues

Under the OFPA, a producer or marketer may not label a product "organic" unless it meets all of the organic production and handling standards set forth by the NOP. The NOP requires the following organic certification requirements: production methods and materials must meet organic standards; production methods and materials must be clearly documented; and producers and handlers must maintain a paper trail that allows a product to be traced back to its production site.

The organic certification standards promulgated by the USDA under the OFPA require that all producers of organic crops and livestock and all subsequent handlers be certified. A "handler" is defined as any operation that "receives, processes, packages, or stores agricultural products." Exempted from the certification requirement are retailers, such as grocery stores, and small producers that engage in direct sales to consumers or retailers.

The NOSB definition of "organic" notes that organic agricultural practices cannot guarantee that all organic products will be free of synthetic fertilizers or pesticides, although NOP standards will attempt to "maintain the integrity of organic agricultural products." Under the OFPA, growers seeking organic certification for the production of crops must grow crops on land that has not had any prohibited substance applied during the previous three years. Organic farmers must maintain buffer zones between land used in organic production and land used for the production of conventional crops. Buffer zones are intended to minimize airborne synthetic fertilizers, pesticides, or other substances from neighboring fields.

A sign in a minneola citrus orchard states "Organic Farm: Please Do Not Spray: Watch Wind Speed and Direction." © *inga spence / Alamy.*

A vendor at a farmer's market in Boca Raton, Florida, displays vegetables bearing the USDA Organic label. © *Jeff Greenberg / Alamy.*

In addition, the USDA regulates livestock and related products, such as dairy products and eggs, under the OFPA. All organic livestock must be fed organic feed; use of growth hormones and the routine use of antibiotics in organic livestock are prohibited. Producers, however, may use synthetic vitamins and minerals on livestock. For organic meat, the OFPA processing requirements prohibit the use of nitrates, nitrites, or sulfites.

The OFPA also addresses the labeling of organic agricultural products. A product labeled "USDA organic" must contain at least 95 percent organic ingredients by weight, excluding water, salt, and air. All producers and handlers of the product and its components must be certified organic. In certain situations, the USDA allows producers and marketers to use the word "organic" on the labels of products that do not meet the 95 percent organic requirement. The front panel of a product label may claim that the product "contains organic ingredients" if the product contains more than 50 percent organic ingredients. Products that contain less than 50 percent organic ingredients may specify which ingredients are organic in the product's ingredient list.

■ Primary Source Connection

The Organic Foods Production Act of 1990 defines organic farming practices and creates minimum standards for certified organic production. It was established that the Act would be administered under the U.S. Department of Agriculture's Agricultural Marketing Service (AMS), which would create funding and a budget for administering the program.

Organic Foods Production Act of 1990

Title XXI of the Food, Agriculture, Conservation, and Trade Act of 1990 (Public Law 101-624)

Title XXI-Organic Certification

SEC. 2101. [7 U.S.C. 6501 note] SHORT TITLE. This title may be cited as the "Organic Foods Production Act of 1990."

SEC. 2102. [7 U.S.C. 6501] PURPOSES.

It is the purpose of this title—

(1) to establish national standards governing the marketing of certain agricultural products as organically produced products;

(2) to assure consumers that organically produced products meet a consistent standard; and

(3) to facilitate interstate commerce in fresh and processed food that is organically produced. . . .

SEC. 2105. [7 U.S.C. 6504] NATIONAL STANDARDS FOR ORGANIC PRODUCTION.

To be sold or labeled as an organically produced agricultural product under this title, an agricultural product shall—

(1) have been produced and handled without the use of synthetic chemicals, except as otherwise provided in this title;

(2) except as otherwise provided in this title and excluding livestock, not be produced on land to which any prohibited substances, including synthetic chemicals, have been applied during the 3 years immediately preceding the harvest of the agricultural products; and

(3) be produced and handled in compliance with an organic plan agreed to by the producer and handler of such product and the certifying agent.

SEC. 2106. [7 U.S.C. 6505] COMPLIANCE REQUIREMENTS.

(a) DOMESTIC PRODUCTS.—

(1) IN GENERAL.-On or after October 1, 1993—

(A) a person may sell or label an agricultural product as organically produced only if such product is produced and handled in accordance with this title; and

(B) no person may affix a label to, or provide other market information concerning, an agricultural product if such label or information implies, directly or indirectly, that such product is produced and handled using organic methods, except in accordance with this title.

(2) USDA STANDARDS AND SEAL.-A label affixed, or other market information provided, in accordance with paragraph (1) may indicate that the agricultural product meets Department of Agriculture standards for organic production and may incorporate the Department of Agriculture seal.

(b) IMPORTED PRODUCTS.-Imported agricultural products may be sold or labeled as organically produced if the Secretary determines that such products have been produced and handled under an organic certification program that provides safeguards and guidelines governing the production and handling of such products that are at least equivalent to the requirements of this title.

U.S. CONGRESS. *ORGANIC GOODS PRODUCTION ACT OF 1990.* WASHINGTON, DC: U.S. GOVERNMENT PRINTING OFFICE, 2005.

SEE ALSO *Agroecology; Farm-to-Table Movement; International Federation of Organic Agriculture Movements; Organics; Pesticides and Pesticide Residue; Phytochemicals (Phytonutrients); Produce Traceability; Slow Food Movement; Sustainable Agriculture; U.S. Department of Agriculture (USDA).*

BIBLIOGRAPHY

Books

Bingen, Jim, and Lawrence Busch. *Agricultural Standards: The Shape of the Global Food and Fiber System.* Dordrecht, The Netherlands: Springer, 2006.

Rawson, Jean M. *Organic Agriculture in the United States: Program and Policy Issues.* CRS report for Congress, RL31595. Washington, DC: Congressional Research Service, 2008.

Williams, Elizabeth M., and Stephanie J. Carter. *The A–Z Encyclopedia of Food Controversies and the Law.* Santa Barbara, CA: Greenwood, 2010.

Web Sites

"National Organic Program." *U.S. Department of Agriculture (USDA).* http://www.ams.usda.gov/AMSv1.0/nop (accessed September 25, 2010).

"Organic Farming." *U.S. Environmental Protection Agency (EPA).* http://www.epa.gov/agriculture/torg.html (accessed September 15, 2010).

Joseph P. Hyder

Organics

■ Introduction

Organic products are grown or raised using only natural inputs, using no chemical fertilizers or pesticides. Organic growers rely on maintaining the natural fertility of soil through crop rotations and by applying amendments such as manure, compost, and naturally occurring minerals. Pest problems are addressed by introducing or encouraging the appearance of beneficial insects, by using disease resistant varieties, and through occasional use of approved chemicals.

Organic meats are producing by raising animals using principles similar to those used by organic fruit and vegetable growers. Organically raised animals are fed only organic feeds, are not given antibiotics or other drugs to promote growth, and are usually raised under humane conditions without overcrowding.

Organic agriculture is designed to eliminate the problems caused by massive use of fertilizers and pesticides. By rotating crops, growing cover crops periodically, and plowing the cover crops into the soil to replenish it, organic farmers are able to avoid chemical fertilizers completely. Minimally processed mineral fertilizers derived from rock may be used in place of highly concentrated and refined chemical fertilizers. Sulfur dust or other natural substances are used for pest control in place of chemical pesticides. Organic agriculture also rejects the use of genetically modified organisms in any aspect of food or commodity production.

Organic farming (to include the raising of food animals) has two major goals. One is to provide high quality, healthful food that is as pure as possible. The other is to farm in a sustainable way that preserves the environment.

■ Historical Background and Scientific Foundations

Organic farming is the oldest kind of farming practiced by humans. The era of chemical fertilizers and industrial scale farming began only slightly more than 100 years ago. Prior to that time, the only way to fertilize crops was with fish or other animal parts, animal manures, and plant waste. Alternatively, entire communities could migrate to new areas when the local soil lost fertility.

Although industrial scale farming driven by technological developments in both chemistry and engineering became the dominant food production model from the mid-twentieth century onward, there has always been a segment of the population committed to the organic approach. Small-scale and family farmers are close to the land they work, and for them sustainable agriculture is not a new idea. "Back-to-the-land" movements have come and gone numerous times over the centuries with notable occurrences during the early 1920s and 1930s, and again in the 1960s and 1970s. The implementation of sustainable agricultural methods along with a desire for self sufficiency have always been a hallmark of such movements, and the current interest in healthy foods and environmental awareness can be considered a related phenomenon.

The term *organic* as used with respect to agriculture was first popularized by Walter E. C. James (1896–1982, Lord Northbourne) in England in the 1940s and by Jerome I. Rodale (1898–1971) in the United States in the 1950s. Although the scientific community greeted the claimed benefits of organic and sustainable methods with skepticism early on, this attitude began to change as research confirmed the relationship between the condition of a soil and its year-on-year productivity. Scientists came to recognize that when the organic content of a soil decreases, its ability to retain nutrients and support a healthy, diverse microbial flora is damaged. This results in eventual nutrient depletion, which leads many farmers into a continuing cycle of chemical fertilizer use.

The majority of the fruit, vegetables, beef, pork, and chicken consumed in the United States continues to be produced using non-organic methods, but more and more land comes into organic production every year. California is the state with the most organic acreage, with Minnesota, Montana, North Dakota, Texas, and

WORDS TO KNOW

CERTIFIED ORGANIC: In the United States, the states manage and regulate the use of the label "certified organic" and associated claims by supervising programs designed to give consumers confidence that products claimed to be organic meet certain standards.

ORGANIC CHEMICAL: Any compound containing carbon is technically referred to as an organic compound, including most chemical pesticides. This use of the term organic should not be confused its use with respect to farming methods.

ORGANIC FARMING: The use of natural and unrefined fertilizers, physical methods, and natural pest controls to produce foods without the use of chemical fertilizers and pesticides.

SUSTAINABLE AGRICULTURE: Agricultural practices designed to preserve the long-term viability of the land and its inhabitants.

THIRD-PARTY CERTIFICATION: A system in which an organization independent of all the companies in a supply chain certifies that a good reaches particular standards or has particular attributes. Most international organic standards, fair trade standards, humane animal treatment standards, and claims of being not genetically modified, as well as a variety of environmental claims are certified using third-party certification.

Wisconsin also having large certified organic acreages. Although the total U.S. acreage under organic production was less than 1 percent in 2008, it grew by 15 percent per year from 2003 to 2008.

Some crops have proven so successful in organic culture that they have a much higher than average portion produced organically. Approximately 25 percent of the U.S. carrot crop and 8 percent of the lettuce crop is organic.

Organic livestock operations continue to expand with about 3 percent of dairy cows and 1.5 percent of egg-producing hens raised under organic conditions. Organically produced pork, turkey, bison, ostrich, and elk are also available in some stores.

■ Impacts and Issues

The specific meaning of what counts as organic or biological or natural varies among the various standards in different parts of the world. Almost all of the commonly used organic standards rely on third-party certification. This means that a regulator or an organization, independent of all the farms or companies in a supply chain, certifies that the farms or the products meet the organic food standard. Certified organic production and sales have grown tremendously since the 1980s when the first third-party certifiers started working on a more commercial basis. Many governments have also enacted national standards for what may be classified as organic. In 1990 the Organic Foods Production Act (OFPA) was enacted by the U.S. Congress to establish national standards for the production, handling, and labeling of organic food in the United States.

Consumer interest in organic products has grown steadily. Although the recession that began in 2008 has slowed growth of the organic sector, the market for organic and sustainably produced food is expected to continue growing at a rate of about 2 to 5 percent per year. In 2009 the total organic market was valued at a bit more than $51 billion, up from $25 billion just five years earlier.

Although non-organic farm productivity increased dramatically with the advent of chemical fertilizers that allowed for controlled applications of essential plant nutrients, the productivity boon has come at a cost. Fertilizer runoff from soil can contaminate both surface waters and groundwater, leading to explosive algal growth and severe damage to aquatic ecosystems. Water supplies contaminated with fertilizer become unfit for human consumption. The use of large quantities of pesticides has resulted in exposure of virtually all consumers to low levels of pesticides in commercially grown fruits and vegetables. Of particular concern are systemic herbicides and insecticides in the tissues of plants. Systemic pesticides cannot be washed off.

For farmers, the advantages of organic farming include reduced pesticide and fertilizer costs, higher market prices, better soil structure and conservation, and in some cases reduced water use. Side benefits include reduced environmental pollution from chemical fertilizers, better integration of farmlands with natural ecosystems, improved prospects for long-term sustainability of agricultural land, and less use of petroleum products for agrochemical production.

From the consumer's perspective, organic products (especially certified organics) offer a choice in what kinds of foods to eat. They also provide for the reduction or even elimination of possibly harmful organic chemicals from the diet and the opportunity to support a sustainable agriculture system.

In many (but not all) cases, organic foods cost more to both produce and to purchase at the retail level. This is because sustainable farming is often more labor-intensive, and crop yields are often not as high as those achieved using highly mechanized and chemically supported methods. The process towards organic certification is also time consuming and expensive for a farmer.

Organic farms are generally small and are not able to meet the food needs of the world's population. They are, however, well positioned to supply local markets with fresh produce on a seasonal basis. Large traditional farming operations can use their economy of scale to transport food over longer distances more efficiently

An organic produce stand sells seasonal fresh fruit and produce from the Center for Urban Agriculture at Fairview Gardens, one of the oldest organic farms in California. Located on over 12 acres, the 100-year-old farm provides the community with organic fruits and vegetables and through educational programs and public outreach demonstrate the economic viability of sustainable agricultural methods. *© Ambient Images Inc. / Alamy.*

than small organic farms. Paradoxically, as organic farms scale up to achieve greater production, they often rely more on mechanization and monoculture (growing one crop), which makes them very similar to non-organic farms in how they operate. Organic farms generally use more land to produce less than non-organic farms.

Despite these disadvantages, organic farming continues to expand. A major reason is that organic produce often tastes better and sometimes has higher nutritional content than non-organic produce. Many consumers consider such taste and nutritional advantages worth the additional cost.

The interest in organics has spawned innovation in other sectors besides food production. All-organic restaurants have arisen to take advantage of the increasing availability of more organically produced fruits, vegetables, meats, and dairy products. Organic restaurants cater to the tastes of consumers who want to eat strictly organic but not have to prepare all their own meals. In addition, organic non-food products such as cotton, linen, pet food, flowers, and cleaners are a small but growing market segment.

As the market for organic goods continues to grow, the selection of products will increase, and prices will continue to fall. This should result in a positive feedback loop creating even more growth in the organic sector. Organic production will probably never be able to compete on price with factory-scale non-organic mass production, but as the price gap shrinks, organically produced foods and other commodities could become an increasingly attractive option for environmentally and health-conscious consumers.

SEE ALSO *Agribusiness; Agroecology; Alice Waters: California and New American Cuisine; Community Supported Agriculture (CSAs); Ecological Impacts of Various World Diets; Edible Schoolyard Movement; Ethical Issues in Agriculture; Family Farms; Farm-to-Table Movement; Humane Animal Farming; International Federation of Organic Agriculture Movements; Locavore; Michael Pollan: Linking Food and Environmental Journalism; Organic Foods Production Act of 1990; Pesticides and Pesticide Residue; Slow Food Movement; Sustainable Agriculture.*

A farmers' market vendor inspects produce before opening his Twinn Bridges Farms stand at the Beaches Greenmarket in Florida. In addition to organic and heirloom variety produce, Twinn Bridges specializes in non-pasteurized eggs from free-roaming chickens. *Adrienne Lerner / Lerner & Lerner / LernerMedia Global Photos.*

BIBLIOGRAPHY

Books

Burke, Cindy. *To Buy or Not to Buy Organic: What You Need to Know to Choose the Healthiest, Safest, Most Earth-Friendly Food.* New York: Marlowe & Company, 2007.

Lappé, Anna, and Bryant Terry. *Grub: Ideas for an Urban Organic Kitchen.* New York: Jeremy P. Tarcher/Penguin, 2006.

Perry, Luddene, and Dan Schultz. *A Field Guide to Buying Organic.* New York: Bantam Books, 2005.

Ronald, Pamela C., and Raoul W. Adamchak. *Tomorrow's Table: Organic Farming, Genetics, and the Future of Food.* New York: Oxford University Press, 2008.

Valentin, Rachel. *Transition into Organic Foods.* Montclair, NJ: Lehcar, 2004.

Weinstein, Jay. *The Ethical Gourmet.* New York: Broadway Books, 2006.

Periodicals

Dangour, Alan D., et al. "Nutritional Quality of Organic Foods: A Systematic Review." *The American Journal of Clinical Nutrition* 90, no. 3 (2009): 680–685.

Rich, Deborah. "Not All Apples Are Created Equal: The Latest Science on Organic Foods." *Earth Island Journal* 23, no. 1 (2008): 26–30.

Web Sites

"National Organic Program." *U.S. Department of Agriculture (USDA).* http://www.ams.usda.gov/AMSv1.0/ams.fetchTemplateData.do?template=TemplateA&navID=NationalOrganicProgram&leftNav=NationalOrganicProgram&page=NOPNationalOrganicProgramHome&acct=AMSPW (accessed October 17, 2010).

"Organic Farming." *U.S. Environmental Protection Agency (EPA).* http://www.epa.gov/agriculture/torg.html (accessed October 17, 2010).

Organic.org. http://www.organic.org/ (accessed October 17, 2010).

Philip McIntosh

Paleolithic Diet

Introduction

Paleolithic diets (also known as paleo diets), primal diets, origin diets, and other nutritional regimes based on a mixture of popular and scientific ideas about ancestral human diets have become popular over the last few decades. Books, Internet discussions, and media accounts of "caveman diets" have multiplied, particularly since 2007. These primarily low-carbohydrate food plans are based on the premise that the healthiest foods for people in the early twenty-first century are those that were consumed by the hunter-gatherers of the past. Most paleo diet advocates argue that modern nutrition is dangerously out of step with human physiology and biochemistry, which evolved during the 2.6 million years before the Neolithic period. After the Neolithic Revolution, which occurred fairly recently in human history (in different areas between 12,000 to 2,000 years ago), agriculture added a few grains, tubers, and legumes to human dietary staples. The Industrial Revolution brought about even greater changes in modern diets over the last few hundred years. New processing techniques, increased trade, and agricultural specialization have made highly refined carbohydrates, sugars, and vegetable fats more commonly consumed than ever before. Although all paleo diets attempt to recreate prehistoric human subsistence, they vary a great deal in their use of the archaeological and anthropological evidence for ancient diets; the types of foods that are forbidden; and recommended amounts and ratios of fruits, vegetables, meat, fat, and fiber.

Historical Background and Scientific Foundations

Paleo diet enthusiasts point to Canadian anthropologist Vilhjalmur Stefansson (1879–1962), whose adventures, in which he subsisted entirely on meat and fat in the Arctic, were published in *Harper's Magazine* in 1935–1936, as one of their intellectual pioneers. Another early forerunner was Weston A. Price (1870–1948), an American dentist who traveled to Switzerland, Africa, Polynesia, Scotland, and South America and published *Nutrition and Physical Degeneration* in 1939. Price's book, currently enjoying a resurgence in popularity, compared the nutrition and health of "Isolated and Modernized" peoples and advocated a diet high in raw milk, eggs, meat, fats, and nuts, with some fermented vegetables and cooked grains to prevent cavities and many of the other "diseases of civilization." American physician Walter L. Voegtlin (1904–?), who published *The Stone Age Diet* in 1975, was also concerned with the link between modern diet and chronic, primarily Western diseases. Voegtlin claimed that humans ate mostly meat and fat for at least two million years before the Neolithic, and that plants were eaten only when prehistoric hunter-gatherers were starving. His "Stone Age" diet prescribed mostly meats and fat with a few fruits and well-cooked vegetables.

More modern interest in paleo diets came in 1985, when doctors S. Boyd Eaton (1938–) and Melvin Konner published an influential article in *The New England Journal of Medicine* that used data from Konner's work among the !Kung of southern Africa to examine the link between "Paleolithic" and hunter-gatherer diets and health. They coauthored *The Paleolithic Prescription* with anthropologist Marjorie Shostak (1945–1996) in 1988, recommending whole grains, fruits, vegetables, and lean meats as the healthiest foods, most like those eaten during the Paleolithic. Their book was moderately popular through the 1990s, and spawned a number of related diet books. Increased interest in traditional foods, low-carbohydrate diets, and recommendations by athletes and fitness trainers produced a renewed surge of popularity for Paleolithic diets after 2007, with a variety of new "paleo lifestyle" books and popular accounts in *Maclean's* and *The New York Times*. Many paleo diet advocates reject foods that would not have been available during the Paleolithic period, including dairy products, most grains and legumes, all refined sugars and starches,

WORDS TO KNOW

HUNTER-GATHERERS: People whose subsistence depends on hunting and gathering or foraging for their food. In the Paleolithic period, all humans were hunter-gatherers, but in the early twenty-first century most of the world's population eats an agriculturally based diet.

PALEOLITHIC: Also known as the Stone Age, this archaeological period of time began when human ancestors and their relatives began making stone tools and ended with the transition to agriculture, from about 2.6 million to 12,000 years ago. The Paleolithic period is concurrent with the Pleistocene geological epoch and is followed by the transitional Epipaleolithic or Mesolithic periods and then the agricultural Neolithic period. The Paleolithic is often divided into overlapping subdivisions: the Lower (2.6 million–100,000 years ago), Middle (300,000–30,000 years), and Upper (50,000–12,000 years) Paleolithic.

SUBSISTENCE: Methods of obtaining food for survival. Subsistence was based on hunting and gathering until the Neolithic period, when plants and animals were domesticated.

Welsh cawl, a stew of meat and vegetables, typifies the Paleolithic diet, which consists of meats, fish and shellfish, vegetables, fruit, nuts, and roots. *Image copyright Monkey Business Images, 2010. Used under license from Shutterstock.com.*

and New World domesticates such as potatoes, corn, tomatoes, many beans, chocolate, and chili peppers.

■ Impacts and Issues

Popular paleo diets have been criticized for the flaws inherent in their scientific and logical assumptions, especially by primate anthropologist Katherine Milton. First of all, Milton demonstrates that humans are omnivores with few specific genetic adaptations to diet. She points out that there is no single modern or historic hunter-gatherer diet, and that many cultures with varied cuisines were free from Western diseases associated with affluence, whether their diets were based largely on wild meat, gathered plants, crops, or some combination of all of these foods. Furthermore, it is problematic for paleo dieters that meat from modern domesticated animals is considerably fattier than meat from wild animals. Some paleo dieters do eat fish, shellfish, bison, and venison instead of beef and pork, along with honey and some foraged wild plant foods. The amounts of fruits and vegetables (and carbohydrates in general) that they consume vary a great deal from diet to diet. It is also clear that people are much more sedentary in the early twenty-first century compared to Paleolithic hunter-gatherers, though some paleo dieters do attempt to emulate the levels of physical activity and even blood loss (through blood donation instead of accidents) that their ancestors may have experienced. Anthropologists have described the "noble savage" and primeval appeal of Paleolithic

diets, and it is notable that many of the current books that advocate meat-based paleo diets are aimed at men.

A few paleo diet advocates take archaeological and paleoanthropological evidence for Paleolithic subsistence into consideration. Many others are unfamiliar with the scientific evidence—and lack of evidence—for prehistoric diets. The Paleolithic period spanned at least 2.6 million years in Africa, Europe, Asia, and Australia, and hunter-gatherer diets were quite varied in both time and space. Plants are not as easily preserved as animal bone, so the archaeological record for subsistence has been heavily skewed towards meat consumption. Recent archaeological research shows much more proof for plant use in the Middle and Upper Paleolithic than previously found. Recent models of human evolution also emphasize the importance of plant foods, especially starchy tubers, during the Paleolithic period.

Although modern paleo diets may be very loosely based on actual Paleolithic diets, there is evidence that some paleo diets are healthier than those followed by many people in industrialized nations in the early twenty-first century. Many paleo diets are quite restrictive and expensive, however, and some of the most extreme paleo diets may lack sufficient carbohydrates, fiber, or nutrients. As with all diets, a basic understanding of nutrition and health is helpful when evaluating them. Unlike most diets, an understanding of anthropology, archaeology, and human evolution also proves useful when examining the foundations, claims, and historical accuracy of paleo diets.

SEE ALSO *Food Fads; History of Food and Man: From Hunter-Gatherer to Agriculture; Meats; Nutrition's Role in Human Evolution.*

BIBLIOGRAPHY

Books

Cordain, Loren. "Implications of Plio-Pleistocene Hominin Diets for Modern Humans." In *Evolution of the Human Diet: The Known, the Unknown, and the Unknowable,* edited by Peter S. Ungar. Oxford, UK, and New York: Oxford University Press, 2007.

Jones, Martin. "Moving North: Archaeobotanical Evidence for Plant Diet in Middle and Upper Paleolithic Europe." In *The Evolution of Hominin Diets: Integrating Approaches to the Study of Paleolithic Subsistence,* edited by Jean-Jacques Hublin and Michael P. Richards. Dordrecht: Springer, 2009.

Knight, Christine. "The Food Nature Intended You to Eat: Low-Carbohydrate Diets and Primitivist Philosophy." In *The Atkins Diet and Philosophy: Chewing the Fat with Kant and Nietzsche,* edited by Lisa Heldke, Kerri Mommer, and Cynthia Pineo. Chicago: Open Court, 2005.

Voegtlin, Walter L. *The Stone Age Diet: Based on In-depth Studies of Human Ecology and the Diet of Man.* New York: Vantage Press, 1975.

Periodicals

Lev, Efraim, Mordechai E. Kislev, and Ofar Bar-Yosef. "Mousterian Vegetal Food in Kebara Cave, Mt. Carmel." *Journal of Archaeological Science* 32, no. 3 (2005): 475–484.

Milton, Katherine. "Hunter-Gatherer Diets: A Different Perspective." *American Journal of Clinical Nutrition* 71, no. 3 (2000): 665–667.

Web Sites

Engelhart, Katie. "Cavemen Who Walk among Us." *Maclean's,* February 26, 2010. http://www2.macleans.ca/2010/02/26/cavemen-who-walk-among-us/ (accessed August 18, 2010).

Gowlett, J.A.J. "What Actually Was the Stone Age Diet?" *Journal of Nutritional and Environmental Medicine,* September 2003. http://pcwww.liv.ac.uk/~gowlett/GowlettCJNE_13_03_02.pdf (accessed August 18, 2010).

Sandra L. Dunavan

Paralytic Shellfish Poisoning

■ Introduction

Paralytic shellfish poisoning refers to the illness that can strike those who consume certain types of shellfish that are contaminated with a neurotoxin produced during the growth of certain marine microorganisms. The toxin, which is not destroyed by the heat of cooking, produces symptoms that can be relatively mild (e.g., tingling or numbness around the lips) or more pronounced (e.g., speech and coordination difficulties). In extreme cases, the paralysis of muscles that function in respiration can be lethal. Monitoring of shellfish marine environments including aquaculture facilities is necessary to ensure that commercial shellfish do not pose a danger to consumers. When necessary, affected fisheries cease operations until the safety of the shellfish is verified. The economic loss to operators can be considerable.

■ Historical Background and Scientific Foundations

Paralytic shellfish poisoning is typically associated with bivalve shellfish such as oysters, scallops, clams, and cockles that are constructed of two shells that are hinged together and that feed on a microscopic form of marine algae called plankton by filtering seawater through a gill-like structure. Whereas the trapping of plankton by the filter is desirable, noxious compounds and disease-causing bacteria and viruses can also accumulate if they are present in the water. In the case of paralytic shellfish poisoning, the explosive growth in marine water of specific species of dinoflagellates and cyanobacteria, which can be evident as a discoloration of the water that is commonly dubbed red tide, results in the filtering of high numbers of these organisms. The organisms contain a neurotoxin called saxitoxin (named for *Saxidomus giganteus*, the species of clam from which the compound was first isolated). The subsequent consumption of the saxitoxin-laden shellfish causes paralytic shellfish poisoning.

Saxitoxin can also build up in the soft green material (tomalley) in lobsters and crabs. The toxin has also been reported in puffer fish and tilapia. Less commonly, other toxins are involved, including neosaxiton and four types of a toxin known as gonyautoxin.

Depending on the local environmental conditions, particularly the water temperature, the growth of saxitoxin-containing dinoflagellates and cyanobacteria can be exuberant, resulting in huge numbers of the organisms in marine water. Typically, conditions in the summer months favor this explosive growth (May through August in northern latitudes, especially along the east coast of the United States and Canada). Shellfish contamination can occur when this growth occurs near the coastline, where shellfish typically dwell, or in waters housing shellfish aquaculture facilities.

Saxitoxin dissolves more readily in lipids (fats) than in water. Following ingestion of the contaminated seafood, saxitoxin is readily absorbed into nerve and muscle cells of the gastrointestinal and respiratory tracts. The toxin also enters epithelial cells in the lips and adjacent tissues that contact the shellfish during eating. By binding to channels in nerve and muscle tissue that are responsible for the movement of sodium in and out of the cells, saxitoxin can block the process by which a cell generates a nerve impulse. As a result, signal transmission between adjacent nerve cells is blocked.

Saxitoxin-contaminated seafood is difficult to detect, as the toxin has no taste or odor. Also, the toxin is not readily destroyed by heat or acid, and so can survive food preparation (i.e., steam cooking of shellfish).

Symptoms of paralytic shellfish poisoning can begin within minutes of ingestion of the contaminated food, or may take hours to appear. Relatively minor symptoms include tingling or numbness of the area around the lips, with subsequent spread to the rest of the face and the neck. Extremities (fingers and toes) can be similarly affected. Some people develop a headache and dizziness. In more severe cases, the affected person may develop speech and coordination difficulties, arm/leg weakness, rapid pulse, and breathing difficulty. In very severe cases, paralysis of respiratory muscles can stop breathing; without prompt treatment the afflicted will die.

The responsible toxins are detected by tests including radioimmunoassay and enzyme-linked immunosorbent assay (commonly known as ELISA) that use antibody to the toxins to detect the presence of the toxin protein. Whereas the tests are accurate and can detect low levels of saxitoxin, they require transport of samples to a laboratory, technical expertise in test performance and interpretation, and communication of results to local officials for any follow-up action. Typically, when an outbreak of paralytic shellfish poisoning is identified, the affected water is closed to fishing until testing determines that the shellfish are toxin-free.

■ Impacts and Issues

Paralytic shellfish poisoning kills 1 to 12 percent of people who are sickened during an outbreak. For the survivors, the neurological damage can persist following recovery from the initial illness. In 2008 in the

United States, more than 800 cases of paralytic shellfish poisoning were reported.

From an economic standpoint, the discovery of contaminated shellfish typically necessitates the closure of the affected fishery or aquaculture facility. If repeated testing of shellfish continues to detect the toxin, the closure may last for weeks. This will have an obvious economic impact on the operator, as shipments to customers will cease until approval for resumption of sales is granted. As well, the reputation of the operation can suffer, especially if repeated incidents occur. Although the basis of the incidents may be out of the control of

A sign in Scotland warns against collecting shellfish because of potential paralytic shellfish poisoning. © *Paul Glendell / Alamy.*

the operator, such as an abnormally warm summer that increases water temperature, the affected operation will bear the brunt of the lasting damage.

On a larger scale, the affected region can also suffer from a downturn in tourism in the aftermath of an outbreak. A related example involves the Canadian province of Prince Edward Island. There, a 1987 outbreak of a related shellfish disease caused by another toxin (domoic acid) killed three people and sickened more than 100. The shutdown of the shellfish industry in late 1987 and into 1988 cost the province millions. Tourism suffered during the next several years, which was a significant economic blow to the province, as its economy relies heavily on tourist dollars. Other outbreaks of domoic acid have occurred on the coasts of Washington state, Oregon, and California, sometimes resulting in year-long beach and fishery closures. A closure of razor clam fisheries in Washington state in 2002–2003 alone is estimated by the Washington Fish and Wildlife Service to have represented a $10.4 million loss to the economies of Washington's coastal communities.

An outbreak will also affect the market price of shellfish: The scarcity of the product drives the price of the untainted shellfish higher. In a 2004 outbreak that occurred along the New England coast, for example, market prices for clams increased by 200 percent.

Studies by institutions including Woods Hole Oceanographic Institution have demonstrated an increasing number of incidents of red tide along the eastern and western seaboards of North America from 1991 onward. One suggested explanation has been the warming of the tropical Atlantic Ocean as a consequence of climate change and the subsequent ferrying of the warm waters northward via the Gulf Stream. A variety of climatic models consistently predict that, even if all human sources of atmospheric warming could be immediately discontinued, the influence of climate change would not diminish until the next century. The influence of climate change on algal and bacterial blooms that drive paralytic shellfish poisoning could, therefore, be a fact of life for the same extended period.

Woods Hole researchers have developed a forecasting model that has been accurate in predicting algal blooms in coastal waters in the New England region. If the model proves to be more generally accurate, it may help protect consumers from inadvertent consumption of tainted shellfish and reveal the environmental factors that help drive the occurrence of the blooms.

SEE ALSO *Aquaculture and Fishery Resources; Climate Change and Agriculture; Food Webs and Food Chains; Foodborne Diseases; Gulf Oil Spill: Food Impacts; Seafood.*

BIBLIOGRAPHY

Books

Botana, Luis M. *Seafood and Freshwater Toxins: Pharmacology, Physiology, and Detection.* Hoboken, NJ: Taylor & Francis, 2008.

Rees, Gareth J. G. *Safe Management of Shellfish and Harvest Waters.* London: International Water Association, 2010.

Periodicals

Etheridge, Stacey M. "Paralytic Shellfish Poisoning: Seafood Safety and Human Health Perspectives." *Toxicon* 56, no. 2 (2010): 108–122.

Fortuine, Robert. "Paralytic Shellfish Poisoning in the North Pacific: Two Historical Accounts and Implications for Today. 1975." *Alaska Medicine* 49, no. 2 (2007): 65–69.

Web Sites

"Marine Toxins." *Centers for Disease Control and Prevention (CDC).* http://www.cdc.gov/ncidod/dbmd/diseaseinfo/marinetoxins_g.htm (accessed October 4, 2010).

U.S. National Library of Medicine. "Poisoning: Fish and Shellfish." *Medline Plus.* http://www.nlm.nih.gov/medlineplus/ency/article/002851.htm (accessed October 4, 2010).

U.S. National Office for Harmful Algal Blooms at Woods Hole Oceanographic Institution. "Paralytic Shellfish Poisoning." *Harmful Algae Page.* http://www.whoi.edu/redtide/page.do?pid=14279 (accessed October 4, 2010).

Brian Douglas Hoyle

Pasta

■ Introduction

Pasta (or noodles) is a processed food made from flour and water that may have originated in China in ancient times. Pasta can be made in two primary forms, dried and fresh. Durum wheat is the primary ingredient in Italian-style pastas and dried pasta. Most often, pasta is cooked by boiling it in salted water, although a variety of other cooking methods exist. Pasta is an extensively traded food commodity. The world's top pasta consumer is Italy, although many other countries consume large quantities of pasta. The convenience of pasta due to its quick cooking time is one reason for its popularity around the world. There are some health concerns about pasta, specifically about many pastas being made from refined flour, which usually lacks the fiber and nutrients found in a cereal grain's germ and bran.

■ Historical Background and Scientific Foundations

Pasta, a flour-based food often cooked in boiling water or broth, is an ancient example of a processed food. Debate on the origins of pasta abound with some pointing to evidence of what appears to be pasta in art by the Etruscans, a group that occupied the Tuscany region in the western part of Italy, a country in Southern Europe, as early as 400 BC. Even earlier, archeological evidence of noodles from China, made of millet, prove at least a 4,000-year old history of noodles and pasta. The story that Marco Polo (1254–1324) brought pasta to Italy from China during his journey appears to only be a myth because pasta was already known in Italy at the time, probably having been reintroduced by Arab traders in the twelfth century.

Pasta comes in many sizes and shapes, and it can be made from many different flours. Pasta, or noodles, can be made from flours milled from rice, millet, corn, beans, buckwheat, wheat, and other grains. Italian-style pastas are typically made with durum wheat flour, or a slightly less milled durum wheat product called semolina. There are two predominate styles of making pasta. Dried pasta, also known as *pasta secca* from the Italian, is made by adding water to flour. The dough is first kneaded or otherwise processed; then it is shaped and dried. Other ingredients such as vegetable extracts or seasonings may be added to the dough. Dried pasta can easily be stored for up to two years. Fresh pasta, known as *pasta fresca* in Italian, is composed of eggs, water, and flour. The processing is the same, but instead of being dried, the pasta or noodles are then either cooked immediately or stored under refrigeration for a few days. The fresh pasta technique is also widely used to make dumplings, a food found across Asia, Europe, the Middle East, and the Americas, where the dough is stuffed with a filling, then boiled, steamed, stewed, baked, or frozen.

Pasta is typically cooked in salted water, then drained to be served. A wide range of other cooking techniques includes steps for frying, cooking in broth, or having the pasta absorb all the water in the pot. Pasta comes in a wide variety of shapes, but the most common are noodles, long and thin strands of pasta. Italian-style pastas are available in more than 350 different shapes. Couscous, small chunks or balls of pasta, is common in North Africa, and this style of pasta has spread to other parts of the world. Other than couscous, most words for pasta shapes in English come from the Italian language, and Asian noodles borrow terms from their original languages. Pastas often are served warm with a sauce, but they are also incorporated into salads, soups, stews, and other dishes.

■ Impacts and Issues

Pasta is a widely traded processed food, probably due to the long shelf life of dried pastas and the popularity of pasta worldwide. As pasta demand often exceeds a country's ability to produce durum wheat—the key

WORDS TO KNOW

BRAN: The outer coating of a cereal grain that contains fiber and a variety of micronutrients.

SEMOLINA: A rougher, uncooked durum wheat product made as a precursor to the final grinding of flour or for use in pastas, breads, or cereals.

SHELF LIFE: The amount of time a food product can be stored without noticeable changes to its quality or significantly increased risks of foodborne illness.

ingredient in Italian-style pastas—durum wheat is also traded. Canada is the largest durum wheat exporter, but the United States and the European Union export significant quantities of durum wheat, durum wheat flours, and semolina. The largest durum wheat importers, making up more than 60 percent of all imports worldwide in most years, are found in North Africa, with Tunisia, Algeria, and Morocco being predominant. Usually planted in the spring, in contrast to winter wheats (which are planted in the late fall), durum wheat is a hard variety of wheat with a color ranging from translucent to light yellow. Its predominance as the ingredient for pasta comes from its high protein content combined with a high gluten content, which makes it easy to work with and its pasta product easy to store.

Pasta has been manufactured in many countries on a commercial basis since the early nineteenth century. According to the Unioni Industriali Pastai Italiani (UNIPI), an Italian trade association for the pasta industry, the largest pasta producer in the world is Italy, producing more than 3 million tons annually. The United States produces more than 2.5 million tons, and Brazil produces more than 850,000 tons. Russia, Turkey, and Egypt produce more than 400,000 tons each. Consumption per capita of pasta varies widely. According to UNIPI, Italians consume the most at 57.2 pounds (26 kilograms) per capita per year. This is more than double the consumption of the next group of consumer countries such as Venezuela, consuming 26.4 pounds (12 kilograms) per capita per year, Tunisia consuming 25.7 pounds (11.7 kilograms) per capita per year, and Greece consuming 22.9 pounds (10.4 kilograms) per capita per year.

Whereas pasta has become an important staple food in much of the world, some nutritionists question the heavy reliance on pasta as a main part of the diet because of the health consequences. Some blame pasta and other foods made from refined flours that have had the bran

A chef makes pasta noodles by hand in Xian, China.   © *Danita Delimont / Alamy.*

and germ, the sources of fiber in a cereal grain, removed during milling for a wide range of health ailments. Others point to the relatively good health of the Italian population as proof that pasta itself is only one component of a diet, and it is a food that provides an inexpensive, easily-stored, and quick-to-prepare food. Per gram, pasta is a high-calorie food, but is also an efficient delivery mechanism for complex carbohydrates. In response to health concerns, more pasta manufacturers are developing whole-wheat pasta and highly nutritive pasta products enriched with tomatoes, spinach, vitamins, omega-3 fatty acids, and added proteins, while other manufacturers are making pasta products with reduced calories and fat content.

SEE ALSO *Asian Diet; Free Trade and Agriculture; Gluten Intolerance; Grains; Nutrient Fortification of Foods.*

BIBLIOGRAPHY

Books

Academia Barilla. *Pasta!* Vercelli, Italy: White Star, 2010.

Hildebrand, Caz, and Jacob Kenedy. *The Geometry of Pasta*. Philadelphia: Quirk Books, 2010.

Kill, Ron. and Keith Turnbull. *Pasta and Semolina Technology*. Chichester, UK: John Wiley & Sons, Ltd., 2007.

Verkaar, Désirée, and Stefano Manti. *Everything You Need to Know about Pasta*. Nijmegen: Miller, 2008.

Zanini De Vita, Oretta. *Encyclopedia of Pasta*. Berkeley: University of California Press, 2009.

Periodicals

Fast, Yvona. "We Heart Pasta." *E: The Environmental Magazine* 21, no. 5 (2010): 45.

Gumbel, Peter. "Dispatches—Pasta Panic—the Price of Wheat Is Up 60% This Year, and in Italy They're Taking to the Streets over the Cost of Tortellini." *Fortune* 156, no. 11 (2007): 47.

"Pasta That's More Than Carbs." *Environmental Nutrition* 30, no. 11 (2007): 5.

Web Sites

"All about Pasta." *National Pasta Association*. http://www.ilovepasta.org/pasta.html (accessed October 25, 2010).

Demetri, Justin. "Italian Pasta through the Ages." *Life in Italy.com*. http://www.lifeinitaly.com/food/pasta-history.asp (accessed October 25, 2010).

"Oldest Noodles Unearthed in China." *BBC News*, October 12, 2005. http://news.bbc.co.uk/2/hi/science/nature/4335160.stm (accessed October 25, 2010).

Blake Jackson Stabler

Pasteurization

Introduction

Pasteurization is a flash heating process used to reduce the number of microorganisms in food products to a safe level. Pasteurization of milk, cheese, juice, beer, eggs, and other products (usually, but not exclusively, liquids) kills the majority of microbes that may be present but does not guarantee complete sterilization. Sterilization, although theoretically desirable, would have a detrimental effect on the texture or taste of many soft or liquid foods.

Pasteurization is designed to kill all potentially pathogenic organisms. Many such organisms find their way into dairy products either by being present in the environment of dairy cows and hence on and in the cows themselves, or they may be introduced during processing. Bacterial species of concern include *Aeromonas hydrophila*, *Bacillus cereus*, *Campylobacter jejuni*, *Coxiella burnetii*, *Echerichia coli* O157:H7, *Listeria monocytogenes*, *Mycobacterium bovis*, *Salmonella* spp., *Staphylococcus aureus*, *Yersinia enterocolitica*, and others. Although many bacteria species may be found in raw dairy products, only those able to grow in them or grow well at the low temperatures (psychrophiles) used for storage present a serious concern.

The processing times and temperatures for pasteurization depend on the product and its ingredients. A wide range of application-specific procedures exist, but typical temperature/time combinations are 151°F (66°C) for 30 seconds; 162°F (72°C) for 15 seconds; 192°F (89°C) for 1 second; and 212°F (100°C) for 0.01 seconds. Ultra-high-temperature (UHT) processing is done at temperatures above 268°F (131°C) for 2–5 seconds. Lower temperatures require longer times and are suitable for bulk processing in vats. Higher temperatures and shorter times are applied in continuous flow systems.

With the exception of UHT, which renders products close to sterile, pasteurized products require immediate and continuous refrigerated storage after processing. This is because the temperatures used are too low and the times too short to render the product sterile. Slow growing and endospore-producing bacteria (such as *B. cereus*) are not killed by pasteurization. The microbial load is reduced, however, to the extent that properly shipped and stored goods maintain an acceptable shelf life before spoilage.

Historical Background and Scientific Foundations

Pasteurization is named after the French scientist Louis Pasteur (1822–1895), who developed the process in the 1860s as a way of killing organisms in wine. The impetus of his work was the need to reduce spoilage of wine during shipping. Pasteur's invention of the process that bears his name was an offshoot of his research into the existence and activity of microorganisms and the relationship between microbes and human disease.

Although Pasteur's method did produce wines that tasted better after shipping (because of reduced spoilage), vintners were divided as to whether or not pasteurization itself changed the flavor. Although wine makers eventually lost interest in pasteurization, the process was applied to other food products, notably beer and milk, as it became clear that it was based on sound scientific principles.

Before the industrial revolution and the growth of urban population centers, rural people had been drinking raw milk ever since the domestication of cows and other milk-bearing animals, largely without ill effect. The industrial revolution led to the rapid expansion of milk production in more urban environments, much of which took place under unsanitary conditions. During the late 1800s, many outbreaks of milk-borne diseases such as typhoid and scarlet fever, diphtheria, and diarrhea, led to wide use of pasteurization (as well as regulation of the dairy industry). Commercial pasteurization of milk and other dairy and non-dairy products came into use in Europe in the late 1800s and in the United States in the early 1900s.

A worker inspects pasteurization equipment at a dairy in Somerset, England. © *Nigel Cattlin / Alamy.*

In 1908 the city of Chicago required all milk sold in the city to be pasteurized. The U.S. federal government became involved in 1924 with the introduction of the Standard Milk Ordinance, which was designed to assist the states with (what were at that time) strictly voluntary pasteurization policies. The first U.S. state to make pasteurization a legal requirement was Michigan in 1947.

The Standard Milk Ordinance evolved into the Grade A Pasteurized Milk Ordinance (PMO) which provides guidance on all aspects of milk production, although each state is responsible for regulating local production.

■ Impacts and Issues

The success of pasteurization in improving the safety of commercially produced milk and milk products is beyond question. The incidences of food and waterborne illnesses caused by contaminated milk have gone from about 25 percent of all cases in 1938 to less than 1 percent in the first decade of the 2000s. Even so, the pasteurization of milk remains controversial.

Natural and raw food advocates argue that unpasteurized milk is healthier and tastier, whereas most health professionals, regulators, scientists, and dairy industry groups claim there is essentially no difference between pasteurized and unpasteurized milk except that pasteurized milk is much safer. The roots of this argument can be traced back to Pasteur's own time. He assumed that all microbes were essentially bad, although not all of his contemporaries agreed. Some, such as Claude Bernard (1813–1878), insisted that disease was caused by an imbalance in the internal environment (which is now known to include beneficial microbes) and not solely by the invasion of organisms from outside the body.

Raw milk proponents claim that pasteurization negatively changes the nutrient makeup of milk, destroys enzymes and hormones, and eliminates beneficial bacteria. Proponents also claim that raw milk boosts metabolism, increases energy, leads to better muscle growth, stimulates the immune system, and ameliorates a host of ailments. Those who oppose the widespread sale of unpasteurized milk make counterclaims, supported by scientific evidence, to all these statements. The U.S. Centers for Disease Control cautions against usage of raw milk, citing documented disease outbreaks caused by unpasteurized milk or cheese in 2001, 2003, and 2004.

Along with the passing of laws requiring pasteurization are laws banning the sale of raw milk products. For many, it has become a question of freedom of personal choice as to what is safe to consume and what is not. Raw milk proponents do not propose that pasteurized dairy products should be banned but wish to make their own decision about what to consume, and they do not want the sale of raw milk products to be criminalized. It is true that small, well-managed dairy operations can produce safe raw milk products. Safety is maintained in such operations by product testing and careful compliance with sanitary procedures. It is also true that the current demand for dairy products cannot be met both safely and economically by small, locally operated dairies, especially in heavily industrialized regions.

As of May 2010, the retail sale of raw milk was legal in 10 U.S. states and banned in 10 others and in the District of Columbia. Sales to individuals for personal consumption (referred to as "incidental sales") are allowed in 15 states. Eleven states either allow or have no laws prohibiting herd shares, a system in which consumers pay a farmer a fee to keep an animal (or share in one) in exchange for receiving fresh raw milk.

Outside of the United States, rural populations routinely consume unpasteurized milk and cheese, and regulations regarding pasteurization vary from non-existent to unenforced to required. In the United States, efforts to increase the availability of raw milk products by grass roots consumer organizations are ongoing. Even when popular sentiment and legislatures side with consumer choice, there is no guarantee of success. In May 2010 the governor of Wisconsin vetoed the legalization of raw milk sales after becoming personally convinced it represented an unnecessary risk to consumers and the state's dairy industry. Despite calls for the deregulation of raw milk sales, many officials remain skeptical of the wisdom of such a move. Legislation currently working its way through the U.S. Congress (HR2749: The Food Safety Enhancement Act of 2009) aims to give greater authority to federal government agencies in many areas of food-related commerce, including raw milk sales.

■ Primary Source Connection

The Milk Question by Milton J. Rosenau, written in 1912, explains the need for pasteurizing milk for the safety of the public. He details that pasteurization will contain or eliminate the outbreak of typhoid fever and other diseases due to infected milk.

Rosenau served as an assistant surgeon in the United States Marine Hospital Service (later to become the U.S. Public Health Service). In 1899, Rosenau was appointed director of the Hygienic Laboratory of the Marine Hospital Service and later helped establish the Harvard University School of Public Health. In 1940, Rosenau was named the first dean of the University of North Carolina School of Public Health.

The Object of Pasteurization

Pasteurization should only be used to destroy the harmful bacteria in milk and for no other purpose. It must not be used as a redemption process. It cannot atone for filth. It should never be used to bolster up bad milk. It should never be used as a preservative; heated milk keeps somewhat longer than raw milk. From the standpoint of the sanitarian, pasteurization is a valuable public health measure because it prevents disease. From the standpoint of the dairyman, it is sometimes favored because it preserves milk. This is a collateral advantage to which the dairyman is entitled commercially. However, when milk is properly pasteurized at the correct temperature and time, it keeps only about twelve to twenty-four

hours longer than it otherwise would. Milk may be kept from souring another twelve or twenty-four hours by pasteurizing it again. This should not be permitted, for milk should be handled in such a way that double pasteurization should not be necessary....

Why Pasteurization Is Forced Upon Us as a Public Health Safeguard

Raw milk is apt to be dangerous milk. Pasteurization is our only safeguard against certain of the dangers conveyed in milk. The question now arises whether these dangers are sufficiently real or sufficiently frequent to justify all the fuss that is made about them. Is the danger from the use of the average raw market milk a serious one? Yes, it is. The numerous outbreaks of typhoid fever, scarlet fever, diphtheria, sore throat, as well as the relation of milk to tuberculosis and other infections, is sufficiently real, sufficiently frequent, and sufficiently serious to arouse sanitarians and the public to a realization of the danger. In our studies on typhoid fever in Washington, for example, we found that the general market milk is, for the most part, old, stale, and dirty. Further, that at least 11.3 per cent of the cases of typhoid fever which occurred during the summer of 1906 in our capital city were due to infected milk; in 1907, 9.18 per cent; and in 1908, about 10 per cent of the typhoid cases were traced to infected milk. Similar conditions have been found in other cities wherever the matter has been investigated. One needs only to make a superficial study of the subject to be impressed with the number of deaths and diseases caused by impure milk. In pasteurization we have a simple and efficient method to prevent these dangers. Pasteurization is justified independently of the question of infant morbidity and mortality.

That is another story.

Until the health officer can assure us that the market supply of milk is clean and safe we are forced to protect ourselves. It is perfectly plain that we cannot get a safe and satisfactory milk supply for our metropolitan cities to meet all sanitary requirements in this generation. Until the health officer can assure us that it is perfectly safe to drink the milk raw, we should pasteurize it just as we should boil drinking-water that we know is liable to contain infection.

M. J. Rosenau

ROSENAU, M. J. *THE MILK QUESTION*. BOSTON, MA: HOUGHTON MIFFLIN COMPANY, 1912.

SEE ALSO *Center for Food Safety and Applied Nutrition; Dairy Products; E. Coli Contamination; Food Safety and Inspection Service; Foodborne Diseases; Pure Food and Drug Act of 1906; Raw Milk Campaign; Staphylococcal Food Poisoning.*

BIBLIOGRAPHY

Books

Gumpert, David E. *The Raw Milk Revolution: Behind America's Emerging Battle over Food Rights.* White River Junction, VT: Chelsea Green Pub, 2009.

Schmid, Ronald F. *The Untold Story of Milk: The History, Politics and Science of Nature's Perfect Food: Raw Milk from Pasture-Fed Cows.* Washington, DC: NewTrends, 2009.

Stratton, Jayne E. *Raw Milk: Why Take the Risk?* Lincoln: Cooperative Extension, Institute of Agriculture and Natural Resources, University of Nebraska-Lincoln, 2004.

Periodicals

"Arguing over Unpasteurised Milk: Raw Deal." *Economist London* (June 10, 2010): 62.

"Sour Feelings on Raw Milk: Health Officials and Farmers Face Off over Safety of Selling the Unpasteurized Form." *U.S. News & World Report* 144, no.12 (2008): 25.

Weir, Erica, Joanne Mitchell, Steven Rebellato, and Dominic Fortuna. "Raw Milk and the Protection of Public Health." *Canadian Medical Association Journal* 177, no. 7 (2007): 721–723.

Web Sites

"The Dangers of Raw Milk: Unpasteurized Milk Can Pose a Serious Health Risk." *U.S. Food and Drug Administration (FDA).* http://www.fda.gov/Food/ResourcesForYou/Consumers/ucm079516.htm (accessed August 19, 2010).

Philip McIntosh

Pesticides and Pesticide Residue

■ Introduction

The use of chemical pesticides to increase crop yields and control pests has caused the amount of food grown per acre to soar since the 1940s. In 1939 Paul Müller (1899–1965), a chemist from Switzerland, created the synthetic pesticide dichlorodiphenyltrichloroethane (DDT). DDT was a broad-spectrum pesticide that was thought to be non-toxic to humans. Nine years after his discovery, Müller won the Nobel Prize in Physiology or Medicine, and DDT was rapidly adopted for a variety of uses, from crop management to delousing prisoners and military troops, to mosquito control.

DDT is a persistent organic pollutant, or POP, an organic compound that does not degrade rapidly and that can accumulate in animal and human tissue. DDT was banned in the United States by the late 1970s and was linked to reduced populations of wild birds and increased cancer rates in humans. In 2002 the United States and 122 other countries signed the Stockholm Convention treaty regulating the use of 12 POPs, including pesticides used in agriculture such as Aldrin, Chlordane, DDT, Dieldrin, Heptachlor, and Toxaphene.

Whereas pesticides have allowed for a sharp increase in crop yield per acre, the environmental and health impact of pesticide use, as well as pesticide residue on food, has provoked controversy from the mid-1960s to the present day. American marine biologist Rachel Carson's (1907–1964) book *Silent Spring*, published in 1962, highlighted the bioaccumulation of multiple pesticides and chemicals in the environment and in the food chain. The effects of bioaccumulation on food can be explained in an example using apples: Eating an apple sprayed with pesticide periodically might cause no harm, but eating a sprayed apple every day for 50 years leads to a larger cumulative exposure to neurotoxins that could cause cell damage and an increased cancer risk. Scientists examining pesticides in the food supply began to discover that women exposed to POPs such as DDT in their youth had higher rates of breast cancer in adulthood than women not exposed to DDT, or who were exposed later in life.

The USDA currently recommends that consumers wash their fruits and vegetables just prior to cooking them or eating them raw. Rinsing vegetables or fruits under running water has been shown to be as effective as using commercially prepared vegetable washes and sprays, and all parts of the vegetable such as the peel should be washed in order to avoid contamination during peeling or trimming. Additional recommendations include avoiding soap, which can leave its own residue on food, and rinsing pre-packaged fruits, vegetables, and salads, even if their labels state they are pre-washed.

■ Historical Background and Scientific Foundations

Agrichemicals and biological pesticides came into widespread use in the United States and western Europe in the nineteenth and twentieth centuries, largely as a measure to manage insects and fungi that destroyed crops and threatened harvests. In his book *The War on Bugs*, American urban farmer and author Will Allen (1949–) notes that the first use of a chemical pesticide in the U.S. was in 1867, when a paint additive with arsenic was used to control the Colorado potato beetle. In 1892 lead arsenate was used to control the gypsy moth, and chemical fertilizer use grew throughout the 1890s and into the early decades of the twentieth century. The Royal Society of London attempted to set standards for lead and arsenic residue on crops in the late 1890s, gaining France's agreement to set similar limits. The United States refused to join the agreement.

Later, the Federal Insecticide Act of 1910 set U.S. standards for the chemical composition of pesticides. Coupled with the Pure Food and Drug Act of 1906, this legislation began to shape federal regulation of the nation's food and chemical supply. The Insecticide Act was seldom concerned with consumer exposure to chemicals or environmental issues, but rather with protecting consumers from receiving substandard products. The introduction of DDT in the 1940s revolutionized the pesticide industry and farming, ushering in a period of increased chemical use on small and large farms. In 1947 Congress passed the Federal Insecticide, Fungicide, and Rodenticide Act, or FIFRA, in response to concerns about widespread DDT use and the need for federal regulation of the product's composition and use. FIFRA, with amendments throughout the 1950s and 1960s, was the foundation for pesticide regulation until the 1970 creation of the Environmental Protection Agency (EPA), which took on the role of enforcing FIFRA.

The first federal laws protecting workers and farmers from pesticide exposure came in 1974, with the EPA-issued Worker Protection Standard for Agricultural Pesticides regulations. These rules protect farm laborers and were updated in 1992 to restrict worker exposure to certain classes of chemicals, set standards for protective equipment, mandate employers to provide safety training and equipment to workers, and provide decontamination sites and emergency medical services as needed.

The 1938 Federal Food, Drug and Cosmetic Act, or FFDCA, established standards for pesticides and food

WORDS TO KNOW

BIOACCUMULATION: A progressive increase in the amount of a substance in an organism due to the inability of the organism to clear the substance from the body faster than it is accumulated.

FOOD QUALITY PROTECTION ACT OF 1996: Also known as the FQPA, this act changed the way the Environmental Protection Agency regulates pesticides and set stricter standards for acceptable exposure levels for infants and children.

INTEGRATED PEST MANAGEMENT: Also known as IPM, this pest-management technique involves balancing the need to increase crop yield and protect crops from damage with the desire to protect the environment and cause the least damage. Rather than never using pesticides, or always spraying regardless of need, IPM seeks a middle ground to reduce the pesticide load as much as possible.

ORGANICALLY GROWN: This term means that no synthetic fertilizers or pesticides are used in the growing of a particular food. Biological pesticides are permitted for food labeled "organically grown" according to U.S. Department of Agriculture (USDA) standards.

A farmer sprays pesticide on a rice field in Taiwan.   *Image copyright PHOTO 999, 2010. Used under license from Shutterstock.com.*

A crop dusting airplane sprays pesticide on wheat fields. *Image copyright David Kay, 2010. Used under license from Shutterstock.com.*

supplies, setting maximum acceptable levels of pesticide use on certain foods and requiring special labeling for pesticide containers. The FDA works with the U.S. Department of Agriculture (USDA) and the EPA to enforce these requirements. Changes since 1938, such as the Miller Amendment, the Food Additives Amendment, and the Delaney Clause, have increased consumer protections with new reforms such as maximum levels of pesticides permitted within agricultural products, processed foods, and a zero tolerance of cancer-causing pesticide residue in the nation's food supply.

■ Impacts and Issues

The Food Quality Protection Act of 1996 updated all prior pesticide regulations. It tightened rules formerly managed by the Delaney clause and required that cumulative chemical exposure, not just from food, but also from water supplies and airborne pesticides, be calculated when examining cancer issues.

The populations most vulnerable to direct pesticide exposure in agriculture are migrant workers and their children. A 2007 metastudy by researchers in Canada looked at non-cancer health effects of prolonged pesticide exposure and found that as pesticide exposure dramatically increased, dermatologic, neurologic, reproductive, and genotoxic effects of pesticide exposure became more pronounced. The study also concluded that pesticides affect the reproductive system and are linked to genetic damage and increased birth defects. The research on the relationship between pesticides in agriculture and cancer is even more dramatic: A February 2010 study published in *Environmental Health Perspectives* links agricultural pesticide exposure to cutaneous melanoma, whereas a host of other studies link pesticides to increased breast cancer and gastroenterological cancers. A 2008 report from the European Union parliament found that children of migrant farmer workers who live on farms have overall higher rates of cancer as well.

Although most agribusiness farms use pesticides in large quantities to increase crop yields, some farmers are turning to Integrated Pest Management (IPM) and organic methods to reduce the health and environmental effects of chemical use. IPM is a middle ground, using small amounts of pesticides as needed, but emphasizing more environmentally friendly, although sometimes more labor-intensive, methods to reduce pests and increase yields. Sometimes referred to as "low spray," IPM combines synthetic pesticides, biological pesticides, and careful non-chemical crop management. Organically grown crops are held to a stricter standard by the USDA, with farmers required to receive certification from USDA-approved certification organizations and to pay annual inspection fees in order to use the organically grown label. Crops can be labeled organically grown even if pesticides are used, but the chemicals must be biological pesticides and not synthetic compounds.

In May 2010 the issue of pesticide residue on food and children's health received tremendous media exposure when research studies revealed that children with detectable pesticides in urine samples are as much as 93 percent more likely to have attention-deficit-hyperactive disorder (ADHD) than counterparts without these high levels. Scientists in Canada and the United States found the relationship between the presence of dimethyl thiophosphate in urine samples and ADHD to be strong, and children with a tenfold increase of metabolites from the pesticide malathion, found in frozen blueberries, fresh strawberries, and in celery, were 55 percent more likely to have ADHD than children without those high concentrations of the pesticide.

Concern over pesticides has led to a focus on organic food production and local food movements such as community supported agriculture and farmers' markets, where consumers can access farmers directly and ask questions about pesticide management and organic food growing practices, ensuring quality control and limiting pesticide exposure in food.

SEE ALSO *Agribusiness; Agroecology; Center for Food Safety and Applied Nutrition; Climate Change and Agriculture; Community Supported Agriculture (CSAs); Consumer Food Safety Recommendations; E. Coli Contamination; Food Inspection and Standards; Food Irradiation; Food Safety and Inspection Service; Foodborne Diseases; Genetically Modified Organisms (GMO); Organics; Produce Traceability; Reportable Food Registry; Salmonella; U.S. Department of Agriculture (USDA).*

BIBLIOGRAPHY

Books

Barton, Russell P. *Food Safety, Fresh Produce and FDA Oversight.* New York: Nova Science Publishers, 2010.

Fan, Xuetong. *Microbial Safety of Fresh Produce.* Chicago: IFT Press, 2009.

James, Jennylynd. *Microbial Hazard Identification in Fresh Fruit and Vegetables.* Hoboken, NJ: Wiley-Interscience, 2006.

Periodicals

Foladori, Guillermo, and Edgar Záyago. "What Lies Beneath." *Science Technology & Society* 15, no. 1 (2010): 155–168.

"Food Safety: Fresh Produce Is Just as Susceptible to Carrying Foodborne Diseases as Meat, Poultry, and Fish." *Contemporary Pediatrics* 25, no. 9 (2008): 96–97.

Little, Christine L., and Iain A Gillespie. "Review Article: Prepared Salads and Public Health." *Journal of Applied Microbiology* 105, no. 6 (2008): 1729–1743.

Okello, Julius J., and Scott M. Swinton. "From Circle of Poison to Circle of Virtue: Pesticides, Export Standards and Kenya's Green Bean Farmers." *Journal of Agricultural Economics* 61, no. 2 (2010): 209–224.

"Processors, Scientists Look to Improve Fresh-Cut Produce Safety." *Food Chemical News* 50, no. 6 (2008): 10.

Quah, Su-Huey, and Andrew Tan. "Consumer Purchase Decisions of Organic Food Products: an Ethnic Analysis." *Journal of International Consumer Marketing* 22, no. 1 (2010): 47–58.

Web Sites

Kramer, Melody Joy. "Lettuce Learn How to Wash Produce." *National Public Radio,* September 21, 2006. http://www.npr.org/templates/story/story.php?storyId=6104414 (accessed October 25, 2010).

"Safe Produce Handling Education Campaign." *Partnership for Food Safety Education.* http://www.fightbac.org/home (accessed October 25, 2010).

Melanie Barton Zoltan

Phytochemicals (Phytonutrients)

■ Introduction

Plants are rich in compounds called phytochemicals, some of which play a valuable role in the human diet as micronutrients. These phytonutrients include vitamin C, lycopene, carotene, and many others. Plant pigments, which give plants their color, are particularly likely to have health benefits. The carotenoids, which are yellow, orange, and red, and the anthocyanins, which are red, purple, and blue, have antioxidant qualities, and can block some of the cellular damage wrought by free radicals, a byproduct of biochemical reactions involving oxygen. Another important group of phytonutrients is the flavonoids, some of which have estrogen-like properties that could help prevent certain cancers. Knowledge of the identity and biological action of phytochemicals is still at an early stage, because many plants have not even been analyzed for their phytochemical content. Furthermore, there are thousands of phytochemicals whose role in the diet is not well understood. It is, however, well established that a diet rich in fruits and vegetables is beneficial to health, and the phytonutrient content of such a diet is part of the benefit. Rather than focus on a few phytonutrients that have been well investigated, it is likely more beneficial to eat a wide variety of fruits and vegetables, as these compounds likely work in synergy.

■ Historical Background and Scientific Foundations

Plants contain thousands of different compounds known as phytochemicals, which contribute to their color, aroma, and nutritional and medicinal properties. Some of these phytochemicals are also micronutrients and are known as phytochemicals. Although people have been using phytochemicals for millennia, it was only in the nineteenth century, with developments in analytical chemistry, that these compounds began to be identified and characterized. Advances in cell biology in the twentieth century enabled the nutritional and health benefits of phytonutrients to be further investigated. Most phytonutrients are beneficial because of antioxidant properties. Some also have estrogenic properties that could help prevent cancer.

Some phytochemicals are colored and some are not. Both types can have nutrient benefits. Plants get their colors from pigments, phytochemicals that absorb specific wavelengths of visible light. Although there is still much to be learned of the phytochemical composition of plants, there is a general rule: The more highly colored a fruit or vegetable, the richer it is in micronutrient phytochemicals. Plants synthesize vitamin C from sugars, which are a product of photosynthesis, so the more light a plant receives, the higher its sugar concentration and the more vitamin C it is likely to contain. Furthermore, the more light a plant receives, the more pigments it has to deal with the energy input and the darker the coloration of its leaves and stem. Therefore dark green or green and red lettuces are richer in vitamin C and in carotenoids than pale iceberg lettuce.

Plant pigments belong to just a few chemical families, although there are hundreds of different phytochemicals from these families present in fruit and vegetables, resulting in a vast array of hues to attract our attention and add to the pleasure, and nutritional value, of eating. Arguably the most important plant pigment is chlorophyll, which traps the energy of sunlight for photosynthesis.

The vast range of greens in fruits and vegetables is attributed to the presence of differing amounts of chlorophyll-a, which is blue-green, and chlorophyll-b, which is yellow-green. Chlorophyll is an antioxidant that reduces DNA damage. Cooking leaches it into the cooking water and it decomposes on prolonged heating; therefore, green vegetables are best cooked sparingly, in the minimum amount of water, or not at all. The carotenoids are yellow, orange, and red pigments found in wide range of fruits and vegetables including apricots, carrots, watermelon, yellow sweet corn, and pink grapefruit. Beta-carotene is important because it is a precursor of vitamin A. Several carotenoids, including vitamin A, have known antioxidant properties. Lycopene, the red pigment found in tomatoes, reduces oxidative DNA damage, and research has suggested that it may protect against prostate and other cancers. Lutein, a yellow pigment found in green leafy vegetables, slows the progress of macular degeneration, a leading cause of blindness.

The anthocyanins are blue, red, and purple pigments that include cyanidin in blueberries and pelargonidin in blood oranges and red cabbage. Anthocyanins are responsible for the color of many berries. They too have antioxidant properties, and blueberries, in particular, are often recommended as a superfood whose regular consumption can prevent heart disease. The anthocyanins are part of a much bigger group of phytochemicals called the polyphenols. Another important family within the polyphenols is the flavonoids, which also have antioxidant properties. They are widely distributed in the plant

WORDS TO KNOW

ANTIOXIDANT: Oxygen is essential to human life, but biochemical reactions involving oxygen generate substances called free radicals that can damage proteins and DNA in cells. Over time this free radical damage increases the likelihood of chronic diseases such as cancer and heart disease. Antioxidants are compounds that can block free radical damage. Many phytochemicals have antioxidant properties.

PHOTOSYNTHESIS: The process by which plants manufacture sugars from carbon dioxide and water, driven by the energy of the sunlight captured by chlorophyll molecules in the plant.

PHYTOESTROGEN: Phytochemicals that mimic the action of human estrogen and so may block its role in activating cells, potentially preventing the development of some cancers.

Fresh carrots on a supermarket counter. Carrots are rich in beta-carotene, a phytochemical. *Image copyright Kristina Postnikova, 2010. Used under license from Shutterstock.com.*

kingdom and are present in cocoa powder. The more bitter the chocolate, the higher its antioxidant content should be. Ideally this would be indicated by the percentage of cocoa on the label of the chocolate, but some manufacturers remove flavonoids from chocolate, believing consumers will not like their bitter taste. Research has suggested that consuming a couple of squares of a high quality high cocoa chocolate daily can help lower blood pressure. The flavonoids present in soy products and lentils likewise have phytoestrogenic properties. They may therefore prevent or slow the progression of some hormone-sensitive breast and prostate cancers. Indeed, high consumption of soy may partially account for why Asian women have lower rates of breast cancer compared to women in the West.

■ Impacts and Issues

There is still a great deal to be discovered about phytochemicals and phytonutrients. Many plants have not yet been explored for their phytochemical content, so there may be thousands of compounds with potential benefit awaiting discovery. Health benefits are claimed for many phytonutrients; for instance, lycopene in tomatoes and sulphophanes in broccoli are said to prevent cancer. But it has to be remembered that much of the evidence for the antioxidant and anticancer properties of phytonutrients comes from experiments on animals or using cancer cells in test tubes. Often experiments are done with the phytonutrient isolated from the plant when the plant itself may act in synergy with other phytonutrients. It is difficult to know what the benefits shown for individual compounds in such experiments mean in terms of diet and human health. However, there are many studies showing that diets rich in fruit and vegetables have many health benefits and this probably comes from consuming hundreds, or even thousands, of different phytochemicals, rather than just a few. This is why taking individual antioxidants as supplements is probably not as healthy as eating a wide variety of fruits and vegetables, particularly those that are brightly colored.

SEE ALSO *Diet and Cancer; Diet and Diabetes; Diet and Heart Disease; Diet and Hypertension; Dietary Guidelines for Americans; Dietary Reference Intakes; Functional Foods; Nutrition; Organics; Standard American Diet and Changing American Diet; Tea; USDA Food Pyramid; Veganism; Vegetables; Vegetarianism.*

BIBLIOGRAPHY

Books

Giardi, Maria T., Giuseppina Rea, and B. Berra. *Biofarms for Nutraceuticals: Functional Food and Safety Control by Biosensors.* New York: Springer, 2010.

Higdon, Jane. *An Evidence-Based Approach to Dietary Phytochemicals.* New York: Thieme Medical, 2007.

Phytochemicals in Food. Oxford: Wiley Blackwell Pub, 2009.

Phytonutrients. Oxford: Wiley Blackwell Pub, 2009.

Periodicals

"A+ for Apples. Short on Traditional Nutrients, but Long on Phytonutrients That Fight Chronic Diseases." *Environmental Nutrition* 29, no. 9 (2006): 8.

Caëtano, B., et al. "Soya Phytonutrients Act on a Panel of Genes Implicated with BRCA1 and BRCA2 Oncosuppressors in Human Breast Cell Lines." *The British Journal of Nutrition* 95, no. 2 (2006): 406–413.

"Check Out Cherries. Sweet or Tart, They're Packed with Disease-Preventing Phytonutrients." *Environmental Nutrition* 31, no. 6 (2008): 8.

"Food-Disease Links: Phytonutrients That Protect against Heart Disease, Cancer, Inflammation, and More." *Environmental Nutrition* 29, no. 12 (2006): 3–6.

Tucker, Greg. "Phytonutrients." *Comparative Biochemistry and Physiology. Part A, Molecular & Integrative Physiology* 146, no. 4 (2007).

Web Sites

Agricultural Research Service, U.S. Department of Agriculture (USDA). "Phytonutrients Take Center Stage." *Agricultural Research,* December 1999. http://www.ars.usda.gov/is/ar/archive/dec99/stage1299.htm (accessed October 4, 2010).

American Cancer Society. "Phytochemicals." *Cancer.org.* http://www.cancer.org/Treatment/TreatmentsandSideEffects/ComplementaryandAlternativeMedicine/HerbsVitaminsandMinerals/phytochemicals (accessed October 4, 2010).

National Library of Medicine. "Phytochemicals." *Medline Plus.* http://www.nlm.nih.gov/medlineplus/ency/imagepages/19303.htm (accessed October 4, 2010).

Susan Aldridge

Pica

Introduction

Pica is the consumption of (or an appetite for) non-food substances, including dirt, clay, chalk, starch, plaster, paper, stone, hair, plastic, coins, matches, and ice. Food ingredients not usually eaten raw or by themselves, such as cornstarch, flour, baking soda, coffee grounds, and raw potatoes may also be eaten or desired by people with pica. Although pica is classified as an eating disorder in most industrialized nations, in many parts of the world the consumption of some clay or dirt is culturally approved and may actually benefit health. This kind of geophagy (eating earthy substances like dirt, clay, or chalk) is most common among children and women, especially pregnant women, and may be related to nutritional deficiencies, immune system development, and protection from environmental toxins, as well as being important in dietary customs and religious rituals.

Pica as a medical disorder, by contrast, occurs when a person eats inappropriate substances for at least a month, and when it is not culturally or developmentally normal. Children under the age of three commonly eat paper, dirt, and other items, but the intentional ingestion of non-food items usually stops by the time they reach age six. People who have suffered psychological trauma—or those with mental illnesses such as schizophrenia, obsessive-compulsive disorder, and pervasive developmental disorders such as autism—are more likely to engage in pica. Depending on the types and amounts of material ingested, the medical consequences of this kind of pica may be severe.

Historical Background and Scientific Foundations

Pica has been recognized as an eating disorder since the Greek physician Hippocrates wrote about pregnant women eating "earth and charcoal" in the fourth century BC. By the sixth century AD, Byzantine physician Aetius Amidenus called this practice pica. The word pica is derived from the Latin name for the magpie, a bird known for collecting miscellaneous items. Spanish novelist Miguel de Cervantes (1547–1616) wrote about "women that by caprice eat soil, plaster, coal, and other disgusting substances" in *Don Quixote* in 1605, and numerous physicians described pica, including amylophagy (eating pure starch, such as cornstarch or laundry starch) and pagophagy (eating ice) in pregnant women, from the sixteenth through the nineteenth centuries. Pica was noted as a predominately female disorder, most characteristic during pregnancy, and was often said to be associated with chlorosis, an anemia-like malady seen in adolescent girls.

As Europeans encountered other cultures with traditions of geophagy in Africa and the Americas, they wrote about this more widespread type of pica as an exotic curiosity, a disease endemic among "primitive" peoples, or possibly the result of extreme hunger. Plantation owners and doctors in the southern United States in the early 1800s attributed malnutrition and infections among their slaves to the practice of eating dirt or "cachexia Africana," which they thought caused weakness, pallor, and death, and attempted to curtail it with drastic measures. The custom of eating chalk or clay was probably brought to the southern United States by African slaves, and some of their descendants still craved the "white dirt" despite decades of social condemnation and ridicule.

Eating clay is still extremely common in many countries in Africa, especially amongst pregnant women. It is not only socially accepted, but is argued to increase fertility, help with morning sickness, and satisfy intense urges. Geophagy has long been associated with female fertility and healing, as illustrated by rock art at many prehistoric sites on every inhabited continent. Anthropologists suggest that the practice of geophagy is ancient and have hypothesized that human ancestors engaged in it, noting that it is also found amongst chimpanzees that

A woman prepares cookies made of dirt for sale in Port-au-Prince, Haiti, where some people prize dirt as a source of calcium and as an antacid. *AP Images.*

appear to use clay medicinally. One contemporary vestige of this is found in the anti-diarrheal medicine Kaopectate, which used kaolin, a type of soft, white clay, as an ingredient until the 1980s.

■ Impacts and Issues

It is not clear how common pica is, especially in the industrialized nations of Europe and North America, where it still carries a social stigma. The fact that pica is most common among people with lower socioeconomic status, frequently occurs during times of stress or trauma, and is sometimes found in conjunction with other mental disorders probably contributes to its hidden nature. Health care professionals declare that pica, especially geophagy, is often unreported and overlooked, except when it causes medical problems, such as constipation, ulcerations, bowel obstructions, or cracked teeth. Furthermore, benign forms of pica among pregnant women and children often stop spontaneously.

Although geophagy in moderation is not harmful, eating polluted or infected soil is a serious problem. Lead is the most common environmental toxin, but infections from toxocariasis (dog and cat roundworms), toxoplasmosis (commonly carried by cat feces), and bacteria can be deadly. These problems are most common among children and disabled adults, because most adults who eat clay as part of a cultural tradition dig or buy their clay from freshly uncovered subsoil sources that are less likely to be contaminated than dirt at the ground surface.

As researchers have become more aware of the ubiquity of pica, examinations of its roles in different cultures and the varied reasons behind it have become more common and more culturally sensitive. Although the percentage of people that engage in pica varies in different populations, it is a universally observed human behavior. Researchers agree that pica is not a simple phenomenon, but a set of practices incorporating questions from many different fields, including anthropology, nutrition, psychology, immunology, and evolutionary biology. In some cases, pica does seem to be associated with inadequate micronutrients, especially minerals, or with celiac disease, but this is not always the case; pica often persists after dietary changes and supplementation have been implemented. Geophagy also plays an important role in the hygiene hypothesis, which suggests that some exposure to microorganisms such as the bacteria found in large quantities in soil may help the immune systems of pregnant women, fetuses, and young children develop, preventing some allergies and autoimmune diseases later in life. Eating something "inedible" as an adult may no longer be considered a shameful abnormality or the disease of the downtrodden, but its occurrence outside its customary context may still be a symptom of something new, physically or psychologically speaking, including pregnancy.

SEE ALSO *Dietary Changes in Rapidly Developing Countries; Eating Disorders; Undernutrition.*

BIBLIOGRAPHY

Books

MacClancy, Jeremy, C. J. K. Henry, and Helen M. Macbeth. *Consuming the Inedible: Neglected Dimensions of Food Choice.* New York: Berghahn Books, 2007.

Young, Sera L. *Craving Earth: Understanding Pica: The Urge to Eat Clay, Starch, Ice, and Chalk.* New York: Columbia University, 2010.

Periodicals

Blinder, Barton J., and Christina Salama. "An Update on Pica: Prevalence, Contributing Causes, and Treatment." *Psychiatric Times* 25, no. 6 (2008): 1–13.

Callahan, Gerald N. "Eating Dirt." *Emerging Infectious Diseases* 9, no. 8 (2003): 1016–1021.

Larrain, Camilo. "Pica, a Strange Symptom Unveiled Even in *Don Quixote*." *Revista Medica de Chile* 133, no. 5 (2005): 609–611.

Web Sites

"Pica Eating Disorder." *Eating Disorder.org*. http://www.eating-disorder.org/pica-eating-disorders.html (accessed September 14, 2010).

Young Sera L., M. Jeffrey Wilson, Dennis Miller, and Stephen Hillier. "Toward a Comprehensive Approach to the Collection and Analysis of Pica Substances, with Emphasis on Geophagic Materials." *PLoS one* 3, no. 9, 2008. http://www.plosone.org/article/info:doi%2F10.1371%2Fjournal.pone.0003147 (accessed September 14, 2010).

Sandra L. Dunavan

Political Food Boycotts

■ Introduction

Consumers and workers may initiate food boycotts for a number of reasons, including social or political beliefs, concerns over food safety, or solidarity with workers over wages or working conditions. Boycotts may be of a short duration, such as boycotting a certain chain or product for one day to send a message to a company or industry and encourage a change in practices. Other boycotts may last for a prolonged period to raise awareness about a particular issue, to encourage change, or punish a company or industry that will not change its practices. The rise of the Internet and social media provide boycott organizers with new tools for coordinating boycotts and spreading the message about their boycotts.

Food boycotts typically call on consumers to cease purchasing a particular product, substitute another product for the boycotted product, or avoid patronizing a particular company or industry. A company or industry targeted by a boycott may respond by changing behavior to meet the demands of the boycott, ignore the demands and wait for consumers to abandon the boycott, or, in rare instances, break the boycott with the use of force or coercion.

■ Historical Background and Scientific Foundations

The boycott of food products in order to make a political statement or influence behavior traces its origins to at least the mid-eighteenth century. Many American colonists boycotted British tea following the passage of the Townshend Revenue Act of 1767, which placed a tax on British tea sold in the American colonies. The Tea Act of 1773 continued the tax on tea, prompting the Boston Tea Party in 1773. British Parliament repealed the tea tax in 1778 after war had broken out between Great Britain and the American colonies.

The term *boycott* is derived from a tactic used by the Irish Land League, a political organization that assisted Irish farmers, to protest the eviction of Irish tenants from land owned by an English landlord. The English Captain Charles Boycott (1832–1897) served as the estate agent for an English farm owner in west Ireland. Boycott attempted to evict 11 tenants from the land. The Irish Land League called on everyone around the farm to ostracize Boycott. Tenants refused to work the fields and local business refused to deal with Boycott, who eventually paid more to harvest the crops than they were worth.

In the early twentieth century, the British were again the target of a boycott by a colony. In 1905, the Indian independence movement launched Swadeshi, a economic movement designed to weaken British control in India. Swadeshi called for the boycott of British products, including food, and focused on reviving domestic production. Mahatma (M. K.) Gandhi (1869–1948) embraced Swadeshi and called it one of the key components of self-rule. In a defining moment of Indian history, in 1930, Gandhi protested the imposition of a tax on salt by leading a 241 mile (388 km) march to the sea to make salt.

By the mid-twentieth century, increased control of the agricultural and food services industries by large corporations decreased the use of food boycotts to protest government policies. Instead, consumer advocacy groups increasingly turned to boycotts as a way to punish or influence the behavior of corporations. One of the most famous and longest-lasting food boycotts involves Nestlé S.A., the world's largest packaged food company. A variety of consumer advocacy and human rights groups have participated in the boycott against Nestlé since 1977. The boycott targets Nestlé over the aggressive marketing of infant formula in developing countries. Nestlé boycott supporters allege that the company's promotion of infant formula over breast milk has resulted in the death and illness of numerous infants in the developing world. They further state that the use of unsafe, local water to mix infant formula increases the risk of infant death from diarrhea by 25 times. The International Nestlé Boycott Committee now coordinates the Nestlé boycott and has garnered the support of more than 200 groups in excess of 100 countries. The boycott calls on consumers to refrain from purchasing any good produced by Nestlé.

■ Impacts and Issues

Consumers may participate in food boycotts for a variety of reasons. Food boycotts enacted to force a company or industry to conform to the social and political beliefs of those engaged in the boycott are one of the most common types of food boycott. Examples of this form of boycott include boycotts against the fast food, beef, or poultry industries to promote vegetarianism or to call attention to animal cruelty issues. People for the Ethical Treatment of Animals (PETA) initiates many boycotts to promote these issues. Whereas industries that involve the sale of meat are obvious targets of such boycotts, in 2007 PETA called for a boycott of confectionery manufacturer Mars, Inc., over charges of product testing that involved cruelty to animals.

Concerns over food safety also prompt many consumer advocacy groups to organize boycotts of certain products or industries. In the late 1980s health and

WORDS TO KNOW

CONSUMER ADVOCACY GROUP: An organization dedicated to protecting consumers from corporate abuses, including unsafe products and false advertising.

LABOR UNION: An organization of workers formed to negotiate terms of employment with employers.

SWADESHI: The Swadeshi movement was a facet of the Indian independence movement that advocated boycotting British goods in favor of strengthening domestic production.

consumer advocacy groups asked consumers to avoid apples produced in the United States that contained Alar, a chemical use to regulate plant growth, due to fears that Alar increased the risk of cancer. In 1989 the U.S. Environmental Protection Agency (EPA) banned the use of Alar. Many consumer advocacy groups have called for boycotts of Monsanto Company, Kellogg Company, and others over the production or use of genetically-modified grains, sugars, or other products.

An activist protests outside of a Starbucks coffee shop in Seattle, Washington, over the company's use of milk made with bovine growth hormone (rBST). A campaign by the Food and Water Watch and the Organic Consumer Association succeeded in persuading Starbucks to stop using milk from cattle treated with hormones. *AP Images.*

Protesters display placards in front of a McDonald's as they launch a campaign Manila, Philippines, to boycott the fast food chain and several other American multinational companies in protest against the U.S.-led Iraq War (2003–2010). *AP Images.*

Groups may also advocate food boycotts to draw attention to the working conditions or low wages of agricultural workers or other food producers. Between 1967 and 2000, the United Farm Workers (UFW) of America, a labor union for agricultural workers, launched a series of three boycotts against table grapes produced in California. The UFW sought to bring attention to the working conditions of agricultural workers and extract labor concessions for growers. At the height of the UFW's second grape boycott, 17 million American consumers supported the action. In 2001 the Coalition of Immokalee Workers (CIW), a group that represents the rights of immigrant farm workers in Florida, initiated a boycott of Taco Bell. The CIW wanted to force Taco Bell, one of the largest purchasers of Florida-grown tomatoes, to take a role in protecting the rights of agricultural workers. In 2005 Taco Bell agreed to the CIW's demands. The CIW conducted a similarly successful campaign against McDonald's Corporation, and Burger King voluntarily agreed to the CIW's demands before they were targeted by a CIW boycott.

SEE ALSO *Agriculture and International Trade; Breastfeeding; Chocolate; Ecological Impacts of Various World Diets; Embargoes; Ethical Issues in Agriculture; Fair Trade; Food Price Crisis; Free Trade and Agriculture; Gender Equality and Agriculture; Genetically Modified Organisms (GMO); Humane Animal Farming; Migrant Labor, Immigration, and Food Production; Veganism; Wage Slavery in Food Production.*

BIBLIOGRAPHY

Books

Simms, Andrew, and Joe Smith. *Do Good Lives Have to Cost the Earth?* London: Constable, 2008.

Street, Richard S. *Photographing Farmworkers in California.* Stanford, CA: Stanford University Press, 2004.

Periodicals

Foster, Robert. "Commodities, Brands, Love and Kula." *Anthropological Theory* 8, no. 1 (2008): 9–25.

Fridell, Mara, Ian Hudson, and Mark Hudson. "With Friends like These: The Corporate Response to Fair Trade Coffee." *Review of Radical Political Economics* 40, no. 1 (2008): 8–34.

Garcia, Matthew. "Labor, Migration, and Social Justice in the Age of the Grape Boycott." *Gastronomica: The Journal of Food and Culture* 7, no. 3 (2007): 68–74.

Köse, Yavuz. "Nestlé: A Brief History of the Marketing Strategies of the First Multinational Company in the Ottoman Empire." *Journal of Macromarketing* 27, no. 1 (2007): 74–85.

Schmelzer, Matthias. "Marketing Morals, Moralizing Markets: Assessing the Effectiveness of Fair Trade as a Form of Boycott." *Management & Organizational History* 5, no. 2 (2010): 221–250.

Stolle, Dietlind, Marc Hooghe, and Michele Micheletti. "Politics in the Supermarket: Political Consumerism as a Form of Political Participation." *International Political Science Review* 26, no. 3 (2005): 245–269.

Tessier, Stacy. "Rethinking the Food Chain: Farmworkers and the Taco Bell Boycott." *Journal of Developing Societies* 23, no. 1 (2007): 89–97.

Web Sites

"The Campaign for Fair Food." *Coalition of Immokalee Workers.* http://www.ciw-online.org/101.html#cff (accessed October 25, 2010).

"Formula versus Mother's Milk: The Boycott Battle Continues." *Food and Agriculture Organization of the United Nations (FAO).* http://www.fao.org/docrep/T3550E/t3550e01.htm (accessed October 25, 2010).

Friedman, Emily. "Health Care Stirs Up Whole Foods CEO John Mackey, Customers Boycott Organic Grocery Store." *ABC News,* August 14, 2009. http://abcnews.go.com/Business/story?id=8322658&page=1 (accessed October 25, 2010).

Joseph P. Hyder

Population and Food

■ Introduction

The global human population exceeded 6.5 billion in 2006. Population growth affects the availability and allocation of necessary resources, including water and food. Regions with large populations must either grow enough food to support the local population or import food from elsewhere. Producing enough food requires sufficient farmland, water, labor, seed, and lack of crop failure. Sufficient access to food demands the availability of markets, reliable means of transporting foodstuffs, and money to purchase food if necessary. A combination of adequate food production, availability, and access to food to sustain a population is known as food security. Food insecurity contributes to incidence of undernourishment, hunger, and famine. The United Nations Food and Agriculture Organization (FAO) estimates that more than one in seven people worldwide, more than 1 billion people, suffered from hunger in 2010.

The global population has increased significantly since the Industrial Revolution of the 1700s. The most dramatic rise, however, occurred in last half of the twentieth century. Better agricultural production, improved access to health care, eradication of diseases, and economic development aided population growth as more people lived until adulthood. This population rise combined with a simultaneous and dramatic increase in urbanization—the movement of people to cities—made more global citizens dependent on purchasing most of their food. Food security in most of the world, therefore, is directly tied to the ability to afford food.

The consensus of agricultural and economic experts is that there is currently enough food produced worldwide to feed everyone. However, the most efficient food production is often concentrated in nations far away from the world's most insecure regions, challenging distribution. Factors that contribute to food insecurity—government instability, corruption, warfare, emergencies, and population migration to escape conflict—also threaten the adequate distribution of food. Similarly, the most productive agricultural technologies are concentrated in developed nations. The FAO has challenged researchers, governments, and aid organizations to develop methods of increasing food production by 50 percent by 2025.

■ Historical Background and Scientific Foundations

British political economist Thomas Malthus (1766–1834) first set forth his theories on the relationships among population, poverty, and agricultural production in his *Essay on the Principle of Population*, which was published in 1798. Malthus claimed that population is limited by mortality from disease and famine, but that population growth could eventually outpace agricultural production.

Malthus was primarily concerned with food assistance preventing what he considered natural checks on population and leading to a dramatic increase in the population of the poor. Subsequent thinkers, many applying Malthus's theory more universally, dubbed the prospect of population severely stressing agriculture as a Malthusian crisis or Malthusian catastrophe. German philosopher Karl Marx (1818–1883) later rejected Malthus's theory, asserting that the technological progress of the Industrial Revolution of the eighteenth and nineteenth centuries would prevent the Malthusian catastrophe of large populations from returning to subsistence farming.

Whereas the Industrial Revolution did make some farms more productive with the advent of mechanization and chemical fertilizers, food security continued to be challenged regionally by crop failure, economic collapse, poverty, and population shifts. Millions of people died in the first half of the twentieth century from famine in Africa, Asia, Central America, and Eastern Europe. Politically motivated changes in agriculture and population resettlement caused millions of famine-related deaths in Russia and China. Forced resettlement of agricultural workers and the state takeover of farms under collectivization, coupled with state-mandated implementation of Lysenkoism (politically influenced, pseudo-scientific agricultural practices), caused agricultural market collapse and massive crop failures in Russia in the 1920s and 1930s. An estimated 4 to 12 million people died from starvation, famine-related disease, or government execution during Russia's collectivization. China collectivized between 1959 and 1962 with similar results. Since then, the worldwide trend has been to decollectivize, but in a way that does not radically shift populations or cause food insecurity.

Crop failure was the predominant cause of localized food insecurity in the twentieth century. In 1943 nearly 4 million people died as result of crop failures and a food price crisis in India and present-day Bangladesh. Inadequate emergency stores of food helped undermine food security in the region. Famine in China following World War II (1939–1945), as well as localized food insecurity in Asia, the Pacific Island nations, and parts of the Americas, prompted researchers to develop new, hardy strains of wheat and rice seeds. The new seeds produced higher yields on existing farmland when coupled with modern agricultural practices such as the use of chemical fertilizers and pesticides. From 1943 to 1970, new hybridized crops enabled wheat and rice production in Asia to increase at least two-fold. This movement became known as the Green Revolution.

From the 1940s through the 1970s, the Green Revolution transformed worldwide agriculture. The movement promoted the development and use of hybridized, improved, or genetically altered seeds to prevent crop disease and improve yields. Improved irrigation, better land clearing practices, and mechanization expanded farmlands. Crop rotation and multi-cropping made farmland more productive and promoted crop variety. However, some note that improvements in agricultural yields may have both fueled rapid population increases in nations such as India and provided an inadequate solution to permanent food security. The number of hungry in India alone climbed by an estimated 30 million between 1995 and 2010.

The Green Revolution had measurable positive impact on food production, especially in Asia and the Americas. In 1950 the world's grain production was slightly less than 700 million tons. By 2010 world grain output approached 2 billon tons per year. Existing farmland became more productive: The amount of land dedicated to agriculture increased by only 600 million hectares from 1950 to 2000.

■ Impacts and Issues

The United Nations Millennium Development Goals call for halving global hunger and poverty by 2015 (compared to 1990 levels).

WORDS TO KNOW

BIOTECHNOLOGY: The manipulation or use of organisms for industrial or agricultural purposes.

DIRECT FOOD AID: The provision of food or rations of food to individuals. Direct food aid can also include providing the infrastructure for delivering and distributing food aid.

FAMINE: A generalized and extreme scarcity of food; prolonged extreme hunger, undernourishment, or lack of food.

FOOD SECURITY: The production and availability of sufficient food.

NONGOVERNMENTAL ORGANIZATION (NGO): An independent organization that is not part of, or administered by, any government.

POPULATION: A group with similar demographic characteristics such as geographic location, species, gender, age, habits, nationality, ethnicity, productive requirements, or needs.

UNDERNUTRITION: A condition that occurs when the body does not get enough nutrients to ensure healthy organ and tissue functions.

YIELD: The amount of a crop produced per planting or per growing season.

Schoolchildren eat lunch at school in Karottukara, Kerala, India.
© Borderlands / Alamy.

Whereas the Green Revolution significantly improved crop yields and helped several regions achieve greater food security, critics assert that the movement's narrow focus on yields ignored other contributors to endemic food scarcity, such as rapidly shifting and urbanizing populations. Similarly, the Green Revolution's emphasis on grains and rice is unlikely to work in the twenty-first century's most food insecure regions. In Africa, as much as 40 percent of all farmland is nutrient-depleted or seriously degraded. Only 8 percent of all agricultural land is irrigated. Few of the continent's varied growing zones are well suited for the staple grains that have worked elsewhere. The Institute for Natural Resources, which is based in Ghana, estimates that if current population and agricultural trends continue, Africa might be able to feed only 25 percent of its population in 2025.

The global population is expected to grow to 9.1 billion by 2050. The United Nations Population Division estimates that the world's population may exceed 10 billion by the close of the twenty-first century. However, others speculate that world population may peak this century. Some assert that as developing nations become wealthier, birth rates will drop as they did in the Western industrialized nations during the latter half of the twentieth century. Conversely, some assert that increasing food scarcity, competition for resources, and increased mortality from acquired immunodeficiency syndrome (AIDS) and other diseases will halt more rapid population growth in the world's poorest regions.

Solutions to food-population problems are roughly divided into three categories: controlling rates of population growth, increasing food production, and fighting poverty. These philosophies are not mutually exclusive. For example, aid programs in a food-insecure region may seek to promote better agricultural practices while also providing information on family planning; direct emergency food aid may be provided to a region in the short-term while longer-term development programs may encourage the establishment of small local businesses.

Hunger continues to be a widespread problem despite sufficient global food resources. Increased local food production can help fight undernutrition and bolster the distribution of food to nearby stressed regions, but it is not a sufficient solution in and of itself. Neither, strictly, is population limitation a solution. Roughly 5 percent of global foreign aid is related to agricultural development; even less is allocated to family planning education or the provision of contraceptives.

The global population replacement fertility rate, the number of children that women must have on average to keep current levels of population steady, is 2.33 children. Women in industrialized nations typically have fewer children than the global replacement rate whereas women in developing nations tend to have more children. Local population replacement fertility rates vary based on life expectancy, infant mortality rates, disease rates, and regularity of access to food and healthcare.

Family planning initiatives can also be controversial. Aid recipients may have cultural or religious taboos about speaking of sex or using birth control methods. Funding of family planning initiatives can spark controversy in donor nations, sometimes leading to reductions in overall aid amounts given to regions in need. State-imposed limitations on population, such as China's One Child Policy, are criticized as violating a basic human right to form a family. Others note that family planning helps women and families in the world's poorest regions have adequate food and other resources while also allowing women more time to become economic producers. Reliable food production and family planning primarily aid global food security by alleviating poverty—the primary cause of hunger worldwide.

Climate change poses additional challenges for global food security as Earth's population continues to grow. Agriculture will likely face new environmental stresses. Sea-level rise could inundate farmlands and salinate freshwater irrigation sources. Changing weather patterns may lengthen growing seasons in some places while shortening growing seasons in others. New outbreaks of crop diseases may emerge. Desertification and land degradation may render sterile formerly productive agricultural lands.

The effects of climate change on food production are most likely to be felt in Earth's middle latitudes, from 35 degrees south to 35 degrees north. This swath of the globe, home to more than 3 billion people, has some of the poorest regions and highest rates of population growth. Without adequate agricultural adaptation, especially in the equatorial belt, half of the world's population could face food shortages in the future. Poverty and underdeveloped modern agriculture already undermine food security in large areas of the equatorial belt, especially in Africa and south-central Asia.

SEE ALSO   *African Famine Relief; Agribusiness; Agricultural Deforestation; Agricultural Demand for Water; Agricultural Land Reform; Agriculture and International Trade; Agroecology; Biodiversity and Food Supply; Biofuels and World Hunger; Climate Change and Agriculture; Decollectivization; Desertification and Agriculture; Disasters and Food Supply; Ecological Impacts of Various World Diets; Ethical Issues in Agriculture; Ethical Issues in Food Aid; Extreme Weather and Food Supply; Famine; Food and Agriculture Organization (FAO); Food First; Food Price Crisis; Food Security; Food Sovereignty; Free Trade and Agriculture; Gender Equality and Agriculture; Genetically Modified Organisms (GMO); Green Revolution (1943); Hunger; International Food Aid; International Fund for Agricultural Development; Land Availability and Degradation; Livestock Intensity and Demand; Malnutrition; Rome Declaration on World Food Security (1996); Subsistence Farming; Sustainable Agriculture; UN Millennium Development*

Goals; Undernutrition; U.S. Agency for International Development (USAID); Wage Slavery in Food Production; War, Conquest, Colonialism, and Cuisine; Water Scarcity; Women's Role in Global Food Preparation; World Food Day; World Trade Organization (WTO).

BIBLIOGRAPHY

Books

Bayart, Jean-Francois. *The State in Africa: The Politics of the Belly.* Cambridge, UK: Polity, 2009.

Laszlo, Ervin, and Peter Seidel. *Global Survival: The Challenge and Its Implications for Thinking and Acting.* New York: SelectBooks, 2006.

Perfecto, Ivette, John H. Vandermeer, and Angus L. Wright. *Nature's Matrix: Linking Agriculture, Conservation and Food Sovereignty.* London: Earthscan, 2009.

Schanbacher, William D. *The Politics of Food: The Global Conflict between Food Security and Food Sovereignty.* Westport, CT: Praeger Security International, 2010.

Periodicals

Beddington, John. "Food Security: Contributions from Science to a New and Greener Revolution." *Philosophical Transactions of the Royal Society of London. Series B, Biological Sciences* 365, no. 1537 (2010): 61–71.

Godfray, H. Charles J., et al. "Food Security: The Challenge of Feeding 9 Billion People." *Science* 327, no. 5967 (2010): 812–818.

"How to Feed a Hungry World." *Nature* 466 (July 29, 2010): 531–532.

Rull, Valenti. "Food Security: Green Revolution Drawbacks." *Science* 328, no. 5975 (April 9, 2010): 169.

Westing, Arthur H. "Food Security: Population Controls." *Science* 328, no. 5975 (April 9, 2010): 169.

Web Sites

MacFarquhar, Neil. "Experts Worry as Population and Hunger Grow." *New York Times*, October 21, 2009. http://www.nytimes.com/2009/10/22/world/22food.html (accessed October 28, 2010).

Sadik, Nafis. "Population Growth and the Food Crisis." *Food and Agriculture Organization of the United Nations (FAO).* http://www.fao.org/docrep/u3550t/u3550t02.htm (accessed October 28, 2010).

Vidal, John. "Artificial Meat? Food for Thought by 2050." *The Guardian*, August 16, 2010. ttp://www.guardian.co.uk/environment/2010/aug/16/artificial-meat-food-royal-society (accessed October 28, 2010).

Adrienne Wilmoth Lerner

Poultry

■ Introduction

In less than 100 years, the poultry industry and the role of poultry in the diets of Americans and those in the developed world have undergone tremendous change. Until the 1920s, poultry was the purview of the small farm, and its primary role was as egg producer. Farmers raised hundreds of different poultry breeds. Roosters and older hens were slaughtered for the occasional dinner or soup pot.

The broadest poultry definition refers to domesticated fowl raised for meat or eggs. Chicken and turkey comprise the vast majority of worldwide poultry consumed. However, poultry can include duck, geese, guinea fowl, pheasant, quail, squab, ostrich, and emu.

Red meat rationing during World War II (1939–1945) coupled with advances in agricultural and food science in the decade after the war gave rise to larger-scale poultry production. Modernization brought greater supply, lower costs, and convenience products to consumers as American lifestyles changed.

Poultry is the most consumed meat in the United States, outpacing beef and pork since the early 1990s. Recent data show that the United States has the second largest per capita chicken consumption behind the United Arab Emirates. Per capita, Israel consumes the most turkey; the United States is second. Annual U.S. poultry production, which includes chicken, turkey, and eggs, exceeds $20 billion.

Health and environmental trends among consumers have increased demand for organic poultry, healthier cuts of meat, and greater understanding of food production practices. Rising obesity rates (partially attributable to consumption of processed foods) and outbreaks of foodborne illnesses are just two of the issues that have contributed to this increased demand.

■ Historical Background and Scientific Foundations

Domesticated chickens (*Gallus domesticus*) originated from wild red junglefowl (*Gallus gallus*) in South or Southeast Asia. They were domesticated for meat and eggs somewhere between 5000–10000 BC, spreading gradually throughout Asia, the Middle East, North Africa, and eventually Europe and the Americas.

Turkey (*Meleagris*), however, is a New World species and was domesticated by the Aztecs at least 2,000 years ago. Research suggests that turkeys originally were domesticated for their feathers and ritual value rather than for meat or eggs, which came later. Since that time, humans have developed hundreds of chicken breeds, selecting favorable meat and egg-producing characteristics to improve domestic production.

Beginning in the mid-nineteenth century, fancy poultry breeds were developed purely for recreational purposes, particularly in Great Britain. Poultry shows gained in popularity, featuring bantam, or miniature, and standard varieties sporting colorful feathers, lavish-appearing headdresses, spotted patterns, or elaborately long tail feathers. Nearly 400 breeds and varieties of ornamental poultry exist in the early twenty-first century. Poultry shows have seen a resurgence in Britain and the United States as raising backyard poultry makes a comeback.

Red meat rationing during World War II opened up the market for chicken, which was not rationed. Farmers raised young chickens called broiler-fryers to supply the growing demand in increasingly larger commercial operations. From the 1920s to mid-1950s, the retail price of poultry decreased whereas that of red meat increased. Cornish-Rock chickens, a cross between male Cornish and female Plymouth Rock birds, became the most commonly used in broiler production.

As the percentage of women in the workforce increased from 29.6 percent in 1950 to 46.6 in 2000, so did the demand for convenience foods. The first Kentucky Fried Chicken outlet was franchised in 1952. In 1954 Swanson foods introduced the first TV dinner. Fried chicken and roast turkey were among the most popular first TV dinner entrees. In 1980 McDonald's restaurants introduced Chicken McNuggets: deep-fried, battered portions made from minced chicken meat. Currently, processed chicken accounts for the largest percentage of chicken consumed in the United States.

Poultry has been at the center of a number of high-profile foodborne illness outbreaks. In 2007, for example, more than 270 individuals in 35 U.S. states were infected with *Salmonella*, most likely attributable to frozen Banquet brand not-ready-to-eat pot pies. A study showed that consumer failure to cook the pot pies thoroughly due to confusing label instructions may have contributed to the outbreak. In 2010, *Salmonella* tainted eggs were linked to two Iowa farms, after sickening over 1,600 people and leading to a national recall of over half a million eggs.

For decades, the U.S. Food and Drug Administration (FDA) has allowed the use of subtherapeutic (low) levels of antibiotics to be added to poultry feed. This practice has been found to speed up growth rates by impeding potential infections. A 1984 study by the U.S. Centers for Disease Control linked these antibiotics in poultry and livestock feed to resistant bacteria found in humans. Further studies found other cases linking antibiotic resistant bacteria in humans to antibiotic use in poultry. In 2001 the FDA released a report directed at poultry producers outlining principles for judicious use of antimicrobials, or antibiotics. By June 2010, the FDA issued more stringent guidelines, stating that "[g]iving animals antibiotics in order to increase food production is a threat to public health and should be stopped." At that time, the FDA issued "draft guidelines" for livestock producers to phase out antibiotics voluntarily, but a spokesperson stated that they had the power to issue an outright ban if necessary.

Since 1990 the demand for organic food has increased markedly in the United States and in the countries that comprise the European Union, reaching more than $35 billion combined in 2003. Of all organic meats, chicken is the most widely available: More than 70 percent of U.S. shoppers purchase natural or organic chicken. To be labeled organic, poultry must meet certain standards that stipulate 100 percent organic feed, certified organic pasture, and acceptable practices for treatment of diseases and pests.

WORDS TO KNOW

FREE RANGE: A food-source animal that is permitted to pasture graze for food rather than being confined to a feed house or feed lot.

HEIRLOOM: A variety of plant or breed of animal that has not been subjected to industrialized modification. Heirloom chickens, for example, include mostly free-range breeds that are slow-growing, as opposed to the fast-growing chickens that are used in conventional poultry operations.

ORGANIC AGRICULTURE: The production of food or fiber crops, livestock, or livestock-related products without the use of synthetic fertilizers, pesticides, or hormones.

PATHOGEN: A disease-causing organism.

POULTRY: General term describing all birds raised for their meat, feathers, or eggs, including chickens, quail, turkeys, ducks, geese, doves, and pheasants.

SALMONELLA: A rod-shaped, Gram-negative bacterium often present in low levels in food sources such as poultry and eggs that is the cause of salmonellosis infection in humans.

■ Impacts and Issues

Enhanced poultry production techniques have increased the availability of poultry worldwide and have lowered the cost relative to beef and pork. But this has not been without consequences: The practice of keeping concentrated numbers of birds in confined spaces contributes to a number of negative health and safety outcomes both for the animals and for consumers. Large flocks of genetically similar birds are more susceptible to infectious disease outbreaks. Insect pests such as mites and lice spread more quickly when poultry are in confined spaces.

The rapid spread of avian influenza among poultry has been attributed to concentrated living quarters and poor hygiene practices. Avian influenza is a naturally occurring virus that infects waterfowl and some shorebirds. Domestic poultry are susceptible to a highly virulent strain of avian influenza known as H5N1 that causes severe disease with high death rates. The World Health Organization reported the first known case of H5N1 in a farmed goose in Guangdong Province, China.

In 2003 the virus swiftly spread to eight Asian countries including the Republic of Korea (South Korea), Vietnam, Japan, Thailand, Cambodia, and China. Since that time the virus continues to be reported in Asia, and has spread to a number of other Asian countries, as well as to Egypt, Africa, and Europe. Transmission to humans occurs primarily

A customer looks at cooked ducks hanging in a restaurant in New York City's Chinatown district. *Adrienne Lerner / Lerner & Lerner / LernerMedia Global Photos.*

from close contact with infected birds, though a few cases of human-to-human transmission have not been ruled out.

The risk of foodborne illness-causing bacteria increases during mechanized processing of poultry carcasses. *Salmonella* and *Campylobacter* are two of the most common bacteria associated with poultry. Bird digestive tracts naturally contain *Salmonella* and *Campylobacter* bacteria. If the intestines are ruptured during processing, the poultry flesh may come in contact with the bacteria. Improper processing or food handling techniques can cause the bacteria to be transmitted to humans. Thorough cooking kills these bacteria.

A method to identify potential food safety risks was developed in the 1960s by the Pillsbury Company. Known by the acronym HACCP (Hazard Analysis Critical Control Points), this method has evolved as a widely accepted industry standard proven to reduce risk of contamination, particularly in the meat and poultry industries when followed.

Current statistics indicate that worldwide, more than one billion adults are overweight or obese, reaching epidemic proportions. In the United States, rates are even more startling: Statistics from the U.S. Centers for Disease Control in 2008 show combined overweight and obese adults to account for 68 percent of all American adults, nearly 73 million people. Scientific evidence

in a 2003 expert report commissioned by the World Health Organization and the Food and Agriculture Organization of the United Nations found that eating energy-rich foods contributes to weight gain. Current U.S. dietary guidelines issued in 2005 recommend curbing total fat intake, often found in energy-rich foods, to no more than 20–35 percent of total calories.

Though lean cuts of poultry cooked in low-fat ways such as baking or broiling can be a healthful part of a balanced diet, processed chicken products such as nuggets, strips, and patties are examples of energy-rich foods that tend to be high in saturated fats. Processed poultry products account for the majority of poultry consumed in the United States, with more than 40 percent of all chicken being sold in a processed form (other than cut-up chicken parts).

Nutrition labels on popular chicken products such as a Banquet brand chicken patty show that 55 percent of the calories in one serving are from fat. One serving of Tyson Buffalo Style Chicken Strips contains nearly 40 percent of its calories from fat and has 52 percent of daily recommended sodium.

Greater awareness among consumers of the potential negative health impacts of factory-farmed poultry, concerns over inhumane treatment of animals in factory farms, and the environmental costs of intensive farming systems have increased demand for organic and free-range poultry. In addition, current trends toward smaller-scale farming, sustainable production methods, backyard poultry keeping, and conserving heirloom poultry breeds have led to greater availability of a wider variety of poultry such as duck, geese, and guinea fowl as well as heirloom varieties of chicken and turkey.

SEE ALSO *Avian Influenza; Eggs; Factory Farming; Fast Food; Food Inspection and Standards; Food Safety and Inspection Service; Humane Animal Farming; International Federation of Organic Agriculture Movements; Livestock Intensity and Demand; Meats; Organics; Poultry Products Inspection Act of 1957; Processed Foods;* Salmonella; *Urban Chicken Movement.*

BIBLIOGRAPHY

Books

Nollet, Leo M. L. *Handbook of Processed Meats and Poultry Analysis.* Boca Raton, FL: CRC Press, 2009.

Peacock, Paul. *The Urban Hen: A Practical Guide to Keeping Poultry in a Town or City.* Oxford: Spring Hill, 2009.

Periodicals

Altekruse, Sean F., et al. "Salmonella Enteritidis in Broiler Chickens, United States, 2000–2005." *Emerging Infectious Diseases* 12, no. 12 (2006): 1848–1852.

Beato, Maria Serema, Ilaria Capua, and Dennis J. Alexander. "Avian Influenza Viruses in Poultry Products: A Review." *Avian Pathology: Journal of the W.V.P.A.* 38, no. 3 (2009): 193–200.

Buzby, Jean, and Hodan Farah. "Chicken Consumption Continues Longrun Rise." *Amber Waves* 4, no. 2 (April 2006): 5.

Web Sites

Oyarzabal, Omar A. "*Campylobacter* in Poultry Processing." *Auburn University Department of Poultry Science.* http://www.ag.auburn.edu/poul/virtuallibrary/oyarzabalcampylobacter.html (accessed October 2, 2010).

"Poultry and Eggs." *Economic Research Service, U.S. Department of Agriculture* updated April 16, 2009. http://www.ers.usda.gov/Briefing/Poultry/ (accessed October 2, 2010).

Andrea Abel

Poultry Products Inspection Act of 1957

■ Introduction

The Poultry Products Inspection Act of 1957 (P.L. 85-172, later amended) required that all domesticated birds intended for slaughter, interstate sales, and human consumption be inspected by the United States Department of Agriculture (USDA) Food Safety Inspection Service (FSIS) for sanitation and purity. The legislation covered chickens, ducks, geese, guinea fowl, and turkeys, whether they were used for butchered meat or in processed foods. The law sought to prevent the adulteration of food products containing poultry, to enforce hygienic slaughtering and processing standards, and to outlaw the mislabeling of products that contained or should have contained poultry.

■ Historical Background and Scientific Foundations

At the turn of the twentieth century, activists, journalists, and government officials embarked on a campaign to expose unsanitary practices in the food industry, especially in meatpacking. Without dependable refrigeration, many non-farm and urban households frequently used potted meat products. Adulterated food—food contaminated with unspecified additives, preservatives, non-food ingredients, chemicals, waste products, rancid ingredients, or harmful bacteria—was commonplace. Robust scientific inspections and industry regulations to ensure food safety, however, were rare.

A series of highly publicized incidents involving contaminated foods and patent medicines, coupled with the publication of graphic stories and books depicting the meatpacking industry, spurred government action to regulate the significant portion of the meatpacking industry that sold its products in interstate commerce (commerce across state lines). Congress passed the Pure Food and Drug Act of 1906 and the Federal Meat Inspection Act of 1906 simultaneously. The laws governed a variety of

food products from popular health tonics to meats; however, poultry was excluded from regulation under both laws. A rhyme from the era, a play on the child's rhyme "Mary Had a Little Lamb," highlighted popular concern over food purity: "Mary had a little lamb, and when she saw it sicken, she shipped it off to packing town and now it's labeled chicken." (U.S. President Lyndon B. Johnson mentioned the rhyme in his speech upon signing the successor to the Poultry Products Inspection Act of 1957, the Wholesome Poultry Products Act of 1968.)

After World War II ended in 1945, consumer demand increased for newly introduced ready-to-cook products and processed foods. Refrigerated transportation and increasing economic prosperity led to a decline in sales of potted meats and a boom in convenient, already-butchered meat cuts. Innovations in home cooking appliances, coupled with the advent of large supermarkets, promised rapid and easy-to-cook meals. In response to changing food consumer behavior, food safety experts and advocacy groups pushed Congress to broaden safety and purity laws governing meats to include poultry.

The Poultry Products Inspection Act of 1957 accomplished essentially the same ends as the 1906 meatpacking laws that proceeded it. Poultry that entered interstate commerce was subject to federal health and safety inspections, new sanitary standards governed slaughterhouses and processing plants, sickly birds and contaminated or rancid poultry was excluded from human consumption, and poultry food products had to be accurately labeled to indicate the types of meats, poultry, and some (but not all) of the additives used.

■ Impacts and Issues

The 1957 act provided the foundation for poultry inspection in the United States, but the body of laws governing inspection changed over the following decades. Regulations on poultry safety and purity generally became more strict and expanded to cover a great number of poultry products.

The Poultry Products Inspection Act of 1957, by providing for the inspection of poultry that entered interstate commerce, ensured that by 1967 USDA regulations covered approximately 87 percent of the nation's poultry food products. However, the act still left 13 percent of all U.S. poultry products—those that remained in intrastate commerce—subject to little, infrequent, or no inspection. Whereas some states had robust inspection programs for poultry products within their bounds, others had no regulation at all.

In August 1968, the federal government closed the loophole excluding poultry that remained in its home state. Under the Wholesome Poultry Act of 1968, all poultry had to meet USDA regulatory standards for food safety, purity, sanitation, and labeling. States were charged with insuring that their inspection programs met or exceeded federal regulations within two years after the passage of the act. If they failed to do so, federal inspectors were permitted to inspect poultry in the state. The law followed a similar law governing meat enacted in 1967, the Wholesome Meat Act, another so-called "Equal to" law because state inspections had to be equal to federal inspections in quality, scope, and frequency. The 2008 Farm Bill permits some meats and poultry that have passed rigorous state inspections to enter interstate commerce without undergoing federal inspection.

Eggs, the most commonly consumed poultry product in the United States, were not regulated at the federal level until 1970. The USDA was then authorized to inspect the contents of eggs used in processed egg products and the shells of eggs sold whole. Regulations were adopted that covered safe storage and transportation of eggs as well as sanitary conditions for egg processing facilities. Regulations governing eggs later expanded to cover pasteurization, grading, labeling, and random sample testing for food-borne illnesses.

As of 2010, issues remain in poultry processing. Despite legal challenges in 2008, poultry continues to be excluded from the 1958 Federal Humane Methods of Slaughter Act. Investigations and reports by the Humane Society of the United States and East Bay Animal Advocates noted alleged instances of routine animal cruelty in poultry processing plants, including shackling, spiking, impaling, electrocuting, limb-breaking, beak cutting, and drowning of live birds. Poultry processing advocates assert that the industry recognizes that good, rapid, and humane slaughtering practices are the norm as they ensure the best quality of meat.

Poultry processing is a dangerous occupation. Workers in poultry processing plants have higher-than-average rates of on-the-job injuries, ranging from catastrophic injuries by machines and cutting devices to repetitive stress injuries from the highly physical assembly line work. In May 2008, the median annual wage for an individual

WORDS TO KNOW

ACT: A statute, rule, or formal lawmaking document enacted by a legislative body or issued by a government.

INTERSTATE COMMERCE: The buying and selling of goods or services across state boundaries.

INTRASTATE COMMERCE: The buying and selling of goods or services within the boundaries of a single state.

POULTRY: Domestic birds raised for consumption of their meat or eggs.

REGULATION: Controlling behaviors, business practices, or industrial practices through rules, restrictions, or laws to encourage preferred outcomes or prevent undesired outcomes that may otherwise occur.

working in poultry or meat processing was $23,030. Labor leaders assert that working conditions and sanitation in all meatpacking professions are closely related. Workers who are tired, in pain, and expected to butcher animals at a rapid rate, may miss signs of contamination

Chickens hang from a line at a chicken processing plant in Tecumseh, Nebraska. The Poultry Products Inspection Act of 1957 requires the U.S. Department of Agriculture to inspect slaughtered and processed poultry. *AP Images.*

in meat. Stressful working conditions may exacerbate worker illnesses or make workers more careless about sanitation precautions.

■ Primary Source Connection

President Lyndon Baines Johnson (1908–1973) issued these remarks when signing the Wholesome Poultry Products Act on August 19, 1968. The Food Safety and Inspection Service (FSIS) continues to inspect meat and poultry products to insure they are correctly labeled, properly packaged, and safely stored.

Statement by the President Upon Signing the Wholesome Poultry Products Act

Eight months ago I signed into law the Wholesome Meat Act of 1967. That landmark bill capped a crusade that had begun 60 years ago—to assure American housewives that the meat they served their families was pure, not harmful or dirty or diseased.

Today I am proud to sign a bill that will extend the same coverage to all poultry products. It is the fulfillment of a promise I made to every housewife—in my first consumer message just after I became President.

In the early days of this century, Americans took for granted that there were risks in buying food. They even joked about it in print. One newspaper printed a little poem:

"Mary had a little lamb,
And when she saw it sicken,
She shipped it off to packing town,
And now it's labeled chicken."

In 1968, we cannot tolerate the image, or the fact, of unwholesome food:

—Not when Americans last year consumed more than 12 billion pounds of poultry.

—Not when a full 13 percent of that supply—or 1.6 billion pounds—was subject to little or no inspection because it didn't cross State lines.

That loophole did not necessarily mean that all, or even most, of those 1.6 billion pounds were unsafe.

But it did mean that shady processors could avoid Federal inspection laws by distributing tainted poultry within the same State.

It did mean that the housewife often took an unnecessary risk—for her children and herself—when she bought a chicken.

The Wholesome Poultry Products Act of 1968 will insure that dirty plants will have to clean up or close down.

It will give a State 2 years to develop an inspection system as good as the Federal system. If, at the end of that time, the State has not done so, then Federal inspection will be imposed.

It will give the States financial and technical assistance in establishing inspection programs and training inspectors.

It will let the Secretary of Agriculture take action against any plant where the State fails to correct conditions endangering the public health.

When I was a year old—the same age as my grandson is now—President Theodore Roosevelt stated a principle which has survived the test of time: that "No man may poison the people for his private profit."

I believe that. I think all Americans believe it. And this bill will help us make sure it becomes a reality.

Lyndon Baines Johnson

JOHNSON, LYNDON BAINES. "LYNDON B. JOHNSON: STATEMENT BY THE PRESIDENT UPON SIGNING THE WHOLESOME POULTRY PRODUCTS ACT." *THE AMERICAN PRESIDENCY PROJECT.* HTTP://WWW.PRESIDENCY.UCSB.EDU/ WS/INDEX.PHP?PID=29084 (ACCESSED OCTOBER 24, 2010).

SEE ALSO *Factory Farming; Food Inspection and Standards; Food Safety and Inspection Service; Humane Animal Farming; Poultry; Urban Chicken Movement.*

BIBLIOGRAPHY

Books

Amundson, Finn J. *Inspection and Protection of U.S. Meat and Poultry.* New York: Nova Science Publishers, 2010.

Grist, A. *Poultry Inspection: Anatomy, Physiology and Disease Conditions.* Nottingham, UK: Nottingham University Press, 2006.

Law, Marc T., and Gary D. Libecap. *The Determinants of Progressive Era Reform: The Pure Food and Drugs Act of 1906.* Cambridge, MA: National Bureau of Economic Research, 2004.

Periodicals

DeHaven, W. Ron, and Ruth Goldberg. "Animal Health: Foundation of a Safe, Secure, and Abundant Food Supply." *Journal of Veterinary Medical Education* 33, no. 4 (2006): 496–501.

Web Sites

"Poultry Products Inspection Act." *U.S. Food and Drug Administration (FDA).* http://www.fda.gov/ RegulatoryInformation/Legislation/ucm148721. htm (accessed September 7, 2010).

Adrienne Wilmoth Lerner

Preservation

■ Introduction

The source of a food and the consumer of that food are often far apart in location and time. Few people can eat their food as soon as it is harvested or ready. Therefore, food storage and preservation play an important role in maintaining regular food supplies and keeping them edible and palatable. Foods such as fruits, vegetables, meat, and fish, have a natural tendency to spoil over time because of the action of enzymes in their tissues. Most fresh foods also attract bacteria and fungi, which present a food safety hazard when they multiply. There are many methods of preserving foods to keep them edible and safe, among which are canning, refrigeration, and freezing. More traditional methods of food preservation, such as drying; curing with salt, nitrite, or smoke; and preserving of fruits and vegetables as jam and pickles are still valued, but more as a way of enhancing the taste of certain foods. Chemical preservatives are also added to foods to prolong their shelf life and increase the number of foods available to consumers. Food preservatives have been criticized because they enable food to be transported many miles while maintaining freshness, thereby increasing carbon emissions and decreasing consumers' purchases of foods from local sources.

■ Historical Background and Scientific Foundations

Before agriculture, when humans relied on hunting and gathering for food, supplies were unpredictable. Even when crops were cultivated, harvests had to last all year round. Therefore there has always been a need for food storage and preservation, with the latter implying some kind of treatment of the food to keep it edible. Food preservation aims to arrest the natural processes of decay of food, which are brought about by enzymes, and also to stop microbial growth, both of which impair the palatability of food by altering its taste and texture, and also

its safety. Different foods lend themselves to different methods of preservation. Drying, curing with smoking and salting, and making jams and jellies are traditional methods of food preservation, and they are still used. However, the advent of canning and refrigeration in the nineteenth century enabled a wide range of foods to be stored and preserved on a large scale and led to the rapid expansion of the food industry.

All methods of preservation aim to deprive spoilage enzymes in food of the conditions they need for optimum activity. Preservation also inhibits the growth of microbes that would otherwise compromise the safety of food. Drying is the simplest method of preservation: It removes enough water from food to make it unattractive to microbes, and a solid skin also forms on the food, which makes it harder for microbes to enter. Drying is carried out either in the sun or in a food dehydrator, which applies gentle heat to the food, which evaporates moisture and removes it from the food's surface. This is the method of drying most often used commercially. Freeze-drying was used thousands of years ago by Peruvian Indians in the high altitudes of the Andes as a way of preserving potatoes. Freeze-drying dehydrates food through sublimation, which turns ice crystals in the frozen food directly

WORDS TO KNOW

CANNING: A process of preserving food by boiling it in a container, creating a vacuum inside that inhibits the growth of bacteria.

PECTIN: A glue-like compound located between plant cell walls. Pectin forms a matrix that traps water into a smooth and viscous gel. It is an essential component in making jams and jellies to preserve fruit.

PRESERVATIVES: A type of food additive that preserves the life of a food. The use of preservatives increases the range of foods available to the consumer by extending their shelf lives and improving food safety.

into water vapor. This technology is used in the manufacture of instant soups, emergency rations, and foods used in camping and space travel. Foods suitable for drying include meat, seafood, fruit, vegetables, and herbs.

Curing is a method of preservation that utilizes salt, nitrite, or smoke to dehydrate foods, depriving spoilage enzymes and microbes of the moisture they need. Salting food has a long history, whereas potassium nitrate preservation was discovered sometime in the Middle Ages. Nitrate is reduced to nitrite by bacteria in food, and this is actually the preserving agent. Nitrite blocks the growth of many bacteria, although the mechanism may be more complex than mere dehydration.

Smoking is a method of curing that dehydrates a food by exposing it to smoke, either directly in hot smoking or indirectly in cold smoking. The source of the smoke must be carefully chosen to ensure the food is not exposed to dangerous amounts of polycyclic aromatic hydrocarbons, which are carcinogens found in some smokes. Smoking adds characteristic flavors to foods such as fish and meat.

Preserves and pickles are traditional ways of preserving fruits and vegetables, still often used by gardeners to deal with a glut of produce. Sweet preserves may be whole preserved fruits, fruit jellies, or jams. Getting the correct balance of sugar, acid, and pectin (a natural gelling agent present in fruit) is the key to making a successful preserve. The high sugar content of sweet preserves draws water out of bacteria and so inhibits growth. Pickles are vegetables placed in a strong acidic solution,

Residents of a hutong in China dry vegetables on a line outside of their home. Drying is a common and easy method of preserving some foods. *Adrienne Lerner / Lerner & Lerner / LernerMedia Global Photos.*

Narwhal meat cures throughout the summer in northwest Greenland. Cured narwhal meat will keep indefinitely.   © *Arcticphoto / Alamy.*

usually vinegar, whose low pH inhibits the growth of many bacteria. Another approach to pickling is fermentation, which involves placing the vegetables with bacteria that produce lactic acid. One of the best known example is sauerkraut, which is a fermented cabbage product.

Refrigeration is now the most widespread and convenient method of food preservation. Most foods can be refrigerated, although the time they can be kept fresh varies. Tropical fruits such as avocado and banana cannot stand chilling and should never be refrigerated.

IN CONTEXT: ACID PRODUCING MICROORGANISMS

Some microorganisms are capable of modifying the pH of their environment. For example, bacteria that utilize the sugar glucose can produce lactic acid, which can lower the pH. The term pH refers to the concentration of hydrogen ions (H+) in a solution. An acidic environment is enriched in hydrogen ions, whereas a basic environment is relatively depleted of hydrogen ions. The hydrogen ion concentration can be determined empirically and expressed as the pH scale ranging from 0 to 14, with 1 being the most acidic and 14 being the most basic. Mathematically, pH is calculated as the negative logarithm of the hydrogen ion concentration. For example, the hydrogen ion concentration of distilled water is $10-7$, and hence pure water has a pH of 7. The pH scale is a logarithmic scale. That is, each division is different from the adjacent divisions by a factor of ten. For example, a solution that has a pH of 5 is 10 times as acidic as a solution with a pH of 6.

Microorganisms can tolerate a spectrum of pHs. However, an individual microbe usually has an internal pH that is close to that of distilled water. The surrounding cell membranes and external layers such as the **glycocalyx** contribute to buffering the cell from the different pH of the surrounding environment. Some microorganisms can actively pump hydrogen ions out of the cell into the environment, creating more acidic conditions. Acidic conditions can also result from the microbial utilization of a basic compound such as ammonia. Conversely, some microorganisms raise the pH of the surrounding mix by releasing ammonia (a base).

The ability of microbes to acidify the environment has been long exploited in the pickling process. Foods commonly pickled include cucumbers (i.e., pickles), cabbage (i.e., sauerkraut), milk (i.e., buttermilk), and some meats. As well, the production of vinegar relies upon the pH decrease caused by the bacterial production of acetic acid.

A variety of homemade pickles and preserved vegetables. *Image copyright Ferencz Teglas, 2010. Used under license from Shutterstock.com.*

Freezing is a more extreme version of refrigeration and involves rapid cooling of the food until its water content becomes ice, which stops all enzymatic and microbial activity. Most foods survive freezing well and can be cooked from the frozen state, however, if freezing is done too slowly, larger ice crystals form that can damage the tissue of the food, impairing its texture. Foods with very high water content, such as lettuce, do not freeze well because they do not regain their texture when thawed.

Canning is the other major method of food preservation and involves heating the food in a hermetically sealed stainless steel can for a time that depends upon the nature of the food. If heating is not thorough, spores of the bacterium *Clostridium botulinum* may survive and cause potentially deadly food poisoning. Any cans that have outward bulges ought to be discarded, as this may be a sign of bacterial activity inside the can.

■ Impacts and Issues

The use of food preservatives is intended to keep food safe for human consumption by stopping its spoilage during storage. Without food preservatives, people would be forced to buy food more frequently and use mainly local sources, so their introduction by the food industry has increased the convenience of shopping and cooking. Common food preservatives include sorbates, benzoates, sulfites, and lactates. As food additives, food preservatives have all been extensively tested for safety. However, critics say that allergic reactions to sulfites and benzoates may occur. It can also be argued that the use of preservatives harms the environment because it encourages international food trade, which increases carbon emissions. Some products, including organic foods, market themselves as more ethically sound because they are preservative-free.

SEE ALSO *Diet and Cancer; Diet and Heart Disease; Diet and Hypertension; Farm-to-Table Movement; Fast Food; Food Additives; Food Allergies; History of Home Cooking; Locavore; Processed Foods; Salt, Nitrites, and Health; Slow Food Movement; Truth in Labeling.*

BIBLIOGRAPHY

Books

Madison, Deborah. *Preserving Food without Freezing or Canning: Traditional Techniques Using Salt, Oil,*

Sugar, Alcohol, Vinegar, Drying, Cold Storage, and Lactic Fermentation: The Gardeners and Farmers of Terre Vivante. White River Junction, VT: Chelsea Green, 2007.

Russell, Nicholas. *Food Preservatives.* New York: Kluwer Academic/Plenum, 2003.

Shepard, Sue. *Pickled, Potted, and Canned: How the Art and Science of Food Preserving Changed the World.* New York: Simon & Schuster, 2006.

Periodicals

Eigenmann, Philippe A., and Charles A. Haenggeli. "Food Colourings, Preservatives, and Hyperactivity." *Lancet* 370 no. 9598 (2007): 1524–1525.

Soubra, Lama, Dolla Sarkis, Christoper Hilan, and Philippe H. Verger. "Dietary Exposure of Children and Teenagers to Benzoates, Sulphites, Butylhydroxyanisol (bha) and Butylhydroxytoluen (bht) in Beirut (Lebanon)." *Regulatory Toxicology and Pharmacology* 47, no. 1 (2007): 68–77.

Web Sites

"Food Ingredients and Colors." *U.S. Food and Drug Administration (FDA).* http://www.fda.gov/food/foodingredientspackaging/ucm094211.htm (accessed October 10, 2010).

"Preservatives; Use in Non-standardized Foods; Label Declaration." *U.S. Food and Drug Administration (FDA).* http://www.fda.gov/ICECI/ComplianceManuals/CompliancePolicyGuidanceManual/ucm074583.htm (accessed October 10, 2010).

Susan Aldridge

Processed Foods

Introduction

Food processing refers to methods used to transform raw ingredients into different forms of food. Food processing often produces foods that have extended shelf lives and contain flavor-enhancing food additives, exhibit enhanced appearances, and/or have undergone processes to inhibit the growth of pathogens. Processed foods comprise the majority of food consumed in developed nations, both at home and in restaurants. In the United States, for example, processed foods account for approximately 90 percent of food consumption.

Processed foods have a number of benefits and drawbacks. They are generally safe due to processes used to destroy pathogens that cause foodborne illnesses. Preservation techniques used in food processing prolong the shelf life of food, which reduces food spoilage and waste. Many of the additives included in processed foods, however, have been linked to various health problems. Processed foods with salts, including certain preservatives, contribute to hypertension and an increased risk of heart disease and stroke. Sugars and fats added to enhance the flavor of processed foods have been linked to increased rates of obesity and diabetes.

Historical Background and Scientific Foundations

Pre-industrial societies around the world developed various food preservation techniques, some of which date back more than 2,500 years, to delay food spoilage and deterioration and enable them to supplement their diets with preserved food during times when seasonal food was scarce. For example, livestock would be slaughtered before winter when grazing land and silage would be in short supply. People would preserve the meat by salt curing, sun drying, or smoking. Pre-industrial societies typically preserved vegetables through fermentation or sun drying.

By the late eighteenth century, European armies and navies began searching for new food preservation methods that would allow them to feed sailors and soldiers on campaigns. In 1795 the French army offered a reward to anyone who developed an improved food preservation method. After 14 years of experimentation, in 1810 French chef and inventor Nicolas Appert (1749–1841) announced that he had developed a method of canning. Appert's canning method involved sealing cooked food in glass jars and submerging the jars in boiling water, which creates a vacuum seal. Appert noted that the canned food would not spoil unless the seal leaked. More than 50 years later, French chemist Louis Pasteur (1822–1895) explained that microbes entering through broken seals caused spoilage and contamination.

Scientists and industrialists in Europe and the United States made numerous improvements on Appert's innovation in the following decades, including replacing the fragile glass jars with metal containers. The cost of canned goods, however, remained prohibitively expensive for the average consumer until manufacturing improvements in the late nineteenth century.

In the mid-nineteenth century, Louis Pasteur revolutionized food processing by applying the results of his research on microbial contamination to the food industry. Pasteur developed a process of heating food to certain temperatures for certain lengths of time and then quickly cooling the food. This process, known as pasteurization, impedes microbial growth in the food by reducing the number of pathogens contained in the product. Although the high temperatures used to pasteurize food affects the taste of some foods, many other foods undergo pasteurization without a noticeable effect on flavor. In the twenty-first century, pasteurization is most closely associated with dairy processing.

In the early twentieth century, food manufacturers established numerous methods of food processing. During the 1920s Clarence Birdseye (1886–1956) developed a method for freezing fish, meat, and vegetables. Birdseye discovered that freezing foods quickly prevented the formation of large ice crystals that damaged the cell walls of food and made food less palatable. By the mid-twentieth century, food manufacturers employed Birdseye's freezing methods to produce a wide array of frozen products, including complete meals known as "TV dinners." At the same time, food manufacturers also expanded the use of food additives, including preservatives, sweeteners, and salts, to produce ready-to-eat convenience foods.

■ Impacts and Issues

Modern processed food has numerous advantages for both consumers and manufacturers. Various processes, including canning and freezing, preserve food, which extends shelf life and delays deterioration. Improved preservation methods benefit consumers by decreasing the amount of food that spoils before consumption. In the United States, for example, only about 3 percent of processed foods are discarded for spoilage. In developing countries with limited food processing, food loss rates of 30 to 50 percent are not uncommon.

Food preservation also enables consumers to consume a wider array of foods and a more varied diet throughout the year, because they do not have to rely solely on seasonal foods. Consumers may obtain quickly perishable

foods, such as fruits and vegetables, from distant regions. Also, because many perishable foods are processed near their points of origin, manufacturers do not have to transport fragile food quickly over great distances. Processed foods, therefore, offer consumers cheaper alternatives to more expensive, perishable, fresh foods.

In some instances, processed foods supply consumers with food that is healthy as well as safe. Modern food preservation and packaging methods have decreased the

Workers at the Hummel Brothers, Inc., hot dog plant in New Haven, Connecticut, inspect hot dogs. © *Peter Casolino / Alamy.*

incidence of foodborne illnesses caused by food contamination. Pasteurization and freezing slow the reproduction of pathogens that cause disease. Many foods, including breakfast cereals, milk, and salt, are also fortified with essential vitamins and minerals. Without food fortification, most consumers would not consume the recommended allowance of many vitamins and minerals.

Despite these health and safety benefits, however, processed foods also have a negative effect on the health of many consumers and have been blamed for rising rates of obesity, diabetes, and heart disease in developed nations. Processed foods typically contain high levels of sugars and fats to improve taste. The consumption of high-calorie, high-fat foods contributes to obesity. The World Health Organization (WHO) states that overconsumption of foods high in calories and fat is the primary cause of increased obesity rates. By 2015, the WHO estimates, 2.3 billion adults will be overweight and more than 700 million adults will be obese. The consumption of high-sugar foods also contributes to diabetes. The WHO estimates that global diabetes rates will increase by 50 percent between 2005 and 2015.

In addition to high levels of sugars and fats, many processed foods contain high levels of sodium, which contributes to hypertension and heart disease. Other preservatives used in processed foods, such as sodium benzoate, also contain high levels of sodium. Sodium inhibits the growth of bacteria, mold, and yeasts that cause food to spoil and become unsafe. Because preservation is one of the primary goals of food processing, many manufacturers add sodium to processed foods. Salt enhances the flavor of food, enhances color, serves as a stabilizer, and covers the flavor of low quality ingredients used in some processed foods. Sodium, however, is one of the leading contributors to hypertension and increases the risk of heart disease and stroke. The Dietary Guidelines for Americans recommends limiting sodium intake to no more than 2,300 milligrams per day with a goal of 1,500 milligrams per day. A cup of canned soup or a frozen dinner, however, may contain as many as 1,200 milligrams of sodium.

Advocates of the consumption of fresh, seasonal foods also lament that processed foods have decreased public awareness about the source of food. Activists such as Michael Pollan (1955–) argue that the proliferation of processed foods has disconnected consumers from the land and an understanding of agricultural production. Consumers have lost touch with the seasonality of ingredients and expect all varieties of food to be available all year. Finally, Pollan and others argue that fast preparation of processed foods has removed many of the social aspects of food preparation and consumption shared among family and friends.

SEE ALSO *Alice Waters: California and New American Cuisine; Diet and Cancer; Diet and Diabetes; Diet and Heart Disease; Diet and Hypertension; Fast Food; Food Additives; Improving Nutrition for America's Children Act of 2010; Michael Pollan: Linking Food and Environmental Journalism; Nutrient Fortification of Foods; Preservation; Raw Milk Campaign; Salt, Nitrites, and Health; Slow Food Movement.*

BIBLIOGRAPHY
Books
Ettlinger, Steve. *Twinkie, Deconstructed: My Journey to Discover How the Ingredients Found in Processed Foods Are Grown, Mined (Yes, Mined), and Manipulated into What America Eats.* New York: Hudson Street Press, 2007.

Fellows, Peter. *Processed Foods for Improved Livelihoods.* Rome: Agricultural Support Systems Division, Food and Agriculture Organization of the United Nations, 2004.

Salt Assault: Brand-Name Comparisons of Processed Foods. Washington, DC: Center for Science in the Public Interest, 2008.

Shahidi, Fereidoon. *Quality of Fresh and Processed Foods.* New York: Kluwer Academic/Plenum, 2004.

Periodicals
Angell, Sonia Y. "Emerging Opportunities for Monitoring the Nutritional Content of Processed Foods." *The American Journal of Clinical Nutrition* 91, no. 2 (2010): 298–299.

Fiocchi, Alessandro, et al. "Clinical Tolerance of Processed Foods." *Annals of Allergy, Asthma & Immunology* 93, no. 5 (2004): 38–46.

"Pros and Cons of Minimally Processed Foods." *Trends in Food Science & Technology* 18, no. 11 (2007): 582.

Webster, Jacqueline L., Elizabeth K. Dunford, and Bruce C. Neal. "A Systematic Survey of the Sodium Contents of Processed Foods." *The American Journal of Clinical Nutrition* 91, no. 2 (2010): 413–420.

Web Sites
Kotz, Deborah. "Wean Yourself off Processed Foods in 7 Steps." *U.S. News and World Report*, June 4, 2010. http://health.usnews.com/health-news/diet-fitness/diabetes/articles/2010/06/04/wean-yourself-off-processed-foods-in-7-steps.html (accessed October 31, 2010).

"Obesity Expert Calls Processed Food 'Toxic.'" *Consumer Affairs.com*, August 14, 2006. http://www.consumeraffairs.com/news04/2006/08/processed_food.html (accessed October 31, 2010).

Zeratsky, Katherine. "Low-Sodium Diet: Why Is Processed Food So Salty?" *Mayo Clinic.com.* http://www.mayoclinic.com/health/food-and-nutrition/AN00350 (accessed October 31, 2010).

Joseph P. Hyder

Produce Traceability

■ Introduction

Traceability refers to the ability to follow a product through each step in a supply chain. A supply chain consists of all the steps, companies, warehouses, and others between a farm and the final consumer who buys the food. Produce traceability refers to the ability to follow fruits and vegetables through the supply chain from farm to table. Traceability can provide several types of information about produce to consumers. However, increased traceability may add additional costs to the production process of produce. Several countries have mandated country-of-origin labeling (COOL) of produce so that consumers know which country is its source. Mandatory and voluntary traceability efforts for produce involve both costs and benefits for the final consumer.

■ Historical Background and Scientific Foundations

Supply-chain management has taken great strides since World War II (1939–1945) ended. Companies once kept large inventories compared to their sales at the beginning of the twenty-first century. As technology, better record keeping, and improved management techniques took hold, companies began to realize that storing inventory cost money for warehouse space, electricity, and other storage requirements. When dealing with perishable food items, unnecessary inventories in storage often cannot be sold even at a deep discount, because they have a short shelf life—the amount of time a food product can sit before being safely used. Companies in manufacturing first started to lower the inventory-to-sales ratio, and the food industry quickly followed. According to the U.S. Department of Agriculture (USDA) Economic Research Service (ERS), in the United States cereal manufacturers went from keeping an 8 percent inventory-to-sales ratio in 1958 to 3 percent by the early 1990s. Just-in-time deliveries and increasing ability

to match inventory of sales quickly led to lower stocks, first within big companies such as Toyota, a Japanese car manufacturer. Later, large food retailers such as Walmart integrated their supply management systems with those of their suppliers.

The technologies and techniques used to control inventory were later applied to track food-borne illnesses, usually in meat or dairy products, to their sources. Produce is only recently joining this trend, starting on a large scale in the 1990s. From 1980 until 1997, the United States increased its produce consumption by 43 percent, so the larger variety and amount of produce provided consumers with new choices. Better traceability meets the desires of consumers who demand more information about the sources of their produce and want information on various attributes that can be traced back to the source.

Many attributes of a food product can be traced. Traceability can be used in a supply chain to better manage inventory and cut costs. Also, traceability can assist in monitoring safety and quality. In the case of the outbreak of a food-borne illness, traceability may enable companies to recall the products that may pose a risk of illness or to identify the source of the outbreak. Traceability increasingly is used to provide information to consumers on particular attributes of food such as produce.

The types of attributes consumers demand generally come in three forms. Some attributes are easy to identify at the point of retail. For example, if consumers like green apples, they can easily identify these apples at an outdoor market, at a produce stand, or at a supermarket. It would be difficult for a produce stand to represent red apples as green apples, because consumers could spot the fraud easily. These types of attributes that consumers can see, feel, or taste are sensory attributes. Consumers also demand credence attributes that they cannot themselves distinguish with their senses. These include content attributes. For example, consumers may prefer fruit that is higher in vitamin content.

They cannot taste this attribute, but the vitamin content could be physically verified in a laboratory. The third attributes are process attributes. These are attributes that could not be verified through a physical, laboratory test because they relate to the process involved in growing and marketing the product, not the physical attributes of the product. Most traceability systems for produce

A farm worker in Salinas, California, washes and packs Romaine lettuce for shipment. *AP Images.*

seek to trace and verify process attributes. For example, consumers may prefer avocados from Mexico to avocados from California. For the same variety of avocados, there is no test for a consumer to see where they were grown. Companies must instead keep records to be able to verify the source of the avocado and inform consumers.

■ Impacts and Issues

Country of origin labeling (COOL) requires that the country where produce is grown be indicated at the point of retail. In 2008, with a final regulation being issued in 2009, COOL for fresh produce became mandatory in the United States. COOL has been required in Japan since 2000, and the European Union has a longer history of mandatory COOL requirements for fresh produce. In addition to these fresh produce markets, Brazil, Costa Rica, Egypt, Mexico, Peru, Russia, South Korea, South Africa, and Switzerland require labeling of some or all fresh produce items by country of origin.

Whereas labeling is intended to provide additional information to consumers and possibly to encourage more consumption of domestic produce instead of imported, it has little use as a traceability device for foodborne illness outbreaks. Outbreaks from fresh produce tend to be from items that are consumed raw and not properly cleaned. Having country of origin information for that produce does not necessarily trace back to an individual farm or a particular practice that leads to contamination, so even with COOL, the source of an outbreak may be difficult or impossible to identify.

More regulation related to traceability or increased private sector-driven traceability tends to be proposed in the press with each new foodborne illness outbreak or food-related news event. However, in the private sector, third-party certification systems can be very expensive as demonstrated by the high prices seen on produce that is certified organic or fair trade. In a third-party system, a certification body, in addition to the farm and the other steps on the supply chain, inspects, audits, and sets standards for recordkeeping to maintain the process attribute.

Government inspection and enforcement of traceability tends to be weak. Inspectors can only catch so many companies cheating, and critics of government regulation state that standardizing how companies trace so that they can be inspected may limit innovation in the field. Those opposed to government regulation charge that mandatory systems foster incentives for companies to hide their mistakes and not share information with inspectors for fear of fines or bad publicity. Also, by requiring one standard, companies have no incentive to exceed this standard or innovate in how they trace their food through the supply chain.

Counterarguments assert that historical abuses associated with self-regulation and enforcement mandate some functional level of government intervention and monitoring. For consumer protection, such intervention is argued to be best applied in efforts to inspect, document, and enforce safety and quality standards. Without government oversight or possible punitive penalties for non-compliance, many industries are replete with examples of companies willfully abandoning standards and misrepresenting the origins and quality of products, especially if the end results of such actions are not easily traceable.

Technological and management innovations may eventually drive down the costs associated with increased traceability. One promising technology already in use is radio frequency identification (RFID) technology. Small radio signal transmitting tags are attached to produce shipments to convey information to retailers, wholesalers, and others along the produce supply chain.

SEE ALSO *Agribusiness; Agriculture and International Trade; Center for Food Safety and Applied Nutrition; Community Supported Agriculture (CSAs); E. Coli Contamination; Food Recalls; Food Safety and Inspection Service; Foodborne Diseases; Organic Foods Production Act of 1990; Sustainable Agriculture; Truth in Labeling; Vegetables.*

BIBLIOGRAPHY

Books

Marsden, Terry. *The New Regulation and Governance of Food: Beyond the Food Crisis?* New York: Routledge, 2010.

Shewfelt, Robert L., Bernhard Brueckner, Stanley E. Prussia, and Wojciech J. Florkowski. *Postharvest Handling: A Systems Approach.* Amsterdam and London: Elsevier/Academic Press, 2009.

Weirich, Paul. *Labeling Genetically Modified Food: The Philosophical and Legal Debate.* Oxford, UK: Oxford University Press, 2007.

Periodicals

Chen, Ruey-Shun, et al. "Using RFID Technology in Food Produce Traceability." *WSEAS Transactions on Information Science and Applications* 5, no. 11 (2008): 1551–1560.

"Survey Shows Moderate Commitment to Produce Traceability Initiative." *Food Chemical News* 10, no. 4 (2010): 12.

"Traceability for All: Top 10 Produce in Salinas, Ca, Offers an Affordable Traceability Option for Small Growers." *American Fruit Grower* 129, no. 10 (2009): 16–17.

Web Sites

"Country-of-Origin Labeling." *Economic Research Service (ERS), U.S. Department of Agriculture (USDA).* http://www.ers.usda.gov/features/cool/ (accessed September 18, 2010).

Dole Organic Program. http://www.doleorganic.com/index.php (accessed September 18, 2010).

Blake Jackson Stabler

Protein and Carbohydrate Metabolism

■ Introduction

Protein and carbohydrate metabolism are essential biochemical processes that enable the body to utilize these vital nutrients. The first stage in metabolism is breaking down food molecules into their components in digestion. Chewing and propelling food through the gastrointestinal tract breaks it into smaller particles, while enzymes break down large protein and carbohydrate molecules into amino acids and glucose. Amino acids are the basic building blocks of proteins, and glucose is the basic unit of carbohydrates. Enzymes ensure a constant supply of amino acids and glucose. Without enzymes, the process of breaking down food molecules would be too slow. Glucose is then broken down to produce ATP, the energy currency of cells that enables all other metabolic reactions to take place. Amino acids are used to build up the many thousands of protein molecules, most of which are enzymes, needed by the body. Protein function depends upon the order of the amino acid units in the long chain that comprises a protein molecule. This sequence is coded in the DNA of the gene for that protein. Assembling a protein molecule involves the DNA code, several enzymes, and the individual amino acids. Increased understanding of protein and carbohydrate metabolism can help gain a better comprehension of conditions such as diabetes and obesity.

■ Historical Background and Scientific Foundations

The understanding of protein and carbohydrate metabolism grew slowly with the advancement of physiology and biochemistry beginning in the seventeenth century; even in the early twenty-first century the complex molecular pathways involved are not fully understood. There are two aspects to protein and carbohydrate metabolism. Catabolic reactions break down protein to amino acids and carbohydrates to glucose. Anabolic reactions then synthesize thousands of different proteins from their amino acid building blocks and extract biochemical energy from glucose. In other words, catabolic reactions break down molecules, and anabolic reactions build them up or use them in some bodily function.

Protein and carbohydrate catabolism cannot be completely understood without knowing something of the digestive process, which begins as soon as food enters the gastrointestinal tract. Starting at the mouth and ending at the anus, the gastrointestinal tract is basically a muscular tube that pushes through the physical and chemical processes of digestion and absorption. In the mouth, food is chewed and moistened with saliva, which both breaks it into manageable particles for digestion to begin and also creates the sensation of taste in the brain. Bread starts to taste sweet when it is chewed because an enzyme called ptyalin in saliva breaks down starch into the sugar maltose. Digestion of protein begins in the stomach, where an acid-resistant enzyme, pepsin, breaks down protein molecules into smaller chains of amino acids, known as peptides. Amino acids are the basic building blocks of proteins.

A meal remains in the stomach for around four hours before being slowly conveyed by the action of the muscles in the wall of the stomach into the duodenum, a C-shaped section in the upper section of the small intestine. The duodenum is where most of the catabolic reactions of digestion take place. A duct joins the pancreas to the duodenum and secretes pancreatic enzymes that break peptides into individual amino acids. The walls of the duodenum secrete enzymes that break down sugars from starch into glucose. These small molecules are absorbed further down the small intestine into the bloodstream, ready for anabolic reactions to take place. The small intestine is around 20 feet long, and its surface area is further extended by the presence of tiny projections called villi, which play a major role in food absorption.

Every cell in the body requires a constant supply of glucose, the body's main fuel, from food digestion. The brain's requirement for glucose is particularly high. If the supply of glucose to the brain, via the blood, is cut off for more than around five minutes, then irreparable brain damage and perhaps death will result. The complex chain of metabolic reactions involved in the constructive metabolism of glucose is known as glycolysis. The end product of breaking down a glucose molecule, with the aid of oxygen, is several molecules of adenosine triphosphate (ATP), which is the biochemical energy currency of cells. With the help of enzymes, ATP is able to transfer energy from cell to cell, driving thousands of metabolic reactions. The byproducts of glycolysis are carbon dioxide and water. Breathing in oxygen and breathing out carbon dioxide and water are important physical processes that help to drive glycolysis. In the bigger picture, glycolysis can be seen as the opposite process to photosynthesis, which uses energy to create sugars from carbon dioxide and water. If glucose is not available, the body instead uses stored fat for energy in a process called ketosis, which occurs in the liver and utilizes fatty acids stored there. Another important reaction in carbohydrate metabolism is the storage of excess glucose as glycogen in the liver through the actions of the hormone insulin. When glucose is needed, glycogen supplies are broken down by another hormone called glucagon. These reactions help smooth out the peaks and troughs of glucose supply through eating and digestion.

WORDS TO KNOW

DIGESTION: The physical and chemical processes that transform the food a person eats into nutrients that the body can use.

ENZYME: Biological catalysts that accelerate chemical reactions, which would otherwise happen very slowly or not at all. The enzymes of protein and carbohydrate metabolism are all proteins, as are most other enzymes.

METABOLISM: The total of all the chemical reactions that keep the body alive. Metabolic reactions include the breakdown of proteins and carbohydrates to their constituent parts and their use in various bodily functions. Metabolism depends upon action of enzymes to achieve reactions at a rate compatible with life.

Protein metabolism is a complex process, the main stages of which were not really understood until after the discovery of the structure of DNA (deoxyribonucleic acid) by James Watson (1928–) and Francis Crick (1916–2004) in 1953. DNA is the chemical from which genes are made, and genes can be regarded as recipes

Adenosine triphosphate (ATP), shown in magnified crystallized form, plays an important role in both protein and carbohydrate metabolism. *© medicalpicture / Alamy.*

IN CONTEXT: PROTEIN FRAUD

Protein levels are often important to food value. Adulteration of food content specifically to evade or mislead agricultural testing in food products directly consumed by humans (such as milk and eggs) or via ingredients used in animal feed to produce meat, is an increasing global concern. In late 2008, China's official Xinhua News Agency carried a story first reported in a Nanfang daily newspaper that referred to the practice of using melamine in animal feeds in China's booming agricultural industry as an "open secret." Melamine is formed into a "protein powder," which is then sold to feed suppliers. A banned animal-feed additive, melamine falsely increases measurements of food protein levels but actually does not increase protein content.

or blueprints for protein molecules. The body requires thousands of different proteins, most of them enzymes, to function correctly. Each protein consists of hundreds, or maybe thousands, of amino acids arranged in the correct order, known as a sequence. DNA is the chemical code that contains the recipe for a protein sequence. Therefore, assembling a protein chain involves a complex interaction between DNA, a number of enzymes, and the individual amino acids required for that particular protein sequence.

■ Impacts and Issues

As understanding of DNA and genes has advanced, particularly since the announcement of the sequencing of the human genome in 2000, knowledge of carbohydrate and protein metabolism has advanced considerably. The roles of enzymes and hormones involved in metabolism are becoming clearer, and individual differences in metabolic activity can be investigated. It is already known that resting or basal metabolic rate (BMR) differs between individuals. The BMR is the speed at which the body uses up energy or ATP. Someone with a low BMR requires less food for bodily functions than someone with a high BMR, who uses it up faster. People who are overweight or obese often blame it on having a low BMR. Research based on a better understanding of genes has suggested that there may indeed be faulty metabolism involved in some obesity. One gene that contributes to obesity has been identified, and it is likely that there are

several more. A better understanding of carbohydrate metabolism is also contributing to new non-insulin drugs for diabetes to help overcome the challenge of keeping blood glucose levels constant.

SEE ALSO *Changing Nutritional Needs throughout Life; Dairy Products; Diet and Diabetes; Dietary Guidelines for Americans; Dietary Reference Intakes; Eggs; Fruits; Grains; Legumes; Nutrition; Nutrition's Role in Human Evolution; Paleolithic Diet; Pasta; Poultry; Sugar and Sweeteners; Therapeutic Diets; USDA Food Pyramid; Vegetables.*

BIBLIOGRAPHY

Books

Christopher, Joseph. *Nutrition and Digestion.* New Delhi, India: Anmol Publications, 2006.

Driskell, Judy A., and Ira Wolinsky. *Nutritional Assessment of Athletes.* Boca Raton, FL: CRC Press, 2011.

Gabius, Hans Joachim. *The Sugar Code: Fundamentals of Glycosciences.* Weinheim, Germany: Wiley-VCH, 2009.

Garg, Hari G., Mary K. Cowman, and Charles A. Hales. *Carbohydrate Chemistry, Biology and Medical Applications.* Oxford, UK: Elsevier, 2008.

Pratt, Charlotte W., and Kathleen Cornely. *Essential Biochemistry.* Hoboken, NJ: Wiley, 2011.

Wang, Minghan. *Metabolic Syndrome: Underlying Mechanisms and Drug Therapies.* Hoboken, NJ: Wiley, 2011.

Periodicals

Beardsall, Kathryn, Barbro M. S. Diderholm, and David B. Dunger. "Insulin and Carbohydrate Metabolism." *Best Practice & Research, Clinical Endocrinology & Metabolism* 22, no. 1 (2008): 41–55.

Web Sites

Bouchez, Colette. "Making the Most of Your Metabolism." *WebMD.* http://www.webmd.com/fitness-exercise/guide/make-most-your-metabolism (accessed October 15, 2010).

Ophardt, Charles B. "Virtual Chembook: Overview of Metabolism." *Elmhurst College.* http://www.elmhurst.edu/~chm/vchembook/5900verviewmet.html (accessed October 15, 2010).

Susan Aldridge

Pure Food and Drug Act of 1906

■ Introduction

The Pure Food and Drug Act of 1906 (34 Stat. 768) was enacted on the same day as its companion bill, the Federal Meat Inspection Act. The two pieces of legislation sought to remedy the adulteration of food, addition of intoxicating ingredients, and unsanitary conditions in the food processing industry that had been brought to light by worker strikes, progressive era reformers, journalists, and authors.

Alcohol, cocaine, heroin, morphine, and cannabis (marijuana) were common additives to popular patent medicines (medicinal concoctions whose ingredients were often kept secret from consumers) prior to passage of the Pure Food and Drug Act. These treatments were not considered illicit substances by government regulators and were legally available without a prescription. The Pure Food and Drug Act required that all foods and drugs sold across state lines carry accurate labels indicating the presence and dosages of these and other substances.

■ Historical Background and Scientific Foundations

At the turn of the twentieth-century, a high-profile scandal exposed the fact that U.S. soldiers serving in the Spanish-American war had been sickened by tainted, preservative-laden, rancid beef. Journalists, authors, social activists, consumers, and government officials became increasingly concerned with the safety and purity of food.

Most individual states had enacted laws regulating food purity and safety by 1900. Overall, such laws were not uniform, were poorly enforced, and only covered food products that were produced and sold in the same state. However, many meatpacking, packaged foods, and patent medicine companies sold their products in several states. There was no overarching federal law to regulate these products. Harvey W. Wiley (1844–1930), chief of the U.S. Department of Agriculture's Bureau of Chemistry, led a campaign to enact federal food legislation. Wiley sought the aid of popular journalists, doctors, the American Medical Association, labor and social activists, women's societies, and scientists to highlight unsanitary and dangerous food industry practices.

In 1905 American investigative journalist Samuel Hopkins Adams (1871–1958) wrote a series of eleven articles on the patent medicine industry. Adams had written about food purity issues before, but his "The Great American Fraud," published in *Collier's Weekly*, exposed the sometimes dangerous contents and misleading advertising of patent medicines. The series garnered significant public attention, especially among female-dominated temperance groups who opposed the secretive inclusion of alcohol, opiates, and other intoxicating substances in patent remedies.

American journalist and author Upton Sinclair's 1906 book *The Jungle* featured a graphic description of the meatpacking industry. From the stench of the stockyards to the filth of the processing plants, Sinclair (1878–1968) described the industry as dirty, disease-ridden, and rife with corruption. Farmers and plant owners bribed stockyard inspectors to let diseased animals pass. Workers ill with tuberculosis processed meat and relieved themselves near their workstations while on long shifts. Potted meat and sausage products were contaminated with insects, rats, hair, hide, sawdust, human urine, and blood, and animal remnants that had been swept from the floors.

The work of Wiley and the muckrakers spurred public outrage. In response, U.S. President Theodore Roosevelt (1858–1919) sent a government inspection team led by labor commissioner Charles P. Neill (1865–1942) and social worker James Bronson Reynolds (1861–1924) to evaluate the meatpacking industry. Their findings, published as the Neill-Reynolds Report, confirmed the hygiene, adulteration, contamination, and corruption problems highlighted in *The Jungle*.

On June 30, 1906, Congress passed the Pure Food and Drug Act and the Meat Inspection Act. They also created, at Roosevelt's request, the Food and Drug Administration (FDA) to oversee federal regulation and inspection of medicines and foods. The Pure Food and Drug Act took effect on January 1, 1907.

■ Impacts and Issues

Both the Federal Meat Inspection Act and the Pure Food and Drug Act set forth legal criteria for "adulterated food" that influenced increasingly vigorous regulation of foods throughout the twentieth century. Adulterated foods under the act included any product that: was packaged with another substance that adversely affects its potency, strength, or quality; contained ingredients that might be substituted for other ingredients; was altered or colored to give the appearance of freshness or hide imperfections; contained poisonous additives; contained the remains of diseased or downer animals (animals that died from a means other than slaughter before processing); contained decomposed animal or plant materials; or was lacking a presumed essential ingredient (for example, a potted meat product that in reality contained no meat).

The Pure Food and Drug Act expanded regulation of foods for safety to include popular, commercially sold health tonics, beverages, and patent medicines. Previously alcohol, cocaine, heroin, morphine, and cannabis were common additives to widely available tonics, remedies, and patent medicines, but the new labeling requirements changed consumer desire for the long-popular products. Some contemporary estimates assert that sales of patent medicines decreased one-third in the year after the Pure Food and Drug Act's mandated labeling entered into force. Few patent medicines gained approval from the newly created FDA, and regulators

A cartoon depicts a slaughterhouse in Chicago, Illinois circa 1880.   © *North Wind Picture Archives / Alamy.*

later banned others for fraudulent labeling. By the time Pure Food and Drug Act regulations were strengthened in 1911–1912, the patent medicine industry had significantly diminished.

Public concern over intoxicating ingredients led to attempts to outlaw the manufacture and sale of the soft drink Coca-Cola. Before 1903, the beverage—initially sold as a health tonic—contained small amounts of cocaine, but caffeine replaced cocaine as the formula's stimulant. The landmark 1909 case *United States v. Forty Barrels and Twenty Kegs of Coca-Cola* upheld the drink manufacturer's right to sell its caffeinated product (which was duly labeled as containing caffeine). Coca-Cola revised its formula to contain less caffeine, however, in response to the trial and public outcry.

The Pure Food and Drug Act of 1906 was amended several times, each time expanding federal requirements for food and drug safety, purity, and quality. It was superseded and replaced by the Food, Drug, and Cosmetic Act of 1938.

Because subsequent laws have replaced the Pure Food and Drug Act of 1906, the law has little bearing on current food and drug regulation other than the precedents it set for federal interest in food safety regulation. However, because the act deals with now illicit substances such as marijuana, opiates, and cocaine in a regulatory framework in which those substances are legal but controlled, several present-day drug policy reform proponents point to the act as a basic model for the decriminalization of some illicit substances.

■ Primary Source Connection

The Pure Food and Drug Act of 1906 became federal law on June 30, 1906. This act provided for federal inspections of meat and meat products as well as requiring drugs to be labeled accurately. It lead the way for the creation of the Food, Drug and Cosmetic Act in 1938, and eventually, the creation of the modern Food and Drug Administration (FDA).

Pure Food and Drug Act of 1906

For preventing the manufacture, sale, or transportation of adulterated or misbranded or poisonous or deleterious foods, drugs, medicines, and liquors, and for regulating traffic therein, and for other purposes.

Be it enacted by the Senate and House of Representatives of the United States of America in Congress assembled, That it shall be unlawful for Columbia any article of food or drug which is adulterated or misbranded, within the meaning of this Act; and any person who shall violate any of the provisions of this section shall be guilty of a misdemeanor . . .

In the case of food:

First. If any substance has been mixed and packed with it so as to reduce or lower or injuriously affect its quality or strength.

Second. If any substance has been substituted wholly or in part for the article.

Third. If any valuable constituent of the article has been wholly or in part abstracted.

Fourth. If it be mixed, colored, powdered, coated, or stained in a manner whereby damage or inferiority is concealed.

Fifth. If it contain any added poisonous or other added deleterious ingredient which may render such article injurious to health: Provided, That when in the preparation of food products for shipment they are preserved by any external application applied in such manner that the preservative is necessarily removed mechanically, or by maceration in water, or otherwise, and directions for the removal of said preservative shall be printed on the covering or the package, the provisions of this Act shall be construed as applying only when said products are ready for consumption.

Sixth. If it consists in whole or in part of a filthy, decomposed, or putrid animal or vegetable substance, or any portion of an animal unfit for food, whether manufactured or not, or if it is the product of a diseased animal, or one that has died otherwise than by slaughter.

Sec. 8. That the term, "misbranded," as used herein, shall apply to all drugs, or articles of food, or articles which enter into the composition of food, the package or label of which shall bear any statement, design, or device regarding such article, or the ingredients or substances contained therein which shall be false or misleading in any particular, and to any food or drug product which is falsely branded as to the State, Territory, or country in which it is manufactured or produced.

CONGRESS OF THE UNITED STATES. *PURE FOOD AND DRUG ACT OF 1906.* WASHINGTON, DC: U.S. GOVERNMENT PRINTING OFFICE, 1906.

SEE ALSO *Food, Drug, and Cosmetic Act of 1938; Food Inspection and Standards; Truth in Labeling; U.S. Food and Drug Administration (FDA).*

BIBLIOGRAPHY

Books

Bethard, Wayne. *Lotions, Potions, and Deadly Elixirs: Frontier Medicine in America.* Lanham, MD: Taylor Trade, 2004.

Law, Marc T., and Gary D. Libecap. *The Determinants of Progressive Era Reform: The Pure Food and Drugs Act of 1906.* Cambridge, MA: National Bureau of Economic Research, 2004.

Periodicals

Lupein, John. "Food Quality and Safety: Traceability and Labeling." *Critical Reviews in Food Science and Nutrition* 45, no. 2 (2005): 119–123.

Parascandola, Mark. "100 Years of Pure Food and Drugs: The 1906 Act and the Foundations of Modern Drug Regulation." *Research Practitioner* 7, no. 6 (2006): 200–208.

Web Sites

"About FDA: Food Standards and the 1906 Act." *U.S. Food and Drug Administration (FDA)*. http://www.fda.gov/AboutFDA/WhatWeDo/History/Product Regulation/ucm132666.htm (accessed September 7, 2010).

Adrienne Wilmoth Lerner

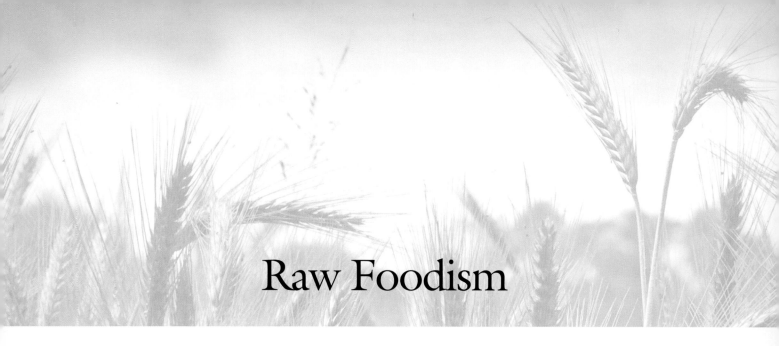

Raw Foodism

■ Introduction

Eating raw vegetables instead of cooked meals has a long tradition in diets devoted to health and religious asceticism, but in the last few decades raw food has gone mainstream—at least in some urban areas. There are raw restaurants, an abundance of raw "cookbooks" or preparation guides, websites, and books devoted to raw food lifestyles, and celebrity endorsements that promote a regime said to be healthier than vegetarian or vegan diets. Although most raw foodists are vegan, some drink raw milk and milk products, whereas others consume raw meats and eggs along with the more usual raw diet of uncooked fruits, vegetables, juices, oils, nuts, fermented foods, and sprouts.

Raw food advocates may differ in the types of food they eat and in the percentages of raw food that make up their diet, but most agree that food is cooked when it is heated above 118°F (47°C). Some specify even lower temperatures. Many raw foodists state that cooked food is toxic due to the chemical processes that occur during cooking. Some rawists also maintain that cooking turns living food into dead food by killing the enzymes and beneficial bacteria present in freshly harvested plants. Many argue that eating raw food is more natural and wholesome, that humans get more nutrition out of uncooked foods, and that many diseases and disorders can be eliminated or at least mitigated by a raw or a partially raw diet of organic foods.

■ Historical Background and Scientific Foundations

American physician and alternative medicine practitioner Herbert M. Shelton (1895–1985) was one of the first modern advocates for raw foods, promoting raw fruits and vegetables as part of his natural hygiene movement in the 1920s and 1930s. Weston A. Price (1870–1948), a dentist who compared the health of indigenous diets to traditional Western diets, also recommended raw fruits

and vegetables in the 1930s and 1940s, and both natural hygienists and Weston A. Price groups remain active in the raw food movement in the early twenty-first century. In the following decades, wheatgrass juice, sprouts, and fresh greens were championed as natural and holistic alternatives to conventional medicine and cuisine. In 1963 Armenian-Iranian Ashavir Ter Hovannessian (also called Aterhov) published a manifesto on the benefits of a raw vegetarian diet called *Raw Eating*, which was not well known in North America or Europe until it was rediscovered several decades later.

Leslie Kenton's *Raw Energy*, which urged readers to "eat your way to radiant health" in 1984, advocated a diet with plenty of fresh fruit and vegetable juices, sprouts, and seeds, and popularized the idea of living enzymes in raw foods. In the 1990s raw foodism gained momentum, and many books promising better health through eating raw were published. Rawists wrote about using the senses to choose raw foods necessary for optimal health instinctively, and some even called cooked food poison. The first raw food restaurant, Raw, opened in San Francisco, California, in 1993. The Living Light Culinary Arts Institute, devoted to raw food preparation, opened in 1998 in Fort Bragg, California, and continues to offer certification for vegan and rawist gourmet chefs. According to an article written by food writer Lessley Anderson in 2009, "Raw food has become glamorous," and this is due at least partially to the creativity of gourmet chefs with both traditional and exotic organic ingredients. Raw foodism has also recently become more accessible, with specialty stores such as Whole Foods offering packaged raw food products including unbaked crackers and coconut water.

■ Impacts and Issues

Many people have given heartfelt testimonials on how eating raw food has improved their health. Rawists often state that eating raw gives them more energy, makes them feel younger, gives them better skin, and helps lose

WORDS TO KNOW

ASCETICISM: A way of life characterized by self-restraint, abstinence, and the rigorous self-denial of earthly pleasures, such as certain foods.

ENZYME: Proteins found in living cells that act as catalysts for chemical reactions, including digestion. Some raw food advocates argue that cooking kills the enzymes found in freshly harvested foods that are beneficial to human health.

RAWIST: A person who consumes a diet of mostly plant-based foods in an uncooked state.

SAD: The Standard American Diet, which is high in fat, meat, sugar, and simple carbohydrates that contribute to many chronic diseases associated with Western civilization including arteriosclerosis and diabetes.

VEGAN: A person who does not eat any animal products, including eggs, milk, cheese, and honey (as opposed to a vegetarian, who does not eat meat).

weight without feeling hungry. Others claim to have cured themselves of cancer, diabetes, and other serious health problems using a raw food diet. Some raw foodists state that they are more conscious of their food choices, feel closer to nature, think that raw foods help detoxify their bodies, and that they enjoy increased feelings of

A raw vegetable salad served with quark dressing. Quark is an acidified cheese made without rennet. © *Bon Appetit / Alamy.*

clarity, lightness, and spirituality when they eat mostly or entirely raw foods. Because most raw foodists are also vegans, the environmental impact of their diet is minimal compared to that of the mainstream American diet. Many raw dishes contain assorted imported ingredients, such as avocados, tropical nuts, and coconut, however, which runs counter to the environmentally inspired movement towards eating more locally produced foods.

Many raw food advocates view their eating habits as more natural than most, often noting that humans are the only animals that engage in cooking. Nevertheless, most rawists take advantage of modern technology to use the cold-pressed and filtered oils, blenders, food processors, juicers, and dehydrators that make raw foods more palatable and interesting. While it is true that human ancestors ate their food raw, there is some debate about when they began using fire to cook. British primatologist Richard Wrangham (1948–), for instance, hypothesizes that the origin of the human genus is linked to the beginning of cooking from 1.8–1.9 million years ago, based on comparisons of human and ape physiology and social behaviors. Wrangham's research shows that unlike chimpanzees and gorillas, humans (with their shorter digestive systems) find it difficult to intake sufficient calories from a totally raw vegan diet. The archaeological evidence for the use of fire is more equivocal, but most anthropologists agree that it was used to cook food well before 200,000 years ago.

Scientists dispute the idea that food contains energy that is destroyed by cooking, and point out that virtually all of the enzymes that are present in food are destroyed by stomach acids before the food is absorbed in the small intestine. Some foods do lose nutritional value during cooking, but many others are more easily digested after being treated with heat. Some kinds of cooked foods may become more carcinogenic when cooked at high temperatures (acrylamide, a potential cancer-causing compound, for example, is a byproduct of carbohydrate-rich foods that are fried, baked, or grilled at high temperatures). The U.S. Food and Drug Administration (FDA) has not yet found in current studies that the low amount of acrylamide formed in cooked foods poses a threat to public health. Bacteria and parasites, especially in meat, are also reduced or eliminated by high temperatures, and raw foodists must take care to avoid foodborne illness from both plant and animal foods.

Raw foodists also must strive to get enough protein, fats, and essential vitamins and minerals in their diets, especially Vitamin B12, Vitamin D, iron, and calcium. The American Dietetic Association does not recommend raw food diets for children, pregnant women, nursing mothers, or people with anemia or who are at risk for osteoporosis. In addition, American physician and alternative medicine specialist Steven Bratman described how the "neoreligious" philosophy associated with some raw food theories can lead to orthorexia—an obsession with eating only certain healthy foods. Raw foodists may become fruitarians, eating predominately fruit, or sproutarians, leading to serious nutritional deficiencies and diseases. Fasting or insufficient caloric intake may promote spirituality, but is clearly not feasible for long periods. Raw food advocates may also alienate family members and friends who do not share their nutritional ideology, especially if their views about cooked food are extreme. In some extreme cases, raw foodism shares many similarities with eating disorders and religious cults.

Another criticism of the raw food movement was expressed by Anthony Bourdain (1956–), a former chef who has become a popular food writer. Angered by what he saw as the culinary chauvinism of an American celebrity who ate only raw food on his visit to Thailand, Bourdain commented in his book *Nasty Bits* in 2007, "What kind of cramped, narrow, and arrogant worldview could excuse shutting oneself off totally from the greater part of an ancient and beautiful culture?" Many chefs and gourmet food lovers agree with Bourdain, viewing the raw food movement as an assault on traditional cuisines and cultures. Others applaud the fact that raw foodists are getting more people to eat a greater variety of fresh, organic fruits and vegetables, which nutritionists agree that most Americans desperately need.

SEE ALSO *Cult Diets; Food Fads; Fruits; Organics; Produce Traceability; Raw Milk Campaign; Veganism; Vegetables; Vegetarianism.*

BIBLIOGRAPHY

Books

Anderson, Lessley. "The Raw Deal." In *Best Food Writing 2009*, edited by Holly Hughes. Philadelphia: Da Capo, 2009.

Bourdain, Anthony. *The Nasty Bits: Collected Varietal Cuts, Usable Trim, Scraps, and Bones.* New York: Bloomsbury, 2007.

Boutenko, Victoria. *12 Steps to Raw Foods: How to End Your Dependency on Cooked Food.* Berkeley, CA: North Atlantic Books, 2007.

Russo, Ruthann. *The Raw Food Lifestyle: The Philosophy and Nutrition behind Raw and Live Foods.* Berkeley, CA: North Atlantic Books, 2009.

Safron, Jeremy. *The Raw Foods Resource Guide.* Berkeley, CA: Celestial Arts, 2005.

Wrangham, Richard. *Catching Fire: How Cooking Made Us Human.* New York: Basic Books, 2009.

Periodicals

Fontana, Luigi, Jennifer L. Shew, John O. Holloszy, and Dennis T. Villareal. "Low Bone Mass in Subjects on a Long-Term Raw Vegetarian Diet." *Archives of Internal Medicine* 165, no. 6 (2005): 684–689.

Song, Moon K., Mark J. Rosenthal, et al. "Raw Vegetable Food Containing High Cyclo (his-Pro) Improved Insulin Sensitivity and Body Weight Control." *Metabolism: Clinical and Experimental* 54, no. 11 (2005): 1480–1489.

Web Sites

"Raw Food Diet." *Science Daily.* http://www.sciencedaily.com/articles/r/raw_food_diet.htm (accessed September 11, 2010).

Robin, Lauren Posnick. "Acrylamide, Furan, and the FDA." *Food Safety Magazine*, June/July 2007. *U.S. Food and Drug Administration (FDA)*. http://www.fda.gov/Food/FoodSafety/FoodContaminants Adulteration/ChemicalContaminants/Acrylamide/ucm194482.htm (accessed September 11, 2010).

Sandra L. Dunavan

Raw Milk Campaign

■ Introduction

All milk is "raw" in its natural form, when first extracted from an animal. The term "raw milk" refers to unpasteurized, unhomogenized milk that is unadulterated. The Campaign for Real Milk triggered the raw milk movement in the United States, calling for greater consumer access to unpasteurized milk and for dairy farmers to have the option to sell raw milk directly to the public. In the United States, 28 states prohibit direct sales of unhomogenized, unpasteurized milk for human consumption to individual consumers. Consumers can obtain raw milk in other ways, purchasing raw milk under the pretense of feeding it to pets, buying part of a "cow share" from a farmer who then provides raw milk to the owners of the cow, and through the creation of a corporation that buys large volumes of milk in a business-to-business transaction with farmers.

The Campaign for Real Milk promotes raw milk sales; promotes initiatives to change local, state and federal policies; and seeks to create greater public awareness of the research behind unpasteurized milk and possible health benefits of the product. As of 2009, the Centers for Disease Control's (CDC) National Center for Zoonotic, Vector-Borne, and Enteric Disease strongly recommends that consumers avoid raw milk and contends that "There are no health benefits from drinking raw milk that cannot be obtained from drinking pasteurized milk that is free of disease-causing bacteria." This directly contravenes the claims made by The Campaign for Real Milk and raw milk proponents and is the center of the debate between the two viewpoints.

■ Historical Background and Scientific Foundations

Milk-related illnesses from tuberculosis, *Listeria*, and *Salmonella* bacteria were part of the reason for the push for pasteurization of milk in the 1930s and 1940s in the United States. Raw milk, fresh from the cow or goat, had long been a staple of the American diet, but as the country urbanized, farmers transported fresh milk across longer distances, creating a breeding ground for bacteria and leading to higher rates of milk-borne illness. By the early 1920s nearly every town, city, or state had some form of milk regulations, and in 1939 the U.S. Public Health Service promoted the Model Milk Health Ordinance, to encourage uniform safety practices and pasteurization. In 1938 contaminated milk represented the source of 25 percent of all reported food-related illnesses; as pasteurization became policy, then law, the percentage declined, reaching less than 1 percent in 2002.

In 1973 the Food and Drug Administration (FDA) banned the cross-state importing of raw milk but left an exception for "certified" raw milk, and by 1987 the FDA banned the shipment and sale of all unpasteurized milk across state lines, declaring all raw milk unsafe, regardless of safety procedures adopted by dairy farmers. The ban did not include activities within states, and over time states developed a patchwork of laws, some banning the sale of raw milk outright, others restricting its sale for animal consumption only. For instance, Massachusetts allows for direct sales to consumers for human consumption, but requires monthly health department inspections of dairy farms selling raw milk.

The Campaign for Real Milk was initiated by Sally Fallon Morell, the co-founder (with nutritionist Mary G. Enig; 1931–) of the Weston A. Price Foundation and co-author of the book *Nourishing Traditions*. Weston A. Price (1870–1948) was a dentist who, in the 1930s, spent time among indigenous peoples in Africa, the South Pacific, North America, and Australia. He found that in cultures that followed a traditional diet, bone structure and overall health appeared superior to that of people among the same groups who ate a more industrialized diet. Price concluded in his book *Nutrition and Physical Degeneration* that the diet of industrialized nations, with an emphasis on refined grains, sugars, and pasteurized dairy products led not only to poor dental health, but to poor health overall. Price's theory was not well-received in his time, but in the early 1990s his work was revived when Morell and Enig created the Weston A. Price Foundation in 1999.

■ Impacts and Issues

The Campaign for Real Milk gained attention by the early 2000s, aided in part by the Internet culture of Web sites and message boards that host discussions of nutrition, natural foods, organic approaches, and other topics related to raw milk. Raw milk advocates claim that the enzymes in unpasteurized, raw milk aid in digestion and calcium absorption. Proponents claim that grass-fed animals produce milk higher in certain fatty acids important for peak neurological functioning, and heating milk through pasteurization kills important peptide segments such as lactoferrin, lysozyme, and lactoperoxidase, which help with iron absorption and have antibiotic and antimicrobial properties. In addition, according to Morell and Enig, people with chronic lactose intolerance often have no problem ingesting raw milk.

Raw milk proponents attend a rally in Boston, Massachusetts, in support of raw milk regulations. *AP Images.*

WORDS TO KNOW

LISTERIA: *Listeria* bacteria can cause listeriosis, a serious condition with a fatality rate of approximately 25 percent. Pregnant women and their fetuses are particularly susceptible to listeriosis, with increased morbidity and mortality rates.

PASTEURIZATION: A process by which food is heated to a high-enough temperature for a specific period of time to kill bacteria. Pasteurization is named after French bacteriologist Louis Pasteur (1822–1895), who developed the process in 1864. By the early 1950s, most milk in the United States was pasteurized, leading to a significant decline in milk-related food-borne illnesses.

TRADITIONAL FOODS: The Traditional Foods movement is a byproduct of the Weston A. Price Foundation and the book *Nourishing Traditions* by Sally Fallon Morell, the co-founder of A Campaign for Real Milk. Using principles from Price's research, Fallon advocates a diet of raw milk, grassfed meats, raw liver, coconut oil, and sprouted grains.

Government health and consumer safety agencies including the CDC, Department of Agriculture, and FDA refute these claims, stating that no research backs them. A 1984 study in the *Journal of the American Medical Association* refers to unpasteurized milk as a "health fetish" and claims that the benefits touted by raw milk proponents remain unsubstantiated. A 2004 study in *Nutrition Research Reviews* notes that conjugated linoleic acid from grass-fed cows is detected at higher levels in raw milk vs. pasteurized milk, but also urges further study to determine the significance of this finding. A 1998 study published in the *American Journal of Public Health* examined food-borne illnesses related to unpasteurized milk from 1973 through 1992, finding that the rate of illness from such bacteria as *Campylobacter, Salmonella, Staphylococci,* and *E. coli O157:H7* was seven-fold higher in states that permit the sale of raw milk; the authors suggest that banning intrastate sales would prevent such outbreaks.

Proper safety procedures on small dairy farms make raw milk as safe, if not safer, than pasteurized milk produced by large-scale factory dairy farms, raw milk advocates claim. Larger outbreaks of *Salmonella* originating with pasteurized milk companies include the 1985 *Salmonella* outbreak that originated with pasteurized milk from Hillfarm Dairy in Melrose Park, Illinois, considered the worst foodborne illness outbreak in U.S. history, with more than 16,000 confirmed food poisoning cases and an estimated total of more than 200,000, leading to between four and 12 deaths. More recent pasteurized milk-related foodborne illnesses such as an August 2010 *Salmonella* outbreak that originated with pasteurized-milk producer Umpqua Farms in Oregon sickened at least 23 people.

The debate over unpasteurized milk continues, as evidenced by protests organized by raw milk advocates

A variety of hard cheeses age in a storage cooler at artisan cheesemakers Sweet Grass Dairy. The dairy must age their raw milk cheeses at least 60 days before selling them in the United States. Stephen Sundlof, director of the FDA Center for Food Safety and Applied Nutrition (CFSAN) said in early 2010 that the FDA is considering raising the aging requirement for raw milk cheeses made in the United States. Most European nations do not place strict limits on raw milk cheeses. *Adrienne Lerner / Lerner & Lerner / LernerMedia Global Photos.*

in Milwaukee, Wisconsin, in February 2010 and in Boston, Massachusetts, in May 2010, when both states' legislatures attempted to pass bills limiting the sale of raw milk. Currently, less than 1 percent of all milk consumed in the United States is unpasteurized.

SEE ALSO *Center for Food Safety and Applied Nutrition; Dairy Products;* E. Coli *Contamination; Food Safety and Inspection Service; Foodborne Diseases; Pasteurization; Pure Food and Drug Act of 1906; Staphylococcal Food Poisoning.*

BIBLIOGRAPHY

Books

Gumpert, David E. *The Raw Milk Revolution: Behind America's Emerging Battle over Food Rights.* White River Junction, VT: Chelsea Green, 2009.

Planck, Nina. *Real Food: What to Eat and Why.* New York: Bloomsbury, 2007.

Schmid, Ronald F. *The Untold Story of Milk: The History, Politics and Science of Nature's Perfect Food: Raw Milk from Pasture-Fed Cows.* Washington, DC: NewTrends, 2009.

Tuberculosis and Queso Fresco: Eat Safe Cheese! San Diego, CA: County of San Diego, Health and Human Services Agency, TB Control Program, 2008.

Periodicals

"CDC Recommends Stricter Rules against Raw Milk Products." *Food Chemical News* 50, no. 46 (2009): 10.

Donnelty, Catherine W. "Perspective—Raw-Milk Cheeses Can Be Produced Safely." *Food Technology* 60, no. 4 (2006): 100.

"Escherichia Coli O157:h7 Infections in Children Associated with Raw Milk and Raw Colostrum from Cows—California, 2006." *Morbidity and Mortality Weekly Report* 57, no. 23 (2008): 625–628.

"FDA Warns of Outbreaks Related to Drinking Raw Milk." *Food Chemical News* 52, no. 4 (2010): 10.

"Got Milk? How Safe Is the Newest Food Fad—Raw Milk?" *Current Science* 93, no. 8 (2007): 10.

Oliver, Stephen P., et al. "Food Safety Hazards Associated with Consumption of Raw Milk." *Foodborne Pathogens and Disease* 6, no. 7 (2009): 793–806.

Paxon, Heather. "Post-Pasteurian Cultures: The Microbiopolitics of Raw-Milk Cheese in the United States." *Cultural Anthropology* 23, no. 1 (2008): 15–47.

Stephenson, Joan. "Studies Probe Microbes in Raw Milk, Swine." *Journal of the American Medical Association* 298, no. 12 (2007): 1388.

Weir, Erica, Joanne Mitchell, Steven Reballato, and Dominic Fortuna. "Raw Milk and the Protection of Public Health." *Canadian Medical Association Journal* 177, no. 7 (2007): 721–722.

West, Harry G. "Food Fears and Raw-Milk Cheese." *Appetite* 51, no. 1 (2008): 25–29.

Web Sites

"The Dangers of Raw Milk: Unpasteurized Milk Can Pose a Serious Health Risk." *U.S. Food and Drug Administration (FDA).* http://www.fda.gov/Food/ResourcesForYou/Consumers/ucm079516.htm (accessed September 9, 2010).

Weston A. Price Foundation. "A Campaign for Real Milk." *Realmilk.com.* http://www.realmilk.com/ (accessed September 9, 2010).

Melanie Barton Zoltan

Religion and Food

◼ Introduction

Practices about food preparation and consumption have existed since the earliest civilizations. These were created out of tradition mainly to protect group health, and many of the rules centering around food were incorporated into religious laws and codes of practice. Ancient societies had limited means of preserving foods and maintaining the potability of water and other liquids, necessitating rules for safe preparation and consumption.

Religious food restrictions are on a continuum ranging from listings of restricted or forbidden foods to specific kitchen set-up and meal preparation instructions to dietary and lifestyle codes to prescriptions for fasting to delineation of types of foods for different holy days and religious festivals. Many of the early dietary laws and restrictions have Biblical or other holy text origins, and they have been carried into the practice of modern religions. In addition, specific dietary practices have been incorporated into many sects, such as use of fasting during particular times, the avoidance of excessive food consumption, the prohibition against the ingestion of caffeine or other stimulants such as tea or chocolate, and the prohibition of tobacco products, alcohol, and other identified foods or food products. Although most organized religions incorporate fasting practices, the duration and strictness of the fast varies by sect and by group. Some groups, such as the elderly, the chronically ill, pregnant or nursing women, and children below a certain age are routinely exempted from fasting requirements. Numerous religions place restrictions on eating different types of meat, fish, and shellfish. Many Hindus, Buddhists, Seventh-Day Adventists, and Rastafarians are strict vegetarians.

◼ Historical Background and Scientific Foundations

Most contemporary religious and spiritual dietary customs evolved from ancient laws/rules concerning food safety. Prior to the development of refrigeration and effective preservation techniques, it was essential to maintain strict processes for food usage in order to prevent widespread illness caused by spoilage or contamination. Over time, those conventions were incorporated into religious laws.

Before the advent of scientific understanding of bacteria and dangerous microorganisms, decisions were made about food and beverage safety based on practical observations: if people became sick or died after eating meat from animals who lived in certain conditions or maintained specific diets, those animals were considered unclean and prohibited from consumption. Pork, for example, is considered unclean in Islamic, Judaic, Rastafarian, and Seventh-Day Adventist traditions.

Many religions have rules about fasting, which can occur for several hours during certain parts of the day (e.g., from sunup to sundown daily during Ramadan for Muslims) to 24-hour or multi-day fasts (many Mormons and Roman Catholics fast on holy days). Abstaining from food is thought to purify the body, enhance spiritual growth, and encourage development of humility and empathy for those who are suffering. Food as spiritual nourishment is also observed in Christianity, with sacramental bread and wine considered a communal symbol of Christ by some Christians and the embodiment of Christ by others. Food restrictions in Christianity are rarely mandated, but are often self-initiated by those who observe Lent or meatless Fridays or avoid alcohol.

For Hindus, cows are considered sacred and cannot be eaten. Consuming pork or camel meat is also prohibited. Dairy products originating from these animals, however, such as yogurt, butter, and milk, are considered to be pure foods and may generally be eaten. Vegetarianism is encouraged; the eating of fish and shellfish is restricted. Fasting occurs on 18 observed holy days, as well as birthdays, wedding anniversaries, and the annual observance of familial death dates. Many Hindus also fast on Sundays.

Seventh Day Adventists may not eat pork or shellfish. They are encouraged to avoid meat and fish and are encouraged to pursue a lacto-ovo-vegetarian diet, meaning that they can consume eggs and dairy products in moderation. They are prohibited from ingesting stimulants such as coffee and tea and may not drink alcohol. Fasting is not a ritual part of this religion.

Buddhists are encouraged to avoid meat, fish, and shellfish. Eggs and dairy products are permitted in moderation, and fasting (followed by feasting) is encouraged during three annual holy periods celebrating the birth, enlightenment, and death of the Buddha. Buddhist monks rarely eat solid foods after midday, and they fast during some phases of the lunar cycle.

Ascetic Indian Rishis, or Yogis, consider spiritual growth to be enhanced by sacrifice and often engage in prolonged fasts. Indians hold the coconut as sacred and begin many religious ceremonies with the breaking of a sanctified coconut. The coconut is symbolic of Ganesh, a deity associated with success and prosperity. Consuming the hard kernel of the coconut is argued to enhance strength as well as success through hard work. Every portion of the coconut, from outer shell to inner milk, is worshipped and utilized by many Indian people.

The coca plant is sacred to many people of the Andes. The coca leaves are gently chewed until they can be formed into a ball, which is placed between the lining

Activists in Mumbai, India, protest the use of beef products in the French fries sold at international fast-food chain McDonald's on May 4, 2001. The protest was staged after McDonald's admitted before a Washington court that their French fries were laced with flavors of beef products. The company was replying to a million-dollar suit filed by a Seattle-based Indian American lawyer who alleged that McDonald's secretly laced the fries with beef and mislead consumers. A significant majority of India's Hindu population observes a religious prohibition on consuming beef products. *AP Images.*

of the mouth and the gum and left there for prolonged periods of time. It is thought that chewing coca leaves enhances physical strength, diminishes the perception of pain, and extends the ability to work under harsh conditions. Chewing coca leaves produces an anesthetic effect in the tongue, mouth, and throat, as well as in the lower gastrointestinal system. It is widely held by Andean people that drinking tea made with coca leaves diminishes altitude sickness.

■ Impacts and Issues

In both Judaism and the Muslim faith, there are rules and laws not only around which foods can be consumed, but also concerning the ways in which certain foods must be prepared. In the kosher tradition of Judaism, the kitchen must be arranged in specific ways, with separate sections for dairy, meat, and foods that are neither dairy not meat. The latter group of foods are called pareve; they can be eaten with either meat or dairy, and include eggs, fish, fruits, and vegetables. In kosher tradition, dairy and meat may not be eaten together at the same meal. Strict kosher dietary laws prescribe different utensils, dishes, and utensils for dairy and meat. Non-kosher foods cannot commingle with kosher foods. Shellfish may not be eaten, and pork is also prohibited. Animals providing meat must be slaughtered according to specific tradition and blessed after slaughter and before preparation for consumption. Animals must be slaughtered by specially trained butchers under Rabbinical supervision, using a special type of knife (specific to the size of the animal). The blade must be extremely sharp, and the animal must killed by a single rapid cut across the throat. The animal must then be hung upside down and all blood drained from the carcass. In late 2003 the Farm Animal Welfare Council (FAWC), which advises the government of the United Kingdom on how to avoid cruelty to livestock, called for an end to both kosher and Islamic methods of animal slaughter.

Foods that are prepared according to the kosher tradition are labeled by the Kashruth Division of the Union of Orthodox Jewish Congregations of America, otherwise known as the Orthodox Union (OU), with an OU symbol. The symbol, a U featured inside a surrounding O, has become the most recognized symbol for kosher-certified foods worldwide. The Orthodox Union has also begun labeling foods that contain dairy or that have been processed on dairy equipment with an OUD symbol, and meat-containing products with an OUM symbol. OU-labeled foods are now considered pareve. The Orthodox Union maintains a website to update information on the latest products certified kosher, and to answer questions submitted about kosher foods. In the United States alone, the market for prepared kosher foods is growing by about 15 percent annually. Large market chains and specialty stores such as Whole Foods are

A rabbi cleans a giant dough mixer at a matzo factory. The rabbi oversees the making of matzo to make sure it complies with kosher dietary laws. *AP Images.*

expanding their kosher lines to include both specialty and organic items.

The ritual butchering of meat-supplying animals is similarly accomplished in the Islamic tradition. Halal is the term for all foods conforming to Islamic dietary codes. Pork and birds of prey are forbidden, and forbidden foods are referred to as haram. Foods that are neither halal nor haram, or that are of questionable status are called mashbooh.

Halal methods of meat preparation in France have come under fire by both local populations and animal rights groups. This is due in large part to a decision by several branches of a French fast food chain called "Quick" to shift to an all-Halal menu in deference to large local Muslim populations. Although the French popular press reports this to be a marketing decision designed to increase business at specific local targets, many comments by non-Muslims have indicated displeasure with what they perceive to be preferential treatment of a religious minority. French animal activists have protested Halal butchering methods that do not use the

IN CONTEXT: SACRED BREW

After the Roman Empire fell in the fifth century AD, brewing technologies were preserved in the west in Christian monasteries. Monks had originally started making their own sacramental wine and brewed beer as a nutritional alternative to meals. This was important during their many fasts because drinking liquid was not considered to break the fast. The excess was sold to raise money for the monastery.

Some religious houses, in fact, made brewing a big business: eleven out of twelve monastic houses in medieval Yorkshire, for example, had brew houses on their premises. It is not only likely that monks discovered the advantages of adding hops to beer, but medieval monasteries such as those in St. Gall in Switzerland also added secret proprietary mixtures of herbs to their brews to widen their public appeal. The beer industry became so important in Germany that the first food purity laws, the *Reinheitsgebot* of 1516, regulated beer purity, requiring that it only contained water, malted barley, malted wheat, and hops.

usual industry standard of stunning the animals prior to slaughter, citing them as painful and inhumane. As of 2010 about 10 percent of Quick's outlets were serving halal-only meat and the company planned to expand the practice. Kentucky Fried Chicken also offers halal chicken in several of its outlets in France. One European market survey estimated the demand for ready-to-eat foods prepared according to halal requirements in France is larger than the demand for organic food and is increasing by almost 20 percent per year as the European Muslim middle class expands.

SEE ALSO *Food as Celebration; Foodways; Humane Animal Farming; Immigration and Cuisine; Indigenous Peoples and Their Diets; Raw Foodism; Veganism; Vegetarianism.*

BIBLIOGRAPHY

Books

Desai, Anita. *Fasting, Feasting.* New York: Houghton-Mifflin, 2000.

Snow, Michelle. *The Wow Diet: Words of Wisdom from Leading World Religions.* Springville, UT: CFI, 2010.

Walters, Kerry S., and Lisa Portmess. *Religious Vegetarianism: From Hesiod to the Dalai Lama.* Albany: State University of New York Press, 2001.

Periodicals

Cabrita, Joel, and Angel F. Mendez-Montoya. "The Theology of Food: Eating and the Eucharist. *Journal of the American Academy of Religion* 78, no. 3 (2010): 824–827.

Meyer-Rochow, Victor B. "Food Taboos: Their Origins and Purposes." *Journal of Ethnobiology and Ethnomedicine* 5, no. 18 (2009): 1–10.

Web Sites

Das, Sita Rama. "FaithandFood Fact Files: Hinduism." *faithandfood.com.* http://www.faithandfood.com/Hinduism.php (accessed October 31, 2010).

Heneghan, Tom. "French Fast Food Chain Expands Its Halal-Only Outlets." *Reuters*, August 21, 2010. http://www.reuters.com/article/idUSTRE67U3BE20100831 (accessed October 31, 2010).

OU Kosher.org. http://www.oukosher.org/ (accessed October 31, 2010).

State Government of Victoria, Australia, Department of Health. "Food Culture and Religion." *Better Health Channel.* http://www.betterhealth.vic.gov.au/bhcv2/bhcarticles.nsf/pages/Food_culture_and_religion?open (accessed October 31, 2010).

Pamela V. Michaels

Reportable Food Registry

■ Introduction

President George W. Bush (1946–) signed the FDA Amendments Act into law on September 27, 2007; the act reformed the Federal Food, Drug and Cosmetic Act of 1938 by creating a Reportable Food Registry (RFR). The FDA Amendments Act "establish[es] a Reportable Food Registry, to which instances of a reportable food may be submitted via an electronic portal and a unique number issued to the person submitting the report upon receipt." The RFR debuted on September 9, 2009, and all food suppliers are mandated by law to participate; failure to do so is a violation of the Federal Food, Drug and Cosmetics Act and can result in serious fines, felony charges, and possible prison sentences for company executives.

The Reportable Food Registry applies to all foods regulated by the Food and Drug Administration (FDA), both domestic and foreign, but does not include infant formula and dietary supplements. Responsible parties must submit information about a reportable food via the electronic portal within 24 hours of discovery of food that may cause serious harm or death to humans or animals.

■ Historical Background and Scientific Foundations

Requiring manufacturers to report tainted or dangerous foods to the FDA is not new, but the Reportable Food Registry system is the first wholly electronic reporting system in the agency's history, requiring responsible parties to report any reportable food within 24 hours of the discovery of a problem. The FDA and the U.S. Department of Agriculture (USDA) have issued food and feed recalls for decades, but the 2009 introduction of the Reportable Food Registry changed the speed with which tainted foods and feed could be managed and illness prevented.

In February 2007, *Salmonella*-tainted peanut butter from a ConAgra plant in Georgia sickened nearly 300 people in 39 states over a six-month period. The *Salmonella* scare prompted a recall of peanut butter products from the identified plant. This incident, one of many food-related product recalls, helped to promote reform of the FDA's reporting procedures for tainted foods and feed.

Less than two years later, in late 2008 and early 2009, another peanut butter-related *Salmonella* outbreak spread throughout the United States. This time the genesis of the tainted product was Peanut Corporation of America's Georgia plant, where peanut butter, peanut paste, and peanut meal sold to more than 360 other food and feed manufacturers made its way into thousands of products, killing nine people and sickening nearly 700 more throughout 46 states.

The Reportable Food Registry was built for industry officials from registered food manufacturers to report directly to the FDA any suspected questionable product to prevent—or at least contain—food-related illnesses such as the *Salmonella* found in these peanut butter products.

■ Impacts and Issues

The registry is not accessible to the public; consumers call a separate hotline to report food product safety and contamination issues. The Reportable Food Registry is designed to be accessed easily and for the reporting process to be smooth. Responsible parties give their registration number, the name of the product in question, the date of the discovery that the food is reportable, details on how the food is adulterated or tainted, an accounting of investigation and discarding procedures, and any product codes necessary for registry officials to identify the plant of origin. An ICSR number is issued, and the responsible party needs to give this number to any suppliers or buyers affected by the product.

The FDA then issues a consumer alert warning the public that there may be a reasonable, or even probable, assumption that the reported product could have

WORDS TO KNOW

ICSR NUMBER: The Reportable Food Registry issues Individual Case Safety Report numbers when a responsible party inputs a reportable food to the registry. Responsible parties and the FDA then use this number to track developments in the case.

REPORTABLE FOOD: Any food item that, if consumed by humans or animals, may be considered to cause serious health problems or death.

RESPONSIBLE PARTY: Any registered food facility or manufacturer, processor, or packager that manages food for human or animal consumption.

serious adverse health effects if consumed. From there, FDA investigators step in and work with the responsible party to contain the spread of the food product to other manufacturing, processing, and/or packaging facilities.

In July 2010, 10 months after the reportable Food Registry began, the FDA issued a press release touting the program's success. According to agency officials, the system logged 125 primary reports from responsible parties, with 1,638 secondary suppliers filing reports based on primary reports. The Reportable Food Registry caught issues such as undeclared sulfites in boxed side dish food products and hydrolyzed vegetable protein (HVP) recalls of more than 177 products with adulteration issues. Thirty-seven percent of the primary reports involved *Salmonella* contamination.

A man reports a problem with a processed food on the U.S. Food and Drug Administration's (FDA) Reportable Food Registry website. The agency created the online reporting tool in 2007 to let industry workers, physicians, health officials, and the general public easily report instances of tainted or adulterated foods. *K. Lee Lerner & Lerner / LernerMedia Global Photos.*

In June 2010 the FDA issued changes to the original 2007 Act that created the Reportable Food Registry. Changes include: requiring any product with an undeclared food allergen outlined by the Food Allergen Labeling and Consumer Protection Act to be a reportable food; mandating that companies file a reportable food even if the entire shipment of the product is for export; requiring that any rejected shipment of reportable food product, even if never unloaded from a supplier's trucks, must be reported; and mandating that all registry reports will remain on file with the FDA, even if an investigation finds that the report was unfounded and the food product safe.

SEE ALSO *Consumer Food Safety Recommendations; Food, Drug, and Cosmetic Act of 1938; Food Inspection and Standards; Food Safety and Inspection Service; Foodborne Diseases; Produce Traceability; Salmonella; U.S. Food and Drug Administration (FDA)*

BIBLIOGRAPHY

Books

Tzia, Constantina. *Quality and Safety Assurance in Food Processing*. Boca Raton, FL: CRC Press, 2011.

Periodicals

"FDA Changes Portal for Reportable Food Registry, Updates Guidance." *Food Chemical News* 52, no. 12 (2010): 10–11.

"FDA Touts Reportable Food Registry as Successful but Industry Wants Changes." *Food Chemical News* 52, no. 20 (2010): 1.

"Food Industry Responds to New Reportable Food Registry." *Food Chemical News* 51, no. 29 (2009): 14.

Stier, Richard F. "Food Safety: Will Reportable Food Registry Law Make Food Safer?" *Food Engineering-American Edition* 82, no. 1 (2010): 26.

Web Sites

"The Reportable Food Registry, FDA's New Early Detection System, Helps Identify 125 Food Safety Problems in First Seven Months." *Center for Food Safety and Applied Nutrition, U.S. Food and Drug Administration (FDA)*, August 3, 2010. http://www.fda.gov/Food/NewsEvents/ConstituentUpdates/ucm220973.htm (accessed September 7, 2010).

Melanie Barton Zoltan

Rice

■ Introduction

A cereal grain, rice is a staple food for more than half the world's population. Rice cultivation originated in China, Thailand, Myanmar, and West Africa around 10,000 BC. Rice is grown in many different ecological environments, usually as an annual crop, and it is typically milled or processed to some extent before being sold. A wide variety of highly processed foods are based on rice. Though rice is a staple food for many, especially in its processed form it is lacking in certain vitamins that are necessary for human nutrition and health. Scientists have created "golden rice," a genetically engineered variety that contains beta-carotene to combat Vitamin A deficiency. However, regulatory approval of golden rice has been slow due to concerns about genetically modified crops. Despite so many people growing and eating rice, only a small percentage of world rice production is traded. Because this percentage is relatively small, rice price increases in the food crisis of 2008 may have been affected by export bans in countries such as India and Vietnam.

■ Historical Background and Scientific Foundations

Rice is the staple food for more than half the population of the world. Archeological evidence indicates that rice, previously gathered from its wild ancestors, was cultivated as early as 10,000 BC in parts of China, Thailand, and Myanmar. This rice, *Oryzo sativa*, is now grown on all continents other than Antarctica. Another very similar plant species, *Oryzo glaberimma*, was estimated to have been cultivated first in West Africa around the same time period. This species has not spread outside of Africa for widespread commercial use. New, high-yielding varieties, known as dwarf varieties because they grow on shorter stalks so that more of the plant's energy is devoted to developing the grain, emerged as a result of Green Revolution technologies in the 1960s.

Almost all rice is *Oryzo sativa*, including heirloom varieties such as black rice (also known as forbidden rice). Wild rice, which grows wild in North America and in parts of China and can be used for food, comes from similar grasses, but they are genetically distinct from rice.

Rice is an annual crop cultivated through five different growing systems. A limited area of rice is cultivated as a perennial in some tropical areas. Irrigated systems provide 75 percent of global rice production. They depend on irrigation to flood paddies and provide moisture. These systems use more water than that necessary for cultivating other major cereal grains. In tropical areas, irrigated rice production can produce two or sometimes three crops annually, though rice is replanted each time. Rain-fed lowland rice systems take up around 34 percent of total rice growing land in the world, but as there is no control over water, rice yields are less than in irrigated systems. These systems are subject to both droughts and floods, depending upon precipitation instead of irrigation. Upland rice is grown on steep slopes or in valleys with significant water runoff problems. Flood-prone systems are also used in some river valleys and coastal areas. Those systems have low yields due to flooding, which may last for months.

According to the U.S. Department of Agriculture (USDA), the average yields were highest in North Africa in 2009, where rice growers averaged 9.8 tons per hectare planted. North America, East Asia, and South America also had relatively high yields per hectare. The lowest yields were in Sub-Saharan Africa (SSA), the countries of Africa south of the Sahara desert, which averaged two tons per hectare in 2009. The USDA's Economic Research Service (ERS) estimates that between 2001 and 2010, the amount of land cultivated for rice increased only by 6 percent, but the total production of rice rose by 14 percent.

When first harvested and completely unprocessed, rice is known as rough rice, paddy rice, or simply paddy. To be eaten as food, the hull must first be removed from the rice. The de-hulled product is brown rice, which may be prepared in this form or made into flour for use in processed foods such as bread, breakfast cereals, or noodles. Some brown rice is then parboiled and dried. This parboiled rice cooks faster than brown rice, while retaining many of the nutrients. To create white rice, the germ and the bran of the rice are removed. White rice may then be further polished to produce a more uniform shape. Red rices are produced by removing the germ, but not all of the bran residue, during polishing.

Long grain varieties of rice are the most popular, but short and medium grain varieties are used in many dishes around the world. Aromatic rice varieties such as basmati and jasmine are known for their smell while they cook. Water must be added to cook rice, though a wide variety of techniques from different cuisines exist using different amounts of water ranging from steaming the rice, having the cooking rice absorb all the water used, boiling the rice in large amounts of water, or even creating a porridge by adding a little more water than necessary. In addition to being cooked at home, rice is further

processed into many food products, ranging from puffed rice ready-to-eat cereals to rice milk to noodles to pastries to sake, a highly alcoholic rice wine from Japan. The hull is not suitable for human consumption, but the bran from milling, or processing, rice is often used to make rice bran oil and a variety of other foods or is used as an ingredient in livestock feed. Riceland Foods, a U.S.

Different varieties of rice, a staple food in many countries, are grown around the world. *Image copyright Monkey Business Images, 2010. Used under license from Shutterstock.com.*

marketing cooperative with more than 9,000 members in Texas, Arkansas, Louisiana, Missouri, and Mississippi, all states in the southern part of the United States, is the world's highest volume rice miller.

■ Impacts and Issues

The International Rice Research Institute (IRRI) estimates that one billion people in the world depend on growing rice. Often, women are the predominate workers in the rice paddies. In recognition of the large role rice plays, both as a source of food and as a source of livelihood, the United Nations (UN) General Assembly (GA) declared 2004 the International Year of Rice. Despite being a major world cereal grain, most rice is consumed in the country in which it is grown. For example, USDA/ERS estimates that in 2009 only 7 percent of rice entered international trade. Thailand, Vietnam, Pakistan, India, China, and the United States are the largest rice exporters. In 2009, according to USDA/ERS, the largest rice importers were the Philippines, Nigeria, Iran, Iraq, Saudi Arabia, Brazil, and Bangladesh. In the food price crisis of 2008, rice played a key role as the price of rice rose to five times its 2003 price in 2008. As very few countries export rice, India's and Vietnam's decisions to ban rice exports temporarily in 2008 may have exacerbated the price rise, though there were no actual shortages of rice on world markets at the time. Whereas price manipulation through limiting trade and hoarding of rice may have occurred during the food price crisis of 2008, some critics of agricultural subsidies draw attention to the low- or no-cost access to irrigation water that rice producers in the United States and Australia enjoy as a hidden subsidy for rice production in those countries.

As rice is a staple food for so many people, not only its price but its nutritional content is critical for much of the world's population. Particularly in Southeast Asia, Vitamin A deficiency has persisted and continues to affect many children. The World Health Organization (WHO) estimates that as many as one half million children may become blind every year due to Vitamin A deficiency. Of these children, half may die within a year of becoming blind. Although commercially-produced white rice is often fortified with nutrients lost during milling or with Vitamin A, the deficiency continues.

To address this problem, two scientists, Ingo Potrykus (1933–), a German plant biologist, and Peter Beyer (1952–), a German biologist and biochemist, created

Workers plant rice in Malaysia.   *Image copyright Sia Chen How, 2010. Used under license from Shutterstock.com.*

golden rice. Employing both traditional breeding methods and genetic modification, these scientists used some genes from corn to create a rice that has beta carotene, which the body can then convert into Vitamin A. By 2001 this research led to viable rice varieties, but golden rice is being grown only in research settings as of 2010. Proponents of golden rice point to its potential to eliminate Vitamin A deficiency in Asia and other rice-dependent regions. However, the approval process to grow golden rice for purposes other than research has been slow. Critics of genetically modified organisms (GMOs) such as golden rice worry about potential allergens, interference with agricultural ecosystems, and other potential problems that may not have been discovered through research and testing.

SEE ALSO *Agricultural Demand for Water; Agroecology; Asian Diet; Climate Change and Agriculture; Ecological Impacts of Various World Diets; Food Price Crisis; Gender Equality and Agriculture; Genetically Modified Organisms (GMO); Grains; Green Revolution (1943); Women's Role in Global Food Preparation.*

BIBLIOGRAPHY

Books

Asia Society. *Never an Empty Bowl: Sustaining Food Security in Asia.* New York: Asia Society, 2010.

Cheung, Sidney C. H., and Chee B. Tan. *Food and Foodways in Asia: Resource, Tradition and Cooking.* London: Routledge, 2007.

Fields-Black, Edda L. *Deep Roots: Rice Farmers in West Africa and the African Diaspora.* Bloomington: Indiana University Press, 2008.

Pesticide Action Network: Asia and the Pacific. *The Great Rice Robbery: A Handbook on the Impact of IRRI in Asia.* Penang, Malaysia: Pesticide Action Network, Teknolohiya, 2007.

Periodicals

Mariyono, Joko, Tom Kompas, and R. Quentin Grafton. "Shifting from Green Revolution to Environmentally Sound Policies: Technological Change in Indonesian Rice Agriculture." *Journal of the Asia Pacific Economy* 15, no. 2 (2010): 128–147.

Web Sites

FreeRice. http://www.freerice.com/ (accessed October 23, 2010).

"Rice Basics." *International Rice Research Institute.* http://irri.org/about-rice/rice-facts/rice-basics (accessed October 23, 2010).

Blake Jackson Stabler

Rome Declaration on World Food Security (1996)

■ Introduction

The Rome Declaration on World Food Security is an international declaration on world hunger and food security issues adopted by delegates from 185 nations at the World Food Summit held in Rome, Italy, in November 1996. The Declaration states the international community's desire to halve the number of people suffering from hunger by 2015 and increase global food security. The Food and Agriculture Organization (FAO) of the United Nations defines food security as the "physical and economic access, at all times, to sufficient, safe and nutritious food to meet dietary needs and food preferences for an active and healthy life."

The Rome Declaration sets forth seven commitments that signatories agreed to undertake in order to increase global food security. These include the following: ensure a political, social, and economic framework that allows for the eradication of poverty; implement policies designed to eradicate poverty and improve access to safe food; pursue sustainable food, agriculture, forestry, fisheries, and rural development policies; strive to ensure that agricultural trade is fair and market-oriented; prepare to meet the food requirements presented by natural and human-made disasters; promote optimal allocation of investments to foster sustainable development; and implement and monitor the action plan to implement the Rome Declaration.

A number of issues continue to threaten food security, including population growth, global climate change, and lack of funding and dedication to hunger eradication by the international community. The roles of food distribution and liberalization of agricultural trade on food security are also issues of debate in the international community and among agricultural policy analysts.

■ Historical Background and Scientific Foundations

The international community has espoused a strong commitment to food security and hunger eradication since the end of World War II (1939–1945). The disruption to the global food supply caused during the war and subsequent food rationing highlighted the need for increased global food security. Less altruistically, food and agricultural aid and subsidies also became political and ideological tools of the West and Eastern Bloc countries during the Cold War as those factions attempted to curry favor with potential allies.

In 1945 members of the nascent United Nations formed the Food and Agriculture Organization (FAO) of the United Nations to coordinate international efforts to decrease hunger and increase global food security. In 1974 the FAO convened the World Food Conference to address issues related to food production and consumption, including hunger, food security, and malnutrition. The declaration of the World Food Conference states that "every man, woman and child has the inalienable right to be free from hunger and malnutrition in order to develop their physical and mental faculties." The World Food Conference also called on the international community to achieve the goal of eradicating hunger, food insecurity, and malnutrition within a decade.

In 1994 Jacques Diouf (1938–), the newly appointed director-general of the FAO, determined that a consensus existed among FAO member nations that a new international food conference should be convened to reaffirm the international community's commitment to increasing food security. In October 1995 the FAO Conference, the agency's governing body, called for convening the World Food Summit in November 1996. The FAO Conference noted that approximately 800 million people faced chronic malnutrition in 1995. Despite the growing need for international food and agricultural assistance, the FAO determined that food and agricultural assistance to developing nations declined by almost 30 percent between 1982 and 1992.

At the World Food Conference, delegates addressed issues related to malnutrition, sustainable development of agriculture, and food security, particularly with regard to the world's ability to meet future food demands as the world's population increases. The delegates ultimately adopted the Rome Declaration on World Food Security and the corresponding World Food Summit Action Plan, which provides greater detail for implementing the goals of the Rome Declaration.

■ Impacts and Issues

The Rome Declaration declares "the right of everyone to have access to safe and nutritious food, consistent with the right to adequate food and the fundamental right of everyone to be free from hunger." It also states that the international community and individual

member nations are dedicated to increasing food security and reducing the number of undernourished by half by 2015. The international community, however, is not on track to achieve the Rome Declaration's goals. Many issues continue to surround efforts to increase global food security.

Although it promulgates goals and ideals, the Rome Declaration does not include concrete strategies for achieving these aims. Even the World Food Summit

A food depot in Inner Mongolia, China, an area that has experienced increased drought and desertification in recent years.
© *Global Warming Images / Alamy.*

Action Plan merely calls on nations to promote, support, or adopt policies to further the Rome Declaration's goals; it does not set hard financial, technical assistance, or other requirements for countries to satisfy. Furthermore, the Rome Declaration is not a legally binding treaty under international law. Signatories to the declaration are under no obligation to enact policies to achieve the goals of decreasing hunger and promoting sustainable development.

A number of issues continue to affect current and future food security, including food distribution, liberalization of agricultural trade, sustainable development, food safety, population growth, and global climate change. Agricultural analysts remain split over the role of food distribution in food security. Some analysts claim that the world produces enough food for proper nourishment for every person and that distribution is the main problem. Others, however, claim that food production is lacking in many areas and that improved food distribution will not supply everyone with adequate, healthy food. Liberalization of agricultural trade—a key component of global food distribution—also poses a dilemma: Whereas liberal agricultural trade supplies many areas with needed food aid, there is the fear that food aid discourages local peoples from developing sustainable, national agricultural sectors.

The world's growing population threatens future food security. The Rome Declaration notes that a larger population will place additional stress on natural resources such as fish stocks, forests, and arable land. A larger population will require increased food production to meet growing demand. The United Nations estimates that the global population will increase from approximately 6.9 billion people in 2010 to 7.3 billion people in 2015 and to more than 8.3 billion people in 2030.

Despite a growing population and limited natural resources, the Rome Declaration states the goal of cutting global hunger in half by 2015. The Millennium Development Goals, a set of eight international development goals set forth by United Nations member nations in 2000, reaffirm the Rome Declaration's 2015 target. Unfortunately, the international community has not yet made progress: In 1996 the World Food Conference noted that approximately 800 million people suffered from hunger, but in 2010 the United Nations estimated that the number had increased to 925 million.

In 2009 the FAO convened the World Summit on Food Security to address the continued increase of food insecurity, particularly in light of the contemporary global economic recession and the food price crisis of 2007 and 2008. This summit again reaffirmed the goal of halving global hunger by 2015 and encouraged nations to increase agricultural funding to promote development of the public and private agricultural sector in developing nations.

■ Primary Source Connection

The 1996 World Food Summit was held November 13–17, 1996, in Rome, Italy. A result of the summit was an international commitment, contained in the Rome Declaration on World Food Security, to reduce world hunger by 50 percent by 2015. By 2010, while experts lauded individual program and local successes, they called for revisions in estimates of the extent of hunger and the need for a longer range plan to reduce hunger.

In 2009, Ban Ki-moon, Secretary General of The United Nations, called for a "single global vision" to tackle world hunger and for coordinated international efforts to mitigate climate change and increase food production. Food and Agriculture Organization (FAO) officials warned that according to current trends, 370 million people could face chronic famine by 2050, and that the world will need to produce 70 percent more food to meet estimated population increases to more than 9 billion people by the same date.

Rome Declaration on World Food Security

We, the Heads of State and Government, or our representatives, gathered at the World Food Summit at the invitation of the Food and Agriculture Organization of the United Nations, reaffirm the right of everyone to have access to safe and nutritious food, consistent with the right to adequate food and the fundamental right of everyone to be free from hunger.

We pledge our political will and our common and national commitment to achieving food security for all and to an ongoing effort to eradicate hunger in all countries, with an immediate view to reducing the number of undernourished people to half their present level no later than 2015.

We consider it intolerable that more than 800 million people throughout the world, and particularly in developing countries, do not have enough food to meet their basic nutritional needs. This situation is unacceptable. Food supplies have increased substantially, but constraints on access to food and continuing inadequacy of household and national incomes to purchase food, instability of supply and demand, as well as natural and manmade disasters, prevent basic food needs from being fulfilled. The problems of hunger and food insecurity have global dimensions and are likely to persist, and even increase dramatically in some regions, unless urgent, determined and concerted action is taken, given the anticipated increase in the world's population and the stress on natural resources.

We reaffirm that a peaceful, stable and enabling political, social and economic environment is the essential foundation which will enable States to give adequate priority to food security and poverty eradication. Democracy, promotion and protection of all human rights and fundamental freedoms, including the right to development, and the full and equal participation of men and women are essential for achieving sustainable food security for all.

Poverty is a major cause of food insecurity and sustainable progress in poverty eradication is critical to improve access to food. Conflict, terrorism, corruption and environmental degradation also contribute significantly to food insecurity. Increased food production, including staple food, must be undertaken. This should happen within the framework of sustainable management of natural resources, elimination of unsustainable patterns of consumption and production, particularly in industrialized countries, and early stabilization of the world population. We acknowledge the fundamental contribution to food security by women, particularly in rural areas of developing countries, and the need to ensure equality between men and women. Revitalization of rural areas must also be a priority to enhance social stability and help redress the excessive rate of rural-urban migration confronting many countries.

We emphasize the urgency of taking action now to fulfill our responsibility to achieve food security for present and future generations. Attaining food security is a complex task for which the primary responsibility rests with individual governments. They have to develop an enabling environment and have policies that ensure peace, as well as social, political and economic stability and equity and gender equality. We express our deep concern over the persistence of hunger which, on such a scale, constitutes a threat both to national societies and, through a variety of ways, to the stability of the international community itself. Within the global framework, governments should also cooperate actively with one another and with United Nations organizations, financial institutions, intergovernmental and nongovernmental organizations, and public and private sectors, on programmes directed toward the achievement of food security for all.

Food should not be used as an instrument for political and economic pressure. We reaffirm the importance of international cooperation and solidarity as well as the necessity of refraining from unilateral measures not in accordance with the international law and the Charter of the United Nations and that endanger food security.

We recognize the need to adopt policies conducive to investment in human resource development, research and infrastructure for achieving food security. We must encourage generation of employment and incomes, and promote equitable access to productive and financial resources. We agree that trade is a key element in achieving food security. We agree to pursue food trade and overall trade policies that will encourage our producers and consumers to utilize available resources in an economically sound and sustainable manner. We recognize the importance for food security of sustainable agriculture, fisheries, forestry and rural development in low as well as high potential areas. We acknowledge the fundamental role of farmers, fishers, foresters, indigenous people and their communities, and all other people involved in the food sector, and of their organizations, supported by effective research and extension, in attaining food security. Our sustainable development policies will promote full participation and empowerment of people, especially women, an equitable distribution of income, access to health care and education, and opportunities for youth. Particular attention should be given to those who cannot produce or procure enough food for an adequate diet, including those affected by war, civil strife, natural disaster or climate related ecological changes. We are conscious of the need for urgent action to combat pests, drought, and natural resource degradation including desertification, overfishing, and erosion of biological diversity.

We are determined to make efforts to mobilize, and optimize the allocation and utilization of, technical and financial resources from all sources, including external debt relief for developing countries, to reinforce national actions to implement sustainable food security policies.

Convinced that the multifaceted character of food security necessitates concerted national action, and effective international efforts to supplement and reinforce national action, we make the following commitments:

- we will ensure an enabling political, social, and economic environment designed to create the best conditions for the eradication of poverty and for durable peace, based on full and equal participation of women and men, which is most conducive to achieving sustainable food security for all;

- we will implement policies aimed at eradicating poverty and inequality and improving physical and economic access by all, at all times, to sufficient, nutritionally adequate and safe food and its effective utilization;

- we will pursue participatory and sustainable food, agriculture, fisheries, forestry and rural development policies and practices in high and low potential areas, which are essential to adequate and reliable food supplies at the household, national, regional and global levels, and combat pests, drought and desertification, considering the multifunctional character of agriculture;

- we will strive to ensure that food, agricultural trade and overall trade policies are conducive to fostering food security for all through a fair and market-oriented world trade system;

- we will endeavour to prevent and be prepared for natural disasters and man-made emergencies and to meet transitory and emergency food requirements.

We pledge our actions and support to implement the World Food Summit Plan of Action.

Rome, 13 November 1996.

FOOD AND AGRICULTURE ORGANIZATION OF THE UNITED NATIONS (FAO). "WORLD FOOD SUMMIT, ROME 1996: ROME DECLARATION ON WORLD FOOD SECURITY AND WORLD FOOD SUMMIT PLAN OF ACTION." *FOOD AND AGRICULTURAL ORGANIZATION OF THE UNITED NATIONS (FAO).* HTTP://WWW.FAO.ORG/DOCREP/003/W3613E/ W3613E00.HTM (ACCESSED OCTOBER 24, 2010).

SEE ALSO *African Famine Relief; Biofuels and World Hunger; Desertification and Agriculture; Ethical Issues in Food Aid; Famine; Famine: Political Considerations; Food and Agriculture Organization (FAO); Food Security; Free Trade and Agriculture; Hunger; Population and Food; Subsistence Farming; Sustainable Agriculture; UN Millennium Development Goals; Undernutrition; U.S. Agency for International Development (USAID); World Food Programme.*

BIBLIOGRAPHY

Books

Food and Agricultural Organization of the United Nations (FAO). *The State of Food Insecurity in the World 2009: Eradicating World Hunger.* Rome: FAO, 2009.

Web Sites

"Monitoring Progress since the World Food Summit." *Food and Agricultural Organization of the United Nations (FAO).* http://www.fao.org/monitoring progress/index_en.html (accessed September 25, 2010).

"Outcomes on Food." *United Nations.* http://www. un.org/en/development/devagenda/food.shtml (accessed September 25, 2010).

"World Food Summit: The Rome Declaration on World Food Security and the World Food Summit Plan of Action." *Food and Agricultural Organization of the United Nations (FAO).* http://www.fao.org/ docrep/003/w3613e/w3613e00.HTM (accessed September 25, 2010).

Joseph P. Hyder

Salmonella

■ Introduction

Bacteria in the genus *Salmonella* are the cause of salmonellosis infection in humans. Contamination of food by the bacteria is a common cause of salmonellosis, a potentially lethal disease. The *Salmonella* bacteria exist in low populations in many foods, resulting in periodic outbreaks manifested in an array of foods. Mild salmonellosis is common and widespread. Of particular concern, *Salmonella* have emerged that are resistant to many commonly used antibiotics.

Salmonellosis due to the contamination of food can be a food infection or a food intoxication, depending on the antigenic type (serotype) of *Salmonella* involved. A food infection relies on the growth of the bacteria to levels capable of causing symptoms. Growth of the contaminating strain is not necessary for a food intoxication because it is a toxin that has already been produced by the contaminating bacteria that cause the illness. Salmonellosis is most often a food infection, but if enough toxin-loaded bacteria are ingested, salmonellosis can be an intoxication.

■ Historical Background and Scientific Foundations

Salmonella is a Gram-negative, rod-shaped bacterium. It is named after Daniel Salmon (1850–1914), who, with Theobald Smith (1859–1934), isolated the bacterium from pigs in 1885. Since then, more than 2,500 different serotypes of the bacterium have been found; the term serotype indicates the protein composition of the bacterial surface, which produces a distinct immune response by the host. The many different serotypes indicate that the surface of *Salmonella* is highly variable.

The bacterium is commonly found in the gastrointestinal tract of humans and other animals. In this environment it is of no concern. However, if food or water contaminated with *Salmonella*-containing feces is ingested, illness can result. Like other fecal bacteria, food contamination most often occurs when the food is handled by someone who has not properly washed their hands after having a bowel movement. Good hygiene is important in minimizing the risk of salmonellosis.

Salmonellosis is caused most often by two strains: *S. typimurium* and *S. enteritidis*. Other serotypes of the bacterium usually cause disease in animals such as cattle and pigs. If these serotypes infect humans, the infection can be severe and even life-threatening.

Poultry carcasses can be contaminated with intestinal contents during slaughter of the bird. The bacteria can remain alive long enough for the carcass to be shipped to a grocery store and sold. The bacteria are readily killed by heat. But if cooking is inadequate, the surviving organisms are capable of causing illness. An egg can also be contaminated if the shell has a crack or break, which allows the bacteria to enter the inside of the egg. Other foods that are often involved in salmonellosis are raw or undercooked meat, processed meat, dairy products, custards and cream-based desserts, and sandwich filling such as tuna salad or chicken salad.

Symptoms of salmonellosis develop within a few hours of eating contaminated food. The symptoms include abdominal cramping, nausea with vomiting, fever, headache, chills and sweating, a feeling of weakness, and loss of appetite. Some people also develop watery diarrhea or—if cells lining the intestine are damaged—bloody diarrhea. The rapid loss of fluids due to diarrhea can be dangerous to infants and the elderly. Less commonly, the infection may spread to the bloodstream. Some people can develop a painful condition called Reiter's syndrome, which can persist for years and can lead to arthritis.

For most people, the infection lasts 4–7 days, and they recover without needing medical attention. However, severe diarrhea usually results in hospitalization.

Outbreaks of salmonellosis can occur due to the consumption of contaminated food in a restaurant or at a social gathering. For example, an outbreak due to *S. typhimurium* that occurred in 21 states in September 2006

WORDS TO KNOW

CONTAMINATED: The unwanted presence of a microorganism or compound in a particular environment. That environment can be in the laboratory setting, for example, in a medium being used for the growth of a species of bacteria during an experiment. Another environment can be the human body, where contamination by bacteria can produce an infection. Contamination by bacteria and viruses can occur on several levels, and their presence can adversely influence the results of the experiments. Outside the laboratory, bacteria and viruses can contaminate drinking water supplies, foodstuffs, and products, causing illness.

ENTEROTOXIN: Enterotoxin and exotoxin are two classes of toxin that are produced by bacteria.

LIPOPOLYSACCHARIDE (LPS): Lipopolysaccharide (LPS) is a molecule that is a constituent of the outer membrane of Gram-negative bacteria. The molecule can also be referred to as endotoxin. LPS can help protect the bacterium from host defenses and can contribute to illness in the host.

SEROTYPES: Serotypes or serovars are classes of microorganisms based on the types of molecules (antigens) that they present on their surfaces. Even a single species may have thousands of serotypes, which may have medically quite distinct behaviors.

TOXIN: A poison that is produced by a living organism.

was traced to the consumption of contaminated tomatoes at restaurants. However, a number of studies have indicated that more than 80 percent of cases occur individually. This is unfortunate, according to the World Health Organization (WHO), because the individual cases do not attract media attention to a serious global problem, especially in developing and under-developed countries.

The *Salmonella* that cause salmonellosis possess what are termed virulence factors—molecules that enable the bacteria to establish an infection. One important virulence factor is called adhesin. This is a molecule that can recognize a target site on the host cell and help the bacterium adhere to the host cell target. One example of a *Salmonella* adhesin is a tube called a fimbriae that sticks out from the bacterial surface. The end of each fimbriae contains a protein that can bind with a specific host cell surface protein.

Another virulence factor is called lipopolysaccharide (LPS). There are many different structures of LPS. Those that are longer can help shield the bacterial surface from host compounds that can damage or kill the bacteria. Furthermore, a part of LPS called lipid A is a toxin.

Some strains of *Salmonella* also produce a toxin called enterotoxin. This toxin is located inside the bacteria, so as the numbers of *Salmonella* increase, the concentration of the enterotoxin in the food increases.

Ingesting the food releases the enterotoxin in the intestine, where it ruptures the intestinal cells by forming a hole in their cell membrane.

Scope and Distribution

Salmonellosis is global in occurrence and common. According to data from the United States Centers for Disease Control and Prevention (CDC), more than 40,000 cases of salmonellosis are reported each year in the United States. Because many more cases are never reported, the actual total is much higher—1.4 million cases, according to the CDC. Approximately 1,000 people in the United States die of salmonellosis-related complications every year.

Treatment and Prevention

Diagnosis of salmonellosis relies on recognition of its symptoms and the identification of *Salmonella* from a stool (fecal) sample. Current tests that detect certain *Salmonella* proteins do not require growth of the bacteria, and thus can be completed within hours.

Identification of the type of *Salmonella* involved usually helps in determining which antibiotics to use. Salmonellosis often responds well to antibiotics; however, serotypes of *Salmonella* that are resistant to a variety of antibiotics exist and are becoming more common.

Prevention involves good hygiene, including hand washing and the cleaning of cooking utensils and equipment that have been used with foods such as poultry and ground meat before reusing them. Foods containing raw eggs should not be eaten; even if the eggs appeared intact, cracks that are not visible to the eye are large enough to allow bacteria to contaminate the egg.

Researchers are exploring the production of a vaccine against salmonellosis. The most promising strategy is to block the adhesion of the bacteria to the intestinal cells. This strategy has proven successful in developing a vaccine that appeared on the market in 2006 for another intestinal bacterium called *Escherichia coli* O157:H7 (*E. coli* O157:H7).

■ Impacts and Issues

Salmonellosis has major economic impacts. Millions of people each year miss work and school because of the illness. Health care dollars are spent looking after those who become hospitalized. Exact figures are difficult to obtain, especially from developing countries, as they do not report on salmonellosis. But in the United States, the estimated 1.4 million annual cases of salmonellosis result in the hospitalization of 15,000 people. The annual total medical cost of dealing with salmonellosis in the United States is estimated to be $1 billion. Other costs due to lost productivity and lost wages push the total cost to an estimated $3 billion.

In February 2007 *Salmonella*-contaminated peanut butter was responsible for a nationwide salmonellosis outbreak in the United States. The FDA warned consumers not to purchase or eat certain brands of peanut butter manufactured at a facility in Georgia. Companies with brands associated with the salmonellosis outbreak recalled all potentially contaminated products, including peanut butter for home use and commercial peanut butter products used by some fast-food chains. The *Salmonella*-contaminated foods associated with the outbreak affected approximately 370 people in more than 40 states. Although salmonellosis is typically associated with poultry products, the 2007 outbreak was not the first associated with peanut butter: A similar salmonellosis event that occurred in Australia in the mid–1990s was traced to contaminated peanut butter.

In 2010 a salmonellosis outbreak traced to contaminated eggs forced a massive egg recall of eggs in the United States. By September of that year, more than 1,600 *Salmonella*-related illnesses in the United States were linked by the CDC to the contaminated eggs. Within just the first month the 2010 outbreak of salmonellosis was the largest in nearly 40 years.

Using both pulsed-field gel electrophoresis (PFGE) and other types of DNA and protein analysis, teams of

---

IN CONTEXT: EFFECTIVE RULES AND REGULATIONS

According to the Division of Bacterial and Mycotic Diseases at the Centers for Disease Control and Prevention (CDC), the CDC "monitors the frequency of Salmonella infections in the country and assists the local and State Health Departments to investigate outbreaks and devise control measures." CDC also conducts research to better identify specific types of *Salmonella*. The Food and Drug Administration (FDA) inspects imported foods and milk pasteurization plants, promotes better food preparation techniques in restaurants and food processing plants, and regulates the sale of turtles, which can carry salmonella. The FDA also regulates the use of specific antibiotics as growth accelerants in food animals. The U.S. Department of Agriculture monitors the health of food animals, inspects egg pasteurization plants, and is responsible for the quality of slaughtered and processed meat. The U.S. Environmental Protection Agency regulates and monitors the safety of drinking water supplies.

SOURCE: *Centers for Disease Control and Prevention (CDC), Coordinating Center for Infectious Diseases, Division of Bacterial and Mycotic Diseases.*

A sign warns customers of the recall of certain lots of eggs that had been previously sold at a supermarket in Los Angeles, California. A *Salmonella* outbreak sickened as many as 1,600 people and led to the recall of a half-billion eggs from two Iowa farms in August 2010. *AP Images.*

---

investigators from several state public health authorities, the CDC, the FDA and the USDA's Food Safety and Inspection Service linked the outbreak to a *Salmonella* serotype subsequently found in high numbers at two Iowa egg companies. Highly contaminated poultry feed and barns were found at both farms. During processing, poultry feed is routinely heated to kill *Salmonella* and other microbes, but it was not initially clear at what stage the feed became infected. By the end of August, the outbreak continued to increase in numbers and in geographic distribution. More than 550 million potentially contaminated eggs sold by the Iowa farms to multiple food producers under approximately 25 different brand names were ultimately recalled, though the majority of these had already been sold and eaten.

The outbreak occurred despite new rules enacted by the Food and Drug Administration (FDA) regarding egg safety on September 8, 2009, which were required to be implemented by producers with 50,000 or more birds or persons who store and/or transport eggs by July 9, 2010, several weeks after the outbreak began. The new rules require registration with the FDA and new standards that include refrigeration of eggs, biosecurity measures (limiting visitors; taking protective measures when moving from building to building of the facility; preventing stray poultry, wild birds, cats, and other animals; not allowing employees to keep birds at home), cleaning and disinfection, fly and rodent control, and testing for *Salmonella enteriditis* in eggs and chickens at various stages. Many alleged infractions of the new regulations were found on

IN CONTEXT: CONFIDENCE IN FOOD SAFETY

Confidence in the food safety systems of developed nations such as the United States is a key ingredient of overall food security because of the great number of food and agricultural products these nations export throughout the world. Some critics have called for an overhaul of the food safety system in the United States in light of major outbreaks of *Salmonella*-related illness.

Food safety in the United States is regulated principally by both the Food and Drug Administration (FDA) and the Food Safety and Inspection Service (FSIS), which is part of the U.S. Department of Agriculture (USDA). After his appointment by President Barack Obama, Secretary of Agriculture Tom Vilsack (1950–) stated in March 2009 that he favored the creation of a single government agency in charge of all food safety.

the Iowa farms where contaminated eggs were found in August. On August 23, 2010, FDA Commissioner Dr. Margaret Hamburg commented on the "unfortunate irony" of the outbreak just weeks before the new rules would "for the first time put specific food safety standards in place so that we can hold companies accountable for taking the right preventive measures to reduce the risk of Salmonella and other foodborne illnesses." Hamburg also pressed for legislation that would allow the FDA more power to inspect and enforce the new rules on farms and to recall eggs rather than relying on egg producers to do so voluntarily. As of September 20, the CDC reported that "[e]valuation of the investigational data, including review of sampling results and records, continues in order to identify potential sources of contamination."

After the outbreak, CDC officials stressed that nearly all cases of salmonella poisoning can be avoided by properly cooking food and by keeping cooked food and the utensils used to handle cooked food away from raw eggs and other raw food sources. Health experts also increased warnings against consumption of raw or undercooked eggs by young children, elderly persons, and persons with weakened immune systems or chronic illness who are at special risk of food poisoning.

Not all the eggs recalled were destroyed. Infected eggs can be pasteurized and the egg product safely used in derivative egg products and processed foods. Restaurants were encouraged to use pasteurized eggs in recipes calling for the use of raw eggs (e.g., Hollandaise sauce or Caesar salad dressing).

The human suffering and economic consequences of salmonellosis are likely to increase with the continuing spread of *Salmonella* serotypes that are resistant to

a variety of commonly used antibiotics. The WHO is trying to determine the global prevalence and antibiotic resistance patterns of the multi-drug resistant *Salmonella* through its Global Salm-Surv program.

SEE ALSO *Eggs; Food Safety and Inspection Service; Food-borne Diseases.*

BIBLIOGRAPHY

Books

Anderson, Rodney P. *Outbreak: Cases in Real-World Microbiology.* Washington, DC: ASM Press, 2006.

Leadbetter, Jared R., ed. *Environmental Microbiology.* Amsterdam and Boston: Elsevier Academic Press, 2005.

Matthews, Karl R. *Microbiology of Fresh Produce.* Emerging Issues in Food Safety. Washington, DC: ASM Press, 2005.

Montville, Thomas J., and Karl R. Matthews. *Food Microbiology: An Introduction*, 2nd ed. Washington, DC: ASM Press, 2008.

Sylvia, David M., et al. *Principles and Applications of Soil Microbiology*, 2nd ed. Upper Saddle River, NJ: Prentice Hall, 2004.

Periodicals

Centers for Disease Control and Prevention (CDC). "Multistate Outbreak of Salmonella Infections Associated with Peanut Butter and Peanut Butter—Containing Products—United States, 2008–2009." *Morbidity and Mortality Weekly Report* 58 (January 29, 2009): 1–6.

Web Sites

"Drug-Resistant Salmonella." *World Health Organization (WHO).* http://www.who.int/entity/mediacentre/factsheets/fs139/en/index.html (accessed September 2, 2010).

"Egg Safety Final Rule." *U.S. Food and Drug Administration (FDA).* http://edocket.access.gpo.gov/2009/pdf/E9-16119.pdf (accessed September 23, 2010).

"Investigation Update: Multistate Outbreak of Human Salmonella Enteritidis Infections Associated with Shell Eggs." *Centers for Disease Control and Prevention (CDC).* http://www.cdc.gov/salmonella/enteritidis/ (accessed September 23, 2010).

"Salmonella." *World Health Organization (WHO).* http://www.who.int/topics/salmonella/en (accessed September 2, 2010).

"*Salmonella* Infection [Salmonellosis]." *Centers for Disease Control and Prevention (CDC).* http://www.cdc.gov/salmonella (accessed September 2, 2010).

Brian Hoyle

Salt

Introduction

Salt comes from two primary sources: salt mines or via solar evaporation of salt water, also called brine. Salt has a long history in shaping civilization, from its use as a food preservative to extend the edible life of meats and other foods to its use as a form of currency in Roman times. The word salary comes the term for salt given to Roman soldiers as part of their pay, and if someone is "worth his salt" it's a testimony to his character: The phrase also goes back to Roman times, when slaves could be traded for salt provisions rather than currency.

As a consumable item, salt was precious throughout history, but since the 1990s has been made a substance worthy of reconsideration in the diet. Also known by its compound name, sodium chloride, salt has been at the center of public health initiatives and education efforts for nearly a century. Adding iodine to common table salt helps to prevent goiter, a swelling of the thyroid gland caused by iodine deficiency. Iodine deficiency affects more than 2 billion people worldwide. In developed countries, where table salt is iodized and cheap, iodine deficiency is less common, but the use of salt has triggered a different public health risk: Too much sodium in the diet can elevate blood pressure and cause cardiovascular problems for some people. Sodium moderation campaigns have become the new version of the 1920s campaign to sell iodized salt in the United States; both were public health initiatives concerning the consumption of salt.

Historical Background and Scientific Foundations

Civilizations formed around salt springs as the Neolithic Revolution developed, and governments quickly created salt reserves, controlled salt trade, and imposed and collected taxes on salt. In the early years of the first century AD, Timbuktu in Mali, Africa, was a center for salt trade, with slaves and salt often exchanged for each other. Salt roads formed around the Adriatic Sea and into western and southern Europe, and salt was even used as a weapon: The Assyrians and Hittites left records of "salting the earth," pouring salt on the planting fields of its opponents, destroying crops, ruining farmland for years, and weakening entire villages and regional food supplies. The practice was retained and later used in Spain and Portugal in the 1600s and 1700s as punishment for traitors.

The Bible contains many references to salt, the most famous being the passage concerning Lot's wife, who defied the directive of angels not to turn around and look at the burning city of Sodom as she and her family fled. When she turned back for one last glance, she was turned into a pillar of salt, a symbol of returning to sin. "Salt of the earth" appears as a form of praise in the gospel of Matthew, a reflection of the importance this compound had in ancient times.

Salt was a crucial preservative for food, enabling the preservation of raw meat and the pickling of various foodstuffs that would otherwise rot. Preserved food permitted food storage, creating a steady supply year-round and allowing for population growth. In addition, preserved food enabled merchants and armies to carry a stable food supply with them on long journeys. This made it possible for traders to develop more extensive networks over larger territories and for armies to travel longer distances for conquest.

In 1930 salt became the focal point of the civil disobedience campaign led by Mohandas K. Gandhi (1869–1948) to help trigger India's independence. British rulers instituted a tax on all salt supplies in India and made it illegal to collect salt from the coasts, forcing Indians to pay extremely high prices and taxes for a formerly easy-to-access dietary staple. On April 5, 1930, Gandhi and 78 fellow satyagrahis (holy men) gathered salt from the Indian coast in violation of British law. Gandhi and some of his fellow protestors were jailed shortly after, but the protests triggered revolts, closing British salt shops and gaining international media attention as

WORDS TO KNOW

GOITER: A swelling of the thyroid gland, located in the neck, that is caused primarily by iodine deficiency.

IODINE: A chemical element required by the thyroid gland in the body to produce thyroid hormone. Iodine is commonly added to table salt to help prevent goiter development.

NaCl: The chemical formula for sodium chloride, or table salt.

the nonviolent protesters experienced severe violence at the hands of British colonial authorities. The Salt March was instrumental in eventual Indian independence.

■ Impacts and Issues

The world market for salt is strong, with more than 240 million tons of salt used each year worldwide. According to the Salt Institute, the United States alone has enough salt reserves to last the world 100,000 years, although China is the world's largest producer of salt. Iodized table salt is not expensive, selling in the United States for as little as 50 cents per pound.

In the developed world, overconsumption of sodium in processed foods is common, and gourmet stores sell countless varieties of specialty salts. Excessive sodium ingestion can exacerbate high blood pressure, and medical research linking the two has led to public health campaigns in the United States designed to educate the public about consuming sodium and salt in moderation. Excess sodium in the blood can overtax the kidneys, leading to an accumulation of sodium in the blood. Sodium attracts water; this increases blood volume and forces the heart to work harder to circulate blood, raising blood pressure and causing hypertension. According to the 2005 Dietary Guidelines for Americans issued by the U.S. Department of Agriculture, adults are encouraged to limit sodium consumption to 2,300 milligrams or less; 1,500 milligrams or less for those with high blood pressure. Currently the average American adult consumes about 4,000 milligrams of salt per day.

Salt sculptures carved by miners out of rock salt in Wieliczka Salt Mine, Krakow, Poland. The miners also carved out an entire chapel in the mine, one of the world's oldest operating salt mines (from the thirteenth century until 2007). It was placed on the original UNESCO roster of World Heritage Sites. *Image copyright puchan, 2010. Used under license from Shutterstock.com.*

Salt harvesters rake dried sea salt into mounds in Thailand. *Image copyright Worachat Sodsri, 2010. Used under license from Shutterstock.com.*

Whereas iodized salt is cheap and plentiful in the developed world, in developing nations more than 2 billion people lack access to iodine in the diet. In countries such as India, salt is collected in small quantities by poor individuals and families who sell the salt in markets or to larger aggregators; these small producers do not have the means to pay for the iodine sprays and equipment used to create iodized salt. In 2006 UNICEF assisted small salt producers in the Indian state of Gujarat, which produces more than 70 percent of India's salt, to work toward the United Nations' stated goal of universal salt iodization by providing technical assistance and equipment necessary to spray and monitor iodine levels in salt supplies.

The amount of iodine needed to prevent iodine deficiency is just one teaspoon, consumed throughout a person's lifetime, with an annual cost of five cents per year per person. Iodine deficiency in pregnant women can result in birth defects in infants ranging from goiter and cretinism to mental retardation; the United Nations' goal for universal salt iodization is an attempt to prevent such birth defects and improve international public health. In 1990 only 20 percent of the developing world's population had access to iodized salt; as of 2006 that figure was 70 percent.

SEE ALSO *Diet and Cancer; Diet and Diabetes; Diet and Heart Disease; Diet and Hypertension; Dietary Guidelines for Americans; Dietary Reference Intakes; Preservation; Processed Foods; Salt, Nitrites, and Health; Standard American Diet and Changing American Diet; USDA Food Pyramid; Vitamins and Minerals.*

BIBLIOGRAPHY

Books

American Heart Association. *American Heart Association Low-Salt Cookbook: A Complete Guide to Reducing Sodium and Fat in Your Diet.* New York: Clarkson Potter/Publishers, 2006.

Kurlansky, Mark, and S. D. Schindler. *The Story of Salt.* New York: G. P. Putnam's Sons, 2006.

Periodicals

Bibbins-Domingo, Kirsten, et al. "Projected Effect of Dietary Salt Reductions on Future Cardiovascular Disease." *The New England Journal of Medicine* 362, no. 7 (2010): 590–599.

Cappuccio, Franco, and Simon Capewell. "Sprinkle with Care: Excess Dietary Salt Is a Big Killer, So Who's

Fighting the Moves to Cut Back." *New Scientist* 2758 (May 1, 2010): 22.

Haddy, Francis J. "Role of Dietary Salt in Hypertension." *Life Sciences* 79, no. 17 (2006): 1585–1592.

"Sea Salt, Kosher Salt—Better Salts?: Here's How These Specialty Salts Stack Up to Everyday Table Salt." *Environmental Nutrition* 32, no. 5 (2009): 7.

Svetkey, Laura P., et al. "Effect of the Dietary Approaches to Stop Hypertension Diet and Reduced Sodium Intake on Blood Pressure Control." *Journal of Clinical Hypertension* 6, no. 7 (2004): 373–381.

Web Sites

Layton, Lyndsey. "FDA Plans to Limit Amount of Salt Allowed in Processed Foods for Health Reasons." *Washington Post*, April 20, 2010. http://www.washingtonpost.com/wp-dyn/content/article/2010/04/19/AR2010041905049.html (accessed October 23, 2010).

National Institutes of Health. "Salt: Too Much of a Good Thing." *Medline Plus: The Magazine*, Spring/Summer 2010. http://www.nlm.nih.gov/medlineplus/magazine/issues/sprsum10/articles/sprsum10pg12-13.html?debugMode=false (accessed October 23, 2010).

"Sodium (Salt or Sodium Chloride)." *American Heart Association*. http://www.americanheart.org/presenter.jhtml?identifier=4708 (accessed October 23, 2010).

Melanie Barton Zoltan

Salt, Nitrites, and Health

■ Introduction

Salt, or sodium chloride, has always been an important ingredient in food because it helps bring out flavor. Indeed, salt is one of the basic taste sensations. Before refrigeration became widespread, salt had an important role in preserving food. Salting is a type of curing that relies on dehydrating a food so bacteria do not grow on it. In the twenty-first century, salting is done more for the characteristic taste and texture it imparts. Potassium nitrate was also found to be useful in food preservation: Bacteria reduce it to potassium nitrite, which then reacts with the meat being cured to produce a characteristic pink color as well as inhibiting bacterial growth and preventing rancidity. Nitrite is used in curing, and modern curing salts contain a mixture of salt and nitrite. Although salt plays an essential role in health, most people eat more than is recommended, which may raise blood pressure. Research has also suggested that nitrites may be carcinogenic, which has led to levels in cured meats being lowered. There are calls for a complete nitrite ban, given that advances in food safety have modified its role to more of a flavor enhancer and coloring than a true preservative.

■ Historical Background and Scientific Foundations

Salt, the common name for sodium chloride, has always been part of the human diet, whether it was evaporated from sea water or extracted from rocks. Its value is reflected in many historical records; for instance, the word *salary* comes from the fact that Roman soldiers were paid a salt allowance called a *salarium*. Salt has been used to preserve food by curing for thousands of years. Typically, meat or fish would be placed in a barrel of brine or covered in salt crystals. The latter were called corns, which is where the term *corned beef* originates. Salting dehydrates food, drawing water out of both bacteria and the food itself. This makes it a far less attractive medium for bacterial growth. Now that refrigerators are almost universally available, salting for preservative purposes has become less significant, but is still done because people like the taste of salt-preserved foods such as bacon, sausage, and ham. Salt also plays a role in the enjoyment of food, as it enhances aroma and flavor and also decreases the intensity of bitter tastes. Salt-free cooking tends to be bland, unless herbs and spices are employed as a substitute. The importance of salt in the diet is underlined by the presence of specific salt receptors in taste buds on the tongue. Like sweetness, salt is one of the basic taste sensations.

Salting also changes the color of meat from gray-brown to the bright pink associated with ham, sausage, and bacon. It is not the salt that causes the color change, but nitrates occurring as a trace compound in the salt. Nitrates are reduced to nitrites by bacteria in the meat. It is nitrites that undergo a complex series of reactions with the myoglobin in meat to form a compound called nitrosylmyoglobin, which gives cured meat its bright color.

Saltpeter, the common name for potassium nitrate, was discovered in the Middle Ages and came to have many uses, including as an essential component of gunpowder. During the sixteenth and seventeenth centuries, it was realized that saltpeter was useful in curing for its effect on flavor and color. From then on, it was a major ingredient in the curing mixture, and the amounts used would have been ten to fifty times the levels that are used today.

Although much has been learned of the chemistry of nitrite in curing, it is still not clear exactly how it works and what its value is. That it preserves the color of meat is well established. It is also accepted that nitrite contributes a characteristic flavor to cured meats and delays the development of rancidity by blocking the oxidation of fat in the meat. Nitrite has been shown, more recently, to inhibit the growth of a wide range of bacteria, including that of *Clostridium botulinum*.

WORDS TO KNOW

BOTULISM: The most deadly form of food poisoning, botulism is caused by the bacterium *Clostridium botulinum*, which produces a potent nerve toxin. Spores of the bacterium can survive cooking. Although botulism has become rare, its most common cause in Europe is cured pork; in Japan it is salt fish; and in North America it is home-canned vegetables.

CURING: A method of food preservation involving salt, smoking, and dehydrating that works by drawing water out of the food so bacteria are less likely to grow on it.

NITRITES: A group of salts, including sodium nitrite, which are derived from nitrates by either chemical or bacterial action. They play a role in curing meats through stopping the growth of bacteria, preventing oxidation of fat, preserving color, and adding flavor.

An ethnic Akha woman adds monosodium glutamate (MSG), a sodium salt used frequently in Asian cooking, to a bowl of soup at a market in Xishuangbanna, China. © *dbimages / Alamy.*

■ Impacts and Issues

Both salt and nitrites have been linked to health risks, which is why healthy eating advice often recommends against frequent consumption of bacon, ham, hot dogs, and other cured meats. Some salt is needed in the diet, because both sodium and chlorine are essential micronutrients. The chemical composition of fluids inside and outside the cell, particularly in blood plasma, must remain constant for essential biochemical reactions to be carried out. This means keeping amounts of sodium, potassium, calcium, magnesium, and chloride in these fluids balanced. Chloride is also a component of stomach acid, and sodium ions play a role in the transmission of nerve impulses. The body requires about one gram of sodium chloride per day to fulfill these physiological roles.

People in some traditional cultures consume much less than this, without any apparent ill effect. But the average daily intake of salt by North Americans is between six and ten grams. It is not so much salt sprinkled on food at the table that is responsible for overconsumption as is its ubiquitous presence in processed foods and restaurant meals. Too much sodium increases the density of blood plasma, which may result in hypertension over time. Hypertension, or high blood pressure, is a major risk factor for heart disease and stroke. However, genetic factors mean that some people are more sensitive to the negative effects of high salt intake than others. At present, there is no quick and simple genetic test to determine whether an individual is salt-sensitive or not. The only way to reduce salt intake is to do more home cooking and to read food labels for salt and sodium content. Fortunately, some food manufacturers and supermarkets have been working to reduce, or even eliminate, salt in their products.

There has been concern over the potentially carcinogenic effect of nitrites since the 1950s when it was shown they can combine with amino acids to form nitrosamines, which are carcinogenic. However, only trace amounts of nitrosamines were found in cured meats, and nitrite from these products only forms about 20 percent of the nitrite available in the body for these reactions, with the rest coming from nitrates present in vegetables raised on high-nitrate fertilizer. Further experiments carried out in 1978 at the Massachusetts Institute of Technology suggested that nitrite itself might be a carcinogen. After some debate, the Food and Drug Administration ordered nitrite levels in cooked meats to be lowered to no more than 200 parts per million. Those who would have nitrite banned altogether argue that its only real use is as a coloring agent, because botulism is a rare occurrence nowadays.

The negative health impacts of nitrites are still being studied, but research has shown a connection between nitrites, which are found in processed red meats, and cancer, diabetes, and heart disease. Processed meats are generally defined as smoked, cured, or preserved with chemical compounds, including salt, nitrates, and nitrites, e.g., bacon, ham, hot dogs and lunch meats. Researchers at the National Cancer Institute in Rockville, Maryland, released results of a multi-year study of over 300,000 people aged 50–71 in the journal *Cancer* in 2010 that linked nitrates to increased risk of bladder, prostate, and other cancers. Results from a study published in 2010 in the journal *Circulation* also linked processed red meats with both diabetes and heart disease. For the study, researchers at the Harvard School of Public Health defined processed red meat as products including pork, beef, and lamb, such as hot dogs, bacon, sausage, and cold cuts. Results showed that the processed red meats contained 50 percent more preservatives and four times more salt than the same meats cooked without processing. Eating one serving per day of processed meat was shown to elevate the risk of developing heart disease by 45 percent and diabetes by 19 percent. Scientists say this research challenges the notion that saturated fat is the lone or most active culprit in linking red meat with heart disease, and that future research should evaluate processed meats separately from unprocessed meats in order to get a clearer idea of the role of preservatives and their effect on health. Researchers in both studies stated more research was necessary.

SEE ALSO *Diet and Cancer; Diet and Diabetes; Diet and Heart Disease; Diet and Hypertension; Dietary Guidelines for Americans; Dietary Reference Intakes; Preservation; Processed Foods; Salt; Standard American Diet and Changing American Diet; USDA Food Pyramid; Vitamins and Minerals.*

BIBLIOGRAPHY

Books

Pegg, Ronald B., and Fereidoon Shahidi. *Nitrite Curing of Meat: The N-Nitrosamine Problem and Nitrite Alternatives.* Trumbull, CT: Food & Nutrition Press, 2000.

Periodicals

Dias-Neto, Marina, Mariana Pintalhao, Mariana Ferreira, and Nuno Lunet. "Salt Intake and Risk of Gastric Intestinal Metaplasia: Systematic Review and Meta-Analysis." *Nutrition and Cancer* 62, no. 2 (2010): 133–147.

Gonzalez, Carlos A., and Elio Riboli. "Diet and Cancer Prevention: Where We Are, Where We Are Going." *Nutrition and Cancer* 56, no. 2 (2006): 225–231.

Katan, Martijn B. "Nitrate in Foods: Harmful or Healthy?" *The American Journal of Clinical Nutrition* 90, no. 1 (2009): 11–12.

Michaud, Dominique S., et al. "Prospective Study of Meat Intake and Dietary Nitrates, Nitrites, and Nitrosamines and Risk of Adult Glioma." *American Journal of Clinical Nutrition* 90, no. 3 (2009): 570–577.

Svetkey, Laura P., et al. "Effect of the Dietary Approaches to Stop Hypertension Diet and Reduced Sodium Intake on Blood Pressure Control." *Journal of Clinical Hypertension* 6, no. 7 (2004): 373–381.

Web Sites

Harvard School of Public Health. "Eating Processed Meats, but Not Unprocessed Red Meats, May Raise Risk of Heart Disease and Diabetes." *Harvard University.* http://www.hsph.harvard.edu/news/press-releases/2010-releases/processed-meats-unprocessed-heart-disease-diabetes.html (accessed October 4, 2010).

Susan Aldridge

School Lunch Reform

■ Introduction

School lunches are meals provided to students while at school, often with some form of government assistance. As of 2010, in the United States, the National School Lunch Program (NSLP) provides federally assisted school lunches in more than 100,000 public and nonprofit, private schools. Lunches are given to more than 31 million children per day. Under the NSLP, participating schools receive federal cash subsidies and agricultural commodities from the U.S. Department of Agriculture (USDA). The program also supplies reduced-cost or free meals to children with financial need. As of 2010, approximately 62 percent of U.S. children served by NSLP qualify for low-cost or free meals.

The USDA requires each meal provided under the NSLP to comply with the Dietary Guidelines for Americans, which recommends that individuals derive no more than 30 percent of calories from fat and no more than 10 percent of calories from saturated fat. Many U.S. policymakers, nutritionists, and health advocates argue that USDA nutritional guidelines for school lunches should be reformed. School lunch reform advocates argue that school lunches are not nutritious, contribute to the rise in childhood obesity and diabetes rates, do not feature enough fresh fruits and vegetables, and rely too heavily on processed, high-fat, and frozen foods.

■ Historical Background and Scientific Foundations

The provision of lunches for schoolchildren traces its roots to the work of Benjamin Thompson, Count Rumford (1753–1814), in Germany in the late eighteenth century. Rumford founded the Poor People's Institute in Munich, Germany, to provide meals to poor factory workers and schoolchildren, who also worked in factories between lessons. Rumford established similar programs in England, Germany, France, and Switzerland.

By the late nineteenth century, numerous charities provided lunches to schoolchildren in Germany and other European countries.

By the beginning of the twentieth century, national governments recognized the need to provide meals to schoolchildren. In 1900 a royal decree made Holland the first nation to adopt national legislation designed to provide school lunches. The law authorized municipalities to provide food and clothing to children who did not attend school, or would cease attending, due to a lack of proper food and clothing. In 1905, Great Britain passed the Education (Provision of Meals) Act, which called on local school councils to provide food for students who did not receive proper nutrition at home. The act was the product of concern over the physical fitness of British schoolchildren and young people. Near the end of the Second Boer War (1899–1902), the English Major-General John Frederick Maurice (1841–1912) lamented that 60 percent of men who sought to enlist in the army were found physically unfit to serve, largely due to malnutrition.

School lunch programs in the United States followed the same development pattern as most European nations. Beginning in the mid-nineteenth century, charitable organizations in a few American cities initiated programs to supply lunches to poor schoolchildren. Works by progressive authors, including Robert Hunter's (1874–1942) *Poverty* (1904) and John Spargo's (1876–1966) *The Bitter Cry of the Children* (1905), detailed the developmental and educational impacts of poor nutrition and highlighted the need for school lunch programs for poor children. Many other cities implemented school lunch programs. Rural schools districts, meanwhile, developed methods to allow children to heat meals brought from home, but few rural school had the facilities or finances to provide lunches.

The Great Depression (1929–1941) increased both concerns and the need for schools to provide lunches for schoolchildren. By 1937, 15 states authorized local school districts to provide lunches for schoolchildren. Most school districts provided meals at cost, because

Schoolchildren in Swindon, England, receive a healthy lunch.
© *Adrian Sherratt / Alamy.*

only four states had programs to provide reduced-cost or free lunches to poor children. In the early 1930s a variety of federal programs assisted school district lunch programs, and by 1934 the Federal Emergency Relief Administration assisted lunch programs in 39 states. During the late 1930s and 1940s, agricultural subsidy programs, under which the government purchased commodities in order to stabilize food prices, transferred government agricultural commodities to schools for lunch programs.

The federal government exerted greater control over school lunch programs under the National School Lunch Act of 1946 (NSLA). The NSLA established the National School Lunch Program and provided federal assistance to schools for the production of food storage and preparation facilities. The NSLA also established nutritional requirements for school lunches to ensure that children received healthy meals while also making use of government agricultural commodities. Amendments to the NSLA provided for school milk programs. The Child Nutrition Act of 1966 (CNA) continued the milk program, provided increased financial assistance to

states, modified nutritional requirements, and launched a trial breakfast program. In the decades since the implementation of the CNA, Congress and the USDA have amended school lunch program laws and regulations several times to reauthorize funding or modify nutritional requirements.

■ Impacts and Issues

School breakfasts and lunches provide an important source of calories and nutrients for many children, for whom breakfasts and lunches supplied through the NSLP provide the majority of the calories they consume each day. Children that qualify for low-cost or free lunches receive 58 percent of their daily calories from food supplied through the NSLP. When the USDA established the current guidelines in the 1970s, school lunches provided many children who otherwise may have been malnourished with needed calories.

In the early twenty-first century, however, low-cost, high-fat food has made obesity—not hunger—a common condition of poor Americans. School lunch reform advocates argue that USDA guidelines need to address increased incidence of childhood obesity. Current regulations mandate only that no more than 30 percent of calories among the array of foods offered may come from fat. Children, however, are free to eat only high-fat foods, such as pizza, French fries, or hamburgers.

Many of the poor nutritional choices presented in school lunches stem from spending requirements placed on school districts. The USDA's National School Lunch Program provides $2.68 funding per child per lunch. With most local school districts unwilling or unable to

IN CONTEXT: SOARING ADOLESCENT OBESITY INTENSIFIES SCRUTINY OF SCHOOL NUTRITION

Public health officials argue that in order to help fight growing rates of childhood and adolescent obesity, schools must offer balanced nutrition and help children establish healthy eating habits.

In May 2010 a report in the journal *Archives of Pediatrics & Adolescent Medicine* estimated that nearly one-third of U.S. children of the ages 10 to 17 years are considered overweight. Approximately half of overweight U.S. children may be clinically obese.

These estimates, derived from telephone surveys conducted in 2007, indicate a rapid increase in obesity during the preceding four years. Since 2003, 36 U.S. states showed a rise in the percentage of children considered overweight or obese.

spend additional money on lunches, school dieticians are faced with the difficult task of supplying nutritious lunches on such a low cost per head. This decision-making typically involves compromising nutrition. A whole-wheat bun, for example, costs about $0.05 more than a white bun, and a mixed green salad costs about $0.13 more than a less nutritious iceberg lettuce salad.

Studies have also raised concerns regarding the quality of agricultural commodities supplied to the National School Lunch Program, which accounts for 15 to 20 percent of the program's total food. A 2009 study by *USA Today* revealed that most beef and chicken commodities supplied to school lunch programs would fail to meet the quality and safety standards of most fast food companies. Most of the chicken supplied to school lunch programs by the USDA consists of spent hens, which are old hens that are unable to continue egg production. Fast food companies tend to reject these chickens because of quality concerns. Whereas all food supplied to school lunch programs meets or exceeds all USDA requirements, fast food companies often establish more

Chef Jamie Oliver's book *Jamie's Food Revolution* contains simple, healthful recipes and was the basis of a television show by the same name that documents his efforts to transform the eating habits of the city of Huntington, West Virginia, particularly its school lunch programs. He met with harsh criticism and resistance from school cooks, city administrators, and the school children.   *AP Images.*

stringent safety and testing standards. Many fast food companies have meat testing that is five to ten times more stringent than the meat supplied to schools by the USDA. A December 2009 study in *The New York Times* also questioned the safety and effectiveness of ground beef treated with ammonia to prevent contamination by *Salmonella* and *E. coli*. American schools used 5.5 million pounds of ammonia-treated ground beef in 2009.

Many school lunch programs also rely on the sale of potato chips, soda, and other junk food to supplement school lunch budgets and supply healthier lunches. A number of states, however, have banned the sale of soda and junk food at schools. Furthermore, most schools districts rely heavily on processed and frozen foods. In fact, approximately 95 percent of the food served in school cafeterias is processed. School lunch reform advocates argue that the government may need to increase funding for school lunch programs in order to offer healthier choices. Chef and Edible Schoolyard advocate Alice Waters (1944–) states that funding may have to be increased to $5 per child per meal in order to provide fresh, nutritious meals for American schoolchildren. Waters and other noted school lunch reform advocates, including British chef Jamie Oliver (1975–), assert that the use of fresh fruits, vegetables, and meats may be more expensive, but will reduce the incidence of childhood obesity and diabetes, thus cutting long-term health care costs.

SEE ALSO *Alice Waters: California and New American Cuisine; Dietary Guidelines for Americans;* E. Coli *Contamination; Edible Schoolyard Movement; Government Food Assistance for Citizens; Improving Nutrition for America's Children Act of 2010; Obesity;* Salmonella; *U.S. Department of Agriculture (USDA).*

BIBLIOGRAPHY

Books

Debnam, Betty. *Healthy Changes on the Menu: Munching on School Lunches.* Kansas City, MO: Universal Press Syndicate, 2006.

Schanzenbach, Diane W. *Do School Lunches Contribute to Childhood Obesity?* Chicago: Harris School of Public Policy, University of Chicago, 2005.

Periodicals

Blades, Mabel. "A Preliminary Study of School Lunches." *Nutrition & Food Science* 38, no. 6 (2008): 534–539.

"Family of Man—School Lunches." *National Geographic* 210, no. 3 (2006): 14.

"History—How Good School Lunches Went Bad, and the Attempt to Make Them Healthier." *Time* (October 19, 2009): 16.

McGray, D. "A Revolution in School Lunches. Getting Kids to Want to Eat Healthy Food Isn't Easy. Serving Wholesome Fare at Fast-Food Prices Is Even Harder. How Revolution Foods Is Helping School Cafeterias Swear Off Frozen Pizza and Fries." *Time* 175, no. 16 (2010): 50–53.

Web Sites

Dakss, Brian. "Expert: School Lunches Failing Kids." *CBS News,* September 21, 2006. http://www.cbsnews.com/stories/2006/09/21/earlyshow/leisure/books/main2028174.shtml (accessed October 18, 2010).

Flanagan, Caitlin. "Cultivating Failure: How School Gardens Are Cheating Our Most Vulnerable Students." *The Atlantic,* January/February 2010. http://www.theatlantic.com/magazine/archive/2010/01/cultivating-failure/7819/1/ (accessed October 25, 2010).

"Good Food for All Kids: A Garden at Every School." *Ideas for Change in America.* http://www.change.org/ideas/view/good_food_for_all_kids_a_garden_at_every_school_2 (accessed October 25, 2010).

"National School Lunch Program." *Food and Nutrition Service, U.S. Department of Agriculture.* http://www.fns.usda.gov/cnd/lunch/ (accessed October 25, 2010).

Joseph P. Hyder

Seafood

■ Introduction

Seafood is the term used for fish and other ocean-dwelling animals consumed as food. Debate on what the term encompasses from inland bodies of water is divided between those who classify all fish as seafood and those who only include fish from saltwater sources. Seafood can be a more inclusive term spanning fish from both oceans and inland bodies of water, sea vegetables such as seaweed, and other products from inland fisheries and from aquaculture. Aquaculture is the raising of fish, shellfish, sea vegetables, and other food products for human consumption or other commercial use. Fish and other seafood items are an important source of animal protein in the diet, especially in Asia.

Overfishing led to the collapse of many fisheries in the 1970s and 1980s. Initial regulatory attempts sought to limit the catch of individual species. More recently, regulatory approaches view fisheries as common pool resources (CPR), which should be regulated by their users or as ecosystems in which more than only commercially viable species must be monitored. Consumer pressures also are changing the seafood industry out of concern for health and the sustainability of seafood.

■ Historical Background and Scientific Foundations

Around 39,000 BC, archeological evidence indicates that humans on Borneo, an island now part of Indonesia between Australia and mainland Asia, were gathering shellfish for food. Archeological evidence of aquaculture appears in Australia as early at 6000 BC, and written instructions on how to conduct aquaculture appear in China from around 500 BC. Seafood from both catch and from aquaculture has long been a part of the human diet. This important food source is a major source of animal protein. In 2006, according to the Food and Agricultural Organization (FAO) of the United Nations in

their *The State of World Fisheries and Aquaculture 2008,* fish alone provided 15 percent or more of animal protein supply for 2.9 billion people. In 1996 this percentage had peaked when fish provided 16 percent of animal protein supply. In 2006 there were 110 million tons of fish used as human food or 36.7 pounds (16.7 kilograms) per capita. By far the largest consumer of seafood for 2006 was China. China's domestic production of fish is estimated to be 64.7 pounds (29.4 kilograms) per capita, representing 67 percent of the of the world's aquacultural production. Asian countries, including China, India, Japan, and Thailand, accounted for 52 percent of all capture fishing in the world in 2006. A common source of animal protein, fish and other seafood appear to provide health benefits because they are low in fat and contain fatty acids thought to protect humans from cardiovascular disease, as well as many micronutrients, vitamins, and minerals.

The scale of fishing increased in the late nineteenth century as new technologies enabled larger catches and growing populations increasingly demanded fish. Also, the technology became available to maintain a cold chain, or a series of chilled, cold, or below-freezing environments to transport frozen fish, chilled fish, or live fresh fish in water tanks. Whereas these technologies allowed fish and other seafood products to enter markets further inland, the industrial-sized fishing operations caused stress on fishery resources. Many of these operations also led to large levels of bycatch, of non-targeted species such as other fish, sea mammals, turtles, and birds becoming caught in fishing equipment. Most bycatch are thrown back into the water as waste, though many animals die in this process.

By the 1970s and 1980s, some fisheries had collapsed. A 10-percent reduction from the highest recorded yield is the threshold used to define a fishery collapse. However, from 1990 until 2007, it appears that the number of overexploited fisheries, both inland and in the ocean, had stabilized. According to estimates from the FAO for 2007, 28 percent of world fisheries are overexploited, depleted, or recovering. A further 52 percent of stocks were calculated to be yielding at their maximum potential and at their maximum sustainable yield (MSY).

■ Impacts and Issues

Managing fisheries, marine resources, and the oceans represents a major challenge for the twenty-first century. As population increases, demand for seafood will increase. Also, as incomes increase, according to Engel's law, many people will consume more expensive sources of calories, decreasing the grain content of their diet and increasing the seafood content among other higher cost sources of calories and protein. Many marine policy approaches begin with what Garrett Hardin (1915–2003), an American ecologist, wrote in his article "The Tragedy of the Commons" in *Science* in 1968. Hardin proposed that a resource, such as a fishery, if left open for every individual to exploit, would become depleted in the absence of rules and rights.

When the oceans are treated as an open access resource like this, overfishing will surely occur, leading

A display of fresh fish in a market in Paris, France.   *Image copyright leaada, 2010. Used under license from Shutterstock.com.*

IN CONTEXT: THE GLOBAL FISHING INDUSTRY

In 2010 officials with the United Nations Environment Programme's (UNEP) Green Economy Initiative estimated that globally, 35 million people work as fisher-folk aboard approximately 20 million fishing boats. Fishing boats range from hand-powered boats and canoes fishing local waters to large vessels operating in international waters. An additional 145 million jobs depend directly on the fishing industry.

to a lower level of fish availability in the future. Policy approaches based on this view attempt to calculate how much can be extracted from the resource, the maximum sustainable yield (MSY), and then limit the ability of fishers to take more than this through rules and regulations. Many national authorities and international treaties attempt to limit the catching of certain fish. The problem with this approach is that fisher-folk will still have an incentive to catch, sell, and consume fish above

the limit. According to the Monterey Bay Aquarium, a quarter of the catch worldwide may be illegal or above statutory limits.

Another approach to managing natural resources sees fisheries and other resources not as open access, but as common pool. A common pool resource (CPR) allows many to access it, but it is not the unregulated, rule-free anarchy as proposed by Hardin in "The Tragedy of the Commons." Instead, social scientists including Elinor Ostrom (1933–), an American political scientist who won the Nobel Memorial Prize in Economic Sciences in 2009 for her work on economic governance of common pool resources, propose that there are a wide variety of governance systems already in existence. These systems include particular rights of access and social limits to access. Most surprisingly, when coming from Hardin's view, in many common pool resources the users regulate each other, preventing each user from taking as much from the common resource as would be dictated purely by short-term self-interest. So fisheries, especially inland fisheries in a small area, may have users who are already aware of the potential damage of overfishing and regulate each other through informal pressures or formal rules. Ostrom's insights have been applied to write

A fleet of shrimping boats docks at Mayport, Florida. Area shrimpers sell some of their catch to local fresh seafood markets, but most is flash-frozen in local plants and sent to commercial seafood distributors and restaurants in the eastern United States. *K. Lee Lerner / Lerner & Lerner / LernerMedia Global Photos.*

community fishery management plans on a small scale in some countries.

Another approach to fishery and marine resource management is referred to as the ecosystem approach. Traditionally, fishing has been regulated on a species-by-species basis, with each variety of fish or seafood having its own limits and sets of rules. This view is that each fish has an equilibrial population, which can be maintained by keeping the catch under the maximum sustainable yield (MSY). However, taking the primary insight of non-equilibrium ecology, the ecosystem approach views the entire ecosystem and realizes that when the population of one species decreases, another may move in and take its place. Non-equilibrium ecology shows that populations are constantly in flux, so there is no pre-set equilibrium for any given species. Instead of using the idea of an equilibrium, which must be maintained for a species, the ecosystem approach attempts to view the various populations within the ecosystem and maintain the entire ecosystem instead of just the population of commercially important varieties of seafood. The approach remains new despite being introduced by the early 1980s, though South Africa, in particular, has worked to integrate this approach into its regulatory system for fisheries.

Environmental and consumer demands have a huge impact on trade and consumption of seafood. In the Tuna Dolphin case between Mexico and the United States, American consumers pushed for legislation to protect marine mammals such as dolphins. American fishers were required to take measures to prevent bycatch of dolphins while fishing for tuna, but Mexican fishers were not. Under the ruling by a panel under the General Agreement on Tariffs and Trade (GATT) in 1991, Mexico was not forced to change its fishing practices to limit bycatch under GATT. However, labeling of dolphin-safe tuna brought an eventual end to these fishing practices as many consumers chose to buy only tuna marked with such a label.

Building on this success, many organizations have sought to provide consumers with information on which fish are fished in a more sustainable manner and which are not. The Monterey Bay Aquarium in Monterey, California, on the Pacific coast of the United States has published since 1997 a list of fish to avoid consuming to prevent their overfishing. Greenpeace, an international environmental group, also publishes a red list of species it recommends not to eat. Also, lists are published in other countries: The World Wide Fund for Nature (WWF; formerly World Wildlife Fund), an international environmental group, published a list for consumers in Malaysia of the most threatened species in 2010. These lists are controversial with fishing personnel and others whose livelihoods are threatened because consumers, restaurants, and retailers have responded by removing some species from sale once they appear on a list. Many consumers and some health scientists express concern at

---

IN CONTEXT: FISHLESS OCEANS

In 2010 officials with the United Nations Environment Programme's (UNEP) green economy initiative warned that the world faced a global seafood shortage and "fishless oceans" by 2050 (i.e., a depletion of fish stocks to the point at which they are not commercially viable) unless there are substantial reductions in fishing fleet allowances so that fish stocks are allowed to recover from decades of overfishing. The UNEP warning came after a failure to secure a worldwide ban on bluefin tuna fishing. UNEP estimates that globally, about 1 billion people rely on fish as their primary source of animal protein. UNEP warns that by 2010 about 30 percent of fish population stocks had already collapsed, with many yielding commercial catches less than 10 percent of documented highs. As of 2010, only a quarter of the world's fish stocks are near normal population numbers.

Awareness of the problem may be key to changing this trend. One notable success story of recovery in a previously declining population of fish is that of the swordfish. In 1998 multiple observations indicated that swordfish populations were in decline, and in an effort to limit the rate and extent of this decline, conservationists and chefs began a boycott that took swordfish off many restaurant menus and put news of the species' peril on the front page. The swordfish became the official symbol of global overfishing for the National Coalition for Marine Conservation, representing dozens of endangered species.

Environmental organizations such as the Natural Resource Conservation Council and Seaweb created a partnership with prominent chefs at famous fine dining establishments across the nation. Participating restaurants, leading the boycott, removed swordfish from their menus while the environmental awareness groups spread the word about swordfish decline. Restaurants in Dallas, Philadelphia, Boston, New York City, and Baltimore were among the cities that led the boycott.

Restaurants also took swordfish off the menu due to fears of high levels of mercury, with some samples showing approximately three times FDA recommended amounts. The FDA and public health officials recommend that women who are (or may become) pregnant and small children avoid eating swordfish.

As of 2010, swordfish are not listed as an endangered species, and stocks in the Atlantic Ocean have returned to expected population levels. In the Pacific, the swordfish population remained slightly below target population levels.

---

high levels of mercury, a heavy metal, in some fish, so consumer taste may eventually move away from predatory fish in which high levels of mercury concentrate such as tuna.

SEE ALSO *Aquaculture and Fishery Resources; Asian Diet; Biodiversity and Food Supply; Convention on*

Biological Diversity (1992); Mediterranean Diet; Shark Harvesting; Water: Water Scarcity.

BIBLIOGRAPHY

Books

Grescoe, Taras. *Bottomfeeder: A Seafood Lover's Journey to the End of the Food Chain.* New York: Bloomsbury USA, 2008.

Halweil, Brian, and Lisa Mastny. *Catch of the Day: Choosing Seafood for Healthier Oceans.* Washington, DC: Worldwatch Institute, 2006.

Johnson, Paul. *Fish Forever: The Definitive Guide to Understanding, Selecting, and Preparing Healthy, Delicious, and Environmentally Sustainable Seafood.* Hoboken, NJ: Wiley, 2007.

Molyneaux, Paul. *Swimming in Circles: Aquaculture and the End of Wild Oceans.* New York: Thunder's Mouth, 2007.

Nesheim, Malden C., and Ann L. Yaktine. *Seafood Choices: Balancing Benefits and Risks.* Washington, DC: National Academies Press, 2007.

World Bank. *Changing the Face of the Waters: The Promise and Challenge of Sustainable Aquaculture.* Washington, DC: World Bank, 2007.

Periodicals

Cressey, Daniel. "Aquaculture: Future Fish." *Nature* 458, no. 7237 (2009): 398–400.

FDA. "Mercury and Seafood Advice Still Current." *FDA Consumer* 40, no. 5 (2006): 2–3.

Hardin, Garrett. "The Tragedy of the Commons." *Science* 162, no. 3859 (December 13, 1968): 1243–1248. Available online at: http://www.sciencemag.org/cgi/content/full/162/3859/1243.

Kuehn, Bridget M. "Gulf Seafood Safety." *JAMA: The Journal of the American Medical Association* 304, no. 4 (2010): 398.

Smith, Martin D., et al. "Sustainability and Global Seafood." *Science* 327, no. 5967 (2010): 784–786.

Web Sites

"MSC Certified Fish to Eat." *Marine Stewardship Council.* http://www.msc.org/cook-eat-enjoy/fish-to-eat (accessed October 23, 2010).

"Seafood Watch: Ocean Issues." *Monterey Bay Aquarium.* http://www.montereybayaquarium.org/cr/cr_seafoodwatch/issues/ (accessed October 23, 2010).

Blake Jackson Stabler

Shark Harvesting

Introduction

The shark (superorder Selachimorpha) is a fish found in every ocean and saltwater environment in the world: There are more than 360 known types of sharks. Notwithstanding the notoriety achieved by species such as the great white, tiger, and bull shark for unprovoked attacks on humans, most sharks pose little or no threat to humans. Sharks have evolved over the past 360 million years, and their fundamental biology has remained largely unchanged for the past 70 million years. Most sharks are predators that occupy the top spot in their food chains. Shark populations play an essential role in marine ecosystems.

Shark harvesting is the general term that describes the commercial shark fishing undertaken in many regions of the world. The immense whale shark is one of the few shark species harvested for its meat. Shark meat is generally considered to have a poor texture and quality when compared with other commercially harvested sea fish. Many shark species are commercially desired for their fins, with the tiger, Mako, and hammerhead species among the most preferred. Shark harvesting is not subject to any binding international convention or treaties that regulate the type or number of sharks that can be harvested in a given year or region. In recent years, shark fin demand in China has grown rapidly. The world shark fishery has expanded in response, placing extreme pressure on many shark populations. The scalloped hammerhead shark is a species designated as globally endangered by the International Union for Conservation of Nature (IUCN).

Historical Background and Scientific Foundations

Sharks have been hunted by humans since prehistoric times. Through most of human history, shark was an unimportant food source, given the lesser quality of its meat and the need to hunt most shark species from boats on the open ocean. In literary works such as Herman Melville's *Moby Dick*, in which the whaling industry is described, the shark was portrayed as a fearsome and highly unpredictable human predator. The general ignorance of the important ecological role played by the species was the chief reason why the sharks were indiscriminately killed by European and North American whalers and fisherman. Shark populations have also been adversely affected by global pollution and other human-caused impacts on natural shark habitats.

Although a secondary human food source, various shark components were highly regarded in Asian cultures. Powdered shark fin is argued to possess aphrodisiac qualities. Shark fin is also revered as an alternative medicine for combating various forms of cancer. The number of shark harvested for these purposes has been relatively small throughout human history.

The increased Chinese demand for shark fin as a soup ingredient is a modern-day pressure that has been exerted on the worldwide shark population. The whale shark (*Rhincodon*) is the largest known fish species. It inhabits most open tropical ocean regions. With an average lifespan of 70 years, the whale shark can grow to as large as 40 ft (12.9 m) in length, with weights exceeding 15 tons (13,600 kg). Its name confirms its whale-like appearance. Whale shark is designated as a vulnerable species by the IUCN. It continues to be extensively hunted for its meat and fins by fishermen based in Taiwan and the Philippines.

Impacts and Issues

The most controversial aspect of shark harvesting techniques is the practice of *shark finning*. When a shark is caught, the fins are removed while the fish is alive. The fins are retained and the shark is dumped overboard as waste. As the shark is unable to swim, it slowly dies and the carcass is consumed by other aquatic life. Shark finning has been attacked as a cruel and barbaric practice by many international environmental advocacy groups, including IUCN and Greenpeace. The practice has been

WORDS TO KNOW

CITES: The Conference of the Parties for the Convention on International Trade in Endangered Species in Wild Fauna and Flora (CITES) is an international agreement that is intended to monitor the international trade of flora and fauna, particularly endangered species. CITES entered into force in 1975 and as of 2010 has more than 170 member nations.

LONGLINE FISHING: Longline fishing is a technique used extensively in the commercial swordfish and tuna fisheries. Monofilament lines equipped with hundreds of baited hooks and flotation devices are extended for up to 100 miles (160 km) over open ocean waters. Longline fishing is controversial because it is indiscriminate; "bycatch" describes the sharks and other aquatic species frequently caught by longlines that are not commercially desirable. As shark is a poorer quality meat relative to tuna or swordfish, sharks are usually discarded once their valuable fins have been removed.

SHARK FIN SOUP: Shark fin soup, *yu chi* (translated Mandarin for shark wing) has been regarded as a delicacy in Chinese food culture for centuries. This soup was a dish traditionally available only to the very wealthy due to the scarcity of shark fins needed for its preparation. The emergence of a consumer middle class in late twentieth century China broadened the soup's appeal as a status symbol. Chinese consumer demand for fins spurred the dramatic growth of the international shark fishery. Shark fin does not add flavor to the soup. The fin gives the soup color and a gelatinous texture.

IN CONTEXT: HUNTING THE OCEAN'S HUNTERS

In March 2010, the Convention on International Trade in Endangered Species—meeting in Doha, Qatar—rejected appeals to extend protection to several shark species, including scalloped hammerhead sharks, oceanic whitetip sharks, and spiny dogfish sharks. Millions of sharks of all species are killed solely to harvest their fins to supply market demands. Environmentalists and marine wildlife activists further claim that some fishermen simply cut off shark fins and then dump the finless sharks back into the sea to die a slow death.

At the same convention, CITES Appendix II protection was extended to the porbeagle shark, a shark species prized by fishermen because of demand for porbeagle fin in the Asian markets. Porbeagle meat is also coveted in Europe. Porbeagle fins and meat, used in soups and alternative medicines, will now require export controls and monitoring.

equated by environmentalists and shark advocacy organizations to the older and now-outlawed practice of killing African elephants for their valuable ivory tusks. An estimated 50 million sharks per year are killed for their fins alone. The market for shark fins is estimated to be increasing at a rate of 5 percent per year.

Shark finning results in two adverse impacts on marine ecology. As a top predator, sharks tend to prey on the weaker elements of the species lower on its food chain, a factor that tends to promote the survival and propagation of the strongest and fittest of shark prey. The removal of sharks from an ecosystem thus removes an important balancing element from optimal system function. Shark harvesting also places disproportionate stress on shark populations relative to other types of fisheries due to the low natural reproductive rates and the slower physical maturation process observed in the species generally.

The conflict between shark conservation efforts and the economic aspects of shark harvesting is brought into clear focus in the Pacific Ocean waters near Hawaii. The state enacted legislation effective July 1, 2010, that rendered shark fin possession, sale, and distribution illegal anywhere within the jurisdiction. The new law prohibits shark fishery vessels from using the island's ports to trans-ship and store fins. Whereas the Hawaii legislation will deter the shark fishery from operating in Hawaii, absent coordinated international enforcement efforts other Pacific islands will be utilized for these purposes by the fishery. Shark fins command prices approaching $500 per pound in Hong Kong, the leading commercial fin market.

The gap between legislative efforts to protect shark populations and practical effects is also evident in Costa Rica. The Central American nation passed strict laws prohibiting shark fishing within its claimed 3-mile territorial waters. International fishing fleets operate without limits, however, on the edge of the Costa Rican waters that are home to a number of shark species. In 2000, many United Nations (UN) member countries agreed to voluntarily formulate plans to protect vulnerable shark species and prohibit shark finning. In 2007, a UN recommitment agreement was drafted, however, a binding agreement has yet to be achieved.

At the 2010 triennial CITES conference, efforts to designate eight different shark species as globally endangered were defeated, despite the estimated 80 percent decline in all global shark populations since 1980. Fishing superpowers Japan and China have been influential in efforts to limit the number of fish species protected by harvest quotas and international trade restrictions.

SEE ALSO *Aquaculture and Fishery Resources; Biodiversity and Food Supply; Seafood.*

Baby sharks being sold in a Dubai fish market.   *Image copyright hainaultphoto, 2010. Used under license from Shutterstock.com.*

BIBLIOGRAPHY

Books

Clarke, Shelley, Eleanor J. Milner-Gulland, and Trond Bjorndal. *Social, Economic and Regulatory Drivers of the Shark Fin Trade*. Portsmouth, UK: Centre for the Economics and Management of Aquatic Resources, University of Portsmouth, 2008.

Grescoe, Taras. *Bottomfeeder: How to Eat Ethically in a World of Vanishing Seafood*. New York: Bloomsbury, 2008.

Periodicals

Brierley, Andrew S. "Fisheries Ecology: Hunger for Shark Fin Soup Drives Clam Chowder Off the Menu." *Current Biology* 17, no. 14 (2007): R555–R557.

Clarke, Shelley. "Use of Shark Fin Trade Data to Estimate Historic Total Shark Removals in the Atlantic Ocean." *Aquatic Living Resources* 21, no. 4 (2008): 373–382.

"Going Green: Shark-Fin Soup, a Symbol of Good Fortune, Means Bad Luck for Sea Life." *Time* (October 4, 2010): 65.

Web Sites

"Governments Agree on New UN-Backed Pact to Protect Sharks." *UN News Centre*, December 13, 2007. http://www.un.org/apps/news/story. asp?NewsID=25056&Cr=UNEP&Cr1 (accessed October 10, 2010).

"Let's Take Shark Fin Soup off the Menu!" *Stop Shark Finning*. http://www.stopsharkfinning.net/ network.htm (accessed October 10, 2010).

"Sharks: Dying for a Bowl of Soup." *Humane Society International*, January 31, 2007. http://www. hsi.org/issues/shark_finning/facts/dying_for_a_ bowl_of_soup.html (accessed October 10, 2010).

Bryan Thomas Davies

Slow Food Movement

Introduction

The Slow Food movement is an international movement dedicated to preserving biodiversity in heirloom plants and heritage breeds of livestock, promoting traditional methods of food production, and preserving traditional cuisines. Tracing their roots to the 1980s in Italy, Slow Food groups have more than 100,000 members in 132 nations in the early twenty-first century.

The Slow Food movement asserts that food should taste good, be produced in a clean and environmentally responsible manner, and result in fair wages for food production workers. Slow Food International, the parent organization of numerous national Slow Food branches, seeks to educate and empower consumers, or "co-producers" in Slow Food parlance, to become active in acquiring their food from sources that meet the movement's criteria.

Historical Background and Scientific Foundations

The Slow Food movement traces its origins to July 1986 when a group of food enthusiasts gathered in the cellar of a restaurant in Fontanafredda, Italy, a small town in the northern Italian province of Friuli-Venezia Giulia. Carlo Petrini (1949–), a freelance food writer, organized the small group in order to inspire its members to defend traditional Italian food from the encroachment of the international corporate food industry. News of the construction of a McDonald's restaurant near the Spanish Steps in Rome was the catalyst for Petrini and other members to meet. After two days of discussions, Petrini and his group formed Arcigola, the forerunner of Slow Food.

In 1989 Petrini and other Arcigola members founded the Slow Food movement. In November of that year, delegates from 15 countries met at the Opéra Comique in Paris, France, and established Slow Food International. The delegates adopted the movement's constitution, which had been written by Petrini and Folco Portinari, a journalist and poet. Slow Food's constitution embraces traditional food production methods and eschews the modern globalization and corporatization of food production. Slow Food's constitution states, "We are enslaved by speed, and have all succumbed to the same insidious virus: Fast Life, which disrupts our habits, pervades the privacy of our homes, and forces us to eat fast foods."

The Slow Food movement spread slowly from its northern Italian stronghold. Slow Food Deutschland opened an office in Germany in 1992, and Slow Food Switzerland was founded in 1993. Slow Food USA was founded in 2000 and comprises more than 200 chapters. Slow Food UK launched in 2005 and by 2010 had more than 2,000 members. Worldwide, by 2010 Slow Food had expanded to more than 100,000 members in 132 nations.

Impacts and Issues

The Slow Food movement seeks to educate consumers about sustainable, local agriculture while promoting and supporting farmers and artisans of traditional food production methods. Slow Food organizes farmers and artisanal producers, then works to link these producers with consumers at farmers' markets and food stores.

Slow Food also focuses on preserving and promoting heirloom varieties of vegetables, fruits, grains, and livestock that might otherwise go extinct. Since 1900, roughly 75 percent of European food diversity has been lost. In America, 93 percent of food species diversity has disappeared since 1900. Slow Food aims to prevent further variety loss through its Ark of Taste program. Ark of Taste is a catalog of heritage foods that are in danger of extinction. Since 1996, Slow Food has cataloged more than 800 products from 50 countries in the Ark of Taste.

The Slow Food movement, particularly its top leadership, closely aligns the movement with environmentalism and leftist politics. Petrini is fond of saying that "a gastronome who isn't an environmentalist is just stupid, and . . . an environmentalist who isn't a gastronome is just sad." Whereas the goals of the Slow Food movement have an obvious connection with the land, including local food production and preservation of biodiversity, the Slow Food movement has a leftist, anarcho-syndicalist origin. The leaders of Slow Food continue to espouse many of these leftist views, including anti-globalism, anti-corporatism, and anti-technologism. Many rank-and-file members, however, participate in Slow Food in order to focus on food and taste. These members either do not espouse similar political beliefs or are unaware of the Slow Food movement's political aspects altogether.

The Slow Food movement has attracted several notable chefs and authors to its cause. Authors Michael Pollan (1955–) and Eric Schlosser (1959–) have written extensively on key aspects of Slow Food's ethos. Pollan's best-selling book, *The Omnivore's Dilemma*, examines various food production chains that have developed since the dawn of humanity, from hunter-gatherer societies to the modern industrial food production system. Pollan argues that the industrialization of food production has severed an important connection between humans and the natural world. Schlosser's *Fast Food Nation: The Dark Side of the All-American Meal* is concerned with the fast food industry, and includes an

in-depth examination of industrial meat packing and the fast food industry's marketing efforts. Chef Alice Waters (1944–) has been a staunch proponent of local, organic eating for decades and founded the Edible Schoolyard program, which seeks to introduce children to healthy eating habits.

The Slow Food movement has a number of critics, particularly in the United States. Many denounce the movement's leftist political philosophy, noting that industrial food production decreased malnutrition and famine in the twentieth-century. Some critics, including artisanal food producers, see Slow Food as too

Food is served at a stall, which is part of the Slow Food Movement, at a farmers market in London. © *Stuart Forster / Alamy.*

Eurocentric. In a July 23, 2008, article in *The New York Times* entitled "Slow Food Savors Its Big Moment," John Scharffenberger (1955–), a noted producer of sparkling wine and chocolate, stated, "I think it [the Slow Food movement] is a really good way to promote Italian food." Scharffenberger noted that he already produces his products using artisanal methods and questioned the need for himself and other successful artisanal food producers to embrace Slow Food.

Other critics assert that the Slow Food movement appears too elitist to appeal to mainstream America. Many of these critics, including Brahm Ahmadi (1975–), the executive director of the People's Grocery, a nonprofit organization dedicated to supplying healthy food to people in inner-city Oakland, California, note that the Slow Food movement lacks economic and racial diversity.

Despite the criticism, the Slow Food movement continues to grow its membership and expand its mission. In 2004 Petrini founded the University of Gastronomic Sciences in Bra, Italy, with a satellite campus in Colorno, Italy. The university, which offers undergraduate and graduate degrees, focuses on the relationship between gastronomy and food and agricultural science. Since 1996, Slow Food International also has hosted a biennial exposition in Turin, Italy, to showcase producers that adhere to Slow Food's principles. In 2008 the Salone del Gusto attracted more than 180,000 attendees. The eighth international Salone del Gusto was scheduled to take place at the Lingotto Fiere exhibition center in Turin from October 21–25, 2010.

SEE ALSO *Agribusiness; Alice Waters: California and New American Cuisine; Biodiversity and Food Supply; Farm-to-Table Movement; Fast Food; Locavore; Organics.*

BIBLIOGRAPHY

Books

Andrews, Geoff. *The Slow Food Story: Politics and Pleasure.* Montreal: McGill-Queen's University Press, 2008.

Fleetwood, Jenni. *Slow Food.* London: Lorenz, 2006.

Kummer, Corby. *Pleasures of Slow Food: Artisan Traditions and Recipes.* San Francisco, CA: Chronicle, 2008.

Petrini, Carlo. *Slow Food Nation: Why Our Food Should Be Good, Clean, and Fair.* New York: Rizzoli Ex Libris, 2007.

Petrini, Carlo, and Gigi Padovani. *Slow Food Revolution: A New Culture for Eating and Living.* New York: Rizzoli, 2006.

Slow Food Movement. *Slow Food U.S.A. 2003.* New York: Slow Food U.S.A., 2003.

Wilk, Richard R. *Fast Food/Slow Food: The Cultural Economy of the Global Food System.* Lanham, MD: Altamira Press, 2006.

Periodicals

Schlosser, Eric. "Slow Food for Thought." *The Nation.* 287, no. 8 (2008): 4.

"The Slow Food Movement Tries to Shed Its Elitist Reputation." *Time—Europe* 172, no. 12 (September 22, 2008): 40.

Waters, Alice. "Slow Food Nation." *The Nation* 283, no. 7 (2006): 13.

Web Sites

Slow Food International. http://www.slowfood.com/ (accessed August 1, 2010).

Joseph Hyder

Social Media and Food

■ Introduction

Social media are media with user-generated content that are generally accessible to everyone, usually through the Internet or mobile communication devices. Examples would be *blogs*, *podcasts*, and social networks such as Facebook, Twitter, Wikipedia, and Flickr. Though a recent phenomenon, social media has impacted many aspects of food culture and learning by connecting people all over the globe who share an interest in cooking.

■ Historical Background and Scientific Foundations

Sharing food is commonly an important aspect of human interaction. People all over the world have exchanged recipes at parties, brought dishes to potlucks, or contributed a dish to a wedding or social gathering. The advent of the Internet removed the barrier of distance from communication, and in doing so greatly accelerated the global exchange of ideas. This exchange included the sharing of ideas about food, often through social media. Social media refers to media in which users generate the content, whereas in classic media professional writers, editors, and producers create the content. Some social media sites, such as Wikipedia, have rigorous community fact checking, review, and debate to try and ensure the accuracy of all the information presented. Other media, such as public forums and blogs, are completely unfiltered. The result is a large amount of information that must be navigated with critical thought.

Along with the development of social media came another new phenomenon, called *micro-communities*. A micro-community is a group of people that share a similar interest and communicate about that interest on the Internet. Similar to a traditional book club or car club, the Internet has enabled people who share similar interests to meet and communicate regardless of where they live. It is via micro-communities of food enthusiasts that recipes and techniques from all over the world have been shared so quickly. There are quite literally millions of cooking forums on the Internet: A quick Google search for "cooking forum" yields more than 25 million hits. Not all are forums, but it demonstrates the popularity of the concept.

■ Impacts and Issues

Whereas the Internet allows access to a wide variety of information and opinions, anyone with access to a computer may post opinions and ideas online. The absence of any kind of review or fact checking process means that there is a great deal of information on the Internet that is false or simply incorrect. The concept of legislating the Internet, however, is a difficult and controversial topic. The debate is much less severe when it comes to food, because the concept of an "incorrect" recipe is debatable. When there are multiple recipes for a certain dish, it is almost impossible to assert which one is the "correct" recipe. What is more important is that a cook finds a recipe that results in the final product he or she desires, and on the Internet one can find many recipes for the same dish, allowing the cook to experiment and try different techniques. Seeing multiple recipes can also be helpful for creating one's own version of a recipe, because seeing different ideas can help spark a new idea of one's own.

Micro-communities have had a wide-ranging impact. Advertisers have discovered that micro-communities have singled themselves out as being interested in certain topics, and marketers constantly work on finding new ways of targeting specific micro-communities with advertisements for products related to their interest. In fact, many forum hosts and bloggers are able to earn income by selling advertising space on their websites. For example, if one were to visit a popular cooking forum, most likely there would be ads on the side of the page for cookbooks or kitchen tools. In addition, some micro-communities allow for certain small businesses to

WORDS TO KNOW

BLOG: Short-hand term for the word weblog, which is a site in which one can write articles, news posts, or diary entries, either to be shared publicly or for only a select few friends.

MICRO-COMMUNITIES: Groups of people who communicate on the Internet and via social media that come together based upon a shared interest regardless of the physical distance between them; for example, people in different countries who are car enthusiasts or fans of an artist that communicate on a public message board.

PODCASTS: Spoken word shows, similar to talk radio shows, that are recorded and posted on the Internet for download. The word is derived from the name of Apple's "iPod" mp3 player. Whereas many podcasts are homemade, some traditional radio stations record their shows and post them as podcasts on the Internet for fans to download.

a single owner-operator, and have only one truck from which they can sell their food. Fans of these vendors sign up to follow the vendor's Twitter feed, and every day the vendor posts on the website where he or she will be operating that day. Those who have signed up will receive the message on their phones or computers, so they will know where to go to find the street vendor's truck.

Another area of traditional media that social media is taking over is reviewing restaurants. Traditionally a restaurant would receive a review from a local newspaper, and that review would stand until the newspaper decided to review the restaurant again. On the Internet there are many different websites that review restaurants, and many of them are simply a collection of reviews written by users of the site. This again encounters the issue of the veracity of information on the Internet. Anyone can post a review, whether they have eaten at a restaurant or not. Sometimes false negative or false positive reviews will be posted for myriad different reasons. However, if a website is popular enough to have a large number of reviews, one can get a picture of average public opinion of the restaurant. Some review sites, such as the user reviews on Google Maps, Yelp!, and OpenTable (which also serves as a means of reserving a table at a restaurant

operate. As an example, there are several independent street-food vendors in New York City that are run by

California dairy farmer Ray Prock uses Twitter while working in order to connect with consumers. Prock and other farmers established AgChat Foundation, which encourages farmers to use Facebook, Twitter, YouTube, and other Web sites to reach out to the public. *AP Images.*

via the Internet) are so popular that they are becoming more trusted than the reviews given by traditional media. This has opened up the market for restaurants that serve simple day-to-day fare, because it avoids the bias in traditional media towards favoring sophisticated cuisine. If a restaurant is reviewed and given no stars, but the reviews online have multiple comments along the lines of "simple food but well cooked," the online reviews may attract customers who, prior to the Internet, would have overlooked the restaurant due to its low rating.

In addition to the blogs about food and cooking, another common blog topic is nutrition. There are numerous blogs that discuss basic nutrition information, tips on what dishes at popular restaurants are healthier choices, and so on. Often nutrition blogs will point out the dangers of eating at fast food restaurants on a regular basis. Whereas fast food restaurants do publish the nutrition facts of all of their meals, most people do not understand the implication of that information and how it should impact their decisions. These blogs are raising awareness about dietary needs in an attempt to persuade people to make more healthful eating choices.

SEE ALSO *Advertising Food; Food and the Internet; Food Critics and Ratings; Gourmet Hobbyists and Foodies; Television and Food.*

BIBLIOGRAPHY

Books

Dooher, Carrie. *Using Social Media in FDA-Regulated Industries: The Essential Guide.* Washington, DC: FDLI, 2010.

Jacob, Dianne. *Will Write for Food: The Complete Guide to Writing Cookbooks, Blogs, Reviews, Memoir, and More.* Cambridge, MA: Da Capo Lifelong, 2010.

Lewis, Sara E., and William T. Ross. *Marketing Health Food: The Strategic and Ethical Marketing Plan Utilizing Social Media.* University Park: Pennsylvania State University Press, 2010.

Powell, Julie. *Julie and Julia: 365 Days, 524 Recipes, 1 Tiny Apartment Kitchen.* New York: Little, Brown and Co, 2005.

Web Sites

"Best of the Food Blogs." *Delish.com.* http://www.delish.com/food/best-of-food-blogs (accessed October 18, 2010).

Open Table. http://www.opentable.com/home.aspx (accessed October 18, 2010).

David Brennan Tilove

Spice Trade

Introduction

The spice trade refers to the specialized, commercial trade of spices and other luxury goods that stretched across Eurasia and North Africa. People have used spices—the aromatic seeds, fruits, roots, or barks of plants—and herbs to season food for thousands of years. People also developed traditional medicines from spices and used spices to embalm bodies. In some parts of the world, people have even used spices as currency.

The spice trade traces its origins to at least 1200 BC, when ancient Egyptians imported spices that were cultivated in South Asia. For more than 3,000 years, empires and fortunes rose and fell with control over land and sea spice trade routes. Traders used these routes to move spices from southern Asia, which continues to be the world's leading spice-producing region, to the Middle East, Europe, and North Africa. As the spices made their journey westward, the prices of the spices increased greatly because of tariffs, middlemen, and the labor involved in transporting the spices.

The influx of flavorful, exotic spices influenced the development of cuisines across Eurasia. The high cost of spices also spurred European powers to venture forth to seek new, cheaper trade routes to Asia. This period, referred to as the Age of Discovery, resulted in Europeans exploring much of the globe, including the Americas. The spice trade also provided a conduit for the transfer of culture, religion, and languages across continents.

Historical Background and Scientific Foundations

The global spice trade can be traced back to ancient Egypt. Records from around 1200 BC document the religious offering of cinnamon that originated in present-day Sri Lanka. The spice trade to Egypt likely predates these documents, however, as the spices noted in the records were likely shipped along existing trade routes that connected Egypt to the Middle East. The Egyptians maintained strong trading links with the Middle East, either overland across the Sinai Peninsula or across the Red Sea, until the Roman conquest of Egypt.

By the third century BC, the Greeks and Romans had forged a complex network of trading routes that connected Europe and North Africa with India via the Middle East. By the first century BC, Alexandria, a coast city on the Nile Delta of northern Egypt, had become the center of the spice trade in the Greco-Roman world. The first century BC *Periplus Maris Erythraei*, a Greco-Roman manuscript that details ports and sailing routes, describes a complex network of land and sea trading routes between the Mediterranean Sea and India that included extensions into present-day China. The Greeks and Romans traded incense, silk, textiles, and ebony along this route in addition to spices. The Roman empire's conquest of much of continental Europe expanded the use of native Indian spices, including black pepper, cardamom, cinnamon, ginger, and turmeric.

Arab traders took over many of the old Roman trade routes in the Middle East beginning around the fifth century AD. The *Periplus Maris Erythraei* describes Indian ports that conducted trade with ports in Java and Borneo to the east. Arab traders strengthened these eastern overseas trade routes. In addition to sending Indian spices east, these trade routes supplied Indian and Arab traders with spices from the Maluku Islands, also known as the Spice Islands, east of Java in present-day Indonesia. By dominating the land trade routes across Central Asia and the Middle East and controlling sea routes from Indonesia to the Red Sea, Arab traders dominated the world spice trade for more than 1,000 years.

Arab traders profited handsomely from their domination of the spice trade. Each kingdom along the trade routes also profited from tariffs placed on spices that passed through their lands. By the time spices reached markets in the West, the price of the spices had increased astronomically. In some areas cinnamon and nutmeg became more valuable than gold. According to a four-teenth-century source, one pound of nutmeg cost seven fattened oxen in Europe.

By the fifteenth century the high cost of spices, par-ticularly black pepper, and other Eastern luxury goods led the maritime powers of Western European to seek alternative trade routes to the East. The spice trade was a driving force behind the Age of Discovery, which led to the discovery of the Americas by Europeans and the establishment of new sea trading routes.

In 1492 Christopher Columbus (1451–1506), sail-ing under the flag of Spain, attempted to reach India by sailing west from Europe. North and South America blocked the western sea route to Asia. The Americas re-vealed a source of spices, fruits, and vegetables unknown to the rest of the world. European traders soon im-ported a wide array of dried chilies, allspice, and vanilla from the Americas along with beans, potatoes, tomatoes, squashes, cocoa, and tobacco.

In 1498, Portuguese explorer Vasco da Gama (1460–1524) became the first European to discover the route connecting the Atlantic and Indian Oceans by sail-ing around the southern tip of Africa. Da Gama's dis-covery broke the domination of the spice trade by Arabs and the Republic of Venice and made Portugal one of the dominant players in the spice trade.

WORDS TO KNOW

AGE OF DISCOVERY: A period from the late fifteenth through early seventeenth centuries, during which European mari-time powers explored, mapped, and claimed previously unexplored parts of the world.

HERB: A plant with aromatic leaves, seeds, or flowers that is used, fresh or dried, to flavor food, scent perfume, or in medicine.

SPICE: Any aromatic part of a plant, including roots, seeds, fruit, or bark, which is dried and used in small quantities to flavor, preserve, or color food.

■ Impacts and Issues

Spices were valued for both their culinary applications and their use in embalming, perfume production, and medicine. Ancient Egyptian texts mention the use of spices during the mummification process but no source lists specific spices. Modern analysis of mummies, how-ever, reveals that Egyptians used a variety of imported spices, including juniper berries from other parts of the Mediterranean and cassia and cinnamon from Sri Lanka and India. The use of spices in embalming was practiced in many Middle Eastern and Asian cultures. Europeans used embalming infrequently until Crusaders returning

A woman looks over a display of spices for sale in Istanbul's famous Spice Market. Istanbul, Turkey, was a key city in the ancient spice trade between Asia and Europe. *Adrienne Lerner / Lerner & Lerner / LernerMedia Global Photos.*

from the Middle East popularized the practice, which had become commonplace by the Renaissance. Spices also have played an important role in the production of medicines for thousands of years. Many cultures continue to use spices in traditional medicine mixtures.

The spice trade also permitted cultural exchanges, including the spread of religion and foreign cuisines. By the tenth century, Arabs had carried Islam along trade routes from the Middle East to Southeastern Asia. The impact of Arab traders can still be seen: The world's three most populous Muslim countries—Indonesia, Pakistan, and Bangladesh—are legacies of centuries of Arab spice trade domination in Asia. While the spice trade spread the ingredients used in foreign cuisines, the tastes and preferences of returning traders led to the popularization of the foreign cuisines themselves. Trade from India popularized Indian cuisine in both Malaysia and Indonesia, where locals adopted and transformed Indian curries. British soldiers and traders returning from India also popularized Indian cuisine in Great Britain by the early nineteenth century.

Spice production remains concentrated to a limited number of countries. According to the Food and Agriculture Organization (FAO) of the United Nations, India continues to lead the world in spice production, producing approximately 1.6 million tons of spices each year—86 percent of the world's total. The remaining top five spice producing nations are located in Asia, as well: India is followed by China, Bangladesh, Pakistan, and Nepal. Together these five nations account for 97 percent of the world's nearly 1.9 million ton spice production. Modern production and shipping methods, however, ensure that spices are not as prohibitively expensive as they were for most of the history of the spice trade.

SEE ALSO *Herbs and Spices; Immigration and Cuisine; Import Restrictions; World Trade Organization (WTO).*

BIBLIOGRAPHY

Books

Freedman, Paul H. *Out of the East: Spices and the Medieval Imagination.* New Haven, CT: Yale University Press, 2008.

Keay, John. *The Spice Route: A History.* Berkeley: University of California Press, 2006.

Rodger, Ellen. *The Biography of Spices (How Did That Get Here?).* New York: Crabtree, 2006.

Wells, Donald. *The Spice Trade.* New York: Weigl, 2005.

Periodicals

Hull, Bradley. "Frankincense, Myrrh, and Spices." *Journal of Macromarketing* 28, no. 3 (2008): 275–288.

Sikora, Ewa, Anna Bielak-Zmijewska, Grazyna Mosieniak, and Katarzyna Piwocka. "The Promise of Slow Down Ageing May Come from Curcumin." *Current Pharmaceutical Design* 16, no. 7 (2010): 884–892.

Tugault-Lafleur, Claire, and Sarah Turner. "The Price of Spice: Ethnic Minority Livelihoods and Cardamom Commodity Chains in Upland Northern Vietnam." *Singapore Journal of Tropical Geography* 30, no. 3 (2009): 388–403.

Web Sites

"Spice Industry Overview." *Spice Trade.* http://www.spice-trade.com/industry-overview.html (accessed October 23, 2010).

Whipps, Heather. "How the Spice Trade Changed the World." *Live Science*, May 12, 2008. http://www.livescience.com/history/080512-hs-spicetrade.html (accessed October 23, 2010).

Joseph P. Hyder

Standard American Diet and Changing American Diet

■ Introduction

The diet of Americans is slowly changing to favor lighter, healthier food over the heavy preparations of the past. The Western dietary pattern, also called the standard American diet (SAD) by authors, nutritionists, and activists working to change it, refers to typical high-fat, high-calorie dietary choices often made by people living in industrialized Western nations. American cuisine and the American diet are somewhat unique in that the country does not have the same deeply rooted culinary traditions as many other countries in the world. For many years, the fast-paced national culture favored easy-to-prepare meals that often included processed and refined ingredients, which pose potential nutrition and health issues. Since the early 1990s, however, a shift in the nation's dietary patterns evolved to include more fresh ingredients and less prepared foods.

■ Historical Background and Scientific Foundations

In most areas of the world, the local cuisine is deeply rooted in history and tradition, based upon the ingredients that are naturally available on a seasonal basis. Whereas the inherent availability of food creates the framework around which cuisine is built, the actual development of a national cuisine is primarily an ancient oral tradition of recipes handed down from one generation of cooks to another, so the origins of many cultural preparations can be difficult to trace.

One of the few countries with an exception to this rule is the United States, because it is a country colonized and shaped by an influx of immigrants from many different countries, each bringing a different cuisine. Very little Native American cuisine exists in modern American cooking; almost all of the modern cuisine of the United States is an amalgam of traditional recipes of immigrants from a wide variety of countries. In addition, by the time the borders of the United States were finalized, it became a relatively large country that spans the width of an entire continent, allowing for easy access to the oceans on either coast while maintaining enormous amounts of grazing plains and farmland in the interior, eventually nullifying the ingredient availability concerns that influenced most other national cuisines. Considering another factor, American cuisine developed in an age in which documentation was common, so historians are able to learn how this cuisine has been evolving from its beginning.

At its earliest, American cuisine was highly regionalized and varied. Due to the amount of time needed to travel across the country, shipping ingredients was not possible, so each region of the country developed cuisine based upon the available local ingredients that same way that most other cuisines began. However, within each region in the United States there existed people of many different backgrounds, so many cuisines fused together. The Southwest regions included areas that at one time were a part of Mexico and New Spain and were therefore heavily influenced by Spanish cooking techniques. However, not too far away, the relocated French-speaking Acadians had settled, and the mixture of Acadian, British, Native American, Spanish, German, and Creole cuisines eventually gave rise to what would be called Cajun cooking.

When cooking in America was fragmented and regionalized, there was no all-encompassing style of food that could truly be called American cuisine. This started to change with the building of railroads and eventually highways across the country that enabled cultures from different areas to mix and blend. However, one event that greatly impacted American cuisine was World War II (1939–1945). During World War II, many countries, including the United States, instituted rations, and heavy industrial food production expanded in order to feed the soldiers overseas. However, those who remained within the United States needed to be fed as well, but now with fewer resources, less time, and less money. It was during this time that commercially prepared foods started to become popular, such as boxed cake mixes for which one

WORDS TO KNOW

CARBOHYDRATES: Molecules composed of carbon, hydrogen, and oxygen. For many animals carbohydrates are a primary source of energy, mainly in the form of starches and sugars. This term can also be used to refer to foods that are high in carbohydrates such as bread and grains.

CREOLE: Refers to the both the people and the culture of French settlements in the Caribbean and Louisiana beginning in the fifteenth century.

LIPIDS: Molecules that include fats such as oils from plants and animal fats such as butter and lard, as well as fat-soluble vitamins.

needed only add water and bake, packaged foods such as dried rice and seasoning mixes, canned meats, and other preserved goods. These goods provided inexpensive, fast meals and rarely needed rationed ingredients such as meat and dairy.

Packaged food products became common in many countries during the years of World War II; the difference in American cuisine occurred in the recovery years afterward. In most countries, after the war and rationing ended and regular production restarted, people returned to their familiar traditional cuisines. America, however, had spent the 1930s suffering through the Great Depression and the early 1940s fighting the war, and had no firm national cuisine to which to return. As a result, packaged and commercial goods remained popular in American cuisine for many years. Cookbooks written and published in the United States in the 1950s often contained preparations including canned and packaged products. Popular dishes regularly included packaged, flavored gelatin combinations made into shaped molds, or sweet potatoes baked with packaged marshmallows. Whereas the 1930s and 1940s were difficult times of personal and economic stress on American culture, it was also a time of technological innovation. One of the effects of the innovation was that the country became fully interconnected with railroads, highways, readily available private automobiles, and telecommunications, making the post-World War II cuisine one of the first truly national American diets.

While local and regional cuisine continued to exist in the United States during the 1950s, much of popular American cuisine maintained elements concerned with

A food aisle of a large American supermarket shows the influence of immigration in the diet of Americans. © *Tina Manley / Alamy.*

Traditional Greek, Italian, and Polish foods for sale at a riverfront festival in Carrabelle, Florida.   © *Pat Canova / Alamy.*

easy-to-use ingredients and methods, which was part of what eventually fueled the creation of fast food restaurants. Because many of the ingredients used during this time were processed industrially, the cuisine included a large amount of refined carbohydrates, lipids or fats, salt, and other food additives and preservatives, which made much of the cuisine heavy, or high in calories. The term "standard American diet" often refers to this phase in the cuisine's development. However, California cuisine (which is rooted in French Nouvelle cuisine) started to develop in the 1970s, and by the 1980s its focus on fresh produce and lighter preparations began to influence all of American cooking.

The national movement away from the heavier foods, often containing processed ingredients, towards lighter fresher fare is called New American Cuisine (NAC). Several major food movements helped spur NAC, including the organic movement and the slow food movement. National interest in food and cooking that has been supported by both traditional mass media and new social media has also helped to spread NAC quickly. Many restaurants in the country could be considered to be NAC restaurants, in that they serve food rooted in the mix of cultures that founded the country but use fresh ingredients and lighter, healthier preparations. The media outlets that have pushed this cuisine

forward have also influenced many people to start utilizing NAC in their home cooking, and the prevalence of this cuisine in regular homes across the country is what makes NAC a national cuisine development as opposed to a cooking genre.

■ Impacts and Issues

The phase of American cuisine that is referred to as standard American cuisine or the standard American diet (SAD diet) has many nutritional flaws. As the diet had its basis in industrial food preparation, it included many processed ingredients. The act of processing an ingredient often strips it of many nutrients. Because fresh ingredients are perishable and therefore cannot be included in prepared foods, much of the standard American diet was made up of processed carbohydrates and fats. Whereas both carbohydrates and fats are necessary for a healthy diet, when processed they become nutrient-degraded and can become empty calories, or calories that provide energy but without regular nutritional value. In addition, the standard diet's tendency towards quick food preparation eventually led to the creation of fast food restaurants, which have been implicated in providing a significant source of empty calories

IN CONTEXT: HEART DISEASE DIET LINKS

Heart disease was the leading cause of death in America by 1960, due in part to Americans' changing diet and lifestyles. Nutritional habits changed as processed, convenience, and fast foods contributed a higher fat and salt content in the diet. Simultaneously, increased urbanization led to a more sedentary lifestyle. As a result, more Americans suffered myocardial infarctions (heart attacks). According to the Centers for Disease Control and Prevention (CDC), 631,636 people died of heart disease in 2006 (26 percent of all deaths). The CDC also estimates that in 2010 heart disease cost the United States $316.4 billion for health care, lost productivity, and medication. Of the five recommendations the CDC gives for preventing heart disease, eating a healthy diet is the first, followed by maintaining a healthy weight, getting regular exercise, not smoking, and limiting alcohol intake.

to children, and in the development of obesity. The standard American diet is also associated with elevated rates of high blood pressure, type-2 diabetes, colon cancer, attention-deficit-hyperactivity disorder, and overall mortality.

In addition to a wealth of innovative chefs and restaurateurs, the movement towards NAC brings with it a change in the American diet by including more fresh ingredients, especially fruits and vegetables, and avoiding processed foods. For many Americans who grew up with the standard American diet, the trend towards New American cuisine seems like a suddenly emerging trend, when in fact it has been developing slowly since the inception of California cuisine in the 1980s. Additionally, NAC utilizes fruits, vegetables, fish, small portions of lean meats, herbs, nuts, and especially olive oil, making it similar to the diet characteristic of people of the northern Mediterranean region for thousands of years. The prevalence of NAC in homes may allow for the next generation of Americans to grow up with more sophisticated palates and a favor for lighter, healthier preparations.

While the American diet is changing along with the cuisine, American culture still retains its busy, fast-paced nature. It is more common now than in previous years that families do not have dinner together, and in many cases parents have difficulty finding time to prepare a complete meal every day. Although the cuisine development and the surge of interest in cooking is pervasive, it is often easier for parents or individuals to eat out or buy prepared meals than it is to spend time cooking. The new American diet is healthier than the standard American diet, but it also lies in direct contradiction with the frenetic lifestyle of many American families.

■ Primary Source Connection

As American society has changed in the past 60 or 70 years, so has when, where, and how the average American eats, especially compared to one's grandparents. Author Tom Hughes was raised in Haddonfield, New Jersey, a small town east of Philadelphia. In the 1950s the area still had many farms and local markets in main street shops. In this primary source, a narrative recollection, Tom Hughes describes meals in the 1950s.

The Foodways of a 50s Childhood

It seems remarkable to think about it now, but I went home for lunch until high school. I dashed home on my bike, about four blocks, sat down with my Mom and ate lunch at the kitchen table. We discussed our mornings. I played with my dog a few minutes and then biked back to play with friends in the schoolyard. Some students brought lunch but not many. Those were the days most moms were homemakers. I didn't encounter a school cafeteria until I was in 9th grade.

Another strong memory of growing up in the 50's was how almost every family had a vegetable garden in the backyard. These were habits formed by wartime victory garden necessity. We would all pour over the seed catalogs that piled up in winter. Parts of every weekend were dedicated to working in the garden with my Dad.

My family, like most families I knew, always sat down for meals together, including breakfast. We were expected to be on time, help serve, clear and clean up. We were also expected to participate in the conversation. Sunday midday dinner was served in the dining room. We wore our best clothes and used the best china.

We all ate the same food, no special menus or diets were considered. We certainly were expected to "clean our plates" and if we balked the "starving Armenians, or Chinese children" were quickly mentioned.

Many of my fondest childhood memories are food related. My parents canning surplus fruits and vegetables, for instance. I loved watching their assembly line. Later they put a big freezer in the basement and froze their excess garden harvest, as well as buying and freezing meat fresh from wholesalers. No wonder I had so many friends—my parents kept a steady supply of popsicles and ice cream sandwiches which were freely distributed.

I can remember enjoying watching my parents cook up huge pots of vegetable soup, Saturday night feasts of "corned beef and cabbage," my Dad sharpening his carving knives for baked hams, and roast beef. My mom grew up on a dairy farm and my dad was a city fellow who enjoyed eating. Once a month or so we went out for dinner. We dressed for this occasion as well. On

Tuesdays, my dad was usually away on business and my Mom took the night off from cooking and we all went to Yvonne's Diner for dinner. Yvonne's menu featured the same things we ate at home. It was all cooked from fresh ingredients and not at all fast. I can't remember ever having Chinese take-out, eating pizza or any other ethnic food until I was away at college.

The type of food my family cooked or ordered out, I guess, could be identified as standard American/British. Meat, potatoes, a green veg, dinner rolls, salad and dessert. Once in a while I got my mom to prepare my favorite—"Spanish rice." This was the most ethnic we ever got. It was pork chops cooked in stewed tomatoes, bell peppers, onion, sugar and some spices poured over rice. The only time we did not have potatoes with a meal was this one dish with rice.

We ate out of our garden from spring to the middle of fall. But we still made regular trips to the farm stands on the edge of town for fried green tomato orgies and, of course, sweet corn. My Dad ate prodigious amounts of corn on the cob and he said we didn't need to bother growing it in our garden. We also ate corn chowder, corn fritters, corn pudding and corn a dozen other ways.

In peach season we sat with our neighbors out on the porch and took turns cranking our own ice cream. We also had fresh strawberry ice cream and later in the summer, blueberry.

A big deal in high school once we all got driving licenses was to drive out of town to the highway and hang out at a place called Gino's Hamburgers. We would buy a bag of silver dollar sized mini hamburgers and a separate bag of fries, all washed down with strawberry milkshakes. We watched as these meals were assembly-line mass produced and passed through a window. We would go back and lean on our cars to eat. Little did any of us know that we were experiencing the birth of the fast food revolution.

In my junior year I lived with an Italian family in Florence, Italy. It was altogether familiar to me that they too, sat down for every meal as a family. Everyone came home from work or school at midday for lunch and a rest. I had developed the hamburger habit, nevertheless, and a big treat to assuage my homesickness was tracking down hamburgers in Milan and Rome.

A lot has changed about how American families eat over this past quarter century. Now in most families, both parents work, kids are required to eat lunch at school, few people have the time or energy to tend much of a vegetable garden; eating out is common, ethnic restaurants and fast food outlets are everywhere, people don't need to know how to cook to feed themselves as packaged convenience foods and microwaves cater to everyone's tastes and habits. Kids spend their time riding in or pushing a grocery shopping cart, not tending the family garden.

What hasn't changed is that early experiences with food imprints habits and tastes that extend into adulthood. Kids who eat well, participate in gardening, cooking and sharing meals with family and friends are more likely to continue these habits as adults with their own families, as my wife and I have done.

Now after several decades of eating conveniently and fast, an alarming percentage of two generations are seriously overweight and out of touch with their food.

Reformers feel the only alternative is to reconnect children at the earliest age possible with food experiences in school settings that were once a universal feature of family life.

(Tom Hughes grew up in Haddonfield, New Jersey, a town or 10,000 people nine miles east of Philadelphia. In those days, Southern New Jersey was still full of farms and small towns each with their main street shops.)

Tom Hughes

HUGHES, TOM. "50'S CHILDHOOD FOOD MEMOIR." *THE FOOD MUSEUM: WHAT'S NEW.* HTTP://WWW. FOODMUSEUM.COM/SLR50CHILDHOODESSAY.HTML (ACCESSED NOVEMBER 2, 2010).

SEE ALSO *Alice Waters: California and New American Cuisine; Cooking Fats; Diet and Cancer; Diet and Diabetes; Diet and Heart Disease; Diet and Hypertension; Dietary Guidelines for Americans; Dietary Reference Intakes; Edible Schoolyard Movement; Ethical Issues in Agriculture; Family Meal Benefits; Farm-to-Table Movement; Fast Food; Food Additives; History of Home Cooking; Junk Food; Mediterranean Diet; Organics; Processed Foods; School Lunch Reform; Slow Food Movement; Sustainable Table; Urban Chicken Movement; Urban Farming and Gardening.*

BIBLIOGRAPHY

Books

Beare, Sally. *50 Secrets of the World's Longest Living People.* New York: Marlowe & Company, 2006.

Pollan, Michael. *In Defense of Food: An Eater's Manifesto.* New York: Penguin Press, 2008.

Periodicals

Erber, Eva, et al. "Dietary Patterns and Risk for Diabetes." *Diabetes Care* 33, no. 3 (2010): 532–538.

Fung, Teresa T., et al. "Dietary Patterns and the Risk of Postmenopausal Breast Cancer." *International Journal of Cancer* 116, no. 1 (2005): 116–121.

Fung, Teresa T., Matthias Schulze, JoAnne E. Manson, Walter C. Willett, and Frank B. Hu. "Dietary Patterns, Meat Intake, and the Risk of Type 2 Diabetes in Women." *Archives of Internal Medicine* 164, no. 20 (2004): 2235–2240.

Gustaw-Rothenberg, K. "Dietary Patterns Associated with Alzheimer's Disease: Population Based Study." *International Journal of Environmental Research and Public Health* 6, no. 4 (2009): 1335–1340.

Thomson, Cynthia A., and Patricia A. Thompson. "Dietary Patterns, Risk and Prognosis of Breast Cancer." *Future Oncology* 5, no. 8 (2009): 1257–1269.

Web Sites

Irwin, Kim. "Pancreatic Cancers Use Fructose, Common in Western Diet, to Fuel Growth, Study Finds." *University of California: UCLA Newsroom*, August 4, 2010. http://newsroom.ucla.edu/portal/ucla/pancreatic-cancers-use-fructose-165745.aspx (accessed November 2, 2010).

Slow Food USA. http://www.slowfoodusa.org/ (accessed November 1, 2010).

"Western Diet Link to ADHD, Australian Study Finds." *Science Daily*, July 29, 2010. http://www.sciencedaily.com/releases/2010/07/100729091454.htm (accessed November 2, 2010).

David Brennan Tilove

Staphylococcal Food Poisoning

■ Introduction

Staphylococcal food poisoning refers to the gastrointestinal illness caused by eating food contaminated by the bacterium *Staphylococcus aureus*. The illness is the result of one of several heat- and salt-resistant toxins produced during growth of the bacteria in the food. The bacteria are typically transferred to the food by handling during food preparation of packaging, because *Staphylococcus aureus* is a common resident on the skin and surrounding the nasal passages. Foods that are especially susceptible to staphylococcal food poisoning are those that are handled during preparation and then consumed without heating. Examples are sliced meat, prepared sandwiches, pudding, and cream-filled pastries.

Staphylococcal food poisoning is an important contributor to the estimated 76 million cases of food poisoning the U.S. Centers for Disease Control (CDC) estimate occur each year in the United States alone. Whereas most cases of staphylococcal food poisoning resolve in a few days without lasting damage, outbreaks can involve many people because the contaminated food can be served in group settings. More ominously, outbreaks that occur in a hospital environment can be more serious, because those who are affected can be already in a weakened state.

■ Historical Background and Scientific Foundations

Even though staphylococcal food poisoning is the result of toxin production, it differs from food intoxication. The latter occurs when pre-formed toxin is ingested. In staphylococcal food poisoning, the production of toxin occurs after the contamination of the food, as the bacteria grow and increase in number. Because the quantity of toxin produced will depend on the number of bacteria present, and so typically on the length of time the food has been contaminated prior to consumption, the severity of the resulting symptoms will vary. Also, the severity of symptoms and their time of onset can vary depending on the particular toxin that predominates. Symptoms can begin in less than 1 hour after eating the contaminated food if the bacterial growth occurs quickly, or may take longer (usually within six hours) to appear.

Typical symptoms are nausea, vomiting, stomach cramps, fever, and diarrhea. Recovery is usually complete after several days of the intestinal upset. However, as with many illnesses, a minority of people can be more severely affected. The onset of nausea with staphylococcal food poisoning can be characteristically sudden, and vomiting can be explosive.

The overwhelming root of the illness is the improper handling of food during preparation or packaging. *Staphylococcus aureus* is a common inhabitant of the skin and nasal passages of healthy individuals, being detected in more than half of the population. In these environments, the bacterium is innocuous, and its presence is usually unnoticed. But in other environments, including the intestinal tract, illness can be produced.

Improper hygiene, such as poor or no handwashing, or failure to wear protective gloves when handling food, can result in the transfer of *Staphylococcus aureus* from the person to the particular food. In the case of foods that are not consumed for some time, the bacteria can grow and multiply and produce the illness-causing toxin(s) in increasing quantity.

Seven different types of *Staphylococcus aureus* toxin that can cause food poisoning have been identified so far. All are similar in that they are enterotoxins (an enterotoxin is a toxin that is released in the intestinal tract). Because the toxins are resistant to heat, salt level in the food, and the pH of the food, the toxin molecules are very hardy and can remain capable of causing illness even in salted food or food that is held at an elevated temperature after preparation. As an example, potato salad is a food product that is typically prepared by heating and cooling prior to serving. If the mayonnaise used in the salad is contaminated with *Staphylococcus aureus* that

WORDS TO KNOW

COMMENSALISM: A relationship involving two organisms, in which one organism benefits, and the other is not affected.

HYGIENE: Actions that help maximize health, particularly by controlling the growth of bacteria on surfaces.

TOXIN: A protein that causes damage on contact with cells.

survive the heating, an increase in bacterial numbers can occur, especially if the food is left at room temperature or a slightly elevated temperature (which is conducive to bacterial growth) following preparation. Enterotoxin can be produced during this time and can sicken those who eat the food.

Other foods associated with staphylococcal food poisoning include salted (cured) ham, meat products, sandwich meat, poultry and egg products, pastries that include cream such as cream pies and éclairs, and milk and dairy products.

Treatment of staphylococcal food poisoning mainly involves rehydration to replace the fluids lost to diarrhea and vomiting. Then, time becomes the healer. Once the toxin has been expelled from the body, recovery is usually quick, although a residual feeling of being unwell can linger for some hours. Within several days, recovery is almost always complete, generally with no lasting damage.

■ Impacts and Issues

Everyone is at risk of food poisoning in general and staphylococcal food poisoning in particular. This fact is reflected in the estimated 76 million foodborne illnesses that occur in the United States every year. The exact toll due to *Staphylococcus aureus* is difficult to determine, because many people do not seek medical attention for treatment. Nevertheless, staphylococcal food poisoning is an important contributor to the total number of cases. Both genders and all ages are susceptible.

Vigilance in food preparation in the home cannot protect someone from food contamination elsewhere, short of avoiding eating suspect food products. The impact of the illness is even greater and potentially more serious when the contaminated food is served to ill patients in hospitals, whose bodies may already be

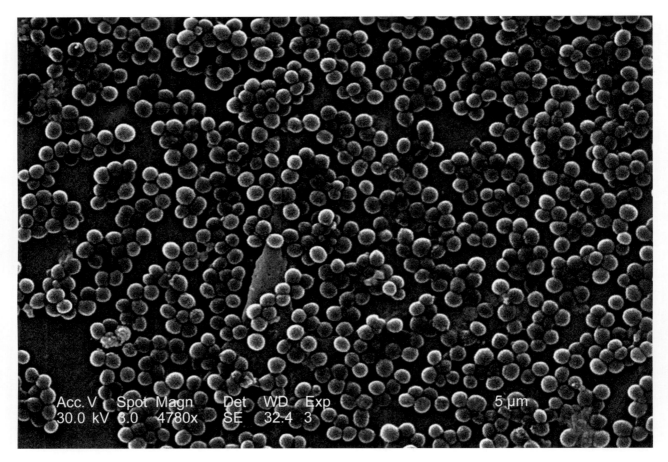

Staphylococcus aureus bacteria, shown in this image taken by a scanning electron microscope, causes staphylococcal food poisoning, a common foodborne illness. © *Scott Camazine / Alamy.*

weakened, making them more susceptible to severe illness and, rarely, death.

Staphylococcal food poisoning outbreaks can affect many people at once, because the affected foods are often served in group settings such as picnics or school cafeterias. Outbreaks that have sickened thousands of people have occurred.

The importance of proper hygiene in the handling and preparation of food cannot be overemphasized. A strategy as simple as handwashing is a powerful way to reduce the incidence of illness. Still, ensuring compliance with handwashing remains a challenge.

SEE ALSO *Consumer Food Safety Recommendations; E. Coli Contamination; Food Safety and Inspection Service; Foodborne Diseases;* Salmonella.

BIBLIOGRAPHY

Books

Juneja, Vijay K., and John N. Sofos. *Pathogens and Toxins in Foods: Challenges and Interventions.* Washington, DC: ASM Press, 2010.

Periodicals

Kitamoto, Miyoko, et al. "Food Poisoning by Staphylococcus Aureus at a University Festival." *Japanese Journal of Infectious Diseases* 62, no. 3 (2009): 242–243.

Larkin, Eileen A., Robert J. Carman, Teresa Krakauer, and Bradley G. Stiles. "Staphylococcus Aureus: The Toxic Presence of a Pathogen Extraordinaire." *Current Medicinal Chemistry* 16, no. 30 (2009): 4003–4019.

Web Sites

National Library of Medicine. "*Staph aureus* Food Poisoning." *Medline Plus.* http://www.nlm.nih.gov/medlineplus/ency/article/000227.htm (accessed October 6, 2010).

"Staphylococcal Food Poisoning." *Centers for Disease Control and Prevention (CDC).* http://www.cdc.gov/ncidod/dbmd/diseaseinfo/staphylococcus_food_g.htm (accessed October 6, 2010).

Brian Douglas Hoyle

Street Food

Introduction

Street food is quick, easy-to-eat food sold by street vendors. Many street foods are finger foods, intended for eating by hand because often there is no dedicated place to sit down near the food vendor stand. Street food plays a large role in the cuisine of many countries, particularly in urban areas, and street food is deeply tied in with the local culture. The Food and Agriculture Organization (FAO) of the United Nations estimates that street food provides up to half of all daily calories consumed by people living in cities in the developing world. Street food can be as simple as fresh fruit sold from a cart, or it can include complete hot dishes served from small stalls on the sidewalk. It exists in almost endless variety in many different countries; some originating from old traditions, whereas others are the result of commingling culinary traditions due to immigration.

Historical Background and Scientific Foundations

Street foods can be traced to the development of urban areas around the globe. As population density grew, enterprising cooks made local dishes that were both easy to eat while standing, and easy to prepare and sell on the streets. Deeply rooted in tradition, some street foods have changed little as time has progressed. However, as people emigrated from one country to another, they would often bring some street food traditions with them, such as the Middle-Eastern immigrants introducing *falafel* from street carts in New York City.

There are a wide variety of dishes that can be made and sold as street food. Some classic examples are Vietnam's *pho*, which is made by pouring boiling broth over thinly shaved meat, vegetables, and noodles. *Pho* varies between Northern and Southern Vietnam: Southern *pho* is offered with a wide variety of garnishes such as freshly chopped herbs, spice pastes, and lime, whereas Northern *pho* ordinarily is served plain. Germany, with its large Turkish population, has many Turkish-inspired street foods; one of the most popular is the *Döner kebab*, which is roasted and sliced lamb served folded into a flatbread sandwich with various toppings and sauces. India is renowned for its diversity of street foods, an example of which is *Pani Puri*, a hollow ball of dough filled with a spicy or sweet *chutney*. Japan's *udon* and *ramen* dishes are well known street foods, consisting of rice noodles in various broths served at small street stalls. *Empanadas*, which are made from fried dough flour filled with meat or vegetables, though originally from Spain, are a popular street food in Latin America and various countries in the Caribbean. Many of these street foods are well-known dishes that can be found all over the world, but what makes them traditional street food of a certain country is the prevalence of cart or stall vendors that one can find. In order to survive as a street food stand, the food being sold must be familiar to most of the pedestrian traffic likely to walk by the stall. In that regard, common street food can be indicative of the culinary traditions of the population of a given neighborhood.

Impacts and Issues

A primary difficulty for street food is ensuring sanitary standards. Many street vendor stands lack refrigeration and need to access fresh ingredients almost every day in order to serve safe food. In industrialized nations, governmental agencies enact regulations and monitor street food vendors. The Food Standards Agency, for example, controls the sanitation standards of all street food vendors in the United Kingdom. In the United States, street food vendors are regulated and licensed by state health departments. Unfortunately, there are some street food health issues that cannot be controlled by regulation. Water in different areas of the world contains different microorganisms, and oftentimes visitors from different regions can get sick by ingesting microbes to which they are not accustomed. Many varieties of street food include water in their preparation, and travelers can ingest the local water unknowingly by eating street food. This even effects expatriates: People who spend long periods of time in countries different than their home country may become acclimated to the water in the new areas, and cannot eat the street food when they visit their home countries without becoming ill.

In the crowded conditions prevalent in parts of the developing world, other diseases such as salmonellosis, hepatitis A, and amebiasis are often spread by the contaminated hands of street food vendors, who have few facilities for washing their hands while preparing food and handling money. In addition, street foods prepared close to the ground are susceptible to contaminants from dust and emissions from vehicle traffic. Fruits, vegetables, and meats used in street preparations are often obtained from unregulated sources, and are sometimes contaminated with pesticide residues, heavy metals, or even textile dyes when harvested from polluted soil or raised on refuse or contaminated feed. While recognizing the vital role street food plays in the economies of developing countries, agencies such as the World Health Organization are working to make street food safer. In one area of Pakistan, for example, helping street food vendors to elevate their cookstoves, increase their workspace, providing

access to clean water, and educating vendors on food safety dramatically reduced the number of contaminated foods and resulting illnesses from street food.

An additional health issue arising from street food is the switch in some countries from street food to fast food. One of the attributes of street food is that it is cheap and quick. In some countries, street food vendors have been replaced by fast food restaurants, which often offer more food for about the same amount of money.

A street food vendor in Xi'an, China, prepares a popular sweet rice and nut confection.   *Adrienne Lerner / Lerner & Lerner / LernerMedia Global Photos.*

One of the biggest health risks in India is infection by hepatitis B and typhoid, the main source being contaminated unclean food, such as street food made, sold, and eaten in unhygienic conditions. © *Travelfile / Alamy.*

However, as opposed to buying a fresh chicken satay kabob, the diner is buying a hamburger and fries made by an industrial process and containing preservatives. The cumulative health impact of fast food versus traditional street food can be enormous, because a healthy street food population increases the demand for local ingredients and agriculture. Street food may not always be healthier than fast food, but it is usually made with fresh ingredients as opposed to processed ingredients. Additionally, the popularity of fast food restaurants makes it more difficult for street food vendors to stay in business, reducing their numbers in some cities.

Despite concerns of health issues and increasing competition from fast food restaurants, street food has a long history and remains quite popular in its respective countries. Street food is tied in closely with national culture, and is still a quick and inexpensive meal. Additionally, in keeping with the current renewed interest in food and cuisine there are certain niche street food vendors with high-end, artisanal street food such as the gourmet ice cream trucks and South American barbeque stands that are starting to appear in New York City and are popular destinations in Los Angeles, Austin, and other cities. With both the new high-end vendors and continued traditional recipes, the street food model of quick food sold from stands or trucks is gaining in popularity in the developed world, while remaining an urban staple for quick, inexpensive nutrition in developing nations.

■ Primary Source Connection

The Food and Agriculture Organization (FAO) of the United Nations has its headquarters in Rome, Italy. The organization's charter is to reduce and eliminate world hunger. It works in four main areas: to provide information; to share policy expertise; to provide meeting places for nations; and to provide knowledge to the projects around the world aimed at reducing hunger. The FAO also prepares studies on the interaction and impacts of food policy on economies and culture. The following is an excerpt from the final report of an FAO technical meeting on street foods held in Calcutta, India, in November 1995.

Socio-economic Aspects of Street Foods

While reviewing the information from various street food projects and activities carried out in Asia, Latin

America and Africa, the meeting recognized the socio-economic, nutritional and cultural significance of street foods. The meeting reiterated that street food vending provided food at the work place as well as at other important locations in the city; and its variety and form depended upon local eating habits, socio-economic environment and trends in style of living.

Street foods, defined as "ready-to eat foods and beverages prepared and/or sold by vendors and hawkers especially in street and other similar public places", can be found in clusters around places of work, schools, hospitals, railway stations, bus terminals etc. They are inexpensive when compared to food from the formal sector and in fact are often less expensive when compared to home cooked food. They also fill the need of providing food at places where people work or otherwise congregate. A major concern is that while they play an important socio-economic role, their tremendous unlimited and unregulated growth has placed a severe strain on city resources and through congestion and littering adversely affected daily life.

The meeting recognized that setting up as a street food vendor involved a low-cost investment. Further, it required no special training other than the domestic experience of preparing food and provided employment. Street food operations often involved entire families in the procurement of raw materials, preparation and cooking of meals and their sale. The role of women in the street food sector and the potential for their employment in this sector was most significant. The overall economic implications of street foods were immense. It was recognized that in many cities of the world, the equivalent of millions of US dollars exchanged hands each day as a result of the vending of street foods. The impact on local agricultural production is in many cases immense.

The meeting discussed how cultural, ethnic and religious differences had influenced the variety and nature of street foods around the world. The food might be cooked at home and distributed or alternately prepared on the spot depending upon the space available. There are fixed stalls, a variety of types of push-carts, road side stands, hawkers with head-loads, and other arrangements depending upon the ingenuity of the individual, resources available, the type of food sold, and the availability of other facilities either acquired officially or appropriated from the city.

The meeting reaffirmed that street foods have significant nutritional implications for consumers, particularly for middle and low income sectors of the population who depend heavily on street foods. In this, a number of factors that influence the consumer's choice play an important role. These include cost, convenience and type of food available, the individual's taste and the organoleptic qualities of the food (smell, texture, colour, appearance). The nutritional value of street foods depends upon the

ingredients used and how they are prepared, stored and sold. The meeting urged the development and use of proper technologies in order to preserve the nutritional value of street foods. On the basis of the information so far available, the meeting was of the opinion that the eating of a combination of street foods did provide the consumer adequate opportunity to meet his or her daily nutritional requirements at an affordable pace.

The meeting pointed out that an important aspect of street foods that deserved particular attention related to their safety. It was recognized that street foods raise concern with respect to their potential for serious food poisoning outbreaks due to microbiological contamination, improper use of additives (in particular the use of unapproved colourings) and the presence of other adulterants and environmental contaminants. Surveys in Africa, Asia, and Latin America suggested that these concerns were real and needed to be addressed to protect consumers. Improper food handling practices could be a serious cause of contamination. There were also problems with potable water supply, the quality of raw materials used (for example rotten vegetables or spoiled meat) and unsuitable environments for street food operations (such as proximity to sewers and garbage dumps). Inadequate facilities for garbage disposal posed further hazards.

FOOD AND AGRICULTURE ORGANIZATION OF THE UNITED NATIONS (FAO). *FAO TECHNICAL MEETING ON STREET FOODS, CALCUTTA, INDIA. III. SOCIO-ECONOMIC ASPECTS OF STREET FOODS, NOVEMBER 1995.* HTTP://WWW.FAO.ORG/DOCREP/ W4128T/W4128T03.HTM (ACCESSED OCTOBER 24, 2010)

SEE ALSO *Cholera; Consumer Food Safety Recommendations;* E. Coli *Contamination; Fast Food; Food and Agriculture Organization (FAO); Foodborne Diseases; Foodways; Immigration and Cuisine; Produce Traceability;* Salmonella; *Water; Water Scarcity; Women's Role in Global Food Preparation.*

BIBLIOGRAPHY

Books

Hester, Elliott. *Adventures of a Continental Drifter: An Around-the-World Excursion into Weirdness, Danger, Lust, and the Perils of Street Food.* New York: St. Martin's Press, 2005.

Kime, Tom. *Street Food: Exploring the World's Most Authentic Tastes.* New York: DK Publishing, 2007.

Menzel, Peter, and Faith D'Aluisio. *What the World Eats.* Berkeley, CA: Tricycle Press, 2008.

Periodicals

Afele, Mawusi. "Street Food Boom in Ghana Spurs Calls for Better Hygiene." *Bulletin of the World Health Organization* 84, no. 10 (2006): 772–773.

"Family of Man—Street Food." *National Geographic* 211, no. 2 (2007): 14.

"Food: Street Food Comes in from the Cold." *Newsweek* (March 29, 2010): 54.

Gurbaxani, M. M. "Street Food Activism." *Ecologist* 37, no. 10 (2007).

Web Sites

Consumers International. "Streetfood." *Streetfood.org.* http://streetfood.org/index.php?option=com_frontpage&Itemid=1 (accessed September 29, 2010).

"Food for the Cities: Ensuring the Quality and Safety of Street Foods." *Food Quality and Standards Service, Food and Agriculture Organization of the United Nations (FAO).* ftp://ftp.fao.org/docrep/fao/011/ak003e/ak003e09.pdf (accessed September 29, 2010).

International Food Safety Authorities Network (INFOSAN). "Basic Steps to Improve Safety of Street-Vended Food." *World Health Organization (WHO).* http://www.who.int/foodsafety/fs_management/No_03_StreetFood_Jun10_en.pdf (accessed September 29, 2010).

David Brennan Tilove

Subsidies

■ Introduction

Agricultural subsidies, which may be one of the least understood of government programs, include any government programs that pay farmers for farming, or for abstaining from farming certain parts of land, or for simply possessing a tract of land. Some critics lump a variety of other agricultural support programs with subsidies such as crop insurance programs in which the government subsidizes part of the bill. Agricultural subsidies expanded greatly during the Great Depression (1929–1941) to increase farmers' incomes by influencing the price of agricultural commodities. The European Economic Community (EEC), formed in 1957, administered subsidies through the Common Agricultural Policy (CAP), as does the European Union (EU) now. Starting with the Uruguay Round negotiations (1986–1994), countries began to experiment with ways to reduce subsidies and lessen their unintended impacts on trade in agricultural commodities. However, even after reducing subsidies, the level remains extremely high, especially in some countries in Asia and Europe, where in some areas subsidies make up a majority of farmers' income. New Zealand, a nation located on several large islands in the Pacific east of Australia, has eliminated agricultural subsidies with positive results for its farm economy and rural areas.

■ Historical Background and Scientific Foundations

In 1933 the United States enacted the Agricultural Adjustment Act (AAA), a set of farm subsidies designed to improve the income of poor farmers. The prices of agricultural commodities were very low in part due to the Great Depression. Because low prices led to low income for farmers, the AAA was an attempt to prevent farmers from abandoning their farms by selling them and becoming destitute. The bill enabled the U.S. Department of Agriculture (USDA) to influence the prices of unprocessed farm commodities by several means. USDA could pay farmers to take land out of cultivation. By reducing the amount of land cultivated and thus the amount of commodities produced, the supply of a commodity would fall. The fall in supply would result in an increased price if demand remained the same. USDA was also allowed to purchase surplus commodities. By taking a surplus out of the commercial market, the supply is reduced, so if demand stays the same, the price will increase. This bill became the first of many bills that were later known as farm bills, enacted usually once every five years in the United States covering farm programs including subsidies. Until the late 1980s, the U.S. approach focused primarily on using prices to ensure farmer income. Subsidies in the United States currently tend to be linked to the production of particular commodities such as corn, wheat, rice, soybeans, and cotton instead of being linked to farmers' incomes. For this reason and others, not all farmers receive subsidies. In the United States, according to the 2007 Census of Agriculture, only 38 percent of farmers received any form of subsidy in the previous five years.

In Europe, similar programs had been launched for various commodities in several countries. When the European Economic Community (EEC) was formed in 1957, though, subsidies were thought to give unfair advantage to farmers in one country compared to farmers in neighboring countries. In a single market, subsidies in one country could affect the price in another. For example, if one country paid its farmers a subsidy to produce wine, those farmers could sell their wine for less. With open markets within the EEC, the less expensive wine could flood into the neighboring market to dispose of its surplus. Most of these subsidies were focused on a single commodity, like those in the United States. To harmonize farm programs and agricultural policy, the European Community launched the Common Agricultural Policy (CAP) in 1962, which standardized the benefits of agricultural subsidies so that no one member's farmers have an unfair advantage.

Pakistani activists of Sustainable Agriculture Action Group protest proposed World Trade Organization cuts to farm subsidies in 2007. *AP Images.*

Subsidies grew ever more expensive, but this trend changed with the founding of the World Trade Organization (WTO) in 1995 following the Uruguay Round of multilateral trade negotiations (1986–1994). Several agreements between WTO member countries fundamentally altered approaches to agricultural subsidies. Under the Agreement on Agriculture, countries were limited to an Aggregate Measure of Support (AMS) on subsidies, which are argued to impact world commodity prices. This level would be reduced over time, though not all forms of subsidies or forms of government spending in the agricultural sector are affected. Export subsidies were to be phased out, but countries could continue to support agriculture in other ways. To comply with the new rules, the United States started income support payments not contingent upon current production of a commodity. In the European Union, income support payments also came into greater prominence, often with requirements for animal welfare and environmental compliance. Though subsidies were only one issue in the Doha Round negotiations in the WTO that began in 2000, subsidies were one of the issues on which further agreement on reform could not be reached when the talks collapsed in 2008.

■ Impacts and Issues

The results of the reforms under the WTO remain unclear. One common way of measuring subsidies and other programs that impact prices is the producer support estimate (PSE), which looks at the difference between world prices and domestic prices in addition to actual spending on subsidies. The PSE captures both the cost to consumers of agricultural policies and subsidies and the cost to taxpayers, and it is often listed both as a spending amount and as a percentage of total farm income. The Organisation for Economic Co-operation and Development (OECD) estimates that their member countries spent 253 billion U.S. dollars supporting agricultural producers in 2009, making up 22 percent of farmer income compared to 37 percent in 1986. There were many different levels of subsidy between these economies. The United States and the European Union are actually in the middle of this range. The United States provided 31 billion U.S. dollars of support worth 10 percent of gross receipts in 2009. That same year, the EU spent 121 billion U.S. dollars providing 24 percent of support for producers.

Some countries have much higher historic and current levels of subsidy, including Japan, whose PSE in 2009 provided 48 percent of farm receipts. Other countries with continued high 2009 PSEs include Iceland at 48 percent, South Korea at 52 percent, Switzerland at 63 percent, and Norway at 66 percent. In contrast, other OECD members have much lower levels of subsidies, such as Australia, which provided 3 percent support in 2009. New Zealand provided 20 percent support in 1986, but following radical reforms of agricultural policy this had been reduced to less than 1 percent by 2009. Almost all of New Zealand's remaining spending is dedicated to agricultural research.

According to many critics, agricultural subsidies continue to encourage overproduction. These commodities from the subsidizing countries come into world markets, driving down prices so that farmers in other countries cannot compete. Increased supply on the market drives down the world price, which may harm poor, limited-resource farmers in developing countries. Advocates for developing world farmers often advocate the elimination of subsidies. The story of New Zealand's experience with agricultural subsidies and then virtual overnight elimination of these subsidies provides an interesting case study into how subsidies work and what the effects of further reform might be for agriculturally productive countries.

By eliminating subsidies, 1 percent of New Zealand's farms were bankrupted overnight and had to sell off their farms and assets. However, New Zealand had 1.5 percent annual productivity increases per year under subsidies from 1972 until 1985, and this has since jumped to 2.5 percent annual productivity increases for the period from 1986 until 2004. New Zealand has maintained the workforce in agriculture, and the population in rural areas. Some forms of farming such as beef production and fruit and vegetable production have greatly increased. New Zealand's farmers are currently more diversified in the crops they grow both between and within farms. Varied interest groups support subsidies, and these well-organized groups make reforms difficult in the democratic countries that continue to have high levels of subsidies.

SEE ALSO *Agribusiness; Agriculture and International Trade; Aid for Agriculture to Replace Illicit Drug Production; Free Trade and Agriculture; U.S.* *Department of Agriculture (USDA); World Trade Organization (WTO).*

BIBLIOGRAPHY

Books

Anderson, Kym. *The Political Economy of Agricultural Price Distortions.* New York: Cambridge University Press, 2010.

Merino, Noël. *Agricultural Subsidies.* Detroit: Greenhaven Press, 2010.

Peterson, E. Weseley F. *A Billion Dollars a Day: The Economics and Politics of Agricultural Subsidies.* Malden, MA: Wiley-Blackwell, 2009.

Periodicals

Elinder, Liselotte S. "Obesity, Hunger, and Agriculture: The Damaging Role of Subsidies." *British Medical Journal* (clinical research ed.) 331, no. 7528 (2005): 1333–1336.

"Industry to Support Agriculture—Subsidies Help Small Farmers." *Beijing Review* 48, no. 15 (2005): 24–25.

Nucci, Mary, Cara Cuite, and William Hallman. "When Good Food Goes Bad." *Science Communication* 31, no. 2 (2009): 238–265.

Web Sites

"Burkina Faso: Cotton Story." *Oxfam International.* http://www.oxfam.org/en/campaigns/trade/real_lives/burkina_faso (accessed September 25, 2010).

"Understanding the WTO: The Agreements: Antidumping, Subsidies, Safeguards." *World Trade Organization.* http://www.wto.org/english/thewto_e/whatis_e/tif_e/agrm8_e.htm#subsidies (accessed September 25, 2010).

Blake Jackson Stabler

Subsistence Farming

■ Introduction

Subsistence farming is agriculture and livestock production that yields all the goods, primarily food, necessary for the survival of a household. Sometimes subsistence farming is referred to as peasant agriculture or smallholder agriculture. Smallholder agriculture would include farmers who produce not only food for subsistence, but all farmers holding less than two hectares (less than five acres) of land. Subsistence farmers often have varied sources of income, which are referred to as a livelihood portfolio. Because subsistence farming and all agriculture faces risks of low yields, subsistence farmers employ coping strategies when confronted with falls in yield and lack of sufficient food. Some economists suggest that economies of scale in agriculture make smallholder agriculture inherently low yielding. However, other economists suggest that the role of economies of scale is minimal in some farming systems and that smallholder farmers can experience productivity gains that can lead to economic growth.

■ Historical Background and Scientific Foundations

Subsistence farming has always existed in the sense that farmers with small amounts of land made a living primarily off of that land by producing food for themselves. However, if subsistence farming is defined as producing all the food necessary for the household to survive, these self-sufficient farms are currently very rare and probably have been so throughout history. In the twenty-first century, subsistence farming in the developed world is primarily thought of as self-sufficiency in food production. Movements such as the back-to-the-land movement in North America in the 1960s and 1970s saw self-sufficiency as a goal for agriculture and an alternative to modern, urban living.

In the developing world, small scale farmers, often called smallholders, may produce primarily for their own consumption but they often also participate in some trade or need to sell their labor in order to buy additional sources of food. In this sense, most contemporary subsistence farmers are actually net buyers of food: They buy more food than they sell. Very few subsistence farmers actually exist entirely outside of the cash economy, producing only food for their own consumption. On the agriculture side, many smallholder farmers produce cash crops in addition to crops for subsistence. For example, they may produce non-food crops such as cotton, food crops that require intensive processing such as oilseeds or sugar cane, or simply produce extra staple crops or horticultural crops or livestock for the market. Households may not obviously participate in a market economy, but they may trade, barter, or possibly give and receive gifts instead of surviving completely and totally off their own subsistence production. According to the World Bank, as of 2008 there were approximately 1.5 billion people living in smallholder rural households in developing countries. Agriculture, including subsistence agriculture, provides a livelihood source for 86 percent of the developing world's 3 billion rural residents.

As most subsistence farmers or smallholder farmers do not survive entirely off their land, they employ a variety of livelihood strategies to support themselves. This group of strategies is referred to as a livelihood portfolio. Like a financial portfolio of stocks, bonds, bank accounts, and other monetary instruments, a diversified livelihood portfolio reduces risk by not depending entirely on smallholder agriculture for subsistence. In addition to producing crops and raising livestock, both for use by the household and for sale or barter, households may gather wild foods or other products from forests or from other nearby areas. They may hunt or fish for some food. They also have a variety of cash handling strategies. They sometimes both take loans and have various forms of savings or insurance including both formal and informal arrangements.

Many farmers will also work for cash wages as day laborers or irregular laborers, sometimes in agriculture but other times in construction and other trades. Some members of the household may migrate, either seasonally for additional agricultural work or to more urban areas for wage labor. A few migrants even travel to other countries seeking work opportunities. Some of the wages earned by these migrants will be sent or brought back to households in the countries of origin, and this form of income is known as a remittance. Remittances are difficult to measure, but for example, remittances in Latin America in 2006 totaled at least $60 billion, according to the World Bank. For poor rural households, remittances can be an important source of income. Also, households may run small businesses such as taking in sewing, conducting various trades, producing handicrafts for sale, or engaging in petty trade. A variety of cash- or food-earning mechanisms will be used, as well as management techniques for money, in an attempt to supplement the food grown and raised by a household and to cover other expenses.

■ Impacts and Issues

Subsistence farmers face a variety of risks related to their dependence on agriculture for their livelihood. Because agricultural production is their primary source

of food, falls in production resulting from bad weather, drought, poor seed quality, crop failure, plant disease, or poor soil conditions can lead to food shortages. Agricultural and livestock yields are variable and not predictable, so households will employ various coping strategies to deal with shortfalls at harvest time. A household may reduce the amount of food its members consume, switch to less expensive foods for purchases, draw down stockpiles and stored food, draw on cash

A farmer works in rice fields using an ancient technique; a domesticated swamp buffalo (carabao) pulls a plow. In many of the world's developing countries people rely on subsistence farming. *Image copyright Hugo Maes, 2010. Used under license from Shutterstock.com.*

savings, send household members away as migrants, seek additional paid labor opportunities, or beg to cope with shortages of food or cash income. Coping strategies may enable households to survive a lean harvest or drought, though some coping strategies such as reducing food consumption may have long-term impacts on the health and the long-term income earning potential of some household members. Children under the age of five and pregnant women have special nutritional needs and are most at risk to suffer negative effects of coping strategies that reduce the household's food consumption.

Whereas most subsistence farmers in the developing world are either already in poverty or at risk of falling into poverty, the relationship between smallholder farming and poverty reduction is an area of intense debate in economics. Some economists suggest that subsistence farming is a practice that holds back agricultural productivity growth and overall economic growth. The smallholders' land holdings are seen as not having much potential for commercialization due to their scale, so larger groupings of land would be necessary to take advantage of economies of scale in agriculture. To do this, some smallholders would need to leave their land and become urban residents. Other economists suggest that economies of scale are not universal for all crops, livestock, and agro-climactic conditions. In their view, other factors unrelated to the size of farms prevent subsistence farmers from increasing their productivity and earning more from their land. However, these economists do not suggest that smallholder farms cannot be commercialized or experience significant gains in productivity under the right conditions. These economists posit that smallholder agriculture can play a key role in reducing poverty through productivity gains and can be a driver of overall economic growth.

SEE ALSO *Agricultural Land Reform; Decollectivization; Ethical Issues in Agriculture; Food Security; Food Sovereignty; Free Trade and Agriculture; Gender Equality and Agriculture; Sustainable Agriculture.*

BIBLIOGRAPHY

Books

Erreygers, Guido, and Tadele Ferede. *The End of Subsistence Farming: Growth Dynamics and Investments in Human and Environmental Capital in Rural Ethiopia.* Antwerp, Belgium: University of Antwerp, 2009.

Waters, Tony. *The Persistence of Subsistence Agriculture: Life beneath the Level of the Marketplace.* Lanham, MD: Lexington Books, 2008.

Periodicals

Finnis, Elizabeth. "Why Grow Cash Crops? Subsistence Farming and Crop Commercialization in the Kolli Hills, South India." *American Anthropologist* 108, no. 2 (2006): 363–369.

Seals, Alan, and Joachim Zietz. "The Decline in Maize Prices, Biodiversity, and Subsistence Farming in Mexico." *The American Economist* 54, no. 2 (2009): 10–20.

Southgate, Douglas, Fabian Rodriguez, and Timothy Haab. "Payments for Sustainability: A Case Study on Subsistence Farming in Ecuador." *Harvard International Review* 31, no. 2 (2009): 52.

Web Sites

Potaka, Elise. "Lao Rice Farmers Move from Subsistence to Cash Crops." *Public Radio International (PRI),* October 5, 2009. http://www.pri.org/business/global-development/lao-rice-farmers1653.html (accessed October 10, 2010).

Redding, Sean. "Structural Adjustment and the Decline of Subsistence Agriculture in Africa." *Amherst College.* http://www3.amherst.edu/~mrhunt/womencrossing/redding.html (accessed October 10, 2010).

"Small-Scale Dairy Production: A Way Out of Poverty." *Food and Agriculture Organization of the United Nations (FAO).* http://www.fao.org/news/story/en/item/44582/icode/ (accessed October 10, 2010).

Blake Jackson Stabler

Sugar and Sweeteners

■ Introduction

Sweet foods have always been popular because they taste good and usually supply quick energy. Sugar's properties mean that it plays an important role in both baking and confectionery. But consuming too much sugar may lead to weight gain. Therefore several low- or no-calorie sweeteners have been developed to help people satisfy their desire for sweetness without ingesting significant calories. For some sweeteners, however, the health risks may outweigh the benefits. There has been controversy over cyclamate, which has been banned in the United States for many years, because studies seemed to suggest it could pose a cancer risk. Lifting this ban, in the light of contradictory and more recent evidence, could widen the choice of low calorie sweeteners available. Meanwhile, hidden sugar in the form of corn syrup and high fructose corn syrup threatens to compound the weight gain problem associated with sugar.

■ Historical Background and Scientific Foundations

The first sweet foods humans encountered were honey and fruit. Eventually they learned how to extract sugar from sugar cane and, later, sugar beet. There is evidence of the extraction of sugar from sugar cane in India around 2,500 years ago. Sugar cane contains 13 percent sucrose in its fluid; it originated in the South Pacific and was then transported to Asia. An extensive trade in sugar developed, with Venice being the hub for exports to the West. At first, sugar was seen as a medicinal remedy in its own right or used to sweeten bitter pills. It was a luxury item until the fifteenth century, when it passed into more general use and the arts of confectionery, in which sugar is used in candy treats and sweet cooking, were established. Trade in sugar boomed in the eighteenth century and was linked to the expansion of colonial rule. The growth of sugar plantations in the West Indies was a driving force

in the slave trade and fortunes made in sugar helped lay the foundations of the Industrial Revolution.

In 1747 the Prussian chemist Andreas Marggraf (1709–1782) found a way of extracting sugar from sugar beet, and by the early nineteenth century sugar beet factories had been built in France. In the early twenty-first century, 30 to 40 percent of sugar comes from sugar beet and the remainder from sugar cane. The main sugar beet operations are in Russia, Germany, and the United States, whereas sugar cane plantations are located chiefly in India and Brazil.

Sugar is refined from beet or cane by a stepwise process. First the beet or cane is shredded to extract a juice that is 10 to 15 percent sucrose. This is then clarified by mixing it with calcium hydroxide and heating it to coagulate proteins before they are removed. Clarified juice is heated in shallow pans to concentrate the sucrose to around 60 percent and further concentrated in

---

WORDS TO KNOW

CORN SYRUP: An aqueous solution composed of glucose chains of different lengths derived from the acidic or enzymatic breakdown of corn starch, a glucose polymer.

SUGAR: The common name for the smaller molecules of the carbohydrate family, known as the monosaccharides and disaccharides, composed of one sugar unit and two sugar units respectively. Glucose is the monosaccharide that is used as the body's fuel. Sugar is also the common name for sucrose, a disaccharide composed of glucose and fructose, which is also known as fruit sugar.

SWEETNESS: One of the five basic tastes, long associated with pleasure. There are taste buds that detect sweet-tasting molecules on the tongue, and these relay messages to the brain, creating the sensation of sweetness. There are many sweet-tasting compounds, both natural and synthetic.

forms a syrup. Seeding with ... ... ing leads to crystallization of the ... golden crystals coated with a thick brown ... ... molasses. The next step is centrifugation to ... ... parate sugar crystals and molasses. Further purification steps, including de-colorization with activated charcoal, are carried out to produce white sugar.

Several varying sizes of sugar crystals are available. Regular granulated sugar, for example, has crystals that are 0.5 mm in diameter, whereas confectioner's sugar, used to make icing, has crystals that are only 0.01 mm in diameter. There are also a number of brown sugars that are either less refined or refined sugars coated with molasses to change the color. The properties of sugar enable it to have many roles in cooking and baking. It blocks the coagulation of proteins such as egg and interferes with gluten formation in flour, so it improves the texture of cakes and pastries. Sugar also stops baked goods from drying out because it is hygroscopic, drawing water from its surroundings, and hydrophilic, bonding to water and hanging onto it. Sugar has long been a commodity item, and most of the United States population consumes 80 to 100 pounds of sugar per year in one form or another.

The nutritional concern of sugar is that it contains calories, but no other significant nutrients. Too much sugar can lead to weight gain and may also make the control of diabetes difficult. Accordingly, a number of artificial sweeteners have been developed, which impart a sweet taste without as many calories as sugar. Sweeteners come from natural or synthetic sources: For instance, glycyrrhizin,

A man works in a sugar cane field.   *Image copyright Eric Isselee, 2010. Used under license from Shutterstock.com.*

from licorice root, and stevia, which comes from a South American shrub in the sunflower family, have been used as sweetening agents for centuries and are many times sweeter per gram than sucrose, so only need be used in trace amounts. The first synthetic sweeter, saccharin, was derived originally from coal tar in 1879 by researchers at Johns Hopkins University. It is about 500 times sweeter than sucrose and stable in both heat and cold. It became very popular during sugar shortages in World Wars I (114–1918) and II (1939–1945) and with dieters in the 1960s, though its popularity waned in the late 1970s when it was linked in animal studies to bladder cancer. This link was disproved by 2000. It is still used in many products, but the negative cancer association and saccharin's slightly bitter aftertaste led to saccharin sales being surpassed by other, later artificial sweeteners. One such sweetener is aspartame, created in 1969 by joining two amino acids together with a methyl ester group. It is 200 times sweeter than sucrose and is currently used in more than 6,000 foods and beverages. Aspartame's main drawback is that it not stable during heating. The leading synthetic sweetener as of 2010 is Sucralose, a chlorinated sugar discovered in 1989 and introduced to the lucrative artificial sweetener market in 1999 that swiftly surpassed aspartame's sales in the decade after its introduction. It is stable during heating and is 600 times sweeter than sucrose. It can be used in baked goods and is found in more than 4,500 foods and beverages. Sucralose is neither absorbed nor digested, so contributes zero calories to the diet.

■ Impacts and Issues

Corn syrup and high-fructose syrup have become ubiquitous in food because they keep products moister and fresher longer. Regular corn syrup consists of 14 percent glucose, 11 percent maltose, and 55 percent oligosaccharides, which are longer sugar chain molecules. The latter are not sweet, but add viscosity to the syrup. Manufacturers can manipulate the composition of a corn syrup to suit the application. High fructose corn syrup was discovered in the 1960s by adding an enzyme to corn starch, which converts much of the glucose into fructose, which is sweeter. This turned out to be a very cost-effective method of sweetening processed foods. Both corn syrup and high fructose syrup can be classed as "hidden sugars" because they add to the calorie and sugar content of foods without explicitly stating on the label that they are a form of sugar. Therefore, people may gain weight and possibly put themselves at risk of adverse health consequences by consuming processed foods in quantity.

The development of artificial sweeteners has also led to controversy. Cyclamates were developed in 1937 by scientists at the University of Illinois and became very popular as additives in soft drinks. Research involving giving rats very high doses suggested that cyclamate might pose a health risk, so the Food and Drug Administration (FDA)

banned their use in commercially available foods and beverages in 1969. Since the ban, additional research has suggested the risks of cyclamate may have been overstated, and a petition for reversal of the ban was presented to the FDA in 1982. More than 100 countries around the world do allow cyclamates in food and drink, and they were declared safe by the World Health Organization Joint Expert Committee on Food Additives and various other authorities. Whether the FDA will bow to their advice and again allow cyclamates in food remains to be seen.

SEE ALSO *Chocolate; Confectionery and Pastry; Diet and Diabetes; Dietary Guidelines for Americans; Processed Foods; School Lunch Reform; USDA Food Pyramid; Wage Slavery in Food Production; War, Conquest, Colonialism, and Cuisine.*

BIBLIOGRAPHY

Books

Abbott, Elizabeth. *Sugar: A Bittersweet History.* London: Duckworth Overlook, 2009.

Hollander, Gail M. *Raising Cane in the 'Glades: The Global Sugar Trade and the Transformation of Florida.* Chicago: University of Chicago Press, 2008.

Kessler, David A. *The End of Overeating: Taking Control of the Insatiable American Appetite.* Emmaus, PA: Rodale, 2009.

Periodicals

Berfield, Susan, and Michael Arndt. "Kraft's Sugar Rush." *Business Week New York*, no. 4164 (January 25, 2010): 36–39. Available online at: http://www.businessweek.com/magazine/content/10_04/b4164036495789.htm.

"The Everglades—Sugar and Grass." *The Economist* 389, no. 8610 (2008): 55.

Keane, Michael G., et al. "Taxing Sugar-Sweetened Beverages." *New England Journal of Medicine* 362, no. 4 (2010): 368–369.

Web Sites

Better Sugar Cane Initiative (BSI). http://www.bettersugarcane.org/ (accessed October 4, 2010).

Charles, Dan. "Sugar Beet Beatdown: Engineered Varieties Banned." *National Public Radio (NPR)*, September 16, 2010. http://www.npr.org/templates/story/story.php?storyId=129891767 (accessed October 4, 2010).

Parker, Hilary. "A Sweet Problem: Princeton Researchers Find That High-Fructose Corn Syrup Prompts Considerably More Weight Gain." *Princeton University*, March 22, 2010. http://www.princeton.edu/main/news/archive/S26/91/22K07/ (accessed October 4, 2010).

Susan Aldridge

Sustainable Agriculture

■ Introduction

Sustainable agriculture includes a group of practices intended to reduce the environmental impact of food and natural fiber production, while preserving natural resources such as soil, water, air quality, agricultural biodiversity, and wildlife for use and enjoyment by future generations. Interest in sustainable agriculture and in sustainability of other industries has increased greatly since the publishing of the Brundtland Report by the United Nations-sponsored World Commission on the Environment and Development in 1987, under the title *Our Common Future*. However, the techniques and environmental and health concerns of sustainable agriculture draw heavily on earlier movements in biodynamic farming, organic farming, and local food production. As the market for sustainable food products has grown around the world, large agribusinesses have become involved, especially in certified organic food marketing and production. Some consumers, producers, and activists question the contribution of agribusinesses to sustainable agriculture, whereas other consumers and producers see agribusinesses as making a positive contribution to sustainability.

■ Historical Background and Scientific Foundations

In 1924 a group of farmers concerned about recent drops in seed and livestock fertility in Silesia, Germany, in an area now part of Poland, invited Austrian philosopher Rudolf Steiner (1861–1925) to give a series of lectures that came to be known as the Agricultural Course. The Agricultural Course proposed that the farm should be treated as a single organism and that the addition of mineral fertilizers and other inputs sourced from outside of the farm degraded that organism. By 1928 Steiner's followers in Europe had founded Demeter, an organization that created the Demeter Biodynamic Farm Standard, the first set of standards for what later would be known as sustainable agriculture.

Concern about pesticides became widespread in many parts of the world in the early 1960s. Specifically, concerns focused on dichlorodiphenyltrichloroethane (DDT) in reaction to *Silent Spring* by Rachel Carson (1907–1964), which was published in 1962. In this book, Carson, an American marine biologist and science writer, details the consequences of DDT used as a pesticide on the environment and wildlife, particularly birds, including effects such as the production of thinner egg shells, reproductive problems, and death. To address the demand for pesticide-free foods due to fear over the potential effects of pesticide residues in food, new marketing channels between farms and households were created in the 1960s. In the mid-1960s, groups of Japanese women worked with farmers to establish *teikei* gardens and farms. The women's groups agreed to purchase a farm's produce or milk if the farmer abstained from using chemical pesticides. Similar arrangements spread to Austria, Germany, North America, and other areas. In the 1970s, food cooperatives emerged in parts of North America and Europe in which consumers formed groups to make bulk purchases of foods grown without chemical fertilizers and pesticides. Also, health foods or natural foods stores emerged along with specialized retail outlets offering foods grown with fewer chemical inputs and those that were argued to be more natural or more healthful.

As more marketing channels for food grown with fewer chemical pesticides, herbicides, and fertilizers formed, consumers demanded to know in increasing detail about how their food was grown, raised, and processed. One way to provide information was through certification to a set of standards. Non-use of artificial pesticides, herbicides, and fertilizer since the 1960s has been called organic farming. A set of standards for farms or for production is laid out, then those farmers that comply with the standards apply to have their farms or products certified. The specific meaning of what counts as organic or biological or natural varies in different parts of the world. Almost all of the commonly used organic standards rely on third-party certification. This means that a regulator or an organization, independent of all the farms or companies in a supply chain, certifies the farms or the products meet the organic food standard. Certified organic production and sales have grown tremendously since the 1980s when the first third-party certifiers started working on a more commercial basis.

Whereas organic certification has been used to help connect producers and consumers, the term *sustainable agriculture* has come to mean much more than simply abstaining from the use of certain inputs prohibited by organic standards. Following the Brundtland Report, *Our Common Future*, sustainable development was defined as "the ability to meet the needs of the present without compromising the ability of future generations to meet their needs." Sustainability, therefore, stresses not only the current farming systems and their waste products, but the equity of natural resource distribution between the present generation and future generations. In agriculture, sustainability includes not only organic farming but also more comprehensive efforts to make agriculture more environmentally aware and beneficial. One focus in marketing has been to encourage consumers to buy locally produced foods to reduce food miles, a way to quantify the energy consumed to move food from the farm to the consumer. Controlling farm waste, erosion, and soil fertility have been other areas of sustainability research and practice. Science has begun to be applied to sustainable agriculture in academic and research settings. For example, the University of California (UC) system started programs on several of its campuses under the Sustainable Agriculture Research and Education Program (SAREP) in 2001. In some of these programs, the social and economic sustainability of agricultural systems are examined in addition to plant, soil, and animal sciences.

■ Impacts and Issues

While the *teikei* sought to link groups of Japanese housewives to individual farmers with more sustainable practices, the natural food, health food, and organic food market has expanded rapidly since the 1970s. In most of the developed countries that are members of the Organisation for Economic Co-operation and Development (OECD), certified organic foods have moved into almost all food retail sectors, not just specialized stores or consumer food cooperatives. In the United States, the market for certified organic foods and beverages has grown from one billion U.S. dollars in 1990 to 24.8 billion U.S. dollars in 2009 according to the Organic Trade Association. Worldwide, the market for certified organic goods is also growing rapidly, including in several developing countries. In 2005 the worldwide market for certified organic foods was estimated as worth 30 billion

---

WORDS TO KNOW

ECONOMY OF SCALE: A reduction in the cost of production of a product attained by producing more. Economies of scale also refer to cost reductions accrued by geographic concentration of an industry.

FOOD MILES: The distance that food products or the raw ingredients used in food travel between the farm gate and the final producer. Food miles are used as a comparative measure of the environmental impact of transportation in the food industry.

THIRD-PARTY CERTIFICATION: A system in which an organization independent of all the companies in a supply chain certifies that a good reaches particular standards or has particular attributes. Most international organic standards, fair trade standards, humane animal treatment standards, and claims of being not genetically modified, as well as a variety of environmental claims are certified using third-party certification.

U.S. dollars. By 2006 the estimated value had grown to 40 billion U.S. dollars, according to a 2007 study cited by the United Nations Conference on Trade and Development (UNCTAD).

Local production sales are more difficult to track, but farmers' markets that tend to feature foods produced locally numbered 1,755 in the United States in 1994. By 2010, 6,132 farmers' markets could be found in all regions of the United States with sales estimated at one billion U.S. dollars according to the U.S. Department of Agriculture's (USDA) Agricultural Marketing Service (AMS).

The huge annual increases in sales, especially of certified organic foods, have attracted larger agribusinesses to certified organic production, fair trade certified products, locally produced foods, and a variety of other ways to appeal to consumers interested in sustainable agriculture. As larger retailers and agribusinesses carry and use certified organic products, two concerns about the sustainability of organic food production emerge. First, concern with food miles or the distance between the farm gate and the final point of retail continues to be expressed by environmental advocates. These advocates are concerned about the impact of transportation on the environment, specifically the effect fossil fuel emissions may play in contributing to global climate change. Also, some activists question whether larger agribusinesses driven by profits can contribute to sustainable agriculture. Another point of concern is whether current organic standards are actually sustainable over the long term. These activists may distinguish between organic farming and sustainable agriculture.

A minority of activists advocate for a return to subsistence agriculture and deindustrialization of the food

Researchers from the University of California Cooperative Extension teach Hmong farmers sustainable agriculture methods in Fresno, California. *AP Images.*

industry. Although many criticisms have been leveled against larger agribusinesses' new interest in sustainable agriculture, agribusiness defenders look to the potential spread in the use of sustainable agricultural technologies, the potential investment in agricultural research related to sustainability, and how economies of scale may be realized by the entry of agribusinesses into certified organic production and other more sustainable practices.

SEE ALSO *Agribusiness; Agricultural Deforestation; Agricultural Demand for Water; Agricultural Land Reform; Agriculture and International Trade; Agroecology; Biodiversity and Food Supply; Biofuels and World Hunger; Climate Change and Agriculture; Commission on Genetic Resources for Food and Agriculture; Community Supported Agriculture (CSAs); Convention on Biological Diversity (1992); Decollectivization; Desertification and Agriculture; Ethical Issues in Agriculture; Factory Farming; Food and Agriculture Organization (FAO); Food Price Crisis; Food Security; Food Sovereignty; Free Trade and Agriculture; Gender Equality and Agriculture; Genetically Modified Organisms (GMO); Green Revolution (1943); Import Restrictions; International Federation of Organic Agriculture Movements; International Fund for Agricultural Development; Land Availability and Degradation; Population and Food; Rome Declaration on World Food Security (1996); Subsidies; Subsistence Farming; UN Millennium Development Goals; U.S. Agency for International Development (USAID); U.S. Department of Agriculture (USDA); Wage Slavery in Food Production; Waste and Spoilage; Water; Water Scarcity; World Trade Organization (WTO).*

BIBLIOGRAPHY

Books

Francis, Charles A., Raymond P. Poincelot, and George W. Bird. *Developing and Extending Sustainable Agriculture: A New Social Contract.* New York: Haworth Food & Agricultural, 2006.

Hahlbrock, Klaus. *Feeding the Planet: Environmental Protection through Sustainable Agriculture.* London: Haus, 2009.

Madden, Etta M., and Martha L. Finch. *Eating in Eden: Food and American Utopias.* Lincoln: University of Nebraska Press, 2006.

Pretty, Jules N. *Sustainable Agriculture and Food.* London: Earthscan, 2008.

Radbill, Amy. *The Davis Food Co-op Cookbook.* Davis, CA: Davis Food Co-op, 2007.

Periodicals

"The Co-op's Innovative Drive to Promote Fresh Food Sales." *Grocer London* (June 5, 2010): 8–11.

Cooney, Catherine M. "Sustainable Agriculture Delivers the Crops." *Environmental Science & Technology* 40, no. 4 (2006): 1091–1092.

Pollock, Chris, and Jules Pretty. "Farming Could Destroy Earth Unless We Rethink What 'Sustainable' Agriculture Is." *New Scientist* (April 21, 2007): 18–19.

Web Sites

"Introduction to Sustainability: What is Sustainable Agriculture?" *Sustainable Table.* http://www.sustainablet able.org/intro/whatis/ (accessed October 4, 2010).

UN World Commission on Environment and Development. "Our Common Future." *United Nations.* http://www.un-documents.net/wced-ocf.htm (accessed October 4, 2010).

Blake Jackson Stabler

Sustainable Table

■ Introduction

The sustainable table does not represent any one agricultural practice or regulatory definition. Rather, it is a conglomeration of practices, tastes, and beliefs rooted in sustainable agriculture.

To understand the sustainable table is to understand sustainability itself, which may be defined as "meeting the needs of the present without compromising the ability of future generations to meet their own needs." Although similar definitions surfaced beginning in the late 1960s, this definition, first reported in 1987 by the Brundtland Commission (formally known as the United Nations World Commission on Environment and Development), is a generally accepted standard.

The sustainable table celebrates the sensory pleasures of eating based on sustainable food systems. Whereas there is no one definition of the sustainable table, a number of different elements are recognized as core components. On a larger scale, these include efforts to create food-secure local economies, provide access to fresh and healthy foods for all socioeconomic groups, and maintain vibrant farming and ranching communities. Personal eating habits focus on eating minimally processed foods, and foods in season that are locally produced. Emphasis is placed on preserving heirloom plant varieties and heritage animal breeds and reviving artisanal food preparation methods.

■ Historical Background and Scientific Foundations

Sustainable agriculture is not a new phenomenon. Agrarian practices that maintain an ecological balance and maximize productivity have been passed down for thousands of years by generations of farmers. Crop rotation, cover crops, organic fertilizer, intercropping, and integrated crop and animal operations were standard methods.

The Industrial Revolution in the eighteenth and nineteenth centuries brought with it advances in machinery, steam engines, metallurgy, and chemicals. With the advent of train travel in the first part of the nineteenth century, agricultural goods could be transported longer distances without spoiling.

By the end of World War II (1939–1945), mechanization, synthetic chemical use, and government policies that rewarded maximum yields became the favored production methods. Food shortages were much reduced compared to the past, and prices fell. Crops were specifically engineered for large-scale production. As a result, farmers relied on a few plant varieties and animal breeds, sacrificing taste and biodiversity for convenience.

Yet as the trend towards factory farming continued, concerns about the negative effects on human health, the environment, and biodiversity were being voiced. In the United States, a handful of writers, farmers, chefs, agrarians, and environmentalists began to solidify a uniquely American form of the sustainable table. J. I. (Jerome Irving) Rodale (1898–1981) founded the Rodale Institute in 1947 to study the relationship between healthy soil, healthy food, and healthy people. An early devotee of organic agriculture, he paired scientific research with writing and a publishing house. Rodale's descendants have continued with his original mission.

Prolific writer and farmer Wendell Berry (1934–), author of *The Unsettling of America and Home Economics*, argues against industrial agriculture and promotes healthy rural communities, appropriate technologies, and the pleasures of good food. Agrarian and writer Wes Jackson (1936–) understood the importance of the prairie ecosystem, creating The Land Institute in 1976 to promote Natural Systems Agriculture through a combination of ecology and agronomy.

In 1971 chef Alice Waters (1944–) opened Chez Panisse Restaurant in Berkeley, California. Waters used the restaurant as a springboard to showcase fine cuisine highlighting fresh local foods. Her philosophy and advocacy have been instrumental in creating entire local food systems in the Bay Area and beyond from farmers producing heirloom fruits and vegetables, to bakeries, to schoolyard gardens.

Since the turn of the twenty-first century, anecdotal evidence shows a rapid growth in the number of components considered integral to creating a sustainable table. Farmers' markets featuring locally produced foods have increased in total number and in number of customers. Small farms, often located near urban areas, comprise one of the fastest growing segments of the agricultural sector. Restaurants featuring locally produced foods have sprouted up across the country. Backyard gardening and backyard poultry-keeping have made a resurgence.

■ Impacts and Issues

It would be easy to dismiss the sustainable table as an issue invented by the wealthy who can afford locally produced foods prepared by artisans. But there is far more involved: The very crux of the sustainable table is the long-term productivity of land, the conservation and quality of natural resources such as water and soil, and biodiversity through preservation of heirloom plant varieties and heritage animal breeds. Healthy ecosystems lead to healthy farms and, therefore, healthy rural

WORDS TO KNOW

AGRARIAN: Rural, agricultural, or a member of an agrarian movement.

AGRONOMY: The science of cultivation of land, soil management, and crop production.

ARTISANAL: Any product made by hand by a skilled craftsperson.

CARBON FOOTPRINT: A measure of the amount of carbon dioxide released into the atmosphere by a single endeavor or by a company, household, or individual through day-to-day activities over a given period.

FOOD MILES: The distance food is transported from the time of its production until it reaches the consumer.

FOOD SECURITY: When all people at all times have access to sufficient, safe, nutritious food to maintain a healthy and active life.

HEIRLOOM PLANT: A plant that was grown historically but has not been used in modern agriculture on a large scale.

HERITAGE BREED: Traditional, genetically distinct livestock and poultry breeds that were raised by farmers in the past before the reduction of breed variety caused by industrial agriculture.

Vendors at a Hong Kong market sell local, organic produce. © *Peter Llwellyn (L) / Alamy.*

economies. Diverse local economies that include food production create greater community food security and overall economic well-being.

Much of European society still places cultural importance on regional produce and artisanal preparations. Produce is eaten in season with grand celebrations feting the annual bounty. When asparagus is at its spring peak, stores sell specialized steaming pots, restaurants feature asparagus dishes, and crowds form at market stalls selling the vegetable during its short season. Some may be pickled or preserved, but when the asparagus is gone, it is gone until the next year.

One important aspect of the sustainable table is devoted to the difficult-to-quantify aspect of simply enjoying food. The Slow Food Movement developed as a way to bring together all aspects of the sustainable table. Initiated in Italy in 1986, the parent organization, Slow Food International, argues "everyone has a fundamental right to the pleasure of good food and consequently the responsibility to protect the heritage of food, tradition and culture that make this pleasure possible."

Slow Food's work is based on the concept of neo-gastronomy that recognizes the linkages between plate, planet, people, and culture. The organization has national offices in eight countries and a network of 1,300 local chapters called convivia. Convivia hold events in their communities to support the concept that enjoying food to the fullest enriches human existence while protecting the environment and strengthening the economy. Some of the most basic elements of the sustainable table are played out through Slow Food Convivia activities. Events might include shared meals, visits to local farms and artisan food producers, film screenings, or conferences and discussions.

Reducing the amount of fossil fuel used is one approach to creating more sustainable agricultural systems. A 2005 report by the Earth Policy Institute analyzes U.S. food system energy use. Data included in the report show that 21 percent of energy in the Unites States goes toward agricultural production, especially fossil fuels used to make synthetic fertilizers and chemicals. Food processing eats up another 16 percent of the energy, and transportation another 13 percent.

Sustainable agriculture avoids synthetic fertilizers and chemicals. Consuming less processed foods further reduces fossil fuel demand. Purchasing foods grown locally decreases the amount of energy required in order to transport food from farm to market. Professor Tim Lang of London's City University coined the term *food miles* to characterize this transportation energy input. Reducing food miles in particular, and food production's carbon footprint in general, have become highly visible components of the sustainable table.

American First Lady Michelle Obama (1964–) has become one of the most visible spokespersons for the sustainable table through her campaign to reduce childhood obesity. Soon after moving into the White House, the First Lady planted an organic kitchen garden, setting an example that backyard gardens provide healthy, tasty fresh produce and an opportunity for regular physical activity. She spearheads the Let's Move campaign, which is designed to reduce childhood obesity within a generation by changing how children think about food and nutrition.

SEE ALSO *Alice Waters: California and New American Cuisine; Community Supported Agriculture (CSAs); Edible Schoolyard Movement; Ethical Issues in Agriculture; Family Farms; Farm-to-Table Movement; Fusion; Improving Nutrition for America's Children Act of 2010; Locavore; Michael Pollan: Linking Food and Environmental Journalism; Organic Foods Production Act of 1990; Organics; School Lunch Reform; Slow Food Movement; Standard American Diet and Changing American Diet; Sustainable Agriculture; Urban Chicken Movement; Urban Farming/Gardening.*

BIBLIOGRAPHY

Books

Berry, Wendell. *Bringing It to the Table: On Farming and Food.* Berkeley: Counterpoint, 2009.

McNamee, Thomas. *Alice Waters & Chez Panisse: The Romantic, Impractical, Often Eccentric, Ultimately Brilliant Making of a Food Revolution.* New York: Penguin Press, 2007.

Web Sites

The Land Institute. http://www.landinstitute.org/ (accessed October 16, 2010).

Let's Move. http://www.letsmove/ (accessed October 16, 2010).

The Rodale Institute. http://www.rodaleinstitute.org/ (accessed October 16, 2010).

Slow Food International. http://www.slowfood.com/ (accessed October 16, 2010).

The Sustainable Table. http://www.sustainabletable. org/ (accessed October 16, 2010).

United Nations World Commission on Environment and Development. http://www.un-documents.net/ ocf-02.htm#I (accessed October 16, 2010).

U.S. Department of Agriculture (USDA). http://www. usda.gov/ (accessed October 16, 2010).

"What is Sustainable Agriculture?" *University of California Davis.* http://www.sarep.ucdavis.edu/concept. htm (accessed October 16, 2010).

Andrea Abel

Tasting Food

■ Introduction

Taste is one of the chemical senses, enabling humans and other animals to evaluate foodstuffs in the surrounding environment. Smell, the other chemical sense, is closely related to taste. Both make it possible for the brain to respond to different taste and smell molecules when these molecules bind chemically to a receptor molecule on the tongue or in the nose. The binding causes electrical impulses to travel to the brain, where a taste or smell sensation is produced. Put simply, many substances that are poisonous tend to taste bad, whereas those giving nourishment and energy tend to taste pleasurable. The four basic taste sensations are sweet, salty, bitter, and sour, with different chemoreceptor molecules responding to each type of taste molecule. Babies have more taste buds, which contain the taste receptor molecules, than adults do, which is why they are more sensitive to taste and tend to prefer blander foods. The number of taste buds declines with age, which may help explain why older people tend to lose their appetite for some foods previously enjoyed. The pleasure of eating, mediated by the sense of taste and smell, has an important role in maintaining health and good nutrition.

■ Historical Background and Scientific Foundations

The taste buds, or basic taste organs within the papillae, were discovered by German scientists Georg Meissner (1829–1905) and Rudolf Wagner (1805–1864) in the nineteenth century. An adult human has around 10,000 taste buds distributed among the different types of papillae in areas of the tongue's upper surface. Vallate papillae, each containing between 90 and 250 taste buds, are found at the back of the tongue. Fungiform papillae, containing only between one and eight taste buds, are scattered singly on the whole surface of the tongue, particularly near the front tip. The foliate papillae are found at the back edges of the tongue, and house a variable number of taste buds, whereas the filiform papillae, which are found all over the tongue, may not contain any taste buds at all.

The four basic types of taste have long been linked to the geography of the tongue, with sweet tastes being detected mainly at the tip, salt at the front edges, sour at the side, and bitter at the back. This is because the taste buds in different types of papillae contain chemoreceptors that respond to different types of taste molecule. However, the discovery of the many different chemoreceptor molecules in recent years has suggested that this mapping of taste onto the tongue is too simple. Researchers at the University of California San Diego, who discovered chemoreceptors for sweet, umami (a savory taste), bitter, and sour tastes, now say that humans detect basic tastes more or less equally all over the tongue's surface.

The neurochemical pathway by which a taste is perceived is well established. A taste molecule is dissolved in saliva and is exposed to chemoreceptors in the taste bud when it passes down a tiny pore between cells in the taste bud. This is lined with tiny projections called microvilli, bearing chemoreceptor molecules. Binding between taste molecules and receptors causes a chain of intracellular reactions, triggering a nerve impulse that travels through the nerves in contact with the taste bud to the medulla oblongata in the base of the brain. From here, the impulse goes to the thalamus, which is the brain's relay station for environmental stimuli such as taste molecules. The impulse then passes to the parietal lobe of the cerebral cortex, which interprets taste through connections to memory and emotional areas of the brain. As a person eats, each taste molecule sends a complex pattern of impulses, generated by thousands of taste bud receptors, to the brain, resulting in the complex experience of tasting the food.

■ Impacts and Issues

Researchers are still trying to understand what the sensation of taste really is. It may be more appropriate to talk about the flavor of a food as being an interaction

WORDS TO KNOW

PAPILLAE: Small projections on the upper surface of the tongue that give it a rough appearance. Each papilla houses 25 to 250 taste buds. Papillae are also located in the throat, sides of the mouth, and soft palate.

TASTE BUD: A group of cells that are responsive to taste molecules. Taste buds consist of a barrel shaped arrangement of alternating taste receptor cells and supporting cells, the latter acting as a source of new taste receptor cells.

UMAMI: Sometimes known as the fifth basic taste, umami is a savory taste triggered by the presence of amino acids in meat or aged cheese.

between taste, smell, and factors such as texture and temperature. Smell and taste are really separate, but parallel, inputs when something is put in the mouth. Odor molecules are released and go up the passage from the back of the mouth, whereas taste molecules adhere to

A man tastes and brands coffee in Addis Ababa, Ethiopia. *AP Images.*

their receptors on the taste buds. Thereafter, inputs are processed by separate brain pathways, but unite in higher areas of the cerebral cortex to give the sensation of flavor. Without a sense of smell, flavor is diminished.

Taste can also be influenced by what is seen. In a classic experiment, French researchers colored a white wine red with an odorless dye and asked a panel of wine experts to describe its taste. The connoisseurs described the wine using words that suggested they thought they were tasting a red wine.

The experience of taste is also influenced by genetic differences. Experiments have been carried out on people's ability to taste a synthetic compound called propylthiouracil (PROP). Around a quarter of the population are "supertasters" and find PROP intensely bitter, half find it moderately bitter, and the remaining quarter cannot taste it at all. Supertasters may have an overall higher level of tasting ability, perhaps because they have a greater number of fungiform papillae on their tongue. The supertasters are more responsive to bitter compounds including coffee, grapefruit juice, and green tea. They find sugar tastes sweeter and chili hotter. This is important, because tasting preferences may affect health: A supertaster will likely find broccoli, which is full of beneficial vitamins and antioxidants, unpleasant. On the other hand, they may avoid obesity and its related problems by not liking sweet things, because they find the taste overwhelming.

Parents are increasingly encouraging their children to experience different tastes at younger ages than previous generations, after evidence linked early exposure to varied flavors with a more varied and healthy diet in later years. Although many children experience a notorious phase of "picky eating," researchers have found that the phase is often of shorter duration and is less extreme in children who were repeatedly exposed to healthy foods varying in taste, texture, and color when they were preschoolers.

SEE ALSO *Foodways; Human Gastrointestinal System.*

BIBLIOGRAPHY

Books

Banes, Sally, and André Lepecki. *The Senses in Performance.* New York: Routledge, 2007.

Brynie, Faith H. *Brain Sense: The Science of the Senses and How We Process the World around Us.* New York: American Management Association, 2009.

Light, Douglas B. *The Senses.* Your Body: How it Works. Philadelphia, PA: Chelsea House, 2004.

Stevenson, Richard J. *The Psychology of Flavour.* Oxford: Oxford University Press, 2009.

Periodicals

Guerrieri, Ramona, Chantal Nederkoorn, and Anita Jansen. "The Interaction between Impulsivity and a Varied Food Environment: Its Influence on Food Intake and Overweight." *International Journal of Obesity* 32, no. 4 (2008): 708–714.

Korsmeyer, Carolyn. "Review of Making Sense of Taste: Food and Philosophy." *Leonardo* 37, no. 1 (2004): 79–80.

Web Sites

"Physiology of Taste." *Colorado State University.* http://www.vivo.colostate.edu/hbooks/pathphys/digestion/pregastric/taste.html (accessed August 25, 2010).

Susan Aldridge

■ Introduction

Tea refers to the beverage, the leaf, and the plant on which the leaf grows. Grown and served in China since ancient times, tea was introduced to Europeans in the seventeenth century. Several varieties of tea exist, all of which are made from the leaves of the same plant but differ in their processing. Tea often is served with additional ingredients, and in many cultures, traditions or special ceremonies may accompany the serving of tea. The tea trade has existed since a taste for tea was acquired in countries that cannot grow tea, but future growth of the trade is uncertain, as demand is not growing in the traditional export markets of Russia and the United Kingdom.

■ Historical Background and Scientific Foundations

The plant *Camellia sinensis* was cultivated as early as the tenth century BC. The first tea cultivation was probably in the area near where the current borders of China, India, and Myanmar intersect. Tea has been a popular beverage in China, India, and Japan for many centuries. Introduced to Europeans in the seventeenth century, tea quickly rose in popularity on that continent. Tea is a tropical or semi-tropical product, so it is grown commercially in only 36 countries. All types of teas are made using the leaves of the *Camellia sinensis*, but the processing varies for different types of teas.

White tea is made from the very young leaves of the plant when they first appear. They are picked before the leaves develop chlorophyll, so the leaves appear to be white or silver in color. Green tea is made from picked mature leaves, which are then left to dry. After these leaves wither, they are steamed and rolled, then dried again. Black tea is the most popular type, comprising 65 percent of production and 80 percent of traded tea in the early twenty-first century according to the Food and Agriculture Organization (FAO) of the United Nations, and it undergoes extensive processing. The tea is picked mature and left to dry, after which it either is rolled in the orthodox method or cut or torn in the unorthodox method. Left to oxidize in a moist environment for several hours, the tea then is dried or fired before packaging or storing.

Several other varieties of tea are popular in Asia, and they have a growing number of drinkers in other areas of the world. Oolong tea is made in the same manner as black tea, but the oxidization period is reduced. Some teas, and probably the earliest teas in China, are made by steaming, then compressing the tea leaves into a block or ball. Fermented or pu-erh tea is made by fermenting the block or ball of tea. Fermented tea is popular in China and other parts of East Asia. Tea processors refer to the oxidization process as fermentation, but most teas are oxidized for only a few hours; the vast majority of teas are not actually fermented with live and active cultures in the manner of yogurt. A wide variety of aromatic ingredients can be added when blending teas to impart particular flavors. Flavored teas include the addition of bergamot, citrus peels, vanilla, lavender, lotus, jasmine, and other aromatics.

Tea in most countries is prepared from loose tea. Sometimes the tea leaves are boiled with water, but usually boiling water is poured over the tea. Some preparers form a strong brew to which they then add hot water to serve. Some strain out the leaves or put the leaves in a metal mesh ball placed in the water so that they can be removed. Others allow the leaves to settle then pour tea from a pot, being careful to retain the leaves in the pot. In some areas of the world, the individual teacups will have tea leaves floating in them. Starting in the 1920s, producers in the United States used gauze and then paper to deliver tea in a ready-to-use package—the teabag. Quickly adopted in the United States, use of the teabag began to spread, first to the United Kingdom in the 1950s and later to other parts of the world. In the 1980s bottled teas appeared in Japan, and afterward these convenience foods expanded into other countries.

Tea is served in a variety of ways. Most tea is consumed hot immediately after it is made, but consumers of tea in the United States often drink cold, iced tea. Tea can be sweetened with sugar, honey, or jam, and is often served with milk or lemon added. In areas of Tibet, Pakistan, Central Asia, Nepal, and Mongolia, all countries in Asia, tea often is served with salt and butter, sometimes with butter made from yak's milk. Tea may undergo a single steeping, the process of allowing the leaves to release their flavor into the water, but in many cultures multiple steepings of the same leaves are common.

Many cultural traditions are built around the serving of tea. Tea ceremonies are common in East Asia, whereas special places for drinking tea or special events known as tea parties are found in other cultures. Since the early 1990s, a variety of evidence of the health benefits of tea drinking has been published. Most studies examine the potential health benefits of the antioxidants found in tea.

WORDS TO KNOW

ANTIOXIDANT: A substance that inhibits oxidization or slows the progress of oxidization.

THIRD-PARTY CERTIFICATION: A system in which an organization independent of all the companies in a supply chain certifies that a good reaches particular standards or has particular attributes. Most international organic standards, fair trade standards, claims of being not genetically modified, and a variety of environmental claims are certified using third-party certification.

TROPICAL PRODUCT: An agricultural product that can be cultivated only in a relatively warm climate. Tropical products include tea, coffee, cocoa, cotton, pineapples, bananas, and a wide variety of other tropical fruits.

Green tea pickers harvest tea leaves in springtime at the foot of Mt. Fuji, Japan. *Image copyright Hiroshi Ichikawa, 2010. Used under license from Shutterstock.com.*

■ Impacts and Issues

As tea is popular in countries in which it does not grow, the tea trade has been important since the seventeenth century. China is the largest exporter of tea. Kenya, India, and Sri Lanka are also major exporters. The largest importers of tea are Russia, the United Kingdom, Pakistan, and the United States, according to the FAO. The largest consumers are India, China, Russia, and Japan. Most tea is grown on plantations, sometimes called estates, but plantation labor conditions have been controversial and labor rights violations have been suspected. Women perform the majority of both field and processing work on tea plantations, which is time-sensitive and labor intensive.

Smallholders, farmers who own or have access to small plots of land, usually less than two hectares, also grow tea. Efforts to encourage smallholder production, especially in East Africa, to be sold in developed countries have been assisted by labeling tea "organic" or "fair trade" through third party certification systems. Tea imports by the large import markets have been relatively stable for many years, revealing saturation of those markets. However, the market for green tea is expected to grow in developed countries due to its purported health benefits. Also, according to the FAO, potential growth in tea-growing regions is largely unexplored, as in these countries, consumers on average use only one tenth of the volume of tea used by consumers in the saturated markets such as Russia and the United Kingdom.

SEE ALSO *Agriculture and International Trade; Asian Diet; Caffeine; Fair Trade; Foodways; Functional Foods; Gender Equality and Agriculture; Gourmet Hobbyists and Foodies; Phytochemicals (Phytonutrients); Religion and Food; Women's Role in Global Food Preparation.*

BIBLIOGRAPHY

Books

Harney, Michael. *The Harney & Sons Guide to Tea.* New York: Penguin Press, 2008.

Heiss, Mary L., and Robert J. Heiss. *The Story of Tea: A Cultural History and Drinking Guide.* Berkeley, CA: Ten Speed Press, 2007.

Ho, Chi-Tang, Jen-Kun Lin, and Fereidoon Shahidi. *Tea and Tea Products: Chemistry and Health-Promoting Properties.* Boca Raton, FL: CRC Press, 2009.

Hohenegger, Beatrice. *Liquid Jade: The Story of Tea from East to West.* New York: St. Martin's Press, 2006.

Hohenegger, Beatrice, and Terese T. Bartholomew. *Steeped in History: The Art of Tea.* Los Angeles: Fowler Museum at UCLA, 2009.

Jolliffe, Lee. *Tea and Tourism: Tourists, Traditions and Transformations.* Clevedon, UK: Channel View Publications, 2007.

Ohki, Sadako. *Tea Culture of Japan.* New Haven, CT: Yale University Art Gallery, 2009.

Rose, Sarah. *For All the Tea in China: How England Stole the World's Favorite Drink and Changed History.* New York: Viking, 2010.

Periodicals

Cole, Thomas B. "The Tea." *JAMA: The Journal of the American Medical Association* 301, no. 9 (2009): 914.

Kuriyama, Shinichi, Yoshikazu Nishino, Yoshitaka Tsubono, and Ichiro Tsuji. "Green Tea Consumption and Mortality in Japan—Reply." *JAMA: The Journal of the American Medical Association* 297, no. 4 (2007): 360.

Schneider, Craig, and Tiffany Segre. "Green Tea: Potential Health Benefits." *American Family Physician* 79, no. 7 (2009): 591–594.

"Tea Drinking." *JAMA: The Journal of the American Medical Association* 293, no. 5 (2005): 632.

Web Sites

Edgar, Julie. "Health Benefits of Green Tea." *WebMD.* http://www.webmd.com/food-recipes/features/health-benefits-of-green-tea (accessed October 25, 2010).

Thibodeaux, Raymond. "India's Tea Trade Features New Brew." *VOANews.com,* September 21, 2010. http://www.voanews.com/english/news/asia/VOA-Indias-Tea-Trade-Features-New-Brew-103424084.html (accessed October 25, 2010).

Blake Jackson Stabler

Television and Food

■ Introduction

Food-related television shows are among the earliest and most enduring shows on television. The first television food shows developed from radio broadcasts were designed to provide homemakers with information on cooking and other topics. Throughout most of television history, food-related shows on television revolved around the concept of providing home cooks with instruction on preparing meals at home. Pioneers of this genre, including James Beard (1903–1985) and Julia Child (1912–2004), used television to introduce and popularize foreign cuisines in the United States.

The number of food-related television shows has grown steadily since the mid-1990s, which is attributable in part to the establishment of cable television channels dedicated to food programming. Food-related television programming moved beyond educational cooking shows and began featuring travel-related food shows, reality-based competitions, and other non-instructional programs. Although these shows have expanded the popular appeal of food-related programming, some chefs and gourmets argue that many television food shows cater to mass consumerism and fall short of the culinary standards established by Beard, Child, and other chefs who sought to elevate home cooking.

■ Historical Background and Scientific Foundations

Television cooking shows evolved from cooking and home economics radio shows of the 1920s. In 1926 the Farm Radio Service launched *Housekeeper's Chat*, a radio program that featured household tips for homemakers, including food preservation and preparation. The radio broadcast featured Aunt Sammy, a fictitious character. By the early 1940s the first locally-produced television cooking shows began to appear. Like *Housekeeper's Chat*, and other radio programs, early television cooking

programs presented recipes that were accessible to most homemakers. World War II-era programs also featured instructions on cooking for a family using rationed food supplies.

The first nationally televised cooking show was *I Love to Eat*, featuring James Beard. *I Love to Eat* premiered on NBC in August 1946 as a 15-minute program before expanding to 30 minutes in April 1947. Only one audio recording from the show exists. Beard, however, went on to host other television cooking shows. In the 1950s Beard introduced American audiences to French cuisine. Beard became the first television celebrity chef, and he is recognized as one of the central figures in the American culinary landscape of the twentieth century.

Although Beard may have introduced American television audiences to French cuisine, Julia Child popularized French cooking and launched a new era of television cooking shows. Child's *The French Chef* first aired in 1962, produced by WGBH in Boston, Massachusetts. Her affable style, enthusiasm, and distinctive voice made Child a celebrity, and her relaxed approach, including her willingness to accept mistakes, made French cuisine accessible to American home cooks and opened the door for other ethnic cuisine programming in the United States. Child focused on using fresh ingredients and preparing meals from scratch. This approach provided a respite from the cooking shows of the 1950s, which focused on the use of processed foods to assemble casseroles and other quick meals.

Whereas Child emerged as an unlikely television celebrity and cultural icon, British chef Graham Kerr (1934–) established the television cooking show model that persisted for nearly three decades. Kerr's *The Galloping Gourmet*, which debuted in 1969, was the first television cooking show to focus on the entertainment aspect of the show over the instructional aspect. Kerr's good looks, comedic purpose, and boundless energy—he ran around the set and leaped over furniture—broadened the appeal of television cooking shows. *The Galloping Gourmet* also featured innovations that became staples of future cooking shows, including a live audience. Most cooking shows throughout the 1970s, 1980s, and early 1990s followed the model established by *The Galloping Gourmet*. During this period, however, television cooking shows presented a wider variety of cuisines, including Chinese, Italian, Cajun, Mexican, and others.

■ Impacts and Issues

Television food programming entered a new era in 1993 with the launch of TV Food Network, the first cable television network devoted solely to food shows. The network featured a collection of cooking shows, largely based on format established by *The Galloping Gourmet*. A full-time network with dedicated food programming, it also spawned a new generation of celebrity chefs, including Emeril Lagasse (1959–), Bobby Flay (1964–), and Mario Batali (1960–). In 2002 the Food Network debuted a travel-related culinary show, *A Cook's Tour*, featuring Anthony Bourdain (1956–). In 2005 Bourdain and the show's concept, reworked as *No Reservations*, moved to the Travel Channel.

Many chefs and gourmets have criticized culinary programming on the Food Network and other networks for focusing too heavily on entertainment value and the appearance and personality of hosts. Critics assert that food programming since the turn of this century has

Chef Hiroyuki Sakai films an episode of *Iron Chef*, a Japanese television cooking show, in 1997. The show was later adapted for American audiences in the series *Iron Chef America*. *AP Images.*

moved away from instructional programming towards entertainment. Furthermore, critics note that the instructional shows that remain on television often emphasis quick, easy cooking that often relies too heavily on processed foods.

Food television programming tends to follow broader television broadcasting trends, and accordingly has added reality show competitions. In May 2005 the American television network Fox launched *Hell's Kitchen*, featuring chefs competing for a position in the kitchen of the restaurant run by British chef Gordon Ramsay (1967–). In June 2005 the Food Network launched its own reality-based competition, *The Next Food Network Star*. The show features chefs and other culinary personalities competing to host a series on the Food Network. In March 2006 Bravo debuted *Top Chef*, a competition among chefs for an editorial feature in a culinary magazine, money, and other prizes. In Britain, *The Restaurant* features non-chef pairs competing for the privilege of opening a restaurant with chef Raymond Blanc (1949–).

Many celebrity television chefs have used their fame to support a number of charities, including those that promote healthy eating, employment for disadvantaged youth, and other causes. British chef Jamie Oliver (1975–) promotes healthy eating habits and decreasing consumption of fast food and other processed foods. Oliver's television shows *Jamie's Ministry of Food* and *Jamie Oliver's Food Revolution* saw Oliver attempt to inspire residents of Rotherham, Yorkshire (United Kingdom), and Huntington, West Virginia, to consume healthy meals. In 2002 Oliver established the Fifteen Foundation, which takes 15 young adults with a history of drug abuse or criminal involvement and trains them to work in the hospitality industry. Gordon Ramsay (1966–) regularly raises money for spina bifida and HIV/AIDS research. American chef Cat Cora (1967–),

who stars on the Food Network's *Iron Chef*, serves as a UNICEF ambassador and established Chefs for Humanity, a charity that supports a number of food-centric charity and educational programs.

SEE ALSO *Advertising Food; Celebrity Chef Phenomenon; Food and the Internet; Food Critics and Ratings; Food Fads; Food Styling; Gourmet Hobbyists and Foodies; Movies, Documentaries, and Food.*

BIBLIOGRAPHY

Books

Collins, Kathleen. *Watching What We Eat: The Evolution of Television Cooking Shows.* New York: Continuum, 2009.

Harris, Patricia, David Lyon, and Sue McLaughlin. *The Meaning of Food: The Companion to the PBS Television Series.* Guilford, CT: Globe Pequot Press, 2005.

Miller, Emily W. *How to Cook Like a Top Chef.* San Francisco: Chronicle Books, 2010.

Pritchard, David. *Shooting the Cook: A True Story about Food, Television, and the Rise of TV's Superchefs.* London: Fourth Estate, 2009.

Web Sites

Cooking Channel. http://www.cookingchanneltv.com/ (accessed October 31, 2010).

Food Network.com. http://www.foodnetwork.com/ (accessed October 31, 2010).

Rogers, Thomas. "How Food Television Is Changing America." *Salon.com,* February 26, 2010. http://www.salon.com/food/feature/2010/02/26/food_network_krishnendu_ray (accessed October 31, 2010).

Joseph P. Hyder

Texas Beef Group v. Winfrey

■ Introduction

Texas Beef Group v. Winfrey (11 F.Supp.2d 858, N.D.Tex.1998 and 201 F.3d 680, 5th Cir. 2000) was a United States court case presented under state food libel and disparagement laws. Libel is the false or malicious publication of an untrue statement that injures the reputation of a person or business. In the context of food, libel is a legal claim that can arise when someone falsely and publicly states that a certain food is somehow "not fit for human consumption."

Texas Beef Group v. Winfrey contested statements made on the popular U.S. daytime talk show, the *Oprah Winfrey Show* in 1996 about the safety of beef raised in the United States and the alleged risk of contracting the human form of mad cow disease (bovine spongiform encephalopathy) from consuming U.S. beef. The beef industry blamed slumping beef sales on Winfrey's emphatic on-air statement that what she learned putting the show together and from the comments of her guests had "stopped [her] cold from eating another hamburger!" Winfrey eventually prevailed, declaring afterward the decision of the Court of Appeals that "free speech doesn't just live, it rocks."

■ Historical Background and Scientific Foundations

On February 26, 1989, the television editorial news program *60 Minutes* aired a feature in which it claimed that apples grown in the United States were contaminated by the pesticide Alar (daminozide). Environmental advocates interviewed during the segment asserted that Alar posed a serious cancer risk in children. After the program aired, sales of apples plummeted, triggering millions of dollars in losses to apple farms and apple product manufacturers. A group of farmers from the state of Washington sued CBS, the network that broadcast the program. The growers asserted that most apple growers in Washington did not use Alar and even if they did, that the reports used in the broadcast were false and that there was no scientific evidence specifically linking Alar to health problems in humans. The growers lost their suit.

In response to the Alar case, several state legislatures in areas with robust agricultural industries enacted laws that prohibited the disparagement of agricultural and food products. These food disparagement acts, or food libel laws, made it easier for food producers to sue their critics and to protect the reputation of their foods in the media. Critics of the laws noted that many states passed food libel laws that made it easer for a potentially libeled food producer to recover damages than it would be for a potentially libeled person to collect damages.

In 1995 British physicians and researchers documented the first deaths in Britain from a variant form of Creutzfeldt-Jakob disease (CJD or vCJD). In March 1996 the British government announced a suspected link between bovine spongiform encephalopathy (BSE, commonly called mad cow disease) in cows and vCJD in humans. Cattle-feeding practices and meat were linked respectively to the spread of BSE in British cattle and the emergence of vCJD. Britain moved to ban the inclusion of beef remnants in cattle feed and to slaughter livestock most likely to be infected with BSE. British beef was banned from export for more than 32 months. Media attention, however, focused on the victims of vCJD and the possibility of BSE and vCJD appearing in other countries.

In April 1996, nationally syndicated talk show host Oprah Winfrey (1954–) aired a program called "Dangerous Food" in which she discussed BSE and CJD dangers with meat, *E. coli* contamination of hamburgers, food handling practices, restaurant food handling, foodborne illnesses from eating raw oysters, contaminated water supplies, and risks from popular herbal tea drinks.

Winfrey's segment on BSE featured a panel of guests discussing the appearance of CJD in Britain, the effects of the fatal disease on its victims, the impacts on victims' families, cattle farming and slaughter practices, the possibility of BSE and CJD emerging in the United States, and preventive measures that government regulators, food producers, and consumers could take to reduce the risk of the disease. Winfrey's panel included Gary Weber from the National Cattlemen's Beef Association, Will Hueston from the United States Department of Agriculture (USDA), and Howard Lyman, director of the Humane Society's "Eating with a Conscience" vegetarianism and food-source awareness campaign.

During the broadcast, Lyman asserted that BSE was an immediate threat in the United States and that the disease could become epidemic. Hueston and Weber countered that several of Lyman's statements were scientifically inaccurate, factually inaccurate, or misleading. Lyman himself admitted during the taping of the program that at that time, no BSE had been detected in the U.S. beef industry. However, that statement, as well as several arguments about the more rigorous testing and inspection standards for beef in the United States as then compared with Britain, were edited out of the

final broadcast version of the program. Critics note that Weber and Hueston make some misleading arguments in the unbroadcast portions of the taped interviews, as

Texas cattleman Paul Engler reacts to a verdict by an Amarillo, Texas, jury that rejected a libel lawsuit against Oprah Winfrey and Howard Lyman for disparaging comments about beef. *AP Images.*

well, in regards to how many feed producers were participating in a voluntary ban on cattle remnants in livestock feed and the purported efficacy of heating remnants to kill parasites before adding them to feed.

Winfrey's show, which typically boasts millions of regular viewers, allegedly had an immediate, negative economic effect on the U.S. beef industry. Sales of beef decreased. The market price of cattle dropped from almost $62 per hundred weight to around $56 per hundred weight the same day the broadcast aired. However, critics of the so-called "Oprah Cattle Crash Effect" note that the market forces such as increased feed prices and an oversupply of meat for commercial sale may have also significantly contributed to lost revenues in the industry.

Winfrey aired a follow-up to the show two weeks later, allowing government regulators and beef industry representatives to again refute Lyman's claims. Lyman was not invited back for the second show. Despite reassurances that U.S. beef was safe and that no traces of BSE had been found in U.S. herds, the meat industry claimed that sales continued to falter.

In May 1996, just over a month after Winfrey's first "Dangerous Foods" program, a group of Texas cattlemen filed suit against Harpo, the show's production company, Winfrey, Lyman, and others associated with the broadcast. The cattlemen sued under Texas' False Disparagement of Perishable Food Products for $10.3 million in damages. They claimed that Winfrey's show had disparaged U.S. beef by giving consumers the false impression that BSE was present in U.S. beef and that U.S. beef was somehow unsafe and "not fit for human consumption."

Despite their reliance on the state food libel law created after the Alar apples case, the plaintiff cattlemen and the beef industry interests that joined the suit lost at trial in 1998. Two years later, they lost again on appeal. The first court found that cattle before slaughter were not sufficiently perishable—a requirement under Texas' act. The court reasoned that the unslaughtered cows of cattlemen waiting for better prices may have diminished in monetary value, but they were not without some value. The appeals court focused more on the elements of the traditional libel and looked at Lyman's intent in making his statements. They held that the cattlemen could not prove that Lyman knew his statements were false.

■ Impacts and Issues

As of 2009, 13 U.S. states had enacted some form of food libel laws, known colloquially also as "veggie libel laws": Alabama, Arizona, Colorado, Florida, Georgia, Idaho, Louisiana, Mississippi, North Dakota, Ohio, Oklahoma, South Dakota, and Texas.

Libel laws in a food context have been tested in other countries as well. In Britain, the longest running case in the nation's history was one of alleged food libel. The ten-year long "McLibel Case" involved international fast-food giant McDonalds suing two environmental activists, Helen Steel and David Morris, over a pamphlet that criticized the company and its food products. McDonald's actually won two separate hearings of the case in UK courts, but refused to collect the judgment awarded because of the bad press the company had received as a result of the case. However, the European Court of Human Rights found on behalf Steel and Morris, holding that the British government had violated the pair's freedom of expression and fair trail rights.

Many of the legal issues surrounding the Winfrey case turned on there being no recorded case of BSE in the U.S. cattle population at the time the mad cow disease segment aired. Since then, BSE has appeared in cattle in Canada, continental Europe, and Ireland. As of 2010, three cases of BSE had been identified in the United States. On December 23, 2003, the USDA testing confirmed a diagnosis of BSE in a cow that was imported from Canada. In 2004–2005, the first endemic case was confirmed in Texas. One other case was confirmed in Alabama in 2006.

Since BSE was confirmed in the United States, the government has enacted and strengthened bans on including cattle remnants in livestock feed. It maintains its 1997 mammalian-to-ruminant feed ban and screens feed for ingredient adulteration. However, meat producers are still permitted to test for BSE in some products after cows from several sources have been combined into one food product (such as ground beef).

Winfrey has said that she will no longer speak publicly on the issues that spurred the court cases. She has, however, made all of the production notes and recordings of the original, unedited interviews open for review. While shying away from discussing the beef industry, Winfrey aired a show on questionable practices in the poultry industry in 2008.

SEE ALSO *Advertising Food; Agribusiness; E. Coli Contamination; Factory Farming; Food Inspection and Standards; Food Recalls; Foodborne Diseases; Free Trade and Agriculture; Humane Animal Farming; Import Restrictions; Livestock Intensity and Demand; Mad Cow Disease and vCJD; Meat Inspection Act of 1906; Meats; Television and Food; Wholesome Meat Act of 1967.*

BIBLIOGRAPHY

Web Sites

"Bovine Spongiform Encephalopathy." *U.S. Food and Drug Administration (FDA).* http://www.fda. gov/AnimalVeterinary/GuidanceCompliance Enforcement/ComplianceEnforcement/Bovine SpongiformEncephalopathy/default.htm (accessed September 28, 2010).

Collins, Ronald K. L., and Jonathan Bloom. "Win or Lose, Dissing Food Can be Costly." *Foodspeak: Center for Science in the Public Interest,* March 8, 1999. http://cspinet.org/foodspeak/oped/winorloss.htm (accessed September 28, 2010).

Lyman, Howard. "Texas Cattleman vs. Howard Lyman and Oprah Winfrey." *Howard Lyman: Mad Cowboy.* http://www.madcowboy.com/01_BookOP.000.html (accessed September 28, 2010).

"Texas Cattlemen v. Oprah Winfrey." *Media Libel.* http://medialibel.org/cases-conflicts/tv/oprah.html (accessed September 28, 2010).

Adrienne Wilmoth Lerner

Therapeutic Diets

■ Introduction

Therapeutic diets are used for preventing or treating specific diseases. The most extreme form of therapeutic diet is the feeding by tube, which is necessary in cases where people cannot independently consume sufficient nutrition to support body function. The parenteral or enteral feeding regime, which is always performed under medical supervision, saves the patient from malnutrition or starvation. There are also some diseases where strict control of diet is needed. One example is celiac disease, a condition in which gluten in wheat and other grains must be avoided, and another is kidney disease, in which a low-sodium diet may be needed. People with diabetes also eat in a therapeutic fashion, often counting food exchanges or carbohydrates. Athletes have special nutritional needs because of their very high levels of physical activity, which require high-energy input in terms of carbohydrates and a high level of hydration to replace fluid losses. The most popular therapeutic diet is the weight loss diet, of which there are many different versions. Whereas initial weight loss from calorie deficit is easy to achieve, maintaining weight loss is more challenging and most reducing diets are not successful in the long term without a maintenance regime. There is no shortage of dietary advice available, but much is not based upon sound science. Information on therapeutic diets is best obtained from reliable sources.

■ Historical Background and Scientific Foundations

Therapeutic diets have always been part of medical practice and were popular even before the scientific principles of nutrition and medicine were established. A diet is an eating plan that is intended to meet some specific health goal. Diets are available to help prevent cancer and prevent or manage heart disease and high blood pressure. Diet also plays a vital role in the management of Type 2 diabetes. Then there are medically supervised diets, of which the most important are the enteral and parenteral feeding regimes to help people who cannot feed themselves. Enteral nutrition is appropriate when someone's digestive system is functioning normally, but the person cannot swallow, perhaps because of a stroke, or cannot eat normally because of severe burns. The liquid food given in the nasogastric tube should contain all the person's nutrient requirements and is administered either continuously or at intervals. Enteral nutrition can cause various complications, some of which can be life threatening, including aspiration of food into the lungs. When the digestive system is not functioning, as in a malabsorption disorder, or must be kept free of food for some time, as in ulcerative colitis, parenteral nutrition is necessary. Intravenous feeding can also cause problems, including infection, which is always a risk with a catheter.

A gluten-free diet is essential for people who have celiac disease. The autoimmune reaction to gluten in

---

WORDS TO KNOW

CELIAC DISEASE: An autoimmune disease in which exposure to gluten in wheat products causes acute inflammation of the lining of the small intestine. Symptoms of celiac disease include chronic diarrhea, fatigue, and in infants, failure to thrive.

ENTERAL NUTRITION: Feeding through a tube that goes in through the nose and down to the stomach. Long-term enteral nutrition may involve a gastrostomy tube being inserted into the stomach through an incision in the abdomen.

PARENTERAL NUTRITION: Feeding intravenously, bypassing the digestive system entirely. An intravenous tube called a catheter is inserted into a vein, usually under the collarbone, to deliver the food.

celiac disease leads to malabsorption, through destroying the villi on the inner lining of the small intestine. These tiny projections play an essential part in food absorption. Malabsorption causes weakness and weight loss in adults and failure to thrive in infants. There is no cure for celiac disease, and treatment consists of a strictly gluten-free diet, which is important because those who do not follow it are more prone to cancers of the digestive system. Gluten, the complex protein that gives wheat dough its stretchy texture and enables it to rise, is found in wheat, as well as rye, barley, and spelt. A gluten-free diet should exclude all products made from these grains. People with celiac disease are usually also advised to avoid oats as well, as it is thought that avenin, the main protein in oats, provokes an autoimmune response similar to that caused by gluten. There are also some unexpected sources of gluten, including some thickeners and stabilizers used in processed foods, certain food additives such as caramel and maltose, whisky, and gin, which are distilled from grain. Some people with celiac disease will cope with products containing minute amounts of gluten, such as the list above, but other patients are extremely sensitive and will react even to trace amounts. The safest approach may be to rely upon home cooking and baking, with thoroughly vetted gluten-free ingredients.

A low-salt diet may be prescribed for people who have liver disease, kidney disease, heart disease, or hypertension. This means limiting sodium to about 2000 mg or less per day, and sometimes substituting potassium chloride for sodium chloride, or table salt.

Sports nutrition is a specialized type of therapeutic diet that is intended to improve performance rather than treat or prevent disease. In the past, a high-protein diet was assumed to be best for athletes because it would build muscle. In fact, it is now known that excess protein is burned as energy or converted into fat. Because carbohydrates are a more efficient source of energy than protein, the emphasis has switched to eating foods such as pasta before a big game or competition. An athlete may lose much more fluid than a person with a normal level of activity, so adequate hydration is another important

A teenager fixes a plate of salad during dining period at the Academy of the Sierras, a new yearlong therapeutic boarding school for overweight adolescents. The school combines a strict eating plan and a ramped-up activity schedule with counseling and college prep courses to attack students' problems from several angles. *AP Images.*

aspect of sports nutrition. Athletes may need to consume many more calories than the usual requirements, particularly if they are involved in high-intensity activity. They also need to take great care not to consume supplements that are on the list of performance-enhancing drugs, as this could earn them a lengthy ban if detected in a routine urine test.

Perhaps the most common of the therapeutic diets is the weight loss diet. Surveys show that many people are on a reducing diet, yet rates of overweight and obesity in many countries continue to rise. There are many approaches to weight loss, including low carbohydrate, low fat, calorie counting, and food combining. If they lead to a calorie deficit of even 100 or 200 calories per day compared to the calorie intake recommended, then weight loss should occur. The problem seems to be not so much one of losing weight, but of maintaining the weight loss. The vast majority of people on a weight loss diet put the excess weight back on, and often more, within about one year if they do not follow a maintenance regime.

■ Impacts and Issues

There is a great deal of dietary advice available in popular books written by self-styled nutritionists. Claims that specific diets can cure cancer, diabetes, and other diseases should be treated with extreme caution. Therapeutic diets are formulated according to accepted scientific principles of medicine and physiology, and are most effective, along with causing the fewest side effects, when followed under the supervision of a medical professional. Diets that are restrictive are also best approached with medical supervision, either by a doctor or a registered dietitian, in order to avoid nutritional deficiency problems. Where there is a known link between a specific food and a serious allergy or a disease such as celiac disease, then an elimination diet is essential. But for most people, following diets that exclude major food groups, such as wheat or dairy, may offer no health benefit and may be harmful.

Physicians, patients, and often the patient's families face a labyrinth of ethical considerations when enteral tube feedings no longer serve a therapeutic purpose to promote healing or well-being, but become maintenance for people who are otherwise approaching the end of life. Physicians describe a repeating spiral of complications that often occurs when debilitated persons, especially those with dementia, experience long-term tube feeding, including agitation, tube removal, aspiration pneumonia, tube reinsertion, and so on. Persons nearing the end of life often choose to forgo long-term therapeutic tube feedings and have caregivers instead focus on comfort measures. A dying person experiences little hunger or thirst. Ice chips and lubricants have been shown to be more effective than tube feedings to relieve symptoms of end-stage dry mouth and dry lips. Over-treatments including excessive long-term tube feedings were seen as major motivators for the patient's rights movement of the 1970s and 1980s, which ultimately resulted in the 1995 Patient's Bill of Rights. Many people have a living will or advanced directives that outline their wishes in case they become unable to express them and long-term tube feeding becomes necessary to sustain their life. Persons can also designate a trusted healthcare proxy to make healthcare decisions on their behalf. Ethical and legal standards have been developed to assist physicians and their patients in making informed decisions about withholding or withdrawing treatments, including long-term nutrition administered via feeding tube.

SEE ALSO *Changing Nutritional Needs throughout Life; Diet and Cancer; Diet and Diabetes; Diet and Heart Disease; Diet and Hypertension; Food Allergies; Gluten Intolerance; Lactose Intolerance; Nutrition; Salt, Nitrites, and Health.*

BIBLIOGRAPHY

Books

Lutz, Carroll A., and Karen R. Przytulski. *Nutrition & Diet Therapy*. Philadelphia: F. A. Davis Co, 2011.

Mahan, L. Kathleen, and Sylvia Escott-Stump. *Krause's Food, Nutrition, & Diet Therapy*. St. Louis: W.B. Saunders, 2008.

Payne, Anne, and Helen M. Barker. *Advancing Dietetics and Clinical Nutrition*. Edinburgh, Scotland: Churchill Livingstone, 2010.

Periodicals

Chan, Lingtak-Neander. "A 'Gutsy Move': Tackling Enteral Feeding Intolerance in Critically Ill Patients." *Nutrition in Clinical Practice* 25, no. 1 (2010): 10–12.

Haub, Mark D. "Sports Nutrition: Energy Metabolism and Exercise." *JAMA: The Journal of the American Medical Association* 299, no. 19 (2008): 2330–2331.

Körner, Uwe, et al. "Ethical and Legal Aspects of Enteral Nutrition." *Clinical Nutrition* 25, no. 2 (2006): 196–202.

McCauley, Sharon M., and Mary H. Hager. "Why Are Therapeutic Diet Orders an Issue Now and What Does It Have to Do with Legal Scope of Practice?" *Journal of the American Dietetic Association* 109, no. 9 (2009): 1515–1519.

Web Sites

American Dietetic Association. http://www.eatright.org/default.aspx (accessed October 15, 2010).

Susan Aldridge

Truth in Labeling

■ Introduction

Food labels provide important information to consumers regarding ingredients, nutritional content, and production processes. Without accurate food labels, consumers would have difficulty ascertaining a product's nutrition content or whether a product contains preservatives or other additives, allergens, trans fats, or other ingredients. Until the early twentieth century, food manufacturers could add deleterious ingredients without providing any information about these harmful, or even deadly, ingredients to consumers. Over the past century, governments have enacted a number of laws establishing standards for food labeling in order to protect consumers.

Food labeling remains a prominent topic as consumers seek ever more information about food ingredients, nutrition, and manufacturing. The truth-in-labeling movement calls for food labels to express information about food products in an open manner so consumers may have the knowledge to make more informed decisions about food consumption. Truth-in-labeling advocates argue that food labeling regulations must keep pace with scientific research that reveals the health benefits or drawbacks of certain ingredients.

■ Historical Background and Scientific Foundations

Laws regulating the labeling of food products date back more than 100 years. In 1906 the U.S. Congress passed the United States' first major food and drug regulatory law—the Pure Food and Drug Act of 1906. The Act prohibited the manufacture, transportation, or sale of adulterated food or drug products. The Act also enacted a labeling requirement for the manufacturers of drugs that contain habit-forming ingredients, such as cannabis, cocaine, heroin, or morphine. Previously, companies did not have to disclose whether food or drug products contained these ingredients. In 1913 the Gould Amendment required that food packages be "plainly and conspicuously marked on the outside of the package in terms of weight, measure, or numerical count."

The Federal Food, Drug, and Cosmetics (FD&C) Act of 1938 expanded the FDA's authority and instituted new food and drug labeling requirements. The FD&C granted the FDA authority to regulate food, drugs, medical devices, food additives, and dietary supplements on its own authority. The Act defined and regulated which food colorings and additives manufacturers could include in foods and established labeling requirements for such additives. It also authorized the FDA to establish standards for the identity and quality of foods.

Over the last several decades, nutrition has become the primary focus of food and package labels. In the United States, the Nutrition Labeling and Education Act of 1990 (NLEA) requires food packages to contain nutrition labels that are consistent with FDA standards. NLEA also standardizes serving sizes presented on nutritional labels and regulates the use of terms such as "low fat" and "light." In Canada, Health Canada and the Canadian Food Inspection Agency regulate a nutritional labeling system similar to that of the United States.

WORDS TO KNOW

ALLERGEN: Any substance that causes an allergic reaction. Typically, various proteins are the most common food allergens.

ANAPHYLAXIS: A life-threatening, multi-symptom allergic reaction to an allergen.

TRANS FATS: Trans fats are a form of unsaturated fat found in hydrogenated oils and often contained in processed foods and fast foods. Research has linked trans fats with an increased risk of coronary heart disease and other health problems.

In the United Kingdom, food labeling requirements are spread across numerous acts of Parliament. The *Codex Alimentarius*, a collection of food standards and practices promulgated by a joint commission of the World Health Organization (WHO) and the Food and Agriculture Organization of the United Nations (FAO), contains recommended international food labeling and nutritional standards.

■ Impacts and Issues

Food labeling laws and regulations have provided consumers with protection from false or misleading claims by unscrupulous food manufacturers. Food labeling, however, has critics that question whether such labels constitute government intrusion into the rights of the individual. Even during the debate over the Pure Food and Drugs Act of 1906, U.S. Senator Nelson Aldrich (1841–1915) questioned whether the government should penalize individuals who eat foods that the government does not find desirable. Advocates for truth in labeling, however, note that food labeling regulations do not infringe upon the liberty of individuals, but rather, provide individuals with the information needed to make informed decisions about nutrition and health.

A major concern of the truth-in-labeling movement concerns government-mandated labeling of products that contain allergens. Food allergies are adverse immune responses to a component of food, typically certain proteins. People with food allergies may experience reactions ranging from a mild rash to the potentially deadly anaphylaxis. Because even trace amounts of allergens may trigger allergic responses in some people, information about the content of possible allergens could prevent allergic reactions.

In the United States, the Food Allergen Labeling and Consumer Protection Act of 2004 seeks to inform consumers about potential allergens contained in food products. All food labels must provide notice if the product contains or may contain a protein derived from cow's milk, eggs, fish, peanuts, shellfish, soybeans, tree nuts, or wheat. In the Europe, EU Directive 2003/89/EC requires food manufacturers to list 12 potential allergens, regardless of quantity, if used as ingredients. EU regulations require manufacturers to list the following allergens: fish, crustaceans, eggs, peanuts, soy, milk and dairy products including lactose, cereals containing gluten, nuts, celery, mustard, sesame seed, and sulfites. Proponents of truth in labeling argue that manufacturers should be required to list all potential allergens on food labels. The allergens that must be listed under U.S. law,

Carol Goland, executive director of Ohio Ecological Food and Farming Association, speaks against a proposed Ohio law that would prevent labeling milk as hormone free. *AP Images.*

for example, comprise only about 90 percent of food allergies in the United States.

Truth-in-labeling advocates also propose stricter labeling requirements for trans fats in the United States, Canada, and other countries. Researchers have linked trans fats, a form of fat found in hydrogenated oils, with an increased risk of coronary heart disease. The American Heart Association, therefore, recommends limiting trans fat intake to less than 1 percent of total daily calories. A person with a 2,000-calorie per day intake, for example, should limit trans fat consumption to 2 grams or less per day. Canadian regulations require food manufacturers to list trans fat content of food products. Products with less than 0.2 grams of trans fat per serving, though, may be labeled as "trans fat free." In the United States, manufacturers may label products "trans fat free" or "no trans fats" if they contain less than 0.5 grams per serving. Under these regulations, consumers could exceed recommended trans fat consumption levels solely by consuming foods labeled "trans fat free." Legislative efforts in Canada and the United States seek to strengthen these regulations.

SEE ALSO *Advertising Food; Center for Food Safety and Applied Nutrition; Dietary Guidelines for Americans; Food Allergen Labeling and Consumer Protection Act of 2004; Food Allergies; Food Packaging; Produce Traceability.*

BIBLIOGRAPHY

Books

Stewart, Kimberly L. *Eating between the Lines: The Supermarket Shopper's Guide to the Truth behind Food Labels.* New York: St. Martin's Griffin, 2007.

Taub-Dix, Bonnie. *Read It before You Eat It: How to Decode Food Labels and Make the Healthiest Choice Every Time.* New York: Penguin Group, 2010.

Weirich, Paul. *Labeling Genetically Modified Food: The Philosophical and Legal Debate.* Oxford, UK: Oxford University Press, 2007.

Periodicals

Geiger, Constance, and Mary H. Hager. "Truth in Labeling: It's a Matter of Principle." *Journal of the American Dietetic Association* 107, no. 12 (2007): 2055.

Khoury, Lara, and Stuart Smyth. "Reasonable Foreseeability and Liability in Relation to Genetically Modified Organisms." *Bulletin of Science, Technology & Society* 27, no. 3 (2007): 215–232.

Nestle, Marion, and David S. Ludwig. "Front-of-Package Food Labels: Public Health or Propaganda?"

IN CONTEXT: FUNNY HONEY

Since Florida first adopted a law in 2009 to combat adulterated "funny honey," a number of states have joined in efforts to ensure that representations of "pure honey" do not mislead consumers. Counterfeit and adulterated honey, in many cases labeled "pure honey" may contain varying amounts of corn syrup or other additives. Beekeepers and honey packers also continue to lobby Congress for tough national standards to require disclosure of additives to honey. Americans consume an estimated 350 million pounds of honey per year, an amount far in excess of the 150 million pounds produced in the United States. Advocates of stricter regulation of honey sales argue that increased oversight and enforcement of tighter safety and labeling regulations will, therefore, also offer consumer protections against adulterated imports.

In September 2010, the U.S. Attorney's office in Chicago disclosed grand jury indictments of executives at six import companies charged with evading honey tariffs and of selling honey containing banned antibiotics. Local beekeepers who often sell their honey locally at farmer's markets and roadside stands argue that stricter enforcement and standards are needed to maintain consumer confidence. However, adulterated honey can also be found in local honey outlets.

JAMA: The Journal of the American Medical Association 303, no. 8 (2010): 771–772.

Web Sites

"Food Labeling Guide." *U.S. Food and Drug Administration (FDA).* http://www.fda.gov/Food/GuidanceComplianceRegulatoryInformation/GuidanceDocuments/FoodLabelingNutrition/FoodLabelingGuide/default.htm (accessed November 3, 2010).

"How to Understand and Use the Nutrition Facts Label." *U.S. Food and Drug Administration (FDA).* http://www.fda.gov/food/labelingnutrition/consumerinformation/ucm078889.htm (accessed November 3, 2010).

"Understanding FALCPA (The Food Allergen Labeling & Consumer Protection Act of 2004)." *Food Allergy Initiative.* http://www.faiusa.org/?page_id=DA172110-99EA-335F-3D2A5BA8DFE1C21D (accessed November 3, 2010).

Joseph P. Hyder

UN Millennium Development Goals

■ Introduction

In 2000, United Nations delegates from 192 nations and 23 international organizations signed the Millennium Declaration. The Millennium Declaration contains eight chapters that address key objectives for the United Nations (UN) to pursue in the twenty-first century. The UN subsequently adopted the Millennium Development Goals (MDGs) from the principles and objectives contained in the Millennium Declaration. The MDGs contain eight goals with 21 targets for the international community to achieve by 2015. The goals primarily address assisting people living in poverty by increasing income, gaining equality for women, increasing access to education, improving healthcare, promoting sustainable development and environmental responsibility, and reducing hunger.

Since the adoption of the MDGs, the UN, governments, non-governmental organizations (NGOs), and other groups have worked together to achieve the MDGs by their target date. The ambitious goals set forth in the MDGs, however, call for projects that require considerable financial commitments from partner nations and organizations. Financial contributions by developed nations and international NGOs have been a concern since the implementation of the MDGs, and many MDG targets remain underfunded. Despite progress toward achieving some MDG objectives, most of them remain off-target for achievement by the intended date.

■ Historical Background and Scientific Foundations

In February 1999, the United Nations General Assembly adopted a resolution that called on member nations to convene to strengthen the UN and articulate a vision for the UN in the twenty-first century. In September 2000, representatives from UN member states convened at the UN headquarters in New York City to attend the Millennium Summit, including the largest collection of world leaders ever assembled and more than 8,000 other delegates. Over three days the delegates expressed their desires for the development of the UN and the role that the international community should play in the twenty-first century.

At the conclusion of the Millennium Summit, the delegates adopted the Millennium Declaration. It contained the following objectives: values and principles; peace, security, and disarmament; development and poverty eradication; protecting the common environment; human rights, democracy and good governance; protecting the vulnerable; meeting the special needs of Africa; and strengthening the United Nations.

Following the Millennium Summit, the Organisation for Economic Co-operation and Development (OECD), an international economic NGO, reworked the eight chapters of the Millennium Declaration and devised the Millennium Development Goals (MDGs). The MDGs were adopted and promoted by the United Nations.

The MDGs comprise eight goals containing 21 quantifiable targets. Goal 1 calls on the international community to eradicate extreme poverty and hunger. Goal 1 includes three targets: halve the proportion of people living on less than $1 per day, achieve full and productive employment for all, and halve the proportion of people living in hunger. Goal 2 targets the achievement of universal primary education. Goal 3 calls on UN member nations to promote gender equality and empower women, primarily by eliminating gender inequality in education.

MDG Goals 4 through 6 address health-related issues. Goal 4 aims to reduce child mortality by two-thirds among children under five years of age. Goal 5 focuses on improving maternal health; it includes targets of reducing the maternal mortality ratio by three-quarters and achieving universal access to maternal health. Goal 6 calls on the international community to combat HIV/AIDS, malaria, and other diseases. In regard to HIV/AIDS, the objective is for nations to halt and begin to reverse the spread of HIV/AIDS by 2015 and achieve universal access to treatment for people living with HIV/AIDS. Goal 6 also focuses on reversing the incidence of malaria, tuberculosis, and other major diseases.

Goal 7 of the MDG addresses environmental and sustainable development issues through several targets. First, Goal 7 calls on nations to integrate the principles of sustainable development into their policies and to reverse the loss of environmental resources. Second, Goal 7 targets reducing biodiversity loss, including achieving a significant reduction in the rate of loss by 2010. Third, Goal 7 seeks to reduce the proportion of people without access to safe drinking water and basic sanitation. Finally, Goal 7 aims to achieve significant improvement in the lives of at least 100 million slum dwellers by 2020. Goal 8 of the MDG calls for a global partnership for development, which addresses trading and financial issues, the needs of least developed countries, the special needs of landlocked and island nations, and debt problems facing developing nations.

■ Impacts and Issues

The international community's funding of and commitment to achieving the ambitious MDGs has been an issue since their inception. In 2005 and 2010, the UN convened summits to review the progress toward achieving the MDGs. Despite a lack of progress in many areas, in September 2010 attendees to the Summit on the Millennium Development Goals expressed optimism at meeting most of the MDGs by the 2015 deadline.

The international community has made progress toward some of the targets set forth in the MDGs. According to the World Bank, 45 out of 84 nations are on track to meet the target of Goal 1 of halving the number of people living in poverty, and 25 out of 55 countries have cut child malnutrition rates in half or are on track. Under Goal 2, nations decreased the number of children not attending school by 37 million children within the first 10 years after adoption of the MDGs. As of 2009, however, only three of 22 fragile states had achieved all of Goal 2's targets. Efforts to achieve Goal 3's push for gender equality have resulted in 31 million more girls enrolled in school since 1999.

However, the international community and individual governments have not made significant progress toward achieving the healthcare-related MDGs 4 and 5. According to the World Bank, one in 14 children in developing nations dies before the age of five. Only 107 out of 145 developing nations, including only two fragile states, are on track to achieve Goal 4. The progress toward Goal 5 has been even more dismal: Only 23 out of 181 nations are on track to reduce the maternal mortality ratio by three-quarters. The international community has made significantly greater progress toward achieving the targets of Goal 6. Efforts have produced

---

WORDS TO KNOW

INTERNATIONAL MONETARY FUND (IMF): An international non-governmental organization that supervises the global financial system with the objectives of stabilizing exchange rates and facilitating economic development through liberal economic policies.

ORGANISATION FOR ECONOMIC CO-OPERATION AND DEVELOPMENT (OECD): An economic forum of 33 countries focused on promoting democracy and market economies.

SUSTAINABLE DEVELOPMENT: Sustainable development involves economic development and the fulfillment of human requirements in an environmentally responsible manner.

WORLD BANK: The World Bank is part of a group of international financial institutions that provides loans and other financial assistance to developing nations to promote economic growth and reduce poverty.

---

an 18-percent decline in the number of children infected with HIV and four million people in low- and middle-income countries have received antiviral drugs to treat HIV/AIDS. The number of children who die from malaria each year has decreased significantly, in large part because of the efforts of the Gates Foundation and other non-profit partners. Approximately 3,000 children, however, still die every day from malaria.

Although the international community has made progress toward achieving the environmental and sustainable development goals of MDG 7, much work remains. Since 1990, 1.6 billion people have gained access to clean drinking water. The UN and other organizations accelerated many of their clean water programs to satisfy the MDGs. However, 2.5 billion people—more than one-third of the world's population—do not have access to basic sanitation. Ecosystem and biodiversity loss continue at an alarming pace, often in the name of development.

Funding by the international community and the financial ability of developing nations to meet the MDGs continues to be a significant issue. In 2005 the G-8 launched an initiative whereby the World Bank, International Monetary Fund (IMF), and the African Development Bank (ADB) would forgive $40–55 billion in debt owed to those institutions by Heavily Indebted Poor Countries (HIPCs), or nations with unsustainable debt burdens. The G-8 hoped the debt forgiveness would assist many developing nations in meeting the MDGs.

In addition to debt forgiveness, governments have worked to achieve the MDGs through direct aid to governments and aid to non-profit and NGOs. Many NGOs, including the World Bank and IMF, have contributed financially to achieving the MDGs. Funding for

Villagers in Mwandama, Malawi, gather water. Mwandama is one of 14 villages in 10 African nations chosen to be a Millennium Village. Various UN agencies and non-governmental organizations work with Millennium Villages to achieve the eight Millennium Development Goals. *Ron Haviv/VII via AP Images.*

MDG programs, while chronically lacking, experienced significant difficulties because of the world financial crisis that began in 2007 as many nations cut foreign aid in order to balance budgets. At the 2010 Summit on the Millennium Development Goals, several nations, including France and Spain, called for innovative financing, including a tax on global capitalism, to fund the MDGs. Delegates to the summit did not approve a tax or similar financing mechanism, but many nations pledged to increase their financial support toward the MDGs.

SEE ALSO *African Famine Relief; Biofuels and World Hunger; Ethical Issues in Agriculture; Ethical Issues in Food Aid; Fair Trade; Famine; Food and Agriculture Organization (FAO); Food Security; Food Sovereignty; Gender Equality and Agriculture; Hunger; International Fund for Agricultural Development; Malnutrition; Population and Food; Women's Role in Global Food Preparation; World Food Day; World Food Programme; World Trade Organization (WTO).*

BIBLIOGRAPHY

Books

Food and Agriculture Organization (FAO) of the United Nations. *The State of Food Insecurity in the World 2009: Eradicating World Hunger.* Rome: FAO, 2009.

Web Sites

"Millennium Development Goals: Goal 1: Eradicate Extreme Poverty and Hunger." *United Nations Development Program.* http://www.undp.org/mdg/goal1.shtml (accessed October 4, 2010).

"Monitoring Progress since the World Food Summit." *Food and Agriculture Organization (FAO) of the United Nations.* http://www.fao.org/monitoring progress/index_en.html (accessed October 4, 2010).

"Outcomes on Food." *United Nations.* http://www.un.org/en/development/devagenda/food.shtml (accessed October 4, 2010).

Joseph P. Hyder

Undernutrition

■ Introduction

Undernutrition is often argued to be primarily a problem of underdeveloped countries where famine and poverty are common. In fact, undernutrition is a risk in any situation where not enough food is eaten to meet the body's nutrient needs for carbohydrate, protein, fat, vitamins, and minerals. A person may have access to food but be unable to eat or absorb it for some reason. Undernutrition is a type of malnutrition, in which the body's need for nutrients is not balanced by intakes. Malnutrition can also occur when food supplies are adequate, but a person eats foods that are low in nutrients. Long-term undernutrition, also known as starvation, affects every part of the body, as essential tissues are broken down to meet nutrient needs. Undernutriton can be successfully treated but more may be needed than just giving the person food. Children are at most risk of long-term effects from undernutrition because of their nutrient needs for growth and development. The elderly, in all parts of the world, are at risk of undernutrition for a number of reasons, including the aging process, illness, the effects of medication, and social isolation.

■ Historical Background and Scientific Foundations

Undernutrition has always been a part of the human condition. In order to remain healthy, human bodies need regular supplies of the macronutrients, which include carbohydrates, fats, and proteins, along with the micronutrients, vitamins and minerals. When any are lacking for a period of time, the body falls into a state of malnutrition, in which the need for a nutrient is greater than its supply. Malnutrition can develop easily from undernutrition, in which a person is not eating enough to meet nutrient needs. It can also arise if a person is eating too many empty calories—food intake supplies calories without nutrients. Empty calorie foods include sugar

and alcohol. There are many causes of undernutrition. Lack of access to food may occur because of poverty, famine, inability to obtain food due to physical impairment, or voluntary restriction through a very low calorie diet. There are also many disorders that can increase the risk of undernutrition, including AIDS, malabsorption disorders, depression, alcoholism, and drug abuse. Some drugs interfere with the intake, metabolism, and absorption of nutrients, such as those used to treat cancer, anxiety, and heart failure. There are also conditions that increase the body's needs for nutrients, so the usual diet may lead to undernutrition; such conditions include injury, surgery, overactive thyroid, pregnancy, and breastfeeding.

Various types and degrees of undernutrition exist among populations. Protein-calorie undernutrition from chronic lack of food is particularly common among children in developing countries and is a major contributor to childhood mortality. Severe protein-calorie malnutrition manifests as marasmus, which develops in young children and infants and results in weight loss and dehydration. Breastfeeding normally prevents marasmus. Starvation is the most extreme form of marasmus and results from severe, or no, food intake over a period of time. When protein (rather than calories) is lacking, a form of undernutrition called kwashiorkor may develop. This happens mainly in regions of the world where staple foods are deficient in protein. Examples of such foods include cassava, yams, sweet potatoes, rice, and green bananas. Kwashiorkor is common in children when they are weaned, although it can develop in anyone whose diet source is mainly from carbohydrates. People who have kwashiorkor tend to retain fluid, making them look puffy and swollen. The abdomen may protrude, creating the image that is often associated with undernourished children in famine areas.

When the body is undernourished, the body first breaks down its own fat to use as calories, rather like burning furniture to keep the house warm in the absence of external fuel. After these stores are used, the

WORDS TO KNOW

MALNUTRITION: A condition in which a person is not consuming or absorbing adequate and balanced nutrients in order to sustain a healthy, active life. Diets with caloric deficits, deficits of protein or fat, or deficits of key vitamins and minerals cause malnutrition. Obesity is also sometimes considered a form of malnutrition if it contributes to a state of decreased health or disease.

STARVATION: The most extreme form of undernutrition, in which there is a partial or total lack of nutrients for a long time. Total starvation, in which no food is consumed, is usually fatal within 8 to 12 weeks.

UNDERNUTRITION: A deficiency of calories or lack of access to sufficient food sources. If a person regularly consumes less than 1,000 calories per day, he or she is likely to develop undernutrition, and the lack of calories will inevitably lead to deficiency in nutrients such as protein, vitamins, and minerals.

body may start to break down other tissues. This begins to happen during starvation, when undernutrition and lack of food are chronic and severe. Many parts of the body are affected in starvation. The stomach shrinks and diarrhea becomes frequent, leading to potentially fatal dehydration. The heart also shrinks, leading to heart failure. Lung capacity reduces, leading to respiratory failure. Body temperature lowers; skin and hair become thin and dry; and the immune system becomes impaired. Severe undernutrition is readily diagnosed from a person's appearance. Treatment of undernutrition is usually based upon gradually increasing the number of calories consumed. Liquid food supplements may be needed if there are problems in digesting solids. Tube or enteral feeding through a tube fed from the nose to the stomach might be needed if someone cannot eat, but has normal gastrointestinal function. If the digestive tract cannot absorb nutrients, then the food is given parenterally, through an intravenous drip into the bloodstream. Undernutrition may have long-lasting effects in children, even when they are successfully treated: Behavioral development

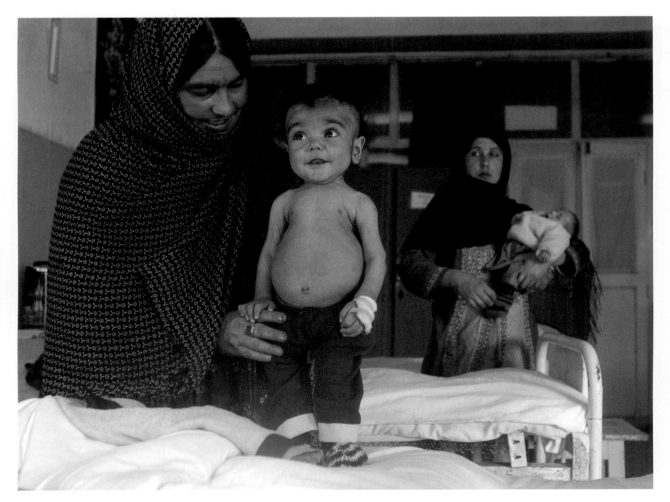

A severely undernourished boy from Khost, Afghanistan, receives treatment at a hospital in Kabul. His development skills have been severely stunted due to malnutrition; even at two years of age he is still unable to crawl or walk. *AP Images.*

may be slow and impairments in mental and digestive function may persist. Adults treated for undernutrition usually make a full recovery.

■ Impacts and Issues

Undernutrition is most common in underdeveloped countries because of higher rates of famine and poverty, which restrict access to food. According to the United Nations Children's Fund (UNICEF) undernutrition plays a role in more than one third of deaths of children globally. Although undernutrition does not cause death directly, when undernutrition exists alongside malaria, tuberculosis, measles, or other diseases common to children in developing countries, death rates are higher. A UNICEF report found that 195 million children under five in developing countries are undernourished and more than 90 percent of these children are in Africa and Asia. The risk of child undernutrition is far greater when the mother is undernourished, so efforts to improve maternal nutrition are as important as those to help children.

The elderly are also at risk of undernutrition. In developed countries one older person in seven is affected; the figure rises to around half among those in long-term care. Older people tend to have less appetite and soon feel full. Lack of appetite may arise from disorders such as depression and cancer. The ability to taste and smell also decreases with age, robbing eating of some of its enjoyment. Furthermore, a stroke may cause eating and swallowing problems, and people with dementia may forget to eat. Medication can also contribute to undernutrition by changing the way nutrients are absorbed or decreasing appetite. Older people living alone may not feel motivated to cook, eat, or shop. These issues can be addressed by caregivers, health professionals, and the individuals themselves, but they must first be made aware of the barriers that may prevent adequate nutrition.

SEE ALSO *Biofuels and World Hunger; Breastfeeding; Famine; Famine: Political Considerations; Food Security; Hunger; International Food Aid; Malnutrition; Nutrient Fortification of Foods; Nutrition and U.S. Government Food Assistance; Rome Declaration on World Food Security (1996); UN Millennium Development Goals.*

BIBLIOGRAPHY

Books

Haddad, Lawrence J., and Sushila Zeitlyn. *Lifting the Curse: Overcoming Persistent Undernutrition in India.* Oxford: Wiley-Blackwell, 2009.

Leathers, Howard D., and Phillips Foster. *The World Food Problem: Toward Ending Undernutrition in the Third World.* Boulder, CO: Rienner Publishers, 2009.

United Nations Standing Committee on Nutrition. *Working Together to End Child Hunger and Undernutrition.* Geneva: United Nations, 2007.

Periodicals

White, Howard. "Tackling Childhood Undernutrition." *Lancet* 371, no. 9612 (2008): 539–541.

Web Sites

"Ending Child Hunger and Undernutrition Initiative." *World Food Programme.* http://documents.wfp. org/stellent/groups/public/documents/resources/ wfp111813.pdf (accessed October 2, 2010).

"UNICEF: Progress for Children. Nutrition, Survival and Development: What Is Undernutrition?" *UNICEF.* http://www.unicef.org/progressfor children/2006n4/index_undernutrition.html (accessed October 2, 2010).

Susan Aldridge

Urban Chicken Movement

Introduction

Chickens have long been a fixture on family and commercial farms. However, chickens are increasingly appearing in neighborhoods where previously the dominant domestic animals have been dogs and cats. The keeping of poultry in urban areas is a trend on the rise.

New or updated resources appear every year on chickens, chicken husbandry, coop construction and "return to basic roots" topics. Specialty magazines and Web sites such as *Backyard Poultry*, *Home Grown Poultry*, and Backyardchickens.com have grown in number since 2004. Backyardchickens claims more than 30,000 members, with more than 100 added each day. U.S. cities that allow chickens within city limits include New York; Chicago; Albuquerque, New Mexico; Portland, Oregon; and Seattle.

Several factors contribute to the increasing interest in city chickens. The primary motivation for the phenomenon can be traced to a rising awareness of and interest in self-sufficiency and permaculture.

Historical Background and Scientific Foundations

Although the exact date cannot be known, chickens were probably domesticated sometime around 3,000 BC in India, or the region including parts of modern day Burma, Thailand, and Singapore. From its South Asian origin, the domestic chicken spread to Egypt and Greece, into China, Africa, and Europe, and eventually throughout the rest of the world.

Charles Darwin (1809–1882) considered chickens to be directly descended from the red jungle fowl native to Southeast Asia. Others are not so sure, claiming that chickens are related to several other species of jungle fowl and include some influence from wild grouse and the extinct dodo bird. Chickens are members of the pheasant family, and they are known to science by their sub-species name *Gallus gallus domesticus.*

A highly efficient mechanized industry exists for the production of chicken eggs and meat in most industrialized nations. Until recently, however, it has usually been illegal to keep poultry or other farm animals within city limits in the United States. As grass-roots interest in chickens grows, town leaders are increasingly convinced that there is no harm in keeping a small number of fowl in backyards. This has led to a relaxing of laws so that many municipalities have begun to allow the keeping of chickens, ducks, pheasants, geese, game hens, and in some cases even other small farm animals such as pigs and goats.

Regulations usually limit the number of fowl to 20 or less, and roosters are prohibited because of the noise they create. In most cases, there is no application or approval process, but some cities charge a small fee for a permit. Laws also generally include a provision that the birds' living space be kept clean.

Impacts and Issues

There are many reasons why chickens are an attractive addition to a backyard environment. Some people are interested in the "do-it-yourself" and self-sufficiency aspects. Keeping live animals provides educational opportunities for families with children. Others are concerned with the safety and security of their food supply or are animal welfare activists who do not want to support the commercial chicken farming industry. Some people attempt to reduce their carbon footprint by cutting out their share of the transportation and production costs associated with commercial chicken farming. However, there is too much uncertainty in such calculations to be sure there is a measurable environmental benefit to raising chickens locally.

Among urban residents who keep chickens, fresh eggs are cited as a major plus; there are no fresher eggs than those just collected from a nest. Chickens are also easy to keep in a small area. They are not choosy about what they eat and will dispose of nearly any kitchen food waste offered. Chickens also are voracious consumers of insects. Their manure is an excellent fertilizer for gardens and lawns. There is an opportunity for creativity and design expression in constructing a habitat (coop and fenced yard) for chickens. Many people are charmed by their appearance and behavior and enjoy watching them and keeping them as pets.

Raising a small number of chickens to supply a household with fresh eggs is rarely economical. The cost of building a chicken coop can vary from almost free (if found or salvaged materials are used) to well over $1,000 for commercially available kits or custom built units. Without considering the cost of the coop, if organic feed is used, the cost of eggs will usually exceed the cost of purchasing them at a local organic grocer. Factory-produced, non-organic eggs are relatively inexpensive and homegrown eggs usually cannot compete with their price. Still, the combination of advantages (whether real or perceived) is enough to keep a growing number of people interested in urban chickens.

A backyard chicken flees the coop that her owner built in a residential neighborhood in Portland, Oregon. © *Green Stock Media / Alamy.*

A number of economic benefits do result from allowing chickens in urban areas. Local feed suppliers realize an increase in business from the sale of chicken feed, watering devices, and other goods needed for keeping hens. In areas without an established agricultural base, pet stores can expand their inventory to meet the demand for such items. Building suppliers provide wood, sheet metal, fencing, and other construction materials. City laws usually disallow the slaughter of chickens for their meat. In these locales, mobile slaughtering services may spring up, or establishments outside of city limits may cater to the needs of those who wish to eat freshly killed chickens. Mail order suppliers of chicks have reaped the benefits of the chicken boom (millions of baby chicks are delivered by mail every year), and business has increased for local suppliers of baby chicks for the urban market.

Although the trend is in favor of relaxing civic ordinances, a minority seeks to prevent the spread of city chickens. Some resistance stems from a desire of residents to keep their urban environment urban in nature. In the absence of such sentiments, the main arguments brought against urban chickens are the smell, noise, disease, and enforcement costs.

In seeking the passage of favorable laws, chicken advocates often prevail with counter arguments. A small flock of chickens produces no more waste or odor, for example, than a pet dog or a few cats. Unlike dog and cat waste, chicken manure is a valuable fertilizer. As roosters are seldom allowed in urban areas, there is little noise from keeping chickens. Hens will occasionally squawk, but barking dogs usually cause more noise in towns than chickens. Chicken keepers are generally environmentally conscious, responsible citizens. There is little evidence that chickens result in increased animal control enforcement costs. Chickens do sometimes harbor *Salmonella* bacteria, which can cause illness in humans. However, *Salmonella* is a concern in commercial eggs and chicken meat as well. The problem is generally one of improper handling of chicken products, which is not exacerbated by the presence of live birds in a yard.

The most successful argument against allowing chickens in urban areas is usually that they present a risk of contributing to the spread of avian influenza viruses such as the H5N1 influenza virus, the so-called "bird flu." There is no indication that small flocks of backyard chickens present an influenza threat in North America. A few simple precautions are sufficient to safely raise birds: keeping birds penned, avoiding contact with wild fowl, keeping the pen covered to protect it from the droppings of wild birds passing overhead, and disinfecting footwear after visiting the chicken area. If a local outbreak of avian influenza occurs, birds should not be moved to a new location and new birds should not be introduced to a flock.

SEE ALSO *Eggs; Locavore; Poultry; Urban Farming/ Gardening.*

BIBLIOGRAPHY

Books

Hatcher, Mike. *Keeping Chickens: Self-Sufficiency.* New York: Skyhorse, 2010.

Hobson, J. C. Jeremy. *Backyard Poultry Keeping.* Ramsbury, UK: Crowood Press, 2007.

Kilarski, Barbara. *Keep Chickens!: Tending Small Flocks in Cities, Suburbs, and Other Small Spaces.* North Adams, MA: Storey, 2003.

Megyesi, Jennifer Lynn, and Geoff Hansen. *The Joy of Keeping Chickens: The Ultimate Guide to Raising Poultry for Fun or Profit.* New York: Skyhorse Pub, 2009.

Paul, Johannes, and William Windham. *Keeping Pet Chickens: Bring Your Backyard to Life and Enjoy the Bounty of Fresh Eggs from Your Own Small Flock of Happy Hens.* Hauppauge, New York: Barron's, 2005.

Peacock, Paul. *The Urban Hen: A Practical Guide to Keeping Poultry in a Town or City.* Oxford: Spring Hill, 2009.

Periodicals

Neuman, William. "Keeping Their Eggs in Their Backyard Nests." *New York Times* (August 4, 2009): B1.

Web Sites

Carver, Donna K. "Preventing Avian Influenza in Backyard Poultry Flocks." *North Carolina State University.* http://www.ces.ncsu.edu/depts/ poulsci/tech_manuals/preventing_avian_influenza_ backyard.pdf (accessed August 1, 2010).

Philip McIntosh

Urban Farming and Gardening

Introduction

An urban farm is more than just a backyard garden used for personal consumption, but individually these farms do not produce the level of output seen from modern industrial farms. The growing numbers of urban farmers and backyard producers have a combined total output, however, that gives buyers a local alternative to what is found in mainstream grocery stores. Those who choose to grow and consume food from local urban farms are doing so for a variety of reasons, including boosting the local economy, decreasing their environmental footprint, and preserving heirloom or less mainstream food varieties. Urban farmers often choose a garden or small-scale production plot as a hobby. However, urban farming does have the potential to turn a profit and create jobs. Neighborhood and community organizations form small groups of urban farms as a way to strengthen social cohesion and make nutritious foods more readily available to area residents.

Historical Background and Scientific Foundations

Convenient access to inexpensive fruits, vegetables, eggs, and other foods in twentieth-century supermarkets made household production and home gardens less of a necessity. However, there typically has been a surge in small household production during times of war and economic downturn, as individuals feel the need to be more self-sustaining. Those who have always carried on the tradition of gardening have typically done so out of the enjoyment of being outdoors, as well as from the satisfaction of eating food they have produced themselves. Urban farming involves more space than a backyard garden, and often entails converting front and back lawns and vacant lots into growing areas. Urban farmers often set out with the intention to grow enough produce to share with or sell to others and earn a profit. The growing popularity of buying local is helping to accomplish this.

Urban farmers use unique intensive methods to maximize the productive potential of plots limited in land area. An intensive method calls for seeds to be planted closer together than standard planting, while keeping the plants staggered to avoid overcrowding. Frequently concerned about sustainability, urban farmers use environmentally friendly farming methods. Rainwater may be captured for irrigation, to avoid using scarce drinking water sources. Pest control is carried out with non-toxic methods, including the use of ladybugs, which can consume 50 to 60 aphids per day. Soil quality is maintained with manure or other organic fertilizers. Raised plant beds are often utilized to further maximize resource use, allowing better containment of soil, organic nutrients, water, and mulch to keep weeds to a minimum. Urban farming may also include a small number of chickens, which provide eggs and a natural defense against insects. Many urban areas have adopted ordinances permitting the keeping of a limited number of backyard poultry. Other urban farms raise fast-growing fish varieties such as tilapia or catfish in small ponds.

Heirloom varieties are commonly planted by urban farmers and gardeners in order to maintain a high level of diversity. This is in contrast to industrial farms, which typically plant a narrower selection of food varieties that transport well and have a longer shelf life. Industrial farms also choose crops that are marketable to national shoppers, who expect standardized shapes and appearances of food. Not restricted by such concerns, urban farmers and gardeners typically deliver foods fresh or directly to their customers, who are often drawn to the diverse varieties available. Many gardeners claim that the flavor of heirlooms is superior to that of their supermarket cousins. The growth of rare varieties helps to maintain agricultural diversity. Diversity is important for ensuring food varieties that will survive current and future diseases. Many urban farmers are uninterested in

WORDS TO KNOW

FOODSHED: Conceptually similar to a watershed, a foodshed is the flow of food feeding a particular community, from the farm to the table, including the transportation and vendor from which it is purchased.

HEIRLOOM PLANTS: Traditional plant varieties often passed down from family to family and not currently used by large agribusiness.

INTENSIVE PLANTING: Planting seeds more densely than traditional methods to increase yields.

using genetically modified organisms, in order to further maintain agricultural diversity.

■ Impacts and Issues

Community urban farms function as a tool to decrease poverty, crime, and other social problems faced by youth and adults in poor or blighted neighborhoods.

These farms aim to empower youth and young adults to grow sustainable farms that provide healthy food options to area residents. The experiences of farming impart leadership skills, emphasizing the importance of community cohesion. Neighborhood urban farms may be diverse, bringing together young people, seniors, the working class, immigrants, and professionals with the aim to build a sense of pride for communities while caring for the natural environment. The farms may be developed on a donated parcel of land, or may include a collection of yards in a neighborhood. Volunteers sign up to learn and complete the needed tasks on a farm, such as clearing land, planting and irrigating crops, administering pest control, harvesting, and marketing the produce. Urban farms may also have an educational component that visits local urban schools to expose children to agriculture science and nutrition. In some areas, families or individuals are able to rent small plots or rows in an urban community farm to grow their own food. This is of particular benefit to individuals who live in apartments, or other dense urban housing, which does not have outdoor space available for gardening. Community gardens are showing up in many places, including high school and college

An urban community garden situated in a neighborhood park allows nearby residents to grow vegetables, fruits, and flowers. Participants share gardening duties, rainwater, compost, tools, and a greenhouse. *K. Lee Lerner / Lerner & Lerner / LernerMedia Global Photos.*

campuses, poor downtown areas, suburban areas, and on church lots.

The success of urban farms and gardens depends upon the ability to find markets for locally grown food. There is a growing movement among individuals who recognize the environmental impact of producing food in unsustainable ways. These consumers are concerned with minimizing the use of pesticides and fertilizers on food, as well as maintaining agriculture diversity. Transporting goods grown at locations that are long distances away, often in other countries, to the final market, increases the release of greenhouse gases and other pollution. Bringing in low-cost produce from out of the area makes it difficult for local farmers to compete in the mainstream market. To address this issue, some consumers advocate buying food in local markets, often referred to as a local foodshed. This surge in the demand for local, sustainably-grown food works to the advantage of gardeners and urban farmers. Local farmers' markets are a popular venue for urban farmers and gardeners to sell food. They may be open once per

IN CONTEXT: URBAN ECOSYSTEMS

Ecologists define an urban ecosystem as a dependent ecosystem, meaning that it depends on other ecosystems, outside energy, and resources to function. In contrast, a natural ecosystem generally has an even balance between its energetic inputs and outputs. Although there are exceptions, urban food systems usually must be artificially maintained, reflecting the state of urban ecosystems in general. Canadian population ecologist William Rees (1943–), a researcher at the University of British Columbia, created an analytical tool to measure the dependency of an urban ecosystem. Termed the ecological footprint, it roughly measures how much land is required to maintain a city's activities. Rees found that Vancouver, British Columbia, for instance, had a footprint 180 times its own size in 1996, meaning that much more land, in terms of extractable resources, is required to support its inhabitants.

A young person works on an urban farm in Flint, Michigan, as part of the Urban Community Youth Outreach farm.   *AP Images.*

The Brooklyn Grange commercial farm is planted on the roof of a building in the Long Island City neighborhood in the borough of Queens, New York. The rooftop farm, which occupies one acre, is constructed with 1.2 million pounds of soil and produces 15 different crops including bok choy, kale, lettuce, and Swiss chard. The urban farm is the largest commercial farming initiative in New York. Their produce is sold at their "farm stand" in LIC and to restaurants around the city.   © *Richard Levine / Alamy.*

IN CONTEXT: MAKING ROOM FOR URBAN GARDENS

Urban gardens have been planted in a diverse range of urban spaces: patios and balconies, abandoned plots of land, rooftops, schoolyards, and more. Urban gardening initiatives have occasionally been fraught with land-use planning or zoning issues but in some places urban gardening has a mandate backed by law and policy and provides valuable resources.

The city of Esslingen, Germany, adopted a bylaw requiring flat and sloping roofs—up to 15 degrees—to be vegetated. In Switzerland, a law stipulates that all new buildings must relocate the green space taken up by the building's footprint to their rooftops. Even existing buildings—some centuries old—are required to vegetate 20 percent of their roof surfaces.

In addition, urban gardening and agriculture can be harnessed to provide food for urban and suburban populations. Cuba is frequently cited as an excellent example of utilizing city space for vital food supplies. The collapse of the Soviet Union in 1991 drastically reduced agricultural inputs sent to Cuba. In the years immediately following, the national caloric intake of Cubans declined by one-third. In response, during the decade following the withdrawal of Soviet support, the number of urban gardens in Cuba surged, and statistics indicated that by the year 2000 urban agriculture produced more than half of the country's vegetables.

week or more and provide entertainment and educational booths in addition to buying local produce. In some cases, small local grocery stores also stock locally grown food.

SEE ALSO *Agribusiness; Agroecology; Alice Waters: California and New American Cuisine; Biodiversity and Food Supply; Community Supported Agriculture (CSAs); Ethical Issues in Agriculture; Locavore; Michael Pollan: Linking Food and Environmental Journalism; Neighborhood Food Cooperatives; Organics; Slow Food Movement.*

BIBLIOGRAPHY

Books

Fox, Thomas. *Taking Root: Urban Farming in the Modern Cityscape.* Irvine, CA: Hobby Farms, 2010.

Neville, Jayne. *Flowerpot Farming: Creating Your Own Urban Kitchen Garden.* Preston, UK: Good Life, 2008.

Van Veenhuizen, Rene. *Cities Farming for the Future: Urban Agriculture for Green and Productive Cities.* Ottawa, Ontario, Canada: International Development Research Centre, 2006.

Zdruli, Pandi, et al., eds. *Land Degradation and Desertification: Assessment, Mitigation and Remediation.* Dordrecht, The Netherlands: Springer, 2010.

Periodicals

Drechsel, Pay, and Stefan Dongus. "Dynamics and Sustainability of Urban Agriculture: Examples from Sub-Saharan Africa." *Sustainability Science* 5, no. 1 (2010): 69–78.

Dregne, Harold E. "Land Degradation in the Drylands." *Arid Land Research and Management* 16, no. 2 (2002): 99–132.

Flisram, Greg. "A Serious Flirt with Dirt: Urban Farming Is Making a Comeback—and Describes Some Potential Spinoff Businesses." *Planning Chicago* 75, no. 8 (2009): 14–19.

Frail, Thomas A. "Farms Go to Town: The U.S. Will See an Upward Trend in Urban Farming." *Smithsonian* 41, no. 4 (2010): 56–57.

Web Sites

Urban Farming. http://www.urbanfarming.org/ (accessed October 16, 2010).

Urban Farm Online. http://www.urbanfarmonline.com/ (accessed October 16, 2010).

Steven Joseph Archambault

U.S. Agency for International Development (USAID)

■ Introduction

The United States Agency for International Development (USAID) is an independent U.S. government agency that administers foreign aid. USAID follows the nation's foreign policy priorities as established by the Secretary of State while providing economic and humanitarian assistance worldwide.

USAID missions address global issues and provide assistance in education and job training, food aid and disaster relief, poverty relief, democracy and good governance, infrastructure construction, and environmental integrity. The agency also supports economic growth incentives including small-enterprise loans, budget support, enterprise funds, credit guarantees, and programs to increase gender and ethnic equality in development benefits. USAID programs focusing on food and agriculture are diverse, ranging from the provision of emergency direct food aid to development incentives for farmers. USAID also provides technical support for manufacturers in developing countries to create safer food products, such as pasteurized milk.

Headquartered in Washington, DC, USAID maintains a network of field missions in more than 100 countries, including 50 developing countries, which work with local officials and populations to carry out aid and development projects. The agency also partners with more than 4,000 advocacy groups, corporations, faith organizations, nongovernmental organizations (NGOs), universities, United Nations agencies and projects, and other governments worldwide.

■ Historical Background and Scientific Foundations

USAID grew out of U.S. experiences with both civilian and military foreign aid after the conclusion of World War II (1939–1945). The United States embarked on an ambitious international aid plan to assist in the reconstruction and redevelopment of war-torn Europe. Through the European Recovery Program (ERP), commonly known as the Marshall Plan, the United States invested $13 billion in redevelopment and aid efforts between 1948 and 1951. An additional $12 billion had been given in aid from the end of the war to the start of the Marshall Plan. The plan focused not only on reconstructing European industry, but also in making it more efficient and economically viable for the future. As a matter of policy, the plan strove to model new European industrial and business practices after those in American corporations. By the end of the Marshall Plan, the economies of participating nations had largely recovered: Economic output in Western Europe was more than 30 percent higher than it was before the war.

Tensions over the postwar divided city of Berlin between the Soviet Union and the other allied powers led to a Soviet blockade of supply lines into the city. The air forces of the United States and Great Britain embarked on a massive military-led aid mission to supply the people of Berlin with food, fuel, and necessities. During what became known as the Berlin Airlift, more than 200,000 flights in 11 months provided the Berliners with needed aid.

On September 4, 1961, Congress passed the Foreign Assistance Act. The legislation separated military-provided and non-military provided foreign aid. To meet the requirements of the act and oversee non-military aid programs, U.S. President John F. Kennedy (1917–1963) established the USAID by executive order that November. The newly formed USAID joined the existing non-military foreign aid operations into one agency. USAID assumed responsibility for coordinating not only development aid and loan programs, but also emergency relief and direct food aid.

USAID programs are organized by individual countries and specific missions within those countries. Roughly half of the Foreign Service members who work for the agency are deployed on a rotation of foreign assignments and assignments at headquarters. When on field missions, these officers work with a predominantly local staff and other organizations to achieve their development or aid objectives.

In the world's poorest regions, USAID provides poverty assistance in the areas of public health, education, funds, and loans to local relief organizations, as well as food aid. USAID supplies direct food aid to people in crisis through its Food for Peace program. Food for Peace has benefited more than 3 billion people in 150 countries over the course of its existence. To ease food shortages or localized food price crises, USAID also manages and distributes agricultural commodity assistance that is provided by the U.S. Department of Agriculture. In developing regions, USAID provides technical assistance and economic incentives to foster economic growth, improve economic productivity, make products and workplaces safer, promote good environmental practices, and prevent corruption and illicit trade.

■ Impacts and Issues

USAID decreases or increases its presence in a given area with the level of need. The end goal of USAID assistance projects is for a mission area to progress to a point at which aid is no longer required. Since 1961, USAID

has closed missions in several countries where U.S.-led aid programs were no longer needed to support local efforts. Costa Rica, South Korea, Tunisia, and Turkey all formerly had USAID missions.

In fiscal year 2010, the U.S. budget for foreign affairs agencies, including USAID and the Department

Afghan workers pack honey jars at a facility in Jalalabad, Afghanistan, that received funding and technical support from USAID. *AP Images.*

of State, totaled $36.7 billion. USAID allotted more than $6.6 billion of those funds for programs to foster economic growth, rebuild infrastructure, and provide necessary aid for individuals in Iraq.

USAID's stated mission is to advance the foreign policy interests of the United States. While USAID provides aid to some of the world's neediest regions, it also uses aid to incentivize outcomes beneficial to U.S. foreign interests. USAID may provide financial grants to policy allies. Its operations also bolster U.S. soft power military aid operations in areas of the world where the United States is trying to build support networks, undermine support for insurgent or terrorist groups, and gain the trust of local populations.

Critics assert that its adherence to U.S. policy aims undermines the organization's ability to distribute aid without significant bias. They note that the largest beneficiaries of USAID are nations who are political or military allies of the United States or areas where the United States is engaged in active military operations. Others have objected to requirements of USAID projects such as one that stipulates participating communities meet the requirements of U.S. anti-terrorism funding laws by declaring themselves "terrorist free zones."

USAID programs that employ economic incentives to keep farmers from growing plants for the illegal drug trade have also come under fire from critics. In 2008, Bolivian President Evo Morales (1969–) banned more than 100 aid personnel working with USAID from conducting operations in a farming region in Bolivia. USAID attempted to persuade local farmers to eliminate their coca crops (in the hopes of preventing cocaine manufacture) and plant alternatives such as coffee and cocoa (for chocolate). Aid to farmers was conditioned on not planting any crops that could enter into the international illegal drug trade. The Bolivian president criticized the aid program for not responding to the economic realities of crop prices and for not providing reasonable, economically viable alternative crops. Critics noted that success of such a program would require alternative crops that would produce a living wage for a farmer within one growing season. USAID asserts that similar programs targeting the unrestricted growing of opium poppy in central Asia have successfully produced living wages for farmers.

USAID is funded primarily by the U.S. government, comprising less than one-half of one percent of the federal budget. When working with NGOs and other contractors, USAID has a stated policy of preferring to hire local contractors from the target mission nation or region when possible. However, independent NGO analysis of USAID hiring during the first decade of the twenty-first

century found that as much as 40 percent of economic aid in Afghanistan worked its way back to donor nations through contract hiring of donor nation firms at prices normalized for the donor, not recipient, nations.

SEE ALSO *Aid for Agriculture to Replace Illicit Drug Production; Ethical Issues in Food Aid; Food Security; International Food Aid; International Fund for Agricultural Development; Sustainable Agriculture; UN Millennium Development Goals; World Food Programme.*

BIBLIOGRAPHY

Books

Carothers, Thomas. *Revitalizing U.S. Democracy Assistance: The Challenge of USAID.* Washington, DC: Carnegie Endowment for International Peace, 2009.

Committee on Evaluation of USAID Democracy Assistance Programs. *Improving Democracy Assistance: Building Knowledge through Evaluations and Research.* Washington, DC: National Academies Press, 2008.

Perkins, John. *The Secret History of the American Empire: Economic Hit Men, Jackals, and the Truth about Global Corruption.* New York: Dutton, 2007.

USAID. *Family Planning: Improving Lives in the Democratic Republic of Congo.* Washington, DC: United States Agency for International Development, 2006.

USAID. *Indila's Story: One Girl's Fight to Stop Child Marriage.* Washington, DC: United States Agency for International Development, 2007.

USAID. *USAID Primer: What We Do and How We Do It.* Washington, DC: U.S. Agency for International Development, 2006.

Periodicals

Fariss, Christopher J. "The Strategic Substitution of United States Foreign Aid." *Foreign Policy Analysis* 6, no. 2 (2010): 107–131.

Frumin, Amy B. "Diagnosing USAID." *Foreign Affairs* 88, no. 2 (March/April 2009).

Web Sites

Feed the Future. http://www.feedthefuture.gov/ (accessed October 14, 2010).

"U.S. Aid from the American People." *U.S. Agency for International Development (USAID).* http://www.usaid.gov/ (accessed October 14, 2010).

Adrienne Wilmoth Lerner

U.S. Department of Agriculture (USDA)

■ Introduction

The U.S. Department of Agriculture (USDA) is the United States cabinet-level department responsible for formulating and implementing all U.S. agricultural and food policies. The USDA administers or regulates agricultural subsidy programs, soil conservation, rural development, forest management, and other environmental programs. It also focuses on hunger and food safety issues in the United States, including distributing domestic and some foreign food aid, inspecting meat and other food products, and promoting nutrition.

With an annual budget of more than $100 billion, the USDA engages in a wide array of agriculture-related activities, including promoting agricultural trade, conserving natural resources, protecting the environment, addressing hunger through public food aid programs, researching agricultural science, and promoting rural development. The USDA's influence over agriculture often draws criticism from the international community and environmental groups over policies that are perceived to harm non-U.S. farmers or the environment.

■ Historical Background and Scientific Foundations

The USDA traces its roots to the formation of the Agricultural Division of the Patent Office, which Congress established in 1839. Under the leadership of Henry Leavitt Ellsworth (1791–1858), the Agricultural Division of the Patent Office focused on collecting, preserving, and distributing seeds from heirloom and new hybrid varieties of plants. In 1862, facing calls for an independent agricultural agency, President Abraham Lincoln (1809–1865) established the Department of Agriculture as an independent, non-cabinet level agency. In 1889 Congress passed legislation, which was subsequently signed by President Grover Cleveland (1837–1908), that elevated the Department of Agriculture to cabinet level.

The passage of the Hatch Act of 1887 laid the foundation for one of the USDA's primary objectives—scientific research to benefit farmers and ranchers. The Hatch Act granted federal land to each state for the establishment of agricultural research stations. Most states chose to associate their agricultural research stations with their land-grant colleges or universities established under the Morrill Act of 1862. The Morrill Act itself focused on establishing land-grant universities for the purpose of furthering agricultural education. Most of the agricultural research stations established under the Hatch Act became part of the cooperative extension service under the Smith-Lever Act of 1914, which continues to provide agricultural education services to agricultural professionals and the public.

The USDA provided considerable assistance to American farmers during the Dust Bowl and Great Depression (1929–1941) years of the 1930s. The Dust Bowl was period of agricultural and ecological degradation in the American and Canadian prairie lands in the early and mid-1930s. Poor agricultural practices combined with drought

---

WORDS TO KNOW

FARM BILL: A comprehensive omnibus bill adopted by the United States Congress that sets the agricultural and food policy of the United States.

GENETICALLY MODIFIED ORGANISM (GMO): Any living organism, including plants, animals, and bacteria, that has had genetic material altered to express desired traits.

SUBSIDY: A form of financial assistance granted by the government to assist a particular business or industry, usually to maintain a competitive price of a commodity.

created conditions that resulted in wind-driven clouds of dust. President Franklin Roosevelt (1882–1945) established the USDA's Soil Erosion Service, now known as the Natural Resources Conservation Service, in 1933 to address soil erosion in American prairie states. The USDA taught farmers soil conservation techniques, which, combined with the planting of 200 million trees to serve as windbreaks, has prevented a repeat of the Dust Bowl in the United States.

The Agricultural Adjustment Act (AAA) of 1933, considered to be the first U.S. farm bill, restricted and controlled agricultural production in the United States in order to stabilize agricultural prices, which had tumbled due to increased surplus. To increase farm prices, the federal government paid farmers to destroy crops or take farmland out of production. By decreasing supply, agricultural prices rose. The government paid farmers set prices to reduce crop yields, which made the AAA the first large-scale agricultural subsidy program administered by the USDA.

USDA officials confiscate a herd of sheep suspected of carrying a prion disease similar to mad cow disease. One of the functions of the USDA is maintaining food safety, including the inspection of meat. *AP Images.*

■ Impacts and Issues

As the head agricultural agency for one of the world's largest agricultural producers, the USDA wields enormous influence over domestic and international agricultural policies and practices. The USDA's agricultural subsidy programs have a significant impact on food prices, food supplies, and agricultural markets in the United States and around the world. Congress adjusts agricultural policy approximately every five years through a comprehensive omnibus farm bill. Between 1995 and 2009, the USDA provided U.S. farmers with more than $245 billion in agricultural subsidies.

Agricultural subsidies represent an increasingly large percentage of U.S. agricultural income. In 1974, for example, agricultural subsidies only accounted for 2 percent of total U.S. agricultural income. By 2000 this figure had increased to 47 percent of total U.S. agricultural income. Subsequent increases in global food prices have reduced the percentage of subsidies to between one-quarter and one-third of total U.S. agricultural income. Critics note that USDA subsidies tend to favor large-scale producers. Between 1995 and 2009, the top 10 percent of U.S. agricultural producers received almost three-quarters of all subsidies.

The international community opposes U.S. subsidies for U.S. farmers, on the grounds that the subsidies create an unequal playing field for agricultural goods. Foreign governments and the World Trade Organization (WTO) argue that U.S. subsidies drive down the global price of agricultural commodities. Whereas lower prices help provide consumers with cheaper food, lower commodity prices adversely impact non-U.S. farmers who cannot compete in a low-priced commodities market. Farmers in developing nations, which generally cannot afford to provide subsidies to their farmers, are at a particular disadvantage. In 2005 the WTO told the United States to stop providing its farmers with subsidies that manipulate the global agricultural markets. The United States' refusal to lower agricultural subsidies ultimately led to the collapse of the Doha round of negotiations over a new WTO international trade agreement.

The USDA has also received considerable domestic and international criticism over its support of genetically modified organisms (GMOs). Many foreign governments oppose the importation of genetically modified (GM) food from the United States. They raise concerns over the safety of GM food for human consumption and the potential impact on the environment. Under international trade agreements, countries may not prohibit the importation of processed foods containing GM products. Under the Cartagena Protocol on Biosafety, an international agreement that addresses GM and living modified organism (LMO) food products, a country may prohibit the importation of some LMO products if the country has concerns about any potential risk to humans or the environment.

U.S. environmental and consumer advocacy groups also oppose the USDA's support of GM foods, citing concerns over potential health and environmental concerns.

In the 1980s and 1990s, the USDA faced criticism for longstanding discrimination against African-American farmers in its agricultural loan and disaster payment practices. More than 400 African-American farmers brought a class-action lawsuit, *Pigford v. Glickman*, against the USDA for discrimination in its loan and payment practices between 1983 and 1997. The U.S. government agreed to settle the lawsuit before trial. The government offered African-American farmers a choice between a $50,000 payout for any farmer who had applied for and been denied USDA aid or filing a claim for a larger payout if the farmer could substantiate the higher award. The U.S. government has paid out more than $1 billion in claims to African-American farmers as a result of the Pigford settlement.

SEE ALSO *Agribusiness; Agriculture and International Trade; Agroecology; Aid and Subsidies to Promote Agriculture and Reduce Illicit Drug Production; Climate Change and Agriculture; Commission on Genetic Resources for Food and Agriculture; Community Supported Agriculture (CSAs); Embargoes; Ethical Issues in Agriculture; Extreme Weather and Food Supply; Factory Farming; Family Farms; Farm-to-Table Movement; Food Inspection and Standards; Food Safety and Inspection Service; Gender Equality and Agriculture; Genetically Modified Organisms (GMO); International Fund for Agricultural Development; Organic Foods Production Act of 1990; Organics; Produce Traceability; Subsidies; Sustainable Agriculture; USDA Food Pyramid; Wage Slavery in Food Production.*

BIBLIOGRAPHY

Books

Tamayo, Efren J. *America's Family Farms*. New York: Nova Science Publishers, 2010.

U.S. Department of Agriculture (USDA) and U.S. Department of Health and Human Services. *Nutrition and Your Health: Dietary Guidelines for Americans*, 6th ed. Washington, DC: U.S. Government Printing Office, 2005.

Periodicals

Broadway, Michael, and Donald Stull. "The Wages of Food Factories." *Food and Foodways* 18, no. 1–2 (2010): 43–65.

Holden, Joanne M., Linda E. Lemar, and Jacob Exler. "Vitamin D in Foods: Development of the US Department of Agriculture Database." *American Journal of Clinical Nutrition* 87, no. 4 (2008): S1092–S1096.

"Insights—Department of Justice and USDA Officials Examine Monsanto's Hold on the Heartland." *Chemical and Engineering News* 88, no. 13 (2010): 16.

"Organic—USDA Announces $50 Million Initiative for Organic Agriculture." *Food Chemical News* 51, no. 12 (2009): 31.

"USDA to Conduct First-Ever On-Farm Energy Production Survey." *Resource: Engineering & Technology for a Sustainable World* 17, no. 5 (2010): 29.

Web Sites

"Country-of-Origin Labeling." *Economic Research Service (ERS), U.S. Department of Agriculture (USDA)*. http://www.ers.usda.gov/features/cool/ (accessed October 16, 2010).

U.S. Department of Agriculture (USDA). http://www.usda.gov/wps/portal/usda/usdahome (accessed October 16, 2010).

Joseph P. Hyder

U.S. Food and Drug Administration (FDA)

■ Introduction

The Food and Drug Administration (FDA) is an agency of the U.S. Department of Health and Human Services (HHS) that is responsible for protecting consumers by regulating and ensuring the safety and effectiveness of food, drugs, cosmetics, tobacco, and other products. The FDA is organized into six product centers, one research center, and two offices. Each product center regulates one category of products or processes under the purview of the FDA, including the Center for Food Safety and Applied Nutrition. The FDA maintains 223 field offices and 13 laboratories in the United States and foreign field offices in several countries. Each year, the FDA regulates more than $1 trillion of products in the United States.

The FDA exercises broad regulatory powers, including the ability to approve whether certain goods may be sold in the United States. The FDA may also issue recalls for products that it determines to be unsafe. Approximately 3,000 products per year are recalled in the United States upon the recommendation of the FDA, and an additional 30,000 foreign products are detained at U.S. ports on FDA orders. Despite the FDA's efforts to protect American consumers, numerous consumer advocacy, public interest, and environmental groups criticize the FDA for issues ranging from new drug approvals to food regulations.

■ Historical Background and Scientific Foundations

The United States did little to regulate food or drug safety prior to the twentieth century. The Vaccine Act of 1813, which encouraged smallpox vaccinations and sought to prevent the use of fraudulent vaccines, was the first law in the United States to regulate food or drug safety. Congress repealed the Vaccine Act in 1822 to allow states to regulate the efficacy and distribution of the smallpox vaccine. In 1862 U.S. President Abraham Lincoln (1809–1865) established the Bureau of Chemistry, the predecessor of the FDA, within the newly established U.S. Department of Agriculture (USDA). In 1880 the USDA recommended that Congress pass a national food and drug law to regulate the adulteration of food and drugs. Congress did not pass the legislation. Over the next 25 years, more than 100 food and drug safety laws came before Congress, but Congress failed to pass a comprehensive food and drug law.

In 1883 American scientist Harvey Wiley (1844–1930) became chief chemist of the Bureau of Chemistry. Wiley was one of the foremost proponents of a federal law to regulate food and drug adulteration and safety. In 1902 Congress authorized Wiley to conduct a scientific investigation into the use of chemical preservatives, additives, and colors in food production. Wiley's investigation showed widespread food and drug adulteration and led to greater public demand for a food and drug law.

In 1906, years of work by Wiley and others culminated in Congress passing the Pure Food and Drug Act of 1906, the United States' first comprehensive food and drug regulatory law. The act prohibited the manufacture, transportation, or sale of adulterated food or drug products. The act also required manufacturers of drugs that contain habit-forming ingredients, such as cannabis, cocaine, heroin, or morphine, to label the product's ingredients. In addition, the act authorized the USDA, which was the Bureau of Chemistry's parent agency, to inspect meat products, a function that the USDA continues to perform. Although the Pure Food and Drug Act only expanded the powers of the Bureau of Chemistry and did not found a new agency, the FDA considers 1906 as its founding date. In 1927 Congress reorganized the Bureau of Chemistry within the USDA and moved the bureau's regulatory functions to the newly created Food, Drug, and Insecticide Administration. In 1930 an agricultural appropriations act changed the agency's name to the Food and Drug Administration.

The Federal Food, Drug, and Cosmetics (FD&C) Act of 1938 greatly expanded the FDA's powers and transformed the FDA into the regulatory agency that exists in the early twenty-first century. The FD&C granted the FDA authority to regulate food, drugs, medical devices, food additives, and dietary supplements. It mandated that manufacturers prove to the FDA that new drugs are safe before marketing or selling the drugs. The Kefauver-Harris Amendment of 1962 required that manufacturers also prove the efficacy of new drugs before marketing or selling them. The FD&C also gave the FDA regulatory powers over the food industry, defining and regulating which food colorings and additives manufacturers could include in foods. The FDA was authorized to establish standards for the identity and quality for foods.

WORDS TO KNOW

FOOD ADDITIVE: A substance, not normally consumed by itself, that is added to a food product to increase shelf life, appearance, or taste.

NUTRITION LABEL: A listing of all ingredients and nutritional information, including calories, fat, sodium, protein, and carbohydrates, contained in the product.

RECOMBINANT BOVINE GROWTH HORMONE (rBGH): A genetically engineered hormone given to cattle to increase milk production.

■ Impacts and Issues

Under the FD&C and subsequent amendments and legislation, the FDA has strong regulatory powers in a broad range of areas. With a staff of more than 9,000 employees and an annual budget of exceeding $2 billion, the FDA regulates the following products or processes: food; dietary supplements; new, generic, and over-the-counter (OTC) drugs; tobacco products; cosmetics; animal and veterinary products; therapeutic and assistive

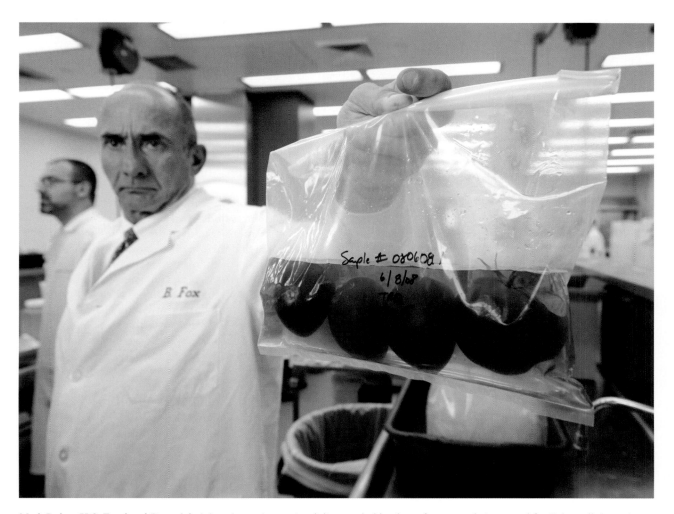

Mark Roh, a U.S. Food and Drug Administration acting regional director, holds a bag of tomatoes being tested for *Salmonella* bacteria at the FDA's southwest regional research lab in Irvine, California, in 2008.   *AP Images.*

A restaurateur in New Orleans, Louisiana, shucks a raw oyster. After protests from restaurateurs and oystermen, the U.S. Food and Drug Administration abandoned a plan that would have required all oysters harvested from the Gulf of Mexico in the summer to be treated to destroy harmful bacteria. *AP Images.*

devices; medical devices; vaccines; biotechnology and related products; blood and tissue products; and radiation-emitting devices, including cellular telephones, lasers, televisions, and microwave ovens.

The FDA protects consumers through one of the world's most stringent food and drug regulatory systems. Nevertheless, the agency attracts frequent criticism over many of its policies and actions. Any deficiency in the FDA's regulatory policies or enforcement could have significant consequences for the health of consumers. Critics often cite the FDA's drug safety and efficacy evaluation procedures of new drugs as a shortcoming of the agency, contending that the FDA takes too long to approve new drugs to the detriment of people in need of new treatments. Others criticize the agency for approving drugs that may harm consumers. In 2004, Merck, a pharmaceutical company, withdrew Vioxx, a non-steroidal anti-inflammatory (NSAID) drug that had received FDA approval in 1999. The FDA estimates that Vioxx contributed to between 88,000 and 139,000 heart attacks, of which 30 to 40 percent were fatal.

The FDA also attracts criticism from consumer advocacy and some environmental groups over regulations that allow the use of certain additives or processes in food production. In 2002 the FDA endorsed the use of carbon monoxide to treat meat and tuna. Carbon monoxide-treated meats keep their red color longer, which consumers find appealing. The FDA also endorses USDA regulations regarding the routine use of antibiotics in animals and the use of hormones, including recombinant bovine growth hormone (rBGH), in dairy cattle. Many consumer advocacy groups have raised concerns about the use of antibiotics and hormones in dairy cattle. Every country in the European Union (EU) has prohibited the use of rBGH since 1993 due to potential health concerns. After years of research by scientists on the routine use of antibiotics to promote growth in livestock and poultry, the FDA announced on June 28, 2010, that routine use of antibiotics may lead to antibiotic-resistant strains of diseases in humans. Some critics of the FDA felt the announcement did not go far enough, because the FDA did not ban or choose to regulate the practice of using antibiotics for animal growth. Instead, the FDA recommended that the industry voluntarily halt the use of antibiotics for growth and use them only for animal health under the supervision of a veterinarian. Those in the livestock industry protested the announcement, questioning the science behind the FDA's conclusions.

Under legislation enacted in 1990, the FDA also became responsible for regulating food nutrition labels. The Nutrition Labeling and Education Act of 1990 requires all food packages to contain nutrition labels that conform to FDA standards. The law also requires all food health claims to be consistent with FDA and HHS standards. Furthermore, the Nutrition Labeling and Education Act standardizes serving sizes for use on nutritional labels and regulates the use of terms such as "low fat" and "light." The Food Allergen Labeling and Consumer Protection Act of 2004 seeks to inform consumers about potential allergens contained in food products: All food labels must list if the product contains or may contain a protein derived from cow's milk, eggs, fish, peanuts, shellfish, soybeans, tree nuts, or wheat. Labeling regulations administered by the FDA are aimed at giving consumers the knowledge about food contents required to make informed nutrition decisions.

SEE ALSO *Center for Food Safety and Applied Nutrition; Codex Alimentarius; Consumer Food Safety Recommendations; Food Additives; Food Allergen Labeling and Consumer Protection Act of 2004; Food, Drug, and Cosmetic Act of 1938; Food Inspection and Standards; Food Recalls; Food Safety and Inspection Service; Meat Inspection Act of 1906; Poultry Products Inspection Act of 1957; Pure Food and Drug Act of 1906; U.S. Department of Agriculture (USDA); Wholesome Meat Act of 1967.*

BIBLIOGRAPHY

Books

Hilts, Philip J. *Protecting America's Health: The FDA, Business, and One Hundred Years of Regulation.* New York: Alfred A. Knopf, 2003.

McSwane, David Z., Richard Linton, and Nancy R. Rue. *2005 FDA Food Code Update: What You Need to Know.* Upper Saddle River, NJ: Pearson Prentice Hall, 2007.

Morrone, Michele. *Poisons on Our Plates: The Real Food Safety Problem in the United States.* Westport, CT: Praeger, 2008.

Periodicals

"FDA Food Compliance Chief Warns of Further Enforcement Uptick." *Food Chemical News* 51, no. 33 (2009): 1.

"Food Safety: Discussions to Overhaul FDA, Food-Safety System Begin." *Quality Progress* 42, no. 5 (May 1, 2009).

"OIG to Audit FDA Food Oversight Programs." *Food Chemical News* 51, no. 33 (2009): 11.

"Washington Trade Forum Focuses on FDA Food Import Safety." *Food Chemical News* 51, no. 4 (2009): 12.

Web Sites

"Food." *U.S. Food and Drug Administration (FDA).* http://www.fda.gov/Food/default.htm (accessed October 18, 2010).

"The Reportable Food Registry, FDA's New Early Detection System Helps Identify 125 Food Safety Problems in First Seven Months." *Center for Food Safety and Applied Nutrition, U.S. Food and Drug Administration (FDA).* http://www.fda.gov/Food/NewsEvents/ConstituentUpdates/ucm220973.htm (accessed October 18, 2010).

Joseph P. Hyder

USDA Food Pyramid

Introduction

The Improved American Food Guide Pyramid, known informally to the public as simply the "food pyramid," is the most recent set of advice for public nutrition issued by the United States government. First issued in 1992 and updated in 2005, the food pyramid provides a structure for understanding optimal food choices for a healthy diet and lifestyle. In 1994 the Center for Nutrition Policy and Promotion was formed to promote the food pyramid under the auspices of the U.S. Department of Agriculture (USDA). The food pyramid organizes a healthy diet via a pyramid schema, with five food groups: milk, grains, vegetables, fruits, and meat and beans. The pyramid also incorporates discretionary calories—calories for non-healthy foods—and physical activity into the schema.

According to a 1996 survey of adults in the United States, 40 percent claimed that it is difficult to know how to eat a healthy diet, given a wide variety of conflicting information in the media on the subject. This survey came on the heels of the 1994 Nutrition Labeling and Education Act, which changed nutrition information on product labels, ushering in the current, standardized food label on products sold in the United States. The nutrition labels and the food pyramid were designed to provide the public with more transparency about food ingredients, and how those ingredients and food composition of micronutrients fit into a healthy diet.

Historical Background and Scientific Foundations

Since 1894 the federal government in the United States has issued dietary guidelines in some form for public nutrition education. The USDA published a "composition of different food materials" table in the 1894 Yearbook of Agriculture that outlined the percentage of water, protein, fat, carbohydrates, and "mineral matters," along with a calorie count, for various foods ranging from beef to bread crackers to turnips.

In 1916 the USDA released a food and nutrition guide for public use, organized by food groups. The author, Caroline L. Hunt (1865–1927), created food groups in the Food for Young Children guide: milk and meat, vegetables and fruits, fats and fatty foods, sugars and sugary foods, and cereals. The guide made suggestions regarding the types of food in each group and the allocations of servings of food per day based on micronutrients and health. In 1921 Hunt published a new guide that made specific suggestions for foods to purchase and prepare each week, and the guide was popular among the public.

The Great Depression (1929–1941) led to more interest in the government's role in helping to prevent malnutrition and helping the public to develop better nutrition habits. In 1933 the USDA published food plans for four different income ranges, each designed by a food economist. These food plans continue to be published in the twenty-first century. For example, the August 2010 plan estimates that a family of four, with two children in the 6–11 age range, could spend between $579.20 for the "thrifty" plan per month for food, up to $1,143 per month for the "liberal" plan for food. These food plans, from 1933 to the present, offer shopping tips and meal planning as well.

The National Nutrition Conference of 1941, spearheaded by President Franklin D. Roosevelt (1882–1945), examined the nation's nutritional health and needs, sparked in part by the National Defense Advisory Commission's 1940 report about the need to find physically qualified soldiers to fight in World War II (1939–1945). Many were malnourished, experienced severe dental decay and infection, and were underweight and unable to fight. The National Nutrition Conference established the first Minimum Daily Requirement (MDA) charts for specific micronutrients (vitamins and minerals). The Food and Drug Administration (FDA) subsequently called for the enrichment of flour and other foodstuffs with B vitamins and iron to meet identified nutrition deficiencies among the public. The MDA designation was replaced by the Recommended Daily Allowance (RDA).

The "Basic Seven" food groups were developed by the USDA in 1943, later modified to the "Basic Four": fruits and vegetables, grains, dairy, and meats. USDA advisories on nutrition emphasized a proper balance of these four food groups. This campaign extended through the 1970s, when a fifth group was added: fats, sugars, and alcohol, a food group to be consumed sparingly. In 1992 the USDA revamped the food group education program and introduced the food pyramid.

■ Impacts and Issues

The food pyramid is not a meal plan, but rather a guide to healthy eating. The 1992 pyramid used a graphic that showed 6 to 11 servings of grains as the base of the pyramid, with the next level split between 3 to 5 servings of vegetables and 2 to 4 servings of fruits. Above this level, the guide recommends 2 to 3 servings of dairy products, and 2 to 3 servings of meat, legumes, eggs, and nuts. The very tip of the pyramid is reserved for fats, oils, and sweets, "to be used sparingly" according to the graphic. In 2005 the USDA revised the food pyramid and created My Pyramid, along with the Web site MyPyramid.gov,

to update recommendations to include issues related to alcohol and physical activity.

The current food pyramid recommends that Americans consume 5 to 9 servings of fruits and vegetables per day, and the Centers for Disease Control and Prevention (CDC) promotes a campaign called "Five a Day" as part

A student plays a computer game with Eric Bost, Under Secretary for Food, Nutrition, and Consumer Services, to learn about the food pyramid. *AP Images.*

of the National Fruit and Vegetable Program to encourage Americans to eat the minimum number of servings.

The 2005 version of the food pyramid does not specify the number of servings adults need per food group, but instead provides general guidelines based on caloric intake. This has led critics to complain that My Pyramid promotional materials and public health education efforts are confusing. Unlike the 1992 food pyramid, which stated the ranges for servings per food group, the 2005 My Pyramid adjusts the number of servings per food group based on 12 different caloric intake levels ranging from 1,000 calories per day to 3,200 calories per day, and uses a series of charts and Web site tools to help individuals calculate specific nutritional needs. The Web site is a requirement for calculating individual needs, leaving those without technical savvy or easy access to the Internet unable to participate. This variability does not deliver enough specificity to provide a consistent, simple nutrition message that promotes health, according to some food consultants and nutrition professors.

A 2010 report released by the CDC revealed that 32.5 percent of adults eat two or more servings of fruit each day, and only 26.3 percent eat three or more servings of vegetables (not including French fries). CDC goals for 2009 were 75 percent for fruits and 50 percent for vegetables, leaving a serious gap between public health goals and actual dietary and nutrition behaviors among the American public.

SEE ALSO *Calories; Changing Nutritional Needs throughout Life; Cooking Fats; Dairy Products; Diet and Cancer; Diet and Diabetes; Diet and Heart Disease; Diet and Hypertension; Dietary Guidelines for Americans; Dietary Reference Intakes; Eggs; Family Meal Benefits; Fruits; Grains; Hydrogenated Fats and Trans Fats; Improving Nutrition for America's Children Act of 2010; Legumes; Meats; Nutrient Fortification of Foods; Nutrition; Nuts and Seeds; Obesity; Processed Foods; Salt; Seafood; U.S. Department of Agriculture (USDA); Vegetables; Vitamins and Minerals; Water.*

BIBLIOGRAPHY

Books

Burstein, John. *The Shape of Good Nutrition: The Food Pyramid.* St. Catharines, Ontario, Canada: Crabtree Publishing, 2008.

D'Elgin, Tershia. *What Should I Eat?: A Complete Guide to the New Food Pyramid.* New York: Ballantine Books, 2005.

Periodicals

"America's New 'Food Pyramid.'" *Lancet* 365, no. 9470 (2005): 1516.

"Kid-Friendly Food Pyramid." *FDA Consumer* 39, no. 6 (2005): 4–5.

Mitka, Mike. "Government Unveils New Food Pyramid: Critics Say Nutrition Tool Is Flawed." *JAMA: Journal of the American Medical Association* 293, no. 21 (2005): 2581–2852.

Web Sites

U.S. Department of Agriculture (USDA). "MyPyramid. gov: Steps to a Healthier You." *MyPyramid.gov.* http://www.mypyramid.gov/ (accessed October 18, 2010).

Melanie Barton Zoltan

Veganism

■ Introduction

Humans are capable of eating and digesting both plant and animal foods. However, vegetarians prefer to avoid consuming meat, fish, and poultry on health, ethical, religious, or environmental grounds, or a combination of these reasons. Vegans follow a vegetarian diet that also excludes all animal products such as eggs and dairy products like milk, cheese, and yogurt. Strict vegans will not use anything that has been derived from an animal, so they will not eat honey, wear leather, use toiletries with lanolin, or consume any other animal products. Veganism is not widespread, but it does have a long history. Vegans need to eat a wide variety of plant proteins from legumes, grains, fruits, and vegetables to be sure of getting essential amino acids compared to those who eat at least some animal protein. With a few exceptions, plant proteins do not contain all the essential amino acids, whereas animal protein does. Vegans may also go short on micronutrients, particularly vitamin B12, and must seek out foods containing these or, if they are not available from plant sources, consider taking dietary supplements. A vegetarian or vegan diet can be very healthy though, because it is low in saturated fat and high in fiber, both of which can help prevent heart disease and cancer.

■ Historical Background and Scientific Foundations

Veganism has its roots in vegetarianism, the practice of avoiding the consumption of meat and fish. Vegetarianism was first mentioned by the Greek philosopher and mathematician Pythagoras around 2,500 years ago. Pythagoras argued in benevolence toward all species, which meant not killing animals for food. Followers of Buddhism, Hinduism, and Jainism also advocate vegetarianism because animal welfare is a key concept in their philosophies. The first vegetarian society was formed in 1847 in England, and three years later, Presbyterian minister Sylvester Graham (1795–1851) co-founded the American Vegetarian Society. Graham also advocated the consumption of whole grains and was one of the pioneers of breakfast cereals. In 1944 Donald Watson (1910–2005), a British woodworker, first coined the word vegan, arguing that vegetarians often ate products that came from animals such as eggs and milk. Thus veganism is a stricter form of vegetarianism. Watson observed that tuberculosis had been found in nearly half of Britain's cows, and therefore argued it would be prudent to avoid animal products altogether. By the time of Watson's death in 2005, there were a quarter of a million vegans in Britain and around two million in the United States.

The main difference between the diets of those who eat animal protein, whether from animal meat or animal-derived products, and those who do not, is in the type of protein they consume. The body requires an adequate supply of the eight essential amino acids from food. These come from the digestion of protein in the diet and are used to build up the proteins that the body needs for growth, repair, and correct functioning. Humans are omnivores who can digest both plant and animal foods. Because animal proteins are complete proteins, non-vegetarians will have adequate amounts of essential amino acids, assuming they eat sufficient food. Plant proteins are usually deficient in one or more essential amino acids, with the exception of the grains amaranth, quinoa, and buckwheat, whose proteins are complete. This means that strict vegetarians must mix and match to get the essential amino acids they require. Popular vegan sources of protein include soy foods, such as tofu and soy milk, along with chickpeas, lentils, peanut butter, nuts, and rice.

A strict vegan differs from an ovo-lacto vegetarian (a vegetarian who eats eggs and dairy products) in that in addition to avoiding animal foods, the vegan does not eat any animal-derived products, including eggs or egg products (such as mayonnaise), milk or other dairy products (such as cheese and yogurt), nor honey or anything containing gelatin, which is derived from animal connective tissue. A vegan

WORDS TO KNOW

COMPLETE PROTEINS: Protein sources that contain all eight amino acids in adequate amounts. Animal foods are complete proteins but many plant foods are not.

ESSENTIAL AMINO ACIDS: All the proteins in the body are made from 20 different amino acid building blocks. Humans can synthesize 12 of these but eight need to be obtained from the diet. These eight are known as essential amino acids.

OMNIVORE: An animal that derives food from both plant and animal sources.

lifestyle extends beyond diet to not using any clothing or object made from leather, wool, silk, pearls, or anything else derived from animals, such as toiletries and cosmetics containing products such as lanolin, an animal fat.

Reasons for adopting veganism vary. Some vegans consider the vegan diet genuinely healthier than one containing animal protein. Others are vegan for religious or ethical reasons connected with animal welfare concerns. Even eating eggs and milk, although not consuming animals directly, promotes the meat industry, vegans argue, because the poultry and dairy animals are often killed eventually for their meat. In addition, many dairy animals are kept in conditions that vegans and vegetarians consider inhumane, such as on factory farms. Veganism is also, arguably, better for the environment, because it takes eight pounds of grain to produce one pound of beef. Therefore, more food would be available if people ate only plant food, and there would be fewer carbon dioxide emissions.

■ Impacts and Issues

A vegan diet has both health risks and health benefits. Getting sufficient protein, with an adequate amount of essential amino acids, should not be difficult if a varied diet is eaten along with a range of nuts, pulses, legumes, and grains. Vegans are at risk of missing out on some of the micronutrients. The American Dietetic Association advises that those who are not eating any animal products should take care not to go short on vitamin B12, vitamin D, iodine, calcium, and omega-3 fatty acids. Vitamin B12 is needed only in microgram amounts each day, but is found only in animal foods and products. A lack of B12 can lead to damage to the nervous and digestive systems, and a severe form of anemia. Vegans may need to consider supplementation if they are unwilling to even consider adding eggs or milk to their diet. However, some vegetable oils such as flaxseed and hemp are rich in omega-3 fatty acids.

Stop sign with sticker "Eating Animals" added as a political protest.   *Image copyright Matt McClain, 2010. Used under license from Shutterstock.com.*

Animal rights activists promote the environmental benefits of a vegan diet.   *AP Images.*

A vegan diet is naturally low in saturated fat because of the lack of animal foods. This should help lower the risk of heart disease and cancer. The high fruit and vegetable content means a vegan diet is high in fiber and in many micronutrients. Such diets have also been shown to be protective against heart disease, cancer, and other diseases and, indeed, form the mainstay of most healthy eating plans. There is some documented clinical evidence for the health benefits of a long-term vegetarian diet, but so far, less evidence exists documenting the benefits of a long-term vegan diet.

SEE ALSO   *Agroecology; Diet and Cancer; Diet and Diabetes; Diet and Heart Disease; Diet and Hypertension; Dietary Guidelines for Americans; Dietary Reference Intakes; Ecological Impacts of Various World Diets; Ethical Issues in Agriculture; Factory Farming; Foodways; Grains; Legumes; Nuts and Seeds; Organics; Phytochemicals (Phytonutrients); Sustainable Agriculture; Vegetables; Vegetarianism; Vitamins and Minerals.*

BIBLIOGRAPHY

Books

Guihan, Vincent. *New American Vegan.* Oakland, CA: PM Press, 2010.

Periodicals

Barnard, Neal D., et al. "A Low-Fat Vegan Diet and a Conventional Diabetes Diet in the Treatment of Type 2 Diabetes: A Randomized, Controlled, 74-Wk Clinical Trial." *The American Journal of Clinical Nutrition* 89, no. 5 (2009): 1588–1596.

Dunn-Emke, Stacey R., et al. "Nutrient Adequacy of a Very Low-Fat Vegan Diet." *Journal of the American Dietetic Association* 105, no. 9 (2005): 1442–1446.

Keane, Michael. "Taxing Sugar-Sweetened Beverages." *New England Journal of Medicine* 362, no. 4 (2010): 368–369.

"Vegan Diet Helps Treat Type 2 Diabetes." *Environmental Nutrition* 29, no. 10 (2006): 1.

Web Sites

Norris, Jack. "Staying Healthy on Plant-Based Diets." *VeganHealth.org.* http://www.veganhealth.org/ (accessed October 4, 2010).

"Why Vegan?" *Vegan Outreach.* http://www.veganoutreach.org/whyvegan/ (accessed October 4, 2010).

Susan Aldridge

Vegetables

■ Introduction

Vegetables have long played an important part in the human diet for their flavor, texture, and nutritional value. Some, such as the potato, are as significant as grains as a staple crop because they provide energy. Vegetables include many different botanical classes, which can be conveniently classified in broad groups of roots, stems, leaves, and flowers, depending on what part of the plant is eaten. Most plants create sugars, stored as starch, through photosynthesis, providing both sweetness and calories. Vegetables are also a source of vitamins, minerals, fiber, as well as phytochemicals, which may help prevent cancer. The storage characteristics and culinary properties of vegetables vary widely. Leaf vegetables such as lettuce soon wilt and are best eaten raw, whereas potatoes store well and can be cooked in a variety of ways. Plant pests, such as potato blight and insects, can devastate vegetable crops causing economic ruin and hardship, as in the Irish potato famine (1845–1849). Modern farming methods use high yielding varieties and agrochemicals, and many people enjoy growing their own vegetables, often using organic growing methods.

■ Historical Background and Scientific Foundations

Vegetables have probably formed part of the human diet since prehistory. Many are easy to grow and harvest and are good to eat, as well as having high nutritional value. Cabbage, beetroot, carrot, and potato are among the many vegetables known to have been cultivated for thousands of years. The simplest vegetables are the fungi, which are related to yeasts and molds. They do not have the ability to photosynthesize and often live off decaying matter such as the bark of dead trees. Some live in symbiosis with the roots of trees, providing the root with minerals from the soil while benefiting from the sugars present in the roots. Mushrooms are also unusual in that their cells are strengthened with chitin, rather than the cellulose that forms the walls of most plant cells.

The root vegetables include beets, the carrot family, and radishes and turnips (which belong to the cabbage family). Roots store nutrients from the soil and also starch and sugars made by photosynthesis in the leaves and conducted down the stem to the root. Hence root vegetables tend to taste sweet. Their tissue is composed of vacuoles filled with starch interspersed with fibers. As the root matures, the vacuoles expand, making it sweeter to the taste. But if left in the ground too long, the woodiness of the fibers starts to predominate in the texture. Thus, root vegetables have to be harvested at the right time for palatability.

The tubers include potatoes, sweet potatoes, water chestnuts, and yams. All are from different botanical families. The potato, which was a staple food of the Incas, is a true tuber or swollen tip of an underground stem and is a member of the tobacco, tomato, and deadly nightshade family. Although the sweet potato resembles the yam, it actually belongs to the morning glory family whereas the yam is the tuber of a plant related to grasses and lilies. The water chestnut is a corm, or swollen underwater stem tip of a plant from the sedge family.

The only vegetable that is solely a stem is rhubarb, which is actually a culinary fruit. Celery consists of leaf and stem and is more correctly described as a bunch of leaf stalks or petioles. Onion, which belongs to the lily family, like asparagus and leek, is both stem and leaf. The concentric rings of onion tissue are the swollen bases of the previous year's leaves and contain food reserves for the next year's growth. The flower vegetables include broccoli and cauliflower and globe artichoke, which is a kind of thistle.

Leafy vegetables include spinach, lettuce, and cabbages. They are the most perishable of all vegetables. As the organ of photosynthesis, leaves tend to be broad and flat to maximize surface area for trapping sunlight and carbon dioxide, and releasing oxygen as a photosynthesis by-product. They are full of air pockets; this increases the number of cells coming into contact with the air, which improves the efficiency of photosynthesis. It is this porosity that makes the leaf vegetables so prone to wilting. Most of a leaf vegetable is actually only air and water. If lettuce or spinach is heated, its structure readily collapses, which is why the volume of cooked spinach is so much less than raw. Finally, there is a diverse group of fruits that are culinary vegetables, including tomatoes, squashes, olives, peppers, and eggplants.

■ Impacts and Issues

Like any other food crop, vegetables are prone to attacks by disease and predators. The potato, a native of Central and South America, was introduced into Europe by Spanish explorers around 1570 and arrived in Britain and Ireland around 1610. Many poor people became dependent on the potato as a staple food because it is cheap and nutritious, being rich in starch and vitamin C and also containing about 3 percent protein, which is high for a vegetable. When blight struck Irish potato crops, famine was the result. Between 1845 and 1849, one million people died and 1.25 million people emigrated from Ireland, mainly to the United States. These events shaped the history of both countries.

In the early twenty-first century, nutrition guidelines call for the consumption of more vegetables. It is now recommended that to maintain good health and to prevent chronic diseases a minimum of five portions of fruits and vegetables should be eaten per day. The more brightly colored the vegetables are, the better they are in

A variety of vegetables is displayed in an open air market. *Image copyright Baloncici, 2010. Used under license from Shutterstock.com.*

nutritional terms. Some of the colored phytochemicals, such as carotene, chlorophyll, and anthocyanins, have antioxidant properties. Sulphoranes, which give broccoli and cabbage their characteristic taste, are phytochemicals, which have been shown to have anti-cancer properties, at least in laboratory experiments. There are many more phytochemicals whose biological properties are being investigated, in order that the health-giving properties of specific vegetables can be evaluated.

Crossbreeding and hybridization have commonly been used to alter and improve plant products including vegetables, and increasingly this process is also accomplished by genetic engineering. Most genetically engineered vegetables are used in livestock food, although some varieties of genetically modified vegetables such as beets, squash, potatoes, and corn are sold in supermarkets. Genetic engineering has produced fruits, vegetables, and grains that are more resistant to pests, viruses, and drought. However, some food advocates question their long-term safety. The Food and Drug Administration (FDA) evaluates and clears for consumption each GM (genetically modified) food product variety before it is made available for sale to the public, but does not require specific labeling that identifies the food as GM. On the other side of the spectrum, heirloom vegetables and fruits are growing in popularity among both food producers and consumers. Heirloom fruits and vegetables are diverse, vintage varieties that are usually organically grown and pollinated by natural means in the open environment.

■ Primary Source Connection

Mary Frances Kennedy Fisher (1908–1992) was an American culinary writer who captivated audiences with the first popular American essays on food. Under the moniker M.F.K. Fisher, her essays and short stories appeared in food and literary magazines including *Gourmet, The New Yorker, House Beautiful* and *Atlantic Monthly.* Among her popular books were *Serve It Forth* (1938), *Consider the Oyster* (1941), and *How to Cook a Wolf* (1942).

Fisher was influenced by the culinary traditions of Dijon, France, where she lived as a newlywed beginning in 1929. Many of her works feature personal experiences, journal entries, and references to food as a metaphor for cultural or societal commentary. "The Social Status of a Vegetable" was first published in *Harper's Magazine* in 1937.

The Social Status of a Vegetable

It is constantly surprising, this vegetable snobbism. It is almost universal.

My mother, who was raised in the county too crowded with Swedish immigrants, shudders at turnips, which they seem to have lived on. And yet there she ate, week in and week out, corn meal mush and molasses, a dish synonymous to many Americans with poor trash of the pariah-ridden South.

And my grandmother . . . I remember hearing her dismiss some unfortunate person as a vulgar climber by saying, quietly, "Oh, Mrs. Zubzub is the kind of woman who serves artichokes!"

Of course, to a child reared within smelling distance, almost, of the fog-green fields of those thistly flowers, such damnation was quite meaningless; but I suppose that to a Midwestern woman of the last century, it meant much.

Just a few years ago, the same class consciousness was apparent in a small college in Illinois, where students whispered and drew away from me after I innocently introduced a box of avocados from my father's ranch into a dormitory "feast." From that unfortunate night, I was labeled a stuck-up snob.

The first time, though, that I ever felt surprise at the social position of a vegetable was when I was a lower-class-man in a boarding school. Like most Western private schools, it was largely filled with out-of-state children whose families wintered in California, and the daughters of the newly-rich.

Pretension and snobbishness flourished among these oddly segregated adolescents, and nowhere could such stiff cautious conventionality be found as in their classrooms, their teas, their sternly pro-British hockey matches.

One girl, from Englewood in New Jersey or maybe Tuxedo Park, was the recognized leader of the Easterners, the "bloods." She was more dashing than the rest; she used with impressive imitation her mother's high whinnying gush of poise and good breeding. She set the pace, and with a certain surety too, for such an unsure age as sixteen. She was daring.

The reason I know she was daring, even so long ago, is that I can still hear her making a stupendous statement. That takes courage any time, but when you are young, and bewildered behind your affectation of poise, and surrounded by other puzzled children who watch avidly for one wrong move, it is as impressive as a parade with trumpets.

We were waiting for the lunch bell. Probably we were grumbling about the food, which was unusually good for such an institution, but, like all food cooked *en masse,* dull. Our bodies clamored for it, our tongues rebelled.

The girl from Englewood or Tuxedo Park spoke out, her hard voice clear, affectedly drawling, to hide her own consciousness of daring. She must have known that what she said, even while aping her mother's social sureness, was very radical to the children around her, the children fed from kitchens of the *haute bourgeoisie* and in luxurious hotels. . . .

"I know it's terribly, terribly silly of me," she said, with all she could summon of maternally gracious veneer, "but of course I was brought up near Pennsylvania, and the customs there are so quaint, and I know you'll all be terribly, terribly shocked, but I *love,* I *adore* wieners and sauerkraut."

Yes, it was surprising then and still is. All round are signs of it, everywhere, little trickles of snobbish judgment, always changing, ever present.

In France, old Crainquebille sold leeks from a cart, leeks called "the asparagus of the poor." Now asparagus sells for the asking, almost, in California markets, and broccoli, that strong age-old green, leaps from its lowly pot to the *Ritz's* copper saucepan.

Who determines, and for what strange reasons, the social status of a vegetable?

M.F.K. Fisher

FISHER, M. F. K. "THE SOCIAL STATUS OF A VEGETABLE" IN *THE MEASURE OF HER POWERS: AN M.F.K. FISHER READER*, EDITED BY DOMINIQUE GIOIA. WASHINGTON, DC: COUNTERPOINT, 1999.

SEE ALSO *Agribusiness; Biodiversity and Food Supply; Climate Change and Agriculture; Community Supported Agriculture (CSAs); Consumer Food Safety Recommendations; Dietary Guidelines for Americans; Dietary Reference Intakes; Ecological Impacts of Various World Diets; Family Meal Benefits; Fruits; Functional Foods; Genetically Modified Organisms (GMO); Hydroponics; Immigration and Cuisine; Improving Nutrition for America's Children Act of 2010; Legumes; Phytochemicals (phytonutrients); Produce Traceability; USDA Food Pyramid; Veganism; Vegetarianism.*

BIBLIOGRAPHY

Books

Li, Thomas S. C. *Vegetables and Fruits: Nutritional and Therapeutic Values.* Boca Raton, FL: CRC Press, 2008.

Nichols, Mike, and Martin Hilmi. *Growing Vegetables for Home and Market.* Rome: Rural Infrastructure and Agro-Industries Division, Food and Agriculture Organization of the United Nations, 2009.

Watson, Ronald R., and Victor R. Preedy. *Bioactive Foods in Promoting Health: Fruits and Vegetables.* Amsterdam: Academic Press, 2010.

World Cancer Research Fund, American Institute for Cancer Research (AICR). *Food, Nutrition, Physical Activity, and the Prevention of Cancer: A Global Perspective.* Washington, DC: AICR, 2007.

Periodicals

Allen, Kimberly Jordan. "Eating Right Edible History: Heirloom Fruits and Vegetables." *E: The Environmental Magazine* 16, no. 3 (2005): 42–43.

Kavanaugh, Claudine J., Paula R Trumbo, and Kathleen C. Ellwood. "The U.S. Food and Drug Administration's Evidence-Based Review for Qualified Health Claims: Tomatoes, Lycopene, and Cancer." *Journal of the National Cancer Institute* 99 (2007): 1074–1085.

Nishino, Hoyoky, et al. "Cancer Prevention by Phytochemicals." *Oncology* 69, supplement 1 (2005): 38–40.

Web Sites

Harvard School of Public Health. "Nutrition Source: Fruits and Vegetables—The Bottom Line." *Harvard University.* http://www.hsph.harvard.edu/nutritionsource/what-should-you-eat/vegetables-and-fruits/index.html (accessed September 29, 2010).

Susan Aldridge

Vegetarianism

■ Introduction

Vegetarianism is a widespread phenomenon of people choosing or otherwise abstaining from eating meat. Some vegetarians avoid other animal products such as dairy products, eggs, and honey, or non-food products such as leather. Vegetarians may choose this diet for religious reasons, and many religions recommend a vegetarian diet. Other people choose vegetarianism for ethical reasons related to animal welfare or animal rights. In addition, some vegetarians cite health reasons or environmental reasons for their diet. As personal incomes around the world increase, the demand for meat increases. The environmental problems of current production practices, especially in concentrated animal feeding operations (CAFOs) lead some dietary activists to advocate a vegetarian diet to protect the environment from the growing human population. Whereas many vegetarians choose to abstain from meat and other animal products for a variety of reasons, many of the world's poor adopt a grain-based, vegetarian diet out of economic necessity.

■ Historical Background and Scientific Foundations

Religious prescriptions of vegetarianism began in ancient times and persist to this day. For example, many branches of Hinduism, some branches of Buddhism, some Seventh Day Adventists, and followers of Jainism prescribe a vegetarian diet. Jainism, a religion practiced in India and in other regions in the world, primarily among the Indian diaspora, disallows the harm of animals, and some Jainists even avoid root crops in addition to animal products, because digging up these crops would disturb worms, insects, and other animals in the soil. For similar reasons, many branches of Hinduism adhere to principles of nonviolence and include nonviolence toward animals, thus limiting or excluding the slaughter of animals for meat.

Dietary restrictions can be found in most religions and religious traditions. One common dietary restriction may require a vegetarian diet for a length of time for observance of a particular religious period or event. For example, in some branches of Orthodox Christianity, adherents will eat a vegetarian diet during Lent, a religious season. A vegetarian diet is also common for religious ascetics, those who choose to dedicate their lives entirely to religious study or practice such as monks.

Other individuals choose to be vegetarian on ethical grounds. Whereas meat eating or use of other animal products may not be restricted by religion for these individuals, they find the harming of animals to provide food for humans to be ethically unacceptable. Some vegetarians who follow very strict diets, such as vegans, do not consume any animal product. Vegans may avoid meat, honey, leather, eggs, all dairy products, foods containing gelatin, and other products produced by animals or derived from their slaughter. Some vegans frame, for example, the collection of honey from bee hives as exploitation of the bees and equate such use of livestock animals and wild animals with human slavery. Others protest against what they refer to as the pain and suffering of livestock.

Some ethical arguments are based in opposition to the environmental and animal welfare standards in what they term factory farms, what is known in the livestock industry as concentrated animal feeding operations (CAFOs). Two groups of ethical arguments concern livestock practices. The first argument is that the animal welfare conditions in CAFOs and other livestock operations are insufficient to protect livestock from pain and harm. Vegetarians who accept this argument may abstain from eating meat and other animal products now, but presumably, they would eat meat and other animal products produced with improved animal welfare measures. Others view an ethical problem with any use of livestock as human food. For these people, many of whom argue that animals have rights, any consumption of meat or other animal products presents an ethical wrong.

A woman at a London market prepares vegetarian food typical of Gujarat State, India. *© Jenny Matthews / Alamy.*

WORDS TO KNOW

CONCENTRATED ANIMAL FEEDING OPERATION (CAFO):
A single facility that confines a large number of animals. Legally, in the United States, the Environmental Protection Agency (EPA) defines a CAFO as a farm that has at least 1,000 beef cattle, 700 dairy cows, 2,500 hogs, or 125,000 broilers.

ENGEL'S LAW: As a household's income increases, it will spend a lower percentage of income on food though its actual food expenditures may increase. The increase spending is due to a shift in the diet away from grain to more expensive foods such as meat, dairy, fruits, and vegetables. Engel's law is named after Ernst Engel (1821–1896), the German economist and statistician who first wrote about it.

MICRONUTRIENTS: Vitamins and minerals necessary for growth, metabolic functions, and other biological processes in humans, other animals, and plants.

VEGAN: The strictest type of vegetarian, refraining from eating not only meat and fish, but also eggs, dairy products, and all other food containing or derived from animals, often including honey. A vegan diet contains no cholesterol and very little fat, so it is quite healthy as long as sufficient nutrients are obtained, especially vitamins B12 and D, calcium, and quality protein. Most vegans also avoid wearing or using animal products of any kind, including fur, leather, and even wool. Vegans are often motivated primarily by a humane and ethical concern for the welfare of animals and by a desire to avoid unhealthy food products. Vegans generally argue that many industrial and commercial methods of raising livestock and other food animals are not only harmful and cruel to animals but also damage the natural environment.

A philosophy of animal rights was laid out by Peter Singer (1946–), Australian ethical philosopher, in his book *Animal Liberation* in 1975. Some activist groups such as People for the Ethical Treatment of Animals (PETA) also adhere to an animal rights standpoint that a vegan diet is the only way to protect these rights.

Vegetarians also may chose their diet for health and medical reasons. Consumption of meat, especially what is known as red meat from cattle, hogs, sheep, and goats, has been linked to a variety of health problems. These foods and other animal derived foods can be high in saturated fats and cholesterol, both of which medical studies show contribute to cardiovascular diseases and higher incidence of various forms of cancer. Doctors may prescribe a vegetarian diet for either short-term or long-term use to combat specific health problems. Many dietary activists have recommended vegetarianism for general health reasons, including the Reverend Alexander Graham (1794–1851), an American reformer and Presbyterian minister best known as the inventor of the Graham cracker, a high-fiber, honey-sweetened cracker popular in the United States. Graham recommended a vegetarian diet both to cure and prevent alcoholism and

sexual desire. More modern dietary activists point to evidence from various health studies of the benefits of a diet high in fiber, low in fat, and based in fruit, nuts, vegetables, and grains.

As environmental awareness has grown in the developed countries since the 1960s, various environmental advocates have put environmental reasons forward for adopting a vegetarian diet. Concerns about the amount of water used to produce meat on CAFOs and about the amount of land used to grow grain to feed livestock in CAFOs are used to show the lessened environmental impact of a vegetarian diet. Water use by CAFOs can be intensive: For example, in a 1997 study from the journal *Bioscience*, one pound of grain-fed broiler chicken meat required 420 gallons (1590 liters) of water to produce. Others point to the fact that livestock animals at CAFOs consume grain. For every six kilograms of vegetable protein consumed, livestock

Hundreds of vegetarians gather in the meatpacking district of New York City for the 2nd Veggie Pride parade. It is patterned after a similar parade that takes place in Paris, France. © *Frances Roberts / Alamy.*

in the United States generally produce one kilogram of animal protein, according to studies conducted in 1997 by a Cornell University professor. These advocates say that these grains could be better used to feed people than livestock. Concern about global climate change also leads to criticisms of livestock production systems, as livestock and their manure from CAFOs are a significant source of methane, nitrous oxide, and other pollutants.

■ Impacts and Issues

According to Engel's law, as incomes increase, people worldwide will spend a smaller percentage of their income on food. However, the real spending will increase, primarily as the diet shifts from low-cost calories from grain and legumes to higher cost calories from fruit, vegetables, meat, and dairy products. As population and income of the world are both expected to grow, the impact of livestock on the environment and the need for more overall calories and the desire for more expensive forms of calories will remain. Some fear that population growth will outstrip the ability of agriculture and livestock production to feed the planet. Paul Ralph Ehrlich

(1932–), an American entomologist and biologist, in his 1968 best seller *The Population Bomb*, emphasized the environmental harm of a growing population and warned of mass starvation. Some environmental activists point out that switching to vegetarian diets would reduce the impact of livestock production on the environment and help accommodate a growing population. Others view the tremendous increases in both livestock and crop productivity in the twentieth century as evidence that technology can continue to provide for a growing population without having to undertake significant dietary changes. However, this view may underestimate how much diets will shift as poor populations move out of poverty and consume more livestock products.

The American Dietetic Association and the Canadian Dietetic Association, both professional groups of dieticians, along with many other groups have shown that either a vegetarian diet or a vegan diet can contain all micronutrient and macronutrients needs equally as well as a diet that includes animal products. In fact, many health benefits have been shown for diets, vegetarian and otherwise, that include a diverse selection of fruits, vegetables, and whole grains. However, for many vegetarians in the developing world who do not consume meat or animal products due to poverty, their diets may lack adequate protein or have a variety of micronutrient deficiencies. Poverty can be either endemic, meaning that it persists for a long time, often across many generations, or transitory, meaning an unexpected shock causes a household to temporarily fall into poverty. Both forms of poverty may cause households to cope by reducing food consumption or consuming less costly sources of food. Currently, the Economic and Social Research Institute estimates that worldwide, up to 1.5 billion people are either vegetarians or lacto-vegetarians (those who do not eat meat but consume dairy products) out of economic necessity. These poor households usually survive on a very limited vegetarian diet with little variety. This grain-based diet often lacks essential micronutrients and adequate protein, and in its most extreme form may lack sufficient calories. For these who are involuntary vegetarians, nutritional assistance may be necessary to prevent malnutrition.

SEE ALSO *Agroecology; Climate Change and Agriculture; Diet and Cancer; Diet and Diabetes; Diet and Heart Disease; Diet and Hypertension; Dietary Guidelines for Americans; Dietary Reference Intakes; Eggs; Ethical Issues in Agriculture; Factory Farming; Fruits; Functional Foods; Grains; Legumes; Livestock Intensity and Demand; Meats; Nuts and Seeds; Obesity; Phytochemicals (Phytonutrients); Population and Food; Rice; Sustainable Agriculture; Veganism; Vegetables; Vitamins and Minerals.*

BIBLIOGRAPHY

Books

Carlson, Peggy. *The Complete Vegetarian: The Essential Guide to Good Health.* Urbana: University of Illinois Press, 2009.

Horsman, Jennifer, and Jaime Flowers. *Please Don't Eat the Animals: All the Reasons You Need to Be a Vegetarian.* Sanger, CA: Quill Driver/Word Dancer, 2007.

Keith, Lierre. *The Vegetarian Myth: Food, Justice and Sustainability.* Crescent City, CA: Flashpoint Press, 2009.

Lappé, Frances Moore, and Anna Lappé. *Hope's Edge: The Next Diet for a Small Planet.* New York: Putnam, 2003.

Perry, Cheryl L., Leslie A. Lytle, and Teresa G. Jacobs. *The Vegetarian Manifesto.* Philadelphia: Running Press, 2004.

Singer, Peter, and Jim Mason. *The Way We Eat: Why Our Food Choices Matter.* Emmaus, PA: Rodale, 2006.

Stuart, Tristram. *The Bloodless Revolution: A Cultural History of Vegetarianism from 1600 to Modern Times.* New York: W.W. Norton & Co., 2007.

Vegetarian Network Victoria. *Eating Up the World: The Environmental Consequences of Human Food Choices.* Melbourne, Australia: Vegetarian Network, 2009.

Wells, Troth. *The Global Vegetarian Kitchen.* Oxford, UK: New Internationalist, 2010.

Periodicals

Fraser, Gary E. "Vegetarian Diets: What Do We Know of Their Effects on Common Chronic Diseases?" *The American Journal of Clinical Nutrition* 89, no. 5 (2009): S1607–S1612.

Lindbloom, Erik J. "Long-Term Benefits of a Vegetarian Diet." *American Family Physician* 79, no. 7 (2009): 541–542.

Mann, Jim. "Vegetarian Diets." *British Medical Journal* 339 (2009): b2507.

"Poultry, Food Security and Poverty in India: Looking Beyond the Farm-Gate." *World's Poultry Science Journal* 66, no. 2 (2010): 309–320.

Van der Kooi, Merle E. "The Inconsistent Vegetarian." *Society and Animals* 18, no. 3 (2010): 291–305.

Web Sites

American Dietetic Association. "Appropriate Planned Vegetarian Diets Are Healthful, May Help in Disease Prevention and Treatment, Says American Dietetic Association." *American Dietetic Association Press Release,* July 1, 2009. http://www.eatright.org/Media/content.aspx?id=1233&terms=vegetarian (accessed October 22, 2010).

U.S. Department of Agriculture (USDA). "Vegetarian Diets." *MyPyramid.gov.* http://www.mypyramid.gov/tips_resources/vegetarian_diets.html (accessed October 22, 2010).

Vegetarian Resource Group. http://www.vrg.org/ (accessed October 22, 2010).

Blake Jackson Stabler

Viniculture

Introduction

Viniculture is the cultivation of grapes for the production of wine by fermentation. All of the chemical elements to make wine are in the grape itself: Grape pulp or flesh has water, sugar, and pectin, and the skin provides yeast, tannins, and pigments that give wine its characteristic color. In order to make wine, the grapes must be crushed so the sugar in the juice comes into contact with the yeast, and the juice must be kept at a constant temperature to allow fermentation to occur. The yeast consumes the sugar and produces carbon dioxide and alcohol. To preserve its quality and prevent it from turning into vinegar, the wine must be protected from air by being stored in tanks, barrels, or bottles. Though the chemical process to make wine itself is simple, the quality and character of the final product is influenced by a score of complex decisions that comprise the art of viniculture. The winemaker or *vigneron* not only attempts to optimize the result of a particular variety of grape in a specific location or *terroir*, but tries to attain a level of sugar concentration, yield, and other qualities to satisfy the legal, aesthetic, and cultural requirements of the market for the specific wine. Wine is not only a product, but a global commodity and sociocultural icon with its own history and politics.

Historical Background and Scientific Foundations

The earliest verification of winemaking has been found in archaeological evidence dating from the Neolithic Period (8500 to 4000 BC), in the Zagros mountains in western Iran. Ancient jars contained remnants of tartaric acid and calcium tartrate, the remnants of fermented grape juice from the wild Eurasian species of grape (*Vitis vinifera sylvestris*), which is the source of 99 percent of the world's wine in the twenty-first century.

The "Noah hypothesis" refers to the quest, using DNA analysis, to discover where and when the wild Eurasian grape was first cultivated, named after the patriarch described in the Bible as the first winemaker. Noah was said to have established vineyards at the foot of Mount Ararat in Eastern Turkey, where the Ark came to rest after the Flood. His wine-drinking proclivities and the flood story were also paralleled by the Mesopotamian flood described in the *Epic of Gilgamesh*, dating from the seventh century BC. In the tale, Gilgamesh was described as entering a grove of grapevines and meeting Siduri, a barmaid possessing vessels for drinking wine. Gilgamesh's half-wild companion, Enkidu, was also portrayed as drinking seven goblets of a strong beverage offered to him by a temple prostitute, an indulgence to mark him as "civilized" and "human." The *Epic* supports the fact that there is clear evidence of simultaneous production of wine in the mountainous areas of Mesopotamia around 5000 BC.

From the northern mountains of the Near East, viniculture spread across the region to the eastern edge of the Mediterranean Sea and across Europe. According to Rod Philips's *Short History of Wine*, the spread of wine technology between 5000 BC and the collapse of the Western Roman Empire in the 5th century AD was due to four main factors. First, viniculture spread due to the trade and colonization movements of wine-producing societies, such as the ancient Greeks who introduced winemaking to southern Italy. Second, viniculture spread because wine had powerful religious and cultural meanings. Wine was used as an offering to a deity or in religious rituals such as the Christian sacrament or the drinking contests of the Dionysian Anthesteria (the Festival of the Vine Flower). As a luxury drink, wine was also a symbol of status among elites. As the ancient Greek dramatist Aristophanes (c.446–386 BC) wrote in his play *The Knights*, "When men drink, then they are rich and successful and win lawsuits and are happy and help their friends. Quickly, bring me a beaker of wine, so that I may wet my mind and say something clever." Third, because it initially was a commodity of luxury, wine production and trade became extremely profitable and the object of vast commerce in the Mediterranean, Europe, Asia, and Africa. Particular areas in Spain, Germany, France, and Italy also arose whose economies became dependent on viniculture. This led to the fourth reason, the spread of wine consumption throughout society, from a drink only enjoyed by the wealthy in ancient Mesopotamia or Egypt to a commodity drunk by all social classes in Imperial Rome.

Though the collapse of the Western Roman Empire would seem to have threatened viniculture and the wine markets, evidence indicates that the Goths, Vandals, and Franks who occupied Western Europe valued the vineyards. Apart from the shock waves of initial invasion, winemaking continued to flourish, supported by the Christian Church, some of whose monastic and Episcopal vineyards were substantial. Wine was also accepted for church tithes because it was a commodity easily converted into cash. In Germany, Martinmas, the feast day for St. Martin, the patron of wine-growers, was the day for payment of tithes in kind. Some monastic communities had a daily wine ration—the Benedictines allowed a *hemina* of wine (.27 liter) per meal—and there was the need for sacramental wine as well as provisions for travelers who stayed at monasteries or patients at the monastic hospitals. As Benedict stated in his book of monastic rules, "Better to take a little wine of necessity than a great deal of water with greed."

Though Islam forbade the production and consumption of alcoholic beverages, viniculture was not eradicated in the areas that Muslim armies conquered in the eighth century such as Northern Africa, Spain, and Portugal. In the heart of the Muslim Empire, prohibitions against wine drinking were more rigorously enforced, but in more distant regions such as Spain, rulers took a more permissive attitude toward alcohol and Spanish Muslims drank at wine symposiums, where the evening was devoted to discussion, poetry, and entertainment.

With the rise of towns in the twelfth century in the medieval West came the establishment of major international wine routes: (1) the Mediterranean network that traded wine in the region itself, as well as by sea to England and northern Europe; (2) the German wine trade that exported products to Northern Germany, Scandinavia, and to England; and (3) the French wine trade, where wines from western France had markets in Spain, Eastern Europe, England, and Flanders. The establishment of the great Italian vineyards in Tuscany and the major French vineyards such as Bordeaux and Burgundy took place in the medieval era. The English grew to love Bordeaux wine, retaining for it the name of claret, anglicized from the French clairet, meaning "clear wine." Burgundy was already known in the late fourteenth

WORDS TO KNOW

APPELLATION D'ORIGINE CONTRÔLÉE: Translated as "controlled designation of origin," AOC is a French certification designed to protect the geography and quality of wines.

FERMENTATION: The metabolic process by which yeast consumes carbohydrates and produces carbon dioxide and alcohol.

GENETICALLY MODIFIED OR "GM" FOODS: Foods derived from genetically modified organisms that have had changes introduced into their DNA by techniques in genetic engineering to introduce a new trait that does not occur naturally in the species.

TANNINS: Astringent chemical compounds found in the skins, stems, and seeds of wine grapes that produce a sense of bitterness and tactile drying sensation in wine. As a wine ages, tannins form long polymerized chains resulting in the wine "mellowing" its taste and mouth feel.

TERROIR: The special characteristics of soil, weather, and techniques of farming that contribute to the unique qualities of wine.

VIGNERON: A person who cultivates grape vines.

VINICULTURE: Cultivation of grapes for the production of wine by fermentation.

VINTNER: A person who makes wine.

century for its wines produced from pinot noir grapes. Wine made in Beaune in Burgundy was considered the most exquisite and favored by the papal courts during their residence in Avignon during the Great Schism. The papal courts also enjoyed less expensive Rhone wines, later to be known as the famous Châteauneuf-du-Pape (new castle of the Pope).

Religion and wine continued to have close connections with the advent of the Protestant Reformation in the sixteenth century. Although Protestants did not forbid the drinking of wine (though they criticized overconsumption), historical evidence indicates that some wine growers during the French Reformation were among the most resistant to the new Protestant religion. Burgundian vintners in particular considered that the fruit of their labor was chosen by God over everything else to become Christ's blood. For them, wine sustained the Catholic faith.

Viniculture was also affected by the Scientific Revolution of the seventeenth century. Developments in chemistry and metallurgy led to better design of furnaces, which were coal-fired rather than wood-fired and much hotter. This allowed for improvements in glass making and the development in England of a new type of bottle with thicker walls that was more

Grapes in a vineyard in the Douro Valley in Portugal are ripe for the autumn harvest. *Image copyright Antonio Jorge Nunes, 2010. Used under license from Shutterstock.com.*

durable and cheaper. Cork stoppers, rather than those of leather, wood, or textiles, led to an airtight seal. Both of these technologies made possible the development of champagne. Sparkling wine was therefore actually invented not by Dom Pierre Pérignon in 1668, but it was being produced by English wine coopers at least six years earlier. Christopher Merret (1614–1695) described in a paper presented to the Royal Society on December 17, 1662, that English wine makers added sugar and molasses to a finished wine to make it taste "brisk and sparkling." This was because the French did not have the technology to produce sparkling wine in 1662, but the English did. English glass was also used to make wine glasses with their characteristic stem. The French then of course went on to refine the *methode champenoise.*

Colonialism in the New World also led to new wine-producing areas and new markets in the seventeenth and eighteenth centuries. Spanish Franciscan missionary efforts from Loreto in 1697 to Sonoma in northern California in 1823 involved the planting of vineyards and viniculture. However, the mission grape, which had been brought from Mexico to Baja California, was a poor variety, deficient in acidity and color with little keeping quality.

It was not until the Spanish authorities abandoned the expansion of the missions along the El Camino Real and secularized them in the 1820s and 1830s that commercial viniculture began. Jean Louis Vignes (1780–1862), a Frenchman from Bordeaux, was the first to import not only orange trees but also European varieties of grapes into California in 1831, growing them in his vineyard (which is now a part of downtown Los Angeles). Vignes invited other Frenchmen to come to California, and by the mid-nineteenth century Los Angeles was a major wine growing region. Agoston Haraszthy (1812–1869), "the father of the California Wine Industry" and founder of the Buena Vista Vineyards, would challenge their dominance in the wine markets, importing Zinfandel and Muscat grapes and showing the feasibility of growing them on non-irrigated land in Sonoma County. In 1861 Haraszthy was named by Governor John G. Downey (1827–1894) to visit Europe as an agricultural commissioner where he learned all he could about grape growing and wine production; on his return he reported to the California legislature that California's climate made it a superior wine-growing region to Europe, and he claimed he purchased 10,000 vines to cultivate and test. His energy and enthusiasm encouraged others to establish vineyards, a momentum sustained by the Gold Rush (1848–1855), which brought a rapid influx of Europeans knowledgeable about viniculture to Northern California.

At approximately the same time that the Californian wine industry was being established, sustained viniculture had started in Australia. In 1788 Governor Arthur Phillip (1738–1814) on the First Fleet brought vine cuttings from the Cape of Good Hope to the penal colony of New South Wales. Australian wine was exported for the first time in the 1820s, and as in California, European emigrants used their knowledge to establish premier wine regions. By the 1880s Australian wines were winning medals at French wine exhibitions, some judges refusing to accept their provenance. New World Wines in Chile, Argentina, and New Zealand also entered the market.

■ Impacts and Issues

Winemakers had experienced relative prosperity throughout most of the nineteenth century with market expansion and more consistent production of high-quality wines. A series of crises from 1870 until 1950, however, affected the wine industry for nearly a century. *Phylloxera* aphids devastated vineyards; anti-alcohol movements gained momentum, resulting in Prohibition in the United States; two world wars caused a lack of labor supply; and the Great Depression (1929–1941) and ensuing tariff barriers reduced demand.

Phylloxera is a small yellow aphid that feeds on the roots of a grapevine, infecting it until it swells into growths called galls, causing the root to shrivel, killing the plant. It is prolific in reproduction, migrating via cracks in the soil and on the wind, but mostly through human migration, attaching itself to boots, tools, and machinery. Although it is indigenous to North America, from 1858 to 1862 large numbers of vines were brought to Europe from the United States. By 1890 most of France's wine region showed evidence of *phylloxera*, and some areas such as the Gard lost four-fifths of their wine production. France, embroiled in the Franco-Prussian war of 1870 and social revolution the following year, was slow to respond. At an international conference on *phylloxera* held in Bordeaux in 1881, it was decided to graft resistant American rootstocks onto French vines, and by 1900 more than 66 percent of French vines had American roots. The aphid also reached Italy, Spain, and Australia, leading to widespread replanting with grafted vines, and to disrupted wine production for the last two decades of the nineteenth century.

In the short term, at the beginning of the twentieth century, the *phylloxera* epidemic encouraged wine fraud and adulteration because supplies were low. Dubious blending and misrepresentation led to coherent wine regulations being developed in France in 1905, 1919, and 1927. A large unsold surplus of wine during the economic depression of the 1930s, however, made these laws ineffective in controlling fraudulent merchants until the efforts of Baron Pierre Le Roy de Boiseaumarié (1890–1967), a vintner near Avignon. Boiseaumarié influenced *vignerons* to consider wine provenance. He proposed a series of restrictive measures to define wine from his region, Châteauneuf-du-Pape, that included acceptable grape varieties, alcohol content, geographical delimitation, and viticultural method. Boiseaumarié's efforts led to the founding in 1935 of the entity that became the *Institut National des Appellations d'Origine* (INAO), which oversees a complex series of regulations pertaining to the production and character of wine from each French *terroir*. To compete against New World wine producers, the *Appellation d'Origine Contrôlée* (AOC) regulations ensure, for example, that no sparkling wine can be called "champagne" unless it is from that particular region of France, and Cote de Beaune can contain only pinot-noir grapes from Burgundy. Italy followed suit with its own set of regulations, the DOC (*Denominazione de Origine Controllata*) in the 1930s.

New World wineries have responded by abandoning geographical references, describing their wines by the varieties of grape utilized, such as a Californian merlot or an Australian shiraz. Ironically, as French and Italian producers have marketed their products to America, Australia, and Canada, they are finding they also need to specify the varieties of grapes from which their wines are made to appeal to their customer base. Nonetheless the AOC designations have dovetailed with rise of the "slow food" movement founded in 1989 to counter "fast food" and "fast life" and the disappearance of local food and wine traditions.

Another form of regulation has arisen with the use of the designation of "organic," the first wines labeled organic having appeared on the market in the 1980s. Although the specific definition of "organic farming" varies from country to country, it typically excludes pesticides, fungicides, herbicides, and chemical fertilizers. In the case of wine, this should mean that "organic" wine should have no sulfur dioxide or sulfite added as a preservative to reduce oxidation and spoilage. Although technical developments have made it possible to significantly reduce the amount of sulfites added to wine, many winemakers doubt it is feasible to eliminate them completely. Therefore, organic wine generally is defined as being produced with organically grown grapes and marketed much as organic food for its perceived health benefits. In fact, the National Restaurant Association in the United States identified organic wine as one of the "hottest drink trends for 2009."

Some of the interest in organic wines may also be due to fears about the use of GM or genetically modified grapes resistant to diseases such as powdery mildew, *Clostridium*, nepovirus, or grapevine fanleaf virus. The disease-resistant genes include antimicrobial peptides encoded by synthetic genes, and field testing of GM grapevines has occurred in several countries, including the United States, Australia, and France. Whereas the American agricultural industry is pushing for worldwide acceptance of GM food, resistance to GM crops is stronger in European countries. Moet and Chandon, the French Champagne maker, dropped work on genetically engineered vines in 1999 in response to public and industry pressure.

On August 16, 2010, *Le Figaro* reported that a group of protesters locked themselves in a field of genetically modified grapevines at France's National Institute for Agronomic Research near Colmar and uprooted all 70 plants before submitting to arrest. The protesters condemned the use of public funds for open-field testing of the GM grapevines designed to be resistant to grapevine fanleaf virus. A group of winemakers called *Terre et Vin du Monde* feared that the test vineyard could contaminate French vineyards and affect their reputation in the wine market. Ironically, in the case of Colmar, it is only the rootstock that is genetically modified, because the fanleaf virus, like *Phylloxera*, infects only the root. The top of the vine, and hence the pollen, has not been modified by genetic engineering so the modified DNA has no way of contaminating anything. At the same time, many winemakers see genetic engineering as a threat to the idea of *terroir* and the artisan crafting of wine. Much public debate will have to take place to determine the future of GM grapes in viniculture.

SEE ALSO *Agribusiness; Agriculture and International Trade; Agroecology; Fermentation: Alcohol; French Paradox; Gastronomy.*

BIBLIOGRAPHY

Books

Bird, David. *Understanding Wine Technology: The Science of Wine Explained*, 3rd ed. San Francisco: Wine Appreciation Guild, 2005.

Cowen, Ruth. *Relish: The Extraordinary Life of Alexis Soyer, Victorian Celebrity Chef.* London: Phoenix, 2007.

Nossiter, Jonathan. *Liquid Memory: Why Wine Matters.* New York: Farrar, Straus and Giroux, 2009.

Robertson, Carol. *The Little Red Book of Wine Law: A Case of Legal Issues.* Chicago: American Bar Association, 2008.

Sommers, Brian J. *The Geography of Wine: How Landscapes, Cultures, Terroir, and the Weather Make a Good Drop.* New York: Plume, 2008.

Periodicals

Geraci, Victor W. "Fermenting a Twenty-First Century California Wine Industry." *Agricultural History* 78, no. 4 (Autumn 2004): 438–465.

Web Sites

"Chef Survey: What's Hot in 2009." *National Restaurant Association.* http://www.restaurant.org/pdfs/research/2009chefsurvey.pdf (accessed October 7, 2010).

Students of HIST 452. "Terroir and the Perceived Value of Regional Origin." *Cornell University History Department,* Fall 2005. http://courses.cit.cornell.edu/his452/Alcohol/terroirandorigin.html (accessed October 7, 2010).

Wineculture: A Hip Guide to Wine on the Web. http://www.wineculture.com/home.html (accessed October 7, 2010).

Anna Marie Eleanor Roos

Vitamins and Minerals

◼ Introduction

Vitamins and minerals are nutrients that are essential for the healthy functioning of the body, but are needed in far smaller amounts than the carbohydrates, fats, and proteins that form the bulk of the diet and are used for energy and growth. Therefore, vitamins and minerals are often referred to as micronutrients, whereas carbohydrates, fats, and proteins are the macronutrients. Vitamins are organic molecules that play a role in the body's biochemical activities, or metabolism, often supporting the activity of enzymes. Minerals are naturally occurring inorganic elements, such as sodium and calcium, which are essential for a wide range of functions, from transmission of nerve impulses to building strong bones and teeth. Vitamin and mineral deficiencies may cause serious disease. For instance, lack of B vitamins can affect nerve function, and iron deficiency may cause anemia. There is ongoing research into whether vitamin deficiency contributes to common chronic diseases such as heart disease and cancer. A healthful diet should contain all the vitamins and minerals needed for good health. However, there may be some groups, such as pregnant women or the elderly, who could benefit from vitamin or mineral supplementation.

◼ Historical Background and Scientific Foundations

Cases of vitamin and mineral deficiencies, and their remedies by introducing certain foods, were known long before the compounds responsible were discovered. Perhaps the best known example is scurvy, the vitamin C deficiency disease, which was common among sailors undertaking long voyages in the sixteenth and seventeenth centuries. Scurvy, which is rare in the early twenty-first century, is characterized by anemia and susceptibility to infection. In the mid-eighteenth century, Scottish physician James Lind (1716–1794) discovered that oranges and lemons could both cure and prevent scurvy. Accordingly, the British Navy ordered supplies of limes to be taken onboard ships to keep sailors healthy. Limes, like other citrus fruits, are rich in vitamin C, but it was not until 1925 that Hungarian biochemist Albert Szent-Györgi (1893–1986) discovered vitamin C, or ascorbic acid, in plants. Its chemical structure was deduced by Charles G. King (1896–1988) and his team at the University of Pittsburgh in 1932.

Similarly, two other major deficiency diseases, pellagra and beriberi, became common when people's dietary habits suddenly altered. Pellagra, which is a deficiency disease of vitamin B3, or niacin, spread throughout Europe with the introduction of Indian corn from the Americas. Corn, which is low in both niacin and tryptophan (converted to niacin in the body), became a staple of the poor, who were not processing it with lime (the alkali) to make the niacin available (as was done by indigenous people in the Americas) and who ate little or no protein-rich food to counteract the niacin deficiency. Beriberi, a vitamin B1 or thiamine deficiency, resulted when mechanized rice milling was introduced into Asia. Polish chemist Casimir Funk (1884–1967) showed that an extract of rice hulls, which were lost with the new milling process, was able to prevent the disease. He named the active ingredient "vitamine," which is short for *vital amine*. The term Funk coined became *vitamin* when it was realized that vitamin B1 was not actually an amine. Meanwhile, E. V. McCollum (1879–1967) and Marguerite Davis (1887–1967) at the University of Wisconsin found that rats whose only fat source was lard did not grow and developed eye problems. When they added egg yolk to the animals' diet, the disorder was corrected. They called their active ingredient vitamin A to distinguish it from Funk's water-soluble vitamin B. During the next decade, several other vitamins were isolated and identified.

The importance of the trace element iodine became apparent through studies of the so-called goiter belt of the American Midwest between 1907 and 1920. Goiter

WORDS TO KNOW

DIETARY REFERENCE INTAKES (DRIs): The Institute of Medicine of the National Academy of Sciences has developed this set of reference values, which includes the RDA and also the tolerable upper intake levels (UL) that represent the maximum daily intake unlikely to result in adverse health effects. The DRIs are intended as guidelines for planning and assessing nutrient intake for healthy people.

RECOMMENDED DIETARY ALLOWANCE (RDA): Sometimes known as the recommended daily allowance, RDA is the level of intake of a vitamin or mineral required to prevent deficiency disease. In real life, people will tend to consume more of a vitamin or mineral on one day than another, so it is probably best to think in terms of average, rather than daily, intakes.

TRACE ELEMENTS: Including elements such as copper, molybdenum, boron, selenium, chromium, iron, and manganese, the trace elements are the minerals that the body requires in much smaller amounts than calcium, for instance, or phosphorus. There are only a few grams of each trace element in the body.

is an enlargement of the thyroid gland, accompanied by profound fatigue, which is caused by iodine deficiency. Iodine is essential for normal thyroid gland function. In mountainous and inland areas, iodide salts in the soil are washed by rainfall into rivers and then into the sea, leaving the population short of this mineral. Iodine deficiency is practically unknown in populations living near the sea because vegetables and animals raised in these areas are rich in the mineral. Researchers at Case Western Reserve University discovered the link between goiter and iodine deficiency in their experiments and, in 1924, Michigan began to enrich table salt with iodine and Rochester, New York, added it to the municipal water supply. Goiter is very rare in developed countries in the early twenty-first century.

The fat-soluble vitamins are vitamins A, D, E, and K. In the diet they tend to be found in oily fish, liver, vegetable oils, and animal fats. The body can store them in the liver and in fatty tissue; the liver alone can hold a year's supply of vitamin A. Because of this, it is not necessary to include the fat-soluble vitamins in the diet every day. However, accumulation of these vitamins in the body does raise the potential for toxic effects. An excess of vitamin A can cause swelling of the liver and spleen.

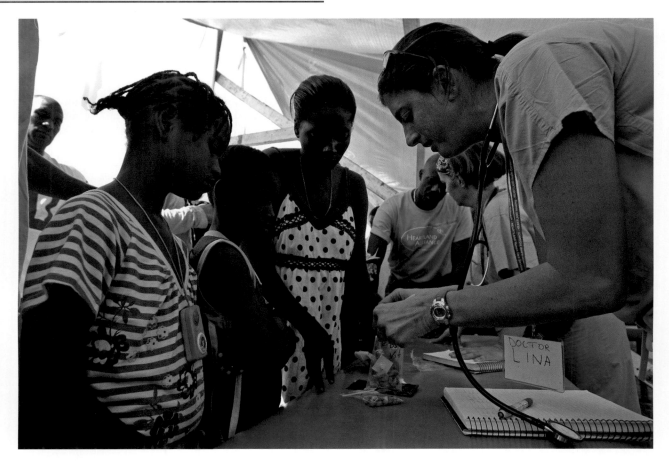

An aid worker distributes vitamin supplements to children in Port-au-Prince, Haiti, following the devastating earthquake of January 12, 2010. *AP Images.*

Vitamin A, also known as retinol, is essential for good vision, as it is used to synthesize the pigments of the retina. Vitamin D is actually a group of compounds related to cholesterol. The best source of vitamin D is sunlight, as this converts one of the body's natural cholesterol-like compounds into the vitamin. Vitamin D works with calcium to ensure strong bones and teeth. A lack of vitamin D can lead to the childhood disease rickets, characterized by a softening of the bones that leads to bowed legs, and its adult version osteomalacia. Vitamin E, or tocopherol, is an antioxidant molecule whose role in health is not yet fully defined.

The water-soluble vitamins are the B vitamins and vitamin C. These are found mainly in fruits and vegetables and in whole grains. Water-soluble vitamins are excreted in the urine and are not stored in the body, so are unlikely to exert toxic effects. They are also prone to break down on exposure to light and heat, so storage and overcooking can deplete foods of their water-soluble vitamin content.

The B vitamins are a group of eight different vitamins: thiamine (B1), riboflavin (B2), niacin (B3), pyridoxine (B6), cobalamin (B12), folic acid, pantothenic acid, and biotin. They play a number of roles in metabolism. For instance, folic acid is important for the formation of DNA, the genetic material, whereas riboflavin helps in the generation of biochemical energy from glucose. Vitamin C aids in wound healing and in the synthesis and maintenance of collagen, a major component of the connective tissue that holds the body together.

Salt is the major source of the minerals sodium and chloride, and phosphorus and potassium are present in most foods. Calcium is most readily available in dairy foods. It is present in vegetables such as spinach and also in whole grains, but its binding to oxalic acid and phytic acid respectively in these foods make it less readily absorbed by the body. Sodium, chloride, and potassium help maintain the body's fluid and chemical balance and are involved in the transmission of nerve impulses. Calcium and phosphorus are present in higher amounts. There are about three pounds of calcium and four pounds of phosphorus in the body. Calcium is responsible for hardening bones and teeth, whereas phosphorus is a major component of DNA, RNA, adenosine triphosphate (the body's biochemical energy molecule), and the phospholipid molecules of cell membranes. Sulfur is found in the amino acids that make up skin and nails, in the hormone insulin, and in heparin, an anticoagulant molecule. Deficiencies of the main minerals are rare.

Iron is perhaps the most significant of the trace elements. It is required to make hemoglobin, the protein that transports oxygen throughout the body. Iron deficiency anemia, characterized by fatigue and pallor, is relatively common in the United States, particularly among younger women who do not eat red meat, which is a major source of iron. Another trace element, copper, is important for bone development, and fluoride helps to prevent tooth decay. Magnesium and zinc are important in maintaining enzyme functioning.

IN CONTEXT: VITAMINS AS PROSTATE CANCER PREVENTATIVES

In recent years, high dosage regimes of vitamin C or E have been popularized as alternative medicine prostate cancer preventatives. However, two studies—one conducted by researchers from University of Texas, the other independently by researchers at the Cleveland Clinic Lerner College of Medicine—published in the *Journal of the American Medical Association* concluded that supplements of vitamin C or E do not reduce the risk of prostate cancer.

■ Impacts and Issues

The United States National Health and Nutrition Examination Survey has shown that vitamin and mineral deficiencies do occur in the American population, despite the widespread availability of these nutrients in foodstuffs. Iron and vitamin D deficiencies, particularly among younger people, women, and the elderly are the deficiencies that seem to be the most common. One possible solution is to take supplements of the vitamins and minerals that are lacking in the diet. Approximately half of the U.S. population ingests some kind of supplement, including vitamins and minerals. Some groups, such as the elderly, may benefit from calcium and vitamin D supplements in terms of reduced risk of brittle bones and falls. However, it is less clear whether taking a vitamin supplement will lower the risk of other diseases. A report from the Women's Health Study concluded that vitamin E did not prevent cardiovascular events, cancer, or other causes of mortality. There have also been studies that show that vitamins can even be harmful, such as a classic study of beta-carotene (a precursor of vitamin A) and vitamin E in Finnish male smokers, which suggested that the supplements actually increased mortality in this group.

Another approach is for the government or food companies to fortify foods with vitamins or minerals. Examples include margarines with added vitamin D or water supplies with added fluoride. The latter in particular has proved controversial, even though fluoridated water supplies have been shown to reduce rates of childhood tooth decay, because they remove the element of choice from the consumer. A more radical approach is exemplified by the "golden rice" invented by German scientists Peter Beyer (1963–) and Into Potrykus (1933–). The rice is genetically modified to produce sufficient beta-carotene to meet a child's daily needs for vitamin A in one serving. Between 250,000 and 500,000 children go blind each year in less developed countries because of vitamin A deficiency. The golden rice program is intended to be put into operation in India, Vietnam, and Bangladesh, although it is still far from achieving its goals because the development of the project has been hampered by the controversy surrounding the safety and environmental impact of genetically modified foods, as well as the involvement of a multinational corporation.

An emerging health issue is high consumption of salt, as excess sodium intake is linked to high blood pressure, which is a risk factor for heart and kidney disease. Much of the salt consumed is hidden in processed foods, although some manufacturers have initiated efforts to reduce the amount of salt in their products. The American Heart Association recommends that salt intake correspond to calorie intake (for every 1000 calories consumed, salt should be limited to 1000 mg), and should not exceed 3000 mg per day. Currently, adults in most developed countries consume an average of 4000–9000 mg of salt per day.

There is still much to be learned about the role vitamins and minerals play in protecting and maintaining health. For instance, there is evidence that vitamin D deficiency may be a factor in cancer and other chronic diseases. RDAs need to be kept under review in light of the latest scientific evidence to ensure that levels are not too low for optimal health. At the same time, people should seek advice from their healthcare professional to avoid wasting money on supplements that are without value or may be harmful. Experts in nutrition agree that food should always come first when it comes to maintaining an optimal vitamin and mineral status, although there may be a role for supplementation to improve the health of those at risk of deficiencies.

SEE ALSO *Center for Food Safety and Applied Nutrition; Changing Nutritional Needs throughout Life; Diet and Cancer; Diet and Diabetes; Diet and Heart Disease; Diet and Hypertension; Dietary Guidelines for Americans; Dietary Reference Intakes; Functional Foods; Nutrient Fortification of Foods; Salt.*

BIBLIOGRAPHY

Books

Blake, Steve. *Vitamins and Minerals Demystified.* New York: McGraw-Hill, 2008.

Combs, Gerald F. *The Vitamins: Fundamental Aspects in Nutrition and Health,* 3rd ed. Amsterdam and Boston: Elsevier Academic Press, 2008.

Frankenburg, Frances R. *Vitamin Discoveries and Disasters: History, Science, and Controversies.* Santa Barbara, CA: Praeger, 2009.

Hurley, Dan. *Natural Causes: Death, Lies, and Politics in America's Vitamin and Herbal Supplement Industry.* New York: Broadway, 2006.

Sharon, Michael. *Nutrients A to Z: A User's Guide to Foods, Herbs, Vitamins, Minerals & Supplements,* 5th ed. London: Carlton Books, 2009.

Periodicals

"Diet Coke with a Shot of Vitamins." *Newsweek* 149, no. 20 (2007): 60–61.

Hobson, Katherine. "The Skinny on Vitamins." *U.S. News & World Report* 146, no. 1 (2009): 78–80.

Holick, Michael F. "Vitamin D Deficiency." *The New England Journal of Medicine* 357, no. 3 (2007): 266–281.

Kittisupamongkol, Weekitt. "Effect of Folic Acid and B Vitamins on Cardiovascular Disease in Women." *JAMA: Journal of the American Medical Association* 300, no. 12 (2008): 1410.

Matthews, Rowena G. "A Love Affair with Vitamins." *The Journal of Biological Chemistry* 284, no. 39 (2009): 26217–26228.

Web Sites

"Fortify Your Knowledge about Vitamins." *U.S. Food and Drug Administration (FDA).* http://www.fda.gov/ForConsumers/ConsumerUpdates/ucm118079.htm (accessed August 20, 2010).

"Vitamins and Minerals." *UK Food Standards Agency.* http://www.eatwell.gov.uk/healthydiet/nutritionessentials/vitaminsandminerals/ (accessed August 20, 2010).

Susan Aldridge

Wage Slavery in Food Production

■ Introduction

Wage slavery is the condition of being completely dependent on a wage and thus dependent on an employer. As artisan trades gave way to manufacturing in the eighteenth and nineteenth centuries, the vast majority of workers in developed countries could be classified as wage slaves. Some critics of labor conditions would argue all wage labor or day labor is exploitative of the worker, though more moderate critics may designate specific contemporary labor situations as problematic, including the continued existence of slavery, debt bondage, sharecropping, child labor, and human trafficking. Although possibly no more exploitative than other manufacturing processes, agriculture and the food industry have many low-paid laborers and widely condemned labor practices.

■ Historical Background and Scientific Foundations

Slavery, the practice of one human being owning another, is at least as old as recorded history. Slave labor has often been employed in agriculture and food production. Large plantations in many parts of the world depended on slaves or on minimally paid laborers to plant and harvest crops before mechanization began in the late nineteenth century. As slaves, serfs, and other slave-like peoples gained legal rights, slavery slowly became illegal around the world. The anti-slavery movement gained momentum after slavery was banned in the British Empire in 1833. In fact, all countries except China have ratified bans against forced labor, such as the International Labor Organization (ILO) Convention 29. Of course, slavery continues to exist in the early twenty-first century, and estimates are that as many as 12 million people continue to live in slavery in parts of West Africa such as Mauritania, Mali, and Niger; in India; and in other countries, according to Anti-Slavery

International, a human rights organization based in the United Kingdom. Because contemporary slavery tends to be in rural settings, many of these slaves provide agricultural labor.

In the developed world, situations that could be characterized as wage slavery accompanied the development of industrial food processing facilities. Poor working conditions were the norm in many early aspects of the food industry, with conditions in meatpacking plants in the late nineteenth century being one area that attracted attention from media and labor activists. In addition to industrial settings in the food industry, many forms of bondage and of coerced labor continue to exist in agriculture itself in the developed world. Human trafficking plays a role in agricultural labor, especially during the harvest.

Migrant labor is common in the United States, especially for less mechanized horticultural crops such as lettuce and tomatoes. Some of these laborers have been trafficked into the United States with their employers holding on to their passports or other identification documents. They tend to be paid very low wages, usually at a per-piece rate, and may be paid far below the minimum wage. Many of these people are indigenous peoples from Central America, Mexico, and the Caribbean who claim they have no alternative to working the lettuce harvest in California or the winter tomato harvest in Florida. They seldom protest the work because they may not have legal rights to work in the United States. A conservative estimate of the size of the human trafficking problem by the United Nations Office of Drugs and Crime (UNODC) puts the number at 2.5 million victims at any time.

Migrant harvest labor is also found in Europe, especially in production of the same horticultural crops as in the United States such as the citrus industry in Italy. Food processors in Southern European countries such as Italy, Spain, and Greece may also depend on migrants from Africa, Asia, and the Middle East to undertake poorly paid work, some living in abandoned factories and experiencing the same problem of being

WORDS TO KNOW

ECONOMY OF SCALE: A reduction in the cost of production reached by producing more. Economy of scale also refers to cost reductions accrued by geographic concentration of an industry.

HUMAN TRAFFICKING: To move a person, often from one country to another, for the purpose of exploiting that person.

WAGE SLAVERY: The practice of being dependent on a wage from hiring out of a person's labor. For some critics of capitalism, all workers who receive wages and live by hiring out their labor are wage slaves. For others not opposed to wage employment *per se*, wage slavery usually denotes forms of indebtedness or other forced systems in which a worker is unable to leave a poor work environment for fear of the consequences.

lower wages due to their illegal status or to their lack of knowledge of labor laws. Agriculture and the restaurant industry also commonly employ child labor in both the developed and developing world. Some child labor practices may be legal within certain countries, with children working on the family farm or in the family restaurant.

In the developing world, both land rental and sharecropping are common for both the landless rural poor and for those wanting to expand their operations. Sharecropping refers to the situation in which a farmer rents land that is paid for by a share of the crop being produced by the renter. Although not based in wages, sharecropping is often prevalent in systems in which the landlord also provides credit. Once the sharecropper is indebted to the landlord, leaving this relationship may become nearly impossible. Debt bondage such as that to a landlord is one source of agricultural labor. Very common in the South Asian countries of India, Pakistan, and Bangladesh, some form of debt bondage also exists in most parts of the developing world. In Pakistan alone, there are argued to be 1.8 million bonded laborers according to Anti-Slavery International. At the end of the hungry season—the time before the first early harvesting crops are available

undocumented. Due to frequently paying in the form of hard-to-track cash wages and the low-wage nature of the work, the restaurant industry around the world is another common place of employment for poorly paid, poorly documented migrant laborers who may accept

Members of the Coalition of Immokalee Workers protest in Tampa, Florida, for farm worker rights and increased wages. *AP Images.*

but after most from the previous harvest have been removed—a household may trade promises of a future crop to cover basic needs such as receiving a cash loan or perhaps simply a bag of flour, wheat, or maize. This indebtedness is hard to escape because the pre-selling of some or all of the harvest out of desperation to meet basic needs reduces the household's future ability to survive subsequent hungry seasons by storing adequate amounts of food from the harvest or accumulating enough cash resources. Also, another situation of forced labor may exist on some of the remaining collective farms around the world, the administrators of which may be unable or unwilling to properly compensate all of the members.

■ Impacts and Issues

Debt bondage, forced labor, wage slavery, and various other forms of exploitive labor relations in agriculture have proved to be difficult to eradicate. Some critics of modern agriculture claim these forms of labor are necessary because the economies of scale of large farms, agribusinesses, and plantation crops demand large amounts of cheap labor. These critics argue that the economies of scale that lower costs in agriculture and food production are possible only because of exploitative labor practices. However, in many of these countries, the vast majority of short-term labor needs are met through day laborers. Though often compensated at low wages, these are voluntary labor relationships, frequently of a short-term nature that poor rural households seek out to supplement their other sources of income and livelihood. Day laboring for cash by working on farms is common in the developing world and in the developed world. Although the food processing industry may also be criticized for its labor practices, they do not differ substantially from the practices of manufacturers that produce other low cost goods.

Studies of exploitative labor practices tend to identify several characteristics of the targeted source population. Foremost, the population is very poor. They are often ethnic, linguistic, or religious minorities or people of a lower caste who may be excluded from other, more profitable economic opportunities. These populations may be poorly educated and unaware of alternatives to wage slavery practices. Also, they may be so far into debt that they feel they have no alternative to exploitative labor practices such as slavery, child labor, and debt bondage. Discrimination may prevent others in a community from alerting authorities of the existence of these labor practices or it may desensitize authorities from caring about or taking action on exploitive labor practices. Also, lack of opportunities may make people more likely to be trafficked to another country to serve as agricultural labor or another purpose. Agriculture and the food industry are not the largest recipients of human trafficking, but the practice continues to be easily hidden

and confused with what the International Organization for Migration estimates to be 214 million international labor migrants.

■ Primary Source Connection

Viji Srinivasan was an Indian social worker and the former managing director of ADITHI, a non-governmental organization (NGO) dedicated to the advancement of women. Srinivasan devoted her career to working with the poor, challenging female infanticide, and promoting education for girls.

In the primary source that follows, a reporter's contemporaneous notes of an interview, Srinivasan comments on the hardships of sharecroppers and explains what ADITHI was doing to improve their situation.

Srinivasan died in Bhopal, India, on June 13, 2005, at the age of 67.

Interview: Late Ms. Viji Srinivasan

REPORTER: What exactly is the sharecropper issue and who do you target and assist the farmers?

MS. SRINIVASAN: The Sharecroppers are considered—

- Invisible and denied recognition—Government and administration deny their existence
- Illegal
- Denied access to credit

The sharecroppers or the landowners do not take the initiative of improving the land, which results in low productivity.

ADITHI aims to expose the hidden sharecroppers and present the Government with a concrete data of the total number of sharecroppers existing in the state of Bihar. This is to—

- To sensitize and impress upon the officials of formal financial institutions to make suitable amendments for the benefit of the women sharecroppers, that is to look at other factors than repayment, sharecroppers are unable to repay when there are floods.
- To provide recognition to the sharecroppers as a special category so that they get priority over others especially where getting bank loan is concerned.
- To expose the unfair treatment meted out to the sharecroppers by seeking data on the percentage of share of sharecroppers and landowners respectively in cereals, straws and bran.
- To expose the common problems in this work (relationship with landowners, gender disparity, opportunity for self-sustenance, quantum of work and quantum of money they earn, extent of technical expertise).

ADITHI's work with the sharecroppers:

- ADITHI is presently working with 1087 sharecroppers

- Sharecroppers' yield of wheat has increased many folds as compared with 30 kg. per khatta in 1992. The Rabi crop output by the sharecropper women for 2003–2004 had been phenomenal. The Kharif crop (paddy) output for 2004 had been 6260 kg. Yet all in waste. Nature played its havoc. The major culprit is the flood ravaging North Bihar now. 100% of the crops were destroyed in the flood.

- The sharecroppers own a tractor, which is being used to its full capacity by the women.

- ADITHI's continuous advocacy has given recognition to the sharecroppers, who earlier according to the Government were non-existent. The banks are giving them loans now (though to very small numbers). The women sharecroppers have reached the point of sustainable food security. Earlier the practice of sharecropping was insecure in both ways, mankhap (land lease) and bataiya because the landlord had been changing the plot. ADITHI convinced the landlords to continue every sharecropper in the same allotted plot so that they could go in for manuring with compost, oil cakes and green manuring with leguminous plants for nitrogen fixation, vermicompost. The farmers were also convinced towards the economics of crop cultivation and were requested to share the inputs as much as possible. This model is now being replicated.

- Sharecroppers now have security of tenure. This is being replicated in other blocks and districts.

- The development of "barefoot researchers" from the sharecroppers has been significant in the development of the programme.

- Sharecropper women, under the aegis of Mahila Krishi Vigyan Kendra (a partner organization of ADITHI) are authorized distributors of urea, which they get at a landed cost of Rs.4.25/-per kg.

- Vermicompost, started in a small way some years ago is now made on a larger scale.

- The women sharecroppers have been recognized by National Seeds Corporation and Indian Farmer's Fertiliser Corporation Ltd.

Viji Srinivasan

SRINIVASAN, VIJI. "INTERVIEW: LATE MS. VIJI SRINIVASAN." *DEVELOPEDNATION.ORG.* OCTOBER 24, 2010. HTTP://WWW.DEVELOPEDNATION.ORG/INTERVIEWS/VIJISRINIVASAN.HTM (ACCESSED NOVEMBER 15, 2010).

SEE ALSO *Agriculture and International Trade; Ethical Issues in Agriculture; Fair Trade; World Trade Organization (WTO).*

BIBLIOGRAPHY

Books

Burton, Alvin W., and Irwin B. Telpov. *Farm Labor: 21st Century Issues and Challenges.* New York: Nova Science Publishers, 2008.

Martin, Philip L., Michael Fix, and J. E. Taylor. *The New Rural Poverty: Agriculture & Immigration in California.* Washington, DC: Urban Institute Press, 2006.

Pearce, Fred. *Confessions of an Eco-Sinner: Tracking Down the Sources of My Stuff.* Boston: Beacon Press, 2008.

Pearson, Elaine, et al. *The Mekong Challenge: Underpaid, Overworked, and Overlooked: The Reality of Young Migrant Workers in Thailand.* Bangkok, Thailand: ILO, 2006.

Periodicals

Donohue, Caitlin. "Out of Reach: How the Sustainable Local Food Movement Neglects Poor Workers and Eaters." *San Francisco Bay Guardian* 44, no. 9 (2010): 12–14.

Parenti, Christian. "Fortune—Chocolate's Bittersweet Economy—The Industry Agreed to Abolish Child Labor Seven Years Ago, But Little Progress Has Been Made." *Fortune International* 157, no. 2 (2008): 24–31.

Rye, Johna Frederick, and Joanna Andrzejewska. "The Structural Disempowerment of Eastern European Migrant Farm Workers in Norwegian Agriculture." *Journal of Rural Studies* 26, no. 1 (2010): 41–51.

Weigel, M. Margaret, et al. "The Household Food Insecurity and Health Outcomes of U.S.-Mexico Border Migrant and Seasonal Farmworkers." *Journal of Immigrant and Minority Health/Center for Minority Public Health* 9, no. 3 (2007): 157–169.

Web Sites

"Facts on Migrant Labor." *International Labour Organization,* June 2004. http://www.ilo.org/public/english/bureau/inf/download/factsheets/pdf/migrants.pdf (accessed September 23, 2010).

"Stop Child & Forced Labor: Cocoa Campaign." *International Labor Rights Forum.* http://www.laborrights.org/stop-child-labor/cocoa-campaign (accessed September 23, 2010).

Blake Jackson Stabler

War, Conquest, Colonialism, and Cuisine

■ Introduction

Food is often ignored in histories of war and colonization. Yet food is one of the many material and cultural elements that help to shape the new social, economic, and political orders that grow out of conquest. Food is arguably more critical to the success of colonization than military tactics or administrative structures. To survive, native peoples and colonists had to produce, distribute, and consume a sufficient amount of calories. Out of the mixing of cultures, new nutritional regimes emerged, which typically proved more satisfying than those that had existed prior to conquest.

The impact of war and conquest can be seen in the cuisines of the world. The cooking styles of Asia are largely based on the Chinese model, which came to such places as Korea and the Philippines via conquest and trade. Before Christopher Columbus (1451–1506) traveled to the New World in 1492, three main staples of the modern diet were unknown in the Old World: corn, potatoes, and many kinds of beans (including snap beans, kidney, lima, and others). Native Americans were unfamiliar with pigs, chickens, cattle, sheep, and goats, all of which became essential elements of New World cooking.

■ Historical Background and Scientific Foundations

The Chinese and the Spanish are the leaders in spreading their cuisines through conquest and colonization. However, political and economic links often brought foods from one country to another. As one example, a foreign influence is indicated by the names of such popular medieval French dishes as Saracen Broth, German Broth, Subtle English Broth, and Norse Pasties. Much of African cuisine, including most of the domesticated animals, initially came from Asia or Egypt.

In Asia, Chinese traders sailed across the South China Sea around AD 300. By the year 1000 they traded regularly with people in the coastal ports and colonies that they had established. By 1400 they had made their way inland. Evidence of the Chinese impact can be seen in noodle dishes, egg rolls, and stir-frying in the Philippines, Indonesia, Japan, Korea, and other Asian countries.

Meanwhile, Christopher Columbus sailed to the New World in 1492 and returned to Spain with many new foods. The white potatoes that subsequently became the major source of calories for the Irish are a South American crop that came to Europe only because of the Columbian Exchange. Other New World food plants that reached Europe via the Columbian Exchange are tomatoes, peanuts, squash, peppers, tomatoes, pumpkins, pineapples, papayas, guavas, and avocados. The Spanish introduced the New World to wheat, rice, and barley, as well as peaches, pears, figs, cherries, grapes, and sugar cane. Many of these foods also made their way to Asia via the Spanish, while trade from Africa spread millet, sorghum, and ginger. As an example of the impact of conquest and colonization, about 80 percent of present-day Filipino dishes can be traced to Spain.

WORDS TO KNOW

COLUMBIAN EXCHANGE: The products and ideas that were traded between the New World and the Old World as the result of Christopher Columbus' voyage to the Americas.

DESERTIFICATION: The process by which fertile land, typically semi-arid dryland, degrades and turns into arid desert.

FUSION: Fusion cuisine blends the ingredients and traditions of food preparation from different cultures into hybrid dishes.

When the Spanish conquered the Philippines, they introduced tomatoes and garlic, along with the technique of sautéing them with onions in olive oil. Many Filipino-baked goods and desserts, such as egg custard, derive from Spanish recipes but have been adapted to local tastes and ingredients.

The United States, one of the last countries to acquire colonies, has also spread a number of foods through war. It acquired the Philippines from the Spanish in 1898 as a result of the Spanish-American War and introduced a number of foods to this island nation, including potato and macaroni salads, baked fruit pies, and canned foods. Much of the American influence upon world cuisine, however, has come through cultural domination rather than through war.

■ Impacts and Issues

The initial impact of conquest upon cuisine generally has been favorable. People have a greater variety of foods to eat and an easier time of obtaining sufficient

In this reproduction of a nineteenth century illustration, Native Americans gather maize (corn) and squash. Corn, beans, and squash (called "The Three Sisters") were staples of the Native American diet prior to colonization. © *North Wind Picture Archives / Alamy.*

calories. In the sixteenth century, it was unlikely that any other region in the world had the diversity of staples and abundance of animal protein that could be found in Spanish America. As a result, the basic food needs of both Europeans and Native Americans were satisfied easily. The agricultural surplus created by the Columbian Exchange would help the Europeans in the eighteenth century to break through old ceilings on growth. The American foods of corn and potatoes helped to ensure that hunger seldom turned into famine and starvation. The Irish Potato Famine of the 1840s is a notable exception, but it occurred because the Irish had become so dependent upon potatoes for all of their nutritional needs that they were devastated by a potato blight. Most people had more than one primary subsistence food in the wake of the Columbian Exchange.

Not until the late twentieth century did the effects of introducing non-native plants and animals become recognized as a significant environmental threat. Pigs that were introduced to the Caribbean islands overran and ate the local fauna and flora. Rabbits in Australia, introduced by the conquering British, decimated the countryside. Water in semi-arid regions went toward watering cattle or irrigating thirsty non-native crops. The standard reclamation projects of the nineteenth and early twentieth centuries aimed primarily to convert wetlands, viewed as worthless, into productive farmland. Agricultural expansion was behind much habitat loss and served as a major contributor to water pollution.

In the Americas, cattle and sheep reshaped the land, opened it for invasion through overgrazing, and threatened or replaced native plants and animals. Predators of domestic stock, such as wolves, were targeted for extinction, which led to an explosion in the populations of rodents and deer that such carnivores had once kept in check. Cattle raising has become one of the primary factors in the destruction of the world's remaining tropical rain forests. The clearing of forests to create grazing pastures in forested developing nations is contributing both to world desertification and global warming. Organic runoff from feedlots has become a major source of pollution in groundwater. Lastly, the meat-heavy diet of people in the developed world has been blamed for contributing to ailments such as obesity and diabetes. The expansion of the diet as a result of conquest, the ultimate in food fusion, therefore, has been a phenomenon with both success and resultant difficulties.

SEE ALSO *Agricultural Deforestation; Biodiversity and Food Supply; Chocolate; Desertification and Agriculture; Foodways; Gastronomy; History of Food and Man: From Hunter-Gatherer to Agriculture; History of Home Cooking; Immigration and Cuisine; Indigenous Peoples and Their Diets; Livestock Intensity and Demand; Women's Role in Global Food Preparation.*

BIBLICGRAPHY

Books

Civitello, Linda. *Cuisine and Culture: A History of Food and People.* Hoboken, NJ: John Wiley, 2007.

Kiple, Kenneth F. *A Movable Feast: Ten Millennia of Food Globalization.* Cambridge, UK: Cambridge University Press, 2007.

Smith, Andrew F. *Eating History: Thirty Turning Points in the Making of American Cuisine.* New York: Columbia University Press, 2009.

Stark, Miriam T., Brenda J. Bowser, Lee Horne, and Carol Kramer. *Cultural Transmission and Material Culture: Breaking Down Boundaries.* Tucson: University of Arizona Press, 2008.

Xu, Wenying. *Eating Identities: Reading Food in Asian American Literature.* Honolulu: University of Hawaii Press, 2008.

Periodicals

Lyons, Diane. "Integrating African Cuisines." *Journal of Social Archaeology* 7, no. 3 (2007): 346–371.

Sengupta, Jayanta. "Nation on a Platter: The Culture and Politics of Food and Cuisine in Colonial Bengal." *Modern Asian Studies* 44 (2010): 81–98.

Web Sites

"New Orleans: Gumbo as History." *PBS.org,* December 1, 2006. http://www.pbs.org/wgbh/amex/neworleans/sfeature/food.html (accessed October 18, 2010).

Owels, Kahled Yacoub. "Ancient Aleppo Cuisine Tastes of Conquest and Trade." *Reuters,* October 24, 2007. http://www.reuters.com/article/idUSL2450249520071024 (accessed October 18, 2010).

Caryn E. Neumann

Seminole Indian fast food for sale at a festival in Lake City, Florida. Prior to colonization, the Seminoles farmed crops such as corn, beans, and squash, and hunted deer, wild turkeys, rabbits, and even alligators. The changes in cuisine have been implicated in health problems among Native Americans, including diabetes and obesity-related illnesses. *© Pat Canova / Alamy.*

Waste and Spoilage

■ Introduction

Food spoilage refers to the deterioration in the structure and the nutritional quality of a food due to the growth of microorganisms, which use components of the food as nutrients, or the degradation of the food material as a result of the activity of enzymes. Food spoilage may merely be inconvenient, necessitating the disposal of the perhaps-unidentifiable item discovered in the refrigerator. But spoilage by microorganisms can involve the production of noxious compounds that can contaminate the food. If the food is consumed, illness can result.

Food waste refers to raw or prepared food in a commercial establishment such as a supermarket that is disposed of, and the disposal of household food as trash rather than for composting. Food that may still be edible is disposed of as trash, although some establishments do participate in programs that help distribute the food that can no longer be sold to those in need.

Even if a commercial foodstuff remains edible, if it has exceeded certain benchmarks, such as a certain shelf date for sale, supermarkets and other food service establishments can be mandated to remove the product from the shelves for disposal. As well, some establishments will dispose of food if it presents a less-than-ideal appearance. Other criteria for waste food, which vary municipally and from state-to-state in the United States, include the composition of the material and the establishment involved. Both food spoilage and food waste can also occur during the transport and processing of food from its point of origin (e.g., crop field, ocean) to its final destination (e.g., supermarket, restaurant).

A huge amount of food is discarded by consumers. A 2008 survey of more than 2,000 households in the United Kingdom revealed that almost 30 percent of purchased food is discarded. In Toronto, Canada, 210 million kilograms of food—equivalent in weight to 35,000 African elephants—is disposed of every year. Whereas 75 percent of organic waste in Toronto is composted, 32,000 tons are disposed of in landfills.

■ Historical Background and Scientific Foundations

Food spoilage is a natural process of degradation by microorganisms, typically bacteria and fungi, that generally adhere to the surface of the food and degrade the food as a source of nutrients for their own growth and multiplication. Enzymes produced by the microbes or that originate from other sources (including the food) break apart bonds holding food components together. With enough time and continued enzyme activity, the result for some food can be a near liquefied product that hardly resembles the original.

As well, fats in food can be oxidized, which causes the food to become rancid. Other changes include discoloration and growth of surface mold.

The resulting growth and division of the microorganisms can also lead to the production of compounds that are toxic if consumed. Consumption can be accidental, for example when the food is handled during disposal and one's unwashed hands are placed in the mouth.

Typically, several parameters are involved in food spoilage. One that is fulfilled by the nature of food is the requirement for proteins, carbohydrates, and other

---

WORDS TO KNOW

DECOMPOSITION: Breakdown of cells and tissues.

EDIBLE: The ability to be used as a source of nutrients.

FOOD PRESERVATION: Techniques of food handling, processing, or packaging that slow down the decomposition of the food.

organic compounds. The temperature needs to be sufficient to allow at least microorganism activity. An excessively high temperature will destroy microbial enzymes that are vital for survival of the organisms. Refrigeration temperature often slows down or halts microbial activities. But even refrigeration temperature can be sufficient to promote food spoilage by organisms that can tolerate the lower temperature. Examples include bacteria of the genera *Aeromonas*, *Chryseobacterium*, and *Pseudomonas*. Cold-tolerant molds include *Cladosporium*, *Sprotrichum*, *Geotricum*, and *Penicillium*. Other parameters include the presence of moisture and an appropriate pH.

Once a food is contaminated, removal of the microbes is virtually impossible, short of physically removing the visibly contaminated regions. Even then it cannot be excluded that products produced during microbial growth had not permeated more widely through the food. The ultimate prudent action is to dispose of the entire item.

Efforts to reduce the spoilage of packaged foods have focused on providing an environment in the package that retards microbial growth. Traditionally the canning of foods has enabled the longer-term storage of some foods that would otherwise perish. Other preservation examples include drying, rapid freeze-drying, removal of air from the package (vacuum packing), replacement of air in a package with an inert gas such as carbon dioxide, and exposure to radiation. Packaging material that is antimicrobial has also been developed.

■ Impacts and Issues

Whereas the past two generations in many developed countries have begun to embrace the concepts of composting and recycling, much remains to be done to ensure that food that is still edible is not thrown out. The 2007 survey conducted in the United Kingdom, for example, revealed that a staggering amount of unopened or whole food is disposed of every day. The list includes 660,000 eggs, 1.2 million sausages, almost 3 million tomatoes, and 260,000 packages of cheese. The subsequent rotting of the food in landfills produces methane and more than 18 tons of carbon dioxide, which are both drivers of atmospheric warming. Curbing this emission would be equivalent to reducing the number of carbon dioxide-emitting vehicles by 20 percent. Estimates in the United States are that consumers throw out 60–100 billion pounds of food as trash every year.

IN CONTEXT: COMPOSTING

In addition to the health benefits of organic gardening, composting lays a foundation for pest control and landscape health. Composting provides gardeners with nutrient-rich materials to support plant growth. A natural process, composting enables nutrients to be cycled back into an ecosystem.

Composting is the conversion of organic material, such as plant material and household foodstuffs that would likely otherwise be wasted, into a material having a soil-like consistency. This material is called compost. The composting process, which is one of decomposition, relies upon living organisms. Insects and earthworms participate; bacteria and fungi are of fundamental importance. The end products of decomposition are compost, carbon dioxide, water, and heat.

The decomposition process is achieved mainly by bacteria and fungi. Bacteria predominate, making up 80 percent to 90 percent of the microorganisms found in compost. There are several phases to the composting process, each involving different microorganisms. The first phase, which lasts a few days after addition of the raw material to the compost pile, is a moderate temperature (mesophilic) phase. As microbial activity produces decomposition and byproducts, including heat, a high-temperature (thermophilic) phase takes over. The dominant microorganisms become those that are adapted to life at higher temperature, the so-called thermophiles. This high-temperature (thermophilic) phase will last anywhere from a few days to a few months. Finally, as decomposition activity of the microbial population slows and ceases, a cooling-down phase ensues over several months.

Initially, the mesophilic microorganisms break down compounds that readily dissolve in water. This decomposition is rapid, causing the temperature inside the compost pile to rise quickly. The microbes involved at this stage tend to be those that predominate in the soil. One example is *Actinomyces*, which resemble fungi but which are actually bacteria composed of filaments. They are what give the soil its earthy smell. Enzymes in *Actinomyces* are capable of degrading grass, bark, and even newspaper. Species of fungi and protozoa can also be active at this stage.

As the internal temperature of the pile exceeds 104°F (40°C), the mesophiles die off and are replaced by the thermophilic microbes. A decomposition temperature of around 131°F (55°C) is ideal, as microbial activity is pronounced and because that temperature is lethal to many human and animal microbial pathogens. Thus, the composting process is also a sterilizing process, from an infectious point of view. However, temperatures much above this point can kill off the microbes involved in the decomposition. For this reason, compost piles are occasionally agitated or "turned over" to mix the contents, allow oxygen to diffuse throughout the material (efficient decomposition requires the presence of oxygen), and to disperse some of the heat. The ideal blend of microorganisms can be established and maintained by the addition of waste material to the compost pile so as to not let the pile become enriched in carbon or nitrogen. A proper ratio is about 30 parts carbon (brown waste, such as dried leaves) to one part nitrogen (generally green waste, such as kitchen scraps like fruit and vegetable peels) by weight.

A woman searches for food in a food waste dump in Dhaka, Bangladesh.   *AP Images.*

Food waste also carries an economic cost involved in transport to landfills. In Toronto, transport of waste food alone costs almost 10 million Canadian dollars annually.

The global distribution of food that has evolved results in more than 30 percent of food spoiling or being unacceptably damaged prior to reaching the marketplace. One of the arguments for a more local distribution of food is the avoidance of transport-associated food loss. At the heart of food waste in many developed countries is the mindset that views food as a commodity, rather than a valuable necessity of life.

Some organizations are trying to change this situation by collecting still-edible food from supermarkets and distributing to those in need. As of 2008, a food distribution agency called Second Harvest/Feeding America was redirecting almost 6.6 million pounds (3 million kilograms) of food that would have otherwise being thrown out.

■ Primary Source Connection

Yukako Ichikawa is the chef and owner of Wafu restaurant in Sydney, Australia. Wafu emphasizes what it considers eco-conscious and socially responsible food, catering to vegetarians, vegans, and people with severe food allergies. Chef Ichikawa has also instituted an anti-food waste policy to encourage patrons to be mindful about how much food they order and consume. Patrons who over-order and fail to consume all of their food, including most garnishes, are sometimes asked not to return to Wafu.

Staffing issues and increased media attention over its anti-waste policy overwhelmed the 30 seat restaurant in 2010. Chef Ichikawa announced on the restaurant's Web site that Wafu would limit its service mostly to its members as well as patrons with health concerns addressed by the special menu.

Japanese 'Iron Chef' Ruffling Feathers in Australia with Her Anti-waste Movement

Mom's old adage of finishing everything on your dinner plate has been given a new, hard-line interpretation by one brave Japanese chef in Australia.

Failure to sufficiently clean your plate at Yukako Ichikawa's restaurant "Wafu" will see you banned from returning to the popular Sydney eatery. "When they try to return, if I remember their face, I say no," Ichikawa told Kyodo News.

Just over two months ago, Ichikawa, 42, became so dismayed at the increasing amount of food being wasted by diners that she temporarily closed her three-year-old restaurant.

According to Ichikawa, a favorable newspaper review of Wafu last December was behind the sudden influx of wasteful consumers. However, spurred on by loyal customers and some legal advice, the Nagoya native adopted a new policy which rewards good eaters and sees "picky people" banished indefinitely.

Diners able to polish off their old-fashioned Japanese meal receive a 30% discount off their bill and an invitation to join Ichikawa's exclusive list of more than 800 regulars.

No other restaurant owner in Australia has gone to the same length to reduce food waste.

Still, Sydney's only organic, dairy-free, refined sugar-free, gluten-free and wheat-free restaurant is so popular that Ichikawa is trying not to take any new customers. The indefatigable owner-chef-waitress has also begun restricting regulars to visiting on a one or two-person basis only.

Like Jerry Seinfeld's "Soup Nazi" from the 1990s, Ichikawa's tasty cuisine has customers queuing up to get in, despite often being turned away. Ichikawa and her staff direct all diners to the front door, where they must read and, importantly, agree to the new restaurant policy.

The guidelines recommend ordering "just the right amount of food" and suggest sharing meals to reduce food wastage and to increase the number of dishes an individual can experience. "If after reading this, you feel uncomfortable and find yourself unwilling or unable to respect our philosophy, we will not be offended if you choose to leave," the policy reads.

Patrons refused entry often find themselves dining at Ichikawa's ex-husband's restaurant, just 100 meters away. Menus also lay down the rules, dictating everything except "lemon slices, gari (pickled ginger) and wasabi" must be consumed.

"Sometime people can't use chopsticks (and leave) three or four pieces of rice, I can't complain," Ichikawa chuckles.

Keen to bring the Japanese concept of "mottainai" to Australia, Ichikawa works hard to conserve the environment through a number of different measures. Stemming from Buddhist philosophy, "mottainai" essentially involves making the most of limited resources and avoiding wastefulness.

The concept has also redefined the term "BYO" (Bring Your Own). Wafu customers keen on grabbing a takeaway meal must bring their own plastic container, or face a surcharge or refusal of service.

Ichikawa said she has already noticed a significant reduction in the amount of garbage she throws away. These days she has to remind herself to take out the trashcan because it takes so long to fill.

IN CONTEXT: MANAGING RESTAURANT WASTE

Most restaurants have a par sheet to keep track of the amount of food in storage and reduce food waste. Par—in food as in golf—means average or suggested amount. Every restaurant has stores of food, and when the quantity for a particular item falls below par, it needs to be reordered.

Knowing yield on products and how long food can be kept enables managers to order food in the correct quantities. This minimizes spoilage, as does a common method known as FIFO (first in, first out). FIFO is a basic rule in which storage shelves are stocked with the newest food being placed in the back. In this way, food is used in the order in which it arrives at the restaurant. Minimizing waste is key to a successful restaurant operation.

Whatever the education or background of a restaurant manager, the primary strategy for a successful manager is to ensure that the mathematics add up for a profitable business. This includes making sure everything comes together at the right time and place, including the prime components of fresh food, advertising, employees, and customers.

One of Ichikawa's customers also takes the restaurant's food waste and uses it as compost and to feed his worm farm.

Dubbed the "Iron Chef" by local media for her rigid stance on food wastage, Ichikawa has made both friends and foes with her new approach. "I get letters, so many emails, even phone calls not for reservations but just to say thank you," Ichikawa said.

While she has received an overwhelmingly positive response to her anti-waste movement, there has also been some grumbling about the way the policy is communicated to diners. Unhappy customers have gone online to the diner-review restaurant guide "Eatability" to lament their treatment.

"I'm all for the sustainable approach too, but managing your customers in a respectful way is surely doable within this framework?!," wrote "taraw" on April 14. "Their treatment was totally unnecessary, patronizing, and downright rude," "taraw" added.

"Love the concept . . . in reality the way the philosophy/rules were communicated made for rude and to be honest very weird customer service," "JRJG" wrote.

However, Ichikawa said people simply need to be better educated on food wastage, with restaurants, schools and families bearing the brunt of this responsibility.

The New South Wales government, under which the municipality of Sydney falls, has recently started a "Love Food, Hate Waste" website designed to educate locals about how to reduce food waste. According to the website, NSW,

Australia's most populous state, throws away A$2.5 billion (about U.S.$2 billion) worth of food every year.

Australians waste around 3 million tons of food a year, (according to Australian action group "Do something!") and NSW throws away 1.1 million tons, according to Love Food Hate Waste. The website adds the food supply chain accounts for 23% of the country's greenhouse gas emissions—the second highest contributor after power stations.

Looking at the bigger picture, Ichikawa believes there is more than enough food in the world and that with better education, as well as a more equitable distribution of food, everyone can "share the good feeling."

"In India, Africa, many people die . . . every three seconds see people die without food, if we can change to four or five seconds I am happy," the chef said with her characteristic iron.

"JAPANESE 'IRON CHEF' RUFFLING FEATHERS IN AUSTRALIA WITH HER ANTI-WASTE MOVEMENT." *JAPAN TODAY: JAPAN NEWS AND DISCUSSION*, OCTOBER 18, 2010. HTTP://WWW.JAPANTODAY.COM/CATEGORY/LIFESTYLE/VIEW/JAPANESE-IRON-CHEF-RUFFLING-FEATHERS-IN-AUSTRALIA-WITH-HER-ANTI-WASTE-MOVEMENT (ACCESSED NOVEMBER 15, 2010).

SEE ALSO *African Famine Relief; Agribusiness; Agriculture and International Trade; Agroecology; America's Second Harvest/Feeding America; Biofuels and World Hunger; Cooking, Carbon Emissions, and Climate Change; Ethical Issues in Agriculture; Extreme Weather and Food Supply. Famine; Food Safety and Inspection Service; Foodborne Diseases; Preservation.*

BIBLIOGRAPHY

Books

Kosovska, Halyna. *The Biological Treatment of Organic Food Waste.* Stockholm: Royal Institute of Technology, 2006.

Morgan, Sally. *Leftover Food.* London: Franklin Watts, 2006.

Scott, Nicky. *How to Make and Use Compost: The Ultimate Guide.* Totnes Devon, UK: Green Books, 2009.

Stuart, Tristram. *Waste: Uncovering the Global Food Scandal.* New York: W.W. Norton & Co, 2009.

Ventour, Lorrayne. *The Food We Waste.* Banbury, UK: WRAP, 2008.

Periodicals

Brody, Aaron L. "How Green Is Food Waste?" *Food Technology* 62, no. 6 (2008): 121.

Griffin, Mary, Jeffery Sobal, and Thomas Lyson. "An Analysis of a Community Food Waste Stream." *Agriculture and Human Values* 26, no. 1–2 (2009): 67–81.

Web Sites

Oliver, Rachael. "All About: Food Waste." *CNN.com/Asia*, January 22, 2008. http://edition.cnn.com/2007/WORLD/asiapcf/09/24/food.leftovers/#cnnSTCText (accessed October 7, 2010).

"Waste Not, Want Not." *Environmental Protection Agency (EPA).* http://www.epa.gov/wastes/conserve/materials/organics/pubs/wast_not.pdf (accessed October 7, 2010).

Brian Douglas Hoyle

Water

■ Introduction

Water is an essential part of food production and preparation. Everything humans consume as food is produced using water or contains water. Without fresh, safe-to-consume water resources, farming, livestock raising, cooking, and sustaining human life are not possible.

For individual use in cooking, drinking, and cleaning, the recommended daily per person minimum of clean water is 5.3 gallons (20 liters) per day. Only one in five people in developing nations receives this amount. More than 99 percent of all people in developed nations have access to this much water daily. Citizens of the United States, Canada, Australia, and Europe typically use 52.8–158.5 gallons (200–600 liters) per day.

More than 1.1 billion people worldwide, 400 million of whom are children, lack daily access to clean water. Approximately 2.6 billion lack basic sanitation, putting local communal water supplies at increased risk of contamination and local populations at greater risk of waterborne disease. One in five children in the world's developing regions have no access to either potable water or sanitation.

■ Historical Background and Scientific Foundations

Water is the most abundant resource on Earth, covering approximately 71 percent of the Earth's surface. Water consists of one oxygen atom and two hydrogen molecules held together by covalent bonds in which the oxygen and hydrogen atoms share electrons. Water generally exists as a tasteless, virtually colorless, and odorless liquid at ambient temperatures. The presence of various minerals, either as elements or compounds, may alter the taste, color, or odor of water. In addition to a liquid phase, water may exist in solid or gaseous phases.

Approximately 98.4 percent of all water on Earth is found on the surface, while 1.6 percent of water is located in underground aquifers. Liquid water accounts for 97.6 percent of all surface water on Earth, with oceans accounting for 97 percent of all surface water. Surface freshwater, as found in lakes, ponds, and rivers, comprises only 0.6 percent of all surface water on Earth. Most of the Earth's freshwater exists as ice in glaciers and polar ice caps, which account for 2.4 percent of all surface water. Water vapor, in the form of clouds and suspended vapor, and precipitation accounts for 0.001 percent of all water.

Although water vapor comprises a miniscule percentage of the Earth's water, it plays a significant role in the movement of water through the process known as the hydrologic cycle, also called the water cycle. The hydrologic cycle involves the transition of water molecules from one state to another. Although the total amount of water on Earth remains relatively constant, water constantly transitions from one state to another. Liquid water evaporates from oceans and other surface bodies of water and forms water vapor. Vegetation also expels water vapor through a process known as transpiration. The water vapor returns to the surface of land or oceans as rain or snow. Surface water reaches the ocean as run-off from rivers or other surface sources. Ice contributes to the process by melting to form liquid water. Liquid surface water, either from existing bodies or as fallen rain, also recharges aquifers.

Although most precipitation falls on the oceans, the water cycle releases 107 trillion metric tonnes (118 trillion short tons) of precipitation over land each year. People, plants, and animals rely on the freshwater discharged by the hydrologic cycle to sustain life. Humans use this freshwater for drinking, agriculture, sanitation, industry, recreation, and other purposes. With the rise of agriculture, people developed a need to provide a constant supply of freshwater to crops, which was not possible given the unreliability of precipitation. Around the sixth millennium BC, the Egyptians and Mesopotamians developed the earliest irrigation techniques. In the second decade of the twenty-first century, agriculture accounts for about 70 percent of global freshwater use.

■ Impacts and Issues

Lack of access to water is closely tied to geography and poverty. Most of the people without access to freshwater live in rural areas of developing countries and survive on less than $2 per day. One-third of those without clean water live on less than $1 per day. Most safe freshwater resources are disproportionately consumed by residents of the world's wealthiest nations. Twelve percent of the global population, almost all of whom live in developed nations, use 85 percent of all water consumed by people worldwide each day.

Whereas people in the poorest rural regions are more likely not to have access to water, the world's poorest residents are least likely to be able to afford to purchase fresh, clean water. The United Nations Development Programme (UNDEP) stated in a 2006 report that residents of urban slum areas of developing nations often paid five to ten times more for water that those in wealthier areas with piped, constant water resources. The report declared that people living in slums in Manila pay more for water than people living in London.

Millions of people rely on consistent supplies of water for food production. Crop farmers, livestock ranchers, herders, and fishing enterprises all rely on water. Here again, the global distribution of water resources is uneven. In Asia, approximately 70 percent of freshwater utilized for crop irrigation is used exclusively for growing rice. In Egypt, the demand for irrigation water from the Nile River and its tributaries—in addition to the needs of the country's cities and people—exceeds

A woman in Karnataka, India, waters her vegetable crop by hand. © *Eye Ubiquitous / Alamy.*

the amount of available water. Irrigation channels are thus treated as community water sources, serving as a place to wash clothes, obtain cooking water and water for livestock, and discharge waste. In Ethiopia, large, predominantly foreign-owned, intensive farms can use as many water resources as 100,000 of the country's citizens. Technological innovations have decreased the amount of water required for irrigation, but the irrigation systems that conserve water are prohibitively expensive in many parts of the world.

Diet also affects global water consumption. Raising plant crops requires less water than raising livestock. A global increase in meat consumption increases the amount of water used to produce a person's daily meals. On average, people who consume a large amount of meat in their diets require approximately 5,000 liters (1,321 gallons) of water input to produce the food they consume each day. People in developing countries who adhere to predominantly vegetarian diets require only 1,000 to 2,000 liters (264 to 528 gallons) of water to produce their daily food supply.

Water scarcity, a condition in which demand for water exceeds the availability of freshwater, is likely to worsen over the next century. Population growth,

---

IN CONTEXT: LIVESTOCK RUNOFF POLLUTION

According to a 2004 report on water safety by the World Health Organization (WHO), diarrheal diseases kill 1.8 million people per year. The WHO attributes 88 percent of these deaths to unsafe drinking water. Higher levels of bacteria or other pathogens may produce increased incidence of waterborne diseases. Increased levels of bacteria and pathogens are usually attributable to contamination by livestock and the release of effluent, or wastewater, into the water supply.

Unwanted hormones and other pharmaceutical agents from discarded medicines used in managing livestock are also an increasing source of water contamination.

---

conflict, urbanization, increased industrial and agricultural water use, and global climate change will all impact the amount of Earth's freshwater resources available for human use. By 2025, 1.8 billion people will live in regions facing chronic water scarcity. Since 1990 water

A man in south India drinks clean water from a tank. Though 16 percent of the world's population resides in India, the renewable water resource there is only about 4 percent of the world's freshwater resources. *Image copyright Paul Prescott, 2010. Used under license from Shutterstock.com.*

IN CONTEXT: AGRICULTURAL RUNOFF AND AQUATIC DEAD ZONES

Water pollution carries many risks for humans and other living organisms. Silt and chemical water pollution, including fertilizers, herbicides, and insecticides, can lead to eutrophication, an over-enrichment of water with nutrients, usually nitrogen or phosphorus. Increased levels of nutrients encourage plant and algae growth, which then deplete the water of dissolved oxygen. Depleted oxygen levels harm fish and other aquatic organisms.

Pollution, especially from nitrogen rich fertilizer runoff, can create transient "dead zones" in bodies of water. Dead zones are hypoxic areas that contain oxygen levels too low to support many life forms. Dead zones normally form as a result of intense bacterial feeding on algae blooms in agricultural and other chemical runoff. Such dead zone areas off the coasts of Louisiana and Texas vary from season to season, especially in areas near where the Mississippi River flows into the Gulf of Mexico. The Gulf's dead zone phenomena is one of approximately 250 known hypoxic aquatic areas (both freshwater and marine) in U.S. waters.

use has grown at more than twice the rate of the global population. More water is being used worldwide per capita, on average, than at any other time in recorded history.

SEE ALSO *Agricultural Demand for Water; Agroecology; Aquaculture and Fishery Resources; Biodiversity and Food Supply; Bottled Water; Cholera; Consumer Food Safety Recommendations; Desertification and Agriculture; Dietary Guidelines for Americans; Dietary Reference Intakes; Disasters and Food Supply; Ecological Impacts of Various World Diets; Ethical Issues in Agriculture; Extreme Weather and Food Supply; Hydroponics; Infant Formula and Baby Food; Oral Health and Diet; Sustainable Agriculture; UN Millennium Development Goals; Water Scarcity.*

BIBLIOGRAPHY

Books

Molden, David. *Water for Food, Water for Life: A Comprehensive Assessment of Water Management in Agriculture.* London: Earthscan, 2007.

Myers, Daniel J. J. *Food Water Energy and Human Survival.* Oakland, OR: Red Anvil Press, 2008.

Parris, Kevin. *Sustainable Management of Water Resources in Agriculture.* Paris, France: OECD, 2010.

Pascual, Unai, Amita Shah, and Jayanta Bandyopadhyay. *Water, Agriculture, and Sustainable Well-Being.* New Delhi, India: Oxford University Press, 2009.

Wolter, Hans W. *Overcoming the World Water Crisis: Achieving Water, Food, and Environmental Security.* Colombo: Dialogue Secretariat, 2003.

Periodicals

"Early Warning—The Energy-Food-Water-Security Matrix." *Defense & Foreign Affairs* 36, no. 6 (2008): 2.

Rosegrant, Mark W., Claudia Ringler, and Tingju Zhu. "Water for Agriculture: Maintaining Food Security under Growing Scarcity." *Annual Review of Environment and Resources* 34 (2009): 205–222.

Tarver, Toni. "'Just Add Water': Regulating and Protecting the Most Common Ingredient." *Journal of Food Science* 73, no. 1 (2008): 1–13.

Web Sites

Water.org. http://water.org/ (accessed November 4, 2010).

"Water for Life, 2005–2015." *United Nations.* http://www.un.org/waterforlifedecade/index.html (accessed November 4, 2010).

"World Water Day." *IRC International Water and Sanitation Center.* http://www.worldwaterday.org/ (accessed November 1, 2010).

Adrienne Wilmoth Lerner
Joseph P. Hyder

Water Scarcity

Introduction

The world has more than doubled its human population since 1950. In general, people are wealthier, consume more calories, and eat more meat and thus require more water to produce food. More pressure is placed on the environment and as a result, the quality of the water that is available for drinking, food production, and marine life is depleting.

In many regions, further appropriation of water for human use is not possible because limits have been reached and in many cases breached, either as a result of a lack of available freshwater, or as a consequence of a lack of investment in infrastructure such as dams and reservoirs. According to the International Water Management Institute (IWMI), "current estimates indicate that we will not have enough water to feed ourselves in 40 years time."

Greater competition for water resources raises challenging questions about water rights and allocations. And when water becomes an expensive commodity, and by extension food supplies diminish and food prices rise, then social cohesion erodes as basic rights become privileges. Organizations such as Food & Water Watch (FWW), a non-profit, U.S.-based organization, advocate for policies that encourage access to healthy food and safe drinking water worldwide. Food & Water Watch has waged a 10-year campaign at the United Nations to promote a legally binding recognition of the human right to water.

Historical Background and Scientific Foundations

Although 70 percent of the earth's surface is covered by water, almost all of that is saltwater found in the oceans. Only 3 percent is freshwater, and of this most is frozen in ice caps and glaciers or present in underground aquifers.

Of the remaining surface water, a very large part must stay in the rivers and streams to ensure effluent dilution and safeguard the integrity of the aquatic ecosystem. But exactly how large this part should be is little understood. It varies with the time of year, and each watershed has its own specific ecological limit below which the system will degrade.

Agriculture is the principal user of all water resources—rainfall and ground and surface waters. It accounts for about 70 percent of all withdrawals worldwide, with domestic use amounting to about 10 percent and industry using some 21 percent.

Because water and population are distributed unevenly throughout the world, the water situation is already critical in various countries and regions and likely to become so in several more. In India, for example, where 16 percent of the world's population resides, the maximum renewable freshwater resource is about 4 percent of the world's freshwater resources.

Impacts and Issues

The concept of water stress or water scarcity is relatively simple. It applies to situations in which there is not enough water for all uses, whether agricultural, industrial or domestic, according to the World Business Council for Sustainable Development.

Defining thresholds for stress, however, is complex. Nevertheless, hydrologists have proposed that when annual per capita renewable freshwater availability drops below 1,700 cubic meters, countries begin to experience periodic or regular water stress. Below 1,000 cubic meters, water scarcity begins to hamper economic development and human health and well-being. Below 500 cubic meters, countries face conditions of absolute water scarcity.

The contributors to water scarcity are many: a growing population, urbanization, dietary habits, water pollution, climate change, and regional droughts. In some

WORDS TO KNOW

AQUIFER: An underground layer of water-bearing permeable rock or unconsolidated materials (clay, silt, sand, or gravel) from which groundwater can be readily extracted.

BLUE WATER: A term used to refer to all bodies of ground and surface waters together: rivers, lakes, and aquifers.

EUTROPHICATION: A scientific term describing the overfertilization of lakes with nutrients and the changes that occur as a result. In particular it is the "bloom" or excessive simple plant growth in a water body.

FERTILIZERS: Fertilizers are soil amendments applied to promote plant growth and are usually directly applied to soil, and also sprayed on leaves.

GREEN WATER: A term used to refer to rainwater.

GROUNDWATER: The water that settles between rocks and directly underneath the earth's surface.

POTABLE: Potable water (or drinking water) is water fit for human consumption. Water that is not potable may be made potable by filtration or distillation, or by a range of other methods.

WATERSHED: The surface waters or streams, rivers, deltas, wetlands, and lakes that share sources of water from both above and below the ground.

regions, underground water levels are falling because water is being extracted through wells faster than it is naturally replaced by rainfall. When groundwater disappears, pumping from wells becomes harder and more expensive. Rivers, lakes, streams and wetlands dry up, and even the land itself can cave in.

Industrial waste and agricultural contaminants contribute to water scarcity by polluting freshwater sources. Both deliberate discharge and accidental spillage from industrial and agricultural sources are serious detriments to local water supplies. Such contaminants may reach the surface or groundwater directly, e.g., being discharged directly into surface waters and traveling through drainage ditches and pipes to surface waters, or indirectly by leaching into groundwater. Contaminants include industrial wastes like heavy metals and toxic chemicals, artificial fertilizer residues, insecticides, herbicides, pesticides, and farmyard waste.

Though fertilizers increase crop yields, high application rates of inorganic nitrogen fertilizers, which are highly soluble, lead to increased runoff into surface water as well as leaching into groundwater. Other types of agricultural pollution can also be highly damaging: Undiluted animal manure (slurry) is 100 times more concentrated than domestic sewage and can carry parasites that are difficult to detect.

Agricultural return water flows to rivers and aquifers are only about 50 percent of the water withdrawn, compared to 90 percent from domestic and 95 percent from industry. But poor-quality return flows from urban and industrial areas are easier to treat before being returned to watercourses.

The non-point character of agricultural pollution—pollution originating from a distance source—makes treatment difficult. In the early twenty-first century, non-point source pollution remains the largest water quality problem in countries such as the United States because it is the main reason that approximately 40 percent of rivers, lakes, and estuaries are not clean enough to meet basic uses such as fishing or swimming.

Developing Countries

Water scarcity already predominantly affects developing countries where the majority of the world's 840 million undernourished people live without regular access to safe water. Urbanization in the developing countries is also responsible for loss of agricultural land, depletion, and pollution of water resources.

Population growth, the majority of which will occur in Africa, parts of Asia, and Latin America, will intensify these stresses. A recent report suggests that by 2030, in some developing regions of the world, water demand will exceed supply by 50 percent.

The required food productivity increases will demand investment in knowledge, infrastructure, and capacity. More and better water storage systems, such as dams and reservoirs; improved management of irrigation systems; and increasing water productivity in both irrigated and rain-fed farming systems will all contribute. The need is critical and will necessitate the redesign of both the physical and institutional arrangements of some large and often dysfunctional agricultural schemes. Safe, risk-free re-use of wastewater from growing cities will also be needed. And these actions will need to be performed in parallel with further developments of drought-tolerant crops and the provision of infrastructure and facilities to get fresh food to markets.

SEE ALSO *Agricultural Deforestation; Agricultural Demand for Water; Agricultural Land Reform; Agriculture and International Trade; Agroecology; Biofuels and World Hunger; Bottled Water; Desertification and Agriculture; Ethical Issues in Agriculture; Extreme Weather and Food Supply; Food and Agriculture Organization (FAO); Food Security; Hunger; Population and Food; Rome Declaration on World Food Security (1996); UN Millennium Development Goals; Water.*

Water pollution from a copper mine. Industrial and agricultural emissions of chemicals into freshwater deplete global supplies of clean drinking water. *Image copyright Rechitan Sorin, 2010. Used under license from Shutterstock.com.*

BIBLIOGRAPHY

Books

Aswathanarayana, Uppugunduri. *Food and Water Security in Developing Countries.* London: Taylor & Francis, 2008.

Food and Agriculture Organization (FAO) of the United Nations. *The State of Food Insecurity in the World 2009: Eradicating World Hunger.* Rome: FAO, 2009.

Periodicals

Kortmann, Karin. "The Human Rights to Food and Water." *Environmental Policy and Law* 39, no. 1 (2009): 2–3.

Rosegrant, Mark W., Claudia Ringler, and Tingiu Zhu. "Water for Agriculture: Maintaining Food Security under Growing Scarcity." *Annual Review of Environment and Resources* 34 (2009): 205–222.

Web Sites

FAO Newsroom. "FAO Urges Action to Cope with Increasing Water Scarcity." *Food and Agriculture Organization of the United Nations (FAO),* March 22, 2007. http://www.fao.org/newsroom/en/news/2007/1000520/index.html (accessed October 6, 2010).

Food & Water Watch. http://www.foodandwaterwatch.org/ (accessed October 6, 2010).

"Special Programme on Food Security." *Food and Agriculture Organization of the United Nations (FAO).* http://www.fao.org/spfs/en/ (accessed October 6, 2010).

Melissa Carson

Whaling

■ Introduction

Whaling refers to the practice of killing whales, primarily for meat and whale oil, along with other products. People in coastal communities around the world have engaged in whaling for nearly 8,000 years. Throughout most of whaling history, people killed whales close to shore in order to provide food for communities: A single small whale could provide enough food after simple preservation to feed a community for weeks or months. Whale meat was one of the few types of food available for many people living in harsh climates, such as the Arctic.

By the late nineteenth century, however, large-scale commercial whaling operations decimated global whale populations. Most commercial whaling operations used whale products, such as whale oil for lamps or baleen (whalebone) for dressmaking, while discarding much of the whale meat. By the early twentieth century, the international community took action to regulate whaling in order to preserve whales for future generations. In the early twenty-first century, the International Whaling Commission (IWC), an international body established to regulate whaling, has imposed a global moratorium on whaling. Several important exceptions to the moratorium have generated considerable friction between pro-whaling and anti-whaling governments and organizations.

■ Historical Background and Scientific Foundations

Archaeological evidence indicates that humans have engaged in whaling for thousands of years. Archaeologists have uncovered harpoons and other whaling implements on the Korean Peninsula dating to 6000 BC. Similar whaling implements from North America indicate that the Inuit and other Arctic indigenous groups began whaling before 3000 BC. The Basque people of Spain and France, Scandinavian peoples, and Japanese had thriving whaling communities before AD 1600.

Throughout the early history of whaling, communities relied on whaling for food and whale oil for lamps and candles. Whale meat provided energy and nutrients for many people living in harsh climates. According to Denmark's Department of Nutrition, a 3.5 ounce (100 gram) portion of lean whale meat provides 117 calories, 23.5 grams of protein, and 2.4 grams of fat compared to 187 calories, 29.8 grams of protein, and 6.6 grams of fat in lean beef. Whale blubber, a thick layer of fat found under the skin of whales, provides calorie-laden fat to sustain people in harsh climates who have few carbohydrates in their diets. Blubber also contains vitamin D, which for centuries helped prevent rickets among Arctic peoples.

By the nineteenth century, the demand for whale oil, which was also used in the production of machine lubricants, soap, cosmetics, and leather, led to new developments in whaling technology. The use of explosive harpoons enabled whalers to kill large species of whales, including blue and fin whales. At the same time, steam-powered ships enabled commercial whalers to venture far from shore and remain at sea for months.

WORDS TO KNOW

BIOACCUMULATION: The process by which a substance becomes concentrated in an organism, because the substance is absorbed at a greater rate than it is secreted or removed.

CETACEAN: Any member of marine mammal order Cetacea, including whales, dolphins, and porpoises.

DIOXINS: A group of highly toxic, carcinogenic compounds produced during the manufacturing process of various substances, such as herbicides.

Commercial whale hunting for non-agricultural purposes decimated global whale populations. Between the mid-nineteenth century and the 1960s, the global population of blue whales fell from approximately 275,000 to between 650 and 2,000 whales. The global humpback whale population fell from 125,000 to 80,000 during the same period. The International Union for Conservation of Nature (IUCN), a nongovernmental organization dedicated to conservation issues, estimates that the Northwest Pacific stock of gray whales has fallen from thousands of whales to about 100 whales in the early twenty-first century.

By the 1930s and 1940s, scientists realized that modern commercial whaling was decreasing whale populations at an unsustainable rate. In 1937 nine nations signed the International Agreement for the Regulation of Whaling, which established regulations on the number, size, species, and location of whales that may be killed commercially. In 1946, 42 nations signed the International Convention for the Regulation of Whaling, which required the member nations to establish the IWC to implement the economic and conservation goals of the convention. The IWC has the power to establish whale sanctuaries, set limits on the size and number of catches, set seasons, prohibit catching certain species, and regulate the equipment used in whaling. The IWC currently has 88 member nations.

■ Impacts and Issues

Despite the establishment of the IWC, global whale populations continued to decline after World War II. In 1972 the United Nations Conference on the Human Environment adopted the Stockholm Action Plan, which called for a ten-year moratorium on commercial whaling. In 1982 the IWC voted to implement a five-year moratorium on commercial whaling. The moratorium went into effect in 1986. Japan, Norway, Peru, and the Soviet Union registered formal objections to the moratorium, but Japan and Peru subsequently withdrew their objections. The 1986 moratorium subsequently became a permanent moratorium on whaling activities with several important reservations.

The IWC's whaling moratorium does not apply to either aboriginal subsistence whaling or whaling performed for scientific research. The IWC views aboriginal subsistence whaling as a non-commercial form of whaling undertaken by groups that traditionally have

The whale hunt has been part of the culture of the Faroe Islands for centuries. These pilot whales were killed during the July 2010 hunt. *Image copyright Kitti, 2010. Used under license from Shutterstock.com.*

practiced whaling. Furthermore, as the name implies, communities use subsistence whaling to supplement their diets. IWC regulations permit certain native peoples in Greenland, Siberia, St. Vincent and the Grenadines, and Alaska to engage in aboriginal subsistence whaling. The people of the Faroe Islands also continue traditional whaling practices, but their activities are not regulated under the IWC moratorium, which does not apply to taking small cetaceans.

The scientific exception to the IWC whaling moratorium remains the most significant controversy over whaling practices. Japan continues whaling operations under the scientific exception to IWC's moratorium through Japan's Institute for Cetacean Research (ICR). The ICR has killed up to 1,000 whales per year in the name of scientific research. Since 1987, the ICR has given more than 180 presentations to IWC's Scientific Committee and published more than 90 journal articles. In 2005 the IWC passed Resolution 2005-1, which noted that Japan killed 6,800 minke whales for scientific research after the moratorium compared to 840 whales in the 31 years before the moratorium. The resolution called on the Japanese government to abandon or revise their scientific whaling program.

Many nations and conservation organizations have criticized Japanese whaling under the scientific exception and note that the ICR has produced little important research and that much of the research could have been gathered without killing whales. Critics argue that Japan is in violation of the IWC moratorium. They argue that the ICR does not engage in true scientific research but instead serves as a cover for Japan's lucrative commercial whale meat industry.

Both Iceland and Norway have lodged objections to IWC's moratorium on commercial whaling, which exempts them from regulation under the moratorium. Norway resumed commercial whaling in 1993. Iceland began whaling under the scientific research exception in 2003. In 2006, Iceland resumed commercial whaling.

Whale meat continues to appear in fish markets and at restaurants in Japan, Iceland, Norway, Greenland, and the Faroe Islands. Whale meat may pose a health risk to consumers: A large percentage of whale meat contains unacceptably high levels of mercury, dioxins, and other toxins that bioaccumulate in whales. The Japanese government claims that meat from minke whales harvested near Antarctica, which comprises the

Japanese school children watch whalers butcher a Baird's Beaked whale on a port deck in Wada, Japan, on June 21, 2007. *AP Images.*

majority of whale meat consumed in Japan, meets government standards for mercury and other toxins. A 2003 study in the Journal of Environmental Science and Technology contradicts this assertion. Japanese researchers evaluated the mercury levels contained in 137 samples of fresh and frozen whale meat collected from various parts of Japan. Their study revealed that all samples contained mercury above the government limit of 0.4 parts per million, and some samples exceeded the government limit by 160 to 200 times the allowable amount of mercury.

SEE ALSO *Biodiversity and Food Supply; Ecological Impacts of Various World Diets; Indigenous Peoples and Their Diets; Protected or Threatened Species as Food.*

BIBLIOGRAPHY

Books

Estes, James A. *Whales, Whaling, and Ocean Ecosystems.* Berkeley: University of California Press, 2006.

Great Britain Department for Environmental, Food & Rural Affairs. *The International Whaling Commission: The Way Forward.* London: DEFRA, 2008.

Happynook, Kathy. *Whaling for Food.* Qualicum Beach, British Columbia: WCW Publications, 2005.

Kraus, Scott D., and Rosalind Rolland. *The Urban Whale: North Atlantic Right Whales at the Crossroads.* Cambridge, MA: Harvard University Press, 2007.

Periodicals

Marker, Michael. "After the Makah Whale Hunt." *Urban Education* 41, no. 5 (2006): 482–505.

Parsons, E. Chris, Naomi A. Rose, Claire Bass, Clare Perry, and Mark P. Simmonds. "It's Not Just Poor Science—Japan's 'Scientific' Whaling May Be a Human Health Risk Too." *Marine Pollution Bulletin* 52, no. 9 (2006): 1118–1120.

Web Sites

Kuze, Motofume. "Whaling Just Part of the Food Chain." *The Japan Times* May 2, 2010. http://search.japantimes.co.jp/cgi-bin/rc20100502a7.html (accessed October 16, 2010).

"Status of Whales." *International Whaling Commission.* http://iwcoffice.org/conservation/status.htm (accessed October 16, 2010).

Joseph P. Hyder

Wholesome Meat Act of 1967

■ Introduction

The Wholesome Meat Act of 1967 is a U.S. federal law that amended the Federal Meat Inspection Act (1906), the first law in the United States to mandate sanitary standards for the meatpacking industry and regulate the inspection of meat. The Wholesome Meat Act is also known as the "Equal To" Act because it requires individual states to have meat inspection programs that are equal to or better than the federal standards. It charged the U.S. Department of Agriculture (USDA) and the Food Safety Inspection Service (FSIS) with promulgating federal inspection and food safety standards for meat.

Under the 1906 act, only meat that crossed state lines for butchering, distribution, or sale was subject to uniform inspections and regulation. Passage of the Wholesome Meat Act ensured that all meat in the United States intended for commercial sale would be inspected for safety and that such inspections would conform to a minimum standard. Under the 1967 act, however, meat processing facilities that choose to use only state inspection programs are limited to selling their meat within that state, whereas those that choose federal inspection programs can sell throughout the country and export their products.

■ Historical Background and Scientific Foundations

American journalist and author Upton Sinclair's 1906 book *The Jungle* featured a graphic description of the meatpacking industry. From the stench of the stockyards to the filth of the processing plants, Sinclair (1878–1968) described the industry as dirty, disease-ridden, and rife with corruption. Farmers and plant owners bribed stockyard inspectors to let diseased animals pass. Workers ill with tuberculosis processed meat.

Workers relieved themselves near their work stations. Potted meat and sausage products were contaminated with insects, rats, hair, hide, sawdust, human urine and blood, and animal remnants that had been swept off of the floors.

Sinclair's book spurred public and media outrage. In response, U.S. President Theodore Roosevelt sent a government inspection team led by labor commissioner Charles P. Neill (1865–1942) and social worker James Bronson Reynolds (1861–1924) to evaluate the meatpacking industry. Their findings, published as the Neill-Reynolds Report, confirmed the hygiene, adulteration, contamination, and corruption problems highlighted in *The Jungle*. On June 30, 1906, Congress passed the Pure Food and Drug Act and the Meat Inspection Act. Under the Meat Inspection Act, livestock were submitted to a mandatory inspection before slaughter and a subsequent inspection after slaughter but before processing. All meatpacking facilities that bought, sold, or transported meat across state lines were subject to government regulations dictating cleanliness standards and sanitary practices.

The 1906 act governed U.S. meat processing for decades, but after World War II (1939–1945), the industry changed significantly, rendering the old act less effective. Meatpacking and slaughter facilities moved out of the cities as developments in refrigerated warehousing and trucking permitted them to take advantage of cheaper land. The newly constructed interstates facilitated rapid transport. Plants became increasingly mechanized for packing, but retained much of the same difficult assembly line work in slaughtering and butchering that had been developed 50 years before.

As meat became cheaper and more reliably processed, Americans started eating more poultry and beef. At the same time, however, some manufacturers began adding fillers to their products such as wheat, oats, vegetable proteins, flours, and chemicals to improve appearance or reduce consumer costs. No law required meat processors to label these additions and alterations to their products, and a new generation became concerned with the integrity of meat products. In response to public concern, in 1958 Congress amended the Federal Food, Drug and Cosmetic Act of 1938 with the Food Additive Amendment to ensure the safety and integrity of additives and ingredients used in processed foods. The act included screening meat for levels of animal drugs such as antibiotics and other additives such as chemical feed enhancers, which had been introduced into agricultural use since the passage of the 1938 act.

When Congress passed the Wholesome Meat Act of 1967, states were required to inspect meat that stayed within state lines. Meat must be inspected under the 1967 act to certify that it is free of disease, sanitary, unadulterated, and truthfully labeled. The following year, the Wholesome Poultry Products Act of 1968 imposed the same requirements on the poultry industry and created a unified meat inspection division for all meats subject to federal inspection.

■ Impacts and Issues

As of 2010, there were more than 6,000 meatpacking plants in the United States that were subject to either state or federal regulations. Regulations still exempt specialty shops that butcher animals for licensed hunters. The laws also exclude farms that slaughter and process meats for their own or guest consumption.

Critics assert that labeling of meat continues to be misleading. Though most consumers confuse them, there is no regulatory relationship between meat inspection for health and safety and meat quality grading. Whereas health and safety inspections are mandatory, meat grading is a voluntary program for which meat processors must pay. Many leading meatpackers submit to the grading program in order to fetch higher market prices for their best quality meats.

Regulation of the meat industry continues to be controversial. Labor and workers' rights activists heavily supported the initial meatpacking industry regulations in 1906, only to have the final legislation leave out any worker concerns. When the Pure Food and Drug Act and the Federal Meat Inspection Act were subsequently reformed, the emphasis of the reforms was again on food purity and not on industry working conditions. However, labor leaders assert that working conditions and sanitation are closely related. Slaughter-house workers who are tired, in pain, and expected to butcher animals at a rapid rate, may miss signs of contamination in meat. Stressful working conditions may exacerbate worker illnesses or make workers more careless about sanitation precautions.

In 2001, Congress overturned reforms intended to reduce repetitive stress injuries among meatpackers. In 2005, the international watchdog group Human Rights

WORDS TO KNOW

ACT: A statute, rule, or formal lawmaking document enacted by a legislative body or issued by a government.

MEATPACKING: The process of slaughtering animals and preparing meat for sale to consumers.

REGULATION: Controlling behaviors, business practices, or industrial practices through rules, restrictions, or laws to encourage preferred outcomes or prevent undesired outcomes that may otherwise occur.

Watch concluded in its report "Blood, Sweat, and Fear: Workers' Rights in U.S. Meat and Poultry Plants" that working conditions in the U.S. meatpacking industry violated labor laws and basic human rights. The report cited dangerous working conditions, long shifts, repetitive work, unfair wage practices, anti-union actions, and abuses toward the significant population of recent immigrant workers in the industry. Labor rights activists have reported that some workers in meat processing plants wear adult diapers in order to maintain their stations for the long hours required or to avoid being monetarily penalized for slowing down the assembly line with breaks. Industry workers and advocates also report instances in which meat may have been contaminated by blood, tissue, or fluids from injured workers who were not removed from the processing line as required by law. In 2006, the U.S. Bureau of Labor Statistics reported an average injury and job-related illness rate of 12.6 percent for full-time meatpacking plant employees, twice as high as the national average of all manufacturing jobs.

Despite over a century of reform in the U.S. meatpacking industry, there remain consumer questions about the quality and safety of meat products. Labeling laws do not require notifying consumers when meats have been adulterated with simple additives such as water and salt. There are no labeling requirements for meats from animals that have received antibiotics or growth hormones, though products are allowed to truthfully advertise the absence of them in their beef-source animals.

Testing meats for disease and food-borne illness also remains an issue. The USDA currently tests around 1 percent of all U.S.-raised and processed meat for bovine spongiform encephalopathy (BSE or "mad cow disease"). The USDA asserts that this number is scientifically adequate to ensure a safe food supply, and that the test does not work as well in the younger animals preferred in the meat industry. In 2004, a small beef producer, Creekstone Farms, built a testing facility on its slaughterhouse site and announced its intention to test all of its meat for BSE so that they could affix special "100% tested" labeling to their products. In 2006

A USDA inspector examines, grades, and stamps sides of beef in Colorado.   © *Stock Connection Blue / Alamy.*

Creekstone sued the USDA when the USDA declined to sell Creekstone the government-approved test kits. The USDA denial of the test kits prohibited Creekstone from testing all of their animals and adding the special labeling. Representatives from the meatpacking industry argued that Creekstone's plan could influence consumer patterns such that full-testing would become an international standard and would significantly raise the cost to industry and the price of meat. Creekstone argued that their costs to consumers increased by only 0.10 USD per pound of beef sold. On August 29, 2008, the Court of Appeals for the District of Columbia Circuit ruled that the USDA could prevent Creekstone from testing its animals for BSE.

■ Primary Source Connection

In the United States, individual states are permitted their own food safety policies and legislation provided it is at least as stringent as that of the federal standards often enforced by the Food and Safety Inspection Service (FSIS). The following excerpt is part of a Congressional Research Service (CRS) report on the issue of whether or not the individual state inspection programs can ensure the same level of safety as federal regulation and oversight.

State-Inspected Meat and Poultry: Issues for Congress

Approximately 2,100 meat and poultry establishments in 27 states are subject to state-conducted rather than federal inspection programs. However, these state programs are operated in accordance with cooperative agreements that USDA's Food Safety and Inspection Service (FSIS) has with each of the states; the federal government also provides 50 percent of the cost of state programs. The "Federal and State Cooperation" provisions of the FMIA (21 U.S.C. 661) were added by the Wholesome Meat Act of 1967 (P.L. 90–201).

Congressional Quarterly (CQ) at the time of the 1967 legislation observed that the state cooperation provision was "[t]he farthest-reaching portion [of the measure] . . . aimed at helping—or, if necessary, forcing—states to strengthen their own meat inspection systems." All plants providing meat for interstate and foreign commerce had been subject to federal inspection regulations basically since passage of the Meat Inspection Act of 1907 [sic; the law was passed in 1906].

However, plants that limited their product sales within a state were covered by what critics described as a patchwork of varying, often inadequate laws and regulations;

seven of them had no inspection at all, according to CQ. "Revelations in the press and during committee hearings about slaughter and packing practices at some state plants made meat inspection the most emotional consumer issue of 1967."

Currently, the Secretary of Agriculture (hereafter, USDA or FSIS) is authorized to approve a cooperative program in any state if it has enacted a "law that imposes mandatory ante mortem and post mortem inspection, reinspection and sanitation requirements that are *at least equal to* those under Title I of [the FMIA], with respect to all or certain classes of persons engaged in the State in slaughtering amenable species [i.e., cattle, sheep, swine, goats, equines], or preparing the carcasses, parts thereof, meat or meat food products, of any animals for use as human food solely for distribution within such State" (21 U.S.C. 661(a)(1); emphasis added by CRS). Section 661 also requires USDA to assume federal inspection of state plants whenever a state decides to terminate its own program, or USDA determines that FMIA requirements are not being met.

Pursuant to the FMIA as amended by the Wholesome Meat Act, USDA-FSIS must receive a formal request for a program from the governor, and review the state's laws, regulations, and performance plan (including funding, staffing, training, labels and standards, enforcement, laboratory and testing procedures, and other aspects). To ensure continued compliance, FSIS annually certifies state programs based on a review of materials (like performance plans and an annual report submitted by the state); FSIS also conducts a more comprehensive review of each state every one to five years.

Geoffrey S. Becker

BECKER, GEOFFREY S. "STATE-INSPECTED MEAT AND POULTRY: ISSUES FOR CONGRESS." *CRS REPORT* *FOR CONGRESS.* WASHINGTON, DC: U.S. GOVERNMENT PRINTING OFFICE, MAY 22, 2008.

SEE ALSO *Food Safety and Inspection Service; Humane Animal Farming; Meat Inspection Act of 1906; Meats; U.S. Department of Agriculture (USDA).*

BIBLIOGRAPHY

Books

Amundson, Finn J. *Inspection and Protection of U.S. Meat and Poultry.* New York: Nova Science Publishers, 2010.

Becker, Geoffrey S. *USDA Meat Inspection and the Humane Methods of Slaughter Act.* Washington, DC: Congressional Research Service, Library of Congress, 2008.

Sinclair, Upton. *The Jungle.* New York: Simon & Schuster, 2004.

Singh, Vijender. *Meat Inspection for Public Health.* New Delhi: Maxford Books, 2007.

Web Sites

Apuzzo, Matt. "Court: US Can Block Mad Cow Testing." *Washington Post,* August 29, 2008. http://www.washingtonpost.com/wp-dyn/content/article/2007/03/29/AR2007032901795.html (accessed September 13, 2010).

"Federal Meat Inspection Act." *U.S. Department of Agriculture (USDA).* http://www.fsis.usda.gov/regulations/federal_meat_inspection_act/index.asp (accessed August 3, 2010).

Adrienne Wilmoth Lerner

Women's Role in Global Food Preparation

■ Introduction

According to the Food and Agriculture Organization (FAO) of the United Nations, women produce between 60 and 80 percent of all food consumed in developing countries and half of all food produced globally. The balance worldwide is extremely uneven, with fewer women involved in food production in developed countries: In the United States women constitute just 19 percent of all agricultural laborers, according to a 2004 U.S. Department of Labor National Agricultural Workers Survey. Of those women in the United States who work in agriculture, most work in low-paid seasonal jobs, and 48 percent are foreign-born migrant workers.

Lack of access to credit and land rights hampers women's efforts in many developing regions. Less than 2 percent of the world's land is owned by women, notes the United Nations International Development Fund for Women, whereas in some regions, such as Sub-Saharan Africa, women produce as much as 80 percent of all food yet comprise only 5 to 15 percent of farmers with access to agricultural extension services. In terms of access to capital to buy equipment, fertilizers, and other food production supplies, the average woman in both developed and developing countries has less access to business and personal credit lines, though the situation in the developing world is much more severe: African women in five countries studied in 1998 received less than 10 percent of credit extended to male counterparts.

■ Historical Background and Scientific Foundations

In rural societies, women have always shared the labor of agricultural production with men, cultivating the household's food supply, preparing meals, and contributing to field work for cash crops or surplus. Women handle the majority of household food production, procurement, and preparation worldwide, though the process involved in these tasks has varied greatly over time. The Industrial Revolution of the eighteenth and nineteenth centuries, along with its accompanying urbanization, shifted labor from the field to the factory in industrialized nations, making an urban woman's earning power an important factor in household income and food procurement. Meanwhile, in rural settings and less developed nations, women often lacked income-earning opportunities outside of agricultural activities.

In developed countries, women own a very small percentage of agricultural land. According to the U.S. National Agricultural Statistics Service, as of 2002 women owned only 5 percent of commercial farms in the United States, whereas in the European Union (EU) the number of farms owned or co-owned by

---

WORDS TO KNOW

FOOD SECURITY: The ability to access, produce, and distribute food for optimal physical and financial health. Many female food producers in developing countries lack access to basic credit, equipment, and land rights, weakening food security.

MICROCREDIT: Loan programs that give people (often women) access to small sums of money by developed-nation standards (often less than $100) but that enable those who are unable otherwise to access capital to buy equipment necessary for creating surpluses to sell in a small business or at market.

MICRONUTRIENT MALNUTRITION: Different from general malnutrition, micronutrient malnutrition occurs largely in women and children in developing countries with low food security and with low food variety, evidenced by conditions such as anemia and vitamin A deficiency.

women is on the rise. The daily burden of food preparation and production for women in developed nations is radically different from the experiences of women in developing nations, with access to freshwater, indoor plumbing, and steady year-round food supplies in grocery stores and at markets. The average household in the EU spends less than 18 percent of household income on food, whereas households in countries such as Bulgaria, Slovenia, and Greece may spend as much as 53 percent of income on food. Women tend to be the shoppers and cooks in families, and women in poorer countries, even in the developed world, spend considerable effort securing fresh, healthy, and affordable food.

This task is radically different for women in the developing world, where the poorer the family, the more important the woman's role in food preparation and production. The 1996 Rome World Food Summit set a 2015 goal to reduce by half the number of undernourished people in the world. The role of women in this United Nations Millennium Development Goal is critical, as women in developing nations where food security is least stable are pivotal for household survival. When women in poor households in Africa, Asia, and Latin America see income increases, nutrition improves; women tend to spend available income on more and better-quality food in areas where malnutrition is common.

■ Impacts and Issues

The enormous burden women face as majority food producers is heaviest in Africa. A 2004 report from the World Health Organization and UNICEF notes that only 58 percent of sub-Saharan Africans live within a 30-minute walk of safe water supplies; getting and transporting safe water represents an enormous output of labor for women in Africa, with the average woman spending 30 minutes each day simply retrieving water for use in the home and in growing food. For those 42 percent who live more than a half hour from safe drinking water, the burden is worse, and many turn to contaminated water that carries bacteria and disease, increasing mortality rates for women and children. Women are vulnerable to violence during food and water labor as well: A 2005 study from Doctors Without Borders concluded that 82 percent of women in West and South Darfur treated for rape were victimized while collecting water, firewood for stoves, or thatching material to repair roofs.

Women in Africa also face the most entrenched cultural obstacles to land ownership and credit access. In Swaziland, for instance, women have no property rights of any kind; in other African countries women cannot inherit land, and if they do not produce sons, male relatives can give women's land away when they become

Women use a mortar and pestle to prepare cassava, also known as yucca or manioc, in Liberia. *© Jacques Jangoux / Alamy.*

widows. The lack of basic land ownership hampers agricultural production for markets, which in turn makes accumulating capital for equipment and expansion extremely difficult.

Asia and Latin America have different agricultural labor profiles for the rural poor. Although women in these regions handle the majority of household food matters, as members of the agricultural labor force participating in the market their numbers pale in comparison to Africa. A 2010 report on micronutrient malnutrition in Asia centered on programs to help encourage diversity in household agriculture. Through education and training of women in Bangladesh, Nepal, Cambodia, and the Philippines, malnutrition issues such as vitamin A deficiency and anemia were improved by helping families to improve dietary diversification in home-grown food.

Microcredit access helps women in developing nations to improve food quantity, quality, security, and to reduce vulnerability to disease and violence. Studies of microcredit programs, in which small sums of money (typically less than $100) are lent to women to launch businesses or buy agriculture equipment, show that women become less dependent on husbands as a result of these microloans and business expansion.

Women work in a ricefield in Myanmar.   *Image copyright Pozzo Di Borgo Thomas, 2010. Used under license from Shutterstock.com*

IN CONTEXT: GLOBAL ALLIANCE FOR CLEAN COOKSTOVES

In Africa alone, an estimated two million people rely on wood fires for cooking. In the developing world, indoor cooking stoves fueled by wood, coal, waste, and animal dung are not uncommon and can create dangerous levels of toxic smoke and fumes. Because women still do the majority of cooking in the developing world, they have the highest cumulative risk from such exposure. Children constitute a second vulnerable group. In these groups there are significantly elevated cases of pneumonia, cancers (including lung cancers), pulmonary diseases, and cardiovascular disease. In 2010, the United States committed to a global partnership designed to provide 100 million cleaner-burning stoves to Africans. The partnership, titled the Global Alliance for Clean Cookstoves, will pool and coordinate government and private contributions. The alliance also intends to foster self-sufficiency by promoting the development of waste reprocessing facilities.

Women in Bangladesh, for instance, experienced higher levels of autonomy and authority in some microcredit studies. Critics point to studies that show that microcredit programs may have the unintended consequence of victimizing women once again as husbands and sons could potentially use the women as fronts, forcing women to channel the capital to male heads of household.

SEE ALSO   *Agriculture Brings Hierarchical Societies; Building Better Ovens; Ethical Issues in Agriculture; Family Farms; Family Meal Benefits; Food and Agriculture Organization (FAO); Food Sovereignty; Foodways; Gender Equality and Agriculture; UN Millennium Development Goals; World Food Programme.*

BIBLIOGRAPHY

Books

Jacobs, Susie M. *Gender and Agrarian Reforms.* New York: Routledge, 2010.

Kristof, Nicholas D., and Sheryl WuDunn. *Half the Sky: Turning Oppression into Opportunity for Women Worldwide.* New York: Knopf, 2009.

Periodicals

de Brauw, Alan, Qiang Li, Chengfang Liu, Scott Rozelle, and Linxiu Zhang. "Feminization of Agriculture in China? Myths Surrounding Women's Participation in Farming." *China Quarterly London* 194 (June 2008): 327–348.

Giarracca, Norma, and Miguel Teubal. "Women in Agriculture." *Latin American Perspectives* 35, no. 6 (2008): 5–10.

Gill, Jatinderjit Kaur, M. K. Dhillon, and Muninder K. Sidhu. "Women in Agriculture." *International Journal of Rural Studies* 14, no. 1 (2007): 2–6.

Motzafi-Haller, Pnina, and Paul J. Kaldjian. "Geographical Reviews—Women in Agriculture in the Middle East." *Geographical Review* 96, no. 4 (2006): 721–722.

Ngowi, Aiwerasia Vera Festo. "Women's Work in Agriculture." *African Newsletter on Occupational Health and Safety* 18, no. 3 (2008): 48–49.

Web Sites

"Agriculture and Achieving the Millennium Development Goals." *International Food Policy Research Institute.* http://www.ifpri.org/publication/agriculture-and-achieving-millennium-development-goals (accessed October 25, 2010).

Sustainable Development Department, Food and Agriculture Organization of the United Nations (FAO). "Asia's Women in Agriculture, Environment, and Rural Production: India." *SD Dimensions.* http://www.fao.org/sd/wpdirect/WPre0108.htm (accessed October 25, 2010).

Melanie Barton Zoltan

World Food Day

■ Introduction

World Food Day (WFD) is a United Nations–sponsored international day of recognition dedicated to food and hunger issues. It is celebrated annually worldwide through related events in more than 150 countries, on October 16 each year.

The stated objectives of World Food Day are to promote agricultural production, facilitate government and international cooperation and support for agricultural production, encourage the sharing of agricultural technology and knowledge, and empower rural agricultural workers and farmers, especially women. World Food Day is also dedicated to highlighting issues of malnutrition, hunger, poverty, and food scarcity worldwide.

■ Historical Background and Scientific Foundations

At the twentieth annual meeting of the United Nations Food and Agriculture Organization (FAO) in November 1979, delegates voted to establish an international World Food Day to highlight agricultural production

and women's issues. October 16 was chosen as the annual day of observance to commemorate the founding of the FAO on that date in 1945.

Beginning in 1981, World Food Day events adopted a different theme each year. Organizers hoped that the annual themes would provide a clear focus for public information, participation, and fundraising. In 2000 "A Millennium Free from Hunger" was the theme of World Food Day. WFD that year highlighted the food security and anti-hunger aims of the UN Millennium Development Goals (MDGs), a set of goals that all UN member states and 23 international organizations pledged at the Millennium Summit in September 2000 to help achieve by 2015. The MDGs, which are aimed at improving living conditions in the world's poorest regions, include: combating treatable and preventable diseases, fighting other epidemics such as HIV/AIDS, reducing infant and child mortality, fostering cooperation for development, increasing participation of underrepresented or marginalized peoples, eradicating hunger, and eliminating extreme poverty. World Food Day events tied to the adoption of the MDGs emphasized the global prevalence of hunger and undernourishment, the portion of the global population who was then living on less than one dollar per day, and the prevalence of underweight children under five years of age.

In 2006 WFD sought to promote international, private sector (non-government) investment in agriculture. The theme "Invest in Agriculture for Food Security" promoted investment in agricultural education and projects. WFD also emphasized the need for increased government action by highlighting the global decline in foreign aid to agriculture over the preceding 20 years.

Whereas the FAO sets the theme for World Food Day, sponsors related UN events, provides information on world agriculture and hunger, and aids local WFD programs, there is no set international schedule. Most events are planned and hosted at the national and local levels. WFD events may include academic symposia, public debates, agricultural themed celebrations, seminars and workshops for agricultural workers, public information campaigns, protests, 24-hour voluntary hunger strikes, charity football (soccer) matches, and fundraising campaigns for hunger relief.

World Food Day has been observed every year since its adoption in 1979. The United Nations also annually recognizes October 16 as Food Engineer Day.

■ Impacts and Issues

Although World Food Day has brought increased global attention to food and hunger issues, the number of undernourished people worldwide grew to 1.02 billion in 2009. From 2007 to 2010, the global recession and rising food and energy costs increased the number of global hungry by more than 100 million people.

The World Food Day theme for 2010 was "United against Hunger." Events were scheduled in more than 150 countries. The theme was chosen to recognize the efforts of UN agencies, governments, non-governmental organizations, and aid groups in fighting hunger at the global, national, and local levels. The FAO encouraged individuals who support WFD to continue participating in the global anti-hunger campaign begun in 2009, One Billion Hungry. The project includes a petition, a social media campaign, and action opportunities.

The World Food Prize is an independent prize recognizing significant contributions to agriculture, distribution, economics, production, policy, quality, quantity, security, or science of the global food supply. The prize is not connected to the United Nations or formally attached to World Food Day, but is formally presented to the announced recipient on October 16 in support of World Food Day's message.

■ Primary Source Connection

The Food and Agriculture Organization of the United Nations has its headquarters in Rome, Italy. Its purpose is to reduce and eliminate world hunger. It works in four main areas: to provide information; to share policy expertise; to provide meeting places for nations; and to provide support to projects around the world aimed at reducing hunger. Mr. Ban Ki-moon, Secretary General of the United Nations, delivered this message for World Food Day on October 16, 2009.

A child decorated with artificial fruits is pictured during celebrations to mark World Food Day in Khartoum, Sudan, 2008.
© STR/Reuters/Corbis.

Achieving Food Security in Times of Crisis

Food and nutritional security are the foundations of a decent life, a sound education and, indeed, the achievement of all the Millennium Development Goals. Over the past two years, volatile food prices, the economic crisis, climate change and conflict have led to a dramatic and unacceptable rise in the number of people who cannot rely on getting the food they need to live, work and thrive. For the first time in history, more than one billion people are hungry.

Throughout the developing world, food prices remain stubbornly high. We must respond to the needs of the hungry, first by ensuring adequate political and financial support for emergency food assistance. "Achieving food security in times of crisis" is the theme for this year's World Food Day and for the TeleFood campaign of the Food and Agriculture Organization of the United Nations. It emphasizes the need for even greater efforts to respect the dignity of those affected by poverty and hunger, and to support the committed women and men who often risk their lives to deliver help.

Second, we must invest in food production and distribution. Last year, I set up a High-Level Task Force on the Global Food Crisis. Its Comprehensive Framework for Action outlines a strategy to provide safety nets and assistance for smallholder farmers and to support longer-term agricultural productivity and resilience, social protection schemes, market access and fair trade.

Nations are mobilizing for action. In July, 26 countries and 14 multilateral organizations agreed to work together under the umbrella of the L'Aquila initiative on food security. Next month's World Summit on Food Security in Rome is a further opportunity to focus on country-led and regional strategies, country-level partnerships and increased levels of assistance.

The challenges of food security demand multilateral commitment, creativity and leadership. At this time of crisis, I encourage all nations to pursue coordinated and comprehensive strategies for agricultural development and effective social protection so that vulnerable people—women and children in particular—can get the food they need for nutritional security and well-being.

Ban Ki-moon

KI-MOON, BAN. "KI-MOON, BAN: 'ACHIEVING FOOD SECURITY IN TIMES OF CRISIS.' A MESSAGE ON WORLD FOOD DAY, 2009." *FOOD AND AGRICULTURE ORGANIZATION OF THE UNITED NATIONS (FAO)*. HTTP://WWW.FAO.ORG/ FILEADMIN/TEMPLATES/GETINVOLVED/PDF/WFD_2009_ LEAFLET-EN_WEB.PDF (ACCESSED OCTOBER 24, 2010).

SEE ALSO *Food and Agriculture Organization (FAO); Food Security; Hunger; Malnutrition; UN Millennium Development Goals; Undernutrition; Women's Role in Global Food Preparation; World Food Prize; World Food Programme.*

Web Sites

Dag Hammarskjöld Library. "World Food Day: 16 October." *United Nations.* http://www.un.org/ depts/dhl/food/index.html (accessed September 14, 2010).

"Get Involved against Hunger: World Food Day." *Food and Agriculture Organization of the United Nations (FAO).* http://www.fao.org/getinvolved/ worldfoodday/en/ (accessed September 14, 2010).

World Food Day USA. http://www.worldfooddayusa. org/ (accessed September 14, 2010).

Adrienne Wilmoth Lerner

World Food Prize

■ Introduction

The World Food Prize is an international award that recognizes individuals or organizations that have promoted development and eased human hunger through improving the availability, quantity, and quality of food supplies. The prize is intended to promote food security, encourage research and development in food production that could alleviate hunger, draw attention to worldwide food issues, and inspire others to work toward solving the world's food problems.

Nominees for the World Food Prize may be involved in any aspect of human food supply, including academia, aid work, biotechnology, distribution, economics, farming, manufacture, marketing, nutrition, policy development, political leadership, transport, and research. Nobel laureate and agronomist Norman Borlaug (1914–2009) created the prize, which is now granted annually by the World Food Prize Foundation. The prize's honorariums are funded by the estate of American businessman John Ruan (1914–2010).

The World Food Prize has been awarded to recipients from Bangladesh, Brazil, China, Cuba, Denmark, Ethiopia, India, Mexico, Sierra Leone, Switzerland, the United Kingdom, the United Nations, and the United States. The prize is awarded in a ceremony in Des Moines, Iowa, and is followed by the Borlaug International Symposium, or "Borlaug Dialogue," a conference that brings together worldwide experts on agricultural development, hunger, food policy, and food security issues.

The recipient of the World Food Prize is announced in the spring of each year, but the prize's official award ceremony occurs on October 16, the United Nations (UN) recognized international World Food Day. The prize is not sponsored by the UN nor is the UN formally attached to the World Food Prize. World Food Prize organizers chose the ceremonial day to highlight the agricultural development and anti-hunger themes of World Food Day.

■ Historical Background and Scientific Foundations

In 1970, U.S. agronomist, plant geneticist, and humanitarian advocate Norman E. Borlaug won the Nobel Peace Prize for, according to his award citation, "providing bread for a hungry world." Borlaug was known as the father of the Green Revolution for his pioneering work on the development of high-yield and disease-resistant wheat crops. During the mid-twentieth century, use of Borlaug's crops in India, Pakistan, and Mexico helped reduce endemic, regional food shortages and averted famine. Upon receipt of the Peace Prize, Borlaug asked the Nobel committee to institute a prize for agriculture and food. The committee rejected the proposal.

Borlaug asserted that many people working in the fields of agriculture, food production, and food aid deserved as much recognition as he had received. He then sought to establish an international prize for food on the same scale as the Nobel prizes. In 1986 Borlaug convinced the General Foods Corporation, a U.S.-based food producer, to sponsor his prize.

The first World Food Prize was given in 1987. Its recipient, Indian agronomist Monkombu Sambasivan Swaminathan (1925–), led the successful introduction of high-yield wheat and rice varieties to farmers in India. The high-yield crops nearly doubled the nation's wheat production between 1965 and 1970.

General Foods withdrew its sponsorship in 1990 after the company was purchased by Philip Morris Companies in 1988 and then merged with Kraft Foods in 1990. During that year, the prize committee raised money from several corporations to be able to award the prize. In order to keep the World Food Prize solvent, U.S. businessman, financier, and trucking magnate John Ruan donated funds to establish the World Food Prize Foundation. Ruan's gift allowed for the continuation of the $250,000 cash award to recipients or their designated organizations. He specified that the foundation

WORDS TO KNOW

AGRIBUSINESS: Any entity involved in food production and the raising, distribution, and processing of crops. The term is also narrowly used as a synonym for corporate farming or industrial farming by opponents of large, corporate-run farms.

AGRONOMIST: A scientist who applies soil and plant sciences to agriculture.

NONGOVERNMENTAL ORGANIZATION (NGO): An independent organization that is not part of, or administered by, any government.

SMALLHOLDER: The owner of a small agricultural parcel.

and award ceremony for the prize move from Washington, DC, to Iowa, his and Borlaug's home state. After Ruan's death in 2010, his grandson John Ruan III assumed leadership of the World Food Prize Foundation.

■ Impacts and Issues

The World Food Prize has been recognized by international leaders and non-governmental organizations (NGOs) as a valuable incentive for the funding of agricultural development and aid programs. The award has recognized individuals with diverse food production backgrounds, from lab scientists to NGO leaders and government officials to the United Nations World Food Programme. In 2010, the World Food Prize was given to two individuals in recognition of the work of their respective international NGOs and aid organizations: Jo Luck, president of Heifer International, and David Beckmann, president of Bread for the World.

The U.S. government, in conjunction with the announcement of the 2010 World Food Prize laureates, introduced the Feed the Future partnership between the U.S. Agency for International Development (USAID) and the U.S. Department of Agriculture (USDA) and the establishment of the Norman Borlaug Commemorative Research Initiative. The program intends to facilitate partnerships between U.S. agricultural scientists and research entities with smallholders and small farmers and organizations in developing nations. In a USAID press release from June 6, 2010, Secretary of State Hillary Rodham Clinton (1947–) stated, "In a few decades, the world's population will grow to 9 billion people. If we are to feed the future without leveling the forests, draining the aquifers, and depleting the soil of all its nutrients, we need science."

However, some critics assert that the World Food Prize places too singular an emphasis on biotech

In 2000 Evangelina Villegas (1924–) became the first woman to be awarded the World Food Prize. Here, she stands next to the high-yield, high-protein corn that she helped develop. *AP Images.*

IN CONTEXT: WALTER PLOWRIGHT (1923–2010)

By mid–2011, rinderpest, a lethal disease in cattle caused by the Rinderpest virus (RPV), is expected to join smallpox as a globally eradicated disease. Elimination of the disease, responsible for centuries of famine and economic hardship, is greatly credited to a vaccine developed by British veterinary surgeon and scientist Walter Plowright (1923–2010).

Plowright served in Kenya as an officer in the Royal Army Veterinary Corps and later in the Colonial Veterinary Service. In 1956 he assumed leadership of the department of pathology at the East African Research Laboratory (EAVRO). His work at EAVRO, later in conjunction with the Animal Virus Research Institute, ultimately produced the rinderpest vaccine. In 1971 Plowright returned to the United Kingdom, ultimately finishing his academic career at the Institute for Research on Animal Diseases.

Plowright's work often took him from the lab into areas of discomfort and danger. Far from the order of the laboratory environment, Plowright collected samples from tick-infested burrows and personally inoculated test species (including wild wildebeest) in remote and harsh field conditions. In the lab, Plowright was one of the first to employ tissue culture techniques to successfully prepare an effective vaccine. Plowright's laboratory used cell-culture techniques developed by polio vaccine researchers to produce a live attenuated (weakened, non-pathogenic) virus as an antigen for the rinderpest vaccine. Disease experts credit Plowright's work and methodology with significantly advancing the study of viral animal diseases.

Plowright's work was widely honored for its scientific and humanitarian achievements. According to the United Nations Food and Agriculture Organization, Plowright's rinderpest vaccine helped produce much needed food, especially in Africa and India, and increased production for subsistence farmers around the world. In 1999 Plowright was honored with the World Food Prize, awarded for advancing human development and health by "improving the quality, quantity or availability of food in the world."

---

solutions to international food crises. Whereas the Food Prize has spurred initiatives such as Feed the Future to empower small farmers worldwide with access to technology, critics assert that such farmers themselves are absent from the Borlaug Dialogue. Critics also note that the World Food Prize Foundation has received donations from large, Western agribusiness companies, food manufactures, and agricultural lobbying groups including Philip Morris Companies, Kraft Foods, International Minerals Corp., International Life Sciences Institute, McCormick Co., RJR Nabisco, Archer Daniels Midland (ADM), General Mills, the Iowa Corn Growers Association, the Iowa Soybean Association, Land O'Lakes, Syngenta AG, and others.

In 2009, while speaking at the Borlaug International Symposium following the award ceremony, Bill Gates (1955–), U.S. business leader and co-chair of the Bill & Melinda Gates Foundation, spoke out against critics of GMO foods, asserting that GMO projects should receive funding and "have the potential to address farmers' challenges more efficiently than conventional techniques." Critics of GMO, large corporate agribusinesses, and the World Food Prize seized upon the remarks as evidence that the award overlooks work on sustainable agricultural development and promotes developing world farmers' dependence on costly products from Western biotech companies. However, Gates also admonished large agribusiness, representatives of which were present at the symposium, for not buying more food crops from small farmers.

SEE ALSO *Ethical Issues in Agriculture; Famine; Famine: Political Considerations; Food Security; Genetically Modified Organisms (GMO); Green Revolution (1943); Heifer International; International Food Aid;* *U.S. Agency for International Development (USAID); World Food Day; World Food Programme.*

BIBLIOGRAPHY

Books

World Food Prize Foundation. *The Borlaug Dialogue: The 2006 Norman E. Borlaug International Symposium "The Green Revolution Redux."* Des Moines, IA: World Food Prize Foundation, 2006.

World Food Prize Foundation. *The World Food Prize: Twentieth Anniversary 1986–2006.* Des Moines, IA: World Food Prize Foundation, 2006.

Periodicals

"Food Scientist Wins World Food Prize." *Food Technology Champaign Then Chicago* 61, no. 7 (2007): 59–60.

Klapthor, James N. "Word of the World Food Prize Laureate Travels the Globe." *Food Technology* 61, no. 7 (2007): 115–116.

"Negroponte Urges Biotech Solutions in World Food Prize Speech." *Food Chemical News* 50, no. 18 (2008): 8.

Web Sites

Heifer International. http://www.heifer.org/site/c.edJRKQNiFiG/b.183217/ (accessed October 22, 2010).

The World Food Prize. http://www.worldfoodprize.org/ (accessed October 22, 2010).

World Food Programme. http://www.wfp.org/ (accessed October 22, 2010).

Adrienne Wilmoth Lerner

World Food Programme

■ Introduction

The World Food Programme (WFP) is a branch of the United Nations (UN) that provides humanitarian assistance in the form of food and agricultural development aid worldwide. WFP is headquartered in Rome, Italy, and maintains offices in approximately 80 countries.

WFP's core mission has five objectives, including saving lives and livelihoods during crises, preparing for emergencies, and restoring and rebuilding the lives of citizen after emergencies. The organization aims to reduce chronic hunger and alleviate undernutrition as a means of improving people's health, especially that of infants, pregnant women, and those suffering from diseases such as human immunodeficiency virus (HIV) and acquired immunodeficiency syndrome (AIDS). WFP not only provides direct food aid, but also works to build capacity for reducing hunger at its sources through sustainable economic development programs, food-for-work initiatives, and farming support.

In 2010 WFP aided 90 million people, 58 million of whom were children. WFP delivered approximately 3.7 million tons of food to beneficiaries in 73 countries. Beneficiaries were victims of conflict, economic distress, natural disasters, government collapse, and crop failures.

■ Historical Background and Scientific Foundations

The World Food Programme was formed by the UN Food and Agriculture Organization (FAO). At the 1960 FAO international conference, the director of the United States Food for Peace Program, George McGovern (1922–), proposed that the FAO help establish an international food aid program. McGovern wanted to create a central organization that could coordinate the administration and distribution of aid from participating countries. The United Nations and the FAO agreed to establish and fund the WFP on an experimental basis starting in 1963. Two years later, WFP became a permanent mission.

The WFP is governed by a board of representatives from its member states. The organization maintains a staff of around 10,000 people, 90 percent of whom work in the field. Operations of the WFP are funded by voluntary donations from participating governments and the private sector. The WFP partners with national governments, national and international aid agencies such as USAID and the Red Cross/Red Crescent, other UN agencies such as the FAO, nongovernmental organizations (NGOs), agribusinesses, and food producers to supply and distribute food aid. These partner organizations also assist the WFP in its development and provision of agricultural development programs. Because timely distribution of food aid is critical, the WFP also maintains the Fast Information Technology and Telecommunications Emergency and Support Team (FITTEST), a group of logistics specialists who help emergency response teams rapidly establish communication and distribution networks.

To bring attention to hunger and food issues, the WFP sponsors or participates in several international events. WFP participates in World Food Day, the annual United Nations sponsored international day of recognition dedicated to food and hunger issues (October 16). WFP's Fill the Cup campaign raises awareness and funds by encouraging donations of as little as $.25, the amount needed to fill one of the red cups used in WFP emergency food aid missions with nutrient-fortified porridge.

In 2010 WFP spent more than $3 billion on aid, most of which went toward responding to emergencies and natural disasters.

◼ Impacts and Issues

In 2009 the largest active WFP operation was in the northeast African nation of Sudan. Providing emergency food aid to large populations of persons displaced by years of endemic conflict comprises the significant majority of WFP's operations in the region. In 2010 WFP's Sudan mission utilized $690 million and reached 5.5 million beneficiaries (2.8 million in the Darfur conflict region alone). WFP not only provides direct food aid to the nation, but also helps regional farmers by purchasing foodstuffs. In 2008 WFP purchased 100,000 metric tons of food from Sudanese farmers outside of the conflict region to incorporate into emergency food aid elsewhere in Sudan.

Devastating flooding in Pakistan in 2010 threatened to create an emergency food aid need larger than 2010 operations in Sudan. WFP anticipated that Pakistan's floods created food need for as many as 6 million people per month in 2010–2011.

Although WFP missions have successfully delivered food aid to millions of people worldwide, the agency has also received criticism. WFP estimates that roughly half of the population in Somalia needs aid. A 2010 UN report claimed that a significant portion, ranging from one-third to one-half, of all food aid to Somalia had not

reached its intended beneficiaries. The report noted that food aid had been diverted by corruption of local officials, warlords, and contractors. Food aid was found

Unloading sacks of World Food Programme supplies for distribution in Burundi. © *Alan Gignoux / Alamy.*

IN CONTEXT: SOMALI REBELS BAN WORLD FOOD PROGRAMME (WFP)

World Food Programme (WFP) workers often face difficult and dangerous conditions in unstable areas. In 2010 WFP workers were accused of acting in a covert scheme to subjugate the Somali people, and the Islamist rebel group al Shabaab issued a proclamation banning the UN food agency. The fundamentalist rebels also demanded that the WFP halt its food distribution programs and leave Somalia. An al Shabaab statement subsequently declared that anyone helping the WFP would be punished as an accomplice.

The rebel proclamation caught WFP workers in the middle, facing criticism by both government and rebel forces. (Government officials had accused WFP officials of diverting food to rebel forces.) Despite the proclamation and criticism, WFP officials vowed to stay as long as the safety of aid workers could be ensured. In 2009 the United Nations Food and Agriculture Organization estimated that Somalia has the highest malnutrition levels in the world, with nearly half the population requiring some form of food aid.

being sold on the black market, and distribution contractors were found to be using aid transport vehicles for arms trading. Similarly, the U.S. State Department estimated that in 2008 only 12 percent of its food aid administered by the WFP reached its intended recipients in neighboring eastern Ethiopia.

The WFP focuses much of its aid, especially emergency aid, on women and children. The WFP has a stated priority of addressing and ending child hunger and lowering infant mortality rates linked to hunger. Distribution of direct food aid is often aimed at getting food into homes by giving aid to female heads of families and women responsible for communal cooking. WFP initiatives also provide children with meals at school or give children take-home food rations to share with their family in an effort to encourage school attendance. However, WFP operations have also excluded men at distribution centers or from receiving some forms of direct food aid in attempt to stem corruption, violence, or the theft of food aid. Proponents of the women-only distribution strategy claim that it is the most secure, effective way to get food aid to families. In their response to the 2010 Haiti earthquake, WFP

Refugees from Somalia's civil war wait for a World Food Programme food aid distribution at a camp for internally displaced Somalis in Abdi Aziz district, north Mogadishu, Somalia. *AP Images.*

distributed almost all of its direct food aid to women only. Critics noted that many men, especially young single men, faced famine conditions as a result of ineffective alternative means of food distribution (such as through soup kitchens).

In 2008 WFP officials failed to sufficiently take into account the effects of a severe winter in the former Soviet republic of Georgia. Direct food aid did not contain enough calories to sustain recipients according to international minimum standards for aid. When the WFP began issuing credits for aid recipients to purchase foods, most recipients used the credits to bolster their supply of basic grains instead of supplementing their rations with vegetable and fruits as hoped. The WFP stated that it and its partner NGOs would work to be more sensitive to special climate conditions that may require changes in the types and amounts of aid provided.

The FAO asserts that in 2010, 925 million people worldwide lived in chronic huger. Whereas the number of people living in hunger declined in 2010, the global economic and food price crises of 2008–2009 had increased the number of global hungry in the preceding years. WFP identified 22 nations as suffering from protracted food crises, including Afghanistan, Chad, Ethiopia, Haiti, North Korea (Democratic People's Republic of Korea), Somalia, and Sudan. Approximately one-fifth of the world's undernourished people live in a nation experiencing a long-term food crisis.

SEE ALSO *African Famine Relief; Agribusiness; Aid and Subsidies to Promote Agriculture and Reduce Illicit Drug Production; Disasters and Food Supply; Ethical Issues in Agriculture; Ethical Issues in Food Aid; Extreme Weather and Food Supply; Famine; Famine: Political Considerations; Food and Agriculture Organization (FAO); Food Price Crisis; Food Security; Hunger; International Food Aid; International Fund for Agricultural Development; Malnutrition; Rome Declaration on World Food Security (1996); UN Millennium Development Goals; Undernutrition; U.S. Agency for International Development (USAID); Water Scarcity; World Food Day.*

BIBLIOGRAPHY

Books

Climate Change and Hunger: Responding to the Challenge. Rome: World Food Programme, 2009.

Concrete Steps towards a Millennium Free from Hunger: The World Food Programme and the Millennium Development Goals. Rome: World Food Programme, 2006.

Fighting Hunger Worldwide. Rome: World Food Programme, 2010.

Hunger and Health. London: Earthscan, 2008.

Web Sites

Roman, Nancy. "How We Can End Hunger: A Billion for a Billion." *Human Rights: Change.org*, October 11, 2010. http://humanrights.change.org/blog/view/how_we_can_end_hunger_a_billion_for_a_billion (accessed October 16, 2010).

World Food Programme. http://www.wfp.org/ (accessed October 16, 2010).

World Trade Organization (WTO)

Introduction

Established in 1995 in Geneva, Switzerland, the World Trade Organization (WTO) is a leading international driver of economic globalization. The WTO administers trade agreements, arbitrates trade disputes, monitors national trade policies, and provides technical assistance to developing countries. According to the WTO, 97 percent of world trade is governed by WTO trade agreements.

At regular meetings, its 153 member states and observer nations negotiate and resolve policies governing global trade. In October 2010 the United States and a number of European governments pledged to accelerate Russia's 17-year-long quest to join the WTO.

Historical Background and Scientific Foundations

Since the 1950s the world has experienced an unparalleled movement of currency, capital, trade, and human resources between countries. This flow across borders, called globalization, has fueled debates regarding development and economic theory, largely due to its impact on workers and the environment in low-income countries. Supporters of globalization argue that this free flow of trade and currency has facilitated the expansion of economic growth and opportunities worldwide. Dissenters in the globalization debate assert that globalization has promoted unfair labor practices and environmentally detrimental policies in low-income countries, as well as an increase in the income gap between wealthier and poorer nation-states. In the globalization discourse, low-income and developing nations are referred to as the Global South due to the geographic location of most of these nations south of the equator, including areas in Latin America, Africa, and Asia. Likewise, developed countries are often referred to as the Global North. This difference in globalization experiences in the Global North and Global South embodies the globalization debate.

WTO is the successor to GATT, the General Agreement on Tariffs and Trade, a multilateral treaty drafted at the end of World War II (1939–1945). The final round or series of talks between representatives from states signatory to GATT was the Uruguay Round that took place from 1986 to 1993. The WTO was created by the 123 countries that participated in this round of talks. The stated purpose of the WTO, like that of GATT before it, was to enhance free trade by reducing barriers to international trade.

Since the late 1990s, a vigorous debate has divided the U.S. government and biotech corporations from states in Africa and the European Union (EU) that block the importation of genetically modified organism (GMO) crops. The United States has sought, through several legal actions including appeals to the World Trade Organization (WTO), to compel European states to drop barriers to GMO foods. In 2006, in a major victory for U.S. GMO policy, the WTO ruled that Europe's moratorium on new licenses to grow GMO crops was a violation of global trade agreements. The WTO also ruled that Austria, France, Germany, Greece, Italy, and Luxembourg broke WTO rules by banning the importation and marketing of GMO foods. In May 2008 Austria became one of the last European countries to succumb to WTO pressure when it lifted its ban on importing and processing GMO corn from the United States. Despite the decisions of the WTO, other countries, including Japan and Australia, continue to prohibit or restrict GMO use.

Impacts and Issues

The activities of the WTO are controversial, with many critics charging that it systematically favors the interests of the wealthiest countries of the world at the expense of the poor. The WTO responds that its work produces multiple benefits for the entire world. WTO's official position is that its goal is "to help producers of goods and services, exporters, and importers conduct their business," so the interests of workers are explicitly not represented by the organization.

The WTO remains a target of anti-globalization activists who view the organization as manipulating international trade in order to steal from the poor and give to the rich on a global scale. Such activists see the WTO's policies—often, but not exclusively, dealing with food and agriculture—as systematically undermining environmental, consumer, labor, and other protections in order to protect the profits of multinational corporations. Defenders of the WTO and the neoliberal economic policies it promotes argue that unrestricted international corporate activity—often referred to as free trade—actually produces greater prosperity, on average, for poorer as well as for wealthier countries.

Supporters of WTO's globalization drive assert that globalization has also facilitated the spreading of knowledge and democracy, which facilitates a stronger, more widely employed workforce and therefore a peaceful future. At the helm of the globalization movement are multinational corporations (MNCs) and trans-national corporations (TNCs). Dissenters in the globalization

> ## WORDS TO KNOW
>
> **GLOBALIZATION:** The integration of national and local systems into a global economy through increased trade, manufacturing, communications, and migration.
>
> **SMALLHOLDER:** The owner of a small agricultural parcel.
>
> **SUBSIDY:** Monetary assistance given by a government in support of a certain enterprise.
>
> **TARIFF:** A duty or tax imposed on imports or exports.
>
> **TRADE AGREEMENT:** An accord or contract among participating nations or trade groups that establishes rules for trade, including taxes, import fees, tariffs, duties, levies, subsidies, or restrictions on the exchange of goods and money.

debate suggest that these corporations are the cause of a decline in standards in developing countries. The dissenters assert that the integration of global markets has enabled MNCs and TNCs to pressure low-income countries in the Global South to relax environmental regulations and labor standards or risk losing jobs and international investment. Critics of the WTO argue that phrases such as "free trade" and "lowering barriers to

South Korean farmers protest the World Trade Organization conference held in Hong Kong, 2005. © *Ron Yue / Alamy.*

trade" are not neutral, but misleading labels for policies that selectively favor rich countries and large corporations. For example, Noam Chomsky (1928–), a famous U.S. critic of globalization and U.S. foreign policy, wrote in the May 1997 issue of *Z Magazine* that what advocates of "free trade" really means is "for you, market discipline, but not for me, unless the 'playing field' happens to be tilted in my favor, typically as a result of large-scale state intervention."

Proponents of WTO policies argue that the WTO's drive to eliminate agricultural subsidies and tariffs will lift millions out of poverty, but critics argue that the WTO's ongoing trade liberalization will serve to benefit large corporate farms at the expense of independent, smallholder farmers in the poorer countries. Critics further assert that the WTO promotes food protectionism, the favoring of one nation's food production and exports at the expense of other nations, and unfair subsidies that primarily benefit the wealthiest nations. However, the WTO's Development Round of negotiations, which began in 2001 and broke down in 2008, failed to reach a member consensus on agricultural subsidies. Several member states argued for a reduction or an end to certain agricultural subsidies, whereas other nations refused to end subsidy programs.

Agricultural subsidy opponents cite U.S. corn subsidies as a prominent market influence that lowers raw corn prices in neighboring markets. During the 2007–2008 global food price crisis, while food prices rose compared to previous years, processed corn food products (such as ready-made cereals or tortillas) made in the United States were less expensive in domestic and some neighboring markets than raw corn produced in neighboring markets. The price neighboring-market farmers—especially in Mexico and Central America—received for their corn declined while food prices rose. The resulting diminished wages threatened food security in some smallholder households. Similarly, subsidies to turn food crops into biofuels, including ethanol, threaten to drive up the price of food as less corn is planted for consumption. Competing nations are thus left in what critics call the double-subsidy trap. Agro-economists, however, may counter that this argument exaggerates the limited role that corn and biofuel subsidies played in the global food price crisis. Some claim that import tariffs intended to protect the prices of national food production against imports have a larger negative impact on global food prices than do direct subsidies paid to agricultural interests.

SEE ALSO *Agribusiness; Agriculture and International Trade; Codex Alimentarius; Embargoes; Food and Agriculture Organization (FAO); Food Price Crisis; Food Security; Genetically Modified Organisms (GMO); Sustainable Agriculture.*

BIBLIOGRAPHY

Books

Echols, Marsha A. *Food Safety and the WTO: The Interplay of Culture, Science and Technology.* London: Kluwer Law International, 2001.

Karapinar, Baris, and Christian Haberli. *Food Crises and the WTO: World Trade Forum.* Cambridge, UK: Cambridge University Press, 2010.

Sampson, Gary P. *The WTO and Sustainable Development.* New York: United Nations University Press, 2005.

Voigt, Christina. *Sustainable Development as a Principle of International Law: Resolving Conflicts between Climate Measures and WTO Law.* Leiden, Holland: Martinus Nijhoff Publishers, 2009.

Wallach, Lori, and Patrick Woodall. *Whose Trade Organization?: A Comprehensive Guide to the WTO.* New York: New Press, 2004.

Periodicals

Connolly, Rebecca. "The World Trade Organization Biotechnology Products Dispute: A New Era for Genetically Modified Food?" *Environmental and Planning Law Journal* 26, no. 5 (2009): 363–374.

Kelly, Trish. "Is the WTO a Threat to the Environment, Public Health, and Sovereignty?" *Challenge* 51, no. 5 (2008): 84–102.

Veggeland, Frode, and Svein O. L. E. Borgen. "Negotiating International Food Standards: The World Trade Organization's Impact on the Codex Alimentarius Commission." *Governance* 18, no. 4 (2005): 675–708.

Winickoff, David, and Douglas Bushey. "Science and Power in Global Food Regulation: The Rise of the Codex Alimentarius." *Science, Technology, & Human Values* 35, no. 3 (2010): 356–381.

Web Sites

"Agriculture: Work in the WTO." *World Trade Organization.* http://www.wto.org/english/tratop_e/agric_e/negoti_e.htm (accessed November 3, 2010).

Adrienne Wilmoth Lerner

Yeast and Leavening Agents

■ Introduction

Leavening is the process by which dough is increased in volume and made soft, puffy, or flaky. Baked goods made of unleavened dough are hard, thin, and more difficult to chew. Leavening can be done before or during baking.

Natural leavening agents include yeast, carbon dioxide, air, and water. Yeast is a one-celled fungus that reacts with sugars in dough to form carbon dioxide bubbles, which become trapped within the dough and, when baked, give breads and other baked products their distinctive light and airy texture. Leavening is also accomplished chemically by combining the base sodium bicarbonate (baking soda) and an acid to form carbon dioxide as a reaction product. Baking powder works in the same way, but includes both sodium bicarbonate and tartaric acid (cream of tartar), which react upon the addition of water. Although it is not necessary for the production of carbon dioxide, some baking powders include starch to absorb moisture and improve the flow characteristics of the powder. Double-acting baking powders contain an additional acid that only reacts at high temperature so that additional leavening takes place during baking.

Whatever the leavening agent, the basic means by which leavening occurs is through the formation and expansion of gas bubbles. Gas bubbles form tiny voids in the dough that make it lighter and fluffier.

■ Historical Background and Scientific Foundations

Probably the first leavening agent intentionally used by humans was the carbon dioxide generated by the action of yeast. Evidence suggests that leavened bread was produced in Egypt around 1500 BC, although alcoholic fermentation was practiced much earlier.

Fermentation has been used to produce foods and beverages for millennia, but it was not until the discovery and study of microorganisms that the biological mechanisms of leavening and alcohol production were understood. Early bakers knew that samples of successful batches of dough had to be transferred to make a new batch rise, but they did not know why.

French chemist and biologist Louis Pasteur (1822–1895) was the founder of the science of zymurgy (the study of fermentation), and it was his work during the middle of the nineteenth century that led to the connection between yeast and leavening. At about the same time, baking powder came into use, followed shortly thereafter by baking soda.

Baker's yeast is the fungus *Saccharomyces cerevisiae*, which is naturally found on grapes and other sugary fruits. Dried yeast is added to dough before baking. When water is added, the yeast activates and begins to grow by cell division. The yeast ferments sugar in the dough, resulting in the formation of alcohol and carbon dioxide. The carbon dioxide creates tiny bubbles in the dough, expanding it to several times its original volume over a period of hours. The heat of baking kills the yeast and drives off the carbon dioxide and alcohol, leaving behind voids where the carbon dioxide bubbles originally formed. This results in a soft, fluffy product that is pleasing to the palate and easy to chew.

Although carbon dioxide produced by yeast fermentation remains the leavening agent of choice for

---

WORDS TO KNOW

FERMENTATION: Biological process performed by many microorganisms in which sugars are converted to carbon dioxide and alcohol.

LEAVENING: The volume expansion of baking dough caused by the formation and inclusion of gas bubbles.

YEAST: Single-celled fungus that ferments sugar to produce carbon dioxide bubbles to leaven dough.

IN CONTEXT: PASTEUR EFFECT

Louis Pasteur (1822–1895), at the time Dean of Sciences at the University of Lille, was asked for help by an industrialist who was producing beer from beet sugar. The batches continually were going sour. By examining the brewer's samples under the microscope, Pasteur realized that correctly aged beer contained spherical yeast, but sour batches contained yeasts that were elongated. Pasteur also noted that the desirable globe-shaped yeasts produced alcohol, but the rod-shaped yeasts produced lactic acid, making the batches go sour. These findings made him realize 1) yeasts were responsible for fermentation, 2) different types of yeasts made different byproducts, and 3) yeasts did not need oxygen to metabolize. Anaerobic respiration (without oxygen) to this day is sometimes referred to as the "Pasteur effect."

A chef adds yeast into a bowl of flour. © *Andre Martin / Alamy.*

most breads, products that do not require as much expansion can be made more quickly by other means. Denser products such as thin breads, pancakes, muffins, fruit cakes, pie crusts, and other pastries are produced without yeast.

Water transitions from a liquid to a gas when heated to its boiling point. Gaseous water, better known as steam, forms small voids in dough during baking and thus performs some expansion in all baked goods but the results are unpredictable. In small, relatively flat pastries, steam can suffice as the sole leavening agent.

Air is also present in all dough, and tiny air bubbles contribute to leavening. However, air leavening is made more effective by intentionally increasing the air content of the dough. Aggressive mixing or beating of dough prior to baking introduces more air. The effect is enhanced by the addition of whipped egg whites, which can hold a lot of air. Too much whipping of egg whites, however, will remove air and produce unsatisfactory results.

Whereas the leavening methods described earlier can be considered "natural" because they involve only natural products or additional work, chemical reactions can produce significant quantities of carbon dioxide in dough in much less time than is achievable with yeast. This is accomplished by using either baking soda or baking powder. The choice of one or the other depends on the other ingredients in the recipe and the final taste requirements. If an acidic ingredient such as buttermilk, fruit juice, or vinegar is called for, then baking soda is used. If no acids are introduced, then the acid-base combination of baking powder works. These chemical leavening agents generally do not produce as good a rise or as fluffy a product as yeast does, so are more commonly employed in non-bread baking.

It seems reasonable to think that much time could be saved by injecting carbon dioxide gas directly into dough before baking, and indeed that has been done on a commercial level. However, the process requires specialized equipment so it is seldom used.

■ Impacts and Issues

Although dough is commonly called unleavened if it does not include yeast, baking powder, or baking soda, by the strict definition of leavening, this is not exactly correct because some gas bubbles are formed in all dough during baking. Indeed, if this were not the case, "unleavened" bread would be almost inedibly hard.

Some unleavened products remain popular for specific cultural, religious, or ceremonial purposes. Examples of this include the matzo (or matsah), eaten during the Jewish Passover, and the use of unleavened bread during the Eucharist in the western Catholic Church.

Many people overwhelmingly prefer the taste and texture of baked goods produced with leavened dough. The use of leavening agents has greatly increased the kinds of baked goods enjoyed by humans. Unleavened dough presents limited possibilities and produces a thin, hard product, although it does have better storage properties.

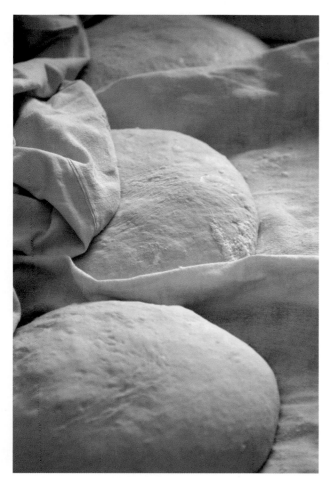

Dough rises in preparation for cooking. *Image copyright fd,meo, 2010. Used under license from Shutterstock.com.*

One acid often used in double-acting baking powder is aluminum sodium sulfate. Some consumers avoid this type of baking powder because they are concerned that aluminum is a factor in causing Alzheimer's disease. It is true that Alzheimer's plaques in the brains of affected individuals often do contain an elevated aluminum concentration, however, current research suggests that the aluminum is concentrated as a result of the disease, but is not a cause of the disease. People exposed to high levels of aluminum do not contract the disease at a higher rate than the population as a whole. Aluminum occurs naturally in the environment and as a trace contaminant in many foods and some water supplies, but less than one percent is absorbed by the digestive system when ingested. Most of the aluminum that is absorbed is rapidly excreted in urine. Although it was an open question when it was first proposed that there might be a causal relationship between aluminum and Alzheimer's, the majority of the medical community now refutes any correlation between exposure to aluminum in the diet and the incidence of Alzheimer's disease.

SEE ALSO *Baking Bread; Food Preparation Methods.*

BIBLIOGRAPHY

Books

Boekhout, Teun, and Vincent Robert. *Yeasts in Food: Beneficial and Detrimental Aspects.* Cambridge: Woodhead, 2003.

Figoni, Paula. *How Baking Works: Exploring the Fundamentals of Baking Science,* 2nd ed. Hoboken, NJ: Wiley, 2008.

Schünemann, Claus, and Günter Treu. *Baking, the Art and Science: A Practical Handbook for the Baking Industry.* Weimar, TX: Chips Books, 2007.

Periodicals

Mannie, Elizabeth. "Phosphates and Yeasts in Baking." *Prepared Foods* 176, no. 8 (2007): 47.

Web Sites

Manthey, David. "A Comparison of Leavening Agents." *Orbitals Central,* 2002. http://www.orbitals.com/self/leaven/leaven.pdf (accessed August 20, 2010).

Philip McIntosh

Organizations

CENTER FOR SCIENCE IN THE PUBLIC INTEREST

The Center for Science in the Public Interest seeks to educate the public and policymakers in the United States and Canada by providing science-based information on food and nutrition issues. Their newsletter *Nutrition Action Health-letter* is the most circulated health newsletter in North America with over 900,000 subscribers.

> 1220 L St. NW
> Washington, DC
> 20005
> Phone: (202) 332-9110
> Fax: (202) 265-4954
> cpsinews@cpsinet.org
> http://www.cspinet.org/about/
>   contact_us.html

CONFEDERATION OF THE FOOD AND DRINK INDUSTRIES IN THE EU

The Confederation of the Food and Drink Industries in the EU is an organization that promotes the interests of the food and beverage industries in the European Union.

> Ave. des Arts 43
> 1040 Brussels
> Belgium
> Phone: 32 2 5501740
> Fax: 32 2 5501759
> info@fevia.be
> http://www.fevia.be

COOPERATIVE GROCERS' INFORMATION NETWORK

The Cooperative Grocers' Information Network is a business association that supports the growth of food cooperatives.

> PO Box 399
> Arcata, CA 95518
> Phone: (866) 709-2667

Fax: (866) 910-0652
admin@cgin.coop
http://www.cgin.coop

CORN REFINERS ASSOCIATION

The Corn Refiners Association is a trade association that represents the interests of corn refiners.

> 1701 Pennsylvania Ave., Ste. 950
> Washington, DC 20006
> Phone: (202) 331-1634
> Fax: (202) 331-2054
> http://www.ccrn.org

CROPLIFE AMERICA

Founded in 1933, CropLife America is a federation of companies that produce or sell biotechnology and crop protection products.

> 1156 15th St. NW
> Washington, DC 20005
> Phone: (202) 296-1585
> Fax: (202) 463-0474
> ldismuke@croplifeamerica.org
> http://www.croplifeamerica.org

EARTHSAVE INTERNATIONAL

EarthSave International is a non-profit organization that addresses hunger and obesity issues in a sustainable manner.

> PO Box 96
> New York, NY 10108
> Phone: (718) 459-7503
> Phone: (800) 362-3648
> Fax: (718) 228-2491
> info@earthsave.org
> http://www.earthsave.org

ECOLOGICAL FARMING ASSOCIATION

The Ecological Farming Association is a non-profit organization that promotes sustainable agriculture education.

406 Main St., Ste. 313
Watsonville, CA 95076
Phone: (831) 763-2111
info@eco-farm.org
http://www.eco-farm.org

ENVIRONMENTAL WORKING GROUP

Founded in 1993, Environmental Working Group is a non-profit organization that promotes public and environmental health with a particular focus on toxic chemicals and corporate accountability.

> 1436 U St. NW, Ste. 100
> Washington, DC 20009
> Phone: (202) 667-6982
> Fax: (202) 232-2592
> info@ewg.org
> http://www.ewg.org

FAMILY FARM DEFENDERS

Family Farm Defenders is a non-profit organization that promotes the interests of small, family-owned farms.

> PO Box 1772
> Madison, WI 53701
> Phone: (608) 260-0900
> Fax: (608) 260-0900
> familyfarmdefenders@yahoo.com
> http://www.familyfarmdefenders.org

FARMERS MARKET COALITION

The Farmers Market Coalition is a non-profit organization that seeks to promote and strengthen farmers markets in the United States.

> PO Box 4089
> Martinsburg, WV 25402
> Phone: (304) 263-6396
> Phone: (877) 362-0553

info@farmersmarketcoalition.org

http://www.farmersmarketcoalition.org

FOOD ADDITIVES AND INGREDIENTS ASSOCIATION

Founded in 1977, the Food Additives and Ingredients Association is a trade association that represents the interests of food additive manufacturers in the United Kingdom.

> *10 Whitchurch Close*
> *Maidstone,*
> *Kent MEI6 8UR*
> *United Kingdom*
> *info@faia.org.uk*
> *http://www.faia.org.uk*

FOOD ALLERGY AND ANAPHYLAXIS NETWORK

The Food Allergy and Anaphylaxis Network is a civic and social association dedicated to raising awareness about food allergies, promoting food allergy research, and advocating on behalf of food allergy sufferers.

> *11781 Lee Jackson Hwy., Ste. 160*
> *Fairfax, VA 22033-3309*
> *Phone: (703) 691-3179*
> *Phone: (800) 929-4040*
> *Fax: (703) 691-2713*
> *faan@foodallergy.org*
> *http://www.foodallergy.org*

FOOD ALLERGY INITIATIVE

The Food Allergy Initiative is an organization that promotes medical research of food allergies and seeks to increase public awareness about food allergy issues.

> *1414 Ave. of the Americas, Ste. 1804*
> *New York, NY 10019*
> *Phone: (212) 207-1974*
> *Fax: (917) 338-5130*
> *info@faiusa.org*
> *http://www.faiusa.org*

FOOD ALLIANCE

Food Alliance is an organization that promotes sustainable and humane agriculture, primarily through a food certification program.

> *1829 NE Alberta, Ste. 5*
> *Portland, OR 97211*
> *Phone: (503) 493-1066*
> *Fax: (503) 493-1069*
> *info@foodalliance.org*
> *http://www.foodalliance.org*

FOOD AND AGRICULTURE ORGANIZATION (FAO) OF THE UNITED NATIONS

Founded in 1945, the Food and Agriculture Organization (FAO) of the United Nations (UN) is a specialized agency of the UN dedicated to hunger issues, including improving agricultural and fisheries practices in developing nations.

> *Viale delle Terme di Caracalla*
> *00153 Rome, Italy*
> *Phone: 39 06 57051*
> *Fax: 39 06 57053152*
> *fao-hq@fao.org*
> *http://www.fao.org/about/en*

FOOD AND DRUG LAW INSTITUTE

The Food and Drug Law Institute is a non-profit organization that provides a forum for the discussion of food and drug law issues.

> *1155 15th St. NW, Ste. 800*
> *Washington, DC 20005-4903*
> *Phone: (202) 371-1420*
> *Phone: (800)956-6293*
> *Fax: (202) 371-0649*
> *comments@fdli.org*
> *http://www.fdli.org*

FOOD AND NUTRITION BOARD

The Food and Nutrition Board of the Institute of Medicine studies U.S. food safety and security, nutrition, and disease prevention issues.

> *c/o Institute of Medicine*
> *500 5th St. NW*
> *Washington, DC 20001*
> *Phone: (202) 334-2352*
> *Fax: (202) 334-1412*
> *iomwww@nas.edu*
> *http://www.iom.edu/CMS/3788.aspx*

FOOD AND WATER WATCH

Food and Water Watch is a non-profit organization dedicated to ensuring the safety and sustainability of global food and water supplies.

> *1616 P St. NW, Ste. 300*
> *Washington, DC 20036*
> *Phone: (202) 683-2500*
> *Fax: (202) 683-2501*
> *foodandwater@fwwatch.org*
> *http://www.foodandwaterwatch.org*

FOOD ANIMAL CONCERNS TRUST

Founded in 1982, the Food Animal Concerns Trust is an organization focused on the welfare of farm animals and the safety of farm animal products.

> *PO Box 14599*
> *Chicago, IL 60614*
> *Phone: (773) 525-4952*
> *Fax: (773) 525-5226*
> *info@foodanimalconcerns.org*
> *http://www.foodanimalconcerns.org*

FOOD INSTITUTE

Founded in 1928, the Food Institute is a business association that provides information about the food industry to the food manufacturers, distributors, and consumers.

> *10 Mountainview Road, Ste. S125*
> *Upper Saddle River, NJ 07458*
> *Phone: (201) 791-5570*
> *Fax: (201) 791-5222*
> *questions@foodinstitute.com*
> *http://www.foodinstitute.com*

FOOD MARKETING INSTITUTE

The Food Marketing Institute is a trade association that represents and promotes the interests of food retailers and wholesalers.

> *2345 Crystal Dr., Ste. 800*
> *Arlington, VA 22202-4801*
> *Phone: (202) 452-8444*
> *Fax: (202) 429-4519*
> *http://www.fmi.org*

FOOD RESEARCH AND ACTION CENTER

The Food Research and Action Center is a non-profit organization that works to eradicate hunger and malnutrition in the United States by improving public policies and fostering public-private partnerships.

> *1875 Connecticut Ave. NW, Ste. 540*
> *Washington, DC 20009-5728*
> *Phone: (202) 986-2200*
> *Fax: (202) 986-2525*
> *foodresearch@frac.org*
> *http://www.frac.org*

FOOD SAFETY CONSORTIUM

The Food Safety Consortium brings together researchers from U.S. universities to investigate all areas of meat and poultry production.

> *University of Arkansas*
> *110 Agriculture Bldg.*
> *Fayetteville, AR 72701*
> *Phone: (479) 575-5647*
> *Fax: (479) 575-7531*
> *dedmark@uark.edu*
> *http://www.uark.edu/depts/fsc*

FOOD SECURITY WORKING GROUP

The Food Security Working Group is a network of non-profit organizations and non-governmental organizations that promote food security in Myanmar.

> *Room (205), Tower (B), 2nd Floor,*
> *Diamond Condominium,*
> *497, Pyay Road,*
> *Kamaryut Township*
> *Yangon, Myanmar*
> *Phone: 95 1 523930 ext. 3205*
> *fswg.coordinator@gmail.com*
> *http://www.myanmarfswg.net*

FOOD TRADE SUSTAINABILITY LEADERSHIP ASSOCIATION

The Food Trade Sustainability Leadership Association is a non-profit trade organization that promotes that expansion of organic and sustainable agricultural practices.

> PO Box 51267
> Eugene, OR 97405
> Phone: (541) 852-0745
> nwhite@organicgrown.com
> http://www.ftsla.org

FOODFIRST INFORMATION AND ACTION NETWORK

Founded n 1986, the FoodFirst Information and Action Network is a human rights organization that promotes access to food for all individuals.

> Willy-Brandt-Platz 5
> 69115 Heidelberg
> Germany
> Phone: 49 6221 6530030
> Fax: 49 6221 830545
> fian@fian.org
> http://www.fian.org

FOODSERVICE PACKAGING INSTITUTE

The Foodservice Packaging Institute is a business association specializing in sanitary food containers.

> 201 Park Washington Ct.
> Falls Church, VA 22046
> Phone: (703) 538-3552
> Fax: (703) 241-5603
> fpi@fpi.org
> http://www.fpi.org

GLOBAL AQUACULTURE ALLIANCE

Founded in 1997, Global Aquaculture Alliance is an organization dedicated to promoting environmentally and socially responsible aquaculture.

> 5661 Telegraph Rd., Ste. 3A
> St. Louis, MO 63129
> Phone: (314) 293-5500
> Fax: (314) 293-5525
> homeoffice@gaalliance.org
> http://www.gaalliance.org

GROCERY MANUFACTURERS ASSOCIATION

Founded in 1908, the Grocery Manufacturers Association is the world's largest trade association and represents the interests of many of the world's largest food and beverage corporations.

> 1305 I St. NW, Ste. 300
> Washington, DC 20005
> Phone: (202) 639-5900
> Fax: (202) 639-5932
> info@gmaonline.org
> http://www.gmaonline.org

HEALTH FOOD MANUFACTURERS' ASSOCIATION

Founded in 1965, the Health Food Manufacturers' Association is a trade association that promotes the interests of the natural products industry in the United Kingdom.

> 1 Wolsey Rd.
> E Moleysey
> Surrey KT8 9EL
> United Kingdom
> Phone: 44 20 84817100
> Fax: 44 20 84817101
> hfma@hfma.co.uk
> http://www.hfma.co.uk

HEALTHY CHILD HEALTHY WORLD

Healthy Child Healthy World is a civic and social association that seeks to protect children from harmful chemicals through education and policy promotion.

> 12300 Wilshire Blvd., Ste. 320
> Los Angeles, CA 90025
> Phone: (310) 820-2030
> Fax: (310) 820-2070
> http://healthychild.org

HECTOR KOBBEKADUWA AGRARIAN RESEARCH AND TRAINING INSTITUTE

The Hector Kobbekaduwa Agrarian Research and Training Institute is an organization that promotes sustainable rural development through research and technical training.

> 114 Wijerama Mawatha
> Colombo 07,
> Sri Lanka
> Phone: 94 11 2696981
> Fax: 94 11 2692423
> hartilib@sltnet.lk
> http://www.harti.lk

HEIFER INTERNATIONAL

Founded in 1944, Heifer International is a non-profit charitable organization that relieves hunger and poverty through livestock donations and sustainable agriculture programs.

> 1 World Ave.
> Little Rock, AR 72202
> Phone: (800) 422-0474
> Fax: (501) 907-2902
> info@heifer.org
> http://www.heifer.org

HERB RESEARCH FOUNDATION

The Herb Research Foundation is an organization focused on improving health through the promotion of herbs and herbal remedies.

> 5589 Arapahoe Ave., Ste. 205
> Boulder, CO 80303

> Phone: (303) 449-2265
> Fax: (303) 449-7849
> info@herbs.org
> http://www.herbs.org

HOME BAKING ASSOCIATION

Founded in 1943, the Home Baking Association is a non-profit organization dedicated to promoting home baking.

> 2931 SW Gainsboro Rd.
> Topeka, KS 66614-4413
> Phone: (785) 478-3283
> Fax: (785) 478-3024
> hbapatton@aol.com
> http://www.homebaking.org

HOME ORCHARD SOCIETY

The Home Orchard Society is a membership organization that assists orchardists by providing education and technical support.

> PO Box 230192
> Tigard, OR 97281-0192
> Phone: (503) 293-1468
> masonbees@homeorchardsociety.org
> http://www.homeorchardsociety.org

HUMANE FARM ANIMAL CARE

Humane Farm Animal Care is a non-profit organization that works to improve the care of farm animals by establishing standards of care and conducting inspections.

> PO Box 727
> Herndon, VA 20172
> Phone: (703) 435-3883
> info@certifiedhumane.org
> http://www.certifiedhumane.org

INSTITUTE FOR AGRICULTURE AND TRADE POLICY

The Institute for Agriculture and Trade Policy is an organization that promotes policies that benefit family farmers and rural communities, including fair trade policies, health and safety standards, human rights policies, and environmentally-responsible actions.

> 2105 1st Ave. S.
> Minneapolis, MN 55404
> Phone: (612) 870-0453
> Fax: (612) 870-4846
> iatp@iatp.org
> http://www.iatp.org

INSTITUTE FOR FOOD AND DEVELOPMENT POLICY

The Institute for Food and Development Policy is an organization that promotes agricultural policies that eliminate hunger.

> 398 60th St.
> Oakland, CA 94618

Phone: (510) 654-4400
Fax: (510) 654-4551
info@foodfirst.org
http://www.foodfirst.org

INSTITUTE OF FOOD SCIENCE AND TECHNOLOGY—UK

Founded in 1964, the Institute of Food Science and Technology—UK is a professional organization that qualifies and regulates food professionals in the United Kingdom.

5 Cambridge Ct.
210 Shepherds Bush Rd.
London W6 7NJ
United Kingdom
Phone: 44 20 76036316
Fax: 44 20 76029936
info@ifst.org
http://www.ifst.org

INTERNATIONAL ASSOCIATION OF CULINARY PROFESSIONALS

Founded in 1978, the International Association of Culinary Professionals is a professional organization dedicated to the development of culinary professionals and the exchange of culinary ideas.

1100 Johnson Ferry Rd., Ste. 300
Atlanta, GA 30342
Phone: (404) 252-3663
Phone: (800) 928-4227
Fax: (404) 252-0774
info@iacp.com
http://www.iacp.com

INTERNATIONAL BABY FOOD ACTION NETWORK—AFRICA

Founded in 1981, International Baby Food Action Network—Africa is a public interest group that works to decrease infant mortality and improve childhood health through the promotion of breastfeeding.

PO Box 781
Mbabane, Swaziland
Phone: 268 4045006
Fax: 268 4040546
ibfanswd@realnet.co.sz
http://www.ibfanafrica.org.sz

INTERNATIONAL BLUE CRESCENT RELIEF AND DEVELOPMENT FOUNDATION

The International Blue Crescent Relief and Development Foundation is a non-governmental organization dedicated to reducing world hunger, increasing literacy rates, and reducing human suffering.

Bostanci Mah. Cami Sk.; Cesur Apt.
No: 11/3 Bostancı - Kadıköy
TR-81110 Istanbul, Turkey

Phone: 90 216 4646881
Fax: 90 216 3615745
ibc@bluecrescent.net
http://www.ibc.org.tr/ana.htm

INTERNATIONAL CENTRE OF INSECT PHYSIOLOGY AND ECOLOGY

The International Centre of Insect Physiology and Ecology is a professional organization focused on reducing the impact of insect-borne diseases on livestock, crops, and people.

PO Box 30772-00100
Nairobi, Kenya
Phone: 254 20 8632000
Fax: 254 20 8632001
icipe@icipe.org
http://www.icipe.org

INTERNATIONAL COCOA ORGANIZATION

Founded in 1973, the International Cocoa Organization is an international group that promotes the interests of cocoa producers around the world.

Commonwealth House
1-19 New Oxford St.
London WC1A 1NU
United Kingdom
Phone: 44 20 74005050
Fax: 44 20 74215500
info@icco.org
http://www.icco.org

INTERNATIONAL COMMISSION FOR AGRICULTURAL AND FOOD INDUSTRIES

Founded in 1936, the International Commission for Agricultural and Food Industries is an intergovernmental agency recognized by the United Nations dedicated to fostering international cooperation on and the promotion of agriculture and food industries.

42 Rue Scheffer
75116 Paris
France
Phone: 33 1 53702246
Fax: 33 1 53702054
ciia@wanadoo.fr
http://www.ciia-c.com

INTERNATIONAL CULINARY TOURISM ASSOCIATION

The International Culinary Tourism Association is a business association specializing in the promotion of culinary tourism.

c/o Erik Wolf, Pres./CEO
4110 SE Hawthorne Blvd., Ste. 440
Portland, OR 97214
http://www.culinarytourism.org

INTERNATIONAL FEDERATION OF COMPETITIVE EATING

The International Federation of Competitive Eating serves as the governing body for competitive eating and develops and promotes competitive eating competitions.

151 W 25th St., 4th Floor
New York, NY 10001
Phone: (212) 352-8651
Fax: (212) 627-5430
info@ifoce.com
http://www.ifoce.com

INTERNATIONAL FOOD AND AGRIBUSINESS MANAGEMENT ASSOCIATION

The International Food and Agribusiness Management Association is a business association that promotes information sharing and industry development among its agribusiness membership.

PO Box 14145
College Station, TX 77841-4145
Phone: (979) 845-2118
Fax: (979) 862-1487
iama@tamu.edu
http://www.ifama.org

INTERNATIONAL FOOD SAFETY COUNCIL

The International Food Safety Council is a foodservice coalition that promotes food safety education.

c/o National Restaurant Association
Educational Foundation
175 W Jackson Blvd., Ste. 1500
Chicago, IL 60604-2814
Phone: (312) 715-1010
Phone: (800) 765-2122
info@restaurant.org
http://www.nraef.org

INTERNATIONAL FOOD, WINE AND TRAVEL WRITERS ASSOCIATION

Founded in 1956, the International Food, Wine and Travel Writers Association is a network of journalists dedicated to food, wine, and hospitality issues.

1142 S Diamond Bar Blvd., No. 177
Diamond Bar, CA 91765-2203
Phone: (909) 860-6914
Phone: (877) 439-8929
admin@ifwtwa.org
http://www.ifwtwa.org

INTERNATIONAL FUND FOR AGRICULTURAL DEVELOPMENT

The International Fund for Agricultural Development (IFAD) is a specialized agency of the United Nations dedicated to eradicating rural poverty.

Via Paolo di Dono, 4
00142 Rome, Italy
Phone: 39 0654591
Fax. 39 065043463
ifad@ifad.org
http://www.ifad.org

INTERNATIONAL ORGANIZATION OF THE FLAVOR INDUSTRY

The International Organization of the Flavor Industry is a non-governmental organization of national associations of flavor manufacturers that promotes scientific research and legislation to benefit the flavoring industry.

Rue du Rhône, 100
1204 Geneva
Switzerland
Phone: 41 22 3104421
Fax. 41 22 7163075
secretariat@iofiorg.org
http://www.iofi.org

INTERNATIONAL RICE COMMISSION

Established in 1949 by the Food and Agriculture Organization of the United Nations, the International Rice Commission promotes the production, distribution, and conservation of rice.

AGPC/FAO; Viale delle Terme di Caracalla
153 Rome, Italy
Phone: 39 6 57056265
Fax. 39 6 57056347
nguu.nguyen@fao.org
http://www.fao.org/ag/agp/agpc/doc/
    field/commrice/index_en.htm

INTERNATIONAL SEED FEDERATION

The International Seed Federation is a non-profit organization that represents the interests of the seed industry.

Chemin du Reposoir 7
1260 Nyon, Switzerland
Phone: 41 22 3654420
Fax. 41 22 3654421
isf@worldseed.org
http://www.worldseed.org/isf/home.html

INTERNATIONAL SPICE INDUSTRY ASSOCIATION

The International Spice Industry Association is a European association of spice and flavoring manufacturers.

Reuterstrasse 151
D-53113 Bonn, Germany
Phone: 49 228 216162
Fax. 49 228 229460
info@gewuerzindustrie.de
http://www.gewuerzindustrie.de

ISLAMIC FOOD AND NUTRITION COUNCIL OF AMERICA

The Islamic Food and Nutrition Council of America is a non-profit organization dedicated to the promotion of halal food.

777 Busse Hwy.
Park Ridge, IL 60068
Phone: (847) 993-0034
Fax: (847) 993-0038
http://www.ifanca.org

JAMES BEARD FOUNDATION

Founded in 1986, the James Beard Foundation is a non-profit organization that promotes the celebration, preservation, and development of American cuisine.

167 W 12th St.
New York, NY 10011
Phone: (212) 675-4984
Phone: (800) 36-BEARD
Fax: (212) 645-1438
info@jamesbeard.org
http://www.jamesbeard.org

KITCHEN GARDENERS INTERNATIONAL

Kitchen Gardeners International is a non-profit organization that promotes kitchen gardening, home cooking, and sustainable food production.

3 Powderhorn Dr.
Scarborough, ME 04074
Phone: (207) 883-5341
info@kitchengardeners.org
http://www.kitchengardeners.org

LES AMIS D'ESCOFFIER SOCIETY OF NEW YORK

Founded in 1936, Les Amis d'Escoffier Society of New York is a professional organization that promotes haute cuisine and the culinary tradition of Auguste Escoffier (1846–1935).

787 Ridgewood Rd.
Millburn, NJ 07041
Phone: (212) 414-5820
Fax: (973) 379-3117
http://www.escoffier-society.com

LOCALHARVEST

LocalHarvest is an information resource for local and organic family farms and community supported agriculture (CSA).

PO Box 1292
Santa Cruz, CA 95061
Phone: (831) 515-5602
Fax: (831) 401-2418
http://www.localharvest.org

MOTHERS WITHOUT BORDERS

Founded in 1996, Mothers Without Borders is a non-profit volunteer organization that promotes the interests of orphaned children around the world, including nutrition, medical care, and housing.

125 E Main St., Ste. 402
American Fork, UT 84003
Phone: (801) 796-5535
mail@motherswithoutborders.org
http://www.motherswithoutborders.org

NATIONAL CATTLEMEN'S BEEF ASSOCIATION

Founded in 1922, the National Cattlemen's Beef Association is a business association that represents the interests of the beef industry, from farming to meat sales, and promotes consumer meat consumption.

9110 E Nichols Ave., Ste. 300
Centennial, CO 80112
Phone: (303) 694-0305
Phone: (866) 233-3872
Fax: (303) 694-2851
membership@beef.org
http://www.beefusa.org

NATIONAL CENTER FOR FOOD SAFETY AND TECHNOLOGY

The National Center for Food Safety and Technology, based at the Illinois Institute of Technology, fosters the exchange of scientific research, industry practices, and regulatory policy on food safety. The center aims to brings together disparate voices in the food production, research, and regulation sectors.

6502 S Archer Rd.
Summit, IL 60501-1957
Phone: (708) 563-1576
Fax: (708) 563-1873
nnoka@iit.edu
http://www.ncfst.iit.edu

NATIONAL COALITION FOR FOOD AND AGRICULTURAL RESEARCH

Founded in 2001, the National Coalition for Food and Agricultural Research is dedicated to supporting and enhancing government funding of agricultural research, agricultural extension projects, and university-based and community agricultural education programs.

2441 Village Green Pl.
Champaign, IL 61822
Phone: (217) 356-3182
Fax: (217) 398-4119
ncfar@assochq.org
http://www.ncfar.org

NATIONAL COUNCIL OF CHAIN RESTAURANTS

The National Council of Chain Restaurants is a business association of multi-location, commercially-branded eating establishments.

325 7th St. NW, Ste. 1100
Washington, DC 20004
Phone: (202) 783-7971
Phone: (800) 673-4692
whipplej@nccr.net
http://www.nccr.net

NATIONAL EATING DISORDER INFORMATION CENTRE

Founded in 1985, the National Eating Disorder Information Centre is a social services organization in Canada that provides the public with information on various eating disorders and encourages treatment regimes for those with eating disorders.

200 Elizabeth St., ES 7-421
Toronto, Ontario M5G 2C4
Canada
Phone: (416) 340-4156
Phone: (866) 633-4220
Fax: (416) 340-4736
nedic@uhn.on.ca
http://www.nedic.ca

NATIONAL FROZEN AND REFRIGERATED FOODS ASSOCIATION

The National Frozen and Refrigerated Foods Association is a trade and industry lobbying organization dedicated to promoting the sale and consumption of frozen and refrigerated foods.

PO Box 6069
Harrisburg, PA 17112
Phone: (717) 657-8601
Fax: (717) 657-9862
info@nfraweb.org
http://www.nfraweb.org

NORMAN BORLAUG INSTITUTE FOR INTERNATIONAL AGRICULTURE

The Norman Borlaug Institute for International Agriculture is part of the international agricultural program of Texas A&M University and seeks to strengthen sustainable agriculture in developing nations through research and scientific training.

2935 Research Parkway, Room 337
College Station, TX 77843
Phone: (979) 845-4164
Fax: (979) 845-5663
borlauginstitute@tamu.edu
http://borlaug.tamu.edu

OK KOSHER CERTIFICATION

OK Kosher Certification, established in 1935, is a company that certifies food as kosher according to the religious food laws and dietary restrictions expressed in the Torah.

391 Troy Ave.
Brooklyn, NY 11213
Phone: (718) 756-7500
Fax: (718) 756-7503
info@ok.org
http://www.ok.org

ORGANIC FOOD FEDERATION

Founded in 1986, the Organic Food Federation provides UK-based companies and individuals involved in the processing, trading or importing of organic foods with relevant trade information and assistance obtaining international organic certifications.

31 Turbine Way
EcoTech Business Park
Swaffham
Norfolk PE37 7XD
United Kingdom
Phone: 44 1760 720444
Fax: 44 1760 720790
info@orgfoodfed.com
http://www.orgfoodfed.com

OXFAM

Founded in 1942, Oxfam is an international confederation of organizations working in almost 100 countries to fight poverty and injustice, including addressing issues such as food insecurity, agricultural land rights, and unjust allocation of food resources.

Oxfam House,
John Smith Drive,
Cowley,
Oxford OX4 2JY
United Kingdom
Phone: 44 1865 472602
http://www.oxfam.org.uk

RUDD CENTER FOR FOOD POLICY AND OBESITY

The Rudd Center for Food and Policy and Obesity is a non-profit organization located at Yale University that is dedicated to obesity prevention, diet improvement, and other food issues.

PO Box 208369
New Haven, CT 06520
Phone: (203) 432-6700
http://www.yaleruddcenter.org

SCHOOL NUTRITION ASSOCIATION

Founded in 1946, the School Nutrition Association is a professional organization specializing in advancing good nutrition for children.

700 S Washington St., Ste. 300
Alexandria, VA 22314
Phone: (703) 739-3900
Fax: (703) 739-3915
servicecenter@schoolnutrition.org
http://www.schoolnutrition.org

SLOW FOOD USA

An active part of the international Slow Food movement, Slow Food USA is a grassroots organization dedicated to promoting sustainable, locally-grown, whole foods prepared without industrial processing or adulteration.

20 Jay St., Ste. M04
Brooklyn, NY 11201
Phone: (718) 260-8000
Fax: (718) 260-8068
info@slowfoodusa.org
http://www.slowfoodusa.org

SOCIETY FOR THE ANTHROPOLOGY OF FOOD AND NUTRITION

The Society for the Anthropology of Food and Nutrition provides a forum for the exchange of ideas and scientific research on behavioral, cultural, economic, and political issues related to food and nutrition.

c/o Janet Chrzan, President
University of Pennsylvania
Anthropology Dept.
323 Museum
Spruce St. and S. 33rd St.
Philadelphia, PA 19104
Phone: (215) 898-7461
Fax: (215) 898-7462
info@nutritionalanthro.org
http://www.nutritionalanthro.org

SOCIETY FOR THE RESPONSIBLE USE OF RESOURCES IN AGRICULTURE AND ON THE LAND

Founded in 1983, the Society for the Responsible Use of Resources in Agriculture and on the Land (RURAL) is a U.K.-based organization that promotes constructive dialog, often among adversarial parties, about issues affecting the countryside, rural, and agricultural lands.

c/o Brigadier John Hickman, CBE, Director
Chester House, Hillbury Rd., Alderholt
Fordingbridge SP6 3BQ
United Kingdom
Phone: 44 1425 652035
http://www.rural.org.uk

SOCIETY OF RHEOLOGY

The Society of Rheology is a professional organization of scientists and mathematicians interested in applying rheology, the science of deformation and flow of matter. Rheology has practical culinary applications, especially in cheese making.

c/o A. Jeffrey Giacomin, Secretary; University of Wisconsin; Rheology Research Center
Madison, WI 53706
Phone: (608) 262-7473
Fax: (608) 265-2316
giacomin@wisc.edu
http://www.rheology.org/sor

SUSTAIN: THE ALLIANCE FOR BETTER FOOD AND FARMING

Sustain is a network of over 100 public interest groups. It promotes socially-just, environmentally-responsible, humane, and sustainable farming practices.

> 94 White Lion St.
> London N1 9PF
> United Kingdom
> Phone: 44 20 78371228
> Fax: 44 20 78371141
> sustain@sustainweb.org
> http://www.sustainweb.org

TRUE FOOD NETWORK

Sponsored by the Center for Food Safety, the True Food Network is a grassroots action network with over 130,000 U.S. members dedicated to providing a public forum in which people can voice opinions and coordinate advocacy on critical food safety issues and promote sustainable, socially-just food systems.

> 2601 Mission St., Ste. 803
> San Francisco, CA 94110
> Phone: (415) 826-2770
> Fax: (415) 826-0507
> info@truefoodnow.org
> http://www.truefoodnow.org

UNITED NATIONS CHILDREN'S FUND

The United Nations Children's Fund (UNICEF) works to improve social outcomes for children worldwide through development, education, emergency aid, health, and nutrition programs.

> 3 United Nations Plaza
> New York, NY 10017
> Phone: (212) 326-7000
> Fax: (212) 887-7465
> http://www.unicef.org

UNITED NATIONS DEVELOPMENT PROGRAMME

The United Nations Development Programme (UNDP) is part of the United Nations dedicated to global development and capacity building.

> One United Nations Plaza
> New York, NY 10017
> Phone: (212) 906-5000
> Fax: (212) 906-5001
> http://www.undp.org

UNITED NATIONS ENVIRONMENT PROGRAMME

The United Nations Environment Programme (UNEP) is the agency responsible for developing and implementing the United Nations' environmental activities.

> United Nations Avenue, Gigiri
> PO Box 30552, 00100
> Nairobi, Kenya
> Fax: 254 20 7624489
> unepinfo@unep.org
> http://www.unep.org

UNITED NATIONS SYSTEM NETWORK ON RURAL DEVELOPMENT AND FOOD SECURITY

Founded in 1997, the UN System Network on Rural Development and Food Security addresses interagency policy on rural agricultural development, agricultural land rights, and food availability issues.

> Viale delle Terme di Caracalla
> 00100 Rome, Italy
> Fax: 39 6 57053250
> rdfs-net@fao.org
> http://www.rdfs.net

UNITED NATIONS SYSTEM STANDING COMMITTEE ON NUTRITION

The United Nations System Standing Committee on Nutrition is an interagency forum on UN policy on malnutrition and food issues worldwide.

> c/o World Health Organization
> 20, Ave. Appia
> CH-1211 Geneva
> Switzerland
> Phone: 41 22 7910456
> Fax: 41 22 7988891
> scn@who.int
> http://www.unscn.org

UNITED STATES AGENCY FOR INTERNATIONAL DEVELOPMENT

The United States Agency for International Development (USAID) is the U.S. agency responsible for administering and distributing all non-military foreign aid for the United States.

> Ronald Reagan Building
> Washington, DC 20523-1000
> Phone: (202) 712-0000
> Fax: (202) 216-3524
> http://www.usaid.gov

UNITED STATES DEPARTMENT OF AGRICULTURE

The United States Department of Agriculture (USDA) is a cabinet level agency responsible for developing and implementing U.S. food and agricultural policy.

> 1400 Independence Ave., SW
> Washington, DC 20250
> Phone: (202) 720-2791
> http://www.usda.gov

VEGAN ACTION

Vegan Action is a membership-based advocacy organization that educates the public on the vegan lifestyle and mobilizes members in support of animal rights and environmental issues.

> PO Box 4288
> Richmond, VA 23220
> Phone: (804) 502-8736
> Fax: (804) 254-8346
> information@vegan.org
> http://www.vegan.org

VEGETARIAN RESOURCE GROUP

Founded in 1982, the Vegetarian Resource Group works with other organizations to promote vegetarianism. The group maintains an extensive online portal with nutrition information, news and feature articles, recipes, and advocacy projects.

> PO Box 1463
> Baltimore, MD 21203
> Phone: (410) 366-8343
> Fax: (410) 366-8804
> vrg@vrg.org
> http://www.vrg.org

W.K. KELLOGG FOUNDATION

Founded in 1930, the W.K. Kellogg Foundation is dedicated to creating healthy places where all children thrive. The organization supports agricultural development, nutritional education, and food system improvement in areas where food insecurity threatens the well-being of children.

> 1 Michigan Ave. E
> Battle Creek, MI 49017-4012
> Phone: (269) 968-1611
> Fax: (269) 968-0413
> wkkfbr@wkkf.org
> http://www.wkkf.org

WESTON A. PRICE FOUNDATION

The Weston A. Price Foundation is an organization dedicated to promoting research in the tradition of pioneering nutritional researcher Weston A. Price. The Price Foundation supports the reintroduction of nutrient-dense, whole foods into individuals' daily diets.

> PMB 106-380
> 4200 Wisconsin Ave. NW
> Washington, DC 20016
> Phone: (202) 363-4394
> Fax: (202) 363-4396
> info@westonaprice.org
> http://www.westonaprice.org

WOMEN, FOOD AND AGRICULTURE NETWORK

The Women, Food and Agriculture Network is an international association of women involved in sustainable agriculture. The group promotes gender equity in food production and allocation worldwide.

> PO Box 611
> Ames, IA 50010
> Phone: (515) 460-2477
> info@wfan.org
> http://www.wfan.org

WOMEN'S FOOD AND FARMING UNION

Founded in 1979, the Women's Food and Farming Union is a British membership organization for women who work in farming, food production, and food sales.

> Cargill Plc.
> Witham St Hughs,
> Lincoln LN6 9TN
> United Kingdom
> Phone: 44 844 3350342
> Fax: 44 844 3350342
> secretary@wfu.org.uk
> http://www.wfu.org.uk

WORLD FOOD DAY USA

World Food Day USA coordinates U.S. events connected to worldwide World Food Day, observed annually on October 16th, which seeks to increase worldwide awareness of global hunger issues and promote anti-hunger campaigns year-round.

> 2175 K St. NW
> Washington, DC 20437
> Phone: (202) 653-2404
> Fax: (202) 653-5760
> patricia.young@fao.org
> http://www.worldfooddayusa.org

WORLD FOOD LAW INSTITUTE

The World Food Law Institute at the Howard University School of Law promotes social development through the development of agriculture and agribusiness legal policy worldwide.

> 2900 Van Ness Street NW
> Houston Hall, Room 310
> Washington, DC 20008
> Phone: (202) 806-8039
> worldfoodlaw@law.howard.edu
> http://www.law.howard.edu/
>   worldfoodlaw/

WORLD FOOD PROGRAMME

The World Food Programme (WFP) is a branch of the United Nations that addresses hunger and food security issues around the world

> Via C.G. Viola 68
> Parco dei Medici
> 00148 Rome
> Italy
> Phone: 39 06 65131
> Fax: 39 066590632
> http://www.wfp.org

WORLD HUNGER YEAR

Founded in 1975, World Hunger Year (WHY) is a grassroots organization dedicated to finding community-based solutions to hunger worldwide.

> 505 8th Ave., Ste. 2100
> New York, NY 10018
> Phone: (212) 629-8850
> Phone: (866) 348-6479
> Fax: (212) 465-9274
> development@worldhungeryear.org
> http://www.yhunger.org

WORLD TRADE ORGANIZATION

The World Trade Organization (WTO) is an international body that helps formulate and regulate trade agreements among its participating nations.

> Centre William Rappard,
> Rue de Lausanne 154,
> CH-1211 Geneva 21,
> Switzerland
> Phone: 41 22 739 51 11
> Fax: 41 22 731 42 06
> enquiries@wto.org
> http://www.wto.org/

YUM-O ORGANIZATION

Founded in 2006 by celebrity cook and television personality Rachael Ray, Yum-O Organization seeks to empower children to develop healthy eating and cooking habits.

> 132 E. 43rd St., No. 223
> New York, NY 10017
> info@yum-o.org
> http://www.yum-o.org

ZAGAT SURVEY

The Zagat Survey compiles and publishes customer ratings and reviews of restaurants in various cities.

> 4 Columbus Circle, 3rd Floor
> New York, NY 10019
> Phone: (800) 540-9609
> Fax: (212) 977-9760
> http://www.zagat.com

Sources Consulted

BOOKS

Aaron, Shara, and Monica Bearden. *Chocolate: A Healthy Passion.* Amherst, NY: Prometheus, 2008.

Abbott, Elizabeth. *Sugar: A Bittersweet History.* London: Duckworth Overlook, 2009.

Abdel-Aal, Elsayed, and Peter J. Wood. *Specialty Grains for Food and Feed.* St. Paul, MN: American Association of Cereal Chemists, 2005.

Academia Barilla. *Pasta!* Vercelli, Italy: White Star, 2010.

Achterbosch, Thom. *Consumer Health Hazards in International Food Trade.* The Hague, The Netherlands: LEI, 2007.

Adam, Katherine L. *Community Supported Agriculture.* Fayetteville, AR: National Sustainable Agriculture Information Service, 2006.

Agroecology for Food Sovereignty. Cincinnati: Food First Books, 2009.

Albert, Janice. *Innovations in Food Labelling.* Rome: Food and Agriculture Organization of the United Nations, 2010.

Alcabes, Philip. *Dread: How Fear and Fantasy Have Fueled Epidemics from the Black Death to Avian Flu.* New York: PublicAffairs, 2009.

Alinovi, Luca, Günter Hemrich, and Luca Russo. *Beyond Relief: Food Security in Protracted Crises.* Warwickshire, UK: Practical Action Publishing, 2008.

Allen, Lindsay. *Guidelines on Food Fortification with Micronutrients.* Geneva: World Health Organization, 2006.

American Academy of Child and Adolescent Psychiatry: Task Force for Diagnostic Criteria: Infants and Children. *Diagnostic Classification of Mental Health and Developmental Disorders of Infancy and Early Childhood.* Washington, DC: Zero to Three Press, 2005.

American Cancer Society. *American Cancer Society's Complete Guide to Cancer and Nutrition.* Atlanta, GA: American Cancer Society, 2008.

American Diabetes Association. *What to Expect When You Have Diabetes: 170 Tips for Living Well with Diabetes.* Intercourse, PA: Good Books, 2008.

American Heart Association. *American Heart Association Low-Salt Cookbook: A Complete Guide to Reducing Sodium and Fat in Your Diet.* New York: Clarkson Potter/Publishers, 2006.

———. *An Eating Plan for Healthy Americans: Our American Heart Association Diet.* Dallas: American Heart Association, 2005.

American Psychiatric Association. *Diagnostic and Statistical Manual of Mental Disorders,* 4th ed. text revision. Arlington, VA: American Psychiatric Association, 2000.

America's Second Harvest—The Nation's Food Bank Network: Ending Hunger. Chicago: America's Second Harvest, 2007.

Amundson, Finn J. *Inspection and Protection of U.S. Meat and Poultry.* New York: Nova Science Publishers, 2010.

Anderson, Jennifer E. L., L. Young, and E. Long. *Diet and Hypertension.* Fort Collins: Colorado State University, Cooperative Extension, 2005.

Anderson, Kym. *The Political Economy of Agricultural Price Distortions.* New York: Cambridge University Press, 2010.

Anderson, Lessley. "The Raw Deal." In *Best Food Writing 2009,* edited by Holly Hughes. Philadelphia: Da Capo, 2009.

Anderson, Lynn Christie. *Breaking Bread: Recipes and Stories from Immigrant Kitchens.* Berkeley: University of California Press, 2010.

Anderson, Patricia, Nancy Clark, and Jan Temple. *Eating Well—Moving More for Healthier Blood Pressure, Blood Cholesterol, and Weight: I Lowered My Blood Pressure, So Can You.* Ames: Iowa State University, 2008.

Anderson, Rodney P. *Outbreak: Cases in Real-World Microbiology.* Washington, DC: ASM Press, 2006.

Anderson, Shauna, and Elizabeth L. Place. *Offal Great: A Memoir from the Queen of Chitlins.* Erie, PA: First Place Publishing Company, 2006.

Anderson, Warwick. *The Collectors of Lost Souls: Turning Kuru Scientists into Whitemen.* Baltimore, MD: Johns Hopkins University Press, 2008.

Andrée, Peter. *Genetically Modified Diplomacy: The Global Politics of Agricultural Biotechnology and the Environment.* Vancouver: UBC Press, 2007.

Andrews, Geoff. *The Slow Food Story: Politics and Pleasure.* Montreal: McGill-Queen's University Press, 2008.

Ansell, Christopher K., and David Vogel. *What's the Beef?: The Contested Governance of European Food Safety.* Cambridge, MA: MIT Press, 2006.

Aratow, Paul, and E. Saint-Ange. *La Bonne Cuisine de Madame E. Saint-Ange: The Original Companion for French Home Cooking.* Audiobook. Los Angeles: Los Angeles Public Library, 2006.

Arnold, Carrie, and B. Timothy Walsh. *Next to Nothing: A Firsthand Account of One Teenager's Experience with an Eating Disorder.* Oxford, UK: Oxford University Press, 2007.

Ash, Michael, and Irene Ash. *Handbook of Food Additives.* Endicott, NY: Synapse, 2008.

Asia Society. *Never an Empty Bowl: Sustaining Food Security in Asia.* New York: Asia Society, 2010.

Aswathanarayana, Uppugunduri. *Food and Water Security in Developing Countries.* London: Taylor & Francis, 2008.

Australian Farm Institute. *China—Emerging Opportunity or Emerging Threat?* Surry Hills, New South Wales: Australian Farm Institute, 2007.

Avramescu, Catalin. *An Intellectual History of Cannibalism.* Princeton, NJ: Princeton University Press, 2009.

Babe, Robert E. *Culture of Ecology: Reconciling Economics and Environment.* Toronto, Ontario, Canada: University of Toronto Press, 2006.

Bagchi, Debasis. *Nutraceutical and Functional Food Regulations in the United States and around the World.* Amsterdam: Elsevier/Academic Press, 2008.

Bals, Christoph, Sven Harmeling, and Michael Windfuhr. *Climate Change, Food Security and the Right to Adequate Food.* Stuttgart, Germany: Diakonisches Werk der Evangelischen Kirche, 2008.

Banes, Sally, and André Lepecki. *The Senses in Performance.* New York: Routledge, 2007.

Bannerman, Colin. *Seed Cake and Honey Prawns: Fashion and Fad in Australian Food.* Canberra: National Library of Australia, 2007.

Barrett, Christopher B., and Daniel G. Maxwell. *Food Aid after Fifty Years: Recasting Its Role.* London: Routledge, 2005.

Barton, Russell P. *Food Safety, Fresh Produce and FDA Oversight.* New York: Nova Science Publishers, 2010.

Bass, Scott. *The Dietary Supplement Health and Education Act: Regulation at a Crossroads.* Boston: American Society of Law, Medicine & Ethics (ASLME), Boston University School of Law, 2005.

Batello, Caterina, Marzio Marzot, and Adamou Harouna Touré. *The Future Is an Ancient Lake: Traditional Knowledge, Biodiversity, and Genetic Resources for Food and Agriculture in Lake Chad Basin Ecosystems.* Rome: Food and Agriculture Organization of the United Nations, 2004.

Bau, Frédéric, and Jean B. Lassara. *Fusion Chocolate: Chocolate in Cuisine.* Barcelona: Montagud, 2006.

Baur, Gene. *Farm Sanctuary: Changing Hearts and Minds about Animals and Food.* New York: Simon & Schuster, 2008.

Bayart, Jean-Francois. *The State in Africa: The Politics of the Belly.* Cambridge, UK: Polity, 2009.

Beare, Sally. *50 Secrets of the World's Longest Living People.* New York: Marlowe & Company, 2006.

Beck, Leslie, and Michelle Gelok. *Heart Healthy Foods for Life: Preventing Heart Disease through Diet and Nutrition.* Toronto: Penguin Canada, 2009.

Becker, Geoffrey S. *USDA Meat Inspection and the Humane Methods of Slaughter Act.* Washington, DC: Congressional Research Service, Library of Congress, 2008.

Beckett, Stephen T. *The Science of Chocolate.* Cambridge, UK: RSC Publishing, 2008.

Begon, Michael, Colin R. Townsend, and John L. Harper. *Ecology: From Individuals to Ecosystems,* 4th ed. Malden, MA: Blackwell, 2006.

Benardot, Dan. *Advanced Sports Nutrition*. Champaign, IL: Human Kinetics, 2006.

Bender, David A. *A Dictionary of Food and Nutrition*. New York: Oxford University Press, 2009.

Bennet, Gregory S. *Food Identity Preservation and Traceability: Safer Grains*. Boca Raton, FL: CRC Press, 2010.

Berdanier, Carolyn D. *CRC Desk Reference for Nutrition*. Boca Raton, FL: CRC/Taylor & Francis, 2006.

Bernstein, Melissa, and Ann S. Luggen. *Nutrition for the Older Adult*. Sudbury, MA: Jones and Bartlett, 2010.

Berry, Wendell. *Bringing It to the Table: On Farming and Food*. Berkeley, CA: Counterpoint, 2009.

Bethard, Wayne. *Lotions, Potions, and Deadly Elixirs: Frontier Medicine in America*. Lanham, MD: Taylor Trade, 2004.

Bethe, Marilyn R. *Global Spread of the Avian Flu: Issues and Actions*. Hauppauge, NY: Nova Science, 2006.

Bhote, Tehmina. *Medieval Feasts and Banquets: Food, Drink, and Celebration in the Middle Ages*. New York: Rosen Central, 2004.

Bingen, Jim, and Lawrence Busch. *Agricultural Standards: The Shape of the Global Food and Fiber System*. Dordrecht, The Netherlands: Springer, 2006.

Bird, David. *Understanding Wine Technology: The Science of Wine Explained*, 3rd ed. San Francisco: Wine Appreciation Guild, 2005.

Birnbaum, Charlotte, and Christa Näher. *A Journey Within: Cooking with Offal*. Köln, Germany: König, 2009.

Black, Henry R., and William J. Elliott. *Hypertension: A Companion to Braunwald's Heart Disease*. Philadelphia: Elsevier Saunders, 2007.

Blake, Steve. *Vitamins and Minerals Demystified*. New York: McGraw-Hill, 2008.

Blakeney, Michael. *Intellectual Property Rights and Food Security*. Wallingford, Oxfordshire, UK: CABI, 2009.

Blank, Grant. *Critics, Ratings, and Society: The Sociology of Reviews*. Lanham: Rowman & Littlefield, 2007.

Boekhout, Teun, and Vincent Robert. *Yeasts in Food: Beneficial and Detrimental Aspects*. Cambridge: Woodhead, 2003.

Botana, Luis M. *Seafood and Freshwater Toxins: Pharmacology, Physiology, and Detection*. Hoboken, NJ: Taylor & Francis, 2008.

Boutenko, Victoria. *12 Steps to Raw Foods: How to End Your Dependency on Cooked Food*. Berkeley, CA: North Atlantic Books, 2007.

Bower, Anne L. *African American Foodways: Explorations of History and Culture*. Urbana: University of Illinois Press, 2007.

Bower, Anne L., ed. *Reel Food: Essays on Food and Film*. New York: Routledge, 2004.

Bower, Sylvia Llewelyn, Mary Kay Sharrett, and Steve Plogsted. *Celiac Disease: A Guide to Living with Gluten Intolerance*. New York: Demos Medical Pub, 2007.

Brancato, Robin F. *Food Choices: The Ultimate Teen Guide*. Lanham, MD: Scarecrow, 2010.

Brand, Stewart. *Whole Earth Discipline: Why Dense Cities, Nuclear Power, Transgenic Crops, Restored Wildlands and Geoengineering Are Necessary*. New York: Penguin, 2010.

Bray, Tamara L., ed. *The Archaeology and Politics of Food and Feasting in Early States and Empires*. New York: Kluwer Academic/Plenum, 2003.

Bread for the World Institute. *A Just and Sustainable Recovery: Hunger 2010: 20th Annual Report on the State of World Hunger*. Washington, DC: Bread for the World Institute, 2009.

Brette, Isabelle. *The French Paradox*. Monaco City, Monaco: Alpen, 2010.

Brown, Lester R. *Outgrowing the Earth: The Food Security Challenge in an Age of Falling Water Tables and Rising Temperatures*. New York: W.W. Norton & Company, 2004.

Brown, Simon, and Dragana Brown. *Macrobiotics for Life: A Practical Guide to Healing for Body, Mind, and Heart*. Berkeley, CA: North Atlantic Books, 2009.

Brynie, Faith H. *Brain Sense: The Science of the Senses and How We Process the World around Us*. New York: American Management Association, 2009.

Bucklin-Sporer, Arden, and Rachel Pringle. *How to Grow a School Garden: A Complete Guide for Parents and Teachers*. Portland, OR: Timber Press, 2010.

Burke, Cindy. *To Buy or Not to Buy Organic: What You Need to Know to Choose the Healthiest, Safest, Most Earth-Friendly Food*. New York: Marlowe & Company, 2007.

Burnside, Robin. *Farm to Table*. Salt Lake City, UT: Gibbs Smith, 2010.

Burrows, Ian. *Food from the Wild*. London: New Holland, 2005.

Burstein, John. *The Shape of Good Nutrition: The Food Pyramid*. St. Catharines, Ontario, Canada: Crabtree Publishing, 2008.

Burton, Alvin W., and Irwin B. Telpov. *Farm Labor: 21st Century Issues and Challenges.* New York: Nova Science Publishers, 2008.

Caballero, Benjamin, and Barry M. Popkin. *The Nutrition Transition: Diet and Disease in the Developing World.* Amsterdam: Academic Press, 2006.

Cahill, Jamie. *The Patisseries of Paris: Chocolatiers, Tea Salons, Ice Cream Parlors, and More.* New York: Little Bookroom, 2007.

Cairns, Malcolm. *Voices from the Forest: Integrating Indigenous Knowledge into Sustainable Upland Farming.* Washington, DC: Resources for the Future, 2007.

Calaguas, Belinda. *Failing the Rural Poor: Aid, Agriculture, and the Millennium Development Goals.* Johannesburg: ActionAid International, 2008.

Canavan, Orla, Maeve Henchion, and Seamus O'Reilly. *An Assessment of Irish Specialty Food Enterprises' Use of the Internet as a Marketing Tool.* Dublin: Teagasc, 2005.

Cardinale, Bradley J. *Microbial Ecology.* Sudbury, MA: Jones & Bartlett Learning, 2011.

Carey, Diana, and Judy Large. *Festivals, Family and Food: Guide to Seasonal Celebration.* Lansdown, Stroud, UK: Hawthorn Press, 2005.

Carlson, Bruce M. *Human Embryology and Developmental Biology,* 4th ed. Philadelphia: Mosby/Elsevier, 2009.

Carlson, Peggy. *The Complete Vegetarian: The Essential Guide to Good Health.* Urbana: University of Illinois Press, 2009.

Carothers, Thomas. *Revitalizing U.S. Democracy Assistance: The Challenge of USAID.* Washington, DC: Carnegie Endowment for International Peace, 2009.

Carpenter, Daniel P. *Reputation and Power: Organizational Image and Pharmaceutical Regulation at the FDA.* Princeton, NJ: Princeton University Press, 2010.

Carper, Steve. *Planet Lactose: Reports from the Worlds of Lactose Intolerance, Milk Allergies, and Dairy-Free Alternatives: The Best of the Planet Lactose Blog.* Rochester, NY: Planet Lactose Publishing, 2009.

Carson, Walter P., and Stefan A. Schnitzer. *Tropical Forest Community Ecology.* Chichester, UK: Wiley-Blackwell Pub, 2008.

Cartere, Jason Y. *TV, Food Marketing and Childhood Obesity.* New York: Nova Science, 2009.

Castell-Perez, Elena, Ljubica Dokic, and Petar Dokic. *Rheology Applications to Food Quality and Product Development.* Oxford, UK: Blackwell, 2008.

Center for Food Safety and Applied Nutrition. *100 Years: Working to Keep Food and Cosmetics Safe and Promote Good Nutrition.* Washington, DC: Food and Drug Administration, Center for Food Safety and Applied Nutrition, Department of Health and Human Services, 2006.

Chamabati, Walter, and Sam Moyo. *Land Reform and the Political Economy of Agricultural Labour in Zimbabwe.* Harare, Zimbabwe: African Institute for Agrarian Studies, 2007.

Chambers, Kenneth P. *Caffeine and Health Research.* New York: Nova Biomedical Books, 2009.

Chartier, François, and Levi Reiss. *Taste Buds and Molecules: The Art and Science of Food with Wine.* Toronto: McClelland & Stewart, 2010.

Chat, Mingkwan. *Vietnamese Fusion: Vegetarian Cuisine.* Summertown, TN: Book Publishing Company, 2007.

Chen, Nancy N. *Food, Medicine, and the Quest for Good Health: Nutrition, Medicine, and Culture.* New York: Columbia University Press, 2008.

Chen, Viola. *The Evolution of the Baby Food Industry 2000–2008.* Washington, DC: Bureau of Economics, 2009.

Chesterton, Carrie M. *Food Allergies: New Research.* New York: Nova Science, 2008.

Cheung, Sidney C. H., and Chee Beng Tan. *Food and Foodways in Asia: Resource, Tradition and Cooking.* London and New York: Routledge, 2007.

Chiellini, Emo. *Environmentally Compatible Food Packaging.* Boca Raton, FL: CRC, 2008.

Chisholm, Anthony H., and Robert Dumsday. *Land Degradation: Problems and Policies.* Cambridge, UK: Cambridge University Press, 2009.

Chomitz, Kenneth M., and Piet Buys. *At Loggerheads?: Overview: Agricultural Expansion, Poverty Reduction, and Environment in the Tropical Forests.* Washington, DC: World Bank, 2007.

Christopher, Joseph. *Nutrition and Digestion.* New Delhi, India: Anmol Publications, 2006.

Civitello, Linda. *Cuisine and Culture: A History of Food and People.* Hoboken, NJ: John Wiley, 2007.

Clark, Stephanie, Michael Costello, and Maryanne Drake. *The Sensory Evaluation of Dairy Products,* 2nd ed. New York: Springer, 2009.

Clark, Taylor. *Starbucked: A Double Tall Tale of Caffeine, Commerce, and Culture.* New York: Little, Brown, 2007.

Clark, Val. *The Parisian Café: A Literary Companion.* New York: Universe, 2002.

Clarke, Shelley, Eleanor J. Milner-Gulland, and Trond Bjorndal. *Social, Economic and Regulatory Drivers of the Shark Fin Trade.* Portsmouth, UK: Centre for the Economics and Management of Aquatic Resources, University of Portsmouth, 2008.

Clay, Jason. *World Agriculture and the Environment: A Commodity-by-Commodity Guide to Impacts and Practices.* Washington, DC: Island Press, 2003.

Claybourne, Anna. *Healthy Eating: Diet and Nutrition.* Chicago: Heinemann Library, 2008.

Clements, David, and Anil Shrestha, eds. *New Dimensions in Agroecology.* Binghamton, NY: Food Products Press, 2004.

Cliggett, Lisa. *Grains from Grass: Aging, Gender, and Famine in Rural Africa.* Ithaca, NY: Cornell University Press, 2005.

Climate Change and Hunger: Responding to the Challenge. Rome: World Food Programme, 2009.

Codex Alimentarius Commission. *Understanding the Codex Alimentarius.* Rome: World Health Organization, 2006.

Coffee, Neil. *The Commerce of War: Exchange and Social Order in Latin Epic.* Chicago: University of Chicago Press, 2009.

Cohen, Jan. *Memoirs of a Travelling Foodie.* Hamilton, New Zealand: J. Cohen, 2007.

Cohen, Marc J., and Jennifer Clapp. *The Global Food Crisis: Governance Challenges and Opportunities.* Waterloo, Ontario, Canada: Wilfrid Laurier University, 2009.

Cohen, Mark N., and Gillian M. M. Crane-Kramer, eds. *Ancient Health: Skeletal Indicators of Agricultural and Economic Intensification.* Gainesville: University of Florida Press, 2007.

Cohen, Rhoda, Myoung Kim, and James C. Ohls. *Hunger in America 2006: A Project of America's Second Harvest—The Nation's Food Bank Network: Full Report, March 2006.* Chicago: America's Second Harvest, 2006.

Collin, Robin M., and Robert W. Collin. *Encyclopedia of Sustainability.* Santa Barbara, CA: Greenwood Press, 2010.

Collins, Kathleen. *Watching What We Eat: The Evolution of Television Cooking Shows.* New York: Continuum, 2009.

Combs, Gerald F. *The Vitamins: Fundamental Aspects in Nutrition and Health,* 3rd ed. Amsterdam and Boston: Elsevier Academic Press, 2008.

Committee on Evaluation of USAID Democracy Assistance Programs. *Improving Democracy Assistance: Building Knowledge through Evaluations and Research.* Washington, DC: National Academies Press, 2008.

Conner, Mary T. *Farm Bill of 2008: Major Provisions and Legislative Action.* New York: Nova Science Publishers, 2010.

Connor, Elizabeth. *Internet Guide to Food Safety and Security.* New York: Haworth Information Press, 2005.

Convention on Biological Diversity. *Handbook of the Convention on Biological Diversity: Including Its Cartagena Protocol on Biosafety.* Montreal, Canada: Secretariat of the Convention on Biological Diversity, 2005.

Cooper, Frank A., and Charles T. McGee. *Cholesterol and the French Paradox.* Burleigh, Queensland, Australia: Zeus Publications, 2006.

Cordain, Loren. "Implications of Plio-Pleistocene Hominin Diets for Modern Humans." In *Evolution of the Human Diet: The Known, the Unknown, and the Unknowable,* edited by Peter S. Ungar. Oxford, UK, and New York: Oxford University Press, 2007.

———. *The Paleo Diet: Lose Weight and Get Healthy by Eating the Foods You Were Designed to Eat.* New York: Wiley, 2002.

Costin, Carolyn. *The Eating Disorder Sourcebook: A Comprehensive Guide to the Causes, Treatments, and Prevention of Eating Disorders.* New York: McGraw-Hill, 2007.

Cotler, Amy. *The Locavore Way: Discover and Enjoy the Pleasures of Locally Grown Food.* North Adams, MA: Storey, 2009.

Cowen, Ruth. *Relish: The Extraordinary Life of Alexis Soyer, Victorian Celebrity Chef.* London: Phoenix, 2007.

Crocombe, Angela. *Ethical Eating: How to Make Food Choices That Won't Cost the Earth.* Camberwell, Victoria, Australia: Penguin Books, 2008.

Culture 21: Agenda 21 for Culture. Barcelona, Spain: Institut de Cultura de Barcelona, 2007.

Custer, Delores. *Food Styling: The Art of Preparing Food for the Camera.* Hoboken, NJ: Wiley, 2010.

Cycon, Dean. *Javatrekker: Dispatches from the World of Fair Trade Coffee.* White River Junction, VT: Chelsea Green, 2007.

D'Amore, Joseph, and Lisa D'Amore-Miller. *Just What the Doctor Ordered Diabetes Cookbook: A Doctor's Approach to Eating Well with Diabetes.* Alexandria, VA: American Diabetes Association, 2010.

Damrosch, Phoebe. *Service Included: Four-Star Secrets of an Eavesdropping Waiter.* New York: William Morrow, 2007.

Danforth, Arn T. *Corn Crop Production: Growth, Fertilization and Yield.* New York: Nova Science Publishers, 2009.

Darling, Katherine. *Under the Table: Saucy Tales from Culinary School.* New York: Atria Books, 2009.

Davies, Glyn, and David Brown. *Bushmeat and Livelihoods: Wildlife Management and Poverty Reduction.* Oxford, UK: Blackwell, 2007.

Davies, H. Dele, Hiram E. Fitzgerald, and Vasiliki Mousouli. *Obesity in Childhood and Adolescence.* Westport, CT: Praeger, 2008.

Davies, Lee, et al. *Dynamic Changes in Marine Ecosystems: Fishing, Food Webs and Future Options.* Washington, DC: National Academies Press, 2006.

Davis, Christina L. *Food Fights over Free Trade: How International Institutions Promote Agricultural Trade Liberalization.* Princeton, NJ: Princeton University Press, 2005.

Davis-Gibson, Katonya. *Plantation Sweetness: The True History of African-American Home Cooking.* Baltimore: PublishAmerica, 2008.

De, Dipak, Basavaprabhu Jirli, and K. Kiran. *Empowerment of Women in Agriculture.* Varanasi, India: Ganga Kaveri, 2010.

de Ruiter, Peter C., Volkmar Wolters, and John C. Moore, eds. *Dynamic Food Webs: Multispecies Assemblages, Ecosystem Development and Environmental Change.* Burlington, MA: Academic Press, 2005.

De Waal, Alex. *Famine Crimes: Politics & the Disaster Relief Industry in Africa.* London: African Rights, 2006.

———. *Famine That Kills: Darfur, Sudan.* Oxford, UK: Oxford University Press, 2005.

Debnam, Betty. *Healthy Changes on the Menu: Munching on School Lunches.* Kansas City, MO: Universal Press Syndicate, 2006.

DeJean, Joan E. *The Essence of Style: How the French Invented High Fashion, Fine Food, Chic Cafés, Style, Sophistication, and Glamour.* New York: Free Press, 2005.

D'Elgin, Tershia. *What Should I Eat?: A Complete Guide to the New Food Pyramid.* New York: Ballantine Books, 2005.

Desai, Anita. *Fasting, Feasting.* New York: Houghton-Mifflin, 2000.

Desmarais, Annette, Nettie Wiebe, and Hannah Whitman, eds. *Food Sovereignty: Reconnecting Food, Nature and Community.* Oakland, CA: Institute for Food & Development Policy, 2010.

Devaney, Barbara L. *Review of Dietary Reference Intakes for Selected Nutrients: Challenges and Implications for Federal Food and Nutrition Policy.* Washington, DC: USDA Economic Research Service, 2007.

Devereux, Stephen. *The New Famines: Why Famines Persist in an Era of Globalization.* London: Routledge, 2007.

Diamond, Jared M. *Collapse: How Societies Choose to Fail or Succeed.* New York: Viking, 2005.

Diaz, Laia, and Marta Perez. *Ecology Research Trends.* New York: Nova Science Publishers, 2008.

Dooher, Carrie. *Using Social Media in FDA-Regulated Industries: The Essential Guide.* Washington, DC: FDLI, 2010.

Doornbos, Martin R. *Complex Emergencies, Food Security and the Quest for Appropriate Institutional Capacity.* The Hague, The Netherlands: Institute of Social Studies, 2006.

Drake, Richard L., ed. *Gray's Anatomy for Students,* 2nd ed. Philadelphia: Elsevier/Churchill Livingstone, 2010.

Dreiss, Meredith L., and Sharon Greenhill. *Chocolate: Pathway to the Gods.* Tucson: University of Arizona Press, 2008.

Driskell, Judy A., and Ira Wolinsky. *Nutritional Assessment of Athletes.* Boca Raton, FL: CRC Press, 2011.

D'Silva, Joyce, and John Webster. *The Meat Crisis: Developing More Sustainable Production and Consumption.* London: Earthscan, 2010.

Du Bois, Christine M., and Chee B. Tan. *The World of Soy.* Urbana: University of Illinois, 2008.

Duyff, Roberta L. *American Dietetic Association Complete Food and Nutrition Guide.* Hoboken, NJ: John Wiley & Sons, 2006.

Echols, Marsha A. *Food Safety and the WTO: The Interplay of Culture, Science and Technology.* London: Kluwer Law International, 2001.

Edge, John T. *Foodways.* Chapel Hill: University of North Carolina, 2007.

Eguaras, Louis, and Matthew Frederick. *101 Things I Learned in Culinary School.* New York: Grand Central Pub, 2010.

Emerton, Victoria, and Eugenia Choi. *Essential Guide to Food Additives.* Surrey, UK: Leatherhead, 2008.

Emmeluth, Donald. *Botulism (Deadly Diseases and Epidemics).* New York: Chelsea House Publications, 2005.

Erlich, Reese W. *Dateline Havana: The Real Story of U.S. Policy and the Future of Cuba.* Sausalito, CA: PoliPoint, 2009.

Gregson, Bob, and Bonnie Gregson. *Rebirth of the Small Family Farm: A Handbook for Starting a Successful Organic Farm Based on the Community Supported Agriculture Concept.* Austin, TX: Acres, 2004.

Grescoe, Taras. *Bottomfeeder: A Seafood Lover's Journey to the End of the Food Chain.* New York: Bloomsbury USA, 2008.

Grilo, Carlos, and James E. Mitchell. *The Treatment of Eating Disorders: A Clinical Handbook.* New York: Guilford, 2010.

Grist, Andrew. *Poultry Inspection: Anatomy, Physiology and Disease Conditions.* Nottingham, UK: Nottingham University Press, 2006.

Grivetti, Louis, and Howard-Yana Shapiro. *Chocolate: History, Culture, and Heritage.* Hoboken, NJ: Wiley, 2009.

Grogan, Sarah. *Body Image: Understanding Body Dissatisfaction in Men, Women and Children.* New York: Routledge, 2007.

Guha-Khasnobis, Basudeb, S. S. Acharya, and Benjamin Davis. *Food Security: Indicators, Measurement, and the Impact of Trade Openness.* Oxford, UK: Oxford University Press, 2007.

Guihan, Vincent. *New American Vegan.* Oakland, CA: PM Press, 2010.

Gullino, Maria Lodovica. *Crop Biosecurity: Assuring Our Global Food Supply.* Dordrecht: Springer, 2008.

Gumpert, David E. *The Raw Milk Revolution: Behind America's Emerging Battle over Food Rights.* White River Junction, VT: Chelsea Green Pub, 2009.

Gura, Trisha. *Lying in Weight: The Hidden Epidemic of Eating Disorders in Adult Women.* New York: HarperCollins, 2007.

Gursche, Siegfried. *Good Fats and Oils: Why We Need Them and How to Use Them in the Kitchen.* Summertown, TN: Alive Books, 2007.

Gustafsson, Kerstin. *Retailing Logistics & Fresh Food Packaging: Managing Change in the Supply Chain.* London: Kogan Page, 2006.

Guynup, Sharon. *State of the Wild 2006: A Global Portrait of Wildlife, Wildlands, and Oceans.* Washington, DC: Island Press, 2005.

Haddad, Lawrence J., and Sushila Zeitlyn. *Lifting the Curse: Overcoming Persistent Undernutrition in India.* Oxford: Wiley-Blackwell, 2009.

Haggard, Stephan, and Marcus Noland. *Famine in North Korea: Markets, Aid, and Reform.* New York: Columbia University Press, 2007.

Hahlbrock, Klaus. *Feeding the Planet: Environmental Protection through Sustainable Agriculture.* London: Haus, 2009.

Halford, Nigel. *Plant Biotechnology: Current and Future Applications of Genetically Modified Crops.* Chichester, UK: John Wiley, 2006.

Halweil, Brian, and Lisa Mastny. *Catch of the Day: Choosing Seafood for Healthier Oceans.* Washington, DC: Worldwatch Institute, 2006.

Hamilton, Lisa M. *Deeply Rooted: Unconventional Farmers in the Age of Agribusiness.* Berkeley, CA: Counterpoint, 2009.

Han, Jung H. *Innovations in Food Packaging.* San Diego, CA: Elsevier Academic, 2005.

Happynook, Kathy. *Whaling for Food.* Qualicum Beach, British Columbia: WCW Publications, 2005.

Hargreaves, Ben. *Eat Me: Delicious, Desirable, Successful Food Packaging Design.* Mies, Switzerland: RotoVision, 2004.

———. *Successful Food Packaging Design.* Crans-Près-Céligny, Switzerland: RotoVision, 2006.

Harney, Michael. *The Harney & Sons Guide to Tea.* New York: Penguin Press, 2008.

Harris, Patricia, David Lyon, and Sue McLaughlin. *The Meaning of Food: The Companion to the PBS Television Series.* Guilford, CT: Globe Pequot Press, 2005.

Hartog, Adele P., Wija A. Staveren, and Inge D. Brouwer. *Food Habits and Consumption in Developing Countries: Manual for Field Studies.* Wageningen, The Netherlands: Wageningen Academic, 2006.

Hatcher, Mike. *Keeping Chickens: Self-Sufficiency.* New York: Skyhorse, 2010.

Hatfield, Jerry L., ed. *The Farmer's Decision: Balancing Economic Agriculture Production with Environmental Quality.* Ankeny, IA: Soil and Water Conservation Society, 2005.

Hauck-Lawson, Annie, and Jonathan Deutsch. *Gastropolis: Food and New York City.* New York: Columbia University Press, 2009.

Health Canada. *Caffeine.* Ottawa: Health Canada, 2007.

Heinrich, Michael, Walter E. Müller, and Claudio Galli. *Local Mediterranean Food Plants and Nutraceuticals.* Basel, Switzerland: Karger, 2006.

Heiss, Mary Lou, and Robert J. Heiss. *The Story of Tea: A Cultural History and Drinking Guide.* Berkeley, CA: Ten Speed Press, 2007.

Helou, Anissa. *The Fifth Quarter: An Offal Cookbook.* Bath, UK: Absolute, 2004.

Helstosky, Carol. *Food Culture in the Mediterranean.* Westport, CT: Greenwood Press, 2009.

Hempel, Sandra. *The Strange Case of the Broad Street Pump: John Snow and the Mystery of Cholera.* Berkeley: University of California Press, 2006.

Henderson, Elizabeth, and En R. Van. *Sharing the Harvest: A Citizen's Guide to Community Supported Agriculture.* White River Junction, VT: Chelsea Green, 2007.

Hesse-Biber, Sharlene N. *The Cult of Thinness.* New York: Oxford University Press, 2007.

Hester, Elliott. *Adventures of a Continental Drifter: An Around-the-World Excursion into Weirdness, Danger, Lust, and the Perils of Street Food.* New York: St. Martin's Press, 2005.

Hewitt, Ben. *The Town That Food Saved: How One Community Found Vitality in Local Food.* Emmaus, PA: Rodale, 2010.

Hewlings, Susan J., and Denis M. Medeiros. *Nutrition: Real People, Real Choices: Food Composition Table and Dietary Reference Intakes (DRIs): Recommended Intakes for Individuals of Elements.* Upper Saddle River, NJ: Pearson Prentice Hall, 2009.

Heyhoe, Kate. *Cooking Green: Reducing Your Carbon Footprint in the Kitchen: The New Green Basics Way.* Cambridge, MA: Da Capo Lifelong, 2009.

Higdon, Jane. *An Evidence-Based Approach to Dietary Phytochemicals.* New York: Thieme Medical, 2007.

Hildebrand, Caz, and Jacob Kenedy. *The Geometry of Pasta.* Philadelphia: Quirk Books, 2010.

Hilts, Philip J. *Protecting America's Health: The FDA, Business, and One Hundred Years of Regulation.* New York: Alfred A. Knopf, 2003.

Ho, Chi-Tang, Jen-Kun Lin, and Fereidoon Shahidi. *Tea and Tea Products: Chemistry and Health-Promoting Properties.* Boca Raton, FL: CRC Press, 2009.

Hobson, J. C. Jeremy, and Rupert Stephenson. *Backyard Poultry Keeping.* Ramsbury, UK: Crowood Press, 2007.

Hoeller, Suzie L. *Recall: Food and Toy Safety: An American Crisis.* Charleston, SC: BookSurge, 2007.

Hoffmann, Sandra A., and Michael R. Taylor. *Toward Safer Food: Perspectives on Risk and Priority Setting.* Washington, DC: Resources for the Future, 2005.

Hohenegger, Beatrice. *Liquid Jade: The Story of Tea from East to West.* New York: St. Martin's Press, 2006.

Hohenegger, Beatrice, and Terese T. Bartholomew. *Steeped in History: The Art of Tea.* Los Angeles: Fowler Museum at UCLA, 2009.

Holden, Stacy E. *The Politics of Food in Modern Morocco.* Gainesville: University Press of Florida, 2009.

Hollander, Gail M. *Raising Cane in the 'Glades: The Global Sugar Trade and the Transformation of Florida.* Chicago: University of Chicago Press, 2008.

Holthaus, Gary H. *From the Farm to the Table: What All Americans Need to Know about Agriculture.* Lexington: University Press of Kentucky, 2006.

Horowitz, Roger. *Putting Meat on the American Table: Taste, Technology, Transformation.* Baltimore: Johns Hopkins University Press, 2006.

Horsfield, Alan, and Elaine Horsfield. *Talking about Food and the Environment.* New York: Gareth Stevens, 2010.

Horsman, Jennifer, and Jaime Flowers. *Please Don't Eat the Animals: All the Reasons You Need to Be a Vegetarian.* Sanger, CA: Quill Driver/Word Dancer, 2007.

Hosking, Richard. *Eggs in Cookery: Proceedings of the Oxford Symposium of Food & Cookery 2006.* Totnes, UK: Prospect, 2007.

Hovorka, Alice, Henk de Zeeuw, and Mary Njenga. *Women Feeding Cities: Mainstreaming Gender in Urban Agriculture and Food Security.* Warwickshire, UK: Practical Action, 2009.

How to Use Your SNAP Benefits at Farmers' Markets. Oklahoma City: OK-SNAP, Supplemental Nutrition Assistance Program, Oklahoma OKDHS, 2010.

Huang, Bochao. *Diet, Nutrition and Optimal Health: From Food Supply to Nutrigenomics, the 10th Asian Congress of Nutrition, September 2007.* Middle Park, Victoria, Australia: HEC Press, 2008.

Hublin, Jean-Jacques, and Michael P. Richards. *The Evolution of Hominin Diets: Integrating Approaches to the Study of Paleolithic Subsistence.* Dordrecht: Springer, 2009.

Hughes, Kathryn. *The Short Life and Long Times of Mrs. Beeton.* New York: Knopf, 2006.

Hunger and Health. London: Earthscan, 2008.

Hurley, Dan. *Natural Causes: Death, Lies, and Politics in America's Vitamin and Herbal Supplement Industry.* New York: Broadway, 2006.

Hussain, Azmal. *Malnutrition: Issues and Combat Strategies.* Hyderabad, India: Icfai University Press, 2007.

Implementing Agenda 21. Geneva, Switzerland: United Nations Economic and Social Council, 2002.

Intergovernmental Panel on Climate Change (IPCC). *Climate Change 2007: Synthesis Report*. Geneva: IPCC, 2008.

International Atomic Energy Agency. *Irradiation to Ensure the Safety and Quality of Prepared Meals: Results of the Coordinated Research Project*. Vienna: International Atomic Energy Agency, 2009.

Iverson, Jon. *Home Winemaking, Step-by-Step: A Guide to Fermenting Wine Grapes*. Medford, OR: Stonemark, 2000.

Jacob, Dianne. *Will Write for Food: The Complete Guide to Writing Cookbooks, Blogs, Reviews, Memoir, and More*. Cambridge, MA: Da Capo Lifelong, 2010.

Jacobs, Susie M. *Gender and Agrarian Reforms*. New York: Routledge, 2010.

Jaffa, Tony, and Brett McDermott. *Eating Disorders in Children and Adolescents*. Cambridge, UK: Cambridge University Press, 2007.

Jaffee, Daniel. *Brewing Justice: Fair Trade Coffee, Sustainability, and Survival*. Berkeley: University of California Press, 2007.

Jain, H. K. *Green Revolution: History, Impact and Future*. Houston: Studium Press LLC, 2010.

James, Jennylynd. *Microbial Hazard Identification in Fresh Fruit and Vegetables*. Hoboken, NJ: Wiley-Interscience, 2006.

Jamison, Cheryl A., and Bill Jamison. *American Home Cooking: Over 300 Spirited Recipes Celebrating Our Rich Tradition of Home Cooking*. New York: William Morrow, 2005.

Janer, Zilkia. *Latino Food Culture*. Westport, CT: Greenwood Press, 2008.

Jansen, Kees, and Sietze Vellema. *Agribusiness and Society: Corporate Responses to Environmentalism, Market Opportunities and Public Regulation*. London: Zed Books, 2004.

Jarvis, Devra I., and Christine Padoch. *Managing Biodiversity in Agricultural Ecosystems*. New York: Columbia University Press, 2007.

Jensen, Heather. *Reevaluating U.S. Food Aid to Africa: Food Aid for Food Security*. Cambridge, MA: John F. Kennedy School of Government, 2007.

Joanna Briggs Institute. *Minimising Undernutrition in the Older Patient*. Carlton, Victoria, Canada: Blackwell, 2007.

Johnson, Douglas L., and Laurence A. Lewis. *Land Degradation: Creation and Destruction*. Lanham, MD: Rowman & Littlefield, 2007.

Johnson, Paul. *Fish Forever: The Definitive Guide to Understanding, Selecting, and Preparing Healthy, Delicious, and Environmentally Sustainable Seafood*. Hoboken, NJ: Wiley, 2007.

Johnson, Renee, and Geoffrey S. Becker. *The 2008 Farm Bill: Major Provisions and Legislative Action*. CRS Report for Congress, RL34696. Washington, DC: Congressional Research Service, Library of Congress, 2008.

Joint FAO/WHO/UNU Expert Consultation on Human Energy Requirements (2001: Rome, Italy). *Human Energy Requirements: Report of a Joint FAO/WHO/UNU Expert Consultation: Rome, 17–24 October 2001*. Rome: Food and Agriculture Organization, 2004.

Jolliffe, Lee. *Coffee Culture, Destinations and Tourism*. Bristol, UK: Channel View Publications, 2010.

———. *Tea and Tourism: Tourists, Traditions and Transformations*. Clevedon, UK: Channel View Publications, 2007.

Jones, J. Benton. *Hydroponics: A Practical Guide for the Soilless Grower*, 2nd ed. Boca Raton, FL: CRC Press, 2005.

Jones, Martin. "Moving North: Archaeobotanical Evidence for Plant Diet in Middle and Upper Paleolithic Europe." In *The Evolution of Hominin Diets: Integrating Approaches to the Study of Paleolithic Subsistence*, edited by Jean-Jacques Hublin and Michael P. Richards. Dordrecht, The Netherlands: Springer, 2009.

Joshi, Satish V. *Agriculture as a Source of Fuel: Prospects and Impacts, 2007 to 2017*. Washington, DC: U.S. Dept. of Agriculture, Office of Energy Policy and New Uses, 2007.

Juneja, Vijay K., and John N. Sofos. *Pathogens and Toxins in Foods: Challenges and Interventions*. Washington, DC: ASM Press, 2010.

Kallen, Stuart A. *Is Factory Farming Harming America?* Detroit: Greenhaven Press, 2006.

Kamp, David. *The United States of Arugula: How We Became a Gourmet Nation*. New York: Broadway Books, 2006.

Kaplan, Steven L. *Good Bread Is Back: A Contemporary History of French Bread, the Way It Is Made, and the People Who Make It*. Durham, NC: Duke University, 2006.

Karapinar, Baris, and Christian Haberli. *Food Crises and the WTO: World Trade Forum*. Cambridge, UK: Cambridge University Press, 2010.

Kastner, Justin, and Jason Ackleson. "Global Trade and Food Security: Perspectives for the Twenty-First Century." In *Homeland Security: Protecting America's Targets, Vol. 1: Borders and Points of*

Entry. Westport, CT: Praeger Security International, 2006.

Kaufman, Sheilah, and Sheri Coleman. *Canola Gourmet: Time for an Oil Change!* Sterling, VA: Capital, 2008.

Kaushal, Neeraj, and Qin Gao. *Food Stamp Program and Consumption Choices*. Cambridge, MA: National Bureau of Economic Research, 2009.

Keay, John. *The Spice Route: A History*. Berkeley: University of California Press, 2006.

Keith, Lierre. *The Vegetarian Myth: Food, Justice and Sustainability*. Crescent City, CA: Flashpoint Press, 2009.

Kessler, David A. *The End of Overeating: Taking Control of the Insatiable American Appetite*. Emmaus, PA: Rodale, 2009.

Kessler, J. Raymond. *Hydroponics for Home Gardeners*. Auburn, AL: Alabama Cooperative Extension System, 2006.

Kidd, Jerry S., and Renee A. Kidd. *Agricultural versus Environmental Science: A Green Revolution*. New York: Chelsea House, 2006.

Kilarski, Barbara. *Keep Chickens!: Tending Small Flocks in Cities, Suburbs, and Other Small Spaces*. North Adams, MA: Storey, 2003.

Kill, Ron, and Keith Turnbull. *Pasta and Semolina Technology*. Chichester, UK: John Wiley & Sons, Ltd., 2007.

Kime, Tom. *Street Food: Exploring the World's Most Authentic Tastes*. New York: DK Publishing, 2007.

Kingsolver, Barbara. *Animal, Vegetable, Miracle: A Year of Food Life*. New York: HarperCollins, 2007.

Kiple, Kenneth F. *A Movable Feast: Ten Millennia of Food Globalization*. Cambridge, UK, and New York: Cambridge University Press, 2007.

Klapp, Emilia. *Your Heart Needs the Mediterranean Diet: Learn How Mediterraneans Have Kept a Healthy Heart for Centuries*. South Pasadena, CA: Preventive Nutrition Press, 2007.

Knasmüller, Siegfried. *Chemoprevention of Cancer and DNA Damage by Dietary Factors*. Weinheim, Germany: Wiley-VCH, 2009.

Knight, Christine. "The Food Nature Intended You to Eat: Low-Carbohydrate Diets and Primitivist Philosophy." In *The Atkins Diet and Philosophy: Chewing the Fat with Kant and Nietzsche*, edited by Lisa Heldke, Kerri Mommer, and Cynthia Pineo. Chicago: Open Court, 2005.

Koeppel, Dan. *Banana: The Fate of the Fruit That Changed the World*. New York: Hudson Stuart Press, 2008.

Kohlstadt, Ingrid, ed. *Scientific Evidence for Musculoskeletal, Bariatric, and Sports Nutrition*. Boca Raton, FL: CRC/Taylor & Francis, 2006.

Kopelman, Peter G., Ian D. Caterson, and William H. Dietz, eds. *Clinical Obesity in Adults and Children*. Malden, MA: Blackwell, 2005.

Kosovska, Halyna. *The Biological Treatment of Organic Food Waste*. Stockholm: Royal Institute of Technology, 2006.

Krasner, Deborah. *Good Meat: The Complete Guide to Sourcing and Cooking Sustainable Meat*. New York: Stewart, Tabori & Chang, 2010.

Kraus, Scott D., and Rosalind Rolland. *The Urban Whale: North Atlantic Right Whales at the Crossroads*. Cambridge, MA: Harvard University Press, 2007.

Kristof, Nicholas D., and Sheryl WuDunn. *Half the Sky: Turning Oppression into Opportunity for Women Worldwide*. New York: Knopf, 2009.

Kuhnlein, Harriet V., Bill Erasmus, and Dina Spigelski, eds. *Indigenous Peoples' Food Systems: The Many Dimensions of Culture, Diversity and Environment for Nutrition and Health*. Rome: Food and Agriculture Organization of the United Nations, Centre for Indigenous Peoples' Nutrition and Environment, 2009.

Kummer, Corby. *Pleasures of Slow Food: Artisan Traditions and Recipes*. San Francisco, CA: Chronicle, 2008.

Kurlansky, Mark, and S. D. Schindler. *The Story of Salt*. New York: G. P. Putnam's Sons, 2006.

Kutz, Gregory D. *Investigation: Military Meals, Ready-to-Eat Sold on Ebay*. Washington, DC: U.S. Government Accountability Office, 2006.

Lacey, Hugh. *Values and Objectivity in Science and Current Controversy about Transgenic Crops*. Lanham, MD: Lexington Books, 2005.

Lankford, Ronald D. *Can Diets Be Harmful?* Detroit: Greenhaven Press, 2007.

Lappé, Anna, and Bryant Terry. *Grub: Ideas for an Urban Organic Kitchen*. New York: Jeremy P. Tarcher/Penguin, 2006.

Lappé, Francis Moore, and Anna Lappé. *Hope's Edge: The Next Diet for a Small Planet*. New York: Putnam, 2003.

Larsen, Kurt, Ronald Kim, and Florian Theus. *Agribusiness and Innovation Systems in Africa*. Washington, DC: World Bank, 2009.

Larson-Meyer, D. Enette. *Vegetarian Sports Nutrition*. Champaign, IL: Human Kinetics, 2007.

Laszlo, Ervin, and Peter Seidel. *Global Survival: The Challenge and Its Implications for Thinking and Acting.* New York: SelectBooks, 2006.

Law, Marc T., and Gary D. Libecap. *The Determinants of Progressive Era Reform: The Pure Food and Drugs Act of 1906.* Cambridge, MA: National Bureau of Economic Research, 2004.

Lawley, Richard. *Food Safety and Traceability Strategies: Key Hazards, Risks and Technological Developments.* London: Business Insights, 2010.

Lawrence, Geoffrey, Kristen Lyons, and Tabatha Wallington. *Food Security, Nutrition and Sustainability.* Sterling, VA: Earthscan, 2010.

Lawrence, Ruth A., and Robert M. Lawrence. *Breastfeeding.* St. Louis, MO: Elsevier Mosby, 2005.

Leadbetter, Jared R., ed. *Environmental Microbiology.* Amsterdam and Boston: Elsevier Academic Press, 2005.

Leathers, Howard D., and Phillips Foster. *The World Food Problem: Toward Ending Undernutrition in the Third World.* Boulder, CO: Rienner Publishers, 2009.

Lee, Dong S., Kit L. Yam, and Luciano Piergiovanni. *Food Packaging Science and Technology.* Boca Raton, FL: CRC Press, 2008.

Lerman, Zvi. *Russia's Agriculture in Transition: Factor Markets and Constraints on Growth.* Lanham, MD: Lexington Books, 2008.

Leung, PingSun, Cheng-Sheng Lee, and P. J. O'Bryen. *Species and System Selection for Sustainable Aquaculture.* Ames, IA: Blackwell, 2007.

Lew, Kristi. *Food Poisoning: E. Coli and the Food Supply.* New York: Rosen, 2011.

Lewis, G. P. *Legumes of the World.* Richmond, UK: Royal Botanic Gardens, Kew, 2005.

Lewis, Sara E., and William T. Ross. *Marketing Health Food: The Strategic and Ethical Marketing Plan Utilizing Social Media.* University Park: Pennsylvania State University Press, 2010.

Li, Thomas S. C. *Vegetables and Fruits: Nutritional and Therapeutic Values.* Boca Raton, FL: CRC Press, 2008.

Liang, George H., and Daniel Z. Skinner, eds. *Genetically Modified Crops: Their Development, Uses, and Risks.* Binghamton, NY: Food Products, 2004.

Light, Douglas B. *The Senses.* Philadelphia: Chelsea House, 2004.

Lipski, Elizabeth. *Digestive Wellness.* New York: McGraw-Hill, 2005.

Lipton, Michael. *Land Reform in Developing Countries: Property Rights and Property Wrongs.* London and New York: Routledge, 2009.

Lopez, Gail Woodward, ed. *Obesity: Dietary and Developmental Influences.* Boca Raton, FL: CRC/Taylor & Francis, 2006.

Louv, Richard. *Last Child in the Woods: Saving Our Children from Nature-Deficit Disorder,* updated and expanded. Chapel Hill, NC: Algonquin Books, 2008.

Lovegren, Sylvia. *Fashionable Food: Seven Decades of Food Fads.* New York: Macmillan, 1995.

Lozano, Jorge E. *Fruit Manufacturing.* New York: Springer, 2006.

Lumpkin, Thomas A., et al. *Proceedings of the 1st International Conference on Indigenous Vegetables and Legumes Prospectus for Fighting Poverty, Hunger and Malnutrition: Hyderabad, India, December 12–15, 2006.* Leuven, Belgium: International Society for Horticultural Science, 2007.

Luning, Pieternel A., Frank Devlieghere, and Roland Verhe, eds. *Safety in the Agri-Food Chain.* Wageningen, The Netherlands: Wageningen Academic Publishers, 2006.

Lurquin, Paul. *High Tech Harvest: Understanding Genetically Modified Food Plants.* Boulder, CO: Westview Press, 2004.

Lutz, Carroll A., and Karen R. Przytulski. *Nutrition & Diet Therapy: Evidence-Based Applications.* Philadelphia: F.A. Davis Co., 2006.

Lyon, Sarah, and Mark Moberg. *Fair Trade and Social Justice: Global Ethnographies.* New York: New York University Press, 2010.

Lyson, Thomas A. *Civic Agriculture: Reconnecting Farm, Food, and Community.* Medford, MA: Tufts University Press, 2004.

MacClancy, Jeremy, and Helen Macbeth. *Researching Food Habits: Methods and Problems.* The Anthropology of Food and Nutrition, Series 5. New York: Berghahn Books, 2004.

MacClancy, Jeremy, C. J. K. Henry, and Helen M. Macbeth. *Consuming the Inedible: Neglected Dimensions of Food Choice.* New York: Berghahn Books, 2007.

Mack, Glenn R., and Asele Surina. *Food Culture in Russia and Central Asia.* Westport, CT: Greenwood Press, 2005.

Maczulak, Anne E. *Pollution: Treating Environmental Toxins.* New York: Facts on File, 2010.

Madden, Etta M., and Martha L. Finch. *Eating in Eden: Food and American Utopias.* Lincoln: University of Nebraska Press, 2006.

Madison, Deborah. *Preserving Food without Freezing or Canning: Traditional Techniques Using Salt, Oil, Sugar, Alcohol, Vinegar, Drying, Cold*

Storage, and Lactic Fermentation: The Gardeners and Farmers of Terre Vivante. White River Junction, VT: Chelsea Green, 2007.

Mahan, L. Kathleen, and Sylvia Escott-Stump. *Krause's Food, Nutrition, & Diet Therapy.* St. Louis: W.B. Saunders, 2008.

Majahara, Pharahada. *Food Sovereignty and Uncultivated Biodiversity in South Asia: Essays on the Poverty of Food Policy and the Wealth of the Social Landscape.* New Delhi: Academic Foundation in Association with International Development Research Centre, Ottawa, Canada, 2007.

Maleki, Soheila J., A. Wesley Burks, and Ricki M. Helm. *Food Allergy.* Washington, DC: ASM Press, 2006.

Manning, Ivy. *The Farm to Table Cookbook: The Art of Eating Locally.* Seattle: Sasquatch Books, 2008.

Manning, Richard. *Against the Grain: How Agriculture Has Hijacked Civilization.* New York: North Point Press, 2005.

Marchant, John, Bryan G. Reuben, and Joan P. Alcock. *Bread: A Slice of History.* Stroud, UK: History, 2008.

Marcus, Joyce, and Charles Stanish, eds. *Agricultural Strategies.* Los Angeles: Cotsen Institute of Archaeology, 2005.

Marczinski, Cecile A., Estee C. Grant, and Vincent J. Grant. *Binge Drinking in Adolescents and College Students.* Hauppauge, NY: Nova Science, 2009.

Marquart, Len. *Whole Grains and Health.* Ames, IA: Blackwell, 2007.

Marsden, Terry. *The New Regulation and Governance of Food: Beyond the Food Crisis?* New York: Routledge, 2010.

Martin, Philip L., Michael Fix, and J. E. Taylor. *The New Rural Poverty: Agriculture & Immigration in California.* Washington, DC: Urban Institute Press, 2006.

Mason, John. *Commercial Hydroponics,* 2nd ed. Pymble, New South Wales, Australia: Kangaroo Press, 2005.

Masson-Matthee, Marielle D. *The Codex Alimentarius Commission and Its Standards.* The Hague, The Netherlands: T.M.C. Asser Press, 2007.

Masters, Lesley. *The Global Food Crisis and the Challenge of Food Security.* Pretoria: Africa Institute of South Africa, 2008.

Matthews, Karl R. *Microbiology of Fresh Produce.* Washington, DC: ASM Press, 2005.

Mattila-Sandholm, Tiina, and Maria Saarela, eds. *Functional Dairy Products,* 2 vols. Cambridge, UK: Woodhead, 2003 and 2007.

Maxwell, Daniel. *Emergency Food Security Interventions.* London: Humanitarian Practice Network, 2008.

McDonald, Bryan. *Food Security.* Cambridge, UK: Polity, 2010.

McGee, Harold. *Modern Gastronomy A to Z: A Scientific and Gastronomic Lexicon.* Boca Raton, FL: CRC, 2010.

McInerny, Ralph. *The Green Revolution.* New York: St. Martin's Minotaur, 2008.

McKibben, Bill, and Albert Gore. *American Earth: Environmental Writing since Thoreau.* New York: Literary Classics of the United States, 2008.

McNamee, Gregory. *Moveable Feasts: The History, Science, and Lore of Food.* Westport, CT: Praeger, 2007.

McNamee, Thomas. *Alice Waters & Chez Panisse: The Romantic, Impractical, Often Eccentric, Ultimately Brilliant Making of a Food Revolution.* New York: Penguin Press, 2007.

McSwane, David Z., Richard Linton, and Nancy R. Rue. *2005 FDA Food Code Update: What You Need to Know.* Upper Saddle River, NJ: Pearson Prentice Hall, 2007.

McWilliams, James E. *Just Food: Where Locavores Get It Wrong and How We Can Truly Eat Responsibly.* New York: Little, Brown & Co., 2009.

Mead, Geoffrey C. *Microbiological Analysis of Red Meat, Poultry and Eggs.* Boca Raton, FL: CRC Press, 2007.

Medical Economics Company. *PDR for Nutritional Supplements.* Montvale, NJ: Thomson Reuters, 2008.

Megyesi, Jennifer Lynn, and Geoff Hansen. *The Joy of Keeping Chickens: The Ultimate Guide to Raising Poultry for Fun or Profit.* New York: Skyhorse Pub, 2009.

Mela, David J., ed. *Food, Diet, and Obesity.* Boca Raton, FL: CRC Press, 2005.

Menzel, Peter, and Faith D'Aluisio. *What the World Eats.* Berkeley, CA: Tricycle Press, 2008.

Merino, Noël. *Agricultural Subsidies.* Detroit: Greenhaven Press, 2010.

Merkaz Peres Leshalom (corporate author). *Peacebuilding through Regional Agriculture, Water, Agrotechnology and Food Security Programs.* Tel-Aviv: Peres Center for Peace, 2007.

Metcalfe, Dean D., Hugh A. Sampson, and Ronald A. Simon. *Food Allergy: Adverse Reactions to Foods and Food Additives.* Malden, MA: Blackwell, 2008.

Miller, Daphne. *The Jungle Effect: The Healthiest Diets from around the World—Why They Work and How to Make Them Work for You.* New York: Harper, 2009.

Miller, Emily W. *How to Cook Like a Top Chef.* San Francisco: Chronicle Books, 2010.

Miller, Frederic P., Agnes F. Vandome, and John McBrewster. *Industrial Agriculture: Factory Farming, Livestock, Aquaculture, Agribusiness, Monoculture, Agroecology, Organic Farming, Urban Agriculture.* Beau Bassin, Mauritius: Alphascript Pub, 2009.

Miller, G. Tyler, Jr., and Scott Spoolman. *Living in the Environment,* 16th ed. Pacific Grove, CA: Brooks Cole, 2008.

Miller, Gregory D., Judith K. Jarvis, and Louis D. McBean. *Handbook of Diary Foods and Nutrition,* 3rd ed. Boca Raton, FL: CRC Press, 2007.

Millington, A. C., and Wendy Jepson. *Land-Change Science in the Tropics: Changing Agricultural Landscapes.* New York: Springer, 2008.

Millstone, Erik, and Tim Lang. *The Atlas of Food: Who Eats What, Where, and Why.* Berkeley: University of California Press, 2008.

Minich, Deanna. *An A–Z Guide to Food Additives: Never Eat What You Can't Pronounce.* San Francisco: Conari, 2009.

Mintel International Group, Ltd. *Nuts, Seeds and Dried Fruit.* London: Mintel, 2008.

Mitchell, James E. *Binge-eating Disorder: Clinical Foundations and Treatment.* New York: Guilford, 2008.

Moberg, Mark. *Slipping Away: Banana Politics and Fair Trade in the Eastern Caribbean.* New York: Berghahn Books, 2008.

Molden, David. *Water for Food, Water for Life: A Comprehensive Assessment of Water Management in Agriculture.* London: Earthscan, 2007.

Molyneaux, Paul. *Swimming in Circles: Aquaculture and the End of Wild Oceans.* New York: Thunder's Mouth, 2007.

Montville, Thomas J., and Karl R. Matthews. *Food Microbiology: An Introduction,* 2nd ed. Washington, DC: ASM Press, 2008.

Moore, N. Anthony, and William A. Roy. *Gross and Developmental Anatomy,* 2nd ed. Philadelphia: Mosby Elsevier, 2007.

Morgan, Diane, and Leigh Beisch. *The New Thanksgiving Table: An American Celebration of Family, Friends, and Food.* San Francisco: Chronicle Books, 2009.

Morgan, Kevin, Terry Marsden, and Jonathan Murdoch. *Worlds of Food: Place, Power, and Provenance in the Food Chain.* Oxford, UK: Oxford University Press, 2006.

Morgan, Sally. *Leftover Food.* London: Franklin Watts, 2006.

Morris, Scott A. *Food Packaging Engineering.* Ames, IA: Blackwell, 2006.

Morrone, Michele. *Poisons on Our Plates: The Real Food Safety Problem in the United States.* Westport, CT: Praeger, 2008.

Murray, Sarah. *Moveable Feasts: From Ancient Rome to the 21st Century, the Incredible Journeys of the Food We Eat.* New York: St. Martin's Press, 2007.

Myers, Daniel J. J. *Food Water Energy and Human Survival.* Oakland, OR: Red Anvil Press. 2008.

Nabhan, Gary Paul. *Where Our Food Comes From: Retracing Nikolay Vavilov's Quest to End Famine.* Washington, DC: Island Press, 2009.

———*Why Some Like It Hot: Food, Genes, and Cultural Diversity.* Washington, DC: Island Press/Shearwater, 2004.

Nandi, Sukdeb. *Avian Influenza or Bird Flu.* Delhi, India: Daya Pub. House, 2009.

Nassauer, Joan I., Mary V. Santelmann, and Donald Scavia. *From the Corn Belt to the Gulf: Societal and Environmental Implications of Alternative Agricultural Futures.* Washington, DC: Resources for the Future, 2007.

National Corn Growers Association. *Corn: Nature's Sustainable Resource.* Washington, DC: National Corn Growers Association, 2006.

National Dairy Council. *Lactose Intolerance and Minorities: The Real Story.* Rosemont, IL: National Dairy Council, 2005.

National Institutes of Health. *Your Digestive System and How it Works.* Bethesda, MD: National Institute of Diabetes and Digestive and Kidney Diseases, 2004.

Nehlig, Astrid. *Coffee, Tea, Chocolate, and the Brain.* Nutrition, Brain, and Behavior, vol. 2. Boca Raton, FL: CRC Press, 2004.

Nesheim, Malden C., and Ann L. Yaktine. *Seafood Choices: Balancing Benefits and Risks.* Washington, DC: National Academies Press, 2007.

Nestle, Marion. *What to Eat.* New York: North Point Press, 2006.

Netter, Frank H. *Atlas of Human Anatomy,* 4th ed. Philadelphia: Saunders Elsevier, 2006.

Neville, Jayne. *Flowerpot Farming: Creating Your Own Urban Kitchen Garden.* Preston, UK: Good Life, 2008.

Newson, Malcolm D. *Land, Water and Development: Sustainable and Adaptive Management of Rivers.* London: Routledge, 2009.

Nguyen, Andrea Q. *Into the Vietnamese Kitchen: Treasured Foodways, Modern Flavors.* Berkeley, CA: Ten Speed Press, 2006.

Nicholls, Alex, and Charlotte Opal. *Fair Trade: Market-Driven Ethical Consumption.* London: Sage, 2008.

Nichols, Mike, and Martin Hilmi. *Growing Vegetables for Home and Market.* Rome: Rural Infrastructure and Agro-Industries Division, Food and Agriculture Organization of the United Nations, 2009.

Nierenberg, Danielle, and Lisa Mastny. *Happier Meals: Rethinking the Global Meat Industry.* Washington, DC: WorldWatch Institute, 2005.

Niman, Nicolette H. *Righteous Porkchop: Finding a Life and Good Food beyond Factory Farms.* New York: Collins Living, 2009.

Nimji, Noorbanu. *A Spicy Touch, Volume III: A Fusion of East African and Indian Cuisine.* Calgary: Spicy Touch Publishing, 2007.

Nollet, Leo M. L. *Handbook of Processed Meats and Poultry Analysis.* Boca Raton, FL: CRC Press, 2009.

Northern Clay Center. *Eat with Your Eyes: A Celebration of the Art and Design and Pleasure of Sharing Food.* Minneapolis: Northern Clay Center, 2007.

Norton, Ian T. *Practical Food Rheology: An Interpretive Approach.* Oxford, UK: Wiley-Blackwell, 2011.

Nossiter, Jonathan. *Liquid Memory: Why Wine Matters.* New York: Farrar, Straus and Giroux, 2009.

Nuffer, David. *The Walkable Feast: (Left Bank Communion with Ernest): Five Café to Café Walks to the Places of Ernest Hemingway in His Early Years in Paris.* San Diego, CA: Bookman Publishing Marketing, 2005.

Nützenadel, Alexander, and Frank Trentmann. *Food and Globalization: Consumption, Markets and Politics in the Modern World.* Oxford, UK, and New York: Berg, 2008.

Nzioki, Akinyi. *Land Policies in Sub-Saharan Africa.* Nairobi, Kenya: Center for Land, Economy and Rights of Women, 2006.

O'Donnell, Ryan W. *Intellectual Property in the Food Technology Industry: Protecting Your Innovation.* New York: Springer, 2008.

Off, Carol. *Bitter Chocolate: The Dark Side of the World's Most Seductive Sweet.* New York: New Press, 2008.

Ogle, Maureen. *Ambitious Brew: The Story of American Beer.* Orlando: Harcourt, 2006.

Ohki, Sadako. *Tea Culture of Japan.* New Haven, CT: Yale University Art Gallery, 2009.

Ojiem, John O. *Exploring Socio-Ecological Niches for Legumes in Western Kenya Smallholder Farming Systems.* Wageningen, The Netherlands: Wageningen University and Research Center, 2006.

Oliver, J. Eric. *Fat Politics: The Real Story behind America's Obesity Epidemic.* Oxford, UK: Oxford University Press, 2006.

Ondetti, Gabriel A. *Land, Protest, and Politics: The Landless Movement and the Struggle for Agrarian Reform in Brazil.* University Park: Pennsylvania State University Press, 2008.

Otten, Jennifer J., Jennifer P. Hellwig, and Linda D. Meyers. *DRI, Dietary Reference Intakes: The Essential Guide to Nutrient Requirements.* Washington, DC: National Academies Press, 2006.

Overview of Progress towards Sustainable Development: A Review of the Implementation of Agenda 21, the Programme for the Further Implementation of Agenda 21 and the Johannesburg Plan of Implementation: Report of the Secretary-General. New York: United Nations, 2010.

Owens, Jasper T. *The Farm Bill and Its Far-Ranging Impact.* New York: Nova Science Publishers, 2008.

Oyeyinka, Banji, and Padmashree G. Sampath. *The Gene Revolution and Global Food Security: Biotechnology Innovation in Latecomers.* Basingstoke, UK: Palgrave Macmillan, 2009.

Palm, Cheryl A. *Slash-and-Burn Agriculture: The Search for Alternatives.* New York: Columbia University Press, 2005.

Palmer, Carole A. *Diet and Nutrition in Oral Health.* Upper Saddle River, NJ: Pearson, 2007.

Palmer, Gabrielle. *The Politics of Breastfeeding: When Breasts Are Bad for Business,* 3rd ed. London: Pinter & Martin, 2009.

Pampel, Fred C. *Threats to Food Safety.* New York: Facts on File, 2006.

Park, Young W. *Bioactive Components in Milk and Dairy Products.* Ames, IA: Wiley-Blackwell, 2009.

Parkin, Katherine J. *Food Is Love: Food Advertising and Gender Roles in Modern America.* Philadelphia: University of Pennsylvania Press, 2006.

Parkinson, Eleanor. *The Complete Confectioner, Pastry-Cook, and Baker.* Charleston, SC: BiblioLife, 2010.

Parris, Kevin. *Sustainable Management of Water Resources in Agriculture*. Paris, France: OECD, 2010.

Parsons, Russ. *How to Pick a Peach: The Search for Flavor from Farm to Table*. Boston: Houghton Mifflin, 2007.

Pascual, Unai, Amita Shah, and Jayanta Bandyopadhyay. *Water, Agriculture, and Sustainable Well-Being*. New Delhi, India: Oxford University Press, 2009.

Patel, Raj. *Stuffed and Starved: The Hidden Battle for the World Food System*. Brooklyn, NY: Melville House Pub. 2008.

Paul, Johannes, and William Windham. *Keeping Pet Chickens: Bring Your Backyard to Life and Enjoy the Bounty of Fresh Eggs from Your Own Small Flock of Happy Hens*. Hauppauge, NY: Barron's, 2005.

Payne, Anne, and Helen M. Barker. *Advancing Dietetics and Clinical Nutrition*. Edinburgh, Scotland: Churchill Livingstone, 2010.

Peacock, Paul. *The Urban Hen: A Practical Guide to Keeping Poultry in a Town or City*. Oxford: Spring Hill, 2009.

Pearce, Fred. *Confessions of an Eco-Sinner: Tracking Down the Sources of My Stuff*. Boston: Beacon Press, 2008.

———. *When the Rivers Run Dry: Water, the Defining Crisis of the Twenty-First Century*. Boston: Beacon Press, 2006.

Pearson, Elaine, et al. *The Mekong Challenge: Underpaid, Overworked, and Overlooked: The Reality of Young Migrant Workers in Thailand*. Bangkok, Thailand: ILO, 2006.

Peck, Pamela. *Tales from Cannibal Isle: The Private Journals of an Anthropologist in Fiji*. Bloomington, IN: Trafford On Demand, 2010.

Pegg, Ronald B., and Fereidoon Shahidi. *Nitrite Curing of Meat: The N-Nitrosamine Problem and Nitrite Alternatives*. Trumbull, CT: Food & Nutrition Press, 2000.

Pennington, Thomas Hugh. *When Food Kills: BSE, E. Coli, and Disaster Science*. Oxford and New York: Oxford University Press, 2003.

Percival, Steven, et al. *Microbiology of Waterborne Diseases: Microbiological Aspects and Risks*. New York: Academic Press, 2004.

Perfecto, Ivette, John H. Vandermeer, and Angus L. Wright. *Nature's Matrix: Linking Agriculture, Conservation and Food Sovereignty*. London: Earthscan, 2009.

Perkins, John. *The Secret History of the American Empire: Economic Hit Men, Jackals, and the Truth about Global Corruption*. New York: Dutton, 2007.

Perry, Cheryl L., Leslie A. Lytle, and Teresa G. Jacobs. *The Vegetarian Manifesto*. Philadelphia: Running Press, 2004.

Perry, Luddene, and Dan Schultz. *A Field Guide to Buying Organic*. New York: Bantam Books, 2005.

Pesticide Action Network: Asia and the Pacific. *The Great Rice Robbery: A Handbook on the Impact of IRRI in Asia*. Penang, Malaysia: Pesticide Action Network, Teknolohiya, 2007.

Peterson, E. Weseley F. *A Billion Dollars a Day: The Economics and Politics of Agricultural Subsidies*. Malden, MA: Wiley-Blackwell, 2009.

Petrini, Carlo. *Slow Food Nation: Why Our Food Should Be Good, Clean, and Fair*. New York: Rizzoli Ex Libris, 2007.

Petrini, Carlo, and Gigi Padovani. *Slow Food Revolution: A New Culture for Eating and Living*. New York: Rizzoli, 2006.

Phytochemicals in Food. Oxford: Wiley Blackwell Pub., 2009.

Phytonutrients. Oxford: Wiley Blackwell Pub., 2009.

Pimbert, Michel. *Towards Food Sovereignty*. London: International Institute for Environment and Development, 2009.

Planck, Nina. *Real Food: What to Eat and Why*. New York: Bloomsbury, 2007.

Planet Aid, USDA. *5 Years of Rural Empowerment: Planet Aid in Partnership with USDA*. Columbia, Maryland: Planet Aid, 2009.

Pollan, Michael. *Food Rules: An Eater's Manual*. New York: Penguin Books, 2009.

———. *In Defense of Food: An Eater's Manifesto*. New York: Penguin Press, 2008.

———. *The Omnivore's Dilemma: A Natural History of Four Meals*. New York: Penguin Press, 2006.

Powell, Julie. *Julie and Julia: 365 Days, 524 Recipes, 1 Tiny Apartment Kitchen*. New York: Little, Brown and Co., 2005.

Prakash, M., and S. Murugan. *Legumes, Their Production, Improvement and Protection*. Delhi, India: Satish Serial Pub. House, 2009.

Pratt, Charlotte W., and Kathleen Cornely. *Essential Biochemistry*. Hoboken, NJ: Wiley, 2011.

Preedy, Victor R., and Ronald R. Watson. *Olives and Olive Oil in Health and Disease Prevention*. Amsterdam and Boston: Elsevier, 2010.

Presilla, Maricel E. *Cooking from Sun Country: A Cookbook of Latin American Cuisine*. New York: Scribner, 2009.

Pretty, Jules N. *Sustainable Agriculture and Food.* London: Earthscan, 2008.

Pritchard, David. *Shooting the Cook: A True Story about Food, Television, and the Rise of TV's Superchefs.* London: Fourth Estate, 2009.

Procter, Sandy. *Everyone to the Table: Family Meals Serve Us Well.* Manhattan: Kansas State University, 2007.

Pyle, George. *Raising Less Corn, More Hell: The Case for the Independent Farm and against Industrial Food.* New York: Public Affairs, 2005.

Quiles, José L., M. Carmen Ramirez-Tortosa, and Parveen Yaqoob. *Olive Oil and Health.* Wallingford, UK, and Cambridge, MA: CABI, 2006.

Radbill, Amy. *The Davis Food Co-op Cookbook.* Davis, CA: Davis Food Co-op, 2007.

Rao, M. Anandha. *Rheology of Fluid and Semisolid Foods: Principles and Applications.* New York: Springer, 2007.

Rao, Mamatha. *Legumes in India: Applications in Food, Medicine, and Industry.* New Delhi: Ane Books India, 2008.

Rathore, Narendra S. *Consumer Awareness for Food & Dairy Products.* Udaipur, India: Apex Pub. House, 2006.

Raviv, Michael, and Johann Heinrich Lieth. *Soilless Culture: Theory and Practice.* Amsterdam and Boston: Elsevier Science, 2008.

Rawson, Jean M. *Organic Agriculture in the United States: Program and Policy Issues.* CRS report for Congress, RL31595. Washington, DC: Congressional Research Service, 2008.

Rayner, Lisa. *The Sunny Side of Cooking: Solar Cooking and Other Ecologically Friendly Cooking Methods for the 21st Century.* Flagstaff, AZ: Lifeweaver, 2007.

Raynolds, Laura T., Douglas L. Murray, and John Wilkinson. *Fair Trade: The Challenges of Transforming Globalization.* London: Routledge, 2007.

Reeder, Kevin, Jonathan Tisdall, and Arne Cartridge. *Catalyst for Action: Towards an African Green Revolution.* Oslo, Norway: Yara International ASA, 2007.

Reeder, Richard, and Faqir Bagi. *Geographic Targeting Issues in the Delivery of Rural Development Assistance.* Washington, DC: U.S. Department of Agriculture, Economic Research Service, 2010.

Rees, Gareth J. G. *Safe Management of Shellfish and Harvest Waters.* London: International Water Association, 2010.

Reilly, Katherine V. *Food Aid Policy and Challenges.* New York: Nova Science Publishers, 2009.

Renewable Energy Programs in the 2008 Farm Bill. Little Rock: University of Arkansas, Division of Agriculture, Public Policy Center, 2009.

Richer, Alice C. *Food Allergies.* Westport, CT: Greenwood Press, 2009.

Ricketts, Cliff, and Kristina Ricketts. *Agribusiness: Fundamentals and Applications.* Clifton Park, NY: Delmar Cengage Learning, 2009.

Risk-Based Food Inspection Manual. Rome: Food and Agriculture Organization (FAO), 2008.

Robertson, Carol. *The Little Red Book of Wine Law: A Case of Legal Issues.* Chicago: American Bar Association, 2008.

Robinson, Nicholas A. *Strategies toward Sustainable Development: Implementing Agenda 21.* Dobbs Ferry, NY: Oceana Publications, 2004.

Rodger, Ellen. *Reducing Your Foodprint: Farming, Cooking, and Eating for a Healthy Planet.* St. Catherines, Ontario, Canada: Crabtree, 2010.

———. *The Biography of Spices (How Did That Get Here?).* New York: Crabtree, 2006.

Rogers, Heather. *Green Gone Wrong: How Our Economy Is Undermining the Environmental Revolution.* New York: Scribner, 2010.

Ronald, Pamela C., and Raoul W. Adamchak. *Tomorrow's Table: Organic Farming, Genetics, and the Future of Food.* New York: Oxford University Press, 2008.

Rosbottom, Betty. *Coffee.* San Francisco: Chronicle, 2007.

Rose, Sarah. *For All the Tea in China: How England Stole the World's Favorite Drink and Changed History.* New York: Viking, 2010.

Rosillo, Callé F., and Francis X. Johnson. *Food versus Fuel: An Informed Introduction to Biofuels.* London: Zed, 2010.

Roush, Margaret. *U.S. National Debate Topic, 2009–2010: Social Services for the Poor.* New York: H.W. Wilson Company, 2009.

Royte, Elizabeth. *Bottlemania: Big Business, Local Springs, and the Battle over America's Drinking Water.* New York: Bloomsbury, 2009.

Russell, Nicholas. *Food Preservatives.* New York: Kluwer Academic/Plenum, 2003.

Russo, Ruthann. *The Raw Food Lifestyle: The Philosophy and Nutrition behind Raw and Live Foods.* Berkeley, CA: North Atlantic Books, 2009.

Ryberg, Roben. *The Gluten-Free Kitchen: Over 135 Delicious Recipes for People with Gluten Intolerance or Wheat Allergy.* New York: Prima Health, 2000.

Safron, Jeremy. *The Raw Foods Resource Guide*. Berkeley, CA: Celestial Arts, 2005.

Sahi, Sarabjit S. *Rheological and Other Techniques and Methods Used in the Characterisation of Food Systems*. Campden, UK: Campden & Chorleywood Food Research Association, 2007.

Salt Assault: Brand-Name Comparisons of Processed Foods. Washington, DC: Center for Science in the Public Interest, 2008.

Sampson, Gary P. *The WTO and Sustainable Development*. New York: United Nations University Press, 2005.

Samuelson, Sheila, and Ed Williams. *The Feel-Good Heat: Pioneers of Corn and Biomass Energy*. North Liberty, IA: Ice Cube Press, 2007.

Satin, Morton. *Food Alert!: The Ultimate Sourcebook for Food Safety*, 2nd ed. New York: Facts on File, 2008.

Savage, Brent, and Nick Hildebrandt. *Bentley: The New Gastronomy*. London: Murdoch, 2010.

Saxen, Ron. *The Good Eater: The True Story of One Man's Struggle with Binge Eating Disorder*. Oakland, CA: New Harbinger, 2007.

Schünemann, Claus, and Günter Treu. *Baking, the Art and Science: A Practical Handbook for the Baking Industry*. Weimar, TX: Chips Books, 2007.

Schanbacher, William D. *The Politics of Food: The Global Conflict between Food Security and Food Sovereignty*. Westport, CT: Praeger Security International, 2010.

Schanzenbach, Diane W. *Do School Lunches Contribute to Childhood Obesity?* Chicago: Harris School of Public Policy, University of Chicago, 2005.

Schlosser, Eric. *Fast Food Nation: The Dark Side of the All-American Meal*. New York: Harper Perennial, 2005.

Schmid, Ronald F. *The Untold Story of Milk: The History, Politics and Science of Nature's Perfect Food: Raw Milk from Pasture-Fed Cows*. Washington, DC: NewTrends, 2009.

Schmitz, Andrew. *International Agricultural Trade Disputes: Case Studies in North America*. Calgary, Alberta, Canada: University of Calgary Press, 2005.

Schoenwolf, Gary C., and William J. Larsen. *Larsen's Human Embryology*, 4th ed. Philadelphia: Churchill Livingstone/Elsevier, 2009.

Scott, Nicky. *How to Make and Use Compost: The Ultimate Guide*. Totnes, UK: Green Books, 2009.

Seekamp, Gail, and Pierce Feiritear. *The Irish Famine*. Phibsboro, Dublin: Pixie Books, 2008.

Seeking Safer Packaging: Ranking Packaged Food Companies on BPA. Boston: Green Century Capital Management, 2009.

Shahidi, Fereidoon. *Quality of Fresh and Processed Foods*. New York: Kluwer Academic/Plenum, 2004.

Shapiro, Laura. *Perfection Salad: Women and Cooking at the Turn of the Century*. Berkeley: University of California Press, 2009.

———*Something from the Oven: Reinventing Dinner in 1950's America*. New York: Viking, 2004.

Sharlin, Judith, and Sari Edelstein. *Essentials of Life Cycle Nutrition*. Sudbury, MA: Jones and Bartlett, 2011.

Sharon, Michael. *Nutrients A to Z: A User's Guide to Foods, Herbs, Vitamins, Minerals & Supplements*, 5th ed. London: Carlton Books, 2009.

Shaw, Clare. *Nutrition and Cancer*. Chichester, West Sussex, UK: Blackwell, 2011.

Shaw, D. John. *World Food Security: A History since 1945*. Basingstoke, UK: Palgrave Macmillan, 2007.

Shepard, Sue. *Pickled, Potted, and Canned: How the Art and Science of Food Preserving Changed the World*. New York: Simon & Schuster, 2006.

Sherrow, Victoria. *Food Safety*. New York: Chelsea House, 2008.

Shetty, Kalidas. *Functional Foods and Biotechnology*. Boca Raton, FL: CRC/Taylor & Francis, 2007.

Shewfelt, Robert L., Bernhard Brueckner, Stanley E. Prussia, and Wojciech J. Florkowski. *Postharvest Handling: A Systems Approach*. Amsterdam and London: Elsevier/Academic Press, 2009.

Shrivastava, Mohan P. *Second Green Revolution vs. Rainbow Revolution*. New Delhi, India: Deep & Deep Publications, 2010.

Siegel, Michele, Judith Brisman, and Margot Weinshel. *Surviving an Eating Disorder: Strategies for Families and Friends*. New York: Collins Living, 2009.

Simms, Andrew, and Joe Smith. *Do Good Lives Have to Cost the Earth?* London: Constable, 2008.

Sinclair, Upton. *The Jungle*. New York: Simon & Schuster, 2004.

Singer, Peter, and Jim Mason. *The Way We Eat: Why Our Food Choices Matter*. Emmaus, PA: Rodale, 2006.

Singh, Dharm, and Devender Pratap Singh. *Hydroponics: Soilless Culture of Plants*. Jodhpur: Agrobios, 2009.

Singh, Ram J., and Prem P. Jauhar. *Grain Legumes.* Boca Raton, FL: Taylor & Francis, 2005.

Singh, Satya Narayan. *Climate Change and Crops.* Berlin: Springer, 2009.

Singh, Vijender. *Meat Inspection for Public Health.* New Delhi: Maxford Books, 2007.

Sinha, Archana, and T. A. John. *Food Security Matters: Social Dynamics and Determinants of Food Security.* New Delhi, India: Indian Social Institute, 2010.

Siva, Kumar M. V. K, and Ndegwa Ndiang'ui. *Climate and Land Degradation.* Berlin: Springer, 2007.

Slow Food Movement. *Slow Food U.S.A. 2003.* New York: Slow Food U.S.A., 2003.

Smith, Alisa, and J. B. MacKinnon. *Plenty: One Man, One Woman, and a Raucous Year of Eating Locally.* New York: Harmony Books, 2007.

Smith, Andrew F. *Eating History: Thirty Turning Points in the Making of American Cuisine.* New York: Columbia University Press, 2009.

———. *Encyclopedia of Junk Food and Fast Food.* Westport, CT: Greenwood Press, 2006.

———. *The Oxford Companion to American Food and Drink.* Oxford, UK, and New York: Oxford University Press, 2007.

Smith, Barry D., Uma Gupta, and Bhupendra S. Gupta. *Caffeine and Activation Theory: Effects on Health and Behavior.* Boca Raton, FL: CRC Press, 2007.

Smith, Drew. *Food Industry and the Internet: Making Real Money in the Virtual World.* Chichester, UK: John Wiley & Sons, Ltd., 2007.

Smith, Elspeth. *Healthy Heart.* London: Simon & Schuster, 2005.

Smith, Jeremy N., Chad Harder, and Sepp Jannotta. *Growing a Garden City: How Farmers, First Graders, Counselors, Troubled Teens, Foodies, a Homeless Shelter Chef, Single Mothers, and More Are Transforming Themselves and Their Neighborhoods through the Intersection of Local Agriculture and Community—and How You Can, Too.* New York: Skyhorse Publishing, 2010.

Smith, Wendy. *Give a Little: How Your Small Donations Can Transform Our World.* New York: Hyperion, 2009.

SNAP Can Make a Big Difference in Feeding Your Family. Salem, OR: DHS, Children, Adults and Families Division, Supplemental Nutrition Assistance Program, 2010.

SNAP: Supplemental Nutrition Assistance Program. Indianapolis, IN: Family and Social Services Administration, 2010.

Snow, Michelle. *The Wow Diet: Words of Wisdom from Leading World Religions.* Springville, UT: CFI, 2010.

Soetaert, Wim, and Erick J. Vandamme. *Biofuels.* Chichester, UK: Wiley, 2009.

Soluri, John. *Banana Cultures: Agriculture, Consumption, and Environmental Change in Honduras and the United States.* Austin: University of Texas Press, 2005.

Sommers, Brian J. *The Geography of Wine: How Landscapes, Cultures, Terroir, and the Weather Make a Good Drop.* New York: Plume, 2008.

Sommers, Christopher H., and Xuetong Fan. *Food Irradiation Research and Technology.* Ames, IA: Blackwell, 2006.

Sorai, Michio, ed. *Comprehensive Handbook of Calorimetry and Thermal Analysis.* Hoboken, NJ: John Wiley & Sons, 2004.

Sorte, Joanne, Inge Daeschel, and Carolina Amador. *Nutrition, Health, and Safety for Young Children: Promoting Wellness.* Boston: Pearson, 2011.

Sosa-Morales, Maria E., and Jorge F. Vélez-Ruiz. *Food Processing and Engineering Topics.* New York: Nova Science Publishers, 2009.

Soyinka, Wole. *Changing Attitudes and Behaviors: The Role of Africa's Cultural Leaders.* Washington, DC: International Food Policy Research Institute, 2007.

Spellman, Frank R. *Food Supply Protection and Homeland Security.* Lanham, MD: Government Institutes, 2008.

Spiller, Gene A. *Caffeine.* Boca Raton, FL: CRC Press, 1998.

Spurlock, Morgan. *Don't Eat This Book: Fast Food and the Supersizing of America.* New York: G. P. Putnam's Sons, 2005.

Staller, John E., Robert H. Tykot, and Bruce F. Benz. *Histories of Maize in MesoAmerica: Multidisciplinary Approaches.* Walnut Creek, CA: Left Coast Press, 2010.

Standage, Tom. *An Edible History of Humanity.* New York: Walker, 2009.

Stanfield, Maggie. *Trans Fats: The Time Bomb in Your Food.* London: Souvenir, 2008.

Stanford, Claire, ed. *World Hunger.* New York: H.W. Wilson, 2007.

Stark, Miriam T., Brenda J. Bowser, Lee Horne, and Carol Kramer. *Cultural Transmission and Material Culture: Breaking down Boundaries.* Tucson: University of Arizona Press, 2008.

Steinman, Harris. *Legumes, Nuts & Seeds: Allergy—Which Allergens?* Milnerton, South Africa: Allergy Resources International, 2008.

Stevenson, Richard J. *The Psychology of Flavour.* Oxford, UK: Oxford University Press, 2009.

Stewart, Kimberly L. *Eating between the Lines: The Supermarket Shopper's Guide to the Truth behind Food Labels.* New York: St. Martin's Griffin, 2007.

Stiglitz, Joseph E., and Andrew Charlton. *Fair Trade for All: How Trade Can Promote Development.* Oxford, UK: Oxford University Press, 2005.

Stone, Dori. *Beyond the Fence: A Journey to the Roots of the Migration Crisis.* Oakland, CA: Food First Books, 2009.

Strange, Marty. *Family Farming: A New Economic Vision.* Lincoln: University of Nebraska Press, 2008.

Stratton, Jayne E. *Raw Milk: Why Take the Risk?* Lincoln: Cooperative Extension, Institute of Agriculture and Natural Resources, University of Nebraska-Lincoln, 2004.

Street, Richard S. *Photographing Farmworkers in California.* Stanford, CA: Stanford University Press, 2004.

Stuart, Tristram. *The Bloodless Revolution: A Cultural History of Vegetarianism from 1600 to Modern Times.* New York: W.W. Norton & Co., 2007.

———. *Waste: Uncovering the Global Food Scandal.* New York: W.W. Norton & Co, 2009.

Sullivan, Dana, and Maureen Connolly. *Unbuttoned: Women Open Up about the Pleasures, Pains, and Politics of Breastfeeding.* Boston: Harvard Common Press, 2009.

Sunderland, John P., and Tsutomu Ichiki. *Genetically Engineered Mice Handbook.* Boca Raton, FL: CRC Press, 2004.

Sylvia, David M., et al. *Principles and Applications of Soil Microbiology,* 2nd ed. Upper Saddle River, NJ: Prentice Hall, 2004.

Tamayo, Efren J. *America's Family Farms.* New York: Nova Science Publishers, 2010.

Tamime, Adnan Y. *Structure of Dairy Products.* Oxford, UK: Blackwell, 2007.

Tansey, Geoff, and Tasmin Rajotte. *The Future Control of Food: A Guide to International Negotiations and Rules on Intellectual Property, Biodiversity and Food Security.* London: Earthscan, 2008.

Taub-Dix, Bonnie. *Read It before You Eat It: How to Decode Food Labels and Make the Healthiest Choice Every Time.* New York: Penguin Group, 2010.

Techamuanvivit, Pim, and Jenny Acheson. *The Foodie Handbook: The (Almost) Definitive Guide to Gastronomy.* San Francisco: Chronicle, 2009.

Teuscher, Eberhard, Ulrike Bauermann, and Monika Werner. *Medicinal Spices: A Handbook of Culinary Herbs, Spices, Spice Mixtures, and Their Essential Oils.* Boca Raton, FL: CRC Press, 2006.

Thaxton, Ralph A. *Catastrophe and Contention in Rural China: Mao's Great Leap Famine and the Origins of Righteous Resistance in Da Fo Village.* Cambridge, UK: Cambridge University Press, 2008.

Thomas, Harmon C. *Trade Reforms and Food Security: Country Case Studies and Synthesis.* Rome: Food and Agriculture of the United Nations (FAO), 2006.

Thompson, Kevin J. *Body Image, Eating Disorders, and Obesity in Youth: Assessment, Prevention, and Treatment,* 2nd ed. Washington, DC: American Psychological Association, 2008.

Thomson, Jennifer A. *Seeds for the Future: The Impact of Genetically Modified Crops on the Environment.* Ithaca, NY: Comstock Publishing Associates, 2007.

Tiess, Frederick J. *The Culinary Reference Guide: A Quick Resource for Chefs and Apprentices of over 700 Recipes, Formulas, Practical Cooking Methods, Applications and Terminology.* Matthews, NC: Le Guild Culinaire, 2006.

Toldrá, Fidel. *Safety of Meat and Processed Meat.* New York and London: Springer, 2009.

Travis-Henikoff, Carole A. *Dinner with a Cannibal: The Complete History of Mankind's Oldest Taboo.* Santa Monica, CA: Santa Monica Press, 2008.

Trubek, Amy B. *The Taste of Place: A Cultural Journey into Terroir.* Berkeley: University of California Press, 2008.

Tuberculosis and Queso Fresco: Eat Safe Cheese! San Diego, CA: County of San Diego, Health and Human Services Agency, TB Control Program, 2008.

Tzia, Constantina. *Quality and Safety Assurance in Food Processing.* Boca Raton, FL: CRC Press, 2011.

U.S. Agency for International Development. *Family Planning: Improving Lives in the Democratic Republic of Congo.* Washington, DC: United States Agency for International Development, 2006.

———. *Indila's Story: One Girl's Fight to Stop Child Marriage.* Washington, DC: United States Agency for International Development, 2007.

———. *USAID Primer: What We Do and How We Do It.* Washington, DC: U.S. Agency for International Development, 2006.

U.S. Department of Agriculture and U.S. Department of Health and Human Services. *Nutrition and Your Health: Dietary Guidelines for Americans*, 6th ed. Washington, DC: U.S. Government Printing Office, 2005.

U.S. Department of Health and Human Services. *2006 Guide to Surviving Bird Flu: Common Sense Strategies and Preparedness Plans—Avian Flu and H5N1 Threat*. Mount Laurel, NJ: Progressive Management, 2006.

U.S. Food and Drug Administration. *Draft Assessment of Bisphenol A for Use in Food Contact Applications*. Bethesda, MD: U.S. Food and Drug Administration, 2008.

U.S. Institute of Medicine. *Addressing Foodborne Threats to Health: Policies, Practices, and Global Coordination*. Washington, DC: National Academies Press, 2006.

U.S. Institute of Medicine, Forum on Microbial Threats. *Addressing Foodborne Threats to Health: Policies, Practices, and Global Coordination*. Washington, DC: National Academies Press, 2006.

U.S. National Library of Medicine and U.S. National Institutes of Health. *Caffeine*. Washington, DC.: U.S. National Library of Medicine, 2000. Also available at http://www.nlm.nih.gov/medlineplus/caffeine.html (accessed October 19, 2010).

Ungar, Peter S., ed. *Evolution of the Human Diet: The Known, The Unknown, and the Unknowable*. Oxford, UK: Oxford University Press, 2007.

United Nations. *Addressing the Global Food Crisis*. New York and Geneva: United Nations, 2008.

———*Extreme Weather Events, Water, and Health*. Geneva: United Nations ECE Secretariat, 2005.

——— *Necessity of Ending the Economic, Commercial and Financial Embargo Imposed by the United States of America against Cuba: Report of the Secretary-General*. New York: United Nations, 2004.

United Nations Standing Committee on Nutrition. *Working Together: To End Child Hunger and Undernutrition*. Geneva: United Nations, 2007.

United Nations World Food Programme: Indian Ocean Tsunami Emergency Operation. Colombo, Sri Lanka: United Nations World Food Programme, 2006.

Valentin, Rachel. *Transition into Organic Foods*. Montclair, NJ: Lehcar, 2004.

Veenhuizen, Rene. *Cities Farming for the Future: Urban Agriculture for Green and Productive Cities*. Ottawa, Canada: International Development Research Centre, 2006.

Vegetarian Network Victoria. *Eating Up the World: The Environmental Consequences of Human Food Choices*. Melbourne, Australia: Vegetarian Network, 2009.

Ventour, Lorrayne. *The Food We Waste*. Banbury, UK: WRAP, 2008.

Verkaar, Désirée, and Stefano Manti. *Everything You Need to Know about Pasta*. Nijmegen, The Netherlands: Miller, 2008.

Veryha, Wasyl. *A Case Study of Genocide in the Ukrainian Famine of 1921–1923: Famine as a Weapon*. Lewiston, NY: Edwin Mellen, 2007.

Vesler, Lyman W. *Malnutrition in the 21st Century*. New York: Nova Science Publishers, 2007.

Voegtlin, Walter L. *The Stone Age Diet: Based on Indepth Studies of Human Ecology and the Diet of Man*. New York: Vantage Press, 1975.

Voigt, Christina. *Sustainable Development as a Principle of International Law: Resolving Conflicts between Climate Measures and WTO Law*. Leiden, Holland: Martinus Nijhoff Publishers, 2009.

Walker, Marsha. *Breastfeeding Management for the Clinician: Using the Evidence*, 2nd ed. Sudbury, MA: Jones and Bartlett, 2011.

Walker, W. Allan, and Courtney Humphries. *The Harvard Medical School Guide to Healthy Eating during Pregnancy*. New York: McGraw-Hill, 2006.

Wallach, Lori, and Patrick Woodall. *Whose Trade Organization?: A Comprehensive Guide to the WTO*. New York: New Press, 2004.

Walters, Kerry S., and Lisa Portmess. *Religious Vegetarianism: From Hesiod to the Dalai Lama*. Albany: State University of New York Press, 2001.

Wang, Minghan. *Metabolic Syndrome: Underlying Mechanisms and Drug Therapies*. Hoboken, NJ: Wiley, 2011.

Wang, Wuyi, Thomas Krafft, and Frauke Kraas. *Global Change, Urbanization and Health*. Beijing: China Meteorological Press, 2006.

Wangen, Stephen. *Healthier without Wheat: A New Understanding of Wheat Allergies, Celiac Disease, and Non-Celiac Gluten Intolerance*. Seattle: Innate Health Pub, 2009.

Warner, Keith. *Agroecology in Action: Extending Alternative Agriculture through Social Networks*. Cambridge, MA: MIT, 2007.

Waterlow, John C., Andrew Tomkins, and Sally M. Grantham-McGregor. *Protein-Energy Malnutrition*. New Barnet, UK: Smith-Gordon, 2006.

Waters, Alice. *The Art of Simple Food: Notes, Lessons, and Recipes from a Delicious Revolution.* New York: Clarkson Potter, 2007.

———. *Edible Schoolyard: A Universal Idea.* San Francisco: Chronicle Books, 2008.

———. *In the Green Kitchen: Techniques to Learn by Heart.* New York: Clarkson Potter, 2010.

Waters, Tony. *The Persistence of Subsistence Agriculture: Life beneath the Level of the Marketplace.* Lanham, MD: Lexington Books, 2008.

Watson, Ronald R., and Victor R. Preedy. *Bioactive Foods in Promoting Health: Fruits and Vegetables.* Amsterdam and Boston: Academic Press, 2010.

Watts, Martin. *Corn Milling.* Oxford, UK: Shire, 2008.

Weber, Karl. *Food, Inc.: How Industrial Food Is Making Us Sicker, Fatter and Poorer—and What You Can Do about It.* New York: PublicAffairs, 2009.

Weinberg, Bennett Alan, and Bonnie K. Bealer. *The World of Caffeine: The Science and Culture of the World's Most Popular Drug.* New York: Routledge, 2001.

Weinstein, Jay. *The Ethical Gourmet.* New York: Broadway Books, 2006.

Weinstein, Miriam. *The Surprising Power of Family Meals: How Eating Together Makes Us Smarter, Stronger, Healthier and Happier.* Campbell, CA: Paw Prints, 2010.

Weirich, Paul. *Labeling Genetically Modified Food: The Philosophical and Legal Debate.* Oxford, UK: Oxford University Press, 2007.

Weis, Anthony J. *The Global Food Economy: The Battle for the Future of Farming.* London: Zed Books, 2007.

Wells, Donald. *The Spice Trade.* New York: Weigl Publishers, 2005.

Wells, Troth. *The Global Vegetarian Kitchen.* Oxford, UK: New Internationalist, 2010.

Werth, Nicolas. *Cannibal Island: Death in a Siberian Gulag.* Princeton, NJ: Princeton University Press, 2007.

Wesseler, Justus. *Environmental Costs and Benefits of Transgenic Crops.* Dordrecht, The Netherlands: Springer, 2005.

Whitley, Andrew. *Bread Matters: Why and How to Make Your Own,* new ed. London: Fourth Estate, 2009.

Wietersheim, Erika. *This Land Is My Land!: Motions and Emotions around Land in Namibia.* Windhoek, Namibia: Friedrich Ebert-Stiftung, 2008.

Wild, Alan. *Soils, Land and Food: Managing the Land during the Twenty-First Century.* Cambridge, UK: Cambridge University Press, 2003.

Wild, Antony. *Coffee: A Dark History.* New York: W.W. Norton, 2005.

Wiley, James. *The Banana: Empires, Trade Wars, and Globalization.* Lincoln: University of Nebraska Press, 2008.

Wilk, Richard R. *Fast Food/Slow Food: The Cultural Economy of the Global Food System.* Lanham, MD: Altamira Press, 2006.

Williams, Elizabeth M., and Stephanie J. Carter. *The A–Z Encyclopedia of Food Controversies and the Law.* Santa Barbara, CA: Greenwood, 2010.

Wilson, Michael. *Food Constituents and Oral Health: Current Status and Future Prospects.* Oxford, UK: Woodhead, 2009.

Wilson, William. *Wilson's Practical Meat Inspection.* Chichester: John Wiley & Sons, 2007.

Wilt, Timothy J. *Lactose Intolerance and Health.* Rockville, MD: Agency for Health Care Policy and Research, U.S. Dept. of Health and Human Services, 2010.

Winter, Ruth. *A Consumer's Dictionary of Food Additives.* New York: Three Rivers, 2009.

Witherly, Steven A. *Why Humans Like Junk Food.* New York: iUniverse, 2007.

Wolf, Joan B. *Is Breast Best?: Taking on the Breastfeeding Experts and the New High Stakes of Motherhood.* New York: New York University Press, 2011.

Wolin, Kathleen Y., and Jennifer M. Petrelli. *Obesity.* Santa Barbara, CA: Greenwood Press, 2009.

Wolter, Hans W. *Overcoming the World Water Crisis: Achieving Water, Food, and Environmental Security.* Colombo, Sri Lanka: Dialogue Secretariat, 2003.

Wood, Andrew G. *On the Border: Society and Culture between the United States and Mexico.* Lanham, MD: SR Books, 2004.

World Bank. *Changing the Face of the Waters: The Promise and Challenge of Sustainable Aquaculture.* Washington, DC: World Bank, 2007.

———. *Environmental Health and Child Survival: Epidemiology, Economics, Experiences.* Washington, DC: World Bank, 2008.

World Cancer Research Fund, American Institute for Cancer Research (AICR). *Food, Nutrition, Physical Activity, and the Prevention of Cancer: A Global Perspective.* Washington, DC: AICR, 2007.

World Commission on Environment and Development. *Our Common Future.* New York: Oxford University Press, 1987.

World Food Prize Foundation. *The Borlaug Dialogue: The 2006 Norman E. Borlaug International*

Symposium "The Green Revolution Redux". Des Moines, Iowa: World Food Prize Foundation, 2006.

———. *The World Food Prize: Twentieth Anniversary 1986–2006.* Des Moines, Iowa: World Food Prize Foundation, 2006.

World Food Programme. *Concrete Steps towards a Millennium Free from Hunger: The World Food Programme and the Millennium Development Goals.* Rome: World Food Programme, 2006.

World Trade Organization Agreement: Significance to Food Trade. Geneva: AFIST, 2005.

Wrangham, Richard W. *Catching Fire: How Cooking Made Us Human.* New York: Basic Books, 2009.

Wright, Simon, and Diane McCrea. *The Handbook of Organic and Fair Trade Food Marketing.* Oxford, UK: Blackwell Pub, 2007.

Xu, Wenying.*Eating Identities: Reading Food in Asian American Literature.* Honolulu: University of Hawaii Press, 2008.

Yam, Philip. *The Pathological Protein: Mad Cow, Chronic Wasting, and Other Deadly Prion Diseases.* New York: Springer, 2006.

Yellow Fats, Butter and Spreads. London: Mintel International, 2006.

Young, Sera L. *Craving Earth: Understanding Pica: The Urge to Eat Clay, Starch, Ice, and Chalk.* New York: Columbia University, 2010.

Young, Sophie, and Anuradha Mittal. *Food Price Crisis: A Wake up Call for Food Sovereignty.* Oakland, CA: Oakland Institute, 2008.

Young, Tomme. *Genetically Modified Organisms and Biosafety: A Background Paper for Decision-Makers and Others to Assist in Consideration of GMO Issues.* Gland, Switzerland: World Conservation Union, 2004.

Zanini De Vita, Oretta. *Encyclopedia of Pasta.* Berkeley: University of California Press, 2009.

Zdruli, Pandi, et al., eds. *Land Degradation and Desertification: Assessment, Mitigation and Remediation.* Dordrecht, The Netherlands: Springer, 2010.

Zimmern, Andrew. *The Bizarre Truth: How I Walked out the Door Mouth First and Came Back Shaking My Head.* New York: Broadway Books, 2009.

PERIODICALS

"A+, for Apples. Short on Traditional Nutrients, but Long on Phytonutrients That Fight Chronic Diseases." *Environmental Nutrition* 29, no. 9 (2006): 8.

Abbott, Alison. "European Disarray on Transgenic Crops." *Nature* 457, no. 7232 (2009): 946–947.

Adam, Rachelle. "Missing the 2010 Biodiversity Target: A Wake-Up Call for the Convention on Biodiversity?" *Colorado Journal of International Environmental Law and Policy* 21, no. 1 (2010): 123–166.

"Addiction: Junk-Food Junkies." *Nature* 464, no. 7289 (2010): 652.

Afele, Mawusi. "Street Food Boom in Ghana Spurs Calls for Better Hygiene." *Bulletin of the World Health Organization* 84, no. 10 (2006): 772–773.

"Agribusiness Is Booming." *Business Week New York* (October 20, 2008): 50–51.

Ahn, Sam S., et al. "Consumer Attitudes and Response to New Food Allergen Labeling." *The Journal of Allergy and Clinical Immunology* 121, no. 2, supplement 1 (2008): S182.

Akamatsu, Rie. "A Content Analysis of the Japanese Interpretation of 'Eating a Balanced Diet'." *Psychological Reports* 100, no. 3 (2007): 727–730.

Allen, Kimberly Jordan. "Eating Right Edible History: Heirloom Fruits and Vegetables." *E: The Environmental Magazine* 16, no. 3 (2005): 42–43.

Alonso, Alvaro, and Miguel A. Martinez-Gonzalez. "Mediterranean Diet, Lifestyle Factors, and Mortality." *JAMA: The Journal of the American Medical Association* 293, no. 6 (2005): 674.

Alonso, Alvaro, Valentia Ruiz-Gutierrez, and Miguel A. Martinez-Gonzalez. "Monounsaturated Fatty Acids, Olive Oil and Blood Pressure: Epidemiological, Clinical and Experimental Evidence." *Public Health Nutrition* 9, no. 2 (2006): 251–257.

Altekruse, Sean F., et al. "Salmonella Enteritidis in Broiler Chickens, United States, 2000–2005." *Emerging Infectious Diseases* 12, no. 12 (2006): 1848–1852.

Altieri, Miguel A. "Agroecology, Small Farms, and Food Sovereignty." *Monthly Review New York* 61, no. 3 (2009): 102–113.

American Academy of Pediatrics Committee on Nutrition. "Prevention of Pediatric Overweight and Obesity." *Pediatrics* 112, no. 2 (2003): 424–430.

———. "Soft Drinks in Schools." *Pediatrics* 112, no. 1 (2004): 152–154.

"America's New 'Food Pyramid.'" *Lancet* 365, no. 9470 (2005): 1516.

Anderson, Bridget. "Migration, Immigration Controls and the Fashioning of Precarious Workers."

Work, Employment and Society 24, no. 2 (2010): 300–317.

Anderson-Fye, Eileen P., and Jielu Lin. "Belief and Behavior Aspects of the Eat-26: The Case of Schoolgirls in Belize." *Culture, Medicine, and Psychiatry* 33, no. 4 (2009): 623–638.

Angell, Sonia Y. "Emerging Opportunities for Monitoring the Nutritional Content of Processed Foods." *The American Journal of Clinical Nutrition* 91, no. 2 (2010): 298–299.

Angell, Sonia Y., et al. "Cholesterol Control beyond the Clinic: New York City's Trans Fat Restriction." *Annals of Internal Medicine* 151, no. 2 (2009): 129–134.

Anslow, Mark. "News Focus — Can We Really Grow Good Food without Soil? Mark Anslow Looks into Hydroponics." *The Ecologist* 38, no. 4 (2008): 12–13.

Archibald, John M. "Genomics: Green Evolution, Green Revolution." *Science* 324, no. 5924 (2009): 191–192.

"Arguing over Unpasteurised Milk: Raw Deal." *Economist London* (June 10, 2010): 62.

Auad, Sheyla, and Paula S. Moynihan. "Nutrition & Oral Health—Diet and Dental Erosion." *Quintessence International* (February 2007): 130–133.

Bagla, Pallava. "A Guru of the Green Revolution Reflects on Borlaug's Legacy." *Science* 5951 (2009): 361.

Bales, Connie W. "What Is the 'Right Diet' for a Healthy Old Age?" *Journal of Nutrition for the Elderly* 29, no. 1 (2010): 2–3.

Barham, Peter, et al. "Molecular Gastronomy: A New Emerging Scientific Discipline." *Chemical Reviews* 110, no. 4 (2010): 2313–2365.

Barnard, Neal D., et al. "A Low-Fat Vegan Diet and a Conventional Diabetes Diet in the Treatment of Type 2 Diabetes: A Randomized, Controlled, 74-Wk Clinical Trial." *The American Journal of Clinical Nutrition* 89, no. 5 (2009): 1588–1596.

Barrett, Jennifer. "The Gurus' Guide to Daily Nutrition." *Newsweek* 147, no. 3 (2006): 64–69.

Beardsall, Kathryn, Barbro M. S. Diderholm, and David B. Dunger. "Insulin and Carbohydrate Metabolism." *Best Practice & Research, Clinical Endocrinology & Metabolism* 22, no. 1 (2008): 41–55.

Beato, Maria Serema, Ilaria Capua, and Dennis J. Alexander. "Avian Influenza Viruses in Poultry Products: A Review." *Avian Pathology: Journal of the W.V.P.A.* 38, no. 3 (2009): 193–200.

Beddington, John. "Food Security: Contributions from Science to a New and Greener Revolution." *Philosophical Transactions of the Royal Society of London. Series B, Biological Sciences* 365, no. 1537 (2010): 61–71.

Benhin, James K. A. "Agriculture and Deforestation in the Tropics: A Critical Theoretical and Empirical Review." *Ambio* 351 (2006): 9.

Bennett, Elizabeth, L., et al. "Hunting for Consensus: Reconciling Bushmeat Harvest, Conservation, and Development Policy in West and Central Africa." *Conservation Biology* 21, no. 3, (2006): 884–887.

Berfield, Susan, and Michael Arndt. "Kraft's Sugar Rush." *Business Week New York*, no. 4164 (January 25, 2010): 36–39.

Bergstresser, Sara M. "Cannibal Talk: The Man-Eating Myth and Human Sacrifice in the South Seas." *Ethos* 38, no. 1 (2010): 1–3.

Bertrand, Sue. "Heifer International: Passing on the Gift." *UN Chronicle* 41, no. 2 (2004): 65.

Besky, Sarah. "Can a Plantation Be Fair? Paradoxes and Possibilities in Fair Trade Darjeeling Tea Certification." *Anthropology of Work Review* 29, no. 1 (2008): 1–9.

Betts, Bryan. "Beer Comes Clean. Brewing Processes Old and New." *Engineering and Technology* 5, no. 10 (2010): 59–61.

Bibbins-Domingo, Kirsten, et al. "Projected Effect of Dietary Salt Reductions on Future Cardiovascular Disease." *The New England Journal of Medicine* 362, no. 7 (2010): 590–599.

Binswanger-Mkhize, Hans, Alex McCalla, and Praful Patel. "Structural Transformation and African Agriculture." *Global Journal of Emerging Market Economies* 2, no. 2 (2010): 113–152.

"Biofuels: Food, Fuel and Climate Change." *OPEC Bulletin* 40, no. 5 (2009): 72–75.

"Biotechnology—Key Patent for Roundup Ready Trait Could Be Revoked." *Food Chemical News* 49, no. 6 (2007): 6.

Blades, Mabel. "A Preliminary Study of School Lunches." *Nutrition & Food Science* 38, no. 6 (2008): 534–539.

Blair, Dorothy. "The Child in the Garden: An Evaluative Review of the Benefits of School Gardening." *Journal of Environmental Education* 40, no. 2 (2009): 15–38.

Blinder, Barton J., and Christina Salama. "An Update on Pica: Prevalence, Contributing Causes, and Treatment." *Psychiatric Times* 25, no. 6 (2008): 1–13.

"Blood Risk of vCJD Highlighted." *New Scientist* 2582 (December 16, 2006): 7.

Bobrow-Strain, Aaron. "White Bread Bio-Politics: Purity, Health, and the Triumph of Industrial Baking." *Cultural Geographies* 15, no. 1 (2008): 19–40.

Boddiger, David. "Boosting Biofuel Crops Could Threaten Food Security." *Lancet* 370, no. 9591 (2007): 923–924.

Bone, Eugenia. "Sweet Temptations—What Goes into Our Passion for Chocolate?" *Forbes* 39 (2006): 162.

Borchers, Andrea T., Frank Hagie, Carl L. Keen, and M. Eric Gershwin. "The History and Contemporary Challenges of the US Food and Drug Administration." *Clinical Therapeutics* 29, no. 1 (2007): 1–16.

Borre, Kristen, Luke Ertle, and Mariaelisa Graff. "Working to Eat: Vulnerability, Food Insecurity, and Obesity among Migrant and Seasonal Farmworker Families." *American Journal of Industrial Medicine* 53, no. 4 (2010): 443–462.

Borzekowski, Dina L. G., Summer Schenk, Jenny S. Wilson, and Rebecka Peebles. "E-Ana and E-Mia: A Content Analysis of Pro-Eating Disorder Web Sites." *American Journal of Public Health* 100, no. 8 (2010): 1526–1535.

"Bottled-Water Industry—Tap v. Bottle." *The Economist* 388, no. 8589 (2008): 85.

Bourne, Joel K., Jr. "The End of Plenty—Our Hot and Hungry World Could Face a Perpetual Food Crisis." *National Geographic* 215, no. 6 (2009): 26–59.

Bowne, Mary. "A Comparative Study of Parental Behaviors and Children's Eating Habits." *ICAN: Infant, Child, & Adolescent Nutrition* 1, no.1 (2009): 11–14.

"Breastfeeding—Still Not Reaching the Target." *Public Health Nutrition* 13, no. 6 (2010): 749–750.

Brett, John. "The Political-Economics of Developing Markets versus Satisfying Food Needs." *Food and Foodways* 18, nos. 1–2 (2010): 28–42.

Brierley, Andrew S. "Fisheries Ecology: Hunger for Shark Fin Soup Drives Clam Chowder off the Menu." *Current Biology* 17, no. 14 (2007): R555–R557.

Broadway, Michael, and Donald Stull. "The Wages of Food Factories." *Food and Foodways* 18, nos. 1–2 (2010): 43–65.

Brodie, Mollyann, et al. "Experiences of Hurricane Katrina Evacuees in Houston Shelters: Implications for Future Planning." *American Journal of Public Health* 96, no. 8 (2006): 1402–1408.

Brody, Aaron L. "How Green Is Food Waste?" *Food Technology* 62, no. 6 (2008): 121.

Brown, Cheryl, and Stacy Miller. "The Impacts of Local Markets: A Review of Research on Farmers Markets and Community Supported Agriculture (CSA)." *American Journal of Agricultural Economics* 90, no. 5 (2008): 1296–1302.

Brown, David, J. Christopher, and Scott Desposato. "Who Gives, Who Receives, and Who Wins?" *Comparative Political Studies* 41, no. 1 (2008): 24–47.

Brown, Molly E., and Christopher C. Funk. "Climate: Food Security under Climate Change." *Science* 319, no. 5863 (2008): 580–581.

Bryant-Waugh, Rachel, Laura Markham, Richard E. Kreipe, and R. Timothy Walsh. "Feeding and Eating Disorders in Childhood." *International Journal of Eating Disorders* 43, no. 2 (2010): 98–111.

Burklow, Kathleen A., and Thomas Linscheid. "Rapid Inpatient Behavioral Treatment for Choking Phobia in Children." *Children's Health Care* 33, no. 2 (2004): 93–107.

Butler, Declan. "Food Crisis Spurs Research Spending." *Nature* 453, no. 7191 (2008): 1–2.

Buzby, Jean, and Hodan Farah. "Chicken Consumption Continues Longrun Rise." *Amber Waves* 4, no. 2 (April 2006): 5.

Cabrita, Joel, and Angel F. Mendez-Montoya. "The Theology of Food: Eating and the Eucharist. *Journal of the American Academy of Religion* 78, no. 3 (2010): 824–827.

Cade, Janet E., E. Faye Taylor, Victoria J. Burley, and Darren C. Greenwood. "Common Dietary Patterns and Risk of Breast Cancer: Analysis from the United Kingdom Women's Cohort Study." *Nutrition and Cancer* 62, no. 3 (2010): 300–306.

Caëtano, B., et al. "Soya Phytonutrients Act on a Panel of Genes Implicated with BRCA1 and BRCA2 Oncosuppressors in Human Breast Cell Lines." *The British Journal of Nutrition* 95, no. 2 (2006): 406–413.

Callahan, Gerald N. "Eating Dirt." *Emerging Infectious Diseases* 9, no. 8 (2003): 1016–1021.

Cannuscio, Carolyn C., Eve E. Weiss, and David A. Asch. "The Contribution of Urban Foodways to Health Disparities." *Journal of Urban Health: Bulletin of the New York Academy of Medicine* 87, no. 3 (2010): 381–393.

Cao, Xu-Liang, Jeannette Corriveau, and Svetlana Popovic. "Migration of Bisphenol A from Can Coatings to Liquid Infant Formula during

Storage at Room Temperature." *Journal of Food Protection* 72, no. 1212 (2009): 2571–2574.

Cappuccio, Franco, and Simon Capewell. "Sprinkle with Care: Excess Dietary Salt Is a Big Killer, So Who's Fighting the Moves to Cut Back?" *New Scientist* 2758 (May 1, 2010): 22.

Carnegie, Michelle. "Reviews: Family Farms: Survival and Prospect. A World-Wide Analysis." *Geographical Research* 47, no. 3 (2009): 339–340.

Carpenter, Daniel, and Gisela Sin. "Policy Tragedy and the Emergence of Regulation: The Food, Drug, and Cosmetic Act of 1938." *Studies in American Political Development* 21, no. 2 (2007): 149–180.

Carr, David. "Population and Deforestation: Why Rural Migration Matters." *Progress in Human Geography* 33, no. 3 (2009): 355–378.

Carr, Edward. "The Millennium Village Project and African Development." *Progress in Development Studies* 8, no. 4 (2008): 333–344.

Carrasco, Elena, Fernando Perez-Rodriguez, Antonia Valero, Rosa M. Garcia-Gimeno, and Gonzalo Zurera. "Risk Assessment and Management of *Listeria Monocytogenes* in Ready-to-Eat Lettuce Salads." *Comprehensive Reviews in Food Science and Food Safety* 9, no. 5 (2010): 498–512.

Casotti, Leticia. "He Who Eats Alone Will Die Alone? An Exploratory Study of the Meanings of the Food of Celebration." *Latin American Business Review* 6, no. 4 (2005): 69–84.

Cassel, Chris, Joseph Miller, Todd Biddle, and Michael Benner. "Food to Me: A Farm-to-Table Program for Middle School Children." *Agricultural Education Magazine* 77, no. 1 (2004): 19–22.

"CDC Recommends Stricter Rules against Raw Milk Products." *Food Chemical News* 50, no. 46 (2009): 10.

Centers for Disease Control and Prevention (CDC). "Multistate Outbreak of Salmonella Infections Associated with Peanut Butter and Peanut Butter-Containing Products—United States, 2008–2009." *Morbidity and Mortality Weekly Report* 58 (January 29, 2009): 1–6.

Chan, Lingtak-Neander. "A 'Gutsy Move': Tackling Enteral Feeding Intolerance in Critically Ill Patients." *Nutrition in Clinical Practice* 25, no. 1 (2010): 10–12.

Chang, Huan J., Alison E. Burke, and Richard M. Glass. "Food Allergies." *JAMA: The Journal of the American Medical Association* 303, no. 18 (2010): 1876.

Charles, Dan. "U.S. Courts Say Transgenic Crops Need Tighter Scrutiny." *Science* 315, no. 5815 (2007): 1069.

Charney, Madeleine K. "FoodRoutes Network and the Local Food Movement." *Journal of Agricultural and Food Information* 10, no. 3 (2009): 173–181.

"Check Out Cherries. Sweet or Tart, They're Packed with Disease-Preventing Phytonutrients." *Environmental Nutrition* 31, no. 6 (2008): 8.

"Chemistry in Cooking: Molecular Gastronomy." *The Economist* 385, no. 8560 (2007): 140.

Chen, Guanyi, Ming Ying, and Weizhun Li. "Enzymatic Conversion of Waste Cooking Oils into Alternative Fuel-Biodiesel." *Applied Biochemistry and Biotechnology* 132, nos. 1–3 (2006): 129–132.

Chen, Ruey-Shun, et al. "Using RFID Technology in Food Produce Traceability." *WSEAS Transactions on Information Science and Applications* 5, no. 11 (2008): 1551–1560.

Chin, Gilbert. "Dark Chocolate." *Science* 329, no. 5989 (2010): 259.

Chiu, Ching-Ju, and Linda A. Wray. "Factors Predicting Glycemic Control in Middle-Aged and Older Adults with Type 2 Diabetes." *Preventing Chronic Disease* 7, no. 1 (2010).

"Chocolate Helps Your Brain." *Psychology Today* 40, no. 4 (2007): 54.

Christian, Thomas. "Grocery Store Access and the Food Insecurity-Obesity Paradox." *Journal of Hunger & Environmental Nutrition* 5, no. 3 (2010): 360–369.

Chyau, James. "Casting a Global Safety Net—a Framework for Food Safety in the Age of Globalization." *Food and Drug Law Journal* 64, no. 2 (2009): 313–334.

Ciftcioglu, Gurhan, et al. "Survival of *Escherichia Coli* O157:H7 in Minced Meat and Hamburger Patties." *Journal of Food, Agriculture and Environment* 6, no. 1 (2008): 24–27.

Clark, Maggie L., et al. "Indoor Air Pollution, Cookstove Quality, and Housing Characteristics in Two Honduran Communities." *Environmental Research* 110, no. 1 (2010): 12–18.

Clarke, Shelley. "Use of Shark Fin Trade Data to Estimate Historic Total Shark Removals in the Atlantic Ocean." *Aquatic Living Resources* 21, no. 4 (2008): 373–382.

Cole, Thomas B. "The Tea." *JAMA: The Journal of the American Medical Association* 301, no. 9 (2009): 914.

Collinge, John, et al. "Kuru in the 21st Century—an Acquired Human Prion Disease with Very Long Incubation Periods." *Lancet* 367, no. 9528 (2006): 2068–2074.

Collison, Kate S., et al. "Sugar-Sweetened Carbonated Beverage Consumption Correlates with BMI, Waist Circumference, and Poor Dietary Choices in School Children." *BMC Public Health* 10, no. 234 (2010): 34ff.

Connolly, Rebecca. "The World Trade Organization Biotechnology Products Dispute: A New Era for Genetically Modified Food?" *Environmental and Planning Law Journal* 26, no. 5 (2009): 363–374.

Contreras, Joseph. "Failed Plan: After Five Years and Billions of U.S. Aid in the Drug War, Cocaine Production Still Thrives." *Newsweek International* (August 29, 2005): 40.

Cooney, Catherine M. "Sustainable Agriculture Delivers the Crops." *Environmental Science & Technology* 40, no. 4 (2006): 1091–1092.

"The Co-op's Innovative Drive to Promote Fresh Food Sales." *Grocer London* (June 5, 2010): 8–11.

"Could You Have an Eating Disorder? Learn the Signs—and Get the Help You Need." *Seventeen* (August 2008): 158.

Cousins, John, Kevin O'Gorman, and Marc Stierand. "Molecular Gastronomy: Cuisine Innovation or Modern Day Alchemy?" *International Journal of Contemporary Hospitality Management* 22, no. 3 (2010): 399–415.

Cox, Andrew, Daniel Chicksand, and Martin Palmer. "Stairways to Heaven or Treadmills to Oblivion?: Creating Sustainable Strategies in Red Meat Supply Chains." *British Food Journal* 109, no. 9 (2007): 689–720.

Cressey, Daniel. "Aquaculture: Future Fish." *Nature* 458, no. 7237 (2009): 398–400.

Culp, Jennifer, Robert A. Bell, and Diana Cassady. "Characteristics of Food Industry Web Sites and Advergames Targeting Children." *Journal of Nutrition Education and Behavior* 42, no. 3 (2010): 197–201.

Dalton, Craig B., Michelle A. Cretikos, and David N. Durrheim. "A Food 'Lifeboat': Food and Nutrition Considerations in the Event of a Pandemic or Other Catastrophe." *The Medical Journal of Australia* 188, no. 11 (2008): 679.

Dangour, Alan D., et al. "Nutritional Quality of Organic Foods: A Systematic Review." *The American Journal of Clinical Nutrition* 90, no. 3 (2009): 680–685.

Daponte, Beth, and Shannon Bade. "How the Private Food Assistance Network Evolved: Interactions between Public and Private Responses to Hunger." *Nonprofit and Voluntary Sector Quarterly* 35, no. 4 (2006): 668–690.

Darnhofer, Ika. "Strategies of Family Farms to Strengthen Their Resilience." *Environmental Policy and Governance* 20, no. 4 (2010): 212–222.

Dauvergne, Peter, and Kate Neville. "Forests, Food, and Fuel in the Tropics: The Uneven Social and Ecological Consequences of the Emerging Political Economy of Biofuels." *Journal of Peasant Studies* 37, no. 4 (2010): 631–660.

Day, Michael. "Deadline to End World Hunger by 2025 Is Being Allowed to 'Quietly Wither Away.'" *BMJ: British Medical Journal* 339 (2009): b4977.

de Leiris, Joël, and Francois Boucher. "Does Wine Consumption Explain the French Paradox?" *Dialogues in Cardiovascular Medicine* 13, no. 3 (2008): 183–192.

de Solier, Isabelle. "Liquid Nitrogen Pistachios: Molecular Gastronomy, Elbulli, and Foodies." *European Journal of Cultural Studies* 13, no. 2 (2010): 155–170.

Debevec, Liza, and Blanka Tivadar. "Making Connections through Foodways: Contemporary Issues in Anthropological and Sociological Studies of Food." *Anthropological Notebooks* 12, no. 1 (2006): 5–16.

DeHaven, W. Ron, and Ruth Goldberg. "Animal Health: Foundation of a Safe, Secure, and Abundant Food Supply." *Journal of Veterinary Medical Education* 33, no. 4 (2006): 496–501.

Denton, Fatma. "Climate Change Vulnerability, Impacts, and Adaptation: Why Does Gender Matter?" *Gender & Development* 10, no. 2 (2002): 10–20.

DePaola, Dominick, and Riva Touger-Decker. "Nutrition and Dental Medicine: Where Is the Connection?" *Journal of the American Dental Association* 137, no. 9 (2006): 1208–1210.

Derenne, Jennifer, and Eugene Beresin. "Body Image, Media, and Eating Disorders." *Academic Psychiatry* 30 (May–June 2006): 257–261.

Despommier, Dickson. "The Rise of Vertical Farms." *Scientific American* 301, no. 5 (2009): 80–87.

Devadoss, Stephen. "Optimal Tariff Analysis of India's Apple Import Restrictions." *Journal of Food Products Marketing* 13, no. 1 (2006): 45–59.

Di Genova, Tanya, and Harvey Guyda. "Infants and Children Consuming Atypical Diets: Vegetarianism and Macrobiotics." *Paediatrics & Child Health* 12, no. 3 (2007): 185–188.

"Diabetes and Cancer: A Dietary Portfolio for Management and Prevention of Heart Disease." *Proceedings of the Nutrition Society* 69, no. 1 (2010): 39–44.

Dias-Neto, Marina, Mariana Pintalhao, Mariana Ferreira, and Nuno Lunet. "Salt Intake and Risk of Gastric Intestinal Metaplasia: Systematic Review and Meta-Analysis." *Nutrition and Cancer* 62, no. 2 (2010): 133–147.

"Diet Coke with a Shot of Vitamins." *Newsweek* 149, no. 20 (May 14, 2007): 60–61.

"Dietary Supplements—Patent Protections Called Key to New Dietary Ingredient Safety." *Food Chemical News* 47, no. 14 (2005): 17.

Dietler, Michael. "Alcohol: Anthropological/Archaeological Perspectives." *Annual Review of Anthropology* 35, no. 229 (2006): 229–249.

Diouf, Jacques. "Food Security and the Challenge of the MDGs—the Road Ahead." *UN Chronicle* 44, no. 4 (2007): 17–18.

"Do Handouts Harm?: Rethinking Food Aid." *Time New York, American Edition* 169, no. 26 (2007): 64–66.

Donnelty, Catherine W. "Perspective—Raw-Milk Cheeses Can Be Produced Safely." *Food Technology* 60, no. 4 (2006): 100.

Donohue, Caitlin. "Out of Reach: How the Sustainable Local Food Movement Neglects Poor Workers and Eaters." *San Francisco Bay Guardian* 44, no. 9 (2010): 12–14.

Dowlah, Caf. "The Politics and Economics of Food and Famine in Bangladesh in the Early 1970s—with Special Reference to Amartya Sen's Interpretation of the 1974 Famine." *International Journal of Social Welfare* 15, no. 4 (2006): 344–356.

Drechsel, Pay, and Stefan Dongus. "Dynamics and Sustainability of Urban Agriculture: Examples from Sub-Saharan Africa." *Sustainability Science* 5, no. 1 (2010): 69–78.

Dregne, Harold E. "Land Degradation in the Drylands." *Arid Land Research and Management* 16, no. 2 (2002): 99–132.

Drummond, Sandra. "Bringing the Sense Back into Healthy Eating Advice." *The Journal of Family Health Care* 16, no. 5 (2006): 143–145.

Duffy, Christine, Kimberly Perez, and Ann Partridge. "Implications of Phytoestrogen Intake for Breast Cancer." *CA: A Cancer Journal for Clinicians* 57, no. 5 (2007): 260–277.

Dullo, Esther, Michael Greenstone, and Rema Hanna. "Cooking Stoves, Indoor Air Pollution and Respiratory Health in Rural Orissa." *Economic and Political Weekly* 43, no. 32 (2008): 71–76.

Dunn-Emke, Stacey R., et al. "Nutrient Adequacy of a Very Low-Fat Vegan Diet." *Journal of the American Dietetic Association* 105, no. 9 (2005): 1442–1446.

Dupin, Chris. "Finding a Way into Cuba: Despite Embargo, U.S. Is Cuba's Largest Supplier of Food Products." *American Shipper* 48, no. 10 (2006): 78–79.

"Early Warning—the Energy-Food-Water-Security Matrix." *Defense & Foreign Affairs* 36, no. 6 (2008): 2.

Eastwood, Robert, Johann Kirsten, and Michael Lipton. "Premature Deagriculturalisation? Land Inequality and Rural Dependency in Limpopo Province, South Africa." *The Journal of Development Studies* 42, no. 8 (2006): 1325–1349.

Ebrahim, Shah, et al. "The Effect of Rural-to-Urban Migration on Obesity and Diabetes in India: A Cross-Sectional Study." *Plos Medicine* 7, no. 4 (2010): e1000268.

"E-business: Internet Food Sales Rise by 50 Percent at Tesco." *Computer Weekly* (April 22, 2008): 4.

"The Effects of a Mediterranean Diet on Risk Factors for Heart Disease." Summaries for Patients. *Annals of Internal Medicine* 145, no. 1 (2006): 1–11.

"Egypt: Not by Bread Alone." *Economist* 387, no. 8575 (2008): 47.

Eigenmann, Philippe A., and Charles A. Haenggeli. "Food Colourings, Preservatives, and Hyperactivity." *Lancet* 370, no. 9598 (2007): 1524–1525.

Einarsen, Kari, and Reidar Mykletun. "Exploring the Success of the Gladmatfestival (the Stavanger Food Festival)." *Scandinavian Journal of Hospitality and Tourism* 9 (2009): 225–248.

Eisenberg, Marla E., et al. "Correlations between Family Meals and Psychosocial Well-being among Adolescents." *Archives of Pediatrics & Adolescent Medicine* 158, no. 8 (2004): 792–796.

El Masri, Firas, et al. "Is the So-Called French Paradox a Reality?" *Journal of Bone and Joint Surgery. British Volume* 92, no. 3 (2010): 342–348.

Elias, Merrill F., and Amanda L. Goodell. "Diet and Exercise: Blood Pressure and Cognition: To Protect and Serve." *Hypertension* 55, no. 6 (2010): 1296–1298.

Elinder, Liselotte S. "Obesity, Hunger, and Agriculture: The Damaging Role of Subsidies." *BMJ:*

British Medical Journal (clinical research ed.) 331, no. 7528 (2005): 1333–1336.

Erber, Eva, et al. "Dietary Patterns and Risk for Diabetes." *Diabetes Care* 33, no. 3 (2010): 532–538.

"Escherichia Coli 0157:h7 Infections in Children Associated with Raw Milk and Raw Colostrum from Cows—California, 2006." *Morbidity and Mortality Weekly Report* 57, no. 23 (2008): 625–628.

Esposito, Katherine, Miryam Ciotola, and Dario Giugliano. "Low-Carbohydrate Diet and Coronary Heart Disease in Women." *The New England Journal of Medicine* 356, no. 7 (2007): 750–752.

Etheridge, Stacey M. "Paralytic Shellfish Poisoning: Seafood Safety and Human Health Perspectives." *Toxicon* 56, no. 2 (2010): 108–122.

"EU Embargo Jolts South American Beef Trade." *Food Chemical News* 49, no. 51 (2008): 17.

"EU Parliament Panel Votes to Ban Food from Clones." *Food Chemical News* 52, no. 9 (2010): 6–7.

"EU—GMOs: Commission Defeated on Food Bans." *Environmental Policy and Law* 35, nos. 4–5 (2005): 201–202.

"European Food Safety Authority Dismisses Safety Concerns over Bisphenol A." *Pesticide and Toxic Chemical News* 35, no. 15 (2007): 1.

"European Food Safety Authority Plans to Review Bisphenol A." *Pesticide and Toxic Chemical News* 36, no. 27 (2008): 11–12.

"The Everglades—Sugar and Grass." *The Economist* 389, no. 8610 (2008): 55.

Evers, Catharine, F. Marijn Stok, and Denise T. D. de Ridder. "Feeding Your Feelings: Emotion Regulation Strategies and Emotional Eating." *Personality and Social Psychology Bulletin* 36, no. 6 (2010): 792–804.

"The Fad for Functional Foods: Artificial Success." *Economist* 392, no. 8650 (2009): 84.

"Fair Trade?" *Nature* 455, no. 7216 (2008): 1008.

Fairlie, Simon, and Richard Young. "Meat: Eco Villain or Victim of Spin?" *The Ecologist* 38, no. 8 (2008): 14.

"Family of Man—School Lunches." *National Geographic* 210, no. 3 (2006): 14.

"Family of Man—Street Food." *National Geographic* 211, no. 2 (2007): 14.

"Famine, Prices, and Aid—Food for Thought." *The Economist* 386, no. 8573 (2008): 63.

Fariss, Christopher J. "The Strategic Substitution of United States Foreign Aid." *Foreign Policy Analysis* 6, no. 2 (2010): 107–131.

"The Farm Bill—A Harvest of Disgrace." *The Economist* 387, no. 8581 (2008): 61.

"The Farm Bill—Long Time in Germination." *The Economist* 386, no. 8573 (2008): 52.

"Farm Bill Reduces Support for Corn Ethanol." *Nature* 453, no. 7193 (2008): 270.

"Fast Food: Good and Hungry." *Economist London Economist Newspaper Limited* no. 8687 (June 19, 2010): 65.

Fast, Yvona. "We Heart Pasta." *E: The Environmental Magazine* 21, no. 5 (2010): 45.

"FDA Changes Portal for Reportable Food Registry, Updates Guidance." *Food Chemical News* 52, no. 12 (2010): 10–11.

"FDA Food Compliance Chief Warns of Further Enforcement Uptick." *Food Chemical News* 51, no. 33 (2009): 1.

"FDA Touts Reportable Food Registry as Successful but Industry Wants Changes." *Food Chemical News* 52, no. 20 (2010): 1.

"FDA Warns of Outbreaks Related to Drinking Raw Milk." *Food Chemical News* 52, no. 4 (2010): 10.

Feagans, Jacob M., Darius A. Jahann, and Jamie S. Barkin. "Meals Ready to Eat: A Brief History and Clinical Vignette with Discussion on Civilian Applications." *Military Medicine* 175, no. 3 (2010): 194–196.

Feart, Catherine, Cecelia Samieri, Virginie Rondea, et al. "Adherence to the Mediterranean Diet, Cognitive Decline, and Risk of Dementia." *JAMA: The Journal of the American Medical Association* 302, no. 6 (2009): 638–648.

"Features—News & Trends—America's Second Harvest." *Dairy Foods* 101, no. 12 (2000): 19.

Febriani, Yossi, et al. "Association between Indicators of Livestock Farming Intensity and Hospitalization Rate for Acute Gastroenteritis." *Epidemiology and Infection* 137, no. 8 (2009): 1073–1085.

"Feminization of Agriculture in China? Myths Surrounding Women's Participation in Farming." *China Quarterly London* (2008): 327–348.

Ferguson, Priscilla . "Michelin in America." *Gastronomica: The Journal of Food and Culture* 8, no. 1 (2008): 49–55.

Ferrières, Jean. "The French Paradox: Lessons for Other Countries." *Heart* 90 (2004): 107–111. Available online at http://www.ncbi.nlm. nih.gov/pmc/articles/PMC1768013/pdf/ hrt09000107.pdf (accessed October 9, 2010).

Finnis, Elizabeth. "Why Grow Cash Crops? Subsistence Farming and Crop Commercialization in the

Kolli Hills, South India." *American Anthropologist* 108, no. 2 (2006): 363–369.

Fiocchi, Alessandro, et al. "Clinical Tolerance of Processed Foods." *Annals of Allergy, Asthma & Immunology* 93, no. 5 (2004): 38–46.

Fito, Montserrat, Rafael de la Torre, and Maria-Isabel Covas. "Olive Oil and Oxidative Stress." *Molecular Nutrition & Food Research* 51, no. 10 (2007): 1215–1224.

Fitzpatrick, Mike. "Food Fads." *Lancet* 363, no. 9405 (2004): 338.

Flisram, Greg. "A Serious Flirt with Dirt: Urban Farming Is Making a Comeback." *Planning Chicago* 75, no. 8 (2009): 14–19.

Foladori, Guillermo, and Edgar Záyago. "What Lies Beneath." *Science Technology & Society* 15, no. 1 (2010): 155–168.

Fonseca, Vanessa. "Nuevo Latino: Rebranding Latin American Cuisine." *Consumption, Markets and Culture* 8, no. 2 (2005): 95–130.

Fontana, Luigi, Jennifer L. Shew, John O. Holloszy, and Dennis T. Villareal. "Low Bone Mass in Subjects on a Long-Term Raw Vegetarian Diet." *Archives of Internal Medicine* 165, no. 6 (2005): 684–689.

"Food Aid for Africa: The Politics of Hunger." *The Economist* 394, no. 8674 (2010): 58.

"Food Aid Needs Reform." *Lancet* 369, no. 9580 (2007): 2134.

"Food: Celebrity-Chef Endorsements: Are Brand Ambassadors Losing Their Cachet?" *Marketing* (May 19, 2010): 16.

"The Food Crisis—Shortages Could Inspire Some Long-Term Solutions." *Business Week* (May 12, 2008): 26.

"Food–Disease Links: Phytonutrients That Protect against Heart Disease, Cancer, Inflammation, and More." *Environmental Nutrition* 29, no. 12 (2006): 3–6.

"Food Fighter—Jeremy Preston Has Spent His Life Working in the Food Industry and Is Now Defending Its Rights in the Face of Potential Bans." *Marketing* (March 11, 2004): 22.

"Food for Thought." *Nature* 445, no. 7129 (2007): 683–684.

"Food Industry Responds to New Reportable Food Registry." *Food Chemical News* 51, no. 29 (2009): 14.

"Food Irradiation: A Technology Wasted or Simply Unwanted?" *Food Engineering and Ingredients* 33, no. 2 (2008): 16–19.

"Food Safety: Fresh Produce Is Just as Susceptible to Carrying Foodborne Diseases as Meat, Poultry, and Fish." *Contemporary Pediatrics* 25, no. 9 (2008): 96–97.

"Food Scientist Wins World Food Prize." *Food Technology* 61, no. 7 (2007): 59–60.

"Food: Street Food Comes in from the Cold." *Newsweek* (March 29, 2010): 54.

"Food—The Latest Fad in Healthy Food Additives Is Good Wishes. Can Meals "Embedded" with Love Actually Make You Feel Better?" *Time* (April 6, 2009): 58.

"Food to Blow Your Mind: 'Molecular Gastronomy' Has Attracted Chefs and Plain Foodies with an Appetite for Extreme Experimentation." *Business Week New York* 4000 (September 11, 2006): 104–105.

"Food World—From Stamping Out Counterfeit Food Products, to Lifting UK Beef Bans, Food World Provides a Round Up of News from around the Globe." *Food Processing* 74, no. 12 (2005): 12.

Fortuine, Robert. "Paralytic Shellfish Poisoning in the North Pacific: Two Historical Accounts and Implications for Today. 1975." *Alaska Medicine* 49, no. 2 (2007): 65–69.

Foster, Rebecca, Claire S. Williamson, and Joanne Lunn. "Briefing Paper: Culinary Oils and Their Health Effects." *Nutrition Bulletin* 34, no. 1 (2009): 4–47.

Foster, Robert. "Commodities, Brands, Love and Kula." *Anthropological Theory* 8, no. 1 (2008): 9–25.

Fra, Molinero B., Charles I. Nero, and Jessica B. Harris. "When Food Tastes Cosmopolitan: The Creole Fusion of Diaspora Cuisine: An Interview with Jessica B. Harris." *Callaloo* 30, no. 1 (2007): 287–303.

Frail, Thomas A. "Farms Go to Town: The U.S. Will See an Upward Trend in Urban Farming." *Smithsonian* 41, no. 4 (2010): 56–57.

Fraser, Gary E. "Vegetarian Diets: What Do We Know of Their Effects on Common Chronic Diseases?" *The American Journal of Clinical Nutrition* 89, no. 5 (2009): S1607–S1612.

"Fresh Market to Supermarket: Nutrition Transition Insights from Chiang Mai, Thailand." *Public Health Nutrition* 13, no. 6 (2010): 893–897.

Fridell, Mara, Ian Hudson, and Mark Hudson. "With Friends like These: The Corporate Response to Fair Trade Coffee." *Review of Radical Political Economics* 40, no. 1 (2008): 8–34.

"From Nouvelle Cuisine through Fusion Confusion to Modern Habits." *Asian Hotel and Catering Times* (April 2006): 68–71.

Frumin, Amy B. "Diagnosing USAID." *Foreign Affairs* 88, no. 2 (March/April 2009).

"Fuelled by Coffee." *Economist* 390, no. 8621 (2009).

Fulkerson, Jayne A., et al. "Adolescent and Parent Views of Family Meals." *Journal of the American Dietetic Association* 106, no. 4 (2006): 526–532.

Fung, Teresa T., et al. "Adherence to a Dash-Style Diet and Risk of Coronary Heart Disease and Stroke in Women." *Archives of Internal Medicine* 168, no. 7 (2008): 713–720.

Fung, Teresa T., et al. "Dietary Patterns and the Risk of Postmenopausal Breast Cancer." *International Journal of Cancer* 116, no. 1 (2005): 116–121.

Fung, Teresa T., Matthias Schulze, JoAnne E. Manson, Walter C. Willett,, and Frank B. Hu. "Dietary Patterns, Meat Intake, and the Risk of Type 2 Diabetes in Women." *Archives of Internal Medicine* 164, no. 20 (2004): 2235–2240.

"The Future of Confectionery Lies in Chocolate." *Food Manufacture* 84, no. 12 (2009): 43.

Garcia, Matthew. "Labor, Migration, and Social Justice in the Age of the Grape Boycott." *Gastronomica: The Journal of Food and Culture* 7, no. 3 (2007): 68–74.

Gebbers, Robbin, and Viacheslav I. Adamchuk. "Precision Agriculture and Food Security." *Science* 327, no. 5967 (2010): 828–831.

Geiger, Constance, and Mary H. Hager. "Truth in Labeling: It's a Matter of Principle." *Journal of the American Dietetic Association* 107, no. 12 (2007): 2055.

Geraci, Victor W. "Fermenting a Twenty-First Century California Wine Industry." *Agricultural History* 78, no. 4 (Autumn 2004): 438–465.

Geraghty, Maureen E., Jody Bates-Wall, and Christopher A. Taylor. "The Factors Associated with Dietary Supplement Use in College Students." *Journal of the American Dietetic Association* 108, no. 3 (2008): A29.

Getz, Christy, and Aimee Shreck. "What Organic and Fair Trade Labels Do Not Tell Us: Towards a Place-Based Understanding of Certification." *International Journal of Consumer Studies* 30, no. 5 (2006): 490–501.

Getz, Christy, Sandy Brown, and Aimee Shreck. "Class Politics and Agricultural Exceptionalism in California's Organic Agriculture Movement." *Politics & Society* 36, no. 4 (2008): 478–507.

Ghatak, Maitreesh, and Sanchari Roy. "Land Reform and Agricultural Productivity in India: A Review of the Evidence." *Oxford Review of Economic Policy* 23, no. 2 (2007): 251–269.

Giarracca, Norma, and Miguel Teubal. "Women in Agriculture." *Latin American Perspectives* 35, no. 6 (2008): 5–10.

Gill, Jatinderjit Kaur, M. K. Dhillon, and Muninder K. Sidhu. "Women in Agriculture." *International Journal of Rural Studies* 14, no. 1 (2007): 2–6.

Gillespie, Gilbert W. "2009 AFHVS Presidential Address: The Steering Question: Challenges to Achieving Food System Sustainability." *Agriculture and Human Values* 27, no. 1 (2010): 3–12.

Godfray, H. Charles J., et al. "Food Security: The Challenge of Feeding 9 Billion People." *Science* 327, no. 5967 (2010): 812–818.

Godwin, Sandria, Richard Coppings, Leslie Speller-Henderson, and Lou Pearson. "Scholarship—Study Finds Consumer Food Safety Knowledge Lacking." *Journal of Family and Consumer Sciences* 97, no. 2 (2005): 40–44.

"Going Green: Shark-Fin Soup, a Symbol of Good Fortune, Means Bad Luck for Sea Life." *Time* (October 4, 2010): 65.

Gombay, Nicole. "Shifting Identities in a Shifting World: Food, Place, Community, and the Politics of Scale in an Inuit Settlement." *Environment and Planning D: Society and Space* 23, no. 3 (2005): 415–433.

Gonzalez, Carlos A., and Elio Riboli. "Diet and Cancer Prevention: Where We Are, Where We Are Going." *Nutrition and Cancer* 56, no. 2 (2006): 225–231.

Gonzalez, Carlos A., and Jordi Salas-Salvadó. "The Potential of Nuts in the Prevention of Cancer." *The British Journal of Nutrition* 96, supplement 2 (2006): 87–94.

Gonzalez, Vivian M., and Kelly M. Vitousek. "Feared Food in Dieting and Non-Dieting Young Women: A Preliminary Validation of the Food Phobia Survey." *Appetite* 43, no. 2 (2004): 155–173.

"The Good Life—Offal Good." *Newsweek* 154, no. 19 (2009): 65.

"Gordon Ramsay Shares a Few Choice Words on Becoming a Celebrity Chef." *People Weekly* (July 24, 2006): 67.

Gorman, Christine. "The Avian Flu: How Scared Should We Be?" *Time* (October 17, 2005): 30–34.

"Got Milk? How Safe Is the Newest Food Fad—Raw Milk?" *Current Science* 93, no. 8 (2007): 10.

"Gourmet Food Trends: Mighty Special." *The Progressive Grocer* 86, no. 6 (2007): 88–91.

"Green Eggs and *Salmonella*?" *Smithsonian* (June 2010): 92.

Griffin, Mary, Jeffery Sobal, and Thomas Lyson. "An Analysis of a Community Food Waste Stream." *Agriculture and Human Values* 26, nos. 1–2 (2009): 67–81.

"Grilling Basics: Don't Char the Meat." *Consumer Reports* 73, no. 8 (2008): 52.

Grimond, John. "China's Peasants Look to the Skies." *Economist* 395, no. 8683 (May 22, 2010).

Groves, Rachel M. "E. Coli Outbreak." *The American Journal of Nursing* 107, no. 10 (2007): 16.

"Growth Spurt Continues for Organic Baby Food and Infant Formula Sales." *Nutrition Business Journal* 13, nos. 3–4 (2008): 26–28.

Guerrieri, Ramona, Chantal Nederkoorn, and Anita Jansen. "The Interaction between Impulsivity and a Varied Food Environment: Its Influence on Food Intake and Overweight." *International Journal of Obesity* 32, no. 4 (2008): 708–714.

Gumbel, Peter. "Dispatches—Pasta Panic—The Price of Wheat Is Up 60%, This Year, and in Italy They're Taking to the Streets over the Cost of Tortellini." *Fortune* 156, no. 11 (2007): 47.

Gupta, Vikrant, et al. "Genome Analysis and Genetic Enhancement of Tomato." *Critical Reviews in Biotechnology* 29, no. 2 (2009): 152–181.

Gurbaxani, M. M. "Street Food Activism." *Ecologist* 37, no. 10 (2007).

Gurven, Michael, and Kim Hill. "Why Do Men Hunt? A Reevaluation of 'Man the Hunter' and the Sexual Division of Labor." *Current Anthropology* 50, no. 1 (2009): 51–74.

Gustaw-Rothenberg, Katarzyna. "Dietary Patterns Associated with Alzheimer's Disease: Population Based Study." *International Journal of Environmental Research and Public Health* 6, no. 4 (2009): 1335–1340.

Guthman, Julie. "Commentary on Teaching Food: Why I Am Fed Up with Michael Pollan et al." *Agriculture and Human Values* 24, no. 2 (2007): 261–264.

Haas, Jere H., and Dennis D. Miller. "Overview of Experimental Biology 2005 Symposium: Food Fortification in Developing Countries." *The Journal of Nutrition* 136, no. 4 (2006): 1053–1054.

Haddy, Francis J. "Role of Dietary Salt in Hypertension." *Life Sciences* 79, no. 17 (2006): 1585–1592.

Haile, Menghestab. "Weather Patterns, Food Security and Humanitarian Response in Sub-Saharan Africa." *Philosophical Transactions: Biological Sciences* 360, no. 1463 (2005): 2169–2182.

Hambidge, K. Michael. "Micronutrient Bioavailability: Dietary Reference Intakes and a Future Perspective." *American Journal of Clinical Nutrition* 91, no. 5 (2010): 1430S–1432S.

Hamer, Ed. "Bananas." *The Ecologist* (September 2007): 24.

Hardin, Garrett. "The Tragedy of the Commons." *Science* 162, no. 3859 (December 13, 1968): 1243–1248.

Harmon, Katherine. "Shelling Out for Eggs." *Scientific American* 301, no. 5 (2009): 20–21.

Harris, William. "Omega-6 and Omega-3 Fatty Acids: Partners in Prevention." *Current Opinion in Clinical Nutrition and Metabolic Care* 13, no. 2 (2010): 125–129.

Hartwig, Bob. "Bob Hartwig, Chef Instructor at the French Pastry School in Chicago, Gives His Take on Industry Trends, Pastry versus Confectionery and the Trials of Making Chocolate." *Candy Industry* 174, no. 3 (2009): 20–23.

Hasler, Clare M., and Amy C. Brown. "Position of the American Dietetic Association: Functional Foods." *Journal of the American Dietetic Association* 109, no. 4 (2009): 735–746.

Haub, Mark D. "Sports Nutrition: Energy Metabolism and Exercise." *JAMA: The Journal of the American Medical Association* 299, no. 19 (2008): 2330–2331.

"Health Effects of Olive Oil and the Mediterranean Diet." *Nutrition Reviews* 64, no. 10 (2006): pt. 2.

Hemphill, Thomas A. "Globalization of the U.S. Food Supply: Reconciling Product Safety Regulation with Free Trade." *Business Economics: The Journal of the National Association of Business Economists* 44, no. 3 (2009): 154–168.

Henry, C. Jeya. "Functional Foods." *European Journal of Clinical Nutrition* 64, no. 7 (2010): 657–659.

Herbold, Nancie H., and Elizabeth Scott. "A Pilot Study Describing Infant Formula Preparation and Feeding Practices." *International Journal of Environmental Health Research* 18, no. 6 (2008): 451–459.

Heyman, Melvin B. "Lactose Intolerance in Infants, Children, and Adolescents." *Pediatrics* 118, no. 3 (2006): 1279–1286.

Hinderliter, Justine D. "From Farm to Table: How This Little Piggy Was Dragged through the Market." *University of San Francisco Law Review* 40, no. 3 (2006): 739–768.

"History—How Good School Lunches Went Bad, and the Attempt to Make Them Healthier." *Time* (October 19, 2009): 16.

Hite, Adele H., et al. "In the Face of Contradictory Evidence: Report of the Dietary Guidelines for Americans Committee." *Nutrition* 26, no. 10 (2010): 915–924.

Hobson, Katherine. "The Skinny on Vitamins." *U.S. News & World Report* 146, no. 1 (2009): 78–80.

Hoffman, Richard E. "Preventing Foodborne Illness." *Emerging Infectious Diseases* 11, no. 1 (2005): 11–16.

Holden, Joanne M., Linda E. Lemar, and Jacob Exler. "Vitamin D in Foods: Development of the US Department of Agriculture Database." *American Journal of Clinical Nutrition* 87, no. 4 (2008): S1092–S1096.

Holdrege, Craig. "Blame Factory Farming, Not Organic Food." *Nature Biotechnology* 25, no. 2 (2007): 165–166.

Holick, Michael F. "Vitamin D Deficiency." *The New England Journal of Medicine* 357, no. 3 (2007): 266–281.

Holmes, Bob. "Meat-Free World." *New Scientist* 207, no. 2769 (2010): 28–31.

Holt, Robert D. "Ecology: Asymmetry and Stability." *Nature* 442, no. 7100 (2006): 252–253.

"The Horn of Africa—Famine Looms Again." *The Economist* 389, no. 8604 (2008): 44.

Horton, Sue. "The Economics of Food Fortification." *The Journal of Nutrition* 136, no. 4 (2006): 1068–1071.

"How It Works: Food Irradiation." *Restaurant Business* 106, no. 8 (2007): 74.

"How to Feed a Hungry World." *Nature* 466 (July 29, 2010): 531–532.

Hu, Jinfu, et al. "Nutrients and Risk of Prostate Cancer." *Nutrition and Cancer* 62, no. 6 (2010): 710–718.

Hull, Bradley. "Frankincense, Myrrh, and Spices." *Journal of Macromarketing* 28, no. 3 (2008): 275–288.

"Hurricane Katrina Response—Food Processors, America's Second Harvest Help." *Food Processing* 66, no. 10 (2005): 11.

Ilea, Ramona Cristina. "Intensive Livestock Farming: Global Trends, Increased Environmental Concerns, and Ethical Solutions." *Journal of Agricultural and Environmental Ethics* 22, no. 2 (2009): 153–167.

"Indigenous Peoples' Food Systems for Health: Finding Interventions That Work." *Public Health Nutrition* 9, no. 8 (2006): 1013–1019.

"Industry to Support Agriculture—Subsidies Help Small Farmers." *Beijing Review* 48, no. 15 (2005): 24–25.

"Insights—Department of Justice and USDA Officials Examine Monsanto's Hold on the Heartland." *Chemical and Engineering News* 88, no. 13 (2010): 16.

"International—Six More Brazilian States Escape Russia's Meat Embargo." *Food Chemical News* 47, no. 5 (2005): 17.

"International—World Food Prices—Whatever Happened to the Food Crisis?" *The Economist* 392, no. 8638 (2009): 53–54.

Issar, Sukriti. "Multiple Program Participation and Exits from Food Stamps among Elders." *The Social Service Review* 84, no. 3 (2010): 437–459.

Jabs, Lorelle. "Where Two Elephants Meet, the Grass Suffers." *American Behavioral Scientist* 50, no. 11 (2007): 1498–1519.

Jayatissa, Renuka, Aberra Bekele, C. L. Piyasena, and S. Mahamithawa. "Assessment of Nutritional Status of Children under Five Years of Age, Pregnant Women, and Lactating Women Living in Relief Camps after the Tsunami in Sri Lanka." *Food and Nutrition Bulletin* 27, no. 2 (2006): 144–152.

Jevsnik, Mojca, Valentina Hlebec, and Peter Raspor. "Consumers' Awareness of Food Safety from Shopping to Eating." *Food Control* 19, no. 8 (2008): 737–745.

Jochelson, Karen. "Nanny or Steward? The Role of Government in Public Health." *Public Health* 120, no. 12 (2006): 1149–1155.

Just, David R., Brian Wansink, and Calum G. Turvey. "Biosecurity, Terrorism, and Food Consumption Behavior: Using Experimental Psychology to Analyze Choices Involving Fear." *Journal of Agricultural and Resource Economics* 34, no. 1 (2009): 91–108.

Kaiser, Jocelyn. "Resurrected Influenza Virus Yields Secrets of Deadly 1918 Pandemic." *Science* 310 (2005): 28–29.

Katan, Martijn B. "Nitrate in Foods: Harmful or Healthy?" *American Journal of Clinical Nutrition* 90, no. 1 (2009): 11–12.

Kaufman, Frederick. "World Hunger: A Reasonable Proposal." *BMJ: British Medical Journal* 339 (2009): b5209.

Kavanaugh, Claudine J., Paula R. Trumbo, and Kathleen C. Ellwood. "The U.S. Food and Drug Administration's Evidence-Based Review for Qualified Health Claims: Tomatoes, Lycopene, and Cancer." *Journal of the National Cancer Institute* 99 (2007): 1074–1085.

Keane, Michael G., et al. "Taxing Sugar-Sweetened Beverages." *New England Journal of Medicine* 362, no. 4 (2010): 368–369.

Kelly, Bridget, et al. "Television Food Advertising to Children: A Global Perspective." *American Journal of Public Health* 100, no. 9 (2010): 1730–1736.

Kelly, Trish. "Is the WTO a Threat to the Environment, Public Health, and Sovereignty?" *Challenge* 51, no. 5 (2008): 84–102.

Kennedy, Shaun. "Why Can't We Test Our Way to Absolute Food Safety?" *Science* 322, no. 5908 (2008): 1641–1643.

Khatamzas, Elham, et al. "The Increasing Prevalence of Listeriosis—What Are We Missing?" *QJM: An International Journal of Medicine* 103, no. 7 (2010): 519–522.

Khoury, Lara, and Stuart Smyth. "Reasonable Foreseeability and Liability in Relation to Genetically Modified Organisms." *Bulletin of Science, Technology & Society* 27, no. 3 (2007): 215–232.

"Kill King Corn." *Nature* 449, no. 7163 (2007): 637.

Kirby, Midge, and Elaine Danner. "Nutritional Deficiencies in Children on Restricted Diets." *Pediatric Clinics of North America* 56, no. 5 (2009): 1085–1103.

Kislev, Mordechai E., Anat Hartmann, and Ofer Bar-Yoself. "Early Domesticated Fig in the Jordan Valley." *Science* 312, no. 5778 (2006): 1372–1374.

Kitamoto, Miyoko, et al. "Food Poisoning by Staphylococcus Aureus at a University Festival." *Japanese Journal of Infectious Diseases* 62, no. 3 (2009): 242–243.

Kittisupamongkol, Weekitt. "Effect of Folic Acid and B Vitamins on Cardiovascular Disease in Women." *JAMA: Journal of the American Medical Association* 300, no. 12 (2008): 1410.

Klapthor, James N. "Word of the World Food Prize Laureate Travels the Globe." *Food Technology* 61, no. 7 (2007): 115–116.

Klass, Perri. "The Fast-Food Fund." *The New England Journal of Medicine* 360, no. 3 (2009): 209–211.

Kleinman, Sharon S. "Cafe Culture in France and the United States: A Comparative Ethnographic Study of the Use of Mobile Information and Communication Technologies." *Atlantic Journal of Communication* 14, no. 4 (2006): 191–210.

Klemmer, Cynthia D., Tina M. Waliczek, and Jayne M. Zajicek. "Growing Minds: The Effect of a School Gardening Program on the Science Achievement of Elementary Students." *HortTechnology* 15 (2005): 448–452.

Koester, Veit. "The Compliance Mechanism of the Cartagena Protocol on Biosafety: Development, Adoption, Content and First Years of Life." *Review of European Community & International Environmental Law* 18, no. 1 (2009): 77–90.

Kontogianni, Meropi D., et al. "The Impact of Olive Oil Consumption Pattern on the Risk of Acute Coronary Syndromes: The Cardio2000 Case-Control Study." *Clinical Cardiology* 30, no. 3 (2007): 125–129.

Körner, Uwe, et al. "Ethical and Legal Aspects of Enteral Nutrition." *Clinical Nutrition* 25, no. 2 (2006): 196–202.

Korsmeyer, Carolyn. "Review of Making Sense of Taste: Food and Philosophy." *Leonardo* 37, no. 1 (2004): 79–80.

Kortmann, Karin. "The Human Rights to Food and Water." *Environmental Policy and Law* 39, no. 1 (2009): 2–3.

Kosa, Katherine M., Sheryl C. Cates, Shawn Karns, Sandria L. Godwin, and Delores H. Chambers. "Consumer Food Safety and Home Refrigeration Practices: Results of a Web-Based Survey." *Journal of the American Dietetic Association* 106, no. 8 (2006): A68.

Köse, Yavuz. "Nestlé: A Brief History of the Marketing Strategies of the First Multinational Company in the Ottoman Empire." *Journal of Macromarketing* 27, no. 1 (2007): 74–85.

Kotz, Deborah. "Anxieties in a Bottle (or a Can)." *U.S. News & World Report* 145, no. 7 (September 29, 2008): 84.

Kuehn, Bridget M. "Aid Groups Target 'Silent' Malnutrition." *JAMA: The Journal of the American Medical Association* 300, no. 17 (2008): 1983–1985.

———. "Food Allergies Becoming More Common." *JAMA: The Journal of the American Medical Association* 300, no. 20 (2008): 2358.

———. "Gulf Seafood Safety." *JAMA: The Journal of the American Medical Association* 304, no. 4 (2010): 398.

———. "Surveillance and Coordination Key to Reducing Foodborne Illness." *JAMA: The Journal of the American Medical Association* 294, no. 21 (2005): 2683–2684.

Kume, Tamikazu, et al. "Status of Food Irradiation in the World." *Radiation Physics and Chemistry* 78, no. 3 (2009): 227–226.

Kummerer, Klaus, Martin Held, and David Pimentel. "Sustainable Use of Soils and Time." *Journal of Soil and Water Conservation* 65, no. 2 (2010): 141–149.

Kummerow, Fred A. "The Negative Effects of Hydrogenated Trans Fats and What to Do about Them." *Atherosclerosis* 205, no. 2 (2009): 458–465.

Kuriyama, Shinichi, Yoshikazu, Nishino, Yoshitaka Tsubono, and Ichiro Tsuji. "Green Tea Consumption and Mortality in Japan—Reply." *JAMA: The Journal of the American Medical Association* 297, no. 4 (2007): 360.

La Vecchia, Carlo. "Association between Mediterranean Dietary Patterns and Cancer Risk." *Nutrition Reviews* 67, supplement 1 (May 2009): 126–129.

"Lactose Intolerance and African Americans: Implications for the Consumption of Appropriate Intake Levels of Key Nutrients." *Journal of the National Medical Association* 101, no. 10 (2009): S5–S23.

Lang, Tim. "Functional Foods." *BMJ: British Medical Journal* (clinical research ed.) 334, no. 7602 (2007): 1015–1016.

Lanou, Amy J., Susan E. Berkow, and Neal D. Barnard. "Calcium, Dairy Products, and Bone Health in Children and Young Adults: A Reevaluation of the Evidence." *Pediatrics* 115, no. 3 (2005): 736–743.

Larkin, Eileen A., Robert J. Carman, Teresa Krakauer, and Bradley G. Stiles. "Staphylococcus Aureus: The Toxic Presence of a Pathogen Extraordinaire." *Current Medicinal Chemistry* 16, no. 30 (2009): 4003–4019.

Larrain, Camilo. "Pica, a Strange Symptom Unveiled Even in *Don Quixote*." *Revista Medica de Chile* 133, no. 5 (2005): 609–611.

Lee, Jennifer, et al. "Beyond the Hazard: The Role of Beliefs in Health Risk Perception." *Human and Ecological Risk Assessment: An International Journal* 11, no. 6 (2005): 1111–1126.

Lee, Mendoza R. "Breast Milk versus Formula." *Infant, Child, & Adolescent Nutrition* 2, no. 1 (2010): 7–15.

Lee, Thomas H. "Good News for Coffee Addicts." *Harvard Business Review* 87, no. 6 (2009): 22–24.

Lele, Uma. "Food Security for a Billion Poor." *Science* 327, no. 5973 (2010): 1554.

Lerman, Zvi. "Land Reform, Farm Structure, and Agricultural Performance in CIS Countries." *China Economic Review* 20, no. 2 (2009): 316.

Lev, Efraim, Mordechai E. Kislev, and Ofar Bar-Yosef. "Mousterian Vegetal Food in Kebara Cave, Mt. Carmel." *Journal of Archaeological Science* 32, no. 3 (2005): 475–484.

Levin, Susan. "Dairy Products and Bone Health." *Journal of the American Dietetic Association* 107, no. 1 (2007): 35.

Lichtenstein, Alice H. "Diet, Heart Disease, and the Role of the Registered Dietitian." *Journal of the American Dietetic Association* 107, no. 2 (2007): 205–208.

Lindbloom, Erik J. "Long-Term Benefits of a Vegetarian Diet." *American Family Physician* 79, no. 7 (2009): 541–542.

Linden, Erik, David McClements, and Job Ubbink. "Molecular Gastronomy: A Food Fad or an Interface for Science-Based Cooking?" *Food Biophysics* 3, no. 2 (2008): 246–254.

Lindenbaum, Shirley. "Cannibalism, Kuru, and Anthropology." *Folia Neuropathologica* 47, no. 2 (2009): 138–144.

Little, Christine L., and Iain A. Gillespie. "Review Article: Prepared Salads and Public Health." *Journal of Applied Microbiology* 105, no. 6 (2008): 1729–1743.

Liu, Aimee. "The Perfect Pantomime: What Is Our Body Telling Us When We Have an Eating Disorder?" *MS New York* 19, no. 2 (2009): 74–78.

Liu, Yifan, and Lawrence M. Wein. "Mathematically Assessing the Consequences of Food Terrorism Scenarios." *Journal of Food Science* 73, no. 7 (2008): 346–353.

Lomer, Miranda C., Gareth C. Parkes, and Jeremy D. Sanderson. "Review Article: Lactose Intolerance in Clinical Practice—Myths and Realities." *Alimentary Pharmacology & Therapeutics* 27, no. 2 (2008): 93–103.

Lopez-Garcia, Esther, et al. "The Relationship of Coffee Consumption with Mortality." *Annals of Internal Medicine* 148, no. 12 (2008): 904–914.

"Lose Weight with Chocolate?" *Health* 20, no. 1 (2006): 114.

Lukacs, Gabriella. "Iron Chef around the World." *International Journal of Cultural Studies* 13, no. 4 (2010): 409–426.

Lupein, John. "Food Quality and Safety: Traceability and Labeling." *Critical Reviews in Food Science and Nutrition* 45, no. 2 (2005): 119–123.

Lyons, Diane. "Integrating African Cuisines." *Journal of Social Archaeology* 7, no. 3 (2007): 346–371.

MacDonald, Rhona. "Save Somalia!" *Lancet* 373, no. 9682 (2009): 2184.

Machado, Antonio E. "Preventing Foodborne Illness in the Field." *Journal of Environmental Health* 72, no. 3 (2009): 56.

"Major North American Pet Food Recall." *Animal Pharm* 610 (March 30, 2007): 8.

Maki, Dennis G. "Coming to Grips with Foodborne Infection—Peanut Butter, Peppers, and Nationwide Salmonella Outbreaks." *The New England Journal of Medicine* 360, no. 10 (2009): 949–953.

Maldonado, Marta M. "'It Is Their Nature to Do Menial Labour': The Racialization of 'Latino/a Workers' by Agricultural Employers." *Ethnic and Racial Studies* 32, no. 6 (2009): 1017–1036.

"Malnutrition—the Starvelings." *The Economist* 386, no. 8564 (2008): 56–57.

Mann, Jim. "Vegetarian Diets." *BMJ: British Medical Journal* 339 (2009): b2507.

Mannie, Elizabeth. "Phosphates and Yeasts in Baking." *Prepared Foods* 176, no. 8 (2007): 47.

Marcason, Wendy. "What Is the Latest Research Regarding the Avoidance of Nuts, Seeds, Corn, and Popcorn in Diverticular Disease?" *Journal of the American Dietetic Association* 108, no. 11 (2008): 1956.

Marchione, Thomas, and Ellen Messer. "Food Aid and the World Hunger Solution: Why the U.S. Should Use a Human Rights Approach." *Food and Foodways* 18, nos. 1–2 (2010): 10–27.

Mariyono, Joko, Tom Kompas, and R. Quentin Grafton. "Shifting from Green Revolution to Environmentally Sound Policies: Technological Change in Indonesian Rice Agriculture." *Journal of the Asia Pacific Economy* 15, no. 2 (2010): 128–147.

Marker, Michael. "After the Makah Whale Hunt." *Urban Education* 41, no. 5 (2006): 482–505.

Martinez, Maria E., James R. Marshall, and Edward Giovannucci. "Diet and Cancer Prevention: The Roles of Observation and Experimentation." *Nature Reviews: Cancer* 8, no. 9 (2008): 694–703.

Masamitsu, Emily. "Apocalypse Chow—Hungry Taste-Testers Scarf MREs—Meals Ready-to-Eat—to Find Out If Survival Grub Can Fuel the Body and Boost Morale." *Popular Mechanics* (October 2009): 78.

Matthews, Rowena G. "A Love Affair with Vitamins." *Journal of Biological Chemistry* 284, no. 39 (2009): 26217–26228.

Mauer, Whitney A., et al. "Ethnic-Food Safety Concerns: An Online Survey of Food Safety Professionals." *Journal of Environmental Health* 68, no. 10 (2006): 32–38.

Maunula, Leena. "Norovirus Outbreaks from Drinking Water." *Emerging Infectious Diseases* 11 (2005): 1716–1722.

May, Kidd. "Food Safety—Consumer Concerns." *Nutrition & Food Science* 30, no. 2 (2000): 53.

McCally, Michael, and Martin Donohoe. "Irradiation of Food." *The New England Journal of Medicine* 351, no. 4 (2004): 402–403.

McCauley, Sharon M., and Mary H. Hager. "Why Are Therapeutic Diet Orders an Issue Now and What Does It Have to Do with Legal Scope of Practice?" *Journal of the American Dietetic Association* 109, no. 9 (2009): 1515–1519.

McCullough, Marjorie L., and Edward L. Giovannucci. "Diet and Cancer Prevention." *Oncogene* 23, no. 38 (2004): 6349–6364.

McGray, D. "A Revolution in School Lunches. Getting Kids to Want to Eat Healthy Food Isn't Easy. Serving Wholesome Fare at Fast-Food Prices Is Even Harder. How Revolution Foods Is Helping School Cafeterias Swear Off Frozen Pizza and Fries." *Time* 175, no. 16 (April 26, 2010): 50–53.

McLaren, Anne. "Free-range Eggs?" *Science* 316, no. 5823 (April 20, 2007): 339.

McMichael, Anthony J., John W. Powles, Colin D. Butler, and Ricardo Uauy. "Food, Livestock Production, Energy, Climate Change, and Health." *Lancet* 370, no. 9594 (2007): 1253–1263.

"Me & My Factory: MD David Rixon Talks about the Art of Baking and Getting a Slice of the Artisan Bread Market." *Food Manufacture* 84, no. 9 (2009): 24–25.

"Meals, Ready-to-Eat—Innovations in Food Chemistry and Packaging Provide Soldiers on the Battlefield with Tastier, More Nutritious Food." *Chemical and Engineering News* 88, no. 18 (2010): 40.

"Meat Cutback Could Prolong Life." *Science News* 174, no. 9 (2008): 17.

Medina, Widman, et al. "Dental Caries in 6–12-Year-Old Indigenous and Non-Indigenous Schoolchildren in the Amazon Basin of Ecuador." *Brazilian Dental Journal* 19, no. 1 (2008): 83–86.

"Mediterranean Diet: Good Snacking." *Consumer Reports on Health* 20, no. 3 (2008): 7.

Megiorni, Francesca, Barbara Mora, Monica Bon-amico, et al. "HLA-DQ and Susceptibility to Celiac Disease: Evidence for Gender Differences and Parent-of-Origin Effects." *American Journal of Gastroenterology* 103 (2008): 997–1003.

Mehta, Darshan H., Paula M. Gardine, Russell S. Phillips, and Ellen P. McCarthy. "Herbal and Dietary Supplement Disclosure to Health Care Providers by Individuals with Chronic Conditions." *Journal of Alternative and Complementary Medicine* 14, no. 10 (2008): 1263–1269.

Melillo, Edward D. "Kathleen Mapes, Sweet Tyrany: Migrant Labor, Industrial Agriculture, and Imperial Politics." *Business History Review* 84, no. 2 (2010): 390.

Mellentin, Julian. "Why the Beauty Food Fad Is Finished." *Dairy Industries International* 74, no. 3 (2009): 14–15.

"Mercury and Seafood Advice Still Current." *FDA Consumer* 40, no. 5 (2006): 2–3.

"Methodological Issues in Oral Health/Diet Linkage." *Dental Abstracts* 54, no. 5 (2009): 262–263.

"Mexico Mulls Dairy Import Restrictions." *Food Chemical News* 50, no. 50 (2009): 18.

"Mexico's Shrimp Sector Questions U.S. Import Restrictions." *Food Chemical News* 52, no. 1 (2010): 25.

Meyer-Rochow, Victor B. "Food Taboos: Their Origins and Purposes." *Journal of Ethnobiology and Ethnomedicine* 5, no. 18 (2009): 1–10.

Michaud, Dominique S., et al. "Prospective Study of Meat Intake and Dietary Nitrates, Nitrites, and Nitrosamines and Risk of Adult Glioma." *American Journal of Clinical Nutrition* 90, no. 3 (2009): 570–577.

Mietje, Germonpré, et al. "Fossil Dogs and Wolves from Palaeolithic sites in Belgium, the Ukraine and Russia: Osteometry, Ancient DNA and Stable Isotopes." *Journal of Archaeological Science* 36, no. 2 (2009): 473–490.

Miglierini, Giuliana. "Regulatory Focus—Center for Food Safety and Applied Nutrition (CSFAN)." *Agrofoodindustry Hi-Tech* 16, no. 1 (2005): 6.

Miglio, Christina, et al. "Effects of Different Cooking Methods on Nutritional and Physicochemical Characteristics of Selected Vegetables." *Journal of Agricultural and Food Chemistry* 56, no. 1 (2008): 139–147.

Milius, Susan. "Cannibal Power." *Science News* 169, no. 9 (2006): 131–132.

Mills, James L., and Tonia C. Carter. "Invited Commentary: Preventing Neural Tube Defects and More via Food Fortification?" *American Journal of Epidemiology* 169, no. 1 (2009): 18–21.

Milton, Katherine. "Hunter-Gatherer Diets: A Different Perspective." *American Journal of Clinical Nutrition* 71, no. 3 (2000): 665–667.

Mishra, Vinod, Xiaolei Dai, Kirk R. Smith, and Lasten Mika. "Maternal Exposure to Biomass Smoke and Reduced Birth Weight in Zimbabwe." *Annals of Epidemiology* 14, no. 10 (2004): 740–747.

Mitka, Mike. "BPA Ban Proposed." *JAMA: The Journal of the American Medical Association* 301, no. 18 (2009): 1868.

———. "Government Unveils New Food Pyramid: Critics Say Nutrition Tool Is Flawed." *JAMA: The Journal of the American Medical Association* 293, no. 21 (2005): 2581–2852.

Mitra, Saswata. "Patent & Food Security—Opening the Pandora's Box." *Journal of Intellectual Property Rights* 13, no. 2 (2008): 145–151.

Mochly-Rosen, Diana, and Samir Zakhari. "Focus On: The Cardiovascular System: What Did We Learn from the French (Paradox)?" *Alcohol Research and Health* 33, nos. 1–2 (2010): 76–86.

Moeller, Lorena, and Kan Wang. "Engineering with Precision: Tools for the New Generation of Transgenic Crops." *Bioscience* 58, no. 5 (2008): 391–401.

Mohtadi, Hamid, and Antu P. Murshid. "Risk Analysis of Chemical, Biological, or Radionuclear Threats: Implications for Food Security." *Risk Analysis* 29, no. 9 (2009): 1317–1335.

Molony, Thomas, and James Smith. "Biofuels, Food Security, and Africa." *African Affairs* 109, no. 436 (2010): 489-498.

"Monsanto Alleges Patent Infringement in Pioneer GAT Soybeans." *Food Chemical News* 51, no. 9 (2009): 10.

Mooney, Chris. "Things Can Get Pretty Murky When You Start Thinking about the Virtues of Bottled Water." *New Scientist* no. 2659 (June 7, 2008): 49.

Moore, Simon C., Lisa M. Carter, and Stephanie van Goozen. "Confectionery Consumption in Childhood and Adult Violence." *The British Journal of Psychiatry* 195, no. 4 (2009): 366–367.

Morgan, Maria, et al. "A Content Analysis of Children's Television Advertising: Focus on Food and Oral Health." *Public Health Nutrition* 12, no. 6 (2009): 748–755.

Morin, Karen H. "Organic Baby Food: What Do You Tell Parents?" *American Journal of Maternal Child Nursing* 34, no. 2 (2009): 129.

Mostafavi, Hossein A., Hadi Fathollahi, Farahnaz Motamedi, and Seyed M. Mirmajlessi. "Food Irradiation: Applications, Public Acceptance, and Global Trade." *African Journal of Biotechnology* 9, no. 20 (2010): 2826–2833.

Motzafi-Haller, Pnina, and Paul J. Kaldjian. "Geographical Reviews—Women in Agriculture in the Middle East." *Geographical Review* 96, no. 4 (2006): 721–722.

Mourao, Denise M., Josefina Bressan, Wayne W. Campbell, and Richard D. Mattes. "Effects of Food Form on Appetite and Energy Intake in Lean and Obese Young Adults." *International Journal of Obesity* 31, no. 11 (2007): 1688–1695.

Moynihan, Paula, et al. "Researching the Impact of Oral Health on Diet and Nutritional Status: Methodological Issues." *Journal of Dentistry* 37, no. 4 (2009): 237–249.

Müller, Keith F., Dawn VanLeeuwen, Keith Mandabach, and Robert J. Harrington. "The Effectiveness of Culinary Curricula: A Case Study." *International Journal of Contemporary Hospitality Management* 21, no. 2 (2009): 167–178.

Mullin, Gerard. "Popular Diets Prescribed by Alternative Practitioners—Part 2." *Nutrition in Clinical Practice* 25, no. 3 (2010): 308–309.

"My Kitchen: Locavore Pioneer Alice Waters." *Vanity Fair* (October 2010): 148.

Nauänez-Caordoba, Jorge M., Faelix Valencia-Serrano, Estefanaia Toledo, Alvaro Alonso, and Miguel A. Martinez-Gonzalez. "The Mediterranean Diet and Incidence of Hypertension." *American Journal of Epidemiology* 169, no. 3 (2009): 339–346.

"Negroponte Urges Biotech Solutions in World Food Prize Speech." *Food Chemical News* 50, no. 18 (2008): 8.

Nepusz, Táma, Andrea Petróczi, and Declan P. Naughton. "Worldwide Food Recall Patterns over an Eleven Month Period: A Country Perspective." *BMC Public Health* no. 8 (2008): 308.

Nestle, Marion, and David S. Ludwig. "Front-of-Package Food Labels: Public Health or Propaganda?" *JAMA: The Journal of the American Medical Association* 303, no. 8 (2010): 771–772.

Nettleton, Jennifer A., et al. "Dietary Patterns and Risk of Incident Type 2 Diabetes in the Multi-Ethnic Study of Atherosclerosis." *Diabetes Care* 31, no. 9 (2008): 1777–1782.

Neumark-Sztainer, Diane, et al. "Family Weight Talk and Dieting: How Much Do They Matter for Body Dissatisfaction and Disordered Eating Behaviors in Adolescent Girls?" *Journal of Adolescent Health* 47, no. 3 (2010): 270–276.

Neumark-Sztainer, Diane, et al. "Overweight Status and Weight Control Behaviors in Adolescents: Longitudinal and Secular Trends from 1999 to 2004." *Preventative Medicine* 43, no. 1 (2006): 52–59.

"The Next Green Revolution." *The Economist* 386, no. 8568 (2008): 67.

"New Twists on Latin American Foods: Latin American Cuisine Is a Mix of Worlds, Old and New, Near and Far, Native and Imported." *Prepared Foods* 172, no. 7 (2003): 57–64.

Newbold, K. Bruce, Marie McKeary, Robert Hart, and Robert Hall. "Restaurant Inspection Frequency and Food Safety Compliance." *Journal of Environmental Health* 71, no. 4 (2008): 56–61.

Newell, Alexa. "USDA Launches Searchable Database of Foods." *AWHONN Lifelines / Association of Women's Health, Obstetric and Neonatal Nurses* 10, no. 2 (2006): 167–169.

Ngowi, Aiwerasia Vera Festo. "Women's Work in Agriculture." *African Newsletter on Occupational Health and Safety* 18, no. 3 (2008): 48–49.

Nishinari, Katsuyoshi. "Rheology, Food Texture and Mastication." *Journal of Texture Studies* 35, no. 2 (2004): 113–124.

Nishino, Hoyoky, et al. "Cancer Prevention by Phytochemicals." *Oncology* 69, supplement 1 (2005): 38–40.

Noèel, Harold, et al. "Consumption of Fresh Fruit Juice: How a Healthy Food Practice Caused a National Outbreak of Salmonella Panama Gastroenteritis." *Foodborne Pathogens and Disease* 7, no. 4 (2010): 375–381.

Nucci, Mary, Cara Cuite, and William Hallman. "When Good Food Goes Bad." *Science Communication* 31, no. 2 (2009): 238–265.

"Nutrition and Health: Food, Glorious Food." *The Economist* 393, no. 8655 (2009): 103.

"Nutrition—Food for Thought." *The Economist* 378, no. 8461 (2006): 14.

Ochs, Elinor, and Merav Shohet. "The Cultural Structuring of Mealtime Socialization." *New Directions for Child and Adolescent Development*, no. 111 (2006): 35–49.

O'Flynn, Michael. "Food Crisis and the Ghost of Malthus." *Journal of Marxism and Interdisciplinary Inquiry* 3, no. 1 (2009): 33–41.

OIG to Audit FDA Food Oversight Programs." *Food Chemical News* 51, no. 33 (2009): 11.

Okello, Julius J., and Scott M. Swinton. "From Circle of Poison to Circle of Virtue: Pesticides, Export Standards and Kenya's Green Bean Farmers." *Journal of Agricultural Economics* 61, no. 2 (2010): 209–224.

Oliver, Stephen P., et al. "Food Safety Hazards Associated with Consumption of Raw Milk." *Foodborne Pathogens and Disease* 6, no. 7 (2009): 793–806.

Olson, Kory. "Maps for a New Kind of Tourist: The First Guides Michelin France (1900–1913)." *Imago Mundi* 62, no. 2 (2010): 205–220.

Olstad, Dana, and Linda McCargar. "Prevention of Overweight and Obesity in Children under the Age of 6 Years." *Applied Physiology, Nutrition, and Metabolism* 34 (August 2009): 551–570.

"Organic Confectionery Market." *Candy Industry* 169, no. 12 (2004): 40–46.

"Organic—USDA Announces $50 Million Initiative for Organic Agriculture." *Food Chemical News* 51, no. 12 (2009): 31.

Out of Africa: Famine-Ridden Ethiopia Is Home to New Commercial Farms Growing Fresh Tomatoes and Lettuce-for Export." *Maclean's* 123, no. 32 (2010): 46–47.

Pacheco, Pablo. "Smallholder Livelihoods, Wealth and Deforestation in the Eastern Amazon." *Human Ecology* 37, no. 1 (2009): 27–41.

Paik, HeeYoung. "The Issues in Assessment and Evaluation of Diet in Asia." *Asia Pacific Journal of Clinical Nutrition* no. 17 (2008): 294–295.

Palacio, Herminia, et al. "Norovirus Outbreak among Evacuees from Hurricane Katrina—Houston, Texas, September 2005." *Morbidity and Mortality Weekly* 54 (2005): 1016–1018.

Palmer, Amanda, and Keith West. "A Quarter of a Century of Progress to Prevent Vitamin A Deficiency through Supplementation." *Food Reviews International* 26, no. 3 (2010): 270–301.

Parascandola, Mark. "100 Years of Pure Food and Drugs: The 1906 Act and the Foundations of Modern Drug Regulation." *Research Practitioner* 7, no. 6 (2006): 200–208.

Parenti, Christian. "Fortune—Chocolate's Bittersweet Economy—The Industry Agreed to Abolish Child Labor Seven Years Ago, but Little Progress Has Been Made." *Fortune International* 157, no. 2 (2008): 24–31.

Parry, Jovian. "Gender and Slaughter in Popular Gastronomy." *Feminism and Psychology* 20, no. 3 (2010): 381–396.

Parsons, E. Chris, Naomi A. Rose, Claire Bass, Clare Perry, and Mark P. Simmonds. "It's Not Just Poor Science—Japan's 'Scientific' Whaling May Be a Human Health Risk Too." *Marine Pollution Bulletin* 52, no. 9 (2006): 1118–1120.

"Pasta That's More Than Carbs." *Environmental Nutrition* 30, no. 11 (2007): 5.

Patel, Raj. "Food Sovereignty." *Journal of Peasant Studies* 36, no. 3 (2009): 663–706.

Paxon, Heather. "Post-Pasteurian Cultures: The Microbiopolitics of Raw-Milk Cheese in the United States." *Cultural Anthropology* 23, no. 1 (2008): 15–47.

Pearson, Helen. "The Dark Side of E. Coli." *Nature* 445, no. 7123 (2007): 8–9.

Peck, Jason. "The Courage of Farmers: In Our Transient Society, Few People Stay Put in One Place." *The Piedmont Virginian* 2, no. 4 (2008): 54–60.

Pelucchi, Claudio, et al. "Selected Aspects of Mediterranean Diet and Cancer Risk." *Nutrition and Cancer* 61, no. 6 (2009): 756–766.

Pengue, Walter. "Agrofuels and Agrifoods." *The Bulletin of Science, Technology & Society* 29, no. 3 (2009): 167–179.

Petrick, Gabriella M. "Manly Meals and Mom's Home Cooking: Cookbooks and Gender in Modern America." *Journal of Social History* 38, no. 2 (2004): 515–517.

Petrick, Martin, and Michael R. Carter. "Critical Masses in the Decollectivisation of Post-Soviet Agriculture." *European Review of Agricultural Economics* 36, no. 2 (June 2009): 231–252.

Petrini, Carlo. "The New Gastronomy." *Resurgence* 236 (May/June 2006): 17.

Pham, Vu H. "Secret Kitchen & Trade: An Amalgam of Family, Fortune, and Fusion Food in Asian American Cuisine." *Amerasia Journal* 32, no. 2 (2006): 37–48.

Pimentel, David. "Ethical Issues of Global Corporatization: Agriculture and Beyond." *Poultry Science* 83, no. 3 (2004): 321–329.

Pimentel, David, Harold Brookfield, Helen Parsons, and Muriel Brookfield. "Producing Food, Protecting Biodiversity." *Bioscience* 55, no. 5 (2005): 452–453.

Plahuta, Primo, Zora Korosec-Koruza, Peter Stanovnik, and Peter Raspor. "Current Viticulture and Winemaking Technology versus GMO Viticulture and Winemaking Technology." *Journal of Wine Research* 17, no. 3 (2006): 161–172.

"Plate of Nations: Canada's Culinary Variety and Fusion Cuisine Are Not to Be Missed." *Successful Meetings: SM* 53, supplement 5 (2004): 4–7.

Pluhar, Evelyn B. "Meat and Morality: Alternatives to Factory Farming." *Journal of Agricultural and Environmental Ethics* 23, no. 5 (2010): 455–468.

Pollock, Chris, and Jules Pretty. "Farming Could Destroy Earth Unless We Rethink What 'Sustainable' Agriculture Is." *New Scientist* (April 21, 2007): 18–19.

Pope, Harrison G., et al. "Binge Eating Disorder: A Stable Syndrome." *The American Journal of Psychiatry* 163, no. 12 (2006): 2181–2183.

Posey, Lee. "The Farm Bill: Planting Farm, Rural and Food Assistance Policy for America." *Legisbrief* 16, no. 37 (2008).

"Poultry, Food Security and Poverty in India: Looking beyond the Farm-Gate." *World's Poultry Science Journal* 66, no. 2 (2010): 309–320.

"Power from Chocolate—The Mighty Bean." *The Economist* 390, no. 8624 (2009): 50.

"The Price of Foodborne Illness in the USA." *The Lancet* 375, no. 9718 (2010): 866.

"Processors, Scientists Look to Improve Fresh-Cut Produce Safety." *Food Chemical News* 50, no. 6 (2008): 10.

"Pros and Cons of Minimally Processed Foods." *Trends in Food Science & Technology* 18, no. 11 (2007): 582.

"Protection, Promotion and Support of Breast-Feeding in Europe: Progress from 2002 to 2007." *Public Health Nutrition* 13, no. 6 (2010): 751–759.

Prudhomme, Paul. "Herbs and Spices Can Help Restore a City." *U.S. News & World Report* 140, no. 7 (2006): 72–73.

Psaltopoulou, Theodora, Ioannis Ilias, and Mana Alevizaki. "The Role of Diet and Lifestyle in Primary, Secondary, and Tertiary Diabetes Prevention: A Review of Meta-Analyses." *Review of Diabetic Studies* 7, no. 1 (2010): 26–35.

Puglisi, Gregory, and Marianne Frieri. "Update on Hidden Food Allergens and Food Labeling." *Allergy and Asthma Proceedings* 28, no. 6 (2007): 634–639.

Purdy, Isabell B. "Social, Cultural, and Medical Factors That Influence Maternal Breastfeeding." *Issues in Mental Health Nursing* 31, no. 5 (2010): 365–367.

Quah, Su-Huey, and Andrew Tan. "Consumer Purchase Decisions of Organic Food Products: An Ethnic Analysis." *Journal of International Consumer Marketing* 22, no. 1 (2010): 47–58.

Rahn, Millie. "Laying a Place at the Table: Creating Public Foodways Models from Scratch." *Journal of American Folklore* 119, no. 471 (2006): 30–46.

Ramirez, W. Fred, and Jan Maciejowski. "Optimal Beer Fermentation." *Journal of the Institute of Brewing* 113, no. 3 (2007): 325–333.

Razzaq, Samiya. "Hemolytic Uremic Syndrome: An Emerging Health Risk." *American Family Physician* 74, no. 6 (2006): 991–996.

"Reforming the Food Safety System: What If Consolidation Isn't Enough?" *Harvard Law Review* 120, no. 5 (2007): 1345–1366.

Reinhard, Karl J. "A Coprological View of Ancestral Pueblo Cannibalism." *American Scientist* 94, no. 3 (2006): 254–261.

Reisin, Efrain. "The Benefit of the Mediterranean-Style Diet in Patients with Newly Diagnosed Diabetes." *Current Hypertension Reports* 12, no. 2 (2010): 56–58.

Resnik, David. "Trans Fat Bans and Human Freedom." *The American Journal of Bioethics* 10, no. 3 (2010): 27–32.

Reuben, Bryan, and Tom Coultate. "On the Rise — The Ancient Tradition of Bread Baking Depends on a Cascade of Chemical Reactions." *Chemistry World* 6, no. 10 (2009): 54–57.

Rich, Deborah. "Not All Apples Are Created Equal: The Latest Science on Organic Foods." *Earth Island Journal* 23, no. 1 (2008): 26–30.

"The Risks of Not Breastfeeding." *Journal of Acquired Immune Deficiency Syndromes: JAIDS* 53, no. 1 (2010): 1–4.

Rodriguez-Marval, Mawill, Patricia A. Kendall, Kenneth E. Belk, and John N. Sofos. "Inactivation of *Listeria Monocytogenes*." *Food Protection Trends* 30, no. 1 (2010): 16–24.

Roehm, Eric. "The Evidence-Based Mediterranean Diet Reduces Coronary Heart Disease Risk, and Plant-Derived Monounsaturated Fats May Reduce Coronary Heart Disease Risk." *American Journal of Clinical Nutrition* 90, no. 3 (2009): 697–698.

Rose, Natalie, Sabrina Koperski, and Beatrice A. Golomb. "Mood Food: Chocolate and Depressive Symptoms in a Cross-Sectional Analysis." *Archives of Internal Medicine* 170, no. 8 (2010): 699–703.

Rosegrant, Mark W., Claudia Ringler, and Tingju Zhu. "Water for Agriculture: Maintaining Food Security under Growing Scarcity." *Annual Review of Environment and Resources* 34 (2009): 205–222.

Rosenberg, Andrew A. "Aquaculture: The Price of Lice." *Nature* 451, no. 7174 (2008): 23–24.

Rosenberg, Norman J. "Climate Change, Agriculture, Water Resources: What Do We Tell Those That Need to Know?" *Climatic Change* 100, no. 1 (2010): 113–117.

Rosolen, Deanna. "Industry and Consumers Are Still Hearing Mixed Messages about the Use of Bisphenol-A in Food Packaging." *Food in Canada* 69, no. 2 (2009): 25.

Roth, Aleda V., Andy A. Tsay, Madeline E. Pullman, and John V. Gray. "Unraveling the Food Supply Chain: Strategic Insights from China and the 2007 Recalls." *Journal of Supply Chain Management* 44, no. 1 (2008): 22–39.

Rowe, William. "Agrarian Adaptations in Tajikistan: Land Reform, Water and Law." *Central Asian Survey* 29, no. 2 (2010): 189–204.

Rublin, Lauren R. "A Special Report on Philanthropy—Animal Spirits—Through the Gift of Livestock, Heifer International Nurtures Self-Reliance." *Barron's* (December 1, 2004): 26.

Ruhlman, Michael. "Forget Molecular Gastronomy. Michael Ruhlman Explains What's Really Going on in Cutting-Edge Kitchens around the Globe." *Restaurant Hospitality* 91, no. 5 (2007): 26.

Rull, Valenti. "Food Security: Green Revolution Drawbacks." *Science* 328, no. 5975 (2010): 169.

Ruxton, Carrie H. S., Elaine J. Gardner, and Helene M. McNulty. "Is Sugar Consumption Detrimental to Health? A Review of the Evidence 1995–2006." *Critical Reviews in Food Science and Nutrition* 50, no. 1 (2010): 1–19.

Rye, Johna Frederick, and Joanna Andrzejewska. "The Structural Disempowerment of Eastern European Migrant Farm Workers in Norwegian Agriculture." *Journal of Rural Studies* 26, no. 1 (2010): 41–51.

Saar, Ellu, and Marge Unt. "Falling High: Structure and Agency in Agriculture during the Transformation." *Journal of Baltic Studies* 41, no. 2 (2010): 215–235.

Sachs, Jeffrey D. "The African Green Revolution." *Scientific American* 298, no. 5 (2008): 42.

———. "The Promise of the Blue Revolution: Aquaculture Can Maintain Living Standards While Averting the Ruin of the Oceans." *Scientific American* 297, no. 1 (2007): 37–38.

Saldanha, Leila. "The Dietary Supplement Marketplace: Constantly Evolving." *Nutrition Today* 42, no. 2 (2007): 52–54.

Sanchez, Pedro A., and Monkombu S. Swaminathan. "Cutting World Hunger in Half." *Science* 5708 (2005): 357–360.

Sanders, Tom A. B. "The Role of Fat in the Diet—Quantity, Quality, and Sustainability." *Nutrition Bulletin* 35, no. 2 (2010): 138–146.

Sawhney, Aparna. "Quality Measures in Food Trade: The Indian Experience." *The World Economy* 28, no. 3 (2005): 329–348.

Schlosser, Eric. "Slow Food for Thought." *The Nation* 287, no. 8 (2008): 4.

Schmelzer, Matthias. "Marketing Morals, Moralizing Markets: Assessing the Effectiveness of Fair Trade as a Form of Boycott." *Management & Organizational History* 5, no. 2 (2010): 221–250.

Schmid, Heinrich O. E. "Biofuels, Food and Population." *World Watch* 21, no. 1 (2008): 2–3.

Schneider, Craig, and Tiffany Segre. "Green Tea: Potential Health Benefits." *American Family Physician* 79, no. 7 (2009): 591–594.

Schnell, Steven M. "Food with a Farmer's Face: Community-Supported Agriculture in the United States." *Geographical Review* 97, no. 4 (2007): 550–564.

Schooler, Deborah. "Real Women Have Curves." *Journal of Adolescent Research* 23, no. 2 (2008): 132–153.

"Sea Salt, Kosher Salt—Better Salts?: Here's How These Specialty Salts Stack Up to Everyday Table Salt." *Environmental Nutrition* 32, no. 5 (2009): 7.

Seals, Alan, and Joachim Zietz. "The Decline in Maize Prices, Biodiversity, and Subsistence Farming in Mexico." *The American Economist* 54, no. 2 (2009): 10–20.

See, Siao W., and Rajasekhar Balasubramanian. "Chemical Characteristics of Fine Particles Emitted from Different Gas Cooking Methods." *Atmospheric Environment* 42, no. 39 (2008): 8852–8862.

Sengupta, Jayanta. "Nation on a Platter: The Culture and Politics of Food and Cuisine in Colonial Bengal." *Modern Asian Studies* 44 (2010): 81–98.

Setola, Roberto, and Maria Carla De Maggio. "Security of the Food Supply Chain." *Proceedings: Annual International Conference of the IEEE Engineering in Medicine and Biology Society* (2009): 7061–7064.

Shah, Dimpy J., et al. "Hand Problems in Migrant Farmworkers." *Journal of Agricultural Safety and Health* 15, no. 2 (2009): 157–169.

Shaukat, Aasma, et al. "Systematic Review: Effective Management Strategies for Lactose Intolerance." *Annals of Internal Medicine* 152, no. 12 (2010): 797–803.

Shreck, Aimee. "Resistance, Redistribution, and Power in the Fair Trade Banana Initiative." *Agriculture and Human Values* 22, no. 1 (2005): 17–29.

Shute, Nancy. "The Scoop on Carbs and Fats. A New Study Tries to Make Sense of Diet and the Risk of Heart Disease." *U.S. News & World Report* 141, no. 19 (2006): 89–90.

Sikora, Ewa, Anna Bielak-Zmijewska, Grazyna Mosieniak, and Katarzyna Piwocka. "The Promise of Slow Down Ageing May Come from Curcumin." *Current Pharmaceutical Design* 16, no. 7 (2010): 884–892.

"The Simplicity Diet Fad—After a Variety of Hot Diet Books Extolling Extreme Nutritional Approaches, Common Sense Returns to the Table." *Publishers Weekly* 252, no. 45 (2005): 28.

Singh, Neeta. "Expert System Prototype of Food Aid Distribution." *Asia Pacific Journal of Clinical Nutrition* 16 (2007): 116–121.

Slegers, Monique F., and Leo Stroosnijder. "Beyond the Desertification Narrative: A Framework for Agricultural Drought in Semi-Arid East Africa." *Ambio* 37, no. 5 (2008): 372–380.

"The Slow Food Movement Tries to Shed Its Elitist Reputation." *Time* 172, no. 12 (2008): 40.

Smith, Martin D., et al. "Sustainability and Global Seafood." *Science* 327, no. 5967 (2010): 784–786.

Snow, Michelle. "On the Lookout for Listeriosis." *Nursing* 39, no. 7 (2009): 59.

Snyder, Carolyn, and Tandalayo Kidd. "Quality of Life Factors Influencing Health Behaviors in Young Adult Families." *Journal of Nutrition Education and Behavior* 42, no. 4 (2010).

So Good, It's Offal—Top Chefs Are Bringing New Finesse to Old Bistro Fare: Organ Meats." *Business Week* (March 28, 2005): 116.

Sofi, Francesco, Francesca Cesari, Rosanna Abbate, Gian Franco Gensini, and Alessandro Casini. "Adherence to Mediterranean Diet and Health Status: Meta-Analysis." *BMJ: British Medical Journal* 337 (2008): a1344.

Solomon, Diane. "The Devil's Fruit: The Strawberries That You Get at the Supermarket Come at a Cost to Pickers." *The Progressive* 72, no. 1 (2008): 22–24.

Solomons, Noel W. "Food Fortification with Folic Acid: Has the Other Shoe Dropped?" *Nutrition Reviews* 65, no. 11 (2007): 512–515.

Soltis, Cassandra A. "FDA Enforcement of the Food Allergen Labeling Law." *Regulatory Affairs Focus* 11, no. 10 (2006): 28–31.

Song, Moon K., Mark J. Rosenthal, et al. "Raw Vegetable Food Containing High Cyclo (his-Pro) Improved Insulin Sensitivity and Body Weight Control." *Metabolism: Clinical and Experimental* 54, no. 11 (2005): 1480–1489.

Soubra, Lama, Dolla Sarkis, Christoper Hilan, and Philippe H. Verger. "Dietary Exposure of Children and Teenagers to Benzoates, Sulphites, Butylhydroxyanisol (bha) and Butylhydroxytoluen (bht) in Beirut (Lebanon)." *Regulatory Toxicology and Pharmacology* 47, no. 1 (2007): 68–77.

"Sour Feelings on Raw Milk: Health Officials and Farmers Face Off over Safety of Selling the Unpasteurized Form." *U.S. News & World Report* 144, no. 12 (2008): 25.

Southgate, Douglas, Fabian Rodriguez, and Timothy Haab. "Payments for Sustainability: A Case Study on Subsistence Farming in Ecuador." *Harvard International Review* 31, no. 2 (2009): 52.

Spitz, Janet. "CEO Gender and the Malt Brewing Industry: Return of the Beer Witch, Ale-Wife, and Brewster." *Forum for Social Economics* 39, no. 1 (2010): 33–42.

Srinath, Reddy K., and Martin B. Katan. "Diet, Nutrition and the Prevention of Hypertension and Cardiovascular Diseases." *Public Health Nutrition* 7 (2004): 167–186.

Stephenson, Joan. "Malnutrition in Darfur." *Journal of the American Medical Association (JAMA)* 299, no. 7 (2008): 755.

———. "Studies Probe Microbes in Raw Milk, Swine." *Journal of the American Medical Association* 298, no. 12 (2007): 1388.

Stier, Richard F. "Food Safety: Will Reportable Food Registry Law Make Food Safer?" *Food Engineering—American Edition* 82, no. 1 (2010): 26.

Stiner, Mary C. "Carnivory, Coevolution, and the Geographic Spread of the Genus *Homo*." *Journal of Archaeological Research* 10 (2002): 1–63.

Stokstad, Erik. "Could Less Meat Mean More Food?" *Science* 327, no. 5967 (2010): 810–811.

Stolle, Dietlind, Marc Hooghe, and Michele Micheletti. "Politics in the Supermarket: Political Consumerism as a Form of Political Participation." *International Political Science Review* 26, no. 3 (2005): 245–269.

Stringam, Betsy B., John Gerdes, and Dawn Vanleeuwen. "Assessing the Importance and Relationships of Ratings on User-Generated Traveler

Reviews." *Journal of Quality Assurance in Hospitality & Tourism* 11, no. 2 (2010): 73–92.

"Study Links Bisphenol A to Heart Disease in Adults." *Food Chemical News* 51, no. 46 (2010): 12.

Sturm, Roland, and Doborah Cohen. "Fast-Food Bans: The Authors Respond." *Health Affairs* 29, no. 1 (2010): 219.

Suchy, Frederick J., et al. "National Institutes of Health Consensus Development Conference: Lactose Intolerance and Health." *Annals of Internal Medicine* 152, no. 12 (2010): 792–796.

"Sudan—Over Six Million People Need Food Aid." *UN Chronicle* 43, no. 1 (2006): 57.

"Summaries for Patients: The Effects of a Mediterranean Diet on Risk Factors for Heart Disease." *Annals of Internal Medicine* 145, no. 1 (2006): 1–11.

"Survey Shows Moderate Commitment to Produce Traceability Initiative." *Food Chemical News* 10, no. 4 (2010): 12.

"A Sustainable Ally—Food Alliance Wants to Help Growers Differentiate and Add Value to Their Fruit Crops through Sustainable Agriculture Practices and Certification." *American Fruit Grower* 129, no. 2 (2009): 16–17.

Svetkey, Laura P., Denise G. Simons-Morton, et al. "Effect of the Dietary Approaches to Stop Hypertension Diet and Reduced Sodium Intake on Blood Pressure Control." *Journal of Clinical Hypertension* 6, no. 7 (2004): 373–381.

"Sweeteners Focus: Opportunities in Sugar-Free Confectionery Market." *Food Manufacture* 82, no. 11 (2007): 69–70.

"Taiwan Bans Food Plastics." *ICIS Chemical Business: Europe, Middle East, Asia* (November 27, 2006): 13.

"Talking Pictures—Community Supported Agriculture." *World Watch* 22, no. 3 (2009): 18–19.

Tanne, Janice Hopkins. "FDA Says That Bisphenol A in Food Is Safe, Despite Controversy." *BMJ: British Medical Journal* 337 (2008): a1429.

Tarantino, Maria, and Sabina Terziani. "A Journey into the Imaginary of Sicilian Pastry." *Gastronomica: The Journal of Food and Culture* 10, no. 3 (2010): 45–51.

Tarver, Toni. "Just Add Water": Regulating and Protecting the Most Common Ingredient." *Journal of Food Science* 73, no. 1 (2008): 1–13.

Tasevska, Natasa, et al. "A Prospective Study of Meat, Cooking Methods, Meat Mutagens, Heme Iron, and Lung Cancer Risks." *The American Journal of Clinical Nutrition* 89, no. 6 (2009): 1884–1894.

"Taste a Food Fight in the World of Molecular Gastronomy." *Maclean's* 119, no. 25 (2006): 60.

"Taste Everyone's Restaurant Critic on Chowhound." *Maclean's* 123, no. 13 (2010): 62.

Taylor, Cathy. "Lactose Intolerance in Infants." *Nursing Times* 102, no. 17 (2006): 43–44.

Taylor, Michael R., and Jerry Cayford. "Changing U.S. Biotech Patent Policy Could Bring Food Security to Sub-Saharan Africa." *Resources* no. 152 (2004): 3.

"Tea Drinking." *JAMA: The Journal of the American Medical Association* 293, no. 5 (2005): 632.

Tenenbaum, David. "Food vs. Fuel: Diversion of Crops Could Cause More Hunger." *Environmental Health Perspectives* 116, no. 6 (2008): A254–A257.

Tessier, Stacy. "Rethinking the Food Chain: Farmworkers and the Taco Bell Boycott." *Journal of Developing Societies* 23, no. 1 (2007): 89–97.

This, Hervé. "Food for Tomorrow? How the Scientific Discipline of Molecular Gastronomy Could Change the Way We Eat." *Embo Reports* 7, no. 11 (2006): 1062–1066.

Thomson, Cynthia A., and Patricia A. Thompson. "Dietary Patterns, Risk and Prognosis of Breast Cancer." *Future Oncology* 5, no. 8 (2009): 1257–1269.

Thulier, Diane. "Breastfeeding in America: A History of Influencing Factors." *Journal of Human Lactation* 25, no. 1 (2009): 85–94.

Tillotson, James. "Agribusiness—The Backbone of Our Diet for Better—or for Worse, Part 1." *Nutrition Today* 41, no. 5 (2006): 233–238.

Timmer, Peter C. "Staving Off the Global Food Crisis." *Nature* 453, no. 7196 (2008): 722–723.

Tirado, Reyes, and Paul Johnston. "Food Security: GM Crops Threaten Biodiversity." *Science* 328, no. 5975 (2010): 171–172.

Tiwari, Rakesh, et al. "Land Use Dynamics in Select Village Ecosystems of Southern India: Drivers and Implications." *Journal of Land Use Science* 5, no. 3 (2010): 197–215.

Todd, Betsy. "Outbreak: E. Coli O157:h7." *The American Journal of Nursing* 107, no. 2 (2007): 29–32.

Tolley-Stokes, Rebecca. "Appalachian Home Cooking: History, Culture, & Recipes." *Gastronomica: The Journal of Food and Culture* 7, no. 1 (2007): 118–119.

"The Top 10 Functional Food Trends." *Food Technology* 62, no. 4 (2008): 24–44.

Touger-Decker, Riva. "Diet, Cardiovascular Disease and Oral Health: Promoting Health and Reducing Risk." *Journal of the American Dental Association* 141, no. 2 (2010): 167–170.

"Traceability for All: Top 10 Produce in Salinas, CA, Offers an Affordable Traceability Option for Small Growers." *American Fruit Grower* 129, no. 10 (2009): 16–17.

Trang, Tran T. T. "Social Differentiation Revisited: A Study of Rural Changes and Peasant Strategies in Vietnam." *Asia Pacific Viewpoint* 51, no. 1 (2010): 17–35.

"Trends: Food Miles." *Marketing Week* (August 24, 2006): 28–30.

"The Trends—How the Housewares Show Provokes Food Trends." *Food Processing* (May 2008): 14.

Trentmann, Frank. "Before Fair Trade: Empire, Free Trade, and the Moral Economies of Food in the Modern World." *Environment and Planning D: Society & Space* 25, no. 6 (2007): 1079–1102.

Trevors, Jack T. "Climate Change: Agriculture and Hunger." *Water, Air & Soil Pollution* 205, supplement 1 (2010): 105.

Tucker, Greg. "Phytonutrients." *Comparative Biochemistry and Physiology. Part A, Molecular & Integrative Physiology* 146, no. 4 (2007).

Tuei, Vivian C., Geoffrey K. Maiyoh, and Chung-Eun Ha. "Type 2 Diabetes Mellitus and Obesity in Sub-Saharan Africa." *Diabetes Metabolism Research and Reviews* 26, no. 6 (2010): 433–445.

Tugault-Lafleur, Claire, and Sarah Turner. "The Price of Spice: Ethnic Minority Livelihoods and Cardamom Commodity Chains in Upland Northern Vietnam." *Singapore Journal of Tropical Geography* 30, no. 3 (2009): 388–403.

Tumlison, Katie M., Margaret Harris, Reza Hakkak, and Polly A. Carroll. "Student Behavior Outcomes of an Expanded Nutrition Curriculum in Culinary School of Apprenticeship." *Journal of the American Dietetic Association* 107, no. 8 (2007): A56.

Tyagi, Sanjay. "E. Coli, What a Noisy Bug." *Science* 329, no. 5991 (2010): 518–519.

Uauy, Ricardo, Cecilia Albala, and Juliana Kain. "Obesity Trends in Latin America: Transiting from Under to Overweight." *Nutrition* 131 (2001): 893S–899S.

"UK Beef Embargo to Be Lifted." *Fleischwirtschaft International* no. 1 (2006): 8–9.

"United States—Winemaking—the French Touch." *The Economist* 379, no. 8478 (2006): 51.

U.S. Centers for Disease Control and Prevention. "Vital Signs: State-Specific Obesity Prevalence among Adults—United States, 2009." *Morbidity and Mortality Weekly Report (MMWR)* 59 (August 3, 2010): 1–5.

U.S. Food and Drug Administration. "Kid-Friendly Food Pyramid." *FDA Consumer* 39, no. 6 (2005): 4–5.

"USDA to Conduct First-Ever On-Farm Energy Production Survey." *Resource: Engineering & Technology for a Sustainable World* 17, no. 5 (2010): 29.

"USDA—FSIS Permanently Bans Downer Cattle from U.S. Food Supply." *Food Chemical News* 49, no. 22 (2007): 1.

"The Use of Low-Glycemic Index Diets in Diabetes Control." *British Journal of Nutrition* 104, no. 6 (2010): 797–802.

van den Berg, Patricia, Dianne Neumark-Sztainer, Peter J. Hannan, and Jess Haines. "Is Dieting Advice from Magazines Helpful or Harmful? Five-Year Associations with Weight-Control Behaviors and Psychological Outcomes in Adolescents." *Pediatrics* 119, no. 1 (January 2007): e30–e37.

Van der Kooi, Merle E. "The Inconsistent Vegetarian." *Society and Animals* 18, no. 3 (2010): 291–305.

Van Heel, David A., and J. West. "Recent Advances in Celiac Disease." *Gut* 55 (2006): 1037–1046.

Van Horn, Linda. "Diet and Heart Disease: Continuing Contributions." *Journal of the American Dietetic Association* 108, no. 2 (2008): 203.

———. "Nutritional Research: The Power behind the Fad-Free Diet." *Journal of the American Dietetic Association* 107, no. 3 (2007): 371.

"Vegan Diet Helps Treat Type 2 Diabetes." *Environmental Nutrition* 29, no. 10 (2006): 1.

Veggeland, Frode, and Svein O. L. E. Borgen. "Negotiating International Food Standards: The World Trade Organization's Impact on the Codex Alimentarius Commission." *Governance* 18, no. 4 (2005): 675–708.

Venkataraman, Chandra, et al. "The Indian National Initiative for Advanced Biomass Cookstoves: The Benefits of Clean Combustion." *Energy for Sustainable Development* 14, no. 2 (2010): 63–72.

Verrill, Linda, and Conrad J. Choiniere. "Are Food Allergen Advisory Statements Really Warnings? Variation in Consumer Preferences and Consumption Decisions." *Journal of Food Products Marketing* 15, no. 2 (2009): 139–151.

Vidavalur, Ramesh, Hajime Otani, Pawan K. Singa, and Nilanjana Maulik. "Significance of Wine and Resveratrol in Cardiovascular Disease: French

Paradox Revisited." *Experimental and Clinical Cardiology* 11, no. 3 (2006): 217–225.

Voelker, Rebecca. "FDA Tries to Catch Up on Food Safety." *JAMA: The Journal of the American Medical Association* 303, no. 18 (2010). 1797.

———. "NIH Panel Tackles Lactose Intolerance." *JAMA: The Journal of the American Medical Association* 303, no. 13 (2010): 1240–1242.

vonHoldt, Bridgett M., et al. "Genome-Wide SNP and Haplotype Analyses Reveal a Rich History Underlying Dog Domestication." *Nature* 464 (2010): 898–902.

Ward, Lorna A., et al. "Health Beliefs about Bottled Water: A Qualitative Study." *BMC Public Health* 9 (June 19, 2009): 196.

Warehousing & Distribution—Do Something— America's Second Harvest Is Working to See That No One in America Goes Hungry." *Material Handling Management* 59, no. 7 (2004): 46.

"Washington Trade Forum Focuses on FDA Food Import Safety." *Food Chemical News* 51, no. 4 (2009): 12.

Waters, Alice. "Slow Food Nation." *The Nation* 283, no. 7 (2006): 13.

Waugh, Irma M. "Examining the Sexual Harassment Experiences of Mexican Immigrant Farmworking Women." *Violence against Women* 16, no. 3 (2010): 237–261.

Weber, Christopher L., and H. Scott Matthews. "Food-Miles and the Relative Climate Impacts of Food Choices in the United States." *Environmental Science & Technology* 42, no. 10 (2008): 3508–3513.

Weber, Kristi, Mary Story, and Lisa Harnack. "Internet Food Marketing Strategies Aimed at Children and Adolescents: A Content Analysis of Food and Beverage Brand Web Sites." *Journal of the American Dietetic Association* 106, no. 99 (2006): 1463–1466.

Webster, Jacqueline L., Elizabeth K. Dunford, and Bruce C. Neal. "A Systematic Survey of the Sodium Contents of Processed Foods." *The American Journal of Clinical Nutrition* 91, no. 2 (2010): 413–420.

Weigel, M. Margaret, et al. "The Household Food Insecurity and Health Outcomes of U.S.-Mexico Border Migrant and Seasonal Farmworkers." *Journal of Immigrant and Minority Health/Center for Minority Public Health* 9, no. 3 (2007): 157–169.

Weir, Erica, Joanne Mitchell, Steven Reballato, and Dominic Fortuna. "Raw Milk and the Protection of Public Health." *Canadian Medical Association Journal* 177, no. 7 (2007): 721–722.

Weiss, Ehud, Mordechai E. Kislev, and Anat Hartmann. "Autonomous Cultivation before Domestication." *Science* 312, no. 5780 (2006): 160–161.

West, Harry G. "Food Fears and Raw-Milk Cheese." *Appetite* 51, no. 1 (2008): 25–29.

Westing, Arthur H. "Food Security: Population Controls." *Science* 328, no. 5975 (2010): 169.

White, Howard. "Tackling Childhood Undernutrition." *Lancet* 371, no. 9612 (2008): 539–541.

Wieck, Christine, and David Holland. "The Economic Effect of the Canadian BSE Outbreak on the US Economy." *Applied Economics* 42, no. 8 (2010): 935–946.

Wilde, Parke E., Lisa M. Troy, and Beatrice L. Rogers. "Food Stamps and Food Spending: An Engel Function Approach." *American Journal of Agricultural Economics* 91, no. 2 (2009): 416–430.

Wilkins, Jennifer. "Heifer International: Ending Hunger, Caring for the Earth." *Journal of Nutrition Education and Behavior* 39, no. 6 (2007): 358.

Willett, Walter C. "Diet and Cancer: An Evolving Picture." *Journal of the American Medical Association* 293, no. 2 (2005): 233–234.

Williams, Christina D., et al. "Associations of Red Meat, Fat, and Protein Intake with Distal Colorectal Cancer Risk." *Nutrition and Cancer* 62, no. 6 (2010): 701–709.

Wilson, G. Terence, Denise E. Wilfley, W. Stewart Agras, and Susan W. Bryson. "Psychological Treatments of Binge Eating Disorder." *Archives of General Psychiatry* 67, no. 1 (2010): 94–101.

Wilson, James. "GM Crops—Patently Wrong?" *Journal of Agricultural and Environmental Ethics* 20, no. 3 (2007): 261–283.

Winickoff, David, and Douglas Bushey. "Science and Power in Global Food Regulation: The Rise of the Codex Alimentarius." *Science, Technology, & Human Values* 35, no. 3 (2010): 356–381.

Wolfe, Nathan D., et al. "Bushmeat Hunting, Deforestation, and Prediction of Zoonotic Disease." *Emerging Infectious Diseases* 11, no. 12 (2005): 1822–1827.

Woo, Jean, Chi Shun Leung, and Yeung Shan Samuel Wong. "Impact of Childhood Experience of Famine on Late Life Health." *The Journal of Nutrition, Health, and Aging* 14, no. 2 (2010): 91–95.

"The World: Food Crisis—The Hefty Dinner Bill." *Time* (May 19, 2008): 34.

"The World: Hunger Levels in the U.S. Rise to an All-Time High." *Time* (November 30, 2009): 16–17.

Writing Committee of the World Health Organization Consultation on Human Influenza A/H5. "Avian Influenza A (H5N1) Infection in Humans." *New England Journal of Medicine* 353 (September 29, 2005): 1374–1385.

Wu, Anna H., Mimi C. Yu, Chiu-Chen Tseng, Frank Z. Stanczyk, and Malcolm C. Pike. "Dietary Patterns and Breast Cancer Risk in Asian American Women." *The American Journal of Clinical Nutrition* 89, no. 4 (2009): 1145–1154.

Wurgaft, Benjamin. "Economy, Gastronomy, and the Guilt of the Fancy Meal." *Gastronomica: The Journal of Food and Culture* 8, no. 2 (2008): 55–59.

Yek, Grace S., and Kurt Struwe. "Deconstructing Molecular Gastronomy: Part Food Science and Part Culinary Art, Molecular Gastronomy and Its Offshoots Are Revolutionizing Food Preparation, Presentation, and Eating and Sensory Experiences." *Food Technology* 62, no. 6 (2008): 34–45.

Yetley, Elizabeth A., et al. "Dietary Reference Intakes for Vitamin D: Justification for a Review of the 1997 Values." *The American Journal of Clinical Nutrition* 89, no. 3 (2009): 719–727.

Youn, Hyewon, Robert Woods, Xun Zhou, and Christian Hardigree. "The Restaurant Industry and Illegal Immigrants: An Oklahoma Case Study." *Journal of Human Resources in Hospitality & Tourism* 9, no. 3 (2010): 256–269.

Zarocostas, John. "New Network of Weather Stations in Africa Aims to Improve Food Security and Health." *BMJ: British Medical Journal* (clinical research ed.) 338 (2009): b2555.

Zevenbergen, Hans, et al. "Foods with a High Fat Quality Are Essential for Healthy Diets." *Annals of Nutrition & Metabolism* 54, supplement 1 (2009): 15–24.

WEB SITES

"The 1938 Food, Drug, and Cosmetic Act." *U.S. Food and Drug Administration (FDA).* http://www.fda.gov/AboutFDA/WhatWeDo/History/ProductRegulation/ucm132818.htm (accessed October 15, 2010).

"2008 Farm Bill Side-by-Side." *Economic Research Service (ERS), United States Department of Agriculture.* http://www.ers.usda.gov/FarmBill/2008/ (accessed September 26, 2010).

"2009 Food Aid Flows." *World Food Programme.* http://home.wfp.org/stellent/groups/public/documents/newsroom/wfp223562.pdf (accessed October 20, 2010).

Abend, Lisa. "The Cult of the Celebrity Chef Goes Global." *Time,* June 21, 2010. http://www.time.com/time/magazine/article/0,9171,1995844,00.html (accessed October 6, 2010).

Abend, Lisa. "Debating the Merits of Molecular Gastronomy." *Time,* January 23, 2009. http://www.time.com/time/arts/article/0,8599,1873579,00.html (accessed September 21, 2010).

"About FDA: Food Standards and the 1906 Act." *U.S. Food and Drug Administration (FDA).* http://www.fda.gov/AboutFDA/WhatWeDo/History/ProductRegulation/ucm132666.htm (accessed September 7, 2010).

"About the Center for Food Safety and Applied Nutrition." *Center for Food Safety and Applied Nutrition (CFSAN), U.S. Food and Drug Administration (FDA).* http://www.fda.gov/AboutFDA/CentersOffices/CFSAN/default.htm (accessed August 30, 2010).

"About the Commission." *Commission on Genetic Resources for Food and Agriculture, United Nations Food and Agriculture Organization (FAO).* http://www.fao.org/nr/cgrfa/cgrfa-about/cgrfa-history/en/ (accessed September 14, 2010).

"Afghanistan: Drug Industry and Counter-Narcotics Policy." *The World Bank. World Bank.* http://www.worldbank.org/ZTCWYL49P0 (accessed September 9, 2010).

"Afghanistan Opium Survey 2007: Executive Summary (August 2007)." *United Nations Office on Drugs and Crime.* http://www.unodc.org/documents/crop-monitoring/AFG07_ExSum_web.pdf (accessed September 9, 2010).

"Agenda 21." *United Nations Department of Economic and Social Affairs, Division for Sustainable Development.* http://www.un.org/esa/dsd/agenda21/ (accessed October 18, 2010).

"Agribusiness." *College of Agriculture, Food Systems, and Natural Resources, North Dakota State University.* http://www.ndsu.edu/ndsu/academic/factsheets/ag/agbus.shtml (accessed September 9, 2010).

Agricultural Research Service, U.S. Department of Agriculture (USDA). "Phytonutrients Take Center Stage." *Agricultural Research,* December 1999. http://www.ars.usda.gov/is/ar/archive/dec99/stage1299.htm (accessed October 4, 2010).

"Agriculture." *U.S. Agency for International Development (USAID).* http://www.usaid.gov/

our_work/agriculture/ (accessed October 6, 2010).

"Agriculture." *World Trade Organization.* http://www.wto.org/english/tratop_e/agric_e/agric_e.htm (accessed October 18, 2010).

"Agriculture and Achieving the Millennium Development Goals." *International Food Policy Research Institute.* http://www.ifpri.org/publication/agriculture-and-achieving-millennium-development-goals (accessed October 25, 2010).

"Agriculture: Fairer Markets for Farmers." *World Trade Organization.* http://www.wto.org/english/thewto_e/whatis_e/tif_e/agrm3_e.htm (accessed September 30, 2010).

"Agriculture: Work in the WTO." *World Trade Organization.* http://www.wto.org/english/tratop_e/agric_e/negoti_e.htm (accessed November 3, 2010).

"All about Pasta." *National Pasta Association.* http://www.ilovepasta.org/pasta.html (accessed October 25, 2010).

"Allergens." *The Food Allergy & Anaphylaxis Network.* http://www.foodallergy.org/section/allergens (accessed October 2, 2010).

al-Mughrabi, Nidal. "Israel Eases Gaza Embargo to Allow Snack Food In." *Reuters,* June 9, 2010. http://www.reuters.com/article/idUSTRE65820E20100609 (accessed October 25, 2010).

"Alternative Development: Myanmar." *United Nations Office on Drugs and Crime .* http://www.unodc.org/unodc/en/alternative-development/Myanmarprogramme.html (accessed September 6, 2010).

American College of Obstetricians and Gynecologists. "Media and Body Image: A Fact Sheet for Parents." *Tool Kit for Teen Care, Second Edition.* http://www.acog.org/departments/adolescentHealthCare/TeenCareToolKit/mediabody_4_parents.pdf (accessed October 20, 2010).

American Dietetic Association. http://www.eatright.org/default.aspx (accessed October 15, 2010).

American Dietetic Association. "Appropriate Planned Vegetarian Diets Are Healthful, May Help in Disease Prevention and Treatment, Says American Dietetic Association." *American Dietetic Association Press Release,* July 01, 2009. http://www.eatright.org/Media/content.aspx?id=1233&terms=vegetarian (accessed October 22, 2010).

American Dietetic Association. "Improving Nutrition for America's Children Act." *American Dietetic Association Press Release,* June 11, 2010.

http://www.eatright.org/Media/content.aspx?id=6442452566 (accessed July 20, 2010).

AmpleHarvest.org. http://www.ampleharvest.org/LP/Pantry.php?gclid=CKy6_sXC1qQCFc5i2godzkNnJQ (accessed October 18, 2010).

"Antioxidants, Phytochemicals, and Functional Foods." *U.S. Department of Agriculture (USDA).* http://fnic.nal.usda.gov/nal_display/index.php?info_center=4&tax_level=3&tax_subject=358&topic_id=1610&level3_id=5947&level4_id=0&level5_id=0&placement_default=0 (accessed November 30, 2010).

"Aquaculture." *Fisheries and Aquaculture Department, Food and Agriculture Organization of the United Nations (FAO).* http://www.fao.org/fishery/aquaculture/en (accessed October 8, 2010).

"Aquaculture." *U.S. Food and Drug Administration (FDA).* http://www.fda.gov/AnimalVeterinary/DevelopmentApprovalProcess/Aquaculture/default.htm (accessed October 8, 2010).

Aretaeus the Cappadocian. *The Extant Works of Aretaeus the Cappadocian,* edited and translated by Francis Adams. *Google Books.* http://books.google.com/books?id=v4gIAAAAIAAJ (accessed July 20, 2010).

Askin, Jennifer. "Starbucks Set to Rock Italy's Cafe Culture." *ABC News.* http://abcnews.go.com/Business/story?id=88256&page=1 (accessed October 17, 2010).

Associated Press. "Companies Send Goods to Cuba under Embargo Exception." *NewsMax.com,* June 26, 2004. http://archive.newsmax.com/archives/articles/2004/7/25/174317.shtml (accessed October 25, 2010).

"Avian Influenza." *Centers for Disease Control and Prevention (CDC).* http://www.cdc.gov/flu/avian (accessed September 23, 2010).

"Avian Influenza." *World Health Organization (WHO): Global Alert and Response (GAR).* http://www.who.int/csr/disease/avian_influenza/en/index.html (accessed September 23, 2010).

"Avian Influenza (Bird Flu)." *World Health Organization: Medical Centre.* http://www.who.int/entity/mediacentre/factsheets/avian_influenza/en/index.html (accessed September 23, 2010).

"Avian Influenza: Current H5N1 Situation." *Centers for Disease Control and Prevention (CDC).* http://www.cdc.gov/flu/avian/outbreaks/current.htm (accessed September 23, 2010).

"Ban on Fast Food TV Advertising Would Reverse Childhood Obesity Trends, Study Shows." *Science*

Daily, November 29, 2008. http://www.science daily.com/releases/2008/11/081119120149. htm (accessed October 31, 2010).

Bays, Jan Chozen. "Mindful Eating: The French Paradox." *Psychology Today*, March 21, 2009. http:// www.psychologytoday.com/blog/mindful-eating/200903/mindful-eating-the-french-paradox (accessed October 9, 2010).

Bays, Jan Chozen. "Mindful Eating: Rediscovering a Healthy and Joyful Relationship with Food: Fear of Food." *Psychology Today*, February 23, 2010. http://www.psychologytoday.com/blog/mindful-eating/201002/fear-food (accessed September 23, 2010).

Becker, Jeffrey S. "Humane Treatment of Farm Animals: Overview and Issues." *U.S. Department of Agriculture (USDA) CRS Report for Congress*, updated August 28, 2008. http://www.ncseon line.org/nle/crsreports/08Sept/RS21978.pdf (accessed October 19, 2010).

Bennett, Lisa. "The School Garden Debate: To Weep or Reap?" *Center for Ecoliteracy*. http://www.ecoliteracy.org/essays/school-garden-debate-weep-or-reap (accessed July 11, 2010).

"Best of the Food Blogs." *Delish.com*. http://www.delish.com/food/best-of-food-blogs (accessed October 18, 2010).

Better Sugar Cane Initiative (BSI). http://www.bettersugarcane.org/ (accessed October 4, 2010).

"Biodiversity for a World without Hunger." *Commission on Genetic Resources for Food and Agriculture, United Nations Food and Agriculture Organization (FAO)*. http://www.fao.org/fileadmin/templates/nr/documents/CGRFA/commissionfactsheet.pdf (accessed September 14, 2010).

"Bisphenol A (BPA)." *U.S. Food and Drug Administration (FDA)*. http://www.fda.gov/newsevents/publichealthfocus/ucm064437.htm (accessed September 20, 2010).

"Black Carbon Implicated in Global Warming." *Science Daily*, July 30, 2010. http://www.science daily.com/releases/2010/07/100729144225. htm (accessed November 1, 2010).

Black, Jane. "What's in a Number: How the Press Got the Idea That Food Travels 1,500 Miles from Farm to Plate." *Slate*, September 27, 2008. http://www.slate.com/id/2200202 (accessed July 31, 2010).

Bliss, Rosalie Marion. "Molecular Biology Provides Clues to Health Benefits of Olive Oil." *U.S. Department of Agriculture (USDA)*, June 28, 2010.

http://www.ars.usda.gov/is/pr/2010/100628. htm (accessed September 22, 2010).

Blount, Hagan. "The Final Word on Foodies." *The Wandering Foodie*, November 16, 2009. http://wanderingfoodie.com/2009/the-final-word-on-foodies/# (accessed October 15, 2010).

"Body Image: Loving Your Body Inside and Out." *National Women's Health Information Center. womenshealth.gov*. http://www.womenshealth.gov/bodyimage/ (accessed October 9, 2010).

"Bottled Water." *National Resources Defense Council*. http://www.nrdc.org/water/drinking/qbw.asp (accessed September 5, 2010).

"Bottled Water: Get the Facts." *Food and Water Watch*. http://www.foodandwaterwatch.org/water/bottled/ (accessed September 5, 2010).

"Botulism." *Centers for Disease Control and Prevention (CDC)*. http://www.cdc.gov/nczved/divisions/dfbmd/diseases/botulism/ (accessed October 8, 2010).

"Botulism." *World Health Organization*. http://www.who.int/entity/mediacentre/factsheets/fs270/en/index.html (accessed October 8, 2010).

Bouchez, Colette. "Making the Most of Your Metabolism." *WebMD*. http://www.webmd.com/fitness-exercise/guide/make-most-your-metabolism (accessed October 15, 2010).

Bourlaug, Norman. "Biotechnology and the Green Revolution." *Action Bioscience*. http://www.actionbioscience.org/biotech/borlaug.html (accessed October 25, 2010).

"Bovine Spongiform Encephalopathy." *U.S. Food and Drug Administration (FDA)*. http://www.fda.gov/AnimalVeterinary/GuidanceCompliance Enforcement/ComplianceEnforcement/Bovine SpongiformEncephalopathy/default.htm

"Bovine spongiform encephalopathy." *World Health Organization*. http://www.who.int/entity/mediacentre/factsheets/fs113/en/index.html (accessed October 21, 2010).

Bowen, R. "Physiology of Taste." *Colorado State University*, updated December 10, 2006. http://www.vivo.colostate.edu/hbooks/pathphys/digestion/pregastric/taste.html (accessed August 25, 2010).

Branson, Kyle. "Slave-Free Chocolate." *Stop Chocolate Slavery*. http://vision.ucsd.edu/~kbranson/stopchocolateslavery/main.html (accessed October 23, 2010).

Bread Bakers Guild of America. http://www.bbga.org/ (accessed September 14, 2010).

"Breastfeeding." *World Health Organization.* http://www.who.int/topics/breastfeeding/en/ (accessed October 8, 2010).

"Breastfeeding: Impact on Child Survival and Global Situation." *UNICEF.* http://www.unicef.org/nutrition/index_24824.html (accessed October 8, 2010).

Brewers Association. "Craft Beer: Celebrating the Best of American Beer." *craftbeer.com.* http://www.craftbeer.com/ (accessed November 3, 2010).

"BSE (Bovine Spongiform Encephalopathy, or Mad Cow Disease)." *Centers for Disease Control and Prevention (CDC).* http://www.cdc.gov/ncidod/dvrd/bse/ (accessed October 21, 2010).

"Burkina Faso: Cotton Story." *Oxfam International.* http://www.oxfam.org/en/campaigns/trade/real_lives/burkina_faso (accessed September 25, 2010).

Bushmeat Crisis Task Force. http://www.bushmeat.org/ (accessed October 30, 2010).

"The Cartagena Protocol on Biosafety." *Convention on Biological Diversity.* http://bch.cbd.int/protocol/ (accessed August 1, 2010).

Celiac Sprue Association. http://www.csaceliacs.org/index.php (accessed July 20, 2010).

Centers for Disease Control and Prevention (CDC). Division of Foodborne, Bacterial and Mycotic Disease. http://www.cdc.gov/nczved/dfbmd/disease_listing/cholera_gi.html (accessed September 7, 2010).

"Chadians Face a Threefold Emergency of Hunger, Floods, and Cholera." *Médecins Sans Frontières (Doctors without Borders),* October 3, 2010. http://www.msf.org/msf/articles/2010/10/chadians-face-a-threefold-emergency-of-hunger-floods-and-cholera.cfm (accessed November 30, 2010).

Charles, Dan. "Sugar Beet Beatdown: Engineered Varieties Banned." *NPR: National Public Radio,* September 16, 2010. http://www.npr.org/templates/story/story.php?storyId=129891767 (accessed October 4, 2010).

"Chef Survey: What's Hot in 2009." *National Restaurant Association.* http://www.restaurant.org/pdfs/research/2009chefsurvey.pdf (accessed October 7, 2010).

Childs, Dan. "Take It or Leave It? The Truth about 8 Mediterranean Diet Staples." *ABC News,* June 24, 2009. http://abcnews.go.com/Health/MensHealthNews/story?id=7911505 (accessed November 4, 2010).

"Chimpanzees and Bushmeat 101." *Jane Goodall Institute.* http://www.Janegoodall.org/Chimpanzees-And-Bushmeat-101 (accessed October 30, 2010).

"Cholera." *World Health Organization.* http://www.who.int/entity/mediacentre/factsheets/fs107/en/index.html (accessed September 7, 2010).

Clifford, Carolyn, et al. "Diet and Cancer Risk." *National Cancer Institute.* http://rex.nci.nih.gov/NCI_Pub_Interface/raterisk/risks73.html (accessed September 6, 2010).

"Climate Change and Food Security: A Framework Document." *Food and Agriculture Organization of the United Nations (FAO),* 2008. http://www.reliefweb.int/rw/lib.nsf/db900sid/PANA7KADCQ/$file/fao_may2008.pdf?openelement (accessed October 27, 2010).

"Climate Change: Food Security." *Food and Agriculture Organization of the United Nations (FAO).* http://www.fao.org/climatechange/49357@152835/en/ (accessed October 27, 2010).

"Climate Change—Health and Environmental Effects: Agriculture and Food Supply." *U.S. Environmental Protection Agency (EPA).* http://www.epa.gov/climatechange/effects/agriculture.html (accessed October 1, 2010).

"Codex Alimentarius." *Codex Alimentarius Commission.* http://www.codexalimentarius.net/web/index_en.jsp (accessed October 16, 2010).

"Codex Alimentarius." *Food Safety and Inspection Service (FSIS), U.S. Department of Agriculture (USDA).* http://www.fsis.usda.gov/codex_alimentarius/index.asp (accessed October 16, 2010).

"Coffee Production." *Coffee Science Information Centre.* http://www.cosic.org/background-on-coffee/coffee-production

College of Agriculture and Natural Resources. "How to Make a Transgenic Plant." *University of Delaware.* http://www.ag.udel.edu/agbiotech/transgenic-tomato-cc.php (accessed November 1, 2010).

Collins, Ronald K. L., and Jonathan Bloom. "Win or Lose, Dissing Food Can be Costly." *Foodspeak: Center for Science in the Public Interest,* March 8, 1999. http://cspinet.org/foodspeak/oped/winorloss.htm (accessed September 28, 2010).

"Community Supported Agriculture." *Local Harvest.* http://www.localharvest.org/csa/ (accessed October 16, 2010).

"Concentrated Animal Feeding Operations (CAFOs)." *Environmental Health Services (EHS), U.S. Centers for Disease Control and Prevention (CDC).* http://www.cdc.gov/nceh/ehs/Topics/CAFO.htm (accessed September 20, 2010).

Consumers International. "Streetfood." *Streetfood.org.* http://streetfood.org/index.php?option=com_frontpage&Itemid=1 (accessed September 29, 2010).

Cooking Channel. http://www.cookingchanneltv.com/ (accessed October 31, 2010).

"Cooking in the 1940s." *Retro-Housewife.com.* http://www.retro-housewife.com/1940-cooking-and-recipes.html (accessed October 27, 2010).

"Corn." *Economic Research Service, U.S. Department of Agriculture (USDA),* updated September 23, 2010. http://www.ers.usda.gov/Briefing/Corn/ (accessed October 23, 2010).

"Corn Cam." *Iowa Farmer Today.* http://www.iowafarmertoday.com/corn_cam/ (accessed October 23, 2010).

"Countries: Sudan." *World Food Programme.* http://www.wfp.org/countries/sudan (accessed October 18, 2010).

"Country-of-Origin Labeling." *Economic Research Service (ERS), U.S. Department of Agriculture (USDA).* http://www.ers.usda.gov/features/cool/ (accessed October 16, 2010).

Culinary Herb Guide. http://culinaryherbguide.com/index.html (accessed September 21, 2010).

Culinary Online: Your Roadmap to the Culinary Internet. http://www.culinary-online.com/ (accessed October 6, 2010).

"The Current State of World Hunger." *East Africa Famine,* March 19, 2010. http://www.eastafricafamine.com/ (accessed October 18, 2010).

Dag Hammarskjöld Library. "World Food Day: 16 October." *United Nations.* http://www.un.org/depts/dhl/food/index.html (accessed September 14, 2010).

Dakss, Brian. "Expert: School Lunches Failing Kids." *CBS News,* September 21, 2006. http://www.cbsnews.com/stories/2006/09/21/earlyshow/leisure/books/main2028174.shtml (accessed October 18, 2010).

"The Dangers of Raw Milk: Unpasteurized Milk Can Pose a Serious Health Risk." *U.S. Food and Drug Administration (FDA).* http://www.fda.gov/Food/ResourcesForYou/Consumers/ucm079516.htm (accessed August 19, 2010).

Darwin, Roy. "Climate Change and Food Security." *U.S. Department of Agriculture Economic Research Service,* June 2001. http://www.ers.usda.gov/publications/aib765/aib765-8.pdf (accessed October 27 2010).

Das, Sita Rama. "FaithandFood Fact Files: Hinduism." *faithandfood.com.* http://www.faithandfood.com/Hinduism.php (accessed October 31, 2010).

Demetri, Justin. "Italian Pasta through the Ages." *Life in Italy.com.* http://www.lifeinitaly.com/food/pasta-history.asp (accessed October 25, 2010).

"Desertification." *Food and Agriculture Organization of the United Nations (FAO).* http://www.fao.org/desertification/default.asp?lang=en (accessed October 15, 2010).

Desmond, Daniel, James Grieshop, and Aarti Subramanian. "Revisiting Garden Based Learning in Basic Education: Philosophical Roots, Historical Foundations, Best Practices and Products, Impacts, Outcomes, and Future Directions." *United Nations Food and Agriculture Organization (FAO),* May 2003. http://www.fao.org/sd/2003/kn0504_en.htm (accessed July 10, 2010).

"The Developing World's New Burden: Obesity." *Food and Agriculture Organization of the United Nations (FAO).* http://www.fao.org/FOCUS/E/obesity/obes1.htm (accessed October 15, 2010).

"Diet and Lifestyle Recommendations." *American Heart Association.* http://www.heart.org/HEARTORG/GettingHealthy/Diet-and-Lifestyle-Recommendations_UCM_305855_Article.jsp (accessed September 10, 2010).

"Dietary Guidelines for Americans." *U.S. Department of Health and Human Services.* http://www.health.gov/dietaryguidelines/ (accessed October 19, 2010).

"Dietary Supplement Health and Education Act of 1994." *Office of Dietary Supplements, National Institutes of Health.* http://ods.od.nih.gov/About/DSHEA_Wording.aspx (accessed September 26, 2010).

"Dietary Supplements." *U.S. Food and Drug Administration (FDA).* http://www.fda.gov/food/dietarysupplements/default.htm (accessed September 26, 2010).

"Digestive System." *National Geographic Society.* http://science.nationalgeographic.com/science/health-and-human-body/human-body/digestive-system-article.html (accessed September 29, 2010).

Dirks, Tim. "The History of Film." *AMC Filmsite.* http://www.filmsite.org/pre20sintro2.html (accessed October 21, 2010).

Diverseeds: Plant Genetic Resources for Food and Agriculture. http://www.diverseeds.eu/DVD/Home.html (accessed October 18, 2010).

Doheny, Kathleen. "Eating Red Meat May Boost Death Risk." *WebMd*, March 23, 2009. http://www.webmd.com/diet/news/20090323/eating-red-meat-may-boost-death-risk (accessed September 28, 2010).

Dole Organic Program. http://www.doleorganic.com/index.php (accessed January 18, 2011).

Dr. Temple Grandin's Web Page: Livestock Behavior, Design Facilities, and Humane Slaughter. http://www.grandin.com/index.html (accessed October 19, 2010).

"Drug-Resistant Salmonella." *World Health Organization.* http://www.who.int/entity/mediacentre/factsheets/fs139/en/index.html (accessed September 2, 2010).

"Early Agriculture and Development." *Oregon State University.* http://oregonstate.edu/instruct/css/330/one/index.htm#EarlyAgriculture (accessed October 22, 2010).

The Earth Institute. "Toll of Climate Change on World Food Supply Could Be Worse Than Thought, Predictions, Already Daunting, Fail to Account for Extreme Weather, Disease and Other Complications." *Columbia University*, December 3, 2007. http://www.earth.columbia.edu/articles/view/2001 (accessed October 1, 2010).

"Eating Disorders." *National Institute of Mental Health.* http://www.nimh.nih.gov/health/publications/eating-disorders/complete-index.shtml (accessed October 8, 2010).

"Ecosystems: Agroecosystems: Agriculture." *U.S. Environmental Protection Agency (EPA).* http://www.epa.gov/ebtpages/ecosagroecosystemsagriculture.html (accessed August 4, 2010).

Edgar, Julie. "Health Benefits of Green Tea." *WebMD.* http://www.webmd.com/food-recipes/features/health-benefits-of-green-tea (accessed October 25, 2010).

The Edible Schoolyard. http://www.edibleschoolyard.org/ (accessed October 4, 2010).

"Egg Safety Final Rule." *U.S. Food and Drug Administration (FDA).* http://edocket.access.gpo.gov/2009/pdf/E9-16119.pdf (accessed September 23, 2010).

"The End of India's Green Revolution?" *BBC News*, May 29, 2006. http://news.bbc.co.uk/2/hi/south_asia/4994590.stm (accessed October 25, 2010).

"Ending Child Hunger and Undernutrition Initiative." *World Food Programme.* http://documents.wfp.org/stellent/groups/public/documents/resources/wfp111813.pdf (accessed October 2, 2010).

Engelhart, Katie. "Cavemen Who Walk among Us." *MacLeans*, February 25, 2010. http://www2.macleans.ca/2010/02/26/cavemen-who-walk-among-us/ (accessed August 18, 2010).

Epstein, Rebecca L. "Food on Film." *Gastronomica.* http://www.gastronomica.org/foodfilms.html (accessed October 21, 2010).

"*Escherichia coli* O157:H7." *National Center for Zoonotic, Vector-Borne, and Enteric Diseases, U.S. Centers for Disease Control and Prevention.* http://www.cdc.gov/nczved/divisions/dfbmd/diseases/ecoli_o157h7/ (accessed September 1, 2010).

Escoffier On Line: The Culinary Resource. http://www.escoffier.com/ (accessed October 6, 2010).

Evans, Dale. "Documentaries: New Film Links Food to Immigration." *Rochester City Newspaper*, May 29, 2007. http://ns.rochestercitynewspaper.com/entertainment/movies/DOCUMENTARIES-New-film-links-food-to-immigration/ (accessed October 21, 2010).

"Fact Sheet: Plan Columbia." *U.S. Bureau of Western Hemisphere Affairs, U.S. Department of State*, March 28, 2000. http://www.state.gov/www/regions/wha/colombia/fs_000328_plancolombia.html (accessed September 6, 2010).

"Factory Farming." *HFA: The Humane Farming Association.* http://www.hfa.org/factory/index.html (accessed October 19, 2010).

"Facts about Farm Animal Welfare Standards." *Farm Sanctuary.* http://www.upc-online.org/welfare/standards_booklet_FINAL.pdf (accessed October 17, 2010).

"Facts about Noroviruses on Cruise Ships." *U.S. Centers for Disease Control and Prevention (CDC).* http://www.cdc.gov/nceh/vsp/pub/norovirus/norovirus.htm (accessed November 1, 2010).

"Facts on Migrant Labor." *International Labour Organization*, June 2004. http://www.ilo.org/public/english/bureau/inf/download/factsheets/pdf/migrants.pdf (accessed September 23, 2010).

Fairfood International. http://www.fairfood.org/?gclid=COG0l8WCyqQCFcTt7Qod9VcqDA (accessed October 19, 2010).

Fairtrade Foundation. http://www.fairtrade.org.uk/products/default.aspx (accessed October 19, 2010).

"Family Farms." *Sustainable Table.org.* http://www.sustainabletable.org/issues/familyfarms/ (accessed October 19, 2010).

Famine Early Warning Systems Network (FEWS-Net), U.S. Agency for International Development (USAID). http://www.fews.net/Pages/default.aspx (accessed September 9, 2010).

"FAO and the Eight Millennium Development Goals." *Food and Agriculture Organization of the United Nations (FAO).* http://www.fao.org/mdg/en/ (accessed September 30, 2010).

FAO Newsroom. "FAO Urges Action to Cope with Increasing Water Scarcity." *Food and Agriculture Organization of the United Nations (FAO),* March 22, 2007. http://www.fao.org/newsroom/en/news/2007/1000520/index.html (accessed October 6, 2010).

FAO Newsroom. "The Gene Revolution: Great Potential for the Poor, but No Panacea." *Food and Agriculture Organization of the United Nations (FAO),* May 17, 2004. http://www.fao.org/newsroom/en/news/2004/41714/index.html (accessed November 1, 2010).

Farm to Table (New Mexico). http://www.farmtotablenm.org/ (accessed October 23, 2010).

Farm to Table: The Emerging American Meal. http://www.farmtotableonline.org/ (accessed October 16, 2010).

"Farmers Protected against GM Patent Lawsuits." *European Public Health Alliance.* http://www.epha.org/a/3404 (accessed October 28, 2010).

farmingsolutions: Success Stories for the Future of Agriculture. http://www.farmingsolutions.org/ (accessed October 9, 2010).

"Fast Food Nutrition Facts." *FastFoodNutrition.org.* http://www.fastfoodnutrition.org/ (accessed October 17, 2010).

Feed the Future. http://www.feedthefuture.gov/ (accessed October 14, 2010).

Feeding America. http://feedingamerica.org/ (accessed October 18, 2010).

Ferguson, Priscilla Parkhurst. "Babette's Feast: A Fable for Culinary France," from *Accounting for Taste: The Triumph of French Cuisine,* University of Chicago Press, 2004. http://www.press.uchicago.edu/Misc/Chicago/243230.html (accessed October 21, 2010).

"Fermentation Process." *VirtualWine.com.au.* http://www.virtualwine.com.au/wine-making/fermentation.asp (accessed November 3, 2010).

"Fifth Annual New York Food Film Festival: 2011." *NYC Food Film Festival & Grease Bomb LLC.* http://www.nycfoodfilmfestival.com (accessed October 21, 2010).

"Fish and Omega-3 Fatty Acids." *American Heart Association.* http://www.americanheart.org/presenter.jhtml?identifier=4632 (accessed September 10, 2010).

"Five Freedoms." *Farm Animal Welfare Council.* http://www.fawc.org.uk/freedoms.htm (accessed October 17, 2010).

Flanagan, Caitlin. "Cultivating Failure: How School Gardens Are Cheating Our Most Vulnerable Students." *The Atlantic,* January/February 2010. http://www.theatlantic.com/magazine/archive/2010/01/cultivating-failure/7819/1/ (accessed October 25, 2010).

"Food." *U.S. Food and Drug Administration (FDA).* http://www.fda.gov/Food/default.htm (accessed October 18, 2010).

Food & Water Watch. http://www.foodandwaterwatch.org/ (accessed October 6, 2010).

"Food Additives." *U.S. Food and Drug Administration (FDA).* http://www.fda.gov/food/foodingredientspackaging/foodadditives/default.htm (accessed October 7, 2010).

"Food and Soil." *Global Education Project.* http://www.theglobaleducationproject.org/earth/food-and-soil.php (accessed October 30, 2010).

"Food Coops." *Local Harvest.* http://www.localharvest.org/food-coops/ (accessed October 4, 2010).

"Food Crisis: What the World Bank Is Doing." *The World Bank.* http://www.worldbank.org/foodcrisis/ (accessed September 18, 2010).

"Food Defense & Emergency Response." *Food Safety and Inspection Service (FSIS), U.S. Department of Agriculture (USDA).* http://www.fsis.usda.gov/Food_Defense_&_Emergency_Response/FSIS_Security_Guidelines_for_Food_Processors/index.asp (accessed September 11, 2010).

Food First: Institute for Food & Development Policy. http://www.foodfirst.org/ (accessed October 9, 2010).

"Food for the Cities: Ensuring the Quality and Safety of Street Foods." *Food Quality and Standards Service, Food and Agriculture Organization of the United Nations (FAO).* ftp://ftp.fao.org/docrep/fao/011/ak003e/ak003e09.pdf (accessed September 29, 2010).

"Food, Genetically Modified." *World Health Organization.* http://www.who.int/topics/food_genetically_modified/en (accessed November 1, 2010).

"Food Ingredients & Packaging." *U.S. Food and Drug Administration (FDA)*. http://www.fda.gov/Food/FoodIngredientsPackaging/default.htm (accessed October 30, 2010).

"Food Ingredients and Colors." *U.S. Food and Drug Administration (FDA)*. http://www.fda.gov/food/foodingredientspackaging/ucm094211.htm (accessed October 10, 2010).

"Food Irradiation." *U.S. Centers for Disease Control and Prevention (CDC)*. http://www.cdc.gov/ncidod/dbmd/diseaseinfo/foodirradiation.htm (accessed September 11, 2010).

"Food Labeling Guide." *U.S. Food and Drug Administration (FDA)*. http://www.fda.gov/Food/GuidanceComplianceRegulatoryInformation/GuidanceDocuments/FoodLabelingNutrition/FoodLabelingGuide/default.htm (accessed November 3, 2010).

Food Network.com. http://www.foodnetwork.com/ (accessed October 31, 2010).

"Food Recalls and Alerts." *FoodSafety.gov*. http://www.foodsafety.gov/keep/recalls/index.html (accessed October 10, 2010).

"Food Safety Education: Be Food Safe." *Food Safety and Inspection Service, U.S. Department of Agriculture (USDA)*. http://www.fsis.usda.gov/Be_FoodSafe/index.asp (accessed October 19, 2010).

"Food Security." *World Health Organization*. http://www.who.int/trade/glossary/story028/en/ (accessed October 30, 2010).

"Food Stamps and Other Nutrition Programs." *Social Security Administration*. http://www.ssa.gov/pubs/10100.html (accessed November 2, 2010).

"Food Standards under the 1938 Food, Drug, and Cosmetic Act: Bread and Jam." *U.S. Food and Drug Administration (FDA)*. http://www.fda.gov/AboutFDA/WhatWeDo/History/ProductRegulation/ucm132892.htm (accessed October 15, 2010).

Food Trends. http://www.foodtrends.com/ (accessed October 25, 2010).

"Foodborne Diseases." *World Health Organization*. http://www.who.int/topics/foodborne_diseases/en/ (accessed October 2, 2010).

"Foodborne Illness." *U.S. Centers for Disease Control and Prevention (CDC)*. http://www.cdc.gov/ncidod/dbmd/diseaseinfo/foodborneinfections_g.htm (accessed October 2, 2010).

"Foodborne Illness: What Consumers Need to Know." *Food Safety and Inspection Service (FSIS), U.S. Department of Agriculture (USDA)*. http://www.fsis.usda.gov/Fact_Sheets/Foodborne_Illness_What_Consumers_Need_to_Know/index.asp (accessed October 19, 2010).

FoodSHIELD.org. http://www.foodshield.org/ (accessed September 11, 2010).

"Forging Food Sovereignty for Human Rights and Sustainable Livelihoods." *Food First*. http://www.foodfirst.org/about/programs (accessed October 17, 2010).

"Formula versus Mother's Milk: The Boycott Battle Continues." *Food and Agriculture Organization of the United Nations (FAO)*. http://www.fao.org/docrep/T3550E/t3550e01.htm (accessed October 25, 2010).

"Fortify Your Knowledge about Vitamins." *U.S. Food and Drug Administration (FDA)*. http://www.fda.gov/ForConsumers/ConsumerUpdates/ucm118079.htm (accessed August 20, 2010).

Fox, Nick. "Chicago Overturns Foie Gras Ban." *The New York Times*, May 14, 2008. http://dinersjournal.blogs.nytimes.com/2008/05/14/chicago-overturns-foie-gras-ban/ (accessed November 1, 2010).

FreeRice. http://www.freerice.com/ (accessed October 23, 2010).

Friedman, Emily. "Health Care Stirs Up Whole Foods CEO John Mackey, Customers Boycott Organic Grocery Store." *ABC News*, August 14, 2009. http://abcnews.go.com/Business/story?id=8322658&page=1 (accessed October 25, 2010).

"The Future of World Food Security." *IFAD: International Fund for Agricultural Development*. http://www.ifad.org/hfs/ (accessed October 30, 2010).

Gadsby, Patricia. "Cooking for Eggheads." *Discover*, February 2006. http://discovermagazine.com/2006/feb/cooking-for-eggheads (accessed September 21, 2010).

Gambrell, John. "10 Million Face Famine in West Africa." *The Independent*, May 30, 2010. http://www.independent.co.uk/news/world/africa/10-million-face-famine-in-west-africa1986875.html (accessed October 17, 2010).

Gates, Melinda. "Celebrating the Simple, Lifesaving Act of Breastfeeding." *Bill & Melinda Gates Foundation*, August 30, 2010. http://www.gatesfoundation.org/foundationnotes/Pages/melinda-gates-100830-celebrating-breastfeeding.aspx (accessed October 8, 2010).

Gayot: The Guide to the Good Life. http://www.gayot.com/restaurants/ (accessed October 30, 2010).

Genauer, Ethan. "Ideas for Change in America: Good Food for All Kids: A Garden at Every School." *Change.org.* http://www.change.org/ideas/view/good_food_for_all_kids_a_garden_at_every_school_2 (accessed October 25, 2010).

George Ohsawa Macrobiotic Foundation. http://www.ohsawamacrobiotics.com/ (accessed October 15, 2010).

"Get Involved: World Food Day 16 October 2010: United against Hunger." *Food and Agriculture Organization of the United Nations (FAO).* http://www.fao.org/getinvolved/worldfoodday/en/ (accessed September 23, 2010).

Gibbs, Nancy. "The Magic of the Family Meal." *Time,* June 4, 2006. http://www.time.com/time/magazine/article/0,9171,1200760,00.html (accessed October 1, 2010).

Global Alliance for Clean Cookstoves. http://cleancookstoves.org/ (accessed November 1, 2010).

"Global Consultation on Oral Health through Fluoride." *World Health Organization.* http://www.who.int/oral_health/events/Global_consultation/en/index.html (accessed October 15, 2010).

Global Crop Diversity Trust. http://www.croptrust.org/main/ (accessed October 18, 2010).

"The Global Food Crisis: The Silent Tsunami." *The World Bank.* http://go.worldbank.org/TLTXLXZE00 (accessed September 18, 2010).

"Global Status Report on Alcohol 2004." *World Health Organization (WHO).* http://www.who.int/substance_abuse/publications/globalstatusreportalcoholchapters/en/ (accessed November 3, 2010).

"Global Task Force on Cholera Control." *World Health Organization (WHO).* http://www.who.int/entity/cholera/en (accessed September 7, 2010).

Gluten Intolerance Group of North America. http://www.gluten.net/ (accessed July 20, 2010).

"Go West, Early Man: Modeling the Origin and Spread of Early Agriculture." *PLoS Biology* 3, no. 12, December 2005. http://www.ncbi.nlm.nih.gov/pmc/articles/PMC1287510/ (accessed October 22, 2010).

"Governments Agree on New UN-Backed Pact to Protect Sharks." *UN News Centre,* December 13, 2007. http://www.un.org/apps/news/story.asp?NewsID=25056&Cr=UNEP&Cr1 (accessed October 10, 2010).

Gowlett, J. A. J. "What Actually Was the Stone Age Diet?" *Journal of Nutritional and Environmental Medicine,* September 2003. http://pcwww.liv.ac.uk/~gowlett/GowlettCJNE_13_03_02.pdf (accessed August 18, 2010).

"Grain Market Report: 26 August 2010." *International Grains Council.* http://www.igc.int/downloads/gmrsummary/gmrsumme.pdf (accessed September 21, 2010).

Greene, Gael. "What's Nouvelle? La Cuisine Bourgeoise." *Insatiable Critic,* June 2, 1980. http://www.insatiable-critic.com/Article.aspx?id=1131 (accessed October 15, 2010).

Haggard, Stephen, and Marcus Noland. "Hunger and Human Rights: Politics and Famine in North Korea." *U.S. Committee for Human Rights in North Korea.* http://www.hrnk.org/download/Hunger%20and%20Human%20Rights.pdf (accessed October 17, 2010).

Handman, Gary. "Food and Eating in the Movies." *Library, University of California, Berkeley,* updated November 29, 2010. http://www.lib.berkeley.edu/MRC/foodmovies.html (accessed October 21, 2010).

Harris, Jennifer L., John A. Bargh, and Kelly D. Brownell. "Priming Effects of Television Food Advertising on Eating Behavior." *Health Psychology* 28, no. 4 (2009). http://www.yale.edu/acmelab/articles/Harris_Bargh_Brownell_Health_Psych.pdf (accessed October 31, 2010).

Harvard Medical School. "Red Meat and Colon Cancer." *Harvard Medical School Family Health Guide,* March 2008 update. http://www.health.harvard.edu/fhg/updates/Red-meat-and-colon-cancer.shtml (accessed September 28, 2010).

Harvard School of Pubic Health. "Nutrition Source: Fruits and Vegetables-The Bottom Line." *Harvard University.* http://www.hsph.harvard.edu/nutritionsource/what-should-you-eat/vegetables-and-fruits/index.html (accessed September 29, 2010).

Harvard School of Public Health. "Eating Processed Meats, but Not Unprocessed Red Meats, May Raise Risk of Heart Disease and Diabetes." *Harvard University.* http://www.hsph.harvard.edu/news/press-releases/2010-releases/processed-meats-unprocessed-heart-disease-diabetes.html (accessed October

Harvard School of Public Health. "Health Gains from Whole Grains." *Harvard University.* http://www.hsph.harvard.edu/nutritionsource/what-should-you-eat/health-gains-from-whole-grains/ (accessed September 21, 2010).

"Hazard Analysis Critical Control Point System (HACCP)." *World Health Organization.* http://www.who.int/foodsafety/fs_management/haccp/en/ (accessed September 25, 2010).

"A Healthy Nutrition Environment: Linking Education, Activity, and Food through School Gardens." *California Department of Education.* http://www.cde.ca.gov/LS/nu/he/gardenoverview.asp (accessed July 20, 2010).

"Healthy Youth! Food Allergies." *National Center for Chronic Disease Prevention and Health Promotion, U.S. Centers for Disease Control and Prevention.* http://www.cdc.gov/healthyyouth/foodallergies/ (accessed October 2, 2010).

Heifer International. http://www.heifer.org/site/c.edJRKQNiFiG/b.183217/ (accessed August 18, 2010).

Hensrud, Donald. "Coffee and Health: What Does the Research Say?" *Mayo Clinic.* http://www.mayoclinic.com/health/coffee-and-health/AN01354 (accessed December 12, 2010).

"Hepatitis A." *World Health Organization.* http://www.who.int/entity/mediacentre/factsheets/fs328/en/index.html (accessed September 6, 2010).

"Hepatitis A Vaccination." *Centers for Disease Control and Prevention (CDC).* http://www.cdc.gov/vaccines/vpd-vac/hepa/default.htm (accessed September 6, 2010).

"Herbs at a Glance." *National Center for Complimentary and Alternative Medicine.* http://nccam.nih.gov/health/herbsataglance.htm (accessed September 21, 2010).

Hispanic Foodways. http://hispanicfoodways.com/ (accessed October 9, 2010).

"The History of Beer." *Beer Brewing.org.* http://www.beerbrewing.org/the-history-of-beer/ (accessed November 3, 2010).

Hochman, Karen, Rowann Gilman, and Ruth Katz, eds. "Letters to the Editor: FAQs about Food." *The Nibble.* http://www.thenibble.com/nav2/letters/food.asp (accessed October 15, 2010).

Hoppe, Robert A., David E. Banker, and James M. MacDonald. "America's Diverse Family Farms, 2010 ed." *U.S. Department of Agriculture (USDA).* http://www.ers.usda.gov/publications/eib67/ (accessed October 19, 2010).

"Honduras: Cashews Create Stable Income For Poor Communities." *World Food Programme.* http://www.wfp.org/stories/honduras-cashews-create-stable-income-poor-communities (accessed October 2, 2010).

Horovitz, Bruce. "Pepsi Is Dropping Out of Schools Worldwide by 2012." *USA Today,* March 17, 2010. http://www.usatoday.com/money/industries/food/2010-03-16-pepsicutsschoolsoda_N.htm (accessed November 4, 2010).

"How Safe are Color Additives?" *U.S. Food and Drug Administration (FDA).* http://www.fda.gov/ForConsumers/ConsumerUpdates/ucm048951.htm (accessed October 7, 2010).

"How to Understand and Use the Nutrition Facts Label." *U.S. Food and Drug Administration (FDA).* http://www.fda.gov/food/labelingnutrition/consumerinformation/ucm078889.htm (accessed November 3, 2010).

Howard, Mike. "Is Your Diet a Cult?" *Dietblog.* http://www.diet-blog.com/08/is_your_diet_a_cult.php (accessed September 6, 2010).

Humane Farm Animal Care. "Frequently Asked Questions." *CertifiedHumane.org.* http://www.certifiedhumane.org/index.php?page=frequently-asked-questions" (accessed October 17, 2010).

Humane Research Council. "Animal Tracker—Wave 1, an HRC-Managed Research Study." *HumaneSpot.org.* http://www.humanespot.org (accessed October 17, 2010).

"Hunger." *World Food Programme.* http://www.wfp.org/hunger (accessed October 9, 2010).

"Illegal Bushmeat Trade Rife in Europe, Research Finds." *Science Daily,* June 18, 2010. http://www.sciencedaily.com/releases/2010/06/100617210641.htm (accessed October 30, 2010).

"Import Alerts." *U.S. Customs and Border Protection.* http://www.cbp.gov/xp/cgov/trade/trade_programs/agriculture/import_alert/ (accessed October 23, 2010).

"Indoor Air Pollution and Cookstove Efforts at NIH." *John E. Fogarty International Center, National Institutes of Health.* http://www.fic.nih.gov/news/resources/cookstoves.htm (accessed November 2, 2010).

"Infant Feeding & Nutrition." *International Formula Council.* http://www.infantformula.org/ (accessed October 4, 2010).

"Infant Formula." *Food and Drug Administration (FDA).* http://www.fda.gov/Food/FoodSafety/Product-SpecificInformation/InfantFormula/default.htm (accessed October 4, 2010).

"Influenza." *Centers for Disease Control and Prevention (CDC).* http://www.cdc.gov/flu (accessed September 23, 2010).

Institute for Agriculture and Trade Policy. http:// www.iatp.org/ (accessed September 18, 2010).

International Federation of Organic Agriculture Movements. http://www.ifoam.org/ (accessed October 9, 2010).

International Food Safety Authorities Network (INFOSAN)."Basic Steps to Improve Safety of Street-Vended Food." *World Health Organization,* June 30, 2010. http://www.who.int/ foodsafety/fs_management/No_03_StreetFood_ Jun10_en.pdf (accessed September 29, 2010).

International Fund for Agricultural Development. http://www.ifad.org/ (accessed October 6, 2010).

International HACCP Alliance. http://www. haccpalliance.org/sub/index.html (accessed September 25, 2010).

International Soil Reference and Information Centre (ISRIC). "Degraded Soil." *United Nations Environmental Programme.* http://maps.grida.no/ go/graphic/degraded-soils (accessed October 30, 2010).

"Introduction to Sustainability: What Is Sustainable Agriculture?" *SustainableTable.org.* http://www. sustainabletable.org/intro/whatis/ (accessed October 4, 2010).

"Investigation Update: Multistate Outbreak of Human Salmonella Enteritidis Infections Associated with Shell Eggs." *Centers for Disease Control and Prevention (CDC).* http://www.cdc.gov/ salmonella/enteritidis/ (accessed September 23, 2010).

"Irradiation and Food Safety." *Food Safety and Inspection Service (FSIS), U.S. Department of Agriculture (USDA).* http://www.fsis.usda.gov/ Fact_Sheets/Irradiation_and_Food_Safety/ index.asp (accessed September 11, 2010).

Irwin, Kim. "Pancreatic Cancers Use Fructose, Common in Western Diet, to Fuel Growth, Study Finds." *University of California: UCLA Newsroom,* August 4, 2010. http://newsroom.ucla.edu/portal/ucla/ pancreatic-cancers-use-fructose-165745.aspx (accessed November 2, 2010).

"It's Over: France Lifts 'Illegal' Embargo on British Beef." *Food Navigator.com,* October 3, 2002. http://www.foodnavigator.com/Legislation/ It-s-over-France-lifts-illegal-embargo-on-British-beef (accessed October 25, 2010).

The Journal of Culinary Education. http://culinary education.org/ (accessed September 17, 2010).

"Kibale Chimpanzee Project." *Harvard University.* http://www.fas.harvard.edu/~kibale/ (accessed August 1, 2010).

Kleim, Brandon. "Fast Food Just Another Name for Corn." *Wired Science,* November 10, 2008. http://www.wired.com/wired-science/2008/11/fast-food-anoth/ (accessed October 23, 2010).

Kleinerman, Rachel. "Functional Foods?" *American Council on Science and Health.* http://www.acsh. org/factsfears/newsID.396/news_detail.asp (accessed October 15, 2010).

Kotz, Deborah. "Wean Yourself off Processed Foods in 7 Steps." *U.S. News and World Report,* June 4, 2010. http://health.usnews.com/health-news/ diet-fitness/diabetes/articles/2010/06/04/ wean-yourself-off-processed-foods-in-7-steps. html (accessed October 31, 2010).

Kramer, Melody Joy. "Lettuce Learn How to Wash Produce." *National Public Radio,* September 21, 2006. http://www.npr.org/templates/story/ story.php?storyId=6104414 (accessed October 25, 2010).

Kuze, Motofume. "Whaling Just Part of the Food Chain." *The Japan Times,* May 2, 2010. http:// search.japantimes.co.jp/cgi-bin/rc20100502a7. html (accessed October 16, 2010).

La Chaîne des Rôtisseurs—International Gastronomic Association. http://www.chaine-des-rotisseurs. net/ (accessed September 25, 2010).

"Lactose Intolerance." *National Institute of Diabetes and Digestive Disorders.* http://digestive.niddk. nih.gov/ddiseases/pubs/lactoseintolerance/ (accessed October 25, 2010).

The Land Institute. http://www.landinstitute.org/ (accessed October 16, 2010).

"Land Tenure." *Food and Agriculture Organization of the United Nations (FAO).* http://www.fao. org/nr/tenure/lt-home/en/ (accessed August 23, 2010).

Landsberg, Mitchell, and Monte Morin. "School Soda, Junk Food Bans Approved." *The Los Angeles Times,* September 7, 2005. http://articles. latimes.com/2005/sep/07/local/me-junkfood7 (accessed November 1, 2010).

"Large Agribusiness Hurting Small Landholders, Says UN Rights Expert." *UN News Centre,* March 5, 2010. http://www.un.org/apps/news/story.as p?NewsID=33984&Cr=agriculture&Cr1= (accessed September 9, 2010).

Latin Fast Food Growth, Latin Business Chronicle. http://www.latinbusinesschronicle.com/ (accessed October 17, 2010).

Layton, Lyndsey. "FDA Plans to Limit Amount of Salt Allowed in Processed Foods for Health Reasons." *Washington Post,* April 20, 2010. http://

www.washingtonpost.com/wp-dyn/content/article/2010/04/19/AR2010041905049.html (accessed October 23, 2010).

Le, C. N. "Asian Cuisine & Foods." *Asian-Nation: The Landscape of Asian America.* http://www.asian-nation.org/asian-food.shtml (accessed October 21, 2010).

Le Procope. http://www.procope.com/ (accessed October 17, 2010).

Lee-Thorp, J., and B. R. Ackerman. "Lactose Intolerance is Normal!" *Science in Africa*, June 2002. http://www.scienceinafrica.co.za/2002/june/lactose.htm (accessed October 25, 2010).

Let's Move. http://www.letsmove/ (accessed October 16, 2010).

"Let's Take Shark Fin Soup off the Menu!" *StopSharkFinning.net.* http://www.stopsharkfinning.net/network.htm (accessed October 10, 2010).

"Lifecycle Nutrition." *U.S. Department of Agriculture (USDA)*. http://fnic.nal.usda.gov/nal_display/index.php?info_center=4&tax_level=1&tax_subject=257 (accessed October 17, 2010).

Linus Pauling Institute. "Micronutrient Center: Legumes." *Oregon State University.* http://lpi.oregonstate.edu/infocenter/foods/legumes/ (accessed September 29, 2010).

"Listeriosis." *U.S. Centers for Disease Control and Prevention (CDC).* http://www.cdc.gov/nczved/divisions/dfbmd/diseases/listeriosis/ (accessed October 21, 2010).

"Livestock Impacts on the Environment." *Food and Agriculture Organization of the United Nations (FAO).* http://www.fao.org/ag/magazine/0612sp1.htm (accessed October 15, 2010).

Locavore Network. http://www.locavorenetwork.com/ (accessed July 31, 2010).

Lombardi, Candace. "Compostable Food Packaging on its Way to Europe." *Green Tech*, September 15, 2010. http://news.cnet.com/8301-11128_3-20016471-54.html (accessed October 30, 2010).

Lord, Ashley. "Selective Eating May Be a Food Phobia in Disguise." *Tulane University*, February 6, 2003. http://tulane.edu/news/releases/archive/2003/selective_eating_may_be_food_phobia_in_disguise.cfm (accessed September 23, 2010).

Lothar, Corrina. "Chinese Food in America." *Washington Times*, August 13, 2008. http://www.washingtontimes.com/news/2008/aug/31/chinese-food-in-america/ (accessed October 21, 2010).

Luchetti, Emily. "The Life of a Pastry Chef." *SFGate*, July 21, 2010. http://insidescoopsf.sfgate.com/eluchetti/2010/07/21/the-life-of-a-pastry-chef/ (accessed November 4, 2010).

Lyman, Howard. "Texas Cattleman vs. Howard Lyman and Oprah Winfrey." *Howard Lyman: Mad Cowboy.* http://www.madcowboy.com/01_BookOP.000.html (accessed September 28, 2010).

MacFarquhar, Neil. "Experts Worry as Population and Hunger Grow." *New York Times*, October 21, 2009. http://www.nytimes.com/2009/10/22/world/22food.html (accessed October 28, 2010).

MADD. http://www.madd.org/ (accessed November 3, 2010).

Makabila, Stephen. "Politics of Relief Food Get Worse as Famine Strikes." *The Standard*, October 2, 2010. http://www.standardmedia.co.ke/InsidePage.php?id=2000019547&cid=4 (accessed October 17, 2010).

"Make Your Calories Count." *U.S. Food and Drug Administration (FDA).* http://www.fda.gov/Food/LabelingNutrition/ConsumerInformation/ucm114022.htm (accessed October 9, 2010).

"Malnutrition." *World Health Organization.* http://www.who.int/child_adolescent_health/topics/prevention_care/child/nutrition/malnutrition/en/index.html (accessed September 6, 2010).

Manthey, David. "A Comparison of Leavening Agents." *Orbitals Central*, 2002. http://www.orbitals.com/self/leaven/leaven.pdf (accessed August 20, 2010).

"Marine Toxins." *Centers for Disease Control and Prevention (CDC).* http://www.cdc.gov/ncidod/dbmd/diseaseinfo/marinetoxins_g.htm (accessed October 4, 2010).

Mayo Clinic Staff. "Bird Flu (Avian Influenza)." *Mayo Clinic.com.* http://www.mayoclinic.com/health/bird-flu/DS00566 (accessed September 23, 2010).

Mayo Clinic Staff. "Low-Sodium Diet: Why Is Processed Food So Salty?" *Mayo Clinic.com.* http://www.mayoclinic.com/health/food-and-nutrition/AN00350 (accessed October 31, 2010).

Mayo Clinic Staff. "Healthy Cooking Techniques." *Mayo Clinic.com.* http://www.mayoclinic.com/health/healthy-cooking/NU00201 (accessed October 2, 2010).

Mayo Clinic Staff. "Mediterranean Diet: Choose This Heart-Healthy Diet Option." *Mayo Clinic.com.* http://www.mayoclinic.com/health/mediterranean-diet/CL00011 (accessed November 4, 2010).

"Meal, Ready-to-Eat (MRE)." *Defense Logistics Agency: Troop Support.* http://www.dscp.dla. mil/subs/rations/programs/mre/mreabt.asp (accessed October 9, 2010).

"Meat and Meat Products in Human Nutrition: Meat and Health." *Agriculture and Consumer Protection Department, Food and Agriculture Organization of the United Nations (FAO).* http:// www.fao.org/docrep/t0562e/t0562e05.htm (accessed September 28, 2010).

Medecins Sans Frontieres (Doctors without Borders). "Starved for Attention." *StarvedforAttention.org.* http://www.starvedforattention.org/ (accessed September 9, 2010).

Media Centre. "Towards a More Sustainable Livestock Sector." *Food and Agriculture Organization of the United Nations (FAO),* February 18, 2010. http://www.fao.org/news/story/pt/ item/40117/icode/en/ (accessed September 20, 2010).

"Mediterranean Diet." *American Heart Association.* http://www.americanheart.org/presenter. jhtml?identifier=4644 (accessed November 4, 2010).

"Meet the Fats." *American Heart Association.* http://www.heart.org/HEARTORG/ GettingHealthy/FatsAndOils/MeettheFats/ Meet-the-Fats_UCM_304495_Article.jsp (accessed October 2, 2010).

"Millennium Development Goals: Goal 1: Eradicate Extreme Poverty and Hunger." *United Nations Development Program.* http://www.undp.org/ mdg/goal1.shtml (accessed October 4, 2010).

"Monitoring Progress since the World Food Summit." *Food and Agriculture Organization of the United Nations (FAO).* http://www.fao.org/ monitoringprogress/index_en.html (accessed October 4, 2010).

Monsanto vs. Schmeiser. http://www.percyschmeiser. com/ (accessed October 28, 2010).

Mousseau, Frederic. "Food Aid or Food Sovereignty? Ending World Hunger in Our Time." *Oakland Institute,* October 2005. http://www. oaklandinstitute.org/pdfs/fasr.pdf (accessed October 17, 2010).

"MSC Certified Fish to Eat." *Marine Stewardship Council.* http://www.msc.org/cook-eat-enjoy/ fish-to-eat (accessed October 23, 2010).

"Myths & Facts about Fighting the Opium Trade in Afghanistan." *U.S. Department of State, International Narcotics and Law Enforcement Affairs.* http:// www.state.gov/documents/organization/ 142643.pdf (accessed September 9, 2010).

National Agricultural Library. "Community Supported Agriculture." *U.S. Department of Agriculture.* http://www.nal.usda.gov/afsic/pubs/csa/ csa.shtml (accessed October 16, 2010).

National Cancer Institute. "Red Meat Consumption." *U.S. National Institutes of Health.* http:// progressreport.cancer.gov/doc_detail.asp?pid=1 &did=2007&chid=71&coid=731&mid=#cancer (accessed September 28, 2010).

National Center for Food Protection and Defense. http://www.ncfpd.umn.edu/Ncfpd/ (accessed September 6, 2010).

National Eating Disorder Association (NEDA). http://www.nationaleatingdisorders.org/index. php (accessed October 8, 2010).

National Family Farm Coalition. http://www.nffc. net/ (accessed October 19, 2010).

National Institutes of Health. "Salt: Too Much of a Good Thing." *Medline Plus: The Magazine,* Spring/Summer 2010. http://www. nlm.nih.gov/medlineplus/magazine/ issues/sprsum10/articles/sprsum10pg12-13. html?debugMode=false (accessed October 23, 2010).

National Institutes of Health, National Institute on Alcohol and Alcoholism, College Drinking— Changing the Culture. "A Snapshot of Annual High-Risk College Drinking Consequences." *CollegeDrinkingPrevention.gov.* http://www. collegedrinkingprevention.gov/StatsSummaries/ snapshot.aspx (accessed November 3, 2010).

National Library of Medicine. "*Staph aureus* Food Poisoning." *Medline Plus.* http://www.nlm.nih. gov/medlineplus/ency/article/000227.htm (accessed October 6, 2010).

National Library of Medicine. "Phytochemicals." *Medline Plus.* http://www.nlm.nih.gov/ medlineplus/ency/imagepages/19303.htm (accessed October 4, 2010).

"National Organic Program." *U.S. Department of Agriculture (USDA).* http://www.ams.usda. gov/AMSv1.0/ams.fetchTemplateData.do?tem plate=TemplateA&navID=NationalOrganicProg ram&leftNav=NationalOrganicProgram&page= NOPNationalOrganicProgramHome&acct=AM SPW (accessed November 30, 2010).

"National School Lunch Program." *Food and Nutrition Service, U.S. Department of Agriculture (USDA).* http://www.fns.usda.gov/cnd/ lunch/ (accessed October 25, 2010).

Nebehay, Stephanie. "WHO Targets Childhood Obesity with Market Curbs." *Reuters,* May 20, 2010. http://www.reuters.com/article/

idUSTRE64J6A520100520 (accessed October 31, 2010).

The Nemours Foundation. "Teens Health: Body Image and Self Esteem." *kidshealth.org.* http://kidshealth.org/teen/exercise/problems/body_image.html# (accessed October 9, 2010).

"New Orleans: Gumbo as History." *PBS.org.* http://www.pbs.org/wgbh/amex/neworleans/sfeature/food.html (accessed October 18, 2010).

"Norovirus Infection [Calicivirus]." *Centers for Disease Control and Prevention (CDC).* http://www.cdc.gov/ncidod/dvrd/revb/gastro/norovirus.htm (accessed September 6, 2010).

"Norovirus: Technical Data" *Centers for Disease Control and Prevention (CDC).* http://www.cdc.gov/ncidod/dvrd/revb/gastro/norovirus-factsheet.htm (accessed September 6, 2010).

Norris, Jack. "Staying Healthy on Plant-Based Diets." *VeganHealth.org.* http://www.veganhealth.org/ (accessed October 4, 2010).

"NOW with Bill Moyers: Migrant Labor in the United States." *PBS.org.* http://www.pbs.org/now/politics/migrants.html (accessed November 3, 2010).

NPR Staff. "What's Healthier: Raw Milk or Regulation?" *All Things Considered, National Public Radio (NPR).* http://www.npr.org/templates/story/story.php?storyId=128912799 (accessed September 2, 2010).

"Nutrition." *Centers for Disease Control and Prevention (CDC).* http://www.cdc.gov/nccdphp/dnpa/nutrition.htm (accessed October 9, 2010).

"Nutritional Support." *National Institutes of Health, U.S. Department of Health and Human Services.* http://health.nih.gov/topic/Nutritional Support (accessed October 9, 2010).

Nutrition.gov. http://www.nutrition.gov/nal_display/index.php?info_center=11&tax_level=1 (accessed October 17, 2010).

"Obesity." *National Institutes of Health, U.S. Department of Health and Human Services.* http://health.nih.gov/topic/Obesity (accessed November 3, 2010).

"Obesity and Genetics." *Centers for Disease Control and Prevention (CDC).* http://www.cdc.gov/genomics/resources/diseases/obesity/index.htm (accessed November 3, 2010).

"Obesity and Overweight." *Centers for Disease Control and Prevention (CDC).* http://www.cdc.gov/nccdphp/dnpa/obesity/index.htm (accessed November 3, 2010).

"Obesity and Overweight." *World Health Organization (WHO).* http://www.who.int/mediacentre/factsheets/fs311/en/index.html (accessed November 3, 2010).

"Obesity Expert Calls Processed Food Toxic." *ConsumerAffairs.com,* August 14, 2006. http://www.consumeraffairs.com/news04/2006/08/processed_food.html (accessed October 31, 2010).

"Of Hearth and Home: Cooking In the Late 18th Century." *Minisink Valley Historical Society.* http://www.minisink.org/hearthhome.html (accessed October 27, 2010).

Oger, Genevieve. "French Cafe Culture Struggles to Stay Alive." *Deutsche Welle,* August 14, 2009. http://www.dw-world.de/dw/article/0,,4562836,00.html (accessed October 17, 2010).

"Oldest Noodles Unearthed in China." *BBC News.* http://news.bbc.co.uk/2/hi/science/nature/4335160.stm (accessed October 25, 2010).

Oliver, Rachael. "All About: Food Waste." *CNN.com/Asia,* January 22, 2008. http://edition.cnn.com/2007/WORLD/asiapcf/09/24/food.leftovers/#cnnSTCText (accessed October 7, 2010).

Olver, Lynne. "Popular Twentieth-Century American Foods." *Food Timeline.* http://www.foodtimeline.org/fooddecades.html (accessed October 25, 2010).

Open Table. http://www.opentable.com/home.aspx (accessed October 18, 2010).

Ophardt, Charles B. "Virtual Chembook: Overview of Metabolism." *Elmhurst College.* http://www.elmhurst.edu/~chm/vchembook/5900verviewmet.html (accessed October 15, 2010).

"Oral Health." *World Health Organization (WHO).* http://www.who.int/mediacentre/factsheets/fs318/en/index.html (accessed October 15, 2010).

"Organic Chocolate." *organic-nature-news.com.* http://www.organic-nature-news.com/organic chocolate.html (accessed October 23, 2010).

"Organic Farming." *U.S. Environmental Protection Agency (EPA).* http://www.epa.gov/agriculture/torg.html (accessed October 17, 2010).

Organic.org. http://www.organic.org/ (accessed October 17, 2010).

OU Kosher.org. http://www.oukosher.org/ (accessed October 31, 2010).

"Our Common Future." *United Nations World Commission on Environment and Development*, March 20, 1987. http://www.un-documents.net/wced-ocf.htm (accessed October 4, 2010).

"Outcomes on Food." *United Nations.* http://www.un.org/en/development/devagenda/food.shtml (accessed October 4, 2010).

Owels, Kahled Yacoub. "Ancient Aleppo Cuisine Tastes of Conquest and Trade." *Reuters,* October 24, 2007. http://www.reuters.com/article/idUSL2450249520071024 (accessed October 18, 2010).

"Oxfam Calls for Radical Shake-Up of Aid System to Break Cycle of Hunger in Ethiopia." *Oxfam International,* October 22, 2009. http://www.oxfam.org/en/pressroom/pressrelease/2009-10-22/aid-system-break-cycle-hunger-ethiopia (accessed September 9, 2010).

"Oxfam International's Position on Transgenic Crops." *Oxfam International.* http://www.oxfam.org/en/campaigns/agriculture/oxfam-position-transgenic-crops (accessed November 1, 2010).

Oyarzabal, Omar A. "*Campylobacter* in Poultry Processing."*Auburn University Department of Poultry Science.* http://www.ag.auburn.edu/poul/virtuallibrary/oyarzabalcampylobacter.html (accessed October 2, 2010).

"Pakistan Emergency." *World Food Programme.* http://www.wfp.org/crisis/pakistan (accessed October 15, 2010).

Parker, Hilary. "A Sweet Problem: Princeton Researchers Find That High-Fructose Corn Syrup Prompts Considerably More Weight Gain." *Princeton University,* March 22, 2010. http://www.princeton.edu/main/news/archive/S26/91/22K07/ (accessed October 4, 2010).

Partnership for Food Safety Education. "Safe Produce Handling Education Campaign." *fightbac.org.* http://www.fightbac.org/home (accessed October 25, 2010).

Pearce, Fred. "The Battle to Save Russia's Pavlovsk Seed Bank." *The Guardian,* September 20, 2010. http://www.guardian.co.uk/environment/2010/sep/20/campaign-russia-pavlovsk-seed-bank (accessed October 18, 2010).

Penland, James G. "Dietary Reference Intakes (DRIs)—New Dietary Guidelines Really Are New!" *U.S. Department of Agriculture (USDA),* October 23, 2006. http://www.ars.usda.gov/News/docs.htm?docid=10870 (accessed September 29, 2010).

People for the Ethical Treatment of Animals. http://www.peta.org/ (accessed October 17, 2010).

Phillips, Melissa Lee. "No Cannibalism Signature in Human Gene." *The Scientist,* January 9, 2006. http://www.the-scientist.com/templates/trackable/display/news.jsp?type=news&o_url=news/display/22927&id=22927 (accessed October 14, 2010).

"Phytochemicals." *American Cancer Society.* http://www.cancer.org/Treatment/TreatmentsandSideEffects/ComplementaryandAlternativeMedicine/HerbsVitaminsandMinerals/phytochemicals (accessed October 4, 2010).

"Pica Eating Disorder." *Eating Disorder.org.* http://www.eating-disorder.org/pica-eating-disorders.html (accessed September 14, 2010).

Pittman, Ginevra. "What Do Food Allergy Labels Really Mean?" *Reuters Health,* August 11, 2010. http://www.reuters.com/article/idUSTRE67A4RP20100811 (accessed January 20, 2010).

Podmolick, Mary Ellen. "Trade Group Seeks Name Change for High-Fructose Corn Syrup." *Los Angeles Times,* September 15, 2010. http://articles.latimes.com/2010/sep/15/business/la-fi-corn-sugar-20100915 (accessed October 23, 2010).

Pollan, Michael. "The Food Movement, Rising" from *The New York Review of Books,* May 20, 2010. *MichaelPollan.com.* http://michaelpollan.com/articles-archive/the-food-movement-rising/ (accessed August 24, 2010).

"Pollutants/Toxics: Toxic Substances: Persistent Bioaccumulative Toxic Pollutants (PBTs)." *U.S. Environmental Protection Agency (EPA).* http://oaspub.epa.gov/webimore/aboutepa.ebt4?search=9,45,345 (accessed October 27, 2010).

Potaka, Elise. "Lao Rice Farmers Move from Subsistence to Cash Crops." *Public Radio International (PRI),* October 5, 2009. http://www.pri.org/business/global-development/lao-rice-farmers1653.html (accessed October 10, 2010).

"Poultry and Eggs." *Economic Research Service, United States Department of Agriculture (USDA),* updated April 16, 2009. http://www.ers.usda.gov/Briefing/Poultry/ (accessed October 19, 2010).

"Poultry Products Inspection Act." *U.S. Food and Drug Administration (FDA).* http://www.fda.gov/RegulatoryInformation/Legislation/ucm148721.htm (accessed September 7, 2010).

"Preservatives, Use in Non-standardized Foods, Label Declaration." *U.S. Food and Drug*

Administration (FDA). http://www.fda.gov/
ICECI/ComplianceManuals/CompliancePolicy
GuidanceManual/ucm074583.htm (accessed
October 10, 2010).

"Progress for Children. Nutrition, Survival and
Development: What is Undernutrition?"
UNICEF. http://www.unicef.org/progress
forchildren/2006n4/index_undernutrition.html
(accessed October 2, 2010).

"Protect Your Baby and Yourself From Listeriosis."
*Food Safety and Inspection Service (FSIS), U.S.
Department of Agriculture (USDA).* http://
www.fsis.usda.gov/Fact_Sheets/Protect_Your_
Baby/index.asp (accessed October 21, 2010).

"Putting It All Together for Food Co-ops." *National
Cooperative Grocers Association.* http://www.
ncga.coop/ (accessed October 4, 2010).

"Rapid Growth of Selected Asian Economies: Lessons and Implications for Agriculture and Food
Security." *Regional Office for Asia and the Pacific, Food and Agriculture Organization of the
United Nations (FAO).* http://www.fao.org/
docrep/009/ag087e/AG087E00.htm (accessed
August 24, 2010).

"Raw Food Diet." *Science Daily.* http://www.sci-
encedaily.com/articles/r/raw_food_diet.htm
(accessed September 11, 2010).

Redding, Sean. "Structural Adjustment and the
Decline of Subsistence Agriculture in Africa."
Amherst College. http://www3.amherst.
edu/~mrhunt/womencrossing/redding.html
(accessed October 10, 2010).

Reichl, Ruth. "The Ruth of the Matter." *Time Out
New York,* January 24, 2008. http://newyork.
timeout.com/articles/tv/25772/the-ruth-of-
the-matter (accessed October 15, 2010).

Reid, T. R. "Caffeine—What's the Buzz?." *National Geographic Society.* http://science.nationalgeographic.
com/science/health-and-human-body/human
body/caffeine-buzz.html (accessed October 19,
2010).

"The Reportable Food Registry, FDA's New Early
Detection System Helps Identify 125 Food Safety
Problems in First Seven Months." *Center for
Food Safety and Applied Nutrition, U.S. Food and
Drug Administration (FDA).* http://www.fda.
gov/Food/NewsEvents/ConstituentUpdates/
ucm220973.htm(accessed October 10, 2010).

"Restaurant Reviews: Personal Experience vs. Professional Opinions." *Open Table,* May 27, 2009.
http://blog.opentable.com/2009/restaurant-
reviews-personal-experience-vs-professional
opinions/ (accessed October 30, 2010).

Restione, Dan. "A Call for Revolution." *Food Mus-
ings,* March 17, 2009. http://www.mynorth-
west.com/?nid=408&sid=146250 (accessed
October 15, 2010).

Revkin, Andrew C. "Buried Seed Vault Opens
in Arctic." *The New York Times,* February
26, 2008. http://dotearth.blogs.nytimes.
com/2008/02/26/buried-seed-vault-opens-in-
arctic/ (accessed October 18, 2010).

"Rice Basics." *International Rice Research Institute.*
http://irri.org/about-rice/rice-facts/rice-basics
(accessed October 23, 2010).

Robin, Lauren Posnick. "Acrylamide, Furan, and
the FDA" from *Food Safety Magazine,* June/
July 2007. *U.S. Food and Drug Administration
(FDA).* http://www.fda.gov/Food/FoodSafety/
FoodContaminantsAdulteration/Chemical
Contaminants/Acrylamide/ucm194482.htm (ac-
cessed September 11, 2010).

The Rodale Institute. http://www.rodaleinstitute.
org/ (accessed October 16, 2010).

Rogers, Thomas. "How Food Television Is Changing
America." *Salon.com,* February 26, 2010. http://
www.salon.com/food/feature/2010/02/26/
food_network_krishnendu_ray (accessed October
31, 2010).

Roman, Nancy. "How We Can End Hunger: A Billion
for a Billion." *Human Rights: Change.org,* October 11, 2010. http://humanrights.change.org/
blog/view/how_we_can_end_hunger_a_billion_
for_a_billion (accessed October 16, 2010).

Rose, Joel. "I-95 a Trap for Migrant Fruit Pickers."
National Public Radio (NPR), September 4,
2010. http://www.npr.org/templates/story/
story.php?storyId=129580744&ft=1&f=1006
(accessed September 7, 2010).

Rosegrant, Mark W., Siwa Msangi, Timothy Sulser,
and Rowena Valmont-Santos. "Biofuels and
the Global Food Balance." *International Food
Policy Research Institute,* December 2006.
http://www.globalbioenergy.org/uploads/
media/0612_IFPRI_-_Biofuels_and_the_
Global_Food_Balance_01.pdf (accessed September 9, 2010).

Roy, Sandip. "Indian Mangoes—Now in America."
National Public Radio (NPR), June 11, 2009.
http://www.npr.org/templates/story/story.
php?storyId=104881449 (accessed September
11, 2010).

Ruby, Jeff. "Why the Professional Restaurant Critic
Will Survive the Age of Yelp." *Chicago Mag.
com,* October 2010. http://www.chicagomag.
com/Chicago-Magazine/October-2010/

The-Professional-Restaurant-Critic-in-the-Age-of-Yelp/ (accessed October 30, 2010).

"Rural Poverty Report 2011." *International Fund for Agricultural Development (IFAD)*. http://www.ifad.org/rpr2011/index.htm (accessed October 22, 2010).

Sadik, Nafis. "Population Growth and the Food Crisis." *Food and Agricultural Organization (FAO)*. http://www.fao.org/docrep/u3550t/u3550t02.htm (accessed October 28, 2010).

"Safe Handling of Raw Produce and Fresh-Squeezed Fruit and Vegetable Juices." *U.S. Food and Drug Administration (FDA)*. http://www.fda.gov/Food/ResourcesForYou/Consumers/ucm114299 (accessed September 7, 2010).

"Safeguarding Traditional Foodways." *Bioversity International*. http://www.bioversityinternational.org/announcements/safeguarding_traditional_foodways.html (accessed October 27, 2010).

"Safer Food, Better Business." *UK Food Standards Agency*. http://www.food.gov.uk/foodindustry/regulation/hygleg/hyglegresources/sfbb/ (accessed October 21, 2010).

Salisbury, David. F. "Exploration: Brief History of Cannibal Controversies." *Vanderbilt University*, August 15, 2001. http://www.vanderbilt.edu/exploration/news/news_cannibalism_pt2.htm (accessed October 14, 2010).

"Salmonella." *World Health Organization (WHO)*. http://www.who.int/topics/salmonella/en (accessed September 2, 2010).

"*Salmonella* Infection [Salmonellosis]." *Centers for Disease Control and Prevention (CDC)*. http://www.cdc.gov/salmonella (accessed September 2, 2010).

Schalch, Kathleen. "All Things Considered: U.S. Food Aid Critics Call on Congress for Overhaul." *National Public Radio (NPR)*, November 6, 2007. http://www.npr.org/templates/story/story.php?storyId=16053196(accessed October 17, 2010).

Schulte, Brigid. "Once Just a Sweet Birthday Treat, the Cupcake Becomes a Cause." *The Washington Post*, December 11, 2006. http://www.washingtonpost.com/wp-dyn/content/article/2006/12/10/AR2006121001008.html (accessed November 1, 2010).

"Seafood Watch: Ocean Issues." *Monterey Bay Aquarium*. http://www.montereybayaquarium.org/cr/cr_seafoodwatch/issues/ (accessed October 23, 2010).

Sekuler, Robert. "Texture and Mouthfeel." *Brandeis University*, revised 2004. http://people.brandeis.edu/~sekuler/SensoryProcessesMaterial/rheology.html (accessed October 17, 2010).

Severson, Kim. "Film Food, Ready for Its 'Bon Appetit.'" *The New York Times*, July 28, 2009. http://www.nytimes.com/2009/07/29/dining/29movie.html (accessed September 28, 2010).

Shah, Anup. "Food Patents—Stealing Indigenous Knowledge?" *Global Issues*, September 26, 2002. http://www.globalissues.org/article/191/food-patents-stealing-indigenous-knowledge (accessed October 28, 2010).

Shapiro, Ari. "Americans' Insatiable Hunger for Celebrity Chefs." *National Public Radio (NPR)*, March 5, 2005. http://www.npr.org/templates/story/story.php?storyId=4522975 (accessed October 6, 2010).

"Sharks: Dying for a Bowl of Soup." *Humane Society International*, January 31, 2007. http://www.hsi.org/issues/shark_finning/facts/dying_for_a_bowl_of_soup.html (accessed October 10, 2010).

Sherman, Lauren. "Up-and-Coming Celebrity Chefs." *Forbes.com*, April 1, 2008. http://www.forbes.com/2008/04/01/chef-celebrity-food-forbeslife-cx_ls_0401food.html (accessed October 6, 2010).

"Since You Asked: Bisphenol A (BPA)." *National Institute of Environmental Health Sciences*. http://www.niehs.nih.gov/news/media/questions/sya-bpa.cfm (accessed September 20, 2010).

Slow Food International. http://www.slowfood.com/ (accessed August 1, 2010).

Slow Food USA. http://www.slowfoodusa.org/ (accessed November 1, 2010).

"Small-Scale Dairy Production: A Way Out of Poverty." *Food and Agriculture Organization of the United Nations (FAO)*. http://www.fao.org/news/story/en/item/44582/icode/ (accessed October 10, 2010).

Smith, David. "Change Beckons for Billionth African." *Guardian.co.uk*, December 28, 2009. http://www.guardian.co.uk/world/2009/dec/28/billionth-african-future (accessed October 15, 2010).

"SNAP/Food Stamps." *Food Research and Action Center*. http://frac.org/federal-foodnutrition-programs/snapfood-stamps/ (accessed November 2, 2010).

"Sodium (Salt or Sodium Chloride)." *American Heart Association*. http://www.americanheart.org/presenter.jhtml?identifier=4708 (accessed October 23, 2010).

Soldier System Center. "Nanotechnology Applied to Ration Packaging." *U.S. Army*, June 4, 2004. http://www.natick.army.mil/about/pao/2004/04-21.htm (accessed October 9, 2010).

Soller, Kurt. "Head to Hoof: A Butcher Helps Lead a New Carnivore Movement." *Newsweek*, January 28, 2009. http://www.newsweek.com/2009/01/27/head-to-hoof.html (accessed October 21, 2010).

Southern Foodways Alliance. http://www.southernfoodways.com/ (accessed October 9, 2010).

"Special Programme for Food Security." *Food and Agriculture Organization of the United Nations (FAO).* http://www.fao.org/spfs/en/(accessed October 30, 2010).

"Spice Industry Overview." *Spice-Trade.com.* http://www.spice-trade.com/industry-overview.html (accessed October 23, 2010).

Spiller, Gene A., and Bonnie Bruce. "Nuts and Healthy Diets." *Vegetarian Nutrition: An International Journal*, 1, no. 1, 1997. http://www.fao.org/inpho/content/documents/vlibrary/ac307e/pdf/ac307e05.pdf (accessed October 2, 2010).

"Staphylococcal Food Poisoning." *Centers for Disease Control and Prevention (CDC).* http://www.cdc.gov/ncidod/dbmd/diseaseinfo/staphylococcus_food_g.htm (accessed October 6, 2010).

State Government of Victoria, Australia, Department of Health. "Food and Celebrations." *Better Health Channel.* http://www.betterhealth.vic.gov.au/bhcv2/bhcarticles.nsf/pages/Food_and_celebrations (accessed November 1, 2010).

State Government of Victoria, Australia, Department of Health. "Food Culture and Religion." *Better Health Channel.* http://www.betterhealth.vic.gov.au/bhcv2/bhcarticles.nsf/pages/Food_culture_and_religion?open (accessed October 31, 2010).

"Status of Whales." *International Whaling Commission.* http://iwcoffice.org/conservation/status.htm (accessed October 16, 2010).

Steel, Tanya. "Epicurious's Top 10 Food Trends for 2010." *Shine.yahoo.com*, November 30, 2009. http://www.epicurious.com/articlesguides/blogs/editor/2009/11/epicurious-predicts-top-ten-food-trends-for-2010.html (accessed October 25, 2010).

Steffe, James D. "Rheological Methods in Food Process Engineering, 2nd ed." *Michigan State University*, 1996. http://www.egr.msu.edu/~steffe/Freebooks/Rheological%20Methods.pdf (accessed October 17, 2010).

Stein, Joel. "Extreme Eating." *Time*, January 10, 2008. http://www.time.com/time/magazine/article/0,9171,1702353,00.html (accessed October 16, 2010).

Stoddard, Ed. "Agriculture Dependent on Migrant Workers." *Reuters*, July 23, 2007. http://www.reuters.com/article/idUSN1526113420070723 (accessed November 3, 2010).

"Stop Child & Forced Labor: Cocoa Campaign." *International Labor Rights Forum.* http://www.laborrights.org/stop-child-labor/cocoa-campaign (accessed September 23, 2010).

Students of HIST 452. "Terroir and the Perceived Value of Regional Origin." *Cornell University History Department*, Fall 2005. http://courses.cit.cornell.edu/his452/Alcohol/terroirandorigin.html (accessed October 7, 2010).

"Supplemental Nutrition Assistance Program (SNAP)." *Food and Nutrition Service, U.S. Department of Agriculture (USDA).* http://www.fns.usda.gov/snap/ (accessed October 30, 2010).

"Sustainable Agriculture Will Help Stop Desertification, UN Agency Says." *UN News Center*, June 17, 2008. http://www.un.org/apps/news/story.asp?NewsID=27048&Cr=desert&Cr1 (accessed October 15, 2010).

Sustainable Table. http://www.sustainabletable.org/issues/ (accessed October 15, 2010).

Team Planet Green. "Eating Head-to-Tail? Dressing Up Less Popular Cuts of Meat." *PlanetGreen.com.* http://planetgreen.discovery.com/food-health/eating-head-tail.html (accessed October 21, 2010).

"Texas Cattlemen v. Oprah Winfrey." *Media Libel.* http://medialibel.org/cases-conflicts/tv/oprah.html (accessed September 28, 2010).

Thibodeaux, Raymond. "India's Tea Trade Features New Brew." *VOANews.com*, September 21, 2010. http://www.voanews.com/english/news/asia/VOA-Indias-Tea-Trade-Features-New-Brew-103424084.html (accessed October 25, 2010).

"Tips for the Savvy Supplement User: Making Informed Decisions and Evaluating Information." *U.S. Food and Drug Administration (FDA).* http://www.fda.gov/Food/DietarySupplements/ConsumerInformation/ucm110567.htm (accessed September 26 2010).

"Tips to Reduce Your Risk of Salmonella from Eggs." *Centers for Disease Control and Prevention (CDC).* http://www.cdc.gov/Features/SalmonellaEggs/ (accessed October 19, 2010).

"Top Issues Today." *National Confectioners Association.* http://www.candyusa.com/PublicPolicy/IITopIssueToday.cfm?navItemNumber=2671 (accessed November 4, 2010).

"Trade and Agriculture." *Food and Agriculture Organization of the United Nations (FAO).* http://www.fao.org/english/newsroom/focus/2003/wto.htm (accessed October 4, 2010).

"Trade and Markets: Bananas." *Food and Agriculture Organization of the United Nations (FAO).* http://www.fao.org/es/esc/en/15/190/index.html (accessed September 6, 2010).

"Trans Fats." *American Heart Association.* http://www.heart.org/HEARTORG/GettingHealthy/FatsAndOils/Fats101/Trans-Fats_UCM_301120_Article.jsp (accessed October 2, 2010).

Turecamo, David. "The Art of Baking Bread." *CBS News*, March 28, 2010. http://www.cbsnews.com/video/watch/?id=6341065n (accessed September 14, 2010).

"U.S. Aid from the American People." *U.S. Agency for International Development (USAID).* http://www.usaid.gov/ (accessed October 14, 2010).

"USAID: Agriculture: Overview." *U.S. Agency for International Development (USAID).* http://www.usaid.gov/our_work/agriculture (accessed August 4, 2010).

"USAID Responds to Global Food Crisis." *U.S. Agency for International Development (USAID).* http://www.usaid.gov/our_work/humanitarian_assistance/foodcrisis/ (accessed September 18, 2010).

U.S. Bureau of Census. http://www.census.gov/ (accessed October 17, 2010).

U.S. Department of Agriculture (USDA). http://www.usda.gov/ (accessed October 16, 2010).

U.S. Department of Agriculture (USDA). "Inside the Pyramid: How Are Oils Different from Solid Fats?" *MyPyramid.gov.* http://www.mypyramid.gov/pyramid/oils_how.html (accessed October 2, 2010).

U.S. Department of Agriculture (USDA). "What Are Oils?" *MyPyramid.gov.* http://www.mypyramid.gov/pyramid/oils.html?debugMode=false (accessed September 2, 2010).

U.S. Department of Agriculture (USDA). "Life Stages." *Nutrition.gov.* http://riley.nal.usda.gov/nal_display/index.php?info_center=11&tax_level=1&tax_subject=395 (accessed August 30, 2010).

U.S. Department of Agriculture (USDA). "MyPyramid.gov: Inside the Pyramid: Meats and Beans." *MyPyramid.gov.* http://www.mypyramid.gov/index.html (accessed September 28, 2010).

U.S. Department of Agriculture (USDA). "MyPyramid.gov: Steps to a Healthier You." *MyPyramid.gov.* http://www.mypyramid.gov/ (accessed October 17, 2010).

U.S. Department of Agriculture (USDA). "MyPyramid.gov: Vegetarian Diets." *MyPyramid.gov.* http://www.mypyramid.gov/tips_resources/vegetarian_diets.html (accessed October 22, 2010).

U.S. Government: Unified Command's Joint Information Center. *Restore the Gulf.gov.* http://www.restorethegulf.gov/ (accessed October 31, 2010).

U.S. Government: Unified Command's Joint Information Center. "Seafood Safety." *Restore the Gulf.gov.* http://www.restorethegulf.gov/health-safety/seafood-safety (accessed October 31, 2010).

U.S. National Commission on the BP Deepwater Horizon Oil Spill and Offshore Drilling. "Media Advisories." *oilspillcommission.gov.* http://www.oilspillcommission.gov/news#media-alerts (accessed October 31, 2010).

U.S. National Library of Medicine. "*E. coli* Enteritis." *Medline Plus.* http://www.nlm.nih.gov/medlineplus/ency/article/000296.htm (accessed September 1, 2010).

U.S. National Library of Medicine. "Poisoning: Fish and Shellfish." *Medline Plus.* http://www.nlm.nih.gov/medlineplus/ency/article/002851.htm (accessed October 4, 2010).

U.S. National Office for Harmful Algal Blooms at Woods Hole Oceanographic Institution. "Paralytic Shellfish Poisoning." *Harmful Algae Page.* http://www.whoi.edu/redtide/page.do?pid=14279 (accessed October 4, 2010).

"Understanding FALCPA (Food Allergen Labeling & Consumer Protection Act of 2004)." *Food Allergy Initiative.* http://www.faiusa.org/?page_id=DA172110-99EA-335F-3D2A5BA8DFE1C21D (accessed August 23, 2010).

"Understanding the WTO: The Agreements: Anti-dumping, Subsidies, Safeguards." *World Trade Organization.* http://www.wto.org/english/thewto_e/whatis_e/tif_e/agrm8_e.htm#subsidies (accessed September 25, 2010).

United Nations World Commission on Environment and Development. http://www.un-documents.net/ocf-02.htm#I (accessed October 16, 2010).

"Unsaturated Fats." *American Heart Association.* http://www.heart.org/HEARTORG/

GettingHealthy/FatsAndOils/Fats101/
Monounsaturated-Fats_UCM_301460_Article.jsp
(accessed September, 2010).

Urban Farm Online. http://www.urbanfarmonline.
com/ (accessed October 16, 2010).

Urban Farming. http://www.urbanfarming.org/
(accessed October 16, 2010).

USDA Foreign Agricultural Service. http://www.fas.
usda.gov/ (accessed October 17, 2010).

USDA Food Safety and Inspection Service. http://
www.fsis.usda.gov/ (accessed September 20,
2010).

"vCJD (Variant Creutzfeldt-Jakob Disease)." *Centers for Disease Control and Prevention (CDC).*
http://www.cdc.gov/ncidod/dvrd/vcjd/ (accessed October 21, 2010).

Vegetarian Resource Group. http://www.vrg.org/
(accessed October 22, 2010).

Vidal, John. "Artificial Meat? Food for Thought by
2050." *The Guardian,* August 16, 2010. ttp://
www.guardian.co.uk/environment/2010/
aug/16/artificial-meat-food-royal-society (accessed October 28, 2010).

"Vitamins and Minerals." *UK Food Standards Agency.*
http://www.eatwell.gov.uk/healthydiet/nutrition
essentials/vitaminsandminerals/ (accessed August
20, 2010).

"Waste Not, Want Not." *Environmental Protection
Agency (EPA).* http://www.epa.gov/wastes/
conserve/materials/organics/pubs/wast_not.
pdf (accessed October 7, 2010).

"Water for Life, 2005–2015." *United Nations.*
http://www.un.org/waterforlifedecade/index.
html (accessed November 4, 2010).

Water.org. http://water.org/ (accessed November 4,
2010).

"Welcome to the Controlled Environment Agriculture Center." *University of Arizona.* http://
www.ag.arizona.edu/ceac/ (accessed July 20,
2010).

"Western Diet Link to ADHD, Australian Study Finds." *Science Daily,* July 29,
2010. http://www.sciencedaily.com/
releases/2010/07/100729091454.htm (accessed November 2, 2010).

"What Can I Eat?" *American Diabetes Association.*
http://www.diabetes.org/food-and-fitness/
food/what-can-i-eat/ (accessed October 6,
2010).

"What Is Food for Peace?" *U.S. Agency for International Development (USAID).* http://www.
usaid.gov/our_work/humanitarian_assistance/
ffp/ (accessed October 15, 2010).

"What is Sustainable Agriculture?" *University of California, Davis.* http://www.sarep.ucdavis.edu/
concept.htm (accessed October 16, 2010).

"What Is the Asian Diet Pyramid?" *Oldways.* http://
www.oldwayspt.org/asian-diet-pyramid (accessed
October 21, 2010).

Whipps, Heather. "How the Spice Trade Changed
the World." *Live Science,* May 12, 2008. http://
www.livescience.com/history/080512-hs-
spicetrade.html (accessed October 23, 2010).

"Why Vegan?" *Vegan Outreach.* http://www.
veganoutreach.org/whyvegan/ (accessed October 4, 2010).

Wiebe, Keith. "Linking Land Quality, Agricultural
Productivity, and Food Security." *U.S. Department of Agriculture (USDA),* June 2003. http://
www.ers.usda.gov/Publications/AER823/ (accessed October 30, 2010).

Wineculture: A Hip Guide to Wine on the Web. http://
www.wineculture.com/home.html (accessed November 3, 2010).

Wise, Timothy. "Policy Space for Mexican Maize:
Protecting Agro-biodiversity by Promoting Rural Livelihoods." *Tufts University,* February
2007. http://ase.tufts.edu/gdae/Pubs/wp/07-
01MexicanMaize.pdf (accessed October 17,
2010).

"Women, Agriculture, and Food Security." *Food and
Agriculture Organization of the United Nations
(FAO).* http://www.fao.org/worldfoodsummit/
english/fsheets/women.pdf (accessed September
30, 2010).

Woods Institute for the Environment. "The Impacts
of Large Scale Use of Biofuels on Food, Agriculture, and Trade." *Stanford University.* http://
woods.stanford.edu/docs/biofuels/Biofuels3a.
pdf (accessed September 9, 2010).

Working Group on Indigenous Food Sovereignty.
Indigenous Food Systems Network. http://www.
indigenousfoodsystems.org/#content (accessed
October 27, 2010).

World Food Day USA. http://www.worldfooddayusa.
org/ (accessed September 14, 2010).

"World Food Insecurity and Malnutrition: Scope,
Trends, Causes, and Consequences." *Food and
Agriculture Organization of the United Nations
(FAO).* ftp://ftp.fao.org/docrep/fao/010/
ai799e/ai799e02.pdf (accessed September 6,
2010).

The World Food Prize. http://www.worldfoodprize. org/ (accessed October 22, 2010).

World Food Programme. http://www.wfp.org/ (accessed October 15, 2010).

"World Food Programme: Fighting Hunger Worldwide." *World Food Programme.* http://www.wfp. org/ (accessed October 17, 2010).

"World Food Summit: The Rome Declaration on World Food Security and the World Food Summit Plan of Action." *Food and Agriculture Organization of the United Nations (FAO).* http:// www.fao.org/docrep/003/w3613e/w3613e00. HTM (accessed September 25, 2010).

"World Water Day." *IRC International Water and Sanitation Center.* http://www.worldwaterday. org/ (accessed November 1, 2010).

Wrigt, Andy. "Finally, Candy Makers Market Directly to Women with Food Issues." *Mother Jones,* February 13, 2009. http:// motherjones.com/media/2009/02/ finally-candy-makers-market-directly-women-food-issues (accessed November 4, 2010).

"You Are What You Eat!" *Food Alliance.* http:// foodalliance.org/information-for/for-consumers (accessed October 17, 2010).

Young Sera L., M. Jeffrey Wilson, Dennis Miller, and Stephen Hillier. "Toward a Comprehensive Approach to the Collection and Analysis of Pica Substances, with Emphasis on Geophagic Materials." *PLoS one* 3, no. 9, 2008. http://www.plosone. org/article/info:doi%2F10.1371%2Fjournal. pone.0003147 (accessed September 14, 2010).

"Your Guide to Lowering Your Blood Pressure with DASH." *National Institutes of Health, U.S. Department of Health and Human Services.* http:// www.nhlbi.nih.gov/health/public/heart/hbp/ dash/new_dash.pdf (accessed September 1, 2010).

Zagat. http://www.zagat.com/ (accessed October 30, 2010).

General Index

Page numbers in **boldface** indicate the main essay for a topic, and primary source page numbers are in **boldface and italics**. An *italicized* page number indicates a photo, illustration, chart, or other graphic.

A

AAP (American Academy of Pediatrics), 1:495, 2:604

Abdi Aziz district, Somalia, refugees, 2:862

Aboriginal peoples, 2:516, 843–844

Academy of the Sierras boarding school, 2:771

Achieving Food Security in Times of Crisis (Ban Ki-moon), 2:856

ACOG (American College of Obstetricians and Gynecologists), 1:303

Acquired immunodeficiency syndrome (AIDS). *See* HIV/AIDS

Action Against Famine's Feeding Center, 1:273

ADA (American Diabetic Association), 1:195

ADA (American Dietetic Association), 2:674

Adams, Hopkins, 2:669

Adaptation, 1:133–134

Addis Ababa, Ethiopia, 2:758

Additionality (food aid), 1:504

Adenosine triphosphate (ATP), 2:667, 667

ADHD (Attention-deficit-hyperactive disorder), 2:632

Adolescent and Parent Views of Family Meals (Fulkerson), 1:263

Adolescents
body image, 1:303–305
family meals, 1:263–264

junk food, 2:512
nutritional needs, 1:122, 123, 212
overweight, 1:2
therapeutic boarding schools, 2:771
underage drinking, 1:285
urban farm worker, 2:787

Adrià, Ferran, 2:568, 569, 570

Adventures in Diet (Stefansson), 1:491–492

Advertising food, 1:1–4, *2, 3*
celebrity chefs, 1:116
documentary regarding, 2:576
food fads, 1:326
junk food, 2:511
Pollan, Michael, 2:561, 562

Aeromonas bacteria, 2:831

Aeroponics, 1:479

Afghanistan
Afghan workers packing honey jars, 2:791
bread, 1:62
breastfeeding, 1:91
opium poppy production, 1:40–41
undernourished boy, 2:780
USAID, 2:792
World Food Programme, 2:863

Africa
agriculture, 1:301
bananas, 1:400
black carbon emissions, 1:160
bushmeat, 1:98–101, 230
cacao bean production, 1:125–126
celiac disease, 1:423
chicken domestication, 2:782
cholera, 1:129

climate change, 1:133
coffee trade, 1:138
consumption of dirt and clay, 2:637
deforestation, 1:16
domestication of animals, 1:275
fair trade production, 1:259
famines, 1:187, 266–267, 273, 2:644
farmland degradation, 2:646
food safety, 1:156
food waste, 1:330
GMO crops, 1:420
grain production, 1:356
grains, 1:432
Green Revolution, 1:438
herbs used in cooking, 1:453
influenza, 1:58, 252
land reform, 1:25, 26, 28
migrant workers, 2:823
obesity, 2:602
overgrazing and land degradation, 2:519
rainforests, 1:189
raw milk, 2:676
rice cultivation, 2:686
rise of agriculture, 1:275
roundworm infection, 1:467
slave labor, 2:823
tea, 2:762
USAID, 1:28
wheat imports, 2:624
wine, 2:815
women and food, 2:851
women's land ownership, 2:850
women's unequal work burden, 1:244–245
See also African famine relief; developing countries; *specific countries*

African, Caribbean, and Pacific (ACP) banana-producing nations, 1:65–68

African-Americans
food advertising stereotypes, 1:3
lactose intolerance, 2:516
obesity rates, 1:210, 2:603
Southern cooking, 1:386
U.S. Food Stamp Program, 2:592
USDA discrimination against, 2:795

African Development Bank (ADB), 2:777

African famine relief, 1:**5–8,** *6, 7,* 187
See also Famine

AgChat Foundation, 2:722

Agenda 21, 1:**9–11,** *10,* 142

Aggregate Measure of Support (AMS), agricultural subsidies, 2:742

Agreement on Trade Related Aspects of Intellectual Property Rights (TRIPS), 1:344–345

Agribusiness, 1:**12–15,** *14*
indigenous peoples, 1:16, 18
irrigation, 1:21–23
sustainable agriculture, 2:751–752
World Food Price Foundation, 2:747
See also Factory farming;
Industrial agriculture

Agricultural Adjustment Act (AAA) of 1933, 1:316, 2:741, 794

Agricultural commodities, 2:707, 791

Agricultural Course (lectures), 2:750

Agricultural deforestation, 1:**16–19,** *17,* 2:*518*

Agricultural demand for water, 1:**20–24,** 2:836

Agricultural Division of the Patent Office, 2:793

Agricultural land reform, 1:**25–29,** 330–331

Agricultural policies and famine, 1:271–273

Agricultural subsidies, 1:**40–42,** 486–487, 2:741, 794

Agricultural Trade Development and Assistance Act of 1954, 1:503

Agriculture
climate change, 1:132–134
employment sector, 1:370
ethical issues, 1:243–245, 2:823–825
food laws, 2:766
food security, 2:690, 691, 692
foreign aid, 1:369
gender equality, 1:412–415
history, 1:275, 456–458
land degradation, 1:370, 2:517–519, *518*
migrant labor and immigration, 2:**564–567,** *566,* 823
population, 2:645

Agriculture and international trade, 1:**30–33**

Agriculture brings hierarchical societies, 1:**34–36,** *36*

Agroecology, 1:**37–39,** *38*

Agronomists, 2:858

Agronomy, 1:37–38, 2:755

Agroterrorism, 1:78

Agroterrorism: Threats and Preparedness (CRS), 1:80

Ahmadi, Brahm, 2:720

Aid for agriculture to replace illicit drug production, 1:**40–42**

Aid workers, 2:*820*

AIDS. *See* HIV/AIDS

Air pollution, indoor, 1:95–97

Akha woman, 2:*704*

Alabama, 1:*441, 442,* 2:768

Alaska, 1:430, 2:844

Albania, 1:185

Albuquerque, New Mexico, urban chicken movement, 2:782

Alcohol fermentation, 1:**282–287**

Alcoholic beverages, 1:282–287, 312–313
See also Beer and wine

Aldrich, Nelson, 2:774

Aleurone, 1:433

Algeria, 2:624

Alice Waters: California and New American cuisine, 1:**43–45,** *44*
See also Waters, Alice

Allen, Will, 2:630

Allergens, food labels, 1:291–293, 2:773–775, 799

Allergies
dairy products, 1:179, 236
eggs, 1:236
food, 1:152, 294–296, 404
food labels, 1:*292,* 2:774, 799
GMO products, 1:419
regulation regarding, 1:291–293, 2:684
skin tests, 1:*295*

Almonds, 1:107, 2:*600*

Alms, 1:428

Alzheimer's disease, 1:166, 2:557, 869

Amaranth, 1:432

Amazon
animal production, 1:229
Brazil nuts, 2:598, 600
deforestation, 1:18, 27, 98
rainforest burning, 1:*17*
Yanomamo Indians, 1:201

American Academy of Pediatrics (AAP), 1:495, 2:604

American Cancer Society, 1:104, 2:538

American College of Obstetricians and Gynecologists (ACOG), 1:303

American Diabetic Association (ADA), 1:195

American Dietetic Association (ADA), 2:674, 804, 812

American Heart Association (AHA), 1:199, 201, 2:572, 775, 822

American Journal of Clinical Nutrition, 2:606

American Journal of Public Health, 2:677

American Southern Foodways Alliance, 1:385

American Veal Association, 1:470

American Vegetarian Society, 2:803

America's Second Harvest/Feeding America, 1:**46–48**

America's Second Harvest/Feeding America food bank, 1:*47*

Amherst, Massachusetts, 1:145–146

Amylophagy, 2:638

Anaphylaxis, 1:291, 294, 2:773

Anasazi Pueblo site, 1:110

Ancient Greece. *See* Greece (ancient)

Andean dietary customs, 2:680–681

Anderson, Lessley, 2:673

Andrzewski, Elizabeth, 1:*482*

Animal, Vegetable, Miracle (Kingsolver), 2:534–535

Animal Liberation (Singer), 2:811

Animal Machines (Harrison), 1:469

Animal right activists, 2:*805*

Animal waste, 2:531, 840

Annakut Darshan celebration, 1:*310*

Anorexia nervosa, 1:225, *226,* 226–228

Anorexia Nervosa (Gull), 1:*227–228*

Antananarivo, Madagascar, 1:*130*

Antarctica, whaling, 2:845–846

Anthrax attacks of 2001, 1:78

Anthropophagy, 1:**109–111**

Antibiotics, 1:254, 255, 2:531, 649, 695

Antibodies, 1:58, 90, 423, 496

Antioxidants
beans, 2:523
cancer, 1:193
chlorophyll-a, 2:634
flavonoids, 1:152
fruits, 1:399, 400, 401
vegetables, 2:807–808
wine, 2:558

Appellation d'Origine Contrôlée (AOC), 2:817

Appert, Nicolas, 1:339, 460, 2:660

Apples, 1:*277, 427*
　　Alar, 2:641, 766
　　calories, 1:107
　　symbolic importance, 1:399
Appliances, 1:459–460, *461*
Apricots, 1:399
Aquaculture and fishery resources,
　　1:**49–52,** *50, 51,* 56, 2:710–714
Aquaponics, 1:479
Aquifers, 1:22–23, 2:835, 840
Archer Daniels Midland (ADM), 2:859
Archives of Internal Medicine, 2:554,
　　557
*Archives of Pediatrics and Adolescent
　　Medicine,* 1:263–264
Areas for Municipal Level Alternative
　　Development (ADAM), 1:40
Arens, William, 1:109
Arequipa, Peru, 1:*143*
Aretaeus of Cappodocia, 1:422
Argentina
　　bacterial blight, 1:31
　　ban on the use of gavage, 1:314
　　corn production, 1:169, 171
　　family farms, 1:260
　　wine, 2:817
Aristophanes, 2:814
Arizona, food libel laws, 2:768
Ark of Taste program, 2:718
Armenia, land reform, 1:27
Armstrong, Lance, 1:*192*
Arnon, Daniel, 1:478
Aromatic oils, 1:452
*The Art of Cookery Made Plain and
　　Easy* (Glasse), 1:*460–461*
Artisan products
　　cheese, 1:*426*
　　liquors, 1:*284*
　　sustainable table, 2:754
　　in the U.S., 1:*426*
Ascetic dietary rules, 2:680
Aseptic packaging, 1:460
Asia
　　agricultural subsidies, 2:741
　　allergies, 1:294
　　aquaculture and fishery resources,
　　　1:56
　　avian influenza, 2:649
　　bananas, 1:400
　　black carbon emissions, 1:160,
　　　162–163
　　breast cancer rates, 2:636
　　bushmeat, 1:98
　　cancer rates, 1:192
　　chicken domestication, 2:782
　　chicken species, 2:782
　　cholera, 1:129
　　citrus fruits, 1:399
　　cuisine history, 2:827
　　deforestation, 1:16, 2:519

domestication of animals, 1:275
　　early agriculture, 1:457
　　fair trade production, 1:259
　　famines, 2:644
　　food insecurity, 1:53–54
　　grains, 1:432
　　Green Revolution, 1:437, 438
　　hunger, 1:470
　　lactose intolerance, 2:516
　　land reform, 1:25, 26, 28
　　migrant workers, 2:823
　　modern ovens, 1:459
　　obesity, 1:55–56, 2:602
　　open cook stoves, 1:460
　　rise of agriculture, 1:275
　　roundworm infection, 1:467
　　seafood production, 2:710
　　spice production and trade, 2:724
　　sugar trade, 2:747
　　tea, 2:760
　　USAID, 1:28, 2:792
　　water usage, 1:22–23
　　wine, 2:815
　　women and food, 2:851
Asian diet, 1:**53–56,** *54, 55,* 2:523, 599
Asian fusion cooking, 1:406
Asian pastries, 1:*407*
Asia's Dirty Little Secret (Coates),
　　1:*162–163*
Aspartame, 2:749
Aterhov, 2:673
Atherosclerosis, 1:477
Atlantic Monthly, 2:808
Attention-deficit-hyperactive disorder
　　(ADHD), 2:632
Aunt Jemima, 1:3
Aurochs, 1:276
Australia
　　agricultural subsidies, 2:741,
　　　742–743
　　beer consumption, 1:284
　　bioterrorism, 1:80
　　breastfeeding, 1:92
　　climate change, 1:133
　　daily water access, 2:835
　　food waste, 2:833–834
　　GMO ban, 2:864
　　migrant workers, 2:565
　　modern ovens, 1:459
　　raw milk, 2:676
　　salmonellosis outbreak, 2:697
　　wine, 2:817, 818
Australopithecines, 2:596
Austria, 1:284, 2:750, 864
Ausubel, Kenny, 1:69
Autotrophs, 1:377, 378
Avenin, 2:771
Average Crop Revenue Election
　　(ACRE) program, 1:316, 317
Avian influenza, 1:**57–60,** 252,
　　2:649–650, 784

Azerbaijan, 1:27, 58
Aztec civilization
　　animal domestication, 2:648
　　cannibalism, 1:109
　　chocolate, 1:125
　　corn, 1:169
　　diet, 2:520
　　hydroponic systems, 1:478

B

Baba Budan, 1:138
Babette's Feast (movie), 2:574–575
Baby bottles, 1:*82,* 83, 86
Baby food and infant formula. *See*
　　Infant formula and baby food
BAC (blood alcohol concentration),
　　1:285
Backyard chickens, 2:*783,* 784, 785
Backyard Poultry (Web site), 2:782
Backyardchickens.com, 2:782
Bacon, 1:327–332
Bacon, Sir Francis, 1:478
Bacteria, 1:360, 2:**526–528,** *527,*
　　550, 676, 677
　　bacterial blights, 1:31
　　refrigeration, 2:831
　　soil bacteria, 2:523, 524
　　waste and spoilage, 2:831
　　See also E. coli contamination;
　　　specific bacteria
Baird, John, 1:*82*
Baird's Beaked whale, 2:*844*
Bake sale ban protest, 1:*313*
Baked bread, 2:582
Bakers, 1:*36*
Baking bread, 1:**61–64,** *62, 63,* 351,
　　432
Baking foods, 1:352
Baking powder, 1:3
BAL (blood alcohol level), 1:285
Baldwin Park, California, 1:*280*
Balik, Julia, 1:*482*
Banana trade wars, 1:**65–68**
Bananas, 1:*14, 66,* 400
Bangkok, Thailand, 1:*55, 450*
Bangladesh
　　cholera, 1:128
　　famine, 1:272, 436–437, 2:645
　　food waste dump, 2:*832*
　　hunger and malnutrition, 1:54
　　malnourished child, 2:*545*
　　rice, 2:688, 822
　　sharecropping, 2:824
　　spice production, 2:726
　　spice trade, 2:726
　　women and food, 1:*433,* 2:851, 852
　　World Food Prize, 2:857

Banquet chicken patties, 2:650

Banquet pot pies, 2:649

Bans
blowfish, 1:313
genetically modified organisms,
1:314, 486, 2:864
recombinant bovine growth
hormone, 1:314
trans fats, 1:165, 314, 2:572

Banting, Frederick, 1:194

Banting, William, 1:176

Barbecuing and grilling, 1:351, 353

Barcelona, Spain, 1:150, *400*

Barley, 1:432, 433, 2:771

Basal metabolic rate (BMR), 2:668

Basic food groups, 2:801

BASIS, 1:28

Batali, Mario, 1:116, 2:764

Battery cage, 1:468, 470

Battle Creek Sanitarium, 1:176

Baum, Joseph, 1:426

BBB (Better Business Bureau), 1:447

Beaches Greenmarket, Florida, 2:*616*

Beak trimming, 1:468

Bean curds, 1:*333*

Beans, 2:*538, 828*
hydroponic, 1:479
macrobiotic diet, 2:537
patents, 1:345

Beard, James, 1:115, 2:763

Beatrice's Goat, 1:447

Becker, Geoffrey S., 2:*848–849*

Beckmann, David, 2:858

BedZed eco development, 1:*10*

Beef, 2:766, 768, *848*

Beer and wine
barley, 1:432
fermentation process, 1:282–287
heart disease, 1:396
lager, 1:481
Mediterranean diet, 2:558
organics, 2:817
pasteurization, 2:626
religion and food, 2:682, 814, 815
science, 2:815–816
yeast and leavening agents, 2:868
See also Alcoholic beverages;
winemaking

Beijing, China, 1:*86, 161, 404*

Beira, Mozambique, 1:131

Belarus, decollectivization, 1:184

Belen, Costa Rica, 1:*139*

Belgium, beer consumption, 1:284

Benjamin, Regina, 1:441

Bentham, Jeremy, 1:469

Berkeley, California, 1:232, *233*

Berlin Airlift, 2:790

Berries, 1:399, 401

Berry, Wendell, 2:754

Best, Charles, 1:194

Better Business Bureau (BBB), 1:447

Beverage Marketing Corporation,
1:84

Beyer, Peter, 1:55, 2:688, 822

Bhagavad Gita, 1:312

Bicycle race, 1:*192*

Big Night (movie), 2:575

Big pharma, 1:137

Bile, 1:450, 465, 466

Bill & Melinda Gates Foundation,
2:859

Binge eating, 1:225

Bio-security law protest, 1:*419*

Bioaccumulation, 2:631, 842

Biodiesel, 1:74, 75

Biodiversity
CGRFA, 1:142–144
deforestation, 1:18
human actions that affect,
1:157–158
monocultures, 1:372

Biodiversity and food supply, 1:**69–73**

Biofuels and world hunger, 1:**74–77,**
355

Biofuels industry, U.S. government
encouragement, 1:316

Biomass, 1:95, 377–378

Biopiracy, 1:71, 345

Biosafety, Cartagena Protocol on,
1:**112–114**

Biosafety Clearing-House, 1:113

Bioscience, 2:811

Biotechnology, 1:244, 438, 2:645

Bioterrorism, food as a weapon,
1:**78–80,** *79,* 89

Biotoxins, 2:621

Bipedalism, 2:595, 596

Bird flu. *See* Avian influenza

Birdseye, Clarence, 1:460, 2:660–661

Birth defects, 1:104, 324, 2:607,
632, 701

Birthday celebrations, 1:310–311

Bisphenol A, 1:**81–83,** 496–497

The Bitter Cry of the Children
(Spargo), 2:706

Black carbon, 1:96, 160–161, 162

Blakely, Georgia, 1:*361*

Blanc, Raymond, 2:765

Blanding, Michael, 1:327

Blogs, 2:721, 722, 723

*Blood, Sweat, and Fear: Workers' Rights
in U.S. Meat and Poultry Plants*
(Human Rights Watch), 2:550, 847

Blood alcohol concentration (BAC),
1:285

Blood alcohol level (BAL), 1:285

Blowfish bans, 1:313

Blue Diamond Growers, 1:257

Blueberries, 1:152, 401, 2:632, 635

Blumenthal, Heston, 2:569, *569*

BMI (body mass index), 1:397,
2:601–602, 604

Boca Raton, Forida, 2:*611*

Bocuse, Paul, 2:568

Body image, food and, 1:**303–305**

Body mass index (BMI), 1:397,
2:601–602, 604

Boiling food, 1:351–352

Bok choy, 2:*788*

Bolivia
coca trade, 1:*41*
food aid, 1:*247*
food sovereignty principles, 1:374
natural vegetation loss, 1:18–19

Bonaparte, Napoleon, 1:339

Bonobo, 1:98

Borlaug, Norman E., 1:436, 437,
2:857

Borlaug International Symposium,
2:857

Bosenberg, Henry F., 1:343

Bosnia and Herzegovina, 1:185

Bost, Eric, 2:*801*

Boston, Massachusetts, raw milk
rally, 2:*677*

*The Botany of Desire: A Plant's-Eye
View of the World* (Pollan), 2:561

Botswana, 1:492

Bottled water, 1:**84–87,** *86*

Botulism, 1:80, **88–90,** *89,* 359, 2:704

Bourdain, Anthony, 1:116, *117,*
2:675, 764

Boussingault, Jean Baptiste, 1:478

Bovine spongiform encephalopathy
(BSE), 2:**540–543,** 767
embargoes, 1:240
food inspections, 1:333–334
food libel laws, 2:766–768
infective agent, 1:381
meat testing, 2:847–848
See also Creutzfeldt-Jakob Disease
(CJD); Variant Creutzfeldt-
Jakob Disease (vCJD)

Boycott, Charles, 2:640

Boycotts, political food, 2:**640–643,**
641, 642

Boyer, Herbert, 1:112

BP *Deepwater Horizon* oil spill,
1:**440–442**

Brambell, Roger, 1:469

Brambell Report, 1:469

Bran, 2:624, 687

Brandenberger, Jacques, 1:340

Bratman, Steven, 1:177, 2:674
Brazil, 2:*520*
  agricultural subsidies, 1:486–487
  coffee, 1:138
  deforestation, 1:16, *17*
  family farms, 1:260
  farmer spraying herbicide, 1:*345*
  indoor air quality, 1:95
  natural vegetation loss, 1:18–19
  pasta production, 2:624
  rice, 2:688
  rice field, 1:*417*
  social safety net, 1:357
  World Food Prize, 2:857
Brazil nuts, 1:419
Bread, 1:107, 2:*582*
Bread, baking, 1:**61–64**, *62, 63,* 351, 432
Breastfeeding, 1:**91–94**, *93*
  advocacy, 1:497
  allergies, 1:295
  infant formula, 1:13, 91–92, 495, 496
  nutritional needs of women, 1:212
  rates, 1:496
  undernutrition, 2:779
  WIC program, 1:488, 489
Breastfeeding: Biocultural Perspectives (Dettwyler), 1:91
Bremstrahlung, 1:336, 337
Brigade system, 1:174
Briggs, Annalise, 1:*92–93*
Brillat-Savarin, Jean Anthelme, 1:409
Brittany, France, 2:*555*
Broiler barns, 2:*530*
Broiler chickens, 1:254
Bronson Reynolds, James, 2:846
The Brooklyn Grange commercial farm (Queens, New York), 2:*788*
Browning, 1:164, 351, 352, 2:554
Browning agents, 1:375
Bruch, Hilde, 1:227
Brundtland Commission, 2:754
Brundtland Report (WCED), 1:9, 244, 2:750, 751
Bruni, Frank, 1:307
The Bruni Digest (Langbein), 1:307
Bryant-Waugh, Rachel, 1:347
BSE. *See* Bovine spongiform encephalopathy
Buckwheat, 2:538
Buddhist dietary rules, 2:680
Buena Vista Vineyards, 2:816
Building better ovens, 1:**95–97**, *96, 97*
Building Sustainable Organic Sectors (Källander & Rundgren), 1:**500–502**

Bulgaria, 1:184, 2:851
Bulimia nervosa, 1:225, 226–227
Bureau of Chemistry, 2:796
Burger King, 2:522, *642*
Burgundy, France, 1:*283*
Burma, chicken domestication in, 2:782
Burundi, food supplies, 2:*861*
Bush, George W., 1:316, 317, 2:683
Bushmeat, 1:**98–101**, *99,* 229, 230
Bushmeat Smuggling Widespread in Paris (Cheng & Okello), 1:**100–101**
Butchers, 2:*541*
BYO (Bring Your Own) concept, 2:833

C

C-reactive protein (CRP), 1:126
Cabbage family, 1:452
CABI (Commonwealth Agricultural Bureaux International), 1:18
Cadbury-Schweppes, 1:360
Café (Montpelier, France), 1:*397*
Café culture, 1:**393–395**
Café culture, French, 1:**393–395**
Café de Flore (Paris, France), 1:*394*
Café Procope (Paris, France), 1:393
Caffeine, 1:**102–105**, *103*
CAFOs. *See* Concentrated animal feeding operations (CAFOs)
Calcium, 1:403
Calgene, 1:112
California
  almonds, 2:*600*
  ban of foie gras, 1:314
  ban of trans fats, 1:314
  California State Polytechnic University, 1:*479*
  egg recall, 2:*697*
  FDA research lab, 2:*797*
  fishery closures, 2:622
  genetically altered goat, 1:*421*
  grape harvests, 1:311
  Hmong farmers, 2:*752*
  In-N-Out Burger, 1:*280*
  lettuce washing, 2:*664*
  migrant workers, 2:566, 823
  organic produce stand, 2:*615*
  wine, 2:816
California Almond Growers Exchange (CAGE), 1:257
California cuisine, 1:**43–45**, 2:576, 729
California Department of Education and the Cornell Garden-Based Learning program, 1:234
California organic acreage, 2:613

California State Polytechnic University, 1:479, *479*
Calorie sign, Panera, 1:*107*
Calories, 1:**106–108**, 123, 177, 472, 474, 2:779
Calumet baking powder, 1:3
Cambodia, 1:54, 58, 59, 2:851
Camellia sinensis, 2:760
Cameroon, 1:71
The Campaign for Real Milk, 2:676, 677
Campbell's reduced sodium soup, 1:*202*
Campylobacter bacteria, 1:381, 2:550, 650, 677
Canada
  alcohol prohibition, 1:313
  botulism toxin-based weapons, 1:89
  bovine spongiform encephalopathy (BSE), 2:768
  BPA use in baby bottles, 1:82, 497
  breastfeeding, 1:497
  BSE cases, 2:541
  daily water access, 2:835
  durum wheat exports, 2:624
  E. coli outbreaks, 1:223
  farmed mussels, 1:*50*
  food aid provided by, 1:246, 503, 504–505
  food recalls, 1:360
  food safety, 1:155
  food waste, 2:830, 832
  fortification of milk, 2:586
  Invialuit people, 1:491–492
  migrant workers, 2:565
  obesity, 2:603
  paralytic shellfish poisoning, 2:622
  patent law, 1:344
  trans fats ban, 1:314
  wine, 2:817
Canadian Dietetic Association, 2:812
Canadian Food Inspection Agency, 2:773
Cancer
  Alar, 2:641
  caffeine, 1:104
  diet, 1:191–193
  digestive system, 2:771
  food testing, 1:324
  lycopene, 1:353
  macrobiotic diet, 2:538
  meat consumption, 2:554
  Mediterranean diet, 2:557
  obesity, 1:1, 191, 193, 2:603
  patents on human genes, 1:420
  patients and listeriosis, 2:526
  pesticides, 2:632
  phytochemicals, 2:808
  processed meats, 2:705
  raw food, 2:674
  saturated fats, 2:571

Cancer (*continued*)
  soybeans, 2:523, 524–525, 538, 636
  sugar and sweeteners, 2:749
  undernutrition, 2:779
  veganism, 2:803, 805
  vegetarianism, 2:811
  vitamins and minerals, 2:821
Cancer (journal), 2:795
Cancer Research (journal), 2:554
Canned vegetables, 2:658
Cannibalism, 1:**109–111**
Canning, 1:339, 460, 2:655, 658, 660, 661
Canola oil, 1:199, 2:571
Canola plants, 1:*199*, 418
Cape of Good Hope, 2:817
Capitalism, 1:484
Capsaicin, 1:453–454
Carabao (swamp buffalo), 2:*745*
Carbohydrates
  diabetes, 1:194–195
  diets, 1:75, 2:617, 772
  display, 1:*328*
  energy density, 1:106
  metabolism, 2:666–667, 668
  nutritional needs, 1:122, 2:590
Carbon emissions, cooking and climate change, 1:96, **160–163**
Carbon footprint, 2:756
Carcinogens, 1:191
  See also specific cancer causing agents
Cardiff, Wales, U.K., 1:*427*
Carême, Marie-Antoine, 1:115
Caribbean
  banana trade wars, 1:65–68
  cacao plantations, 1:125
  cholera, 1:128
  coffee, 1:138
  deforestation, 1:16
  migrant workers, 2:823
  obesity, 2:602
  street vendors, 2:736
  weddings, 1:309
Carpenter, Karen, 1:225
Carrots, 1:*331*, 452, 2:614, *635*
Carrying capacity, 1:268
Carson, Rachel, 1:469, 2:630, 750
Cartagena Protocol on Biosafety (2000), 1:**112–114**, 2:794
Castro, Raul, 1:27
Caterers, 1:309
Cattle, 1:*79*, 2:*518*, 531
Cattle industry, 1:79, 2:530, 766
Cave painting (Valencia, Spain), 1:*458*
CCAs (Community conserved areas), 1:18
CDC. *See* U.S. Centers for Disease Control and Prevention (CDC)

Celebration, food as, 1:**309–311**
Celebrity chef phenomenon, 1:**115–118**, *116, 117,* 326, 2:763–765
Celery, 2:632, 806
Celiac disease, 1:**422–424**, 2:770–772
Celiac Sprue Association, 1:424
Center for Food Safety and Applied Nutrition (CFSAN), 1:**119–121**, 365, 2:796
Center for Nutrition Policy and Promotion, 2:800
Center for Urban Agriculture (Fairview Gardens, California), 2:615
Central America
  bushmeat, 1:98
  cacao bean, 1:125
  coffee cultivation, 1:102
  deforestation, 1:16
  famines, 2:644
  grains, 1:432
  illicit drugs, 1:40
  migrant workers, 2:823
  sugar fortification, 2:586
  World Trade Organization (WTO), 2:866
  See also specific countries
Cereals, 1:432, 434
Certified organic label, 2:614
Cervantes, Miguel de, 2:637
Cetaceans, 2:844
CFSAN (Center for Food Safety and Applied Nutrition), 1:**119–121**, 365, 2:796
CGRFA (Commission on Genetic Resources for Food and Agriculture), 1:72, **142–144**
Chad, 1:71, 2:863
Changing nutritional needs throughout life, 1:**122–124**
Charles II (king), 1:393
Charlie and the Chocolate Factory (movie), 1:152
Chaudhary, Sitapati, 1:447–448
Chávez, César, 2:564
Cheese
  artisan, 1:426
  calories, 1:107
  Cheez Whiz, 1:326
  hard, 2:*678*
  Italian, 1:*407*
  listeriosis, 2:528
  making, 1:180, *180*
  poem, 1:182
  quark, 2:*674*
  veganism, 2:803
Cheese Festival (Cardiff, Wales, U.K.), 1:*427*
Cheese making, 1:*364*
Chefs, 1:**115–118**, 2:*624*, 763–765, 868

Chefs for Humanity, 2:765
The Chemistry of Cooking and Cleaning (Richards and Elliot), 1:166–167
Chemosynthetic autotrophs, 1:378
Cheney, Ian, 2:575
Cheng, Maria, 1:*100–101*
Cherries, 1:399
Chez Panisse Restaurant (Berkeley, California), 1:43, 44, 233, 425, 2:754
Chicago, Illinois
  foie gras ban, 1:314, 470
  government food assistance, 1:429
  pasteurization requirement in, 2:627
  slaughterhouse (1880), 2:*670*
  stockyards and meatpacking, 2:548, 550–552
  trans fats ban, 2:572
  urban chicken movement, 2:782
Chicken, 1:*58, 237,* 2:530
  backyard, 2:*783, 784, 785*
  broiler, 1:254
  calories, 1:107
  domestication, 1:275, 2:782
  foodborne illness, 1:381
  fried, 1:*165*
  patties, 2:650
  processing plant, 2:*653*
  school lunches, 2:708
  urban farming, 2:785
  See also Eggs; Poultry
Chicken coops, 2:*783*
Chicken farming, 1:*255*, 468, 469, 2:529, 530
Chickpeas, 2:523, 525
Child, Julia, 1:115, *116*, 425, 2:575, 763
Child labor, 2:566, 824
Child Nutrition Act of 1966, 1:488, 2:707
Childe, V. Gordon, 1:34
Children, 1:2, *234, 290, 295, 348, 370, 473, 489, 493,* 2:*513, 535, 545, 578, 590, 707, 801, 820, 844, 855*
  allergies to foods, 1:236, 291, 294–295
  bisphenol A, 1:82–83, *82,* 86
  breastfeeding, 1:91–94, *93*
  child labor, 2:566, 824
  child trafficking and slavery, 1:13
  daily water access, 2:835
  deaths from pollution relating to open cookstoves, 1:460
  diabetes, 2:709
  dietary reference intakes, 1:212
  dirt consumption, 2:637
  E. coli, 1:222
  eating, 1:*348,* 2:645
  edible schoolyard movement, 1:232–235, *234*
  family meals, 1:263–264
  famine, 1:*273*
  fasting, 2:679

fish consumption, 1:198, 2:713
food advertising, 1:1–3, 2, *2*
food phobias, 1:347, *348*
gluten intolerance, 1:422
hunger, 1:472, *473*, *590*
infant botulism, 1:88
iron deficiency, 2:588
junk food, 2:511–513, *513*
listeriosis, 2:528
marasmus, 1:369
nutrition legislation in the United
    States, 1:488–490, *489*
nutritional needs, 1:122–123, 2:688
obesity, 1:151–152, 2:603–605,
    709, 756, *771*
oral health, 2:606, 607
overweight, 1:311, 490, 2:511,
    512–513
overweight rates, 1:303
pesticides, 2:632, 766
raw food diets, 2:674
roundworm infection, 1:467
school lunch reform, 2:706–709,
    707
taste sensation, 2:757, 758
undernourished, 1:*473*, 2:*780*
undernutrition and malnutrition,
    2:544, *545*, 546, *590*, 779, 781
in U.S. Food Stamp Program,
    2:592
World Food Programme (WFP),
    2:525, 860
See also Infant formula and baby
    food
Chile (country), 1:145, 2:817
Chiles, 2:520
Chimpanzees, 1:98, 109
China
    Akha woman and MSG, 2:*704*
    aquaculture, 1:49, 2:710
    avian influenza, 2:649
    bean curd shop vendor, 1:*333*
    biofuels, 1:74, 77
    bird domestication, 1:236
    bottled water, 1:84, *86*
    chicken domestication, 2:782
    coal fire stoves, 1:*161*
    corn imports and exports, 1:171
    cuisine history, 2:827
    deforestation, 1:17
    dried fruit display, 1:*401*
    dried vegetables, 2:656
    eggs, 1:*238*
    family meals, 1:263
    famine, 1:271, 272, 274, 2:645
    farming, 1:183–184, *185*,
        185–186, *188*
    fish species protection, 2:716
    food aid provided by, 1:505
    food depots, 2:*691*
    food safety laws, 1:136
    fortification of soy sauce, 2:587, *587*
    GMO ban, 1:486
    hypertension rates, 1:206

infant formula made in, 1:496
influenza, 1:58, 59
irrigation systems, 1:20, 2:686
land reform, 1:26, 27, 184–185
melamine tainted milk, 1:136
migrant workers, 2:565
obesity, 1:55–56
oldest domesticated rice, 1:457
One Child Policy, 2:646
pasta, 2:623, *624*
plant patents, 1:343
restaurants in eleventh century,
    1:319
rice, 2:686, 688
seafood production, 2:710
seafood street market, 1:*382*
shark fin demand, 2:715, 716
spice production, 2:726
spring rolls, 1:406
street food vendors, 1:*353, 382,
    401*
supermarket, 1:*404*
tea, 2:760, 762
wheat production, 1:437
World Food Prize, 2:857
Chinese law enforcement officers,
    1:*136*
Chinese Ministry of Health, 2:587
Chiquita Brands International, 1:65
Chocolate, 1:**125–127**
    advertising, 1:1
    caffeine, 1:102
    calories, 1:108
    flavonoids, 1:151
    history in Latin America, 2:520
    hypertension, 2:636
    macrobiotic diet, 2:537
    recall of chocolate bars, 1:360
Cholera, 1:80, **128–131**
Cholesterol, 1:199
Chomsky, Noam, 2:866
Choux pastry, 1:151
Christie, Agatha, 1:176
Chryseobacterium bacteria, 2:831
Chutney, 1:406, 2:737
Cibophobia. *See* Food Phobias
CIC (Council of Islamic Courts), 1:6
Cinema, movies, documentaries, and
    food, 2:**574–576**
Circulation (journal), 2:705
Cisgenic organisms, 1:112
CITES. *See* entries beginning with
    Convention on International Trade
    in Endangered Species
Citrus orchard, 2:*610*
Ciudad Obregon, Mexico, 1:*437*
Civet coffee, 1:326
CIW (Coalition of Immokalee
    Workers), 2:642
Cladosporium mold, 2:831

Claiborne, Craig, 1:425
Clay, consumption of, 2:637
Clean Air Act of 1963, 2:574
Clean Water Act of 1972, 2:574
Clear wine, 2:815
Cleveland, Grover, 2:793
Climate change
    aquaculture and fishery resources,
        1:51
    cooking, 1:95, 160–163
    deforestation, 1:17–18
    desertification, 1:187, 188
    extreme weather, 1:252
    factory farming, 1:255
    famine, 1:6
    food insecurity, 1:370, 2:646,
        690, 692
    Green Revolution, 1:438
    meat consumption, 1:230
    red tide, 2:622
Climate change and agriculture,
    1:**132–134**
Clinton, Hillary Rodham, 2:858
Cloaca, 1:58
Coal fire stoves, 1:*161*
Coalition of Immokalee Workers
    (CIW), 2:642
Coates, Karen, 1:*162–163*
Coca
    crops, 1:40–42, 2:792
    leaves, 1:*41*, 2:680–681
Coca-Cola, cocaine and caffeine in,
    2:671
Coca-Cola Company, 1:3, 327,
    2:513
Cochabamba, Bolivia, 1:*247*
Cochrane, Josephine, 1:460
Cocoa, 1:102, 2:792
Cocoa beans, 1:125–126, *126, 244*
Cocoa farmers and workers, 1:*126, 244*
Codex Alimentarius, 1:**135–137**, *136*
    food labeling and nutritional
        standards, 2:774
    formation, 1:333, 365
    infant formula, 1:496
    overview, 1:119–120, 496
Codex Alimentarius Austriacus,
    1:135, 154
Coffee, 1:**138–141**, *139*
    advertising, 1:1
    caffeine, 1:102
    calories, 1:108
    civet, 1:326
    fair trade, 1:*258*
    history of coffee and
        coffeehouses, 1:393
    organic, 1:*298*
    planting, 2:792
    tasting, 2:*758*
Coffee (Fisher), 1:*140–141*

Cohen, Stanley, 1:112

The Coke Machine (Blanding), 1:327

Colas, caffeine and, 1:102, 2:671

Colbert, Stephen, 2:566

Cold waves, 1:250

Collective agriculture, 1:183–185

Collective farm workers, 1:*184*

Collectivization, 1:25–26, *26*

Collier's Weekly, 2:669

Colorado, 1:*21,* 2:603, 768, *848*

Columbia, 1:40

Columbian Exchange, 2:827–828, *828*

Columbus, Christopher, 1:109, 236, 386, 2:725, 827

Combine (agricultural machinery), 1:*434*

Coming Home to Eat (Nabhan), 2:534

Commis (assistant), 1:173

Commission on Genetic Resources for Food and Agriculture (CGRFA), 1:72, **142–144**

Common Agricultural Policy (CAP), 2:741

Common pool resource, 2:710, 711

Commonwealth Agricultural Bureaux International (CABI), 1:18

Commonwealth fund, 1:303

Communist Party of India (Marxist), 1:26

Community conserved areas (CCAs), 1:18

Community gardens (New Orleans, Louisiana), 2:*581*

Community supported agriculture (CSAs), 1:**145–148,** 2:535

Comparative advantage, 1:30, 389

The Composition of Foods (McCance and Widdowson), 2:590

Composting, 2:831

Computers, 2:*801*

ConAgra plant (Georgia), 2:683

Concentrated animal feeding operations (CAFOs), 1:237, 2:530–532, 561, 562, 810
    See also Factory farming

Confectionery and pastry, 1:**149–153**
    Asian, 1:*407*
    consumption in France, 1:396
    cooking fats, 1:164–165
    displays, 1:*150, 151*
    India, 1:*205*
    students preparing, 1:*174*

Conference Report of the House Committee on Appropriations (1987), 1:208

Congo, Democratic Republic of, 1:98, *99*

Congressional Research Service (CRS), 2:848

Connecticut, 1:*251,* 2:*661*

Connective tissue, 2:553

Conquistadors, 2:520, 521

Consider the Oyster (Fisher), 2:808

Consultative Sub-Committee on Surplus Disposal (CSSD), 1:246

Consumer advocacy group, 2:641

Consumer food safety recommendations, 1:**154–156**

Consumer price index, 2:592, 593

Contract Use Continues to Expand (MacDonald & Perry), 1:*14–15*

Convenience foods
    advertising, 1:1, 3
    developing countries, 1:204, 206, 207
    women in the workforce, 1:3, 204, 459, 460

Convenience stores, 2:594

Convention Concerning the Protection of the World Cultural and Natural Heritage (1972), 1:71

Convention on Biological Diversity (CBD) (1992), 1:71, 72, 112, 142, **157–159**

Convention on International Trade in Endangered Species (CITES) (2006), 1:314

Convention on International Trade in Endangered Species (CITES) (2010), 2:716

Convention on International Trade in Endangered Species of Wild Fauna and Flora (CITES) (1973), 1:71, 99

Convention on the Conservation of Migratory Species of Wild Animals (CMS or Bonn Convention) (1979), 1:71

Convention on Wetlands of International Importance (1971), 1:71

Converging Patterns in Global Food Consumption and Food Delivery Systems (USDA), 1:*206–207*

Cookbooks, 1:307, 376, 2:575, 728

Cookies made of dirt, 2:*638*

Cooking
    celebrity chef phenomenon, 1:115–118, 326, 2:763–765
    evolution, 2:596
    methods, 1:350–354
    raw food lifestyles, 2:673, 674
    television and food, 2:763–765

Cooking, carbon emissions, and climate change, 1:96, **160–163**

Cooking fats, 1:**164–168**

A Cook's Tour (Bourdain), 2:764

COOL (Country of origin labeling), 2:663, 664

Cooley, Heather S., 1:85

Cooperative greenmarkets, 1:*38*

Cooperatives, 1:257

Copeland, Royal S., 1:324

Coping with Water Scarcity: Challenge of the Twenty-First Century (FAO), 1:*23–24*

Cora, Cat, 2:*535,* 765

Le Cordon Bleu (Paris, France), 1:173

Corn, 1:*113,* **169–172,** *170, 184, 267,* 2:*828,* 858
    agricultural subsidies, 2:741
    allergies, 1:292
    biofuel production, 1:74, 76, 77
    cultivation history, 2:520
    food aid using GMO, 1:248
    global consumption, 2:521
    grits, 2:576
    herbicide-resistant, 1:*345*
    hydroponic, 1:479
    laws, 1:389
    low genetic variability, 1:69
    movie regarding, 2:575
    organic, 1:*501*
    planting, 1:*413*
    price, 1:355
    protests, 1:*373, 391, 419*
    rainforest burning, 1:17
    trade impact, 2:522
    vitamins and minerals, 2:819

Corn oil, 2:571, 572

Corn syrup, 1:288, 2:747

Cornell University, 1:53, 151

Coronary heart disease. *See* Heart disease

Corporate farming. *See* Industrial agriculture

Cortés, Hernán, 1:125

Cosmetics, 1:18–19, 323–325, *324, 390,* 2:671

Costa Rica
    banana plantation, 1:*14*
    coffee, 1:*257*
    coffee plantation, 1:*139*
    country of origin labeling (COOL) requirements, 2:664
    family farms, 1:260
    shark fishing prohibition, 2:716
    USAID and, 2:791

Côte d'Ivoire, 1:189

Cotton, agricultural subsidies, 2:741

Council of Islamic Courts (CIC), 1:6

Country of origin labeling (COOL), 2:663, 664

Couscous, 2:623

Cows, 1:*471*

Cracker Jacks, 2:511

Cream of Wheat, 1:3

Creekstone Farms, 2:847, 848

Creole cuisine, 1:406–407, 2:728

Creutzfeldt-Jakob Disease (CJD), **2:540–543**
brains from cows, 1:444
deaths and costs, 1:111
epidemic, 1:334, 381
Texas Beef Group v. Winfrey, 2:766–768
See also Bovine spongiform encephalopathy (BSE)
Crick, Francis, 2:667
Crisco, 1:166–168
Croatia, 1:185
Crop rotation, 2:517, 518
CRP (C-reactive protein), 1:126
CRS (Congressional Research Service), 2:848
Cruise ships, norovirus infections and, 2:584
CSAs (Community supported agriculture), 1:**145–148**, 2:535
CSD (United Nations Commission on Sustainable Development), 1:9
Cuba, 1:27, 239, 240, 241, 2:857
Cuchamatanes Mountain community (Guatemala), 2:607
Cucumbers, 1:479
Culinary education, 1:**173–175**, 410
Cult diets, 1:**176–178**, 178
Cultivar, 2:521
Cultivating Failure: How School Gardens Are Cheating Our Most Vulnerable Students (Flanagan), 1:234
Cured meat, 2:657
Curry, 1:406
Cyclamate, 2:747, 749
Czech Republic, 1:184, 284, 314

D

Dairy Ode (McIntyre), 1:182
Dairy products, 1:**179–182**
factory farms, 1:255
foodborne disease, 2:734
Pasteurization, 2:626–628
religious rules regarding, 2:680
richer populations' consumption, 1:355
standards, 1:135
unpasteurized, 2:528
vitamins added to, 1:403
See also Cheese; Milk
Dangerous Food (Winfrey), 2:766, 768
Darfur, Sudan, 1:5, 273
Darwin, Charles, 1:34, 456, 2:782
DASH (Dietary Approaches to Stop Hypertension), 1:202
Dauphin Island Sea Lab, 1:380
Davis, Marguerite, 2:819

De Beauvoir, Simone, 1:393, 394
Debeaking, 1:468
Declaration of Nyéléni (2007), 1:372
Decollectivization, 1:**183–186**
Decolonization, 1:26
Deepwater Horizon, 1:380, 440
Deforestation
agricultural, 1:**16–19**, 17
global land degradation, 2:519
logging, 1:99, 2:518
zoonotic disease, 1:99
DEKALB® corn sign, 1:317, 345
Del Monte, 1:46
Demeter Biodynamic Farm Standard, 2:750
Democratic People's Republic of Korea (DPRK), 1:272, 273, 505, 2:863
Democratic Republic of Congo, 1:98, 99
Denbies Wine Estate (Dorking, England), 1:133, 133
Deng Xiaoping, 1:184
Denmark
ban on the use of gavage, 1:314
beer consumption, 1:284
fortification of margarine, 2:586
trans fat bans, 1:165, 314
whale consumption, 2:842
World Food Prize, 2:857
Dental caries or cavities, 2:606, 607, 607
Deoxyribonucleic acid (DNA), 1:416, 2:668
Department of Nutrition (Denmark), 2:842
Des Moines, Iowa, 2:857
Descartes, René, 1:468
Desertification and agriculture, 1:5, **187–190**, 2:519, 691
Detritus, 1:379
Dettwyler, Kathryn, 1:91
Developed/industrial countries
agricultural technologies, 1:369
allergies, 1:291
animal-based product demand, 1:230
birth rates, 2:646
botulism, 1:90
breastfeeding, 1:91–92
cooking schools and classes, 1:174
diet, 1:63, 491, 493, 2:676–677
eating disorders, 1:225
emergency preparedness, 1:218
environmental concerns and vegetarian diet, 2:811
family farms, 1:261
family size, 2:646
food abundance, 1:304
food packaging, 1:339

food spoilage rates, 2:661
food surplus and food aid, 1:503
Green Revolution technologies, 1:437
grocery stores, 1:276
heart disease, 1:199
Hepatitis A infections, 1:449, 450
iodized salt, 2:699
Kyoto Protocol, 1:134
labeling for calorie content, 1:107
meat consumption, 1:443, 2:828
Millennium Development Goals, 2:776
nutritional needs, 1:124
obesity, 2:602
oral health, 2:606, 607
organic foods, 2:751
plant biodiversity, 1:142
processed food, 1:326.2.660, 2:662, 700
salt, 1:201, 2:700, 822
street food, 2:738
subsidies, 1:486–487
tea market, 2:762
trade, 1:31–32, 257–259
undernourishment of elderly, 2:781
wage slavery, 2:823–824, 825
water, 2:835, 836
welfare programs, 1:428
wet nursing, 1:91, 495
women and food preparation, 1:460, 2:850, 851
See also specific countries
Developing countries
agriculture employment, 1:370
agroecology, 1:37
barriers to trade, 1:32
convenience foods, 1:204, 206, 207
demand for food, 1:355
diet of grains, 1:434
dietary changes in rapidly, 1:204–207
fair trade, 1:257–259
family farms, 1:260
food assistance, 1:428, 430
food insecurity, 1:330, 2:691, 692, 693
food sovereignty, 1:372–374
free trade, 1:486
head-to-tail eating, 1:443
heart disease, 1:199
hunger, 1:369, 472
IFAD activities, 1:507–509
infant formula, 1:495, 496
international food aid, 1:503–506
iodized salt, 2:701
lactose intolerance, 1:179
local food movement, 2:535
obesity, 2:602
open-hearth cooking, 1:95–97, 162–163, 353, 460
organic agriculture, 1:501–502
plant biodiversity, 1:142
poverty, 1:369
protectionism, 1:486–487

Developing countries (*continued*)
    roundworm infection, 1:467
    trade liberalization, 1:390–391
    undernutrition, 2:781
    water scarcity, 2:840
    women, 1:412
    World Trade Organization
      (WTO), 1:31–32
    See also specific countries
Dewey, John, 1:232
Dhaka, Bangladesh, food waste
    dump, 2:*832*
Diabetes, 2:602
    advertising, 1:1
    diet, 1:194–197
    indigenous peoples diet, 1:493
    Mediterranean diet, 2:559
    middle-income countries, 1:206
    obesity, 1:264
    processed meats, 2:705
    raw food, 2:674
    therapeutic diets, 2:770–772
Diabetic supplies, 1:*196*
Diba, 1:93
Dichlorodiphenyltrichloroethane
    (DDT), 2:630, 631, 750
Dicke, Willem-Karel, 1:422
Diemer, Walter, 2:511
Diesel, Rudolf, 1:74
Diet and cancer, 1:**191–193**
    See also Cancer
Diet and diabetes, 1:**194–197**
    See also Diabetes
Diet and heart disease, 1:194–197,
    198–200, 201, 202
    See also Heart disease
Diet and hypertension, 1:**201–203**
    See also Hypertension
Diet and infectious diseases, 2:544
Diet and oral health, 2:**606–608**
Dietary Approaches to Stop
    Hypertension (DASH), 1:202
Dietary changes in rapidly developing
    countries, 1:**204–207**
Dietary Goals for the United States,
    1:208
Dietary Guidelines for Americans,
    1:122, **208–211,** 2:662, 700, 707
Dietary reference intakes (DRIs),
    1:**212–214,** 2:578, 591
Dietary Supplement Health and
    Education Act of 1994 (DSHEA),
    1:120, **215–217**
Dietary Supplement Safety Act of
    2010 (bill withdrawn), 1:217
Dietary supplements, 1:*216*
    dietary reference intakes (DRIs),
      1:213
    food labels, 2:773
    veganism, 2:804
    vitamin and minerals, 2:819–822

Diets, cult, 1:**176–178,** *178*
Digestion, 2:591, 666, 667
Dijon, France, 2:808
Dinesen, Isak, 2:574
Diouf, Jacques, 2:690
Dioxins, 2:842
Direct food aid, 2:645, 791, 861
Dirt, consumption of, 2:637, 638, *638*
Disasters and food supply, 1:**218–221,**
    219
Discourse on the Method (Descartes),
    1:468
Diseases
    Alzheimer's, 1:166
    autoimmune conditions, 1:422
    botulism, 1:88–90, *89*
    bushmeat, 1:99, 100
    deficiency, 2:515
    diet-related, 1:1–2, 53
    Ebola, 1:100
    embargoes and, 1:239, 240
    extreme weather, 1:252
    foot and mouth, 1:79
    germ theory, 1:78, 128
    gingivitis, 2:606, 607
    gluten intolerance, 2:770
    goiter, 1:403, 2:586, 587, 700,
      819–820
    increase in chronic and life-
      threatening, 2:602
    indoor air quality, 1:95
    infectious, 2:544
    legume related, 2:523–524
    Minamata, 1:381
    obesity, 2:602
    oral, 2:607
    paralytic shellfish poisoning,
      2:620–622
    periodontal, 2:607
    prions, 1:109, 110–111
    raw food lifestyles, 2:674–675
    rickets, 2:586
    therapeutic diets, 2:770–772
    trans fatty acids, 1:165
    trichinellosis, 1:383
    ulcerative colitis, 2:770
    zoonotic, 1:98, 2:541
    See also specific diseases
Djibouti, influenza in, 1:58
DNA, recombinant, 1:112, 113
DOC *(Denominazione de Origine
    Controllata),* 2:817
Doctors Without Borders, 2:851
Documentaries, movies and food,
    2:**574–576**
*Does SNAP Decrease Food Security:
    Untangling the Self-Selection Effect*
    (Nord & Golla), 1:*430*
Dogs, 1:457
Doha Round negotiations,
    agricultural subsidies, 2:742
Dole banana plantation, 1:*14*

Domestication
    animals, 1:236, 275, 443, 457,
      2:648, 782
    hierarchical societies, 1:34, 35
Dominican Republic, 1:*244*
Don Quixote (Cervantes), 2:637
Donetske, Ukraine, 1:*184*
Donuts, 1:108, *210*
Dorgan, Byron, 1:217
Dorking, England, 1:133, *133*
Dotterweich, U.S. v., 1:119
Dough, 2:*869*
Dough mixers, 2:*681*
Downey, John G., 2:816
DPRK (Democratic People's
    Republic of Korea), 1:272, 273,
    505, 2:863
The Drawbacks of Women's Equality
    (Briggs), 1:*92–93*
Dried fruits, 1:*401*
Dried vegetables, 2:656
*Drinking and Driving: A Road
    Safety Manual for Decision-Makers
    and Practitioners* (GRSP), 1:285
Drought
    agricultural demand for water,
      1:20, 23
    climate change, 1:132
    commodity price increases, 1:77
    desertification, 1:187, 189, 2:691
    embargoes, 1:240
    famine relief, 1:5, 7, 8
    food supply, 1:218, 250, 252
    impacts, 1:250, 2:686
    increase in heat waves, 1:252
    resistant plants, 1:*75,* 76, 112
Drugs
    food labels, 2:773
    illicit, 2:669
    regulation, 1:323–325, 2:796, 797
Drunk driving, 1:282, 284–285
Dry nursing, 1:91, 495
DSHEA (Dietary Supplement Health
    and Education Act of 1994), 1:120,
    215–217
Dubai fish market, 2:*717*
Dubble Bubble gum, 2:511
Ducks (cooked), 2:*650*
Dujiangyan irrigation system, 1:20
Dumping, 1:372
Durand, Peter, 1:339
Dust Bowl, 2:793–794
Dysphagia, 1:347

E

E. coli contamination, 1:**222–224,** *223*
    bioterrorism, 1:80
    cookie dough, 1:342

food production processes, 1:359
hamburger meat, 2:550
lettuce testing, 1:120, *120*
meats, 2:766
nano-scale technology, 2:550
overview, 1:381
raw milk, 2:677
reporting systems, 1:382
symptoms, 1:382
See also Bacteria
Earth Policy Institute, 2:756
Earthen furnace, 1:*162*
East Bay Animal Advocates, 2:653
Easter meal, 1:*311*
Eat Well and Stay Well the Mediterranean Way (Keys), 2:557
Eating Behaviors and Attitudes Following Prolonged Exposure to Television among Ethnic Fijian Adolescent Girls, 1:303–304
Eating disorders, 1:**225–228**, *226, 305*
    anorexia nervosa, 1:225, 226–227, 227–228, 304
    binge eating, 1:225, 226, 304
    bulimia nervosa, 1:225, 226–227, 304
    family meals, 1:263–264
    obesity, 1:303
    orthorexia, 1:176, 177, 225–226, 2:562. 674
    pica, 2:637–638
    raw food lifestyles, 2:675
Eating habits, 1:264
Eating with a Conscience campaign, 2:767
Eaton, S. Boyd, 1:492, 2:617
Ebola, 1:99, 100, 101
Ecological impacts of various world diets, 1:**229–231**, 2:674
Ecological pyramids, 1:**377–380,** *379*
Economic and Social Council (ECOSOC), 1:500
Economic and Social Research Institute, 2:813
Economic Research Service (ERS), 2:686
Economy of scale, 1:459, 2:530, 745, 751
ECOSOC (Economic and Social Council), 1:500
Ecuador, 1:66, 374
Edible schoolyard movement, 1:44, **232–235,** *233, 234,* 2:709, 719
Edinburgh, Scotland, 1:*284*
EEC (European Economic Community), 2:741
EEG (Electroencephalogram), 1:102

Eggs, 1:**236–238,** *237, 238*
    allergies, 1:294
    allergy warning labels, 1:291, 292, 2:774, 799
    cooking, 1:461
    factory farms, 1:254–255
    foodborne disease, 1:383, 2:734
    free-roaming chickens, 2:616
    government oversight regarding, 1:365, 366
    inspection, 1:*366*
    irradiation, 1:337
    non-pasteurized, 2:616
    omega-3 fatty acids, 1:236–237, 327, 404
    recall, 1:120, 360, 2:697
    regulation governing, 2:653
    religious rules regarding, 2:680
    Salmonella, 1:366–367, 2:695, 696, 697–698
    veganism, 2:803
Egremont, Massachusetts, 1:145
Egypt
    bread, 1:61, 63
    chicken domestication, 2:782
    country of origin labeling requirements, 2:664
    GMO ban, 1:486
    influenza, 1:58, 59
    pasta production, 2:624
    wheat shortage, 1:434
    wine, 2:815
    yeast and leavening agents, 2:867
Egypt (ancient)
    baking, 1:363
    cheese making, 1:179
    confections and pastry making, 1:149, 150
    eggs, 1:236
    ovens for bread baking, 1:351
    spice trade and uses, 2:724, 725
    wine and beer, 1:285
Ehrlich, Paul, 1:37, 472, 2:812
Eijkman, Christiaan, 2:589
El Bulli (Catalonia, Spain), 2:568, 570
El Salvador, 1:66, 260
Elderly persons
    E. coli, 1:222
    fasting, 2:679
    listeriosis, 2:528
    nutritional needs, 1:122, 123, *123*
    undernutrition, 2:779, 781
    U.S. Food Stamp Program, 2:592
Electroencephalogram (EEG), 1:102
Electrolytes, 1:129
Electromagnetic radiation, 1:336
Electron beams, 1:335–336
Elixir sulfanilamide, 1:323–324
Elkington, John, 1:298
Elliott, S. Maria, 1:167
Ellis, Curt, 2:575
Ellis, Michael, 1:216

Ellsworth, Henry Leavitt, 2:793
Embargoes, 1:**239–242**
Empty calories, 2:779
Encephalopathy, 2:540, 541, 542
Endangered species
    beluga sturgeon, 1:314
    bonobos, 1:100
    chimpanzees, 1:100
    CITES, 1:71, 99, 314, 2:716
    fish, 2:713
    gorillas, 1:100
    green sea turtles, 1:*158*
    laws regarding, 1:71, 98, 99, 314, 2:716
    shark harvesting, 2:715–718
    sharks, 2:716
    sturgeon caviar, 1:314
    See also Extinction/extinct species
Endocannibalism, 1:109, 110
Energy, bottled water and, 1:85
Energy drinks, 1:105
Energy Implications of Bottled Water (Gleick and Cooley), 1:85
Energy Security and Independence Act of 2007, 1:74
Engel's law, 1:53, 204, 206, 2:530, 711, 812
England
    animal welfare legislation, 1:469
    BedZed eco development, 1:*10*
    biofuels protest, 1:*76*
    cholera, 1:128
    film projection inventions, 2:574
    food co-ops, 2:580
    pasteurization equipment, 2:*627*
    patents, 1:343
    school lunch programs, 2:706
    spice trade, 1:452
    vegan activists, 1:*230*
    winemaking, 1:133, *133,* 2:816
Engler, Paul, 2:*767*
Enig, Mary G., 2:676, 677
Enriching the Landscape (Fairhead & Leach), 1:*189*
Enteral nutrition, 2:770
Enteropathogenic, 1:222, 223
Enterotoxin, 2:696
Entitlement programs, 2:592
Envirofit, 1:97
Environmental degradation
    agriculture, 1:370, 2:517–519, *518*
    food sovereignty movement, 1:372–374
    Green Revolution, 1:437–438
    land availability, 2:517–519
Environmental Health Perspectives (journal), 2:632
Environmental Working Group, 1:85
Enzymes, 2:667, 674

EPA. *See* U.S. Environmental
Protection Agency (EPA)

Ephedra, 1:216, 217

EPIC (European Prospective
Investigation of Cancer), 1:191

Epic of Gilgamesh, 2:814

Epoxy resins, 1:81

Epperson, Frank, 2:511

Equal to Act. *See* Wholesome Meat
Act of 1967

Eritrea, 1:267, 2:564

ERP (European Recovery Program),
2:790

ERS (Economic Research Service),
2:686

Escherichia coli. See E. coli
contamination

Escoffier, Georges-Auguste, 1:173

Essay on the Principle of Population
(Malthus), 1:472, 2:644

Essential oils, 1:452

Estonia, 1:184, 285

Estrogenic, 1:21

Ethanol, 1:74, 75, 317–318

Ethical issues in agriculture,
1:**243–245**

Ethical issues in food aid, 1:**246–249**

Ethiopia
famines, 1:5, 7–8, 267, 272
man tasting coffee, 2:*758*
World Food Prize, 2:857
World Food Programme, 2:862,
863

Ethnobiology, 1:491

Ethnocentrism, 1:385

EU Hazard Analysis and Critical
Control Point (HACCP), 1:156

EU Union Food Safety Authority,
1:171

Europe
agricultural land ownership,
1:412
agricultural subsidies, 2:741
allergies, 1:294
banana trade wars, 1:65–68
biofuels, 1:74, 75
bovine spongiform
encephalopathy (BSE), 2:541,
768
bushmeat, 1:98, 99, 100–101
chicken domestication, 2:782
chocolate, 1:125
climate change, 1:133
coffee, 1:138
CSAs, 1:145
daily water access, 2:835
deforestation, 1:16, 2:519
domestication of animals, 1:275
embalming with spices, 2:725–726
famines, 2:644

food aid provided by, 1:503,
504–505
food co-ops, 2:580
food diversity, 2:718
food safety regulations, 1:365
functional food market, 1:344
GMO crops, 2:818
grains grown, 1:432
grape harvests, 1:311
influenza, 1:58, 252
lactose intolerance, 2:516
land reform, 1:25
modern ovens, 1:459
norovirus infection, 2:584
obesity, 2:601, 603
pasteurization, 2:626
pesticide use, 2:630
potato consumption, 2:521, 807
restaurants, development, 1:319
rise of agriculture, 1:275
school gardens, 1:232
sustainable agriculture, 2:750
tea, 2:760
tomatoes, 1:386
USAID, 1:28
water usage, 1:23
wine, 2:814, 815
See also specific countries

European Court of Human Rights,
2:768

European Economic Community
(EEC), 2:741

European Union (EU)
agricultural subsidies, 1:486–487
animal welfare regulation, 1:370
banana trade wars, 1:65–68
biofuels, 1:355
blood alcohol concentration
limits, 1:285
CAFOs regulation, 2:531
country of origin labeling
requirements, 2:664
embargoes on beef, 1:240
foie gras policies, 1:470
food aid provided by the, 1:246
food bans, 1:213, 314
food safety, 1:156
food safety regulation and
inspection, 1:332, 333
fortified food regulations, 2:588
functional foods, 1:403, 405
GMO crops, 1:171, 420
migrant workers, 2:565
organic food market, 2:649
recombinant bovine growth
hormone (rBGH), 2:798
U.S. farm subsidies, 1:317
wheat exports, 2:624

Eutrophication, 1:229, 2:838

Evapo-transpiration, 1:187

Evidence-based guidelines, 1:208

Evolution (human), nutrition's role
in, 2:**595–597**, *597*

Exocannibalism, 1:109

Extinction/extinct species
aurochs, 1:276
biodiversity, 1:157
dodo bird, 2:782
domesticated animals, 1:35, 457
livestock breeds, 1:143
natural and human causes, 1:157
predators of domestic stock, 2:828
rate, 1:69, 71
slow food movement, 2:718
vegetable varieties, 1:69
wild game, 1:230
See also Endangered species

Extra virgin olive oil, 1:164, 2:558

Extreme weather and food supply,
1:**250–253**

Exxon Valdez, 1:440

F

FAC (Food Aid Convention), 1:246

FACT. *See* Food, Agriculture,
Conservation, and Trade Act
(FACT) of 1990

Factory farming, 1:**254–256**, *255*
animal treatment, 1:468, 469,
470
family farm *vs.,* 1:260
Food Alliance, 1:297
food safety, 1:361
poultry, 2:650
See also Agribusiness;
Concentrated animal feeding
operations (CAFOs); Industrial
agriculture

Fad diets, 1:**176–178**, *178*, 326–329

FAED (Food avoidance emotional
disorder), 1:347

Fair Labor Standards Act (FLSA) of
1938, 2:564

Fair trade, 1:138–139, **257–259**,
2:581

Fair trade coffee, 1:*258*

Fairhead, James, 1:*189*

Fairtrade Labeling Organization
(FLO), 1:258–259

Fairview Gardens, California, 2:615

Falafel, 2:*524,* 737

FALCPA. *See* Food Allergen
Labeling and Consumer Protection
Act (FALCPA) of 2004

False Disparagement of Perishable
Food Products Act, 2:768

Family farms, 1:256, **260–262**, *262*

Family meal benefits, 1:**263–265**,
264, 304

Famine, 1:**266–270**, *267, 268–269*
desertification, 1:187
embargoes, 1:239

government actions, 1:355, 357, 2:644–645

Irish potato, 1:158, 2:806, 807, 828

Famine, political considerations, 1:**271–274**, *272, 273,* 355, 357, 2:644–645

Famine Early Warning Systems Network (FEWSNet), 1:267

Famine relief, African, 1:*5–8, 6, 7,* 187

Fanar, Lebanon, 2:*524*

FANTA (Food and Nutrition Technical Assistance Program), 2:545

FAO. *See* Food and Agriculture Organization (FAO)

FAO: The Challenge of Renewal, 1:301

FAO Technical Meeting on Street Foods, Calcutta, India. III. Socio-economic Aspects of Street Foods (FAO), 2:*738–739*

Farm Animal Welfare Council (FAWC), 1:469, 2:681

Farm bills (U.S. laws), 1:316–318

Farm Radio Service, 2:763

Farm Security and Rural Investment Act of 2002, 1:316

Farm stands, 1:*146, 147, 261*

Farm subsidies, 1:*40–42,* 486–487, 2:741, *742,* 794

Farm to school programs, 1:488

Farm-to-table movement, 1:**275–278**

Farm workers
  protest, 2:*824*
  washing lettuce, 2:*664*

Farmer, Fannie Merritt, 1:166

Farmers
  Cuban, 1:*27*
  in field, 1:*437*
  harvesting wheat, 1:*434*
  plowing, 2:*745*
  spraying herbicide, 1:*345*
  spraying pesticide, 2:*631*
  subsistence, 1:*331*
  tractor, 1:*262*
  using Twitter, 2:*722*

Farmer's markets, 1:*44, 147,* 2:*611, 616*

Farming, factory, 1:237, **254–256,** *255*

Farming, industrial. *See* Industrial agriculture

Farmland degradation. *See* Environmental degradation

Farms
  experimental, 1:*75*
  fair trade, 1:257–259

Faroe Islands, 2:*843,* 844

Fast food, 1:**279–281,** *280*
  advertising, 1:*1*
  allergies, 1:295
  documentary, 2:575
  income and consumption, 1:204

Latin America, 2:522

meat testing, 2:709

protest, 2:*680*

sign, 2:*829*

super-sizing, 2:511

trans fats and, 1:476

Fast Food Nation (Schlosser), 1:279, 2:719

Fast Information Technology and Telecommunications Emergency and Support Team (FITTEST), 2:860

Fat, body, 2:601, 602

Fats
  balanced diet, 2:590
  calories, 1:164
  cancer, 1:192
  digestion, 2:591
  energy density, 1:106
  heart disease, 1:198
  high-fat diets, 2:571
  poultry, 2:650
  processed foods, 2:662
  school lunches, 2:707

Fatty acids, 1:475

FDA. *See* U.S. Food and Drug Administration (FDA)

FDA Amendments Act (2007), 2:683

Feasts, 1:35, 309

Fecal-oral route, 1:129, 130, 449, 450

Federal Emergency Relief Administration, 2:707

Federal Food, Drug and Cosmetics Act of 1998, 2:683

Federal Food, Drug and Cosmetics Act (FD&C) of 1938, 1:119, 2:631–632, 773, 797, 847

Federal Food and Drugs Act of 1906. *See* Pure Food and Drug Act of 1906

Federal Insecticide, Fungicide, and Rodenticide Act of 1947, 2:631

Federal Insecticide Act of 1910, 2:630–631

Federal Meat Inspection Act of 1906, 1:323, 332, 2:652, 669, 846, 847

Federal Trade Commission (FTC), 1:324

Feed the Future, 2:858, 859

Feeding America/America's Second Harvest, 1:**46–48,** *47*

Feeding disorders. *See* Food phobias

Feltman, Charles, 1:279

Fermentation, alcohol, 1:**282–287,** 2:814

Fermentation, baking, 1:61, 2:867

Fertilizers
  biological dead zones, 1:372
  Green Revolution, 1:436–438
  overuse, 2:518
  sustainable agriculture, 2:750
  urban farming, 2:785, 786

Fiber
  in a balanced diet, 2:590
  cancer, 1:191, 2:589
  colon health, 2:589
  diabetes, 1:195, 2:589
  fruits, 1:399, 400
  macrobiotic diet, 2:537

Fifteen Foundation, 2:765

Le Figaro, 2:818

Fiji, 1:303–304

Film festivals, 2:576

Finland, 1:284, 313, 314

Fish. *See* Seafood

Fish farms, 1:*50, 51*

Fish markets, 1:*54,* 2:*717*

Fisher, M. F. K., 1:*140–141,* 409, 410, 2:*808–809*

Fishery resources, aquaculture and, 1:**49–52,** *50, 51*

Five a Day program, 2:801–802

Flanagan, Caitlin, 1:232, 233–234

Flavonoids, 1:152, 2:634

Flay, Bobby, 2:764

Fleer Chewing Gum, 2:511

Fletcher, Horace, 1:176

Flint, Michigan, 2:*787*

FLO (Fairtrade Labeling Organization), 1:258–259

Floating market, 1:*55*

Floods
  climate change, 1:252
  flood water for irrigation, 1:20, 2:612
  flooded farm, 1:*251*
  food aid, 1:248
  food supply, 1:250–251

Florida
  Beaches Greenmarket farm stand, 2:*616*
  cooperative greenmarket, 1:*38*
  farm stand, 1:*146*
  farm workers protest, 2:*824*
  fast food sign, 2:*829*
  food libel laws, 2:768
  grocery store display, 1:*341*
  migrant workers, 2:823
  riverfront festival, 2:*729*
  shrimping boats, 2:*712*
  tomatoes, 2:642
  Tommy's Brick Oven Pizza in Jacksonville, 1:*423*

Flour, 2:*868*

FLSA (Fair Labor Standards Act of 1938), 2:564

Foie gras, 1:314, 396, 397, 470

Folklore, 1:385, 386

Food, Agriculture, Conservation, and Trade Act (FACT) of 1990, 2:609, 674, 766, 768, 827–828

Food, Conservation, and Energy Act of 2008, 1:**316–318**

Food, Drug, and Cosmetic Act of 1938 (as amended), 1:290, **323–325**, 2:671

Food, Inc. (movie), 1:237, 2:576

Food & Water Watch (FWW), 2:*641*, 839

Food Additive Amendment, 2:847

Food additives, 1:**288–290**, 324, 2:771, 773, 797

Food aid, 1:473
 ethical issues, 1:246–249
 food price crisis, 1:356
 Kendekeza, Malawi, 1:*6*
 World Food Programme supplies, 1:*247*, 2:*861*
 See also International food aid

Food Aid Convention (FAC), 1:246

Food Allergen Labeling and Consumer Protection Act (FALCPA) of 2004, 1:**291–293**, 296, 2:684, 774, 799

Food allergies, 1:152, **294–296**, 404

Food allergy warning labels, 1:*292*, 2:774

Food Alliance, 1:**297–299**

Food and Agriculture Organization (FAO), 1:**300–302**
 agricultural output and hunger, 1:331
 aquaculture production, 1:51–52
 BPA safety, 1:86
 CGRFA, 1:142–144
 Codex Alimentarius, 1:135, 300, 333
 deforestation, 1:16
 embargoes and food prices, 1:240
 ethics principles used by the, 1:243
 fisheries, 2:710–711
 food balance sheets, 1:473
 food labeling, 2:774
 food price crisis and hunger, 1:357, 2:692
 food safety, 1:156, 301
 food security, 1:300, 301, 2:690–691
 foreign aid, 1:42
 genetic food diversity, 1:70, 72
 hunger, 1:368, 370, 472, 473, 2:546, 644, 690, 692
 International Federation of Organic Agriculture Movements (IFOAM), 1:500
 land degradation, 2:518
 malnutrition, 2:544, 545, 546–547
 nutrition, 1:300
 processed food, 1:205
 purpose, 2:855
 spices, 2:726
 street food, 2:738–739
 tea, 2:760, 762

 traditional foodways, 1:494
 undernutrition, 2:544
 water scarcity, 1:23
 women and agricultural extension services, 1:413
 women and food preparation, 2:850
 women in Africa, 1:244–245, 412
 women's access to land, 1:414
 World Food Day (WFD), 2:854, 855
 World Food Programme (WFP), 2:860

Food and body image, 1:**303–305**

Food and Cookery for the Sick and Convalescent (Farmer), 1:166

Food and Financial Crisis: Implications for Agriculture and the Poor (von Braun), 1:357

Food and Nutrition Board of the National Academy of Science, 1:212

Food and Nutrition Technical Assistance Program (FANTA), 2:545

Food and population. *See* Population and food

Food and religion. *See* Religion and food

Food and the Internet, 1:**306–308**
 foodie phenomenon, 1:427
 fusion cooking, 1:406
 indigenous peoples, 1:494
 locavores, 2:535
 restaurant reviews and ratings, 1:319, 427
 social media, 2:721–723

Food as celebration, 1:**309–311**

Food assistance, 1:316, 317, 428–431, *429*

Food aversion, 1:410

Food avoidance emotional disorder (FAED), 1:347

Food banks, 1:46, *47*, 2:593

Food bans, 1:**312–315**

Food-borne illness. *See* Foodborne diseases

Food boycotts, political, 2:**640–643**, *641*, *642*

Food colorings, 1:290

Food Crises and the Ghost of Malthus (O'Flynn), 1:472

Food critics and ratings, 1:307, **319–322**

Food depots, 2:*691*

Food Engineer Day, 2:855

Food fads, 1:**326–329**, 2:568–569

Food festivals, 1:232, 311, *386*, *427*, 2:576, *729*

Food Fight (movie), 2:576

Food First, 1:**330–331**

Food First: Beyond the Myth of Scarcity, 1:330

Food for Peace program, 2:791

Food groups, basic, 2:801

Food guides, 1:319, 320

Food insecurity
 climate change, 2:690, 692
 developing countries, 1:472, 2:691, 692, 693
 factors that contribute to, 2:644
 food production, 2:693
 government assistance, 1:430
 poverty, 2:690, 693
 in the U.S., 1:47
 See also Food security

Food inspection and standards, 1:**332–334**

Food intolerance, 1:291, 294

Food irradiation, 1:289, **335–338**

Food libel laws, 2:766–768

Food miles, 1:373, 2:535, 751, 756

The Food Movement, Rising (Pollan), 2:563

Food of the Gods (movie), 2:574

Food packaging, 1:**339–342**, 460

Food patents, 1:**343–346**

Food phobias, 1:**347–350**

Food photographer, 1:*376*

Food poisoning. *See* Foodborne diseases

Food preparation methods, 1:**351–354**, 2:674, 681, 828

Food price crisis, 1:**355–358**, 369, 474, 2:692

Food prices, 1:*6*, 74, 75–77, 240

Food pyramids, 2:800–802, *801*, 810–812

Food Quality Protection Act of 1996, 2:631, 632

Food recalls, 1:147, **359–362**, 366

Food rheology, 1:**363–364**

Food Rules: An Eater's Manual (Pollan), 2:561, 562

Food Safety and Inspection Service (FSIS), 1:**365–367**, 2:652, 654, 846

Food Safety Enhancement Act of 2009, 2:628

Food Safety Modernization Act (FSMA), 1:276–277, 360–361

Food safety recommendations for consumers, 1:**154–156**

Food security, 1:**368–371**
 agriculture, 2:690, 691, 692
 depots, 2:*691*
 ethical food aid, 1:246–248
 hunger, 1:47, 2:690
 population and food, 2:690, 692
 Rome Declaration, 2:690–694
 sustainability, 2:690

World Food Day (WFD), 2:854
World Food Prize, 2:857
See also Food insecurity
Food sovereignty, 1:**372–374**
Food Stamp Act of 1964, 2:592
Food stamps, 1:46, 147, 357, 429
Food standards, 1:135–137
Food styling, 1:**375–376**
Food supply and extreme weather, 1:**250–253**
Food texture, 1:363
Food waste, 1:330, 331, 2:*830–831, 832*
Food webs and food chains, 1:**377–380**, *379*, 442
Food workers in the U.S., 1:331
Foodborne diseases, 1:154, 155, 276, **381–384**
   food handling, 1:333, 2:766
   listeriosis, 2:**526–528**
   milk, 2:626, 628, 676, 677
   nano-scale technology, 2:550
   new pathogens, 1:333–334
   norovirus infection, 1:310, 2:583–585
   poultry, 2:649, 650
   processed foods, 2:661–662
   product traceability, 2:663, 664
   raw milk, 2:677
   safety recommendations, 1:154–156
   Salmonella, 1:78, 80, 100, 120, 236, 237, 359–361, 366–367, 381–382, 2:550, 649, 650, 683–684, **695–698**, 783
   staphylococcal food poisoning, 2:677, 733–735
   in U.S., 1:333, 2:550
Foodies, 1:326, 409, **425–427**
Foods for specified health use (FOSHU), 1:403, 405
Foodshed, 2:787
Foodways, 1:**385–388**, 491, 493, 2:562, 730–731
The Foodways of a 50s Childhood (Hughes), 2:*730–731*
Foot and mouth disease, 1:79
Ford, Henry, 1:74
Ford Foundations, 1:438
Foreign Assistance Act (1961), 1:28, 2:790
Fortified foods, 2:**586–588**, *587*, 662
   See also Functional foods
Forty Barrels and Twenty Kegs of Coca-Cola, U.S. v., 2:671
Fourth Assessment Report: Climate Change 2007 (IPCC), 1:188–189
France
   arrondissements, 1:394
   ban on U.K. beef, 2:542
   bottled water usage, 1:397
   café culture, 1:393–395

Café de Flore, 1:*394*
café in Montpelier, 1:*397*
cake shop, 1:*151*
film projection inventions, 2:574
fish farm, 1:*51*
fresh fish display, 2:*711*
GMO ban, 2:864
herbs used in French cooking, 1:453
migrant workers, 2:565
obesity, 1:398
olive oil press, 2:*572*
school lunch programs, 2:706
slaughterhouse, 2:555
sugar production, 2:747
University of Paris South, 1:*277*
walnut oil, 2:599–600
whaling, 2:842
wine, 1:*283*, 2:815, 818
Franchise, fast food, 1:279
Frankenfood, 1:51
Free and reduced lunch, 1:488
Free range, 1:254, 256, 2:581, 649
Free trade
   agriculture, 1:389–392
   developing countries, 1:486
   NAFTA (North American Free Trade Agreement), 1:390, 391
   protest, 1:*32*
   world preference, 1:484–485
   WTO (World Trade Organization), 1:485
   See also Trade
Free trade and agriculture, 1:**389–392**
French café culture, 1:**393–395**
The French Chef (Child), 2:763
French cooking, 1:115, 173, 320, 321, 2:763
French fries, 1:*476*, 2:575
The French Laundry Cookbook (Keller), 1:307
French paradox, 1:**396–398**
Fresh Del Monte Produce, 1:65
Fresh Fruit and Vegetable Program, 1:488
Fresno, California, 2:*752*
Frozen foods, 1:460, 482
Fruit displays, 1:*400, 401*
Fruitarians, 2:674–675
Fruits, 1:**399–402**, *400, 401*
   dried, 1:*401*
   food preparation methods, 1:353
   foodborne illness, 1:224, 382
   macrobiotic diets, 2:537
   micronutrients, 2:590
   norovirus infection, 2:583
   organic, 2:*615*
   pesticides, 2:630
   phytonutrient content, 2:634
   traceability, 2:663–665
   See also specific fruits
Frying foods, 1:352

FSMA (Food Safety Modernization Act), 1:276–277, 360–361
FTC (Federal Trade Commission), 1:324
Fugu (puffer fish) bans, 1:313
Fujimoto, Terry, 1:479, *479*
Fukuoka Cancer Study, 2:554
Fulani peoples, 2:514
Functional foods, 1:344, **403–405**
   heart disease, 1:200
   patents, 1:344
   See also Fortified foods
Fungible, 1:241
Funk, Casimir, 2:819
Fusion, 1:43, **406–408**, 483
The Future is an Ancient Lake, 1:70–71

G

GACC. *See* Global Alliance for Clean Cookstoves (GACC)
Galliformes, 2:783
The Galloping Gourmet (Kerr), 2:763–764
Gallup-Healthways survey, 1:195
Gallus gallus domesticus, 2:782
Gama, Vasco da, 2:725
Gamma rays, 1:335
Gandhi, Mohandas, 2:640, 699
Gansu province, China, 1:*188*
GAO (Government Accountability Office), 1:85
Garbanzo beans, 2:523, 525
Garcia, Deborah Koons, 2:575
Gardens
   community, 2:*581*, 786
   school, 1:232, *233, 234*
   sharing, 2:581
Garlic, 1:452, 453
Garner, Dwight, 1:*321–322*
Gastroenteritis, 2:583
Gastrointestinal system, human, 1:**463–467**, *465*
Gastronomy, 1:**409–411**, 2:720
Gâteau Saint Honoré, 1:*174*
Gates, Bill, 1:438, 2:859
GATT (General Agreement on Tariffs and Trade), 1:30, 31, 65, 389, 485, 2:864
Gaud, William S., 1:*438–439*
Gault, Henri, 1:319
Gault Millau, 1:319
Gayot Guides, 1:319
Gee, Samuel, 1:422, 424
Gender and Land Rights Database, 1:414
Gender equality and agriculture, 1:**412–415**

Gender mainstreaming, 1:414

Gender stereotypes, food advertising, 1:3

General Agreement on Tariffs and Trade (GATT), 1:30, 31, 65, 389, 485, 2:864

General Foods Corporation, 2:857

General Mills, 2:859

Genetically modified organisms (GMO), 1:13–14, **416–421**
  aquatic species, 1:51
  bans, 1:314, 486, 2:864
  boycotts, 2:641
  Cartagena Protocol, 1:112, 2:794
  corn, 1:169, 170, 171
  cotton, 1:169
  criticism, 2:794, 859
  ecological impacts, 1:229
  food aid, 1:248
  foods using, 1:344
  fruits, 1:401
  golden rice, 1:55–56, 2:686, 687, 689, 822
  grains, 1:432
  grape vines, 2:816
  Green Revolution, 1:**436–438**
  patents, 1:343–344
  protests regarding, 1:*418, 419*
  soybeans, 1:169
  urban farming, 2:785–786
  World Trade Organization (WTO), 2:864

Geneva, Switzerland, 2:864

Genocide, 1:271

Geophagy, 2:637, 638

Georgia (U.S.)
  food libel laws, 2:768
  peanut plant, 1:*361*
  peanut recall, 1:361, 367, 2:696–697
  Sweet Grass Dairy, 1:181, *181, 364, 426,* 2:*677*

Geotricum mold, 2:831

Gerber baby foods, 1:496

Gericke, William, 1:478

Germany
  ban on the use of gavage, 1:314
  beer consumption, 1:284
  film projection inventions, 2:574
  food and service regulation history, 1:309
  genetically modified crops, 1:171
  genetically modified organism (GMO) ban, 2:864
  migrant workers, 2:565
  open hearth and kitchen, 1:*461*
  overweight population, 1:284
  school lunch programs, 2:706
  slow food movement, 2:718
  street vendors, 2:736
  sugar operations, 2:747
  sustainable agriculture, 2:750
  wine, 2:815

Germplasm, 1:69, 70, 71–72

Gestation crates, 1:468, 470

Ginger, 1:406, 452

Gingivitis, 2:606, 607

Ginseng, 1:*404*

Glasse, Hannah, 1:*460–461*

Gleick, Peter H., 1:85

Global Alliance for Clean Cookstoves (GACC), 1:97, 460, 2:852

Global Alliance for Improved Nutrition, 2:587

Global Biodiversity Outlook 3 (United Nations), 1:18

Global Hunger Index report (GHI), 1:54

Global Interdependency for Local Sustainability (FAO), 1:*72*

Global Road Safety Partnership (GRSP), 1:282, 285

GlobalGAP standard, 1:334

Globalization
  dietary changes, 1:204
  food industry, 1:207
  hunger, 1:330
  Internet, 1:306–307

Glucose, 1:194, 195

Glutamate (MSG), 2:*704*

Gluten, 1:61, 62, 2:771, 774

Gluten-free pizza, 1:*423*

Gluten intolerance, 1:**422–424,** 2:770–772

Gluten Intolerance Group, 1:424

Glycemic index (GI), 1:195

Glycyrrhizin, 2:748–749

GMO. *See* Genetically modified organisms (GMO)

Goats, 1:*181, 421, 446*

Goiter, 1:403, 2:586, 587, 700, 819–820

Goland, Carol, 2:*774*

The Golden Cage (Bruch), 1:227

Golden rice, 2:686, 687, 689, 822

Golla, Ann Marie, 1:*430*

Gorillas, 1:71, 98

Gould Amendment, 2:773

Gourmet (magazine), 2:808

Gourmet hobbyists and foodies, 1:326, 409, **425–427**

Government Accountability Office (GAO), 1:85

Government food assistance for citizens, 1:**428–431,** *429*

Gracchus, Tiberius, 1:25

Grade A Pasteurized Milk Ordinance (PMO), 2:627

Graham, Alexander, 1:403, 2:811

Graham, Sylvester, 1:176, 434, 2:803

Grain Inspection Act of 1916, 1:332

Grains, 1:**432–435,** 2:538
  grain reserves, 1:355–356
  laws regarding, 1:389
  meat production, 2:554–555
  macrobiotic diet, 2:537
  price, 1:355
  storage building, 1:*370*
  world production, 1:437

Gram calorie, 1:106

Gran Dolina (Spain), 1:109–110

Grape harvests, 1:311

Grape workers' strikes, 2:564–565, 642

Grapefruit, 1:399

Grapes, 1:*283,* 2:564–565, *566, 816*

The Great American Fraud (Adams), 2:*669*

Great Britain. *See* United Kingdom

Great British Cheese Festival (Cardiff, Wales, U.K.), 1:*427*

Great Depression, 1:484, 2:793

Great Leap Forward Program (China), 1:26, 27

Great Society, 1:46

Greece
  chicken domestication, 2:782
  genetically modified organism (GMO) ban, 2:864
  migrant workers, 2:565, 823
  pasta consumption, 2:624
  villagers' Easter meal, 1:*311*
  waterwheels, 1:20
  women and food, 2:851

Greece (ancient)
  bakers and pastry-makers, 1:150
  beans for voting, 2:523
  confections, 1:149
  food inspection systems, 1:135
  Hippocrates, 1:403, 2:514, 637
  inns and hostels, 1:309
  salt, 1:288
  spice trade, 2:724
  trade, 2:557, 724

Green coffee, 1:138

The Green Consumer Guide (Hailes and Elkington), 1:298

Green consumers, 1:298

Green Economy Initiative (UN), 2:712, 713

Green Giant's Jolly Green Giant, 1:1

Green Revolution, 1:71, 368, 434, **436–439,** 2:645, 857

The Green Revolution: Accomplishments and Apprehensions (Gaud), 1:*438–439*

Green sea turtles, 1:*158*

Green tea picking, 2:*761*

Greene, Gael, 1:426

Greenhouse effect, 1:132

Greenhouse gases, 1:17, 18, 74, 132, 133, 2:553, 555
Greenhouses, 1:*188*
Greenland, 2:*657*, 844
Greenleaf, Kansas, 1:*262*
Greenmarkets, 1:*38*, 145, *146*
Greenpeace, 2:713
The Greens restaurant, 1:44
Grenadines, whaling, 2:844
Grilling and barbecuing, 1:351, 353
Grimod, Alexandre, 1:409
Grits, 2:576
Grocery stores
    breakfast cereal display, 1:*341*
    China, 1:*404*
    development, 1:145
    farm-to-table movement, 1:276
    vs. farmers' markets and CSAs, 1:146, 147
    food co-ops, 2:581
    Internet, 1:307
    low carbohydrate products display, 1:*328*
    middle-income countries, 1:207
    quality and safety standards, 1:334
    in the U.S., 2:*728*
Groundwater, 1:23, 2:840
GRSP (Global Road Safety Partnership), 1:282, 285
Guangxi province, China, 1:*185*
Guatemala, 1:*66*, 357, 2:586, *607*
Guatemala City, Guatemala, 1:*66*
Guest worker programs, 2:564
Le Guide Culinaire (Escoffier), 1:173
Gulf of Mexico oil spill food impacts, 1:**440–442**
Gull, William Whitney, Sir, 1:225, *227–228*
Gum, 1:152
Gustatory cannibalism, 1:109
Guthman, Julie, 2:562
Guyomard, Hervé, 1:*67–68*

H

Haas, Sydney, 1:422
Habilines, 2:596
HACCP (EU Hazard Analysis and Critical Control Point), 1:156
Haditha, Iraq, 2:*578*
Hailes, Julia, 1:298
Haiti
    dirt consumption, 2:638, *638*
    earthquake of 2010 and relief, 1:*219*, 220, 248, 2:820
    wet nursing, 1:92
    World Food Programme, 2:863
Halal foods, 1:386, 2:578, 679, 681–682

Ham, 1:*485*
Hamburg, Margaret, 1:367, 2:698
Hamburgers, 1:279
Happy Meals, 1:*2*
Haraszthy, Agoston, 2:816
Hard cheese, 2:*678*
Hardin, Garrett, 1:37, 2:517
Harkin, Tom, 1:*317*
Harkin-Engle Protocol, 1:13
Harmonization of food standards, 1:136
Harper's Magazine, 1:426, 491, 2:617, 808
Harpo Productions, 2:768
Harrington, Michael, 1:46
Harrison, Ruth, 1:469
Harrison Act of 1914, 1:323
Harshberger, John, 1:491
Harvard Faculty Club, 2:585
Harvard University School of Public Health, 1:53, 2:557, 705
Harvest of Shame (Murrow), 2:564
Hatch, Orrin, 1:217
Hatch Act of 1887, 2:793
Hawaii, 1:*328*, 430, 2:716
Hazard Analysis and Critical Control Point (HACCP), 1:332, 365–366, *366*, 2:650
HDL (High-density lipoprotein), 1:166, 200, 2:558
HDRs (Humanitarian Daily Rations), 2:578
Head-to-tail eating, 1:**443–445**
Health Canada, 2:773
Health Food Junkies (Bratman), 1:177
Health food store herb tea display, 1:*405*
Healthy Start, 1:92
Heart disease
    American diet, 2:730
    chocolate, 1:126
    coronary, 1:396
    diet, 1:194–197, 198–200, 201, 202
    gingivitis, 2:607
    meat consumption, 2:554
    Mediterranean diet, 2:557
    obesity, 1:2, 264
    olive oil, 2:557–558
    processed meats, 2:705
    salt, 1:201, 202, 2:699
    saturated fats, 1:166, 2:571
    therapeutic diets, 2:770–772
    trans fats, 1:476
    veganism, 2:803, 805
    wine, 1:396
Heat waves, 1:250, 252
Heavily Indebted Poor Countries (HIPCs), 2:*777*

HEB (High energy biscuits), 1:7, 504
Heifer International, 1:**446–448**
Heimlich maneuver, 1:466, *466*
Heirloom plants, 2:649, 718, 719, 755, 786
Hell's Kitchen (Ramsay), 2:765
Hemolytic uremic syndrome (HUS), 1:222
Henderson, Fergus, 1:443, 444
Hepatitis A, 1:**449–451**
Herb tea, 1:*405*
Herbicide tolerance (HT), 1:417, 418, 420
Herbs and spices, 1:**452–455**
    dietary supplements, 1:215, 216
    Indian market, 1:*453*
    medicinal properties, 1:453–454
    plants, 1:*454*
    spice trade, 1:452, 2:724–726
Heterotrophs, 1:378
HFCS (High-fructose corn syrup), 2:561, 562
HHS (U.S. Department of Health and Human Services), 1:208
Hierarchical societies, agriculture and, 1:**34–36**, *36*
High blood pressure. *See* Hypertension
High-density lipoprotein (HDL), 1:166, 200, 2:558
High energy biscuits (HEB), 1:7, 504
High-fructose corn syrup (HFCS), 2:561, 562
Hillfarm Dairy (Melrose Park, Illinois), 2:*677*
Hindu dietary laws, 1:312, 2:680
Hindu New Year celebration, 1:*310*
Hippocrates, 1:403, 2:514, 637
Hiroyuki Sakai, 2:*764*
Hispanic-Americans
    obesity rates, 1:210, 2:522, 603
    urban farming, 2:581, *581*
    in U.S. Food Stamp Program, 2:592
Hispanic ancestry and lactose intolerance, 2:516
History of food
    bread, 1:61
    coffee and coffeehouses, 1:138, 393
    confections, 1:149–151
    corn, 1:169
    dairy products, 1:179
    eggs, 1:236
    fats and oils, 1:164
    fermentation, 1:282, 285
    food additives, 1:288–289
    food codes, 1:135–136

History of food (*continued*)
  grains, 1:432
  irrigation, 1:20–21
  legumes, 2:523
  meal ready to eat (MRE), 2:577
  meat eating, 1:443, 2:553
  packaging, 1:339–340
  restaurants, 1:319
  salt, 1:201
  spice trade, 2:724–725
  See also Egypt (ancient); Greece
    (ancient); Middle Ages; Middle
    East; Rome (ancient)
History of food and man from
  hunter-gatherer to agriculture,
  1:456–458
History of home cooking, 1:**459–462**
HIV/AIDS
  awareness training, 1:448
  food safety, 1:156
  listeriosis, 2:526, 528
  macrobiotic diet, 2:537, 538
  Millennium Development Goals,
    2:776, 777, 854
  population, 2:646
  Ramsay, Gordon, 2:765
  World Food Programme, 2:860
  zoonotic viral diseases, 1:99, 101
Hmong farmers, 2:*752*
Hoagland, Dennis, 1:478
Hoge, Warren, 1:321
Hogs, 2:529, 530, *555*
Holistic development, 1:446
Holland, 1:452
Hollin Meadows Elementary School
  students (Alexandria, Virginia), 2:*535*
Holocene, 1:187
Home Grown Poultry (magazine),
  2:782
Homeopathic medicines, 1:324
Hominins, 2:595, 596
Honduras, 1:91, 125
Honey, 2:537, 775, *791,* 803
Hong Kong, 2:*755,* 865
Hong Kong flu, 1:57–58
Hopkins, Frederick, 2:589
Horizontal integration, 1:13, 204
Horse meat, 1:*349*
Hostels, 1:309
Hot dogs, 1:279, 481, 2:527, 528, *661*
House Beautiful (magazine), 2:808
Housekeeper's Chat (radio show),
  2:763
Hovannessian, Ashavir Ter, 2:673
How to Cook a Wolf (Fisher), 2:808
Huerta, Dolores, 2:564
Huerto, Garcia del, 1:128
Hueston, Will, 2:767
Hughes, Tom, 2:*730–731*

Human evolution, nutrition's role in,
  2:**595–597**
Human gastrointestinal system,
  1:**463–467,** *465*
Human immunodeficiency virus. *See*
  HIV/AIDS
Human Rights Watch (HRW),
  2:550, 566
Humana Milchinion, 1:496
Humane animal farming, 1:**468–471,**
  471
Humane Farm Animal Care, 1:468
Humane Methods of Livestock
  Slaughter Act, 1:470
Humane Research Council, 1:470
Humane Society of the United
  States, 2:653
Humanitarian Daily Rations
  (HDRs), 2:578
Hume, David, 1:484
Hummel Brothers, Inc. hot dog
  plant (New Haven, Connecticut),
  2:*661*
Hungary, alcohol prohibition, 1:313
Hunger, 1:**472–474**
  biofuels, 1:74–77
  elimination, 1:507
  Food First, 1:330–331
  food security, 2:690
  in the United States, 1:46–48
  poverty, 1:46–47, 330, 369,
    2:690
  World Food Day (WFD), 2:854,
    855
  World Food Prize, 2:857
Hunger in America 2010, 1:47
Hunt, Caroline L., 2:800
Hunter, Robert, 2:706
Hunter-gatherers
  agriculture, 1:20, 34, 227, 432,
    2:544
  diet, 1:492, 2:534, 553, 597,
    598, 617–619
  division of labor, 2:595
  evolution, 2:595–596
Huntington, West Virginia, 2:708,
  765
HUS (Hemolytic uremic syndrome),
  1:222
Hydrogenated fats and trans fats,
  1:**475–477,** *477,* 2:775
Hydrologic cycle, 2:835–836
Hydrolyzed vegetable protein recalls,
  2:684
Hydroponics, 1:**478–480,** *479*
Hygiene, 2:733, 734
Hypertension
  chocolate, 2:636
  diet, 1:201–203
  Mediterranean diet, 2:558

  obesity, 1:2, 177, 264
  salt, 1:201–203, 289, 2:699, 822
  therapeutic diets, 2:770–772

I

I Love to Eat (Beard), 2:763
I-tal, 2:679
IAASTD (International Assessment
  of Agricultural Knowledge, Science,
  and Technology for Development),
  1:261, 372–373
IATP (Institute for Agriculture and
  Trade Policy), 1:248
Ice cream, 1:*290*
Iceland, 1:313, 2:742, 844
Ichikawa, Yukako, 2:832–833
ICSR number, 2:684
Idaho, food libel laws, 2:768
Ideology, food, 1:177
IDPs (Internally displaced persons),
  1:*273,* 503
IFAD (International Fund for
  Agricultural Development),
  1:**507–509**
IFOAM (International Federation of
  Organic Agriculture Movements),
  1:**499–502**
IFPRI. *See* International Food Policy
  Research Institute
Illicit drug production, 1:**40–42**
Illicit drugs, 2:669
Illinois. *See* Chicago, Illinois
ILO (International Labor
  Organization), 2:565–566, 823
IMF (International Monetary Fund),
  1:330, 2:777
Immigrants and immigration, 1:*482,*
  2:593, 642, 728, 736
  See also Migrant labor, immigration,
    and food production
Immigration Act of 1924, 1:268
Immigration Act of 1965, 1:481
Immigration and cuisine, 1:**481–483**
Immune globulins, 1:450
Import restrictions, 1:**484–487**
*Improving Gender Equality in Access
  to Land* (Nichols), 1:*414*
Improving Nutrition for America's
  Children Act of 2010, 1:**488–490**
*In Defense of Food: An Eater's
  Manifesto* (Pollan), 2:561, 562
In-kind donations, 1:247, 248
In-N-Out Burger (Baldwin Park,
  California), 1:*280*
INAO (Institut National des
  Appellations d'Origine), 2:817
Independent contractors, 2:565

India, 1:*205*
  biofuels, 1:75, 77
  bird domestication, 1:236
  charcoal stoves, 1:*96*
  chicken domestication, 2:782
  cholera, 1:128
  deaths from pollution relating to
    open cookstoves, 1:460
  diabetes, 1:205
  domestication of animals, 1:275
  famines, 1:274, 436–437
  food protest, 2:*680*
  fortification of curry powder, 2:587
  genetically modified organism
    (GMO) ban, 1:486
  genetically modified organism
    (GMO) crops, 1:420
  Green Revolution, 2:857
  herbs used in cooking, 1:453
  hunger and malnutrition, 1:53–54,
    369
  migrant workers, 2:565
  obesity, 1:205
  open fire stoves, 1:*162*
  protests, 1:*356*, 2:640, 699
  rice, 2:686, 688, 822
  rice production, 1:437
  school children eating lunch,
    2:*645*
  sharecropping, 2:824
  slave labor, 2:823
  spice production, 2:726
  spices in a market, 1:*453*
  street vendors, 2:736
  tea, 2:760, 762
  water scarcity, 2:*837*, 839
  water usage, 1:23
  watering vegetables, 2:*836*
  wheat production, 1:437
  World Food Prize, 2:857
Indian Line Farm (Egremont,
  Massachusetts), 1:145
Indigenous peoples, 1:16, 18, 109
Indigenous peoples and their diets,
  1:**491–494**
Indonesia
  avian influenza, 1:58
  coffee cultivation, 1:102
  cuisine history, 2:827
  deforestation, 1:16–17
  diets, 1:56
  E. coli outbreaks, 1:223
  early fishing, 2:710
  influenza, 1:58, 59
  Korowai tribe member, 1:*110*
  roundworm infection, 1:467
  spice trade, 2:726
Industrial agriculture
  agrochemical, 1:372
  beginning, 2:613
  biodiversity, 1:71, 143, 2:785
  corn production, 2:575
  documentary regarding, 2:576
  ecological impacts, 1:229, 2:575

Food Alliance, 1:298
  irrigation, 1:21
  land reform, 1:26
  Pollan, Michael, 2:561, 719
  processed foods, 1:275
  subsidies, 1:317
  World Trade Organization
    (WTO), 2:866
  World War II, 2:727
  See also Agribusiness; Factory
    farming
Industrialized countries. *See*
  Developed/industrial countries;
  specific countries
Infant formula and baby food,
  1:**495–498**, *497*
  breastfeeding, 1:13, 91–92, 495,
    496, 497
  developing world, 2:640–641
  government oversight, 1:120
  marketing, 1:13
  PBA and baby bottles, 1:82, 497
  recall, 1:360, 496
  See also Children
Infants
  caffeine, 1:102, 104
  daily calorie allowance, 1:122
  marasmus, 1:369
  taste sensation, 2:757
  World Food Programme (WFP),
    2:860
Infectious diseases and diet, 2:544
Influenza, avian, 1:**57–60**
Ingo Potrykus, 1:55, 2:688
Inner Mongolia, China food depots,
  2:*691*
*Innovating Institutions to Help Land
  Reform Beneficiaries* (Lyne &
  Roth), 1:*28–29*
Insect resistance (IR), 1:417, 418
Institut National des Appellations
  d'Origine (INAO), 2:817
Institute for Agriculture and Trade
  Policy (IATP), 1:248
Institute for Natural Resources, 2:646
Insulin, 1:194, 195, *196*
Integrated pest management (IPM),
  2:631, 632
Intellectual property rights (IPR),
  1:243
Intergenerational equity, 1:10, 244
Intergovernmental Panel on Climate
  Change. *See* United Nations
  Intergovernmental Panel on
  Climate Change (IPCC)
Internally displaced persons (IDPs),
  1:*273*, 503
International Agreement for the
  Regulation of Whaling, 2:843
International Assessment of
  Agricultural Knowledge, Science,

and Technology for Development
  (IAASTD), 1:261, 372–373
International Code of Marketing of
  Breast-milk Substitutes, 1:496
International Coffee Organization,
  1:138–139
International Convention for the
  Regulation of Whaling, 2:843
International Culinary Schools at
  the Art Institutes (Pittsburgh,
  Pennsylvania), 1:*174*
International Dairy Federation,
  1:135
International Federation of Organic
  Agriculture Movements (IFOAM),
  1:**499–502**
International food aid, 1:**503–506**,
  504
International Food Policy Research
  Institute (IFPRI), 1:54, 206, 357,
  390
International Fund for Agricultural
  Development (IFAD), 1:**507–509**
International Labor Organization
  (ILO), 2:565–566, 823
International Life Sciences Institute,
  2:859
International Minerals Corporation,
  2:859
International Monetary Fund (IMF),
  1:330, 2:777
International Nestlé Boycott
  Committee, 2:640–641
International Organization for
  Standardization (ISO), food
  standards, 1:334
International Rice Research Institute
  (IRRI), 1:54, 72, 437, 438, 2:688
International trade, agriculture and,
  1:**30–33**
International Treaty of Plant Genetic
  Resources for Food and Agriculture
  (ITPGRPA), 1:72, 142
International Union for
  Conservation of Nature and
  Natural Resources (IUCN), 1:71,
  157, 2:843
International Water Management
  Institute (IWMI), 1:22, 444, 2:839
International Whaling Commission
  (IWC), 2:842
International Year of Rice, 2:688
Internet and food. *See* Food and the
  Internet
Interstate commerce, 2:653
Intestinal motility, 1:464
Intrastate commerce, 2:653
Invialuit people, 1:491–492
Iowa Corn Growers Association, 2:859

Iowa egg farms, 2:697–698
Iowa Soybean Association, 2:859
IPCC. *See* United Nations Intergovernmental Panel on Climate Change (IPCC)
IPR (Intellectual property rights), 1:243
Iran, 2:688, 814
Iraq
  boy with MREs, 2:*578*
  influenza, 1:58
  rice, 2:688
  seed bank, 1:70
  USAID, 2:791
Ireland
  beer consumption, 1:284
  bovine spongiform encephalopathy, 2:768
  boycotts, 2:640
  caloric consumption, 1:206
  food recall, 1:360
  gavage regulation, 1:314
  potato famine, 1:158, 266, 268–269, 368, 2:544, 806, 807, 828
Irish Land League, 2:640
Iron Chef, 2:*764,* 765
Iron Chef America, 2:764
Iron-fortified soy sauce, 2:587, *587*
Irradiation of food, 1:289, **335–338**
IRRI. *See* International Rice Research Institute (IRRI)
Irrigation
  history, 1:20–21
  impacts from, 1:21–23, 2:517–518
  inefficient methods, 1:20
  pivot farming, 1:*22*
  political structure, 1:34
  sprinkler, 1:*21*
  systems, 2:686
  types, 1:21–22
  urban farming, 2:785
Irvine, California, FDA research lab, 2:*797*
Ishizuka, Sagen, 2:537
Islamic dietary laws, 1:312, 2:679
ISO (International Organization for Standardization), food standards, 1:334
Israel, 1:78, 314, 496, 2:648
Italian cheese, 1:*407*
Italy, 1:198
  ban on the use of gavage, 1:314
  family meals, 1:263
  genetically modified organism (GMO) ban, 2:864
  horse meat display, 1:*349*
  migrant workers, 2:565, 823
  pasta, 2:623, 624, 625
  slow food groups, 2:718
  slow food movement, 2:756

spice trade, 1:452
St. Mark's Square, 1:*410*
  sugar trade, 2:747
  walnut oil use, 2:599–600
  wedding cake tradition, 1:309
  wine, 2:814, 815, 817
It's Grits (movie), 2:576
IUCN (International Union for Conservation of Nature and Natural Resources), 1:71, 157, 2:843
IWC (International Whaling Commission), 2:842
IWMI (International Water Management Institute), 1:22, 444, 2:839

J

Jackson, James Caleb, 1:434
Jackson, Wes, 2:754
Jacksonville, Florida, 1:*423,* 2:*554*
Jakarta, Indonesia, 1:92
Jalalabad, Afghanistan, 2:*791*
Jamaican Blue Mountain coffee, 1:140
James, Walter E. C., 2:613
James Beard Foundation, 1:43
Jamie Oliver's Food Revolution (television show), 2:765
Jamie's Food Revolution (Oliver), 2:708, *708*
Jamie's Ministry of Food (Oliver), 2:765
Jamon Iberico, 1:*485*
Jamor, 1:162–163
Japan
  agricultural subsidies, 2:742
  blood alcohol concentration limits, 1:285
  caloric consumption rate, 1:206
  community farming movement, 1:145
  country of origin labeling requirements, 2:664
  cuisine history, 2:827
  diet and disease, 1:53
  fish species protection, 2:716
  food aid provided by, 1:246, 505
  food safety regulation and inspection, 1:333
  functional foods, 1:344, 403, 404
  genetically modified organism (GMO) ban, 2:864
  green tea picking, 2:*761*
  restaurant reviews, 1:320
  street vendors, 2:736
  tea, 2:760, 762
  television and cooking, 2:764, 765
  whale butchering, 2:*844*
  whaling, 2:842, 843, 844
Japan Today (magazine), 2:*832–834*

Japanese "Iron Chef" Ruffling Feathers in Australia with her Anti-waste Movement, 2:*832–834*
Japanese Standards Association (JIS), 1:333
Japan's Institute for Cetacean Research (ICR), 2:844
Jatropha plants, 1:*75, 76*
Jell-O, 1:326
Jepma, C. J., 1:163
Jewish ancestry and lactose intolerance, 2:516
Jewish dietary rules, 1:168, 312, 313, 2:679, 681
Johns Hopkins University, 2:749
Johnson, Lyndon B., 1:46, 488, 2:652, *654*
Jolly Green Giant, 1:1
Joseph Project feeding program, 1:6
Joule, 1:106
Journal of Adolescent Health, 1:304
Journal of Communication, 1:303
Journal of Environmental Science and Technology, 2:845
Journal of Food Protection, 2:527
Journal of the American Medical Association, 2:677
Juices, 1:224, 403
Julie and Julia (movie), 1:376, 2:575
The Jungle (Sinclair), 1:119, 332, 365, 2:548–549, *550–552,* 669, 846
Junk food, 2:**511–513,** *603*
  advertising, 1:1, 2:511
  calories, 1:108
  fast food, 1:279
Just Food, 1:147

K

!Kung San peoples, 1:492, 2:617
Kailua, Hawaii, 1:*328*
Kaimowitz, David, 1:*18–19*
Kaldi, 1:138
Kale, 2:*788*
Källander, Inger, 1:*500–502*
Kamp, David, 1:426, 2:534
Kansas farm, 1:*262*
Kaopectate, 2:638
Kaplan, Hillard, 2:595
Karam's Lebanese restaurant (Jacksonville, Florida), 2:*554*
Karnataka, India, 2:*836*
Karottukara, Kerala, India, 2:*645*
Kashrut, 2:679
Katrina (Hurricane), 1:129, 220, 2:585
Kaufman, Phil, 1:*3*
Kayunga District, Uganda, 1:*370*

Kefauver-Harris Amendment of 1962, 2:797
Keller, Thomas, 1:307
Kellogg, John Harvey, 1:176
Kellogg Company, 2:641
Kendekeza, Malawi, 1:6
Kennedy, John F., 2:592, 790
Kenner, Robert, 2:576
Kenton, Leslie, 2:673
Kentucky Fried Chicken (KFC), 2:649, 682
Kenya, 1:78, *446*, 2:762
Kern County, California, 2:566
Kerr, Graham, 2:763–764
Keys, Ancel B., 1:198, 2:557
KFC (Kentucky Fried Chicken), 2:649, 682
Khartoum, Sudan, World Food Day (WFD) celebration, 2:855
Khost, Afghanistan, 2:780
Ki-moon, Ban, 2:692, 855, *856*
Kilogram calorie, 1:106
King, Charles G., 2:819
King Corn (movie), 2:575
Kingsolver, Barbara, 2:534–535
Kissidougou, Republic of Guinea, 1:189
KitchenAid, 1:460
Kneading, 1:62
Koch, Robert, 1:128–129
Kolkata, India, 1:162
Konner, Melvin, 1:492, 2:617
Kopi Luwak coffee, 1:140
Korean Peninsula, whaling, 2:842
Korowai tribe member, 1:110
Kosher food, 1:168, 312, 2:679, 681
Kowalcyk, Barbara, 1:223
Kowalcyk, Kevin, 1:223
Kraft Foods, 2:859
Krakow, Poland, 2:700
Kroger, food advertising, 1:3
Krugman, Paul, 1:486
Kuru, 1:109, 110–111
Kushi, Michio, 2:537
Kwashiorkor, 2:779
Kyaing Tong, Myanmar, 1:103
Kyoto Protocol, 1:134
Kyrgyz, Kyrgyzstan, 1:504
Kyrgyz Republic, 1:28
Kyrgyzstan, 1:504

L

La Leche League, 1:497
La Paz, Bolivia, 1:41

La Terminal market (Guatemala City, Guatemala), 1:66
La Tomatina festival (Bunol, Spain), 1:386
Lactase, 2:514, 515, 516
Lacto-vegetarians, 2:813
Lactose, 2:774
Lactose intolerance, 1:179, 180–181, 294, 2:**514–516**, *515*, 677
Lagasse, Emeril, 1:116, *116*, 2:764
Lake City, Florida, fast food sign, 2:829
Lancaster, Chet S., 2:595
Lance Armstrong Foundation's Livestrong Web site, 1:192
Land availability and degradation, 2:**517–519**
   See also Environmental degradation
The Land Institute, 2:754
Land O'Lakes, 2:859
Land O'Lakes butter, 1:3
Land reform, agricultural, 1:**25–29**, 330–331
Land tenure, 1:412, 413
Landraces, 1:169, 2:521
Lang, Tim, 2:756
Langbein, Julia, 1:307
Lasègue, Charles, 1:225, 227
Lask, Bryan, 1:347
Latin America
   banana trade wars, 1:65–68
   black carbon emissions, 1:160
   cholera, 1:128
   climate change, 1:133
   fair trade production, 1:259
   history of food, 2:520
   land reform, 1:26, 27
   street vendors, 2:736
   subsistence farming, 2:745
   USAID, 1:28
   women and food, 2:851
   See also Developing countries; *specific countries*
Latin American diet, 2:**520–522**, 523
Latino Farmers Cooperative community garden (New Orleans, Louisiana), 2:581
Latvia, 1:184
Lavoisier, Antoine, 2:589
LDL (Low-density lipoprotein cholesterol), 1:166, 200, 2:558
Le Mouël, Chantal, 1:67–68
Leach, Melissa, 1:189
League of Nations, 1:300
Leakage (food aid), 1:504
Leavening. *See* Yeast and leavening agents
Lebanon, 2:524

Legumes, 2:**523–525**
Lehrer, Jim, 2:*604–605*
Lemongrass, 1:406
Lenin, Vladimir, 1:25, 183
Lentils, 2:523
Lesotho, 1:331
Let's Move initiative, 1:233, 489, 2:604, 756
Letter on Corpulence (Banting), 1:176
Lettuce, 1:120, 2:788
   E. coli outbreaks, 1:223
   organic, 2:614
   washing, 2:664
Levert, Fabrice, 1:67–68
Levy, Paul, 1:426
Lex Sempronia Agraria, 1:25
Liberalization of trade, 1:389, 390–391
Liberia, women preparing food, 2:851
Liebig, Justis von, 1:91
Life Cycle Assessment (LCA), 2:535
Lightner, Candy, 1:285
Like Water for Chocolate (Esquivel), 2:575
Lincoln, Abraham, 2:793, 796
Lincoln, Blanche, 1:488
Lind, James, 2:819
Link, David, 1:276
L'Inspecteur se met à table (Rémy), 1:321
Lipids, 2:728
Lipopolysaccharide (LPS), 2:696
Liquors, artisan, 1:284
Listeria, 1:360, 2:**526–528**, *527*, 550, 676, 677
Lithuania, 1:184
Livestock
   bioterrorism, 1:79
   corn feed, 1:170, 171
   desertification, 1:187
   domestication of wild breeds, 1:275
   embargoes regarding, 1:240
   genetic diversity, 1:143
   heritage breeds, 2:718
   monocultures, 1:372
   organic, 2:611, 614
   overgrazing, 2:517, 518–519
   water usage, 1:20, 22
Livestock intensity and demand, 2:**529–533**
Livestrong bicycle race, 1:192
The Living Light Culinary Arts Institute (Fort Bragg, CA), 2:673
Living modified organisms (LMO), 1:112, 113–114, 2:794
Local and regional procurement (LRP), 1:504–505
Local food movement. *See* Locavore

Locavore, 2:**534–536**
   food additives, 1:289
   macrobiotic diet, 2:538
   See also Waters, Alice
Lombana, F. Jahir, 1:*67–68*
London, England, 1:*230*
   BedZed eco development, 1:*10*
   biofuels protest, 1:*76*
   butcher shop, 2:*541*
   protest against genetically
     modified crops, 1:*418*
The London (Manhattan restaurant),
   1:*117*
London market, 2:*811*
Lorenz, Nathan, 1:*97*
Los Angeles, California, 2:*697*
Louisiana, 1:*47*, 2:*581*, 768, *798*
Love Food, Hate Waste (Web site), 2:833
Low carbohydrates
   diets, 1:75, 2:617, 772
   product display, 1:*328*
Low-density lipoprotein cholesterol
   (LDL), 1:166, 200, 2:558
LPS (Lipopolysaccharide), 2:696
LRP (Local and regional
   procurement), 1:504–505
Lubin, David, 1:300
Luck, Jo, 2:858
Lumiere, Auguste, 2:574
Lumiere, Louis, 2:574
Luxembourg, 1:284, 314, 2:864
Lycopene in tomatoes, 1:353
Lyman, Howard, 2:767, 768
Lyne, Mike, 1:*28–29*

M

Maccioni, Sirio, 1:321
MacDonald, James, 1:*15*
Macedonia, 1:185
Maclean's, 2:617
Macrobiotic diet, 2:*538*
Macrobiotics, 2:**537–539**
Macronutrients, 2:589, 590, 779
Mad cow disease and vCJD,
   2:**540–543**
   See also Bovine spongiform
     encephalopathy (BSE);
     Creutzfeldt-Jakob Disease
     (CJD); Variant Creutzfeldt-
     Jakob Disease (vCJD)
Madagascar, 1:*130*
MADD (Mothers Against Drunk
   Driving), 1:285
Madison, Deborah, 1:44
Madre, 1:248
Magnetic resonance imaging (MRI),
   1:102

Maize, 2:*828*
   See also Corn
Malabsorption, 2:770, 771, 779
Malawi, villagers gathering water,
   2:*778*
Malaysia, 1:56, 2:*688*, 726
Mali, 1:187, 374, *473*, 2:823
Malnourished child, 2:*545*
Malnourished man, 2:*564*
Malnutrition, 2:**544–547**, 779
   eradication, 2:690
   famine, 1:266
   feeding regimes, 2:770
   nutritional deficiencies, 2:591
   prehistoric people, 1:35
   therapeutic diets, 2:770–772
   in the United States, 1:46
   World Food Day (WFD), 2:854
Malthus, Thomas, 1:10, 34–35, 266,
   268, 472, 2:518, 644
Mama Ekila's Inzia restaurant
   (Congo), 1:*99*
The Man-Eating Myth (Arens), 1:109
Mangos, 1:*336*, 337, *337*
Manila, Philippines, 1:*497*, 2:*642*
Mannerino, Helen, 1:*482*
Mao Zedong, 1:26, 272
Maple Leaf Foods, 1:360
Marasmus, 1:369, 2:779
Marbling (meat), 2:553
Margarine, 1:475, 476–477, 2:586
Marggraf, Andreas, 2:747
Marinkina City, Philippines, 1:*93*
Market access, 1:412–413
Market power, 1:170, 171
Marketing Daily, 1:404
Mars, Inc., 2:641
Marseille, France, 1:*51*
Marshall, Kirstie, 1:*92*
Marshall Plan, 1:246, 2:790
Martin, Richard, 1:469
Martin Luther King Jr. Middle
   School (Berkeley, California),
   1:232, *233*
Martinez, Steve, 1:*3*
Marx, Karl, 2:644
Mass media, weight control
   behaviors and, 1:303–304
Massachusetts
   Panera bread store sign, 1:*107*
   raw milk, 2:676, *677*, 677–678
Matzo factory, 2:*681*
Mauritania, 1:187, 2:823
Maximum sustainable yield,
   2:711, 712
Mayan society, 1:*36*, 125, 169, 500,
   2:520
Mayport, Florida, 2:*712*

McCain, John, 1:217
McCance, Robert, 2:590
McCollum, E. V., 2:589, 819
McCormick Co., 2:859
McDonald's
   boycotts, 2:642, *642*
   Chicken McNuggets, 2:649
   food libel case, 2:768
   founding, 1:279
   Happy Meal, 1:*2*
   Latin America, 2:522
   packaging, 1:281
   protest, 2:680
   slow food movement, 2:718
McGovern, George, 1:208, 2:860
McIntyre, James, 1:*181–182*
McKees Rocks, Pennsylvania,
   pierogie shop, 1:*482*
"McLibel Case," 2:768
MDA (Minimum Daily
   Requirement), 2:800
MDGs. *See* United Nations Millennium
   Development Goals (MDGs)
Meal, ready-to-eat (MREs),
   2:**577–579**, *578*
Mearns, Robin, 2:*532*
Meat and Poultry Pathogen
   Reduction Act of 2003 (unpassed),
   1:223
Meat Inspection Act of 1906,
   2:**548–552**, 846
Meatpacking
   inspections of facilities, 1:332,
     2:846, 847
   Meat Inspection Act, 2:548–552,
     846
   Sinclair, Upton, 1:119, 332, 365,
     2:548, *550–552*, 669, 846
   See also Pure Food and Drug Act
     of 1906
Meat thermometers, 1:*155*
Meats, 1:*155*, 2:**553–556**
   allergies, 1:291
   beef, 2:766, 768, *848*
   bovine spongiform encephalopathy,
     1:240, 2:766–768
   cancer, 1:191
   cost, 2:529
   cured, 2:657
   diabetes, 2:828
   E. coli outbreaks, 1:223, 224
   ecological impacts, 1:229–230
   environmental costs, 2:554–555
   factory farming, 1:254–256, *255*
   fast food, 2:709
   food additives, 2:846–847
   food libel, 2:766, 768
   foodborne illness, 1:382, 383,
     2:766, 847
   government oversight regarding,
     1:365–366
   hamburger, 1:223, 224

heart disease, 1:198
hominin meat consumption, 2:595–596
horse meat, 1:*349*
income and consumption, 1:204
inspection, 1:365–366
irradiation, 1:337
junk food, 2:512
obesity, 2:828
organic, 2:613
Paleolithic diet, 2:618
Pollen, Michael, 2:561, 562
pork, 2:554
preparation methods, 1:351, 352, *352*
processed, 2:705, 734
rainforest burning and production, 1:17
recalls, 1:360
religious rules regarding, 1:312, 2:679, 680
richer populations consumption, 1:355
sales, 2:768
Salmonella, 1:154–155
salt as preservative, 1:288, 2:703
satay, 2:737
school lunches, 2:708–709
on shawarma grill, 2:*554*
smoked, 1:386
sodium nitrate, 1:90, 288, 289
Medan, Indonesia, 1:*58*
Medications, 1:102, 2:781
Mediterranean diet, 1:166, 198, 200, 2:523, **557–560,** 815
Mège-Mouriés, Hippolyte, 1:475
Meissner, Georg, 2:757
Melamine, 1:289
Melons, 1:399, 479
Mendez, Dionidas, 1:*27*
Menes (pharaoh), 1:20
Merck, 2:798
Mercy Corps, 1:92
Merret, Christopher, 2:816
Mesoamerica, 2:520, 521
Mesolithic period deforestation, 1:16
Methode champenoise, 2:816
Metz, France, 1:*151*
Mexican dip, 1:*407*
Mexico
    bottled water usage, 1:84, 85
    corn protest, 1:*113, 373, 391*
    early agriculture, 1:456, 457
    farmer in Ciudad Obregon, 1:*437*
    fat consumption, 1:206
    Green Revolution, 1:436, 438, 2:857
    indoor air quality, 1:95
    maize crop variety, 2:522
    migrant workers, 2:823
    wheat crops, 1:436

wine, 2:816
World Food Prize, 2:857
World Trade Organization (WTO), 2:866
Mexico City, Mexico, 1:*113, 373, 391, 419*
Miami, Florida, 1:*341*
MIC. *See* Middle-income countries
Michael Pollan: linking food and environmental journalism, 1:327, 2:534, **561–563,** *562,* 662, 719
Michelin, André, 1:319
Michelin Guide, 1:115, 319–321
Michigan, 2:586, 627, *787*
Micro-communities, 2:721–722, *722*
Microcredits, 2:851–852
Microloans, 1:41, 42
Micronutrient deficiency, 2:544
Micronutrients. *See* Vitamins and minerals
Microvilli, taste sensation, 2:757
Microwave cooking, 1:351, 459, 460
Middle Ages
    assistance to the poor, 1:428
    beer consumption, 1:282
    breastfeeding, 1:91
    catering and hospitality, 1:309
    confections and pastry, 1:149, 150
    disease theories, 1:78
    frying of food, 1:164
    meats, 2:553
    pea as protein source, 2:523
    potassium nitrate preservation, 2:656, 703
    street food, 1:279
Middle East
    coffee, 1:138
    domestication of animals, 1:275, 443, 457
    early agriculture, 1:456, 457
    embalming with spices, 2:725
    grains grown, 1:432
    Halvah, 1:149, 150
    influenza, 1:58, 252
    migrant workers, 2:823
    oil, 1:74
    spice trade, 2:724–725
    USAID, 1:28
Middle-income countries (MIC), 1:53, 56, 204–207
Migrant and Seasonal Agricultural Worker Protection Act (MSPA) of 1983, 2:565
Migrant labor, immigration, and food production, 1:13, 2:**564–567,** *566,* 632, 745, 823
    See also Immigrants and immigration
Military rations, 2:577
Milk, 1:179, 180–181
    allergies, 1:291, 294

allergy warning labels, 2:774, 799
bovine growth hormone, 2:641
contaminated, 1:136
decreased consumption, 2:513
E. coli, 1:224, 2:677
evaporated, 1:495–496
food-related illness, 2:676, 677
irradiation, 1:335
lactose intolerance, 1:179, 180–181, 294, 2:514–516
melamine, 1:289
milk-borne illness, 2:676
pasteurization, 1:495, 2:677
price, 1:355
raw, 2:627–628
raw milk campaign, 2:676–678
religious rules regarding, 2:680
Salmonella outbreak, 2:677
vitamins added to, 1:403, 2:586
See also Dairy products
The Milk Question (Rosenau), 2:*628*
Millau, Christian, 1:319
Millennium Declaration, 2:776
Millennium Summit, 2:776
Millennium Villages, 2:*778*
Miller, George, 1:489
Millers, 1:*36*
Milton, Katherine, 2:617
Minimum Daily Requirement (MDA), 2:800
Minnesota organic acreage, 2:613
Mint family, 1:452, 453
Miso, 1:406, 2:537, 538
Mississippi, 2:603, 768
Mobile Bay, oil spill booms, 1:*441*
Model Milk Health Ordinance, 2:676
Moët and Chandon, 2:818
Mogadishu, Somalia, refugees, 2:*862*
Moldova, 1:27
Molecular gastronomy, 2:**568–570**
Mongolia, tea, 2:761
Monkey head, 1:*99*
Monks, 2:*558*
Monoculture, 1:143, 158, 372, 378, 379–380
Monomers, 1:81
Monosodium glutamate (MSG), 1:288, 2:*704*
Monounsaturated and polyunsaturated oils, 1:164, 166, 2:558, **571–573**
Monsanto Company, 1:13–14, 171, 344, 2:641
Montaigne, Michel de, 1:110
Montenegro, 1:185
Monterey Bay Aquarium, 2:713
Montessori, Maria, 1:232

Monteverde, Costa Rica, 1:*258*

Montezuma II, 1:125

Montpelier, France, 1:*397*

Morales, Evo, 2:792

Morell, Sally Fallon, 2:676, 677

Morgan, Lewis Henry, 1:34

Morocco, 2:624

Morrill Act of 1862, 2:793

Morris, David, 2:768

Mortar and pestle, 2:*851*

Moses, 1:312

Mothers Against Drunk Driving
(MADD), 1:285

Moula-Guercy (France), 1:110

Mountain Dew, 1:3

Movies, documentaries, and food,
2:**574–576**

Mozambique, 1:131

Mr. Peanut, 1:1

MREs (meal ready-to-eat), 2:**577–579,**
578

MRI (Magnetic resonance imaging),
1:102

MSG (Monosodium glutamate),
1:288, 289, 2:*704*

MSPA (Migrant and Seasonal
Agricultural Worker Protection Act
of 1983), 2:565

Mt. Fuji, Japan, green tea picking,
2:*761*

Muckrakers, 2:549, 669, 670

Mugabe, Robert, 1:26

*Mukta-Kamaiya—Discovering True
Freedom* (Singh), 1:*448*

Müller, Paul, 2:630

Mumbai, India, 1:*96,* 2:*680*

Murrow, Edward R., 2:564

Mussels, 1:*50*

Mwandama, Malawi, villagers
gathering water, 2:*778*

Myanmar, 1:*103, 314,* 2:686, 760, *852*

Myoglobin, 2:553

MyPyramid.gov, 2:801–802

N

Nabhan, Gary Paul, 1:492, 2:534

NAFTA (North American Free Trade
Agreement), 1:390, 391

Nano-scale technology, 2:550

Napoleon Bonaparte, 2:577

Napoleon III, 1:475

NASA (National Aeronautics and
Space Administration), 1:332

Nasty Bits (Bourdain), 2:675

National Aeronautics and Space
Administration (NASA), 1:332

National Agricultural Law Center,
1:316

National Broadcasting Company
(NBC), 2:763

National Cancer Institute (NCI),
2:554

National Cattlemen's Beef
Association, 2:767

National Center for Complementary
and Alternative Medicine
(NCCAM), 1:454

National Center for Food Protection
and Defense (NCFPD), 1:80

National Center for HIV/AIDs,
1:450

National Center for Zoonotic,
Vector-Borne, and Enteric Disease,
2:676

National Defense Advisory
Commission, 2:800

National Institute for Food and
Nutrition Research, 1:151

National Institute of Environmental
and Health Sciences, 1:191

National Institutes of Health (NIH),
1:467

National Nutrition Conference of
1941, 2:800

National Nutrition Monitoring and
Related Research Act of 1990, 1:209

National Oceanic and Atmospheric
Administration (NOAA), 1:441

National Organic Program (NOP),
2:609

National Organic Standards Board
(NOSB), 2:609–610

National Restaurant Association,
2:817

National School Breakfast Program,
1:488

National School Lunch Act of 1946,
2:592, 707

National School Lunch Program,
1:209, 488–489, 490, 2:592–593,
706, 707–709

National Survey on Drug Use and
Health, 1:285

National Toxicology Program
(NTP), 1:83

National Veterinary School and
Natural History Museum of
Toulouse, 1:99

Native Americans, 2:*828*
cannibalism, 1:110
Columbian Exchange, 2:827–828
food advertising stereotypes, 1:3
influence on American cuisine,
1:385, 482, 2:727
lactose intolerance, 2:516
traditional crops, 1:275

Natural Resources Conservation
Service, 2:794

Natural Resources Defense Council
(NRDC)
bottled water survey by the, 1:84

Nature et Progrès, 1:499

NBC (National Broadcasting
Company), 2:763

Neanderthals, 2:596

Nebraska, 2:*653*

Neighborhood food cooperatives,
2:**580–582**

Neil, Marion Harris, 1:*166–168*

Neill, Charles P., 2:669, 846

Neill-Reynolds Report, 2:669, 846

Nelson, Philip E., 1:460

Neolithic, 1:457

Neolithic Revolution, 1:456

Nepal
Heifer International Inc.,
1:447–448
hunger and malnutrition, 1:54
spice production, 2:726
tea, 2:761
women and food, 2:851

Neptune Beach, Florida, 1:*38, 146*

Nerva (emperor), 1:428

Nestlé, 1:13, 342, 495, 496,
2:640–641

Nestlé, Henri, 1:91, 495

Netherlands, 1:*444*

Netherlands, gavage regulation, 1:314

Neurotoxin, 1:89, 2:621

New American cuisine (NAC),
1:**43–45,** 2:729–730

New Delhi, India, 1:*205, 356*

*New Directions for Child and
Adolescent Development,* 1:263

New England Journal of Medicine,
1:195, 2:603, 617

New England region, algal blooms
model for, 2:622

New Guinea, 1:109

New Haven, Connecticut, 2:*661*

New Orleans, Louisiana, 1:*47,* 2:*581,
798*

New Oxford American Dictionary,
2:535

New South Wales, 2:817

New York City, New York, 1:*165,* 313
The Brooklyn Grange commercial
farm, 2:*788*
cooked ducks, 2:*650*
restaurant reviews, 1:320, 321
street vendors, 2:722, 736
trans fats ban, 2:572
urban chicken movement, 2:782
urban farming, 2:788
Veggie Pride parade, 2:*812*

New York City Film Festival, 2:576

New York Department of Education, 1:313

New York Magazine, 1:426

The New York Times, 2:535, 617, 709

The New Yorker, 2:808

New Zealand
agricultural subsidies, 2:741, 743
climate change, 1:133
grape harvests, 1:311
H5N1 infection in animals, 1:59
wine, 2:817

News Hour (Lehrer), 2:*604–605*

The Next Food Network Star, 2:765

NGOs. *See* Non-governmental organizations (NGOs)

Nicaragua, 1:66

Nichols, Susan, 1:*414*

Niger, 1:6, 71, 187, 2:823

Nigeria, 1:71, 189, 467, 2:531, 688

NIH (National Institutes of Health), 1:467

Nitrates, 1:288, 289, 2:703–705

Nixon, Richard, 2:574

No Reservations (Bourdain), 1:116, 2:764

NOAA (National Oceanic and Atmospheric Administration), 1:441

Noah hypothesis, 2:814

Nobel Peace Prize, 2:857

Nomadic peoples, 2:514, 515

Non-governmental organizations (NGOs), 1:136, 2:645
Millennium Development Goals (MDGs), 2:776
World Food Prize, 2:858

Non-tariff barrier, 1:30, 31, 390

Nord, Mark, 1:*430*

Norman Borlaug Commemorative Research Initiative, 2:857, 858

Norovirus infection, 1:310, 2:**583–585,** *585*

North America
cholera, 1:128
climate change, 1:133
early agriculture, 1:457
modern ovens, 1:459
raw milk, 2:676
red tide along seaboards, 2:622
subsistence farming, 2:744
sustainable agriculture, 2:750
whaling, 2:842
wild rice, 2:686
See also specific countries

North American Free Trade Agreement (NAFTA), 1:390, 391

North Amherst Community Farm (Amherst, Massachusetts), 1:145–146

North Carolina, 1:*210*, 2:531

North Dakota, 2:613, 768

North Korea, 1:272, 273, 505, 2:863

Northwest Food Alliance, 1:297

Norwalk virus, 1:382

Norway
alcohol prohibition, 1:313
ban on the use of gavage, 1:314
Svalbard Global Seed Bank, 1:70, *70, 72,* 143
whaling, 2:843, 844

Nose-to-tail eating. *See* Head-to-tail eating

A Note on Rising Food Prices (World Bank), 1:76

Nourishing Traditions (Morell), 2:676, 677

Nouvelle cuisine, 2:568–569

NRDC (Natural Resources Defense Council), 1:84

Nursing homes, 1:122, *123*

Nutraceutical, 1:403

Nutrient film technique, 1:479

Nutrient fortification of foods, 2:**586–588,** *587*
See also Functional foods

Nutrition, 2:**589–591**
food pyramid, 2:800
raw food lifestyles, 2:673, 674
raw milk, 2:677
taste and smell, 2:757, 758

Nutrition and Physical Degeneration (Price), 1:492, 2:617, 676

Nutrition and U.S. government food assistance, 2:**592–594**

Nutrition and Your Health: Dietary Guidelines for Americans (1985), 1:208–209

Nutrition Labeling and Education Act of 1990, 2:773, 799, 800

Nutrition labels, 2:590, 773
Food and Drug Administration (FDA), 2:799
food pyramid, 2:800
sugar and sweeteners, 2:749

Nutrition Research Reviews, 2:677

Nutrition Work with Children (Roberts), 1:46

Nutritional Business Journal, 1:404

Nutritional needs throughout life, 1:**122–124**

Nutrition's role in human evolution, 2:**595–597**

Nuts and seeds, 2:**598–600,** *599, 600*
advertising, 1:1
allergies, 1:291
allergy warning labels, 2:774
almonds, 2:598, *600*
in a balanced diet, 2:599–600
Brazil nuts, 1:419, 2:598, 599, 600
calories and fat, 1:108, 2:599
coconut, 2:598
cooperatives, 1:257
fruit classification, 1:399
oils, 2:598, 599–600
peanuts, 2:598–599
pine nuts, 2:599
walnuts, 2:599–600

O

Oats, 1:292, 432, 433, 2:771

Obama, Barack, 1:137, 152, 233, 440, 488, 2:550

Obama, Michelle, 1:233, 489, 2:*604–605,* 756

Obesity, 2:**601–605**
advertising, 1:1–2
Asia, 1:55
baked goods ban, 1:313
basal metabolic rate, 2:668
body mass index (BMI), 1:103, 397, 2:601–602, 604
caffeine as treatment, 1:104–105
calorie consumption, 1:123
cancer, 1:1, 191, 193
candy, 1:150–151
childhood, 1:233, 489, 2:603–605, 756
contributing factors, 2:602
death and obesity related conditions, 2:601
developing countries, 1:204
diabetes, 1:194, 195, 196, 264
discrimination against overweight people, 2:603
eating disorders, 1:303
epidemic, 1:209
fast food, 1:279–280
hypertension, 1:2, 177, 264
increase, 1:303
increase in chronic and life-threatening diseases, 2:602
junk food, 2:511
Let's Move initiative, 1:233, 2:756
malnutrition, 1:473, 2:545–546, 546–547
middle-income countries, 1:206
processed foods, 2:662
taste sensation, 2:758
therapeutic diets, 2:770–772
United States, 1:210
See also Overweight

Obukhow, Ukraine, 1:*272*

OECD. *See* Organisation for Economic Co-operation and Development (OECD)

Of Cannibalism (Montaigne), 1:110

Offal, 1:443, 444

The Official Foodie Handbook (Levy), 1:426

O'Flynn, Michael, 1:472

Ohio, food libel laws, 2:768

Ohio Ecological Food and Farming Association, 2:774

Ohsawa, George, 2:537

Oil spill, BP *Deepwater Horizon,* 1:**440–442,** *441*

Oils, 1:*136,* 2:557–558, 590, *765*
  See also specific oils

Okello, Christina, 1:*100–101*

Oklahoma, food libel laws, 2:768

Okra, 1:386, 479

Olive oil, 2:557–558, 571

Olive oil windmill press, 2:*572*

Oliver, Jamie, 2:708, 709, 765

Omega-3 fatty acids, 1:198
  eggs, 1:236–237, 327, 404
  health, 2:571–572
  nuts and seed oils, 2:598

The Omnivore's Dilemma: A Natural History of Four Meals (Pollan), 2:534, 561, 719

The Omnivore's Dilemma for Kids: The Secrets behind What You Eat (Pollan), 2:562

On the Mode of Communication of Cholera (Snow), 1:128

On the Origin of Species (Darwin), 1:456

On the Relations Existing between Oxygen and Yeast (Pasteur), 1:*285–286*

The 100-Mile Diet (Smith and MacKinnon), 2:535

Onion family, 1:452

Open air markets, 2:*807*

Open fire stoves, 1:*161, 162,* 459, 460

Oprah Cattle Crash Effect, 2:768

Oprah Winfrey Show (Winfrey), 2:766

Oral diseases, 2:607

Oral health and diet, 2:**606–608**

Orange juice, 1:108

Orchestra, 1:*410*

Oregon
  backyard chickens, 2:*783*
  bioterrorism, 1:78
  chicken coop, 2:*783*
  fishery closures, 2:622
  Salmonella outbreak, 2:677

Oregon State University, 1:297

Oreo cookies, 1:*340*

Organic agriculture. *See* Organics

Organic citrus orchard and no spray sign, 2:*610*

Organic Consumer Association, 2:641

Organic Foods Production Act of 1990, 2:**609–612,** 614

Organic Foods Production Act of 1990 (U.S. Congress), 2:*611–612*

Organic produce, 2:*615, 755*

Organics, 1:146, 500–502, 2:**613–616**
  advertising, 1:3
  certified, 2:614, *615, 751*
  coffee, 1:298
  corn, 1:*501*
  developing countries, 1:501–502
  ecological impact, 1:230–231
  factory farms, 1:298
  family farms, 1:260
  food co-ops, 2:581
  International Federation of Organic Agriculture Movements (IFOAM), 1:499–502
  labels, 1:298, 2:614, 631
  organically grown designation, 2:631
  poultry, 2:649
  school food, 1:488
  tea, 2:762
  third-party certification, 1:499, 500, 2:751
  vs. traditionally grown produce, 1:44–45
  USDA requirements, 1:45, 2:581
  Waters, Alice, 1:425
  wine, 2:817

Organisation for Economic Co-operation and Development (OECD), 2:742, 751, 776, 777

Orthodox Union (OU), 2:681

Orthorexia, 1:176, 177, 225–226, 2:562, 674

Oryzo glaberimma, 2:686

Oryzo sativa, 2:686

OSHA (U.S. Department of Labor's Occupational Safety & Health Administration), 2:564

Osteoporosis, 1:104

Ostrom, Elinor, 2:712

The Other America: Poverty in the United States (Harrington), 1:46

Our Common Future (UNCED), 1:9, 244, 2:750, 751

Ovary, plant, 1:399, 400

Oven spring (baking), 1:62–63

Ovens, 1:95–97, *96, 97,* 459–460

Overweight
  basal metabolic rate, 2:668
  beer consumption, 1:284
  junk food, 2:511
  See also Obesity

Ovo-lacto vegetarian, 2:803

Owner-member of a food co-op, 2:581

P

Pacific region, hunger, 1:472

Paddy rice, 2:687

Pakistan
  chickpea paste and food aid, 2:525
  farm subsidies protest, 2:*742*
  floods 2010, 1:219–220
  food insecurity, 1:54
  Green Revolution, 2:857
  rice, 2:688
  sharecropping, 2:824
  spice production, 2:726
  spice trade, 2:726
  tea, 2:761
  wheat production, 1:437
  World Food Programme, 2:861

Palate Revolt (Reichl), 1:*321–322*

Paleolithic diet, 1:492, 2:597, **617–619,** *618*

The Paleolithic Prescription (Eaton et al.), 1:492, 2:617

Pan American Health Organization, 1:92

Panama, 1:66, 260

Pandemics, 1:57, 128

Panera calorie sign, 1:*107*

Papillae, 2:757

Paralytic shellfish poisoning, 2:**620–622,** *621*

Parenteral nutrition, 1:349, 2:770

Paris, France
  bushmeat, 1:99, *100–101*
  café culture, 1:393–395
  Café de Flore, 1:*394*
  fresh fish display, 2:*711*

Parkinson's disease, 2:557

Pasta, 2:**623–625,** *624*

Pasteur, Louis
  cheese and yogurt cultures, 1:179
  fermentation, 1:*285–286,* 2:867, 868
  germ theory, 1:128
  pasteurization, 1:180, 2:626, 660, 677

Pasteur effect, 2:868

Pasteurization, 2:**626–629,** 676, 677

Pasteurization equipment, 2:*627*

Pastry and confectionery, 1:**149–153**
  Asian, 1:*407*
  consumption in France, 1:396
  cooking fats, 1:164–165, *174, 205*
  displays, 1:*150, 151*
  students preparing, 1:*174*

Patent medicines, 2:669, 670

Patents, food, 1:**343–346**

Pathogens, 1:78, 79–80, 154, 2:649, 661

Pav bhaji, 1:*482*

Pavlosk Experimental Station, 1:72

PBDE (Polybrominated diphenyl ethers), 1:92

PCB (Polychlorinated biphenyls), 1:92

Peaches, 1:399

Peanut allergy skin test, 1:*295*

Peanut Corporation of America, 1:*361*, 2:683

Peanut processing plant, 1:*361*

Peanuts and peanut butter
    allergies, 1:291, 294, 295
    allergy warning labels, 1:291, 292, 2:774, 799
    recall, 1:120, 361, 367, 2:683, 696–697
    veganism, 2:803

Pears, 1:399

Peasants' War (1524–1525), 1:25

Pectin, 2:655, 656

Pediatrics (journal), 1:304, 2:512–513

Pedregal, Venezuela, 1:*126*

Penicillium mold, 2:831

Pennsylvania, 1:*174, 482*

People for the Ethical Treatment of Animals (PETA), 1:446, 470, 2:641, 811

Pepin, Jacques, 1:116

Peppers, 1:*348, 376*, 479

PepsiCo, 2:513

Perfect Pierogie shop (McKees Rocks, Pennsylvania), 1:*482*

Pérignon, Pierre, 2:816

Periodontal disease, 2:607

Periplus Maris Erythraei, 2:724

Perkins, Jacob, 1:460

Perry, Janet, 1:*15*

Persia, waterwheels, 1:20

Persistent organic pollutant (POP), 2:630

Peru, 1:*32, 143*, 2:664, 843

Pesticides and pesticide residue, 2:**630–633**, *632*, 750, 766, 785, 786

PET (Polyethylene terephthalate), 1:84, 340

Petrini, Carlo, 2:718

Phenols, 2:558

Phenylethylamine, 1:126

Philip Morris Companies, 2:857, 859

Philippines
    breastfeeding mothers, 1:*93*
    cacao tree colonies, 1:125
    cuisine history, 2:827
    fortification of margarine, 2:586
    golden rice, 1:55–56
    infant formula, 1:*497*
    rice, 2:688
    women and food, 2:851

Philips, Rod, 2:814

Phillip, Arthur, 2:817

Phobias, food, 1:**347–350**

Photography, food, 1:**375–376**

Photosynthesizing autotrophs, 1:378

Phylloxera, 2:817, 818

The Physiology of Taste (Brillat-Savarin), 1:409

Phytochemicals (phytonutrients), 2:**634–636,** 808

Phytoestrogens, 2:538

Pica, 2:**637–639**

Pickled tea leaves, 1:*314*

Pickles, 2:*645*

Pictographs, 1:*36*

Pig, roasted, 1:*352*

Pigford v. Glickman, 2:795

Pillsbury Company, 1:332, 2:650

Pilot whales, 2:*843*

Pittsburgh, Pennsylvania, 1:*174*

Pizza, gluten free, 1:*423*

A Place of My Own: The Education of an Amateur Builder (Pollan), 2:561

Plan Colombia, 1:40

Plant Patent Act of 1930, 1:343

Plant Variety Protection Act of 1970 (PVPA), 1:343

Planters Nuts, 1:1

Plenty (Smith and MacKinnon), 2:535

Plums, 1:399

Poaching, 1:98

Podcasts, 2:722

Point Clear, Alabama, 1:*442*

Poland, 1:185, 314, 2:*700*, 750

Political food boycotts, 2:**640–643,** *641, 642*

Pollan, Michael, 1:327, 2:534, 561–563, *562*, 662, 719

Polybrominated diphenyl ethers (PBDE), 1:92

Polycarbonate plastic, 1:81

Polychlorinated biphenyls (PCB), 1:92

Polyethylene terephthalate (PET), 1:85, 340

Polymers, 1:81

Polyunsaturated and monounsaturated fats, 1:164, 2:558, **571–573**

Pomona, California, 1:*479*

POP (Persistent organic pollutant), 2:630

Population and food, 2:**644–647**
    agroecology, 1:37
    desertification, 1:188
    famines, 1:266, 268, 2:692
    food security, 2:690, 692
    livestock demand, 2:530
    water scarcity, 2:837–838, 839, 840

The Population Bomb (Ehrlich), 1:*37*, 472, 2:812

Port-au-Prince, Haiti, 1:*219*, 2:*638*, 820

Portinari, Folco, 2:718

Portland, Oregon
    backyard chickens, 2:*783*
    chicken coop, 2:*783*
    urban chicken movement, 2:782

Portugal, 1:452, 2:815, 816

Pot pies, 2:649

Potatoes, 1:*143*, 161, 2:520, *521*

Potrykus, Ingo, 1:55, 2:688, 822

Poultry, 2:**648–651**, 653, 695, 697
    See also Chicken

Poultry farming, 1:*255*, 2:*530*

Poultry plant workers, 2:653–654

Poultry Products Inspection Act of 1957, 2:**652–654**

Poverty
    famines, 1:7–8, 472
    food insecurity, 2:690, 693
    food prices, 1:355, 357
    hunger, 1:46–47, 330, 369, 2:690
    International Fund for Agricultural Development (IFAD) activities regarding, 1:507–509
    subsistence farming, 2:746
    trap, 1:6
    urban farming, 2:786
    vegetarianism, 2:812–813
    water, 1:23
    World Food Day (WFD), 2:854

Poverty (Hunter), 2:706

Poverty and Famines: An Essay on Entitlement and Deprivation (Sen), 1:*7*, 472

Prebisch, Raúl, 1:257

Precautionary principle, 1:112, 157, 243–244

Pregnant women
    cholera, 1:131
    cult diets, 1:177
    fish consumption by, 1:198, 2:713
    folic acid, 1:124
    iodine deficiency, 2:671
    iron deficiency, 2:588
    listeriosis, 2:526, 527, 528, 677
    malnutrition, 2:544
    pica, 2:637, 638
    raw food diets, 2:674

Preservation, 2:**655–659**
    advertising, 1:1
    canning, 1:339, 340, 460, 2:655, 658, 660, 661
    curing, 2:656, 703, 704
    drying, 2:655–656
    foodborne diseases, 1:154
    salt and nitrates, 2:655, 656, 662, 699, 703, 704

Preservatives, 2:655, 660, 661

Preserved vegetables and meats, 2:*656, 657, 658*

Price, Weston A., 1:492, 2:617, 673, 676–677

Price Waterhouse Coopers, 1:404

Prince Edward Island (Canada), 1:*50*

Prions, 1:109, 110–111, 2:540–541

Processed foods, 2:**660–662**
  advertising, 1:1, 3
  diseases and obesity, 1:199, 2:660
  food fads, 1:326–327
  gluten, 2:771
  home cooking, 1:460
  increase in use, 1:204, 205
  irradiation, 1:335, 336
  Pollen, Michael, 2:561
  sustainable table, 2:754
  television, 2:765

Prock, Ray, 2:*722*

Proctor & Gamble, 1:166

Produce traceability, 2:**663–665**

Producer support estimate (PSE), 2:742

Program on Science Technology, and Development (PROCIENTEC), 2:522

Progressive Era, 2:548, 549, 670

Proofing, 1:62

Propylthiouracil (PROP), 2:758

Protectionism, 1:317, 486–487

Protein
  balanced diet, 2:590
  dairy products, 1:179
  digestion, 2:591
  energy density, 1:106
  legumes, 2:523
  meat, 2:553
  nutritional needs, 1:122
  seafood, 2:710
  veganism, 2:803, 804

Protein and carbohydrate metabolism, 2:**666–668**

Protests
  bake sale ban, 1:*313*
  biofuels, 1:*76*
  corn, 1:*373, 391*
  farm subsidies, 2:*742*
  farm workers, 2:*824, 865*
  fast food, 2:*680*
  food prices, 1:*356*
  free trade, 1:*32*
  genetically modified crops, 1:*113, 418, 419*
  outside a Starbucks, 2:*641*
  salt tax, 2:640, 699
  U.S.-led war on Iraq, 2:*642*

PSE (Producer support estimate), 2:742

Pseudomonas bacteria, 2:831

Psychrophiles, 2:626

Public Health Service Act of 1944, 2:606

Puck, Wolfgang, 1:406

Pueblo site, Anasazi, 1:110

Puffer fish bans, 1:313

Pulses, 2:524

Pure Food and Drug Act of 1906, 1:119, 323, 2:548, **669–672**
  food and drug safety, 2:796
  food labeling, 2:773, 774
  meatpacking, 2:846, 847
  pesticides, 2:630
  poultry, 2:652
  See also Meatpacking

Pure Food and Drug Act of 1906 (U.S. Congress), 2:*671*

Putin, Vladimir, 1:434

PVPA (Plant Variety Protection Act of 1970), 1:343

Pyramids, ecological, 1:**377–380**, *379*

Pyramids, food, 2:800–802, *801,* 810–812

Pythagoras, 2:803

Q

Quaker Oats Man, 1:1

Quark cheese, 2:*674*

Queens, New York, 2:*788*

Quinoa, 1:432

Quotas, 1:65, 66, 67–68, 484

Quran, 1:312, 386

R

Rabbi, 2:*681*

Racial stereotypes, food advertising, 1:3

Radio frequency identification (RFID), 2:665

Rainforest Alliance, 1:298

Rainforests, 1:*17*, 189

Ramadan, 2:679

Ramesh, Jairam, 1:420, 486

Ramsay, Gordon, 1:*117*, 2:765

Ranking systems, restaurant, 1:116

Rations, military, 2:577

Raw Eating (Aterhov), 2:673

Raw Energy (Kenton), 2:673

Raw foodism, 2:**673–675**

Raw milk campaign, 2:627–628, **676–678**

Raw milk rally, 2:*677*

Raw oysters, 2:*798*

Raw vegetables, 2:*673, 674, 807*

Rawists, 2:674

Ray, Rachael, 1:426

Raytheon, 1:459

RDA (Recommended Daily Allowance), 1:212, 2:801, 820

Ready-to-eat (RTE), 1:14, 2:527

Ready-to-use foods (RTUFs), 1:7, 459, 460, 2:525

Reagan, Ronald, 1:285

Recombinant bovine growth hormone (rBGH), 1:314, 2:797, 798

Recombinant DNA, 1:112

Recommended Daily Allowance (RDA), 1:212, 2:801, 820

Red Cross/Red Crescent societies, 1:218

Reducing Emissions from Deforestation and Forest Degradation (REDD), 1:18

Reduction (cooking), 1:43

Rees, William, 2:787

Refrigeration and freezing, 2:657–658, 660–661, 831

Refrigeration machines, 1:460, *461*

Refugees, 2:*862*

Reichl, Ruth (interview), 1:*321–322*

Reinheitsgebot, 2:682

Religion and food, 1:386, 2:**679–682**
  fasting, 2:675, 679
  food aid for the poor, 1:428
  food bans, 1:312
  veganism, 2:804
  vegetarianism, 2:679, 810
  wine and beer, 2:682, 814, 815
  yeast and leavening agents, 2:868

Rémy, Pascal, 1:320–321

Report of the Technical Committee to Enquire into the Welfare of Animals kept under Intensive Livestock Husbandry Systems (Brambell), 1:469

Reportable Food Registry (RFR), 1:237, 2:674, **683–685**, *684*

Republic of Guinea, 1:189

The Restaurant (Blanc), 2:765

Restaurants and restaurant industry, 1:319, 326, *353*
  books about, 1:426–427
  celebrity chefs, 1:116
  gluten free food, 1:424
  migrant labor, 2:824
  organic, 2:615
  outdoor restaurant, 1:*353, 410*
  reviews, 1:307, 319–322, 320, 321, 427, 2:722–723
  waste and spoilage, 2:832–833
  See also specific restaurants

The Resurgence of Breastfeeding at the End of the Second Millennium (Wright & Schanler), 1:92

A Return to Cooking (Ripert), 1:307

Réunion Island, Africa, 1:*158*

Reynolds, James, 2:669

RFID (Radio frequency identification), 2:665
Rheology, food, 1:**363–364**
Rhizobia bacteria, 2:523, 524
Ricardo, David, 1:389
Rice, 1:*185, 417*, 2:**686–689**
  agricultural subsidies, 2:741
  allergies, 1:294
  Asian diet, 1:53
  black rice, 2:686
  embargoes, 1:239–240
  fields, 1:*417, 508*, 2:*631, 745, 852*
  golden, 1:55–56, 2:686, 687, 689, 822
  Green Revolution, 1:438–439, 2:686
  growing systems, 2:686
  husk, 1:433, 2:686–687
  leftover after harvest, 1:*433*
  oldest domesticated, 1:457
  patents, 1:345
  planting, 2:*688*
  price, 1:355, 2:686, 688
  rice germplasm and biodiversity, 1:70, 72
  rice grassy stunt virus, 1:143, 158
  rice production in India, 1:437
  varieties, 2:686–687, *687*
Rice grassy stunt virus (RGSV), 1:143, 158
Rice Krispies, 1:1
Riceland Foods, 2:687–688
RiceTec, 1:345
Richards, Ellen H., 1:166
Rickets, 2:586
Rinderpest, 2:531, 859
Rio Earth Summit, 1:9
Rio Grande do Sul, Brazil, 1:*345*
Ripert, Eric, 1:307
Rising Food Prices Intensify Food Insecurity in Developing Countries (Rosen & Shapouri), 1:*77*
Riverfront festival (Carrabelle, FL), 2:*729*
RJR Nabisco, 2:859
Roasting foods, 1:352
Roberts, Lydia, 1:46
Robinson Crusoe (Defoe), 1:110
Rochdale Equitable Pioneers Society (England), 2:580
Rockefeller Foundation, 1:438, 439
Rodale, Jerome I., 2:613, 754
Rodale Institute, 1:145, 147, 2:754
Roh, Mark, 2:*797*
Romania, 1:*63*, 184
Rome (ancient)
  beans for voting, 2:523
  confections, 1:149
  cooking oils, 1:164
  crop rotation, 2:524

  dairy products, 1:179, 2:514
  eating disorders, 1:227
  eggs, 1:164, 236
  fast food, 1:279
  food additives, 1:2
  food assistance, 1:428
  food laws, 1:154
  food packaging, 1:339
  land reform, 1:25
  Mediterranean diet, 2:557
  salt, 1:201, 288, 2:699, 703
  spice trade, 2:724
  waterwheels, 1:20
Rome, Italy, 2:855, 860
Rome Declaration on World Food Security (1996), 2:**690–694**
Rome Declaration on World Food Security (FAO), 2:**692–694**
Rooftop farm, 2:*788*
Roosevelt, Franklin D., 1:300, 316, 2:794, 800
Roosevelt, Theodore, 2:548–549, *549*, 551, 669, 846
Rosen, Stacey, 1:*77*
Rosenau, Milton J., 2:*628*
Roth, Michael, 1:*28–29*
Rotherham, Yorkshire, 2:765
Roundup Ready Canola, 1:344
Roundup Transorb® sign, 1:*417*
Roundworm infection, 1:467
Rousseau, Jean-Jacques, 1:468
Roux, 1:43
Royal Society of London, 2:630
Royal SPCA, 1:469
Royal Veterinary College (RVC), 1:99
Rozin, Paul, 1:453–454
RTE (Ready-to-eat), 1:14, 2:527
RTUFs. *See* Ready-to-use foods
Ruan, John, 2:857–858
Ruan, John, III, 2:858
Rueckheim, Frederick, 2:511
Rueckheim, Louis, 2:511
Rundgren, Gunnar, 1:**500–502**
Rural development, 1:507, 508
Rural Poverty Report (IFAD), 1:**507–508**
Russia
  alcohol prohibition, 1:313
  blood alcohol concentration limits, 1:285
  country of origin labeling, 2:664
  famines, 2:644–645
  food safety regulation and inspection, 1:333
  land reform, 1:26–27, 184
  pasta production, 2:624
  seed banks, 1:72
  sugar operations, 2:747
  tea, 2:760, 762
  wheat embargoes, 1:240

  wheat exports, 1:63, 434
  wheat harvest, 1:434
  World Trade Organization (WTO), 2:864
Rye, 1:432, 2:771

S

Saccharin, 2:749
Saccharomyces cerevisiae, 2:867
Sachs, Julius von, 1:478
Sacred brew, 2:682
Sacred foods, 1:*310*
Sahara desert, 1:5
Sakai, Hiroyuki, 2:*764*
Salad, 2:*674, 771*
Salinas, California, 2:*664*
Salmon, 1:51
  botulism outbreak, 1:359
  genetically modified organism (GMO), 1:420, 421
Salmon, Daniel, 2:695
Salmon, S. Cecil, 1:436
Salmonella, 1:360, 2:**695–698**
  animals, 1:381–382
  bioterrorism, 1:78, 80
  bushmeat, 1:100
  chicken, 2:783
  eggs, 1:236, 237, 2:649, 695, 696, 697–698, 783
  factory farms, 1:361
  food production processes, 1:359–360
  food recalls, 1:360, 366–367
  nano-scale technology, 2:550
  poultry, 2:649, 650, 695
  raw milk, 2:676, 677
  recall of contaminated products, 1:120
  reporting systems, 1:382, 2:683–684
  symptoms, 1:382, 2:695
  urban chicken movement, 2:783
  See also Bacteria
Salone del Gusto exposition, 2:720
Salsa, 2:520
Salt, 2:**699–702**
  in the bible, 2:699
  cancer, 1:192
  chemical formula, 2:700
  food additive, 1:288, 289
  heart disease, 1:201, 202, 2:699
  hypertension, 1:201–203, 289, 2:699, 822
  iodized salt, 1:403, 2:586–587, 699, 700–701, 820
  Mediterranean diet, 2:558
  processed foods, 2:660, 662
  therapeutic diets, 2:770–772
Salt, nitrites, and health, 2:**703–705**
Salt harvesters (Thailand), 2:*701*

Salt sculptures, 2:*700*
Salted herring, 1:*444*
Sandwich, Lord, 1:279
Sanitary and phytosanitary measures (SPS), 1:30, 31, 239, 309–310, 390
SAPs (Structural adjustment policies), 1:330
Sartre, Jean-Paul, 1:393, 394
Satay, 2:737
Saturated fats, 1:164, 165, 166, **2:571–573**
   veganism, 2:803, 805
   vegetarianism, 2:811
Saudi Arabia, 1:246, 2:688
Sautet, Marc, 1:393
Saxitoxin, 2:620, 621
Scharffenberger, John, 2:720
Schlosser, Eric, 1:279, 2:719
School lunch reform, 2:**706–709**, *708*
School lunches
   fast and junk foods, 2:512, 513, 709
   gluten-free diets, 1:424
   government aid, 1:46, 317
   guidelines, 2:594, 707
   India, 2:*645*
   Latin culinary influences, 2:520
   National School Lunch Program, 1:209, 488–489, 490, 2:592–593, 706, 707–709
   Oliver, Jamie, 2:709
   Singapore, 1:56
   Waters, Alice, 1:44, 2:709
Science fiction films, 2:574, 575
Scotland, 1:223, *284*, 2:*621*
Scotts Miracle-Gro Company, 1:344
Scrapie, 2:540, 542
Scrimshaw, Nevin, 2:544
S.E. Massengill, Corp., 1:324
Sea lice, 1:50
Seafood, 2:**710–714**
   allergies, 1:294
   allergy warning labels, 1:291, 292, 2:774, 799
   aquaculture and fishery resources, 2:710–714
   aquaponics, 1:479
   aquatic food web, 1:*379*
   Asian diet, 1:53
   bans, 1:314
   brain health, 2:571
   common pool resources, 2:710, 711
   dolphin-safe tuna, 2:713
   ecological impacts, 1:229, 230
   fresh fish display, 2:*711*
   genetic diversity, 1:143
   Gulf of Mexico oil spill, 1:440–442
   heart disease, 1:198, 2:571
   irradiation, 1:336

maximum sustainable yield, 2:711, 712
   macrobiotic diet, 2:537, 538
   norovirus infection, 2:583
   overfishing, 2:710, 711–712, 713
   Paleolithic diet, 2:618
   paralytic shellfish poisoning, 2:620–622
   religious rules regarding, 1:312, 2:680
   salt as preservative, 1:288
   salted herring, 1:*444*
   shark harvesting, 2:715–717
   smoked fish, 1:386
   street market, 1:*382*
   urban farming, 2:785
Seattle, Washington, 2:*641*, 782
Second Harvest/Feeding America, 2:832
Second Nature: A Gardener's Education (Pollan), 2:561
Seed banks, 1:69–70, *70, 72,* 143
Seeds and Nuts. *See* Nuts and Seeds
Seeds of Change (Ausubel), 1:69
Self (magazine), 1:226
Semolina, 2:624
Sen, Amartya, 1:*7–8,* 268, 271, 273, 472
Senegal, 1:301, *301*
Senossa, Mali, 1:*473*
Serbia, 1:91, 185
Serewa food station, 1:*267*
Serotypes, 1:222, 223, 2:696
Serve It Forth (Fisher), 2:808
Sesame seeds, 1:292
Seven-Eleven convenience store chain, 2:511
Seven Ms, 1:446
Seventh Day Adventists' dietary rules, 1:176, 2:680
Shakraba, Olga, 1:*482*
Shapouri, Shahla, 1:*77*
Sharecropping, 2:824–825
Shark harvesting, 2:**715–717**
Sharks, 2:*717*
Shawarma grill, 2:*554*
Sheep, 1:*79,* 2:*794*
Sheeran, Josette, 1:76
Shellfish poisoning, paralytic, 2:**620–622**, *621*
Shelton, Herbert M., 2:673
Short History of Wine (Philips), 2:814
Shostak, Marjorie, 1:492, 2:617
Shovondaha, Bangladesh, 1:*433*
Shrimping boats (Mayport, Florida), 2:*712*
Shweiry, Ramzi, 2:*524*
Siberia, 2:844
Sierra Leone, 1:98, 2:857
Sikinos, Greece, 1:*311*

Silent Spring (Carson), 1:469, 2:630, 750
Silesia, Germany, 2:750
Similac, recall, 1:120, 360, 497
Sinclair, Upton, 1:119, 332, 365, 2:548, *550–552,* 669, 846
Singapore, 1:56, 2:542, 782
Singer, Peter, 2:811
Singh, Puja, 1:*448*
60 Minutes, 2:766
Skin test for peanut allergy, 1:*295*
Skulls, evolution, 2:*597*
Slash-and-burn, 1:16, 161, 162
Slaughterhouses, 2:*555, 670*
Slave labor, 1:13, 126, 2:823
Slavery, cannibalism and, 1:109
Slovakia, 1:184
Slovenia, 1:184, 185, 2:851
Slow Food International, 2:756
Slow food movement, 1:43, 44, 2:**718–720,** 756
Slow Food Savors Its Big Moment (Scharffenberger), 2:720
Smallholder, 1:6, 2:744, 746, 858
Smith, Adam, 1:484
Smith, George, 1:284
Smith, Joyotee, 1:*18–19*
Smith, Theobald, 2:695
Smith-Lever Act of 1914, 2:793
Smithsonian Folklife Festival (Washington, DC), 1:232
Smoot-Hawley Tariff Act of 1930, 1:484
SNAP (Supplemental Nutrition Assistance Program), 1:357, 429–430, 2:592–594
Snap, Crackle, and Pop, 1:1
Snow, John, 1:128, 129
Social media and food, 2:**721–723**
Social safety net (SSN), 1:6, 357
The Social Status of a Vegetable (Fisher), 2:**808–809**
Society for the Prevention of Cruelty to Animals (SPCA), 1:469
Socio-economic Aspects of Street Foods (FAO), 2:*738–739*
Sodium chloride. *See* Salt
Sodium nitrate, 1:90, 289
Soft drinks
   calcium, 1:403
   consumption, 2:513
   super-sizing, 2:511, 513
Soil acidification, 2:517
Soil erosion, 2:517, 519
Soil salination, 2:517, 518, 519
Somalia, 1:5–6
   refugees, 2:*862*
   World Food Programme, 2:861–862, 863

Somerset, England, 2:627

The Song of the Famine (Anonymous), 1:*268–269*

Sonoma County, California, 2:816

Soot, 1:95, 160, 161, 162

Sorghum, 1:423, 432

Soup, 1:*202*

Soup Nazi (*Seinfeld*), 2:833

South Africa
  ban on U.K. beef, 2:542
  country of origin labeling, 2:664
  grape harvests, 1:311
  !Kung San diets, 1:492
  land reform, 1:28

South America
  coffee cultivation, 1:102
  deforestation, 2:519
  early agriculture, 1:457
  grape harvests, 1:311
  illicit drugs, 1:40
  modern ovens, 1:459
  obesity, 2:602
  See also specific countries

South Dakota, 2:768

South Korea
  activists, 1:*272*
  agricultural subsidies, 2:742
  ban on U.K. beef, 2:542
  country of origin labeling, 2:664
  farmers protest, 2:*865*
  influenza, 1:58
  United States Agency for International Development (USAID), 2:791

South Pacific, 2:676, 747

Southern corn leaf blight, 1:69

Soviet Republic of Georgia, World Food Programme, 2:863

Soviet Union
  alcohol prohibition, 1:313
  decollectivization, 1:26–27, 183
  famine, 1:271–272
  United States Agency for International Development (USAID), 2:790
  whaling, 2:843

Sow pens, 1:468, 470

Soy sauce, 2:587

Soybean Technology and the Loss of Natural Vegetation in Brazil and Bolivia (Kaimowitz & Smith), 1:*18–19*

Soybeans
  agricultural subsidies, 2:741
  allergies, 1:291, 294, 419
  allergy warning labels, 1:292, 2:774, 799
  biofuels, 1:75, 77
  cancer, 2:524–525
  genetically modified organism (GMO), 1:419

natural vegetation loss, 1:18–19
  products, 2:524–525
  rainforest burning, 1:17
  veganism, 2:803

Soyer, Alexis, 1:115

Soylent Green (movie), 2:574

Space program (U.S.), 1:327, 332

Spain, 1:109–110, 125
  cave painting, 1:*458*
  confectionery display, 1:*150*
  cuisine history, 2:827
  fruit display in Barcelona, 1:*400*
  jamon, 1:*485*
  migrant workers, 2:565, 823
  post Spanish Civil War development, 1:446
  spice trade, 1:452
  whaling, 2:842
  wine, 2:815, 817

Spanish flu, 1:57

Spargo, John, 2:706

SPCA (Society for the Prevention of Cruelty to Animals), 1:469

Special Milk Program, 1:488

The Spectrum of Malnutrition (FAO), 2:*546–547*

Spelt, 2:771

Spencer, Percy, 1:459

Spice trade, 1:452, 2:*724–726*
  See also Herbs and spices

Spores, 1:88–89, 286, 2:658

Sports nutrition, 1:104, 2:771–772

Spring rolls, 1:406

Spring water, 1:84

Sprotrichum mold, 2:831

Sproutarians, 2:674–675

Spurlock, Morgan, 2:575, *575*

Squash, 2:*828*

Sri Lanka, tea in, 2:762

Srinivasan, Viji (interview), 2:*825–826*

SSA (Sub-Saharan Africa), 1:5

SSN (Social safety net), 1:6, 355

St. Bartholomew's Hospital Reports, 1:422

St. John Restaurant (London, England), 1:444

St. Mark's Square (Venice, Italy), 1:*410*

St. Mary's Food Bank, 1:46

St. Vincent, 2:844

Stage (kitchen work), 1:174

Stalin, Josef, 1:183, 271

Standard American Diet (SAD), 2:674, 801

Standard American diet and changing American diet, 2:*727–732*

Standard Fruit Company, 1:65

Standard Milk Ordinance, 2:627

Staphylococcal food poisoning, 2:677, **733–735**

Staphylococcus aureus bacteria, 2:*734*

Starbucks, 1:395, 2:641, *641*

Starvation, 2:779–780

State-Inspected Meat and Poultry: Issues for Congress (Becker), 2:*848–849*

The State of World Fisheries and Aquaculture 2008 (FAO), 2:*51–52*, 710

Statement by the President Upon Signing the Wholesome Poultry Products Act (Johnson), 2:*654*

Steel, Helen, 2:768

Stefansson, Vilhjalmur, 1:491–492, 2:617

Steiner, Rudolf, 1:145, 500, 2:750

Sterilization, 2:626, 627

Stevia, 2:749

Stew, 2:*618*

Stewart, Martha, 1:116

Stockholm Action Plan, 2:843

Stockholm University, 1:279

Stomach flu. *See* Norovirus infection

The Stone Age Diet (Voegtlin), 2:617

Stop sign, 2:804

The Story of Crisco (Neil), 1:*166–168*

Strains, avian influenza, 1:57

Strategic Plan of Action for Food Safety in Africa, 1:156

Strawberries
  biodiversity, 1:72
  false fruit, 1:399
  hydroponic, 1:479
  ice cream and milk shakes, 2:731
  pesticides, 2:632
  phenolic compounds, 1:152
  photographing, 1:375

Street food, 2:**736–740**
  Asian diet, 1:56
  fast food, 1:279
  health issues, 1:450, 2:736–738
  hygiene, 1:451
  social media, 2:722
  socio-economic aspects, 2:*738–739*
  urbanization, 1:204, 2:736

Street food vendors, 1:*353, 382, 401, 450*, 2:*737, 738, 755*

Structural adjustment policies (SAPs), 1:330

Sub-Saharan Africa (SSA), 1:5, 26

Sub-tropical fruits, 1:399

Subsidies, 2:**741–743**
  agricultural, 1:**40–42**, 316, 317, 486–487, 2:741, 794
  illicit drug prevention, 1:40–42
  livestock, 2:532

Subsistence farming, 1:17, *331*, 2:*744*, **744–746**

Substrates, 1:479

Sucralose, 2:749

Sucre, Bolivia, 2:*521*

Sudan
 aid, 1:*7,* 370
 civil war, 1:5
 IDP women and a child, 1:*273*
 World Food Day (WFD)
  celebration, 2:*855*
 World Food Programme, 2:861,
  863

Sugar and sweeteners, 2:**747–749**
 aspartame, 1:289
 brown sugar, 2:748
 diabetes, 1:195, 2:748
 fermentation process, 1:282
 food additive, 1:288, 2:749
 food labels, 2:749
 fortification of sugar, 2:586
 medical remedy, 2:747
 macrobiotic diets, 2:537
 oral health, 2:606
 processed foods, 2:662
 sugar cane, 1:*241,* 317, 2:747
 weight gain, 2:747, 748, 749

Sugar cane field, 2:*748*

Sulfa drugs, 1:323–324

Summit on the Millennium
 Development Goals, 2:777

Sundlof, Stephen, 2:678

Sunflower seeds, 1:292

Super Size Me (movie), 2:575

Supplemental Nutrition Assistance
 Program (SNAP), 1:357, 429–430,
 2:592–594

Surplus food, 1:43, 456, 503

Sushi, 1:406

Sustainable agriculture, 2:**750–753**
 fertilizers, 2:750
 food security, 2:690
 food sovereignty approach, 1:373
 intergenerational equity, 1:244
 pesticides and pesticide residue,
  2:750
 sustainable table, 2:754
 third-party certification, 2:751
 urban farming, 2:785

Sustainable Agriculture Action
 Group, 2:742

Sustainable Agriculture Research and
 Education Program (SAREP), 2:751

Sustainable development, 1:9–11,
 142, 372, 2:691

Sustainable table, 2:**754–756**

Svalbard Global Seed Bank, 1:70, *70,*
 72, 143

Swadeshi movement, 2:640, 641

Swaminathan, Monkombu
 Sambasivan, 2:857

Swamp buffalo, 2:*745*

Swanson, C.A., 1:460

Swanson foods, 2:649

Sweden
 drinking and driving, 1:285
 gavage regulation, 1:314
 organic farming, 1:502

Sweet Grass Dairy (Thomasville,
 Georgia), 1:181, *181, 364, 426,* 2:*677*

Sweetwater Organic Coffee Roasters,
 1:*298*

Swiss chard, 2:*788*

Swiss Federal Institute of
 Technology, 1:279

Switzerland, 1:126
 agricultural subsidies, 2:742
 country of origin labeling, 2:664
 gavage regulation, 1:314
 iodized salt, 2:586
 school lunch programs, 2:706
 slow food movement, 2:718
 trans fat bans, 1:165
 World Food Prize, 2:857

Syngenta AG, 2:859

Synthetic fertilizers, 2:609, 610

Synthetic pesticides, 2:609, 610

Syria, 1:434

Szent-Györgi, Albert, 2:819

T

Taco Bell, 2:642

Taiwan, 2:*631*

Tampa, Florida, farm workers
 protest, 2:*824*

Tap water, 1:84

Tariffs, 1:65, 66, 67, 389
 banana trade wars, 1:67
 General Agreement on Tariffs and
  Trade (GATT), 1:30, 31, 65,
  389, 485, 2:864
 non-tariff barrier, 1:30, 390

Tasmania, Australia, 2:*518*

Taste buds, 2:758

Tasting food, 2:**757–759,** 758

Taylor, Christopher, 2:576

Tea, 2:**760–762**
 advertising, 1:1
 caffeine, 1:102
 fair trade, 2:762
 green tea and weight loss, 1:105
 herb, 1:*405*
 organic, 2:762
 picking, 2:*761*
 pickled tea leaves, 1:*314*

Tea Act of 1773, 2:640

Tecumseh, Nebraska, 2:*653*

Teenagers. *See* Adolescents

Teikei gardens, 1:145, 2:750, 751

Television and food, 1:426,
 2:**763–765**

Temple-Wilton Community farm
 (Wilton, New Hampshire), 1:145

Terre et Vin du Monde, 2:818

Terroir, 2:817

Texas Beef Group v. Winfrey, 2:**766–769**

Texas Farm-to-Table Café, 1:*277*

Texas organic acreage, 2:613

Texture of food, 1:363

Thailand
 chicken domestication, 2:782
 diets, 1:56
 floating market, 1:*55*
 rice, 2:686, 688
 salt harvesters, 2:*701*
 street food vendor, 1:*450*

Thalidomide, 1:324

Thanksgiving, 1:311

The International Maize and Wheat
 Improvement Center (CIMMYT),
 1:72

The Knights (Aristophanes), 2:814

Theobromine, 1:126

Therapeutic boarding schools, 2:*771*

Therapeutic diets, 2:**770–772**

Third-party certification, 1:257, 258,
 333, 2:761
 humane animal farming, 1:468
 organic standards, 1:500, 2:610,
  614, 751
 sustainable agriculture, 2:751

39 False Food Fads (Washington Post),
 1:176

Thomasville, Georgia, 1:*364*

Thompson, Benjamin, 2:706

Thompson, Tommy, 1:79

The Three Sisters, 2:*828*

Thrombocytopenic purpura (TTP),
 1:222

Tibet, 2:761

Time magazine, 1:227, 2:535, 561

Timor-Leste, hunger and
 malnutrition, 1:54

TNG (Transitional National
 Government), 1:6

To Make a Grand Dish of Eggs
 (Glasse), 1:*460–461*

Tofu, 2:537, 538

Tomatoes, 2:*797*
 European cuisine, 1:386
 festival, 1:*386*
 fruit classification, 1:399
 genetically engineered, 1:112, 417
 history of Latin American
  cultivation, 2:520
 hydroponic, 1:479
 lycopene, 1:353
 Salmonella, 2:696

Tommy's Brick Oven Pizza
 (Jacksonville, Florida), 1:*423*

Tool Kit for Teen Care, Second Edition (ACOG), 1:303
Tootsie Rolls, 2:511
Top Chef, 2:765
Torah, 1:312
Toronto, Canada, 2:830, 832
Toys "R" Us, 1:82
Traceability, produce, 2:**663–665**
Trade
    agriculture, 1:30–33
    banana trade wars, 1:65–68
    coca leaves, 1:*41*
    coffee, 1:138–139
    fair, 1:138–139, 257–259, 2:581
    food sovereignty approach,
        1:373–374
    indigenous peoples diets, 1:491
    living modified organisms, 1:112
    loss of plant biodiversity,
        2:521–522
    preservation, 2:658
    salt, 2:699
    spice, 1:452, 2:724–726
    See also Free trade
Trade barriers, 1:30, 31
Traditional foods
    food preparation, 1:204, 206
    indigenous peoples diets, 1:491–494
    movement, 2:677
    Paleolithic diet, 2:617
    slow food movement, 2:718
    Weston A. Price Foundation's
        diet, 1:177, 492
Traditional knowledge, 1:37, 38
Tragedy of the Commons (Hardin),
    1:37, 2:517, 712
Trajan (emperor), 1:428
A Tramp Abroad (Twain), 1:*386–387*
Trans fats, 1:164, 165
    bans, 1:314, 2:572
    cholesterol levels, 1:166, 2:512,
        572
    fast food, 1:476
    food labels, 2:773, 775
    sign regarding, 1:*477*
Transgenic crops, 1:113, 416–417
Transitional National Government
    (TNG), 1:6
Transmissible spongiform
    encephalopathies (TSEs), 1:110,
    2:540, 542
Travel, Hepatitis A and, 1:449–451
Trichinella spiralis, 1:*383*
Trichinellosis, 1:383
Triglycerides, 1:198, 199, 2:572
Troigros, Pierre, 2:568
Trophic level, 1:377, 378
Tropical Deforestation (Jepma), 1:163
Tropical fruits, 1:399, 479
Truth in labeling, 2:773–775

TSEs (Transmissible spongiform
    encephalopathies), 1:110, 2:540, 542
tTG test (for celiac disease), 1:423
TTP (Thrombocytopenic purpura),
    1:222
Tunisia, 2:624, 791
Turbidity, 1:17, 18
Turkey (country)
    influenza, 1:58
    pasta production, 2:624
    United States Agency for
        International Development
        (USAID), 2:791
    wheat shortage, 1:434
Turkey domestication, 2:648
Turmeric, 1:453
TV dinners, 1:326, 460, 2:649, 661
TV Food Network, 2:764
Twain, Mark, 1:*386–387*
*Twenty Years of Competition Reshape
    the U.S. Food Marketing System*
    (Martinez & Kaufman), 1:*3*
Twiggy, 1:227
Twinkies, 2:511
Twinn Bridges Farms farmer's
    market stand, 2:*616*
Tyson Buffalo Style Chicken Strips,
    2:650

U

Uganda, 1:*370*
Ukraine, 1:184, *184,* 272, *272*
Ulcerative colitis, 2:770
Ultraviolet (UV) radiation, 1:335, 336
Umami, 2:757
Umbrella organization, 1:500
Umpqua Farms (Oregon), 2:677
UN-OCHA (United Nations
    Office for the Coordination of
    Humanitarian Affairs), 1:218
UN World Food Programme, 2:858
UNCCD (United Nations
    Convention to Combat
    Desertification), 1:187
UNCED (United Nations
    Conference on the Environment
    and Development), 1:9
Uncle Ben's rice, 1:3
UNCOD (United Nations Conference
    on Desertification), 1:187
UNCTAD (United Nations
    Conference on Trade and
    Development), 1:257, 2:751
Undernutrition, 1:266, 301,
    2:**779–781**
    children, 1:*473,* 2:*780*
    malnutrition, 2:544

oral health, 2:606
World Food Day (WFD), 2:855
Undocumented workers, 2:565
UNDP (United Nations
    Development Programme), 1:23,
    2:564, 836
UNEP. *See* United Nations
    Environment Programme (UNEP)
UNICEF. *See* United Nations
    Children's Fund (UNICEF)
Unioni Industriali Pastai Italiani
    (UNIPI), 2:624
United Arab Emirates (UAE), 1:85,
    2:648
United Farm Workers of America
    (UFWA), 2:564–565, 565, 566, 642
United Fruit Company, 1:65
United Kingdom
    animal slaughter, 2:681, 766
    animal welfare laws and
        regulations, 1:370, 469
    beer consumption, 1:284
    boycotts, 2:640
    bovine spongiform
        encephalopathy (BSE) and
        Creutzfeldt-Jakob disease,
        2:540–543
    Café Culture campaign, 1:395
    cattle industry, 2:766
    cheese festival, 1:*427*
    corn laws, 1:389
    Creutzfeldt-Jakob disease, 1:381,
        2:766
    drunk driving, 1:284
    food additive regulation, 1:289
    food allergy warning labels,
        1:292, 2:774
    food assistance, 1:428
    food bans, 2:766
    food libel laws, 2:768
    food phobias, 1:348
    food recalls, 1:360
    food waste, 2:830
    free-range egg usage, 1:237
    gavage regulation, 1:314
    girl with an eating disorder, 1:*305*
    Indian cuisine, 2:726
    Irish potato famine, 1:266
    migrant workers, 2:565
    overweight population, 1:284
    poultry shows, 2:648
    school lunch programs, 2:706
    slow food movement, 2:718
    tea, 2:760, 762
    United States Agency for
        International Development
        (USAID), 2:790
    wheat flour fortification, 2:586
    World Food Prize, 2:857
United Kingdom. Food Standards
    Agency, 2:542
United Kingdom. Meat and
    Livestock Commission, 2:542

United Nations
    biodiversity, 1:18
    deforestation efforts, 1:18
    elimination of hunger goal, 1:507
    embargoes, 1:239
    food aid provided by the, 1:246
    poverty and hunger, 2:776
    World Food Day (WFD),
        2:854–856
    World Food Prize, 2:857
United Nations Children's Fund
    (UNICEF), 1:92, 2:765, 781, 851
United Nations Codex Alimentarius
    Commission, 1:119–120, 135,
    136, 137
    See also Codex Alimentarius
United Nations Commission on
    Sustainable Development (CSD), 1:9
United Nations Conference on
    Environment and Development in
    1992, 1:71
United Nations Conference on Food
    and Agriculture (1943), 1:300–301
United Nations Conference on the
    Environment and Development
    (UNCED), 1:9
United Nations Conference on the
    Human Environment, 2:843
United Nations Conference on Trade
    and Development (UNCTAD),
    1:257, 2:751
United Nations Convention to
    Combat Desertification (UNCCD),
    1:187
United Nations Development
    Programme (UNDP), 1:23, 2:564,
    836
United Nations Environment
    Programme (UNEP), 1:71, 157,
    251, 370, 2:712, 713
United Nations Food and Agriculture
    Organization. *See* Food and
    Agriculture Organization (FAO)
United Nations Framework
    Convention on Climate Change, 1:16
United Nations Intergovernmental
    Panel on Climate Change (IPCC),
    1:132–133, 188, 252, 438
United Nations International
    Development Fund for Women,
    2:850
United Nations Millennium
    Development Goals (MDGs),
    1:474, 2:645, 692, 776–778, 854
United Nations Office for the
    Coordination of Humanitarian
    Affairs (UNOCHA), 1:218
United Nations Office on Drugs and
    Crime (UNODC), 1:40, 2:823
United Nations World Commission
    on the Environment and
    Development, 2:750

United Nations World Meteorological
    Organization, 1:252
United Nations World Summits,
    2:518
United States
    agricultural subsidies, 1:486–487,
        2:741, 742
    alcohol prohibition, 1:312–313
    allergies, 1:294
    animal welfare opinion and
        regulation, 1:470
    antibiotic use, 1:255
    assistance to Columbia, 1:40
    banana trade wars, 1:65–68
    beer consumption, 1:284
    biofuels, 1:74, 77, 355
    bioterrorism, 1:79–80
    birthday celebrations, 1:311
    blood alcohol concentration
        limits, 1:285
    bottled water usage, 1:84, 85, 397
    botulism, 1:88, 89–90
    botulism toxin-based weapons, 1:89
    bovine spongiform encephalopathy
        (BSE), 2:541, 768
    boycotts, 2:640, *641*, 642
    BPA-containing baby bottles,
        1:497
    breastfeeding, 1:81, 82, 92, 496,
        497
    caloric consumption rate, 1:206
    caloric content labeling, 1:107
    cannibalism, 1:110
    carbon and soot emissions, 1:160
    cattle industry, 1:79
    celiac disease, 1:423, 424
    cereal industry, 2:663
    certified organics, 2:751
    children's nutrition legislation,
        1:488–490
    chocolate consumption, 1:126
    cholera, 1:129, 130
    Codex Alimentarius, 1:137, 365
    coffee, 1:138, 139
    coffee houses, 1:395
    cooking technology aid, 1:97
    corn production and exports,
        1:169, 170–171
    corn subsidies, 1:171, 2:741
    community supported agriculture
        (CSA), 1:145–147
    Cuba embargo, 1:239
    cuisine history, 2:828
    cyclamate ban, 2:747, 749
    daily water access, 2:835
    diabetes, 1:194, 195–196
    dietary guidelines, 1:123,
        208–211, 2:662, 700, 707
    drunk driving, 1:284–285
    E. coli outbreaks, 1:223
    early agriculture, 1:456
    eating disorders, 1:225, 227
    embargoes, 1:239, 240–241
    family farms, 1:260, 261, 262, *262*
    family meals, 1:263

    farm subsidies, 1:32
    farm-to-table movement, 1:275,
        276–277
    fast food, 1:279
    film projection inventions, 2:574
    foie gras policies, 1:314, 470
    food additive regulation, 1:289
    food aid, 1:246, 247, 248, 503,
        504, 505–506
    food allergies, 1:291
    food allergy warning labels,
        1:292, 2:774–775, 799
    food assistance (domestic),
        2:592–594
    food bans, 1:212–213, 314,
        2:768
    food diversity, 2:718
    food inspections and standards,
        1:332
    food recalls, 1:360, 2:683
    food spoilage rates, 2:661
    food stamps, 1:429–430
    food waste, 2:830
    food workers, 1:331
    foodborne illness, 2:550, 734
    foodborne illness and death,
        1:381, 2:677
    fortification of milk, 2:586
    free-range egg usage, 1:237
    functional foods, 1:344, 403,
        404–405
    genetically modified organism
        (GMO) crops, 1:417, 420,
        2:794
    grain crops and meat, 2:554–555
    heart disease, 1:199, 2:730
    Hepatitis A infection, 1:449
    herbal or botanical supplement
        use, 1:454
    holiday weight gain, 1:310
    hunger, 1:46–47
    immigration, 1:268, 481–483
    influenza deaths, 1:57
    iodized salt, 2:586, 820
    Irish potato famine, 2:807
    irradiation of foods, 1:335
    junk food, 2:511–513
    kosher food, 2:681
    Kyoto Protocol, 1:134
    Latino descent population, 2:520
    malnutrition, 2:544, 545
    meat consumption, 2:648, 649
    meat production, 2:529–530,
        548–552
    migrant labor, 1:13, 2:564–565,
        565–566, 823
    norovirus infection, 2:584–585
    nutrition facts labels, 2:590
    obesity, 1:210, 2:512–513, 601,
        603–605, 650
    oral health, 2:606
    organic food market, 2:649
    organic production, 2:613–614
    organics regulation, 2:609–612
    overweight population, 1:284

packaging waste, 1:341
paralytic shellfish poisoning, 2:621, 622
pasta production, 2:624
pasteurization, 2:626–627
peanuts, 2:598–599
pesticide use, 2:630
pica, 2:637
portion size, 1:396–397
poultry shows, 2:648
produce consumption, 2:663
raw milk, 2:627–628, 676
recommended daily energy intake, 1:108
regional cuisine, 1:385–386, 411, 481, 482
restaurant development, 1:319
rice, 2:688
roundworm infection, 1:467
salmonellosis, 2:696–697
salt consumption, 2:699, 700
school gardens, 1:232, 233
slow food movement, 2:718
standard American diet, 1:326, 2:674, 727–732, 801
sugar consumption, 2:748
sushi, 1:406
tea, 2:760, 761
television and food, 2:763
trans fat bans, 1:165
United States Agency for International Development (USAID), 2:790, 792
vegetable costs, 2:564
water usage, 1:23
wheat exports, 2:624
wheat flour fortification, 2:586
wheat harvest, 1:434, *434*
wine, 2:816, 818
women and food preparation, 2:850
World Food Prize, 2:857
See also U.S. entries
United States National Heart, Blood, and Lung Institute, 1:202
The United States of Arugula (Kamp), 1:426, 2:534
United States School Garden Army, 1:232
University of California San Diego, 2:757
University of California Davis, 1:*421*
University of Gastronomic Sciences (Italy), 2:720
University of Michigan family farm study, 1:260–261
University of Minnesota family connectedness study, 1:264
University of North Carolina, 1:226
University of Paris South (France), 1:*277*
University of South Alabama, 1:380
University of Wisconsin, 2:819

UNODC (United Nations Office on Drugs and Crime), 2:823
Unsaturated oils, 2:571, 572
The Unsettling of America and Home Economics (Berry), 2:754
Urban chicken movement, 1:237, **2:782–784**
Urban Community Youth Outreach farm (Flint, Michigan), 2:*787*
Urban ecosystems, 2:787
Urban farming and gardening, 2:581, *581*, **785–789**, *786*
Urbanization, 1:205–206
Uruguay, 1:206
Uruguay Round negotiations, 2:741, 742, 864
U.S. Agency for International Development (USAID), 1:436, **2:790–792**
    Afghan workers packing honey jars, 2:*791*
    agricultural programs, 1:40–41
    creation, 1:28, 2:790
    famine relief, 1:267, 2:791
    Food for Peace program, 2:791
    hiring practices, 2:792
    malnutrition, 2:545
    purpose, 1:28, 2:790
    World Food Prize, 2:858
U.S. Agricultural Division of the Patent Office, 2:793
U.S. Centers for Disease Control and Prevention (CDC), 2:676, 677, 801–802
    antibiotic use in poultry, 2:649
    bioterrorism, 1:78
    botulism, 1:89–90
    BPA studies by, 1:82, 86
    cholera, 1:130, 131
    E. coli outbreaks, 1:223
    food allergies, 1:294–295
    food poisoning, 2:733
    heart disease, 2:730
    irradiation, 1:337
    lettuce inspections, 1:120
    listeriosis, 2:526
    norovirus infection, 2:583
    obesity, 1:210, 303, 2:522, 601, 603, 650
    overweight or obese children, 2:511
    raw milk, 2:627
    salmonellosis, 2:696
U.S. Coast Guard, 1:220
U.S. Conference of Mayors, bottled water and energy usage, 1:85
U.S. Department of Agriculture (USDA), **2:793–795**
    agricultural subsidies, 2:741
    Amber Waves journal, 1:*3, 14, 77, 206*
    basic food groups, 2:801
    biofuels and food insecurity, 1:77

blueberries, 1:401
campaign for federal food legislation, 2:669
cereal inventory-to-sales ratio, 2:663
corn production, 1:169, 170
dietary changes due to income, 1:204
dietary guidelines. 1:122, 208, 209
Dust Bowl, 2:793
family farms, 1:260, 261
farm size and ownership, 1:13
food advertising, 1:3
food and drug safety, 2:796
food insecurity, 1:47, 330
food pyramid, 2:800
food regulation, 1:119
food safety, 1:154–155
Food Safety and Inspection Service (FSIS) division, 1:**365–367**, 2:846
fruit and vegetable washing, 2:630
genetically modified organisms (GMOs), 1:344
global food trends, 1:206–207
Great Depression, 2:793
inspector, 2:*848*
Japanese food costs, 1:53
labeled food (natural), 2:581
labeled food (organic), 2:581, *611*
liberalization of trade, 1:390
local produce for schools program, 2:535
malnutrition measure, 2:545
meatpacking facilities, 2:548, 845
officials, 2:*794*
organic requirements, 1:45, 2:609–612, 631
pesticides, 2:632
poultry inspection, 2:653, 654
raw milk, 2:677
rice, 2:686
school lunch guidelines, 2:707
SNAP program, 1:430
sodium consumption, 2:700
soft drink consumption, 2:513
Soil Erosion Service, 2:794
supplied rolled oats and walnuts, 2:593
World Food Prize, 2:858
U.S. Department of Agriculture food pyramid, 1:209, 2:**800–802**
U.S. Department of Defense, 2:577
U.S. Department of Health, Education, and Welfare, 1:208
U.S. Department of Health and Human Services (HHS), 1:208, 209, 2:796
U.S. Department of Labor, 2:565
U.S. Department of Labor National Agricultural Workers Survey, 2:850
U.S. Department of Labor's Occupational Safety & Health Administration (OSHA), 2:564

U.S. Environmental Protection
Agency (EPA), 2:574
  Alar ban, 2:641
  Concentrated Animal Feeding
    Operation (CAFO), 1:254
  extreme weather events, 1:252
  municipal water systems
    regulation, 1:84, 85
  oil dispersant usage, 1:440–441
  pesticides, 2:631, 632
U.S. Food and Drug Act of 1958,
  1:289
U.S. Food and Drug Administration
  (FDA), 2:796–799
  antibiotic use in poultry, 2:649
  ban of sweeteners, 2:749
  bottled water regulation, 1:84, 85
  BPA safety, 1:83, 86, 497
  caffeine, 1:104
  caloric content labeling, 1:107
  CFSAN subdivision, 1:119–121,
    365
  creation, 2:670
  dietary supplement regulation,
    1:215–217, 2:797
  drug regulation, 2:796, 797
  eggs, 1:236, 2:697–698
  food additives regulation, 1:288,
    2:796, 797
  food allergies regulation, 1:293,
    2:684, 799
  food contamination, 1:342
  food labels, 2:799
  food recalls, 1:90, 2:683, 796
  food safety, 1:154, 2:796
  history, 1:118, 2:796–797
  lycopene, 1:353
  medical device regulation,
    2:797–798
  olive oil, 1:166
  pesticides, 2:632
  raw food, 2:674, 676, 677
  raw milk, 2:676, 677
  recombinant bovine growth
    hormone (rBGH), 2:798,
    847–848
  responsibilities, 1:276, 323,
    2:796–799
  technology regulation, 2:798
  trans fats, 1:477, 2:572
  transgenic salmon species, 1:51
U.S. General Accounting Office, 1:79
U.S. Immigrant Reform and Control
  Act of 1986, 2:565
U.S. Institute of Medicine, 2:578,
  591
U.S. National Agricultural Statistics
  Service, women and land
  ownership, 2:850–851
U.S. Public Health Service, raw milk,
  2:676
USDA. *See* U.S. Department of
  Agriculture (USDA)

V

Vaccine Act of 1813, 2:796
Vaccine Act of 1822, 2:796
Valencia, Spain, 1:458
Valle de los Ingenios, Cuba, 1:241
Value chain, 1:12
Van Hengel, John, 1:46
Vanilla, 1:452
Variant Creutzfeldt-Jakob Disease
  (vCJD), 2:540–543
Vavilov, Nikolai, 1:69, 456
Vavilov Research Institute, 1:69, 72
Veal, 1:468, 469, 470
Vegan activists, 1:230, 2:805
Veganism, 2:674, 803–805
  ecological impact, 1:230, 2:674
  religion and food, 2:804
  vs. vegetarianism, 2:803, 810
Vegetables, 2:538, 806–809, 836
  canned, 2:658
  cost, 2:564
  dried, 2:656
  food preparation methods, 1:353,
    353
  foodborne illness, 1:224, 382
  garlands, 1:356
  Mediterranean diet, 2:558
  macrobiotic diet, 2:538
  micronutrients, 2:590, 807
  norovirus infection, 2:583
  organic, 2:611, 615
  pesticides, 2:630
  phytonutrient content, 2:634
  raw, 2:674, 807
  richer populations' consumption,
    1:355
  traceability, 2:663–665
  varieties, 2:806–807
  See also specific vegetables
Vegetarianism, 2:810–813, 811
  alcoholism, 1:403, 2:811
  Buddhists, 1:312, 2:679, 803, 810
  campaign, 2:767
  ecological impact, 1:230,
    2:811–812
  Hindus, 2:680, 803
  Jainism, 2:803, 810
  Rastafarians, 2:679
  religion and food, 2:679, 810
  Seventh Day Adventists, 1:176,
    2:679, 810
  sexual desires, 1:403, 2:811
  vs. veganism, 2:803, 810
  water usage, 1:22, 2:811–812, 837
"Veggie libel laws," 2:768
Veggie Pride parade, 2:812
Venezuela, 1:126
  cacao bean production, 1:125
  native maize, 1:170
  pasta consumption, 2:624

Venice, Italy, 1:349, 410, 2:747
Vermont, 2:593
Via Campesina, 1:372
*The Vicious Cycle of Water &
  Poverty—An Issue of Life &
  Livelihood* (FAO), 1:23–24
Victor Emmanuel III (king), 1:300
Victoria (queen), 1:469
Vietnam
  fish market, 1:54
  fortification of fish sauce, 2:587
  influenza, 1:58, 59
  rice, 2:686, 688, 822
  spring rolls, 1:407
Vignerons, 2:814, 817
Vignes, Jean Louis, 2:816
Villagers gathering water
  (Mwandama, Malawi), 2:778
Villegas, Evangelina, 2:858
Vilsack, Tom, 1:367, 2:698
Viniculture, 1:310, 2:814–818
Vintners, 2:815
Vineyards, 2:816
Vioxx, 2:798
Virginia, 1:471
Vitamins and minerals, 1:216,
  2:819–822
  allergies, 1:295
  boiling foods, 1:353
  cancer, 2:821
  deficiencies, 2:544
  deficiencies in Asia, 1:54–55
  deficiencies in nursing home
    residents, 1:122
  deficiencies in the United States,
    1:123, 2:821
  deficiency diseases, 2:819
  dietary reference intakes (DRIs),
    1:212–214, 2:820
  digestive process, 1:463, 465
  factory farming, 1:254
  fortified foods, 1:288, 403, 404,
    2:586–588
  fruits, 1:399, 400
  macrobiotic diet, 2:538
  micronutrients, 1:404, 2:545,
    811, 819
  milk additives, 1:403
  oral health, 2:606
  phytonutrients, 2:634–636
  pica, 2:638
  raw food lifestyles, 2:674–675
  roles in the body, 2:590, 819
  types, 2:820–821
  veganism, 2:803, 804, 812
  vegetarianism, 2:812
Vitis vinifera sylvestris, 2:814
Voegtlin, Walter L., 2:617
Voit, Carl, 2:589
Von Braun, Joachim, 1:357
Von Liebig, Justis, 1:495, 2:589